The Maki of English I
King Alfred to the Twelfth Century

Volume I

For Jenny, Tom and Luke

The Making of English Law:
King Alfred to the Twelfth Century

Volume I
LEGISLATION AND ITS LIMITS

Patrick Wormald

BLACKWELL
Publishers

First published 1999
Reprinted 2000

First published in paperback 2001

Blackwell Publishers Ltd
108 Cowley Road
Oxford OX4 1JF
UK

Blackwell Publishers Inc.
350 Main Street
Malden, Massachusetts 02148
USA

British Library Cataloguing in Publication Data

A CIP catalogue record for this book is available from the British Library.

Library of Congress Cataloging-in-Publication Data

Wormald, Patrick.
  The making of English law : King Alfred to the twelfth century /
Patrick Wormald.
     p.   cm.
  Includes bibliographical references and index.
  Contents: v. 1. Legislation and its limits—
  ISBN 0–631–13496–4 (hdbk); 0–631–22740–7 (pbk)
  1. Law—England—Sources. 2. Law—England—History.
3. Legislation—England—History—Sources. I. Title.
KD554.W67 1999
349.42—dc21
                                                    98–50476
                                                       CIP

Contents

Tables and Map

Tables

Map

Preface

This is in many ways an old-fashioned book. That is because, for reasons explained in its Prologue, it was not written when it could and should have been a century ago. The founders of English Constitutional History thought that law and order was the business of effective government. But they did not expect much from Anglo-Saxon kings. They pictured the founders of England as free, traditionally Germanic, and in want of licking into shape by their island's last conquest. With the retreat of such conceptions there came ways of thinking about early medieval society which have other reasons to expect little of rulers. Nowadays, authority's disciplines are seen to have done less to resolve social tensions than feud and negotiation between parties. Victorians encountering such mechanisms in colonial societies thought them benighted. Anthropologists have taught today's historians to respect them. In the English case, however, this approach has tended to work best when 'bouncing off' the unreal rigidities of constitutionalists. Those rigidities were never put in place for the first phase of English legal history. The anthropological model has had nothing to offset it.

Yet to leave it at that is to intensify the central problem in English law's early history. This is, to borrow Maitland's typically unforgettable phrase, the 'marvellous suddenness' with which the Common Law appeared: bursting, with all the qualities of Athena, from the head of King Henry II (1154–89). Though set in motion by an Angevin king, the new system was far more palpable in England than Anjou. It established itself when Roman Law was making a comeback on the continent but was native not Roman. Professor Milsom, Maitland's most eminent critic, has sought to reduce these improbabilities by making Henry an innovator *malgré lui*. But this relocates rather than solves the riddle. Angevin justice was undeniably more active, however clumsily or unwittingly, in the northern kingdom than the southern homeland. The natural explanation of the fact that it could operate in England as it could not elsewhere in the Angevin condominium is that there was something about its English inheritance which was lacking elsewhere. That something has a *prima facie* connection with the fact that in the tenth and eleventh centuries English kings laid down the law as no other western rulers did. If so, a model of Anglo-Saxon law on loan to historians from analysts of Third World societies where authority historically had little power is unlikely to hold all the answers. Constitutionalists will not have expected too much of early English government but not enough.

The argument of this book is that the story of the birth of the Common Law with which historians and lawyers have lived since Maitland told it is probably – not certainly but probably – wrong. Put crudely, the view defended here is that England's law is distinctive because it is as old as the English kingdom. What above all distinguishes the history of England from that of its neighbours and counterparts is that the power of government has been longer and more consistently felt throughout the area it has claimed to rule. English law has been the instrument and expression of that power ever since it was exercised by King Alfred (871–99) and his heirs. Henry II made law like no other twelfth-century king, because he inherited a system of royal justice that was already uniquely old and active.

Maitland was the greatest legal historian of all time. If the view here offered in opposition to his were clearly right, he would have put that view, not his own. But among (mostly good) reasons why he formed his opinion of Old English law was that he did not quite know what to make of the evidence from the pre-conquest kingdom. He several times compared the law-codes of Alfred's successors with the capitularies of the Carolingian Frankish kings, while still remaining (fairly) sure that the visibly Carolingian apparatus of Angevin justice was imported after rather than before 1066. Anglo-Saxon laws (which he liked, like many others, to call 'dooms', though the Old English legal term *dom* means neither more or less than 'judgement/law') were an unknown, perhaps an unknowable, quantity. Felix Liebermann, their definitive editor, who knew them better than anyone ever has or will, was inclined, because he was trained, to look to them not for links with the Common Law of the future but with the Germanic Law of Antiquity. Since his colossal edition, Anglo-Saxon law has become a statuesque monument to an absorbingly interesting but irretrievably lost past. It could cast no more than a shadow over the brightly lit and vibrant twelfth century. The possibilities of Old English legislation have not been explored and found wanting. This (changing the metaphor) was thought such difficult terrain that the map provided by Liebermann has stayed on the wall.

It is difficult. So difficult as to dictate the eccentric as well as outsize dimensions of these volumes. Pollock and Maitland's classic legal history began in its second edition with a superb *aperçu* of the European background. It then offered a narrative 'Sketch of Early English Legal History', which is essentially an account of texts, before proceeding to a discussion of 'The Doctrines of English Law in the Early Middle Ages', where Maitland was at his brilliant best. This book starts, after a historiographical prologue meant to give substance to the assertions in the foregoing paragraphs, with detailed attention to the continental setting. If Carolingian influence was somehow at work behind the scenes of Common Law's *debut*, it *deserves* close study. Furthermore, Maitland's method of probing the obscurities of early periods was to 'work back from known to unknown': to proceed chronologically backwards within an English framework. Given the inherent teleology of this approach, an equally legitimate angle is to 'work *across* from the known (continental) to the unknown (English)': the 'alien' need no more mislead than the anachronistic. Chapter 2 of this book thus sets a scene that is ninth-century Frankish as well as seventh-century English. Following the classical model, the next step is an account of the texts: the legislation of English rulers from Alfred to Henry I. But whereas the texts of Maitland's 'luminous' Angevin period needed no more than a 'sketch', the more dimly perceptible laws of the pre-conquest era must take up all the rest of this first volume.

A central thesis of this book is that the texts have proved so baffling because they have been read with the expectation that a ninth- or tenth-century law-code would be like one of the twelfth or nineteenth. Codes must instead be approached as artefacts of their own time. That means so far as possible examining them through the eyes of their own time. The method adopted here is to proceed from the most external to the most internal evidence. Chapter 3 asks what would be known of English law-making from historians and law-reports if *no* law-codes were extant. Chapter 4 then enquires what can be learned of the perception and application of legislation from the manuscripts wherein it survives. Next, chapter 5 analyses the codes themselves, in as close as possible to chronological order. That, however, is not the end of the story, because Anglo-Saxon law-codes leave many puzzles as regards their transmission, arrangement, modes of address, and coverage. One has an impression of materials hard at work, yet not doing the job one would expect them to. Chapter 6, therefore, the last in Volume I before a summary of its findings, considers the rationale they might have as manifestos of the new political society, the English kingdom, brought so recently into being. Progress is thus through successive layers of the evidence's materialization: its context in space and time; its appearance as reported by observers, then as reproduced by scribes; its behaviour, oddities and all, as text; and its possible core in the quasi-ideological tenets of its compilers. The premium is on digesting the evidence as it stands rather than flavouring it into something more palatable to modern taste. In Parts III and IV speculation will have a freer rein. In this volume it is limited to whatever seems to make the material *inherently* intelligible. Nor will it form steps in a staircase of conjecture. No stage in the argument should be found to rest gingerly on rickety conclusions reached at a prior stage.

To anticipate chapter 7's conclusions here is a temptation that cannot be resisted. In sum, just as historians never saw the signs of government power in Anglo-Saxon legislation because they were looking for something else, so the reason why they have not found easily recognizable law-making in early English codes is that law was not only, and perhaps not mainly, made that way. Old English legislation came from before the time when law in northern Europe was *ever* systematically expounded or preserved. Hence, the pivotal paradox of this whole project. Because the legislation of kings from Alfred to Cnut was never going to give the full picture of their law-making, it becomes possible to divine an accelerating ambition and activity that legislative texts could not reveal if left alone to do so. The long struggle through the arid tracts of codicology and textual analysis in this volume will make way for a Volume II on 'Doctrines', due in no more than a year, where the eye will be at liberty to range more widely, and so pick up what can look like green shoots of the Common Law. A volume on the 'making of law' in the literal sense from Alfred to the twelfth century will make way for one arguing that it was these centuries that saw 'The Making' of the Law of England.

For all that, some aspects of the subject are barely addressed in this volume. They include what might be called the 'constitutional' rights and wrongs of the law-making process, the question of who was entitled to make law and how; and the roots (if any) of Old English legal notions in practices or ideas shared by other peoples of Germanic – or even Indo-European – speech. These, as chapter 1 explains, are precisely the issues that have attracted most notice hitherto. Attention here focuses, to repeat, on what can be made of the extant texts as such, and how they were handled by their authors and audience. The related problem of the existence of any sort of class of specialists in legal matters is deferred until the Epilogue at the very end of Volume II, when it will be possible to examine the expertise of two successive and crucially different generations.

This book is long enough as it is; not only long but also, especially in 'core' chapters 4 and 5, very technical. If it were less technical it would be longer, and if it were shorter it would be more technical. As it is, some complexities have been hived off into papers, a collection of which will be published more or less simultaneously with this volume. The crucial preliminary definition is that *legislation* here means *written* law-making; 'law-making' on its own may mean that, but need not. King Alfred's *domboc* was legislation. But he probably made other law and in other ways. Further conventions are covered in the notes and bibliography. There is a very full range of reference to secondary literature, because the intention is to open up enquiry in a field where it has for so long been almost closed. That does not mean that I have always remembered to cite works that have advanced my understanding, and I apologize herewith to any who feel themselves unjustly overlooked. These pages also and properly contain a lot of translated text. Renditions are my own, but I have kept close to the hold of Dorothy Whitelock's splendid *English Historical Documents* whenever it was on offer. When I have let go, that was in the cause of inserting into the text as little meaning not already patent there as modern English usage would abide. In the same connection, I have had unstinted guidance from the skills of the lamented Chris Fell, Malcolm Godden and (at very short notice) Eric Stanley; since, however, I have not *always* taken their advice, they should not answer for infelicities that remain.

The Making of English Law has been an altogether unwarrantably long time in coming, so acquiring an ever-expanding list of credits. Liebermann was never distracted by the other pressures of academic life. I have been correspondingly fortunate in the patronage of four distinctive and distinguished institutions. All Souls College Oxford made me a Prize Fellow, and its special commitment to the study of History and Law perhaps set me on the path toward writing this book. As I scurried under the gaze of Blackstone's statue and Holdsworth's portrait, I fancied I could hear mutters about whatever the whipper-snapper would think up next. On the other hand, David Daube and Tony Honoré fostered my youthful heresies long before I ever read in Maitland's inaugural that 'orthodox history' is 'a contradiction in terms'. I particularly thank Norma Potter, who tirelessly fed my appetite for the gems in the Codrington collection. My first full employer was the University of Glasgow's Department of Medieval History. This department pioneered a scheme of sabbaticals when other disciplines were less lucky; the school of McKechnie, Sayles, Chrimes and Brown had its own illustrious record in the study of good old-fashioned 'constitutional history'; and anyone with the merest knowledge of this field will envy me that Michael Clanchy was in the room next door. The first draft of some chapters was written when I was in receipt of one of the British Academy's priceless Readerships in the Humanities. I owe them not just gratitude for what their award made feasible, but contrition for how long it took to fulfil what I promised more speedily. Finally, I have been able to finish this book as a Student of Christ Church Oxford, because its legendary largesse now extends as warmly to its hard-pressed tutors as it ever did to its grandest guests. I am indebted to all my colleagues, but especially wish to thank William Thomas, a Senior History Tutor whose forbearance was sorely tried but never witheld.

More people have answered queries, and even cast an eye over portions of text, than can possibly be thanked individually. But like so many early medievalists of my generation, I am hugely obliged to the inspiration of the late Michael Wallace-Hadrill, my first teacher in Anglo-Saxon history and supervisor of the (abortive) thesis with which this work began; to the genius of Peter Brown; to the disciplined vision of the late Karl Leyser; to the intellectual courage of James Campbell; latterly too to the enthusiastic support of Rees Davies. I have a more personal debt to Maurice Keen and Henry Mayr-Harting, one once my tutor the other now my colleague, both pre-eminently friends. Then, Malcolm Parkes and David Dumville shared their views with me when we were hammering out our respective lines on the idiosyncracies of the 'Parker' Chronicle and Laws. Ray Page, Milly Budny, Tim Graham, Patricia Stirnemann and Father Leonard Boyle eased my access to manuscripts in their care. Hubert Mordek generously kept me abreast of his own work and that of his pupils, as did Rosamond McKitterick. Stephen Baxter made an indispensable contribution to the bibliographical index. Wendy Davies' 'Bucknell Group' was a fount of ideas and a foil to my conceptual and stylistic extravagances. Five people read all or much of this book, sometimes more than once. That Nicholas Brooks, David Ganz, Simon Keynes, Jinty Nelson and Chris Wickham are great scholars as well as discriminating judges of what books like this may and may not say has enabled me to avoid countless errors, ignorances and obscurities; and their faith in the project down all its years has given me confidence to persevere. An obligation of a related kind is owed to John Davey and Tessa Harvey; Blackwell Publishers have hardly fewer letters promising the 'forthcoming' completion of this book than there are undertakings to the same effect in the footnotes of my articles; but they never ceased to believe that they would receive it, nor to wish that one day they should. Lastly, a modern scholar's home can rarely be as placid as the image that phrase conjures up. Mine, doubly a scholar's home inasmuch as it was shared by another of great distinction (who read an unfair share of drafts as crude as the technology that churned them out), suffered more than its due of creative tension. This was endured by my family with bottomless patience and affection. The result can only be dedicated to them.

Patrick Wormald
Christ Church, Oxford
Easter 1998

Abbreviations

Order is primarily alphabetical and secondarily that of an Abbreviation's following or next distinguishable letter, *whether or not acronymic*; i.e. CCSL (Corpus Christianorum) precedes CDL (Codice Diplomatico Longobardo), *DB* (*Domesday Book*) precedes *Dec. Ch.* (*Decretio Childeberti*), etc.

Ab. Ch.	*Charters of Abingdon*, ed. Kelly.	*Bede, Hist. Eccl.*	*Bede's Ecclesiastical History*, ed. Colgrave and Mynors.
Abt	Laws of Æthelberht, ed. *Gesetze.*	*BIHR*	*Bulletin of the Institute of Historical Research*
Af	Laws of Alfred, ed. *Gesetze.*	*BJRL*	*Bulletin of the John Rylands Library.*
AGu	Alfred's Treaty with Guthrum, ed. *Gesetze.*	*Blas.*	*Be Blaserum*, ed. *Gesetze.*
ANS	[*Proceedings of the Battle Conference on Anglo-Norman Studies* I–IV (1978-81), edited by R.A. Brown;] *Anglo-Norman Studies* V– (1983-).	*BNJ*	*British Numismatic Journal.*
		Burt. Ch.	*Charters of Burton*, ed. Sawyer.
		Can. Eg.	*Wulfstan's Canons of Edgar*, ed. Fowler.
Ans.	*Collectio Capitularium Ansegisi/Kapitularien-sammlung des Angsegis*, ed. Schmitz.	*Cap.*	*Capitularia Regum Francorum*, ed. Boretius and Krause.
App. AGu	'Appendix to the Alfred–Guthrum Treaty', ed. *Gesetze.*	CCCM	Corpus Christianorum Continuatio Medievalis (Turnhout).
Arch. Dip.	*Archiv für Diplomatik.*	CCSL	Corpus Christianorum Series Latina (Turnhout).
Arch. SNSL	*Archiv für das Studium der neueren Sprachen und Litteraturen.*	CDL	*Codice Diplomatico Longobardo* I–V, ed. Schiaparelli, Brühl, Zielinski.
ASC	'Anglo-Saxon Chronicle'.		
ASE	*Anglo-Saxon England.*	CHn cor	Coronation Charter of Henry I, ed. *Gesetze.*
[I–VI] As	Laws of Æthelstan, ed. *Gesetze.*		
[+ As Alm]		*ChLA*	*Chartae Latini Antiquiores*, ed. Brückner *et al.*
[I–X] Atr	Laws of Æthelred, ed. *Gesetze.*		
Að,	ed. *Gesetze*	*Chron. Ram.*	*Chronicon Abbatiae Rameseiensis*, ed. Macray.
BCS	*Cartularium Saxonicum*, ed. Birch.	*CLA*	*Codices Latini Antiquiores*, ed. Lowe.
Becwæð	*Hit Becwæð*, ed. *Gesetze.*	[I–II] Cn	Laws of Cnut, ed. *Gesetze.*

Cn 1018	Kennedy (ed.), 'Cnut's law code of 1018'.		*Documents I*, ed. Whitelock.
Cn 1020	Cnut's Letter to England (1020), ed. *Gesetze*.	EHD II	*English Historical Documents II*, ed. Douglas.
Cn 1027	Cnut's Letter to England (1027), ed. *Gesetze*.	EHR	*English Historical Review*.
Cod. Iust.	*Codex Iustinianus*, see *Corp. Iur*.	[I–III] Em	Laws of Edmund, ed. *Gesetze*.
Cod. Theod.	*[Codicis] Theodosiani*, ed. Mommsen, etc.	EME	*Early Medieval Europe*.
Coll. Can. Hib.	*Collectio Canonum Hibernensis = Irische Kanonensammlung*, ed. Wasserschleben.	EMH	Wallace-Hadrill, *Early Medieval History*.
		EMK	Sawyer and Wood (eds), *Early Medieval Kingship*.
Concil.	*Concilia Aevi Karolini*.	Episc.	*Episcopus*, ed. *Gesetze*.
'Conf.'	Fowler (ed.), 'Late Old English Handbook for use of a Confessor'	Epist. Bede ad Ecgb.	Epistola Bede ad Ecgbertum Episcopum, *Baedae Opera*, ed. Plummer.
Cons. Cn	*Consiliatio Cnuti*, ed. *Gesetze*.	[I–II] Ew	Laws of Edward the Elder, ed. *Gesetze*.
Corp. Iur.	*Corpus Iuris Civilis*, ed. Mommsen, etc.	Exc. Can.	'Excerptiones de Canonibus', i.e. 'Excerptiones Ecgberhti', in
CP	Maitland, *Collected Papers*, ed. Fisher.		*Ancient Laws*, ed. Thorpe; or in Aronstam, 'Latin Canonical Tradition'.
Crawf. Coll.	*Crawford Collection of Early Charters*, ed. Napier and Stevenson.	Excom.	*Excommunicationes*, ed. *Gesetze*.
DA	*Deutsches Archiv für die Erforschung des Mittelalters*.	FMS	*Frühmittelalterliche Studien*.
		Formul.	*Formulae Merowingici et Karolini Aevi*, ed. Zeumer.
DB	*Domesday Book*, ed. Farley, etc.	Forf.	*Forfang*, ed. *Gesetze*.
DBB	Maitland, *Domesday Book and Beyond*.	Ger.	*Gerefa*, ed. *Gesetze*.
		Gesetze	*Die Gesetze der Angelsachsen*, ed. Liebermann.
Dec. Ch.	*Decretio Childeberti*, ed. Eckhardt, *Lex Sal*.		
DHII	*Heinrici II et Arduini Diplomata*, ed. Breßlau.	Gebyn.	*Gebyncðu*, ed. *Gesetze*.
Dig.	*Digesta*, see *Corp. Iur*.	Glanvill	*Treatise commonly called Glanvill*, ed. Hall.
Disputes	Davies and Fouracre (eds), *Settlement of Disputes*.	Grið, H[no.]	ed. *Gesetze*. Hübner, 'Gerichtsurkunden': see *III MODERN COMMENTARY s.n.*
Duns.	*Dunsæte*, ed. *Gesetze*.		
ECf	'Leges Edwardi Confessoris', ed. *Gesetze*.	Had.	*Hadbot*, ed. *Gesetze*.
Ed. Ch.	*Edictum Chilperici*, ed. Eckhardt, *Lex Sal*.	HaSD	*Select English Historical Documents*, ed. Harmer.
Ed. Ro.	*Edictum Rothari*, ed. in *Leg. Lang*.	HaWr	*Anglo-Saxon Writs*, ed. Harmer.
EEMSF	Early English Manuscripts in Facsimile (Copenhagen).	Hist. Abb.	Bede, 'Historia Abbatum', *Baedae Opera*, ed. Plummer.
EETS	Early English Texts Society.	Hl	Laws of Hlothere and Eadric, ed. *Gesetze*.
[I–IV] Eg	Laws of Edgar, ed. *Gesetze*.		
EGu	'Peace of Edward and Guthrum', ed. *Gesetze*.	Hn	'Leges Henrici Primi', ed. *Gesetze*.
EHD I	*English Historical*		

Hn com	Henry I's writ on Courts, ed. *Gesetze*.
Hn Lond	Henry I's London Charter, ed. *Gesetze*.
Hom.	Homilies of Wulfstan, ed. Bethurum.
HomN	*Wulfstan, Sammlung Homilien*, ed. Napier.
Hu.	*Hundred*
HZ	*Historische Zeitschrift*.
Ine	Laws of Ine, ed. *Gesetze*.
Inst. Cn	*Instituta Cnuti*, ed. *Gesetze*.
Inst. Pol.	*Die 'Institutes of Polity'*, ed. Jost.
IRMAe	*Ius Romanum Medii Aevi*.
Iud. Dei	*Iudicia Dei*, ed. *Gesetze*.
Iudex,	ed. *Gesetze*.
JEGP	*Journal of English and Germanic Philology*.
JEH	*Journal of Ecclesiastical History*.
JThS	*Journal of Theological Studies*.
JW	*Chronicle of John of Worcester*, ed. Darlington and McGurk.
KCD	*Codex Diplomaticus*, ed. Kemble.
La Giustizia I	*Sett. Spol.* XLII (1995).
La Giustizia II	*Sett. Spol.* XLIV (1997).
Laws (At)	*Laws of the Earliest English Kings*, ed. and tr. Attenborough.
Laws (Ro)	*Laws of the Kings of England from Edmund*, ed. and tr. Robertson.
Leg. Alam.	*Leges Alamannorum*, ed. Lehmann/Eckhardt.
Leg. Burg.	*Leges Burgundionum*, ed. de Salis.
Leg. Lang.	*Leges Langobardorum*, ed. Bluhme (with Boretius).
Leg. Liutpr.	*Leges Liutprandi*, ed. in *Leg. Lang*.
Leg. Rat.	*Leges Ratchis*, ed. in *Leg. Lang*.
Leg. Vis.	*Leges Visigothorum*, ed. Zeumer.
Leis Wl	'Leis Willelme', ed. *Gesetze*.
Lex Bai.	*Lex Baiwariorum*, ed. de Schwind.
Lex Fris.	*Lex Frisionum*, ed. Eckhardt and Eckhardt.
Lex Rib.	*Lex Ribuaria*, ed. Beyerle and Buchner.
Lex Sal.	*Pactus Legis Salicae, Lex Salica*, ed. Eckhardt (MGH).
Lex Sax.	*Lex Saxonum*, in *Gesetze des Karolingerreiches* III, ed. Eckhardt.
Lex Thur.	*Lex Thuringorum (Angliorum et Werinorum)*, in *Gesetze des Karolingerreiches* III.
Lib. Æth.	*Anglo-Saxon Ely*, ed. Keynes and Kennedy.
Lib. El.	*Liber Eliensis*, ed. Blake.
LQR	*Law Quarterly Review*.
LRV	*Lex Romana Visigothorum (Breviarium Alarici)*, ed Hänel.
LS	Wormald, 'Handlist of Anglo-Saxon Lawsuits': see *III MODERN COMMENTARY s.n.*, and 'Summary Concordance' in Subsidiary Source Index (i)
Med. Arch.	*Medieval Archaeology*.
Med. Stud.	*Medieval Studies*.
MGH	Monumenta Germaniae Historica (Hannover, unless stated otherwise).
Mirc.	*Mircna laga*, ed. *Gesetze*.
MÖIG	*Mitteilungen des österreichischen Instituts für Geschichtsforschung*.
Nor grið,	ed. *Gesetze*.
Norðl.	*Norðleoda laga*, ed. *Gesetze*.
Northu.	'Northumbrian Priests' Law', ed. *Gesetze*.
OEN	*Old English Newsletter*.
Ord.	*Ordal*, ed. *Gesetze*.
Pact.	*Pactus pro tenore pacis (regum Childeberti et Chlotharii)*, ed. Eckhardt, *Lex Sal*.
Pax	ed. *Gesetze*.
PBA	*Proceedings of the British Academy*.
Penit. Ps.Th.	*The Penitential of (pseudo-)Theodore*, in *Ancient Laws*, ed. Thorpe.
PL	*Patrologia Latina*.
PM	Pollock and Maitland, *History of English Law*.
PP	*Past and Present*.

Quad.	*Quadripartitus*, ed. Liebermann, *Englisches Rechtsbuch*, or *Gesetze*.
Rec. ChII	*Recueil des Actes de Charles II le chauve*, ed. Tessier *et al.*
Rec. Eud.	*Recueil des Actes d'Eudes roi de France*, ed. Tessier and Bautier.
Rec. LII	*Recueil des Actes de Louis II le Bègue, Louis III et Carloman*, ed. Bautier *et al.*
Rec. S. Ben.	*Recueil des Chartes de Saint-Benôit-sur-Loire*, ed. Prou and Vidier.
Rect.	*Rectitudines Singularum Personarum*, ed. *Gesetze*.
Reg. Conc.	*Regularis Concordia*, ed. and tr. Symons.
RoASCh	*Anglo-Saxon Charters*, ed. Robertson.
Roch. Ch.	*Charters of Rochester*, ed. Campbell.
Romscot	ed. *Gesetze*.
RRAN	*Regesta Regum Anglo-Normannorum*, ed. Davis *et al.*
RS	Rolls Series (London).
S	*Anglo-Saxon Charters*, ed. Sawyer.
S*	Sawyer's *Anglo-Saxon Charters*, revised Kelly and Keynes.
SE	Maitland, *Select Historical Essays*, ed. Cam.
Sels. Ch.	*Charters of Selsey*, ed. Kelly.
Sett. Spol.	*Settimane di Studio del Centro Italiano di Studi sull' alto Medioevo* (Spoleto).
Shaft. Ch.	*Charters of Shaftesbury*, ed. Kelly.
Sherb. Ch.	*Charters of Sherborne*, ed. O'Donovan.
Swer.	*Swerian*, ed. *Gesetze*.
TR	*Textus Roffensis*: see I MANUSCRIPTS: Rochester
TRHS	*Transactions of the Royal Historical Society*.
Urk. Arn.	*Urkunden Arnolfs*, ed. Kehr.
Urk. LoI, *Urk. LoII*	*Urkunden Lothars I und Lothars II*, ed. Schieffer.
Urk. LudII	*Urkunden Ludwigs II*, ed. Wanner.
Urk. Lud. dt.	*Urkunden Ludwigs des deutschen, etc.*, ed. Kehr.
Urk. Pipp., Karl.	*Urkunden Pippins, Karlmanns und Karl des Grossen*, ed. Mühlbacher.
Wal.	*Walreaf*, ed. *Gesetze*.
Wer.	*Wergeld*, ed. *Gesetze*.
WhW	*Anglo-Saxon Wills*, ed. Whitelock.
Wi	*Laws of Wihtræd*, ed. *Gesetze*.
Wif.	*Wifmannes Beweddung*, ed. *Gesetze*.
Wl art.	William I, 'Articles', ed. *Gesetze*.
Wl ep.	William I, 'Episcopales Leges', ed. *Gesetze*.
Wl lad	William I, 'On Exculpation', ed. *Gesetze*.
Wl Lond	William I, writ for London, ed. *Gesetze*.
ZSS	*Zeitschrift der Savigny Stiftung für Rechtsgeschichte*.

PART I

Preliminaries

CHAPTER 1

Prologue: Early English Law and the Historians

> I must confess that the study of the Anglo-Saxon laws often reduces me to a state of mental chaos. I may know, as a rule, the meaning of individual words; I can construe, though not invariably the separate sentences. But what it all comes to is often a total mystery.

Such was Charles Plummer's reflection when turning in his fine book on King Alfred to the king's law-code.[1] Several things about his comment are interesting. Plummer delivered the Oxford Ford lectures, the basis of his book, in the later part of 1901. By then, the chapter on Anglo-Saxon law in Pollock and Maitland's great *History of English Law* (Pollock's sole contribution of substance to the enterprise) had been available for six years. Since the second edition of 1898, it had been prefaced by 'The Dark Age in Legal History', a characteristic Maitland setting of the continental scene. Already in 1897, Maitland's *Domesday Book and Beyond* had brilliantly illuminated the world of pre-conquest justice, even if itself fighting shy of the Anglo-Saxon 'Dooms'. By 1901 too, the first fascicules of Liebermann's titanic *Gesetze der Angelsachsen* were to hand, though Volume I as a whole was published only in 1903.[2] This, then, should have been a time of new enlightenment in the interpretation of the earliest English law. For Plummer at least, it evidently was not.

Plummer was among the greatest of all students of early England. That he should admit defeat is a warning to lesser lights.[3] He was also an honest man. His difficulties in handling pre-conquest legislation have been widely shared, less often admitted. Discussion of Alfred's law-book is rarely among the high spots of the standard Alfredian biography (see chapter 5, pp. 284–5); it is sometimes

1   Plummer, *Life and Times of Alfred*, p. 122.
2   PM I, pp. 25–63 (1st edn, 1–40), 1–24; *DBB*, p. 226 (see below, pp. 16–17: Maitland shared Plummer's hesitancy and may indeed have influenced it). On the publication history of *History of English Law*, see Hudson, 'Maitland and Anglo-Norman Law', pp. 27–32; and for Pollock's role, my own 'Maitland and Anglo-Saxon Law', pp. 2–4. Liebermann's first fascicules came out in 1898–9, though their original scope is now concealed by the binding of the 1903 Vol. I. See further below, pp. 15–16, 21–3.
3   He was to spend the last part of his life performing signal service to the elucidation of early Irish law, a far more rebarbative *corpus* than the Anglo-Saxon: Binchy, 'Linguistic and Historical Value of the Irish Law Tracts', p. 199.

omitted altogether. But dubiety has not on the whole been a salient quality of approaches to Anglo-Saxon legal materials. Maitland was reacting to the complacent nostrums of the Common Lawyers among whom he began his career, and so utterly demolished the claims of any current institution to remote antiquity that scholars largely stopped looking before 1066 for what mattered in English legal history. Liebermann, for his part, cast the memorials of Anglo-Saxon justice in a cement mixed over three previous generations of remorseless German-language reconstruction of 'Germanic' law. The effect was not only to discourage anything more than tinkering with the structure; as often happens to concrete monuments, Anglo-Saxon law became part of an intellectual landscape rather than an object of studied contemplation in its own right. But before examining the new consensus fostered by Maitland and Liebermann, one should look more closely at the older certainties from which their work evolved.

1   Before Maitland

> The English jury has been so highly prized by Englishmen ... that its origin has been sought in many different directions. At the present day, however, there can be little doubt ... [that] ... we must look to the ... prerogative rights of the Frankish kings ... Such is now the prevailing opinion, and it has triumphed ... over the natural disinclination of Englishmen to admit that this "palladium of our liberties" is in its origin not English but Frankish, not popular but royal.

Maitland's pithy sentences were the formative moment in modern study of Anglo-Saxon law.[4] Their significance was that the jury had till then epitomized what Englishmen had done for themselves to protect their freedoms from innovating and foreign or foreign-influenced despots. To show that this cynosure of legal liberty was itself introduced by conquering French-speakers was to undermine the whole tradition that took Common Law back into the mists of pre-conquest time. Maitland was baiting his legally learned but historically illiterate ex-colleagues at the Bar. So whom did he have in mind when disabusing Englishmen of notions about 'this "palladium of [their] liberties"'?

The answer, predictably, is Blackstone. The great eighteenth-century jurist had concluded his *Commentaries*, the Bible of the Common Law, with an account of the 'Rise, Progress, and gradual Improvements, of the Laws of England'.[5] The path of ineluctible progress heralded by this chapter's title had been rudely interrupted by the Norman Conquest; so 'eclipsed' indeed was 'English liberty' that its 'complete restitution' came only with the Restoration of Charles II.[6] As to the

---

4   PM I, pp. 140–2.

5   I cite the reprint of the first (1765–9) edition, ed. Katz *et al.*, where the historical 'Account' is Vol. IV, pp. 400–36. For this and a lot that follows I have been lucky to have pre-publication access to Professor Stanley's learned and amusing 'Angelsächsische Rechtspflege'; see too his 'Glorification of Alfred', and 'Trial by Jury'.

6   *Blackstone, Commentaries* IV, p. 431; cf. his 'peroration', p. 435. What he had in mind were the removal under Charles of the last 'slaveries' of 'the feudal system' (i.e. 'military tenures'), and the Act of *Habeas Corpus*, which completed the work of restoring English liberties that was only begun by *Magna Carta* itself (pp. 416–17).

jury, he was in no doubt that 'the general constitution of this admirable criterion of truth, and most important guardian both of public and private liberty, we owe to our Saxon ancestors'; and he thought that, in contrast to the position in 'France or Turkey', 'the liberties of England cannot but subsist, so long as this *palladium* remains sacred and inviolate'.[7] Blackstone evidently had some direct knowledge of the sources for Anglo-Saxon law. He was not ready to credit the devising of trial by jury to Alfred personally, as others were.[8] But it was Alfred's achievement:

> to new-model the constitution ... This he effected by reducing the whole kingdom under one regular and gradual subordination of government wherein each man was answerable to his immediate superior for his own conduct and that of his nearest neighbours; for to him we owe that masterpiece of judicial polity, the subdivision of England into tithings, and hundreds, if not into counties ... which wise institution has been preserved for near a thousand years unchanged ... He also, like another Theodosius, collected the various customs that he found dispersed in his kingdom, and reduced and digested them into one uniform system or code of laws, in his **dombec**, or *liber judicialis*. This he compiled for the use of the ... tribunals which he established, for the trial of all causes civil and criminal, in the very districts wherein the complaint arose: all of them subject however to be inspected, controlled and kept within the bounds of the universal or common law, by the king's own courts ... [9]

Much later in this book, it will appear that Blackstone's belief in the Alfredian origin of tithing responsibilities had more substance than Maitland or any historian of his or later times have been ready to allow (chapter 9). The point for now is that Alfred's laws were given a central role in the establishment of constitutional law which was already recognizably that expounded by Blackstone himself. If Edward I was 'our English Justinian', Alfred played the role of his Theodosian harbinger, in consolidating a legal system as ancient and illustrious as Rome's (chapter 2, pp. 36–7).[10]

In various ways, Blackstone followed the lead of Sir Matthew Hale, Common Law's first diachronic historian.[11] Hale, however, devoted many pages of a short book to showing that, legally speaking, the Norman Conquest had been no Conquest at all.[12] Crucial to his case were not merely jurisprudential lines of argument but also what passed for historical evidence.[13] An extant code under the title 'Laws of Edward the Confessor' recorded that William had ascertained and

---

7 *Commentaries* IV, pp. 407, 343.
8 He cited III Atr 3:1, the critical pre-conquest evidence (below, pp. 17–18), from Wilkins's edition (below, pp. 21–2): *Commentaries* III, pp. 349–50; continuing: 'we are apt to impute the invention of this, and some other pieces of juridical polity, to the superior genius of Alfred the Great, to whom, on account of his having done much, it is usual to attribute everything'.
9 *Commentaries* IV, p. 404.
10 *Commentaries* IV, pp. 405–7, gives an account of the legal institutions already in place by 1066: they of course include parliament. See p. 418 for Edward as 'our English Justinian'; the conceit was already familiar to Lambarde, *Archion*, p. 67.
11 Posthumously published in 1713; I cite Gray's 1971 edition.
12 *Hale, History*, pp. 47–71; the next chapter goes on to argue that the 'Similitude of the Laws of both Countries did in greater Measure arise from (Norman) Imitation of our Laws, rather than from our Imitation of theirs' (p. 81).
13 *Hale, History*, pp. 61–4, 68–9.

confirmed these on the basis of depositions by twelve sworn men from each county. Meanwhile, a short text put into circulation by Sir Henry Spelman told how Edwin, a Dane who had come to England with Cnut, vindicated his title to the Norfolk estates of which he had been dispossessed in favour of William d' Aubigny and William de Warenne, by proving that he had never fought against the Conqueror; the result was another Inquest 'throughout England', the outcome of which was that all those who had not supported Harold were confirmed in their possessions and were henceforward to have the title of 'drengs'. Neither episode was historical. The 'Laws of Edward' was a twelfth-century tract (not under that title) which provided a fictive historical prologue and epilogue to what is otherwise a reasoned statement of twelfth-century law.[14] The case of 'Edwin of Sharnborn' was apparently a local tradition which Spelman wrote up out of Norfolk *pietas*.[15] But faith in them was very widely shared in the seventeenth century.

Blackstone and Hale were both in fact drawing on the powerful polemical current that had made the antiquity of English law a central issue in the politics of Stuart England.[16] There is no need to rehearse here that very well-told tale. The main point is the inspiration derived by the king's opponents from the conviction that English law was rooted in an immemorial and more specifically Anglo-Saxon past. That view was not confined to lawyers. Foxe's *Acts and Monuments* had supposed that Edward the Confessor fused the 'divers laws ... in divers countries of this realm' into 'one universal and common law for all people through the whole realm, called King Edward's laws'; which 'the Conqueror, at his coming in, did swear to use and practise ... for the common laws of the realm'; though 'afterwards being established ... , he foreswore himself, and placed his own laws in their room, much worse and obscurer than the others were'.[17] But Common lawyers were foremost in arguing the venerability of English law, because even those of royalist convictions needed to put their speciality beyond the reach of Stuart, as of Norman, kings.

The case was already argued in the fifteenth century by Fortescue, and earlier still by the *Mirror of Justices*, a tendentious tract incorporated in an important early-fourteenth-century collection of Old English law.[18] William Lambarde, first

---

14   ECf Pr. – Pr.:1, 34 – 35:2; on this text, see chapter 5, pp. 409–11.

15   Spelman, *Glossarium*, p. 184, *s.v.* 'Drenches, Drengus'; 'Historia Familiae de Sharnburn', in *Reliquiae Spelmannianae*, ed. Gibson, pp. 189–90 (the story survived to become no. 1 in Bigelow's *Placita Anglo-Normannica*). Spelman claimed to have taken his material on the Sharnborn family 'ex veteri MS'; however that may be, there is no Domesday record of William of Warenne's giving up land to its pre-1066 tenant at Shernborne or elsewhere in Norfolk (but cf. *DB* ii 133a, 162a, 166a, 172b, 276b, *Norfolk* 1:195, 8:36,71,138, 66:64, etc.) – though, oddly enough, Ælmer, a Bedford burgess, recovered his father's property at Sharnbrook through a writ of King William: *DB* i 218b, *Bedfordshire* 56:6. I have learned much about the story's seventeenth-century exploitation from Greenberg and Marin, 'Politics and Memory: Sharnborn's case'; and for the more general issue, cf. also Greenberg, 'The Confessor's Laws'.

16   Classic discussions are Pocock, *Ancient Constitution*, especially chapters II – III, VII – IX; and Hill, 'Norman Yoke', especially pp. 57–93.

17   *Acts and Monuments of John Foxe* II, pp. 89–90. Blackstone himself saw the introduction of the 'chicaneries and subtilties of Norman jurisprudence' as another of the Conquest's adverse consequences: *Commentaries* IV, p. 410.

18   *Fortescue, In Praise of the Laws of England* xvii, pp. 26–7; *Mirror of Justices* I ii–iii, pp. 6–8 (and

editor of the Anglo-Saxon laws, wrote in his *Archion* (1592) that 'truly the Normans ... did not so much alter the substance, as the name of the Saxons order'; the structure of County and lesser Courts, once again Alfred's creation, survived a period of disturbance at the Conquest to continue thereafter.[19] Old English 'Parliamentary' history was traced from Edwin of Northumbria (627) through the law-making *witan* of Anglo-Saxon kings to the Conquest and after.[20] Two luminaries of the early-seventeenth-century conflict possessed Old English legal manuscripts: Sir Edward Coke, a pocket copy of *Quadripartitus*, the early-twelfth-century translation of Anglo-Saxon laws into Latin; and John Selden, vernacular copies of Edgar's and Cnut's codes, which he gave to Simonds D'Ewes (chapter 4, pp. 185–6, 253). Spelman was another editor, printing in his *Concilia* the first extracts of early Kentish law from *Textus Roffensis* (chapter 4, pp. 244–53). He probably did more than anyone to give respectability to the proposition that King Alfred had introduced Trial by Jury, perpetuated as this was in the *Life of Alfred* by his royalist son, John.[21] At this stage, then, remoter legal history was more than an intellectual interest. It was part of an ideological battle which lawyers felt they had to win.

Even at this stage, however, the lawyerly construction on the past was not the only one. The remarkable Samuel Daniel was a poet patronized by James I's Queen Anne of Denmark, to whom he dedicated his *Collection of the History of England*. He too was persuaded of Alfred's role in the organization of Shires, Hundreds and Tithings, but he made much less than did lawyers of the contribution of Alfred's council to his legislation. Predictably, given the identity of his patron, he awarded Cnut an equally positive appraisal; his law-code is represented as an act of constructive royal benevolence.[22] William I was found to have been no conqueror in spirit; the Sharnborn saga was recycled; and the king was said to have been prevailed upon to order his judges to observe the 'Lawes of Saint Edward'. But there was no word of his empanelling twelve jurors per shire to ascertain what these were. The object of the exercise was rather:

> to acquit the people with a show of the continuation of their ancient customs and liberties than that they enjoyed them in effect ... And though there might be some veins issuing from former originals, yet the main stream of our Common Law ... flowed out of Normandy. For before ... there was no universal law of the kingdom, but every several Province held their own customs ... By these passages we see ...

---

cf. IV xviii, p. 143, V 108, pp. 166–71, where most of the forty-four unjust judges hanged by Alfred are given more or less plausibly Anglo-Saxon names); for its copying if not composition by Andrew Horn, and for his legal collection (chapter 4, pp. 237–8), see Catto, 'Andrew Horn', pp. 373–4.

19 Lambarde, *Archion*, pp. 9, 15, 21; cf. the citation of III Eg 2 – 2:1 on the right of appeal to the king's person, pp. 115–16.

20 *Archion*, pp. 239–40 (with some appalling mistranscriptions of Old English lettering). Robert Talbot, one of the first Tudor collectors of Old English materials, glossed his copy of V Atr (1008), 'An act of parlament as ytt were': BL. Cotton MS Nero A.i, f. 89r; *Wulfstan Manuscript*, ed. Loyn, p. 40.

21 Spelman, *Glossarium, s.v.* 'Jurata', p. 328: he cautiously noted that judgement of twelve was older than Henry II but rare before his time, citing the crucial III Atr passage and of course ECf Pr (above, nn. 8, 14), but also more questionably AGu 3, which speaks only of 'oath-helpers' (chapter 9). (J.) Spelman, *Ælfredi Vita* ii 13, pp. 71–2 (English edn, ii 15, p. 106); this was for 175 years the standard life of the king (Stanley, 'Glorification', pp. 412–13).

22 Daniel, *Collection of the History of England*, pp. 12–13, 19–21.

the furthest end we can discover of the original of our Common Law, and to strive to look beyond this is to look into an uncertain Vastness beyond our discerning. Nor can it detract from the glory of good Customs, if they bring but a pedigree of 600 years to approve their gentility, seeing that it is the equity, not the Antiquity of laws that makes them venerable.[23]

Judgement of 'actions both criminal and real ... by the verdict of twelve men' was itself 'according to the custom of Normandy, where the like form is ... called by the name of Inquest'; the 'twelve senior thegns' required by Æthelred's Wantage code (?997) to denounce malefactors under oath were deemed irrelevant. The one significant native element was the system for keeping the peace, which Daniel called the 'Borough law', and by which he evidently meant the system of tithing surety (or 'borh') later known as 'Frankpledge' (chapter 9). This formed 'so strong a chain to hold the whole frame of the State together in peace and order as all the most politic regiments on earth cannot show us a straiter form of combination'. Thus, the major legacy of pre-conquest law was a system which Daniel very reasonably thought might explain how easily the Anglo-Saxons were conquered.[24] Fifty years later, the Tory Robert Brady, in a history dedicated to the new King James II, launched an all-out assault on the apparatus of legal traditionalism. There is no word of Alfred and the Jury; Æthelred's twelve were no such thing. 'Trial by ... the oaths of twelve good lawful men of the neighbourhood ... seems to have been introduced, or at least brought into more frequent practice in the time of King Henry II'.[25] 'The bulk and main of our Laws ... were brought hither from Normandy'. The 'pretended Plea of Sharnburn' was 'fabulous'. The 'Laws of Edward' were not traditional, but bore the feudal imprint of the conquerors.[26]

Daniel in the 1620s and Brady in the 1680s had got close to the view of the Conquest's legal effects that would be taken in modern times.[27] Norman law was feudal and was imposed upon the English. Their own legal inheritance was neither here nor there. The demonstration (going back to Spelman) of the Conquest's 'feudal' innovations may underlie Blackstone's picture of an English law recovering down the ages from consequences of 1066 that Hale had in effect denied. But in the short term, seventeenth-century orthodoxy was reasserted. Rapin de Thoyras, a Huguenot exile who fought at the Boyne, dedicated a ten volume *Histoire d' Angleterre* to George I, which was as influential in its time as it is now unknown. He was confident of Alfred's responsibility for the jury as well as for shires, hundreds and tithings – though as reformer of pre-existent local

---

23   Daniel, *Collection*, pp. 37, 39, 43.
24   Daniel, *Collection*, pp. 45–6; his account is taken mostly from ECf 20 – 20:3. Professor John Gillingham kindly drew my attention to this striking thesis.
25   Brady, *Complete History*, pp. 76, 78, 116–17.
26   Brady, *History*, pp. 143, 147, 155, 180–4; in his introduction (p. xxx), Brady (taking Spelman's hint, *Glossarium, s.v.* 'balivus', p. 57) became the first to declare that 'those laws put forward under [Edward's] name were none of his, they are an incoherent farce and mixture, and a heap of nonsense put together by some unskilful bishop, monk or clerk many years after his death'. See Pocock, *Ancient Constitution*, pp. 196–206; O'Brien, *God's Peace*, pp. 123–6.
27   A possible effect of Brady's diatribe (if hardly of it alone) was the removal of the express reference to 'St Edward's Laws' from the 1689 Coronation Oath: Greenberg, 'Confessor's Laws', pp. 615, 634.

units, not their creator.[28] William was again no conqueror, was again induced to respect the Law of 'son Bienfaicteur' (Edward). When the Normans discovered its beneficial import, they too rallied to Edward's Law as underwritten by Henry I's Coronation Charter, so procuring Magna Carta.[29] David Hume's position on Anglo-Saxon law was not dissimilar, though he took a more positive (and cynical) view of the contributions of the Conqueror, Henry I and Henry II.[30] But a more important feature of his work was the rising tide of the Enlightenment in his native Scotland. In so far as it encouraged attention to the savagery (albeit streaked with nobility) of barbarian culture, it of course reduced the relevance of the law of remote eras to a civilized present. The effect is more clearly seen in Burke's 'Abridgement of English history'. There was no question of an Alfredian or even Anglo-Saxon jury. Above all, 'what a visionary nature those systems are, which would settle the ancient constitution in the most remote times exactly in the same form in which we enjoy it at this day; not considering that such mighty changes in manners, during so many ages, always must produce a considerable change in laws'.[31] The classical Whig theory of progress was at odds with the notions of ancestral freedom that gave Whiggery birth. Yet in Burke's time and after, the antiquity of the Constitution remained a cause beloved of political radicals as well as professional lawyers. Turner's generally reputable though sentimental *History of the Anglo-Saxons* (1799–1805) defended the Alfredian jury with reference to the *Mirror of Justices*, Coke and Spelman, while inclined to think this and others institutions 'of progressive growth' from early roots.[32]

The paradigm began to shift, at times in unexpected directions, during the post-Napoleonic era. An easy mistake for a professional historian writing from the perspective of the late-twentieth century is to underrate the learning of leisured amateurs in the first half of the nineteenth. Outstanding works of this period were Hallam's *View of the State of Europe during the Middle Ages*, Allen's *Inquiry into the Rise and Growth of the Royal Prerogative in England*, and Palgrave's

28   Rapin de Thoyras, *Histoire d' Angleterre* I, pp. 316, 486–8 (this work was at once translated by Nicholas Tindal and much reprinted).
29   Rapin de Thoyras, *Histoire* II, pp. 16, 46, 82, 223–4, 327–9. Rapin's case was that Anglo-Saxon law was like barbarian law in general, which everywhere in Europe displaced the Roman system with one where monarchy was in origin marginal and elective: *Histoire* I, pp. 475–8; but (with an eye to another newly arrived foreign sovereign) only the providence of God would explain the unparalleled ease of a conquest that ensured England's 'rise to grandeur and glory'.
30   Hume, *History of England* I, pp. 98–101, 217–24, 233–5, 261, 270–1, 275–9, 309–12, 344–6, 380, 492–6, 509–10. It should be noted that Hume (I, pp. 101–2) was among a number of seventeenth- and eighteenth-century historians who followed Spelman, *Ælfredi Vita* ii 2–36, pp. 63–89, in supposing that Alfred's *real* laws must be lost, in that the law-making described by William of Malmesbury (chapter 3, pp. 137–40), and to which later ages attached such importance, did not and could not correspond to the king's extant code – which itself is a deduction of some significance (chapter 5, pp. 280–5).
31   Burke, 'Abridgement', pp. 260, 294–5, and cf. pp. 311, 325. The fragment of 'an Essay towards a history of the laws of England' that concludes the 'Abridgement' itself breaks off at 1066, but is notably more critical (pp. 413–15) of 'the persuasion hardly to be eradicated from the minds of our lawyers, that the English law has continued very much in the same state from an antiquity to which they will allow hardly any bounds', than of the 'very absurd consequence drawn from the Norman Conquest', that 'all our national rights and liberties ... have arisen from the grants, and [are] therefore to be revocable at the will, of the sovereign'.
32   Turner, *History of the Anglo-Saxons* I, pp. 328–30 (with hesitant reference to Alfred's law-book, cf. n. 30); II, pp. 258–62, 270–5.

Rise and Progress of the English Commonwealth. All of them knew the primary evidence to modern enough standards to be able to distinguish what Old English law actually said about *witan*, shire or jury from what it was supposed to have said, and were unembarrassed by the 'Laws of Edward the Confessor'; though the first and third remained impressed by Frankpledge.[33] All were equally *au fait* with the evidence from continental Europe and were not afraid to draw constructive analogies with it. Hallam and Palgrave made a clearer case than any yet for Henry II's importance in English legal history.[34] None, however, deserted the faith that there was something fundamentally populist about Old English institutions; hence that, however transformed by Norman and Angevin initiatives, they had a basic role in the preservation/evolution of English freedoms.[35] The greatest though nowadays least honoured of the three was Palgrave. After a century and three quarters, his remains the only monograph solely devoted to Old English law and government. His argument was vitiated by wilful refusal to observe a chronological or almost any other perceptible plan. His views are often eccentric (though his notorious conviction that much about early England had Romano-Celtic or common Northern roots looks less absurd in the light of some modern views of the *Adventus Saxonum* than it once did). But his crucial virtue was that he was not put off by the inevitable holes in the legal evidence. 'Being regulations adapted to existing institutions', he wrote, 'the Anglo-Saxon statutes are concise and technical, alluding to the law ... rather than defining it ... Consequently, the appearance of a law, seemingly for the first time, is by no means ... proof that the matter which it contains is new.'[36] The value of this assessment, the greater for the fact that the missing material is *not* equated with a mass of rooted Custom, will be repeatedly underlined throughout this volume.[37]

It is important to realize how far historians had got before Maitland. A salutary reminder of how much remained to be done is the only previous formal 'History of English Law'. Reeves's book, published in 1787, was not an analytical history at all, but a descriptive account of institutions and processes which was both numbingly dull and utterly at sea with pre-conquest texts.[38] Its digestibility was far from aided by Finlayson's reissue of 1869, which as good as doubled its length by notes denouncing its 'errors' – among them that Reeves had wrongly doubted the substantial authenticity of the *Mirror of Justices* as well as the 'Laws of Edward the Confessor', and that he had failed to see that the bulk of unwritten

---

33   Thus, Hallam, *State of Europe* (1st edn) II, pp. 136–51, 160–9, 175–6 (11th edn) II, pp. 377–9, 384–9, 403–4; Allen, *Royal Prerogative*, pp. 65, 88–9; Palgrave, *English Comonwealth* I, pp. 46–8, 54–7, 96–137, 191–204, 213–18, 231–3, 239–63.
34   Hallam (1st edn) II, pp. 190–4 (admitting significant debts here and elsewhere to learning made available a century before by Hickes and Madox), 11th edn II, pp. 387–9, 403–4; Palgrave I, pp. 241–3.
35   Hallam (1st edn) II, pp. 201–3 (11th edn) II, pp. 367–8, 404; Allen, pp. 7–8, 156–9; Palgrave, pp. 3–6, 243, 276–7.
36   Palgrave, p. 58. His remarks on the difficulties of translation are also *à point* (cf. above, p. xiii).
37   A comparable scholar of the next generation was the astonishing E.W. Robertson, whose learning was yet greater, as its presentation was still less penetrable, than Palgrave's; I am indebted to an unpublished paper by James Campbell for a literally indispensable guide around his work. He had less to say about law as such, but his view of the making of the classical English shire, *Essays*, pp. 112–30, comes closest to that taken in chapter 10.
38   Reeves, *History* I, pp. 1–27, and cf, pp. 28–58.

early English law was of course Roman.[39] Still, one's main impression even from Reeves is of the degree to which English legal history was already launched on the path where Maitland would find it. In particular, it was far gone in the obsessive teleology that is the Original Sin of English historians, and whose inexorable corollary was that Anglo-Saxon law was the start of a long story with a happy ending. Whether immediately or only distantly relevant to a liberal present, it was primordial. Its aboriginal status was now to be reinforced from the direction taken by legal studies elsewhere.

It was in earlier-nineteenth-century Germany that Europe's post-Roman law first came under professional historical scrutiny. But the intellectual movement involved derived its unparalleled impact from the fact that its (relatively) scrupulous handling of evidence was infused with a deep faith in the existence, and more important the recoverability, of a primal 'Germanic' law.[40] Its founding father was in effect Jakob Grimm. It is no accident – and to say so is no gibe – that his *Fairy Tales* have everlasting fame where his *German Legal Antiquities* has become an dusty relic of nineteenth-century German mentalities. The *Rechtsalterthümer* (1828) was born of belief that a people's law was inlayed in its 'spirit (*Geist*)' and endowed with a commensurate potential for immortality. It would therefore find the same ubiquitous expression as folk-tales. The roots of this conviction in European Romanticism are obvious enough. Less immediately apparent are its debts to philological discoveries at the turn of the eighteenth and nineteenth century and to contemporary studies in Roman law. The revelation that a common 'Indo-European' language was spoken from the Ganges to the North Cape created an irresistible impression that law, hardly less basic to human sociability, could spread to all corners of the world, yet retain its essential identity.[41] Grimm's first great work was his *Deutsche Grammatik* of 1819. He was also the pupil and friend of the stupendously learned Friedrich von Savigny, whose *History of Roman Law in the Middle Ages* was the companion to his even lengthier *System of Modern Roman Law*. In the glad confident morning of German nationalism, it seemed quite feasible that German law could be reconstructed to a level where it could sustain comparison with Roman.[42]

The scholars who wrote compendious, and within the limits of their approach still extremely valuable, accounts of all conceivable aspects of 'German legal history' thus concocted a *system* of Germanic law, by boiling up evidential ingredients from allotments as diverse as Tacitean Rome and Snorre Sturlasson's

---

39   *Reeves' History*, ed. Finlayson, I, pp. xvii–cxxviii (an introduction putting the Romanist case with nothing if not assiduity), and (e.g.) pp. 5–8, 24–6, 39–46, 51–9. It can be said in Finlayson's defence that he was at least aware of the potential of Old English law's silences; that what he said *à propos* Reeves' bafflement over Alfred's *domboc* is pertinent (above, n. 30); and that, as already noted for Palgrave, faith in a meaningful Roman legacy no longer seems such patent lunacy as it has for most of the last 200 years.
40   This impressive movement still awaits its historian. Aside from Grimm's own *Deutsche Rechtsalterthümer*, its approach is perhaps best sampled in Brunner's still in its way definitive *Deutsche Rechtsgeschichte*. For a shattering critique which had less impact than it merited, see the final section of this chapter.
41   An illuminating account of this intellectual revolution, knowledge of which I owe to my colleague William Thomas, is Aarsleff, *Study of Language*, especially pp. 115–65.
42   See Grimm's seminal words in his 'Vorrede', pp. viii–xii, xvii–xx. Both Palgrave and the hapless Finlayson also cited Savigny with reverence.

Iceland. It needs emphasis that continuities of that order are indeed traceable in Celtic law. The startling similarities in structure and vocabulary between Irish and Welsh kinship can scarcely be otherwise explained.[43] Those societies had a class to serve as the requisite cultural conduit: one-time Druids, latterly *filid* or in their specialized legal function 'brehons/*brithemain*', who entrusted themselves with the preservation (which is to say adaptation) of traditional lore, whether in saga, custom or medicine.[44] The *Rechtsschule* were unabashed by the fact that, as Caesar was the first to note, the Germans had no Druids.[45] They were also of course unaware of what anthropologists have taught the modern mind about the pliability of any oral tradition, law included. On the contrary, it was quite plausible that all German-speaking peoples had held on to a legal heritage since whenever the ancestors of Goths, Lombards, Franks, Saxons and Norse were neighbours. The importance of this for Anglo-Saxon law was that its texts were, alone among those of the Barbarian West, written in the vernacular, and almost uniquely uncontaminated by the breath of imperial Rome. In consequence, they were quarried above all for whatever was archaically Germanic. It was a short step thence to the view that most of what was in them *was* archaic.

The force of this approach was felt in three Anglophone authorities of the mid-to-later-nineteenth century. The first was Kemble, who had actually sat at Grimm's feet in Göttingen. Kemble did not edit the Anglo-Saxon laws as he did *Beowulf* or the corpus of pre-conquest charters. But his *Saxons in England* was 'an account of the principles on which the public life of our Anglosaxon forefathers was based, and of the institutions in which these principles are most clearly manifested'.[46] It was in many ways a commentary on Anglo-Saxon custom, as synchronically manifested in law-codes and any other available evidence from poetry to place-names. Analogies with other Germanic cultures, and more rarely with those further afield, flowed compulsively into the argument. The mode of thinking was Grimm's, though Kemble's analysis was more structured. His second volume was professedly more chronological than the first. It was 'devoted to the historical development of [the] principles ... upon which the original settlement of the Anglosaxons was founded'.[47] But the approach remained analytical. 'Development' featured slightly in his argument, because he did not think that there had been that much. It is nowhere really suggested that the 'rights of royalty' increased, even under Offa, Edgar or Cnut. 'In the later times of the Anglosaxon monarchy, a more immediate interference of the king in the administration of justice is discernible', in the issue of writs commanding court hearings; Kemble quoted part of an important Berkshire case of 990 (chapter 3, pp. 151–3).[48] But

---

43   Charles-Edwards, *Early Irish and Welsh Kinship*, pp. 33–61, 181–200 (especially pp. 191–2).
44   The now very considerable literature on Celtic learned orders and their cultural hoard has recently been sifted by 'revisionism', notably in McCone, *Pagan Past and Christian Present* (especially chapters 1, 4); for the class's legal role, see Charles-Edwards, *Kinship*, pp. 3–17; and Stacey, 'Law and Order in the Very Old West'.
45   Caesar, *Gallic War* vi 21, pp. 344–5; a valuable and regrettably unpublished exploration of the contrast is Moisl, 'Some Aspects of the Relationship between Secular and Ecclesiastical Learning'.
46   Kemble, *Saxons in England* I, p. v.
47   Kemble, *Saxons* II, pp. 1–2.
48   Kemble, *Saxons* II, pp. 29–103, at pp. 46–9.

the point is chiefly and uncontroversially that historical kings had more power than their counterparts in the settlement phase. Kemble's account of Frankpledge is in Volume I; he saw it not as an Alfredian innovation but as an institution whose origin was not much less ancient than kin itself.[49] He did not directly address the issue of what freedoms passed across the 1066 barrier and beyond, but his view was clear enough: 'If it should appear that a gradually diminishing share of freedom remained to the people, yet ... we finally retained a great amount of rational and orderly liberty, full of the seeds of future development'.[50] It is a point of great symbolic weight that Kemble's preface credited England's escape from 1848 revolution to the persistence of its ancient institutions, within months of Macaulay's *History* making the identical claim for the 'conserving' Revolution of 1688.[51]

In 1876, four young American scholars, one of them the son and grandson of Presidents, another the grandfather of the 1960 Republican candidate for Vice-president, produced a set of *Essays in Anglo-Saxon Law*.[52] These were serious, though now rarely cited, studies. The bibliography and footnotes are replete with the names of *Rechtsschule* protagonists. Ready recourse is had to Germanic phenomena in mainland Europe, Scandinavia and Iceland. The approach, in other words, is like Kemble's. Henry Adams, in his lastingly important essay on 'The Anglo-Saxon Courts of Law', was not unaware of change. But he was chiefly struck by the 'conservatism' of Anglo-Saxon law, perhaps attributable to the fact that its rulers 'unlike Charlemagne, were constitutional kings ... controlled in their policy by the Witan'. 'England has always moved slowly, and has been reluctant to abandon established institutions'.[53] When real change came with the growth of private jurisdictions under Edward the Confessor, it was the prelude to collapse into feudalism.[54] The emphasis, in other words, had shifted decisively to what was *unfamiliar* in Old English law. The *Rechtsschule*'s telescopic vision resolved the dichotomy in English Whiggery between the urges to foreshorten and to spin out the course of progress. There was no worry about the jury's postdating the Conquest. Anglo-Saxon law was of course archaic. The 'philosophic continuity' in English institutions resided in 'a slender thread of political thought' that can be traced 'safely and firmly back', through 'the confusion of feudalism', and 'out on to the wide plains of northern Germany'.[55]

The third and in the end most important (before Maitland) of the *Rechtsschule*'s English disciples was Stubbs. He was in personal contact with some of its exponents, but had more respect than Kemble or the centennial Americans for the English writers reviewed earlier in this section. His brilliant achievement was to reconcile contemporary scholarship's focus on the ancient with the English tradition's sense that the earliest phase was of abiding

49   Kemble, *Saxons* I, pp. 228–66, especially pp. 229–31, 239–40.
50   Kemble, *Saxons* II, p. 28.
51   Kemble, *Saxons* I, p. v.
52   Adams *et al.*, *Essays*; in the circumstances, the 1876 publication date seems unlikely to be co-incidental.
53   *Essays*, pp. 24–5, 21.
54   *Essays*, pp. 45–54.
55   *Essays*, pp. 187–8, 1–2.

importance to the history of law and government; to show what Kemble could be taken to mean when claiming that his subject was 'the childhood of our own age, – the explanation of its manhood'. Again, there is relatively little development in the early chapters of the *Constitutional History*, though more than in Kemble. Sixty-five pages pass before the barbarians cross the North Sea. Exactly two-thirds of those on Anglo-Saxon government go to the 'System', with only the residue allotted to 'Development'. The essential argument, which is often at crucial stages left cloudy, almost mystical, is that the resources for Englishmen's long struggle with would-be tyrants were being stored during these centuries in the barns of local institutions. Growth in central government, in national consciousness, was sluggish; the energies of the political nation lurked at a barely visible level, to be brought to the fore by the demands of Norman and later regimes.[56] More precisely, one of Stubbs's two heroes, Henry II, might call the Jury into life; but whether it was 'native or Norman, ... there is no doubt as to the character of the machinery by which it is to be transacted'; 'we may be inclined to claim for the institutions, which like trial by jury came to full growth on English soil, a native or at least a common Germanic origin'.[57] He was the first to doubt not only Alfred's creation of Frankpledge but whether the system was ever fully worked out by the Anglo-Saxons.[58] There was no need to hurry the steady tread of constitutional evolution.

The scholarship of the three centuries from Lambarde to Stubbs matters, not just because gifted men who were in this area no less learned than Maitland could see different – or the same – things, but because it set perceptions of Anglo-Saxon law in a groove from which neither Maitland nor anyone since has dislodged them. In the third quarter of the nineteenth century, as Freeman was penning his Wagnerian volumes, its importance lay where it always had: in forming the bedrock not of the English State but of English Liberty.[59] It was ancient; and antiquity belonged to the people. The point is not that its populist associations were necessarily misconceived, so much as that pre-twentieth-century historians were as yet blessedly innocent of the sort of state muscle that could be packed by a broad political frame: ruling ideology hardly interested one of the scholars so far discussed, nor any of those whose turn is to come. Government power could not have sprung from the sources laid bare in Old English legislation. It was not inherited but imposed by post-conquest kings. Since that is how Anglo-Saxon law was perceived, from whatever set of preoccupations, it went down with most of the Anglo-Saxon 'democratic' array before the guns of John Horace Round. Much in twentieth-century study of early England has hung on the fact that Round was the patron of a grateful young Frank Stenton.

---

56   E.g. Stubbs, *Constitutional History* I, pp. 242–8. See Campbell, *Stubbs*, pp. 6–11.
57   *Constitutional History* I, pp. 531, 237. Stubbs, who knew as well as Maitland himself how to keep intellectual options open, could contemplate the possibility that Carolingian influence which Brunner and Maitland thought to have made itself felt from the later-eleventh century (below) was exerted in the tenth (*History* I, pp. 234–8); this will be discussed in chapter 13.
58   *Constitutional History* I, pp. 97–105, 114–15.
59   Freeman's account of Old English law and institutions differs from those of Kemble and Stubbs chiefly in the reckless gallantry of his phrasing: *Norman Conquest*, I, pp. 69–117.

2   Maitland (and Pollock)

Frederic William Maitland was fluent in German and detested Greek. The revolution in English historical writing wrought by the rise of professional academia is summed up in that double fact. Few historians have ever written so well, but history was not a literary exercize for Maitland, still less a course in citizenly duty.[60] He was not the pupil of any German luminary, but he corresponded with his counterparts in universities across the North Sea more intensively, it seems, than Stubbs. He wrote with awe of 'the tons of books concerning legal history which Germany produced in the nineteenth century', and with shame of his fellow-countrymen's failure to measure up.[61] So, if Grimm was Kemble's model, Maitland's (perhaps less affectionately regarded) was Brunner.[62] Brunner's prodigious output marks the climax of the *historische Rechtsschule*; and it was his most celebrated monograph that put Maitland onto the 'prerogative rights of the Frankish kings' as the germ of the English jury.

Anglo-Saxon law hardly features in Brunner's *Deutsche Rechtsgeschichte*. However valuable as a treasury of Germanic antiquities, its development took place on 'foreign soil', and would anyway have to be broken off when it was 'denationalized (*entnationalisiert*)' – by which Brunner meant when it was de-Germanized, presumably after the Conquest.[63] Brunner did, however, write an account of the 'Sources of English Law' (from Æthelberht to Blackstone); and what he said about the nature and limitations of the Anglo-Saxon materials was echoed in a paper by Maitland which ultimately appeared between the same covers.[64] Both authors stressed the value of the Old English codes to the history of German or 'Teutonic' law generally. For both, their special importance was that they were in the vernacular, that they were free of Roman 'taint', and that they formed a continuous series from the later ninth century, 'when on the continent the voice of law has become silent'.[65] Here again, then, Anglo-Saxon law mattered most as a 'Testament of Antiquitie'. The word 'archaic' was rarely in Maitland's vocabulary, probably because it smacked of Maine's way of thinking

---

60   *Letters of Maitland*, ed. Fifoot, p. 269; Wormald, 'Frederic William Maitland', p. 25 (pp. 68–9). Much of the following distils what that paper argues, itself expanding my 'Maitland and Anglo-Saxon Law'.

61   CP iii, pp. 462–3; see *Letters*, ed. Fifoot, pp. 89–90 for the procuring of some of this tonnage, and *Letters*, ed. Zutshi, p. 229, for his special heroes. Cf. 'Frederic William Maitland', pp. 5, 8–9 (pp. 48, 52–3). Was Maitland (born 28 May 1850) named after the king of Prussia?

62   He was among the few to emerge with credit from Maitland's 'Law of Real Property', his first published paper: CP I, pp. 174–5.

63   Brunner, *Deutsche Rechtsgeschichte* I, p. 2 (n. 2), and 'Sources' (as next nn.), p. 8. von Amira, *Germanisches Recht*, in a short but well-informed account of early English law, declares (I, p. 80) that 'the extinction of Anglo-Saxon legal life (*Rechtsleben*) is to be regarded as accomplished under Henry II'; Anglo-Saxon texts are quite copiously used to throw light on 'Germanic' law in Vol. II.

64   Brunner's paper first appeared in a German Legal Encyclopedia (1877); Maitland's (notably less dry) 'Materials for the History of English Law' was first published in 1889, and reappeared in CP II, pp. 1–60, as well as beside Brunner's in the 1908 *Select Essays*; it in fact cites Brunner's paper, though with reference to 'Norman Law'.

65   (Citing the 1908 versions:) Brunner, 'Sources', p. 8; Maitland, 'Materials', pp. 66–7 (from which the quotes come).

about legal history, which he deplored.[66] But it was often at the tip of Pollock's pen, and a great deal of Anglo-Saxon law was duly stigmatized as such in his chapter for 'Pollock and Maitland' (above, p. 3).[67] Thus, 'trial of questions of fact in anything like the modern sense, was unknown', as 'archaic rules of evidence make no attempt to apply any measure of probability to individual cases'. A king's judicial function was 'to exercize a ... reserved power which a man must not invoke unless he has failed to get his cause heard in ... his own hundred'; in which case 'the process was barely distinguishable from combating an open rebellion'. The 'subject-matters of Anglo-Saxon jurisdiction ... [show] what may be called the usual archaic features ... offences and wrongs'.[68]

One reason why Maitland did not much like what Pollock wrote was that it prevented him from talking about Anglo-Saxon law later in their book.[69] Yet he never said much when free to do so elsewhere.[70] Among possible explanations of his reticence, three stand out. First, he was unsure of his touch with Anglo-Saxon materials. A good indication is that he rightly or wrongly attributed the same unease to Stubbs.[71] The reason can hardly be linguistic. However slight he thought his talent for languages, a man who taught himself to edit 'Law French' had little to fear from Anglo-Saxon. More likely is that he, like Plummer, found it hard to work out what early medieval *Volksrechte* were trying to do. 'As to what [the Dooms] imply it is but too easy for different men to form different opinions'. He was among the first to make himself at home with the documentation of royal justice from the late-twelfth century onwards. Early medieval legislation or lawsuits were by that very token a country where different things were done. For all the limitations upon which he liked to descant, post-conquest law-books, especially *Leges Henrici Primi*, offered safer terrain, because this at least aspired to be a 'legal text-book'.[72] Secondly, the fact that Old English law was 'a slip of German law', occupying, in Brunner's words, 'about the same relative position as the so called "folk-laws" and other legal monuments of the Frankish period in the history of ... Western Teutonic nations' meant that it had been or would be better done by *Volksrechte* specialists: above all Liebermann, or Brunner himself.[73]

---

66   See Burrow, 'The "Village Community"', pp. 273–80; White, 'Maitland on Family and Kinship', pp. 92–102; and references in my 'Frederic William Maitland', n. 78.

67   E.g. PM I, pp. 38–47. I made these remarks the target of my discussion in 'Charters, Law and the Settlement of Disputes', pp. 149–50 (p. 288), erroneously ascribing them to Maitland himself.

68   PM I, pp. 38–9, 40–1, 43.

69   *Letters*, ed. Fifoot, p. 103; see above, n. 2.

70   PM II, pp. 449–58, 503–4, 513–14; the major accounts otherwise are *DBB*, pp. 220–356, *CP* II, pp. 418–30, *SE*, pp. 97–101; fuller references in my 'Maitland and Anglo-Saxon Law', nn. 5, 12, or 'Frederic William Maitland', n. 7. I should stress that I am only tangentially concerned here with his noble discussion of Old English Land Law, which, like the rest of the 'Bookland' controversy, is best taken with the topic itself in chapter 11.

71   *CP* III, p. 506; further, 'Frederic William Maitland', pp. 5–6 (p. 49).

72   *DBB*, p. 226 (see n. 2 above); PM I, pp. 100–1; further, 'Frederic William Maitland', nn. 9, 10, 81; and cf. Hudson, 'Maitland and Anglo-Norman Law', pp. 44–5. In reviewing Liebermann's first volume, he moved almost as soon as he decently could to the 'surer ground' of the Anglo-Norman lawbooks: *CP* III, pp. 466–72.

73   (Cf. n. 64:) Maitland, 'Materials', p. 66; Brunner, 'Sources', pp. 7–8; further (very revealing) remarks by Maitland: 'Frederic William Maitland', p. 5 (p. 49).

A third possible explanation comes closer to the nub of the matter, while again conjuring up the (in Maitland's eyes) gibbering shade of the *Leges Henrici* author. In one respect, Maitland certainly saw Old English law as obsolescent. There were as yet not nearly enough 'true punishments'. Compensation in money would still redeem 'many bad crimes', above all homicide itself. From such atavism, England under Henry II was freed 'with marvellous suddenness'.[74] Maitland was entirely right that the old system belonged to 'a great family', its scions scattered through many historical and geographical climes. He was less clearly right in his lawyerly sense that punishment of the offender without compensating the victim is inherently more civilized than exposing offenders to vengeance *unless* they compensate their victims. But he was anyway quite probably wrong that late Anglo-Saxon law retained 'a scheme of *wer* and bloodfeud, of *bot* and *wite* (blood-price ... amendment and fine)'.[75] What persuaded him that it did was the presence of almost all the old apparatus of compensation in *Leges Henrici* and other twelfth-century law-books. Though he did not rule it out that these had an agenda which fell short of (or went beyond) providing a statement of English law as currently in force, he could not reconcile himself to 'setting aside a theory which writers of the eleventh and twelfth centuries regarded as of great importance'.[76]

More generally, Maitland added to the respect for 'canons of evidence' shared by any professional historian (and admired by Maitland in his own grandfather) a quality that made him an Immortal: he thought that the past was important in and for itself. He resisted, even resented, attempts to tug it into the struggles of the present: 'it is to the interest of the Middle Ages themselves that they be not brought into court any more'.[77] No one knew better than he how ruthlessly early English law had been subpoenaed by controversialists from the *Mirror of Justices* to the seventeenth century and beyond. 'What', he mocked in his Liebermann review:

> is one to make of laws which leave it somewhat doubtful whether our Saxon fore-fathers were possessed of our glorious constitution, with trial by jury and "habeas corpus", and all the other bulwarks, palladia [*sic*], checks, balances, commodities, easements and appurtenances? ... The forgeries and the fables, the legends and the lies, were much more to the point than those meagre, enigmatical, and altogether "Gothic" sentences which defied the resources of gentlemanly scholarship.[78]

Maitland was content that Anglo-Saxon law should be archaic. He deeply distrusted the motives of those who would make it relevant.

Which was why he reacted with something like glee to Brunner's demolition of English legends about the origins of the jury. Before he became the *doyen* of *Rechtshistoriker*, Brunner was a specialist in Carolingian justice. His first famous

---

74   PM I, p. 74, II, pp. 452, 458; 'Frederic William Maitland', n. 66.
75   PM II, p. 448; 'Frederic William Maitland', pp. 5 (48), 20 (63–4); and cf. chapter 9.
76   (Cf. n. 64:) Maitland, 'Materials', p. 67; he was here writing about these sources' belief that English law was divided into the three families of 'West Saxon', 'Mercian' and 'Danelaw' (chapter 6, pp. 466), but the same logic applies to '*bot* and *wite*'.
77   *Letters*, ed. Fifoot, p. 95; *CP* I, p. 493; cf. in general 'Frederic William Maitland', pp. 12–17 (56–61), 21 (64–5).
78   *CP* III, pp. 454–5.

work, 'The Origin of the Sworn Panel (*Schwurgerichte*)', established that Carolingian kings summoned sets of the locally knowledgable to report on oath about encroachments against their property or other royal rights; and that this technique could be traced through the tunnel-like centuries that followed until it re emerged in the light of twelfth-century evidence.[79] Henry II's judges could be seen testing local opinion in very much the same way, for the king's benefit and for that of subjects who claimed to have been dispossessed of their tenures. It was by then common ground that the twelve empanelled under oath by the Assize of Clarendon (1166) were a 'Grand Jury', charged with indicting notorious villains of the neighbourhood. It followed that, whatever the jury later became, it began on English soil as a device brought in by Henry with the baggage of his dynasty's Carolingian past, and used as a weapon against miscreants. As a theory, this had one weakness and one real flaw. The weakness was the considerable difficulty of following the sworn inquest's subterranean progress from the ninth to the twelfth century. The flaw, familiar to Englishmen since Lambarde's time and unconvincingly brushed aside by Brunner, was that something that looked very like an indicting jury appeared in Æthelred II's Wantage Code.[80] Maitland was evidently more worried than Brunner by the Wantage twelve. He was also better aware than Brunner of how near the surety and/or policing responsibility of early English 'Frankpledge' tithings came to a jury's duties. But *Leges Henrici* said nothing of any indictment by Frankpledges.[81] Brunner's thesis could be allowed to stand. The results were far-reaching. Anglo-Saxon justice was not only denied credit for inventing the jury. It lost any pretensions to the sort of aggressive concern with 'law and order' manifested by Henry's jury.

Maitland's most distinguished critic has protested that, thanks to him, 'the early history of our criminal law ... has been bedevilled by our mistaking a legislative change in modes of proof for a much grander invention to secure public order'.[82] One could argue, conversely, that the securing of public order had been the concern of English kings for at least two and a half centuries before 1166: a campaign in which Henry's jury amounted to no more than a slight change of tactics.[83] But one thing above all prevented Maitland from believing that: the Norman Conquest. Like nearly all historians till recently, he thought that their 'stupendous failure' was a comment on the shortcomings of those who ran the pre-1066 regime.[84] But his specific diagnosis had a sophistication lacked by any before or indeed after. The argument over whether the Old English kingdom knew feudal tenure was once an aspect of the debate over the origins of English freedoms. By the 1890s (and since) it was generally agreed that the kindom was

---

79   Brunner, *Entstehung der Schwurgerichte*; this followed 'Zeugen und Inquisitionsbeweis', a study of Carolingian judicial techniques.
80   III Atr 3:1; Brunner, *Entstehung*, pp. 402–4.
81   PM I, pp. 138–44, though note the doubts at I, pp. 151–2 and II, pp. 642–3 (other references, 'Frederic William Maitland', n. 38); 'Frederic William Maitland', nn. 39–40.
82   Milsom, 'Maitland', p. 277.
83   Such is the argument of much of Parts III and IV in Vol. II of this book. See, meanwhile, the implications (at least) of Biancalana, 'For Want of Justice'; Hudson, *Land, Law, and Lordship*, pp. 36–51; and Hudson, *Formation of the English Common Law*, pp. 52–117.
84   DBB, p. 103.

weakened in so far as it did not. But Maitland argued that it was riddled by the galloping feudalism that had brought down Frankish imperial power.[85] He wrote many things about feudalism, most of them wise and some very funny.[86] He did not think it inherently 'anti-national or anarchic'. But his analysis brought him closer than anyone before Georges Duby to seeing how lordship could corrode judicial institutions that ostensibly at any rate stood for a more 'public' interest.[87] That was how he persuaded himself that the time of Cnut and Edward the Confessor saw the growth of 'jurisdiction as high as that which any palatinate earl of after ages enjoyed': law-courts 'owned' by lords and immune from a royal official's activity.[88] For once, however, he persuaded few others. Maitland's Edwardian immunist is as dead as the Alfredian jury.

Maitland's exaggeration of the extent of private jurisdiction before 1066 is one crucial reason why he did not see what he otherwise very well might have seen: the significance of the fact that, as he and even Brunner realized, the kingdom where something singular happened to law in the twelfth century was also one where something without European parallel was happening in the tenth and eleventh. Henry II legislated as Alfred, Æthelstan, Edgar and Cnut had, but as the last Carolingians, Ottonians and Capetians did not.[89] Electrifying papers before he was even academically employed showed Maitland alert to the extent of communal responsibility for good order in pre-conquest England and took him within an ace of perceiving how felony came to have so much wider and grislier a meaning in England than in its French homeland.[90] In the *History of English Law*, he wrote:

> In the Anglo-Saxon dooms a general forfeiture of 'all that one has' begins to recur with increasing frequency ... For 'contempts' of king or lord (they) have a special *wite* ... the very serious mulct of 120 shillings. The first stages in the development of the amercement are ... rather Frankish than English; they may be found in forfeiture of goods for the elastic offence of *infidelitas*.[91]

Much of the second part of this book will go to show just how right he was. He was much impressed by the brute power of the Norman and Angevin kings, and 'the exceptional malleableness of a thoroughly conquered and compactly united kingdom'.[92] Yet there is a difficulty in attaching such a role to the conquest of 1066. The post-conquest regime was not run by equivalents of Cromwell's Major-Generals, but by the machinery, and at lower levels presumably the personnel, of the vanquished. If the levers of power were in good enough order to work for William I and Henry I, the likelihood is that they worked quite smoothly for Cnut, Edward the Confessor and Harold II.

85   *DBB*, pp. 263–85.
86   E.g. *CP* I, p. 489; and cf. 'Frederic William Maitland', nn. 27–8.
87   It might therefore have figured more prominently than it did in the very lively and instructive 'Debate' sparked off by Bisson, '"Feudal Revolution"'; see chapter 6, pp. 453–4.
88   *DBB*, p. 283; cf. 'Frederic William Maitland', pp. 6–8 (pp. 49–52).
89   See above, p. 15; Brunner, 'Sources', p. 12; *CP* II, pp. 422–3; 'Frederic William Maitland', n. 75.
90   *CP* I, pp. 230–48, 316–17; see chapter 9.
91   PM II, p. 515, n. 4; the point was already seen by Palgrave, *English Commonwealth* I, pp. 205–6.
92   PM II, p. 559. Cf. the insights of van Caenegem, *Birth of the English Common Law*, chapter 1.

It has been well said of Maitland that 'before – or after – rejecting a theory, he liked to note that it might be true'.[93] But it might always be a revisionist's wishful thinking to imagine that his target had seen some of the force of the case that could be made against him. If Maitland was truly wedded to the belief that most things were made new by Henry II and his judges, one last reason can be suggested, taking the argument neatly back to Germany. Brunner wished to compare the Anglo-Saxon codes with the continental *Volksrechte*; it was for what they had to offer the run of 'Teutonic' law that he cherished them. But the age of the *Volksrechte* made way for one in which 'the voice of law was silent', and (added Maitland) 'the state for a while seems dissolved in feudal anarchy' (above, pp. 15–16). That was in turn succeeded in Europe at large by a spectacular revival of the secular and religious jurisprudence of Rome. Maitland of course knew that twelfth-century English developments owed comparatively little to Canon law, and less to Roman.[94] But just as he found something like 'feudal anarchy' in eleventh-century England, so he could not get out of his mind the image of a chasm between the law of his 'luminous age' and that of the half-lit earlier centuries, its width measured by the distance dividing the mind of the *Leges Henrici* from that of *Glanvill*.[95] And the one scholar whom he would certainly have thought equipped to bridge it ultimately declined to do so.

3   Liebermann

In the spring of 1913, six years after Maitland died, Felix Liebermann lectured on 'The National Assembly in the Anglo-Saxon Period' to the Third International Congress of Historical Studies in London. The Old English 'Witan' had been used and abused in controversy from Elizabeth to Victoria. Liebermann's account was characteristically judicious and much acclaimed. Volume II of his *Gesetze* had just been published and was being warmly reviewed. He took tea with the King. But the disastrously misconceived dedication of Volume III, dated 20 July 1916 (his sixty-fifth birthday), lost him most of his English friends.[96] He never returned

---

93   White, 'Maitland on Family and Kinship', p. 98.
94   Cf. Helmholz, 'The Learned Laws', pp. 151–8.
95   PM II, pp. 672–3. For the *Leges – Glanvill* contrast and its effect, see PM I, p. 165, with 'Frederic William Maitland', n. 9; it had already been spotted by Madox (a special hero of Maitland's), *History of the Exchequer*, pp. 121–2; and cf. Hallam, *State of Europe*, pp. 191–2.
96   'Gratefully dedicated to the Memory of Heinrich Brunner and Frederic William Maitland, the age's greatest researchers into the legal history of medieval England: a token in melancholy memory of the peace-blessed time when this work began, when the German immersed himself admiringly in the political life and literature of Britain, and the Briton ungrudgingly opened the way to German research, including this contribution to the earliest history of his nation; also as a heartfelt expression of confident hope that the storm of hate and the sea of blood which engulf the time of the completion of these pages ...'; there could thus far have been no objection to so graceful a sentiment. Alas, however, Liebermann continued: '... will soon be understandable as essentially caused by the historical necessity of conflict between the heedless claims of a World-empire, familiar with power, to continue to dominate navigation and world trade, and the justified determination of a unified German people to contend peacefully and circumspectly but with freedom and strength for the goods of this earth, and to expand itself to the measure of its inborn life-force'. As blood cascaded on the Somme, not even a conclusion praying that 'today's enemies might again learn to respect each other and help each other as before toward the higher goals of mankind!' could

to England. The tragedy is emblematic of the fate that overtook his great book.

One important thing about Liebermann is that he had sufficient family wealth (until it was destroyed by Germany's post-War inflation) not to need professional employment; and he was deterred from seeking the university professorship that would have been his *métier* by a speech-defect.[97] Nevertheless, he was a *bona fide* member of the academic circles that had transformed the study of Germanic law since the 1820s. His Göttingen tutors were Georg Waitz, the *Rechtsschule*'s 'constitutional' expert, and Reinhold Pauli, author among much else of the first scholarly biography of King Alfred. After a doctoral dissertation on the *Dialogue of the Exchequer*, he worked for over a decade at the 'Monumenta Germaniae Historica' under Waitz's direction. A product of this phase was his edition of the important tract on the 'Saints of England' (1889), the only serious attention it received for almost ninety years (chapter 4, pp. 209–10). The switch to legal material came when his research for *Unprinted Anglo-Norman Historical Sources* (1879) discovered the connection between the prefaces published in Cooper's *Account of the Public Records* as far back as 1832, an unprinted preface that Liebermann then thought went with the *Leges Henrici Primi*, and the Latin text of Old English codes printed by earlier editors as the 'Old Version'; thus was the existence of the early-twelfth-century collection known as *Quadripartitus* first adumbrated.[98] Brunner, since his *Schwurgerichte* the acknowledged master of Anglo-Norman law, and Konrad von Maurer, the accepted expert on Anglo-Saxon jurisprudence, were sufficiently impressed to induce the Savigny-Stiftung to commission from him a corpus of Anglo-Saxon law that met the criteria of modern scholarship (1883).[99] Within a year he made his first trip to English repositories and published a set of additions and corrections to the then standard edition.[100] From 1892 to 1902 flowed a stream of studies of post-conquest law-books, the first and most important of which was his seminal reconstruction of *Quadripartitus* itself.

Anglo-Saxon law has always been relatively lucky in its editors.[101] Lambarde's *Archaionomia*, the *editio princeps* of 1568, drew on edited transcripts by his friend, Laurence Nowell, the pioneer of Anglo-Saxon studies (chapter 4, pp. 174–8, 261–2). Its reissue in 1644 by Whelock was supplemented by Twysden with texts of Anglo-Norman sources, including *Leges Henrici*. The first fairly complete edition, incorporating the Kentish laws from the great Rochester collection unknown to Lambarde in 1568, was that of David Wilkins; he was in

---

redeem that. The episode is rendered the more poignant to later-twentieth-century eyes by the fact that, like many of the greatest legal historians, Liebermann was a Jew.

97   The fullest accounts of Liebermann are the memoirs by Hazeltine and Heymann; see also n. 108. I have attempted a sketch in Cannon *et al.* (eds), *Blackwell Dictionary of Historians*.

98   Liebermann, 'Ungedrucktes Vorwort'; see chapter 4, pp. 236–44, and my '"Quadripartitus"', p. 112(82), n. 4. He had already written a short piece redating the *Leges Henrici*: 'Die Abfassungszeit'.

99   von Maurer's 'Angelsächsische Rechtsverhältnisse', modifying Kemble's views, were published 1853–6; dedicatee and proof-reader of Liebermann's Volume I, he was evidently his special patron.

100   Liebermann, 'Zu den Gesetzen'. Two years later came his *editio princeps* of *Gerefa* (chapter 5, pp. 387–9).

101   Their efforts were reviewed and justly assessed by Liebermann, 'Bearbeitung der Gesetze c. 1550–1900', *Gesetze* I, pp. xlv-liii.

fact a Prussian named Wilke, and dedicated his volume to a fellow-German immigrant, George I.[102] One of the interesting points about this whole story is the way that developments in the editing of the text marched stride for stride with those in the study of their contents. Just as Wilkins was counterparted by Rapin de Thoyras' *Histoire*, so the insights of Hallam, Allen and Palgrave were matched by the Record Commission version of the *Ancient Laws of England* begun by Richard Price and finished by Benjamin Thorpe (1833–40).[103] Similarly, the impact of Grimm and Kemble was paralleled by the extraordinary achievement of Reinhold Schmid, a self-taught Anglo-Saxonist, who was unable to travel to consult the manuscripts but contrived to produce the first truly scholarly edition from the texts and variants printed by his predecessors.[104] His 'Antiquarisches Glossar' was a mine of learning in the idiom of Grimm, whose influence on the whole exercise is patent. It deservedly held the field for forty-five years.

Liebermann's edition, based on more than 180 manuscripts (the vast majority relating to post-conquest materials), was of course an immense advance. One of its qualities was that he printed the texts of each of the main manuscripts in parallel columns, using a system of types devised by himself to bring out the variants between them. No continental laws of the period have yet been as well served.[105] Another quality was a near- (but not quite) superhuman immaculacy.[106] It is probably wise to check his reading against the manuscript itself for any issue that really matters, but one's trust is soon such that one by no means always does. Yet a notable feature of his edition is how close he kept to Schmid. His *Quadripartitus* study presupposed the availability of Schmid's text. His numbering of royal codes followed Schmid's, even where he knew that this was wrong (chapter 5, nn. 129, 262). So did his division of codes into clauses for which there is no manuscript warrant whatsoever.[107] The whole principle of an edition followed by glossary, which, for all its infinitely magnified scale, is what Liebermann's work amounted to, bespoke a cast of mind like that of Schmid or Grimm. Congenitally modest, Liebermann felt unqualified to leave the track laid down by his great forerunners.

The real problems with Liebermann's edition arose from the then comparatively undeveloped state of insular palaeography, his reliance for the dating of

---

102   *Leges Anglo-Saxonicae*, ed. Wilkins (including Spelman's unprinted collection of 'laws' from William I to 1225); editorially, however, this is not much of an improvement on Lambarde/Nowell (where available); e.g. Wilkins did not amend the laws of Ine in ways that *Textus Roffensis* made possible (cf. chapter 4, n. 40), and he corrected few of Lambarde's perversities (chapter 5, nn. 7, 129, 262).
103   *Ancient Laws*, ed. Thorpe; though Price significantly expanded the number of MSS consulted, and Thorpe's translation did its best, many of Wilkins's shortcomings were perpetuated (see previous n.)
104   Schmid's first edition of 1832 (acknowledging his debt to Grimm's *Grammatik*) was based on Wilkins, and on the *Quadripartitus/ Vetus Versio* texts in the Chronicle ascribed to 'John Brompton' and included in Twysden's *Decem Scriptores* (cf. chapter 4, n. 322); the much fuller second edition of 1858 built on the foundations provided by Price and Thorpe.
105   Eckhardt's 1960s' editions of *Lex Salica* (see chapter 2, n. 14) come closest, but also (perhaps unwisely) essay an 'eclectic' text.
106   For a sample of errors, not all trivial, see chapter 4, nn. 261, 352, chapter 5, nn. 160, 358, 360, 414.
107   See chapter 5, nn. 7, 113, 234, 361, 410, etc.; and for these and other criticisms, Dammery, 'Editing Anglo-Saxon Laws', pp. 252–6.

texts on relatively insecure philological criteria, his translations (into German) that habitually expanded the original wording to what he conceived to be its 'true' sense, and worst of all his belief in a substantial manuscript used by Lambarde but since lost (below, and chapter 4, pp. 260–2). These issues, however, are best addressed as they come up in later chapters. What matters for now is the effect of the Grimm approach on Liebermann's perception of law itself. His second volume comprised a glossary broken down into a vocabulary which is almost a concordance, and a '*Sachglossar* (theme/subject-glossary)' discussing legal issues in alphabetical order of topic. Volume III consisted of introductions to each text with notes on individual clauses. The introductions discussed textual transmission (usually with a manuscript 'stemma'), and gave a conscientious account of date, sources, influence, and so on. They did not address Plummer's question of 'what it all comes to'. Liebermann took his codes as he found them: as finished (or scribally damaged) products. He did not ask himself why they were produced, or for that matter why they were damaged. They were just sources, necessarily inadequate given the barbarity of the age. As for the notes, they were mostly textual or cross-references to the *Sachglossar*.

It is to the *Sachglossar*, therefore, that one turns for Liebermann's views on early English law. The very medium chosen shows how far he, like Grimm, saw law as a system inherent in society's soul, to bring out which it sufficed to supply an exhaustive set of references; and Liebermann in fact made much less use of non-legislative evidence than Grimm. To achieve his end within a less than Brobdingnagian compass, he patented a telegraphic style which reduced his 'own concise idiom' of German to a shorthand that Maitland called 'algebraic' (his own rueful comment in writing to Tout was that legal history 'can never be easy or amusing, excepting of course with a master hand, like F.W. Maitland').[108] Even so, one would estimate the *Sachglossar* to total 450,000 words, and a mere fraction of these are given to analysis rather than presentation. In consequence, there is extraordinarily little sense of legal change throughout the long Anglo-Saxon period. H.W.C. Davis shrewdly noted in a generous review that the entry on the Hundred 'contains a theory of institutional development which is in flat opposition to the orthodox reading of the evidence', yet which 'is not altogether an average example of the author's method'. 'As a rule Dr Liebermann is no revolutionary ... his general conception of the Anglo-Saxon system [*sic*] is derived from Stubbs and the Germanists'; but in this case, 'the author (was) under the spell of that acute critic, Professor Munro Chadwick'.[109] Since Chadwick had given the most evolutionary account of Anglo-Saxon institutions till that date (or this), the exception is significant. More typical are the eight and a half columns on theft, a central topic for Old English codes. The entry is in twenty-four numbered sections, of which just one concedes that tenth-century legislators substantially increased the severity of penalties. This section is buried in the middle; nor does the point affect an argument that otherwise draws indiscriminately on evidence from all periods.[110] The Anglo-Saxon law of theft receives

108   *CP* III, pp. 466–7 (referring to Liebermann's 'pamphlets' on the Anglo-Norman law-books); Tout, 'Felix Liebermann', p. 317.
109   *Gesetze* II, pp. 516–22; Davis, 'Anglo-Saxon Laws', p. 427; Chadwick, *Studies*, pp. 202–62.
110   *Gesetze* II, 'Diebstahl' 17) – 17e), pp. 350–1.

juristic, not historical, analysis. A high proportion of evidence, moreover, is taken from the Anglo-Norman law-books. To an important degree, Liebermann's vision of the evidence was, like Maitland's, foreshortened by the twelfth-century perspective from which he began.

In this as in many entries, Liebermann was ready to refer to other Germanic laws, citing Brunner or Wilda's *Strafrecht der Germanen*, another *Rechsschule* classic. But his objective was, as usual since Grimm, recovery of the Common Germanic in the background. That was one reason why he was more inclined to adduce the Icelandic or Scandinavian evidence that was the staple of the 'urgermanisch' than parallels in (for example) Carolingian capitularies.[111] He thought that the jury of Æthelred's code might be 'a daughter of the Nordic or influenced by the Inquest Jury of the Frankish *missus*-court'.[112] The queer thing about this judgement, given that the Frankish evidence is ninth-century and the Scandinavian twelfth-century or later, is that the odds are considered equal. In any case, 'the later Anglo-Norman jury ... is no continuation of the (Anglo-Saxon)'. Old English law's historical function was to supply a relatively pure font of Germanic antiquity. It could hardly be polluted by Frankish any more than by Roman effluent. Nor could so still a surface easily be connected with the dynamic onrush of Angevin Common Law. Because it was pristine, pre-conquest law remained remote.

Davis concluded his review by hoping that Liebermann would one day tell his story 'in a more synthetic form'. Holdsworth thought that he might have done, had he not been killed by a car outside his Berlin home in October 1925.[113] The signs are that Liebermann himself considered that he had done what he could. He told friends that he saw his task as presenting all facts discoverable from laws. German and English obituarists who knew him well thought that his *Sachglossar* had selected just the right key; to have drawn out the lines of development into Angevin times would have put it at risk of going sooner out of date.[114] Much more regrettable is that he had not in fact, as the English obituarist anticipated, 'prepared the way for a fuller understanding of the law of Henry II's time'. His static view of the subject joined with his crabbed mode of expression (and, it must surely be penitently confessed, his language) to deter Anglophone historians from picking up such ends as he did leave loose. It is a remarkable, indeed an appalling, fact that hardly more has been written on early English law since 1916 than in the century before.

4   Since Liebermann

The mould set hard with Sir William Holdsworth's gargantuan *History of English Law*. Of some 9000 pages, barely 150 were assigned to Anglo-Saxon

---

111   Cf. Campbell, 'Observations on English Government', pp. 43–4 (pp. 159–60). It is doubtless relevant that von Maurer was an exponent of Scandinavian even more than of Old English legal antiquities.
112   *Gesetze* II, 'Geschworene' 1), p. 466.
113   Davis, 'Anglo-Saxon Laws', p. 430; Holdsworth, *Historians of Anglo-American Law*, pp. 126–8.
114   Heymann, 'Liebermann', pp. xxxv–xxxvi; Hazeltine, 'Liebermann', pp. 328, 342 (the latter passage echoing Heymann verbally).

law, most of them in a section on 'Anglo-Saxon Antiquities' at the start of Volume II. Volume I opened squarely in 1066, with the statement: 'At the time of the Norman Conquest there was no central court which regularly administered a law common to the whole country'. This was upheld by reference to the 'three main bodies of custom ... the Mercian law, the Dane law and the West Saxon law' – a theory accepted only with reserve by Maitland himself.[115] The Anglo-Saxon system was one of flabbily-knit communities infested by proto-feudal private jurisdictions.[116] The Anglo-Saxons produced the occasional strong man, but these lacked the 'constructive talent' or overseas contacts to 'develop the natural advantages of the country'. 'It was the Norman Conquest which supplied the man and the dynasty'.[117] This was not an unusual picture of pre-conquest England in the earlier twentieth century.

However, this chapter should conclude with such foretastes as there have been of an alternative approach.[118] The first of these can be labelled 'unfinished business'. Julius Goebel's *Felony and Misdemeanour* was originally subtitled 'A study in the History of English Criminal Procedure'. That implies a quest for the origins of the vigorous campaign against crime which is a hallmark of the early Common Law.[119] It is impossible to know how the argument would have developed, because its second volume was never written. What the extant volume argued was that the Carolingian (up to a point, even the Merovingian) regime developed a sense of crime as a threat to the community at large which was not, as Brunner and others had thought, inherent in early Germanic law; that Brunner was right that these procedures survived post-Carolingian chaos; but that Maitland was wrong that Anglo-Saxon royal justice was as eroded as Frankish by jurisdictional grants. One would therefore guess that Goebel aimed to show how Angevin 'felony and misdemeanour' arose from the new weight given by surviving English public jurisdiction to lingering Frankish principles. Among his many insights was an appreciation of the role of a broadly defined 'fidelity' in generating a communal concept of crime (see chapter 9). Erudite, incisive and humane, his is surely the twentieth century's best book in English on early medieval law. But it lacked the impact it deserved, because its subtitle deflected the attention of the continental legal historians who had most to learn from what there is of it, while historians

---

115   Holdsworth, *History* I, pp. 3–4. Cf. n. 76; and also *SE*, p. 99.

116   Holdsworth, *History* I, pp. 15–24. S.B. Chrimes added a useful new chapter to Volume I, jettisoning Maitland's feudalized immunities in favour of the skilfully modified position prepared by Helen Cam. A mark of the extent of Holdsworth's influence is that his editors saw a need to add this chapter, given the importance of his Volume I to the Legal History Syllabus in University and Bar Exams: p. x.

117   Holdsworth, *History* II, pp. 117–18. A very marked feature of this whole section is Liebermann's scant presence in the footnotes; Sir William was perhaps not at ease with his German.

118   It is no part of the purpose of this section to review everything written on pre-conquest law since 1916; but it is worth noting that Plucknett, *Concise History*, is more sympathetic than Holdsworth to Old English legacies, and Milsom, *Historical Foundations*, less. Modern discussions of frankpledge and jury, courts and franchises, and once again of property, are left for consideration of these subjects in chapters 9, 10 and 11. Likewise, the views of the century's most influential Anglo-Saxon historian, Sir Frank Stenton, are considered with reference to his discussion of particular codes and issues (e.g. chapter 5, p. 284, chapter 10 (3(ii)), chapter 11 (1)); on the whole, he followed Maitland's lead.

119   Goebel, *Felony and Misdemeanour*; the 1976 reissue substitutes the sub-title 'A Study in the History of Criminal Law'.

of English law were put off by its extended discussion of Frankish issues. The irony is that if a case is made for a concept of afflictive punishment in pre-conquest England such as Goebel brilliantly elucidated for Francia, he never needed his elaborate Frankish backdrop at all. It may be that his discussion of Anglo-Saxon public jurisdiction let him see that he had pursued a blind alley; which was why he abandoned his project.

An in some ways similar case was Doris Stenton's *English Justice between the Norman Conquest and the Great Charter*. Despite its title this allotted the unusually high proportion of half as much space to 'The Anglo-Saxon Inheritance' as to the 'Angevin Leap Forward'. Her theme was the transition in the 150 years before 1215 from 'blood feud and the ordeal ... justice administered by peasant suitors in immemorial local courts' to 'trial by jury ... before royal judges conscious of an omnipresent king'.[120] It was the standard post-Maitland story. Yet Stenton sharply observed the note of hesitancy in Maitland's commitment to the Brunner thesis. Her husband's famous theory of heavy Scandinavian colonization in England made her more confident than Liebermann in a 'jury common to the Scandinavian peoples on either side of the North Sea'. But she used this as a basis for reformulating the nineteenth-century vision of pre-conquest practices clearing the ground for twelfth-century initiatives.[121] She continued: 'The rich stream of ... case-law flowing through the Anglo-Saxon period reflects the minds and spirits of a people responsive to reason ... with a clear understanding of the sacral virtue of an oath. It was in this atmosphere that the seeds of the English jury grew and flourished'. This was the first hint of the direction in which close attention to lawsuit records could take the argument.[122]

It is not too much to say that understanding of early medieval European law has now experienced a sea-change brought about by analysis of actual disputing.[123] The justice of feud and settlement is no longer seen as a barbarous prelude to that of judgement and penalty but as a system with its own constructive logic. These perceptions have even been trained on the world of medieval Common Law.[124] But this is itself a warning that resolution of disputes by mechanisms other than executive action does not preclude intervention by a powerful judicial apparatus with a political agenda of its own. That 'feud-centred' justice is most visible in relatively 'stateless' societies does not mean that where it is visible there is no 'state'. It could be as mistaken to move over to a bloodfeud model of Old English justice, however sympathetically envisaged, as it would be wholly to substitute the rhythms of settlement for those of judgement in the thirteenth century. How much less power royal justice had in the tenth century than in the thirteenth remains to be seen.

But an important pointer is that few would now subscribe to Holdsworth's

---

120 Stenton, *English Justice*, p. 1.
121 Stenton, *English Justice*, pp. 16–17; she noted that Sir Paul Vinogradoff, *English Society*, pp. 4–11, was a Maitland contemporary who continued to take this line.
122 Stenton, *English Justice*, p. 17. Cf. my 'Charters, Law and the Settlement of Disputes', and 'Handlist of Anglo-Saxon Lawsuits'; also the implications of van Caenegem, *Royal Writs*, especially pp. 69–81.
123 See my review of the historiographical trend and guide to recent literature in 'Giving God and King their Due', pp. 549–53 (pp. 331–4).
124 Notably by Michael Clanchy, 'Law and Love', and Paul Hyams, 'Feud in Medieval England'.

view of the capacities of the Old English state.[125] This chapter has shown that for most of the history of its study, Anglo-Saxon law was seen as (1) the province not of royal power but of popular liberties; (2) part of the history of a receding Germanic past, not of an ongoing English evoluton; (3) almost unchanging in the 500 years from the code of Æthelberht of Kent to the *Leges Henrici Primi*. As a corollary of these points it has by the canons of Angevin Common Law seemed inert and inept. If there was substance in the first three views, the fourth looks less and less compatible with what else is now thought about the making of an English kingdom.

Meanwhile, important things have happened to the study of law-codes as well as law, bearing on Liebermann's legacy as much as Maitland's. Even before he died, Liebermann was confronted by an irrefutable case that Lambarde's 'lost' manuscript was largely a figment (above, p. 23, chapter 4, pp. 260–2). More serious in its implications was the collapse of the position he took on the degree of responsibility for later Anglo-Saxon legislation assignable to the homilist Archbishop Wulfstan of York (1002–23). Liebermann thought it at most marginal.[126] That he was quite wrong was shown partly by palaeographical research and partly by stylistic analysis. Neil Ker not only pushed back his dating of several manuscripts by decades, but also showed that a number bore Wulfstan's actual script (chapter 4, pp. 188–203). At the same time, Dorothy Whitelock and Dorothy Bethurum proved that numerous texts, from regulations for the Danelaw spuriously fathered on Alfred's successor to Cnut's great code, were indeed drafted by him (chapter 5, pp. 330–65, 389–97).[127] Wulfstan emerged as 'Homilist and Statesman'. But there was more to it than that. The intense, almost pleading, tone of Æthelred's later codes was once seen as yet another sign of his government's flailing inadequacy. Yet, as Sir Frank Stenton observed, it is hardly less evident in Cnut's laws.[128] To require that society purge its guilt before God was therefore not just testimony to the afflictions it was suffering. It meant that relations with God could and should be regulated by law. Wulfstan becomes more than a preacher of genius who drafted laws too. He was the new English kingdom's main exponent of the Biblical ideal that God's People be ruled in accordance with His will: the pre-eminent ideal of Charlemagne's kingship. Anglo-Saxon law gains an ideological dimension beyond the constitutional significance which was all that interested its students for so long.

That insight is born of taking Old English legislation seriously as text. So discussion finally returns to the texts that baffled Plummer, and Maitland too. Like Maitland (but not Palgrave), Plummer thought that Anglo-Saxon law was so obscure because so much remained 'unwritten custom ... beyond our reach'. Up to a point he was of course right. Yet that is not all there is to say. The codes

---

125   It is sufficient to refer here to the epoch-making papers of James Campbell, notably 'Observations on English Government', and 'The Late Anglo-Saxon State'; though it should be noted (as, by legal historians, it on the whole has not) that the 'Anglo-Saxonist *revanche*' has been slowly gathering pace ever since Stenton modulated the Roundian views he published in his *William the Conqueror* (1908).
126   Liebermann, 'Wulfstan und Cnut'.
127   Ker, *Catalogue* no. 164; Ker, 'Handwriting of Archbishop Wulfstan'; Whitelock, 'Wulfstan and the Laws of Cnut'; Bethurum, 'Six anonymous Old English codes'.
128   Stenton, *Anglo-Saxon England*, pp. 409–10.

from Alfred to Cnut still need examination as textual artefacts – as not even Liebermann ever examined them. What does it signify that the remit of legislation remained so limited? Why, if so little was written, was anything written? How and why was it recorded? Is it to be seen as flotsam on an ocean of custom, as placid as it is unplumbed? Can legislation be made to show what kings and their councillors were trying to do? Need the fact that it is so much harder to know about law before 1066 or 1166 mean that there was less royal action? Or is it inherent in the sort of historical evidence likely to be left by a culture at this stage of development that change happen before it be fully recorded? Only by first answering these questions can it be decided whether English law's distinctive history truly began under Henry II. To attempt answers to them is the goal of this volume. To assess the implications for English legal history is the aim of its sequel.

CHAPTER 2

The Background and Origin of
Early English Legislation

Among the other benefits which he thoughtfully conferred on his people, he also established enacted judgements for them, following the examples of the Romans (*decreta illi iudiciorum iuxta exempla Romanorum*), with the counsel of his wise men. These were written in English speech, and are held and observed by them to this day. Among them, he set down first of all what amends were due from whoever removed by theft any property either of the Church or of the bishop or of other orders: he wished of course to give protection to those whose persons and teaching he had received.[1]

Thus, the Venerable Bede, the first and greatest of England's historians, on the code of King Æthelberht of Kent, the first monument of the law and language that are English hallmarks. It is among the most quoted and debated passages in Bede's perennially deliberated masterpiece. More must be said later about its apparently accurate account of what Æthelberht had done (pp. 93–101). For now, attention may focus on its most discussed phrase: 'iuxta exempla Romanorum'.

Like so much that Bede wrote, its meaning is both patent and elusive. The 'example of the Romans' ought to mean simply that Æthelberht was following Rome's model in one of its chief sources of pride: the giving of written law (pp. 128–9). To make law in writing was to be like Romans: a consummation devoutly wished by most post-Roman authorities. Yet why, if that were what Bede meant, did he write of *plural* 'examples'? That word could imply that he had in mind the *exemplars*, the actual law-codes, of still more or less recognizably 'Roman' regimes in the fifth- and sixth-century West. Bede did use 'Romanus' to describe identifiably Roman traits in the post-Roman period. His account of the building of the monastery at Monkwearmouth sees Benedict Biscop's hiring of masons and glaziers from Merovingian Gaul as an adoption of 'the Roman custom (*mos*) that he always loved'. 'Romani' might thus be *'sub-Romans'*.[2] At all events, Bede, if not Æthelberht, directed his gaze beyond the shores of Kent to the grander world of law-giving by Rome and its heirs.

---

1 *Bede, Hist Eccl.* ii 5, pp. 150–1.
2 Hist. Abb. 5, p. 368. The major exploration of this angle is Wallace-Hadrill, *Early Germanic Kingship*, pp. 32–44; he reasserted his view in *Bede: a Historical Commentary*, pp. 60–1, but never cited the Hist. Abb. parallel.

That is also the stance adopted by this chapter, and for three reasons. The first is that much is going to be said throughout both volumes of this book about the ways in which the legislation of the new kingdom of the English compared with law-making (or lack of it) by contemporary regimes. It will be argued that Anglo-Saxon law-makers were aware of the example set by those who from the fifth to the tenth century aspired to Roman standards, above all the Carolingians. The second is that among this book's methodological assumptions is that European panoptics lend perspective to English evidence that rarely has two dimensions, let alone three. When it is difficult to be sure what was being done north of the Channel, guidance *may* (the emphasis is important) be had from what was happening to the south. The third is that pronouncements by any regime obviously need to be understood in terms of its own political culture. The political culture of the first English kingdom was European. Continental parallels therefore form the top layer of the context wherein early English legislation is embedded. This chapter is the first of four which seek to dig down through that context to the roots of the Old English legislative tradition. Its earlier and longer section sets the scene for Alfred's law-making by outlining the written law made and experienced in the West down to the 890s, and more particularly in the Carolingian era (750–887). A second section then examines the lessons that the laws of Æthelberht and of his immediate successors may have for the later and more continuous Anglo-Saxon tradition.[3]

1   The Legal World of 'Lupus'

In the third or fourth decade of the ninth century, a dispute broke out between the 'advocates' (i.e. agents-at-law) of the abbeys of St Denis and Fleury over the possession of some serfs.

> Each side assembled a number of legal experts and judges (*legum magistri et iudices*) to dispute on their behalf. In addition, Jonas bishop of Orléans and Donatus count of Melun were present at the plea as emissaries from the king's person (*missi a latere regis*). However, they were unable to bring the suit to a conclusion at that meeting (*placito*), because judges of Salic law could not properly assess ecclesiastical property subject to Roman law (*Salicae legis iudices ecclesiasticas res sub Romana constitutas lege discernere perfecte non possent*). So the royal emissaries decided to adjourn the plea to Orléans. Legal experts and judges therefore came to the agreed place, and vigorously disputed for each party; also present were legal specialists (*legum doctores*) both from Orléans and from the Gâtinais. The judges indeed spun out the case for some time because one side would not yield to the other, nor would

---

3   The following account of the European background to early Anglo-Saxon law-making expands on my '"*Inter Cetera Bona Genti Suae*" ... ', especially pp. 965–8, 986–93 (pp. 180–2, 194–8), largely in turn echoed by '*Exempla Romanorum* ... ', especially pp. 16–17, 23–4. Like those papers, this discussion can be read as a *Retractatio – not* a retraction – of my '*Lex Scripta* and *Verbum Regis*': it aims to clarify what that paper permitted to be misunderstood, to modulate what it over-stated, and above all to take account of the high quantity and quality of work on the topic which began simultaneously in German, and which has continued in German and English ever since (e.g, below, nn. 105–6, 110, 139, 142); manuscripts and lawsuits (sections 1 (ii) and (iii) below) were aspects of which I certainly took inadequate note in 1977.

the other go along with the first. But it was at length adjudged that witnesses stand forward for each side, who, having taken an oath, would fight with shields and staffs, so bringing the dispute to an end. Yet, although that seemed just and lawful (*rectum*) to all, a certain legal specialist from the Gâtinais, who ominously bore a bestial rather than human name, and who turned up corrupted by a gift from the St Denis advocate (who feared that their witness would be discredited if the two fought it out) proposed the opinion (*iudicium*) that it was wrong for witnesses to wage a battle over ecclesiastical property; it would be much better that the advocates should share out the serfs between them. Genesius, the deputy count (*vicecomes*) agreed with this view, saying that it was more lawful for the serfs to be partitioned than for witnesses to wage battle, to which view he won over the whole assembly. St Benedict, however, in no way forgot that judge and lawyer (*legislator*), who first perversely and as brutishly as his name put the case for partitioning the serfs. For no sooner was the partition of the serfs carried out than he was so smitten by a just judgement of God that he could not say anything at all, having utterly lost the use of his tongue. His friends who were present recognized the truth of the matter and led him to the monastery of the holy confessor he had gravely offended, where he spent a month seeking the famous father's help with his prayers. He finally recovered a measure of health and went home; but so long as he lived, he never managed to utter St Benedict's name with his own voice.[4]

This story is one of the few well-known lawsuits of the early medieval West. It owes its fame chiefly to what it supposedly reveals about the principle of 'personality of law': the principle that legal parties were entitled to be judged by their own law.[5] It is a principle rather easier to find in textbooks than in evidence. The Fleury-St Denis suit does little to uphold it. It was not that one party claimed to live by Salic law and the other by Roman, but that judges whose remit was 'Salic' felt unable to handle a case between parties which each, as churches, adhered to Roman law (pp. 64, 71). Nor did the substitution of partition for trial by battle arise from preference for Roman dispensations. The intervention by the Gâtinois with a 'beastly name' was based on a Carolingian royal decree, as will be seen when the case is re-examined later (pp. 70–2).

More immediately interesting is the man whose name presaged his allegedly mindless and predatory intervention. Someone in the early-ninth-century Gâtinais had a name that was indeed beast-like, and he may very well have been *legis doctor*. The learned Servatus Lupus was monk then abbot of Ferrières, forty miles north-east of Fleury and half way between it and Melun.[6] Other leading Gâtinois of the time must have had names with zoomorphic elements.[7] Some of

---

4 [Ex] Miraculis Sancti Benedicti 25, pp. 489–90; the translation is my own, though gratefully based on that of Ganshof into French (as next note). Further discussion of this source and of the literature arising is at pp. 70, 75 and nn. 211, 231–2 below.

5 Vinogradoff, *Roman Law in Medieval Europe*, pp. 26–7. For the 'personality' principle, see Guterman, *From Personal to Territorial Law*, briefly referring to this case, p. 105. The case itself is rightly viewed from a different angle by Ganshof, 'Contribution à l' étude de l' application du Droit Romain et des Capitulaires', pp. 590–601; also by Nelson, 'Dispute Settlement in Carolingian West Francia', p. 63, and 'Literacy in Carolingian Government', p. 290.

6 This suggestion has the authority of Professor Nelson (as previous n.); for its chronological problems see n. 10.

7 Holder-Egger's suggestion, [Ex] Miraculis, p. 490 (n. 3), was 'Vulpis': not a conspicuously fashionable Carolingian name.

them were presumably legally expert. But Lupus of Ferrières was the compiler of a remarkable collection of laws current in the Carolingian empire. It survives in two copies plus a fragment and is notable for its distinctive texts of all the main codes. Near the start of one copy, and just before a striking illustration of the putative authors of Salic law, stand a pair of poems:

> A HEROIC POEM ON THE APPEARANCE OF THIS WHOLE SUPERB VOLUME. The lord (*heros*) Evrard had this book of laws written: a wise man, he purveyed it to all the wise (*prudens prudentibus*). Whoever loves knowledge of all cases that the laws concern, and wishes himself to seem lucid as a judge to all (*cunctas legum cognoscere causas/ arbiter et clarus vult omnibus ipse videri*) will eagerly and longingly explore it with eyes and mind. He will see Salic Franks depicted at the outset, and may then glimpse their actual written law. In the next book he will meet Ripuarians, followed by their law curbing many crimes. The third image to adorn it is of Lombards, you may view their collected law with wondering eye. Then you will see portraits of a host of Alamans and may survey their law which follows at once. And Bavarian law itself takes up the fifth book. Reader, should you wish, you may perceive in such comely forms an abiding figure of the Franks (*Francorum scema per aevum*). Here is Charles with Pippin, how radiant in countenance! Here are Caesar Louis and Lord Lothar, how their laws resound universally! They shine now, they will, as God grants, shine in time to come.
>   ANOTHER ELEGIAC POEM. These well-meaning little verses, wise Evrard, this lowly Lupus has written for you. If Eternal God would prolong the years of life, then I think even I might sing greater things more worthily. May you be guarded, raised, saved, honoured, loved by Father, Father's son and the sweet Spirit.[8]

The Evrard addressed was in all probability the Marquis Eberhard of Friuli, whose will disposed of a volume very like Lupus' collection. Eberhard was in touch with Abbot Hrabanus of Fulda, and Servatus Lupus is known to have been there in the early 830s, so it is usually deduced that the collection introduced by these verses was the work of Servatus himself.[9] There can be no certainty in this identification. Still less secure is the equation of either Servatus or 'Lupus' with the bestially obtrusive know-all who enraged St Benedict.[10] Any argument thereon founded is a conjuring trick. But even *legerdemain* may be instructive. The ensuing account of Carolingian written law adopts the fiction (if so it be)

---

8   The verses were first printed in *Leges Alamannorum et Baiwariorum*, ed. Merkel, pp. 3–4; and later in *Poetae*, ed. Strecker, p. 1059. My rendition is indebted to the German one offered by Mordek (as next n.), pp. 1039–47; see also Schott, 'Zur Geltung der Lex Alamannorum', pp. 101–3.
9   The evidence for this reconstruction is in *Hrabanus, ... Epistolae*, ed. Dümmler, 42 (to Eberhard) and 23 (to Lupus himself), pp. 481–7, 429–30 (and cf. pp. 523, 397*), and *Lupus, Epistolae*, ed. Dümmler, 1, pp. 7–9; also in Levillain, *Loup de Ferrières, Correspondance* 1, pp. 2–11. Professor Mordek endorses the collection's attribution to Servatus Lupus, but gives reason to think that it may have been made in or soon after 836 as a by-product of the negotiatons between Louis and Lothar, which involved both Eberhard and patrons of Lupus, and when Eberhard married Louis' daughter: 'Frühmittelalterliche Gesetzgeber', pp. 1048–9.
10   The obvious objection is chronological: if Servatus Lupus was at Fulda for some years after 828, and if, as Hincmar averred, 'De Villa Novilliaco', ed. Mordek, 'Exemplarische Rechtsstreit', pp. 103–4, Donatus lost the county of Melun in 834 for supporting Lothar against his father, not to regain his position until Charles the Bald's accession (when Bishop Jonas was dead), the case must have taken place when Lupus was in his early twenties and precociously expert indeed. But it is not clear that Donatus' disgrace was as total as Hincmar's retrospect supposed: Krah, *Absetzungsverfahren*, pp. 72–5.

that a leading light of Carolingian culture, the collector of laws, and the court-room busybody were one and the same. The 'Lupus' treatment of legal texts offsets more 'official' Carolingian expositions of *lex scripta*.[11] The Lupus/Eberhard collection serves as a standard by which to measure other law books circulating in the eighth- and ninth-century Frankish realms. The Orléans initiative of the *legis doctor* is compared with the reception that courts generally gave to enacted law. The next three chapters will survey written law in the Old English kingdom from the successive angles of the impression it made on historians and recorders of lawsuits, of its manuscripts, and of texts themselves. They are fore-shadowed here by a review of these phenomena in the Carolingian empire. The lurking background presence of 'Lupus', however contrived, may give the exercise coherence, and perhaps more.

(i) Legal texts

As represented by its surviving copies (pp. 54–6), Lupus' collection comes in two unequal parts.[12] The first three-quarters comprises texts of the Salic, Ripuarian, Lombard, Alaman and Bavarian law-codes, each except the Bavarian with the frontispiece promised by Lupus' verses (p. 32), and each with a preliminary list of chapters. The last quarter is given over to the 'capitularies' of 'the most outstanding Lord Emperor Charles' (768–814), of Pippin (Charlemagne's son and king of Italy 781–810), and 'of the Lord Emperor Lothar' (emperor and ruler of Italy, 817–55). Lothar was the son and increasingly alienated associate of Charlemagne's heir Louis (814–40), so one of his partizans must have excised the legislation by Louis to which Lupus' poem alluded.[13] It will later be pointed out that Lupus' grouping of capitularies under the name of the rulers who issued them is not the normal ninth-century arrangement (pp. 53, 67–8). More important for the moment is what he did with the law-codes.

Pre-eminent among these is *Lex Salica*. Lupus' presentation of it is very striking.[14] *Lex Salica* was an ancient code, with origins at the dawn of the

11   For a continental scholar's parallel (and in fact strictly contemporary) presentation of this evidence to broadly similar effect, see Siems, 'Textbearbeitung und Umgang mit Rechtstexten', especially pp. 50–72.
12   For this, and a great deal of what follows, see the seminal account of the MSS in Mordek, *Bibliotheca*, pp. 131–49, 256–68. Profesor Mordek is supervising an edition by Dr Oliver Münch of the Lupus collection as presented in its extant manuscripts.
13   On the highs and lows of Lothar's relations with his father and brothers see Nelson, *Charles the Bald*, especially pp. 72–159.
14   What follows may be traced with relative ease thanks to the exemplary clarity of Eckhardt's MGH *Lex Sal.* edition of 1962/9: vol. I sets out the Merovingian 'A' and 'C' texts/MSS, alongside Charlemagne's *Karolina* ('K') – 'B', a textual 'ghost', is best ignored – and vol. II the earlier Carolingian 'D' and 'E' versions, with the Lupus revision ('S') printed pp. 198–230 (this colossal enterprise would have been yet more invaluable if equipped with an adequate concordance). But his MGH edition essentially reproduces the texts he established over the previous decade in the series 'Germanenrechte'; his 1953 and 1954 volumes contain, unlike the MGH introductions, a full statement of his case on the origins of the Merovingian and Carolingian texts, while that of 1957 (besides printing the Lupus version) reconsiders his position in the light of the first critical reaction to it; see also below, nn. 24, 28. *The Laws of the Salian Franks*, trans. Fischer Drew basically renders Eckhardt's reconstructed Merovingian text, but additionally that of Lupus (confusingly called '*Lex Salica Karolina*' and attributed not to Lupus but to an early-ninth-century north Italian), pp. 171–225. For more on the history of successive 'official' recensions, see below, pp. 41–2, 46–7, 62.

Merovingian hegemony or before (pp. 40–2). The ordering of its pristine sixty-five titles had never been wholly logical, and was further disturbed by matter slotted into later Merovingian and early Carolingian recensions.[15] Lupus aimed to remedy this defect. The first title, 'On Summons (*De Mannire*)' had led into a set of titles on stealing animals. Lupus stuck to the procedural theme by putting next the titles from later in the code on refusing summons, on injustice by court officials and on accusing innocent or absent men before the king.[16] He then inserted titles on robbing or burning churches and killing clerics that the code had acquired as it evolved.[17] There follow titles on varieties of homicide and assault, which conclude with a juxtaposition of two once quite distinct titles on robbing corpses.[18] Lupus later takes care to group together nearly all clauses on theft – most but far from all of which had originally followed *De Mannire*. Almost all of Lupus' changes meant transferring titles from their customary place in the *lex* to one where they accompany laws on related themes. Not every anomaly is resolved. Titles are moved about but not broken up; those including laws on tangential issues tend to stay that way.[19] It was not actually necessary to have two clauses on corpse-robbery; one was a revision of the other. The resulting contradictions, extending to variant penalties for the same offence, are not ironed out.[20] Nevertheless, the overall effect of Lupus' efforts was a *Lex Salica* in roughly ordered array.

The other text thoroughly overhauled by Lupus was the Lombard edict (p. 39). His rearrangement here went beyond even that of *Lex Salica*. Lombard legislation had begun in 643 with King Rothari's vast and fairly comprehensive *edictum*, and had been supplemented with laws by four of his successors – almost annually so from 720 to 735 under Liutprand.[21] What Lupus crafted was a 'Concordia' of all this law-making. That is to say, he matched the laws of Rothari with those of later kings on similar topics; then, having exhausted Rothari's coverage, he arranged as yet unallocated laws by these later kings according to their own subject-matter.[22] Rothari anyway organized his code so that laws on any one subject were quite easily found. But Lupus improved access to it by grouping all laws in sixty 'capitula', with headings spelled out in a preliminary contents-list. The title he gave the whole exercise expressed a hope that those

15　See my '*Lex Scripta* and *Verbum Regis*', p. 116 (14–15).

16　*Lex Sal.* 'S' ii – v ('A'/'C' lvi, li, lvii, xviii; 'D'/'E' xci, lxxxvii, xcii, xxiv; 'K' lix, liii, lx, xx).

17　*Lex Sal.* 'S' vi (cf. 'C' lv:7; 'D'/'E' lxxvi lxxviii; 'K' lviii:1–3).

18　*Lex Sal.* 'S' xx – xxi ('A'/'C' xiv:9–10, lv:1–5; 'D'/'E' xviii – xix; 'K' xvii, lvii – and on this issue see further nn. 20, 94).

19　Thus *Lex Sal.* 'S' xiii:3 ('A'/'C' xliii:3, 'K' xlv:3) on killing in the open by a 'band', which belongs not in this clause (otherwise on killing at a feast) but in the one before. Cf. Siems, 'Textbearbeitung', p. 61.

20　*Lex Sal.* 'S' xx – xxi. The original Merovingian titles (not represented in all copies of the seemingly earliest text) are 'A' xiv:9–10, lv:1,4–5; the latter was amplified at the 'C' stage by lv:2–3,6–7; 'D'/'E' xviii – xix manage to integrate these clauses into a coherent statement ('C' lv:6–7 moving to 'D' lxxvi – lxxvii); not so 'K', Lupus' immediate source: see below, p. 47, and n. 94.

21　The standard edition is *Gesetze der Langobarden/Leges Langobardorum 643–866*, trans. and ed. Beyerle; but a fuller set of texts, including Lupus', with detailed (if incomplete) account of MSS, is *Leges Langobardorum*, ed. Bluhme (with Boretius). A translation of legislation to 755 is Fischer Drew, *The Lombard Laws*.

22　*Leg. Lang.* (Bluhme), pp. 235–89 (with useful if not wholly accurate synoptic table of distribution of materials, p. 289).

'seeking the law (*legem querentibus* [going to law?]) could more easily find what they want'. There is no reason to doubt that this was his motive; nor, certain slips aside, to question his success.[23]

His revision of other codes was less comprehensive. *Lex Ribuaria* (p. 43) was an earlier-seventh-century text, loosely based on *Lex Salica* itself though with important new matter.[24] It had structural defects like its Salic parent's. But Lupus was this time content to make a few minor relocations, and to provide an expanded chapter-list as better guidance to what each contained.[25] The Bavarian code may also have originated in the earlier-seventh-century but is extant only as recast in the mid-eighth (pp. 43–4).[26] Its sonorous prologue added a summary history of Frankish legislation to Isidore of Seville's account of the world's great codifiers (p. 55), and Lupus used it as the overture to his whole collection. The *Lex* itself had been organized not in relatively brief titles but in booklets of serried laws on widely-defined topics. Lupus dropped this scheme for one like his Ripuarian system, emerging with 120-plus chapters.[27] This was on balance another boon to those wishing to consult the text. Lastly, the Alaman code (p. 43), also eighth-century as extant but with clear traces of a seventh-century origin, is almost untouched by comparison with the others.[28] The likeliest reason is simply that Lupus thought it in least need of attention. It is a generally lucid presentation with fairly explicit headings.

The overall impression left by Lupus' collection is that he had judges' needs in mind, as his introductory verses proclaim. Dr Johnson's comment on women's preaching was to compare it with a dog walking on its hind-legs: 'it is not done well, but you are surprised to see it done at all'. The central point made by Lupus' programme is that it *needed* to be done at all. It was on the initiative of one thoughtful individual that serious steps were taken to facilitate use of the Frankish empire's codes of law. Modest and flawed though it be, this effort was far more radical than anything ever essayed by a Frankish government. Charlemagne reissued *Lex Salica*, probably more than once. So did his father, and at least one Merovingian predecessor. Charlemagne did still less to revise it

23 For defects see Siems, 'Textbearbeitung', pp. 67–70.
24 The standard edition is *Lex Ribuaria*, ed. Beyerle and Buchner. But there is another (with the chapter-numbering of the nineteenth-century edition) by Eckhardt in his habitual Germanenrechte format. *Laws of the Salian and Ripuarian Franks*, trans. Rivers, follows the Beyerle-Buchner text while giving both sets of chapter numbers.
25 Lupus' chaptering (that of MSS 'A6/7') can be compared at a glance with that of most MSS in Beyerle-Buchner's table, pp. 52–72; e.g., tit. '24', p. 54, is transferred to a more logical position. See too Siems, 'Textbearbeitung', pp. 56–7, who again notes lapses.
26 *Lex Baiwariorum*, ed. de Schwind, is the standard edition, but was severely handled by Krusch (cf. n. 28; and for the debate he inspired on the origins of the south German codes, below, nn. 339–40); the most serviceable edition, though of only one MS, is K. Beyerle's; this is the text translated by Rivers, *Laws of the Alamans and Bavarians*.
27 Siems, 'Textbearbeitung', pp. 57–9; the table offered by Merkel's edition (n. 8 above), pp. 358–73, is easier to follow than de Schwind's, pp. 204–60.
28 The basic edition (again much battered by Krusch) is Lehmann, *Leges Alamannorum*, but it should be consulted in the second and corrected edition by the indefatigable Eckhardt (the one translated by Rivers, as n. 26); Eckhardt summarizes, pp. 2–3, the main differences made by his own important edition, *Leges Alamannorum*. Lehmann provides a table of Lupus' chapters (again, '6/7'), pp. 36–53.

than had they. If any early medieval ruler had the ability to realize his objectives it was he. How is his reticence to be explained?

Answering this question requires some consideration of Charlemagne's legislative heritage.[29] The first of its two main elements was the legacy of Roman law, most prominently the mighty bulk of late imperial codification. The decisive influence for the Franks was not Justinian's *Corpus Iuris* (529–34), which before the twelfth century had little measurable impact in the West beyond parts of Italy and areas to the immediate North.[30] Even in Justinian's Byzantium it was above all an encyclopedia of devoted jurisprudential learning, whose peripheral relevance is brought out by the fact that the flow of fresh imperial legislation ('Novels') became a trickle after the death of Tribonian, its chief architect, then dried up almost completely for two centuries.[31] What counted in the West was the *Codex Theodosianus* (438), Theodosius II's codification of the legal pronouncements of emperors since 312.[32] Though nowhere near as ambitious an undertaking as Justinian's, it was still too bulky for regular circulation.[33] But in 506 King Alaric II of the Visigoths issued a *Breviarium* (usually called the 'Lex Romana Visigothorum'), in which an abbreviated Theodosian code was supplemented by a set of Novels down to the end of the western Empire, and by a selection of jurisprudential tracts.[34] Until Roman law studies were taken up in the twelfth-century Schools (chapter 6, pp. 468–71), this was a major source of inspiration to post-Roman rulers, Charlemagne among them.

A more elusive but ultimately more pervasive aspect of Roman law's half-life was what is adhesively if pejoratively labelled 'Vulgar Law'. Its essence was simply that it was Roman law other than that purveyed in the classics of Roman jurisprudence digested by Tribonian's team (it is an open question how far the sophistication of Papinian, Paul and Ulpian ever reflected the experience of ordinary litigants in the provincial courts).[35] One channel of its transmission to the

---

29   Some of what follows is summarized in my '"*Inter cetera bona*"', pp. 967–8 (p. 182), and '*Exempla Romanorum ...*', pp. 16–17. I develop what can itself be no more than a summary here in my forthcoming 'Kings and Kingship'. A useful review of (relatively) recent continental publications is Schott, 'Stand der Leges-Forschung'.

30   See above all Liebs, *Jurisprudenz im spätantiken Italien*, especially pp. 195–282; and cf. below, nn. 144, 207.

31   *Corp. Iur.*, notably for present purposes *Cod. Iust.*, a compilation of imperial decrees since 117 AD. The images of Justinian and of his great Quaestor were recast by Honoré's classic *Tribonian*. Noteworthy is that such '*Novellae* (new laws)' as were issued after the early 540s were in Greek, the speech of Byzantine legal life, not the Latin of the *Corpus Iuris*, vehicle of a cherished but (for Byzantium) receding past; when the legislative flow was restored from the 740s by the Iconoclast emperors' *Ecloga*, this was a truly manageable handbook and of course in Greek.

32   *[Codicis] Theodosiani*, ed. Mommsen and Meyer; the entire sequence of *Cod. Theod.*, eastern and western post-Theodosian 'Novels' 438–68 (vol. III of the Mommsen-Meyer edition) and 'Sirmond Constitutions' is translated by Pharr, *Theodosian Code*. On the nature of late Roman legislation, see Harries, 'Background to the Code', and Matthews, 'Making of the Text'.

33   For the early post-Roman history of *Cod. Theod.*, see Wood, 'Code in the Middle Ages', pp. 164–70, and his 'Roman Law in the Barbarian Kingdoms', pp. 12–14. Only Books VI–XVI survive complete, in two complementary Lyons MSS: Paris BN MS lat. 9643 (*CLA* v 591) and Vatican, Cod. Reg. lat 886 (*CLA* i 110). The chief source for Books I–V is the seriously fragmentary palimpsest Vatican, MS Vat. lat. 5766 (*CLA* i 46). Cf. below, n. 144.

34   The *Breviarium* as such has not been edited since Hänel, *Lex Romana Visigothorum*, which is still indispensable for its non-imperial elements.

post-Roman West was the surviving law-schools of late Antiquity. They are the likely agents of the circulation of texts like the 'Interpretatio' to the contents of Alaric's *Breviarium*.[36] The law-school of Autun, which produced a now much-mutilated copy of Gaius' *Institutes*, is of special interest, in that Autun will tend to reappear in one or another capacity throughout this chapter (pp. 44, 63, 76–9).[37] Another manifestation of vulgarized Roman law is yet more important. The number of western legal documents surviving from 450–650 is exiguous and largely restricted to a corpus of Ravenna papyri that was shamelessly vandalized by early-modern collectors.[38] But it is certain that deeds of exchange, sale, hire, dowry, manumission and indeed judgement went on being drafted as a matter of course. The proof lies in the documentary templates known as Formularies.[39] One is Visigothic, the rest Gallo-Frankish. They survive only in manuscripts of the eighth century or later, but several must have originated in the seventh century or earlier.[40] They represent residues of Roman registrarial activity which, like most one-time municipal responsibilities, had been absorbed into episcopal administration. The transactions prescribed are those of a sub-Roman society habituated to the use of records and the business they articulated.[41] They show that the notarial tradition, the field of the 'town-clerk' or 'country solicitor', was still fecund. Under the Carolingians it would be refertilized (pp. 75–6, 88–9).

Roman legalism was evident not least in the law laid down by barbarian kings themselves. The crucial point is that this activity began as a perpetuation of Roman patterns. Most late Roman edicts were responses to problems brought to the government's attention, and were drafted by Quaestors of the Sacred Palace, who were qualified for the job by a literary as much as a legal training. Barbarian kings likewise issued judgements on submitted petitions, and only later were these assembled into 'Codices'.[42] The fragments that look like remnants of the code attributed by Isidore of Seville to King Euric of the Visigoths (466–84) apparently cite laws made by Euric's father, Theodoric I (419–51). Theodoric would have been reacting to cases brought before him by his subjects, in the accustomed style of Roman emperors or praetorian prefects. Euric's part was to produce a

35   The pioneer of Vulgar Law studies was Ernst Levy, whose most familiar exposition in English is *West Roman Vulgar Law*, and whose most powerful statement was perhaps 'Weströstlisches Vulgarrecht und Justinian'. A telling account of the overall situation is Wieacker, *Allgemeine Zustände und Rechtszustände*.

36   E. Volterra, 'Western post-classical Lawschools'; Riché, *Enseignement du Droit en Gaule*, pp. 4–12; Levy, 'Vulgarization of Roman Law in the Early Middle Ages, as illustrated by *Pauli Sententiae*'.

37   Autun, Bib. Mun., MS 24 (*CLA* vi 726); and compare Montpellier MS 84 (*CLA* vi 793), an assuredly Autun copy of the Breviary of the late-eighth century: cf. Wallace-Hadrill, '*Gothia* and *Romania*', pp. 37–8.

38   Tjäder, *Nichtliterarischen ... Papyri*. The post-700 emergence of a related Italian documentary tradition can be charted in *ChLA* XX–XLV

39   The main series are in *Formul.*, ed. Zeumer. See also Buchner, *Rechtsquellen*, pp. 49–55.

40   For the two oldest Gallic collections, see respectively Bergmann, 'Formulae Andecavenses', and Wood, 'Disputes in late fifth and sixth-century Gaul', pp. 12–14; on the notarial tradition overall, see Bergmann, 'Fortleben des antiken Notariats'.

41   Ganz and Goffart, 'Charters Earlier than 800', pp. 911–12.

42   The rhythms of Roman imperial legislation are expounded as never before by Millar, *Emperor in the Roman World*, especially pp. 203–72, 375–447, 491–549. See also Honoré, *Emperors and Lawyers*; and for the Late Antique pattern, Honoré, 'Making of the Theodosian Code', and Turpin, 'Law Codes and Late Roman Law'.

code of these, of his own decrees, and doubtless of much besides.[43] Visigothic kings had advisers to coach them in the desired role.[44] At this level, the 'examples of the Romans' meant neither more nor less than doing as the emperors had done. There need therefore have been nothing very 'Germanic' about the law of the first barbarian codes. There is little to suggest that these were directed only at society's 'barbarian' element. The Burgundians produced a *Lex Romana Burgundionum* which is a dehydrated counterpart to the *Breviarium Alarici*. Its existence in no way excluded Romans from the purview of the main Burgundian code (>517).[45] Of the latter's 110 clauses, about a third explicitly concern Burgundian and Roman, a mere ten Burgundians alone.[46] There is no reason to think that arrangements in Gaul under the Visigoths or in Italy under the Ostrogoths were any different.[47]

In the last two decades, the very concept of a 'Germanic' law, so dominant in the nineteenth century (chapter 1, pp. 11–12), has seemed increasingly marginal. As scholarly *terra firma* becomes ever more the domain of Vulgar Law, what were once identified as Germanic legal life-forms tend to be reclassified as species of Roman provincial custom stripped of classical plumage.[48] Undeniable in any event is that laws in the more southern parts of post-Roman Europe retained emphatically Roman markings. The code assembled by Kings Chindaswinth and Reccaswinth of the Visigoths (642–72), and revised and extended by Erwig (681), was set out in books, titles and chapters like the Theodosian Code.[49] For this period – and for long afterwards – it was uniquely exhaustive; no other sub-Roman law-making took such notice of contracts and wills, doctors and teachers. But the most telling point is that the Visigoths banned the use of Roman laws. Their own law sufficed for any foreseeable contingency. The ban may even have worked. The codes of Euric and (so far as Spain was concerned) of Alaric

---

43 Isidore, *Historia Gothorum* '35', p. 281; '*Codicis Euriciani Fragmenta*' (in *Leg. Vis.*) cclxxvii, cccv, cccxxvii. Cf. Zeumer, 'Zur Geschichte der westgothischen Gesetzgebung', pp. 419–516, especially pp. 469–71 (the standard account still); also Collins, *Early Medieval Spain*, pp. 24–9; for the MS, see below, nn. 50, 344.

44 Some of the evidence is marshalled in my '*Lex Scripta* and *Verbum Regis*', pp. 125–8; for the context making this likely, add (e.g.) Harries, 'Sidonius Apollinaris, Rome and the barbarians', pp. 306–8; and see too the excellent survey by Brugière, 'Réflexions sur la Crise de la Justice', with her study, *Littérature et Droit*.

45 The standard edition of main code and of Roman 'shadow' remains *Leg. Burg.*, ed. de Salis, translated by Fischer Drew, *The Burgundian Code*. On the date and circumstances of its production, see Wood, 'Code in Merovingian Gaul', pp. 170–2; with Schott, 'Traditionelle Formen der Konfliktlösung in der Lex Burgundionum', pp. 942–4.

46 Figures from *Leg Burg.*, p. 11; cf. P. Amory, 'Ethnic terminology in the Burgundian Laws', pp. 10–28.

47 For more of the vast literature on early Visigothic lawgiving (but rather different views), see Wolfram, *History of the Goths*, pp. 194–7, 455–7; and King, 'King Chindasvind'. The position in Italy, for which the main evidence is *Cassiodorus, Variae*, ed. Mommsen (trans. Barnish, *Cassiodorus: Variae*) and 'Edictum Theodorici', ed. Baviera, remains unclear; but both these sources address Goth and Roman alike.

48 See, e.g., Collins, *Early Medieval Spain*, p. 28, on the relevance for barbarian laws of relations between neighbouring farmsteads in the 'Farmer's Law' from (probably) seventh- or eighth-century Anatolia; and on possible Roman origins of celebrated Salic laws, see Murray, *Germanic Kinship Structure*, pp. 67–87, and Anderson, 'Roman military colonies in Gaul'.

49 *Leg. Vis.*, the main text edited by Zeumer, and inadequately though as yet irreplaceably translated by Scott, *Visigothic Code*.

subsided into palimpsests.[50] Justinian was no more successful in repressing what preceded his *Corpus*.

The Visigothic record was exceptional in degree but not in kind. The almost exactly contemporary edict of Rothari was disposed in succint clauses, not books and titles, but had some of the same scope, covering marriage and succession to property more fully than any barbarian *lex* except the Visigothic. As with Theodosius' Code, only copies 'written or recognized or sealed' by a named 'notary' might be cited in any contention.[51] Rothari's laws and those of all his successors are dated; thus, though the edict was never abrogated when revised by Liutprand and others, any resulting contradictions could be resolved by chronology as Theodosius II had prescribed.[52] Lombard law, like Visigothic, is conceivable only in terms of an at least Romanesque legal culture. Roman symptoms may even be detectable further north. The booklets of the Bavarian *lex* recall Visigothic rather than Frankish arrangements; this text was evidently under the influence of Euric's codex (pp. 35, 100). Some Burgundian laws had eschatocols on their date and place of issue, and described the circumstances that called them forth, like Theodosian novels.[53] Like Visigothic and Lombard texts, the Burgundian and Bavarian *leges* did specify that they really be used.[54] The areas where these laws were current would all be ruled by Charlemagne. Their example was accessible to him, as that of 'Romans' was to Æthelberht.

Yet none of this can possibly mean that the warlords and their followings who came to dictate events in the West as the Roman army vapourized had no identifiable customs. To say so much of the *Romanitas* of post-Roman law is to offset what cannot be Roman. Rothari legislated in Latin but his edict is the main source for the Lombardic language. Whereas Visigothic law excluded the liability of kindreds for anyone's crime, Rothari went on record as increasing the sums due for injury 'that feud be deferred (*ut faida postponatur*)'.[55] He thus accepted the answerability of a kingroup for what its members did, only hoping that adequate compensation would avoid further violence. Feud remained central to his vision of law and order. Feud was not a process known or acceptable to Roman law.[56] Yet what is left of the vernacular literature of Germanic aristocracies pulsates to the rhythm of feud. To deny the Germanic origin of feud-centred law verges on perversity. It follows that Rothari must be taken seriously when claiming to have drawn on 'the ancient law of the Lombards'.[57] One thus reaches another sort of

50   *Leg. Vis.* II i 5, 10–11, 14; cf. King, 'King Chindavsind', pp. 139–52. The palimpsests are respectively Paris BN MS lat. 12161 (*CLA* v 626) – on which see further below, n. 344; and León Arch. Cat. 15 (*CLA* xi 1637).

51   *Ed. Ro.* 388; cf. *Cod. Theod.* I i 5, and '*Gesta Senatus*' (*ibid.*) 8.

52   *Cod. Theod.* I i 6.

53   *Leg. Burg.* xlii – lv, lxii, lxxiv – lxxxi, const. extr. xx.

54   *Leg. Burg.* Pr.:2–5, 10–11, *Lex Bai.* ii:14; cf. *Leg. Vis.* II i 5, 10–11, *Ed. Ro.* 388, epilogues to *Leg. Liutpr.* 713, 717, 721, etc.

55   *Ed. Ro.* 74 (and cf. 75, also 45); *Leg. Vis.* VI i 8.

56   Though see the interesting citation of the fifth-century *Querolus* by Brugière, 'Réflexions', pp. 210–12; this might mean that feud-based law was already affecting provincial legal practice in the fifth century, but the author's point seems to be that any offence can be bought off – i.e. it is another dig at corrupt justice in Salvianic mode.

57   *Ed. Ro.* 386. The best introduction to Lombard law-making and legal practice is Wickham, *Early Medieval Italy*, pp. 36–7, 43–4, 115–28.

'Roman example' at work in the sub-Roman world: the codification of traditional practice so as to give it a Roman patina.

It is thus too that one arrives at the second main element in Charlemagne's heritage. The story this time begins with *Lex Salica*, the most contentious as well as celebrated of the *Volksrechte*.[58] This was almost certainly the work of the first great Frankish king, Clovis (481–511). That is what the early Carolingian Establishment believed, and it is strongly indicated by one clause that hardly makes sense unless its author were already master of Neustria but had not yet broken the barriers of the Loire and Ardennes – a period thus delimited as 486–507.[59] Yet the code was not published in Clovis' name. Its first and shorter prologue, which itself appears not in the earliest 'A' version but in a later Merovingian recension ('C'), has quite another notion of the code's genesis:

> It has been accepted and agreed (*Placuit atque convenit*) among the Franks and their leaders (*proceribus*) that for the sake of keeping peace among themselves, all aggravations of disputes (*incrementa rixarum*) should be curtailed, so that just as they stand out among their neighbours for their strength of arm, so also they may excel them in authority of law, and thus put an end to criminal behaviour (?) (*sumerent criminalis actio terminum*) according to the nature of the cases (*iuxta qualitate causarum*). Hence, there came forward among them, chosen from many (*electi de pluribus*) four men by name Wisogast, Arogast, Salegast and Widogast [from estates (*in villis*) beyond the Rhine] who assembling in three courts (*mallos*), and carefully debating the sources of litigation (*causarum origines*) gave judgement (*iudicium decreverunt*) on each [in this manner].[60]

The four gentlemen in question are otherwise quite unknown. The traditionally-minded author of the *Liber Historiae Francorum*, writing in 727 and echoing this passage, locates them beyond the Rhine. They are called 'rectores' in the 'Longer Prologue', to be cited in a moment.[61] They would seem to represent legal specialists from a part of the world where the customs of the Franks had not yet been diluted by settlement among Gallo-Romans.[62]

---

58   For the tortured historiography, see Roll, *Zur Geschichte der Lex Salica-Forschung*, with Krusch (as below, n. 340), and on the extraordinary circumstances surrounding Eckhardt's 'breakthrough', see Nehlsen, 'Karl-August Eckhardt+'. The indubitable merits even of Eckhardt's editions (above, n. 14) have not foreclosed debate: Schmidt-Wiegand, 'Die kritische Ausgabe der Lex Salica'; see also the comments of Murray, *Germanic Kinship Structure*, pp. 119–33.
59   *Lex Sal.* 'D'/'E' Pr.:3: 'Deo favendi rex Francorum Chlodouius ... primus recepit catholicum baptismum, et quod minus in pactum habebatur idoneum ... fuit lucidis emendatum'; this is the 'Longer Prologue' of the 760s (see below), here following the lead of (a) the 'Epilogue' (late Merovingian and questionably 'official', Eckhardt, *Pactus* I, p. 253), and (b) of the 'Shorter Prologue' (see n. 60); the Epilogue itself refers only to 'primus rex francorum', but Carolingians may be trusted to have known whom this designated. The Loire-Ardennes clause is *Lex Sal.* 'A'/'C' xlvii; cf. the tough-minded discussion by Wood, *Merovingian Kingdoms*, pp. 108–14.
60   *Lex Sal.* 'C' Pr.; it may be important that the square-bracketed phrases are *not* in the most authoritative texts, and that they could very well derive from the account in *Lib. Hist. Franc.* (as next n.)
61   *Liber Historiae Francorum* iv, p. 244; *Lex Sal.* 'D'/'E' Pr.:2.
62   That they may have been in some sense historical is suggested by analogy with what Professor Mordek has argued for the comparable Ripuarian figure (below, n. 77). However, to suppose that they were fourth-century Frankish officers in the Roman army (Poly, 'La corde au cou'; cf. Geary, *Before France and Germany*, p. 91) goes beyond the evidence: Wood, 'Roman Law in the Barbarian Kingdoms', pp. 6–8.

There would have been much less scope for debate over the origin of *Lex Salica* had it behaved at all like Visigothic or Lombard legislation. Neither Clovis nor Charlemagne nor any other Frankish legislator made life easier for historians (or judges) by dating their decrees as Lombard kings did. There are no remotely contemporary copies, and superseded versions were allowed to survive to confuse matters, as they were not by the Visigoths.[63] All *Lex Salica* recensions are resolutely anonymous. Nothing makes this plainer than the second, 'longer', prologue, prefacing the 'D' text:

> The outstanding people of the Franks, established by God the Creator, bold in war, loyal to treaties, profound in counsel, noble in body ... bold, swift and tough ... immune from heresy ... questing for the key of knowledge, loving justice, preserving piety. Those who were then *rectores*, chosen from among many, four men named ... [as above] dictated Salic law ... But when at God's pleasure King Clovis of the Franks, restless and comely, first received catholic baptism, [he] and Childebert and Chlothar clearly amended whatever seemed less fitting in the *Pactus* ... Long live he who loves the Franks; may Christ guard their kingdom; may he fill their rulers with the light of his grace, shield their army, buttress their faith; may Jesus Christ, lord of lords, grant them joys of peace and seasons of happiness ... For this is the people who ... in war struck the harshness of the Roman yoke off their necks, and after accepting baptism ... adorned with gold and precious stones the bodies of the holy martyrs whom Romans had burned with fire, carved up with steel or thrown to be torn apart by beasts.[64]

These may be the first chords of the anthemic arrogance that would one day give western Europeans mastery of the world. They certainly make claims that barbarians had shrunk from stating before. More immediately relevant, they add Clovis and his sons to the obscure 'rulers' who allegedly drafted *Lex Salica*. There is little doubt that this text was the work of King Pippin's chaplains.[65] Yet the one thing it does not do is to make any claims for the part played by the dynasty that had now taken charge of Frankish destiny. Pippin, even Charlemagne himself, recedes into the penumbra of Frankish glory, as Clovis once had. To this extent, Frankish law was *barely* royal.

Lex Salica is otherwise much more like Lombard than Visigothic law-making. Its Latin is dotted with German vocabulary, and even equipped with Frankish glosses.[66] Its working assumptions are again those of feud. Coercive intervention by authority in various forms is a last resort – though authority's interest in public

---

63   The oldest of all *Lex Sal.* MSS (Eckhardt's A2) is Wolfenbüttel Weißenburg MS 97, (*CLA* ix 1395), which is certainly datable to the reign of Pippin (751–68) and may well post-date his 'D' text (see next n.); for other early- or even mid-ninth-century 'A' MSS, see below, nn. 173–4, 177, and for MSS of early Carolingian 'D' and E' recensions from well past their 'sell-by date', see nn. 168–9. Near-contemporary manuscripts of the Visigothic Code and of the Lombard Edict are respectively Vatican, Cod. Reg. lat. 1024 (*CLA* i 111) and St Gallen MS 730 (*CLA* vii 949, etc.).

64   I have tried (with the aid of Fischer Drew, *Laws of the Salian Franks*, and, so far as available, Bullough, *Age of Charlemagne*, p. 39) to translate the first 'D' version of this text (Eckhardt, *Lex Salica*, as n. 14, pp. 2–8 – not the 'cleaned-up' versions of the 'E' text or Lupus. But the Latin is decidedly clumsy, and I have at times resorted to paraphrase.

65   For vindication of Eckhardt's view that the language of the 'longer Prologue' was that of Pippin's official Baddilo (cf. *Urk. Pipp.* 16), see Merta, 'Politische Theorie in den Königsurkunden Pippins', p. 127.

66   Schmidt-Wiegand, 'Volksprachigen Wörter der Leges barbarorum'.

order is declared by its taking a share of the payment in certain cases.[67] There is a premium on being a 'Frank or barbarian who lives by Salic law'; one's compensation is double the 'Roman's'. This 'Frank' is a 'free man (*ingenuus*)' with a typical householder's concerns; only the king's guards or guests receive special status.[68] *Lex Salica*, in other words, addresses an audience of 'ordinary' Franks, to which Romans were well-advised to affiliate. The code's language is that of the Franks' new home. It presupposes draftsmanship by the sort of provincial bureaucracy that gave Clovis' father, Childeric, his seal-ring.[69] Some clauses, as in Rothari's edict, suggest that law was being made to cover cases brought to the legislator's notice.[70] But most of *Lex Salica* looks to the past embodied by the four trans-Rhenan 'rectores'. Further, it is by Rotharian standards strikingly selective. Whether the ethnogenesis of the Franks is located in Germanic forests or (as nowadays preferred) in the detritus of the Roman Rhine army, their stated customs might be expected to include sanctions for military indiscipline. Mutiny and desertion are covered by early Rothari clauses. The Visigoths went into the issue in characteristically rhetorical detail.[71] There is no such measure in *Lex Salica*. Yet there *was* a Merovingian penalty for failing to attend the host. In a seventh-century lawsuit, it was 600 *solidi*: the wergeld of an '*antrustio*' (member of the royal guard), i.e the price of a life that would otherwise have been forfeit.[72] Even on critical issues, then, much of the 'ancient law' of the Franks, unlike that of the Lombards, remained unwritten. Nearly everything about *Lex Salica* thus points to the earliest phase of a 'Frankish' population's adjustment to life in a Gallo-Roman province. That makes it all the more extraordinary that so little was done to update it. The 'C' version, which may or may not have had 'official' standing, contented itself with a few insertions (one on illicit degrees of marriage) into the original's sixty-five titles.[73] The 'D' recension, product of the new Carolingian royal chapel, was recast in 100 titles. There were efforts to make it more systematic, for example by homogenizing early decrees on corpse-robbery. There was a new clause on homicide of priests and deacons.[74] Yet it is still the paucity of innovation that catches the eye.

---

67   *Lex Sal.* 'A'/'C' l, lvi; 'A'/'C' xiii:6, xxxv:9, l:3, liii:2,4,8: '*fredus*' is obviously cognate with Old English '*friδ* (peace)'. The fundamental study of Frankish feud remains Wallace-Hadrill, 'Bloodfeud of the Franks'; though cf. Sawyer, 'Bloodfeud in Fact and Fiction'; and White, 'Clotild's Revenge'.

68   The quoted phrase is that of *Lex Sal.* 'A'/'C' xli:1, which is the clause that most clearly distinguishes compensations for the 'Frank', whether 'ingenuus' or 'in truste dominica', from his Roman counterparts, 'homo possessor' or 'conviva regis': xli:5,8–9. 'Homo ingenuus', the standard term for the code's subjects, is identified with 'Salic barbarian' or 'Frank' (and again privileged as against Romans) at xiv:1–3, and with a 'Frank' in later Merovingian insertions at xxxii:3–4, as well as implicitly at xlii:1–4. See now Springer, 'Gab es ein Volk der Salier?'.

69   James, *The Franks*, pp. 61–2.

70   The burden of the fundamental paper by Beyerle, 'Normtypen'; and cf. Wood, *Merovingian Kingdoms*, p. 110. A like case for Rothari was made by Besta, 'Fonti dell' Editto di Rotari'. See also section 2 (ii) – (iii) below.

71   *Ed. Ro.* 6 – 7 (the penalty was death); *Leg. Vis.* IX ii, climaxing in extravagantly worded laws by Wamba and Erwig, where penalties are exile, forfeiture, scalping, enslavement, etc.

72   H39; cf. *Lex Sal.* 'A'/'C' xli:5.

73   *Lex Sal.* 'C' xiii:11 (and cf. above, n. 20) – 'C' supplements can be spotted, as usual, *via* Eckhardt's variegated fonts and scrupulous tabulation of MS readings (cf. n. 14). On the question whether, as Eckhardt thought, 'C' is attributable to King Gunthcramn (561–92) see Wood, *Merovingian Kingdoms*, p. 108.

There was more to early Frankish legislation than the statement and re-statement of *Lex Salica*. In the first place, some kings issued edicts: Novels, as it were, which were more obviously in the Roman tradition. Sixth-century legislation says a lot more about '*latrones* (brigands?)' than does *Lex Salica*. The king's court is generally more active.[75] The *Decretio* of Childebert II (594–6) is detectably aggressive about theft and homicide. It was penned, significantly, by an official with a Roman background, Asclepiodatus – and it was dated.[76] Secondly, law was 'given' to associates or subjects of the Franks. *Lex Ribuaria*, certainly seventh-century, aimed to give Austrasian (eastern) Franks their counterpart to a *Lex Salica* now identified as Neustrian. The Ripuarian equivalent to the Salic *rectores* has recently been identified as a trans-Rhenan *dux* of the period.[77] The earliest form of Alaman law, extant only in fragments, was probably promulgated by Chlothar II (584–629), in that the main text of their *Lex* is often ascribed to Chlothar and an assembly of bishops, dukes and counts (pp. 35, 54), though actually issued by an Alaman *dux* in the early eighth century at a time of transient self-government.[78] The extant text of *Lex Baiwariorum* was the work of mid-eighth-century Bavarian dukes.[79] But its prologue, as already observed (p. 35), gave the credit to Frankish kings, puting these in a tradition stretching back to Antiquity's archetypal lawgivers:

> Moses from the people of the Hebrews first spelled out the laws of God in holy letters ... 'Foroneus' [Greeks] ... Mercurius Trimegistus [Egyptians] ... Solon first gave laws to the Athenians ... Lycurgus [Spartans] ... Numa Pompilius, who succeeded Romulus in the kingdom, first produced laws for the Romans. Then ... they set up *decemviri*, who in twelve tables expounded laws from the book of Solon in Latin speech ... These ten men were chosen (*electi*) to write the law down ... But gradually the old laws went out of date through age and neglect ... New laws began with Caesar Constantine ... but they were muddled and disordered. Then Theodosius the Younger ... made a *codex* of constitutions from Constantine's time with a single title for each emperor ... Then each people selected its law (*elegit legem*) from custom; for long-established custom is held as law ... Theuderic king of the Franks, when he was at Châlons chose wise men from his kingdom who were learned in ancient laws. In his own words he ordered the writing down of the law

---

74   *Lex Sal.* 'D'/'E' (cf. n. 14) xviii – xix. The usual practice was to break up overloaded titles, sometimes adding fresh matter; lxxviii is the new clause on killing priests and deacons.

75   *Lex Sal.* 'A'/'C' xlvii; *Pact.* lxxx, lxxxiii, lxxxvi, lxxxix, xcii; *Ed. Ch.* cxiii, cv – cxvi; *Dec. Ch.* ii:5, iii:1–2,4–5; cf. Murray, 'From Roman to Frankish Gaul'. On the not wholly clear relationship between *Lex Salica* as such and citations of it by these texts, see the important paper of Nehlsen, 'Zur Aktualität', pp. 456–60; and Wood, *Merovingian Kingdoms*, p. 112. Eckhardt, *Lex Sal.* (cf. n. 14) prints as 'Capitulare I', 'III' and 'V' clauses whose status raises unanswered, even unanswerable, questions about the 'legislatores' (see above, p. 31, below, p. 45) who worked on the text of *Lex Salica* between the early-sixth and late-eighth century.

76   *Dec. Ch.* ii:3, and p. 269; Nehlsen, 'Entstehung des öffentlichen Strafrechts'. Roman influence is patent in legislation by Childebert I, Guntchramn and Chlothar II: *Cap.* 2, 5, 8 – 9; cf. Murray, 'Immunity, Nobility and the *Edict of Paris*'. For important light on the background, see Esders, *Römische Rechtstradition* (kindly shown me before publication), especially pp. 268–357; and Liebs, 'Römische Juristen der Merowinger'.

77   Mordek, 'Die Hedenen'.

78   Eckhardt, *Leges Alamannorum* (as n. 28).

79   See n. 26; penetrating analyses are Wallace-Hadrill, *Long-Haired Kings*, pp. 213–17, Wood, *Merovingian Kingdoms*, pp. 115–19.

of the Franks, Alamans and Bavarians, each people that was in his power, according to its custom, adding what needed to be added, and cutting away what was unsuitable and ill-arranged. And what was according to the custom of pagans, he changed according to the law of Christians. And whatever King Theuderic could not change because of the great antiquity of pagan custom, King Childebert later undertook and King Chlothar completed. All these the most glorious King Dagobert renewed through the *viros illustres* Claudius, Chadoind, Magnus and Agilulf, and changed everything old in the laws for the better, and gave to each people the writing they keep to this day.[80]

Lex Salica was a basic inspiration for Alaman and Bavarian as for Ripuarian codes. Yet efforts were made to convey Alaman and Bavarian custom.[81] Their injury tariffs are as distinctive as those of other 'Germanic' *leges*; a possible reason why codes regularly contain these idiosyncratic details is that it was by memorizing them that crystallizing *gentes* fixed the identity of their particular law. The Franks, then, were not so much creating law for subject peoples as coaching them in the value of having written law. As the Bavarian prologue forcefully implied, it was a quintessentially Roman policy.

It is nevertheless misleading to characterize this element in Charlemagne's heritage as Roman, even if it is not helpfully called Germanic. What came to matter more than the differences between Roman and 'barbarian' law were the emergent contrasts between that of southern and of northern Europe. Where lawmaking in Spain, Italy and even areas a little to the north of the Alps was more or less marked by Roman legislative disciplines, the laws of the Frankish kingdom were ossified by Frankish tradition. The *Liber Historiae Francorum* gave *Lex Salica* an ancestral context it may in fact have lacked. Another likely reference to the code is from the *Passio* of Leodegar of Autun (cf. pp. 37, 63, 76–9). It tells how this bishop restored pristine law, removing what was 'in contradiction to the laws of ancient kings and the greater nobility'. The legislative *topos* borrowed by the Visigoths and Lombards from Justinian, and echoed by the Bavarian prologue, stressed, on the contrary, readiness to bring law up to date.[82] Clovis' successors made changes, evidently under Roman influence. But *Lex Salica* itself, though altered just enough to show an ability to countenance reform, is largely untouched by novelty. The legislation of Rothari's successors leaves no doubt that the Italian society they addressed greatly differed from the one he had conjured up. It was now, to mention but one point, allowed to alienate land for the good of one's soul.[83] Gallic society can hardly have changed much less. But copies of *Lex Salica* tempt one to think so. Formulae arrange that daughters

---

80   *Lex Bai.* Pr. For a full translation, see *Laws of the Alamans and Bavarians*, pp. 109–10, though from 'Theuderic . . .' onwards I largely follow Wood, *Merovingian Kingdoms*, pp. 116–17. Most of the passage down to 'Theuderic' is lifted from Isidore, *Etymologiae* V i, iii 24, xx; but the clause on each people's *lex* and custom is not Isidorian.

81   The pulling of a Bavarian witness's ear ('aures tractati', *Lex Bai.* xvi:2) is a feature of Bavarian charters: below, n. 290.

82   *Passiones Leudegarii* ii 5, p. 328, and cf. i 8, p. 289; Wood, *Merovingian Kingdoms*, pp. 113–14 (though cf. also *Late Merovingian France*, trans. Gerberding and Fouracre, pp. 223–5). On Euric, Rothari and Justinian (with *Lex Bai.* Pr. and finally Charlemagne), see Wallace-Hadrill, *Early Germanic Kingship*, p. 34, and below, chapter 5, n. 68.

83   *Leg. Liutpr.* (713) 6; and for its portentous results, Wickham, *Early Medieval Italy*, pp. 43, 126.

should after all inherit 'terra/ alodis paterna'. A text in the Formulary of Marculf, which probably emanates from late-seventh-century circles close to the Neustrian court, calls the notorious masculine bias of the *Lex* 'an ancient but impious custom'.[84] A great Merovingian lady duly disposed by will of lands bequeathed to her by her father 'against my brothers'.[85] But written Salic law stayed stubbornly the same, with historic consequences for Anglo-French relations half a millennium later. Frankish *lex* was to all appearances as inert as it was anonymous. If its enshrinement in writing suggests responsiveness to 'Roman examples', its subsequent fossilization implies that it soon became more a symbol than a tool of Frankish ascendancy.

Charlemagne was the most prolific legislator that the West had seen since Theodosius. A mark of this is that his activity was noted by two contemporary narratives. First the so-called 'Lorsch' Annals:

> In October [802], he convoked a universal synod in [Aachen], and there he had all the canons ... read to bishops, priests and deacons, and ordered these to be fully expounded (*tradi*) ... [Abbots and monks gathered likewise, the Rule of St Benedict being read out and expounded; he then ordered all clergy to live and amend according to the custom appropriate to their station.] Meanwhile ... the emperor himself convoked the dukes, counts and the rest of the Christian people, together with legal experts (*legislatoribus*), and there had all the *leges* in his kingdom read, and for each man he had his own law expounded (*et tradi unicuique homini legem suam*), and had them emended wherever necessary and the emended law written down, and [ordered] that judges were to judge by the written word (*per scriptum*) and not take gifts (*munera*), but all men, rich and poor, were to have justice in his kingdom.[86]

Secondly, Einhard:

> After he had received the imperial title, he noticed that the laws of his people had many defects – for the Franks have two laws, differing greatly in many details (*duas ... leges, in plurimis locis valde diversas*). So he planned to add what was lacking, to reconcile discrepancies, and to correct what was badly or falsely stated (*quae deerant addere et discrepantia unire, prava quoque ac perperam prolata corrigere*). Yet little of this was done by him, except that he added to the laws a few chapters, themselves unfinished (*nisi quod pauca capitula et ea inperfecta legibus addidit*). However, he did have the unwritten law of all the nations under his lordship written down and committed to letters (*omnium nationum ... iura quae scripta non erant describere ac litteris mandari fecit*).[87]

There is much to suggest that these are substantially accurate reports of what

---

84 *Lex Sal.* 'A'/'C' lix (on which *Ed. Ch.* cviii is a significant modification – or gloss – that yet survives in a single MS); Marculf ii 12, *Formul.*, p. 83 (cf. 'Cart. Sen.' 45, p. 205). On the dating and context of Marculf see Wood, 'Administration, Law and Culture', pp. 64–77.

85 Guerout, 'Testament de Ste Fare', p. 818; cf. Murray, *Germanic Kinship*, pp. 201–15, Anderson, 'Roman military colonies', pp. 130–5.

86 *Annales Laureshamenses*, p. 39. I have gone along with the translation of '*tradi*' as 'expounded' (as by King, *Charlemagne. Translated Sources*, p. 145 (and cf. Niemeyer, *Lexicon Minus, s.v.* (2)); such was evidently its meaning in the Edict of Pîtres (below, pp. 50–2 and n. 114), as argued by Bühler, 'Wort und Schrift', pp. 284–6. But see further below, p. 48–9.

87 Einhard, *Vita Karoli* 29, p. 33.

Charlemagne was doing. More than that, they expose the unresolved contradictions of Carolingian law-making.

The first point to note is the symbolism of the moment. Einhard chose words carefully. Here is an explicit correlation of the major legislative effort of Charles's reign with the morrow of his imperial coronation. The 'Lorsch' Annals confirm that it was indeed then that Charlemagne moved. And the great king's most productive legislative phase did in fact open, when he was still in Italy in the months after the Christmas *dénouement*, with a remarkable capitulary that is self-consciously in the tradition of Lombard royal legislation.[88] The number of pages allocated by the standard edition of his capitularies to the next thirteen years is one and a half times the total devoted to the previous thirty-two.[89] What he had issued from 768 to *c.* 800 was already a considerable advance in range of coverage and sophistication of expression on the work of Pippin. The 779 Capitulary of Herstal and the *Admonitio Generalis* with related texts of 789 were among his formative pronouncements. Yet his law-making *sessions* were as yet not much more numerous than his father's. After 800 they were almost annual. It is less certain that the *Leges* of the Frisians, Saxons and Thuringians were also promulgated at or soon after the 802 diet, as the narratives imply, but there is no good reason to doubt it.[90] Einhard had Suetonius to tell him that law-giving was an emperor's job. If his hero needed any further incentive, there was always the precedent of what his Merovingian forerunners did, following Moses, Numa Pompilius and the rest, for the south Germans (pp. 43–4).[91]

What, then, did this new Theodosius do for his own peoples' *lex*? The answer was just as Einhard said: oddly little. Aside from an improvement in the codes' Latin, not noted but presumably applauded by Einhard, change is decidedly marginal.[92] If by the 'two differing laws' Einhard meant the Merovingian ('A'/'C') and early Carolingian ('D'/'E') versions of *Lex Salica*, as is nowadays supposed, these were indeed fused in 802/3 or soon after into a new and much more widely circulated seventy-title text, the 'Karolina' ('K').[93] But the alloy retained striking blemishes. Where 'D' made a single coherent statement out of the two contradictory Merovingian laws on grave-robbery and sacrilege, the *Karolina* simply

---

88   *Cap.* 98:Pr.: 'ea quae ab antecessoribus nostris regibus Italiae in edictis legis Langobardicae ab ipsis editae praetermissa sunt ... addere curavimus'; and there is a particularly interesting statement about compensation for injuries at c. 5. The decree is also dated.

89   This necessarily approximate reckoning is conservative in that Carolingian laws are not normally a lot more thoroughly dated than Merovingian (Wormald, 'Lex Scripta', p. 118 (p. 16), and anything not dated post-800 (by Boretius) is assumed to be earlier, including the 'Capitulare de Villis' (no. 32); but some account is taken of modern redatings, e.g. the Italian nos 92–3 (Patetta, 'Sull' introduzione in Italia ... ', pp. 726–7).

90   *Gesetze des Karolingerreiches ... Sachsen, Thüringer, Chamaven und Friesen*, ed. Eckhardt; *Lex Ribuaria* II, ed. Eckhardt; *Lex Frisionum*, ed. Eckhardt (with discussion of problems, including the chronological, pp. 19–22); Siems, *Studien zur Lex Frisionum*: an exhaustive account of this especially intriguing text, including the dating problem, pp. 368–9, and a facsimile of Herold's 1557 edition, where alone it now survives.

91   *Suetonius* I, pp. 56–61 (Julius), 172–9 (Augustus), II, pp. 26–31 (Claudius) etc.

92   For improved (Carolingian) textual families, see, e.g. *Lex Rib.*, pp. 34, 37–8, 46; *Leges Alamannorum* II, ed. Eckhardt, pp. 9–10.

93   Eckhardt, *Lex Salica: Systematischer text* (as n. 14), pp. 301–8; cf. 'Lex Scripta', p. 128 (29) and n. 130.

restored the Merovingian contradiction, compounding it by adding to the first Merovingian law the clause in which 'D' had doubled the payment levied by the second Merovingian clause (retained by 'K', notwithstanding) for sneaking one corpse into another's coffin.[94] Nor is this the only peculiarity of the *Karolina*. A revised version of the early Carolingian recension ('E') had already cleansed *Lex Salica* of most barbarisms, Frankish glosses included; and since the 'D' text had moved the clause on kin liability to the end of the code, commenting that it was 'observed in the time of pagans', 'E' logically omitted it as redundant. The *Karolina* put it back without further remark.[95] The clause required anyone wishing to involve his kindred in paying compensation owed for a homicide to throw dust gathered from the four corners of their house over his left shoulder onto the relatives in question, then to jump the fence clad in a shirt and brandishing a stake in token that he could pay no more himself. Perhaps the Franks clamoured for their ancestral right to do this. Rather more likely is that any tradition was valued for itself.

What of Einhard's 'few [added] chapters'? That seems a weird comment on a king whom Einhard must have known to have issued up to 100 'capitularies'. Yet it is strictly true if what he meant was the *capitula* that Charlemagne now *required to be added to the lex*. A text that can be dated 803 (though in manuscripts it often is not) usually has some such title as '*capitula* that the lord Augustus Charles ordered to be added/sent into Salic law'. A clause of an accompanying 'capitulary of the *missi*' demands that 'the people be asked about the *capitula* which have been recently added to the law, and after all have consented, they put their subscriptions or manual confirmations on the said *capitula*'. A remarkable passage in one copy describes how Count Stephen 'had them read out at Paris in public court in the presence of … *scabini*; all consented as one … and all *scabini*, bishops, abbots and counts confirmed them by subscribing with their own hand'. This was business to which king and political nation clearly attached considerable significance. What the statute in fact covered was a fuller range of clerical wergelds, the legality of infringing immunities in pursuit of a thief or killer, sanctuary, fraudulent intervention in courts, killing to forestall enslavement, procedure for making gifts to the Church, manumission by charter, surety liability, payment of debts to the king, needlessly reviving a case, and treating opposing witnesses as enemies.[96] One can see that these were matters whose importance thoroughly justified their addition to the *lex*. The puzzle is that Charlemagne singled out these 'few' issues for special treatment, when he laid down so many other laws (pp. 45–6), and when he so often (as in

---

94　See pp. 34, 42 and nn. 20, 74; *Lex Sal.* 'K' xvii:3, lvii:3, lviii:1 (Eckhardt's MGH edition, as n. 14), pp. 69, 209; '*Lex Scripta*', pp. 116–17 (p. 15), is to be amended accordingly.

95　*Lex Sal.* 'D' c /'E' xcix: an intriguing comment by 'E' is that 'as a result [*sc.* of this law] the power of many (*potestas multorum*, amended by Eckhardt to '*multarum*', i.e. 'efficacy of fines') declined'. For one view of the genesis of 'E', see Eckhardt, *Lex Salica: 100-titel Text* (as n. 14), pp. 55–78; and for further comment see Kaufmann, '*Quod paganorum tempore observabant* … ', pp. 387–8.

96　*Cap.* 39 (prefaced by Boretius with a review of MS titles – to be amended in places from Mordek, *Bibliotheca* – and the account of the Paris episode offered by Par. BN Lat. 4995, f. 19v, cf below, p. 61), 40:19. At the same time a capitulary was also added to *Lex Rib.* (*Cap.* 41), and another, perhaps from the same diet, to *Lex Bai.* (68).

the 'Lorsch' Annals account) demanded judgement by 'lex scripta'. Lombard or Visigothic rulers would not have been so reticent.

The pattern of Charlemagne's post-800 legislative effort was repeated throughout the ninth century. The nearest parallel is his son's own period of imperial euphoria. Following hard on Louis' accession, and more especially on his coronation by the Pope in October 816, there was an intense burst of legislation, coinciding with his famous Ordinance for the succession to his 'empire' (817), and no less significantly with the rules made by his spiritual advisers for the collective life of canons and monks (816–19). In 816, there were two capitularies for addition to *Lex Salica* (one basically a partial draft for the other), covering aspects of judicial procedure. Then, at some point in the years 818/19, came a whole series of decrees launched by a remarkable general prologue. It included a set of *Capitula Legibus Addenda* much fuller and with a more explicitly ideological agenda than any yet. Finally, in 819 or 820, there was another set of *capitula* for addition to *Lex Salica* which actually addressed numbered chapters of the ('K') *Lex*.[97] Again in 829, in an ideological climate reheated by an extraordinary address on imperial duties from the bishops congregated in Paris, a body of legislation issued at Wörms included a *capitulare pro lege habendum*, shorter but no less morally laden than that of 818/19.[98] About this time, one diehard imperial ideologist, Archbishop Agobard of Lyons, wrote a vituperative attack on the barbarisms in the Burgundian *lex*, notably ordeal by duel, along with a call for the submergence of the several divergent *leges* of the 'Christian Empire' of the Franks in one Pauline law for all believers.[99]

Like the ideal of imperial unity it reflected, Agobard's dream remained unrealized. Under Louis' son, Charles the Bald (840–77), a keynote of the string of proclamations following his truces with his brothers and ordinations to his nephews' kingdoms is a promise 'to each of his appropriate law (*legem unicuique competentem*), in every *ordo* and *dignitas*'.[100] One cannot of course be sure what the 'lex' of these passages really means.[101] It probably meant different things to different people. But a primary meaning was certainly 'written law', the professed code of each subject. One of the last forms of this proclamation (869) spoke of

---

97   *Cap.* 134–42 (Boretius' datings are largely upheld by the modern expertise of Schmitz, 'Kapitulariengesetzgebung Ludwigs', p. 507). On the coincidence with Louis' canonical and monastic regulations, see Noble, 'Monastic ideal as a model for empire'.

98   *Cap.* 184–93; the chief issue in 139 and 193 is sacrilege; there are also overtones of the Decalogue (as in 789) in their concern with killing, theft, adultery and false witness. Louis' General Prologue (137) echoes the 789/802 revision and *ordines* themes, as does his own *Admonitio* of *c.*825 (*Cap.* 150): see Guillot, 'Ordinatio méconnue'.

99   Agobard, ... *Epistolae*, ed. Dümmler, 3, pp. 158–64, especially p. 159; cf. his 'De Divinis sententiis'; and for savage comment on Louis' imperial failings in the context of his 833 deposition, *Cap.* 198; for analysis, see Boshof, *Erzbischof Agobard*, especially pp. 38–49, and cf. pp. 195–300; and cf. too Semmler, 'Reichsidee'.

100   In chronological order: *Cap.* 254:3 (293:3), 204:5, 205:6 + *Ad. Kar.*, 262:10, 295, 269 (*sacr. reg.*), 270:C3+D4, 243 (*Ad. Lud.*:3, *Ad. Kar.*:3), 272:1 (p. 303) and 4 (p. 310), 275:3 + *Ad. Kar.*:1, 276B, 220 (p. 100), 282:2; cf. also 283:A+C (just after Charles's death).

101   The subject has been much discussed. The pioneer modern approach was Classen, 'Verträge von Verdun'; subsequent insights include: Devisse, 'Essai sur l'histoire', with his *Hincmar Archevêque de Reims* I, pp. 281–310; Magnou-Nortier, *Foi et Fidélité*, pp. 85–121; above all Nelson, 'Political Thought of Hincmar of Rheims'.

'appropriate laws, whether worldly or ecclesiastical'. Plural tense and lay-clergy distinction do imply written codes; and Hincmar, author of most such pronouncements, was surely thinking of the 'leges scriptae' in which he was so expert. If so, and in contradiction to the received view that contrasts Charles the Bald's consensual style with his grandfather's single-mindedness, there is a continuity from the way that Charlemagne gave subject peoples their *lex* or had that of the Franks 'expounded' in 802, and his grandsons' repeated 'grant (*perdonare*)' of *lex* from 843 onwards.[102] To receive one's *lex* not only symbolized the donor's sovereignty but also assured the recipient's political security.

The abiding image left by the Carolingian *leges* is thus one of earnest respect for primal Frankish law. The image is intensified if what the Carolingians did not do is compared with the exertions of Lombard or Visigothic kings – or with what Carolingians themselves did in Italy.[103] The unavoidable conclusion is that Frankish *lex* mattered to them for reasons other than its efficacy in legal administration. The paradox of Carolingian legislation is that it was a supreme manifestation of the force of Roman example, as Einhard showed; yet it was no less important, as in Merovingian times, to restore the 'laws of ancient kings and of the greater nobility' than to 'add … reconcile … and correct … ' (pp. 44–5). Whoever it was that the 'Lorsch' Annals meant by 'legislatores', their rooted wisdom outweighed the royal will. And what does Einhard have Charlemagne himself go on to do in the immediate context of his legal 'reforms'? 'The barbarian and most ancient songs, in which the deeds and wars of kings of old were sung, he had written and memorialized'; while the months and the winds received good Frankish names from this stickler for Frankish ways.[104] The *lex* of the Franks was *more* than Frankish law. It was the Frankish past. It was Frankish identity.

It bears emphasis that the evidence of the manuscripts as well as of narrative reports is that it was *lex*, the primary and traditional statement of law, that mattered most in the ninth century. But the great series of Carolingian capitularies is what dominates the historian's vision. Capitularies repeatedly insist on the centrality of written law.[105] Yet it is extremely hard to know what capitularies themselves amounted to.[106] The word itself, which appears as early as

---

102   Hincmar inserted some of these legislative *démarches* in his Annals: *Annales de Saint-Bertin*, pp. 158–64, 219–21. For the consensual issue, see sensitive discussion (with full range of reference) by Nelson, 'Legislation and Consensus'; and, near-simultaneously, the exhaustive discussion by Hannig, *Consensus Fidelium*.

103   The legislation of Charlemagne, Pippin, Lothar I, Louis II, Charles the Bald, Guy and Lambert (*Cap.* 88 – 103, 105, 157 – 166, 168, 201 – 225) was usually 'added' to the Lombard kings' edicts in Italian MSS (cf. the titles of nos 214 – 215, 224); and much was ultimately included in the Lombardic corpus (chapter 6, pp. 468–70).

104   *Einhard* 29, p. 33; and above, p. 44, and n. 82. Compare the brilliant observations of Moisl, 'Kingship and Orally Transmitted *Stammestradition*', pp. 118–19.

105   A sample of key texts includes: *Cap.* 12:10 (penalty for contumacy 'secundum quod in lege scriptum est', already in 744); 22:63 (*Admonitio Generalis* (789), a judge's first job is to learn the 'lex a sapientibus populo conposita'); 25:5 (early declaration of royal respect for each subject's *lex*); 33:26 (unambiguous demand in Visigothic style by the famous 'Programmatic Capitulary' (802) that judges use 'legem scriptum', not their own 'arbitrium'); 58:2 (*missus* instructed to read Roman or Salic law as alternatives); 77:Pr. (802x3, capitulary issued after consulting Salic, Roman and 'Gombatan' (Burgundian) *lex*); 85:Pr. (*capitularia* to be *re*read); 116:11 (lay knowledge and understanding of *lex* is on a par with a priest knowing his canons, penitential, Roman liturgy or Gospels, or a monk knowing the rule, as at Aachen in

Charles's first major decree at Herstal in 779, clearly enough denotes their arrangement under 'head(ing?)s'.[107] They were so arranged, in almost all copies, and like *Leges* themselves. Obviously too, they were not the same as *leges*, or no distinction would have been drawn between those 'added to the *leges*' and the rest. The problem is what to make of the vast majority of capitularies not so designated. Many can be put into rough categories: conciliar resolutions, like the *Admonitio Generalis*; circulars like the 'Epistle on the cultivation of literature'; directions for the king's roving emissaries ('*missi*') that might be simply admonitory or might be lists of headings for business to be transacted or already agreed.[108] However, a large number of capitularies do not fit easily into any of these classes, and among them are decrees that were clearly meant to carry the utmost weight: Herstal, the Saxon capitularies or the 802 Programmatic Capitulary, Thionville (806) or Boulogne (811), Louis' '*Admonitio* to all *Ordines* of his Realm' (823x5) or Charles the Bald's immense Edict of Pîtres (864).[109] Logically, these should all have been *legibus addenda*. It is the 'off the record' air of such nonetheless ostensibly mandatory texts, the absence of any formal process of 'recognition' from nearly all of them, which persuades some historians that they drew their imperative force not from their written form but from the royal word of command that begot them.[110]

Simple chronological context shows that capitulary production was boosted by heightened ideological aspirations. But more was at stake in capitularies than construction of a civilized image. If the texts are to be given any meaning at all, they express a burning aspiration that the Carolingians' subjects should *really* be peoples of written law. Charlemagne and his Frankish advisers will surely have

---

802); 273:34 (remarkable provision in Edict of Pîtres (864) – see below – that though *Lex Salica* has nothing on self-sale into slavery, it is covered by an Ansegisus capitulary). Such references are commoner, as one would expect, for Italy. On the topic in general, the classic account by Ganshof, 'Use of the written word' may be compared with the yet more upbeat views of Werner, 'Missus – Marchio – Comes', and McKitterick, *Carolingians and the Written Word*, pp. 25–37; with the comment of Campbell, 'Significance of the Anglo-Norman State' (from the same conference as Werner's paper), pp. 128–30 (182–3).

106   The topic is now almost as hotly debated as once was the genesis of *Lex Salica*. The key study remains Ganshof, 'Recherches sur les capitulaires' – there are Flemish and (revised) German versions but regrettably none in English. Also most important, and with full review of post-Ganshof work, is Mordek, 'Karolingische Kapitularien'. The most recent comprehensive study, again with extensive bibliography (and index!) is Bühler, 'Capitularia Relecta'.

107   *Cap.* 20:Pr.; the next securely dated use of the term is in the decrees worked out in 786 by the papal legates, George of Ostia (who was much involved in early Carolingian legislation) and Theophylact of Todi, with English kings and churchmen: see my 'In Search of King Offa's "Lawcode"', pp. 28–34, 42–3 (pp. 205–11), and below, pp. 106–7.

108   *Cap.* 22, 29, 23, 34 (on its variant forms, see below, nn. 164–5), 51 (cf. 52), 53, 61 – 63, 64 – 65, 71 (cf. 72), 186, 257 (texts of 'agenda' type become rarer as the century passes). A new study of a capitulary of 'admonitory' type (*Cap.* 121) is Buck, *Admonitio und Praedicatio*; and on *Cap.* 150, see Guillot, 'Ordinatio méconnue'.

109   *Cap.* 20, 26 – 27, 33, 43 – 44, 74, 150, 273: a small selection, it must be stressed, of the capitularies of which this could be said.

110   The central conclusion of Ganshof, 'Recherches'; cf. my '*Lex Scripta*', pp. 118, 123 (pp. 17, 22–3), with Bühler, 'Wort und Schrift' and 'Capitularia', pp. 467–72; Professor McKitterick's contrary view is supported by Sellert, 'Aufzeichnung des Rechts', especially pp. 91–101; Professor Mordek, wholly cognizant of the contradictions of the evidence, wisely reserves his position: 'Kapitularien', pp. 29–49, and 'Kapitularien und Schriftlichkeit', pp. 35–7, 65–6.

learned from southern visitors like the Spaniard Theodulf and the Italian Paul what a regime of *lex scripta* could and should be like.[111] It is more than probable that the heavy capitulary output of Louis' early years was in part prompted by his having brought so many Aquitainian advisers north with him, notably (the Visigoth?) Benedict of Aniane.[112] Even more importunate than the model of Rome was of course that of the Bible. The *Admonitio Generalis* preface shows Charlemagne pondering what God set down for the first Chosen People: 'We read in the Book of Kingdoms how holy Josiah tried to recall the kingdom given to him by God to the worship of the true God by going about correcting and admonishing'. The capitulary's main burden, once it had finished summarizing the canon collection sent by Pope Hadrian, was a rehearsal of the Ten Commandments in Frankish terms.[113] And if Carolingian law-making could aspire to resemble that of Israel or Rome, it could also develop a momentum of its own. Louis' legislation was more ambitious than his father's. Charles the Bald's Edict of Pîtres was full of cross-references to other laws of this king and his predecessors, replete with vernacular words, and notably devoid of ecclesiastical interest; it was the largest single legislative act by a north European king before Edward I.[114] In the light of all this, it would be absurd to argue that some Carolingians were not deeply serious in the demands they made about the uses of written law. The question that lingers is whether their programme would ever be reified by a political culture which so restricted the innovations that could be formally enrolled as *lex*.[115]

A final point, leading naturally into this chapter's next section, concerns the recording of capitularies. It is another of the topic's mysteries that there is little by way of pattern in capitulary manuscripts. *Capitularia legibus addenda* stood a better chance of being copied than less solemn texts. But the same goes for more informal *capitularia missorum* issued to reinforce them. Anything promulgated at times of special effort is apt to have more copies than often weightier measures from other years. The decrees of 779 and 789 are well preserved. But the fundamental Programmatic Capitulary (802) and Louis' *Admonitio* of the 820s owe their survival to lone volumes, and those Italian.[116] Why, when Frankish *leges* circulated widely in standardized, even over-standardized, form, should capitu-

---

111   Theodulf wrote his famous 'Contra Iudices' on the temptations of law-enforcement, and another 'Comparison of Ancient and Modern [*sc.* Mosaic and Roman] law': *Poetae*, ed. Dümmler, pp. 493–520; for Paul the Deacon's knowledge of Roman and Lombard law, see *Historia Langobardorum*, ed. Bethmann and Waitz, i 25, iv 42, v 33, vi 58.

112   For Benedict's possible impact on one *Leges* MS written at or near Louis' court, see below, p. 64, and n. 175.

113   *Cap.* 22:Pr.,61–9 (note the refrain of '*lex Domini*', etc.).

114   *Cap.* 273: there are references to Roman law as well as Ansegisus (below); see, suggestively, Nelson, *Frankish World*, pp. 96–8.

115   One signal is that the more legislative Latin improved, the further it moved from the speech of those it addressed: McKitterick, *Carolingians*, pp. 7–22; with Wright, *Late Latin and Early Romance*, pp. 122–6. Another is that, considering the Biblical imperatives behind the whole Carolingian campaign for the moral rebirth of Frankish society, so *little* was said to reflect the Church's teaching on economic issues; this is one of the major yields from Professor Siems's immense *Handel und Wucher*, especially pp. 717–848.

116   Cf. the entries for *Cap.* 20, 22, 33, 150 in Mordek, *Bibliotheca*, pp. 1081–3, 1096, with references given: no. 150 is fragmentarily extant in a later-ninth-century Valenciennes MS (*ibid.*, pp. 746–8).

laries have so uneven a distribution? One of the signs of an increasingly sophisticated Carolingian approach to *lex scripta* is that from *c.* 808, steps began to be taken to publish capitularies while retaining an archival master-copy. The culmination is again the Edict of Pîtres, whose sheer bulk must have imposed a severe strain on palatial, never mind provincial, registries.[117] In fact, however, the capitulary collection that came nearest to being authoritative was not made by the government at all.

Abbot Ansegisus of St Wandrille was, to be sure, among the government's best trusted servants, but it seems that he acted on his personal initiative, with neither instruction nor assistance from Court.[118] His preface says that the *capitula* he has collected are 'to be firmly held as useful law (*utili . . . tenenda sunt lege*)' because 'made for the profit of Holy Church' as well as 'for keeping the harmony of peace and love within the Catholic Church'.[119] His worry was that they were 'scattered through various parchments (*in diversis sparsim . . . membranulis*) of various times' and so at risk of being forgotten. The very limitations of his enterprise (827) well illustrate the situation he evoked. Such major decrees of Charlemagne as Herstal found no place. Louis is credited with Roman law excerpts that can never have been a capitulary. His 'Ecclesiastical Capitulary' of 818/19 is found among his father's laws.[120] It looks as if Ansegisus drew mainly on the deposits of his own abbey archives, accumulated perhaps through service as *missi* by him and his predecessors. Their assemblage of 'parchments' was both incomplete and presumably damaged to the point that some had lost the portions that identified their real authors.[121] But a yet more startling reflection on the difficulty of getting access to capitularies *via* royal records is that Ansegisus' collection at once became Louis' chief source of reference for his own pronouncements as well as his father's.[122]

This retrospective royal endorsement was part of the reason for Ansegisus' extraordinary success. Seventy-five copies or partial copies can be listed, more than for any single legislative text until the Twelfth Century Renaissance.[123] Nor is it difficult to see other reasons why his efforts were so appreciated. His division of the material into two books on 'ecclesiastical' issues (one for Charles, one for Louis) and two more on 'worldly law' (again divided between Charles and

---

117   *Cap.* 50:8, 150:26, 273:36, etc.: cf. my '*Lex Scripta*', p. 118 (pp. 16–17) with (e.g.) Schneider, 'Zur rechtlichen Bedeutung', pp. 286–92; and *per contra* Bühler, 'Wort und Schrift', pp. 288–92.
118   This conclusion is not the least among the fruits of the new and authoritative edition by Schmitz, *Kapitulariensammlung des Ansegis*: see especially pp. 10–40, 56–66, 68–70. His conclusion is already forecast in his 'The Capitulary Legislation of Louis the Pious', pp. 425–8; and also reached, in effect independently, by Bougard, *La Justice dans le Royaume d' Italie*, pp. 21–3.
119   *Ans.* Praef., p. 432.
120   *Ans.* (intro.), pp. 15–34.
121   For a record of the 813 deliberations surviving in just this form, see Mordek, *Bibliotheca*, pp. 376–7, and his 'Karolingische Kapitularien', pp. 32–5 and Pl. II; cf., for 'one of the extremely few preserved first-drafts from the process whereby capitularies were generated', his *Bibliotheca*, pp. 112–13, and 'Kapitularien', Pl. III.
122   It is already in use, cited by book and title, for the Wörms 829 legislation: *Cap.* 191:5,9, 192:1,8, 193:1,5,8; and was regularly consulted by Charles the Bald: e.g. *Cap.* 273:1,4,8,13, etc. – though Charles could also cite Wörms directly: 273:27.
123   Cf. the list in Mordek, *Bibliotheca*, pp. 1100–1; a full account of most MSS is given by Schmitz in *Ans.* (intro.), pp. 71–191, with an exhaustive account of their textual affiliations, pp. 191–281.

Louis) meant that Church Councils could quarry it for canonical purposes, while kings knew where to find precedents for what they demanded of their subjects. But this collection's impact, however unparalleled or merited, should not eclipse similar endeavours by others. One was encountered at the outset of this section. Lupus' *Liber Legum* contains a capitulary series comprehensive enough to look systematic and showing signs of arrangement. Not only are each king's decrees so far as possible gathered under a collective title, but they are also equipped with an all-inclusive list of rubrics.[124] There is no knowing whether what logic the *ensemble* possessed was imparted by Lupus himself or derived from prefabricated blocks put together by him. But the way that the collection's division between four kings is mirrored in the iconographical scheme described by Lupus' verses argues that this aspect at least was his work. He and his public, or conceivably his source, made a marketable artefact of Carolingian law-making, just as Ansegisus had.[125] There is little or no sign that the government itself did. Lupus' treatment of capitularies was reflected in Italy but seldom if ever in his Frankish home. System, as always, was southern.

The moral of all this is as easily grasped as morals need to be. What Merovingians and Carolingians did not do with legal texts is just as striking as what they did. Frankish *lex* was so solidly cast in the mould of Frankish tradition that the greatest kings merely adorned its surface. It took an intellectual as gifted as Lupus to rework its shape. Frankish capitularies by contrast were left so plastic by kings that only intellectuals like Lupus could give them real shape. Roman example taught the Merovingians that law should be written. It and the Bible taught the Carolingians that society should live by written law. Neither learned, as did their southern neighbours, how written law might be both mirror and instrument of social change. Whatever the shift in quantity and quality from sixth- to ninth-century law-making, the gulf between impassioned capitulary and stolid *lex* abides. That is the message of texts where the goals of Frankish kings are writ largest. But texts are only one vantage-point from which to view the field of early medieval law. It is high time to ascend others.

(ii) Law books

Marquis Eberhard of Friuli (p. 32) possessed a good library. His extant will bestowed on his offspring a collection of over fifty books.[126] A dozen were liturgical or devotional. Upwards of twenty were broadly theological or moralistic; among them were the *City of God*, favoured meal-time reading of great-grandfather Charlemagne, and Alcuin's no less pertinent *Treatise on*

---

124   Cf. above, p. 33, and the references supplied in n. 12.

125   Quite apart from the Italian and German copies of the whole *Liber Legum*, it may be noted that there were three other south German copies of its capitulary constituent: Mordek, *Bibliotheca*, pp. 132, 159, 257, 445, and especially 289.

126   The will is accessible in Thévenin, *Textes relatifs* no. 99, pp. 138–9; I use the summary version conveniently available with French translation in Riché and Tate, *Textes et documents* no. 122, II, pp. 414–16. Its bibliographical interest is assessed by Riché, 'Les bibliothèques', pp. 97–101, and McKitterick, *Carolingians*, pp. 245–8.

Virtues and Vices written for Count Guy. Another ten or so can be classified as works of edification or entertainment: lives of holy men, the *Gesta* of the Popes and of the Franks, a Bestiary, Vegetius, and the romance of Apollonius of Tyre. This was evidently a thoroughly cultivated household. It was apparently also a public-spirited one. Unroch, the eldest son, was bequeathed a 'book of Frankish, Ripuarian, Lombard, Alaman and Bavarian law' and a 'book of princely constitutions and imperial edicts'. To daughter Judith went a 'Lombard law'. The temptation to equate Lupus' compilation with Unroch's 'book(s) of laws' is irresistible. What Judith was expected to do with her 'Lombard law' is harder to guess.[127] But Unroch, like his father and his brother Berengar (Italian king and emperor 888–924), had major responsibilities in Italian government. Such men were beset by legal business (pp. 87–8). To suppose that their law books had any other end in view is to dig one's own pitfalls.

A contemporary fragment of Lupus' *Liber Legum* survives, but it is best captured in two manuscripts that post-date it by a century and a half.[128] The more faithful, from Modena Cathedral Library, is of *c.* 990. It alone retains Lupus' dedicatory verses and the full cycle of superb illustrations to which they refer (pp. 32, 70). As the sole unambiguous depictions of the legislative process from the early medieval West, these are of no slight interest. The mysterious quartet credited with devising *Lex Salica*, and the hardly less obscure Eddana on whom *Lex Ribuaria* is fathered (pp. 40, 43), each sit in deliberation clasping a rod that may be the *festuca* ubiquitous in Frankish legal procedure, while a tonsured man scribbles away with parchment, pen and inkhorn at a desk below.[129] One Lombard picture is lost; the other shows Kings Ratchis and Ahistulf enthroned and with rods but no scribe. The Alamans have neither king nor scribe but as many as 160 faces, all with slightly varied expressions, who represent the thirty-three bishops, thirty-four *duces* and eighty-two counts enumerated in the code's preface, while eleven more stand for 'the rest of the people' also mentioned: a 'host of Alamans' indeed (pp. 35, 43). The last extant scene shows Charles and Pippin, each with rods, the former crowned and clearly in command, and the tonsured scribe back again at their feet. The conclusion to be drawn from this astonishing gallery can scarcely be missed. Law is pronounced by kings and secular lords. It is a tonsured Lupus who turns it into *lex scripta*.[130]

The collection's original content is established by the Modena manuscript's

---

127   McKitterick, pp. 247–8. Given its association with Alcuin's work on (largely male) virtues and vices and Augustine's sermon on drunkenness, might her father have envisaged an Italian marriage?

128   For what follows, see Mordek, *Bibliotheca*, pp. 125–6, 131–49, 256–68; Professor Mordek first identified and discussed the fragment in 'Ein Freiburger Kapitularienfragment'.

129   For these illustrations, see Mordek, 'Frühmittelalterliche Gesetzgeber', pp. 1038–49 and Pll. XXXII–XXXVIII, and his *Bibliotheca*, pp. 259–62. If not a *festuca*, the rod could conceivably be a 'baculus' in process of metamorphosis into a 'sceptrum'/'virga' of justice/mercy: see Nelson, 'Kings with Justice; Kings without Justice', pp. 821–2.

130   Mordek, 'Kapitularien und Schriftlichkeit', pp. 47–57. Barbarian rulers (as opposed to Roman emperors or Moses) are not often depicted brandishing law-books: Mordek (as previous n.) Pll. IV–VI, XIII–XL, as against (e.g.) the 'Moutier-Grandval Bible' (BL Add. MS 10546), f. 25v; exceptions are the 'Wandalgarius' codex, *ibid.*, Pl. XVI, and the enthroned figure in the Gotha MS (Pl. XXIII and below, n. 134), on which (and on the genre in general) see Mütherich, 'Frühmittelalterliche Rechtshandscriften', especially, p. 82. The vivid scene in the Utrecht Psalter (Utrecht Bibl. Rijksuniv. Script. Eccl. 484, f. 90v),

agreements with its Gotha sibling. Both books preface the legal materials described in section (i) with a list of emperors from Octavian through Justinian II and Pippin of Herstal (his contemporary) to Louis the Pious.[131] It is one more compelling demonstration of the neo-imperial mind-set that underlay commitment to *lex scripta*. Both manuscripts also reproduce Emperor Louis II's legislation of 865; since this was not of course in Lupus' original, it looks as though Eberhard or his son(s) updated it, and to that extent used it as a working tool.[132] Only the Modena manuscript, on the other hand, contains the important selection from Isidore, 'De legibus divinis et humanis', which frequently appears in Carolingian law-books. Like the short 'Admonition of the judge on judgement' offered by the Modena manuscript in another hand, this is likely to be an Italian interpolation.[133]

The second copy of the *Liber legum* is in a Mainz manuscript of c. 1000 now at Gotha. The first of three important things about it is its own illustrations. It opens with a rather half-hearted pastiche of Otto III's court style showing a crowned king. Later, however, comes a clear echo of Modena's Salic *rectores*, except that only the two top-left figures appear, both crowned and one practising the Frankish custom of manumission by 'penny-throw'. Space was left for two further pictures; and though the scribe seems to have lost interest in that aspect of his exemplar, he did enough to show that Modena's miniatures had copied Lupus' with some fidelity.[134] A second point is that Gotha's exemplar may better reflect the use made of the *Liber Legum* by Eberhard and his family. It contains not only Louis II's 865 legislation but also most of his imposing 850s output.[135] The third and for present purposes most important thing about Gotha is what it does with the Lupus collection. Most of it is sandwiched between a Part I, in which the collections of Ansegisus (pp. 52–3) and 'Benedict the Deacon' (the latter largely a forged continuation of the former) are supplemented by canons of a 951 council and a bogus capitulary ascribed to Charlemagne on assailants of clergy, and a Part III given over to the Breviary of Alaric, the Frankish kingdom's standard Roman law source (pp. 36, 63–4). Meanwhile, Lupus' digest of Louis/Lothar legislation is hived off to a Part IV, where it supports a full text of the Lombard code (p. 39), the 818–19 capitularies (p. 48), and a second copy of Ansegisus.[136] It well shows how capitulary dossiers could be assembled out of ready-made building-blocks. Gotha Part I is almost identical with another book of the same provenance and earlier date, whose texts of Ansegisus and Benedict

---

adduced by McKitterick, *Carolingians*, p. 30, as perhaps a *tableau* of Carolingian legislation being (as it were) 'published', is as likely to have envisaged a synod (of clerics) as an assembly (of laity). See too below, p. 64, and nn. 163, 174, 181, 198.

131   The Emperor-list is printed (leaving a gap between Augustus and Justinian II) in the Bethmann-Waitz edition of Paul the Deacon, p. 6.

132   *Cap.* 216 – 217; Mordek, *Bibliotheca*, pp. 148, 266–7.

133   Mordek, *Bibliotheca*, p. 259; the Isidorian selection is edited by Tardif, 'Abrégé Juridique', pp. 673–81.

134   Mordek, *Bibliotheca*, pp. 132, 135–7, and 'Frühmittelalterliche Gesetzgeber', Pll. XXIII–XXIV. On the limitations of Mainz art at this time, see Mayr-Harting, *Ottonian Book Illumination* II, pp. 84–6.

135   *Cap.* 209 – 210, 228, 213, 212 (much of this unique or nearly so); Mordek, *Bibliotheca*, pp. 147–8.

136   Mordek, *Bibliotheca*, pp. 132–4, 140–8.

shared an archetype with a volume from Archbishop Hincmar's Rheims.[137] Whether the Breviary, Lombard code and Ansegisus ingredients were blended into Lupus' *Liber legum* in Italy or at Mainz, this collection combined the fullest attainable anthology of Carolingian law-making with updated canons and Roman law. The book as a whole, from its inaugural ruler-portrait onwards, casts a suggestive glow on the ideological horizons of the Ottonian Establishment.[138]

The prolific law book production of the Carolingian period is the strongest suit of those persuaded that the regime was articulated by written law.[139] The Lupus-Eberhard transaction is among their best cards. Yet contemplation of the personalities engaged may induce hesitation. Servatus Lupus (if it was he) was one of the age's leading intellectuals, who must have known very well what 'Lex' meant for the prototype empire of Rome, and who could (in admittedly conventional terms) urge Charles the Bald that 'no one be allowed to scorn divine nor human laws, provided they are just, because the impunity of evil-doers always leads to an increase in vice'.[140] For his part, Eberhard was a Frankish grandee, close enough to the centre of power to marry Louis' daughter while keeping the trust of Lothar, a step-brother who sought to disgrace her mother and marginalize her brother (p. 33); one of their children would be king of Italy. Eberhard was cultured enough to maintain intellectual contact not only with Hrabanus Maurus and Lupus (p. 32), but also with Sedulius Scottus, the controversial Gottschalk (p. 92) and the learned papal librarian Anastasius.[141] Were any layman likely to take on board the full ramifications of the Carolingian programme, it would be he. Nor is the law book he acquired from Lupus and transmitted to his sons in fact representative of surviving Frankish legal manuscripts. A wider-angled view of the field is now desirable.[142]

It must at once be said that the number of manuscripts coming into question is very large indeed. Some 240 volumes dating from the mid-eighth to the late-eleventh century include secular laws from the Frankish sphere; two-thirds date to the Carolingians' pre-900 heyday (table 2.1).[143] From before 750 there are just

---

137   Vatican MS Pal. Lat. 583, St Gallen MS 727: Mordek, *Bibliotheca*, pp. 797–9, 664–5.

138   For the outlook of Mainz's Archbishop Willigis (975–1011), cf. Mayr-Harting, *Ottonian Book Illumination* I, pp. 162, 194.

139   So McKitterick, *Carolingians*, pp. 40–60 (with table of *Lex Salica* MSS, pp. 48–55); Kottje, 'Die Lex Baiuvariorum'; and his 'Zum Geltungsbereich der Lex Alamannorum'.

140   *Lupus, ... Epistolae* LXIV, p. 64, *Correspondance* 31, I pp. 144–5.

141   Riché, 'Bibliothèques', p. 101. Some of the same considerations may (cf. section (iii)), apply to Eccard, the other Carolingian aristocrat whose will features a law book (Riché, 'Bibliothèques', pp. 101–4, McKitterick, *Carolingians*, pp. 248–9): a magnate of south-of-Loire (Burgundian) domicile, he was also a member of the Carolingian line, descended from a branch that had promoted its cause in writing by the 'Continuation of Fredegar': Levillain, 'Les Nibelungen historiques', especially pp. 338–43; also (e.g.) Collins, 'Deception and Misrepresentation', pp. 236–46.

142   It is facilitated above all by Mordek's magnificent *Bibliotheca* (cited in what follows only when its comments bear directly on the argument). I have also gleaned from McKitterick, *Carolingians*, Bühler, 'Capitularia', especially pp. 340–418, and Bougard, *Justice dans le Royaume d' Italie*, pp. 17–54. I have myself examined only (most) MSS in Leiden, London, Paris and the Vatican, but when I differ over such MSS from any of the above in detail or emphasis, it may be taken to reflect personal observation (for better or worse).

Table 2.1   Numbers and types of western legal MSS from *c*.450

	450–750	750–900	900–1100	C12th–13th	Post-1250 etc.	TOTAL
Only Roman:	16	24	15	( )	( )	55
– [Fragments:	[47]	[3]	[–]	( )	( )	
Only Visigothic	1	2	–	( )	( )	3
– [Fragments:	[1]	[1]	[2]	( )	( )	
Only Lombard:	2	–	1	( )	( )	3
– with Fr. Caps	–	3	5	( )	( )	8
Frankish/Roman	—	5	–	–	–	5
– with Caps	–	5	3	–	–	8
– [Fragments:	[–]	[1]	[–]	[–]	[–]	
Single Frankish	–	12	2	3	5	22
– with Caps	–	10	10	6	2	28
– [Fragments:	[–]	[10]	[3]	[2]	[2]	
Plural Frankish	–	11	1	–	3	15
– with Caps	–	22	8	–	1	31
– [Fragments:	[–]	[4]	[–]	[–]	[–]	
Single Caps	–	29	16	4	3	52
– [Fragments:	[–]	[13]	[4]	[1]	[–]	
Plural Caps	1	36	22	5	5	69
– [Fragments:	[–]	[2]	[1]	[–]	[–]	
TOTAL exc. frags	20	159	83	18	19	**299**

143   Given the plasticity of the definitions used in table 2.1 (to say nothing of datings) its individual totals can only be approximate. Nor have I striven for precision in the category of 'fragments' or early modern copies: so little can be said of the structure of either or the dating of the latters' exemplars that they play a very slight part in the subsequent discussion. Further points to note are: (a) Roman law MSS post-800 lack the benefit of dating by *CLA* or Bischoff (mediated, pending the appearance of his monumental *Catalogue*, *via* Eckhardt's *Lex Sal.* or Mordek's *Bibliotheca*), and the dates given by Mommsen, *Cod. Theod.*, or Dolezalek, *Verzeichnis*, evidently tend to be too late; (b) nearly all pre-750 MSS are fragmentary to an extent: those figuring as such here are the palimpsest slivers or papyri sherds (few of the latter western); (c) no totals are given for Roman law MSS after the 1100 watershed, nor post-1050 MSS of Visigothic or Lombard law, in that these belong to a new intellectual world (chapter 6, pp. 468–74); (d) 'only Roman' MSS include those where Roman is accompanied by canon law; (e) 'Frankish' law means all secular laws current in the Carolingian empire, i.e. those from east of the Rhine and south of the Danube as well as the Burgundian and (in 'plural' law codices) the Visigothic and Lombard; (f) Merovingian capitularies included in *Lex Salica* MSS are counted as if part of *Lex Sal.*: the single entry under pre-750 'plural Caps' is the one early MS where Merovingian edicts are preserved with canon law; (g) MSS of 'single Caps' include single excerpts, and Ansegisus and 'Benedict' are treated as single texts; 'plural' Caps are correspondingly multiple; (h) the distinct classes of 'monastic capitulary' MSS, and of the 816 texts for canons (*Bibliotheca*, pp. 1098–9, 1045–58) are omitted; (i/j) also excluded at this stage of course are MSS of English provenance (chapter 13).

twenty, virtually all of Roman law and just one of Frankish.[144] While it is not unusual for Carolingian copies of a given work to vastly outnumber those from earlier times, so overwhelming an imbalance may seem a fair index of the vigour with which Carolingian authorities pursued their goal of rule by *lex scripta*. At the same time raw figures, however beguiling, should never be swallowed whole. There are obvious constraints on what can be digested here. But it is important for this chapter's purposes to ask how far these books really uphold the thesis that written law was regularly consulted by those responsible for making judgements. Is it actually because the Carolingians insisted on the use of *lex scripta* that they exist in such quantities? Not all possible gauges of a manuscript's use are necessarily helpful. For sure, many books are battered; but this may reflect their experiences since, not during, the ninth century.[145] Some are small and easily portable; but more are large, and some are enormous.[146] The evidence that will be considered here is mainly that of content. What can be learned from the materials put into these books about who made them and why?[147]

It would of course be no great surprise if a high proportion of these codices were at one or another time the property of churchmen. How else were early medieval books to survive if not in a church library? This need not mean that they or their archetypes were never in lay ownership. The Modena and Gotha manuscripts show that volumes that once belonged to laymen could well end up in cathedrals. Another example is a book now split between Leiden and Paris.[148] The Leiden constituent is of *c.* 800. It contains extracts from Isidore on kinship which often appear in law books of the period, followed by an epitome of Alaric's Breviary, Marculf's Formulary interspersed with *comparabilia* from Bourges, and

---

144   *CLA* i 46, 110, v 591, vii 1016, viii 1212 (*Cod. Theod.*); iii 295, 402 (*Dig. Just.*); iv 513, viii 1167 (*Cod. Just.*); iv 495 (*Instit. Just.*); vii 986 (*Epit. Iulian. Nov. Just.*); v 617, [625 frag], 703a, viii 1064, ix 1324, xi 1637 (*LRV*); [i 47 frag] (*Lex Rom. Burg.*); i 111, [v 626 frag] (*Lex Vis.*); iv 471, vii 949 (*Ed. Ro.*); v 619 (canons with Merovingian capitularies).

145   Paris BN MS lat. 18237–8 (Mordek, *Bibliotheca*, pp. 612–19) each belonged to the later-sixteenth century Paris lawyer, Antoine Loisel, *before* going to the library of Notre Dame, and it was probably he who put together the *membra disiecta* that make them up (cf. the operations of Sir Robert Cotton *et al.*, chapter 4 below). Paris BN MS lat. 4788 has two unique capitularies of Louis (in the same hand as an Augustine homily, cf. pp. 60–1), but most is worn quite away.

146   I reckon from personal observation and published data that of the 240 MSS mainly under consideration just over a quarter were *smaller* than 220 x 175 mm, the format of Leiden MS Voss. lat. Q. 119 (n. 166 below), while a third are *bigger* than 270 x 200 mm, the dimensions of Paris BN MS lat. 9654 (below, n. 163), the residue falling between these parameters. Some ninth-century MSS of single codes with relatively few capitularies are notably small (e.g. Paris BN MS lat 8801, *Lex Sal.* alone [Eckhardt K29], 150 x 85 mm); but Paris BN MS lat. 4418 (below, n. 175), surely a court product, is massive at 420 x 300 mm, and capitulary MSS tend to be large, especially if also containing canons – all of which is to make the obvious point that size of MSS bears some relation to the quantity of their contents.

147   Thus, I am *not* much concerned with details of date and provenance, partly because Bischoff's final verdicts are not yet available, and partly because of the likelihood that many MSS are copies of collections assembled earlier and elsewhere (e.g. below, pp. 61, 65). Similarly, Mordek's *Bibliotheca* is now (almost) the last word on issues of MS structure, which can anyway hardly be discussed here in the requisite minuteness. My objectives are merely to pick out patterns and to supply apposite instances of the trends I detect.

148   Leiden, Bibl. Rijksuniv. BPL MS 114, Par. BN MS lat. 4629. For what follows, see Mordek, *Bibliotheca*, pp. 502–7, following Bischoff, 'Manuscripts in the Age of Charlemagne', pp. 32–3, and n. 57. Paris and Leiden were apparently already distinct in the later-tenth century, when most of Paris but not Leiden was copied into Berlin Sttsbib. Phillips MS 1736: Mordek, p. 48.

a letter from a Merovingian Bishop of Tours to an abbess on the misconduct of nuns.[149] This book was soon given a supplement, perhaps always detachable. It comprised a truncated *Lex Salica*, complemented in various hands by the 803 capitularies additional to Salic and Ripuarian laws and the associated *capitulare missorum* (p. 47), by further items of post-800 legislation, by *Lex Ribuaria*, and by a summary of what was payable under *Lex Salica*.[150] Blended in with the legal matter, and also in other hands, are educational tracts on the Trinity and 'Philosophy', sundry *Isidoriana*, a diagrammatic schema of God, Soul and Body, a chapter from Alcuin's *Treatise on Virtues and Vices*, Alcuin's epitaph, a Venantius Fortunatus poem, a Bourges formula and Zodiacal reckonings. One of these items shows that the book may well at one time have been in lay hands: Alcuin's treatise was written for a count, and the selected chapter is the peroration, whose burden is that one need not be a cleric to be sure of a welcome in Heaven.[151]

Yet there are grounds for thinking that these are exceptional cases. Ansegisus' collection certainly brought the Church the solace he hoped it would. It and its supplement by 'Benedict' (p. 55) were key sources for pre-Gratian canonists.[152] The Gotha codex's ancestry is a case in point. Its Ansegisus/'Benedict' section is closely akin to texts in a book from Hincmarian Rheims.[153] This is in turn one of a series that integrate Ansegisus and 'Benedict' into canon collections and line up capitularies with canon or Roman law.[154] Hincmar may also have been responsible for two major sets of Charles the Bald capitularies which are clearly seen as continuations of Ansegisus, and in one case of the 829 decrees and 'Benedict' too: as full a set of Carolingian lawmaking as could be managed *c*.860.[155] Especially interesting is the legal collection from Hincmar's 'last years' in Paris BN MS lat. 10758.[156] In the first of its six parts the *Admonitio Generalis* is accompanied by texts from the 794 Council of Frankfurt and by Alcuin's classroom debate with Pippin son of Charlemagne. The fifth part contains the protocol of Charles the Bald's 875 imperial coronation, and the sixth Einhard's *Life of Charlemagne*.

---

149   Isidore, *Etymologiae*, ed. Lindsay, IX v–vi (cf. the non-Lupus preliminaries to the Modena MS: Mordek, *Bibliotheca*, pp. 257–8); *Epistolae aevi Merovingici collectae* 16, ed. Gundlach, pp. 461–4.

150   *Lex Sal.* ('E') xxiv:3 xxxvii; *Dec. Ch.*; *Lex Sal.* Epil. (cf. n. 59); *Cap.* 39, 41, 43–4, 57:7, 67:12; *Lex Rib.*; *Recapitulatio Solidorum* (ed. Eckhardt, as n. 93, pp. 533–4).

151   Alcuin, 'Liber de virtutibus et vitiis' xxxvi, col. 638 (cf. below, chapter 5, pp. 382–3, and nn. 531–6).

152   Mordek, *Bibliotheca*, pp. 1029–44; *Ans.* (intro.), pp. 282–362. The 'Benedictus Levita' collection, studied over the first third of this century in a long series of articles by E. Seckel, direly needs the scholarly treatment that Schmitz has given Ansegisus; it can still only be consulted as 'edited' by Pertz in 1837.

153   See above, n. 137, with Mordek, *Bibliotheca*, pp. 833–4.

154   E.g. Mordek, *Bibliotheca*, pp. 233–40, 451–6, 801–5, 842–4; note also *ibid.*, pp. 524, 834, on interrelationships of the Gotha and St Gallen MSS (as n. 137) with Paris BN MSS lat. 4634 and 4637, and Vatican, Cod. Reg. lat. 974 (all copies of *Ans.*/'Benedict').

155   Berlin Sttsbib. Phillips MS 1762 + The Hague MS 10 D 2 (its coherence first established by Mordek, *Bibliotheca*, pp. 59–60); Yale Beinecke MS 413; on the Hincmarian significance of the relationship of these MSS to the great lost Beauvais collection relayed by two sixteenth-century transcripts in the Vatican (Mordek, *Bibliotheca*, pp. 810–21, 865–81), see Nelson, 'Legislation and Consensus', pp. 205–8, 223–5 (pp. 94–7, 112–14); and on other members of the 'Rheims group', see Mordek, *Bibliotheca*, pp. 526–33, and his 'Weltliches Recht im Kloster Weißenburg'.

156   Fully described by Mordek, *Bibliotheca*, pp. 587–605.

The other three parts form a curious law compendium with its own list of contents. *Lex Salica* is preceded by the Isidorian legal treatise (p. 55), by Merovingian capitularies, by both *Lex Salica* prologues (p. 35), and by Herstal and the additional legislation of 803; it is followed by further *Lex Salica* appendices, by Ansegisus with extra chapters, by a full 829 series, by the 'lawyer's' *Lex Salica* addition of *c.* 819, by a second *Lex Salica* summary, and finally by Hincmar's plaint on a lost Rheims estate, which itself ushers in canonical and capitulary excerpts on Church lands and military service. The first impression left by this book is one of muddle. A closer look suggests a serious effort to supply a wide-ranging account of 'Salic law' and of ways in which legislation affected ecclesiastical interests; the whole being set in literature that variously highlighted the Carolingian ascendancy. If the historical and legal themes of the collection might indicate a secular patron, it is clear enough from other contents that its concerns were those of the Church, and the Church of Rheims in particular.[157]

Hincmar's Rheims is unusual because its high productivity makes its output identifiable. It may not have been so untypical in other ways. A huge preponderance of the more than eighty books from the ninth, tenth or eleventh centuries containing both codes and capitularies or codes alone are yet more secular in tone than Paris lat. 10758. It does not follow that their owners were laymen.[158] One that apparently was is a now well-known manuscript whose colophon says that it was written by Autramnus, 'unworthy lay advocate'.[159] A more characteristic volume is Paris BN MS lat. 10754, a copy of *Lex Salica* with the 803 'additional' capitulary (one of its clauses tacked on to the *lex*) and those of 805. These legal texts are followed without a break by a short note in celebration of St Maurice and his colleagues in the martyred 'Theban legion', and then by a series of scriptural texts on virtues and vices.[160] Martial saints would be an appropriate topic for a conscientious count. The itemized virtues and vices are like those on which Alcuin discoursed for Count Guy. But the Theban legion were above all patrons

157   The historical angle is sharpened in Paris BN lat. 4628a, a tenth-century reassembly of the same contents from St Denis (Hincmar's 'old school'), by prefixing a list of Frankish kings and Roman lords in Gaul; the same concern appears in two easterly twelfth-century MSS, Schaffhausen Sdtbib. MS Min. 75, and Bonn Univbib. MS S 402, the first linking Ansegisus and 829 with Thegan's *Life of Louis*, the other adding Einhard, *Lex Sal.* etc. with Herstal, and an 'Origo Francorum': G. Schmitz, 'Zur Überlieferung von Thegans Vita Hludowici'; see also next n. The Rheims/St Denis *Lex Sal.* arrangement recurs with the Pippin colloquy in the tenth-century Paris BN lat. 4760, and the colloquy once again in London BL Add. MS 22398, which contains *Ans.*, the Edict of Pîtres, *Lex Sal.* with 803 additions, and *Lex Rib.*

158   E.g. Leiden MS Voss. Lat. O. 86 (Eckhardt K18), a compendium of *Lex Sal.* with *Lib. Hist. Franc.*, selections from (the Carolingian) Marculf, a hagiographical romance on the Invention of the Cross, and the 'Liber Tobias'; there are prayers and masses too, but what suggests that the book (or its exemplar) was from Trier cathedral is one specifically Trier formula, plus the fact that Cyriacus, hero (after Helena) of the True Cross 'dig', was a Trier cult: Holder, *Lex Salica nach dem Codex von Trier-Lejden*, p. 42.

159   Mordek, pp. 516–18 (with printing of the colophon). The colophon has two clichés of scribal exhaustion, a sailor's longing for port and the labour of the whole body concentrated in the three writing fingers (Schmitz, 'Intelligente Schreiber', pp. 79–80). Yet one thing established by its shoddy script and spelling is that its scribe did *not* write the rest of the book, whose fine hand is attributable to St Amand; spellings like 'abet' and 'eclesia' suggest that the 'scribere fecit' construction which would have indicated *commissioning* of the book may have been beyond this draftsman's powers.

160   Mordek, pp. 585–7; the hand changes *during* the moralistic citations (at f. 89r), but probably not where they begin (at f. 79v), and *certainly* not at the start of the Theban legion notice (f. 79r). Cf. the (eleventh-century) Paris BN MS lat. 4626 (Mordek, pp. 477–82).

of Agaune abbey, and the virtues and vices were just those that clerical *missi* could be expected to 'teach others as well as display in themselves by deeds'.[161] Capitularies were above all tools of the *missi* (pp. 50–2): instructions for them to carry into localities, reminders of what they were to do themselves. *Missi* teams were made up, as in the Fleury – St Denis case, of paired clerics and laymen. One might guess from the example of Ansegisus himself that surviving sets of laws and capitularies began as the dossiers of the episcopal or abbatial half of a *missus* duo, before being left and/or copied in his 'home-library'. On balance, it is the clerical partner that is more likely to have contributed *extranea* of the sort found in Paris 10754. A number of collections also contain ordeal rituals. The conduct of ordeals might fall to judicial presidents of either cloth, but the rituals designed to add solemnity, indeed efficacy, to the Judgement of God were priest's work.[162]

For two of the greatest capitulary collections, an ecclesiastical origin is virtually certain. The closely related Vatican MS Pal. lat. 582 and Paris BN MS lat. 9654 have more capitularies than any other.[163] Among them are two, of 802 and 853, that actually define *missatica*; and in each case the Vatican/Paris collection refers only, and uniquely, to the circuit of the then Archbishop of Sens.[164] The inescapable conclusion is that this collection originated in the Sens archives. There are two other copies of that 802 capitulary. One has the reference to Count Stephen's broadcasting of the 803 *capitula addenda* at Paris (p. 47).[165] The temptation to see this copy as descended from Stephen's is resistable: his fellow *missus* was Abbot Fardulf of St Denis. The fourth copy is in one of the most interesting of all collections, the late-ninth-century Leiden MS Voss. lat. Q. 119. Here an exceptionally systematic set of *leges*, with the 'legal treatise', the bishop's letter on misbehaving nuns and the one surviving copy of the Edict of Chilperic (pp. 55, 58–9, 43), is followed (in a new hand, layout and parchment texture) by a distinctive collection of capitularies, two of them explicitly concerning Aquitaine and surviving only here. The book has no known Aquitainian connection. Its capitularies must go back to the 790 mission to Aquitaine, furnished with a text from twenty years before.[166] The odds of course favour a capitulary sequence covering decades being put together in a great church rather than the hall of even the most

161 Cf. *Cap.* 23:37 and n. 151 above; and below, p. 67 on Vatican Cod. Reg. lat. 991.
162 München Sttsbib. MS lat. 14508, ff. 146v–147r (later additions to MS); Paris BN MSS lat. 2796, ff. 152v–153r (*integrated* in early-ninth-century MS of Pippin legislation), 4409, f. 35v (added to MS), 4627, ff. 133rv, 145r–147r (added to MS), 10753, f. 91r (addition to MS – *with Louis' capitularies*); see below, chapter 8.
163 Mordek, *Bibliotheca*, pp. 780–97, 562–80 (the collection is the sole source for *Cap.* 48 – 49, 51, 53, 58 – 59, 64 – 65, 72 – 73, from late in Charlemagne's reign). The Paris MS is one of two vast legal codices compiled at Metz *c.*1000 (Mordek, pp. 1031–2, below, n. 176, and for its frontispiece of a – bookless – king, Mütherich, as n. 130); its Vatican sister is a century older and has a Mainz provenance (cf. pp. 00–00) but a NE French, conceivably Rheims, origin.
164 *Cap.* 34:Pr., 260:*miss*.10; for this crucial point see Bühler, 'Capitularia', pp. 369–72. The Sens *missaticum* also appears (again alone) in Yale Beinecke MS 413 (above, n. 155), f. 72r.
165 For what follows see Eckhardt, 'Capitularia Missorum Specialia', pp. 500–6.
166 *Cap.* 18, 24; Mordek, *Bibliotheca*, pp. 210–17. The Mancio and Eucher addressed in *Cap.* 24 are identified by J. Hannig, 'Pauperiores vassi', pp. 330–1, with the Bishop of Toulouse and with a *Comes Palatii* who was subsequently active in Italy; Theodulf of Orléans (above, p. 51) was later in touch with the former, while the latter had his links with Abbot Fardulf. Bischoff placed the MS at Chartres *c.*1000.

trusted comital dynasty. Most of the confirmatory evidence is only incidental to a manuscript's overall content, and such 'incidents' are sadly rare. But those redolent of truly lay preoccupations are rarer still.

A related issue is raised by the agency that apparently produced and no doubt disseminated an important group of law books, the '*Leges*-scriptorium' active from c. 825.[167] One need not spend long with these manuscripts to perceive their consistency in presentation of clauses, titles and title-lists.[168] But if the series was in any meaningful sense 'official', it has at least two disturbing features. One is that the group twice supplies copies of the 'D' text of *Lex Salica* and thrice of 'E', as against four copies of the 'K' version that ought by the 820s to have been the one in force. Why should any sort of official source more often than not offer a text of the kingdom's basic law which was two decades or more out of date? If the responsible commissioner was afflicted by slow communications or 'cussedness', he was not after all close to the governing mind. Alternatively, that mind had priorities which were by modern standards eccentric.[169] The other point concerns the flotilla's flagship manuscript. Paris BN MS lat. 2178 is an unusual product in many ways, not least in a format wider than it is tall. Among its contents is a full set of Louis' capitularies from 817 to c. 820. The *Ordinatio Imperii* and the *Prooemium generale* introducing Louis' 818/19 diet occur nowhere else. Also restricted to this volume are the *Formulae Imperiales*, drafts for some of Louis' government interventions. Above all, the Formulae and three capitularies are in the Tironian shorthand long practised by Frankish bureaucrats.[170] That the book is from an inner circle of Louis' administration can hardly be doubted. Yet overall it is a theological handbook. The opening set of Formulae and the first of the capitularies follow on from Fulgentius' *De Fide*; the main block of Formulae and capitularies share two quires with a group of Cyprian treatises; and the final series of Formulae is interspersed with works of Caesarius, Augustine and Chrysostom. This seems an odd product for a Chancery. In the circumstances, the manuscript's key text may be its unique copy of a letter in which Charlemagne ordered Alcuin to cooperate with Bishop Theodulf over a fugitive cleric to whom Alcuin had given sanctuary. Alcuin must have received this at Tours. Fridugis, his successor there, was Louis' 'archchancellor'. For all that under his stewardship the abbey was an intimate part of the regime, what pointers there are to the home-base of the '*Leges*-scriptorium' indicate the abbey itself as much as the palace at Aachen.[171]

---

167   This, like so much else in the world of Carolingian books, was a Bischoff discovery: *Latin Palaeography*, p. 205 (and cf. 'Court Library', as n. 175); his case is developed by McKitterick, 'Zur Herstellung von Kapitularien'.

168   These MSS are (in table 2.1 terms): Berlin Sttsbib. MS lat. qu. 150, Paris BN MSS lat. 4408, 4416, Vatican Codd. Reg. lat. 852, 1431 ('only Roman'); Warsaw Bibl. Uniw. MS 1 ('Frankish/Roman'); Vatican Cod. Reg. lat. 846, Montpellier MS H 136 ('Frankish/Roman – with Caps'); Paris BN MS lat. 4627 ('Single Frankish'); Paris BN MS lat. 4418, St Gallen MS 729, Vatican Cod. Reg. lat. 857 ('Plural Frankish'); Paris BN MS lat. n.a. 204, Vatican Cod. Reg. lat. 991 ('Plural Frankish – with Caps'); Paris BN MS lat. 2718 ('Plural Caps'); Paris BN MS lat. 10756 is a Formulae MS.

169   McKitterick, *Carolingians*, p. 42; Eckhardt was aware of the problem (as n. 95, pp. 55–76).

170   Mordek, *Bibliotheca*, pp. 422–30; *Bibliothèque Nationale, Catalogue Général*, ed Lauer *et al.*, III, pp. 22–5; *Cap.* 136–41, 143–5; *Formul.*, pp. 285–328. Cf. Ganz, 'Bureaucratic Shorthand'.

The tendency of this line of argument is to cast a shadow over the chances that extant memorials of Carolingian lawgiving reflect action by the lay aristocrats who were expected to enforce it. The surviving manifestations are likelier to come from those most ideologically committed to life by *lex scripta*, the upper ranks of the clergy. It is always conceivable that the numerous volumes which bear no trace of clerical concerns belonged to laymen like Eberhard. But their secular contents are no proof that they did. It cannot be assumed that the gaze of a cleric in the early medieval West (or in any other time and place) was exclusively trained on a better world. The substantially this-worldly preoccupations of Paris 10758 mislead because Hincmar of all people can hardly be denied the legal and historical interests the book reveals. If it was a Carolingian achievement to create a cadre of users of literacy, some of them laymen, the only 'textual community' securely attested by the law books is the stridently textual community of the Frankish Church.

So much for the evidence of content as to those who made Frankish law books. What does it imply about the reasons for making them? Two of the very earliest *Lex Salica* copies are among those tabulated as 'Frankish/Roman', meaning that a Frankish *Lex* or the like, with or without capitularies, follows a version of the Breviary of Alaric. Three more of the type are 'court' or '*leges*-scriptorium' products.[172] An instance of a similar pattern is the Leiden-Paris codex where *Lex Salica*, a few basic post-800 capitularies and *Lex Ribuaria* are tacked onto a copy of a *Breviarium* epitome (pp. 58–9). Also comparable are books that sound the 'Burgundian' note that has rung before in this chapter and will ring again (pp. 37, 44, 76–9); in the 'Wandalgarius' codex, which is dated (793) as well as signed, the Breviary (and genealogy of Jesus) are followed by a depiction of a law-giver, *Lex Salica* and *Lex Alamannorum*.[173] The trend culminates in two splendid Carolingian law books. One is from Tours itself or somewhere in its 'script province' and dates to Charlemagne's last decade. A copy of the Breviary, with

---

171   *Alcuin, Epistolae* 247, pp. 399–401; Dickau, 'Studien zur Kanzlei II', p. 39. McKitterick, Dickau and Mordek, *Bibliotheca*, p. 422, ascribe the operative Paris 2718 hand to Hirminmaris, cleric of Tours and Fridugis' depute notary; other '*Leges*-scriptorium' products are attributed by Mordek to Tours (Paris BN MS lat. n.a. 204, Warsaw Bibl. Uniw. MS 1), or to the Court circle (or Tours). New light is cast on the issue (as Professor Ganz points out to me) by Folliet, 'Le plus ancien témoin': in so far as the Augustine texts in Paris 2718 are closely related to those in Paris BN MS lat. 12205 (from Corbie), this might suggest that Hirminmaris got access to them through contacts at court; but M. Folliet is unsure (p. 97) that one *directly* copies the other. See also Mordek, 'Kapitularien und Schriftlichkeit', pp. 61–3.

172   Wolfenbüttel Weißenburg MS 97 (above, n. 63) is the oldest *Lex Sal.* MS, and Paris BN MS lat. 4403B (Eckhardt C5) is late-eighth-century from Luxeuil; Vatican Cod. Reg. lat. 846 and Warsaw Bibl. Uniw. MS 1 are '*Leges*-scriptorium' (above n. 168) and Montpellier MS H 136 is from the 'Nähe des Hofes' (*ibid.*): Montpellier has a run of capitularies, but the Vatican MS has Herstal only, the others none. The only late example of the genre is Paris BN MS lat. 4409, part II of which joins *Lex Sal.* and *Brev. Al.*; its 'E' text of *Lex Sal.* is among indications of its early exemplar. Other books tabulated as Franco-Roman are Fulda MS D I (*CLA* viii 1199), linking *Brev. Al.* with the Angers Formulary (*Formul.*, pp. 1–25), and St Gallen MS 722 (*CLA* vii 946), where extracts from Julian's Epitome of Justinian's Novels and the *Lex Romana Curiensis* (a Breviary adapted for the Chur area) are followed by the *Capitula* of Bishop Remedius of Chur (Mordek, pp. 660–4); the remainder include combinations with capitularies and canon law (above, n. 154) or with a south German *lex* (below, n. 205).

173   St Gallen MS 731 (*CLA* vii 950); for the likelihood that the illustrated figure is not Wandalgarius the scribe but a legislating king see Mordek, 'Frühmittelalterliche Gesetzgeber', pp. 1022–4 and Pl. XVI. The same sequence is in St Gallen MS 729, also linked with Louis' Aachen court. More strictly Burgundian

pictures of law-making Roman emperors and jurists carrying books, gives way to hardly less lavish presentations of 'barbarian' leges, opening with an elaborated Merovingian ('A') *Lex Salica*, and furnished in the Alaman case with another illustration. A new quire has more Merovingian additions to *Lex Salica*, and in a different but contemporary hand a brief set of Charlemagne's capitularies.[174] The other book is a product of Louis' court. It is an in every dimension huge edition of most of the empire's *leges*, starting with the Breviary (and Julian's Epitome of Justinian's Novels), going on to Ripuarian, Salic and Burgundian codes, and concluding with *Lex Visigothorum* – a text rare enough in such a context to suggest the influence of Benedict of Aniane (p. 51).[175] There may even once have been a second volume for the realm's remaining laws: Lombard, Alaman and Bavarian.[176]

The manuscripts so far reviewed constitute not the sum total of early law books, but a significant fraction of them.[177] They strikingly uphold the thesis that 'barbarian' law-making replicated an archetypal function of Roman imperial sovereignty. Roman law in the Frankish kingdoms was, as is evident from the Fleury – St Denis case, *par excellence* the law of the Church (pp. 31, 71). It is thus suggestive that in these and other manuscripts the Roman law texts are the most likely to carry any degree of annotation, whereas 'barbarian' *leges* tend to remain unsullied.[178] Whether or not they show what uses were found for written law, these books highlight the ideological spur to the making of it. Other relatively early law books are rather different. One group offer a single *lex* with few or no capitularies or extraneous matter. Striking specimens are a self-contained twenty-nine leaf copy of *Lex Alamannorum*, which may have originated at the Pavia court of Pippin of Italy, and a *portmanteau* volume of *Lex Baiwariorum*.[179] The latter is reasonably connected with the Bavarian code's own stipulation that counts should work with the 'liber legis' beside them (p. 39). Yet single-text copies of mainline Frankish *leges* are never common and become increasingly

---

MSS in this category (their symptom the otherwise far from invariable presence of *Leg. Burg.*) are Paris BN MSS lat. 9653, 10753 (cf. Esders, *Römische Rechtstradition*, pp. 56–78), and Vatican Codd. Reg. lat. 1050, 1128; note also Paris BN MS lat. 4758, with the fragments Lyon MS 375 (Eckhardt K50) and Besançon MS 1348 (Eckhardt K48).

174   Paris BN MS lat. 4404 (Mordek, pp. 456–63 – but according to Professor Bullough's pers. comm. *not* necessarily from Tours); for its illustrations, Mordek, 'Frühmittelalterliche Gesetzgeber', pp. 1026–9 and Pll. XX–XXI; Mütherich, 'Frühmittelaterliche Rechtshandschriften', p. 84); the capitularies included, besides the 803 *legibus addenda*, are that 'to be made known by the *missi*' (*Cap.* 67, also in Paris BN MS lat. 4629, above n. 150), and the rare – and fragmentary – 'On Robbers' (*Cap.* 82); both date soon after 803.

175   Paris BN MS lat. 4418; cf. Bischoff, 'Court Library', pp. 87–8.

176   Mordek, *Bibliotheca*, pp. 1031–2.

177   The most singular break in the early pattern is München Sttsbib. lat. MS 4115, the only MS as early as *c.* 800 to offer a run of *leges* (including *Lex Sal.* 'A') of the sort normal after 825 (below); its S.W. German provenance may well be pertinent (below, pp. 68–9).

178   E.g. Leiden MS Voss. lat. Q. 119, Paris BN MSS lat. 4404, 4409, 4418, 9653, Vatican Codd. Reg. lat. 846, 857, 1050, 1128. The only comparable cases known to me for 'barbarian' *leges* are Paris BN MSS lat. 9654 (p. 61) and 10758 (pp. 59–60), and Vatican MS Pal. lat. 582 (p. 61) and Cod. Reg. lat. 991 (below).

179   Wolfenbüttel Helmst. MS 513 (*CLA* ix 1382); München Univbib. 8° 132 (Mordek, *Bibliotheca*, pp. 353–4: the MS edited by Beyerle, above n. 26).

rare. Among the signs of differing conditions in southern Germany is that their codes were being copied long after 900, and in the Bavarian case well into the twelfth century (pp. 68–9).[180]

A last feature of the pre-825 period is the capitulary on its own or out of legal context. Probably the earliest extant text is a Fulda copy of the *Admonitio Generalis*, followed by sermons of Augustine and a Lord's Prayer with accompanying *expositio*, and preceded by an iconographical evocation of (?)Charlemagne as the Church's protector.[181] A near-contemporary copy of Charlemagne's 'Letter on the cultivation of literature' is added onto the opening page of a rather earlier volume of Augustine on the Trinity.[182] The capitularies for the Saxons appear alongside others on opening and closing leaves of a copy of Alcuin on Genesis.[183] There are copies of the *Admonitio Generalis* and of the linked *missi* capitulary in compilations possibly made with the Adoptionist controversy in mind.[184] Canon collections, including those of Merovingian type, supply full or excerpted texts of early Carolingian edicts.[185] There is nothing surprising here. As well as hoping that his collection would help the Church, Ansegisus feared for the vulnerability of texts not incorporated into a solid frame. His view is sustained by the one capitulary preserved in hypothetically original form, on a piece of parchment roll drafted and carried off by a participant in the 813 deliberations (p. 52). Yet it is noteworthy that only two early capitulary manuscripts are thoroughly 'legal/administrative' in content. One is the unique copy of the *Capitulare de Villis*, which has something of the air of a cartulary text.[186] The other, and the only one approaching the status of a capitulary *collection*, is St Gallen MS 733, a south-west German book with a decidedly Italian horizon (below, pp. 68–9).[187]

Frankish law books before *c.*825, then, tend either to have the Roman model to the fore (as a rule literally so), or to be books whose primary content is not

---

180 As strongly emerges from Professor Kottje's manuscript reviews (above, n. 139); almost half the 'Single Frankish' ninth-century category comprises S. German codes. More or less unaccompanied *Lex Sal.* MSS are Paris BN MSS lat. 8801 (above n. 146) and 18237 (II) (above, n. 145), Leiden MS Voss. lat O. 86 (above, n. 158), and, moving into the tenth century, Bern Bgbib. 442 (Eckhardt K22) and Paris BN MS lat. 4789 (Eckhardt K51); there is an isolated *Lex Burg.* in Paris BN MS lat. 4759(A), but no individual *Lex Rib.* other than Vatican MS Pal lat. 773 (with *Cap. Add.*, Mordek, pp. 799–801). So far as I can see, Geneva Univbib. MS 50 (Eckhardt K23) is a 'ghost'.

181 Wolfenbüttel Helmst. MS 496a; cf. Mordek, 'Frühmittelalterliche Gesetzgeber', pp. 1018–22, Pl. XIV.

182 Oxford, Bodl. MS Laud misc. 126 (Mordek, *Bibliotheca*, pp. 406–8).

183 Vatican MS Pal. lat. 289 (Mordek, pp. 769–71): *Cap.* 42, 118, 78, 26–7 – *Cap.* 42, 118, 78 and 26–7 are each in fresh hands.

184 Brussels Bib. Roy. MS 8654–72, München Sttsbib. MS lat. 14468.

185 Examples selected from Mordek, *Bibliotheca*: pp. 190–1, 195–205, 339–42, 653–8, 751–4, 858–63, 883–8, 911–15. By no means all are in fact early, but their likeness to those that are raises a possibility that they are copies of early exemplars; for two cases (on which Professor Bullough has kindly advised me) of late MSS whose combination of *Cap.* 31 with a letter of Alcuin to Charlemagne and a baptismal *florilegium* argues an early origin, see Mordek, pp. 557–9, 805–7.

186 Wolfenbüttel Helmst. MS 254: there is a facsimile edition by Brühl; it is suggestive that the capitulary *follows* a copy of the returns to which it gave rise (*Cap.* 128, 32).

187 Mordek, pp. 676–80; cf. Bougard, *Justice*, pp. 35–6. The MS is of the first quarter of the ninth century, and contains *Cap.* 20, 89, 22–23, 97, 94 – with a suggestive sequel in a passage from Defensor's *Liber Scintillarum* on tithe-payment.

(secular) legal. From the century's third decade the picture begins to change, with 'leges-scriptorium' manuscripts among the earliest where this occurs. There are now sets of Frankish leges without a Roman ingredient or with Roman law in a subordinate role; there are full capitulary collections; and there are grouped laws alongside current capitularies.[188] For the rest of the ninth century and into the tenth, Frankish law books were usually of one or other of these types. Two in the 'without Caps' category look like attempts to form an anthology of law in 'leges-scriptorium' style from once diverse elements.[189] When 'Single' capitularies appear in canon collections, the text in question is increasingly likely to be Ansegisus. 'Plural' series become commoner: Ansegisus and 'Benedict'; the former or both with the 829 decrees; Ansegisus and 829 with Charles the Bald's legislation.[190] Capitulary collections along these lines were still being made, unlike those of leges, through and after the tenth century (pp. 55–6).[191] Lastly, laws and capitularies were more likely to be found together. The Rheims – St Denis confection (pp. 59–60) had a number of counterparts.[192] The class of 'Plural Frankish – with Caps', only incipient c.825, is boosted by a dozen examples from the Frankish 'core'.[193]

Yet the change in the character of Frankish law books from the second quarter of the century cannot obscure one crucial point: lex and capitulary in the Frankish heartland were never fully integrated. Over a third of pre-1100 leges manuscripts contain no capitularies at all, and only some are so early that they can hardly be expected to. Of thirty-two manuscripts in the 'Single/Plural Frankish – with Caps' classes, just nineteen go beyond (and few much beyond) 803, 818–19 and Ansegisus.[194] In all the Carolingians' northerly dominions, only one volume combines an imposing set of capitularies with a full range of leges. Made in the Carolingian 'home-town' of Metz c.1000, it must have been a relatively recent

---

188   Cf. n. 168: Vatican Cod. Reg. lat. 857 is of the first type, Paris BN MS lat. 2718 of the second, and Paris BN MS n.a. lat. 204 (which is fragmentary and could well have contained more texts) of the third. For earlier, south German, cases of grouped leges and of collected capitularies see nn. 177, 187.

189   Paris BN MS lat. 4759, 4787 (Eckhardt K26, K42): so much might be deduced from changes of scribe and layout between codes but within a generally homogeneous format. For earlier MSS in this category, often of 'Franco-Burgundian' type, see n. 173; other later sets include Bamberg Sttsbib. MS Jur. 35 (Mordek, pp. 17–19, but the capitulary element is nugatory), St Gallen MS 338 (Eckhardt K21), and Wolfenbüttel MS Gud. lat. 327 (Eckhardt K60).

190   Cf. nn. 154–5, 163, and add Mordek Bibliotheca, pp. 29–34, 43–7, 329–33, 545–6, 555–7, 720–3.

191   A few unusually important examples: Barcelona Ripoll 40; Berlin Sttsbib. lat. fol. 626 (cf. Eckhardt, Kapitulariensammlung Ghaerbalds); Berlin Sttsbib. Phillips MS 1737; Paris BN MSS lat. 4761/1+2 and 18239.

192   Cf. nn. 156–7, 96, 145, 160; also 'Single Frankish – with Caps' are (e.g.) Cambrai MS 625 (a tenth-century counterpart is Paris BN MS lat. 3182), Nürnberg Stdbib. MS Cent. V, App. 96, St Petersburg Q.v.II. 11, and Wolfenbüttel MS Aug. 4° 50.2. Into this category fall (probably) the fragmentary Vatican Cod. Reg. lat. 520 (with the same annals as Paris BN lat. 4995, and the other copy of the capitulary 'De Latronibus', cf. n. 174).

193   Cf. nn. 148, 159, 166, 168, 173–4. New examples: Cologny (Geneva) Cod. Bodmer 107; Copenhagen Gl. Kgl. Saml. 1943.4°; Hamburg Stts-Univbib. Cod. 141a; London BL Add. MS 22398; London BL Egerton MSS 2832 + 269 + Paris BN MS lat. 4633; Münster Sttsarch. msc. MS VII. 5201; Paris BN MSS lat. 4417; 4628; St Gallen MS 728; Wolfenbüttel MS Gud. lat. 299. The tabular total is made up by the Italian and S. German MSS (below, pp. 67–9).

194   Of MSS adduced in nn. 192–3: Cologny, Leiden, London Add. and Egerton etc., Montpellier,

conflation, as its capitulary collection survives independently (p. 61). More symptomatic is Vatican Codex Reginensis latina 991. This was an elegantly produced specimen of standard '*Leges*-scriptorium' size and format, which for at least two codes offered high-quality texts. It had a separate quire for each of the Ripuarian, Salic, Alaman and Bavarian codes. Space was left at the end of each quire and also at the front of all after the first. The intention was presumably to fit capitularies into the interstices. But the sole addition made was the capitulary for addition to Bavarian law, duly inserted in the right place by a later hand. The available space was otherwise taken up with a more or less continuous devotional sequence.[195] The book stands as a symbol of the *lack* of contact between the capitularies that were the main vehicle of the Carolingian royal will and the codes encapsulating the acknowledged law of their peoples. François-Louis Ganshof, founder of modern capitulary studies, took the view that capitularies were marginal to the administration of justice.[196] On the evidence of manuscripts (to which he barely referred), he was nearer the truth than his critics. Capitularies as preserved did belong to another sphere of perception from *leges*. Either, therefore, they were as peripheral to day-to-day judicial action as he supposed, or the law-codes were; or, possibly, *both* were.

Law book evidence might be interpreted along traditionally 'constitutional' lines. *Leges*, it could be argued, were *Volksrecht*. Royal legislation as such, *Königsrecht*, had no place among them unless subject to the consent that was sought for capitularies formally designed as 'additions to *lex*'. That would be why only capitularies of that type appear at all often in *leges* manuscripts.[197] However, this discussion started with a collection which did fuse a comprehensive set of *leges* with a full series of capitularies, and drew no perceptible distinction between the authority purveyed by either (pp. 32–5, 55–6). Lupus' anthology found no parallel in the north European world. But it had several counterparts in the southern world of its addressee. The earliest ninth-century Italian law book, probably made at Aquileia for the hapless King Bernard of Italy (811–17), opens with his Mantua capitulary. It then includes all the Frankish *leges* along with four books of an epitomized Breviary.[198] There follows a capitulary series in ninety-two continuously numbered chapters, comprising both complete texts and extracts from the major legislation of Charlemagne and Pippin of Italy between 779 and 810. The series was continued by other hands to include the decrees of

---

Münster, Nürnberg, Paris 4404, 4628, 4629, 4788, 4995, 10754, 10758/4628a and n.a. 204, St Petersburg, Vatican Cod. Reg. lat. 520, Wolfenbüttel Aug. 50.2 and Gud. 299. Additions are often limited to *Cap*. 20 (Herstal), 22 (*Admonitio Generalis*), 43–4 (Thionville, 805), 57, 67 (cf. n. 174), 82 (cf. nn. 174, 192); and even fuller sets are in some sense 'specialized'.

195   Mordek, *Bibliotheca*, pp. 838–41.

196   Ganshof, 'Recherches', e.g. at p. 201.

197   Brunner's classical exposition of the difference (*Deutsche Rechtsgeschichte* I, pp. 405–27, 539–58) made little of MS evidence on the point. On problems of drawing a distinction in any way, see Mordek, 'Kapitularien', pp. 25–31, and my 'Lex Scripta', pp. 109–11 (6–8).

198   Sankt Paul im Lavanttal, 4/1 (familiar as St Paul-in-Kärnten xxv.4.8): Mordek, *Bibliotheca*, pp. 685–95, and 'Frühmittelalterliche Gesetzgeber', pp. 1005–18 (plus Pll. VI–XI) for identification of the frontispiece figure as Bernard. In 'Ein Bildnis König Bernhards von Italien?', Professor Mordek argues that an ascription to Bernard was erased after his 817 revolt and deposition.

818–19, 822–3 and 825, and a list of 169 North Italians taking an oath of fidelity (?in 828/9).[199] The ninety-two chapter collection has an evident if elusive relationship to that of Lupus and its south German cousins.[200] It also foreshadows the way that Frankish legislation in Italy was arranged by the late-tenth-century 'Book of the Law of the Lombards' or *Liber Papiensis* (chapter 6, pp. 468–9). There are three other ninth-century Italian manuscripts of this type, and three more (discounting Modena and *Liber Papiensis*) down to *c*.1000. All subjoined a fairly full set of Italian capitularies and the major transalpine pronouncements to Frankish laws or the Lombard edict or in one case both.[201] This one, Wolfenbüttel Blankenberg MS 130, wins the palm as the fullest assemblage of Carolingian law from the period of Carolingian dominance.[202]

The position can thus be stated bluntly. With the exceptions of the Mainz Lupus offshoot (pp. 55–6), the aforementioned Metz book (pp. 66–7) and some southern German examples to be considered in a moment, *every* manuscript containing a code or codes and more than a dozen capitularies is Italian. Fewer than half the law books from Francia proper have both laws and capitularies. Italy, however, has only two substantial capitulary collections with no code, and a single post-750 copy of an unaccompanied *lex*.[203] A number of Italian books have single or few capitularies beside canons or less pertinent material.[204] But Italy's manuscripts generally supply a guidance to the range of law in force that Frankish manuscripts simply do not.

A final point remains. It has already been hinted more than once that the south German pattern is as distinctive as the Italian. There is a contemporary southwest-German fragment of Lupus' collection and a capitulary collection in three tenth-century codices from central or eastern Bavaria has some connection with his (pp. 33, 53). This area produced the first set of Frankish *leges* and the earliest non-Italian capitulary collection (pp. 64, 65). Its other products include a Franco-Italian capitulary collection related to those at Ivrea and Wolfenbüttel; and a notable Romano-Alaman compound, where the Alaman code is combined not only with Breviary excerpts but also with Justinianic legislation, and whose capit-

---

199   *Cap.* 158:1–14, 165, 181; Mordek, pp. 691–3.

200   Mordek, p. 688, and cf. n. 125 above.

201   Ivrea Bib. Cap. MSS XXXIII, XXXIV (Mordek, pp. 172–85); Wolfenbüttel Blankenb. MS 130 (Mordek, *Bibliotheca*, pp. 920–43, and see next n.); Paris BN MS lat. 4613 (Mordek, pp. 469–76); Cava dei Tirreni Bib. Bad. MS 4 (Mordek, pp. 98–111); and Vatican Chigi MS F.IV. 75 (Mordek, pp. 756–68), with many capitularies and perhaps deriving from an archetype containing the Lombard edict. Two of these have unique texts of crucial northern decrees (above, n. 116).

202   See previous n.; like Lupus and the St Paul MS, this groups its capitularies under headings for the kings responsible, also giving a preliminary table of contents: Bühler, 'Capitularia', pp. 354–7. There was also an attempt by a 'Redaktor' to give a similar sort of ordering to Paris 4613: Mordek, *Bibliotheca*, p. 470.

203   München Sttsbib. MS lat. 29555/1 etc. (Mordek, pp. 369–76), Vatican Cod. Reg. lat. 263 (Mordek, pp. 807–10); Paris BN MS lat. 4635 is a tenth-century Italian MS of Ansegisus and 'Benedict'. For the MS of *Lex Alamannorum* (?from the Italian royal court), see n. 179 (but Vatican MS Vat.lat. 5359 (Mordek, pp. 881–3) is a Lombard edict with only *Cap.* 164–5, 201). Bougard, *Justice dans le Royaume d' Italie*, pp. 37–9, gives a very useful table, which does reveal that the unanimity of the Italian series began to break down post-825.

204   E.g. Mordek, *Bibliotheca*, pp. 219–20, 268–70, 629–30, 855–7, 888–90 (Atto of Vercelli's MS), 891–3; examples of more eccentric collocations are *ibid.*, pp. 270–3, 393–9.

ulary collection contains not only Ansegisus Books III and IV and but also the sole text of Charlemagne's 808 decree on military recruitment.[205] This was also the only part of Europe other than Italy and England where pre-1000 legal texts were still being systematically reproduced in the twelfth century.[206] The easiest way to account for the south German record is in terms of the pervasive Italian influence in the area. That a book should contain Justinianic law is itself an Italian symptom.[207] But there may be more to it than that. The St Gallen volume containing an extract from Justinian's Novels also has a text of the Breviary so distinctive as to amount to a recension in its own right for the special purposes of the diocese of Chur. There are possibilities of a continuity of Roman attitudes in this part of Switzerland that cast new light on St Gallen's own documentary habits down the road on Lake Konstanz.[208] Similar claims have been made for areas of Bavaria.[209] In other words, Alamannia and Bavaria may not only have been in closer touch with Italy; they may have been *more like* Italy. The Danube was as much of a watershed as the Alps.

Ultimately, then, the law book evidence runs with, not across, the grain of the texts themselves. The *Liber legum* again stands apart from the world where Lupus was most at home. With manuscripts as with texts, quantity of material counts for less than qualitative variation within it. Geography is crucial. Law was preserved more systematically, as it was presented more tidily, the more southerly its context. The South is as ever an index of what the North might have done but did not. Changes over time are almost as important. Most early copies of Frankish codes followed the lead of Roman law; several seem to come from Burgundian circles where the study of Roman law had persisted in Merovingian times. Roman example is writ large in manuscripts just as it is in Charlemagne's post-800 redoubling of his law-giving efforts (pp. 45–6). The new sophistication of law book production under Louis the Pious coincides with the apogee of Carolingian law-making in other respects (pp. 48, 51–2, 82). As the century passed, the initiative in capitulary collection passed to bishops, so reflecting the period's vigorous conciliar activity. Great churches became the guardians of Carolingian law, as of so much of Carolingian tradition.

The number of post-750 law books is a powerful expression of the regime's aspirations. But the suspicion lingers that these ran deepest among ideologically programmed clergy. And the content of most *leges*-manuscripts suggests that even for them the programme was held back by a sense of *lex* as the capsule of

---

205   München Sttsbib. MS lat. 19416; Stuttgart MS iur. 4° 134.

206   See Kottje's discussions as per n. 139 above; to be added to his Bavarian examples are Admont MS 712 and Wien Natbib. MS 406.

207   For the Italian provenance of most Justinianic MSS (but the south German context of some), see nn. 144, 172, 205; and cf. (e.g.) *CLA* iii 366, v 557. Paris BN MS lat. 4418 (above, n. 175) and Hincmar's acquaintance with Julian's Epitome (Devisse, *Hincmar*, p. 658, and *Hincmar et la Loi*, p. 22) are strict cases of the exception that proves the rule. Other Italian *vestigia* include the extracts from Rothari in München Sttsbib. MSS lat. 3519 and 5260, and Wolfenbüttel Helmst. MS 532 (III). For that matter, Wolfenbüttel Blankenb. MS 130 (above, nn. 201–2) had reached Augsburg by the eleventh century, while München Sttsbib. MS lat. 29555/1 (above, n. 203) ended up at Benediktbeuren.

208   See n. 172; Mordek, p. 661, elaborates on its Italian connections. See also McKitterick, *Carolingians*, pp. 79–126.

209   Prinz, *Frühes Mönchtum*, pp. 318–45.

Frankish tradition. Royal guarantees of *lex* are couched as concessions, and what was conceded must have been desired. But the *lex* that was desired was the *lex* that was known. If law was 'given' by kings, it was received only patchily and on terms. This was a cultural, not a constitutional, issue. Italy, Alamannia and Bavaria were not more autocratically inclined than Francia itself. The determinant of the contrast was a differentiated inheritance from Rome, whose documentary bent, like its buildings, loomed larger as one tracked southwards. It was not that kings were unable in principle to tamper with their 'people's law'. Rather, pursuit of consensus with their ruling elite restricted their ability to make a reality of reforming ideals. An aristocracy looking to a Frankish past put a premium on the integrity of tradition. That may after all be why there are so many copies of the *leges*. Compilations of laws made in the realm's great churches, each potentially a microcosm of the imperial nobility, reflected their diverse land-holdings and polyethnic membership. Lupus himself saw his *Liber legum* as a 'Francorum scema per aevum' (p. 32). The literal meaning of 'scema' was 'figure'. But so accomplished a grammarian must have known that it also meant a figure of speech.[210] The word may be a pun. Pictures of Frankish law-givers adorned texts that as a group became a metaphor of enduring Frankish power. Even for Lupus, the importance of written law went beyond its utility. It remains to ask what its utility turned out to be in legal practice.

(iii) The conduct of legal cases

The lawsuit between Fleury and St Denis was recorded by Adrewald, monk of Fleury, in his 'Miracles of St Benedict' (pp. 30–1). It is a more detailed account of legal proceedings than is provided by most sources of this type.[211] As a narrative, it certainly lends the case more colour than is furnished by drier documents. Especially revealing, if no surprise, is its evidence of the pressures that parties could bring to bear. The likelihood that the legal specialist had indeed received a sweetener from the St Denis advocate is enhanced by Adrewald's report of another case between the same abbeys. On that occasion the abbot of Fleury, anxious not to seem less 'careful' than his opponent, sent two weighty silver vessels to the *vicarius* who was due to preside, only to find that St Denis had got there first and that the *vicarius* was therefore uninterested in Fleury's offering. So far from giving him credit for consistency rather than double-dealing, Adrewald reported with grim satisfaction that the *vicarius* promptly fell off his horse and died three days later.[212] Carolingian sources, legislative and admonitory, say a lot about the malign effects of '*munera*, gifts' on the quality of justice. Theodulf's 'On Justice' has a long and eloquent passage on the beauty

---

210   Note the differing interpretations of Schott (as n. 8), and Mordek, 'Frühmittelalterliche Gesetzgeber', pp. 1046–7, and n. 184.
211   See n. 4. A new edition is forthcoming by F. Charpin; valuable guidance to the collection is meanwhile available from Rollason, 'Miracles of St Benedict'; and on Adrewald from Lysaght, 'Fleury and St Benedict', pp. 67–117. For *Miracula* and Carolingian Justice in general, see below, nn. 231–2.
212   *Ex Miraculis S. Benedicti* 24, p. 489.

of what could be offered.[213] There was ample precedent for such concern in Roman and Biblical law and literature. Yet to think simply in terms of bribery is unhelpful. The cogs of early medieval society hardly turned unless oiled by exchange of favours. Adrewald's indignation was aroused not by the giving of presents but by their gift in a 'bad' cause. The right modern parallel would be a misdirected, not a bent, judge or jury. Neither Adrewald nor any other ninth-century Frank saw anything amiss in justice being influenced by condign fear of saintly wrath.

Terrestrial and supernatural interference notwithstanding, the case proceeded much as it should have done. In supervising a county court session, Bishop Jonas and Count Donatus did just what capitulary injunctions required.[214] It is not clear (though decidedly interesting) why a court meeting at Orléans should be better qualified to cope with a case involving Roman law than one presumably assembled at the county *caput* of Château-Landon.[215] But it was wholly in order that Roman law be invoked in an inter-church suit.[216] For a case which had reached an *impasse* to be resolved by a duel between opposed witnesses was of course not Roman law, and was objectionable to at least one Carolingian ideologue.[217] All the same, it had been the proposed solution for cases 'where in no way is one side prepared to yield to the other' in Louis' legislation additional to the *leges* of 816 and 818/19.[218] The first of these provisions restricted the device to 'secular cases', and the second added cases between clergy and laity. Intractable disputes between churches were in 816 to be submitted to a singular procedure known as 'Judgement of the Cross'. This ordeal, presumably derived from Moses' means of securing God's support in battle with the Amalekites, required a party's representative to stretch out his arms as if on a cross. It first appeared in a capitulary of Pippin's last years, and was called long-established custom when used to decide a case between the bishop of Paris and St Denis in 775.[219] But it predictably aroused unease in Louis' ideologically sensitized circle. In 818/19 it was in effect declared blasphemous by an 'Ecclesiastical' capitulary, so dropped from the

213 'Contra Iudices' lns 163–204 (cf. n. 111), trans. Godman, *Poetry of the Carolingian Renaissance*, pp. 162–5 – who argues, p. 15, that the poem should be conceived as 'De Iustitia' instead of 'Against Judges'. For capitularies on the snares of gifts, see *Cap.* 22:63, 33:1,25, 35:38, 61:7 and 62:17, 141:21 (citing *Lex Rib.* xci), 150:8, 192:4, and (repeating 192:4 as late as 873) 278:10. Admonitions also include Alcuin, 'De Virtutibus' 20, col. 628; Jonas of Orléans, 'De Institutione Laicali' ii 24, cols 218–21 (of special relevance, given his role as *missus* in the Fleury case); and cf. Hinkmar, *De Ordine Palatii* iii lns 161–79; the prime source of these prescriptions seems to be Isidore, 'Libri Sententiarum' iii 54(7), cols 726–7. Cf. Le Jan, 'Justice royale', pp. 51–61.
214   E.g. *Cap.* 33:28, 40:3, 80:4,12, 150:14, 151:2 (*Ans.* (intro.), pp. 38–9), 192:2–4, repeated in 873. But see also below, nn. 245–6.
215   Ganshof, 'Contribution', p. 595.
216   The basic statement of this principle (though clearly regarding it as one already accepted) is *Lex Rib.* lxi:1 ('legem Romanam, quam ecclesia vivit'). *Cap.* 58:2 envisages a case covered by either Roman or Salic law. Cf. Brunner, *Deutsche Rechtsgeschichte* I, p. 394 and n. 56 (which cites this case).
217   Cf. Wood, 'Disputes in late-fifth and sixth-century Gaul', p. 18, and for Agobard, above n. 99. Good discussions of the whole topic (to only superficially different effect) are Bartlett, *Trial by Fire and Water*, pp. 103–6, 113–18, and White, 'Proposing the Ordeal'.
218   *Cap.* 134:1, 139:10, and cf. 141:12; Ganshof, 'Contribution', pp. 598–601, a discussion which makes most of the points that follow.
219   *Cap.* 16:17 (cf. 20:10 for a more clearly related issue); *Urk. Pipp. Karl.* 102; Exodus 17:11–12. Cf. Bartlett, *Trial by Fire and Water*, pp. 9–10.

accompanying addition to the *leges*.[220] Instead, disputing churches were to come to terms if possible; and if not, the court was to impose a 'legitimate conclusion' upon them.

It follows that the interfering legal expert was wholly right to insist that Fleury and St Denis partition the disputed serfs rather than have their witnesses fight it out. This, however, introduces the crux of the whole episode. He alone of all those gathered at Orléans, whether *missus* or viscount, whether specializing in Roman or in Salic law, knew that this was correct procedure. That Adrewald (or St Benedict) should have been unaware of recent imperial legislation is surprising enough, given Fleury's close links with the regime. That Louis' own *missi* should have needed reminding of it is remarkable. Nor can one fall back on the supposition that the case came too soon after the government's change of mind for this to have registered in the provinces. That should have meant the use of the 'iudicium crucis'. Anyway, Bishop Jonas, appointed in 818, should have been present at the deliberations prompting the change, and as an articulate adherent of the Carolingian ideals, should certainly have been briefed about them. Imperial decrees in the old Roman Empire were promptly assimilated and applied by officials.[221] But Adrewald's case shows Carolingian royal legislation again failing to make contact with law as understood and implemented by pillars of the Frankish Establishment. Lupus or another with a zoomorphic name was once again on the side of ideal rather than reality. The ideal in the end prevailed, but with unhappy consequences for its exponent.

For all of that, Adrewald's is not meant to be a formal record of legal business. An essential point – one, it must be said, markedly under-registered in the cornucopia of scholarly work on Carolingian law – is that a substantial body of what may fairly be called law-reports *is* extant from the Frankish kingdom. It was itemized over a century ago in a comprehensive, if naturally not exhaustive, list.[222] There are at least 369 from East and West Francia (Catalonia included) between *c.* 650 and 900 (Table 2.2), with some 209 from Italy (pp. 86–7). This is no place to launch the thorough investigation the material deserves, and anyway in Italy has at last begun to receive. All that is essayed here is a summary and strictly provisional account of a few of the patterns that emerge. In order to supply some sort of footing amidst the swirling torrents of evidence, attention is concentrated on a selection of cases affecting Fleury itself. What happened in these cases is then

---

220 *Cap.* 138:27, 139:10.
221 Steinwenter, 'Briefe des Symmachus', pp. 11–16; de Marini Avonzo, 'Diritto e Giustizia', pp. 118–22.
222 Hübner, 'Gerichtsurkunden' I, II (henceforth cited as H[000]). This in many ways remarkable achievement appeared with a preface by the august Brunner, announcing that it was to be the basis of a proposed volume of 'Placita' in the 'Leges' section of the Monumenta, and asserting the necessity of such an enterprise. But the volume was never published; twentieth-century work on early medieval legal history would surely have been different if it had been (cf. Keller, 'I Placiti'). As it was, Brunner himself usually ignored the list in an account of legal process, *Deutsche Rechtsgeschichte* II, pp. 435–702, that is dominated, like the rest of his great book, by legislative and formulary evidence. Ganshof, 'Contribution', p. 586, n. 2, commends its use, however out-of-date, and he certainly made more of the material than most commentators (e.g. in 'Charlemagne and the Administration of Justice', pp. 71–97, 161–83); but again, it is capitularies that form his picture. A more obvious exception to these strictures is of course the pioneering work of Professors Nelson and Davies in *Disputes*.

compared with ways that legal proceedings were handled elsewhere in the Carolingian realm. However, something must first be said about the figures in table 2.2 and the list on which they are based.[223]

The tabulated figures entail substantial revision of Hübner's list. Dropped are numerous formulae with no immediate application, forgeries that put the historicity of the events recorded in question, and confirmations of immunities or other rights which, whether or no they involved use of sworn evidence, were not ostensibly disputed so cannot count as lawsuits.[224] On the other hand, a number of tabulated cases escaped Hübner's notice. Some subsequently edited royal charters would surely have been listed by him.[225] Some had been edited in stately Spanish series he did not explore.[226] A more problematic category are those that Hübner must have spotted but ignored because he did not think them 'Gerichtsurkunden'. He listed twenty-six lawsuits from the Redon cartulary but omitted some twenty more in that they did not result in reported *iudicia*.[227] There are comparable instances from Freising.[228] In particular, he had a tendency to disregard records of forfeiture or other penalties for 'crime'. A fuller set is

---

223   For the significance of the 'Narratives' element in table 2.2, see below and n. 230. Other points to note are: (a) 'Neustria' means modern France north of the Loire valley, less Brittany but including Flanders; E. Francia is what would become Louis the German's kingdom 842–70; 'Lotharingia' is likewise Lothar I's 842 share, minus Italy; other geographical categories are largely self-evident, but 'Gothia' is here the whole area south of the Garonne and west of the Rhone plus Catalonia. (b) 'Royal Diplomas' for the purposes of this argument include judgements recorded as clauses in capitularies (one each for 789–99 and 869–77, two for 822–29); like charters, these are assigned to the region of the relevant MS(S). (c) Some cases give rise to more than one record, even type or date of record; they are counted only once, and for the period when the original judgement was issued. So Tassilo's trial is a 'narrative' for 779–88, and neither a relevant royal charter (H126) nor a capitulary clause (H132) are counted in the main totals, whereas the trial of Bishop Peter of Verdun (H133) from the next clause of the Frankfurt capitulary, is reckoned a (Lotharingian) royal judgement. (d) Formulae count as cases in the table only if *evidently* refer-ring (e.g. by use of proper names) to specific instances: this is true of some 'Formulae Imperiales', mostly dated to the 820s, the period of the MS (above, n. 168). (e) Redating of several texts by modern editions means assignment to a different time-frame from Hübner's, e.g. below, n. 238. (f) Lastly, and as is evident from the above, problems of definition, classification and dating make precise figures even less attainable than in Table 2.1: it must be repeated that all that is attempted here is some sense of pattern and trend.
224   'Forgeries': H139, 163, 199, 212, 246, 267 (Brückner (ed.), *Regesta Alsatiae* 484), 272, 281, 286, 290–1, 293–4, 326, 348, 357, 397, 407, 428, 444; *Scheinprozeße*, confirmations, etc.: H32, 37, 52–3, 56, 60, 78, 91–2, 115, 179, 211, 228, 322, 344, 350, 389–91, 393, 422, 425, 438, 443. In addition, H369–370–379 and H414–16 should, like H121–126–132 or H124–125, be reckoned 'same cases', while H233 is covered by a 'narrative' (as below, nn. 230, 270).
225   *Urk. Pipp. Karl.* 198 (802) (but 'same case' as H172), 204 (806); *Urk. Ld. dt.* 66 (?853) [H594 is a forged later version]; *Rec. ChII* 340 (870); *Rec. LII* 17 (878); *Rec. Eud.* 22 (890).
226   Iglesia Ferreirós, 'Creacion del Derecho', pp. 289–400: 3 (843), 6 (849), 26 (893), 27 (893), 28 (898). (My own unfamiliarity with Catalan materials probably means their under-representation in this discussion too).
227   *Cartulaire de Redon* 32, 47, 56, 103, 106–8, 118, 129, 147, 163, 184, 190, 202, 216, App. 20; see Davies, 'People and Places in Dispute', p. 68, n. 10. Among Professor Davies' seminal assessments of Redon material (e.g. 'Disputes, their conduct and their settlement', and *Small Worlds*, pp. 134–60), her 'Composition of the Redon Cartulary', redates the whole sequence of charters, meaning that some are in other columns of table 2.2 than those they would have occupied as dated by de Courson.
228   *Traditionen Freising* 49 (772), 259 (807), 864 (860x9); though the first two of these are in a sense 'criminal', see next n. But it is important to emphasize (and no slight tribute to Hübner's industry) that twentieth-century cartulary editions have a strikingly small effect on the totals, Hübner having elicited *placita* from their inferior forerunners; browsing the 80 per cent of pertinent post-1893 cartularies listed

Table 2.2 Distribution of Frankish lawsuits, 648–899

'Province'	648–751	752–78	779–88	789–800	801–13	814–21	822–29	830–40	841–58	859–69	870–77	878–87	889–99	TOTALS
'Neustria'	19	6	1	3	2	–	1	3	1	3	–	–	1	40
– Roy. Dip.	(18)	(6)	(1)	(3)	(2)		(1)	(3)	–	(3)	–		–	(37)
'Lotharingia'	3	2	2	5	2	4	2	3	1	1	1	1	2	29
– Roy. Dip.	(3)	(2)	–	(4)	(2)	(4)	(2)	(2)	(1)	(1)	(1)	–	(2)	(24)
E.Francia	–	4	2	8	29	12	18	10	16	4	1	2	10	116
– Roy. Dip.		(2)	–	(2)	(4)	(4)	(2)	(5)	(1)	(2)	(1)	–	(7)	(26)
Burgundy	1	–	–	1	1	9	1	–	3	5	7	3	5	36
– Roy. Dip.	(1)	–	–	–	–	(1)	(1)	–	(2)	(3)	(1)	(1)	(3)	(13)
'Gothia'	–	–	1	1	2	5	1	6	6	4	11	6	7	50
– Roy. Dip.	–	–	–	–	–	(2)	(1)	(2)	–	–	(3)	(2)	–	(10)
Provence	–	–	2	–	–	–	–	–	1	–	–	–	–	3
– Roy. Dip.	–	–	–	–	–	–	–	–	–	–	–	–	–	(–)
Loire/Poitou	2	–	2	1	–	1	1	2	2	1	2	3	5	22
– Roy. Dip.	–	–	–	–	–	–	(1)	(1)	–	(1)	–	–	(1)	(4)
Brittany	–	–	–	–	1	–	1	2	14	18	4	–	2	42
– Roy. Dip.	–	–	–	–	–	–	–	–	–	–	–	–	–	(–)
Formulae	–	–	–	–	1	1	8	–	–	–	–	–	–	10
Narratives	[*]	–	2	–	–	3	–	4	1	5	–	1	5	21
TOTALS	25	12	12	19	38	35	33	30	45	41	26	16	37	369
– Roy. Dip.	(22)	(10)	(1)	(7)	(6)	(11)	(8)	(13)	(4)	(10)	(6)	(3)	(13)	(114)

included in the figures of table 2.2 for the sake of consistency with those he did admit.[229] Room is found too for reports of prosecution and forfeiture (or worse) in narrative sources. Hübner did list the famous Royal Annals account of Tassilo's trial in 788, and it is a mystery that he left out such almost equally well-known dramas as the duel that convicted the Gothic Count Bera of treason in 820 or Bernard of Septimania's execution in 844.[230] Less baffling is his by-passing of *Miracula* collections like Adrewald's. Some Carolingian miracles involved the punishment of perjury (it was especially unwise to pledge one's hair and beard; an enemy of St Remaclus retrieved only his body-hair and nails after repentance and went bald and beardless for the rest of his life).[231] But few – a high proportion of them related by Adrewald – reached the forensic stage.[232] Not even these feature in table 2.2; there can as yet be no certainty of their date, location or of course historicity.

Table 2.2 is by no means a cross-section of Frankish judicial action, let alone of Frankish social tensions. Statistics from the early period are overwhelmingly dependent on royal charters from St Denis. The increased total of judgements in

---

by Le Jan (*Famille et Pouvoir*, pp. 466–71) that it was possible to see without a degree of effort un-warranted by an exercise at this level yielded *almost no* cases not listed by him (albeit sometimes late in the day: H112a = 'Chartes de Nouaillé' 5; 325a (*recte* 8.3.819) = *Traditionen Regensburg* 15; H416a = *Cartulaire de Gorze* 78). Thus, while the present survey can make no claim to exhaustivity, it seems unlikely that a more complete account would result in a significantly different pattern.

229   *Urk. Ld. dt.* 5 (831), 96 (859); *Rec. ChII* 242 (862), 347 (871), 428 (877); *Urk. LoII.* 23 (865); *Urk. Arn.* 81 (890), 174 (899). Similar cases listed by Hübner are H33, 39, 80, 113, 123, 124[5], [126], [132], 133–5, 169, 176, 201, 218, 221, 253, 296, 324, 338, 362–3, 421, 439, 442, 445, 453. Compare his omission of the seemingly 'criminal' *Textes relatifs* 67 (819), or Freising cases (n. 228 above), or *Cartulaire Redon* 32, 107, 163, 184, 202 involving compensation for injury. There are also circumstan-tial episodes in Merovingian *miracula* from Fleury (n. 232).

230   H121; *Annales Regni Francorum*, p. 152, etc. In default of a search of 'Scriptores rerum Carolingicarum' which is beyond my current powers or responsibility, I have used Krah, *Absetzungsverfahren*, especially her tabulated results, pp. 379–401, and selected those instances where the language of the sources implies that disgrace was engendered by some sort of formal process; my cases are therefore (her numbering, in part adapted): I.1.6 (Hardrad, 786), I.2.2–5 (Bernard and co-conspirators, 817–18), I.2.7 (Lupus Centulli, 819), I.2.8 (Bera, 820), I.3.2 (Heribert, 830), I.2.14 (Bernard, 832), I.2.17 (Donatus, 834), I.3.4–5 (Sanila and Gozhelm, 834), II.1.1 (Bernard, 844), IV.1.3–6 (Ernest and others, 861), IV.1.7 (Karlmann, 862–3), II.1.10 (Bernard son of Bernard, 864), II.1.10a (Pippin II, 864), IV.1.8 (Werinhar, 865), III.2.2 (Hugh son of Lothar II, 885), II.3.1 (Walcher, 892), IV.2.7 (Engilschalk, 893), IV.2.11 (Isanrich, 899), IV.2.11a (Queen Uota, 899), IV.2.11b (Graman and Ruodpurc, 899).

231   *Miracula S. Remacli*, ed. Holder-Egger (as n. 4) 8, pp. 435–6. Lysaght, 'Fleury', pp. 100–2, usefully tabulates the major ninth-century *Miracula* series (the only ones examined for present purposes), and makes the point that most Carolingian miracles are cures; cf. Chapter 3, below, pp. 158–60.

232   *Ex miraculis S. Benedicti* 24, p. 489 (the other Fleury-St Benedict confrontation, as above, n. 212), 26, pp. 490–2 (burglars of the church fortunate to be spared the gallows that would have been their deserts under 'human law'), 35, p. 496 (dispute at a market taken to the 'market judge'), 38, p. 497 (a 'servant' of Fleury vindicated by its advocate in a dispute with an Aquitainian noble over a vineyard). Other cases of this sort include: *Miracula S. Bertini*, ed. Holder-Egger (as n. 4) 45–7, pp. 518–21; *Miracula S. Reginae*, ibid., 7, p. 451; *Miracula S. Dionysii*, *Acta Sanct. Ord. S. Ben.*, ed. Mabillon, III(2)) i 23, ii 33, pp. 351, 358 (both 'mancipial' cases, see below); *Miracula S. Richarii*, ibid. II, i 17–18, pp. 220–1 (two cases of prisoners loosed from their chains, on the prescription of Graus, 'Die Rolle der Gewalt'). Hübner did go to the *Miracula S. Goarii* for what was evidently a lost document of 782 (H117), but not to Aimoin's Fleury collection for two no less unmistakably Merovingian lost records of criminal forfeiture (*Rec. S. Ben.* 2–3) – these and the appreciable wealth of pre-751 narrative also lie beyond the scope of the present argument; for a good account, see James, '"Beati Pacifici" …'.

the first two decades of the ninth century and in the 860s and 870s is much as might be expected, given the legislative and scribal vigour of the same periods; yet what creates this impression are spectacular bulges in the figures for East Francia (above all Freising, whose overall total of fifty-eight is the biggest from any Carolingian repository) and from Redon.[233] What is reflected here are the efforts of an unusually assertive bishop and abbot rather than any change in the climate of the regime.[234] It is obvious enough that the centrality of clerical archives makes for a preponderance of cases won by churchmen.[235] Just as important is that the evidence is a distillation of prelatical and archival strategies that varied from house to house and from time to time. That is why the material is better classified by area and phase than by reign and kingdom. All of this said, however, it is hard to resist the sense that Carolingian judicial energy is conveyed by the distribution of extant *placita*, as it is by the not dissimilar pattern of law-book production. There is the same exponential growth from 750, and especially 780. Here as with law-making, the first decade of Charlemagne's reign looks like nothing so much as an extension of his father's. The way in which the tentacles of royal justice, in particular the justice imparted by the king's own court, seem to spread out from its mid-eighth-century bases at St Denis and the Lotharingian home of the Arnulfings to the conquered territories east of the Rhine, and even-tually the far south and west, may well be a fair reflection of its developing impact.[236]

But Carolingian lawsuits resist generalization, making it all the more urgent to argue from particulars. The Fleury suits discussed here (most actually heard in Burgundy, as will be explained) are chosen partly to retain contact with this chapter's focal case; but also because the Loire-Saône axis was the cultural as well as physical watershed of the Frankish kingdoms. It is here, as with law-codes and law-books, that one might expect variety and change in legal practice.[237] The series begins with a set of six, four of them forming pairs, in which the great Burgundian family of the (historic) Nibelungs aimed to show that four different parties were serfs of their estates. In the first (February 796), Moses, advocate for Count Hildebrand, summoned (*mallavit*) one Dodo before the *missi dominici*, Ansbert and Hildebrand [suitor to the case], 'at *Botedono villa* on Tuesday'. He claimed that Dodo was 'servus' to Lord Charles on his 'benefice' at Le Jeu in the *pagus* of Autun. Under questioning Dodo could not deny it, prostrated himself before Moses, confessed his servitude, and gave his 'pledge' for the service he had neglected, 'as was his law (*qualiter sua lex est*)'. A certain Fredelo was among those 'present and subscribing'.[238] The second/ third case, of 815–17, deserves quotation *in extenso*:

233   Compare Freising's huge collection, none a royal charter, with the total from Saxony: five royal charters, one Hersfeld (*Urk. Pipp. Karl.* 198), and four Korvey (H201, 221, 277, ?297).
234   For Freising activity (and much apposite comment), see Fouracre, 'Carolingian Justice', pp. 784–91; on domination of Redon evidence by Abbot Conwoion's drive, Davies, 'People and Places', pp. 67–8.
235   As is stressed throughout *Disputes*. But see below, pp. 78, 80.
236   While Redon lawsuits had no manifest official encouragement, the activity of its abbots and scribes may have been inspired by knowledge of what churches to the east and south had achieved.
237   Another factor is that this choice makes maximum use of Professor Nelson's discussion (as n. 5).
238   *Rec. S. Ben.* ix, H371 ('868': Hübner was misled by a seventeenth-century edition). I cite modern

When Count Theodoric was in session in public court at Autun for hearing the cases of one and all and the fixing of correct judgements, along with many *scabini* who were present with him there (*Cum resedisset ... in mallo publico ad universorum causas audiendas vel recta judicia terminandas una cum plures scabineis qui cum eo ibidem aderant*), Fredelo came and summoned a man by name of Maurinus. He put it to him that he was serf to the lord emperor Charles for the estate of Perrecy on his father's side, Madalenus by name; and when this emperor died he endowed Emperor Louis with his rights (*legibus*) in the said Madalenus and his son Maurinus, and bequeathed and invested him with their servitude; and this Maurinus wrongly contested this servitude against the claims of Fredelo in the present year, and said that he had witnesses as such. Then the said Maurinus was asked what law he lived under (*sub quale lege vivebat*), and this man declared himself to be of Salic Law (*et ipsus sibi a lege Salica adnunciabit* [!]), and he denied this case in every way, and said that his father was free by birth. This Fredelo invoked the Lord Emperor for his case, that he was trying to [*or* could] make it legally. They thus decreed such a judgement to Fredelo, that at the next session, which the count would hold in that city in forty nights' time, he would produce testimonies whereby he would more judicially prove what he said, or do what was lawful. Maurinus gave a surety named Autard for his presence, and that if this Fredelo proved his case, Maurinus would do what was lawful for Fredelo's claims; and if Autard did not stand for the afore-said Maurinus, he would keep faith with Fredelo as was lawful (*quod si ipse Fredelum adprobat, faciat Maurinus partibus Fredelono quod lex est. Et si a Autardus jam dicto Maurino non representat faciat partibus Fredelono pro fide facta sicut lex est*).

After one 'subscription', two 'signa' (one by 'viscount Bligarius'), and another subscription by the *vicarius* Girbaud, there is a dating clause for December 815, and a subscription by 'Erembert the clerk'. The sequel transpired not 'forty nights' but sixteen months later. A 'record of how and of who was present (*Notitia qualiter vel quibus praesentibus*)' tells how Fredelo faced viscount Blitgar with *scabini* in court at Autun, and 'in the church of St John, where other oaths proceed, presented twelve testimonies', who are then named. They gave testimony on oath, with hands placed on the altar: 'that we saw that Madalenus, father of this Maurinus, served as a serf in service for Hildebrand or Fredelo', and Charlemagne had left their service to Louis when he died, so that 'Maurinus should lawfully be more a *servus* to Hildebrand or Fredelo for his benefice of Perrecy than remain a free man; so help us God and this saint, we are true witnesses and convey true testimony about the said Maurinus'. There are similar subscriptions and *signa*, including the clerk Erembert, who dates the document.[239]

The next paired case (818–19) is much the same. Theodoric was in session at Cronat 'in mallo publico'; Fredelo arrived as (this time explicitly) the advocate of Hildebrand, to claim the servitude of Adelard at Perrecy, because of his father's status, and because this was Hildebrand's benefice; Fredelo was told to supply his testimony at Autun within forty nights 'according to his Salic law'; there were

---

editions for cases actually discussed in what follows, but it would be impossibly cumbrous to do so for Hübner cases to which I merely allude (the Italian apart).
239   *Rec. S. Ben.* x – xi, H215/217.

signa and subscriptions, including the clerk's, and a dating clause for March 818. Nineteen months later, a 'noticia sacramentale' shows Fredelo 'on Thursday at Autun in St John's', providing the *missus* Blitgar, Theodoric and others with nine named witnesses on oath that Adelard 'by law and right (*dricto*) should rather be *servus* for Lord Louis at the estate of Perrecy ... than free ... We are true witnesses and carry true testimony thereto; so may God and this saint be our helper'. There are two subscriptions, three or more *signa*, with the same scribe as before.[240] A sixth text, dated 820 and drafted by Sererius, has Fredelo pursuing the service of Adalberta, apparently Adelard's sister, but bound by her mother's as well as her father's Perrecy obligations. There is this time no suggestion that Fredelo needed two sessions to make his case.[241]

Like Fleury's disputes with St Denis and a good many more from the Carolingian era, these four cases are about rights to others' labour. A reflection that at once comes to mind is that there would not have been so many if the defendants' prospects were as bleak as appears from the surviving records, which survive *because of* their defeat.[242] But three other issues call for more immediate comment. The first is the nature of the documents. They are evidently the work of '*clerici*', whose function was that of notaries even if they are not so called, and who were presumably based at Autun. If the above translation has its clumsinesses (or mistakes) that reflects a Frankish notarial Latin that did not yet – or ever – aspire to Alcuinian standards. The six documents are of two types. Four introduce themselves as '*notitia* (how or) who was present, and there came ... ';the lumbering syntax shows that 'Noticia qualiter vel quibus praesentibus' was a stock formula; it is found in the Angers Formulary of *c*.600.[243] The other two records open 'when X was in session at Y', a clause canonized by Marculf's formulary, regularly used for judgements of Frankish kings, and fairly widely distributed in imitative formularies.[244] A feature of both documents describing the oaths of Fredelo's witnesses is use of direct speech, though the records of his original suits, and of Adalberta's case where suit and oath are recounted by the same text, are entirely in indirect speech. This will turn out to be a point of some importance.

Secondly, all these hearings were held in the Autun county court, usually called a 'mallus publicus'. The meetings when Fredelo submitted his case against Maurinus and Adelard were chaired by Count Theodoric. The swearing sessions were held by Blitgar, who in each of the first two texts is entitled viscount, and who does not appear at all in the third, but who in the fourth is named ahead of Theodoric and called a 'missus' (the likelihood is that the scribe's grasp of the

240   *Rec. S. Ben.* xii, xvi, H220/226.
241   *Rec. S. Ben.* xvii, H234.
242   See Nelson in *Disputes*, pp. 48–52; it may be significant that H255 is a 'Formula Imperialis' where a plea for freedom succeeds.
243   Form Andeg. 10(b), 11(b), 16, 50(b), *Formul.*, pp. 8, 10, 22. Cf. Form. Tur. 32, 41, pp. 154, 157; Cart. Sen. 8–10, 17, 22, 34, Form. Sen. recent. 1 (close to Autun proceedings), pp. 188–9, 191–2, 194–5, 200, 211; Form. Sal. Merk. 29, p. 252; Form. Flav. 39, p. 479; the 'mid-French' origin of these formulae is *à point*.
244   Marculf i 25, 37, *Formul.*, pp. 58–9, 67; Cart. Sen. 26, Form. Sen. recent. 4, pp. 196, 213; Form. Sal. Big. 7 (close to Autun proceedings), 9, pp. 230–1; Form. Sal. Merk. 27–8, 32 (likewise), pp. 251–2, 253; Form Sal. Lin. 21, p. 282,; Form. Aug. 40, p. 362; Form. S. Emm. i 3, 9, ii 24, pp. 463, 465, 467.

formulary slipped again, and that he should have used the genitive to mean that Blitgar was '*missus*, deputed agent, *of* Theodoric'.[245] On the other hand, the very first case was indubitably heard by 'missi dominici', that is by emissaries of the king, fulfilling the role taken by Jonas and Donatus in Adrewald's confrontation. If it is disturbing that one of these, Hildebrand, was anything but the disinterested observer a *missus* was supposed to be, it is not much less alarming that Count Theodoric was probably Hildebrand's cousin by marriage and Fredelo very possibly his (Theodoric's) brother-in-law. Yet none of this is as unusual as might be gathered from the guidelines of Carolingian authorities and modern commentators.[246]

Third, and of particular moment for this chapter, there is the relationship between these proceedings and *lex scripta*. It was clearly in some way important that Maurinus 'lived under' *Lex Salica* and likewise that Fredelo produce evidence 'secundum legem suam Salicam'. 'Forty night' intervals were indeed laid down by *Lex Salica* in connection with pursuit of fugitive slaves.[247] *Lex Salica* has much to say about slaves and their liabilities: it is reckoned that the topic takes up a third of the text.[248] Yet nothing in it exactly covers what was ordained at Autun and Cronat. Here, as in the Formulae that are regularly echoed by reported lawsuits, it seems that it was the general body of 'Salic' custom, not the actual text of the law, that judges and scribes had in mind.[249] A further and thought-provoking point in this connection is that this sort of tantalizing reference to *lex* is particularly characteristic of the Burgundian area – though commoner after 900 than before.[250]

The Autun records can now be compared with the treatment of 'mancipial' issues elsewhere.[251] In May 846, the redoubtable Archbishop Hincmar summoned what the Rheims record was pleased to call a 'placito publico', but which was presided over by his *missi* (the head of his *schola* and one of his aristocratic vassals), and which was reported by one of his *cancellarii*. The text, which, unusually for this part of Francia, is couched in direct speech, tells how seven 'extremely old (*senissimi*)' witnesses gave evidence that the grandparents of the defendants had been purchased, so that the latter did owe service; eight named *scabini* duly gave judgement.[252] If this was 'public' process, it was yet more

---

245   On the use of deputies in cases involving freedom, see *Cap.* 64:3, 65:15, 80:4, 156:3, with Ganshof, 'Contribution', p. 589, and *Frankish Institutions*, pp. 79–80 and n. 62 (p. 170) – pointing out that the prohibition covered *vicarii* and *centenarii*, not necessarily viscounts.
246   For the ideal and its flaws, see n. 214; with Ganshof, *Frankish Institutions*, pp. 81–3; Werner, 'Missus-Marchio-Comes', pp. 195–230 (following a lead from W-A. Eckhardt (as n. 165)); above all, Hannig, '*Pauperiores vassi* ... ?', pp. 314–39. On Nibelung links for Theodoric and even Fredelo, see Levillain, 'Nibelungen', pp. 6, 23–8.
247   E.g. *Lex Sal.* ('A'/'C') xlvii:1 ('K' xlix:1); *Pact.* lxxxii:1, lxxxiii:1 – though these concern cases between rival owners.
248   See Nehlsen, *Sklavenrecht*, especially pp. 261–73.
249   '*Lex Scripta*', pp. 121–2 (pp. 21–2), Nehlsen, 'Zur Aktualität', pp. 456–83.
250   H382 (870); cf. *Textes Relatifs* nos 117, 137, 176–9; and note H362 (*c.*863), compensation for infringement of immunities, as ordered by Charlemagne's addition to *Lex Sal.*, *Cap.* 39:2. This area also supplies most (non-'Mediterranean') instances of 'personality of the law' (cf. nn. 5, 308): so Brunner, *Deutsche Rechtsgeschichte* I, pp. 389–91, 398.
251   Nelson covers two such cases in detail, *Disputes*, pp. 48–53.
252   H323.

dominated by landlord interests than the Nibelung cases. Ten years later, a *mallus publicus* under the count heard suit by Abbot Grimald of St Gallen, who drew the report up. He too was trying to get a man to admit to the 'yoke of servitude', but settled for freeing him, 'as if born of free parents', in return for a gift of property.[253] Though a 'compromise' that was not uncommon in other types of case, the outcome is unusual enough for this sort of dispute to hint that unrecorded pressures were at work, or that suing for his opponent's service was a litigatory tactic of the abbot designed to have the very result it did. However that might be, neither of these texts took any more notice of formal legislation on the subject than others so far reviewed.[254]

The position to the South was quite different. On 25 April 874, Count Miro (who would shortly lose his job and lands to a charge of *infidelitas*), was 'in judgement with judges who are ordered to hear, direct and rightly judge cases'; these included a *saio* (a Gothic official) and at least one perceptibly Gothic name.[255] Miro's own *mandatarius* claimed that Lawrence was a 'fiscal serf' by descent, and that his kin did fiscal service to Count Sunifred, Miro's father, by virtue of a royal charter. In the ensuing trialogue, conducted throughout in direct speech, Lawrence said that neither he nor even his remotest ancestors owed service, in that, 'as the Law of the Goths contains', they had occupied the homes where they were born for thirty, indeed fifty, years, without ever being pressurized by the 'yoke of servitude'; Sisenand admitted that he had no proof except a 'writ (*breve*)' in his lord's possession, whereby he had freed a female member of that kin, to which Lawrence retorted that her alleged servile condition did not descend to her children from the kin to whom he was related so was beside the point; and the judges looked up the '"Lex Gothorum"', and quoting it verbally asked Lawrence for witnesses 'as law contains'. He produced four named individuals 'without criminal repute (*absque crimine*)' who swore 'as inserted in the set of conditions'. Sisenand admitted that he could not challenge this then or in three future pleas; this concession of defeat was given the technical term 'evacuatio'. The record is dated and attested by the 'signa' of the *mandatarius*, of Miro himself, and two others, one of them probably though not professedly the scribe.

This remarkable document is striking not least for the defeat of a lord and a presiding count at that (it presumably survived because a church ultimately profited by Lawrence's proof of his freedom).[256] The text is from the cartulary of Cuxa in Catalonia. Like other records from this area, it is longer than most, yet was evidently one of at least three written statements generated by the dispute; the others would have been the *conditiones sacramentorum* of Lawrence's witnesses, and Sisenand's *evacuatio*, to both of which the narrative refers. In very few cases, all three types of document survive; most often preserved, for obvious

253   H349 (856).
254   E.g. *Cap.* 33:4 (802), 39:7 (803, 'legibus additum'), 56:4 (803x13, germane for Fredelo), 58:7–8 (801x14), 140:1,6 (818–19), 142:3,11 (819).
255   H396; and for the charter recording Miro's forfeiture, *Rec. ChII* 428. The Gothic name is Sisegutus (Sisenand, the *mandatarius*, was of course another); for the *saio*, see Thompson, *Goths in Spain*, pp. 13, 142, and King, *Law and Society*, pp. 94–5, 116–17.
256   Free men alone could bestow land on a church; see H299 (*recte* 841), and Davies, *Small Worlds*, pp. 96, 97, for a similar Redon case.

reasons, was the *evacuatio*.[257] All these records have a regular and distinctive form. Those not beginning 'In Iuditio' may say 'In mallo publico', or 'Conditiones sacramentorum atque exordinationes de ... '.[258] The final eschatol was often mutilated by cartularists, but scribal attestation was normal. The fifty odd south-western records thus bear witness to a vigorous notarial culture firmly rooted in the Gothic and ultimately Roman past. Its endlessly repetitive and circum-locutory documents read like nothing so much as lawyers' prose.[259] But its most arresting feature compared with *iudicia* so far discussed is its recourse to the text of the *Lex Visigothorum*. This was cited or echoed fourteen times in the ninth century and much more often after 900; it is estimated that sixty of the Gothic code's laws were thus exploited.[260] It is likewise in royal charters of 820 and 835 for far-southern Aniane (the first commissioned by Benedict himself) that there occur the most explicit appeals to the Roman law of Thirty Years' prescription.[261] The *only* two (hence much cited) non-Italian suits when litigants were required to say what *lex* they professed were late-ninth-century hearings at Angoulême and Nimes.[262] In this light, the ambiguities of the Burgundian evidence previously discussed are just what might be expected from a receding outpost of the Deeper South.

The first extant Fleury law-report that immediately concerned the abbey itself is a royal charter of 24 April 835. It opens by adapting a proem from an Immunity Formula in the 'Imperial' collection on the value of lending an ear to petitions from 'servants of God'.[263] Louis then describes how Abbot Boso had informed him that an estate given to Fleury by King Pippin had been vested in his vassal Gislhere 'by beneficiary right', but that Gislhere had usurped several appendant estates on the same pretext, so that they had in time slipped from the abbey's 'right (*iure*)'. The king therefore sent his *missi*, Bishop Jonas of Orléans (again) and Count Hugh to investigate. It being clear from their report and from perusal of his grandfather's charter that the estates had been unjustly removed, he restored them with a prohibition on further alienation. The charter was 'recog-nized' by the notary Hirminmaris on behalf of Hugh, sealed, dated and placed. This type of transaction was especially common under Louis the Pious. As many

---

257   On this see Collins, '"*Sicut lex Gothorum continet*" ... ', especially pp. 492–5, and (in effect) its sequel, 'Visigothic law and regional custom', especially pp. 87–8. Examples of each type from dates near the Miro/Lawrence case are H400 (875), H403 (875) and H410 (878); H318 (843) is a single case from which both narrative and *evacuatio* survive.

258   'Mall. pub.': H400; 'Cond. Sac.': H216 (817), 231 (821), 352 (858), 392 (873), etc.; but H287 (836), 334 (852), 366a (865), 421a (884), Calmette, 'Jugement original', pp. 66–9 (898), etc. have versions of the Marculfian 'Cum resederet ... ' formula.

259   For the important point that a sixth/seventh-century Salamanca slate tablet seems to be a *Conditiones Sacramentorum* phrased like those of the ninth century, see Collins, '"*Lex Gothorum*"', pp. 494–5.

260   H269 (832), 287, 318, 334, 359 (862), 366a, 396, 414–16 (878), 421a; and Iglesia Ferreirós (as n. 226). For this now well-established point, see Collins (as n. 257), and beyond that pre-eminently Kienast, 'Fortleben des Gotischen Rechtes', pp. 151–70; with supporting documentation from Nehlsen, 'Zur Aktualität', pp. 483–502, concluding with the vivid illustration also in 'Lex scripta', p. 121 (p. 21).

261   H225 (820), 282 (835); cf. *Cap.* 76 (812).

262   H419 (880x1), 441 (893/8). Cf. also H321 (845, Marseilles).

263   *Rec. S. Ben.* xix, H283. Form. Imp. 29, *Formul.*, p. 307; and cf. 4, 12, 16, 25, pp. 290, 295, 297, 304; also 36, p. 314.

as thirty-two of his charters contain judgements – forty-one counting Imperial Formulae; for his father there are nineteen and for all his sons seventeen.[264] A high proportion of Louis' cases were, like Fleury's, subjected to local enquiry by *missi* before the king gave judgement.[265] It is usually, if not in Fleury's suit, specified that this entailed putting local opinion under oath: a technique with a famous though as yet distant future (cf. chapter 1, pp. 17–18). The upshot is that Louis' biographers were quite right to stress his interest in 'justice'.[266] The reason why this has sometimes been questioned is that, unlike the *iudicia* of other Carolingians, his did not deploy the format of the Marculf *placitum*, with its implication that all was decided at Court. Yet Marculf's formula is in fact most prominent whenever St Denis dominates the records: till 781, to a lesser extent late in Charlemagne's reign, and briefly under Charles the Bald.[267] Louis' charters therefore proclaim a *more* interventionist approach, by king, chancery or both; his father and descendants were less intrusive.[268]

Few of Louis' judgements raise especially interesting questions about the relationship of written and enforced law.[269] But his charters do have a bearing on the definition and punishment of crime. Four concern the consequences of *infidelitas*, to which can be added nine cases (most, not all, of disloyalty) attested by formulae and narrative notices.[270] There are parallel totals for other reigns.[271] Aside from the preponderant 'infidelity' suits, Charlemagne penalized a case of incest, one imperial formula is about homicide, and one of Charles the Bald's prosecutions was for '*latrocinium*'; less solemn texts supply instances of theft, homicide and mayhem.[272] Written law had much to offer here; not, however,

---

264   See the (bracketed) figures in Table 2.2: it should be remembered that, for Louis alone among Carolingians, there is still no edition of his Diplomata (Johanek, 'Probleme'). This topic is the subject of important unpublished research by Dr Philippe Depreux.

265   Exceptions: H208 (815), 225, 230 (821), 237 (822), 263 (a standard Marculfian *placitum* chaired by Pippin of Aquitaine, Nelson, *Disputes*, pp. 48–9), *Urk. Ld. dt.* 5 (831), H275 (833), 277 (833), 282 (835), 284 (835), 296 (839, a restored forfeiture); H246 is a forged version of 244 (823), to the effect that instead of being investigated by *missi*, the parties are summoned directly to the royal presence!

266   *Thegan, Gesta Hludowici* xiii, pp. 192–5; *Astronomer, Vita Hludowici* xix, pp. 340–1; cf. Johanek, 'Probleme', pp. 419–20.

267   Marculf-St Denis *placita* include H85 (774x6), 93–4 (775), 114 (781), *Urk. Pipp. Karl.* 204 (806) and H197 (812). Post-840 in the same vein are H356 (861) and H372 (868); the latter (a mancipial case) survives in two originals, each with the royal seal, but only the first has the Marculf format, the other being a less formal *notitia qualiter* with more detail; H360 (863) and H436 (892) are Marculfian from Le Mans and Montiéremey; see also nn. 258, 310–11. For a possibility of links even in Francia between a charter's form and its beneficiary, see Ganz, 'Bureaucratic Shorthand', pp. 62–7.

268   But see H126, 314 (841); *Urk. Ld. dt.* 66; 335 (853), 354 (860), 402 (875), 430 (890), 437 (888), 448 (898) (!), 451 (898).

269   Most are about depredations by *fiscalini*: H229 (821), 230, 232 (821), 237, 242 (823), 244, 257 (827), 261 (828), 266, 271, 274, 275 (833), 297 (840). *Cap.* 155:10/H256 is a Louis 'Response to *missi*' about a dispute between a Count Hildebrand, possibly the Nibelung, and *pagenses* of his county about supply of '*paravereda* (horse-transport)': Kasten (as n. 275), p. 298.

270   H218 (818), 221 (819), *Urk. Ld. dt.* 5 (Louis the German), H296 (839); Krah I.2.7, I.2.8, I.3.2 (Lothar), I.2.14, I.2.17, I.3.4–5 (Lothar); Krah I.2.2–5 + H233 (Form. Imp. 8, p. 293); H245 (Form. Imp. 53, pp. 325–6); H253 (Form. Imp. 49, pp. 323–4).

271   For Hübner's cases (and those omitted by him) see n. 229. For less formally recorded 'criminal' cases see next n.

272   H176, 253, *Rec. ChII* 242; *Traditionen Freising* 49, 259, 679 (H324, 846), 738 (H338, 853); *Textes relatifs* 67; H362; *Cartulaire Redon* (as n. 229). Cf Le Jan, 'Justice royale', pp. 61–73.

much impact on the conduct of cases. The sanctions of *lex* and capitulary are never cited even for rhetorical effect. Tassilo's indictment (p. 75) was ostensibly for the same offence as brought Immo low in 677 (p. 42): 'deserting his lord king on campaign, which in the German tongue is called *harisliz*'. As a Bavarian whose *lex* required its use in court, Tassilo might reasonably have hoped to find his crime in written law. But he was no luckier in this respect than Immo. Charlemagne's only known pronouncement on the topic was at Boulogne twenty-three years later.[273] Law reports often refer to *lex*. Procedures not infrequently square with those laid down in *leges*: giving of pledges, 'forty night' adjournments, brandishing a *festuca*. But as in Merovingian times, this is because reports were based on Formulae which themselves bore a vague relationship to the codes.[274] Formulae dictated *iudicia*. *Lex* or capitulary did not.

Fleury's next case was again in the first instance not Fleury's affair. Like Fredelo's suits, it was heard in the county of Autun and concerned the Nibelung estate of Perrecy. Though opposed this time not by fugitive serfs but a formidable churchman, the Nibelungs triumphed again in the person of Count Eccard.[275] It is thus possible to explain why a suite of documents relating to a Burgundian lay estate survive in Fleury's cartulary. The evidence that Eccard won is not the report of the case, which is truncated, but Eccard's bequest of Perrecy to Fleury in his will. The monks fell heir to the documentation as to the land.[276] Shortly before Eccard engrossed his will in the 870s, his ownership of Perrecy was challenged by Archbishop Wulfad of Bourges. The report of the case, longer and more detailed than any from the 810s, tells how it was argued before *missi* despatched by the king to investigate the dispute; this was an *ad hoc* enquiry like those of Louis the Pious, but recorded in a local *notitia* not a royal charter (pp. 81–2). Both sides brought written and spoken evidence. Both, it seems, had a good case. Eccard had law books (above, n. 141). But more important, he had the heavier political artillery.

The Perrecy suit is one of a series in the Carolingian period that were apparently generated by the all-too-well-known Carolingian policy on church lands.[277]

---

273   *Cap.* 74:4; an important reassessment of this episode is Becher, *Eid und Herrschaft*, pp. 21–77. A significant exception to the non-citation rule is H134, defining treason by 'lex Romana'; another, as revealing in its own way, is H293, from the somewhat fevered context of the Le Mans forgeries (Goffart, *Le Mans Forgeries*, pp. 309–20).

274   Fouracre, '"Placita" in later Merovingian Francia', pp. 29–30, 33–4; note that his first sample case (p. 27, and App. V, 691/2) is extremely like H197, from which it is separated by 120 years, three Lex Sal. recensions, numerous capitularies and at least one phase of the Carolingian Renaissance: the formative factor in each case is Marculf's influence at St Denis (above, n. 267).

275   *Rec. S. Ben.* xxiv, H399; translated, printed and discussed by Nelson, in *Disputes*, pp. 53–5 and App. IX. For a suggestive account of the history of Perrecy and its outliers, and an exhaustive review of almost all that arises from Eccard's bequest of it, see B. Kasten, 'Erbrechtliche Verfügungen', especially pp. 318–24, 335–8.

276   Eccard's testamentary dispositions are covered by four documents, *Rec. S. Ben.* xxv – xxviii. For the order and a hypothesis that the childless Eccard favoured Fleury because its Abbot Theodbert was his relative, see Levillain, 'Nibelungen', pp. 352–61, 383–93, 403–7; for his will-making in the wider context of Carolingian testamentary procedures, see Kasten (as n. 275), pp. 247–84, 304–17, 324–38; with Nelson, 'Wary widow', and Le Jan, *Famille et Pouvoir*, e.g. pp. 237–42.

277   The huge literature on this subject should now be read subject to the important correctives entered by Wood, 'Teutsind, Witlaic ... '

It is more than likely that Perrecy *had* once been Bourges property and that in the mid-eighth century it had been 'loaned' to Charles Martel's half-brother, Count Hildebrand as a concommitant of the Carolingian southward offensive. The evidence of the Autun cases in the 810s is that it was still held by the Nibelungs as a 'benefice'. But in 836 it was given to Count Eccard *'ad proprium'* (outright) by Pippin I of Aquitaine, and this donation was confirmed by Louis on his son's death. Eccard was able to cite both these documents (preserved, like the rest of the Perrecy dossier, in the Fleury cartulary) in his defence.[278] Among other cases that raised the same issue, Hincmar's Neuilly plea is best known.[279] However credible the church's case in such disputes, it could hardly expect automatic endorsement. Some churches did better than Wulfad or Hincmar, others as badly.[280] To win required more than good evidence. Wulfad may have been emboldened to move against Eccard by his kinship with the presiding *missus* Adalard, and by the latter's evident favour with the king. Yet Charles the Bald badly needed to retain Nibelung support in Burgundy's heated politics. No more than his half-brother or father could he afford to alienate Eccard.[281]

Eccard's defeat of Wulfad was not quite the end of the Perrecy saga. But before coming to that, Burgundian practice can again be compared with that of other areas. Brittany's might be expected to differ markedly. The forty-plus ninth-century Breton records, a remarkable total given the poverty of the material from other 'provinces', owe their survival to the Redon cartulary. But they are not all *about* Redon. One dispute at least dates from a generation before its 832 foundation.[282] Other post-832 disputes were of no obvious interest to the abbey.[283] This makes the extremely important point that it was not just disputing but the documentation of dispute that happened independently of the Church, even on the margins of the Carolingian world, and in far from exalted social circles. A notariate (though probably not a *lay* notariate) was active on the Breton march. Redon *iudicia* are not scribally attested, but it can be shown that the same agencies were at work as in more formal documents, and most identifiable scribes were *not* members of the Redon community.[284] They used broadly the same formulae as their Autun counterparts. These are less rigidly adhered to and yet more clumsily handled, so that it can be difficult to know what was actually happening. One thing is, however, clear. No Redon text ever referred, even

---

278   *Rec. S. Ben.* xx – xxi; cf. Kasten, 'Erbrechtliche Verfügungen', pp. 299–304, 321–2.
279   ed. and discussed by Mordek, 'Exemplarische Rechtsstreit'; also analysed by Devisse, *Hincmar*, pp. 800–2: the *placitum* at Douzy which reviewed the case might well be enrolled among listed lawsuits.
280   Of possible *comparabilia*, bishops won in H116 (782), 130 (777x91), 358 (861), 361 (863), but only partially in *Rec. Eud.* 22 (890), and not at all in H117 (*Miracula* from Prüm, the ultimate beneficiary of the Archbishop of Trier's defeat, 782).
281   Nelson, in *Disputes*, pp. 54–5. For the wider political position, see *idem, Charles the Bald*, pp. 232–4; with Levillain, 'Nibelungen', pp. 361–85; and (for the 830s background) Airlie, 'Political Behaviour of the Secular Magnates', pp. 103–6.
282   H137 (*recte* 801); cf. *Cartulaire Redon* 129 ('pre 1 May 834'), 147 ('821x39'); these are cases with exclusively secular parties, though there is a hint of a religious interest in *Redon* 129.
283   E.g. H312 (832x8: a case heard by an abbatial deputy?: Davies, *Small Worlds*, p. 149, n. 61); *Cartulaire Redon* 106 (841x51); H385 ('post 866'; cf. Davies, 'Forgery in the Cartulaire de Redon', p. 270).
284   Davies, 'People and Places in Dispute', pp. 68–9.

notionally, to the norms of written law. One extant code might have been cited in cases requiring payment of compensation. But it is ignored, as is any contribution from the class of lawyers so prominent in the jurisprudence of other 'Celtic' societies (p. 12).[285] Justice loomed large in the world of Breton villagers. *Lex* did not.

Even in Breton villages there was a basic tension between the efforts of laymen to make permanent and hereditary, i.e. 'alod', what churches (or sometimes lay lords) liked to regard as precarious, i.e. tenanted. In the time of the litigious Abbot Conwoion, a not negligible sum of twenty *solidi* was disbursed so that Buduoret would quit a claim 'quasi hereditatem'; he accordingly gave sureties that neither he 'nor his seed for ever' would pursue it.[286] A more solemn record of a plea heard in 869 at Nantes before Duke Solomon told how Redon sought through *mediatores* to know with what justification a powerful (perhaps in local terms aristocratic) figure held properties given to it by the late Duke Erispoe. Unsatisfied by his reply, they called him before Solomon, and he caved in, requiring only 'a certain honour' from the abbot, and that he be received into the house's prayers. The abbot was inclined to give him nothing *but* prayers, but was in the end prevailed upon by the mediators to pay 60 *solidi*, and even to yield one of the properties as a lifetime benefice. The compromise may have been a tacit admission of the justice of the opposing case as much as a device to placate a dangerous enemy.[287]

Records exist in similar number and type from the geographically opposite end of the Frankish lands. But the records of the Bavarian far east were as unlike Brittany's as those of the Gothic Deep South were unlike Neustria's. Freising offers the biggest single array of Carolingian *iudicia*. There are a few more from Eichstätt, Kempten, Mondsee, Passau and Regensburg. A large number reflect the forensic aggression of Bishop Atto of Freising either side of 800 (with the enthusiastic connivance of the *missus*, Archbishop Arn of Salzburg), and of his successor Hitto in the early years of Louis the Pious. Many arose from efforts by families to retain or recover property that one of their members had insisted on giving to Freising; not infrequently these ended in a compromise whereby the family retained the property as tenants of the church.[288] A characteristic text relates a case heard by a 'missus dominicus', by a 'publicus iudex' and by the bishop himself. Amidst 'many who had arrived to settle their cases justly', the advocates of Hitto and of the Bishop of Augsburg clashed over a property that the latter claimed to have won from a certain Adalhard before another *missus dominicus*. Freising pointed out that Adalhard had held the land as its benefice,

---

285   A point repeatedly made by Professor Davies. The text is the so-called *Canones Wallici* (better, *Excerpta de libris Romanorum et Francorum*), ed. Bieler; discussed (e.g.) by Dumville, 'On the dating of the early Breton law-codes'.
286   *Cartulaire Redon* 118 (832x68). Cf. the case discussed by Davies, 'People and Places', p. 71 and App. XI; also H376 (833x68).
287   H377 (869). Cf. Davies, 'People and Places', pp. 72–3 and App. XII; also H374 (868) and 387 (871).
288   E.g. H166 (802), 174 (806), 178 (807), 210 (815), 289 (837), 298 (840), 320 (845), 327 (849, where Freising's opponent, like St Denis with Fleury, tried to square the presiding officials), 328 (849). For a vivid example of a set of mancipial disputes, see H219 (818); illuminatingly discussed in an as yet unpublished paper by Dr Carl Hammer, 'The Handmaid's Tale'.

and its case was upheld by multiple oaths from those present when Hitto had ceded the land to Adalhard. The judge, ten counts and a very large number of 'other vassals' were then said to have decreed justice 'according to Bavarian law' and Freising was reinvested.[289] This case, like most, appears to have been heard in a 'publicum placitum', though one's impression that jurisdiction was under the bishop's control is reinforced by the virulent *parti pris* of the recording scribes. But it is the way in which it and the others are drawn up that is most strikingly distinctive. Scribes are nearly always named and usually write at length. They often use direct speech, like the those of Gothia. Sometimes, as here, they cite 'Lex Baiwariorum'.[290] And among their most distinctive habits is one that offers a clue to the inspiration behind everything else. The standard Frankish *Placitum* formula begins 'Cum ... '. In Bavaria, it is regularly 'Dum ... '.[291] So it also was in most of Italy.

From Italy, unlike any other part of the Frankish empire except St Denis, *iudicia* survive in some quantity from the pre-Carolingian period. Comparison of records from either side of Charlemagne's 774 blitzkrieg makes it possible to isolate the Carolingian impact or lack of it: 209 or so can be listed from 673 to 900.[292] There are thirty texts of the Lombard period (only one pre-713, and that one of a mere six which can really be called royal records).[293] For the forty years of Charlemagne's ascendancy, there are forty-three cases, eight of which are recorded in royal charters. Figures thereafter tend to have a similar profile to those from the rest of the empire (table 2.2), except that they peak in the third quarter of the century under Louis II, with over forty cases (ten royal charters). Italian statistics are subject to the same distortions as those north of the Alps. Northern Tuscany is over-represented by the excellence of Lucca's episcopal archive, the Spoleto duchy through Farfa's prodigious cartulary; while Abbot Romanus ensured that there was a clutch of Casauria suits, 873–8.[294]

---

289   H238 (822).
290   *Traditionen Freising* 49 (772), 320 (845, '*mos*'), 328 (849, '*consuetudo*'); and cf. H223 (Regensburg, 819). This issue is penetratingly discussed in two other papers by C. Hammer, '*Lex Scripta* in Early Medieval Bavaria', and 'Land sales in eighth and ninth-century Bavaria' – papers that supersede, but also in a sense bear out, the observations on this point in my '*Lex scripta*', pp. 119–25 (pp. 18–25).
291   E.g. H162, 171 (both Passau, 802, 800x4), 165 (802), 174 (806), 235 (822), 236 (822), 238 (822); though the feature fades after the 820s.
292   This total is reached by the same process as yielded 369 for the areas north of the Alps. Hübner's 211 (H615–824 + 677a) lose 615, 617, 625, 627 and 694 as forgeries (H619, 622 having been vindicated by CDL III 12–13); 635, 653–4, 663–4, 666, 688, 720, 725, 730–1, 735, 737, 750, 789, 795–9 and 802 as essentially non-judicial; and 640, 674, 717, 747 and 749 as basically the same cases as others already listed. Added are (i) placita missed by Hübner but published by Manaresi, *Placiti* – most from Casauria or Piacenza; (ii) royal charters: e.g. CDL III 44 (772); Urk. Pipp. Karl. 160 (788); Urk. LoI 14 (833), Urk. LoII 32 (868); Urk. LudII 29; (iii) *supplementa* edited by Volpini, 'Placiti', pp. 275–302; (iv) Italian forfeitures listed by Krah, *Absetzungsverfahren*, III.2.1 (883x5) III.2.3 (894x 6), III.2.4 (898); (v) Professor Wickham's 'about fifteen' less formal records ('Land disputes', n. 1), which he kindly identified for me, turn out to have nearly all been included by Hübner, but I have added his 764 Farfa case (nn. 25, 29) to maintain consistency with N. European reckonings (cf. above, n. 272). Excluded once again are *miracula*; Italian materials seem to be rather later in date. Note that H693/Cap. 129 is a solitary, exceptionally interesting – and of course Italian – instance of a *iudicium* included in law-books, *viz*. Ivrea XXXIII – XXXIV, Wolfenbüttel Blankenb. MS 130, and München Sttsbib. MS lat. 19416: Mordek, *Bibliotheca*, p. 1093.
293   H616/CDL III 6 (674), H619/CDL III 12 (715), H622/CDL III 13 (715), H631/CDL III 22 (747), H644/CDL III 36 (post-7.765), CDL III 44.

Nevertheless, Italian evidence is more homogeneous and tractable than transalpine materials. Doubtless for that reason, it has been adequately edited and fully discussed.[295] For which reasons in turn, it is unnecessary to say much more here.

The important thing is that here as elsewhere Carolingian rule had more effect on the quantity than on the quality of the records. The period does not seem to have been one of marked institutional change. A typical Lombard case was heard in the king's name at one of 'his' courts, not normally Pavia itself, by royal agents who were variously denominated 'iudex', 'missus', 'gastald' or 'notary', or else by the bishop.[296] They presided with named 'sculdhais', 'gastalds' and other 'adstantes', and it was they who directed proceedings by asking questions of the parties and ordering successive stages in the trial; they might also try to ascertain the facts by commissioning sworn testimony from locals.[297] Under the Carolingians presidents would more likely be a count or his 'assistant/deputy (adiutor/locopositus)'. But many cases were heard by bishops, especially at Lucca, and as many by missi. In any event, the president would often act as a notional king's nominee.[298] From the 790s, and especially after 810, presidents are accompanied not only by their usual coteries but also by royal vassi and by scabini, local men trusted to 'know the law'.[299] Placita do confirm that scabini panels formed in many cities; but they do not suggest that the composition or procedure of courts was substantially changed thereby. Nor does it seem that Lombards needed instruction in their own law.[300] Such procedural changes as might be ascribed to the Carolingian regime seem in most or all cases to have been underway before 774.[301]

The reason why questions about 'reform' are hard to answer with confidence

---

294   H778-9/Manaresi 74–6 (873), H786-7/Manaresi 79, 82 (875, 877), with Manaresi 80 (871x5), 83–6 (877–8).

295   Manaresi's Placiti and CDL, together with Wanner's Urk. LudII, are significantly superior to anything comparable from elsewhere (royal diplomata apart); the same, mutatis mutandis, goes for the discussions of Bougard, Keller and Wickham (as nn. 118, 222, 292). I have profited from a long review of Manaresi by Professor Bullough, which was unfortunately not published, but which he kindly showed me.

296   Courts of the dukes of Spoleto and Benevento were heard as a rule by dukes at headquarters, though those of Spoleto might be held at Rieti (H638-[40]/CDL IV 14–15, V 31, 761); for the Archbishop of Lucca's cases, see H643/CDL II 182 (764), H646/CDL II 255 (771); for a hearing at Pavia not held by a king, see H642/CDL II 163 (762).

297   As in the remarkable sworn (and far from consistent!) depositions on the interminable Arezzo-Siena boundary case: H620–1/CDL I 19–20 (715); for a discussion of this issue that has hardly had the notice it deserves see Bullough, 'Europae Pater ... ', pp. 92–6.

298   E.g. H677a/Manaresi 17 (804), H682/Manaresi 21 (807), H687/Manaresi 25 (812), H692/Manaresi 28 (814), H701/Manaresi 32 (821), H705–6/ Manaresi 35–6 (823, 824), etc.; cf. Bullough, 'Leo et le gouvernement du Regnum Italiae', especially pp. 223–32.

299   The earliest scabini cases date 791: Bougard, Justice, p. 140; thereafter, see H665/Manaresi 9 (796), H673–4/Manaresi 13–14 (801), H678/Manaresi 18 (806), etc.

300   See Bougard, Justice, pp. 140–58, with informative prosopography of active scabini, pp. 347–71; M. Bougard does not understate the importance of the 'scabinate', but even so raises, pp. 153–4, the possibility that its introduction was the fruit of northern immigration as much as systemic change. For knowledge of lex, see nn. 306–8.

301   For 'inquests', see n. 297; and for means of proof, including the fossilization of oath-helping, see Wickham, 'Land Disputes', pp. 113–18.

is that the process of recording changed so little. Italian *acta* exhibit local features, but regional traits are much less differentiated, even as far off as Benevento, than are provincial styles in the rest of Francia. Documents might introduce themselves as 'notitia (iudicati/breve/qualiter)', but by far the greater proportion open with a formula like that of the Marculfian *placitum*: 'while I/we were seated in the palace/at X/in the court of Y, with ... , there came ...'; the difference is that in Italy, the introductory word was 'Dum'.[302] A good index of its durability is that Marculfian 'Cum ... ' is used in a Charlemagne charter issued at Bologna in May 801 (on the way home from the imperial coronation).[303] But eighty years later, the count of Charles the Fat's palace at Pavia judged a claim by Novalesa for the service of a man and his son. The text is couched throughout as an Italian *iudicium*, from inaugural '*dum*' to ratifying *signa* by the count himself, the 'notary of the sacred palace' and the '*iudices* of the lord king'.[304] Frankish influence on Italian usage was nugatory when set beside the enduring integrity of Italian notarial practice.[305] Unlike Charlemagne's 801 charter (apart from one sentence), but like the great majority of texts either side of 774, the Pavia document repeatedly quotes the direct speech of the parties. A further crucial way in which Italian deeds of Lombard or Frankish vintage resemble the Gothic series is in readiness to echo and even cite written law. The law of the Lombards was still followed under the Carolingians, if often less explicitly than under their own kings.[306] In a Casauria case of 873, the sums demanded of a Frank who had (unwittingly?) wedded a nun, and of her Lombard guardian who had let him, reflected what Liutprand laid down, as did the lady's forfeiture.[307] From the end of the ninth century come the first cases of that particularly Italian phenomenon, the *professio legis*, the claim to one's personal law.[308] Written law, however venerable, was 'live' for Italy's judges – and litigants.

For all their variety, then, Carolingian lawsuits conform to a pattern: one of hugely increased action but not on the whole of substantial reform. It is a *problem*

---

302   There is usually an invocation, and in official royal documents an *intitulatio*; less often, a regnal dating clause comes first, in accordance with Justinian's injunctions: Tjäder, *Nichtliterarischen ... Papyri*, p. 251; e.g. H634/*CDL* V 16 (751), H657/Manaresi 6 (785), as for a time thereafter at Lucca. Beneventan documents can begin as outright concessions ('Firmamus nos ... '), H628–9 (745–6), or 'Cum coniunximus ... ', H624 (742), but also 'Dum ...', H637 (756).

303   H672/Manaresi 12 (801); this was the first time, and for a long time the last, when a Carolingian king was required to make a judgement; though H715/*Urk. LoI* 11 (833) is close and generally Marculfian: Bergmann, 'Untersuchungen zu den Gerichtsurkunden', p. 130. Other royal charters concern forfeitures, e.g. H655/*Urk. Pipp. Karl.* 134 (781), *Urk. LoI* 24 (835), H781/*Urk. LudII* 63 (874); or confirm decisions reached by earlier rulers, e.g. H660/*Urk. Pipp. Karl.* 159 (787), H715/*Urk. LoI* 14 (833), H752/*Urk. LudII* 10 (852), etc.

304   H792/Manaresi 89 (880).

305   Cf. Bougard, *Justice*, pp. 119–36.

306   H626/*CDL* I 81 (722x44) (referring to *Leg. Liutpr.* 23 (721:V)) is a striking Lombard case (Wickham, *Early Medieval Italy*, p. 122). Cf. (e.g.) *CDL* III 44, H656/*CDL* IV(1) 35 (781), H662/Manaresi 8 (791).

307   H779/Manaresi 76 (873); the relevant reference is *Leg. Liutpr.* 30 (723:I): see Bougard, *Justice*, pp. 147–8.

308   Manaresi 99 (892), H836/Manaresi 114 (903), H879/Manaresi 139 (Milan, 941), Manaresi 142 (Reggio, 944), etc.; this is the trend in other areas too (nn. 250, 260, and cf. n. 5), but the Italian backdrop is clearly more like the Gothic than the Burgundian.

that the evidence becomes so much richer. One is tempted to see more innovation than there may really have been. This book's readers will meet that problem again. If the spread of Carolingian justice is plausibly tied to the dispersal of *missi a latere regis*, there are few major new departures when the evidence permits comparison with pre-Carolingian policy. Even the 'scabinate' can be made to look newer than it was by the scantiness of pre-Charlemagne materials. In *Formulae*, all that exists in meaningful quantities for the Merovingian era, *scabini* gradually replace *rachinburgii*.[309] But it would be hard to show from them that *rachinburgii* and *scabini* had different jobs. The words are almost interchangeable in *placita*.[310] However defined, the premium was still on 'good', that is to say wise, hence experienced, and so usually senior, citizenship.

What seems beyond doubt is that however much Carolingian energy reactivated the empire's documentary traditions, it did not create them. Their sheer heterogeneity is explicable only if each was already well-founded. Autun drew on Burgundian notarial practice, Freising on Bavarian, Cuxa on Gothic, Redon on that of the lower Loire, Lucca on that of sub-imperial Italy. The *dictamen* of the Merovingian court voiced the Neustrian traditions consolidated in Marculf. No less obviously, all these traditions have a common origin, one that must be ultimately Roman.[311] That the various styles began to branch off a single trunk before 400 is the best explanation of their blend of the standard and the idiosyncratic. Since a persistent feature is the introductory image of king, count or judge of whatever stripe seated in judgement pending the arrival of litigants, their common root is most plausibly sought in the court-reports of Roman provincial governors.[312] The argument may then be extended. Italian and Gothic practice shared a common trait in use of direct speech. It is not easy to see how this could have sprung up independently in each area; rather easier to suppose that it is an original Roman feature, progressively if never wholly abandoned in lands to the North. Two other ways in which Gothic and Italian traditions look nearer to a Roman past are the degree of presidential control of proceedings, down to their verdict issued in the first person, and of course their appeal to written law. A perhaps allowable step leads from there to the conclusion that written law was more prominent in what has aptly been termed the 'olive-belt', because Greco-

309   Cf Zeumer's comments, *Formul.*, pp. 227–8, and Ganshof's seminal discussion, *Frankish Institutions*, pp. 76–9, 167; but it begs the question to date texts on the basis that *scabini* were introduced by Charlemagne, especially as the measure launching the 'reform' is lost.
310   Compare, e.g. Form. Sal. Big. 7, p. 230, with (supposedly Carolingian) Cart. Sen. recent. 6, p. 214, or the much earlier Form. Andeg. 50 (a), (b), p. 22; and note the comments of Nelson, Davies and Fouracre, *Disputes*, pp. 61, 83–4, 217, each critically influenced by the now classic study of Nehlsen–von-Stryk, *Die boni homines*. For Rachinburgii in quite late and otherwise highly 'professional' cases, see H364 (865), 419 (880x1).
311   Curiously, Classen, whose classic papers, 'Kaiserreskript und Königsurkunde' and 'Fortleben und Wandel' did more than anyone to establish the imperial origin of sub-Roman diplomatic, thought that the *placitum* was the least likely documentary form to descend from Roman practice. Not so Bergmann's major account of *placitum* origins, 'Untersuchungen zu den Gerichtsurkunden', pp. 105–48.
312   Professor Goffart is attracted to this hypothesis: Ganz and Goffart, 'Charters earlier than 800', pp. 918–21; Professor Bergmann, 'Untersuchungen', sees the various Frankish traditions following a lead from the royal court, but the Italian parallels (which he traces to 'private' notarial practice) militate against his view. A now famous instance of Italian substitution of 'Dum' for stylistically better 'Cum' is that classic of Italian vulgar Latin, the *Rule of St Benedict*: de Vogüé (ed.), *Règle de Saint Benoît* I, pp. 254–5.

Roman values, like olive-trees, flourished better there. A less escapable conclusion is that written law was cited under the Carolingians where it was apparently cited before 750, but not otherwise. If *lex scripta* did make any difference to the conduct of Carolingian justice, it had only the barest effect on the way in which it was reported.

To return, finally, to Fleury: Eccard's bequest was not secure. The last text in the series tells how Count Theodoric's son and stepson (so probably Eccard's nephews) came before the abbot, monks and assembled noblemen in the 'secretarium' of the church at Fleury, and 'most humbly begged the abbot and monks to pardon the sin they had committed against the Lord and St Benedict', in that two years previously they had been induced by Count Theodoric to seize and exploit what Eccard bequeathed at Perrecy 'as if it were hereditary property'. The abbot, with the monks and nobles (among them the culprits' kinsmen), gave thanks to God that He had prompted them to do penance instead of punishing them. All was then settled amicably at the altar, and a document, drafted by the notary Gauzbert, was attested by the guilty parties, by Fleury's Nibelung allies, and three others.[313] This discussion began with St Benedict angrily rejecting a lawfully imposed agreement. It finishes with his inspiring another, albeit one more favourable to himself. There is more than symbolic balance here. Each agreement exposed underlying realities in early medieval justice. If one resulted from a formal hearing, the other makes the fundamental point that solutions to disputes, then as now, could as well be found out of court as within.[314] And each outcome settled matters by giving at least something to parties that could have raised further trouble if left with nothing. St Benedict's consolation in the first case was that St Denis could feel no more satisfied (or less dissatisfied). In the second, Eccard's nephews not only averted a no doubt nastier and more lasting fate than the bestially named lawman's, but also procured the prayers and goodwill of a great saint and abbey, with which both their own family and the ruling house was ever more closely linked.

Two further considerations thus arise. First, saints were more than a safety-net, a last resort of those desperate for justice. Even the most dramatic miracles 'happened' because they were expected to. To that extent the Holy subsumed general perceptions of what was just, of what would or would not further social peace. A second corollary of Fleury's cases is that the only workable legislative programme was one carrying conviction for those in a position to obstruct it. If Nibelung participation in cases affecting their interests outrages modern (or nineteenth-century) opinion, it merely reflects their indispensability to the regime of kings who were their kinsmen several times over, which they helped to create with sword and pen, and from which they benefited hardly less than their cousins. To pit the Carolingians as kings against the Nibelungs as nobles makes no historical sense, because it would have made no political sense. In so far as there was a Frankish state, it rested on the consensus of its ruling nobility. That consensus need not have been intrinsically hostile to 'reform'. If one reason why

313   *Rec. S. Ben.* xxx.
314   This point, now common ground to workers in the 'Dispute Industry', is put with exemplary force by Geary, 'Extra-judicial means'.

Eccard's nephews gave in was fear of a saint, another may well have been the displeasure of their relatives at what they had done with their uncle's pious intent. But one might guess that a family which not only commissioned and kept books, but littered their genealogy with names from the heroic cycle, had the same sort of reverence for Frankish traditions as Einhard ascribed to the great king. No more than Charlemagne would they really have wished to see ancient Frankish law warped so as to fit new times and purposes.[315]

The place of the written word in Carolingian justice has now been controversial for twenty years. Controversies of this order do not happen unless both sides have a case. The best reaction, even for one who has hitherto been a partisan, is to ask how two strong cases could co-exist for so long. The answer is not hard to find. The evidence is ambiguous, indeed contradictory. Legislation constantly demanded resort to written law. It generated a spectacular response in manuscript output. Yet court records from most of the empire show that *lex scripta* remained marginal. If it were only a matter of antithetical categories of evidence, either could be discounted as vitiated by its inherent constraints: law books as the province of an ultra-literate clerisy, lawsuits as that of a bureaucratically hidebound notariate. However, the conclusion indicated here is that, regionally regarded, the evidence is relatively unequivocal. Carolingian law-making, law-copying and law-reporting were *each* more consistently literate to the South than to the North. The Lombards and Visigoths began with the most fully articulated *lex*. Italian and, so far as they go, Spanish legal manuscripts are comprehensive, ordered, *usable* to an extent unparalleled elsewhere. Italian or Septimanian courts duly use them. The Franks by contrast began with a *lex* that already heralded their past and stuck to it regardless of whatever transformations came over them. No wonder that their law books were a matter of Einhard's *pauca capitula*, however many of the latter kings issued, or that their *placita* were as little touched by *lex* as was their *lex* by capitularies. Between the Franks and the southerners lay Burgundy and Bavaria. It has more than once been suggested in this chapter that these areas contrived to retain links with their Roman past and even to channel its values northwards, howbeit their conception of written law ultimately adjusted itself to that of their Frankish conquerors. Why there should have been so variegated a pattern in the legal life of the post-Roman West has hardly yet been explored, still less explained. But one possibility lies in what has just been hinted about law-reporting. It was where something like a Roman notariate survived best that written law was most effectively made, most thoroughly copied and most regularly used.[316]

The Lupus experience thus epitomizes the fortunes of Carolingian law. The

---

315 One of the first and best statements of what are now truisms is Nelson, 'On the Limits of the Carolingian Renaissance', pp. 53–63; far from truistic thoughts on the same lines are in her 'Kings with Justice', pp. 818–23. See Magnou-Nortier, 'Note sur l' expression *Iustitiam Facere*', and Airlie, 'The Aristocracy', pp. 432–6, 444–9. One might speculate that Louis' curbs on his *fiscalini* (above, p. 82) were meant to placate the noble patrons and members of great churches.

316 It may thus be significant that the instances of legal knowledge highlighted by Hartmann's

land for which he made his *liber legum* knew how to appreciate it. Over the next three centuries Italian lawyers would work out the most sophisticated corpus of post-Roman written law, along lines that his own systematic treatment anticipated. But in the land where he lived he was an isolated figure. His collection had no parallel. When he or someone with a similar name tried to enforce the latest edict from Aachen, he infuriated one of the regime's ideological patrons. That land soon ceased to issue written law, and ultimately stopped copying it. For many centuries yet, it was 'pays du Droit Coutumier'. As for Fulda, the abbey where he made his collection, another of its *alumni*, and a correspondent both of Eberhard (p. 56) and Lupus himself, was Gottschalk, who, to Hincmar's bitter frustration, would lapse into ultra-Augustinian despair at the incapacity of mankind to programme its own behaviour. In a previous dispute over Gottschalk's family property, his 'lex gentis', the *Lex Saxonum*, was a central issue, but it was never cited.[317] There is no doubt that their *lex* mattered a great deal to the Saxons. Yet *Lex Saxonum* (p. 46) was among the most marginal of Frankish *Volksrechte*. There are just two copies, and in the one from Corvey the treason clause that was part of Charlemagne's legislative package was significantly glossed 'lex francorum'.[318] The relevance of this goes beyond the limits of Carolingian legislative action. The view of *lex scripta* taken by the English fellow-countrymen of Fulda's founder Boniface was more likely to resemble the hesitancy of the part of the world east of the Rhine and north of the Danube than the familiarity of the areas south of the Alps and Garonne.[319]

Yet in turning at last to the Anglo-Saxons, it is well to recall that what generated the contradictions of Carolingian evidence was the urge to transform society's image. The earnestness of the endeavour to hammer out a culture of written law befitting a Christian empire is an index of what might have been achieved under more malleable conditions. It may therefore offer a foretaste of a kingdom where written legal culture was pursued with scarcely less dedication, and in circumstances more conducive to the forging of a new society. But before examining what was essayed by the English heirs of the Carolingians, one should consider their inheritance from their Anglo-Saxon forebears.

---

thoughtful paper, 'Rechtskenntnis und Rechtsverständnis', come from Italy, from the Edict of Pîtres, from south Germany or Burgundy ('regionale Unterschiede'), or from later times (cf. Theuerkauf, 'Burchard', and chapter 14).

317   See Freise, *Einzugsbereich*, pp. 1021–9, citing the evidence of Hrabanus' 'Liber de Oblatione Puerorum', cols 431–2. On the juristic dimensions of the Predestination controversy see the powerful discussion by Ganz, 'Debate on Predestination' (pp. 289–91 for Lupus' own attitude to Gottschalk (*Epistolae*, ed. Dümmler, XXX, pp. 36–9, *Correspondance* 80, II, pp. 42–55)).

318   *Lex Sax.* xxiv; Mordek, *Bibliotheca*, p. 379; Theuerkauf, *Lex, Speculum, Compendium Iuris*, pp. 49, 69–97. The equivocal attitude of the Saxon historian, Widukind of Korvey, is nicely conveyed in his observation that the hanging of rebels was 'by Frankish law': *Widukind* ii 11, p. 77. On attitudes to Saxon law, see McKitterick, 'Introduction', p. 16; Goldberg, 'Popular Revolt', pp. 481–3; and Mayr-Harting, 'Charlemagne, the Saxons', p. 1130.

319   Cf. Boniface's famous words, *Briefe ... Bonifatius* 46, pp. 74–5.

2   Seventh-Century Southern England: from 'Æ' to 'Cynedom'

Much less need be said about law-making in England's 'Merovingian' period. Much less *can* be said. There are just four texts, two of them brief. The three Kentish codes survive in a single manuscript over four centuries later than the last of them. Ine's so-called code is extant in many copies, but only as transmitted by Alfred beside his own laws. A mere six lawsuits can be listed before the end of the eighth century, and thirteen more from 801 to 844.[320] The seventh-century codes in any case merit (and will soon receive) monographical attention in their own right.[321] Yet in setting the scene for Alfred's law-giving, it would be perverse to say so much of continental models whose effect upon him and his successors is merely hypothetical, while ignoring legislation whose influence he acknowledged. This chapter began with Bede's implication that there was a European context to Æthelberht's code. What of the code itself?

(i) Æthelberht

Not the least of the surprises in Bede's passage is that it is the only explicit evidence that Æthelberht did issue the code ascribed to him. The sentence introducing the laws in the Rochester codex calls them the '*domas* that King Æthelberht laid down in Augustine's day'. But this is a red-ink rubric such as precede other codes. There is no prologue like those authoritatively identifying the rulers responsible for the rest.[322] Alfred, nearly all later commentators, and Rochester's rubricator followed Bede's lead. So the first question is, was Bede right? That he was can be established by arguments like those connecting Clovis with *Lex Salica* (pp. 40–4). The next Kentish legislation has a prologue, and Kings Hlothere (673–85) and Eadric (685–6) say that they have 'added to the *æ* that their predecessors made before with these, the following *domum*'.[323] Unlike Æthelberht or Clovis, but like Childebert II, these are not rulers likely to have had laws mythically foisted upon them. At the same time, their vocabulary resembles Æthelberht's while their syntax represents the same sort of advance on Æthelberht's as do Merovingian 'novels' compared with *Lex Salica*.[324] And whereas Bede says that Æthelberht's grandson Earconberht ordered the abandonment of idols and observance of Lent, the Æthelberht code merely sets

---

320   On *Textus Roffensis*, see chapter 4, pp. 244–53; and *pro tem*. *Textus Roffensis*, ed. Sawyer. For the lawsuits see chapter 3, pp. 143–61, and my 'Handlist'.

321   Further to cross-references in the previous n., see (e.g.) chapter 5, pp. 278–81. Dr Carole Hough and Dr Lisi Oliver are each preparing new editions of the early codes, and I have greatly profited from consultation of their doctoral dissertations. I myself discussed many of the issues in my 1994 Spoleto paper, '"*Inter cetera bona*" ... ', to which space-saving reference is frequently made below.

322   Abt Inscr.; *Textus Roffensis*, f. 1r; cf., e.g., ff. 9r (Alfred), 42r (Edward), etc.; also below on Hlothere and Wihtræd.

323   Hl Pr. See below for the meanings of *æ* and *dom*.

324   Their word for nobleman is, like Æthelberht's, 'eorl' (Abt 13 – 14, Hl 1), where laws from the 690s until Scandinavian influence made itself felt use 'gesið' (Wi 5, Ine 45, 50 – 51, etc.); Af 4:2 has the formulaic 'ge ceorle ge eorle'. For syntax, see pp. 95, 102.

out graded compensations for the property of successive clerical ranks in laws otherwise as secular as *Lex Salica*.[325] If this code was as official as the Kentish tradition relayed by Bede asserted, it must be almost as early as Æthelberht. It may as well *be* Æthelberht's.

The significance of Æthelberht's anonymity, like that of Frankish legislators, is its demonstration that law-making in the North was not yet the fundamentally royal activity it became (pp. 40–1). Bede highlighted the contribution of Æthelberht's 'counsel of wise men'. This aspect of law-making, common to almost all post-Roman laws and those of many other times and places, was at the core of the Democratic Fallacy, which so ruinously discredited nineteenth-century understanding of early medieval polities (chapter 1, pp. 4–14). However far twentieth-century scholars have retreated from the notion that the 'assembly of the wise' (*witena-gemot* – a word always rare and unattested before 1035) was an elected body with a right to vet legislation and to make or unmake kings, this should not obscure the truth that law-making was the business of the community at large, distilled in its most prominent members; just as judgement was the affair of the court as a body till the advent of expert justices in the late-twelfth century (chapter 14).[326] Much of this chapter's previous section went to show that law somehow belonged to 'the Franks', whoever they might be. Æthelberht's code is best seen as the law of the *Cantwara*; a signal that they had joined Franks and Romans in the ranks of civilized because law-abiding peoples.

Not everything that Bede said withstands scrutiny so well. His puzzling phrase 'decreta … iudiciorum', literally 'decrees of judgements', seems likely to be meant to render the word 'dom'. This word was used to describe their own laws by other seventh-century legislators.[327] Its primary meaning, as implied by etymology as well as usage, is 'judgement'. For Edward the Elder, Alfred's *dom-boc* set the standard for the *domas* that reeves are required to 'judge'. The expectation of Judgement was what made the Last Day into one of Doom.[328] So in what way did Æthelberht decree his judgements? Bede also used 'decreta' in his Letter to Ecgberht for the texts used to create fraudulent monasteries and

---

325 In the first of their trenchant interventions into orthodox early English legal history, Richardson and Sayles, *Law and Legislation*, pp. 1–9, argue that the opening laws on church property are later interpolations (how much later is not specified) and that the code is otherwise the product of a pagan but (thanks to the legacy of Romano-British culture) not wholly illiterate Kentish kingdom. Their case spectacularly anticipates current fashions in interpreting the earliest phases of English history and fits a recent theory on the origins of *Lex Sal.* (above, n. 62), but has to confront the fact that no 'barbarian' people felt a need to commit its laws to writing until firmly within a Romano-Christian orbit; Lombard law's 643 date is uniquely secure (p. 39), yet its christian element was more marginal than Æthelberht's (*Ed. Ro.* 35, 272, 343). Below, pp. 96–101, is an argument that Abt 1 is exactly what to expect in a code of this date.

326 ASC 1035E, p.159, 1050C, p.171, 1051DE, pp. 174–5, 1052CD, pp. 180–1, 1055CE, pp. 184–5; even here, there is no proof that *witena -gemot* was, as it were, not one word but two. But it should be added that *witena* is extremely well-attested in similar contexts by poetry, homiletic prose, laws and charters, and is linked with *gemot* to denote the Roman Senate by Ælfric, 'Epilogue', *The Old English Heptateuch*, p. 415 – some institutionalization may therefore be detectable. Fundamental on medieval ideas of representation is Reynolds, *Kingdoms and Communities*, pp. 302–19 with pp. 245–8.

327 Hl Pr.; Wi Pr., 5; Ine Pr.; for his *cynedom* see below. (This and what follows, nn. 330–1, draws on the microfiches of the new Toronto dictionary, also on the advice of Professor Stanley).

328 I Ew Pr. (the sense of judgement is unmissable in II Ew 3:2), and see chapter 5, pp. 289–90; II Cn 84:1a, the work of the Doomsday specialist, Archbishop Wulfstan, cf. chapter 6, pp. 451–6, 462–4.

more justly deployed to abolish them: in other words, charters (which he also calls 'edicta').[329] It seems that what made these texts 'decrees' was not just royal pronouncement but also endorsement by leading figures in Church and government. *Decreta* entailed the use of writing and the adherence of important men. Bede's phrase conveys that Æthelberht's judgements were both written down and expressive of the community consensus.

But Bede's view was conditioned by what kings were doing in his own time. Hlothere and Eadric's word for what their predecessors had established was 'æ'. This word has strong connotations of *accepted* law.[330] Wihtræd likewise saw himself as adding to the 'rihtum þeawum' of Kentishmen; the meaning of *þeaw* was 'custom'.[331] It need not take long in any culture for innovation to become immutable tradition. Nonetheless, there are many signs that almost all that Æthelberht put in writing was not (innovatory) *dom* but (established) *æ/þeaw*. There are several *hapax legomena* and a striking series of archaisms in orthography, phonology and syntax.[332] The utter simplicity of Æthelberht's syntax sets it apart from all subsequent Old English legislation, while matching very well what is often thought typical of early law in general. Overwhelmingly, his clauses are simple conditionals or statements of simple consequence ('if a free man steal from the king, let him repay ninefold'); '[sc. breach of] king's protection 50 shillings'. Relative clauses, which appear to mark a more 'developed' (i.e. more literate) stage in legal conceptions, number four. There are no statements of principle whence certain consequences follow, believed to mark a more 'advanced' stage yet. An obvious risk of circularity attaches to a mode of argument that makes features of early law into characteristics which then become proof that other such laws are early. But the method in fact works out for Anglo-Saxon legislation (e.g. chapter 5, pp. 271–2, 300–4).[333] Yet this proves only that Æthelberht's laws were earlier than others; not that they were well-established when written down.

---

329   Epist. Bede ad Ecgb. 13, p. 417 (and cf. 12, p. 415).

330   In the general legal sense, the word seems to be used only in the seventh century and in antithesis or parallel to *dom*: Hl Pr., Ine Pr., 1:1. But Af Int 49:1, where it means Christ's Law, and Alfred's preface to his *Gregory's Pastoral Care*, p. 4 ln 25, where it apparently means Holy Writ, usher in its late Saxon usage for almost any aspect of the Divine Law, whether specifically Biblical, Godly precept, or even 'natural law': e.g. *Ælfric's Catholic Homilies, Second Series* XXII, p. 207, God is made known in part to the Jewish people through 'Moses' *æ* and to all mankind through Christ's Incarnation; or *ibid*. XXVI, p. 237, 'ante legem, sub lege, sub gratia' is 'before *æ*, under *æ*, under God's gift', the last being 'the time since Christ's advent to manhood'. Ælfric repeatedly has the word in this sense, and it occurs hundreds of times in glosses to Psalm 119. Æ thus retained a sense of enduring law. For its German cognates, see Schmidt-Wiegand, 'Recht und Ewa'.

331   Cf. *Rect*. 3:3, 4:6, 21:1–2, X Atr Pr.:1.

332   These are illuminated as never before by Oliver, 'Language of the Early English Laws'. None of this is to deny that Abt picked up linguistic features from subsequent Mercian and West Saxon masters of Kent and its churches: Lendinara, 'Kentish Laws', with discussion.

333   These arguments were used, following the lead of Beyerle (above, n. 70), and Daube, *Forms of Roman Legislation*, pp. 43–6, in my '"Inter Cetera Bona" ... ', pp. 969–70 (pp. 183–4). That was before I saw Jurg Schwyter's 'Syntax and Style', which together with his courteously proffered counsel, underlies what follows on this topic here and in chapter 5; I confess to having sought guidance thence rather than direct from Bruce Mitchell's awesome *Old English Syntax* – which anyway has relatively little to say of legal prose. A good general account of Anglo-Saxon legislative style is Richards, 'Elements of a Written Standard'.

Two other considerations do make that likely.[334] One is that Æthelberht's code is well-organized. A set of clauses on the Church (there is no manuscript warrant for modern editors' single clause, any more than for the others into which they subdivide this code) make way for similar blocks on the king, earls, ceorls, enclosure, injury, women, serfs and slaves. System might seem to presuppose a body of material to be organized (as with the great Roman codes). In newly Christian Kent, that pre-existing body of material would have been oral custom.[335] The other point is that Æthelberht did notably little to take his code in the direction that innovation might have encouraged. At most two offences are penalized by what can be called a 'fine' rather than 'compensation' – though the king is compensated for breach of the protection he has extended over an already widening range of persons and places.[336] He gained less than did kings from *Lex Salica* or Rothari from his Edict, and much less than did late-seventh-century English kings (pp. 41–2, 103, 105–6). That he changed little in his own favour implies that he changed little else.

What, then, was the use of codifying a law that must already have been known by practitioners who may not have welcomed guidance from the new-fangled technology of script? Among answers to this question by those who do not take the virtues of writing for granted, the most persuasive suppose that Æthelberht *did* make changes. Thus, the sums decreed as compensation for slaying or injury are *introduced*, as a mutually satisfactory alternative to violent revenge. There is support for this view from King Alfred himself, who appears to have thought that compensation came in with conversion.[337] But that solution would have to hold good for *all* post-Roman legislation, Celtic as well as Germanic, where the same range of payments is almost universal. It would also have to confront the observation of Tacitus that among first-century Germans 'for lighter offences those convicted are fined a number of horses and cattle, part of the fine (*multae*) going to the king or state (*civitati*), part to him who is avenged or his kin'. Tacitus' evidence is upheld by the now familiar anthropological insight that compensation is inseparable from the justice of feud almost anywhere that it applies. Without compensation there can be no 'peace in the feud'. Without the alternative of revenge there is no incentive to pay.[338]

It remains conceivable that Æthelberht sought to allay haggling over payments and the attendant risk of renewed violence by giving written permanence to what offenders owed. This could be why Bede said that the code was still 'kept and observed by [his people]'. But Bede also wrote of 'the examples of the Romans'. One feasible interpretation of this gravid phrase paradoxically increases the chances that the code was not new law but old law encased in a

---

334   Argued in more detail by '"*Inter Cetera Bona*" ...', pp. 970–4, 984 (184–6, 192–3). I would give more weight to the second point than the first.
335   Abt 30–1 are rare cases of laws intrusive enough (like some in *Lex Sal.* and more in *Ed. Ro.*) to be judgements included in the main body of codified custom: '"*Inter Cetera Bona*" ...', p. 973 (184–6).
336   Abt 9, ?84; Abt 2 – 3, 5–8, 10.
337   Thus Simpson, 'The Laws of Ethelbert', pp. 13–15; Af Int 49:7 (chapter 6, pp. 421–3); See also *Ed. Ro.* 74 (above, p. 39).
338   Tacitus, 'De Origine et Situ Germanorum' 12(2), p. 43. For feud, see above, n. 67, with Gluckmann's evergreen 'The Peace in the Feud'.

new legislative frame. Bede's 'Romans' may actually have been Franks, as already noted (p. 29). The options were scouted with characteristic canniness by Wallace-Hadrill. But he missed the possible relevance of a clash of titans in the early-twentieth-century *Rechtsschule*. Brunner argued in 1901 that elements common to the Alaman and Bavarian codes could be traced to a lost law of a Merovingian king, he thought Dagobert (623–39). His thesis was scorned by Bruno Krusch, embittered by the feud between *Leges* and *Vitae* departments of the *Monumenta*, and further enraged by the lofty 'juristic' tone with which the young Franz Beyerle, Brunner's pupil, dismissed his labours on manuscript stemmata.[339] But Eckhardt restored the lost *Königsgesetz* to life, by linking the fragments of an evidently early Alaman code with the striking prologue in some copies of the main *Lex* that appears to stand in the name of Chlothar II and his council (pp. 35, 43).[340] No more than Wallace-Hadrill, however, did adherents of the 'royal law' theory note that the features shared by south German laws extend to Æthelberht's code. A table of the similarities in fact goes far to vindicate both (Table 2.3): Æthelberht's laws follow the pattern of the Alaman and Bavarian, and less closely of the Lombard. It bears emphasis that *only* these *leges* have the structure, howsoever rearranged, of laws on the Church, on political authority, on freemen and their injuries, on lower ranks, and on women. Legislation of the turn of the fifth and sixth century has these elements (if at all) in less recognizable order. The codes issued by Charlemagne in imperial vein set out the same subjects in a generally different scheme (p. 46). The compensations for various grades of clergy (omitted by Rothari as a function, it is at least supposed, of his 'Arianism') can be seen to involve the same sort of proportions, once one notes that theft from Kentish free men was compensated threefold: Æthelberht's ninefold for priests and sixfold for deacons thus match Alaman and Bavarian ratios.[341] In this case, there is little doubt that Frankish influence was at work. Wergelds for priests, deacons and lower clergy were laid down in the undeniably seventh-century *Lex Ribuaria*, and so made their way into the Carolingian *Lex Salica*.[342] These are also the first post-Roman laws other than the Visigothic to deal in a systematic way with the law of

339 Brunner, 'Verschollenes merowingisches Königsgesetz'; Beyerle, (e.g.) 'Die süddeutschen Leges'; Krusch, 'Neue forschungen': Krusch returned repeatedly to the topic (mostly goaded by Beyerle), but this paper conveys the essentials of his position, and must rank among the most spectacular assaults ever mounted by a great scholar on another.
340 Eckhardt, *Leges Alamannorum* (as n. 28), especially *Pactus*, pp. 60–77; Krusch's identification (ironically following Brunner) of the Chlothar in question as the utterly obscure and marginal Chlothar IV (717–19) was one of his less inspired insights.
341 Æthelberht's episcopal elevenfold (and God's twelvefold) is a problem whatever approach one adopts: an early medieval legal system where bishops were accorded higher status than kings is not easily envisaged. It may thus be relevant that *Lex Al.* xi left episcopal compensations open to negotiation, while *Lex Bai.* i 10 has an improbable procedure that in some way relates to the martyrdom of St Emmeram *c.*690: Arbeo, *Vita et Passio S. Haimhrammi* 16–22, pp. 28–39, 90–2. One might then speculate that the Kentish Church negotiated itself into a position of unparalleled strength, or else that the bishop's place was at first equal to a priest's (and king's) and was revised upwards at a later date when kings of Kent were weak (or absent) but its prelates remained strong.
342 Cf. n. 341: bishops are omitted in the revised *Lex Sal.*, though appearing in *Lex Rib.* (and one MS of 'K' *Lex Sal.* lviii:4, p. 209).

Table 2.3 The Code of Æthelberht and the 'lost Merovingian King's Law'

Abt	LAl	LBai	EdRth	Other
1 Compensation of Ch. property in grades: – 'God' ×12 – Bishop ×11 – Priest ×9 – Deacon ×6 [NB theft from Freeman is ×3] – Cleric ×3 – 'Church-peace' ×2 – 'Assembly peace' ×2	vi Theft of Ch. property ×3×9 vii–xi Assault on Church property or personnel ×3 xii Assault on priest ×3; wergeld 600s (×3 freeman's] xiii–xiv Assault on deacon ×2; wergeld 300s [×1.5 free man's] xv Compensation for lesser orders × 1.5	i:3 Church property restored ×9 (or ×3 ×9 for special items) i:8 Lesser orders compensation ×2 i:9 Damage to priest ×3; wergeld 300s, deacon wergeld 200s plus *fredus*	–	*LSal* (D) lxxviii:1–2 has 600s for priests (=×3), 300s for deacons (=×1.5) *LRib* xl:6–8 has subdeacon as freeman (i.e. 200s); 300s for deacon (=×1.5) 600s for priest (=×3), 900s for bishops (=×4.5))
2–12 Compensation of king's property and dependents: – injury to 'leode' ×2 + 50s *mund* – injury where king is drinking ×2 – theft of goods ×9 – killing at king's *tun* 50s – killing smith or messenger: wergeld – king's *mundbyrd* 50s – thefts off free men ×3 + *wite* – sleeping with 'maiden' 50s – with 'grinding slave' 25s, 12s	xxiii–xxxv Laws on the *dux*: – xxiii–xxvi treason and army offences – xxvii neglect of ducal orders – xxviii:1–2 killing in duke's court, or when journeying to or from duke ×3 – xxix killing duke's messenger ×3 – xxx stealing from court ×2 plus *fredus* xxxi stealing from duke ×3×9 – xxxii women in ducal service ×3 xxxiii fights in ducal court ×3	ii:1–18 Laws on the *dux* and army – 1–7 treason and army offences – 10–11 fighting in ducal court 12 stealing in ducal court – 13 disobedience to duke	1–18 Royal Laws – 1–7 treason and army offences 8 *scandalum* at royal court: 900s (= ×3 wergeld) 17–18 assaults on those going to or from king	*LSal* xiv:4 is on travelling with *praeceptum regis*: wergeld for assault *LSal* xli:5, xlii:1 liv:1–3, lxiii all give ×3 penalties for offences v. king

13–14 Compensation of *eorl*		iii Status of great families	20–23 Ducal Government etc	
15–25 Compensation of *ceorl* – breach of *tun* – highway robbery – wergeld – binding	xliv–xlviii types of assault on freemen: – xliv fighting in the open pursued to the house – xlv–xlvi kidnapping – lx wergeld of free man	iv injuries etc to freemen – 7–8, 24 varieties of binding and detention – 23–4 ambushing – 28 wergeld of freemen	41–75 injuries to freemen – 41 assault and ambush on freemen – 42 binding freemen	*LSal* xlii–xliii covers assaults on the home; so also *LRib* xlvii *LSal* xli/*LRib* vii are general homicide *LSal* xxxii/*LRib* xvii are on binding
26 Compensation for killing *læt*		v injury and death of freedmen	76–102, 129 injuring and killing half-free	
27–29 Enclosures – breaking in – seizing property – *Ribthamscyld*	*PAl* xix, xxi:3–5 intruding on others' land and court	xi breaking into another's court	32–3 stealing into another's court	*LSal* xi:3–6, xxxiv:5, xlii:5 all relate to breaking and entering
34–72 Injury List – types of teeth – fingers itemized (more for little finger)	*PAl* i–xi, *LAl* lvii injuries – *LAl* lvii:20–25 – *PAl* x, *LAl* lvii: 41–52	iv:1–6, 9–22, 27 freemen's injuries – 16 – 11	See 43–75 51–2 63–7	*LSal* xvii, xxix, *LRib* i–vi are injury tariffs
– medical treatment	*PAl*:ii:2–3, *LAl* lviii:5–7	v:3	78–9, 82–4 etc.	
73–84 Women – remarriage (79–80) – assault (84)	*LAl* l–lvi women – liv *PAl* xviii:4–6 *LAl* lvi	viii wives etc. – xv:7–8 – viii:3–4	178–223 marriage – 182 – 26	*LSal* xxxi:2 assault on woman on road.
85–90 *Esne*, slaves		vi injuring and killing slaves	103–28, 130 injuring and killing slaves	*LSal* xxxv/*LRib* viii are on killing slaves

women.[343] Allowing that the south German codes were reshaped in the eighth century, and accepting large measures of leeway in the details, it is definitely possible that Kentish law partook of the same influences as the others.

It is not easy to see why it *should* be the case that seventh-century codes are of one sort, those of the fifth/sixth or eighth/ ninth of another, unless (as is generally accepted *c*. 500 and again *c*. 800) a degree of mutual influence was somehow exerted at the relevant stage. The case for the early-seventh-century Merovingians as a common inspiration is grounded in the admitted similarity of south German and Lombard pronouncements, when the former preserved garbled traditions that a Chlothar and a Dagobert had been respectively involved.[344] To fit the Kentish code into this picture is merely to find a historical context for similarities of structure as well as content that have often been recognized but hitherto ascribed to ethnic links that would be unprovable even if they were nowadays less unfashionable.[345] The Bishop of Rochester and the Abbot of Sts Peter and Paul attended Chlothar II's seminal Council of Paris in 614: the largest known assembly of the Merovingian episcopate, and held in the 'basilica of the blessed Apostle Peter' (seemingly another name for Clovis' Constantine-evoking Church of the Holy Apostles) in the year when he restored unitary rule to the Frankish kingdom, and when Isidore of Seville for one knew that Jerusalem fell to the Persians and that the Balkans too were lost to Byzantium; held, in other words, at a time when thoughts of a new (Frankish) Rome may have been as much in suitably sensitized minds as they were 185 years later.[346] The year 614 would have been a highly symbolic moment to give written law to subject peoples who were as yet without it, and the council produced one piece of secular legislation (precariously preserved in a lone battered manuscript), that is thought to have influenced south German codes.[347] Now, Kent of course was not (or no longer) subject to the Franks. Unlike the Alamans and Bavarians, but like the Lombards, its king was in a position to make selections that really reflected its *own* law. It may be pertinent that nothing in this code corresponds to the Lombard, Alaman

---

343   For the meaning of Abt 79 – 80, 84, and their resemblances to these continental laws, see Hough, 'Reappraisal of Æthelberht 84', and 'The early Kentish "divorce laws"'.
344   For Dagobert and *Lex Bai.*, see the code's prologue (as above, pp. 43–4); and for the identification of the four named assistants, see Eckhardt, *Austrasisches Recht* (as n. 24), pp. 127–40. It is not generally appreciated that this initiative might provide a context for the never otherwise plausibly explained influence of early Visigothic law on the Bavarian code. The sole manuscript of *Codex Euricianus* is a fragmentary palimpsest from sixth-century S. Gaul, which must have stayed in Gaul given its use (alongside a text of the Breviary of Alaric) in a (?Corbie) copy of Jerome-Gennadius, *De Viris Illustribus*: *CLA* v 624–7 (above, nn. 50, 144). The *palatini* of the Neustrian court were often from this area (Wood, as n. 84) and might well have found *Codex Euricianus* a more serviceable instrument in the construction of *leges* for others than was *Lex Salica* itself.
345   So Joliffe, *Pre-feudal England*, pp. 111–12; R. Buchner, 'Die römischen und die germanischen Wesenszüge', pp. 258–64.
346   *Concilia Galliae*, pp. 274–85, at p. 282 ('ex civitate Castro ultra mare Iustus episcopus ... Peter abba de Doroverno'); for the identity of the 'basilica beati Petri] postea etiam S. Genouefae dicata' (p. 280, n. to ln 147) with Clovis' Church of the Holy Apostles, see Périn, 'The Undiscovered Grave of King Clovis'; for Isidore on the 614 E. Mediterranean cataclysms, see his *Chronica* 414a, ed. Mommsen, pp. 478–9. (Fredegar had *some* knowledge of the subsequent Byzantine recovery, iv 64–5.)
347   Edictum Chlotharii 6, ed. *Concilia* (as n. 346), p. 284; *Lex Al.* i 2, *Lex Bai.* i 2; Beyerle, 'Süddeutschen Leges', pp. 309–11 (but the link is tenuous); for the MS, Mordek, *Bibliotheca*, pp. 56–7.

and Bavarian treason laws.[348] Except perhaps as regards necessarily new laws for the Church, Frankish law was not copied. Instead, it became appropriate to write down Kentish law on certain matters, because these were matters on which eminent Frankish legislators had pronounced. 'Examples', Roman or Frankish, are an occasion for *emulation*, not imitation.

One final and most important issue needs attention. Bede rightly says that Æthelberht's laws were 'conscripta Anglorum sermone'. But why was native speech possible or proper for Anglo-Saxons, where Latin (of a sort) was used on the continent? Three likely and complementary reasons suggest themselves. The first is that no one at Æthelberht's court was sufficiently *au fait* with both Kentish law and Latin prose to make the necessary conversion.[349] Second, it might be guessed that Gregory's Rome already had a 'Byzantine' toleration for ver- naculars, which in the ninth century led successive Popes to view translations of the Bible and the liturgy into Slavonic more positively than did Frankish missionaries, and which may well have inspired Archbishop Theodore's sympa- thetic approach.[350] A third factor, subsuming the two others, was that the language of the *Cantwara* was not cramped by the cultural ascendancy of Latin, as Frankish or Lombardic were so soon as their speakers were established within Roman frontiers, and as trans-Rhenan tongues must have been by Frankish ascendancy. The alternative to Germanic speech in Britain was (or had become) the language of underling *Wealas*. Æthelberht could stick to the native idiom as to native custom, however much inspired by in-laws who did things differently. The code's language is compatible with what else can be ascertained from Bede's evidence and from the text itself. It is a yet more traditional document than other monuments of sub-Roman law-giving. Æthelberht was moved by the 'examples of the Romans', whoever they might be, to one revolutionary step, the use of writing. But in so doing he launched Anglo-Saxon law on a path where 'Roman' example would soon mean rather more.

(ii) Æthelberht's successors

The sole evidence for what Æthelberht called his laws is Bede's. But the code of Hlothere and Eadric has a prologue describing it as 'domas' added to the 'æ' established by their elders. The kings seem to imply that their 'judgements' supplemented the general body of law whereby society lived. Wihtræd, whose prologue is the only formal text of the entire Old English period to contain a

---

348 Wood, *Merovingian North Sea*. That infidelity legislation was the order of the day by the mid-seventh century is shown not only by *Ed. Ro.* 1 but also by *Lex Rib* lxxii:1. (It should be noted that discrediting of the *Textus Roffensis* rubric with its reference to 'the time of Augustine', above n. 322, removes the need to date the code pre-604, or objections to a date in or just after 614.)

349 Wormald, 'Lex scripta', p. 115 (p. 14). This suggestion was partly a tongue-in-cheek provocation to those tempted to take English law's vernacular heritage for granted – an objective evidently realized in so far as it occasioned something akin to outrage in certain quarters. And since it was only meant to apply to the creation of a vernacular tradition in *Æthelberht's* time, it cannot be countered by dwelling on the Latinity of Theodore's time or later.

350 Wormald, 'Uses of Literacy', pp. 103–4 (a suggestion which, unlike the heresy of the previous n., has hardly been noticed at all); Shepard, 'Slavs and Bulgars', pp. 242–3. See also n. 355.

mensal and regnal date (readable as 6 September 695), likewise says that he and his councillors, among them 'the high bishop of Britain' (i.e Archbishop Berhtwald of Canterbury) and the bishop of Rochester, are adding 'domas' to the 'just customs' of the men of Kent. And the pose adopted by these laws, unlike the one ascribed by Bede to Æthelberht, is this time supported by the texts themselves. A first impression made by these codes is of a much more elaborate syntax than Æthelberht's. Hlothere and Eadric retain a basic conditional structure, but all their clauses contain inserted qualifiers.[351] So they provide that 'if one steal goods from another man, and the owner afterwards attaches it, let him vouch to warranty at the king's hall if he can, and bring along him who sold it to him; if he cannot, he is to let go and the owner take it up'.[352] Legislative prose has become so complex that a double- or even triple-take is needed before one is sure who is to do what. Wihtræd's innovations are different. There are two relative clauses; as his code is much less than half the length of Æthelberht's, there is an evident escalation in this supposed symptom of legislative maturity. More striking is the rise in abstract commands: 'Men living in illicit sexuality are to turn to righteous life with repentance of sins, or be cut off from the church's fellowship ... If it happen that a gesith-born man ... enter an illicit union against the king's and bishop's command and the judgement of books, let him amend that with 100s shillings to his lord (*drihtne*) according to old law (*ald reht*)'.[353] The principle, self-evidently innovatory despite the citation of 'boca dom' and 'ald reht', is announced first, with the penalty consequent upon it.

These codes are not without shape and system. Hlothere's first four clauses are a balanced pair, supplementing Æthelberht's final laws and revealing the nobleman's previously unwritten wergeld. The core of the code is devoted to court process and to quarrels arising from festivities, before it concludes with clauses on transactions in London. Most of Wihtræd's code is about the status of the Church and of churchmen in Kentish society: the implications for the behaviour of others of the rules they have introduced; then procedure whereby different grades of cleric may cope with charges against them. But both legislators include a higher proportion of clauses which have no obvious place in their textual context. Hlothere and Eadric have a clause on the protection of the fatherless child between two on theft procedure.[354] Wihtræd's heavily ecclesiastical code finishes with a set of clauses on the killing or capture of thieves with no obvious rationale in this setting save as textual borrowings from Ine.[355] These features in fact go together. More sinuous syntax and inserted items are alike indications of readier recourse to script as a legal medium. Why should Hlothere's

---

351 '"*Inter cetera bona*" ...', pp. 974–5 (pp. 186–7); Schwyter, pp. 194–5. See also Korte, *Untersuchungen*, pp. 131–4, 137–57.
352 Hl 7.
353 Wi 3, 5.
354 Hl 6.
355 Wi 25–8. Given that Wihtræd's code is so completely unique among earlier codes in giving place and full dating of issue, given its massively ecclesiastical content, and given lastly that it marks a sudden switch in Kentish vocabulary from 'eorlcund' to 'gesiðcund' in as little as ten years (above, n. 324), it is *possible* that this was originally a synodical decree in Latin (somewhat like S 20, of much the same date), and that it was later translated into English.

processual complexities have been any more innovative than his laws on the *eorl*? More probably, his draftsmen had acquired the confidence to put problems in writing, the twists and turns of legal process inevitably tangling the terms in which it was conveyed. Similarly, apparent digressions imply that judgements were being written as and when issued. Law was now made as well as recorded in writing.

It is, then, no surprise that these codes should be more visibly innovatory than the prototype Kentish legislation.[356] Hlothere and Eadric extended fines payable to themselves to cases of drunken brawling in anyone's house, where Æthelberht was compensated for outbreaks in his own presence. Their laws on London business must reflect a growth in urban commerce which is archaeologically well-attested by the end of the seventh century but was probably dormant in Æthelberht's time. Wihtræd revealed the Church's tightening grip on Anglo-Saxon society a decade before Bede began to detect the growth of bogus monasteries in Northumbria, when freeing it from 'tribute (*gafol*)' and equating its 'protection value (*mundbyrd*)' with his own, when implementing at least three of the Ten Commandments as matters of royal law, and when allowing clergy a decided advantage in legal disputes with laity.[357] But he also laid claim to a higher fiscal stake in the punishment of thieves than had his great-great-grand-father. He could significantly refer in almost the same breath to the 'king's command', 'judgement of books' and 'old law'. A king's (and bishop's) *domas* were becoming *æ* or *þeawas*, and were ever more likely to be found in books. The 'decreta iudiciorum' that Bede perhaps mistakenly thought to have been the substance of Æthelberht's laws were what kings were indeed producing by Bede's own lifetime.

(iii) Ine

The earliest non-Kentish legislator was (so far as is known) King Ine of the West Saxons (688–726); and the fact that at least one of his laws was echoed by Wihtræd confirms that his code (or part of it) dates to the first years of his reign.[358] Ine's laws survive only as transmitted in an appendix to those of Alfred. Discussion of some resulting problems is best deferred to the account of Alfred's legislation in chapter 5 (pp. 278–80). But one important conclusion therefrom is that Alfred did not tamper himself with the text that had descended to him. If not all his own work, Ine's code was at least not an Alfredian paraphrase. It has a prologue as long as Wihtræd's; it is undated and unplaced, but likewise acknowledges the help of two bishops, those of London and Winchester.[359] Like

---

356   '"*Inter Cetera Bona*" ...', pp. 976–7, 984–5 (pp. 187–8, 192–3).
357   Wi 1, 2, 16 – 24.
358   Wi 28/Ine 20; and cf. also (e.g.) Wi 9–11/Ine 3–3:2, Wi 25/Ine 12. The date might be pushed back to 688x92, as the prologue mentions Bishop Earconwald of London, who died on 30 April, probably in 693 and certainly by 694.
359   Oddly, it also mentions Ine's father, Cenred, who ruled part of Wessex before him; for a solution to this riddle, see Edwards, *Charters of the early West Saxon Kingdom*, pp. 297–9.

their Kentish contemporaries, Ine and his council were concerned with 'æw' and 'domas'. But his formulation of this doublet differed interestingly from theirs. His prologue intended that 'just law and just royal judgements (*cynedomas*) be established throughout our people'. Accepted Law and potentially innovatory judgements were both his business. The word 'cynedom' is particularly intriguing. In *Beowulf* and Alfredian prose, it means kingdom or perhaps royal rank, and Wulfstan used it alongside 'Cristendom'.[360] Ine's usage never caught on, and may have been his own coinage, later displaced by a different currency. In any case, it highlights the hardening adhesive between kingship and law-making. Ine went beyond Kentish kings in actually demanding that his officials and subjects obey his decrees.

Ine's syntax is so much an 'advance' on that of his counterparts in Kent, as to touch heights of complexity not reached again till *c*.930. A quarter of some 137 clauses are relatives or directive statements.[361] Conditional clauses are so infused with sub-clauses that the sense can be hard to make out: 'if anyone comes to terms about a yard of land or more at an agreed payment and ploughs, if the lord wishes to increase that land for him as regards either labour or payment, he need not accept it from him if he does not give him a house, and let him suffer loss of the crops'.[362] The impression is that Ine is reacting to a particular case. A large number of Ine's laws give that impression. All the circumstances get into writing now that scribes feel, rightly or wrongly, competent to itemize everything bearing on a decision reached. This introduces another point basic to the understanding of Ine's code as it stands.

Ine's is much the least organized post-Roman legal statement. An opening set of clauses on the Church's law and on affronts to the king's peace, closely paralleled in contemporary Kentish legislation, leads into the first of five or more distinct pronouncements on theft, each separated from the next by a minimum of six laws on other topics. This is followed by the first of four or more sets of laws on the relationships and wergelds of English and 'Welsh'. Later in the code, there are decrees on the responsibilities of the *gesith* which are displaced by a dozen or so others (featuring yet again theft and English-'Welsh' disputes) from further laws about *gesith* obligations. A number of these clauses repeat the very words of what had already been said: 'if a *ceorl* has been often charged and is at last caught out (*gefongen*), his hand or foot is to be struck off'; 'the *cierlisc mon* who has been often accused of theft and is at last caught (*gefo*) as guilty in the ordeal or in open guilt, his hand or foot is to be struck off'.[363] A central argument of this book is that it may be a methodological error to read modern assumptions

---

360   *Beowulf* ln 2376; *Old English Bede* ii 16, p. 146, v 7, p. 404; *Old English Orosius* iv 5, p. 90; VIII Atr 42, etc.

361   For more on this, see '"*Inter Cetera Bona*" ...', p. 977 (p. 188), with Schwyter, 'Syntax and Style', and Korte, *Untersuchungen*. It must again be stressed that the '76' clauses (with subdivisions) are modern editorial constructs. My count is based on the distribution of main verbs; for the way in which the code was broken up in Alfred's time, see chapter 5, pp. 267–8.

362   Ine 67.

363   Ine 18, 37. For the tabulated structure of Ine's code, with these and other details, and for the conclusions drawn, see '"*Inter cetera bona*"', pp. 977–83 (pp. 188–92); and for a slightly different version of the same case, my '*Exempla Romanorum* ...', pp. 22–3.

about law-making logic into early medieval legislation. Intellectual relativism must nonetheless have its limits. It is hard to see how Ine's laws could appear in the order that they do, were the code in any way pre-planned. But its current state does make sense if one considers how *Lex Salica* would look if it survived only in manuscripts where later legislation, 'official' and otherwise, is added to the original core, and where chapters yet continue the primary numbering. The Edict of Chilperic, with a reconsideration of the laws on owners' responsibility for thefts by slaves appears as 'LXXVII' in two manuscripts.[364] The Burgundian Code *only* survives in expanded form, and is not much less disorganized than Ine's. The most plausible conclusion is that Ine's so-called code was not a code at all but a series of enactments added to an original core over years or decades. Six or seven successive legislative sessions may perhaps be distinguished. Two other conclusions follow. The less important is that some laws transmitted by Alfred under Ine's name could be laws of his successors. West Saxon kings could have gone on having their *domas* recorded well into the eighth century. The more important conclusion is that West Saxon law-makers are regularly found responding to problems laid before them. Law-making in writing had gone 'live'. *Domas* had become part of the king's job.

What 'Ine' does with the law is consonant with the way he does it. This is still 'feud-centred' law in that its primary concern is compensation of injured by injuring party. One royal role is to act as surrogate kin for visitors whose family is distant or in effect non-existent.[365] But the vocabulary of atonement now encompasses the king as well as a more obvious victim: 'if anyone catches a thief, or is given a captive, and he then let him go or conceal the theft, let him pay for (*forgielde*) the thief with his wergeld'; it looks here as if it is governmental authority not the victim who is paid; but in Kent 'forgieldan' was compensatory terminology.[366] 'Wite', that is a fine to the king, is applied almost as a matter of course: for a lord obliging his slave to work on Sundays, for fighting in the home of a *gebur* (when the latter's compensation is 5 per cent of the fine), for theft and rapine, and so on.[367] Penalty matters for Ine as it never obviously did for Æthelberht. All this suggests that early Anglo-Saxon kings and their advisers had learned more from 'Roman examples' than the symbolic gravity of enshrining their *æ* and *domas* in letters. Like the Merovingian kings who made the same move from codified *lex* to royal *edicta*, they stood to make fiscal gains from disturbers of the stability they proclaimed and embodied. If this is the innovation that extant evidence makes it seem, it is as good a marker as any of how Anglo-Saxon royal power grew in the course of the seventh century. More could be gained than revenue. The way that Ine systematically gave *Wealas* half the legal status of his 'English' subjects recalls the *Lex Salica* discrimination in favour of 'Franks' (p. 42).[368] It is unnecessary in this instance (though by no means

---

364   *Lex Sal.* (ed. Eckhardt), pp. 145–54, 262–3, 16.
365   Ine 23 – 23:2.
366   Ine 36. Cf. (e.g.), Abt 22–3, 26, 32, Hl 14.
367   Ine 3, 6:3, 7, 10, 28:1, etc.
368   Ine 23:3, 24:2, 32 – 33, 46:1. The first to see the significance of this was Chadwick, *Studies on Anglo-Saxon Institutions*, pp. 91–3. See also Charles-Edwards, *Irish and Welsh Kinship*, pp. 364–5.

unreasonable) to suppose that West Saxons learned from Franks how to turn Romano-Celtic subjects into true-born barbarians. The point is that in seventh-century Wessex as in sixth-century Francia, law was at once the vehicle of accepted 'popular' tradition and a tool of aggressive royal policy. English law developed as continental law did. Kings who learned to state laws in writing as emperors were accustomed to, soon learned to make law as they had.

(iv) From Ine to Alfred

The analogy of English with Frankish law-making does not stop there. In England as in Francia, an age of intensifying action makes way for up to two centuries of legislative silence. From the latest likely date of an Ine law to Alfred's is yet longer than from Chlothar II's Edict to the earliest capitularies of the ascendant Arnulfings. The usual explanation for the loss of the Merovingians' voice is that they lost the power to make themselves heard. It is not one easily applied to England, where royal power is usually thought to have grown exponentially at least until the death of Offa (796).

The problem is partially resolved by holding that Offa for one did issue a code. The prime evidence is what Alfred says:

> Afterwards, when it happened that many peoples received the faith of Christ, then were assembled throughout the whole world, as also throughout the English ... , many synods of holy bishops and other celebrated wise men ... They then in many synods fixed compensations for many human misdeeds, and they wrote them in many synod-books (senoðbec) ... Then I, King Alfred, gathered these (þas) together, and commanded to be written down many of those which our predecessors held ... , and many of them that did not please me I rejected ... But those that I found either in the time of Ine my kinsman, or of Offa king of the Mercians, or of Æthelberht, who first among the English received baptism ... , I gathered them herein, and left out the others. Then I, Alfred, king of the West Saxons, showed these to all my wise men, and they then said that it pleased them all to observe them.[369]

Alfred speaks of what Offa produced in the same terms as he uses for Æthelberht and Ine. Offa's might then be a text like theirs, in which case it is lost. Yet what Alfred *implies* is that he had gathered 'senoðbec', among them one 'in the time ... of Offa King of the Mercians'. A 'senoðboc' from 'the time of King Offa' is extant. It is the report by the papal legates, George of Ostia and Theophylact of Todi, of the *capitulare* they laid before Ælfwold's Northumbrian council, then before Offa and the southern English.

Three further considerations, in descending order of importance, suggest that this text, or something very like it, is what Alfred had in mind. First, one of Alfred's laws, disinheriting the offspring of nuns, is closer to the legates' view

---

369   Af. Int. 49:7–9. The passage is translated in full, chapter 5, p. 277, and chapter 6, p. 422. The argument summarized here is expounded by my 'In Search of King Offa's "Law-Code"'; I there unfortunately misrepresented Alfred's words, to the extent that I left out much of Af Int 49:9 ('Then I ... gathered these together ... But those which'), as Mr Hayashi has pointed out to me (cf. his own learned treatment, *Lost Laws of Anglo-Saxon Kings*); but I do not see that this oversight unduly shifted the burden of the argument in my favour. But cf. Stanley, 'On the Laws of King Alfred', p. 211.

of the matter than is any other pair of laws on the subject in the post-Roman corpus.[370] Second, the legatine report was known in tenth-century England, and is not a bit likely to have survived there as now extant, that is as a letter to the pope from his legates.[371] Its English *persona* is more likely to have been conciliar proceedings like the extant records of Clovesho (747) and Chelsea (816). A later observer used to royal dominance of Carolingian-style councils might well have labelled those decrees '*senoðbec* in the time of Æthelbald/Cenwulf king of the Mercians'.[372] Since the proceedings in southern England are said to have been 'read out both in Latin and in the vernacular (*theotisce*)', it is not impossible that the English version was preserved with a more or less continuous gloss, so accentuating its resemblance to the codes of seventh-century kings. Third, Alcuin, who attended the 786 assemblies, seems to urge their importance in letters to Anglo-Saxon authorities. One speaks of 'good, modest and chaste customs (*mores*) that Offa of blessed memory ordered (*instituit*)'.[373] 'Mores' is an odd word to use of legislation, but not much odder than the notion of 'instituting' customs; while 'good, modest and chaste customs' would be a less peculiar description of the 786 *capitulare* (or for that matter of the closely related *Admonitio Generalis* of 789 (pp. 50–1)) than of the average early medieval legislative statement. It is quite possible that Alcuin was thinking of the legatine report when he wrote this. If so, the same might well apply to Alfred's words.

Just as important, in any event, is that the *capitulare* of George and Theophylact is a highly sophisticated piece of legislation, of the type that was becoming a Carolingian speciality. The *Admonitio Generalis* three years later reasserted as royal law a set of fifty-nine canonical decrees that had reached Charlemagne in the Pope's 'Dionysio-Hadriana' collection. *Acta* by papal legates which were then subscribed by kings and their councillors constituted the same sort of legislative process.[374] The legates' decrees are divided into ten on more purely ecclesiastical, and ten on roughly secular, issues. This approach became common in Frankish lawmaking from 805 and was echoed by Ansegisus. New topics raised here, as in contemporary Carolingian law, included differentiation of monks and canons, treason against a 'Lord's Anointed', legitimate as opposed to bastard offpsring, and godparenthood. Whatever the *capitulare* ultimately meant for Alfred and Englishmen after him, it is another reminder that English and continental law-making could proceed in tandem; that the stimuli that produced the one could also inspire the other.

370   Af 8 – 8:2; *Alcuin, Epistolae* 3 (xv–xvi), pp. 19–29, at p. 25.
371   The sole extant MS is a canon collection in Wolfenbüttel MS Helmst. 454, of the early-eleventh-century and probably from Hildesheim. For the influence of the legatine *capitulare* on Archbishop Oda (941–58), see *Councils and Synods* 20, I, pp. 67–74.
372   See the discussions of eighth-century councils by Vollrath, *Synoden Englands*, pp. 124–92; and Cubitt, *Anglo-Saxon Church Councils*, pp. 153–90. Dr Cubitt's case for Alcuin's role in what was decreed is a strong one, at least as good as the one I adumbrated against it in 1991; but we both await the forthcoming verdict on 786 (and the 789 *Admonitio Generalis*) of Professor Bullough's Ford Lectures on Alcuin.
373   *Alcuin, Epistolae* 122, p. 180; cf. 18, pp. 49–52, 123, pp. 180–1; my 'In Search', pp. 28, 34 (204, 211); Cubitt, *Church Councils*, pp. 182–5.
374   *Cap.* 22:1–59. The strong textual resemblances between the scriptural quotations of 786 and 789 are part of the evidence that Alcuin (and/or Bishop George) were involved in both.

There is a further way of showing that eighth- and ninth-century English kings did not entirely lose the momentum built up by their seventh-century predecessors. From the mid-eighth century, Mercian rulers began to issue grants of immunity from services and obligations that were in principle due to them.[375] From *c*.800, these are seen to specify that exemption extended to the judicial fines that would otherwise have gone to the king. What may be the earliest such grant simply says that a large estate in Middlesex is to be free from 'popular assemblies (*popularium conciliorum*)'. Before long the formula took the form that freedom did *not* extend to payment of what was called in Latin 'singulare pretium' and in the vernacular 'angyld'.[376] The meaning seems to be that a beneficiary might collect whatever was paid in fines on the granted lands, but must still ensure that injured parties received restitution of their loss. In a remarkable charter, King Cenwulf (796–821) went on from issuing the now regular qualified immunity to say that 'if a wicked man is three times seized in flagrant crime, he is to be handed over to the royal vill'.[377] It is typical of the discourse of early medieval government that one of its prerogatives should be revealed by texts that gave it away. Power resided in allocating a stake in the system to the potentially obstructive. The fact remains that kings were evidently entitled to collect the profits of justice in the normal course, even if not known to have made this a legislative matter, and even though it is unlikely that this was a perquisite of royal office that they had had in their north German homeland. A king did not need to issue a law-code in order to underwrite law and order, or to profit from it as any underwriter would hope to do.

Which is the ultimate moral of a chapter dedicated to what early medieval rulers in the centuries before 890 achieved by making law in writing. The fact must be faced that strong kings did not *necessarily* make written law, and that those who did were not necessarily stronger in consequence. Neither Edwin of Northumbria (617–33) nor Æthelbald of Mercia (716–57) made written law, though they must have known of Æthelberht. Nor for that matter did Otto the Great (936–73) – except in Italy – though he of course knew of Charlemagne. Not the least of the questions to be faced in this book is why Alfred felt the need to carry on where 'Ine' had left off.

---

375   This topic, and in particular the relevant charters, are reviewed in detail below, chapter 10(iii) and chapter 11(i). The seminal discussion is that of Brooks, 'Development of military obligations', pp. 75–82.
376   S* 106/1186a (an ?801 endorsement to a grant originally of 767); S 171 (814), 185 (814), 183 (821), 186 (822), 188 (831), 206 (855), S* 334/342 (869/70), S 218 (883).
377   S 180 (816).

PART II

The Making and Meaning of Written Law, 886–1135

CHAPTER 3

The Impact of Legislation

The next move in the strategy of working down towards early English law-making through its successive contextual layers is to assess the evidence for legislation in other than legislative sources. What would be known of written law-making in England before Henry II had no law-codes survived? The question is no mere paradox. Something may thereby be learned of how legislation affected those on its receiving end. It may also be possible to see how its reception changed with the dawning of the Angevin Age. Contemporary reactions to lawmaking should help to explain why it was carried out.[1]

1 Historical Narrative

There is very little evidence for the making of written law in English narrative sources before, or for some time after, 1066. This is in part because very little historical writing survives.[2] The only significant English historian before 1100 was Bede. He supplies the one unambiguous reference to extant legislation. The course of events from 731 to 1066 must be reconstructed from the nexus of annals long canonized as the *Anglo-Saxon Chronicle*, eked out with hagiographical and quasi-hagiographical texts, only three of which are concerned with kingship. A second reason why early narratives say so little of law-making may be that continental annals and *vitae* were equally reticent. For historians to describe legislation was another 'southern symptom' (pp. 38–9, 44, 51). Isidore, Paul and Gregory of Tours (for the Burgundians) do so; only the *Liber Historiae Francorum* mentions *Lex Salica* (barely). The 'Lorsch' Annals on 802 are an

---

1 Because my crab-like approach to the evidence makes considerable demands on those who do not have English political chronology from Alfred to Henry II at the point of instant recall, I give a chronology in table 3.1, where political events, significant prelates and literary works cited in this chapter are tabulated beside columns for royal and for 'unofficial' codes; datings for the latter are mainly justified (so far as they can be) in chapter 5, section 9, and for the former in section 2 of chapter 6 (though for Alfred, see chapter 5, section 1(iv) and for Cnut, chapter 5, section 8(i)).

2 Gransden, *Historical Writing in England*, pp. 29–91 does her best for the English sources between Bede and the Conquest; and a healthier picture than that reflected by the extant material is implicit in what she is able to show about some post-conquest sources, pp. 105–35. Nevertheless, several of the most important surviving texts, including the *vitae* of Alfred and Edward the Confessor and the *Encomium Emmae*, are not the work of Englishmen.

Table 3.1   The Kingdom of the English, 871–1166: chronological table

Year	Political Events, etc.	Royal Laws (approximate dates)	Other laws (hypothetical dates)
870	– Accession of Alfred (871)		
875	– Defeat of Guthrum (878)		
880		– Treaty of Alfred and Guthrum (AGu)	
885	– Submission to Alfred of English 'not subjected to Danes' (886) – Arrival of Grimbald etc.		
890	– Death of Guthrum (890) – Asser's *Life of Alfred*		
895		– Alfred's *domboc* (Af)	
900	– Death of Alfred (899); accession of Edward 'the Elder' (899) – Death of Ealhswith, Grimbald (901) – Defeat of Æthelwold's rebellion (903)	– Edward's first code (IEw)	
905		– Edward's second code (IIEw)	
910	– Death of Asser (909) – Defeat of the Northumbrian Danes by Edward at Tettenhall (910)		
915	– Submission to Edward of Essex, E. Midlands, E. Anglia (916–17) – Death of Æthelflæd, Edward's seizure of W. Mercia (918)		
920	– Edward's peace with Ragnall of York, Northumbrians, Strathclyde Welsh (920) – Wulfhelm archbishop of Canterbury (923)		

925
- Death of Edward, accession (924) and coronation (925) of Æthelstan
- Æthelstan's occupation of Northumbria (927)
- Æthelstan's first *rex Anglorum* charters (928), *rex to. bri.* coins

  – *Dunsæte* (*Duns.*)

930
- Flight of Edwin, brother of Æthelstan (933)
- Ælfheah I bishop of Winchester (934)

  – Æthelstan's tithe edict (I As)
  – Æthelstan's Charity edict (As Alm)
  – Æthelstan's Grately code (II As)
  – Æthelstan's Exeter code (V As) Thunderfield, Faversham, London, etc. (III–IV, VI As)
  – Whittlebury modification of Thunderfield (VI As 12)

935
- Battle of *Brunanburh* (937)

940
- Death of Æthelstan, accession of Edmund (939)
- Oda archbishop of Canterbury (941)
- 'Redemption of the 5 Boroughs' (942)

  – 'On Incendiaries' (*Blas.*)

945
- Edmund's reconquest of Northumbria, treaty with Scots, etc. (944–5)
- Murder of Edmund, accession of Eadred (946)

  – Edmund's legislation (I–III Em)

  – 'Ordeal' (*Ord.*)

  – 'Adulterers' (*Ymb Æubricas*)
  – 'Wergeld' (*Wer.*)
  – 'Alfred–Guthrum Appendix' (App AGu)
  – 'Rome-payment' (*Romscot*)
  – *Hundred* Ordinance (*Hu*)

950
- Final Northumbrian submission (952–4)

955
- Death of Eadred, accession of Eadwig (955)
- Edgar king in Mercia, Northumbria (957)
- Death of Eadwig, Edgar's accession to whole English kingdom, Dunstan archbishop of Canterbury (959)

960
- Oswald bishop of Worcester (961)
- Æthelwold bishop of Winchester (963)
- Expulsion of the Winchester 'clerks' (964)

  – Edgar's Andover code (II–III Eg)

  – Judging (*Index*)

965

970
- Refoundation of Ely (970)
- *Regularis Concordia*

Political Events, etc.	Royal Laws (approximate dates)	Other laws (hypothetical dates)
975 – Oswald archbishop of York (972) – Coronation of Edgar at Bath (973) – Lantfred, *Translatio S. Swithuni* – Death of Edgar, accession of Edward 'the Martyr' (975) – Murder of Edward, accession of Æthelred II (978)	– Edgar's *Wihtbordesstan* code (IV Eg)	– 'II Æthelred Appendix' (II Atr 8 – 9:4) – *Forfang* (*Forf.*)
980		
985 – Withdrawal of Ælfthryth (984)		– Rights of People (*Rect.*)
990 – Return of Ælfthryth and reformers, Winchester council (993)		
995	– Æthelred's treaty with Olaf etc. (II Atr) – Æthelred's coinage laws (IV Atr 5 – 9:3) – Æthelred's Woodstock code (I Atr) – Æthelred's Wantage code (III Atr)	– Oaths (*Swer.*)
1000 – Wulfstan bishop of London (996) – Wantage council (997)		
– Wulfstan archbishop of York and bishop of Worcester (1002)		– 'Peace', 'Corpse-robbery' (*Pax*, *Wal.*)
1005 – Ælfheah archbishop of Canterbury (1006)	– Law-making council at Enham, 1008 (V–VI Atr)	– 'Peace of Edward and Guthrum' (EGu)
1010 – Arrival of Thorkell's army (1009)	– Penitential edict at Bath (VII Atr)	– The Reeve (*Ger.*) – Ranks of Men (*Geþyn.* etc.) – *Grið*
– Sveinn's invasion, flight of Æthelred (1013) – Death of Sveinn, Æthelred's return		
1015 – Death of Æthelred, accessions of Edmund Ironside, Cnut (1016)	– Æthelred's 'eighth' code, 1014 (VIII Atr) – Extant texts of V Atr, VI Atr, VIIa Atr, VIII Atr	

		– Bequeathing (*Becw.*) – Marriage (*Wif.*)
		– 'Northumbrian Priests' Law (Northu)
– Reconciliation council at Oxford (1018)	– Cnut's? Oxford code (1018) (Cn 1018)	
1020 – Cnut in Scandinavia (1019–20)	– Cnut's first letter to the English (Cn 1020) – Cnut's Winchester code (I-II Cn)	
– Death of Archbishop Wulfstan (1023)		
1025 – Cnut's journey to Rome; Lyfing bishop of Crediton (1027)	– Cnut's second letter to the English (Cn 1027)	
1030		
1035 – Death of Cnut, Oxford *witena gemot* proclaims Harold I – Lyfing bishop of Worcester (1038/9)		
1040 – Death of Harold I, accession of Harthacnut (1040) – 'Encomium Emmae Reginae' – Death of Harthacnut, accession of Edward 'the Confessor' (1042)		
1045 – Ealdred bishop of Worcester, Leofric bishop of Exeter (1046)		
1050 – Expulsion of Earl Godwine (1051) – Return of Earl Godwine (1052)		
1055		
1060 – Ealdred archbishop of York (1061)		
1065 – Northumbrian rebellion (1065) – Death of Edward, defeat and death of Harold II, accession of William 'the Conqueror' (1066) – (?)Goscelin's *Life of Edward*	– William's writ for London (Wl Lond)	

Political Events, etc.	Royal Laws (approximate dates)	Other laws (hypothetical dates)
1070 – Defeat of English rebellions in Northumbria and the Fenland (1069–71) – Lanfranc's reforming council of Winchester (1072)		
1075	– William's writ on Church courts (Wl ep.) – William's writ on Exculpation (Wl lad)	
1080 – Goscelin's *Life of Edith*		
1085 – Maurice bishop of London (1085/6–1107) – Domesday Book (1086) – Death of William I, accession of William Rufus (1087)		
1090		– *Instituta Cnuti* (*Inst Cn*), Articles of William (Wl Art)
1095 – William II in charge of Normandy		
1100 – Death of William II, accession of Henry I (1100); Gerard archbishop of York (1100–1108)	– Coronation Charter of Henry I (C Hn cor), Henry's coinage writ (Hn mon) (1100)	
1105 – Henry's conquest of Normandy (1106)	– Henry's writ on courts (1108)	
1110 – Eadmer, *Historia Novorum* – Ernulf bishop of Rochester (1114–24)		– "*Quadripartitus*"
1115		– *Leges Henrici Primi*
1120 – Death of Queen Edith/Mathilda (1118) – Death of Ætheling William in the 'White Ship' (1120)		

1125
- Henry's castration of crooked moneyers (1124)
- First editions of William of Malmesbury, *Gesta Regum*, *Gesta Pontificum*
- John of Worcester, *Chronicon*

1130
- First extant Pipe Roll (1130/1)

1135
- Henry of Huntingdon, *Historia Anglorum*
- Death of Henry I, accession of Stephen (1135)
- Outbreak of Civil War with Empress Mathilda (1138)
- Geoffrey of Monmouth, *Historia Regum*, Gaimar, *L' Estoire des Engleis*

1140
- Stephen captured at Lincoln (1141)

1145
- Mathilda's escape from Oxford (1142)

1150
- Treaty of Winchester (1153)

1155
- Death of Stephen, accession of Henry II (1154)

1160

1165

- *Consiliatio Cnuti* (*Cons Cn*)

- *Leis Willelme* (*Leis Wl*)

- 'Laws of Edward the Confessor' (ECf)

- Constitutions of Clarendon (1164)

- Assize of Clarendon (1166)

exception; annals otherwise pass over legislative assemblies, unless written by Hincmar. Einhard's definitive biography of Charlemagne set a half-hearted example so far as concerned the great king's legislation. Even that found no echo in the lives of Louis the Pious, which had still richer material to draw upon.[3] Widukind, the continental historian most nearly contemporary with the great days of early English kingship, implied that legal history was supplementary rather than integral to the celebration of warlike deeds which was his main business.[4] Hence, one can hardly expect accounts of the Anglo-Saxons' struggle for earthly glory and heavenly reward to be interrupted by details of their work for social peace. All the same, more can be learned from the taciturnity of the narratives than that they belonged to particular *genres*. Further, the quiet is broken in the twelfth century, and in significant ways. Finally, the silence is not total even before 1100.

(i) Asser

Much the most telling narrative source for the legal activity of kings of England before Henry II is the final chapter of Asser's *Life of Alfred*. The historiographical fortunes of this famous passage are a microcosm of those of the text as a whole. Historians have never been entirely easy in their minds about Asser, which is one of the reasons why the clouds of suspicion that have gathered about it prove so hard to dispel. Even Stevenson, who rescued the *Life* from its nineteenth-century detractors, found the description of Alfred and the judges difficult to reconcile with the then accepted view that Germanic kings were only tangentially concerned with judicial administration. Asser's critics have hardly bothered to deploy against chapter 106 the ingenuity with which they impugn the rest.[5] At least they have paid Asser's importance the compliment of rejecting in its entirety the book ascribed to him. Others, while accepting or arguing the authenticity of the whole, treat it with the misgiving often reserved for 'excitable Celts'. Yet if, to paraphrase Professor Campbell, Asser is not a fake, he is exceedingly important.[6] His voice is that of someone at least as close to his hero as Einhard was to Charlemagne, and closer than was any other historian to an Anglo-Saxon king. His account may not be dispassionate, but losses in objectivity should be balanced if not outweighed by gains in empathy. The message of Asser's last

3   See chapter 2, nn. 43 (with *Gregory, Decem Libri Historiarum* ii 33, p. 81), 61, 86–7, 102, 111, 266.
4   *Widukind* i 14, p. 24.
5   *Asser* 106, with Stevenson's comments, pp. 342–3. Galbraith, 'Who Wrote Asser's Life of Alfred?', p. 121: 'of chapter 106, it is sufficient to observe that it has not been called into service by our legal historians' – no indeed, and why not? Smyth, *Alfred the Great*, is yet more dismissively silent. This is no place to debate Professor Smyth's resurrection of the case against Asser, and I hope to do so in a projected study of the king. Suffice it to observe here that the weaknesses Professor Smyth detects are by no means so embarrassing if it is appreciated that Asser's is less a biography than a programme – and closer to hagiography than Einhard's carefully worked artefact; so much is argued with great force by Dr Anton Scharer (on the whole, an unlikely recruit to any English intellectual *mafia*): 'The writing of history at King Alfred's court', pp. 185–206.
6   Campbell, 'Asser's *Life of Alfred*', p. 115.

chapter therefore merits more than mere tailoring to fit what else is 'known' of early English law. It should stand where it does in this book: in the forefront of the evidence.

According to Asser, King Alfred regularly heard appeals from both noblemen and commoners, because neither party to a dispute accepted the judgement of 'ealdormen or reeves (*comitum et praepositorum*)'; and those aware of a flaw in their case resisted their legal duty to submit it to the king, because they feared exposure of their 'malice'. Alfred was 'an extremely astute investigator in judicial matters as in everything else'. He carefully reviewed judgements made in his absence; if he detected a miscarriage of justice:

> He would ask the judges concerned politely ... either in person or through his other *fideles*, why they had passed so unfair a sentence: whether through ignorance or because of some other malpractice, that is to say either for love or fear of the one party or hatred of the other, or even greed for a bribe (*per ignorantiam aut propter aliam ... malevolentiam, id est ... pro aliquorum amore vel timore aut aliorum odio aut etiam pro alicuius pecuniae cupiditate*).

If the judges claimed to have known no better, the king, remaining polite, would express amazement at their 'insolentiam': "'through God's authority and my own, you have enjoyed the office and status of wise men (*sapientium ministerium et gradus*), yet you have neglected the study and application of wisdom (*sapientiae ... studium et operam*)'". His officials were given the choice between losing their 'offices of worldly power' and taking 'the pursuit of wisdom (*sapientiae studiis*)' more seriously. Greatly alarmed, the ealdormen and reeves made every effort 'to apply themselves to learning what is just (*ad aequitatis discendae studium*)'. As a result:

> Nearly all the ealdormen and reeves and thegns (who were illiterate from childhood) applied themselves in an amazing way to learning how to read (*literatoriae arti*), preferring rather to learn this unfamiliar discipline ... than to relinquish their offices of power. But if one of them, either because of his age or because of his ... unpractised intelligence, could make no progress in learning to read (*litteralibus studiis*), the king commanded the man's son (if he had one) or some relative of his or (if he had no one else) a man of his own, whether freeman or slave, whom he had caused to be taught to read long before, to read out books in English to him by day and night, or whenever he had the opportunity (*libros ante se die nocteque, quandocunque unquam ullam haberet licentiam, Saxonicos imperabat recitare*). Sighing greatly from the bottom of their hearts, these men regretted that they had not applied themselves to such pursuits in their youth, and considered the youth of the present day to be fortunate, who had the luck to be instructed in the liberal arts (*liberalibus artibus*).[7]

Thus, if Asser may be trusted, Alfred exercised appellate jurisdiction over his officials and investigated their decisions even on cases not formally submitted to him. Dissatisfied with their performance, he obliged them to choose between the acquisition of 'wisdom' and loss of office. The result was an extraordinary

---

7   *Asser* 106, pp. 92–5. I have gratefully (if not invariably) used the translation by Keynes and Lapidge, *Alfred the Great*, pp. 109–10.

struggle by his judges to become literate; like parents of more recent times, they dwelt with reproachful envy on the educational opportunities of the young. Stevenson coped with the clash between this account and prevailing perceptions of early Germanic law by stressing that Asser was a 'foreigner': 'The author, perhaps from ignorance of West Saxon law, describes the ealdormen ... and sheriffs or reeves ... as judges, but, like the king, they had no judicial powers apart from the courts of which they formed part. The judges were really the whole body of the freemen ... The ealdormen and sheriffs and reeves would, no doubt, from their position have great influence in shaping the decisions of these courts ... Thus a foreigner such as Asser might imagine that they were judges ...'. Yet Stevenson himself knew of an actual case that vividly illustrates Alfred's prominence in judicial procedure. It is perhaps the most famous single case of the whole Anglo-Saxon period, and will recur more than once later on (pp. 144–8). Nor, as Whitelock showed, is this the only indication that Asser knew what he was talking about.[8] If, then, his final chapter is evidence neither of a forger's anachronism nor of an alien's confusion, it should have much to say about Alfred's approach to justice.

The first point is that the text as it stands says nothing of the king's law-code. Now, the text as it stands could be defective. Asser was among the sources used to deck out the framework of an *Anglo-Saxon Chronicle* in the 'Annals of St Neots', a Bury St Edmunds compilation of the earlier-twelfth century. The author is said to show 'extreme fidelity to the wording of his sources'; and it seems that the text of Asser he used is sometimes better than that preserved elsewhere. Alfred is here reported to have ordered that his judges' reading should include 'written versions of just judgements between the powerful and the weak and many other things useful to both clergy and people (*scripta iusta iudicia inter potentes et inpotentes et alia multa utilia tam cleri quam plebis*)'.[9] Liebermann thought this sentence was 'demanded by the sense, too good for the compiler, and therefore *Asserisch*'.[10] The suggestion has the virtue that Alfred is thus seen to have done what would be expected, but it remains implausible. The sentence stands in the Annals not as an integral part of what is lifted from Asser but just when this breaks off; so when he wrote it, the compiler may no longer have been transcribing. The antitheses, 'potentes ... inpotentes' and 'clerus ... plebs' do not occur elsewhere in Asser, though there are places where they might have done had they been a feature of his style. Whatever his 'extreme fidelity' and other limitations, the compiler's annal has unparalleled passages on Alfred's porphyry mausoleum at Winchester and his patronage of churches and of society's weaker elements. Were one to take the view that these too were 'too good' by his normal standards, the account of the mausoleum can hardly be 'Asserisch', because nothing else suggests that his text of Asser extended as far as the king's death.[11]

---

8   *Asser*, pp. 342–3, with a footnote to what is now S 1445 (LS 24); cf. Whitelock's comments in her own introduction, pp. cxliii–cxlvii.
9   *Annals of St Neots*, pp. xxxix–xliii, lxiv, 104.
10   Liebermann, review of *Asser*, col. 482; cf. *Gesetze* III, p. 39.
11   *Annals of St Neots*, pp. 99, 102. Again, it is inappropriate and also in fact unnecessary to consider here the case, long championed by Dr Hart (e.g. 'The East Anglian Chronicle') and now espoused by

But the most important point is that it could be wrong to think that a reference to Alfred's law-code is 'demanded by the sense'. Whether Asser did after all refer to it, or did not because it was not yet published when he mysteriously laid down his pen in 893, or else ignored it altogether, the code was only one part of Alfred's educational scheme for his judges, and not necessarily the most important part.

Examination of what Alfred himself said about this programme must wait until chapter 6 (pp. 427–9). According to Asser, he thought it 'insolence' that his judges held 'sapientium ministerium' without 'sapientiae studium'. In their consequent efforts 'ad aequitatis discendae studium', the judges strove to master the 'literatoria ars', and wished that they had been instructed when young in 'liberalibus artibus'. Wisdom, justice and literacy went together for Asser's Alfred; but how, and why ? 'Literatoria ars' may mean more than just 'learning how to read'. Asser also used the phrase for the skills of Alfred's court scholar, John the Old Saxon, which evidently extended beyond mere literacy.[12] But the passage's key concept is 'sapientia'. A possible meaning of this word is indeed legal knowledge: it was with the advice of 'sapientes/witan' that Anglo-Saxon kings from Æthelberht onwards are represented as making law. But both Latin and vernacular words for 'the wise' had a much wider semantic range.[13] It seems that, at least for Asser, the primary connotations of wisdom were as much spiritual as practical.

The crucial thing about Asser's account of Alfred and the judges is that it parallels, sometimes in identical words, what is perhaps the dominant *motif* of the whole work: the king's own lifelong quest for learning and wisdom. Like his officials, Alfred 'sighed' for the missed opportunities of youth, 'when he was of the right age and had the leisure and capacity for learning [but] did not have the teachers'. Like them, he tried to make up for lost time amidst the distractions of adulthood; he too 'die noctuque, quandocunque ... licentiam haberet, libros ante se recitare ... imperabat'. The difference was that, from *his* infancy, Alfred had never ceased to yearn for learning 'with insatiable desire'. And where the ealdormen and reeves had the nerve to exercise power without pursuing wisdom, Alfred resembled Solomon who, 'having come to despise all renown and wealth of this world, sought wisdom from God, and thereby achieved both, namely wisdom and renown in this world (*sapientiam ... et praesentem gloriam*)'.[14] Thus, in Asser's presentation Alfred demanded of his officials what he spontaneously sought for himself: the wisdom of Solomon. This is far from the *vita's* only Solomonic echo.[15]

Professor Smyth (*Alfred the Great*, pp. 158–64), that these Annals are actually an East Anglian chronicle of the early-eleventh century. As soon as it is conceded, as it surely must be, that the extant Bury text contains interpolations, the unsupported references to Alfred's *iudicia* (and porphyry mausoleum) lose their authority. It can be added that the drift of the argument in this whole section is such as to make a mention of Alfred's laws likelier in a twelfth-century product than in one of the tenth/eleventh.

12   *Asser*, p. 63; cf. Keynes and Lapidge, *Alfred*, pp. 93, 110.

13   See chapter 2, pp. 94–5, and *Gesetze* II, pp. 737–8. Contrast the Irish 'mundialis sapiens', from the context clearly a 'brehon' (chapter 1, p. 12) in *Die irische Kanonensammlung* xxi 26, p. 72.

14   *Asser* 25, 76, 77, pp. 19–20, 60–1, 63; Keynes and Lapidge, *Alfred*, pp. 75–6, 92–3.

15   See Scharer, 'Writing of History', p. 191, citing Mayr-Harting's 'Saxons, Danes & Normans: Overview', p. 57, and with particular reference to *Asser* 100, pp. 86–7, and I Kings 5:13–14.

One would not have to know much about Solomon to perceive the relevance of 'sapientia' for the 'aequitatis discendae studium'. Solomon had asked God for 'wisdom to discern judgement (*sapientiam ad discernendum iudicium*)', that he might 'judge (*iudicare*)' God's people and 'discern between good and evil'. History's most famous royal judgement was seen by Solomon's subjects as evidence that 'the wisdom of God was in him to do judgement (*sapientiam Dei ad faciendum iudicium*)'. The Book of Proverbs, then thought to be Solomon's own work, sought to teach men 'to know wisdom (*sapientiam*) ... and to receive ... justice and judgement and equity'. In the words of 'Sapientia' herself, 'by me kings reign, and lawgivers decree just things (*iusta decernunt*), princes rule and the mighty decree justice'. The Book of Wisdom, also attributed to Solomon, was addressed to 'kings and ... judges (*iudices*) of the ends of the earth'; it threatened God's swift and terrible judgement on those who, 'being ministers of his kingdom, have not judged rightly, nor kept the law of justice, nor walked according to the God's will'; whereas 'desire of wisdom bringeth the everlasting kingdom (*concupiscentia sapientiae deducet ad regnum perpetuum*)'. For the Psalms of 'David', as for 'Solomon', 'the fear of the Lord is the beginning of wisdom'; 'the mouth of the just shall meditate wisdom, and his tongue shall speak of judgement, the law of his God (*lex Dei*) is in his heart'.[16]

As was seen in chapter 2, it is hard to exaggerate (though easy for a modern mind to overlook) the impact of the Old Testament as a prescriptive mirror for early medieval societies (pp. 41–2, 51). An Old Testament model is always a likely inspiration for an image cultivated or a policy pursued. Asser all but makes it explicit in his vision of Alfred. No student of ancient Israel could doubt the importance of its law. But the wisdom of Solomon was more than legal knowledge, more even than a sense of what modern jurisprudence calls equity. Essentially, it meant sensitivity to the mind of God (who was of course the Supreme Judge). If that is what Asser had in mind, he represents Alfred as expecting in his judges not legal expertise but moral excellence. 'Literatoria ars', whatever its exact meaning, would lead not so much to mastery of the written law as to awareness of Holy Writ, where God's own justice was manifest for all time.

If the Book of Kings was one of Asser's models, another, more generally acknowledged, was Einhard; and not the least interesting thing about his final chapter is the way that it casts King Alfred in a Carolingian mould. Royal intervention in judicial process, so far from being irreconcilable with Frankish law, was envisaged in the original text of *Lex Salica*.[17] Under pressure from the expectations of Carolingian kingship's ideologists, the supervision of justice became an urgent royal preoccupation. It was a prime function of the royal *missi*, as of Alfred's *fideles*.[18] Carolingian rulers not only allowed but positively encouraged

---

16 I Kings 3:9,11,28; Proverbs 1:2–3; 8:15–16; Wisdom 6:2,5–6,11,21; Psalms 110:10, 36:30–1.
17 *Lex Sal.* 'A'/'C' lvi:1; for evidence of this procedure in Frankish practice, see chapter 2 above, pp. 81–2; and note the later Lombard laws, *Leg. Liutpr.* 27 – 28, *Leg. Rat.* 1 – 2.
18 Ganshof, 'Charlemagne's programme', pp. 63–5, with reference to *Cap.* 33:1; cf. also *Ans.* ii 26–7. The parallel between *missi* and Alfred's *fideles* was already noted by Plummer, *Life and Times of Alfred*, p. 125, and by Hodgkin, *Anglo-Saxons* II, p. 606.

appeals. Louis the Pious announced in 829 that he was sitting one day a week at his palace, 'to hear and judge cases'. Archbishop Hincmar's *Admonitio* on the Organization of the Palace', written just before he died (882) so only eleven years before Asser's *Life*, made the Count of the Palace responsible for the settlement of disputes and the rectification of judicial abuses along the lines of 'aequitas'.[19] Like Asser's Alfred, Carolingian kings went looking for miscarriages of justice. According to Thegan's *Life of Louis*, the king 'sent his agents (*legatos*) throughout all his kingdoms, to enquire and investigate whether any injustice had ever been perpetrated against anyone', and of course 'they found an innumerable multitude of the oppressed', thanks to the 'evil devices' of 'unjust *ministri*, *comites* and local officials'.[20] Hincmar's *Admonitio* expressed a fundamental principle of Carolingian kingship when it averred, following the vastly influential Irish tract 'On the Twelve Abuses of the World', that rulers who failed to put right the sinners among their servants would be punished for such sins themselves.[21] Carolingian legislators blamed injustice on the same vices as Alfred. In words from Isidore's *Sententiae* that seem to have been the source of this ubiquitous catalogue for Carolingians (as possibly for Asser too), human judgement is perverted in four ways: 'timore, cupiditate, odio et amore'. Hincmar laid characteristic extra emphasis on those dangers of ignorance that Asser also stressed.[22]

Behind the judicial ambitions of Carolingian ideologues, behind Gregory, Isidore and their other authorities, lay the same Old Testament inspiration as in Asser. The bishops at Paris in 829 (p. 88) drew the Emperor Louis' attention to King Jehoshaphat:

> And he set judges of the land in all the fenced cities of Judah (*civitatibus Iuda munitis*), and charging the judges he said, take heed ... you exercise the judgement not of man but of the Lord, and whatsoever you judge it shall redound to you. Let the fear of the Lord be with you, do all things with diligence; for with the Lord our God there is no iniquity, nor respect of persons nor desire of gifts (*nec personarum acceptio nec cupido munerum*).[23]

The duty of kingly interference in local justice was writ large in the story of the original People of God, as were the appalling penalties for failure. Above all, for Carolingian scholars as for Asser, there was the prototype of Solomon and his *sapientia*. In the earliest Carolingian 'mirror of princes', Smaragdus has a much longer chapter on *Sapientia*, with extensive quotations from the Books of Proverbs and Wisdom, than on any other royal virtue; he puts it well before the chapters on *Iustitia* and *Iudicium*, though significantly just after that on 'Fear (of

---

19   *Cap.* 185, 192:14; cf., e.g., *Cap.* 64:1, 69:7, 146:3–6. *Hinkmar, De Ordine* v, lns 345–50. See again chapter 2, pp. 81–2.
20   *Thegan, Gesta Hludowici*, as chapter 2, n. 266.
21   *Hinkmar, De Ordine* iii, lns 179–202; the same point previously in his 'De regis persona' ii, cols 835–6; *Pseudo-Cyprianus, De XII abusivis* 9, p. 53: 'Attamen sciat rex quod sicut in throno hominum primus constitutus est, sic et in poenis, si iustitiam non fecerit, primatum habiturus est'.
22   See chapter 2, pp. 70–1 and n. 213; *Hinkmar, De Ordine* iii, lns 121–61.
23   *Cap.* 196:59, II Chronicles 19:5–7. One feels that, quite apart from the issues under discussion here, Jehoshaphat's 'civitatibus munitis' may have had some relevance for Alfred.

God)'.[24] Solomon is prominent in the advice subsequently tendered to kings by Agobard, Jonas, Lupus and Sedulius.[25] At the Council of Tribur (895), perhaps the last of the great Carolingian series, and just two years after Asser wrote, the bishops instructed King Arnulf in the role of king:

> That he outshine all in mercy and modesty, and judge not according to person, and, like Solomon, love *iustitiam, iudicium et aequitatem*; adding the examples of Holy Writ, whereby *sapientia*, instructing the pupils educated in its mysteries, says ' ... By me kings reign, and lawgivers decree just things'.[26]

For Alcuin, 'nothing is more necessary for the rule of peoples, nothing better for the arrangement of life according to the best principles, than the ornament of *sapientia* ... the effect of learning (*eruditio*)'; 'it is the true Wisdom to know what you ought and to perform what you know'. It has been said that Alcuin's *sapientia* was more than purely Biblical wisdom, but the 'reading' on which it was to be based centred on the Gospels, 'other books of canonical authority' and Gregory's *Pastoral Rule*.[27] Alcuin's pervasive influence on the world of King Alfred and his biographer is increasingly evident.[28] His choice of reading needed for the acquisition of wisdom could have some bearing on the bibliography put before Alfred's judges, in that the *Pastoral Rule* was the first of the books translated by the king, 'which may be most necessary for all men to know'.

This is not to say (at least not yet) that Asser and his patron were consciously imitating the Carolingians. The themes they share are so universal in the early medieval West that one could as well trace Asser's language to a single Frankish source as identify the part of the Atlantic that spawns any one European weather system. The suspicion already arises that the ideological climate of Alfred's Wessex belonged to the Carolingian zone. But it is more important at this stage that cross-channel parallels give the English evidence credibility. If such was the perception of justice in ninth-century Francia, it requires a doggedly insular approach to Anglo-Saxon history to deny the *possibility* that Alfred's was the same. Since Asser himself, the king's close confidant, anyway raises this possibility, it indeed becomes a *probability*, even before the evidence of the king's lawbook is examined (pp. 265–85, 416–29). The significance of Asser's chapter is thus fourfold. First, it makes the negative point that a long account of an Anglo-Saxon king's concern with justice can seem to ignore his extant legisla-

---

24   Smaragdus, 'Via Regia' iii–iv, viii–ix, cols 939–45, 947–50; Eberhardt, *Via Regia*, pp. 439–41, 597–601.

25   *Agobard, Epistolae* 10, p. 162; *Jonas, 'De Institutione Regia'* iv, ed. Reviron, pp. 146–7; *Lupus, Epistolae* 33, p. 42 (*Correspondence* 46, I, pp. 196–7); *Sedulius, Liber de Rectoribus* iv, pp. 31–3. There is a Solomonic echo in Theodulf, 'Contra Iudices', lns 615–20, *Poetae* I, ed. Dümmler, p. 509 (see chapter 2, pp. 51, 71 with n. 213). Further examples of the theme are in Anton, *Fürstenspiegel*, pp. 430–2; and for the iconographical equation, see Wallace-Hadrill, *Frankish Church*, pp. 249, 255; the most striking of these *mises-en-scène*, from the Book of Proverbs in the 'Bible of San Paolo', is the frontispiece to Nelson's *Politics and Ritual*.

26   *Cap.* 252:Pr. (II, p. 212).

27   *Alcuin, Epistolae* 121, 309, 39, pp. 177, 475, 83; Edelstein, *Eruditio und Sapientia*, p. 154. Cf. the neat formulation of Riché, *De l'Éducation antique à l'Éducation chevaleresque*, p. 44: 'il ne s'agit plus alors d'apprendre à gouverner un état, mais à se gouverner soi-même'; also Eberhardt, *Via Regia*, p. 599.

28   Wallace-Hadrill, *Early Germanic Kingship*, p. 141; Keynes and Lapidge, *Alfred the Great*, pp. 54–5, 265; Bolton, 'How Boethian is Alfred's *Boethius*?', pp. 160–3; Campbell, 'Asser's *Life*', pp. 117–21.

tion. Second, and on the positive side, it raises, at the very outset of the legislative tradition studied in this book, the question of the place of English legal development in that of Carolingian Europe. Third, more important still, it suggests that one Anglo-Saxon king was deeply embroiled in the details of judicial administration, because justice was central to his view of his kingdom as a new People of God. But the fourth and most crucial point is that Asser's detailed description of Alfred's legal activity is unique. Where Charlemagne's biographer remarked curtly on the limitations of his law-making, Alfred's wrote the most circumstantial and arresting account of a king's sense of responsibility for justice in the entire historical literature of the early medieval West. Traditional attitudes to Asser's chapter can thus be stood on their head. It is the first piece of evidence that something extraordinary was happening in late-ninth-century Wessex. It will not prove to be the last.

(ii) From Alfred to Henry I

The narrative evidence for English legislation written between 893 and 1100 is not only skimpy in the extreme, but also very hard to interpret. Essentially, it consists of two enigmatic entries in the *Anglo-Saxon Chronicle(s)*, and of some cloudy passages in Goscelin and other (often, like him, continental) writers who celebrated some later Anglo-Saxon kings and saints. There is a temptation to include the authors who wrote after 1100 about the pre-conquest past, but it should be resisted. The 'St Neots' annalist, the one twelfth-century writer considered so far, apparently introduced a reference to Alfred's law-book that was not in his source. Others, in principle, could have done the same.

Truly tenth- and eleventh-century material begins with what could be a reference to a contemporary edict. It comes from the account of the 'Translation and Miracles' of Winchester's St Swithun by the continental scholar, Lantfred:

> At the command of the glorious king Edgar, a law (*lex*) ... was promulgated throughout England, to serve as a deterrent against all sorts of crime ... that if any thief or robber were found anywhere in the *patria*, he would be tortured at length (*excruciaretur diutius*) by having his eyes put out, his hands cut off, his ears torn off, his nostrils carved open and his feet removed; and finally, with the skin and hair of his head shaved off, he would be abandoned in the open fields dead in respect of nearly all his limbs, to be devoured by wild beasts and birds and hounds of the night.

An innocent man thus convicted and mutilated (though spared his feet and his scalp), was taken home by his grieving 'friends and kinsmen', one of whom restored a dangling eyeball to its socket. After more than three and a half months in this condition, he was persuaded that the relics of St Swithun might restore his hearing, blocked by cakes of blood, though he had no hope of his sight. The saint duly restored both. The tale was taken up by Wulfstan, Precentor of Winchester, in the versified *Narratio Metrica de Sancto Swithuno* which he brought out in 992x94. He added little to Lantfred beyond a stirring description of the manhunt following the promulgation of the 'lex et sententia', which looks like an echo of other panegyrics on royal peace, not least Bede's.[29] But the story itself remains, by hagiographical standards, unusually credible. It seems closely dated. Lantfred wrote more or less when Edgar died (975). This miracle followed St Swithun's removal to Bishop Æthelwold's new shrine four years earlier. Lantfred's implication that recovery of hearing might have been expected, but not restoration of sight, leaves the impression of a judicious witness.

Alas, the *lex* in question does not appear to survive. Dorothy Whitelock, who first drew attention to the literature, tentatively and plausibly suggested that Edgar referred to it in his '*Wihtbordesstan*' or 'fourth' code.[30] This text seems to make notable concessions to the 'Danelaw', and is extant only in manuscripts from the Worcester/York complex, that is from the centre or centres most concerned with Danelaw areas. It draws an interesting contrast:

> ... I will that secular rights should be in force among the Danes according to such good laws as they best prefer ... However, let that apply among the English which I and my wise men have added to the judgements (*domum*) of my ancestors, to the benefit of all people. Nevertheless, this measure (*ræd*) is to be common to the whole people, whether Englishmen or Danes or Britons, in every part of my dominion, so that ... a thief should not know where to dispose of stolen goods ...

There follows a complex strategy against theft, especially of cattle. Then the Danes are told that they may adopt their own measures against those who obstruct the proposed procedures. But, 'among the English, I and my *witan* have chosen what the punishment (*steor*) shall be'.[31] What Edgar added to his forbears' '*domum*' for the '*steor*' of '*Anglum*' was evidently quite unpleasant. Since the *Wihtbordesstan* code made exceptionally elaborate arrangements for its publication, the same should have applied to any twin text. This could then be the law described by Lantfred.[32] That proposition derives support from laws drafted by Archbishop Wulfstan. In Cnut's code, some capital penalties demanded hitherto made way for sanctions almost equally drastic but less immediately terminal. An 'untrustworthy man' who failed an ordeal the second time would lose not his head but his hands and/or feet, and for a greater crime his eyes, nose, ears and upper lip or scalp. Survival of these mutilations may have been uncertain, and undesired by judges or victim, but there was a chance of the latter living to repent:

---

29   Lantfred's work is being exhaustively edited and set in its Anglo-Latin context by Michael Lapidge; it will be published, with Wulfstan's poem and much else, in his *Cult of St Swithun*. Professor Lapidge has been a helpful pilot through these uncharted waters (his MS providing the quoted text and translation), which is not to say that he endorses the course I have taken. See meanwhile (1) for the episode, *Frithegod, breviloquium; Wulfstan Cantor, narratio*, pp. 154–7 (lns 462–5 on the mother and child walking undisturbed from sea to sea echo Bede, *Hist. Eccl.* on King Edwin, see below, p. 128 and n. 41); (2) for Lantfred and Winchester in the 970s, Lapidge, 'Three Latin poems'; *idem*, 'Æthelwold as Scholar and Teacher', pp. 104–117; *Wulfstan, Life of St Æthelwold*, pp. xiii–xxxix, ci–cxii.
30   Whitelock, 'Wulfstan *Cantor* and Anglo-Saxon law' (she was unaware that Wulfstan's poem was based on Lantfred's text).
31   IV Eg 2:1 – 2:2, 13:1 – 14; for Lantfred and Wulfstan, Edgar's edict applied to the whole kingdom; but even if they drew their impression of its scope from the text, Edgar may not have mentioned concessions to the Danelaw in what he aimed at the rest of his realm; cf. the situation with I and III Atr, chapter 5, below, pp. 321–2, 328–9.
32   IV Eg 15 – 15:1; the *Wihtbordesstan* code is more fully discussed below, chapter 5, pp. 317–20; and at pp. 369–70 is an argument that parts of Edgar's lost edict may in fact survive as fragments.

'thus may one punish and also preserve the soul'.[33] Wulfstan made Edgar's laws a model for Cnut's, yet Edgar's extant codes show no interest in mutilation. The Wulfstan/Cnut policy could have been borrowed from the lost edict to which Lantfred and perhaps the *Wihtbordesstan* code refer. This ghastly law would have aimed to secure the prospects of thieves in the next world by extending their agony in this.[34] Lantfred's evidence would then be in counterpoint to Asser's, telling of a lost code where Asser passes over one that is extant. But before this sensible and symmetrical theory is adopted, one might hesitantly ask whether Lantfred *did* have a written law in mind.

Cnut's measure is unlikely to be a *verbal* quotation of one by Edgar. It is actually a quotation, or rather adaptation, of one by Æthelred II.[35] If Cnut's substitution of corporal for capital penalties were lifted from a lost Edgar code, one would have to suppose that he was correcting one quoted law by quoting another. Æthelred did reverse his father's policies as Cnut changed Æthelred's; but there is no other instance of Old English legislation remaining so verbally stable while its content changed so much. It is more economical to think that Wulfstan revived a known initiative of late in Edgar's reign, but used the wording of an Æthelred decree to the opposite effect.[36] There may be a parallel here with Edgar's now famous coinage-reform. The only written source for it is Roger of Wendover, who was writing in the 1230s. The self-denying ordinance on post-conquest sources adopted so far may this time be waived; Roger's annal was the textual peg for the article in which Michael Dolley and Michael Metcalf argued from purely numismatic evidence that this reform did occur, and inaugurated a policy of regular and planned 'renovation of money'.[37] Sceptics have objected that there ought then to be stipulations along the relevant lines in the laws of Edgar, Æthelred or Cnut. But they concede that the reform and the system thus introduced may have been 'effected by administrative direction', that is (presumably) orally.[38] Later Old English law on coinage was ambitious and cruel, but laws alone would never have enabled historians to grasp its full scope. Thus, while it may, on the one hand, be right to deduce from Lantfred's sort of evidence that

---

33 II Cn 30:3b–5.

34 As noted by Whitelock, 'Wulfstan *Cantor*', pp. 84–5, there is yet nastier evidence of this approach in Wulfstan's 'Peace of Edward and Guthrum' (EGu 10, cf. chapter 5, pp. 389–90): 'if a mutilated maimed man, who might have been ruined (*þe forworht wære*) be abandoned (*forlætan*), and after three days is still alive, one ... may look to (*beorgan*) his wounds and his soul by the bishops's leave': even physical salves for survivors were subject to episcopal licence.

35 II Cn 30:3b–4: 'Gif he þonne ful weorðe, æt ðam forman cyrre bete ðam teonde twygylde ... And æt þam oðrum cyrre, ne si þær nan oðer bot, gif he ful wurðe, butan þæt man ceorfe him ða handa oðð þa fet oðð ægþer ...'; I Atr 1:5–6: 'Gif he þonne ful wurðe, æt þam forman cyrre bete þam teonde twygylde ... And æt þam oþran cyrre ne sy þær oðer bot butan þæt heafod'. For a full account of Cnut's code in relation to its predecessors, see chapter 5, below, pp. 353–64, and table 5.4.

36 Cf. Keynes, *Diplomas of King Æthelred*, pp. 163–208. When Æthelred changed his policy on capital theft he did *not* verbally echo his earlier laws: chapter 5, pp. 305–6.

37 *Matthew Paris, Chronica Maiora* I, p. 467; see *EHD* I, pp. 281–4 for his Anglo-Saxon sources; Dolley and Metcalf, 'The reform of the English coinage under Eadgar'.

38 Grierson, Presidential Address, pp. viii–xiv (cf. p. xi, ' ... no more than a private instruction from the Crown [which] would leave no trace in public documents'); Stewart, 'Coinage and recoinage', pp. 268–9; cf. Sawyer, 'Baldersby, Borup and Bruges', p. 81. For further discussion of what legislation there is, see chapter 5, pp. 306, 328, and chapter 12.

there were many written laws which are now lost, it may, on the other, be that some laws inevitably left few or no traces, because they never proceeded beyond the spoken word.

Other sources dwell briefly on the legal activity of kings. Goscelin had this to say in his *Life of St Edith*:

> Edgar prince of peace, after filling Britain with monasteries, ... after pacifying his people with excellent laws (*optimis legibus*) ... was translated from earthly empire to the heavenly crown reserved for him by the Judge of kings Himself.

Dom Wilmart was sure that the reference was to Edgar's surviving laws.[39] The *Encomium Emmae Reginae* may likewise have had Cnut's code in mind when asserting that he 'suppressed unjust laws and those who applied them, he exalted and cherished justice and equity'.[40] And there could be an allusion to William the Conqueror's legislation (such as it was) in the account of his 'iura' and 'iudicium' by William of Poitiers.[41] But what is then to be made of similar language in the *vita* of Edward the Confessor?

> This goodly king abrogated bad laws, with his council of the wise established good ones (*leges iniquas evellens, iustas sapienti consilio statuens*), and filled with joy all that Britain over which ... he ruled.[42]

So far as is known, Edward made no written law. Legal texts after 1066, official and unofficial, made the 'Law of Edward' the shibboleth of the acceptable to ruler and ruled. By that token, one would expect any laws he actually issued to have been cherished and copied. Instead, the image of Edward as lawgiver inspired the so-called *Leges Edwardi Confessoris* (*c*.1140) which, whatever else it was, was not authentic legislation by this king.[43] If Edward did make laws, as is possible, they must have been lost well before the 'Law of Edward' acquired its talismanic force. Or perhaps his reputation for justice rested on his judgements and pronouncements by word of mouth.

More probably, the passage is a *topos*. This was what a good king was *expected* to have done, just as he was expected to have triumphed in war. One model for these kingly virtues was once again the Old Testament.[44] Another was the self-

---

39   'Vita S. Edithae' i 17, p. 80; cf. i 9, pp. 63–5: 'Sous la banalité des termes, il y a sans doute une refer-ence expresse aux "lois d' Edgar"'. (In the *Vita Oswaldi*, Edgar is 'armipotens ... jura regni bellica potestate ... protegens', *Historians of the Church of York* I, p, 425; this *vita* is also being re-edited by Professor Lapidge, *Byrhtferth of Ramsey*, cf. his 'Byrhtferth and Oswald').
40   *Encomium Emmae Reginae* ii 19, pp. 36–7.
41   *Gesta Guillelmi* ii 33, pp. 158–9 (and cf. i 6, pp. 8–9). The famous tribute to his 'gode frið', ASC 1087E, p. 220 (and cf. the verdict on Henry I, 1135E, p. 263) is presumably an echo of Bede on the peace of King Edwin, *Bede, Hist. Eccl.* ii 16, pp. 192–3; for law-making by Norman kings, see chapter 5, section 10(i).
42   *Life of Edward the Confessor* i 1, p. 13.
43   Barlow, *Edward the Confessor*, p. 178. The position as regards the *Leges Edwardi Confessoris* (ECf), a title which should not strictly be borne by the text that usually bears it, or not by it alone, is complex, and is more fully discussed in chapter 5, pp. 409–11.
44   *Life of Edward* i 1, p. 12, has Godwine as David to Edward's Solomon. Cf. the *Vita Oswaldi*, following the excerpt cited in n. 39: Edgar is 'bellicosus ut egregius Psaltes ... sapiens ut Justus [i.e. Solomon, justifying the MS reading as against Professor Whitelock's emendation, *Councils & Synods*, p. 117] ... misericors ut Moyses ...', etc. In Osbern's 'Vita Sancti Dunstani', p. 103, Edgar is 'proficiens,

proclaimed image of Rome, which had conquered the world by its martial skills, then deigned to civilize it with its legal expertise. These two great Roman 'arts' were singled out by Sallust in what, for the early Middle Ages, was the definitive account of Rome's rise and decline, and even more famously hymned by Vergil in Anchises' resounding prophecy of Rome's greatness.[45] The 'Shorter Prologue' to *Lex Salica* credits the Franks with the same two qualities (p. 40). A phrase about reining in peoples by arms and arms by laws used by William of Poitiers of his hero was applied by Sidonius to King Euric at the birth of barbarian *lex scripta*, exactly six centuries before.[46] If the picture of Edward as law-giver is simply a nod to panegyrical convention, sophisticated *litterati* like Goscelin could have said these things whether or not Edgar, Cnut and William I made written law. Such passages seem evidence of legislation only because relevant codes are anyway extant.

Yet *topoi* could be more than verbiage. The definitive version of the 'war/law' diptych was the opening of the *Constitutio* promulgating Justinian's *Institutes*. By the twelfth century this text was well-known, and was an ideological inspiration as well as a panegyricist's device. It lies behind the opening of *Glanvill*:

> Not only must royal power be furnished with arms against rebels and nations which rise up against the king and the realm, but it is also fitting that they should be adorned with laws (*legibus … ornatam*) for the government of subject and peaceful peoples.[47]

Authorities in the early medieval West, kings of the English among them, had long been exposed to such stimuli, if not in Justinian's words. It is unrealistic as well as cynical to assume that flattering exhortation never affects a ruler's behaviour. Universally approved models may also be widely imitated. Literary convention on the 'artes Romanae' should have reinforced the lesson of Solomonic *sapientia*, that an active judicial role was as important in kingship as Davidic and doubtless more congenial war-making and lyre-playing.

Still to be considered are the two entries in the *Anglo-Saxon Chronicle(s)* that seem to refer to legislation. The first records the 'agreement (*sam mæle*)' reached at Oxford in 1018 between Cnut's conquering Danes and his new subjects. The agreement was '*to Eadgares lage*, according to Edgar's law' (or perhaps 'to observe' it). The second occurs in the story of the 1065 revolt of the Northumbrians against Tostig's rule as earl. King Edward ceded the rebels' demand for Tostig's replacement, 'and he renewed there the law of Cnut (7 *he*

---

ut David … fortitudine, atque ut Solomon sapientia …' (see next n.); this text, though written pre-1100, is more fully discussed alongside Eadmer's writings, below pp. 135–6 and n. 71.

45   *Sallust, Catiline* ix 3; *Vergil, Aeneid* vi 851–3 ('hae tibi erunt *artes*' (my emphasis)); see Southern, 'Aspects of the European Tradition of Historical Writing: 1'. For Goscelin, building on Bede, Æthelberht's code meant 'ut Anglia, sicut alter orbis, ita altera videretur Roma' (itself a neat Vergilism): 'Vita Mildrethae' ii, p. 112. The hugely influential *sapientia-fortitudo topos* (Curtius, *European Literature and the Latin Middle Ages*, pp. 170–9) was surprisingly irrelevant for judicial wisdom, but see previous n.

46   *Gesta Guillelmi*, pp. 160–1; *Sidonius, Letters* VIII iii 3. William's 'Frenans ut populos armis ita legibus arma' is a hexameter, though Sidonius distributes the words in a prose sentence; the line should be classical, but my Latinist friends have failed to trace it.

47   *Glanvill*, Prol., p. 1, compared with *Corp. Iur.* I, p. xxiii. See chapter 2, pp. 36, 59–60, and chapter 14.

niwade þær Cnutes lage)'.[48] Before ascertaining what these annals are likely to mean, one would like to know where and when they were written. But it is one of the trials of Anglo-Saxon studies that, though the *Chronicle* is the central narrative source for English history after 731, there is very slight consensus on its authorship or provenance at any stage. A first vital point is of course that one should not speak of a single *Chronicle* (anyway after its common core was completed in 891/2), but of a series of independent if overlapping *Chronicles*. The next step is to appreciate that the three most important post-975 versions are themselves conflations of two or more earlier texts; 'C' being written around the time of the Conquest (when it gave out), 'D' in the later-eleventh century (its last annal, 1079) and 'E' in the mid-twelfth. Finally, therefore, one needs to recognize that any one entry is as likely to have originated in one of these *Chronicles'* sources, miles and/or years from the time and place at which the extant text was written, as it is to be an indicator of the agency responsible for the version as a whole.[49]

The position regarding the annals in question here is fortunately not as complicated as it might be. The mention of Edgar's law as the basis of the 1018 agreement is only in 'D', together with the twelfth-century Latin *Chronicon* of John of Worcester.[50] This is a suggestive, if not yet decisive, pointer to a Worcester origin for 'D' or at least for its source at this point. More pertinent, it goes with a string of unique 'D' (and John of Worcester) entries for the tenth and eleventh centuries which show special knowledge of West Midland affairs. One cluster in particular centres on the activities of Bishop Ealdred of Worcester (1046–62), who became Archbishop of York in 1061, vainly tried to hold both sees in plurality like a number of his predecessors, and died in 1069. The Worcester–York axis offers a plausible context for most 'D' idiosyncrasies. Ealdred himself is the most prominent non-royal figure in 'D', and one of the foremost in any *Chronicle* recension at any time. There is a thus a good case that one of the clergy who followed him north in 1061/2 was its compiler. As for the account of the pacification of the 1065 Northumbrian rebels by the offer of 'Cnut's law', it comes in both 'D' and 'E' in the annal where they resume contact after half a century apart. This begins a sequence when 'D' and 'E' are close (though with 'D' more detailed on northern matters), till 'D' expires. 'E' as it now stands was certainly written at Peterborough, and almost certainly drew on Canterbury annals for the mid-eleventh century. But as soon as it is appreciated that it is a conflation like 'D', there is no reason why its sources should not have included northern annals after 1065 close to those of 'D'.[51] Again, therefore, an

---

48   ASC 1018D, p. 154; 1065DE, pp. 192–3. See the modification of Whitelock's translation (*EHD I*, p. 251) suggested by Kennedy, 'Cnut's law code of 1018', p. 58, n. 9.

49   In *How do we know so much about Anglo-Saxon Deerhurst?*, I discuss aspects of the current position of *Chronicle* studies (with some key recent bibliography), and present a full case for my view of the 'D' (and up to a point of the 'E') texts, the relevant ones for present purposes. A similar conclusion on 'D' has been reached independently by Cubbin, *Anglo-Saxon Chronicle. MS D.*

50   As now handsomely re-edited and translated by +Darlington and McGurk, II, pp. 504–5.

51   Among its points in common with 'D' are that it too gives a text of the so-called 'Northern recension' down to 959, though this may in fact have been compiled in a southern context and have no direct connection with the post-1065 annals: Hart, 'Byrhtferth's Northumbrian Chronicle'; Lapidge, 'Byrhtferth of Ramsey and the early sections of the *Historia Regum*'.

annalistic reference to a king's law may well have Ealdred associations. This is important. Wulfstan, another holder of both York and Worcester, was almost certainly the author of the 'agreement ... *to Eadgares lage*' at Oxford, as well as of the '*Cnutes lage*' 'renewed' in 1065. Ealdred was heir to Wulfstan's office and manuscripts. He had a known interest in royal promises, and was long afterwards reputed to have held the Conqueror to the terms of the oath he took when crowned (by Ealdred) on Christmas Day 1066.[52] He could well have been involved in the 1065 episode. In short, the 'D'/'E' *Chronicles* may offer inside information. A regrettable corollary is that the *Anglo-Saxon Chronicles*' only references to written law may derive from men whose interest in it was exceptional rather than typical.

How, then, may these annals be understood? A record of the 1018 proceedings fortunately appears to survive. Corpus Christi College Cambridge MS 201, a mid-eleventh-century volume deriving ultimately from York, contains what purports to be a code of Cnut. But its contents seem to place it between Æthelred's decrees and Cnut's code proper. It bears no date, but opens as follows:

> This is the ordinance (*gerædnes*) which wise men determined and devised according to many good precedents (*bisnum*) ... as soon as King Cnut with the advice of his wise men fully established peace and friendship between the Danes and the English ... The first decree of the wise men was that above all other things they would ... honour one God ... and love King Cnut ... and eagerly observe Edgar's laws (*Eadgares lagan geornlice folgian*).[53]

The probability that this refers to the *Chronicle's* Oxford meeting is enhanced by comparison with Cnut's letter to his subjects from Denmark in 1019–20. This urged 'that the whole people ... firmly keep Edgar's law (*fæstlice Eadgares lage healde*), which all men have determined and sworn to at Oxford'.[54] Cnut himself evidently considered that his regime was founded on an agreement at Oxford about 'Edgar's law'. Unless the 'D' *Chronicle* took its gloss from Cnut's letter, the evidence of annal and proclamation is mutually supportive, and confirms that the first was right to relate the Oxford encounter to 'Edgar's law'. It is at the very least corroboration that 'Edgar's law' somehow underpinned the Anglo-Danish accommodation.

Strangely, however, the Corpus text owes very little to Edgar's extant legislation. In fact, it contains very little substantive law at all. Codes penned by Archbishop Wulfstan were always prone to wordy imprecision. This one was undoubtedly his work; and even by his standards it is short on legal content, long on moral exhortation. Its coverage of issues is much the same as that of the earlier

---

52   ASC 1066D, p. 200, '*Chronica Pontificum. Eccl. Ebor.*', pp. 350–3. Ealdred increasingly attracts the notice of historians of the Old English kingdom's final crisis, and recent work by Mr Michael Hare (chapter 6, below, n. 110) further illuminates his interests. See also Lapidge, 'Ealdred of York'; Nelson, 'Rites of the Conqueror', pp. 389–99; King, 'Ealdred, Archbishop of York'.
53   The text was first identified and linked with the 1018 council by Whitelock, 'Wulfstan and the Laws of Cnut', and 'Wulfstan's authorship of Cnut's Laws'; it is now edited, translated and further discussed by Kennedy, 'Cnut's law code of 1018' (Cn 1018); I follow his translation, p. 72. For further discussion of the MS see chapter 4, pp. 206–10; and of the text, chapter 5, pp. 346–7.
54   Cn. 1020 13.

parts of the code promulgated by Cnut from Winchester at Christmas 1020 or 1021, but it wholly lacks the latter's legal sanctions.[55] Its wording is otherwise closest to Æthelred's 1008 code, especially the version known as 'VI Æthelred', but it omits the specific regulations on military service found even there.[56] Edgar's influence does not extend to the inclusion of arrangements for the financial support of minsters, nor to penalties for the evasion of ecclesiastical taxation, though both appear in Cnut's Winchester code.[57] Wulfstan had a high opinion of Edgar's laws, one result of which has already been seen. But that does not explain why Edgar's inspiration is acknowledged here, as in Cnut's letter and the 'D' *Chronicle*, but not in the final form taken by Cnut's laws, where it is in fact more obvious.[58]

Among possible explanations, the likeliest is that the 'law of Edgar' had the same sort of significance in this context as had the 'law of Edward the Confessor' after the Conquest; with the difference that a written law of Edgar did exist.[59] Each offered a symbol of promised continuity at a time when it seemed gravely threatened. The traditions of the English kingdom could not in 1018 be labelled with the name of the discredited Æthelred, any more than they could bear Harold's name after 1066. Edgar, by contrast, had been a brilliant success. Furthermore, his one 'misdeed', in words from the panegyric inserted by Wulfstan into the 'D' and 'E' *Chronicles*, was that 'he loved evil foreign customs (*ælþeodige unsida*), and brought too firmly heathen manners (*hæþena þeawas*) within this land, and attracted hither foreigners ... harmful people ...'. Edgar friend of heathens is a shock: Wulfstan had just praised his 'love of God's law'. The meaning may be that he showed favour to Scandinavians without too much fuss about their life-style.[60] This would make him an even more suitable patron for an Anglo-Danish *entente*. There is evidence, as has been seen, for Edgar's willingness to grant a measure of legal autonomy to his Danish subjects (p. 126).[61]

---

55   Cf. Cn 1018 2:2 and I Cn 2:2 on defiance of 'church *grið*'; on Wulfstan's legislative aims and methods, see chapter 5, pp. 338–45, 352–65.

56   Cnut 1018 17:1, VI Atr 27:1 and V Atr 22:1: thrice-yearly communion laid down in the first two, but not the third; cf. Cn 1018 22 – 23 (generally on the '*trimoda necessitas*') and VI Atr 32:3 – 33, where detailed prescriptions follow, including some on ship-service not in V Atr. The relationship of this code with V/VI Atr is further discussed in chapter 5, below, pp. 346, 354–5.

57   II Eg 2 – 4:3, I Cn. 8:2 – 11:2.

58   In VIII Atr. 43, the only other Wulfstan code to cite specific '*bisnan*', Æthelstan and Eadmund accompany Edgar. For Wulfstan and Edgar, see Whitelock, 'Wulfstan and the Laws of Cnut', pp. 442–3, and 'Wulfstan's authorship', pp. 82–3.

59   It was thus understood by Whitelock (as above); also by Plummer in *Chronicles Parallel* II, p. 202, who rightly drew attention to William of Malmesbury's remarks on Cnut's laws (below, pp. 137–8), and those of ECf on the laws of Edgar (chapter 5, p. 411).

60   ASC 959DE, p. 115. William of Malmesbury evidently knew this passage, and thought it referred to the effects upon the English of Saxon temper, Flemish flabbiness and Danish drinking: *De Gestis Regum Anglorum* ii 148, I, p. 165.

61   Of conceivable relevance is that the one place where Cn 1018 becomes precise (25 – 27) is its one clear echo of Edgar (III Eg 3, cf. II Cn 15:1–3): penalties for the unjust judge are rehearsed in extra detail, including a provision that 'he who violates just law in the Danelaw shall pay *lahslit*'. *Lahslit* was certainly a feature of Danish jurisprudence, however obscure, and 1018 saw perhaps its first appearance in an official context (its *début* may be in Wulfstan's purported 'Peace of Edward and Guthrum' (EGu 3, 3:2, 4:1, 6 – 6:4, 7:1, 9), and though it appears in V Atr 31, it is not in the corresponding VI Atr 38, which in principle argues that it is a later interpolation in the former; see chapter 5, pp. 332–5).

More pertinent still, there are reasons to think that his policy had been reversed by Æthelred.[62] If Wulfstan's original critique was prompted by Edgar's flexibility, he could perhaps now come to terms with it as a basis for the reconciliation of Englishman and Dane.

This explanation would mean that the function of 'Edgar's law' in 1018 was in some sense symbolic. The same rationale could account for the 'renewal' of 'Cnut's law' at the end of the 1065 rebellion. There is this time no extant text to illuminate – or confuse – the issue. If anything written was adduced at all, the assumption is that this was Cnut's code itself, although the part of it aimed directly at redress of grievances (chapter 5, pp. 361–2) may also be meant; and since most twelfth-century legal *apocrypha* claiming to reflect pre-conquest usage were in fact ascribed to Cnut rather than Edward the Confessor, 'Cnut's law' may even have had the same general meaning in 1065 that it had later.[63] Whatever its form, its significance for the Northumbrian rebels was presumably that it represented the pattern of northern rule which Tostig's government had subverted. Cnut might have stood for the days before Tostig brought intensive southern government to the north, as King John did afterwards and with similar results. Alternatively, or concurrently, Scandinavian elements among the rebels could have been thinking specifically of the concessions to their customs enshrined by Cnut. The *Vita Ædwardi*, which is sympathetic to Tostig, and the 'C' *Chronicle*, which is hostile, both imply that his law and order policy cut across northern traditions. In the one recorded lawsuit from pre-conquest Northumbria, Tostig arraigned a man, 'whose kin and friends offered much and promised more to the earl lest he be punished by death [for his evil misdeeds]'; this may imply not bribery but a reparative approach to crime better attuned to northern society.[64]

The importance of the *Chronicle* references to legislation is that they bring out its political relevance. Each sets a king's law in the context of resolved tension. In 1014 Æthelred returned to his subjects promising, in return for their future fidelity, to 'reform (*betan*) everything which they hated'; the promise, as will appear (pp. 342–4) probably bore fruit in a code citing the 'bisnan' of previous kings.[65] The 'D'/'E' *Chronicles* are testimony – if in some degree specialists' testimony – that in 1018 and 1065 legal 'precedents' underwrote a subject's sense of political security as well as of legal rights. However this sense arose, it was

---

62   Chapter 5, pp. 318–19, 328–9; Lund, 'King Edgar and the Danelaw'; also Stenton, *Anglo-Saxon England*, pp. 371–2.

63   On twelfth-century appeals to Cnut's law, Hudson, 'Administration, Family and Perceptions (Appendix)', pp. 94–8. Barlow, *Edward the Confessor*, p. 237, suggests that the DE *Chronicle* (pp. 192–3) should have located the confrontation at Oxford not Northampton (cf. 'C', p. 192), so raising the intriguing question why both the 1018 and 1065 assemblies should have met there.

64   ASC 1065C, p. 192; *Life of Edward* i 5, 7, pp. 32, 50; LS 173. Kapelle, *Norman Conquest of the North*, pp. 94–101, superseding earlier treatments of the 1065 episode, prefers to think of fiscal grievances, citing *JW* II, pp. 598–9, on the 'huge tribute which Tostig had unjustly levied'. It may be noted that, of the three ring-leaders named by John, one had an English name and two had English patronymics: it was not just Danes who were outraged by his regime. In any event, Plummer's understanding of 'Cnut's law' as indicating 'political amnesty', *Chronicles Parallel* II, p. 252, is this time wide of the target.

65   The promises of better 'laga/lage' by William Rufus, ASC 1088E, 1093E, pp. 223, 227, need not of course have any bearing on written legislation.

expressed as respect for a king's laws in general. Codes as wholes may have meant at least as much as the sum of their constituent decrees.

Many political communities have vested their identity in their 'good old law', often without any very clear idea of what it amounted to. But it is again instructive to compare Anglo-Saxon transactions with themes in Carolingian history. Chapter 2 found that Carolingian kings made repeated promises of *lex* to their subjects (pp. 48–9). Whatever meaning *lex* had in this context, three things are relatively clear. First, it embodied a notion of agreement between king and subject; *lex* expressed royal *fidelitas* in return for that of the people. Second, it was to that extent concessionary: *lex* offered something which subjects were entitled to expect. Third, it usually deferred to a similar relationship between the progenitors of king and subject alike, sometimes explicitly to the formers' 'leges' as in 869: it promised continuity. A theme so often echoed at so many crises could have created a need if it did not at first meet one. The evidence does not compel belief that English and Frankish experience was similar. It rarely does. Even so, much can be learned from juxtaposition. In each sphere, the political importance of *lex* is suggested by the critical moments when it was proferred. The *lage* of the Anglo-Saxon episodes are those of kings known to have legislated. Each body of evidence makes a complementary contribution to the impression that on either side of the Channel written royal law played a political role apart from and perhaps above its legal content. It helped to assure a subject of his place in the state.

Charles the Bald's earliest proclamation has been called 'the first Charter of the Middle Ages'. In so far as guarantees about *lex* were then and thereafter linked with undertakings not to remove anyone's *'honor'* without just judgement – a central element in many more medieval 'Charters' than *Magna Carta* itself – the proposition has some force.[66] In the 1810 official publication of the *Statutes of the Realm*, *Magna Carta* lost its accustomed first place to its main model, Henry I's 1100 Charter, which resembled Frankish proclamations in its issue at his Coronation and in its promise of 'law' – the 'laga Eadwardi'.[67] The Record Commission could, perhaps should, have gone further back yet. Beyond Henry's citation of 'Edward's law' lay no more precise but no less serious evocations of the legislation of the latter's grandfather, Edgar, and of his stepfather, Cnut, in the aftermath respectively of a conquest and of a Northerners' revolt. As with gossamer, the mesh is tenuous but visible from a selected angle. If the *lage* of Edgar and Cnut had the concessionary purport of Carolingian *lex*, that is this book's first hint of how far the political dramas of the century and a half after 1066 were already choreographed in the 180 years before.

---

66   Lot and Halphen, *La règne de Charles le Chauve*, p. 97. Cf. *Cap.* 254:3, 205:6, 243 (*Ad. Lud:* 3), 275:3, 282:2; and Reynolds, *Kingdoms and Communities*, pp. 241, 285–96.
67   *Statutes of the Realm* I, pp. xxix, 1–2, 9–13; CHn cor 13. Thus far (but *only* thus far!) Professor Holt's stimulating paper, 'Origins of the Constitutional Tradition in England'.

(iii) The Twelfth Century

One glance at the contents page of Antonia Gransden's *Historical Writing in England c.550 to c.1307* reveals the transformation of the historiographical scene in twelfth-century England. It displays, quite suddenly, 'a wider historical curiosity than had been seen in England, or perhaps anywhere else in Europe, since the time of Bede'; and 'the greatest advances in the study and understanding of Anglo-Saxon history . . . before the nineteenth century'.[68] Chapters 4 and 6 will show (pp. 228–53, 465–75) that the first if not indeed the second of these claims may emphatically be made of approaches to the Anglo-Saxon legal records. That is why a study with a natural terminus of 1066 must give so much attention to the twelfth century. Most historians of the age actually have disappointingly little to say about legislation before their time (or even during it, chapter 14). But there is one exception, and he is most instructive.

'In the . . . reign of the most glorious King Edgar, who strenuously governed the whole realm with holy laws (*sanctis legibus*) . . . '; the opening phrases of Eadmer's *Historia Novorum* sound promising. But confidence that he was thinking of what are now known as Edgar's law-codes evaporates in the face of the famous passage, just a few pages on, about the 'usus atque leges' which William brought from Normandy. By these he seems to mean the king's insistence on his right to supervise contacts with Rome, to endorse the excommunication of his barons, and to vet, even initiate, decrees by primatial councils; in other words, those 'novelties' in relations between *regnum* and *sacerdotium* that inaugurate (as Eadmer intended they should) the wearisome saga of 'Twelfth-Century Church and State'.[69] Liebermann did this passage the honour of inclusion in his *Gesetze*. But there is no trace of such 'laws' in the copious conciliar legislation of Normandy before 1066 or England afterwards, nor in William's extant decrees. When Henry II *did* seek to enforce such 'customs' by a written code in 1164, his mother Mathilda (who was well-placed to comment) opined that this was precisely his error; 'for that was not done in the past (*a prioribus*)'.[70] Even if Eadmer did mean specific legislation by Edgar's 'sanctis legibus', that is no evidence that he knew Edgar's codes. He could have drawn conclusions from the *Vita Oswaldi* or from Osbern's *Vita Dunstani*. Yet Osbern's only reference to written laws is in the context of monastic reform, and may have described the *Regularis Concordia*, whose prologue and epilogue stood in

---

68   Southern, 'Place of England in the Twelfth Century Renaissance', p. 162; Campbell, 'Twelfth-Century Views of the Anglo-Saxon Past', p. 131 (209). What follows owes much to Dr Gransden's prehensile scholarship.

69   Eadmer, *Historia Novorum*, pp. 3, 9–10. *Gesetze* I, p. 520; but cf. *ibid.* III, p. 292.

70   'Epistola' lxxvi, *Materials for the History of Thomas Becket* V, p. 149. The most recent treatment of Eadmer's passage sensibly takes 'leges' to mean 'rules': Barlow, *English Church 1066–1154*, p. 279. For Norman synodical legislation, see Foreville, 'Synod of the Province of Rouen', with Bates, *Normandy before 1066*, pp. 197–99, 204–6, 226–8; on England, *Councils and Synods* I II, pp. 591–624. As the editor notes, the canons of the 1080 Council of Lillebonne use both 'consuetudines' and 'leges' for episcopal 'rights': *Ecclesiastical History of Orderic Vitalis* v 5, III, pp. 30–1, n. 1. For the sense of 'episcopales leges' in Wl ep., see Morris, 'William I and the church courts'.

Edgar's name, and which has a king with a scroll as the focus of its frontispiece in its Canterbury copy.[71]

Eadmer had learned to be wary of kings in leading roles. In any case, his *Historia* was not much concerned with pre-conquest affairs. More might be hoped of John of Worcester, especially given the legal interests of one or more Anglo-Saxon bishops of the see. But John also disappoints. His celebrated paean to Alfred includes 'iustitia' and withholds few other virtues, but offers nothing more concrete than what he excerpted from Asser.[72] Nor is anything made of Cnut's laws. This is the more remarkable given John's inherited version of the 1018 meeting, and his probable part in preserving Cnut's second or 'Roman' letter for posterity.[73] But it is Edgar's case that again raises special problems. No scholar who has failed to escape embroilment in the tussles over what Edgar did or did not do for Worcester Priory needs reminding of its interest in his exploits. Praise for this friend of monks and 'rex pacificus' could not be overdone. John duly plundered the *Chronicle* of Marianus, his framework, so as to make Edgar the English equivalent of Romulus, Cyrus, Alexander and Charlemagne.[74] How seriously, in that light, should one take the possible references to his law-giving?

> Each winter and spring he used to investigate carefully within his kingdom, travelling right through all the English provinces, how the justice of the laws and the statutes he had decreed (*legum iura et statuta decretorum*) were observed by his leading men (*principibus*) lest the poor suffer prejudicial oppression from the powerful.

It can be argued that not all such claims are to be dismissed out of hand. But a degree of doubt is certainly in order, especially given the immediately preceding passage's description of Edgar's annual summer circumnavigtion of the island with a total of 3600 ships, 1200 for each coast. If the allusion to his justice raises fewer eyebrows, it is by that token more conventional. In fact it is an elaboration of the *Vita Oswaldi*. Even the statement, buried in the verbal foliage, that Edgar 'instituted just laws (*leges rectas*)' comes to little. For John, as has been seen, used an *Anglo-Saxon Chronicle* which introduced 'Eadgares lage' into its account of 1018, and his finely-tuned ear for the panegyrical repertoire could do the rest.[75] Nor is faith in his precision enhanced when he says that Harold II

---

71   See nn. 39, 44, and for Eadmer's knowledge of the *Vita Oswaldi*, Southern, *Saint Anselm and his Biographer*, pp. 279–81, 283–4; 'Vita S. Dunstani auct. Osbern.' i 34, 35, pp. 110, 112. The relevant MS of *Regularis Concordia* is BL, Cotton MS Tiberius A. iii (Ker, *Catalogue* no. 186); for the frontispiece see the plate in *Regularis Concordia*, ed. Symons.

72   *JW* II, pp. 352–3, and cf. pp. 332–3 with Asser 106, pp. 92–3. On the construction of this source, I follow (pending the new edition's introductory volume) Brett, 'John of Worcester'.

73   *JW* II, pp. 512–19; Cn. 1027 survives only here and in *William of Malmesbury, Gesta Regum* ii 183, I, pp. 221–4. Dr Brett argues, pp. 113–16, that Worcester (if not its chronicler) was supplying William rather than *vice versa*. For a suggestion that the then bishop of Worcester was the letter's actual author, see chapter 5, pp. 348–9.

74   *JW* II, p. 424–5, and *passim* pp. 408–25. The literature cited for the *Altitonantis* charter and its implications (S 731) will no doubt extend *ad infinitum*; the fundamental point remains the depth of twelfth-century Worcester's interest in Edgar.

75   *JW* II, pp. 424–7, 412–13; above, nn. 39, 48–50.

marked his accession by 'abolishing unjust laws (*leges iniquas*), laying down just ones' and ordering a campaign against all sorts of malefactors and disturbers of the peace.[76] It is not unlikely that Harold followed up his coronation oath with an exemplary law and order policy. It is just possible, but not likely, that he did so by 'laying down just laws' in writing, and that they fell victim to William's conquest. The general impression given by the early-twelfth century is that the historiographical cloudburst irrigated the kind of rhetorical enthusiasm about royal justice seen above, but generated little more interest in written law than the age before.

Attempts to prove negatives are as tedious to write as to read. But one purpose they do serve is to isolate exceptions. William of Malmesbury is so much an exception to the pattern observed so far as to make the reticence of his contemporaries seem stranger still. Like Henry of Huntingdon (though unlike John), he mentioned the laws of Æthelberht, but this could have come from Bede. Again like Henry, he might be thought to refer to Edgar's codes, but neither reference is any more exact than those considered above.[77] Three other passages are a different matter. First there is Ine: signs of his greatness in God's business were patronage of Glastonbury and 'legislation for the correction of his people's behaviour (*leges ad corrigendos mores in populum latae*) which to this day vividly reflect his purity'. Almost four and a half centuries after its promulgation, Ine's code makes its *début* in a non-legal text.[78] Second, Alfred: 'though laws be silent amidst arms, as the man said (*leges inter arma sileant*, a Ciceronian *topos* typical both of William and of the context), he laid down laws amidst the clash of arms which accustomed his men to both divine worship and military discipline'. There follows an account of the institution of hundred, tithing, surety and pledge, designed to curb the criminal habits acquired by natives from invading barbarians, and resulting in such peace that golden arm-rings hung at cross-roads were not seized by even the greediest travellers. The text has aroused near-unanimous derision (chapter 1, pp. 5, 14, 18). Despite the now familiar image of improbable social order, it is very important indeed. But that is best shown by discussing the institutions themselves (chapter 9). All that can be said here is that, at the very least, knowledge of Alfred's first law is implied.[79] Finally, Cnut's 'Roman' letter (which ended by promising strict enforcement of church dues 'secundum leges') is rounded off thus:

76   *JW* II, pp. 600–1; cf. the same source, pp. 570–1, on the consequences of the restoration of Godwine. On the general point, the 'iura' of William I in *Orderic* iv, II, pp. 192–3, and probably the 'leges', *ibid.*, pp. 208–9, come from William of Poitiers: see n. 41.

77   *Gesta Regum* i 9, ii 155, I, pp. 13, 176–7. *Henry of Huntingdon* iii 20, v 26, pp. 166–7, 322–3; Henry's Edgar obituary, a versification presumably inspired by Wulfstan's rhythmical prose in *Chronicle* 'E' (above, n. 60), calls him 'alter Salomon, legum pater, orbita pacis'. Henry's pre-conquest studies, otherwise almost as whole-hearted as William's, led to no further accounts of Anglo-Saxon legislation even as vague as this.

78   *Gesta Regum* i 35, I, p. 34.

79   *Gesta Regum* ii 122, I, pp. 129–30; Af 1 – 1:8. For laws and arms see above, pp. 128–9, nn. 41, 44–7. Cf. Whitelock's appraisal, hardly warmer than Stubbs's or Maitland's, 'William of Malmesbury on the works of King Alfred', pp. 84–5. A point that can be made in William's favour even at this early stage is that the *Quadripartitus* version of Af 1:8, which may be what William saw (see n. 82), speaks of 'plegius' and 'infractura plegii/vadii'.

Action matched word. For he ordered all laws laid down by earlier kings (*omnes leges ab antiquis regibus … latas*), and especially by Æthelred his predecessor, to be observed for all time under threat of the royal fine (*sub interminatione regiae mulctae*); the keeping of which … is sworn under the name of King Edward even now, not because he decreed but because he observed them.[80]

It is almost inconceivable that William could have known what Cnut's laws owed to Æthelred's without reading both. Æthelred's inspiration was never admitted by Cnut, and Wulfstan manuscripts withold his name even from his own codes (chapter 5, pp. 333–4).[81] The passage proves what a knowledge of Ine's and Alfred's laws unparalleled in narrative sources already implies. William's dedicated research into the English past extended to careful perusal of a legal collection.[82]

By almost any standards William of Malmesbury was a great historian. In the panoply of creative gifts needed for the recovery and resurrection of a recalcitrant past, he was unsurpassed by any medieval Englishman except Bede.[83] But he was technically no better equipped to explore pre-conquest law than his

---

80   *Gesta Regum* ii 183, I, p. 224.

81   Æthelred is credited with his own I – III Atr, which feature in at least two of three twelfth-century MSS; but unlike the codes in Wulfstan MSS, these say nothing about church dues. See next n.

82   But if William knew so much about pre-conquest law, why did he not say more? Assuming from the above evidence for his awareness of at least three other legal texts that *his* Edgar passage bespeaks direct knowledge of this king's codes, why are other law-makers (Edward, Edmund, above all Æthelstan, his and Malmesbury's hero) left out? It seems reasonable to think that Wihtræd's laws at least would have featured had William seen the *Textus Roffensis* (cf. *Gesta Regum* i 15, I, p. 17). He could have read either of the other twelfth-century collections, perhaps especially *Quadripartitus* given its circulation and its address to the same court circles as furnished William with patrons (chapter 4, pp. 243–4; see also chapter 5, pp. 411–14); yet these collections also contain laws which he ignored. On the other hand, the first part of BL, Cotton MS Nero A.i (chapter 4, pp. 224–8), which otherwise fits the bill admirably, lacks the Æthelred codes that William must have known; and surviving Wulfstan manuscripts of Æthelred material also contain laws of Æthelstan and Edmund on precisely the issue of church dues that was foremost in William's mind when writing about Cnut (I As, I Em, chapter 5, pp. 295, 309). Common sense suggests that he saw a manuscript or manuscripts restricted to laws of Alfred–Ine, Edgar, Æthelred and Cnut that no longer survive(s). Alternative possibilities are: (i) he used only *Quadripartitus*, but regarded Cnut as subsuming the work of all his predecessors (as in effect he says, and as is more or less the case, chapter 5, pp. 355–6); Alfred–Ine got in as forming the 'base-text' of early English law, and Edgar as one whose law-making was brought out, however vaguely, by William's sources. (ii) William alone of medieval sources cites Æthelweard's *Chronicle*. The only known manuscript of Æthelweard is the burnt BL, Cotton MS Otho A.x, where it was bound up with Paul the Deacon's *Historia Langobardorum*, another text William knew (see n. 86), and with 'IX Atr' (Ker, *Catalogue* no. 170, chapter 4, pp. 258–9). While there is no evidence that these texts originally belonged together, it is remotely conceivable that they did, and that the MS was from Malmesbury. If this were so, William could have put 'IX Atr' alongside some such collection as Nero A.i(A), and so drawn the correct conclusion about Cnut's sources. William's knowledge and handling of Anglo-Saxon law are fully analysed in Professor Thomson's forthcoming edition of *Gesta Regum* for Oxford Medieval Texts.

83   William's standing is now recovering from the 'mixed feeling' with which Stubbs left him in the preface to his edition of *Gesta Regum* II, p. cxli: Southern, 'Aspects of the European Tradition of Historical Writing: 4', pp. 253–6; Thomson, 'William of Malmesbury as historian'; Campbell, 'Some Twelfth-century views', pp. 136–7 (214–15), 145–6 (222–3). Modern historians have a more natural sympathy with writers who constitute 'sources', like Bede. As Stubbs said (II, p. cxxxiii), William's contribution to knowledge of Anglo-Saxon times is 'infinitesimal', in that most of the sources he used survive (cf. Campbell, p. 138 (216); Gransden, p. 178, though also a forthcoming vindication of his lost Æthelstan source by Michael Wood). But this is to imply that he was as badly off as today's historians for post-Bedan materials; which in turn makes his achievement all the more astounding.

contemporaries. Their use of *Chronicles* show that John and Henry were equally *au fait* with the language. Henry might be expected to have had easier access to 'governmental' records and casts of mind through his patron, Bishop Alexander of Lincoln, who has himself been credited with a very interesting glossary of Anglo-Saxon legal terms (chapter 14).[84] Nevertheless, there is one good reason why William's interest in the subject should stand out. He is the first Englishman known to have closely studied a manuscript of Roman law. Bodleian MS Arch. Selden B.16 is largely in his own hand. It consists of a remarkable digest of Roman history, displaying one of William's several 'modern' qualities, his capacity to draw lessons from textual comparison. The story is brought up to date with lists of emperors, Byzantine, Carolingian and German, and of French kings after 840. Then a new section opens as follows:

> Because we are anxious not to omit whatever we could find about the rulers of Italy and Rome, it seems appropriate (*congruum*) to add the laws of the Romans; not those which Justinian made (that would be a huge labour) but those collected by Theodosius the younger, son of Arcadius, from Constantine's time to his own, under the title of each emperor.

It is explained that the collection includes an 'explanatio' of the laws that need one, the Novels of some fifth-century emperors and the *Institutes* of the juris-consults Gaius and Paul. What William in fact presents is a text of the 'Breviary' of Alaric (chapter 2, pp. 36, 55, 63–4), less its first book, its few excerpts from the codes of Gregory and Hermogenian, and its solitary sentence from Papinian (i.e. the beginning and end of the whole).[85]

Fascinating, and potentially very important, questions arise as to how William got hold of a manuscript of the 'Breviary', one moreover which, for all its late date and truncated condition, is among the best texts of the collection to survive. But these questions must be deferred until the possible 'sources' of early English law are reviewed in chapter 13. More immediately relevant is the link between William's conviction that knowledge of its law was 'congruum' in a *florilegium* of the Roman achievement and his investigation of pre-conquest law as one aspect of the *Gesta Regum Anglorum*. As has been said (pp. 111, 118), historians of the early medieval West, however otherwise articulate about royal justice, tended to fight shy of legislation itself. But William took the 'wars/laws' theme to the point of including admittedly limited accounts of royal law-making in the text of his '*Gesta*' ('deeds', usually warlike ones). It is no accident that the parts of Europe where legislation is reported in *historiae* as a matter of course are just those which saw the most precocious development of written 'barbarian' law from the outset, and the most elaborate efforts to set it on a par with Civil and

---

84   'Expositiones Vocabulorum', *Red Book of the Exchequer* III, pp. ccclvi–ccclxv, 1032–9.
85   f. 140a; quoted by Stubbs, *Gesta Regum* I, pp. cxxxvii–cxxxviii, and by Thomson, *William of Malmesbury*, p. 63. Note that in the historical section of the MS William cross-references the emperors responsible for Novels in the legal section: ff. 106r, 108v. For the MS as a whole see Stubbs, pp. cxxxi–cxl; Thomson, pp. 25–6, 30–1, 62–4, 66–7, 92–3, 176–7, 200; it was written in 1129 (Thomson, pp. 176–7), after the first recension of *Gesta Regum*, so the above argument demands that William pondered the material for some years before transcribing it. On at least one explanation of his access to the 'Breviary', that is no problem at all (see reference below).

Canonical traditions during and after William's time (chapter 2, pp. 39, 44–5, chapter 6, pp. 468–70). Historical sensitivity to *lex scripta* was an aspect of a written law culture, another sign of the longer shadows cast over southern Europe by the model of Rome. The implication is that William alone of his contemporaries looked closely at the law-making of Old English kings because he had an unparalleled acquaintance with Roman law itself.

William's work cannot be seen as a symptom of awakening English interest in Roman jurisprudence as early as 1125. The *iurisperiti* who were assembling the three great codices of English law at just this time (chapter 4, pp. 228–53, chapter 6, pp. 465–8) had been exposed to the 'Learned Laws' but of the Canon rather than Civil variety.[86] But it is still instructive to see what two members of William's audience made of Alfred's legislation. A writer who shared his patron, political views and historical genius (even if in the use he made of it he was Lucifer to William's Michael) was Geoffrey of Monmouth. He averred that:

> It was [Dunuallo Molmutius] who established among the Britons the so-called Molmutine laws which are famed among the English to this day ... [He also established sanctuary in the temples and 'cities', a privilege which covered the roads leading to them and apparently the ploughs of peasants too. These were ratified by his son Belinus, who clarified and reconstructed the four roads in question, fixing penalties for violent crime thereon] ... If anyone wishes to know all he decreed on these matters let him read the Molmutine laws which Gildas *historicus* translated from Welsh into Latin and King Alfred from Latin into English.

There is more: the multi-talented Marcia, wife of King Guithelinus, 'laid down a law which the Britons call Marcian. This too King Alfred translated, and it is called *Merchenelage* in English'.[87] Such were the 'Laws of the Ancient Britons' that Coke was to brandish at the Early Stuarts. Exactly what Geoffrey was up to will never be agreed. Too little is known of his life. Massive though his impact was, he never really established a *genre* that might have cast retrospective light on his message and medium. But there is little doubt of the relation borne by these passages to what other writers of the period were saying about English law. The four great roads are an unmistakable echo of Henry of Huntingdon. The 'Mercian' Law picks up the strand in early-twelfth-century legal treatises that dwelt on the variety of English custom; roads and their peace were another of their obsessions; and in either case the contrast with genuine Anglo-Saxon

---

86   Thomson, *William of Malmesbury*, pp. 63–4, gives the (perhaps unintended) impression that William had direct knowledge of the Justinianic *Corpus*. This need not be so: in the Selden MS, f. 135r, to which Thomson refers, William contrasts Hugh of Fleury's unfavourable view of Justinian with Paul the Deacon's; the following passage on Justinian's laws is quoted from Paul, continuing, like Paul, with the building of Santa Sophia.

87   *Historia Regum Britanniae* 34, 39, 47, pp. 24, 26–7, 31. Modern trends in Geoffrey studies, abandoning the hopeless quest for his 'true' sources (among which the Molmutine and Marcian Laws have not been enrolled by even the least sceptical scholars) in favour of setting what he says and does not say in its contemporary cultural context, began with Tatlock's sparkling *Legendary History of Britain* – for law see pp. 278–83. Subsequent landmarks include: Brooke, 'Geoffrey of Monmouth' (law, pp. 79–80); Flint, 'The *Historia Regum* ... parody and its purpose' (law, pp. 450–1); and Gillingham, 'Context and Purposes of Geoffrey of Monmouth' (law, etc., pp. 109–10); but it took a distinguished Welsh holder of the chair of medieval history at Oxford to point out that Geoffrey's was the first great historical work written at Oxford: Davies, *Matter of Britain*, p. 3. See also next n.

material is marked (chapter 5, pp. 409–13).[88] The role of Alfred himself surely reflects his emerging reputation as the 'founder of English laws (*Anglicarum legum conditor*)' in the Ramsey Chronicle's words, a development upon which William of Malmesbury may have been a major influence.[89] It might not go too far to read Geoffrey's remarks as a distorted mirror of live legal debate, though one perhaps confined to a small intellectual world.

The other writer to deserve passing attention in this context is Gaimar. His *Estoire des Engleis* was scarcely a masterpiece of world literature like the *Historia Regum Britanniae*. But its dogged and at times poetic Anglo-Norman versification of the English past is remarkable in its way – not least in offering the nearest one gets to an uncloistered twelfth-century view of English history. One of the things he says about Alfred is that:

> He caused a book to be written in English
> Of adventures and of laws
> (*des aventures e des leis*),
> And of battles in the land,
> And of kings who made war.

It has long been recognized that this sounds uncommonly like the Parker codex, where *Chronicle* and Alfred–Ine law-book are bound together, and more recently seen that the same goes for *Chronicle* 'G', a copy of Parker in this and other respects which was almost certainly made at Winchester (chapter 4, pp. 172–81). Gaimar also describes 'Chronicles, a big book', kept chained at Winchester by order of King Alfred who had owned it. He seems to have begun work in Hampshire. More to the point, Southwick Priory, which possessed 'G' by the thirteenth century, was endowed by Ralph fitz Gilbert, husband of Gaimar's patroness, Lady Constance. This is an odd coincidence, perhaps *too* odd. Gaimar may well have seen, even if he did not use, this *Chronicle*.[90] His reference anyway shows that his knowledge of Alfred's laws went beyond what he could read in Geoffrey. This suffices to rank him with William rather than John of Worcester

---

88 *Henry of Huntingdon* i 7, pp. 22–5. Geoffrey's prominence in the largely Anglo-Norman sources listed for 'Strasse', *Gesetze* II, pp. 673–5, is noteworthy; also his importance to the London collection of 'Leges Anglorum' (cf. chapter 4, pp. 237–8), remarked by Ullmann, 'Influence of Geoffrey of Monmouth', pp. 258–63.

89 *Chron. Ram.* 5, p. 13. But the reference to Alfred's laws in the *Annals of St Neots* (above, p. 120, n. 10) owes no more to William's phraseology than it does to Asser or indeed to the code's contents. Other Bury sources seem to describe the laws of Cnut: Hermann, 'Liber de Miraculis S. Eadmundi' 16, I, p.46 (Winchester misread as Windsor?), and more probably Samson, 'Opus de Miraculis S. Eadmundi' vi, I, p. 126. There may be a house tradition here.

90 *Estoire des Engleis*, pp. ix, li–lv; lns 3445–8, cf. lns 2327–34. Gaimar's Chronicle sources are sifted by Plummer, *Chronicles Parallel* II, pp. lviii–lx, and by Whitelock, *EHD I*, pp. 119–20. Here one can only observe another 'coincidence', that lns 6461–72 cite a 'Book of Washingborough', which granted poetic licence and Gaimar's ability to use Bede, could have been very like a source of *Chronicle* 'E' (above, p. 130), when Washingborough was (i) a cell of Peterborough and (ii) linked with Kirkstead, another recipient of fitz Gilbert benefactions: *Estoire des Engleis*, ed. Bell, p. lv. The issue now needs reassessment in the light of Short, 'Gaimar's Epilogue', pp. 328–36; Professor Short makes a good case for Gaimar's knowledge of one of the 'E' sources, but is needlessly negative about the reference to Alfred's laws, and misses the relevance of 'G's' Southwick provenance. Professor Gillingham has recently turned his insights on Gaimar, to Gaimar's and everyone else's profit, 'Kingship, Chivalry and Love in the earliest history written in French'; see also Short, 'Patrons and Polyglots', pp. 243–4.

or Henry of Huntingdon as a witness to post-conquest interest in pre-conquest legislation.[91]

For all of that, William of Malmesbury was the only historian in the first three-quarters of the twelfth century who made a sustained effort to excavate and reassemble the Anglo-Saxon legislative legacy. One sign of this is that, with Geoffrey, he supplied later ages with what narrative information they had on the subject.[92] To that extent William looked back. Yet in another way he looked ahead. One thesis of this book is that the only unquestionable change in twelfth-century English law was in the nature of the evidence for it. Law by 1200 was a great deal more visible (to the modern eye) than it was in 1100 or even 1150. It is suggested here that William's unique effort to do historical justice to Anglo-Saxon law was sparked off by his personal encounter with that of Rome. If not symptomatic of his own age, therefore, he foreshadows, even symbolizes, what would happen when makers of English law in the next generation came to experience the legal discipline purveyed in universities and ecclesiastical courts by civil and canon lawyers. He signals, that is to say, the way that the 'Common Law' would be articulated in conscious response and ultimate rivalry to the 'Learned Laws' (chapter 6, pp. 474–5, chapter 14).

William apart, the gulf between what is known of justice from narrative evidence and what can be read in legislation itself remains almost as wide in the rich historiography of Henry I's era as in the impoverished Anglo-Saxon output. In the second half of the twelfth century it began to close. But throughout this book as little as possible is said of developments under Henry II until they can finally be set against the background that they have usually been allowed to throw out of focus. Let it suffice for now that one of the clearest marks of changed conditions in the Angevin Age is the appearance of a historian, Roger of Howden, who is also the major, sometimes the sole, source for the edicts of Henry II and Richard I (chapter 14). In the three centuries separating him from Asser, however, there are good reasons to doubt whether *lex scripta* was more than a bright but distant vision for historians. *Lex* and *lagu* can, probably at times do, mean written law. At least as often they can hardly have that meaning. Usually, it is impossible to be sure what they mean. But there are no grounds for doubting the interest of historians in royal justice. This section has aimed to do more than entrench the negative conclusion that, were histories the only evidence available, little would be known about the early history of English law. It is meant also to introduce the four stimuli that incited rulers to accept judicial responsibilities,

---

91   The bizarre verse 'Descriptio Britanniae' in two MSS, not Gaimar's work (Bell, pp. xii–xiii) but printed as an epilogue in his Rolls Series edition, has at lns 70–90 a lawgiving king of Wessex who conquered Northumbria and created the English shires; the context suggests this was Ecgberht, Alfred or Æthelstan (if anyone). Also noteworthy is that Gaimar has passages on laws of Edgar and Edward the Confessor, lns 3562–74, 4855–60; these might invalidate the Alfred reference but for its singular mention of the MS's structure.

92   Thus, the twelfth/thirteenth century 'Annales de Wintonia', pp. 10, 15, make Alfred the translator of 'Leges Britonum', and also the author of the 'leges et iura' endorsed in 1018. The second assertion may be deduced from the first; another possibility is that the author, who did use William (and was probably, not certainly, Richard of Devizes, Gransden, p. 252), could not accept that Cnut was indebted to the wretched 'Ethelred', and accordingly emended to read 'Elured'.

and perhaps to make use of writing in doing so. Foremost among these was the example of God's holy people. A second was the general sense that that other people of destiny, the Romans, specialized in the art of law as in that of war. Third was an awareness that an early medieval people was identified by its law. Last, pulling all four together, was the growing feeling that royal law should *look* like the Learned Laws of God's Church and Rome's Empire. Such forces might prompt intense legalistic activity before they urged any final commitment to written law. In early England they did.

2   Anglo-Saxon Lawsuits

Records of actual cases are the other place where references to written law would be expected. The law should have had a more direct relevance for judgements passed on disputes or crimes than it did for historians before Roger of Howden. Yet it can be said at once that law reports are more deafeningly silent than the narratives considered so far. Not a single legal decision reached in Anglo-Saxon (or indeed Anglo-Norman) England deferred explicitly to an extant decree, let alone quoted one. This is a notable point. Texts from southern Europe in the same period *do* cite law-codes, often by chapter and verse (chapter 2, pp. 81, 88). The contrast between English writers and Isidore or Paul thus has its exact counterpart in the behaviour of those recording lawsuits. Like the historians, however, case-law has other, ultimately more important, lessons. It is the primary referent for Parts III and IV of this book. For that reason, this discussion is concerned with more than what sources do not say. Notice is also taken of the overall shape of this body of information, and how it came to exist. At the same time, select cases are used to introduce the salient themes of Part III.[93]

Legal history without reference to law as applied is nowadays seen as a contradiction in terms. The failure of the Anglo-Saxon lawsuits as a group to attract the study that their importance, not to say fascination, deserves is one of the leading mysteries of the whole subject. There is no shortage of material, even if it is scarce by Frankish standards, and still more by those of southern Europe. Rigid application of the criteria that a case must be seen to involve some sort of judicial process, and must demonstrably have been heard before 14 October 1066, still produces 179 or 180 examples. Ninety-five/six are recorded in charters or *notitiae*, seven come from Domesday Book, there are fifty-one in cartulary chronicles (histories of particular churches which draw on charters and *miracula* in varying proportions), and twenty-six can be extracted from narrative sources

---

93   To save space and duplicated effort, Anglo-Saxon lawsuits are cited throughout this book by their number in my 'Handlist' [LS], and a concordance is provided in the Bibliography's Subsidiary Source Index (i) (as well as full references below for sample 'close-up' cases). LS supplies a summary of each case, an approximate date, and a reference to the most appropriate edition. It fully discusses the criteria for selection, with some attention to episodes thus omitted; it treats in greater detail such issues, more cursorily reviewed here, as the authorship of reports; and there is a more copious bibliography of previous work in the area. My 'Charters, Law and the Settlement of Disputes' takes up particular themes (notably the nature of proof and the role of the 'state') with reference to two sets of cases, *viz.* LS 11–12 and 45–6 + 69, not discussed below.

like the *Chronicles* or the lives and miracles of saints. Each category of evidence has its own problems. But only two cases raise a serious suspicion that they may be fiction rather than fact.[94]

(i) Helmstan

All but nineteen of the 179/80 cases post-date 871, so fall within the period covered by this book. One of the earliest of these 160 is also one of the best-known. The story of Helmstan is told in a letter to King Edward the Elder. It was probably written by the Ealdorman Ordlaf who somewhat incongruously also appears in the narrative in the third person. Helmstan, evidently a figure of social standing, was, in modern constabulary jargon, a 'villain'. When he stole a belt, Æthelhelm Higa was among several to exploit the situation, and laid claim to his land at Fonthill (Wiltshire). Helmstan appealed to Ordlaf, his sponsor at Confirmation, who duly had a word with King Alfred. As a result Helmstan was allowed to put his case, and a body of important figures, including Ordlaf, investigated it. They found that he had a royal charter confirming Fonthill's sale by one Æthelthryth to one Oswulf, and that he was thus 'nearer the oath (*aðe ðæs ðe near*)'. Æthelhelm dissenting, the case came to Alfred, 'who was washing his hands'. In tones reminiscent of Asser, Alfred asked Æthelhelm why he objected to the decision and fixed a day for the oath-taking. But Helmstan's troubles were not over; it seems that he needed Ordlaf's assistance in assembling his team of oath-helpers. Ordlaf obliged, provided his help was never abused ('*næfre to nænan wo*'), and that he acquired ultimate rights in the property. Helmstan thus took the oath in the presence of Æthelhelm and two of those who had originally examined his claim. He then gave the title-deed (*boc*) to Ordlaf, who allowed him a life-interest in the land. Which should have been the end of the matter. But a year or two later:

> he stole the untended oxen at Fonthill, by which he was completely ruined, and drove them to Chicklade, and there he was discovered, and the man who tracked him rescued ... the cattle. When he fled, a bramble scratched him in the face; and when he wished to deny it, that was used in evidence against him. Then Eanwulf son of Peneard, the reeve ... took all his property that he owned at Tisbury (*yrfe ... ðæt he ahte to Tyssebyrig*). When I [Ordlaf] asked him why he did so, he said that he was a thief, and the property was adjudged to the king because he was the king's man (*he wæs cinges mon*).

94   My list has already been found wanting: for no. 177a, see n. 147 below. The total is thus 179 or 180, depending on whether one counts the Wulfgeat cases as separate (see n. 106 below). The probably fictional cases are LS 133, 168. On the first (Abingdon vs. the citizens of Oxfordshire), see Chadwick, *Origin of the English Nation*, pp. 278–82; on the second (Dunstan vs. the 'clerici'), see Vollrath, *Synoden Englands*, pp. 251–8, 424–53, with my reasons for dissent in *Catholic Historical Review* 73 (1987), pp. 431–2. There are, as I note, 'Lawsuits', p. 255 (p. 261), at least nine cases knowledge of which comes from very dubious documents (see also below, n. 104) and four more where later sources have elaborated the story, to say no more; but these considerations do not seem to affect the historicity of the episodes themselves, hence I do not exclude them as I do their Franco-Italian equivalents (chapter 2, nn. 231–2, 292).

Helmstan fled to King Alfred's tomb, and brought back a 'seal' to Ordlaf, who was with the new king Edward, and who used it to persuade him to give Helmstan back his 'home (*eard*)'. Ordlaf had meanwhile hung on to Fonthill, which had not been forfeited in that by then Helmstan held it only on lease. He subsequently swapped it with the bishop of Winchester for another property at the far end of the county. The letter ends with the author's plea that matters should thus stand. An endorsement records that Æthelhelm withdrew his suit at Warminster before the king, Ordlaf and others (again including at least one who had conducted the preliminary enquiry). It therefore seems that Æthelhelm had exploited Helmstan's second disgrace to resurrect his case, with the difference this time that it was Ordlaf who stood to lose had his suit been successful.[95]

There is no such thing as a typical Anglo-Saxon lawsuit. But the Helmstan saga is altogether out of the ordinary. It is among the most protracted of Anglo-Saxon counterparts to continental or post-conquest *placita*: documents in charter style which were chiefly concerned to describe legal proceedings. Of the new series of primarily vernacular records that began in Alfred's time, it is in fact the longest and one of the liveliest.[96] It raises in acute form the early medievalist's eternal problem, whether the curtain has merely parted by chance to give a rare glimpse of the normal, or has been blown briefly open by some abnormal disturbance. But there are certain respects in which it fits the pattern of what follows. Like all such documents from Alfred to 1066, it is almost devoid of formulaic elements. This feature sets Anglo-Saxon texts apart from continental case reports, which tend to follow well-worn grooves. The informality of the material may leave urgent questions unanswered but is also a condition of the impact that tales like Helmstan's have. The study of plea rolls or later Italian *placita* has frustrations caused by the very predictability of the evidence. Like nearly half the English records, this one survives in 'original' form, as is shown by the different script of its endorsement. The script itself lacks a clear indication of a date or place of drafting. It is difficult to tie any texts of this type to particular *scriptoria* on grounds of script alone; the one document in a hand identifiable elsewhere is thereby revealed as a later copy.[97] But in this case the handwriting's experimental quality squares with what can be imagined about the culture of Alfred's court. Ordlaf may even have been one of the *comites* scared by the threat of losing his 'office of worldly power' into taking *sapientia* seriously and learning to write

---

95   LS 23–6 (S 1445). My list treats cases within a single record as separate if they evidently involved distinct sessions of formal pleading or adjudication; so, Helmstan's belt theft, his first dispute over Fonthill with Æthelhelm, his rustling prosecution, and the final settlement referred to in the endorsement, constitute a series of different suits. The best edition of the relevant document is HaSD 18, but I tend to follow the translation in *EHD I* 102. Keynes, 'Fonthill letter', is an exhaustive analysis which supersedes earlier treatments, especially as regards the dating of its script and language (though see too below, n. 98); Dr Keynes's paper reached final form after I first drafted my own account, and my understanding of the document has gained greatly from his, even if we do not entirely agree on all its complexities (below, nn. 98, 100).

96   LS 14 and 18 + 19 are the other outsize texts, but neither has the Helmstan case's intensity of colour.

97   A facsimile of the Helmstan document is in *Facsimiles of Anglo-Saxon Manuscripts,* ed. Sanders, I 13. The case recorded in a hand identifiable elsewhere is LS 83; cf. *Facsimiles of English Royal Writs* no. 4 and plate IV(b).

rather than dictate his letters; the novelty of the exercise could explain his anomalous one-off appearance in the third person.[98]

However, another possibility is that other interests than Ordlaf's became involved. Among the many exceptional features of the Fonthill dispute is that it was initially fought out between laymen. At that date, the first extant plea rolls lay almost exactly three centuries away. Judgements, like other forms of title English and continental, were preserved for distant posterity only if they found their way into an ecclesiastical depository. It follows that the vast majority of known suits had clergy on at least one side. Hardly less obviously, all these documents were composed by the winning party (nearly always a church), and make no pretence of impartiality. Not infrequently, they read more like submissions of a plea than reports of its outcome; Ordlaf's is one of several that seems intended for use in a revived suit. In a revealing instance, Æthelred II impugned the will of an alleged traitor in his own court, and one of the triplicate copies of his judgement that it might after all stand was to be kept in his 'haligdome'. This text seems as likely to have been written by a royal clerk as any; but its wording leaves little doubt that it was the work of a scribe of Christ Church Canterbury, the will's main beneficiary, and Christ Church's copy was the one that survived.[99] Thus, though the Helmstan record stands alone in being couched as a letter (except in so far as royal writs were formally letters too), its unilateral origin and tone are anything but unusual. Ordlaf pleads as well as reports his case:

> Sire, when will any suit be ended if one can end it neither with money nor with an oath? And if one wishes to change every judgement which King Alfred gave, when shall we have finished disputing? ... Now, sire, it is very necessary for me that it may remain as it now is arranged.

The endorsement shows that the issue remained 'live', anyway until the letter took effect; and by then Fonthill was owned by the bishop of Winchester, who would no more than Ordlaf have wished to see their mutually acceptable exchange undone by Æthelhelm's claim. Even here, therefore, an ecclesiastical

---

98   Keynes, 'Royal Government and the Written Word', p. 249, finds it 'wishful thinking to suppose that the document was actually written by Ealdorman Ordlaf himself (since he might not have had the benefit of an Alfredian education)'. Equally, he *might*: for a possible parallel see LS 22, where Æthelwulf *dux* 'recitavit et investigavit hereditarios libros Cenwulfi regis et in privilegiis illius scriptum inveniebat ... ' (in view of its 897 date, I would see this document as evidence of Alfredian achievement, and not, like Morrish, 'King Alfred's letter', p. 96, of the resources on which the king could draw). For a view close to that taken above, see Gretsch's rich discussion of the 'Language of the Fonthill Letter', esp. pp. 95–8. On the other hand, Boynton and Reynolds, 'Author of the Fonthill Letter', suggest that it was written not by Ordlaf but by Helmstan's unnamed godfather (not necessarily a layman) and concerned an estate other than Fonthill that was also put at stake by Helmstan's conduct. This is a possibility, like many other interpretations of so absorbingly elusive a document, but one that arguably raises more difficulties than it solves: above all, the letter's author professes to have exchanged the land with the bishop of Winchester, and there is a Winchester charter (S 1284) describing its exchange of Fonthill with Ealdorman Ordlaf. Even if, as postulated by Boynton/ Reynolds (and conceded by Keynes, though see n. 100), this charter has been tampered with, it still suggests a primordial link between Ordlaf and Fonthill which Winchester scribes had no reason to invent – and given that Ordlaf had no other links with Winchester (S 368, 1205, 1797), and that S 1445 is itself from Canterbury, would have been in no position to imagine.
99   LS 62, with discussion at pp. 275–7 (279–81). Other documents providing for a *haligdom* copy are S 1478, 1520, 1521, plus the spurious S 981; the first and last are agreements, the other two wills.

interest was registered, and this could after all be why there is a written text. If Winchester were helping Ordlaf to make what was by now its own case too, that would explain the wobbly syntax. What defies explanation is the document's preservation not at Winchester but at Canterbury. Perhaps the archbishop was at the Warminster finale too, and took it off for safe keeping.[100]

Helmstan's story is both typical and idiosyncratic in another way. The text exists because at its core was a property dispute. Æthelhelm first challenged Helmstan's title and ultimately that of the Bishop of Winchester and Ordlaf his warrantor. But what made it easier for him to do so was Helmstan's criminal record. On the second occasion the interested parties included the king, to whom all Helmstan's estates (bar those held on lease) were forfeit. This brings into view the most remarkable single feature of Anglo-Saxon lawsuits. As many as eighty-three or eighty-four concern what passed as 'crime' and its penalties. All eighty-three/four date from the late-ninth century onwards, more than half the total for that period. Setting aside cases from the category of chronicles and hagiographies, which may put a premium on the dramas of crime, and concentrating on sources where property was the central issue, the resulting ratio is a hardly less striking sixty-three/four criminal cases in a possible 133/4. The line between 'criminal' and 'civil' justice is not always easily drawn even in modern conditions. The threat posed to Helmstan's lands by his thefts shows how title and behaviour, property and reputation interlocked in early English law. But his forfeiture after exposure as a cattle-thief demonstrates that government was an active agent of retribution, with a direct interest in its outcome. The reason why crime is prominent in later Anglo-Saxon charters is not at all that actions to recover private property and to redress personal injury were hard to separate. It is simply that punishment of crime could involve forfeiture of property. The Helmstan case's one real peculiarity is that Fonthill was not forfeited after all. Patronage put it beyond the king's reach.

Before leaving this crucial point for more detailed discussion in Part III, two final observations must be made. One concerns the crime for which Helmstan was forfeit. In the generally much rarer records of prosecutions on the continent, the offence, if specified at all, was treason or what amounted to treason (chapter 2, pp. 82–3). There is a barely resistible suspicion that behind most charges lie the stern politics of success and failure. Helmstan, if not a victim of politics, may have been their plaything. Ordlaf, Æthelhelm and nearly all those involved in the scrutiny and judgement of the successive cases precipitated by his behaviour feature among regular witnesses to the few extant charters of Alfred and his son.[101] But English cases that can be construed as failed political opposition are vastly outnumbered, even in royal charters, by cases of theft, homicide, mayhem

---

100 Stevenson's suspicions of S 1284 (Ordlaf's exchange of Fonthill with the Bishop of Winchester) were, as was not infrequently the case, excessive; and Dr Kelly, better placed to comment than most, finds little to impugn in it (pers. comm.). For other cases of Canterbury 'safekeeping', see below, n. 118.

101 For this see Whitelock, 'Charters in the Name of King Alfred'. The possible political dimensions of the dispute are rightly stressed by Smyth, *King Alfred*, pp. 393–400, though they no more undermine the credibility of Asser's idealized vision than does Carolingian pursuit of consensus (chapter 2, pp. 48–9) discredit the authenticity of Thegan (pp. 81–2).

and sexual offences (chapter 9). Secondly, Fonthill's five hides would (anyway on later reckoning) give Helmstan a thegn's status, and this was not his sole property. But men of his standing were not the only recorded English defendants. While thirty forfeitures are of five hides or more, some are of much less. The smallest recorded is of thirty acres, the next smallest of seventy.[102] Most of those thus disgraced must have been of relatively low status. It is inherent in the hagiography reviewed later in this chapter that saints intervene on behalf of the oppressed. If the system's lesser victims seldom show up in other evidence, that is because documents of endowment rarely dealt in their sort of property.

A final point, the one most relevant to this chapter's central argument, is that there is at no stage any hint of a reference to a law under which Helmstan was indicted. Ordlaf's question to the reeve at Tisbury was in effect a call for chapter and verse. Chapter 9 will argue that Alfred's law on oaths turned any criminal behaviour into a breach of fealty, which explains why Helmstan should have been forfeit as a 'king's man', and why Ordlaf was puzzled by the novelty. In any event, though forfeiture for theft was not explicitly enjoined by Ine or Alfred, Helmstan could have been covered by Ine's law on those repeatedly accused of theft. As he was not caught in the act (mention of the bramble-scratch showing that the case was investigated), he should have gone to the ordeal, then lost his hand or foot.[103] But written law was apparently irrelevant, though Alfred's imposing *domboc* (incorporating Ine's laws) must have been issued only a few years before the episode. This pattern will recur throughout what follows. And persevering readers will meet Helmstan's case again. Its pertinent issues include the grounds of Æthelhelm's challenge to Æthelthryth's sale of what he appears to have thought family property and she to have been alienable rights; the tension between the jurisdictional spheres of ealdorman and reeve; the role of 'rational' concepts of proof as opposed to 'irrational' modes like oath-helping; and the meaning of Helmstan's acquisition of an *insigle* from Alfred's tomb. There can be no final answer to the question whether the story is one of familiar procedures spotlighted by chance or is itself a sign of exceptional times. But it will be critical for later Parts of this book that here is one of the two earliest charter references to land lost for a criminal offence.

(ii) Leofric of Whitchurch

The forfeiture of Leofric a century later was straightforward. It is described in a Latin diploma of Æthelred II (1012) granting ten hides at Whitchurch (Oxfordshire) to a *minister*, also called Leofric.

---

102   30 acres, LS 100 (*DB*); 70 acres, LS 129 (*Libellus Æthelwoldi*, see n. 127 below, the presumption being that this was the extent of *Berlea*, since the total estate, leased after the dispute, was two hides and 70 acres, and Swaffham was assessed at two hides). Other prosecutions for less than five hides (see also chapter 9, chapter 12) are LS 37, 41, 56, 61, 64 (if Woodperry), 73, 94, ?102, 127, 132. Hagiographical stories where small property seems implied are 154–8, 169, 171, 178. See also n. 129.
103   Ine 37 (a law applicable to 'se cirlisca mon', but presumably adaptable if Helmstan were indeed of higher status).

This estate once ... belonged by right of paternal inheritance to a certain Leofric, but he by living impiously, that is by mutinying against my soldiers on my expedition (*rebellando meis militibus in mea expeditione*) and by unprecedented pillages (*rapinis insuetis*), adulteries and many other wicked crimes, condemned at once his person and his possessions.[104]

Narrative clauses of this sort are a well-known feature of Æthelred's charters. Their presence in a set of grants to various beneficiaries is among the best evidence for the 'centralized production' of his diplomas.[105] There can be no question of informal authorship by the profiting party for such texts, except in so far as forfeiture initially profited the crown (Abingdon, which preserved the Whitchurch charter, only acquired the estate a generation later). Up to twenty similar cases occurred in Æthelred's reign. But the earliest forfeitures date to Alfred's time, there are three in dubious documents of the first half of the tenth century, three in Edgar's charters, and one or two in Cnut's. Sources other than charters show that what was unusual under Æthelred was not forfeiture itself but the regular mention of an estate's prior forfeiture in royal grants.[106] In two cases, perhaps at one time in more, a former owner's crimes were rehearsed in the vernacular, like boundary clauses. That would have enabled them to be read aloud in court; and the wisdom of this is underlined by another clause in the 1012 charter which denies any title to the land based on older documents. Families losing their estates might well hang on to the deeds so as later to adduce prior title before an ignorant court. Unambiguous accounts of their loss could stop them. Clauses to that effect often appear in charters from *c.*900 but once again not before.[107]

Leofric's 'crimes' have a further interest. As in other cases of the time, there is a tendency to throw the (metaphorical) book at an offender. Ealdorman Ælfric *Cild*, whose 985 exile the *Chronicle* notes, is accused in one charter of treason, in another of 'many unheard-of sins (*piacula*) against God and my royal rule (*imperium*)'. Each shows that condemnation followed a formal legal process:

... by the unanimous legal counsel and most just judgement of bishops, ealdormen and all magnates of this realm at the royal vill called Cirencester/when all my magnates met together in ... council at Cirencester, and expelled Ælfric as a traitor and fugitive from this country ... [108]

---

104   LS 76, S 927, KCD 1307, *Ab. Ch.* 136. It poses problems of authenticity as it stands: Keynes, *Diplomas of King Æthelred*, p. 265, but these do not lessen its value for present purposes. Its acquisition by Abingdon is illuminated by Dr Kelly, *Ab. Ch.*

105   Stenton, *Latin Charters*, pp. 74–82; Keynes, *Diplomas*, pp. 95–126.

106   Forfeitures (or potential forfeitures) in Æthelred's Diplomas are LS 44, 48, 54, 56–8, 60–1, 63–4, 68, 70–1, 72ab, 73, 75–6, and cf. 81; I accept Keynes's case, *Diplomas*, pp. 184–5, that the pig-stealing Æthelsige of no. 56 was not the same as the reeve-slayer of no. 60; see 'Lawsuits', n. 29, for the identity of no. 63's Ælfrics, and of no. 71's Leofsiges, and for doubts about that of the Wulfgeats of S 918, 934 (whence the compromise of their being numbered 72a and 72b). Other forfeitures in diplomas are LS 27 (Alfred), 29–31 (earlier-tenth century), 36–7, 41 (Edgar), 79, 81 (Cnut); the totals for Edgar and from 1016–66 are much increased by sources in category three and four: see the table in 'Lawsuits', p. 280 (p. 284).

107   Keynes, *Diplomas*, pp. 130 (n. 158), 201; Wormald, 'Charters, Law', p. 161 (pp. 300–1).

108   LS63.

The Whitchurch charter is less explicit, but Leofric's condemnation no doubt followed similar lines. Unlike Ælfric's, it left no other mark, unless he was the Leofric of Whitchurch killed in 1001.[109] All that can otherwise be said is that one Leofric is prominent as a witness of royal charters throughout the reign, a second appears intermittently till 997 and a third twice in 987; the mutineer could have been any or none of them, so long he was not the beneficiary of the 1012 charter itself.[110] More telling is that a Leofric of Whitchurch is singled out as a locally important figure in a 990 case (the one discussed next). As a person of some consequence, he is as likely as Helmstan to have been a victim of court politics. Political faction was hardly new under Æthelred but the rapid rotation of the wheel of political fortune in his long reign does seem unusual, and may explain the amount of mud (and blood) flying about.[111]

Yet Leofric's was among less vague charges levied by Æthelred, and army unrest in his reign was all too well-attested by the *Chronicle* jeremiad. For the first time since Ine it was addressed by law:

> If anyone without leave deserts the army (*fyrde*) when the king himself is there, he risks his life or *wergeld*.

This law was enacted in 1008.[112] The Leofric charter was issued four years later. Here was a good chance to cite written law with reference to legal business; Ine's decree could have been cited, even if Æthelred's was not yet in force when Leofric offended. The chance was not taken. Just two years afterwards, a sonorous Italian diploma of Emperor Henry II announced the treason of Count Hubert and others:

> ... the *lex Langobardorum* was examined. It orders, 'If anyone plots against the king's life he incurs [mortal] danger, and his property will be confiscated'. Thus, according to their own law, all their goods are ours.

Hubert's actual offence was to back the regime of Arduin, having sworn loyalty to Henry.[113] The facts of political life may have been much the same at one end of Europe as the other. The part played by written law in the language of politics was quite different.

---

109   ASC 1001A, p. 132.
110   Cf. RoASCh., p. 382, and below, p. 151, also table LXIII in Keynes's invaluable 'Atlas of Anglo-Saxon Attestations' (or *Diplomas*, nos 7–8). Since (as Dr Keynes reminds me) there is a Hampshire as well as an Oxfordshire Whitchurch, and since one might expect the charter to gloat about it had the mutineer met his fate in battle like his 1001 namesake, his identity with the latter is improbable.
111   It deserves more emphasis than the 'Chancery' controversy has yet allowed that the political analysis from witness-lists of Keynes, *Diplomas*, pp. 163–231, is not only fundamental for understanding the reign but also a major methodological advance in Anglo-Saxon studies.
112   V Atr 28, VI Atr 35 (the latter text arguably contaminating that in MS 'G¹', for which and for the date see chapter 5, pp. 332–4); Ine 51; also Af 40:1.
113   *DHII* 321; cf. 322, 'lege Italica', 'lege Langobardorum'. The reference is to *Ed. Ro.* 1. See chapter 2, pp. 42, 98, 101.

(iii) Wynflæd and Leofwine

At least a quarter, perhaps as many as a third, of recorded Anglo-Saxon lawsuits date from Æthelred's reign.[114] Figures are swollen not only by the number of forfeitures but also by the struggle of reformed monasteries that had profited from Edgar's power to defend their position after his death. A few cases of the latter type will be examined in the next sub-section. But patterns of Æthelredian litigation are even better brought out by a case of 990 whose context is less clear.[115] The estates of Hagbourne and Bradfield (Berkshire) were disputed by Wynflæd and Leofwine, Wynflæd claiming that Ælfric had exchanged them with her for Datchet (Buckinghamshire). She produced before the king a formidable team of witnesses, including the archbishop of Canterbury and Queen Mother Ælfthryth, but Leofwine riposted by demanding that the suit be heard by the Berkshire 'shire-court (scirgemote)'. It met under Bishops Æthelsige and Æscwig at Cwichelmeshlæw (Scutchamer Knob). The king sent his seal by the abbot of Bath; Archbishop Sigeric and another of Wynflæd's original backers sent 'statements (swutelunga)'. It fell to Wynflæd that 'she brought forth her ownership (gelædde hio þa ahnunga)', which she did with the 'help (fultume)' of Ælfthryth and almost as powerful a range of support as in the first instance; they made up 'the full [number?] (se fulla [? ...]), men and women', and included the abbot of Abingdon, the abbesses of Nunnaminster and Reading and others who seem to have been people of substance, like Eadgifu 'of Lewknor' (an estate assessed by Domesday at seventeen hides, with a 1066 value of £10).

> Then the wise men who were there declared that it would be better that one should leave the oath aside ... because there would afterwards be no friendship, and one would demand of the robbery (reaflaces) that [Leofwine] should give it up, and pay compensation and his wer to the king.

So, without the oath, Leofwine surrendered the land and renounced his claim. Wynflæd was told to produce 'all his father's gold and silver', and, 'as far as she dared to protect her oath', she did. Unimpressed, Leofwine demanded an oath that 'all his property (æhta) was there'. She retorted that 'she could not for her part, nor he for his'. The text then concludes by naming some 'god men' who were witnesses: one was Ælfgar, 'the king's reeve', another Leofric 'of Whitchurch', who, since the Whitchurch granted in 1012 was just on the Berkshire border, was presumably the future mutineer.

Like all cases surveyed in this chapter, the Wynflæd-Leofwine dispute will be pivotal in Part III's account of the operation of early English law. Some of the major issues it raises are therefore best deferred to chapters 9, 10 or 11. But four points can be made briefly at this stage. First, the record survives in original form,

---

114   LS 44?, 46, 47–8?, 49, 50–2?, 54–64, 67–71, 72ab, 73–6, 81, 107?, 108–12, 113–14?, 115, 117, 119–23, 126, 128, 130, 137, 138–9?, 141?, 142–3, 152, 158, 168?, 169, 172, 174?; queries mark possibles, so my 'Lawsuits', pp. 278–9 (p. 283), should be revised accordingly.

115   LS 49, RoASCh. LXVI, S 1454. In 'Giving God and King their due', I discuss this case in greater detail, and in the context of the tenth and eleventh-century disputes of Ely and Ramsey; reference should be made to that paper for what is only adumbrated here.

as does the Helmstan deed. But is not a letter pleading a case like Ordlaf's. It is a chirograph, a report designed to provide authenticated copies to two or more parties. That scribal technique was used in six other dispute settlements.[116] But there is no knowing why, that is for whom, this report was made. It is another rare record of a suit between laymen, and with no apparent clerical interest such as came to be involved in the Fonthill case. All that can be said is that the extant text is from Canterbury cathedral, like Ordlaf's.[117] Wynflæd and Leofwine should each have received a chirograph portion, but the text actually records Wynflæd's attainment of her objective and discharge (more or less) of what was due from her, while the archbishop was among her allies; she is perhaps the likelier to have deposited her copy with him.[118]

A second zone of obscurity is the background of the proceedings thus reported. Wynflæd and Leofwine are otherwise unidentified. It is impossible to say how they related to each other or what brought them into dispute. They could have been Ælfric's (second) wife and son, at odds over what Wynflæd should have received in her marriage agreement. There is reason to think that Queen Mother Ælfthryth was patron to her and several of her supporters.[119] The case's conclusion was then foreseeable, if not forgone. No less murky is the judgement's legal basis. It may have been the extent of her support that entitled Wynflæd to make her case. The phrase, 'the full ... [sc. number]' suggests that they made up a body of a requisite size. Fixed totals were a function of 'oath-helping', testimony to a party's good repute rather than the facts of the case itself; the impression is that oath-helping not evidence was decisive here. Yet the swutelunga of Sigeric and his colleague (also a bishop) seem out of place in a compurgation, and sound more like depositions by witnesses; conceivably, they resembled Ordlaf's submission. Oath-helping and witnessing may not have been such distinct procedures as historians of early medieval law have liked to think.[120]

If so much is obscure, other things are not. A third and critical feature of the case is the way that it follows lines that legislation laid down. When insisting that the suit be heard not by the king but by the Berkshire court, Leofwine did just what was ordered in a law of Edgar, even if the relevant law is no more cited than in any other case discussed here. This is one of thirty-six or more cases in which a shire-court was at work.[121] None pre-date Alfred; the clearest examples post-date the accession of Edgar, whose laws first explicitly mention them. Bishop and ealdorman were then put in charge of shire sessions. It may have been in the

116   *Facsimiles of Ancient Charters* III 37; cf. Keynes, 'Royal Government and the Written Word', p. 250 with n. 94; and 'Giving God and King their due', pp. 568–9 (p. 344) with n. 46; also next n.
117   This provenance is shown by its characteristic (and apposite) twelfth-century endorsement, 'inutile'; cf. S 214, 1194, 1472, 1862.
118   Another possibility worth considering is that, as with Helmstan's record, Canterbury was seen as a suitable guarantor for any transaction; for a reason why it might have been, see chapter 12. Chirographs with portions deposited at Canterbury but of no apparent interest to Christ Church are S. 1368 (ref. in text), 1461 (ref. in text), 1472 (ref. in text, original), 1473 (ref. in text, original); the last three are Kentish.
119   'Giving God and King their due', pp. 565–6, 567–8 (pp. 342–4).
120   'Giving God and King their due', pp. 566–7 (pp. 342–3), with [Fouracre,] 'Conclusions', in *Disputes*, pp. 219–21.
121   III Eg 2, 5:1–2, amplified by II Cn 17 – 19:2. See chapter 10, and 'Giving God and King their due', pp. 569–71 (pp. 344–6); the figure argued there, n. 48, supersedes that of 'Lawsuits', p. 279 (284).

capacity of court-president that Æthelsige received the disputed land from a conceding Leofwine; he was actually bishop of Sherborne, but the local see of Ramsbury was vacant in 990 and Sherborne was the neighbouring diocese.[122] Equally important, the king's involvement in the case was not foreclosed by its adjournment to the shire. Æthelred sent his seal. Another shire-court session in his reign is said to have been launched by despatch of his 'writ and seal (*gewrit 7 his insegl*)'. A writ may have been despatched to Berkshire too.[123] Central supervision is further implied by a fourth and last point. The text's concluding clauses suggest that this was another of the 'compromise' settlements typical of the early Middle Ages. To avoid any threat to 'friendship' admirably fits the emphasis put by modern study of disputing in traditional societies on 'love before law'.[124] About 40 per cent of Anglo-Saxon cases did indeed end in compromise. Yet chapter 9 will argue that the most significant point here is the enormous sum Leofwine would have had to pay the king if the suit had in fact been formally judged against him.[125]

(iv) The Fenland abbeys and their enemies

Conclusions indicated by the Wynflæd-Leofwine case are upheld by the tenth- and eleventh-century disputes of the Fenland abbeys. Fifteen years before Bishop Æthelwold reformed Ely (970), Wulfstan of Dalham convened a court of two hundreds at its north gate. The widow Æscwyn there gave him a marsh and fishery at Stonea. Ogga of Mildenhall then promised that Ely would receive a hide in Cambridge when he died. Wulfstan at once transferred Stonea to Ely and urged Ogga to make his gift immediate. Ogga obliged. But after his death, his kinsman Uvi reclaimed the hide from Ely's Abbot Brihtnoth. Men accordingly came to Cambridge 'from all sides'. Uvi's plea was heard and debated, and 'they judged (*iudicaverunt*) that he give four marks as penalty (*pro forisfactura*) because he was claiming land to which he had never laid claim when Ogga was alive'. Uvi was not finished. When Edgar died, he confronted Abbot Brihtnoth again, 'adding trickeries to trickeries and claims to claims'. The abbot 'took counsel with the two hundreds and ... by their testimony it was decided (*quorum testimonio derationatus est*) that Ogga lawfully bought the land from Uvi, and held it unchallenged while he lived'. Stonea had meanwhile given trouble itself. The Ely clerks leased it back to Æscwyn's kin. Æthelwold kept the agreement when he took over, but Æscwyn's kin renounced it after Edgar's death, 'without adjudication or decree of the citizens and hundredmen (*sine iudicio et sine lege civium et hundretanorum*)'. So Ealdorman Æthelwine came to Ely, and

122   Cf. RoASCh., pp. 380–1. (So was Dorchester, Æscwig's see.)
123   LS 69. For the options, see HaWr, p. 47; and Chaplais, 'The Anglo-Saxon Chancery', pp. 171–2; also Keynes, 'Royal Government and the Written Word', pp. 245–6. To argue that the Berkshire text's phraseology ('7 grette ealle þa witan þe þær gesomnode wæron') implies a writ protocol begs the question whether it would have been otherwise phrased had the message been oral.
124   Chapter 1, pp. 3, 26, chapter 2, pp. 80, 85, 90; 'Giving God and King their due', pp. 550–3, 562–3, 575 (pp. 332, 340–1, 348–9) with n. 64.
125   Cf. also below, p. 155, with n. 132; and 'Giving God and King their due', pp. 575–7 (pp. 349–50).

'summoned [them] to a *placitum* of citizens and hundred-men once, twice, and indeed many times', but to no avail. Eventually, Æthelwine 'held a *grande placitum* of citizens and hundred-men before twenty-four *iudicibus*' on Castle Hill Cambridge. Abbot Brihtnoth presented his case, stressing his opponents' failure to appear;

> Then the judges decided (*iudicantes statuerunt*) that the abbot should have ... Stonea [and] that Beahmund and the kinsmen of the widow should pay his fish for six years to the abbot, and compensate and pay a fine to the king (*et persolverent et regi forisfacturam darent*). If ... not ... they would be entitled to seize their property.[126]

The full implications of these cases too are best analysed in chapters 9–11, but it may be helpful to look at their bearing on the four issues that emerged from the Wynflæd-Leofwine suit. First, then, they introduce a new category of evidence. The Ely pleas are recounted in the *Libellus quorundam insignium operum beati Æthelwoldi episcopi*, an originally vernacular work of *c.*990 by a member of the community on the history of Ely's recent endowment, and extant in an early-twelfth-century Latin version which survives both independently and in the *Liber Eliensis*.[127] Its twenty-six lawsuits constitute the largest single archive of pre-conquest case-law.[128] A 'cartulary-chronicle' of this sort is of course even less likely to take an impartial line than texts of *placita* type. But, quantity aside, there is gain as well as loss. Because it is a narrative as well as a cartulary, the *Libellus* contains details on the context of litigation that seldom get into isolated documents, and smaller-scale transactions than normally justified the preparation, or at any rate preservation, of individual charters. Its closer focus picks out the seventy-acre forfeiture mentioned above as the second smallest on record (p. 148). At least half of its cases involve under five hides. Brihtnoth won one by showing that the single hide at stake had bought the freedom of his opponent's wife and sons, once *innati* of Ely's Hatfield estate; in a later age's parlance, that would mean they had been serfs.[129] Likewise, narrators were more likely than charter draftsmen to keep track of lost property. Scars remain visible where in disarticulated archives they escape notice. Attention to detail might even mean that cartulary-chronicles were more apt to note concessions to losers. Ely supplies up to a quarter of recorded compromises after Alfred's time, usually in the form of money payments to the opposition; sources of the same sort provide nine more.[130]

Hence, a second aspect of Ely cases is that they give a clearer picture of

---

126   LS 116–17 (an apparently continuous episode again dividing into two suits because involving two separate hearings), 120; *Anglo-Saxon Ely*, ed. Keynes and Kennedy, 27–8, 34 (*Liber Eliensis*, ed. Blake, ii 18, 24, pp. 93–4, 97–8).

127   For overdue recognition and elucidation of this crucial source, see *Anglo-Saxon Ely*, the forthcoming edition, translation and commentary by Keynes and Kennedy (successive drafts of which were kindly shown me by Dr Keynes).

128   LS 107–32; *Liber Eliensis* also furnishes LS 135 in its own right.

129   LS 110; other 'minor' cases are 113–17, 120?, 122–3, 127–8, 130, 132.

130   Ely: LS 108, 110, 112, 114–15, 119, 122, 125–6, 135. Cf. nos. 104–5 (Worcester); 136–7, 140–2, 146 (Ramsey, cf. below, pp. 156–8); 152 (Evesham). See also above, n. 124.

pressures making for bilateral settlement. Uvi's refusal to admit defeat, or that of Æscwyn's kin to answer repeated summons, are far from uncommon in pre-conquest cases, in their continental equivalents, or for that matter in Common Law's' medieval heyday.[131] Any pre-modern legal system was vulnerable to the uncooperative and unpersuaded. Agreement was best bought by leaving opponents some self-respect. When quashed, Uvi's plea came back to life. After its second but apparently less harsh defeat, no more was heard of it. It is revealing that the *Libellus* reports concessions to the other side with no *diminuendo* in stridency. Such solutions sprang not from rediscovered goodwill but from resentful acquiescence in the facts of legal life. Yet it should not be overlooked that Uvi and Æscwyn's kin were both required to pay the sort of fine with which Leofwine was threatened in 990.[132] Chapter 9 will suggest that the judicial system before 1066 had at least some of the extractive potential of justice in the age of Glanvill.

A third point is that though the Ely reports are as reticent as others in quoting written law, they show unusual interest in the legal principles whereby cases were judged. This could reflect the twelfth-century intellectual context of the sources as they stand; yet the legislation of the period itself attains a level of juris-prudential reflection (chapter 5, pp. 325–6, 369–70). The rebuttal of Uvi's challenge on the grounds that he had not staked his claim in Ogga's lifetime accorded with a rule going back to Alfred, though his law had a different emphasis, and more directly applicable texts were not on offer before Æthelred's own reign.[133] Similarly, the punishment of Æscwyn's kin more or less squares with stipulations on contumacy in the *Hundred Ordinance* and elsewhere.[134] Extant codes do make sense of what was done, if not to the extent of explicitly justifying the action taken. This aside, Ely's suits offer further valuable testimony to the operation of late-tenth-century courts. That of the shire shows up well throughout, in Hertfordshire and Huntingdonshire as well as Cambridgeshire; and clearly enough in the latter to allow limited prosopography of its members (chapter 10).[135] Cambridge's twenty-four *iudices* may have been set up by a surviving Edgar law (chapter 9).[136] Æthelwine is regularly found in an ealdorman's required role as court president, just as Æthelsige did a bishop's job in Berkshire. Especially useful is the light shed by the *Libellus* on lesser courts, courts of first instance which are ignored by more formal records inasmuch as

---

131   Cf. LS 122, 125–6, and *Lib. Æth.* 46 (*Liber Eliensis* ii 35, p. 110); also LS 32, 57–8, 94, 103, 152. For the continent, see (e.g.) Fouracre, 'Disputes in later Merovingian Francia', in *Disputes*, pp. 28–9; for the high Middle Ages in England, see Saul's vivid *tableau*, 'Murder and Justice Medieval Style'.

132   See above, p. 153, with n. 125.

133   Af 41, III Atr 14, V Atr 32:3 (MS D only); cf. II Cn 72 – 72:1, *Becw.* 3:1 (these later laws also require extrapolation in so far as they do not directly concern alienations beyond the kin).

134   *Hu.* 3:1, 7 – 7:1; cf. I Ew 2:1, II As 20 – 20:1, 25:2 (apart from the second and third, these are refer-ences to disobedience in general, whether of reeves to royal orders or of hundred members to a posse; they also tend to invoke the king's 'oferhyrnesse' of 120 shillings, of which there is no trace in the Ely cases). See also Keynes, 'Crime and Punishment', pp. 70–1.

135   LS 110 (Hertfordshire), 121 (Huntingdonshire); 130 etc. (Cambridgeshire), and cf. 111–12 (Northamptonshire).

136   IV Eg 5.

their judgement was not decisive. Stonea's transfer from a court at Ely to a 'great *placitum*' at Cambridge is plausibly seen as a resort from the lower court of the hundred to the shire, such as Edgar envisaged and Cnut demanded.[137] Most important of all is what the *Libellus* implies about the extent of 'private' jurisdiction. One of its cases is among three possible instances of a lord's court in action. But the judgement of Ealdorman Byrhtnoth's court (if such it was) was repeated at Cambridge, presumably by the shire. Wulfstan at the outset of the Uvi and Stonea affairs, and Æthelwine later on, held a court of two hundreds at Ely's north gate. Post-conquest officials would have found that quite impossible. Ely's was by then among the great judicial liberties of England. Even Angevin kings allowed its abbot his franchise 'within the Isle'. The silence of the *Libellus* on Ely's jurisdictional rights in a period when the subsidence of Carolingian 'public' justice into private hands has become a historiographical *cliché* is eloquent indeed.[138]

Finally, the degree of royal control of justice is as clear in the *Libellus* as in the Wynflæd-Leofwine suit, though highlighted from a different angle. The Uvi and Stonea cases took a new turn at Edgar's death. They are among thirteen in the *Libellus* where much the same occurred, most involving similar attempts to retract agreements made under Edgar.[139] The crisis is familiar as the 'anti-monastic reaction' but was more complex than that. Its targets included Rochester, not yet a monastic chapter; and among its villains (in Ely's view) was the same Ealdorman Æthelwine as was Ramsey's 'amicus Dei'. Other changes of regime encouraged previous losers to revive their suits.[140] That said, the sheer scale of the post-Edgar movement suggests (as of course does other evidence) that a huge upheaval in landed property had taken place. The implication of the recurrence of the date 975 in Ely's cases is that Edgar's support had decisively tipped the scales of justice in the monks' favour beforehand. It may have been almost as hard for landowners to hold their own against them in the 960s and 970s as it was for the English against the Normans a century later.

More explicit evidence of the weight of royal support is given by the litigation of Ælfwine, abbot of Ramsey under Edward the Confessor. Ramsey's total of sixteen recorded pre-conquest lawsuits compares with that of its Fenland neighbour, though there seems to be no question of an underlying Anglo-Saxon text

---

137   See above, n. 121, and LS 112, 114–15, 117, 121. Kennedy, 'Law and Litigation', pp. 141–9, is an admirable discussion of these issues that stresses the relative imprecision of arrangements reflected by the *Libellus*; but one cannot say whether irregularities arise from a lack of institutional definition or from the vagueness of the source itself: 'Giving God and King their due', pp. 569–72 (pp. 344–7).

138   LS 128 (with Whitelock's comment, *Liber Eliensis*, p. xiii, and those of Kennedy, 'Law and Litigation', pp. 142 (n. 44), 149; the other possibles are LS 50–1. On Ely's medieval liberty, see the pioneering article of Hurnard, 'Anglo-Norman Franchises', p. 317; with Cam, 'Evolution of the Medieval English Franchise', pp. 28–9; also Miller, *Abbey and Bishopric of Ely*, pp. 28–33. Cf. chapter 10 (3). below, and 'Giving God and King their due', p. 572 (pp. 346–7).

139   LS 108–11, 115 ('Sumerlede ... dixit ... se coactum fecisse quod fecerat'), 117, 119, 120–2, 126, 130, plus *Lib. Æth.* 46 (*Liber Eliensis* ii 35, p. 110).

140   For other reversals under Æthelred not necessariy connected with anti-monk sentiment, see LS 46, 47? (cf. S 885), 59, 60? (cf. S 864), 67?, 72a, 137, 140?, 152, 172?; also LS 63, S 876, 888, 889, with *Papsturkunden 896–1046* 282, and Keynes, *Diplomas*, pp. 102–4, 176–80. For much the same in other reigns, see LS 34–5, 39.

like Ely's.[141] In one case, Ælfric son of Wihtgar challenged Ælfwine over a deathbed bequest by Æthelwine the Black of four large Bedfordshire estates. As usual, the grounds were that Ælfric was Æthelwine's kin and heir. The text then tells, with relish rather than embarrassment, how the abbot, sizing up the man's eminence and the nobility of his *genus*, 'decided that a suit requiring the outlay of much revenue (*litem quae multarum indigebat impendio facultatum*) would be risky to contest':

> Using therefore a more effective plan and a hidden purpose, he deceived the efforts of the other side by a clever trick, obtained the attention of the king and with modest petition skilfully intimated to him the devotion of the dead and the wickedness of his opponents. He added ... twenty marks of gold wherewith to earn the king's favour (*quibus gratiam regis mercaretur*). He acquired also the support of Queen Edith at the price of five marks, that she might faithfully bring her holy prayers into the royal ears. The king assented, and when Ælfric brought his claim to the king's judgement, Abbot Ælfwine received the estates at the king's hand in the witness of the many and great present.

In the event, only one estate was a Ramsey possession by 1066, though another had been till recently.[142] Despite Ælfwine's manoeuvres, it seems that the case came to court. It is thus evidence not merely of what the ideologists of that time and this would call judicial corruption but also of *coram rege* justice. Though suits were not supposed to be brought before the king unless all lower courts had failed to provide redress, the number shown to have reached his presence compares closely with that of recorded shire-courts.[143]

The other Ælfwine case is in some ways more suggestive still. It arose from a challenge by 'certain malignants' over the soke of *Bichamdic* on the Norfolk coast, which the king had granted to Ramsey. All that can be said of this dispute is that, in the story as told, Ælfwine 'rushed to the known defences of royal clemency, showed ... the rash daring of his adversaries, and acquired a *carta* from him for the refutation of all claims, present and future'. An authentic royal writ of the Confessor is then quoted in Latin translation.[144] Yet the writ says nothing about Ælfwine's dispute with his malignants. Only the fact that the surrounding narrative gives it a context shows it to have been judicial at all.[145] The implications of this are profound. Anglo-Saxon writ formulation is notoriously terse. But two examples of pleas initiated by writ and/or seal have been met already. Three others requiring or upholding judgement survive. Several more read like instructions for proceedings without making this as clear as do post-1066

---

141   *Chron. Ram.*; it is in fact the fourth richest repository of cases, after Ely, Christ Church Canterbury and Worcester: cf. my 'Lawsuits', pp. 271–2 (pp. 276–7).

142   LS 150; *Chron. Ram.* 103, pp. 169–70. Cf. *DB* i 210d, 212a, 217b, 217d [*Bedfordshire* 8:1, 19:1, 53:5, 53:33] and *Chron. Ram.* 105, pp. 171–2.

143   For a list of *coram rege* cases before the Conquest (superseding that of 'Lawsuits', p. 280 (p. 284) see 'Giving God and King their due', nn. 60–1, and chapter 10; on 'corruption', cf. chapter 2, pp. 70–1, with Clanchy, 'Law and Love', pp. 63–4.

144   LS 149, *Chron. Ram.* 97–8, p. 163–4; HaWr. 60.

145   For the *Bichamdic* problem, see HaWr, pp. 246–52; Dr Harmer seemed to think that the genuine writ, no. 60 (as opposed to the forged no. 61) was what first bestowed *Bichamdic* on Ramsey, but Ramsey's chronicler evidently thought that it upheld an earlier grant.

documents. Domesday has several references to King Edward's judicial writs.[146] The use of writs to articulate forensic process may therefore have been commoner before the conquest than extant texts reveal. As so often with cases discussed in this section, the evidence is frustratingly unsystematic. The impression neverthe-less remains that a coherent judicial system was in operation, and that kings retained effective control of it.

(v) St Ecgwine and the Holy Cross

Three final cases come from the category of 'Gesta and Miracula'. This means a return to the narratives of this chapter's first section, but now for material on law in action rather than law-giving. There is little to be said for re-examining the famous confrontations in the Chronicles of the Confessor's reign. They are less informative on political trials than Æthelred's charters. The cases selected instead are from ill-known hagiographies. The possibilities are paradoxically illustrated by Osbert de Clare's Vita Edburgae, which was printed only recently.[147] Taking the unsupported word of so notorious a forger and propagandist on any historical episode is like investing life-savings in a project to cure old age. Nonetheless, his story of how Edburga acquired from her father, Edward the Elder, Nunnaminster's rich estate at All Cannings (Wiltshire) is inherently plausible. The property was disputed in the king's curia by two nobles, who drew their swords and were barely restrained from killing each other. They might have been executed or mutilated but for royal mercy; as it was, they forfeited their 'whole substance'. The penalty for fighting before the king in both Ine's and Alfred's laws was indeed forfeiture, and at the king's discretion death. Osbert spoke of the 'appropriate vengeance of the patrie legis' for the offence. He did not quote or cite these texts but could well have been thinking of them.[148] The episode may best be understood as a further sign of the interest taken in written law by authors of the first half of the twelfth century. Like William of Malmesbury, Osbert perhaps researched Old English legal materials, and drew his own conclusions (he was, to put it mildly, so inclined).

A story in Byrhtferth's Vita Ecgwini is at least of pre-conquest vintage, if hardly more circumstantial. It tells of a dispute, at an unknown date but presumably in the tenth or early-eleventh century, between Wigred, senior of Evesham, and a rusticus who 'raised himself from the mire', and though 'of worldly wealth (terrenis lucris)' tried to seize some abbey land. A day was fixed for one or other to claim the land by oath (cum iuramento terram ... vendicaret)'. Wigred, having

---

146   See above, p. 153 with n. 123, and for cases where writs are direct evidence, LS 87, 89, 92. Writs whose tone if not content hints at a background dispute are (e.g.) HaWr 8–10, 13–14, 16, 18; and for Domesday references, see HaWr, pp. 543–5 (no. 12 is LS 96, but one can envisage a similar context at least for nos. 10, 14).

147   'Life of St Edburga' 6, pp. 270–1, with the editor's comments at pp. 33, 99–101. The case is provisionally numbered LS 177a, having regrettably eluded my trawl in 'Lawsuits'.

148   Ine 6, Af 7. It may be noted that the name of one disputant, 'Alla' (= Ælle?), appears in witness-lists of Edward's charters: e.g. S 369, 1443. On Osbert, see Chaplais, 'Original charters of Herbert and Gervase, abbots of Westminster'.

prayed to the abbey's patron St Ecgwine since dawn, came to the 'place of confrontation (*locum certaminis*)' not with 'crowds who by their numbers could conquer the opposition with fear', but bearing St Ecgwine's relics. For his part, the rustic had taken the precaution of putting earth from his own land in his shoe, so that he could truthfully swear to be standing on his property. But when ordered to take the oath:

> That madman was in utter rage; he raised ... his arrogant hand with which he intended to fix ... in the ground the scythe he was carrying ... But the Judge ... directed the ... malice onto his skull. That rascal fixed the shaft of the scythe so strongly in the ground that with one blow he cut off his own foul head at the neck.[149]

This is not, needless to say, the stuff of a legal historian's dreams. Forensic detail is lost in hagiographical *topoi*, by which standards the rustic's clumsiness has a certain realism.[150] Line upon line of Wigred's prayers to St Ecgwine are no substitute for the account of the court's composition that Byrhtferth fails to supply. Yet positive reactions arise. Intervention from the heavens is to be expected when built into the system *via* ordeals and oaths whose whole point is that God and his Saints are not mocked. And lurking in the verbiage is an intriguing possibility. The 'rustic' is said to have been wealthy. The implication of Wigred's disregard for a loud-mouthed supporters' club may be that his opponent had one. Though the text has Wigred ordering the rustic to take the oath, it previously hinted that either might have had to, implying that this was a suit not of lord and man in the lord's court but of balanced parties in a different forum. The post-1104 account of the case by Dominic of Evesham evokes a 'rusticorum tumultu' and envisages something like a shire-court (as in Ely's aforementioned *innati* case).[151] It may not therefore go too far to see this dispute as a struggle between church and peasant in a public court, of a sort sometimes found in continental texts.[152] The Church always wins; the stories would not otherwise survive. But it may *not* always have won.

Last comes a case from the *Waltham Chronicle*. It is a later-twelfth-century text as it stands but drew on pre-conquest materials. One of its most interesting stories, for which it claims the authority of a 'scriptum', concerns four 'enemies of Christ's Cross' who broke into the church and stole ornaments, including silver vases. They then got totally lost in flight, and after wandering all night through

---

149   LS 159; 'Vita S. Ecgwini' iv 10, *Byrhtferth, Lives of Oswald and Ecgwine*, ed. Lapidge. I am again obliged to Professor Lapidge for pre-publication sight of his text and translation. See in the interim his important papers on 'The Medieval Hagiography of St Ecgwine', and 'Byrhtferth and the *Vita S. Ecgwini*'.

150   A theme featured in LS 172, a closely similar story by Dominic of Evesham (see next note), is that of a perjuror pulling out his beard; cf. LS 145, and chapter 2, n. 231, for this sensation elsewhere in England and on the continent. More straightforward divine reprisal is at work in LS 157 (paralysis), 166 (a faint), 167 (dumbness), 169 (blindness), 171 (madness), 173 (a fit, then death) and 177 (death). Cf. also *Anglo-Saxon Ely* 46, *Liber Eliensis* ii 35, p. 110 (also death). When pondering the limitations of all this evidence, it should be noted that little more would be known of the great Penenden Heath case of the 1070s if Osbern were the sole source: *English Lawsuits*, ed. van Caenegem, 5F, p. 12.

151   Dominic, 'Vita S. Ecgwini' i 19, pp. 96–7 (*Chronicon Abbatiae de Evesham*, ed. Macray, pp. 42–4).

152   Chapter 2, p. 78, and n. 242; also Wickham, 'Land disputes', in *Disputes*, p. 118, and Morris, 'Dispute settlement in the Byzantine provinces', *ibid.*, pp. 132–5.

marshy terrain, arrived next day at a London gate. Here they unluckily bumped into Theodoric, the city's premier gold- and silver-smith, and tried to sell him what he could remember making for the wife of Waltham's founder. Excusing himself as needing to fetch cash, he came back with some hastily summoned neighbours and denounced them as thieves, demanding that they return the goods to Waltham with a posse which would then exact the appropriate 'talio, according to the custom of the country'. So it happened. One, a confessed cleric, was branded in the face with the church key, and the other three were executed.[153] The tale's charm (if that is the *mot juste*) is its plainness. There is no miraculous rescue from penalty or sanctuary, no supernaturally exposed perjury.[154] Waltham's own writer was pushed to find any divine action in the capacity to get lost at night, and in a coincidence no greater than those that have formed the hinge of epic modern novels. Because it is just a good yarn of four crooks caught out by their bad luck and bad management, it is a great rarity in an age without Assize Rolls. It thus sheds the brightest of lights on a justice that was unsophisticated but effective – and brutal.

Examination of Anglo-Saxon lawsuits gratifyingly reinforces the impressions left by contemporary historians in three main respects. First, law-codes are more completely overlooked in sources where this is even more of a surprise. Fornication, theft and treason were crimes for which legislation made texts available. They were also relatively common prosecutions. But the linkage is invariably ignored by the documents. Anglo-Saxon property laws were sparse and crude. But they did cover the rights of kin to alienated property, much the most frequent area of dispute. There is again a 'zone of silence' between the two. Second, as with narratives, sources whose interest in *laws* was marginal still had a very marked interest in *law*. On lawsuit evidence, what is seen to be decreed law is seen to be enforced and in the way decreed. Ely's post-975 trauma or the worldly wisdom of Ramsey's Abbot Ælfwine show that alienations garnered by the church and contested by aristocratic interests were directly affected, either way and right or wrong, by imposed authority. The number of forfeitures, and the scope of crimes and properties that they covered, shows that no one was too big or small to escape them. What made this possible were courts that seem to work as ordered. The critical issue is not that they could be defeated or twisted, because that would remain the case long after the first millennium. It is that as the millennium closed, there is so little sign of any restraints on the interventions or extractions of royally primed justice. Around the year 1000, the French oppressors punished by saintly champions of society's underdogs were usually 'castellans' who acknowledged no higher power in theory or fact. Their counterparts in the nascent English kingdom were almost invariably royal officers.[155] Even hagiography tends to show that the 'state' in England was immanent when in much of Europe it was evanescent. If comparison extends to the period with

153   LS 178; *The Waltham Chronicle* 24, pp. 62–5.
154   LS 157 *is* a case of supernatural arrest; rescues from prison or penalty are 154, 156, 158, 173; sanctuary cases are 169, 171; and perjury, 145, 159, 166–7, 172, 177.
155   Morison, 'The Miraculous and French Society', pp. 195–201; cf. Graus 'Die Rolle der Gewalt'. This contrast is further explored in chapter 7, pp. 483–4; and see also chapter 9.

which the first part of chapter 2 was concerned, a different sort of contrast emerges. English records were less numerous and less regular than Carolingian. There is no suggestion of a notariate at work. The only direct evidence for the production of Anglo-Saxon judicial memoranda made these the responsibility of local bishops. The indirect evidence is that this is what happened.[156] For all that, royal pressure on legal process was at least as marked as elsewhere in Europe, perhaps more so. Forfeitures were commoner. Royal charters make up a larger proportion of the texts. One of this book's main themes thus makes its first appearance. The documentation of the government's justice in the Old English kingdom is as uneven as its impact is unmissable.

Finally, the evidence of Asser and William of Malmesbury for significant legal activity under Alfred are not extravagant fancies by a foreigner and a cloistered romancer. Where reliable information is so scarce, it might of course be a coincidence that its nature changed in Alfred's time. Similar modes of argument would prove that Halley's Comet caused the Norman Conquest. The fact remains that vernacular records, the effects of forfeiture, and reorganized courts, all began to influence law-reporting simultaneously. The case for any connection is as yet *prima facie*; but it surely deserves the further exploration that it will receive in Part III.

---

156   Cubitt, *Anglo-Saxon Church Councils*, pp. 77–82; and 'Lawsuits', pp. 272–8 (pp. 277–82).

CHAPTER 4

The Manuscripts of Legislation

The last of the contextual levels to stand between historians of early English law and their legislative raw material consists of the manuscripts which have fossilized the evidence since its days of active life and made it available for modern inspection. The geological metaphor is apt. What seem barriers to scholars intent on instant wealth of knowledge help others to explain what lies below and how it got there. Like his colleagues in nineteenth-century academia, Liebermann tended to see medieval scribes as obstacles rather than aids to the recovery of the past. Manuscripts were studied chiefly in order to construct elaborate textual *stemmata*. Yet anyone trying to approach legal history without preconceptions of what law ought to be should have much to learn from the context in which legislative texts are found. The character of a legal manuscript – physical appearance, glosses, other contents – has obvious implications for the use made of written law in the circles that produced it (cf. chapter 2, pp. 56–70). Such circles are of course confined to those whose efforts survived; which in England before 1066 and for some time thereafter means that they must have had immediate or ultimate access to a great ecclesiastical library. People like that might be thought untypical of the kind of government official that habitually used law-codes. But to think so is to succumb to two preconceptions: that government officials *did* use law-codes; and that they were different sorts of animal from bishops or abbots. Evidence examined so far in this book casts each preconception into doubt. In any case, the views of written law embodied in legal manuscripts are those of pillars of learning and custodians of vast corporate wealth. Those views are important in themselves.[1]

1 Laws and *Gesta*

Two of the earliest English manuscripts of secular legislation share one significant feature. Each joined the combined laws of Kings Alfred and Ine onto an

---

1 Liebermann lists legal manuscripts in *Gesetze* I, pp. xviii–xlii, but his views have been superseded by subsequent research, above all Ker's great *Catalogue*. The only general review of the material since Liebermann's is Richards, 'Manuscript Contexts of the Old English Laws'; my conclusions differ from hers on some points, but I gratefully acknowledge her insights in print, correspondence and conversation.

Anglo-Saxon Chronicle, along with further historical information like the West Saxon genealogical king-list, and lists of popes and English bishops. That they both did so is in a sense unsurprising. Much of one manuscript was almost certainly copied from the other. Yet this was more than a merely mechanical reproduction. The historical element in the second book is strongly reinforced, in that the complete compendium was added to a text of the vernacular version of Bede's *Ecclesiastical History*. Its legislative content was supplemented by laws of Æthelstan and by other legal and quasi-legal texts. The second collection's compiler could see the force of what had been done in the first. However incongruous it looks to modern eyes, it made sense at the time.

(i) Cambridge, Corpus Christi College, MS 173

Corpus Cambridge MS 173, often known as 'the Parker Manuscript' is among the most-discussed manuscripts in early English studies. This is not at all because it contains the earliest surviving record of English royal legislation. It is because it consists mainly of much the oldest of the *Anglo-Saxon Chronicles*, and the only one that was 'live' in the sense of being currently maintained throughout the period from the original compilation of the 'common-stock' in the early 890s till the late-eleventh century.[2] Palaeographically, codicologically, textually and linguistically as well as historically, it is a treasure-house. Like all treasures, it is hotly contested and tends to become an obsession.

Discussion must start by establishing the structure of the codex. The laws now occupy ff. 33r–52v. These leaves constitute two quires, with no break of any kind at f. 42r where the second begins. The first quire now lacks its opening folio, while the second has 'half-sheets' at ff. 45, 48 and 50; the likeliest reason for the disappearance of the first leaf is that it was blank, while the size of the second quire was probably increased in order to allow completion of the text within it. In other words, the quires containing the law-book were designed in the first instance as a self-contained unit or 'booklet'; the two hands responsible do not recur in the rest of the volume, nor indeed elsewhere.[3] As the book stands, the laws follow the text of the *Chronicle* to 1093. They precede a set of papal and episcopal lists and a text of Sedulius' *Carmen Paschale* which, content notwithstanding, has important links with the earlier part of the manuscript. It was not always so. When the manuscript was copied in the early-eleventh century, the lists apparently preceded the laws and the Sedulius was ignored. By 1600

---

table 4.1 gives a preliminary review of MSS in the order followed by the ensuing discussion, and summarizing its main results.

2   *Gesetze* I, p. xxiv (*siglum* E); Ker, *Catalogue* no. 39. The major discussions are those in n. 3 below. A valuable facsimile is *The Parker Chronicle and Laws*, ed. Flower and Smith.

3   For the collation of the MS, see (further to Ker) *Anglo-Saxon Chronicle MS A*, ed. Bately, pp. xvi, clxviii–clxix. The 'booklet' structure of the MS is stressed and the relevance of the 'booklet' notion explained by Parkes, 'Palaeography of the Parker manuscript', especially pp. 150–3. For reservations about the notion and for the explanation of the second quire's 'singletons' adopted here, see Dumville, 'Anglo-Saxon Chronicle', pp. 135–6 and n. 359.

Table 4.1   Summary review of Anglo-Saxon legal manuscripts

Class I

---

1   Corpus Christi College Cambridge 173 ('Parker' MS) [E]: Winchester (s. x^{med})/
Canterbury (after 1001)
– 'Anglo-Saxon Chronicle', **Af–Ine**, papal and episcopal lists

2   BL, Cotton Otho B.xi [Ot]: Winchester (1001x1015)
– OE Bede, 'Anglo-Saxon Chronicle', papal and episcopal lists, **II As**, **Af–Ine**, *Ymb
Æwbricas*, Burghal Hidage, 'Seasons of Fasting', Medical Recipes

---

Class II

---

3   BL, Cotton Nero E.i [F]: Worcester (s. x/xi)
– ['Passionary', Worcester cartulary], liturgical text, **IV Eg** [other Saints' Lives]

4   BL, Harley 55(A) [A]: Worcester (s. xi¹)
– Medical recipes, **II–III Eg**, Property memorandum

Class III

---

5   BL, Cotton Claudius A.iii [K]: Worcester?/York?? (s. x/xi–xi¹)
– **VI Atr** (**Latin.** & OE), Pontifical/Benedictional 'Claudius I'

6   York Gospels: York (s. x/xi – 1020x1023)
– Gospel-book, property memoranda, Wulfstan homilies, **Cn 1020**

Class IV

---

7   BL, Cotton Nero A.i(B) [G]: Worcester?/York?? (s. xi^{in})
– Wulfstan Homilies, *Inst. Pol.*, **I As, I Em, II–III Eg, V Atr, VIII Atr 1 – 5**, *Grið* //
Inst. Pol., Wulfstan Homilies, **V Atr** // Wulfstan 'Canon Collection' (table 4.4)

8   Corpus Christi College Cambridge 201 [D]: Winchester (s. xi^{med})
– *Reg. Conc.* OE frag. // Wulfstan Homilies, *Inst. Pol.* etc., **VIIa Atr, Northu., II–III
Eg, V Atr, I As, VIII Atr, I Em, Geþyn.** etc., **Cn 1018**, *Apollonius of Tyre* // Saints
Resting-places // OE Genesis (Joseph) // Judgement Day // Lord's Prayer, Gloria //
Confession formulae

Class V

---

9   Corpus Christi College Cambridge 265 [C]: Worcester (s. xi^{med})
– Wulfstan 'Canon Collection' (table 4.4), Excommunication and Penance
formulae, **IV Eg**, Penance Formulae, Ælfric letter to monks of Eynsham, *liturgica*
etc.

10   Corpus Christi College Cambridge 190 [O]: Worcester/Exeter (s. xi¹-xi^{med})
– Wulfstan 'Canon Collection' (table 4.4), Ælfric 'Pastoral Letters' (OE),
Penitential texts, *Mirc., Að, Had.* (table 4.5)

Class VI

---

11   BL, Cotton Nero A.i(A) [G]: Canterbury?? (s. xi^med)
     – I–II Cn, II–III Eg, *Romscot, Iudex,* Af–Ine

12   Corpus Christi College Cambridge 383 [B]: St Paul's (s. xi/xii)
     – ... Af–Ine, *Blas.*, *Forf.*, *Hu*, I Atr, AGu, EGu, II As ... I–II Cn, I–II Ew, I–II Em,
     Swer., AGu, *Wif.*, *Wer.*, Charm, *Becw.*, II Atr, *Duns.*, *Rect.*, *Ger.*, Shipmen, WSax
     genealogical king-list

13   *Quadripartitus* [Q]: MSS various (*c.* 1110)
     – I–II Cn, Af–Ine, *Blas.*, *Forf.*, *Hu*, I As, As Alm, II As, *Norðl.* etc., IV As, V As, III
     As, VI As, *Ord.*, AGu, AGu App., EGu, I–II Ew, I–II Em, *Swer.*, *Wif.*, *Wer.*, I Atr,
     III Atr, *Pax*, *Wal.*, IV Atr, II Atr, *Duns.*, VII Atr, *Iudex*, II–III Eg, III Em, Wl lad,
     [Wl Art.], *Gepyn.*, *Rect.*, CHn cor, Hn com

14   *Textus Roffensis* [H]: Rochester (1123–4)
     – Abt, Hl, Wi, *Had.*, WSax genealogical king-list, Af–Ine, *Blas.*, *Forf.* 1, *Ord.*,
     Wal., II As, V(-IV) As, *Pax*, *Swer.*, *Að*, *Mirc.*, EGu, *Wer.* I–II Ew, I–II Em, I Atr,
     Wl lad, III Atr, Ordeal rituals, *Inst. Cn*, Wl Art., Papal decretals, VI As, *Gepyn.*,
     Norðl., *Wif.*, Charm, *Becw.*, CHn cor, Excom., papal, patriarchal and episcopal
     lists, royal genealogies; Rochester charters and obituaries

---

Class VII

---

15   BL, Harley 55(B) [A]: ??? (s. xii^med)
     – I–II Cn

Class VIII

---

16   Vatican Cod. Reg. lat. 946 [Vr]: ??? (s. xi^1)
     – X Atr

17   BL, Burney 277 [Bu]: ??? (s. xi^2)
     – Af–Ine

18   BL, Cotton A.x [-]: ??? (??)
     – IX Atr

19   Bodl. Vet. A.3 c. 196 [-]: ??? (1811)
     – II–III Eg

20   BL, Additional 43703 [Nw2] (1560s)
     – (Af–Ine?), II As, V As, *Iudex*

the Sedulius preceded the laws.[4] The various 'booklets' seem to have had lives of their own. Liebermann's view that the laws had no original connection with what came before or after was thus far justified.

However, it was almost certainly wrong. At the foot of f. 42r is the quire-signature 'e', and there is a 'c' at the foot of f. 25v; f. 42r is the first page of the second quire of laws, and presumably there was a 'd' on the lost opening folio of the first; f. 25v is the final page of the quire concluding with annal '924'(920).[5] Hence, when these signatures were entered, the laws constituted the collection's fourth and fifth quires. They are now the fifth and sixth, because the quire containing the *Chronicle* from '925'(924) has intervened. The present fourth quire was evidently designed to continue the *Chronicle* as it stood in quires 1–3. It seems to have begun with a block of annals written retrospectively and in one stint at some point after 946, in a script which belongs to a later phase in the history of Anglo-Saxon 'square minuscule' than the hand or hands of the *Chronicle* from 891 to '924', or those of the laws themselves. It follows that the laws were joined to the *Chronicle* between the completion of quires 1–3, which is palaeographically unlikely to have been later than 930, and the addition of quire 4, probably in the 950s but perhaps before 951.[6] As it happens, expert palaeographical verdicts on the hands of the laws are that they are 'intermediate in character' between the hand(s) that wrote the *Chronicle* from 891 to '924' and that which resumed the story in '925'; and that 'they are best assigned to the 930s'.[7] A further and virtually conclusive consideration is that the format of the leaves bearing the laws was designed to match the specifications of those concluding the *Chronicle* to '924'.[8] It is reasonably deduced, then, that the laws were written at about the time when they were added to the *Chronicle*; and it can be argued that they were copied in order to be added to the *Chronicle*.[9] Even the

4   Parkes, pp. 151–3, 168–71. For the Sedulius linkage see below; but Page, 'Parker Register', pp. 9–11, suggests that it *was* a 'sharp-eyed antiquary' who joined it to the MS after Parker's time; if so, the two parts may never have been physically united before *c*.1600.
5   They are clearly visible in the Flower/Smith facsimile; see also n. 9. The repeatedly revised chronology of the Parker *Chronicle* to 942 is a much-debated topic: see *Anglo-Saxon Chronicle MS A*, ed. Bately, pp. xcviii–xcix, with references in her n. 288; and Dumville, 'Anglo-Saxon Chronicle', pp. 99–103. The dates given here in inverted commas are those of the MS as it now stands; dates without are adjusted (i.e., so far as possible, 'real' dates).
6   The evidence that the '925' annalist meant to continue the Parker *Chronicle* itself is not just that he (or she) carried on where the previous scribe left off but also that he made an entry in 710 (f. 9r, *Anglo-Saxon Chronicle MS A*, p. 33), where Scribe 1 left a blank. Like Professor Dumville (pp. 62–4), though unlike Professor Bately (p. xxxiv), I incline to regard the change of ink and layout on f. 27v as evidence that the annals to 946 and annal numbers to (erased) 956 were written before the entry for King Eadred's death (955), and perhaps before Bishop Ælfheah's death (951, entered in another hand).
7   Ker, *Catalogue*, p. 59; Dumville, 'Anglo-Saxon Chronicle', pp. 136–7; as against Ker, Parkes and Bately, Professor Dumville makes a strong case (pp. 67–9, 100–1, 122–3, 137–8) that the *Chronicle* 891–'924' was written by a single scribe but on two widely separated occasions (the break coming at '913'(912) near the foot of f. 21r).
8   Dumville, 'Anglo-Saxon Chronicle', p. 138.
9   The otherwise curious fact that signature 'c' comes at the end, signature 'e' at the forefront, of their respective quires, is explicable if they were inserted when the join was made; their lettering is on the whole closer to that of laws scribe 1 (f. 33r) than of laws scribe 2; in any event, microscopic examination of nib width (in which I was assisted by Dr Mildred Budny) suggests that the signatures were more probably entered by one of the laws scribes than by the *Chronicle* scribe who finishes on f. 25v. Remnants of

most hard-headed scholar can hardly deny that the laws were consciously associated with the *Chronicle* half a century after their composition.

Until recently there was little doubt about where this was done. The Parker
manuscript was at Christ Church Canterbury by the later-eleventh century. But
the apparent Winchester interest of some annals in the '925'–955 stint and afterwards have long suggested that it was 'in origin at least a Winchester book'.[10]
The Winchester thesis reached its high-water-mark between the 1957 publication of Ker's *Catalogue* and that of Malcolm Parkes's celebrated paper nineteen
years later, as more and more of the evidence seemed to fit. The *Sedulius* booklet,
some of whose damaged leaves had been restored in a hand very like that of
Chronicle scribe 1 (responsible for the annals to 891), is headed 'FRIÐESTAN
Diacon ... ', and a Frithestan was bishop of Winchester 909 – 931x3. The hand
of the 951 annal could be that of a 956 charter granting land in Hampshire.[11] It
was one of a series of mid-century charter 'originals', distributed between eight
scribes, of whom Dr Chaplais could claim that '[their] style ... is so alike that
one cannot even be sure that some of the works listed here under different hands
were not in fact written by the same scribe'. The Winchester *scriptoria*, in short,
were the royal 'Chancery' detected by earlier scholars in the palaeography and
diplomatic of documents from Æthelstan to Edgar. The script of the Laws can
be compared with that of some of the charters.[12] In addition, Parker *Chronicle*
scribe 1 could be identified with that of an intra-mural Winchester boundary
entered in the Book of Nunnaminster, which delineated a property belonging to
Ealhswith, Alfred's queen, where Nunnaminster was itself erected.[13] The same
scribe may have written part of a copy of Isidore's *Etymologiae* now at Trinity
College Cambridge. Meanwhile, *Chronicle* scribe 2 (annals 891–911/ 920) was
equated with that of the 'Tollemache' Orosius and probably with that of the
'Junius' Psalter (whose initials were almost certainly by the same artist as those
of the Orosius).[14] As Edmund Bishop had long before argued that the calendar
in the Junius Psalter was based on two others for which he postulated a
Winchester origin, it seemed to follow that Psalter, Orosius and Parker *Chronicle*
could all be traced to Winchester.[15] Finally, the Parker annal recording
Frithestan's accession to the bishopric of Winchester is 'boxed' and marked with

quire-signature 'a' occur on f. 7v, and perhaps of 'b' on f. 15v; they look like the work of Scribe 1, and
though Professor Dumville is generally dismissive of the quire-signature evidence, the second has interesting implications for his argument (pp. 89–96, 116–17) that the 'singleton' f. 16 arose from collaboration
between *Chronicle* scribes 1 and 2. For the usually consistent practice of Anglo-Saxon quire signatures,
see Ker, *Catalogue*, p. xl.

10   *Saxon Chronicles Parallel*, ed. Earle and Plummer, II, pp. xcv–xcvi; *EHD I*, pp. 110, 124.

11   Ker, *Catalogue* no. 40 and p. lix; S 636 (it ended up in the Old Minster archive, but probably in
connection with the grant of the land in 1045 (S 1008)).

12   Chaplais, 'Origin and Authenticity of the Royal Anglo-Saxon Diploma', pp. 59–60, as against
Drögereit, 'Gab es eine angelsächsische Königskanzlei?'. See Parkes, 'Parker Manuscript', pp. 166–7, for
the resemblance of laws scribe 2 and Chaplais 'Scribe (3)'/Drögereit 'Eadmund C' (S 497, 510, 528, 535,
552), and compare 'Scribe (2)'/'Æthelstan C' (S 447, 464, 512). But see too Dumville's comments, 'Anglo-
Saxon Chronicle', pp. 136–7.

13   *Ancient Manuscript belonging to Nunnaminster*, ed. Birch, p. 96 (translation, p. 32).

14   Cf. F. Wormald, 'Decorated Initials in English MSS', pp. 117–19.

15   E. Bishop, *Liturgica Historica*, pp. 254–6; see also below n. 23.

a circled cross in red and silver. A similarly elaborate symbol signals Alfred's 'hallowing' at Rome in 853, and cruder counterparts pinpoint other highlights in his career, concluding with his death and that of his wife.[16] Since a similar mark recurs in the Trinity Isidore, which was itself corrected by a hand very like one recurring in the Junius Psalter, the *Chronicle* once again links up with Winchester *scriptoria*. On this apparently 'fail-safe' basis, it was even possible to resurrect Plummer's case for the Winchester origin of the Alfredian *Chronicle* itself; Alfred's court-scholar, Grimbald, came from Rheims where the value of dynastic historiography was well understood, and was to be given charge of Winchester's New Minster, which for the next quarter century was the royal mausoleum.[17]

Yet the Winchester thesis soon ran into stiff resistance. The Parker text's proximity to the *Chronicle* 'original' seems precluded by the textual defects exhaustively rehearsed in a new edition.[18] There is a strong case that something like a real 'chancery' rather than Winchester's *scriptoria* was the agency responsible for mid-tenth century charters; at any rate, the scribes in question evidently attended the king on his travels.[19] Already in the very issue of the journal where Parkes's paper appeared, Professor Dumville targeted its fatal flaw. The pattern of palaeographical evoluton led Parkes to link Corpus Cambridge MS 183, a copy of Bede's *Lives* of Cuthberht presented by Æthelstan to Chester-le-Street, with Winchester. But it is most unlikely to be from Winchester: its list of Winchester bishops is defective not only in the ninth century but also at the very time of writing in the 930s.[20] A tug at this thread begins to pull the whole tapestry apart. The important thing is not that the scribal stitches so carefully knitted by Parkes can be unpicked. Dumville actually accepts the identity of Parker *Chronicle* scribe 2 with that of the Junius Psalter and Tollemache Orosius, as well as the identity of the scribes appearing in the Psalter and Trinity Isidore; and he can envisage that *Chronicle* Scribe 1, the *Sedulius* restorer and the hand responsible for the Nunnaminster boundary were trained in the same *scriptorium*.[21] Since he also believes that *Chronicle* scribes 1 and 2 collaborated, his position is not in the end far from Parkes's own. What he does do is cast clouds of doubt over the centrality of Winchester. The whole conception of a 'Winchester School'

---

16   The elaborate marks are on ff. 13r (Alfred) and 20v (Frithestan); the cruder ones on ff. 13v, 14r (x 2), 14v, 16r, 20r, 20v. Cf. Trinity College Cambridge MS B.15.33, ff. 20r, 23r, and below, n. 34.

17   For the Rheims link, see chapter 6, pp. 423–6, and for its legal/ historical MS(S), chapter 2, pp. 59–60, and below, p. 181. On the New Minster's 'regalibus usibus', see below, pp. 170–1, and n. 36.

18   *Anglo-Saxon Chronicle MS A*, ed. Bately, pp. lxxii–cxi; cf. her now near-conclusive account of these issues, *The Anglo-Saxon Chronicle, Texts . . .* , especially pp. 2–8, 59–62.

19   Keynes, *Diplomas of Æthelred*, pp. 22–6, 39–83 (a case reinforced in his forthcoming study of the charters ascribed to Drögereit's Æthelstan A, see chapter 6, n. 55). In *Diplomas*, p. 24, Keynes draws attention to S 449, 495, 'originals' from the same mould as those ascribed to Winchester, yet not by any supposed 'Winchester' scribe; S. 495 (as observed in a forthcoming study by Professor Dumville) is 'Mercian' so far as it concerns land in Northants and was copied (in part) into the Evesham cartulary, London BL. Cotton Vespasian B xxiv.

20   Dumville, 'Anglian collection', pp. 25–6, 42–3. Dumville is no longer so inclined to connect CCCC 183 with Glastonbury, in keeping with his retreat from Glastonbury ascriptions in general: 'English Square minuscule, mid-century phases', p. 136, n. 18; and *Liturgy*, pp. 39–65, 106–10. But see below, nn. 23–4.

21   Dumville, 'English Square minuscule, background', p. 170; 'Anglo-Saxon Chronicle', pp. 85–6.

of illumination is now so awash in a critical deluge that it can hardly be buoyed up by inverted commas.[22] Likewise, it seems that faith in a Winchester origin for the metrical calendar said to underlie that in the Junius Psalter was conditioned, like older views of the *Chronicle*, by nineteenth-century belief that Alfred's *court* was at Winchester. The full version of this calendar occurs in three other books, one of which (the famous 'Æthelstan Psalter') has only questionable Winchester connections, while the other two may both be from Canterbury, though Glastonbury and the West Country stand somewhere in the background.[23] Meanwhile, a Trinity College Cambridge copy of Hrabanus' *De Laudibus Sanctae Crucis* was apparently written by the second scribe of Boulogne MS 82, whose first scribe may be the main hand of the Junius Psalter; it has a sixteenth-century south-western provenance, and could have inspired the well-known frontispiece of Dunstan's Glastonbury 'class-book'.[24] If an alternative circle of arguments thus radiates from Glastonbury, whose significance as a 'royalist' foundation was hardly less than Winchester's, Canterbury's involvement is not excluded either. Chaplais 'Scribe (3)' inscribed a gospel-book given by Æthelstan to Christ Church, which was ultimately the depository of four of his five 'originals', as well as of all three written by 'Scribe (2)'.[25] Above all, the vernacular gloss to the Junius Psalter is textually very close indeed to that in the 'Vespasian' Psalter, whose Canterbury provenance is now beyond doubt.[26]

Dumville's main point is thus that emergent square minuscule was 'being practised at a number of centres in southern England'. In successive studies of the script's development, he has put more and more emphasis on the lead given by the 'royal chancery'.[27] Whatever the anachronism of tying the court to any one place, the rapid circulation of books and/or scribes from one library to the next is most easily explained by direction from the top. Alfredian literature leaves no doubt about royal initiative. A king with a *schola* under his eye must have had scribes in attendance and should have had books too. For Æthelstan, the regnant king when the laws were probably incorporated in the Parker manuscript, this is again beyond question.[28] Dumville has described the Trinity Hrabanus as 'a book

22   Wormald, 'Decorated Initials', pp. 115–16 (he was of course well aware of the perils of this label's indiscriminate application: see Appendix I to his paper, pp. 131–3); cf. Temple, *Anglo-Saxon Manuscripts*, pp. 17, 37–8.
23   Compare Professor Dumville's contribution to *An Eleventh-Century Miscellany*, ed. McGurk, with his latest views in *Liturgy*, pp. 1–38.
24   Dumville, 'English Square minuscule, background', pp. 175–6, citing Linda Brownrigg's view as communicated to Keynes, *Anglo-Saxon Manuscripts*, p. 10. On Hrabanus' *De Laudibus* and Dunstan's 'Classbook', see Higgitt, 'Glastonbury, Dunstan ... and Manuscripts', pp. 278–9 and Pll 1–2. Not to be forgotten in this connection (cf. Dumville, 'Anglo-Saxon Chronicle', pp. 71–2) is Stenton's 'South-western element in the Old English Chronicle'; especially interesting are the interpolations in the Parker MS at 688 on Glastonbury (f. 8v) and 726 on Ine's death (f. 9v) (*Anglo-Saxon Chronicle MS A*, pp. xxxviii, xcv, 32, 35), though it seems impossible to date these.
25   For the inscription in BL Cotton Tiberius A. ii see Keynes, 'King Æthelstan's books', pp. 149–50 and Plate III. For the charters see above, n. 12.
26   Dumville, 'Anglo-Saxon Chronicle', pp. 77–8, citing the 1955 view of Helmut Gneuss; cf. his *Liturgy*, p. 38.
27   Dumville, 'English Square minuscule, background', pp. 147 (n. 1), 158–9, 173–5; 'Square minuscule, mid-century phases', pp. 144–7, 152–5; cf. his *Liturgy*, pp. 143–4.
28   See Keynes, 'King Æthelstan's books', with the effectively complementary study by Wood, 'Making of King Æthelstan's Empire', pp. 252–9, 270–1.

fit for a king'.[29] The same might well be said of the Junius Psalter. By these standards, the Parker manuscript is a scruffy product. But the interests it displays could as well be a court's as a royal abbey's; the two are not at all easily distinguished in continental contexts.[30]

On that basis, one might even give respiration to the Winchester thesis. Whatever the caveats, the Parker manuscript by the mid-tenth century looks more like a Winchester book than anything else. The AD dates of Byrnstan's episcopate may be wrong, but calendar dates are supplied for his consecration and death, as also for Bishop Ælfheah's *obit*, Æthelwold's consecration and death, and Ælfheah II's consecration; this is more than is offered for any other see.[31] If Bishop Ælfsige is entirely overlooked, the Parker *Chronicle* can identify a 1001 casualty as his son (and so offer a reason for his omission).[32] All this means that the collection was most probably at Winchester before it moved to Canterbury, which matters for the legal manuscript to be considered next. Tracking back to the beginning of the century, it may be recalled that the first Parker *Chronicle* hand is enough like those of the *Sedulius* 'Frithestan' restorations and the Nunnaminster boundary to have been ascribed to the same *scriptorium*. One might expect the deeds and the obit of King Alfred to have been commemorated throughout a grateful realm; but Ealhswith, consistently obscured by West Saxon attitudes to their queens, is most likely to have been remembered at Nunnaminster (if she was actually its co-foundress) or the New Minster where she was interred with her husband.[33] This attaches significance to the cruciform mark opposite her death in the the Parker *Chronicle* margin, especially given that

29   'English Square Minuscule, background', p. 176; a remark, however, that he now regrets: *Liturgy*, p. 144.
30   Fleckenstein, *Hofkapelle* I, pp. 103–9, II, pp. 119–51; see also below, n. 36.
31   *Chronicle MS A*, pp. 70, 74–5, 78 (cf. ASC 971BC, p. 119, for a singularly localized Archbishop Oskytel). On any argument about the successively altered dates in the Parker MS (above, n. 5), the annalist allowed only two-and-a-half years for Byrnstan's episcopate, where he should have allowed three-and-a-half (O'Donovan, 'Interim revision of episcopal dates', pp. 110–11); as against the argument that the erroneous two-and-a-half years were *calculated* from an error in the annals, it seems equally possible that this mistaken figure (in an episcopal list?) *caused* the *Chronicle* blunder. Such an error is surprising but not inconceivable in local annals entered up to twenty years later, and the overlaps of the early 930s in Winchester's episcopal succession may have confused matters. The original omission of Bishop Ælfheah's obit (f. 27v, pp. xxxv–xxxvi, 74) is easily explained if the annals from '925' to 946 were entered before 951: see above n. 6.
32   *Chronicle MS A*, pp. 79–80; something of a *damnatio memoriae* actually overtook a number of bishops at the critical political juncture between Eadwig's accession and the secure establishment of Edgar's regime; I hope to return to this topic shortly.
33   *Liber Vitae*, pp. 5–6. On the obscurity of West Saxon queens, see Stafford, 'King's Wife in Wessex', pp. 3–4, with the alternative approach of Nelson, 'Reconstructing a royal family'.
34   Bately, *Chronicle MS A*, pp. xliii–xliv, ascribes Parker's marginal crosses to 'medieval hands' without apparently taking the point that the commemoration specifically of Ealhswith and Frithestan is suggestive. She cites a communication from Professor Dumville to the effect that the same mark occurs in Trinity Cambridge MS B.11.2 (an Amalarius from St Augustine's Canterbury: Dumville, *Liturgy*, p. 135), but the symbols there seem neater than those in the Trinity Isidore and Parker MS, which are indeed very alike. It should be noted that Ealhswith's obit is recorded in the BCD as well as A texts of the *Chronicle*, and also in the 'metrical calendar'; this has suggested that the latter may derive from Shaftesbury, where Alfred's and Ealhswith's daughter was abbess (McGurk, *An Eleventh-century Miscellany*, p. 48; Lapidge, 'A tenth-century metrical calendar', p. 346, n. 89). But the signalling of Frithestan seems to preclude this option for the Parker MS itself (and the failure to mark his death in '932' (f. 26r) may even suggest that the mark antedates the addition of the post-'925' annals).

it highlights Frithestan's accession too.[34] On top of that, there *is* evidence that court clergy in Edward the Elder's early years were linked with the Winchester minsters.[35] The New Minster's *Liber Vitae* says that Edward founded it 'for royal purposes (*regalibus usibus*)'. The prompt burial there of his parents, followed later by that of himself and many of his family, suggests that it functioned as a royal chapel at least until 924. On European analogies, supportive 'kingly literature' is a likely product for a centre of this sort.[36]

It transpires, not for the first or last time in this book, that the best response to a controversy is respect for each case. Only the most porous of membranes separated the culture of the court from that of major royal abbeys. The Parker manuscript might be a (rather low-quality) product of either. But the crucial point is that for the purposes of this discussion it does not greatly matter which. Ælfheah had once perhaps been a royal chaplain and was bishop of Winchester at the time when the laws of the West Saxons were added to their *Chronicle*. It is of no great moment whether he taught Dunstan and Æthelwold their political and spiritual duties at court or at his cathedral.[37] Either way, the Parker laws were copied by and for people deeply implicated in the West Saxon dynasty's audacious attempt to persuade the English at large of its claims to leadership.

The fact that there are after all indications of some sort of 'official' context for the Parker *Chronicle* and Laws makes it the more noteworthy that the legal text offered is as far from pristine as that of the accompanying *Chronicle*. Liebermann marked sixteen errors, some blatant; seven might be discounted, but at least two could be added.[38] They cover issues of some importance to the sense. Alfred's first law as it stands in the manuscript reads as follows:

> If anyone is wrongly obligated [*sc.* by oath], either to betrayal of a lord or to any unjust cause, it is more just to repudiate it than to perform it ***, and repudiates it, let him humbly give his weapons and his possessions to his friends' keeping (*þæt is þonne ryhtre to aleoganne þonne to gelæstanne ***, 7 þæt aleoge, selle mid eaðmedum his wæpn 7 his æhta his freondum to gehealdanne*).

35 The evidence is the overlap of attestations between Winchester and royal charters in and soon after 900 (Keynes, 'Atlas of Attestations' no. XXXIV: S 359, 374, 1284–6, 1443; Keynes, 'West Saxon Charters', pp. 1146–7) – though the sample is doubtless weighted by the disproportionate number of Winchester charters from the 900s.
36 *Liber Vitae*, p. 4; and see now *Liber Vitae of the New Minster*, ed. Keynes, pp. 16–19; with Allnatt 'New Minster', pp. 38–41. For the link between such foundations and royalist chronicles on the continent, see (e.g.) Wallace-Hadrill, review of Haselbach, *Aufstieg*, p. 155; and Gerberding, *Rise of the Carolingians*, pp. 146–72.
37 'Vita Sancti Dunstani Auctore B' 7–8, 13, ed. Stubbs, *Memorials*, pp. 13–15, 21–3; *Wulfstan, Life of St Æthelwold* 7–8, ed. Lapidge and Winterbottom, pp. 10–13. Cf. Wood, 'Making of Æthelstan's Empire', pp. 257–8, 271.
38 *Gesetze* III, p. 31 (3). Possible deletions from his list are Af Int. 21, Af 21, 65, Ine 26, 42 (see Torkar, *Altenglische Übersetzung*, pp. 130 (n. 5), 131); also Ine Rb. 62 involving an error duplicated by Ine 62 itself, and Ine 13:1 (faced with an essentially 'illogical' chapter-list (chapter 5, pp. 267–9), it is difficult to declare any one reading better than another). Possible additions to the list are Af Int. 49:5 (omission of 'is'), Af 8 ('munuc' for 'nunnan'); Liebermann cites 'Somner's' text in defence of the Parker reading, but this has no textual authority: below, pp. 261–2. The profusion of error is all the more striking for the fact that, as Dumville observes ('Anglo-Saxon Chronicle', pp. 137–8), the 'manuscript appears to have enjoyed very thorough correction'.

At the point marked ***, the line 'if, however, he pledges what is just for him to perform' has dropped out by *saut du même au même*.[39] If any sense at all could be made of the extant text, its effect would be that those who had *repudiated* a wicked oath should surrender weapons and possessions! Again, in two laws of Ine '*ceape* (stock, goods)' has replaced '*ceace* (cup, pan, basin, hence hot water ordeal)'. The resultant meaning is not complete nonsense, but it is strange that Anglo-Saxon law's only two pre-tenth-century references to ordeal should disappear from a manuscript written when the ordeal was in its heyday (chapter 8).[40] Legal historians may set such blunders aside, but not without noting that they were made.

The overall impression made by the Parker compilation is thus paradoxical. It does not seem to have been made for forensic purposes. Its dominant concern is historical. More can be said of the relevance of law-codes for this sort of historical omnibus after examination of the other manuscript where the combination occurs. It is already obvious that, even if the English kingdom's public servants managed to distentangle its legal element from the enveloping chronological data, they could have been grievously misled by the text they had to work with. Yet one could as well say of this manuscript what Bischoff said of those from the Carolingian '*Leges*-scriptorium' (chapter 2, pp. 62–4): that it may come from 'the neighbourhood of the Court'. The attitude to legal texts implicitly espoused in this compilation was not that of 'remote and ineffectual' clerics. It was that of parties near the centre of events. This is a conundrum that will recur throughout this chapter and the next.

(ii) BL, Cotton MS Otho B.xi + BL, Additional MS 43703

The Otho manuscript once contained a mid-tenth-century copy of the vernacular translation of Bede's *Ecclesiastical History*, followed by an *Anglo-Saxon Chronicle* with prefatory king-list, a set of papal and episcopal lists, Æthelstan's Grately law-code, the Alfred–Ine law-book with an extra clause, a text of the *Burghal Hidage*, a poem on the times and rationale of fasting, and a collection of medical recipes; most or all were copied in the early-eleventh century.[41] In its

39   Af 1:2; the error was spotted by the Otho copyist, which has momentous implications: below, pp. 174–5.
40   Ine 37, 62 (with Ine Rb. 62); Bartlett, *Trial by Fire and Water*, pp. 7–8, n. 8. Though it is early-twelfth-century MSS that preserve the correct reading, it is clear from mistranslations in *Quadripartitus* (below, pp. 236–44) that the clause's meaning had been lost by then, and it did not resurface until Liebermann did some inspired detective-work, 'Kesselfang bei den Westsachsen' (signalled in *LQR* XII (1896), pp. 309–10). 'Ceac' is a metallic vessel for liquid, translating Latin 'caucus/um', whence it directly or indirectly derives (*Ducange*, 1883 edition, II, p. 235, for the Latin word, and *Thesaurus Latinae Linguae* III, col. 624, for Greek, Irish and Welsh cognates). 'Caucos/ceacas' were what King Edwin of Northumbria was said to have set up at springs near roads, which none dared abuse for fear of him (*Bede, Hist. Eccl.* ii 16, pp. 192–3; *Old English Bede* I, pp. 144–5; cf. chapter 3, pp. 125–6, 128, 136–7); so was travellers' refreshment really what made such vessels a symbol of law and order?
41   The MS was Plummer's 'A', but is 'G' for modern *Chronicle* editors, as once for Thorpe: *EHD I*, p. 110, and Lutz, *Version G*. For *Gesetze* I, p. xxxvi and subsequent legal studies, it is 'Ot'. It is Ker no. 180, from which most of this paragraph is taken. But all previous work on the MS (*Chronicle* apart) is

original condition, this compilation might have posed fewer problems than the Parker manuscript. First, it may have had no more than three scribes, responsible for the *Bede*, for the Æthelstan code, and the rest. Second, the conjunction of historical and legal texts was certainly intentional: the same scribe wrote *Chronicle* and lawbook, and began his work by completing the *Bede* with its originally omitted autobiographical conclusion. Third, the collection's origin is relatively straightforward. Apart from the likelihood that its *Chronicle*, lists and law-book were copied from the Parker manuscript, the scribe of the *Bede* was also that of the Parker annals from '925' to 946/55. Granted the conclusions tentatively reached above, the Otho manuscript should also be from Winchester. Finally, the date when the most of the new matter was added to the *Bede* can be pinpointed quite precisely. Its *Chronicle* ended in 1001, at almost exactly the point of the last arguably Winchester entry in the Parker manuscript. Its episcopal lists, originally corresponding with Parker's, were apparently supplemented in another hand with bishops whose latest accessions or obits must be dated 1012x1013. It follows that the main Otho assemblage was made between 1001 and 1012; this date fits what survives of the script; and the hand of the Æthelstan code could be contemporary with the additions to the episcopal lists.

Yet many of these observations have had to be put in the past or conditional tense. Otho B.xi was not annihilated by the Cottonian fire like the unique copies of Asser and Æthelweard (pp. 258–9). But less than quarter of its 231 leaves survived, among them only two of the Æthelstan code and three of the Alfred-Ine law-book. Nothing is left of the episcopal lists or of what came after Alfred-Ine. Every leaf except for one detached in the seventeenth century is more or less severely damaged, and nothing can be known about collation and binding. Much of what can be said, including several of the statements in the preceding paragraph, is possible only because of two exceptionally fortunate circumstances. Almost the whole manuscript was copied in 1562, then glossed in the following years, by Laurence Nowell. His transcript is now BL, Additional MS 43703. A century and a half later the volume was studied by Humfrey Wanley. Not only did he describe it fully in his astoundingly perceptive catalogue of manuscripts in ancient Germanic vernaculars; he also annotated his personal copy of Smith's 1696 catalogue of the Cottonian Library catalogue to the effect that the episcopal lists were continued from *c*.988 to 1012x1013 'by another hand', so establishing a *terminus ad quem* for the rest of the collection.[42] All the same, discussions of

---

superseded by Torkar's study, *Altenglische Übersetzung von Alcuins De Virtutibus et Vitiis*, pp. 37–167; I had independently reached some of the same conclusions as Professor Torkar, but the discussion that follows is much indebted to his analysis. I offer a fuller account of some issues raised by the MS as a whole in 'BL, Cotton MS Otho B. xi: a supplementary note'; and cf. Rumble, 'Known Manuscripts of the Burghal Hidage'.

42   The discovery of the Nowell transcript was first announced by Robin Flower, 'Nowell and a recovered Anglo-Saxon poem', 'Nowell and the discovery of England', and 'Text of the Burghal Hidage'; more recent literature is reviewed by Torkar, *Altenglische Übersetzung*, pp. 44–8, 155–67. The detached genealogical king-list (acquired by the BL in 1894, now Add. MS 34652, f. 2) was given its place in the MS by Ker, 'Membra Disiecta, Second Series', pp. 81–2; see now Torkar, pp. 66–9; Lutz, *Version G*, pp. xxxviii–xlii, 1–2; Dumville, 'West Saxon genealogical regnal list', pp. 5–6. Wanley's discussion of the

Otho are bound to be like 'whodunnits' where the corpse consists only of an arm and a leg. Detection, however inspired, demands a lot of guesswork.

The questions needing an answer here are three: was the Otho text of the Alfred–Ine law-book indeed copied from the Parker manuscript's? What is the relationship of the legal texts found in both the Parker and Otho manuscripts with those only in the latter? And what is the logic (if any) of the collection as a whole? For Plummer, it could 'hardly be doubted' that Otho's *Chronicle* was a copy of Parker's; the discovery of the regnal-list leaf and of Nowell's transcript has made slight doubt into virtual certainty.[43] Liebermann was as confident as Plummer that the same could be said of the Alfred–Ine law-book.[44] Oddly enough, however, the transcript might well have persuaded him, with his taste for complex *stemmata*, that their kinship was that of cousins, not father and son. Most of the Parker errors are blithely reproduced by Otho/Nowell. A feature of the hand of the Parker laws (as of its second *Chronicle* hand) was a tall initial 'i'; one effect was to make 'inne' look like 'hine'. The Otho scribe copied it exactly, with the result that 'hine' is what Nowell initially wrote.[45] It is a very important aspect of Nowell's transcript that he corrected this mistake, and many more, to be blamed on his own shortcomings or those of the Otho scribe rather than Parker or another exemplar, in subsequent marginal or interlinear glosses.[46] These corrections will be considered shortly. And yet Alfred's oath and pledge law is flawless in Nowell. The line missed by the Parker scribe seems to have been present in Otho.[47]

Of possible explanations, perhaps the best in the circumstances is that the Otho manuscript was corrected. There are several word-order blunders in Nowell's copy, each marked by transposition signs consisting of parallel diagonals with a

---

MS is in his *Catalogus*, p. 219; his copy of Smith is Bodleian, Gough London 54, where the relevant annotations are on p. 71. Also important for one or two issues (Torkar, pp. 136–42) is that Otho was the basis of Abraham Whelock's *editio princeps* of the *Chronicle*, published as an appendix to his edition of the vernacular *Bede*, pp. 501–70. Among Professor Torkar's discoveries (pp. 52–60) is that the page-numbers given by Wanley as '231–351' should have read '331–451', so disposing of Ker's problem that a MS recorded in Gough 54 as 'constans foliis 231' should have only 351+ pages in Wanley's *Catalogus*; it must in fact have contained 462 pages, numbered recto and verso. Not the least of Otho's jinxes is that it occasioned Homeric somnolence in Wanley and Ker, two 'all-time greats' of Anglo-Saxon palaeography (e.g. nn. 53, 55 below).

43   *Saxon Chronicles Parallel* II, pp. xcix–c; Lutz, *Version G*, especially pp. xix–xxvi; cf. Torkar, pp. 66–8, 70–6, and Dumville, 'Genealogical Regnal List and Chronology', pp. 28–30.

44   *Gesetze* I, p. xxxvi, III, p. 31 (3).

45   Af 42:1, Parker MS, f. 45r, ln 3; Otho MS, f. 50v, ln 17; Nowell, f. 246v, ln 21; cf. *Chronicle* MS A., p. xxvi, with reference to Parker MS, f. 16v, ln 14 (892, p. 84).

46   A sample of errors in Otho/Nowell for which the Parker scribe was certainly not responsible might include: (i) Af Rb. 26, 'monnes fif'(!); (ii) Af Int. 49, 'bead'; (iii) Af Int. 49:9, omission of '7 manege þara þe me ne licodon' by *saut du même au même*; (iv) Af 5:5, 'þone dæg halgan þunres'(!); (v) Af 11:5, 'borenran men wif'; (vi) Af 36:1, 'be þam wite mid þy wite þæt afylle'; (vii) Af 39:2, 'þryfealdlice be syxhundan þæs bote'; (viii) Ine 39, 'fare he þær'; (ix) Ine 52, 'betwigum'; (x) Ine 74, 'þeof wealh'. One cannot of course be sure which of the Otho scribe or Nowell to blame for some of these; but it should be noted a) that (i) is visible in the Otho MS; and b) that, for reasons given in n. 48, (iv) - (viii) should probably also be ascribed to the Otho scribe. For Nowell's relative reliability, see Lutz, pp. liii–lvii, and Torkar, pp. 162–7. For his corrections, see below.

47   *Councils & Synods* I, p. 15; *Alfred*, tr. Keynes & Lapidge, p. 306. Torkar, pp. 130–1, disposes of all other Parker/Otho discrepancies.

dot between [/·/]. These marks also appear near the end of Nowell's version of the Grately code. Since he later crossed them out, it is difficult to see why he should have entered them at all unless they were in the original, where, as will soon be seen, they are best understood as a means of squeezing extra lines into limited space. If so, the other marks are also unlikely to originate with Nowell, whose transcript does have an air of mechanical reproduction first time around. Nor, if these marks were used on the inserted Æthelstan code, can they easily be attributed to the main Otho scribe.[48] But the corrections they signal could be the work of the hand that penned the Æthelstan code, and used them to fit it all in. It is an attractive speculation that a scribe familiar enough with legal literature to insert one code also reviewed the other, and thus restored the sense of Alfred's first law. That he could do so even when some later blunders escaped him, might be because the law's place in the code – and conceivably its importance – made it readily memorized.[49] Remote as such contingencies might seem, they impose less strain on credulity than suppositions that the correction was made silently by Nowell or Otho's main scribe, who contributed numerous extra blunders between them. Only yet more fiendish ingenuity can find a stemmatic way for the Otho MS to have repeated every Parker peculiarity bar this one.

Nevertheless, one feature of the law-book as presented in the Otho MS was certainly not copied from Parker. Immediately after Ine's last law, Nowell has an important little passage, which looks like an excerpt on the subject of adultery, and which was unknown till the transcript came to light. This text will be examined in chapter 5 (pp. 372–3).[50] It is inconceivable that this text belonged in any formal sense to Ine's code. Yet it is contextually germane in so far as it is legally

---

48   Marks for the Alfred–Ine law-book occur in the Otho MS itself on f. 49r (visible in ultra-violet light), corresponding to [n. 46] error (i); and in Nowell, ff. 236v, 243r, 244r, 246r, 246v, 252r, for errors (i), (iv) – (viii); the placing of these marks in relation to the text, especially at nos. (vii) – (viii), suggests that they did not originate with Nowell. For their presence earlier in the MS, see Lutz, *Version G*, p. xlvii and n. 3. Dr Lutz says that not only the mistakes but also the corrections were 'ganz sicher' the work of the Otho scribe, but does not say why (cf. Torkar, p. 132). If so, one would have to suppose that the Æthelstan scribe imitated his predecessor's marks. But the fact that they otherwise occur only in the Otho scribe's stint may be best explained by supposing that he was exceptionally prone to transposing words! However, a different pair of marks appears in Nowell on f. 246v (Af 42:2, 'circan þonne geierne'): ø; they recur on f. 260v ('Seasons of Fasting', p. 104, ln 220), and on f. 261v ('Leechbook' i 17(1), II, p. 60); these at least may reflect the Otho scribe's corrections of his own blunders.
49   The absence at this point in the transcript of the *signes de renvoi* used at the end of the Æthelstan code would be explained if there were sufficient space to make the insertion at the top or bottom of a page. Calculations based on ratios of the space used by Nowell and the Otho scribe are offered by Torkar, p. 142, and Lutz, pp. xxxvi–xxxvii. As Professor Torkar says, one has to reckon with the different layouts of various parts of the original; his estimate for the continuous prose of the Burghal Hidage texts (Otho, pp. 349–50, Nowell, ff. 255r–256r) suggests a ratio of 29 Nowell lines to 27 Otho (cf. n. 51 below), but Nowell was by this time writing less in each line (so taking up more space) than earlier in his transcript. The Bedan autobiography added by the Otho scribe occupied 88+ lines on extant leaves of the Otho MS (ff. 35r–36v), and 87+ in Nowell (ff. 196v–198r), which suggests very little difference between the two at this stage. Now, there are 211–12 Nowell lines for the almost continuous prose of Alfred's Mosaic preface from the start down to the *saut du même au même* at Af. 1:2 (ff. 238v–242r). If this point were to coincide with the top or bottom of a page in the Otho original, so allowing an insertion without *signes de renvoi*, the equivalent passage would have had to occupy 216 lines, or eight 27-line pages. For what the point is worth, therefore, the ratio calculated from the *Bede* works out almost exactly.
50   The text is elsewhere published only by Flower, 'Text of the Burghal Hidage', p. 62; but cf. Torkar, p. 135, n. 3.

prescriptive. Furthermore, Nowell reproduced it almost as if it *were* part of the law-book. He began it with a bigger initial than he gave to individual clauses, but smaller than the one opening the *Burghal Hidage* directly afterwards. The best parallels are the initials of the last clause of Alfred's preface and of Ine's prologue. Like these passages, and unlike the *Burghal Hidage*, Nowell put it on the very next line.[51] He was probably reflecting the layout of the manuscript itself. Significantly, Wanley failed to notice the piece though he picked up both separate sections of the *Hidage*.[52] There is thus reason to think that the Otho scribe saw the text as an appropriate addition to the law-book. This is a first example among several to come of an important feature of Anglo-Saxon legislation: its habit of acquiring more or less alien appendices in transmission.

More important still, if appreciably more complex, are the issues raised by the Æthelstan code's presence in the volume. Its two surviving leaves establish that it was the work of a third scribe, and that its pages were ruled for twenty-two lines, not twenty-seven like the rest of the book. Wanley's report shows that there were no more than three leaves of 'laws' between the episcopal lists and the Alfred–Ine law-book in the manuscript he saw. This means that it cannot then have contained, as Ker (postulating four leaves) supposed, the 'fifth' (Exeter) code of Æthelstan or the anonymous text known as *Iudex*, which Nowell went on to copy.[53] It is in principle possible that the relevant pages had dropped out by Wanley's time. But Nowell put his texts of V Æthelstan and *Iudex* at the very end of his transcript after his colophon, thereby implying that he came upon them only in his revising phase. In addition, the letter-forms and orthography of his transcription suggest that he took them not from Otho but from a manuscript which is no longer extant (see section 8(v), pp. 261–2). The crucial question is how the text of the Grately code terminated in Otho. When, in other words, did Nowell cease to copy Otho, and when did he become dependent on his second copy? In his transcript the Grately code does not end neatly at the foot of a page, but in mid-sentence, half-way through the first provision of the final clause (II As 26, 'he hæbbe'). It is then that a drawn hand directs attention 'to the end of the book', where another drawn hand ushers in the remaining lines of the clause; the Exeter code follows.[54] The lost manuscript must therefore have supplied the last part of Grately as well as Exeter and *Iudex*. Confirmation comes from the fact that the second extant Æthelstan leaf, the original's third and last, would have had no room for all of II As 26. On that basis, one might suppose that Otho's text of Grately was a fragment bound into it at some point between the early-eleventh century and 1562. Its twenty-two line ruling is after all anomalous, and Wanley did describe it as 'imperfect'.

However, the balance of evidence tilts the other way. To start with, the Æthelstan code was anyway 'imperfect' in that it lacked a prologue, as Wanley

---

51   Nowell, f. 255r; cf. ff. 241v, 249r. Cf. Torkar, pp. 135–40: for there to have been room for all the Burghal Hidage (and probably a blank line before it) on Otho pp. 349–50, two lines of '*Ymb Æwbricas*' at least must have been on the preceding verso; but the text of Ine can hardly have occupied less than twenty-five lines of this page, leaving no scope for a blank line between the two.
52   *Catalogus*, p. 219.
53   *Catalogus*, p. 219; Ker, p. 232, art. 5; Torkar, pp. 81–4.
54   Nowell, ff. 236r, 265r–267v. On this, see Torkar, pp. 84–121.

observed on encountering it in *Textus Roffensis*.[55] Even if he did mean that the text broke off unnaturally, he was not at his formidable best in describing this manuscript, and his verdict carries less weight than usual. In the second place, Nowell's copy suggests that the break came at the end of clause 25:2, 'ure ealra freondscipes'. Before the start of the next is an elaborated capital 'C', such as he used when revising his text of Alfred–Ine to mark a break between chapters which he had earlier missed. From that point, his handwriting changes slightly, for example in employing a dotted 'i' (a feature of his revising phase), and the ink is slightly lighter. Thirdly, Nowell put the double-diagonal marks, whose presence and later erasure was noted before, above 'folgoðe' (II As 25:1), 'v' (in 'v pund') and 'ealles' (II As 25:2). Extrapolation from the extant Otho fragment at twenty-two lines to the page suggests that the leaf should have ended some four lines before the end of the penultimate clause (II As 25:1, 'se biscop amanige'). Nowell's double-diagonals are thus just where they would have been if, in the original manuscript, a twenty-third line had been added to the page, with three more distributed by signes de renvoi around it. Finally, and above all, the penultimate clause of the Grately code does in fact read as if this were its intended conclusion: it concerns the punishment of those disregarding the edict as a whole, whereas the final clause on perjury looks like an afterthought (see chapter 5, pp. 307–8). There is anyway reason to think that Otho's text of Grately differed from other surviving copies. Nowell at first omitted the immediately preceding clause on Sunday trading, which is in fact known to have been altered later in the reign. He entered it marginally, presumably from his second exemplar. All in all, it is much more likely that what Nowell and Wanley saw in Otho was a complete but variant text of the Grately code, which the scribe had struggled to accommodate in the available space.[56]

Compression argues an obstacle ahead. That is what a previously entered text of the Alfred–Ine law-book would have been. If, then, Otho's version of Grately ended where it was meant to and with difficulty, it was present by intention rather than chance. The twenty-two line ruling of these pages is explained if the code was entered onto blank sheets of the quire meant to carry episcopal lists, where a variant ruling might be expected.[57] There need therefore be no doubt that a later scribe accepted the view of the Otho and Parker compilers that written law was at home in an essentially historical context. Another important lesson of the Otho manuscript is that distinctly variant legal texts circulated in pre-conquest England. One or other of Otho's early-eleventh century scribes added a chapter to the Alfred–Ine law-book. Its version of Grately lacked the Sunday trading

---

55   *Catalogus*, p. 274. Wanley preferred to call fragments 'mutilated', 'truncated' or 'lacking', and once or twice used 'imperfect' when unsure: cf. his account of the 'Exeter Book', p. 280: 'nunc imperfectus ... sine titulo ... sine initio, & me iudice, sine fine'.

56   Torkar's trailblazing discussion of the whole issue, pp. 84–105, leaves a choice of the two alternatives posed here, while leaning in his final sentence towards the second. The only argument that he does not use is the rather lighter ink from capital 'C' of Nowell f. 236r, ln 20, onwards: this is actually undetectable on microfilm or in his photograph (p. 103), but is apparent in the MS itself, and (for me) decides the issue.

57   As in Otho's Parker prototype. For further exploration of the mechanics, see 'BL, Cotton MS Otho B. xi', p. 66 (74–5), n. 13.

clause that was later changed and the perjury epiloque that was subsequently tacked on (chapter 5, pp. 291, n. 130). Updated in one way, it was outdated in the other. This tendency to resist revision needs attention. Frankish materials are comparable, those of southern Europe in sharp contrast (chapter 2, pp. 44–9).

However, the logic of the Otho compilation can hardly be upheld without taking account of its last three items: the *Burghal Hidage*, the poem christened 'Seasons of Fasting' by modern scholars, and the medical recipes. All were destroyed in 1731; their one-time presence in the manuscript is deducible only from Nowell's transcript and Wanley's report. The easiest option, denial that they belonged to the original collection at all, is not really available. The *Burghal Hidage* at least must have started part of the way down a page, and was therefore copied into the manuscript, not tacked on later.[58] Moreover, Nowell's transcript of both poem and recipes uses an f-shaped 'y', and occasionally substitutes pre-vocalic 'nȝ' for 'nc'. The latter feature is rare but appears in the extant work of Otho's *Chronicle*/law-book scribe; the former is quite regular there but otherwise unusual after *c*.1000.[59] Hence, it is as likely as not that this scribe added all three items himself. Why?[60]

For the *Burghal Hidage* and recipes, there is no clear answer. The cures offered for blurred vision, 'insects in the ears' (tinnitus?), or an inability to discharge one's bowels even 'when shut in the outhouse' have no correlation with the injuries covered by legal compensation tariffs.[61] The most one can say is that the Otho manuscript is not the only instance where medical texts are associated with historical or legal literature, so the association may have made sense of a sort. Another book to be studied shortly, an episcopal collection from York or Worcester (pp. 186–8), juxtaposes medical and legal tracts. More subtly, the major Old English medical encyclopedia known as 'Bald's Leechbook' contains most of the Otho recipes, and a missing quire arguably included those now unique to the Nowell transcript.[62] *Bald's Leechbook* may have had its historical resonances.[63] It was certainly copied by the same scribe as wrote the '925' annals in the Parker *Chronicle*, and the *Bede* in the Otho volume to which a copy of the Parker annals was later added.[64] That is to say that what the Otho scribe copied together had each been in a (Winchester?) predecessor's repertoire two generations before.

58   Torkar, pp. 138–40.
59   Torkar, pp. 152–3.
60   This issue is the particular concern of my note on the manuscript in the Hill-Rumble *Burghal Hidage* collection, and reference may be made to that for elaboration of points made here.
61   'Leech Book' i 2(1,10–11), 3(11–12), ii 32, *Leechdoms*, ed. Cockayne, II, pp. 26–7, 30–1, 42–5, 236–7. Ker, p. 233, lists the recipes in Nowell with reference to Cockayne's edition, and see next n. for those not printed there.
62   *Bald's Leechbook*, ed. Wright and Quirk, pp. 14–15; Torkar, 'Zu den ae. Medizinaltexten', pp. 323–8. But for signs that Otho had more than one source, see Cameron, 'Bald's *Leechbook*', pp. 166–7, and Meaney, 'Variant versions of OE Medical Remedies', pp. 246–55.
63   For the possibility that the original 'Leechbook' dates to Alfred's time (probably not earlier), see Bately, 'Old English Prose before and during the reign of Alfred', pp. 102–3; and for closer associations with the king, Meaney, 'Alfred, the Patriarch and the White Stone', pp. 65–7, and my 'BL, Cotton MS Otho B. xi', pp. 62–3 (pp. 76–8).
64   Ker, *Catalogue*, pp. 58–9, 233–4, 333.

There ought, by contrast, to be no problem about the presence of the *Burghal Hidage* alongside legal texts. It reads more like a government document than anything before Domesday Book. The burghal statistics are followed in the Otho manuscript by instructions for their application. As is now well-known, the formula applies with stunning accuracy to the actual lengths of wall involved.[65] Because a document like this is found in the company of laws that government officials might be expected to use, it reinforces the instinct that laws *were* so used. Yet most texts in this manuscript are historical; and this version of the hidage was a century out-of-date when it was entered in Otho. An alternative textual tradition enrolled Worcester and Warwick among the Boroughs, and identified the fort at Pilton with thriving Barnstaple; modifications unlikely to be later than Æthelstan's time and perhaps as early as Alfred's.[66] This alternative tradition was represented by the early-thirteenth-century London 'Leges Anglorum', where *Tribal* and *Burghal Hidages* supplemented a preface, 'On the number of provinces, homelands, counties and islands that undoubtedly belong to the crown of the realm of Britain, i.e. what is now called the kingdom of the English' (*sic*). The 'Leges Anglorum' is lawyer's work, but it is also a treatise with a profoundly historical theme, and it was not their administrative function that prompted the inclusion of the *Hidages*.[67] Conceivably, the compiler of the Otho volume also saw the *Burghal Hidage* as a historical monument to a critical stage in the making of an English kingdom, one which in the context of renewed Scandinavian assault was again topical.[68]

A particular reason for thinking the message of the recipes and *Burghal Hidage* historical is that this is so clearly true of the third of Otho's concluding items, the poem on 'Seasons of Fasting'.[69] This poem has an ostensibly legal theme. It is designed to foster observance of the Lenten fast that had been obligatory in Anglo-Saxon law since the seventh century.[70] But another of its concerns is that the English remain faithful to the national tradition of Ember Day fasting that had been given them by Gregory, 'the people's pope'. English practice by then differed from the continental custom promoted by tenth-century reformers. The ordinance of a pope, and national apostle at that, of course took precedence over a rival observance, whether Biblical, Cluniac, or otherwise hallowed.[71] The emphasis of 'Seasons' on a special English spiritual heritage thus squares with

65 RoASCh App II i; Hill, 'Burghal Hidage'; Hill, *Atlas*, pp. 85–6; Hill, 'Nature of the figures', and 'The Calculation and the purpose'.

66 Hill, 'Burghal Hidage', pp. 86, 90 (n. 19); cf. Brooks, 'West Saxon hidage'.

67 Liebermann, *Über die Leges Anglorum*, pp. 4–10, and see below, pp. 237–8. Its 'De Numero Provinciarum ... ' is edited, neither flawlessly nor from the best MS, in *Munimenta Gildhallae*, ed. Riley, II, pp. 624–6, with *Tribal* and *Burghal Hidages*, pp. 626–8. It is an elaboration of the interesting tract, originally written in English at the turn of the eleventh and twelfth centuries and variously extant in Latin, that is, *inter alia*, the source of the so-called 'County Hidage' foisted on Anglo-Saxon scholarship by Kemble, *Saxons* I, pp. 493–5, and immortalized by Maitland, *DBB*, pp. 455–60.

68 See further my 'BL, Cotton MS Otho B.xi', p. 64 (79–80).

69 *Anglo-Saxon Minor Poems*, pp. 98–104, 194–8; seminally assessed by Sisam, *Studies*, pp. 45–60. Cf. Richards, 'Manuscript Contexts', p. 175; and note here Robinson, 'Old English Literature', pp. 26–7.

70 Lns 103–83; cf. *Bede, Hist. Eccl.* iii 8, pp. 236–7, with Wi 14–15.

71 Lns 39–102; for a full quotation of lns 87–94, see 'BL, Cotton MS Otho B.xi', p. 63 (78); and cf. Sisam, *Studies*, pp. 48–50, with his important note, *ibid.*, pp. 278–87, at p. 281.

the central *motif* of the whole volume. In the Parker manuscript, the peace-keeping traditions of the West Saxons were set beside the *Chronicle*'s record of their war-making achievement. It was an echo of the 'wars-laws' counterpoise that inspired the prologue to *Lex Salica* and panegyricists of Anglo-Saxon and continental kings (chapter 2, p. 40, chapter 3, pp. 128–9). More obviously, and here perhaps more consciously, it evoked the Book of Exodus, in which God's people went through their *rites de passage* and were then given His Law.[72] In the Otho collection, this block of material was appended to a work that was a history of the *whole* English people, and one where the equation of English destinies with those of the original Chosen People was almost explicit. The volume thus opened with an account of Englishmen's conversion at Pope Gregory's behest, and drew to a close with a reminder of their Faith's Roman benison. This was a period when one Englishman rebuked another for betraying his 'race (*cynn*)' by adopting a 'foreign' hairstyle.[73] Just because it was now under such painful attack, English consciousness was the flavour of the hour. The Otho scribe partook of the mood.

Even if one were to allow that laws, hidage, recipes and poem served their most obvious purpose, it would still be true that the Otho manuscript was first and foremost a historical collection.[74] The question 'why?' relates closely to the question 'who?' For all their ideological implications, the Parker and Otho collections are more secular in content than other English legal manuscripts before 1066, or most afterwards. Here if anywhere is the chance to argue that law-texts belonged to lay officials. But arguments for the Winchester genesis of each manuscript remain strong if not compelling. Late in the eleventh century, the Parker *Chronicle* was reactivated as a Canterbury text. The Otho scribe made his copy from it soon after 1001. In 1006, the future St Ælfheah was translated from Winchester to the archbishopric. The Parker manuscript's Frithestan associations have suggested it was preeminently 'the bishop's book'. The evidence is covered by supposing that Ælfheah took it with him, after thoughtfully having it copied for his successor.[75] However, so critical an issue should not hang on an unsupported guess. It is therefore important that 'Seasons' is less 'secular' than it at first looks. It has a vivid *tableau* of priests popping down the street after mass to a wine- and oyster-bar, and warns the 'folces mann' to ignore the example and adopt the message. But before and after come stanzas addressed to the priests: 'Who can make a thrall's peace with his lord if he has previously angered him greatly and does not make it good, but daily renews by his actions the injury of the old offence?'[76] Layman, priest and God as counterparts to thrall, intercessor

---

72   Howlett, *British Books in Biblical Style*, pp. 360–3, draws a suggestive parallel between the structure of the Parker MS and the Biblical Books of Chronicles, Ezra and Nehemiah.

73   Kluge, 'Fragment'; Wormald, '*Engla Lond*', p. 18 (p. 379); 'BL, Cotton MS Otho B.xi', p. 64 (p. 80).

74   See my statistics 'BL, Cotton MS Otho B.xi', p. 68 (80), n. 33.

75   Parkes, 'Palaeography', pp. 170–1. Professor Dumville, arch-sceptic in these matters, finds this 'the most economical hypothesis': 'West Saxon Genealogical List', p. 6. According to Wanley, p. 219, the MS was from St Mary's Southwick; for linkage of Winchester, Southwick and what may be this MS, see chapter 3, pp. 141–2.

76   Lns 184–230; Sisam, *Studies*, p. 50.

and lord: it is a decidedly clericalist metaphor. The poem's tone is that of a bishop berating his subordinates and flock.

In a debate with so many unmarked hurdles, the burden of proof should be a decisive handicap. Two last points seem to saddle it on advocates for the lay ownership of these books. First, there is potential episcopal interest in *all* their contents. Bishops presided jointly over shire-courts. They had taken charge of urban defence from before the time of Sidonius Apollinaris. Their medical role was on record since John of Beverley recalled what he had been taught about bleeding by Archbishop Theodore.[77] Second, it may be recalled that a Carolingian book with comparable contents was on those grounds taken to have been owned by a count, and was almost certainly, on the contrary, from Hincmar's Rheims.[78] There is thus a good general case that these manuscripts belonged to bishops, whatever the particular case for Winchester. The collections studied in the pages to follow point to the same conclusion, only more directly.

2   Laws on Loose Leaves

If the practical application of laws was apparently not uppermost in the mind of scribes producing legal manuscripts of *gesta* type, the initial impression made by the next class of manuscripts is different. Both contain copies of codes of Edgar, contemporary with or slightly earlier than the *Chronicle* and Laws in the Otho volume. Each is short. One is found beside a cartulary. The other sandwiches a legal text between medical recipes and a list of lands lost to an allegedly rightful owner. Documentary evidence was used in Anglo-Saxon litigation from the earliest recorded cases; the lands were probably listed here with a view to their recovery at law.[79] One might deduce that the juxtaposed code was intended for forensic use.

Yet initial impressions probably mislead. The crucial point is that these manuscripts consist of loose leaves. It will be suggested later (pp. 248, 263) that sets of laws may have circulated in files of single sheets enclosed within a folder. But there are several signs that what are under review here were pages from larger books. Direct evidence particular to each will be considered below. That apart, the parchment of both is of higher quality than one would expect to find in routine circulation. One would also expect a premium on portability in books meant for consultation in the largely localized arenas of later Anglo-Saxon justice. Two or three manuscripts do have this quality (pp. 198–203, 224–8, 228–36), but the first of the two in this section is the largest (310 x 268 mm), the other the third tallest (291 mm), of all those now extant. A further point is more complex. No one familiar with Anglo-Saxon books can be unaware of how individual leaves and quires were torn from their original homes and scattered to

---

77   *Bede, Hist. Eccl.* v 3, pp. 460–1; cf. Lapidge, 'School of Theodore', p. 50.
78   See chapter 2, pp. 59–60. It is almost *too* neat that Paris BN.Lat. 10758 was copied to form Paris BN. Lat. 4628a, just as Corpus 173 gave rise to Otho B.xi.
79   LS 1–2, 6, 11–13 etc.; cf. my 'Charters, Law and the Settlement of Disputes', pp. 154–7 (pp. 292–6).

different refuges like victims of a brutal diaspora. Pages cast loose when their bibliographical home was demolished in the Middle Ages or later could barely remain consecutive unless conjoined, nor survive at all unless used as bindings. An item in the class of fragmentary or lost MSS reviewed later is a bifolium which served as a wrapper by the thirteenth century (pp. 257–8). But the pages in the present category are consecutive though disjoined and lack binder's traces.[80] It will be suggested that one set may have been a medieval reject and perhaps achieved a refuge within the bosom of another very prestigious book. The other, however, was probably cut loose not after the Conquest by those uninterested in Old English texts, but by those after the Dissolution interested in little else. Be that as it may, neither set of pages would have been removed from its primary setting had this contained law-codes or related matter. To judge from extant twelfth-century books, those who did keep Old English laws kept them together (pp. 224–53). Tudor and Stuart collectors are notorious for the awful things they did to the treasures they so jealously preserved, but they rarely separate similar items.[81] The detachability of manuscripts in this class is not, then, a sign of their use. It implies, if anything, that they had once been stored in unsuitable contexts.

(i) BL, Cotton MS Nero E.i

Two leaves, numbered ff. 185–6 in Cotton MS Nero E.i (volume II), contain a copy of the code known as 'IV Edgar'. The script is dated 's x/xi' by Ker. This makes the manuscript the second oldest of those now surviving, and also, since IV Edgar may date to 973 and can be no earlier than c.962, the closest in time to the code it preserves, apart from three in the special class of 'Wulfstan MSS'.[82] It has few textual errors, and they venial.[83]

All that can be said with certainty about the manuscript as it survives today is that it is not in its original 'home'. Big as the two leaves are, they are smaller than those bound on either side. The text is written across pages previously ruled for two columns. It occupies a verso, then a recto and verso. On the foregoing recto is a liturgical text, in which excerpts from Bede's commentary on Mark alternate with responses occurring elsewhere as lections for a martyr in a thirteenth-century Worcester antiphonary.[84] Its opening line has at some stage been erased, presumably because the sentence it contained began on the previous page. Ker dates this text later than the law-code. In any case, it is clearly incomplete: the last Bedan extract has no responding echo, as if the scribe had found his way

---

80   For the role of medieval binders and their tell-tale traces, see Ker, *Catalogue*, pp. xli–xlii.

81   See Ker, *Catalogue*, pp. liv–lvi, lxii–lxiii, with his 'Membra Disiecta I, II'; and his 'Liber Custumarum'. Add Gneuss, 'Preliminary list' nos 3, 448. Note that these are much more often instances of seemingly *irrelevant* material (like charters in Gospel-books, below nn. 103, 117) being transferred elsewhere: the Guildhall collection, an exceptionally outrageous case, was Tate's responsibility, not Cotton's, who was sinned against as well as sinning (compare the stories behind Ker, *Catalogue*, nos 344, 360).

82   Ker, no. 166. Liebermann's *siglum* for the MS is 'F' (*Gesetze* I, p. xxv).

83   IV Eg 1:5a, 6:2; the scribe corrects himself in 12:1, 15.

84   The Bedan text: *Bede, In Marci Evangelium Expositio*, pp. 538–9 (some verses inserted from else-where); the responses: *Antiphonaire monastique de Worcester*, pp. 416–17.

blocked by the laws already *in situ*, and either moved on to the next leaf but one or else removed the obstructive pages and begun again. Hence, it is at least a warrantable assumption, borne out by two or three of the next manuscripts to be examined, that these pages were once in a fairly imposing liturgical collection.

But one can contemplate the possibility that they were in roughly their present context for a while before Sir Robert Cotton bound them. The manuscript as a whole is mainly an enormous 'Passional', more precisely the first part of a legendary, most of whose second part is in the Parker Library.[85] The contents of the second volume of the Nero MS itself, as already listed in Cotton's handwritten catalogue, were as follows: the last 155 leaves of part I of the legendary proper, with early additions; nine leaves and a fragment in twelfth-century script, containing lives of Saints Frideswide, David and Margaret of Antioch; fifteen leaves from the *second* (Parker) part of the legendary (ff. 166–80), relating to feasts at the end of the year; four leaves from an eleventh-century cartulary of Worcester cathedral (ff. 181–4); the two leaves of laws, with their liturgical prelude; two leaves of a *Life of Bede*, in a hand like the Frideswide section's but smaller; and thirty-four thirteenth-century leaves of *vitae* and *passiones*.[86] An alternative sequence is however indicated by a brown-ink foliation predating Cotton's arrangement. According to this, the later-medieval texts (current ff. 189–222) were numbered '53–86'. They probably followed the fifty-two folios of *Lives* of Oswald, Ecgwine and Swithun that now front the first Nero volume. Next were the leaves from the Parkerian part of the legendary ('87–101'). Then came two cartulary leaves ('10?–1??'), the liturgy/laws pages ('104–5'), those of the *Life of Bede* in reverse order ('106–7' = current ff. 188–7), and finally the last two leaves of the cartulary (ff. '1??–10?'). The laws thus stood between two pairs of cartulary folios.[87] A thirteenth-century hand inscribed the *Bede* with the title 'Passionale a Kl. Jan. usque ii Kl. Octobris'. This corresponds to Cotton's part of the legendary and implies that the Bede pages once prefaced the whole collection.[88]

It thus appears that Cotton or a predecessor first encountered a manuscript made up of the detritus of four or more others: the last pages of part II of the legendary, most of which was by then Parker's; the opening of part I, featuring the *Life of Bede*; the Oswald, Ecgwine and Swithun texts; pages from a Worcester cartulary; two pages of a law-code from a (probably) liturgical MS; and later

---

85   Ker, 'Membra Disiecta II', pp. 82–3; see also below, nn. 87, 91.
86   BL, Harley MS 6018, ff. 101–2; cf. Smith, *Catalogus*, pp. 58–60.
87   Ker's discussion (as n. 85) was not concerned with later ingredients in the MS. For the Oswald/Ecgwine section, see Lapidge, 'Byrhtferth and the *Vita S. Ecgwini*', pp. 332–3; and for the thirteenth-century material, *Wulfstan, Life St Æthelwold*, ed. Lapidge and Winterbottom, pp. clxxvi–clxxvii. The brown ink foliation in the Oswald section runs to f. 49: it seems to be a later hand that carries the pagination on (*after* the leaf was damaged, presumably by the Cottonian fire) through 'Acts of St Andrew' (added in a twelfth-century Worcester hand: McIntyre, 'Early Twelfth-Century Worcester', pp. 70–1, 76–7, 81), and launches into the Cottonian legendary proper at (by its own reckoning) 'f. 53' (now f. 55). There is also a second foliation making the cartulary ff. 387–8, 391–2, the laws ff. 389–90, and the 'Bede' (still reversed) ff. 393–4.
88   Ker, p. 82 (it is among other evidence that the legendary always split at 1st October, its division therefore to be blamed on neither Parker or Cotton). The squeezing of the *Bede* into limited space confirms that it was inserted, and perhaps explains its small script.

medieval *vitae*, which, like the Oswald section, may once have gone with either part of the legendary or neither. These constituents could have been detached and reassembled in any century before 1600. But more can be said of the cartulary. It was probably inserted into one of the two great sister-Bibles of the *Codex Amiatinus* that found its way from Monkwearmouth/Jarrow to Worcester.[89] This may have been the Bible that Worcester believed it had been given by King Offa. It must have disintegrated before the Dissolution, when leaves of Bible and cartulary passed to the Willoughbys of Wollaton. The Edgar code pages occupied the place in the cartulary where one of the Wollaton leaves should appear.[90] Possibly, therefore, they were incorporated in the cartulary at quite an early date, conceivably when the scribe of the liturgical recto removed them as a bar to further progress. Incorporation in the cartulary would explain how they survived the Middle Ages as a pair without a binder's help. And if the cartulary was bound in the 'Offa' Bible, Edgar's code would have swapped a liturgical setting for one more solemn still.

Were that argument to hold, the Worcester provenance of Nero's IV Edgar pages would be certain. The case remains cumulatively strong in any event. Ker cautiously allowed that they might have been 'collected by Joscelyn from another source'. But why should Joscelyn (or whoever) have come up with such unlikely bedfellows as cartulary, laws and *Life of Bede* if they were not found in, as it were, already compromising proximity? That any foliator should have perpetuated the disorder of these leaves is surprising enough; that one should have effected that sequence himself would be extraordinary. The legendary's Worcester origin is beyond serious doubt.[91] The nearest parallel to the *liturgica* on the IV Edgar recto is from later-medieval Worcester. The code's other manuscript, its close kin and perhaps descendant, is surely from Worcester (p. 219). For leaves from elsewhere to link up with Worcester books in the sixteenth or seventeenth century, having already done so in the eleventh and thirteenth, would be a singularly elastic coincidence.

The point needs so much labouring, because it confronts a paradox that recurs throughout these sections of the chapter. To judge by its content, IV Edgar should not be in a Worcester book at all. It concerns the Danelaw. Its important concluding clauses entrust publication and enforcement to officials with responsibilities there.[92] However, one of these was ealdorman of Mercia, and he could well have wished to deposit a copy at Worcester, one of his province's leading bishoprics. Yet more likely to have done so is Oswald, who added the archbish-

---

89   *Catalogus ... by Patrick Young*, ed. Atkins and Ker, pp. 77-9; Ker, 'Hemming's Cartulary', pp. 65-7; Dumville, *Liturgy*, pp. 99-100.

90   *Report on the Manuscripts preserved at Wollaton Hall*, pp. 196, 611-12. Evidence on the 'Offa Bible' includes S 118, an eleventh-century forgery. It may be relevant that Harley 6018, echoed in part by Smith but not Wanley, lists IV Eg as 'Carta Saxonica diversarum terrarum tempore regis Edgari', following the MS title probably attributable to Joscelyn, 'Carta Saxonica tempore regis Edgari'. The code calls itself a 'gewrit', but Joscelyn and Cotton should have been able to identify it as 'Leges', and were perhaps misled by the cartulary context.

91   Ker, as n. 85; for Worcester scribes and the legendary, plus its associated texts, see Ker, *Catalogue* no. 29, Lapidge (as n. 87), McIntyre (as *ibid.*), pp. 70, 143, and Bishop, *English Caroline Minuscule*, p. 20, n. 1.

92   IV Eg 15 15:1; see chapter 5, p. 317.

opric of York to the see of Worcester in 972. He was the first of five Anglo-Saxon prelates to hold both dioceses in plurality.[93] The close connection of Worcester and York throughout the period, especially under Wulfstan (1002–16), makes the interchange of legal manuscripts between them as predictable as that of the *Chronicle* texts reviewed in chapter 3 (pp. 130–1). In a way, it hardly matters which of these *scriptoria* wrote any one book. All the same, the number of Anglo-Saxon libraries with an after-life affects the odds that extant lawbooks are a representative sample of what once existed. If York survivals were significant, those odds improve. Whitelock's survey of Wulfstan manuscripts concluded that several might be from York.[94] But this can be proved rather than argued for one alone (below, pp. 195–7). Ker's list of vernacular books probably at York before 1540, which allowed this possibility for Wulfstan manuscripts, remains puny beside that for Worcester. Professor Gneuss's provisional list of all pre-1100 manuscripts suggests a ratio of 1:27.[95] Whitelock's case is a reminder that few manuscripts can be firmly tied to any one home. Just as important is that York is an inherently less likely provenance than Worcester; nor is seemingly 'northern' content a proof of northern origins. The best one can say is that scribes and/or books may have commuted between the two centres, especially in Wulfstan's time. That applies *a fortiori* to the next manuscript.

(ii) BL, Harley MS 55(A)

The Harleian manuscript is composite.[96] One glance suffices to show that the first four folios, which include an Edgar code, are quite distinct from the laws of Cnut in the nine that follow. The script of the latter is a century and a half later than the scripts in the former. Layout of text, size and quality of parchment, are quite different. Nor is there much sign of their association in the sixteenth century. Cnut's code was copied by Nowell and used by Lambarde, but Lambarde certainly did not know the Edgar text (pp. 261–2). Joscelyn's handling of both parts of the manuscript is a complex issue best left for discussion of the Cnut section in its twelfth-century context (pp. 253–4). All that matters here is that he is unlikely to have encountered the two parts at the same time.[97] The first clear evidence of their association is the addition of titles to each code 'in a hand of s xvi ex'. The next news is in a 1649 letter from Simonds D'Ewes warmly thanking

---

93   Whitelock, 'Dealings of the Kings of England', pp. 73–6.
94   Whitelock, 'Wulfstan at York'.
95   Ker, *Catalogue*, p. 562; Gneuss, 'Preliminary list' nos. 417, 774; the MSS at issue here are counted in neither total. Professor Bullough's forthcoming study of Alcuin casts doubt on Whitelock's argument as to Harley 208, 'Wulfstan at York', pp. 218–19, which Gneuss follows as regards no. 417. Yet the argument is circular in so far as a multiplicity of attributable MSS permits identification of more local scribes, and hence attribution of more MSS.
96   Ker, *Catalogue* nos 225–6; but Liebermann's *siglum* for both parts of the MS is 'A' (*Gesetze* I, p. xviii).
97   The essence of the case is that (i) division into chapters (probably by Joscelyn) was carried out thoroughly in the Edgar code, but only partially for Cnut's; (ii) texts of II–III Edgar and Cnut copied into CCCC 383 (below, p. 230) did both derive from Harley 55, but at different times; (iii) Joscelyn glossed

John Selden for his generous (and allegedly unexpected) gift of 'an old parchment fragment containing Anglo-Saxon laws of Kings Edgar and Cnut, and other things in the same idiom'. It was perhaps Selden who joined the two; it may even have been he who cut them out of their one-time homes.[98]

There are three items in the four half-sheets making up Part A of Harley 55. On the five pages opening at the first recto is a medical text about 'half-dead disease' (hemiplegia). Ker dates its 'rather large and handsome hand' s xi[1]. On the verso overleaf are two pages and a line of the two-part code called 'II–III Edgar'. After a two-line gap, the rest of that verso contains an account by Archbishop Oswald of lands taken from the church of York.[99] There is thus no doubt of the codicological connection between the three items, nor of the order in which they were written. Since the second and third are glossed in the hand now ascribed to Archbishop Wulfstan, Ker's s xi[1] date must hold good for their script too. It is also evident that these folios once concluded a larger manuscript. The last verso is 'rubbed as though from exposure', and has been torn and resewn in two places. As the last page suffered more than the first or any other, it must for a time have brought up the rear of the collection sheltering the rest. Hence, the relationship of legal and non-legal texts in Harley 'A' poses a slightly different problem than the Otho manuscript. The issue is not just the linkage between law, medicine and property, but what sort of book is likely to have had these diverse items tacked on at different times. To ask this question of the medical and property items may give clues to a hypothetical provenance for the code.

The medical text may have the weightier implications in that it was entered first. It is of a different type to those that Nowell copied from the Otho manuscript. Like several of them, it corresponds with something indicated in the contents of Bald's *Leechbook* but now missing from that manuscript (above, p. 178). But as a tract on specific ailments rather than an encyclopedia of disorders, it compares not with the collections of Bald or others but with the isolated remedies and (often indistinguishable) 'charms' scattered through an assortment of pre- and post-conquest manuscripts.[100] Two generalizations may be made about these. First, they are relatively rare in the solemn context of gospel-books,

---

clauses of II–III Eg in Cotton Nero A.i, ff. 42–44v (below, p. 225), from Harley 55, whereas when glossing its text of Cnut, ff. 3r–41r, he usually preferred Lambarde's edition (which was based on Harley 55(B)).

98   Hickes, *Antiquae Literaturae Septentrionalis* I, p. xliii; Watson, *Library of D'Ewes*, pp. 9, 81 (n. 55), and cf. p. 315 (M 71). Lest 'a hand of s xvi ex' seem too early for Selden, it is worth noting that he was working for Cotton in the opening years of the seventeenth century: Berkowitz, *Selden's Formative Years*, pp. 13–19.

99   S 1453, RoASCh LIV.

100   E.g. Ker, *Catalogue* nos. 32 (8), an eyesalve entered, with prayers against disease, charms against cattle-theft and much besides, into the OE *Bede* given by Bishop Leofric to Exeter; 154 (2), a copy, with evident Worcester connections, of the translated *Rule of St Benedict*, where a hand like the main scribe's has inserted eyesalves, a 'nonsense charm' against diarrhoea, and two Latin charms for colds and fevers; and 171 (2), the lost Asser MS, containing (said Wanley), 'Saxonice ... Exorcismus contra Melancholiam ... Exorcismus prolixior contra frigora et febres'. Other MSS with such contents (discounting those devoted largely to 'medical' matters) are Ker nos. 45 (below, pp. 220–3), 67, 139, 146, 156–7, 186, 202, 224, 336, 360, 399; Cockayne edited most texts in *Leechdoms* I, pp. 374–94, III, pp. 292–5, though none is nearly as long as Harley's. See generally Cameron and Meaney (as n. 62); also, for distribution of prog-

missals or pontificals.[101] Secondly, four such books, over quarter of the total, have a schoolroom atmosphere. Computistical collections contained prognostics which linked logically with charms or remedies aimed at foreseen results.[102] The four Harley leaves could, then, be from a school-book.

In near-total contrast is the provenance of property memoranda like the list of York losses. When not found in cartularies or on single sheets, they tend to keep the company of Gospels or similarly numinous writings. About two dozen such codices contain pre-conquest estate memoranda. Subtracting an uncertainty and two *Libri Vitae*, the residue breaks down into thirteen Gospel-books, two pontificals, a missal, a psalter and a prayer-book, with two exceptions, a *Rule of St Benedict* and a Gregory (*Moralia*) from Bury, which, given the status of these authors among the Anglo-Saxons, may not be exceptions after all.[103] One of these, the York Gospels, is fully discussed in this chapter's next section (pp. 195–7), but is relevant here because the entries in it show that lands recorded as lost in Harley were by then back in York's hands (see also pp. 192–3). If a Gospel-book seemed a fit repository for a later chapter of the saga, the same sort of book may have been deemed suitable for an earlier.[104]

It is a comment on the hazards of so speculative an enterprise that one of the Edgar code's companion pieces points toward *liturgica*, while the other indicates a textbook. Powerful support for the latter theory are scribal doodles added in the eleventh century between code and memorandum: 'write thus, or better ride away'; 'Ælfmær Pattafox, you want to flog young Ælfric (*þu wilt swingan Ælfric cild*)'. The schoolroom atmosphere here becomes oppressive. Yet similar phrases occur in the Hatton copy of Alfred's *Pastoral Rule*, and in the 'Lanalet Pontifical' – the latter at least no schoolbook.[105] The statistical probabilities can be variously weighed. Gospel-books stood a better chance of survival. That could mean that Harley's pages weathered the Middle Ages in the shelter of God's Word. But it also makes it safer to assert that medical texts were never inserted in Gospel-books than to deny that schoolbooks were ever used to keep track of church endowments. In that case, the medical tract is better evidence that the Harley

nostics, Jayatilaka, 'The *Regula Sancti Benedicti* in late Anglo-Saxon England: the manuscripts and their readers', pp. 320–31.

101   Exceptions: Ker no. 224, a psalter; and some MSS of more personal (prayer-book) type, nos. 67, 157 and 202.

102   Ker nos. 139, 146, 360 and 399; while Ker no. 202 (above note) has some similar 'educational' elements.

103   See the lists in Dumville, *Liturgy*, pp. 120–2, 123–5, 127, discounting items not concerned with landed property or of likely post-1066 inclusion; the indirect evidence of S 455 and William of Malmesbury, *Early History of Glastonbury* 56, pp. 116–19, may be added to S 813 (Dumville, n. 204); and my 'uncertainty' is Add. MS 61735 (Ker no. 80). At p. 127, Professor Dumville makes very similar suggestions as to the MSS discussed here.

104   RoASCh LXXXIV, cf. no. LIV (S 1453).

105   Sisam, *Studies*, pp. 110–12, cf. Ker, nos. 324, 374 (Lyfing was bishop of Worcester as well as of Crediton, 1038/9x46 (see below, p. 223), so that one might establish a Worcester connection for all MSS with this feature, except that Dumville, *Liturgy*, p. 87, authoritatively dates the book's ownership inscription to the time of Lyfing, Bishop of Wells (998/9–1013) before moving to Canterbury).

leaves were not part of some solemn product than is the list of lands that they were.

Whatever kind of manuscript it was, its provenance raises the same problem as the Nero leaves. The indicators are again contradictory. The memorandum of course argues for York. But three glosses on the Edgar code by Worcester's 'tremulous hand' show that it was there by the thirteenth century. If so, need it ever have been away?[106] It can at least be said that it was from an episcopal library, like the Nero E.i pages, and more surely than the Parker and Otho manuscripts. And this time one can go further. Harley's leaves were marked in one or other library by the 'Wulfstan hand'. The Edgar scribe at one point omitted 'Saturday', so that Sunday observance was nonsensically commanded from (in effect) *Sunday* noon till Monday dawn. The necessary insertion was made above the line. This distinctive script also made changes to York's plaint, adding a title, 'these declarations Archbishop Oswald expounded (*swutelunge ... gedihte*) and had written down'; supplying Oswald's name at the end over a statement of what 'my lord' had given; and stressing that York was the intended beneficiary of what had been 'robbed'. Finally, an imprecation is added: 'may God avenge [the theft] as he will'. This last is a typical 'Wulfstanism'.[107] In the course of a career of distinguished service to medieval English palaeography, Neil Ker became increasingly convinced that the handwriting in question was Wulfstan's own. His final decision to drop the 'probably' did not go unchallenged and has left even the persuaded with a sense of unease at some of the implications. But it is strictly true that it is harder to imagine anyone other than the archbishop penning all entries in this script than to accept that it is his.[108] Although so much of the argument in the present section of this book hangs from that one thread, it is tensile enough to take the strain. The Harley manuscript is the first of a series of four law-books where the most important figure in the history of later Anglo-Saxon legislation can be seen at work.

This at once raises two final and awkward problems about the text of II–III Edgar that it preserves. In the first place, it differs in important ways from copies with no Wulfstan association. Its main hand wrote '↑ freme' above 'feore' in the clause on slander, so that this covered damage to 'property or *interest*', not 'property or life' as in the alternative version. 'Feo oðða feore' is a neat alliterative formula, such as Edgar could well have used. But 'property or interest' arguably makes better sense in a slander case. So does the emendation represent a better text? Or is this 'improvement' arising from scribal, which is here to say

---

106   See chapter 3, pp. 130–1, for northward travel by *Chronicle* MS 'D' before return to Worcester by the twelfth century (probably) and sixteenth (for sure); but this MS is unlikely to have got to York.

107   In his *Wulfstan Manuscript*, Professor Loyn gives facsimiles of ff. 3v–4v of this MS in his Appendix; he also includes most other prominent 'Wulfstan' annotations (see below).

108   Above all, Ker, 'Handwriting of Archbishop Wulfstan', building on arguments signalled in his 'Hemming's Cartulary', etc. The chief sceptical statement is Hohler, 'Some Service Books of the Later Saxon Church', p. 225, n. 59; the strongest post-Ker vindication is by Morrish Tunberg, in the introduction to *The Copenhagen Wulfstan Collection*, pp. 45–7. Reference may also be made to my 'Wulfstan and the Holiness of Society', a statement of the case for the identification using the full range of evidence listed by Ker; for me decisive (amidst much other evidence) is Cotton MS Vespasian A.xiv, where a poem in Wulfstan's honour is glossed by this hand in a way that seems inconceivable except as the archbishop's own work.

archiepiscopal, judgement?[109] Further examination of Liebermann's parallel columns shows a series of clauses where Wulfstan manuscripts ('D' and 'G²' as well as 'A') line up against the others ('G' and *Quadripartitus*) (cf. chapter 5, pp. 313–15). Some are more or less desirable textual changes.[110] Others make a real legal difference. Clauses are inserted on plough-alms, soul-scot and church-peace, while the clauses on weights and measures are extended to make London as well as Winchester a standard authority and to penalize trading in under-weight wool. The problem is especially acute with a clause on Friday fasts, found only in Harley's version, that represents the law decreed by Æthelred and Cnut (and worded more like Cnut than Æthelred).[111] Liebermann was in two minds whether all this represented a 'second edition' or additions by a 'clerical copy-ist'. Wulfstan could have been influential in either eventuality. The extent and mediation of this influence is an issue for the next chapter (pp. 302, 309). But it should be recalled from the example of the Otho manuscript that additions (or subtractions) could arise with law-texts where there is no question of a Wulfstan contribution.

The other point about the Harley manuscript's Edgar text is its clause divisions. The only Old English code consistently set out in recognizable chapters is Alfred–Ine, and the result is a far from consistent guide to content (chapter 5, pp. 267–9). English laws otherwise appear as continuous prose until 1215 and beyond. Neither Liebermann's printed divisions nor those of other editors are consistently warranted by manuscript punctuation. Still, punctuation of sorts is normal. In Nero E.i significant breaks in the text of IV Edgar are usually marked by a *punctus versus* (;) followed by a substantial though not highlighted initial. This is especially striking when clauses begin with '7': for obvious reasons Tironian '*et*/and' is rare as an initial.[112] But the regular use of conjunctives in post-899 legislation (chapter 5, pp. 272, 288, 302, 309) evidently had to be reconciled with guidance for the eye to distinct enactments. The Harley code makes this particularly clear. Its text originally had a *punctus versus* at most major breaks, but outsize initials only at the first clause proper and at the start of the secular section ('III'). An early modern scribe, probably Joscelyn, sought to 'improve' matters by inserting 'L' shapes together with marginal numbers wherever he saw breaks. It can scarcely, then, have been this agent who consistently enlarged '7' and some other initials at some of these points but not all and also at *different* points.[113] Yet these enlargements are clearly not original. Wulfstan or someone close to him will be found marking clause divisions again (chapter 5, pp. 341, 350); these could thus be his work.

---

109   III Eg 4; Liebermann's note, *Gesetze* III, p. 136, reaches a different conclusion.

110   II Eg 1, 1:1, 2:1, 3, 4:1, 4:3, 5, III 1:1, 3, 6:1–2, 7, 7:1.

111   II Eg 2:3, 5:1–3, III Eg 8:1–3; *Gesetze* III, pp. 134 (3), 135 (5:2).

112   IV Eg 2a – 2:1, 6, 13; Liebermann's clause numeration is a consistently poor guide to the behaviour of the MS, which marks significant breaks not only at 2a and 2:1 but also at 2:2 and 14:1, as against nothing very obvious at 7 or 11.

113   'L'-shape/numerals: II Eg 2, 2:3(!), 3:1, 4, 5, III Eg. 1, 3, 4, 5, 6, 7, 8. Enlarged '7': II Eg 2:3, 3, 3:1, 4, 4:2, 5, 5:1 ('7 ælces Frigedæges'), 5:3, III Eg 2, 2:2, 3 (+ '7 amanige'), 4, 5, 5:1, 7:3, 8, 8:1, 8:2; enlarged 'Æ' at II Eg 4:3, and perhaps even 'Ð' at III Eg 1. Ker, 'Handwriting', p. 327, indicated Wulfstan amendments on f. 4r, but listed none: he may have been thinking of these marks.

At all events, they show intervention by someone interested in a more 'usable' text.

The lessons of laws on loose leaves are two. The obvious one is their precarious survival. Even after outliving the Dissolution, they were at high risk. The Nero pages could easily have dropped off the end of the collection where they perched. Harley's, however carefully excised, might not have survived but for Selden and D'Ewes. In a sense these manuscripts belong in the category of 'fragmentary and lost MSS' (below, pp. 255–62): fragmentary they almost are, lost they nearly were. Less obvious is a second lesson. Nero E.i and Harley 55(A) probably owe their preservation, like the Parker and Otho laws, to books whose *raison d'être* was not primarily legal. Laws were written into the Parker and Otho collections because, as historical monuments, they fitted a historically-orientated context. The Nero and Harley laws are less likely to have been included so as to harmonize with neighbouring items, whatever these were. Yet neither context guessed at here suggests that the presence of laws was purely incidental. In a school-book, II–III Edgar would be conveniently placed for consultation. A liturgical setting such as apparently sheltered 'IV' would underline its solemnity. Solemnity is still more strongly suggested by the class of manuscripts reviewed next.

3   Laws in Holy Books

For the two codes of law on loose leaves, incorporation in holy books is respectively a probability and a possibility. For another pair of texts and a text that is a law-code in all but modern designation, it is an undoubted fact. Nor is there any question but that this was deliberately done by an identifiable agency. Each manuscript is of Wulfstan's time. Both contain his handwriting. That the most articulate legal mind of the Old English period should have countenanced this arrangement means that it was intelligible.

(i) BL, Cotton MS Claudius A.iii

Like the Harley manuscript, the Claudius manuscript is composite. And whoever was responsible for the job-lot in Nero E.i (II), there is no doubt that Claudius A.iii was given its present form by Cotton.[114] Cotton's bibliographical instincts were not without a clumsy logic. In this instance he assembled (out of order) a trio of pontificals or bits of pontificals, of the tenth, eleventh and twelfth centuries, which are labelled 'Claudius Pontificals I, II, III' by their modern editor.[115] Their surviving content may be recovered by reordering their pages thus:

---

114   Cotton's construction was brilliantly (if metaphorically) dismantled in its turn by Ker, 'Membra Disiecta I', pp. 130–1. Cf. his *Catalogue* nos. 141, 185, the first of these being this MS, for which Liebermann's *siglum* is 'K'. See also next nn.

115   *Claudius Pontificals*, ed. Turner; Dumville, *Liturgy*, pp. 78–9.

I: ff. 31–8, 106–36, 39–86, 137–150;
II: ff. 9–18, 87–105;
III: ff. 19–29.[116]

Cotton inaugurated this *ensemble* with seven+one pages of charters, writs and property memoranda for Canterbury cathedral, taken from the Gospel-book now Cotton Tiberius A.ii. Pontificals 'II' and 'III' contain coronation *ordines*; Cotton was perhaps influenced by his belief that kings had taken their coronation oath on Tiberius A.ii.[117] The most important of the transplanted charters was a spurious *pancarta* of Æthelred II in Latin and Old English. It matches the opening leaves of 'Claudius Pontifical I', containing the unique text, also in both languages, of the law-code known as 'VI Æthelred'.

At the outset of 'Claudius I' (f. 31v) stood a verbose verse inscription in 'Anglo-Saxon minuscule, s x/xi, probably not much later than the caroline script of the Benedictional itself', in which the *halgungboc* records itself that it was 'bedecked with fair ornament' and 'many treasures' by one Thureth, and calls for his 'eternal reward'.[118] On ff. 32–4 comes the Latin version of VI Æthelred, rounded off at the top of f. 35r by a clause of great importance:

> And so these legal statutes or decrees (*Haec itaque legalia statuta vel decreta*) were urgently issued (*edicta*) at our synodical assembly by King N. All the magnates at that time [*tunc temporis*] promised they would observe them faithfully. And for that reason, I N., archbishop of York by disposition of the grace of the Lord, driven of course by love of the Lord and of neighbour, committed the same to writing (*litteris infixi*) for the memory of posterity and the salvation of present and future.

Wulfstan's hand has inserted Æthelred's name above the first 'N' and his own over the second.[119] The page's remaining twenty-four lines are left blank. On ff. 35v–38v is the far from close vernacular rendering of the Latin that nonetheless shares the 'VI Æthelred' label. Its hand is not the same as the Latin's 'but contemporary with it, s xi¹'. After two dozen more blank lines, the Pontifical proper began on what is now f. 106, with episcopal benedictions for the course of the Church year.

It is the activity of two medieval bookworms, their strength (or appetites) waning as they penetrated beyond VI Æthelred into the episcopal benedictions, which prove that the one did originally precede the other. But there is a further point. The parchment of the pontifical's first quire has a pinkish marbled quality.

---

116   Turner, pp. v–viii (f. 30 is an intrusion of German origin).
117   For the Canterbury provenance of 'II' and, 'III', see Turner, pp. xxix–xlii; and on the charters, Brooks, 'Pre-conquest charters of Christ Church', pp. 73–88, 313–16. On Tiberius A.ii's seventeenth-century reception, see Keynes, 'King Athelstan's Books', pp. 151–3. Cotton's use of paste, like his resort to scissors (n. 81), may have been judged too harshly. The transfer of most Latin (papal) charters in Tiberius A.ii to Faustina B.vi, while Claudius A.iii got the Anglo-Saxon ones, shows discrimination, even if a few of the former are on an inserted and outsize f. 9*. Among other less explicable associations, the fact that Tiberius B.v ended with records (*Eleventh-Century Miscellany*, pp. 16, 25–6) may be why documents from an Ely Gospel-book were added to it (Ker no. 22). All this bears on the presence of the IV Edgar folios in Nero E.i; editing by early modern antiquaries at that level of illogicality would be hard to parallel.
118   *Anglo-Saxon Minor Poems*, p. 97.
119   VI Atr 40:2. For Wulfstan's hand here and elsewhere in the MS, see Ker, 'Handwriting', p. 321.

The same goes for ff. 32–4, bearing Latin VI Æthelred. However, the parchment used for the Old English version on ff. 35–8 is blotchier and two leaves are thinner. Now, f. 31 is a half-sheet, and ff. 32–4 a bifolium followed by a half-sheet, while ff. 35–8 are all half-sheets. The codicology is therefore consistent with a hypothesis that f. 34 became a half-sheet when the original f. 31 was replaced by the leaf with the inscription; that Latin VI Æthelred was entered on the remaining bifolium and a half before the benedictional began; and that ff. 35–8 were half-sheets inserted when it was decided to add the Old English text. The above-quoted conclusion of Latin 'VI Æthelred' is the sole item on the recto of f. 35, the first hypothetically inserted half-sheet. The clause is in the same hand as the rest of the code but was written with a thicker nib.[120] It could have been added nearer to, or at, the time when the Old English was included; and it will be suggested in chapter 5 (pp. 333–5) that Old English VI Æthelred was in fact drafted as the basis for Cnut's legislation of 1018 or 1020/1 (hence a reticence in identifying Æthelred that is not apparent in the Latin's prologue). It is at least strictly true that codicologically the Latin conclusion accompanies the Old English text, not the rest of the Latin.

In determining the provenance of 'Claudius I' and its legal addendum, the decisive factor is of course the Wulfstan hand. This, however, leaves a choice of (at least) York and Worcester. Further progress depends on identifying the Thureth (Thored) responsible for its elaborate binding. As luck had it, one of the Tiberius A.ii pages added by Cotton to the manuscript featured a grant by a certain Thored to Christ Church Canterbury. It also happens that 'Claudius II' and 'III' are from Canterbury, where they were perhaps bound together. 'Claudius I' was once, therefore, attributed to Canterbury too.[121] Discovery of the manuscript's structure and of the Wulfstan hand removed Canterbury from the stage and shifted the spotlight to the Thored who, as earl of Northumbria from the late 970s until *c.*992, seemed likeliest to be linked with a northern archbishop. But the evidence remains cloudy and clarification should be attempted.

On the not unreasonable assumption that a Thored able to afford 'many treasures' should make the odd appearance as a witness to royal charters or the muniments of major churches, there is an irreducible minimum of three Wulfstan contemporaries. The last of them, the Thored of Canterbury's charter, can be ruled out. Though he did give two ornamented Gospel-books to Christ Church, his Canterbury activity dates to the 1030s. He may be the Thorth who witnessed Cnut charters from 1018 (or another Thorth featuring in two charters of 1023–4). But this witness (or the other) lasted till 1045, and looks too recent an arrival to have splashed out for a prelate who died in 1023, let alone to have had this celebrated in script of 's x/xi'.[122] If the Canterbury Thored once allotted this role seems too late, the currently favoured candidate

---

120   Compare 'itaque' in the facing first lines of ff. 34v–35r. Note the implication of Dumville, *Liturgy*, p. 78, that the script of OE 'VI Atr' may be *not quite* contemporary with that of the Latin.

121   S 1222; Turner, as n. 117. Robertson (RoASCh, p. 421) and Dobbie, *Anglo-Saxon Minor Poems*, were both misled. For Liebermann's and Sisam's misconceptions, see chapter 5, pp. 334–6.

122   S 1222, 1465 (1032): Brooks, *Early History of Canterbury*, p. 298; Keynes, 'Atlas of Attestations' LXX(2) (S 951, 953, 956, 980, 959–62, 964, 967–9, 975, 994), LXXV(2) (S 1001–2, 1006–7, 1010,

may be a little too early. Earl Thored of Northumbria, probably the king's father-in-law, vanishes from witness-lists shortly before contributing to one of the reign's military *débacles* in 992. To make the inscription's lavish outlay in Wulfstan's favour ten years later, this Thored must have survived his fall in better shape than most victims of Æthelredian politics (chapter 3, pp. 149–50).[123] Besides, Archbishop Oswald's plaint makes Thored the villain (or his ascendancy anyway the occasion) of York's losses, and Wulfstan's added imprecation suggests that he was still not fondly regarded at York after 1002. If, as is possible, he was the Thored son of Gunnar who ravaged Westmoreland in 966, and whose father was the likely recipient of Edgar's grant of Newbald in 963, then further pieces of the jigsaw fit: Newbald was among the estates that Oswald claimed to have purchased from Edgar and to have lost when 'Th — rath came in'; Thored could have forfeited it for his depredations, then recoverd it after 975 in another variant on the 'Anti-monastic reaction' (chapter 3, pp. 153–6). But this again makes him an improbable patron for Wulfstan.[124] A third Thored was son of Earl Oslac of Northumbria (?963x6–75), and first appears before 971 in the Ely *Libellus* pursuing thieves; in 971 he witnessed a Peterborough charter alongside his father.[125] It could have been this Thored that was Northumbria's earl, succeeding his exiled and forfeited father some time after 975; if so, he would have had disagreements with York not unlike those of Gunnar's son.[126] But the Ely/Peterborough Thored need not in fact have been a northern earl at all. Wulfstan was to be buried at Ely, having himself allegedly preferred Peterborough; and if Oslac's son were born *c.*950, he could just have outlived King Æthelred in relative obscurity, to emerge as the 'optimas regis' who sold land to Peterborough in 1020x3.[127] The decoration of Wulfstan's pontifical would then be a function of no more than an early eastern counties connection.

Occam's razor is a clumsy weapon to wield on the prosopography even of elites. These three figures could be expanded into at least five, and the binding's

---

123   Whitelock, 'Dealings of the Kings of England', pp. 79–80, and 'Wulfstan at York', p. 217; Keynes, *Diplomas*, p. 187 (n. 118), and 'Atlas of Attestations' LXII(1). Compare Stafford, *Queen Emma and Queen Edith*, p. 66 (n. 3). A donation by Earl Thored to St Cuthberht's is S 1660.

124   S 1453; ASC 966DE, p. 119; S 716. Cf. also Keynes (as n. 126).

125   *Lib. Æth.* 42; ASC 966DE, p. 119, 975ABC, p. 120; S 782 (and cf. S 792, the Thorney charter that is partly based upon it: Hart, *Early Charters of Eastern England*, pp. 165–76).

126   S 712 is Edgar's grant of Sherburn to Oslac (963), and parts of Sherburn were also among York's claimed losses (S 1453); the difference with Gunnar/Newbald is that York recovered Oslac's lands before Wulfstan's death, so that some kind of settlement was evidently reached: Keynes, 'Additions in Old English', pp. 86–8. See also chapter 6, pp. 441–2, where the circumstances of Oslac's Northumbrian earldom become critical for the dating of IV Eg.

127   See n. 122 for S 1463 (and note the second Thored of S 960–1, dated 1023–4). For Wulfstan's burial, see *Liber Eliensis* ii 87, pp. 155–7; and for Peterborough's claim, see *Sermo Lupi*, ed. Whitelock, p. 8. While Oslac had his (not entirely happy) Ely connections (*Lib. Æth* 29), and the archbishop might have been related to the friend of Ely and vigorous reformer's aide, Wulfstan of Dalham (*Liber Eliensis* ii 55, pp. 126–7), it may be equally relevant that Wulfstan's immediate predecessor as archbishop of York had been abbot of Peterborough, and S* 1377 (?971x5) reveals another Wulfstan with Peterborough links.

1012). Cf. Lawson, *Cnut*, pp. 164–5; Keynes, 'Cnut's Earls', p. 80; Fleming, 'Christ Church's Sisters and Brothers', p. 122: either Thored might be the 'optimas regis' who sold land to Peterborough (S 1463, 1020x3); but see below.

hero might be none of them. But whether one accepts the argument's premiss or no, the case for the specifically York provenance of 'Claudius I' is weakened.[128] Consideration of its contents has a similar effect. Like the benedictionals which often form part of them, pontificals were bishops' books.[129] They ought to cover the ceremonies of blessing, ordination and confirmation that were a bishop's special concern, and an *arch*bishop's pontifical should have contained the rite for the consecration of bishops. The 'Dunstan', 'Ecgberht', 'Lanalet' and 'Anderson' pontificals did so; 'Claudius I' did not.[130] It is difficult to be categorical here, because at least one gathering is lost after f. 86. Yet there is no obvious gap for nearly fifty folios after the start of the Ordinations section on f. 39r. One could get around this by supposing that the episcopal ceremony preceded ordinations for lesser grades, as in the 'Ecgberht' pontifical, and was lost with another quire before f. 39. But one must then make the same supposition for the Sidney Sussex pontifical, closely akin to 'Claudius I' and slightly earlier, which also begins with lesser ordinations and omits bishops.[131] There is a suspicion that 'Claudius I' lacunae relate to its messily arranged ordinations. 'Egbert', Robert', even 'Lanalet' are more logically structured than 'Claudius I', where the rite for making clerics is several items away from those for consecrating virgins and widows, and where blessings for font and Candlemas candle are widely separated from those for bell, cross and cemetery.[132] In general, 'Claudius I' is found to be less developed both in its benedictions and liturgical ritual than other English pontificals of comparable date.[133] In short, it was already outdated when copied. It could be just such a book as Wulfstan might have had decorated at a local landowner's expense when he became bishop of London in 996. But it is not likely to have satisfied him for long as archbishop of York.[134]

128   *Contra*, e.g., Dumville, *Liturgy*, pp. 78–9, 91 (n. 153), 94.
129   For this paragraph, the general review of the materials by Dumville, *Liturgy*, pp. 66–95, is an indispensable introduction and bibliographical guide (not least to his own copious further work), which also re-dates and re-assigns a significant number of books. But Professor Dumville is not so concerned with their content, which is one reason why we take different views of the history of 'Claudius I'. For the general picture see also Gneuss, 'Liturgical Books in Anglo-Saxon England', especially pp. 131–4.
130   *Claudius Pontificals*, pp. ix, xxiv, 31–41 (though note the brief 'Benedictio episcoporum', pp. 54–5); Lerocquais, *Pontificaux Manuscrits des Bibliothèques publiques* no. 93, II, pp. 6–10 ('Dunstan'); *Pontificale Lanaletense*, ed. Doble, pp. 49–59; *Benedictional of Archbishop Robert*, ed. Wilson, pp. 115–30; Brückmann, 'Latin Manuscript Pontificals', pp. 431–2 ('Anderson'); The *Leofric Missal*, ed. Warren, pp. 215–18, also ends its Ordinations series with a bishop's.
131   'The Egbert Pontifical', ed Banting, *Two Anglo-Saxon Pontificals*, pp. 8–15; 'The Sidney Sussex Pontifical', *ibid.*, pp. 157–67. 'Egbert' begins its *Ordines* on the page where episcopal ceremonial ends, but Sidney Sussex and Claudius begin the *Ordines* on new leaves. See also Reynolds, *Ordinals of Christ*, p. 89.
132   *Claudius Pontificals*, pp. 55, 68–71, 56–61, 66–7; cf. the place of the *Ordo Qualiter in Romana Ecclesia* and associated *Capitulum Gregorii* in *Claudius Pontificals*, pp. 33–4, 'Egbert', pp. 15–18, *Lanalet*, pp. 52–3, and (most ruthlessly logical) *Robert*, pp. 115–30.
133   Turner, *Claudius Pontificals*, pp. ix–xviii, xx–xxviii; but given Professor Dumville's redating of 'Robert' (*Liturgy*, p. 87), this is a significant point only for 'Dunstan', 'Lanalet' and 'Anderson'; equally, however, his reconsideration of Corpus Cambridge 146, p. 72, points a revealing contrast with 'Claudius I'.
134   If it is the case that the closest relative of 'Claudius I' is the Sidney Sussex pontifical (*Two Anglo-Saxon Pontificals*, pp. xli–xlii, xlvii); and if the latter's presence at Durham by the mid-eleventh century is to be ascribed to its being taken to York by Archbishop Oswald (Dumville, *Liturgy*, pp. 75–6), their links may be best explained in terms of a common origin in the Fenland abbeys.

The next chapter (pp. 334–5) will take up the question why the Claudius manuscript should juxtapose Latin and vernacular versions of much the same text. The chief lesson of what has been said here is that the book itself is unlikely to have been in current use. Amidst a plethora of wobbly arguments, those underpinning the allocation of 'Claudius I' to York are less stable than most.[135] Its assembly of texts is hardly what Wulfstan would have wished to have to hand when (as in 1014 and 1020) he consecrated bishops.[136] Nor is a pontifical embossed with 'fair ornaments' and 'many treasures' the sort of volume that would have been kept in a travelling satchel rather than on an altar or in a locked chest. That it became a repository for legal texts (whether at York or Worcester) is not, then, *prima facie* evidence of a need to have ready access to them. What it conveys – which is not a little – is the deep respect in which texts of written law were held.

(ii) The York Gospels

In the tropical jungle that is the library of early English law, the York Gospels come as a welcome clearing.[137] Provenance and date are beyond question. Presentation has much interest but few puzzles. The price payable for this relief is that the only text in the volume with any pretensions to being a law-code is Cnut's first letter to the English.

The Gospel-book has glosses in the Wulfstan hand on three of the pieces incorporated into it. The book has undoubtedly been at York – a traumatic seventeenth-century interlude aside – from that day to this. It was used to administer oaths of office to cathedral clergy in the Middle Ages and beyond. The relevant formulae are among the added matter.[138] The one question about its origin is why a sumptuous codex of the last part of the tenth century should need to have a page filled in by Eadwig Basan, the Christ Church master-scribe of the second and third decades of the eleventh. Even that problem allows a guess that the book was finished for presentation by Canterbury to Wulfstan on the occasion of his consecrating Archbishop Æthelnoth in 1020.[139]

The added pieces requiring attention here are on ff. 158–60. These are the first three leaves of a new and freshly ruled gathering of four. There is therefore no proof that they were written for entry into this volume. Yet the new gathering

---

135   Chapter 5 will also discuss the 'Danelaw' conditions allegedly reflected by VI Atr; even if they were, this would not prove the York provenance of the Claudius MS, as already noted (pp. 184–5).
136   *Sermo Lupi*, ed. Whitelock, p. 13; *Hom.* XVII is a Wulfstan homily especially for an episcopal consecration.
137   Among the pleasures of this stage in the safari is the Marquis of Normanby's Roxburghe Club spectacular, *The York Gospels*; the contribution by Keynes, 'Additions in Old English', is essential for what follows. The MS is Ker, *Catalogue* no. 402, but has no Liebermann *siglum* as such.
138   Keynes, 'Additions', pp. 82–3; Ker, 'Handwriting', pp 318–19, 330–1; Barr, 'History of the Volume', pp. 106–8.
139   McGurk, 'The Palaeography', pp. 40–1; Alexander, 'The Illumination', pp. 75–6; cf. Bishop, *English Caroline Minuscule* nos 24–5, p. 22 (and plate XXII), Dumville, *English Caroline Script*, pp. 122–3; also Pfaff, 'Eadui Basan', pp. 270–1; and Brooks, *Early History of Canterbury*, pp. 256–8, 264–5, 273–4, 288–90 (with pp. 290ff. on Æthelnoth's accession as a triumph for the Christ Church community).

followed the specifications of the Gospel-book so closely that Ker, examining the manuscript before it was rebound, believed ff. 156–61 to be a six-leaf quire. The first additions to the book, concerning the York estates mentioned earlier (n. 126), were put on the blank verso after St John's Gospel and the recto of the hitherto blank final leaf (ff. 156v–157r). Items of similar type and later date, lists of church treasures and of Archbishop Ælfric's *festermen*, are on the last folio of the added gathering (f. 161rv).[140] It very much looks as if the fresh gathering was tacked on as soon as the first new entries were put at the back of the Gospels, in order to make room for more of the same. But what was in fact added next was of a rather different order.

The first three pieces are 'tracts', comprising *catenae* of quotations from Wulfstan's writings and undoubtedly his work (the first is one of relatively few in the Wulfstan corpus actually labelled 'Sermo Lupi'). They are all in the same hand, and each is glossed by Wulfstan's. The first is a discourse on Christian duties, addressed to 'God's servants', by whom Wulfstan meant the clergy, and then to laymen at large, a habitual Wulfstan classification. Its central concern is sexual conduct (and more especially misconduct), and it concludes no less typically with admonitions on protection and – financial – support of the Church. The other two are a matched pair, 'On Heathenism' and 'On Christianity'. Heathenism is very broadly conceived, running to most varieties of sin and crime and including the collapse of traditional social bonds. Christianity, on the other hand, focuses rather narrowly on payment of Church dues.[141] The point is that in style and content these texts are much more like the laws that the archbishop was by then accustomed to drafting than his earlier series of homilies had been. So much is this so that Dorothy Bethurum disallowed their status as homilies and excluded them from her standard edition.[142] It is fair comment on her distinction that Wulfstan's laws are so homiletic that they have been dismissed as 'pseudo-legislation'. The blurring of the *genre* boundaries is just what matters most.[143]

Immediately after the three tracts comes the sole surviving copy of Cnut's letter to the English (1019/20).[144] For the reasons just given, this essentially legislative statement closely resembles the preceding homilies. This is an issue best resumed *à propos* the text in chapter 5 (pp. 347–8). But it should be said here that their resemblances extend to their presentation on the page. The Letter is in the same hand as the tracts and may have been copied at the same time. It lacks the heading they have but instead has a pictorial invocation of a cross that they do not. Otherwise, it is laid out in just the same way. In both, continuous prose is broken up by the *punctus versus*, its impact reinforced by initials shaded in red ink. If these were designed to guide readers to the beginning of new clauses, then the tracts were also meant to be read as sets of clauses. Unanimity of message

---

140   For the codicology see McGurk, 'The Palaeography', pp. 37–8; and Keynes, 'Additions', pp. 81–3 (on the script), pp. 83–91, 96–7, 98–9 (on the estates and lists of church-treasures and *festermen*).
141   *HomN.* LIX – LXI. See the analysis of Keynes, 'Additions', pp. 92–5, and next n.
142   *Hom.*, pp. 38–9 (she did not deny their authenticity, unlike Jost, *Wulfstanstudien*, pp. 266–8).
143   I give a fuller discussion of this issue not only in chapter 5, pp. 338–41, but also in 'Archbishop Wulfstan'.
144   Cn 1020.

outweighed the distinction between 'law' and 'homily', 'official' and 'unofficial'. This is the first sounding of a chord that will reverberate throughout the ensuing sections of this chapter and much of the next. Wulfstan 'homilist' is increasingly indistinguishable from Wulfstan 'statesman'.[145]

Two points remain to be made about the York Gospels. In the first place, the date when Cnut's letter was inserted can be fixed almost exactly. It must have been sent in 1019x20 (chapter 5, pp. 345–6). It was copied in the same hand and at much the same time as tracts glossed by Wulfstan who died in May 1023. More than any other Anglo-Saxon legal statement, therefore, the Letter is, in the parlance of diplomatic, a 'contemporary text'. Even the Æthelred codes in the Claudius manuscript and in the one to be studied next, though also drafted and glossed by Wulfstan, may have been copied in the next reign, after a decade when much had changed. It will not do to reply that neither Cnut's letter nor Wulfstan's codes as they survive should be reckoned law-codes in the normal understanding of that term. Knowledge of most Anglo-Saxon laws comes from copies made in the twelfth century, generations after their issue, when the trauma of conquest was not all that had transformed the climate. What little can be seen of the way that codes, or for that matter royal proclamations, were treated in the immediate context of their promulgation demands close attention. The same goes for the second conclusion suggested by the York Gospels. They are as vivid a demonstration as could be wished of what mentalities prompted legal texts to be included in Holy Books. At one level, this was a counterpart to keeping one's charters with one's '*haligdom*, relics'. The security that property rights were evidently felt to derive from proximity to God's Word was logically extended to what kings wished to make binding on everyone. The York Gospels was itself kept in the cathedral treasury with other books bound in precious metal and jewels.[146] At another level, Holy Writ and royal precept had the same objective: the holiness of God's people. The English kingdom's basic law-book opened with extensive excerpts from the law God gave Moses. Its kings' laws were part of the ongoing story of Divine legislation. To enshrine royal law beside God's was not blasphemy. It was a statement, at once blunt and profound, of their common purpose.

4   Law and Homily

To set law beside Holy Writ was arrestingly symbolic. In the next two manuscripts the implications of that symbolism were worked out. Each replicates the pattern of the York Gospels addenda on a wider scale. Laws drafted by Wulfstan and laying down the norms of Christian behaviour in terms more redolent of homily than of law-giving as usually understood mingle with selections from his programme for a Christian society known as the *Institutes of Polity*, and with exhortations to Christian living identifiable as 'pure' homilies only from the

---

145   Cf. the title of Whitelock's classic paper (1942).
146   Barr, 'History of the Volume', pp. 107–9, and 'Excursus I', p. 121. On such a role for the 'haligdom' in just this period, see Keynes, *Diplomas*, pp. 148–9, and chapter 3 above, p. 146.

forms of address used. Hard to tell apart as regards content, these texts are also almost indistinguishable in appearance on the page. Both books are linked with Wulfstan. One bears his hand on works he composed; it is the third and last legal manuscript that is in this sense contemporary. The other is a generation later. It is not a copy of the first, but it must have been copied from a volume of much the same type. To that extent the two pair up like the Parker and Otho codices. Each testifies to the other's logic.

(i) BL, Cotton MS Nero A.i(B)

Cotton Nero A.i is not so obviously composite as Harley 55. But that is only because the pages of its two parts do not differ in size and quality as the other's do. Liebermann gave it a common *siglum* with few of the reservations he felt when doing the same for the Harley manuscript. Professor Loyn put all of it in his facsimile edition. Yet Loyn stressed how weak is the evidence that its two constituents were joined at any medieval date.[147] There is anyway no denying that the first part (ff. 3–57, 'A') is around fifty years later than the second (ff. 70–177, 'B'). The question whether 'A' was added to 'B' at its time of writing may therefore be left until 'A' is studied later (pp. 224–8); but reasons will then be given for doubting that the two were linked before the late-sixteenth century. 'B' for its part contains a series of laws, homilies and other *Wulfstaniana* from the archbishop's time. And the first point to make is that it is far from clear that 'B' itself constitutes a single manuscript.

The structure of 'B' as displayed in table 4.2 raises immediate doubts about its coherence[148]. Quires 5 and 10 (sections c) and e)) have eccentric layouts. Quire 10/section e) may at least share its scribe with sections b) and d), but quire 5/section c) is again distinct. Quire 5 looks less like the runt of the litter than an adopted stray. Moreover, the end of section a) is so severely damaged as to suggest that it was for some time exposed at the end of a manuscript; so indeed is the end of section c); and so is the start of section d) (f. 122), suggesting that it at some point *fronted* the collection.[149] Assorted supplements and marginalia from the twelfth century onwards show that sections b) – e) were by then together. But section a)'s marginalia are of a different type and more liable to have been erased.[150] It begins to look as though section a) had left the manuscript by the time that c) joined it. Finally, there are oddities about the texts in section

---

147   Siglum 'G', Gesetze I, pp. xxv–xxvi, and cf. p. xviii (see n. 241 below); *Wulfstan Manuscript*, ed. Loyn, pp. 32–44. Ker, *Catalogue*, however, numbers the two parts 163, 164 (and cf. pp. xliv–xlv).

148   Abbreviations in this table are those listed at the outset of the bibliography, plus Fe = *Hirtenbriefe Ælfrics*, Th = *Ancient Laws and Institutes*. For a fuller picture of the content of sections d), e), see table 4.4, with discussion and references *ad loc.*

149   Cf. *Wulfstan Manuscript*, ed. Loyn, p. 23: 'there is no certainty that ... the Latin half has always followed the Anglo-Saxon'.

150   For these additional materials, see Loyn, pp. 33–5. Most marginalia are s xiii[in], s xiii[ex] or s xiv[in], and relate to penance, a main theme of the book's Latin texts; Loyn plausibly suggests that it may have become a confessor's handbook. Erased section a) marginalia are on ff. 84v, 85r, 85v, and especially ff. 88v, 96v. For more ephemeral marginalia, and their bearing on a union of parts 'A' and 'B', see below, pp. 225–6.

b), notably that they have rubrics in Latin like sections d) and e), and that here alone a scribe ('S5') follows the lead of insertions in the Wulfstan hand, where the work of other scribes was *in situ* for the hand to gloss. The details cannot be pursued any further here.[151] But the evidence is compatible with, perhaps best explained by, the following propositions: the manuscript once began with section d) before proceeding to b) and then a); b) was subsequently supplemented by Wulfstan and his *amanunensis*, and a)'s place was at the same time taken by c); then or soon afterwards e) was added to d); it was not until the sixteenth century that section a) re-established contact with the rest of the volume; and only then was the Old English put before the Latin.

The impression made by the manuscript's structure is supported by its contents. The law-code 'V Æthelred' is not the only text to reappear in a variant form. Some *Institutes of Polity* passages in section a) are virtually repeated in b). But it is broadly true (though disentangling the 'publication history' of *Polity* is wearisome labour) that the texts in section c) are more 'evolved' than those in a) or b), which themselves reflect developments since the 'first edition'.[152] The Wulfstan homilies in section c), which include the 'final' version of the great 1014 sermon, are likewise generically late, whereas section a)'s homilies probably pre-date 1014.[153] As for the repeated code itself, 'V Æthelred' is one version of the laws issued in 1008 at King's Enham (Hampshire), the Claudius manuscript's 'VI Æthelred' being another. The Nero manuscript's two texts are similar enough to establish that they represent the same code, but there are also differences. Section c)'s 'G2' has marginal additions by the Wulfstan hand, the second of which looks important, though reduced to unintelligibility by mutilation of the manuscript. Neither appears in section a)'s 'G1', as would be expected had this been the later version. Among changes in the text itself, '*georne*, eagerly' seems more likely, given Wulfstan's cast of mind, to have been added to 'G2' than subtracted from 'G1'.[154] Section c) seems to capture Wulfstan at a more advanced stage in his thinking than other parts of the book.

In summing up, it is helpful to remember that parts A and B of the Nero manuscript may have been reduced to a spurious homogeneity by Cotton's binders, so Part B's quires could once have differed slightly in size (see pp. 224–5). Once that is conceded, there is no longer any compelling reason to regard it as a single book by design as opposed to circumstance. Wulfstan's hand is so widespread that one would expect to find it whether the manuscript was one or several. The next hand

---

151   Cf. *Wulfstan Manuscript*, ed. Loyn, p. 26. A fuller exposition of this and the following points is in my 'Archbishop Wulfstan'. My suggestion about section b)'s original place in the collection is not precluded by the fact that almost half of it was left blank (ff. 105v ln 8 – [*110v]); one lesson of this collection (cf. end of sections c), d), e) and doubtless a)) is that Wulfstan's scribes left space for extra material when they reached what they regarded *pro tem.* as the end of a section.

152   Thus the otherwise closely similar *Inst. Pol.* I 1–7 (section a)) and II 4–9 (section c)) differ in that the latter is preceded by II 1–3 'Be hefenlicum cyninge', which sets the tone of what follows; whereas, though giving a basically 'second edition' text at II 85–93 and II 221–34, section a) four times aligns with the first edition.

153   *Hom.*, pp. 103–4; Godden, 'Apocalypse and Invasion', pp. 143–56.

154   V Atr. 27, 30, 14:1. Other variations seem more or less likely to be textual slips, e.g. 26:1; but it is significant that one can hardly say whether at 34, 35:1, where G2 and D are again in agreement against G1, they represent a more accurate text, or simply revision in one or other direction.

Table 4.2 Structure of Cotton Nero A.i(B)

Quires	Written Space	Lns	Scr	Content	Other Notes
a. 1–3, 70r–96v	135 × 70 mm (max)	24	S3	*Inst. Pol.* I 1–15, II 23–40, II 85–93, I 66–7, I 68–77, I 78–83, I 84–115, II 221–34; *Hom.* Xc, XIX; I As, I Em . . . ; . . . II–III Eg, V Atr (G¹), *Grið*, VIII Atr Pr. – 5:2, *Nor Grið* **f. 83v:** Numerological lore, s xii¹	Bifolium missing from central quire (text of I Em 1 – III Eg 3); quire 3 lacks all after first three leaves, the last heavily worn; corrections by Wulfstan hand to *Pol.* II 36 and (esp.) *Hom.* Xc
b. 4, 97r–108v	135 × 65 mm (max)	24	S4,S5	*Inst. Pol.* I 35–40, II 58–76, VIII, 'Admonition to Bishops' (Jost, pp. 262–7), II 102–29, II 170–84, II 94–101 **f. 98v:** Clerical Dress **ff 105v–108v:** 1156 Easter Table, Grace before food, Allegory of Nebuchadnezzar, s xii; Penance procedure, s xiii[ex]	Originally blank ff. 98v lns 7–24, 105v lns 8–24; two leaves lost after f. 107; glosses by Wulfstan hand to *Pol.* VIII 10, II 102, II 183, II 95, and (esp.) 'Admonition' 1, 14
c. 5, 109r–21v	135 × 70 mm (min) (pricking visible all through quire)	25	S6	*Inst. Pol.* II 41–57; *Hom.* XX(EI), XXI; V Atr (G²); *Inst. Pol.* II 1–9 **ff. 120r–121v:** Rich and Poor, 1156 Easter Table, list of	Originally blank from f. 120r ln 23; f. 121v worn, last leaf of quire lost; corrections and glosses by Wulfstan hand to *Pol.* II 50, 57, *Hom.* XX,

				sacraments and 10 Commandments, litany, s xii[1-2]; baptismal theory, s xiii[ex]	XXI, V Atr 27, 30, and (esp.) *Pol.* II 4–6
d. 6–9, 122r–67v	135 × 65 mm (max)	24	?S4	'De Ven. Sac.'; *Hom.* XVIa; 'De Pastore'; 'De Cleric. Grad.'; *Exc. Can.* 1–140, 146–63; *Penit. Ps.Th.* ii; Fe. Anh. III 34–40; *Hom.* App. I; *Penit. Ps.Th.* xlix-l (these eleven = Fe. Anh. IV 164–74); Fe. Anh. IV 175–6 ff. **148r–149r**: Th. *Exc. Can.* '141–5', s xii f. **167v**: prayer etc., s xii	f 122r heavily rubbed, severe staining at quire change ff. 131v/132r; originally blank ff. 148r ln 4 – 149r (from *Exc. Can.* 140 to 146), and f. 167v lns 9–24; additions by Wulfstan hand to *Exc. Can.* 77, *Penit. Ps.Th.* ii, Fe. Anh. III 39, *Hom.* App. I, Fe. Anh. IV 175, and (esp.) *Hom.* XVIa, Fe. Anh. IV 176.
e. 10, 168r–77v	145 × 70 mm (max)	26	??S4	Fe. Anh. III 41(–2), 45–7; *Penit. Ps.Th.* i; Fe. Anh. III 14 (= Fe. Anh IV 177–80); ff. **174v–177v**: prayers, canons, etc., s xii[1]	Originally blank from f. 174v ln 17 – 177v; no Wulfstan additions.

to feature throughout is Robert Talbot's (cf. pp. 225, 230). He is not known to have put hitherto disparate volumes together. But what came so naturally to scholars soon afterwards was perhaps not beyond him too. Many Anglo-Saxon books have eccentric quires. Another legal manuscript has two texts of the same code (pp. 232, 390). But here recurrent matter coincides with idiosyncratic format. A further Wulfstan codex is now seen to have been separate books only later conjoined.[155] The implications are important. A reduplicated V Æthelred then seems no more anomalous than a II–III Edgar reiterated in the Nero volume's parts A and B. For all one can say to the contrary, they were just coeval copies. More significant still, if Nero 'B' is not an assembly of 'booklets' like the Parker codex but pieces of two or more very similar books, it begins to look like one of a series of books; and books intended not to make a point, like those discussed so far, but to serve a purpose.

What purpose? The Latin sections of Nero 'B' are canon law as conceived by the pre-Gregorian western Church. This is one of a set of collections, all more or less nearly associated with Wulfstan, that are best examined in the next part of this chapter (pp. 210–21). Its immediate relevance is that it supplied some of Wulfstan's sources for his homilies, *Institutes* and laws.[156] In other words, the Latin sections of the manuscript provide the raw material for the Old English. These Old English sections present programmatic statements of the Christian life with, to repeat, scant regard for any differences of *genre*. *Polity* is a blueprint of what Wulfstan thought a Christian society should be. His homilies encourage or warn its members to observe its standards. His laws lend those standards the force of terrestrial sanctions; but Wulfstan's laws tend in fact to be sparing of penal stipulation; and the 1008 decrees especially are apt to lay down what was expected, without being too specific about penalties for failure. Wulfstan's codes do not even have distinctive titles. The 'G²' rubric is '*Be Angolwitena gerednesse* (on the decrees of the English wise men)', as if it too were a homily like *Be cristendome* or a part of *Polity* like *Be cynge*.[157] 'G¹' at least bears the date 1008, but it fails to identify Æthelred as the king responsible; and in fact the 1014 *Sermo Lupi* is also dated in this manuscript and another (see pp. 332–3). The laws of earlier kings are ascribed to them explicitly.[158] But all types of rubric are set in small black capitals with a red wash. And as in the York Gospels, homilies, laws and *Institutes* are all divided into 'clauses' by small colour-washed initials.[159] Nor did the archbishop himself seem to recognize any difference between instructions

---

155   *The Copenhagen Wulfstan*, ed. Cross and Morrish Tunberg, pp. 24–8 (it is itself instructive that Professor Cross and Dr Morrish Tunberg reached their conclusion independently from mine).

156   It was this that identified what has become known (perhaps unfortunately, below, pp. 218–19) as 'Archbishop Wulfstan's Commonplace book': see Whitelock, 'Wulfstan, Homilist and Statesman', pp. 28–35; Bethurum, 'Wulfstan's Commonplace book'.

157   On this aspect of Wulfstan/Æthelred laws, see Lawson, 'Wulfstan and the Homiletic Element', pp. 574–9; also chapter 5, pp. 338–41.

158   E.g. I As (f. 86v), I Em (f. 87v), as compared with V Atr (ff. 89r, 116v), or VIII Atr (f. 95v), or *Inst. Pol.* (f. 70r), *Hom.* Xc (f. 76v), etc. (cf. *Wulfstan Manuscript*, ed. Loyn, pp. 15–18). The *Sermo Lupi* rubric is on f. 110r.

159   Another link between sections b) and d) is that the texts in *Inst. Pol.* VIII are consistently paragraphed, ff. 99r–100r, like most items in the so-called 'Excerptiones Ecgberhti' (ff. 127v–154r).

supposedly endorsed by king and *witan*, and those springing from his own earnest solicitude for the ordering of Christian society. In either case the text was adjusted by insertion (or less often deletion) in his hand. He felt as free to revise laws as anything else he wrote.

The Nero manuscript is the earliest extant English law book that is pocket-sized. It does not follow that it was designed for judges to carry around. Its dominant note was not so much legal as moral. Even its law-codes have a cler-ical slant: the 'first', largely ecclesiastical, codes of Æthelstan and Edmund are not accompanied by their more secular laws. The sanctity of church buildings is a particular preoccupation of other contents.[160] The book or books thus look more like a *vade mecum* for an itinerant preacher than for a judge. Yet from another angle, one close to Wulfstan's own, the purpose they served was urgently practical. They educated citizens of all walks of life in the duties of a People of God. They set out the terms not so much of earthly justice as of divine favour.

A last question to ask about Nero A.i(B) is one that has persisted since Nero E.i: which of Wulfstan's sees produced and/or preserved it? As with Nero, Harley 55 and Claudius A.iii, the case for York is not as strong as it at first looks.[161] All or most of the book was probably written after Wulfstan relinquished the Worcester see in 1016, but this does not prove northern origin.[162] Nor does the specifically northern interest of some items (pp. 184–5, 188). Later medieval marginalia do not help (pp. 225–6). The most interesting point is that Wulfstan's ban on clerical marriage is erased in favour of the resounding sentiment, 'it is right that a priest love a decent woman as a bedmate'.[163] But the argument that this outburst is to be expected of York rather than Worcester may rest on false premises. The hostility to clerical marriage of the second (sainted) Wulfstan of Worcester is vouched for by William of Malmesbury; but William was writing in a twelfth-century climate, and St Wulfstan was actually the son of a priest.[164] The best resolution of the conundrum is to accept, as before, that Wulfstan's books were manufactured in his own circle, wherever that happened to be located at the time.

160   Of VIII Atr, only 1 – 5:2 appears, with *Grið* and *Nor grið*.
161   Whitelock, 'Wulfstan at York', pp. 219–20.
162   Morrish Tunberg, *Copenhagen Wulfstan*. pp. 29–30, esp. p. 30, n. 2; and cf., e.g., S 1384.
163   Whitelock, *ibid*., and *Wulfstan Manuscript*, ed. Loyn, pp. 29–30 (*Inst. Pol.* I 72). The temptation to see this as an intrusion by indignant Reformation scholarship (cf. below, n. 220) should be resisted: Professor Chris Fell and Dr Katie Lowe inform me that 'Riht is þæt preost him lufie clænlicne wimman to gebeddan' is impeccable Old English, nor is there anything suspect in the script, f. 72v lns 14–15.
164   Whitelock herself conceded the weakness of this argument, p. 220. If one rejects the 'Northumbrian Priests' Law' as the work of Archbishop Wulfstan (chapter 5, pp. 396–7), so dispensing with the evidence that he came to terms in the North with what he repudiated in the South, then that code proves no more than that *some* northern archbishop was prepared to accept clerical marriage – as, it might be argued, a pre-conquest bishop of Worcester other than the Wulfstans could also have done. On St Wulfstan's origins and attitude and the problem of his biography, see Mason, *St Wulfstan*, pp. 30–2, 162–4, 286–94. Note that added to CCCC MS 190 at Exeter in the late-eleventh century was a spirited verse 'Invectivum in damnantes coniugium sacerdotum', with a special concern for the sons of priests (table 4.5, p. 222).

Table 4.3 Structure and content of Corpus 201

Scribe 1	Scribe 2	Scribe 3	Scribe 4
a. pp. 1–7 (quire 1): originally blank from p. 7 ln 19. *Reg. Conc.* (frag.)			
b.	pp. 8–145 (quire 1, quires 2–10): missing leaf after p. 64; one or more quires missing after p. 142; quire 10 a bifolium (pp. 143–6), blank from p. 145 ln 26. *Hom.*N 1; *Hom.*N 62; *Hom.* VI; *Hom.* VII lns 1–25, 26–end; *Hom.* XIII lns 1–31, 32–41, 42–52, 53–end + *Hom.*N 24(a); *Hom.*N 25 + *Hom.* VIIa lns 17–end; *Hom.*N 23; *Hom.*N 27; *Hom.* XXI+XIX; *Hom.*N 35; *Hom.*N 38; VIIa Atr; Ælfric *Br.* II; *Inst. Pol.* II 145–69a, II 187–97, II 203, 205–6, 213–19, 209–11; *Norðhu.*; II–III Eg; V Atr + *Inst. Pol.* II 223–36; *Hom.* Xc lns 20–38, 62–71 (+ *Hom.*N 40, pp. 188–9, etc.); I As; *Hom.* Xb + Xc lns 1–26, 39–end; *Hom.* XI to ln 212 . . . . *Hom.* IX from ln 69; *Hom.* Ia + Ib; *Hom.* V; *Hom.* II; *Hom.* III; *Hom.* IV; *Hom.*N 40; *Hom.* XVIb + *Hom.*N 41(b); *Hom.* XX(C); *Hom.* XXI; *Inst. Pol.* I 1–5, 16–128; VIII Atr; I Em; *Can. Eg.*; *Gebyn.*; *Norðl.*; *Mirc.*; *Að*; *Had.*; *Hom.* VIIIa + VIIIc lns		

c.

1–155; *Inst. Pol.* XXIV 1–52; *Ben. Off.*; 'Conf.' I–VI + *Penit. Ps.Tb.* lii; Cn 1018; *Inst. Pol.* II 130–4, 135–54 (pp. 256–61); Apollonius

? Erasure of 'Conf.' I lns 7–21 (text repeated in section **g**, p. 170)

d.

pp. 147–51 (quire 11): a '4' (pp. 147–54); presumably blank from p. 151 ln 3. *Halgan, Secgan*

pp. 151–60 (quire 11, quire 12): quire 12 a '6' (pp. 155–60), with missing leaf at start and two at end. *OE Genesis* 37:1 – 47:18 . . . (frag.)

e. pp. 161–7 (quire 13): originally blank from p. 167 ln 9). *OE De Die Iudicii*, etc.

f.

pp. 167–70 (quire 13): presumably blank from p. 170 ln 8: *OE Lord's Prayer, Gloria*

g.

pp. 170–6 (quire 13): quire is supplemented by bifolium (pp. 171–4) which should be bound after p. 176; pp. 177–8 are blank, as presumably was last leaf of quire now excised. 'Conf.' I lns 3–19, Latin forms of confession and absolution, inc. for women.

(ii) Cambridge, Corpus Christi College, MS 201

Corpus 201 is another complicated manuscript best explored by means of visual display (table 4.3).[165] A few specifics in the table call for comment before the discussion goes any further.[166] For one thing, sixteenth-century interests are again involved. Intervention this time was by Archbishop Parker. He added a quite unrelated Exeter copy of Theodulf's *Capitulary* in Latin and Old English to the end of the book.[167] He also erased the first thirty-eight lines of the opening page, and substituted a contents-list for both (Parkerian) parts of the volume. As a result, the text of the Old English translation of the *Regularis Concordia* opens at a relatively 'natural' break, the commencement of the Palm Sunday liturgies. But it looks as if the erased text began in mid-sentence. At least one preceding quire, and probably several, have therefore gone missing.[168] On the other hand, the text breaks off with a strong punctuation mark half way down p. 7, at a point which, if not mid-sentence, clearly envisaged continuation. Either its exemplar was faulty, and scribe 1 left the rest of the quire blank (to be colonized half a century later by scribe 2) as he went in fruitless quest of a replacement; or the project was aborted for some other reason.[169]

A second prolegomenon is that use of a bifolium for quire 10 looks like a special measure to accommodate the 'Apollonius'; and it is important that the scribe left a page and half of it blank before beginning his lists of 'Saints of England' and their 'Resting-Places' in a fresh quire. Again, he provided an irregular double bifolium, presumably to make space for 'Resting-Places', and was again too generous, leaving almost half of it blank. This, thirdly, was the space used by scribe 3 to begin the *Old English Genesis*, and he too added an irregular quire to complete the text.[170] Fourth, the bifolium added to quire 13 is

---

165   It has *siglum* 'D' for Liebermann (*Gesetze* I, pp. xxii–xxiii) and Jost, *Inst. Pol.*, and 'C' for the Homilies editors, Napier and Bethurum; in Ker, *Catalogue*, it is no. 49 and dated 's xi^{in}' (pp. 1–7, 161–7) or 's xi^{med}' (pp. 8–160, 167–76). My understanding of this manuscript has been advanced by the Corpus seminar on Anglo-Saxon manuscripts, organized by Professor Ray Page and Dr Mildred Budny.

166   This table regretfully abandons Ker's classification ('A', 'B', etc.) so as to clarify the extent to which the manuscript comes in more than two distinguishable sections, and arguably therefore stages; nor can it be assumed at the outset that Ker's parts 'A' and 'B' always belonged in the same book (below). Extra abbreviations (cf. n. 148) are: Apollonius: *Old English Apollonius*, ed. Goolden; *Ben. Off.*: *Benedictine Office*, ed. Ure; *Halgan, Secgan*: *Heiligen Englands*, ed. Liebermann; *OE Genesis*: *Old English Heptateuch*, ed Crawford; *OE De Die Iudicii*, etc., *Gloria, Lord's Prayer*: *Minor Poems*, ed. Dobbie, pp. 58–77; *Reg. Conc.*: here Zupitza, 'Ein weiteres Bruchstück'.

167   The intrusive section was from CCCC 191: Ker, *Catalogue*, p. 75.

168   The visible opening corresponds to *Regularis Concordia* iv 36, p. 34; line counting suggests that the page began well before the start of iv 35 (p. 33). (Presumably because he was using photographs, Zupitza (cf. n. 166) missed the erasure of much of the first page, and was thus misled into thinking that the text was deliberately begun at iv 35, i.e. that its deficient opening was a matter of scribal choice.) In an as yet unpublished paper for the 1997 'Fontes Anglo-Saxonici' convention at King's College London, Professor Joyce Hill noted that cross-references in the OE text that do not correspond to the Latin suggest that the text was a lot fuller (or copied from a MS that was).

169   Given the point at which the text breaks off ('7 cweðe a þæt forme', corresponding to the Latin 'et dicat primam', iv 43, p. 42), one could imagine that the intention was to omit the reference to (lack of) genuflection and launch straight into the prayers, with the text perhaps abandoned because it was hoped to expand them; cf. J. Hill, '"Regularis Concordia"', pp. 309–11.

yet another case of making room; scribe 4's expansive style needed a lot. But the paradoxical outcome was once more that the last four pages were unused, and the final leaf was in due course cut away.[171] The logic of all this, then, is that section b) was a conscious continuation of a), and that scribe 2 deliberately reserved some matter (section f)) for a later part of scribe 1's parent manuscript (section e)); that sections c) and d) were also intended additions to the collection by scribes 2 and 3 respectively; and that scribe 4 was another who built on ground left vacant by scribe 2.

If so, the fifth, final and crucial preliminary concerns the volume's overall unity. Could Part I have been assembled by Parker as he united it to its Exeter Part II? It seems odd that scribe 1 should leave his *Regularis Concordia* unfinished before going on to copy 418 lines of the Old English *Judgement Day* and other devotional verse into a new quire (section e)).[172] It is not immediately obvious why scribe 2 should put his vernacular versifications of the Lord's Prayer and Gloria in a discrete section f). Theoretically, scribe 2 could have taken off the shelf two different pieces of unfinished work by the previous generation's scribe 1, and worked on each at different times. But two strong arguments counter this view. First, so far from repeating each other like those of Nero A.i(B), the Corpus 201 sections take pains to avoid this. Scribe 4 (probably) erased from section b) most of the confessional formula that he added (with prayers) to the end of the book.[173] Nor is it likely to be coincidence that scribe 2 omitted from section b) just those parts of the 'Benedictine Office', the versified 'Gloria' and Lord's Prayer, that he included in section f). One could indeed guess that section b) was limited to prose, with the poetry deferred to a place where it could follow Bede's verses.[174] Secondly, the manuscript as a whole has a very idiosyncratic shape, being unusually tall for its width. It has a constant (large) number of forty-one lines in more or less consistently the same written space.[175] The odds are against so unusual a format being devised for two utterly independent projects. For whatever irretrievable reason, scribe 1 probably meant sections a) and e) to be part of the same book. The activity of scribes 2 and 4 then falls into place.

However, there is no denying the manuscript's sectional character. One of the implications is crucial. Not one of section b)'s fifty-plus items coincides with a new quire. Its layout remains consistent throughout seventy-odd folios, yet differs slightly from that of the same scribe's section c).[176] Why should he have stopped at the end of 'Apollonius', then resumed on a fresh quire, unless he was respecting

---

170   Damage to quire 12, with loss of leaves after p. 160 might imply that this was for a time the 'exposed' end of the volume, hence that sections a) – d) and e) – g) began as separate books; but see below.

171   The confusion here is compounded by an untypical Ker slip: the bifolium, pp. 171–4, is of course misbound after p. 170, not p. 174!

172   An adaptation forms a homily in the sub-Wulfstanian collection, Bodleian Hatton MS 113–14 (Ker, *Catalogue*, no. 331 (22)); on the Bedan original, see Lapidge, *Bede the Poet*.

173   Had this been another Parker erasure (cf. Page, *Parker and his Books*, pp. 46–53), would he have so inefficiently overlooked the text's first lines at the foot of p. 114?

174   Cf. *Benedictine Office*, ed. Ure, pp. 50–5, 83–7, 103–6.

175   The MS's dimensions are 280 mm × 165 mm, and it has not been so shorn by binders that its pricking is not still visible; the length of lines incidentally increases in the detectably cramped OE *Genesis*.

176   There are no colour-washed internal initials in the *Halgan/ Secgan* section, and relatively few coloured main ones; further, the parchment of section c) is detectably rougher and thinner.

the integrity of separate exemplars? Section b) therefore originated as a self-contained unit. What at once emerges is that this was a larger-scale equivalent to sections a) – c) of Nero A.i(B). Here are three-quarters of Wulfstan's 'true' homilies, together with seven more not recognized as such by his editor but beyond doubt his work.[177] Here is the complete first edition of the *Institutes of Polity*, alongside two sets of the ingredients later blended into the second. Here is an even fuller set of laws, especially Wulfstan's own: two variants of the 1009 edict, a complete text of the 1014 code, a series of status-tracts assembled and rewritten by the archbishop, and above all the 'framework-document' that he drew up for the 1018 agreement of English and Danes (chapter 3, pp. 131–3).[178] Here too are prescriptive texts that do not appear in Nero A.i: Wulfstan's 'Canons of Edgar' for his diocesan clergy, and 'Benedictine Office', presumably for his monks. Homily, law and other admonitory works have the same homogeneity of presentation as in Nero. There is more variety in phrasing of rubrics, but these are again in small capitals, with the 'clauses' marked by slightly enlarged and colour-washed initials.[179] In sum, section b) of Corpus 201 is a manual for the drilling of a Christian society like Nero A.i(B), only fuller. It may even be a version, at one or more removes, of a 'master-copy' kept in Wulfstan's cathedral libraries.

Not everything in section b) is attributable to Wulfstan. At least one homily is a pastiche of Wulfstanian elements that can hardly have been concocted by the archbishop himself.[180] Especially relevant here is the case of the 'Northumbrian Priests' Law'. It is influenced by Wulfstan's style and views, but is unlikely to be his work (chapter 5, pp. 396–7). It ought, however, to be the work of an archbishop of York (or member of his staff). Yet no northern archbishop after 1023 was bishop elsewhere for more than a short time (Ælfric Puttoc holding Worcester in 1040/1). The genesis of section b) should therefore lie at York. Ælfric Puttoc, as will be seen, may provide a link between York and the house where Corpus 201 was probably written. Such is the basis on which to assess section b)'s most startling feature, its inclusion of the Old English translation of the tale of Apollonius of Tyre.[181] There is no denying the appeal of this saga of true love, conjugal and parental, surmounting incestuous tyranny, envious greed and perverse fortune through ingenuity and positively Pasternakian coincidence. The Anglo-Saxon was the earliest in a string of vernacularizations, climaxing (for England) in the semi-Shakespearean *Pericles*. But what was it doing in a Wulfstanian primer of Christian standards? If

---

177   The exceptions from *Hom.* are nos VIIIb, Xa, XIV – XVIa, XVII–XVIII; and from those in *Hom.N* that can confidently be attributed to the archbishop (see now Wilcox, 'Dissemination of Wulfstan's homilies', pp. 200–1), nos. 36 (essentially a duplicate of 35), 50–53, 59–61 (the York Gospels trio).

178   VIIa Atr (= *Hom.N* 39) with *Hom.N* 35; VIII Atr; *Geþyn. – Had.*; Cn 1018. But it should be recalled that section a) of Nero A.i(B) is fragmentary, and may have contained other codes, homilies and *Inst. Pol.* selections.

179   More prominent coloured letters are used in *Can. Eg.* (pp. 97–101), 'Conf.' IV (pp. 117–21), and compare the handling of the verse Lord's Prayer etc. (pp. 167–70) with that of *Ben. Off.* (pp. 112–14).

180   *Hom.N* XL; see Wilcox, 'Dissemination', p. 206.

181   Ed. Goolden (as n. 166), and by Raith, *Alt- und mittelenglische Apollonius Bruchstücke*; trans. Swanton, *Anglo-Saxon Prose*, pp. 158–73; most illuminatingly discussed by Archibald, *Apollonius of Tyre*.

broadly edifying in so far as virtue is rewarded and vice finally punished, it is not even obviously Christian. As literature, it may not tend to corrupt, but nor does it do much to instruct. To this riddle, two complementary solutions may be offered. First, it could have been grafted onto the exemplar that reached scribe 2 at any stage of its journey to him, or even in his home *scriptorium* before he set to work.[182] Second, the Apollonius story evidently *was* regarded as exemplary, and not just by laymen like Eberhard of Friuli (chapter 2, pp. 53–4). It appears in the library catalogues of Frankish abbeys. A Cluny copy was catalogued as 'a story about the base lust of Antiochus and the exile of Apollonius', which is quite like the Corpus rubric.[183] If this view was taken within Cluny's (socially as well as spritually) august portals, it is not to be ruled out for English communities. Early medieval monks and nuns would insist on being unsuitably entertained. *Apollonius* was less shocking than some well-known examples.[184]

If section b) of Corpus 201 is a copy of a typical Wulfstan manual of pastoral administration with additions made at York and perhaps elsewhere, neither Wulfstan nor his successors need have had anything to do with the manuscript as it now stands. It was very probably in a different place and with different objectives that the Wulfstanian collection in b) and f) was added to the *Regularis Concordia* and Verse in a) and e), then supplemented by 'Resting-Places' (c), part of Genesis (d), and confessional prayers (g). Is it possible to deduce where this was done and why? At least the first question can be answered. Scribe 4's stately hand has been traced to Winchester's New Minster. It recurs in two other books, one definitely from the New Minster, neither attributable to other centres.[185] Preconquest scribes were not necessarily restricted to one scriptorial sphere, as has been observed (pp. 169, 171); and even if scribe 4 was a New Minster man, he could have added to a book penned somewhere else. All the same, scribes 2–4 look contemporary.[186] And other indicators point to the New Minster. One feature of the *Regularis Concordia* liturgy is typically Winchester.[187] The 'Resting-Places' is close to that in the New Minster *Liber Vitae*.[188] Archbishop Ælfric Puttoc of York, one of only two candidates for author of the 'Northumbrian Priests' Law' between Wulfstan's death and the codex's date, is

---

182   Much has been said about its phonology, West/?East Saxon (Goolden, pp. xxix–xxxi), or 'Middlesex' (Raith, pp. 8–15), but this could in any case have been that of the MS scribe or his most immediate source. The same point applies to section b) as a whole, apart from the fact that York cathedral clergy need have been no more Northumbrian than the archbishops; however, Whitelock, *Sermo Lupi*, pp. 37–43, has interesting suggestions about the speech of Wulfstan's circle.

183   Archibald, *Apollonius*, pp. 93, 218–19 (App. II nos 4–5).

184   Archibald, pp. 15–26, assesses the tale's potential as models for fatherhood, kingship, education and riddle-solving, cogently adducing this last as a factor in its Anglo-Saxon appeal, and proposing, p. 184, that the princess's love-sickness was omitted for reasons of taste; see too Raith, *Apollonius Bruchstücke*, pp. 40–1.

185   Bishop, *English Caroline Minuscule*, p. xv, n. 2. The others are Le Havre MS 330 and BL Stowe MS 2 (but apparently *not* C.U.L. Ii.4.6), and it is the first of these that is diagnostically New Minster.

186   Ker, *Catalogue*, p. 90; Professor Godden points out to me that the neatness with which scribe 4 did his work suggests that the manuscript was then still not fully bound.

187   Hill, '"Regularis Concordia"', p. 311.

188   BL Stowe MS 944; *Heiligen Englands*, pp. xiv–xvi; Rollason, 'Saints' resting-places', pp. 61–8; Keynes, *Liber Vitae*, pp. 99–100.

said to have been 'prior of Winchester'.[189] *If* he was and kept in touch with his 'old school', he could have sent it what became section b). None of these points can alone carry the weight of the argument. Together, they support it quite well.

The wherefore of Corpus 201 is more elusive than the where. It is frustratingly difficult to choose between the options offered by so rich a range of content. Each scribe may have had a different agenda. But two threads run right through the volume. One is devotional. 'Resting-places' was in the first instance a pilgrims' guide. The object of the prayers of confession and absolution in scribe 4's stint was presumably to fill out the penitential element in section b).[190] In this light, scribe 2's motives for copying section b) could have been pietistic, cherishing its homiletic above its directive aspects. On the other hand, 'Resting-places' was also a monument to the spiritual record of the English as a people; it again strikes that note of 'national' consciousness that has been found in other Winchester books of the time (pp. 179–80). Further, the translated Genesis extract is the story of Joseph. This, another tale of triumph over adversity leading to beneficent administration in famine conditions but under God's auspices, may have seemed a fitting alternative to the 'Apollonius'.[191] From that angle, scribe 2 may have been interested in section b) as a textbook on Christian government. Perhaps the most important point, however, is that this could be a false antithesis. Places like the New Minster were nurseries of monk-bishops: men trained to serve kings of both earth and heaven. Corpus 201 would have been well suited to familiarize them with their awesome range of responsibilities.

5   Law and Penance

The next class of manuscripts again and for one last time consists of a pair. It is also the last with a Wulfstan connection, albeit there is no longer any question of the archbishop's perceptible presence. These two books are best known for those parts that have been recognized as specimens of what is not altogether helpfully called 'Archbishop Wulfstan's Commonplace Book'.[192] They are also more. Sections were added to both, turning each into a rather different kind of volume.

---

189   Knowles, Brooke and London (eds), *Heads of Religious Houses*, p. 80; but Dr Keynes kindly points out to me that he cannot have been the *praepositus* of the New Minster whose 19 Feburary *obit* is in Titus D. xxvii (so pre-1031; cf. *Liber Vitae*, ed. Keynes, p. 119); and it must be said that there is something suspect about a good deal of John of Worcester's blithe pre-conquest prosopography.

190   One potentially significant point is that scribe 4's texts provided for women, inasmuch as the *Regularis Concordia* extract was among those vernacular memorials of the Tenth-century Reformation that had been adapted for nuns: Hill, '"Regularis Concordia"', pp. 310–11; Gretsch, 'Benedictine Rule in Old English', pp. 142–54; Jayatilaka, '*Regula Sancti Benedicti*', pp. 282–3. But this need not mean that the book came from a nunnery: gender in *Reg. Conc.* says something only about the origins of this extract (or its source(s)); and as regards scribe 4's work, a bishop would expect to administer absolution to women, even if abbots confined their attention to men.

191   The Joseph story's place in the imaginative world of Anglo-Saxon law comes out in the *Illustrated Hexateuch*, ed. Dodwell and Clemoes, f. 59r, where Pharaoh passes judgement on his butler dressed as an Anglo-Saxon king with *witan*; it forms the dust-jacket of this book.

192   See n. 156; also *Wulfstan's Canons of Edgar*, ed. Fowler, pp. xxxiv–lxi, and in particular Cross, 'Newly Identified Manuscript'.

These additions include the items most directly interesting to students of Anglo-Saxon law.

(i) Cambridge, Corpus Christi College, MS 265

Although Corpus Cambridge 265 is by and large the later of the two manuscripts in this class, it is in several ways a better guide to the impulses underlying their compilation, and may therefore be taken first.[193] In its extant form, it is a compendium of canonical, penitential and liturgical texts, amounting to a comprehensive handbook for an active pastor. But, as with other codices in a Wulfstanian mould, the necessary prelude to the understanding of the whole is an analysis of its parts. Table 4.4 will provide assistance when it is most needed (pp. 214–15).

Section b) of Corpus 265 (pp. 209–36, quires 14–15) contains the code known as 'IV Edgar', and is thus the one of primary concern here. It shows signs of being self-contained. It is mainly in the same hand, which is not the one that wrote all of section a). This is an early warning against assuming that it was designated for membership of the same collection. Another is that section a) finishes with ten blank lines, at the end of a text which itself looks like a supplement.[194] Section b) itself originally began with blank pages. Its second quire has six sheets, an indication (if no more) that there was no original intention to carry the compilation on. It also concludes with over five blank pages; and when the collection resumes, section c) is in similar, but possibly not the same, script.[195] The section's content, IV Edgar aside, is more homogeneous than it at first seems. On pp. 211–13 are formulae to be uttered, and procedural rubrics to follow, when excommunicating 'despisers of the law of the Lord and enemies of God's holy Church.' They are like those that Liebermann actually included among his *Gesetze*.[196] Next stand formulae to absolve 'those who after excommunication come to reconciliation with the grief of penitence'. The theme's immediacy is revealed by an addition in the same hand on previously blank p. 209, with a *signe de renvoi* linking it to the relevant part of the formulary. This condemns 'those rebels against holy Christianity who with madness in their heart came at the start of Lent to the land of St Mary *que æt Christes hala alioque vocabulo æt ontelawe vocatur*, and burnt it, afflicting some men with blows, killing others, and carrying off the goods of

---

193   It was given the *siglum* 'C' by Liebermann (*Gesetze* I, p. xx), Jost and Sauer, 'Zur Überlieferung', but 'X' by editors of the Homilies, and 'Z' by Aronstam, 'Latin Canonical Tradition'; it is Ker, *Catalogue* no. 53, where it is dated 's xi^{med}', with additions (from p. 269) of 's xi², s xi/xii' and '(sc. early) twelfth-century'.
194   The number of lines is the same in each section, but twenty-six is a much less singular quantity than CCCC 201's forty-one. Nor are its overall dimensions eccentric: though not so severely shorn that its pricking has disappeared, these are 265 mm x 165 mm, i.e. the same width as MS 201 but 1.5 cm shorter.
195   Though cf. Ker, p. 94. The 'ð' in 'Athelwold', p. 237 ln 6, is certainly quite like those throughout pp. 222–7; but compare the difference in 'g', as between (e.g.) p. 231 lns 3–4, 8–9, 11, 13, etc., and p. 237 lns 2, 8, 11, etc.
196   *Gesetze* I, pp. 432–41; he printed the formula from CCCC 190 (*Excom.* III), so why did he omit those in CCCC 265? Cf. Treharne, 'Unique Old English formula for excommunication', pp. 201–5, and Sauer, 'Die Exkommunikationsriten'.

all inhabitants of that estate ... Who still persist in that malice, and disdain to come to penitence'.[197] The site of this outrage is not at once identifiable, but it at least appears that formulae of this sort were put to use.

At the end of the section, immediately after IV Edgar and still in the same hand, comes the liturgy for the sanctification of oils on Maundy Thursday. Its relevance here is that Maundy Thursday was the chief occasion in the Church's year for readmitting penitents to its communion. This ritual refers both to the assembly in church of those seeking absolution, and to the use of holy oil in the 'remission of sins'.[198] Section a) of the manuscript contains a homily by Abbo of St Germain about the 'Lord's Supper' reconciliation of penitents, which was the foundation for Wulfstan's own disquisition on the subject.[199] In Corpus Cambridge 190, the other manuscript of the pair now under discussion, Abbo's homily was shortly followed by another version of the liturgy for blessing of the oils.[200] It seems, then, that IV Edgar was bracketed by texts concerned with the condemnation and pardon of God's enemies. The probable reason lies in the code's content. The whole of its long first clause, more than a third of the total, is given over to the subject of compulsory payment of tithes; and its prologue declares that a recent 'pestilence' has been caused by Divine anger at 'disobedience to God's commands'. Like other systems of authority, the Church has seldom had so many enemies as when seeking to finance itself at its subjects' expense. One can well believe that its demands led to many threatened and some implemented anathemas. The object of Edgar's laws, as of others in the Anglo-Saxon series, was to put the weight of royal power behind the Church's dues. The Church was not on that account going to temper its own wrath. Spiritual and secular sanctions, penance and punishment, went side-by-side.

The Abbo sermon is not the only hint that sections a) and b) of Corpus 265 may have been more closely linked than at first appears. There is no obvious point to the unfinished sketch-map of the world's resettlement by the offspring of Noah, which a close associate of section b)'s main scribe entered on a hitherto blank p. 210. Yet its message takes shape when it is noticed that the map was meant to mark the particular parts subsequently evangelized by each apostle: Andrew in 'Achaia', Peter in Caesarea, and presumably others.[201] Apocryphal apostolic Acta were popular throughout the early medieval West, especially in insular spheres. Andrew was initially assigned to 'Achaia' by Cynewulf's *Fates of*

---

197   Quoted in full by James, *Catalogue of Manuscripts at Corpus Christi Cambridge* II, p. 17, and Sauer, 'Die Exkommuniktionsriten', p. 294.

198   *Ordines Romani*, ed. Andrieu, I, p. 99.

199   *Abbo Predigten*, ed. Önnerfors, 13, pp. 123–32; it is on pp. 142–8 of MS 265 (MS 190, pp. 253–8, also Nero A.i, ff. 159v–162v), and is printed facing its OE rendition (pp. 222–3 below) as *Hom.* App. I, while Wulfstan's own adaptation is *Hom.* XV, pp. 236–8.

200   *Hirtenbriefe Ælfrics*, ed. Fehr, Anhang III 48, p. 249. The other (near-identical) copy of this ritual (Fehr, n. 3) is in the Ecgberht Pontifical, ed. Banting, pp. 147–52 – significantly, among 'Orationes ad reconciliandos penitentes feria v caene domini'.

201   See James's reconstruction, *Catalogue* I, p. 17; the script seems to be that of section b)'s second scribe, who wrote the first lines of the excommunications, p. 211, and the absolutions, p. 215.

202   *Andreas and the Fates of the Apostles*, ed. Brooks, pp. 6 (lns 168–9), 56 (ln 16); and for the genre as a whole, see [Biggs,] 'Apocryphal Acts', in Biggs, Hill and Szarmach (eds), *Sources of Anglo-Saxon Literary Culture*, pp. 48–63.

the *Apostles* and in the *Andreas* itself.[202] But here they were perhaps more than edifying yarns. Section a) of Corpus 265 opens with an *Ammonitio Spiritalis Doctrinae* which is largely about pastoral duty. This makes way for an *Admonitio Episcopalis Vitae* that is more explicitly so.[203] If one motif runs through the whole lengthy collection, it is the multifarious burdens of bishops. Peter, Andrew and the rest were prototype bishops.

Such clues to the connection between sections a) and b) of Corpus 265 can be followed up only by examining section a) more closely. This is best done by comparing its content with that of other 'Commonplace-book' manuscripts. The relevant parts of all six are displayed in table 4.4, where it can at once be seen that they include Nero A.i, whose Old English content was studied in the previous section of the chapter, and Corpus 190, which is the pair to Corpus 265 in this one.[204] The most obvious thing to emerge from the comparison is the general similarity of the six volumes. Of the seventy or so canonical, penitential, admonitory and liturgical items grouped into the thirteen blocks analysed in the second part of table 4.4, nearly all appear in at least two columns, most in three or more, and some in all.[205] Hardly less obvious is that the various 'blocks' of associated material were repeatedly redistributed as each of the six collections was compiled. The questions that need answering here are how the Corpus arrangement relates to the other five, and how that arrangement is best understood.[206]

A first point is that it is clearly more closely related to the collections in Barlow 37 and (so far as it goes) Rouen 1382 than to the rest. These three adopt the 'second' recension of the 'Excerpts from the Canons' that are usually known as the 'Excerptiones Ecgberhti', where two others have the 'first' and the sixth neither. They also share some of the 'Block IV' texts, and all or part of the (interpolated) 'Penitential of Ecgberht' (IIIa-c), little or none of which are in the remaining three. Barlow 37 is a twelfth-century manuscript, where a full set of

---

203   The first of these two is ed. Cross, 'Newly Identified Manuscript', pp. 78–80.

204   The first recognition of the relationship between these books (though unaware of Barlow, Rouen and Copenhagen) was Mary Bateson's celebrated if impenetrable paper, 'A Worcester Cathedral Book of Ecclesiastical Collections', which as regards the Corpus 265 text of 'Excerptiones Ecgberti' itself followed a lead from Johnson's neglected and rather remarkable *Collection of Laws and Canons*. The argument was advanced by Whitelock, Bethurum, Cross and others (as nn. 156, 192, and see next n.). I essay a fresh approach in 'Archbishop Wulfstan', to which reference must be made for detailed exposition of what follows. See also my 'LAWS' in Biggs *et al.* (eds), *Sources*, under the heading 'The Worcester Canon Collection'.

205   The first to identify these 'blocks' and to chart their movement through the manuscripts was Sauer, 'Zur Überlieferung': a methodological breakthrough, to which my own accounts are deeply indebted.

206   References used in part II of table 4.4 other than abbreviations in the bibliographical list (and n. 148): ?Alcuin's *De Tribulationibus* and 'Penance and compensation in Saxony' are ed. Bateson, 'Worcester Cathedral Book', pp. 731, 724–7; 'Conc. IV Tol.': *Concilios Visigóticos*, ed. Vives, pp. 186–225; 'Council of Aachen (816)': *Concil.* I, ed. Werminghoff, pp. 307–464; 'Cummean', *Pseudo-Romanum*, etc.: *Bußordnungen*, ed. Wasserschleben, pp. 460–93, 360–77; *De militia seculari*: cf. *Exc. Can.* 155; *Dial. Ecgb.* 'Dialogue of Archbishop Ecgberht', in *Councils*, ed. Haddan and Stubbs, III, pp. 403–13; 'Dionysiana': cf. *Ecclesiae Occidentalis monumenta iuris*, ed. Turner, I, pp. 1–32, 249–73, etc. and *PL* LXVII cols 135–230; *Penit. Ecgb.*: 'Egbert's Penitential', in *Councils*, ed. Haddan and Stubbs, III, pp. 413–31; *Pseudo-Angrilamn*: *Decretales pseudo-isidorianae*, ed. Hinschius, pp. 755–69; *Sermones de Coniugio*: cf. *Exc. Can.* 116–17, 119, 121, etc.; Wulfstan, Penitential Letters, ed. Aronstam. 'Penitential pilgrimages', pp. 70–83. Note that some texts remain unidentified and/or unedited.

Table 4.4 Blocks of material in 'Wulfstan Commonplace-Book' MSS

CCCC 265 (pp. 1–208)

VIIb,e,f,d,c Pastors
XI Bishops
IIIb Priests
I *Exc. Can.* iia
IIIa,e,f(i),c, f(ii) Penance
I *Exc. Can.* iib
V Marriage + …
I *Exc. Can.* iicd

IVb-d,a,e Lay and clerical life (cf. IIId Penance)
IIa-c Assaults on clergy etc.

VI Radulf, Theodulf I
IIIg Penance
VIIIc,d Duty of kings and churchmen
VIIa Pastors
VIIIa-b,e-f Clerical security and status
IXe,g,a,f,h,b Ælfric Br. 2–3, liturgical functions and status of clergy
XII Canonical

Xa Anathema and penance
[cf. Xb IV Eg (tithes), etc.]

Barlow 37 (ff. 1r–45v/47r)

I *Exc. Can.* iia-d
IIa-c Assaults on clergy
IIIa,b,c(i),d,e, f(i),c(ii),f(ii) Penance (inc. Priests *Cap.*)
IVa Lay service
V Marriage
VI Radulf, Theodulf I
VIIa-f Pastors
VIIIa-c Clerical security, king ship
IXa-d Clerical functions and status, four fasts
Xa Anathema and penance
IXe *Ælfric Br.* 2
Xb Burchard on dreams and tithes
IXf Mass, g *Ælfric Br.* 3
Xc Further penitential formula

Rouen 1382 (ff. 173r–198v)

XIIIa-b Liturgica
IXc Four fasts
XIIIc *Reg. Conc.* extracts
IXd Four fasts (*per Reg. Conc.* etc.)
VIIb Pastors
I *Exc.Can.* iia (+ *Exc. Can.* 25)
IV c … d Lay and clerical life
IIIa-b Penance (inc. Priests *Cap.*) . …

Nero A.i (ff. 122r–174v)

???????? …
VIIa,g,h Pastors
IXi/j *De Cler. Ord.*
I *Exc. Can.* i (inc. IIIb and interpolations s xii)
IIIf(iia),i/j Penance (also inc. part of IIb)
IIIg Abbo on penance
IIIf(iib),l/m Penance
VIIi/j Pastoral
IIIk Penance
IXc Four fasts

CCCC 190 (pp. i–xii, 1–294)

(III) Penit. Ps. Th. (complete)
VIIk(b) *Ammonitio*
I *Exc. Can.* 161, 98–9, 44, 33 ++
VIIIb Cleric-lay relations
IXi/j-k *De Cler. Ord.*, Pallium – all intermixed [missing leaves shown by table of contents to include VIIg,h, i/j Pastors, I *Exc. Can.* i Pr., IIIb Priests *Cap.* etc.]
I *Exc. Can.* i (inc. V diagram)
IVf Christian warfare
XIIId Liturgica
IXg *Ælfric Br.* 3
IXa,f etc. Liturgica
VIIb,e,f,d,c,a Pastors
IXe *Ælfric Br.* 2
IXh(exc.),b clerical ranks
XIIIa,c, IXc, IIIn, XIIIb, IXd, IIIh,i/j,k, IXl/m, IIIg, XIIIe, VIII/m, IVg Liturgy, Penance, Antichrist

Copenhagen 1595 (ff. 1r–82v)

XIIIf Liturgica
IXh Clerical ranks
IXc Four fasts
Sermons of Abbo (cf. III, IV, IX)
IIc Wulfstan's penitential letters
Ie Homilies relating to *Exc. Can.*
IVh Homilies on End of Time etc.
Further homilies
IXe *Ælfric Br.* 2
IXg *Ælfric Br.* 3
IXa,f,b(exc.) Liturgical functions and status of clergy

Analysis of 'Blocks'

I *Exc. Can.* (i.e. 'Excerpt. Ecgb.'): (i) as in Nero/CCCC 190, (ii) as in CCCC 265/Barlow 37/Rouen 1382, **a**, **b**, **c** separate sets of 'excerpts' in CCCC 265; **d** *Ans.* i 85–7, ii 34; **e** Sermons on society.

II Protection of clergy: **a** Five 'Irish Canons' (cf. *Exc. Can.* 74, 79, ?62), 'Three Irish Canons' (all concerned with assaults on Church and clergy), *Penit. Ps.Th.* iii 1–8, *Dial. Ecgb.* i, xii (further passages on attacking clergy), *Canones Wallici* 'A' 5–8, 10–15, 17, 19–20, 26–34, 37–57, 59–61 (mostly on injury to dependents of clergy), *Exc. Can.* 152–3 + Syn. I S. Pat. 6 + *Exc. Can.* 154; **b** Penance and compensation in Saxony; **c** Wulfstan's penitential letters on heinous offences.

III Egberht's Penitential and associated texts: **a** *Penit Ecgb.*. Praef.; **b** Ghaerbald *Cap.* I ('De iure sacerdotali'); **c** Theodulf *Cap.* II iii 1–2, ii 1–2, iv – x (mostly penitential); **d** Penitential principles based on 'Cummean', *et al.*; **e** *Penit. Ecgb.*; **f** *Penit. Ps.Th.* li–lii, ii, xlix (penitential admin., etc.); **g** Abbo's penitential sermon for Maundy Thursday (no. 13); **h** More on Penance (Fehr, *Hirtenbriefe* Anh. III 33); i/j Further penitential matter (Fehr, *Hirtenbriefe* Anh. III 34–40); **k** Further penance, including other Abbo sermon (10) (Fehr, *Hirtenbriefe* Anh. III 41–6, IV 179); l/m *De medicamento animarum* (Fehr, *Hirtenbriefe* Anh. IV 175); **n** More penance yet (Fehr, *Hirtenbriefe* Anh. III 15–16).

IV 'Secular service': **a** *De militia seculari;* **b** Handbook of Confessor; **c** *Admonitio Generalis* 61–75, 77–8, 80–2; **d** Council of Aachen (816) 145; **e** Penitential excerpts from *Ps.Rom.*, 'Cummean', *Ps.Th.* on clerical-secular relations (not unlike **III d**); **f** On Christian warfare and tribulation, from Abbo's sermon *ad Milites* (no. 6), Alcuin *Epist.* 16+17 (cf. **VII d**), ?Alcuin, *De Tribulationibus*; **g** Adso, *De Ortu Antichristi;* **h** Homiletic matter on impending Apocalypse (some overlap with **g**).

V *Sermones de Coniugio* , *Penit. Ps.Th.* xx 12, 11, 19(pt), Consanguinity, Gregory *Responsa* V, *Vita Gregorii* ii 37–8 (*Exc. Can.* 132–3).

VI Radulf *Cap.* 1–2(pt), 5–7(pts), 8–9, 12, 14, 17(pt), 18–19, 20(pt)+22 (pt), 21, 23–5; Theodulf *Cap.* I.

VII 'De Pastoribus': **a** *De Past. Eccl./De Ven. Sac.;* **b** *Ammon. Spirit. Doct.;* **c** Isidore *Sent.* iii 36–8; **d** Alcuin *Epist.* 114 (York); **e** *Ammon. episc. util.;* **f** Alcuin *Epist.* 17 (Canterbury); **g** Wulfstan *Hom.* XVIa ('Verba Ezechielis'); **h** *De past. et praedic.;* i/j *De cotidianis operibus episcoporum* (Fehr, *Hirtenbriefe* Anh. IV 176); **k** 'Primo omnium admonemus' (cf. Wulfstan, *Hom.* Xb); l/m Defensor, *Liber Scintillarum.*

VIII Cleric-lay relations: **a** *De blasphemia;* **b** Atto of Vercelli *De pressuris ecclesiasticis* I – III (exc.); **c** Sedulius Scottus *De Rect. Christ.* x, *Coll. Can. Hib.* xxv 3–4, 7, 15, Isidore *Sent.* iii 62(4); **d** 'Paulus dixit' (on pastoral duties); **e** *Exc. Can.* 161; **f** Council of Aachen (816) 145.

IX Mainly liturgical: **a** Wulfstan, *Hom.* VIIIa + *De Crismate;* **b** Hrabanus *De Inst. Cler.* ii 1–10; **c** *De ieiunio quattuor tempora* (cf. Fehr, *Hirtenbriefe* Anh. III 14); **d** *Item de quattuor temporibus* (= *Reg. Conc.* IX, Amalarius *De eccl. offic.* ii 1:1, 3:12) (cf. Fehr, *Hirtenbriefe* Anh. III 32); **e** Ælfric *Brief* 2; **f** *Officium missae;* **g** Ælfric *Brief* 3; **h** Ælfric Digest of Aachen (816) on clerical ranks (Fehr, *Hirtenbriefe* Anh. V); i/j *De cler. sive eccles. ord.;* **k** Bede, *Hist. Eccl.* i 23 etc. on 'Pallium'; l/m Abbo Lenten sermon (no. 12).

X Excommunication and reconciliation etc.: a unedited rituals of anathema and repentance [followed by **b** Burchard of Wurms on dreams and tithes; **c** further penitential formula etc.]

XI *De variis observationibus episcopi* (= *Coll. Can. Hib.* i 10).

XII Formal canon law extracts: from *Dionysiana, Pseudo-Angrilann* 71–2, and IV Conc. Tol. (634) 28.

XIII Liturgica: **a** *Ordo Romanus* xiii; **b** Extracts of Amalarius *De eccl. offic.* (Fehr, *Hirtenbriefe* Anh. III 17–31); **c** *Reg. Conc.* III–VI, VIII (cf. Fehr, *Hirtenbriefe* Anh. III 1–13); **d** *Expos. offic. sanct. miss.;* **e** Maundy Thursday liturgy (Fehr, *Hirtenbriefe* Anh. III 46–8); **f** Amalarius *Eclogae* (also later in CCCC 265).

'Commonplace-book' ingredients are followed by extracts from Burchard of Worms and Ivo of Chartres.[207] Rouen 1382 is a fragment in early-eleventh-century English script appended to a later-eleventh-century manuscript from Jumièges; an unascertainable but perhaps considerable amount of 'Commonplace-book' material is missing at the end, and not improbably some from the start.[208] As a result of the relatively recent discovery of these two witnesses, Corpus 265 turns out to have (so to speak) a close as well as an extended family, and it becomes possible to see what its place in that family was. In the Barlow and Rouen manuscripts, the early-ninth century capitulary of Bishop Ghaerbald of Liège for his priests is inserted between the preface and main body of the (perhaps genuine) Penitential of Archbishop Ecgberht (**IIIabc**). This was its place in Bodley 718, a mid-tenth-century English copy of a Carolingian manual of penitential and canon law, which is how it was transmitted beside Ecgberht's preface in three English pontificals.[209] In Nero A.i, it no longer accompanies any part of the penitential, but is prefixed instead to 142 excerpts of Church law (**I i**); yet a trace of its origin remains in that opposite the start of Ghaerbald's capitulary, which immediately follows a pair of introductory canons, stands the rubric 'Excerptiones ... Ecgberhti ... de sacerdotali Iure'.[210] In Corpus 265, the capitulary continues to front the excerpts, here (rightly) called 'Excerptiones de libris canonicis' (**I ii**) and with no mention of Ecgberht, whose penitential comes later (preface *in situ*) in a succession of pieces on penance. In other words, Corpus 265 is the final stage in the picking apart of the tangle created by Bodley 718's Frankish exemplar; in Barlow and Rouen, by contrast, disentanglement had barely begun.[211]

The more closely one looks at Corpus 265 in relation to the other collections in this series, the more sense it seems to make.[212] It opens with a set of admonitions and comments on the pastoral role, symbolically including letters of Alcuin to archbishops of Canterbury and York. In Barlow, these are buried in a series on clerical status later on; and that they had originated there is implied by the

---

207   Its significance was (in effect) first spotted by Sauer, 'Zur Überlieferung', who christened it 'D'. See further discussion in 'Archbishop Wulfstan' (pp. 233–4).

208   It was discovered (and labelled 'R') by Dr Robin Aronstam, 'Latin Canonical Tradition', pp. 21–3, who elicited confirmation of its English origin from Ker. Its fragmentary state and range of content were demonstrated by Cross, 'Newly Identified Manuscript'. But I argue in 'Archbishop Wulfstan' that the CNRS report there quoted is misleading in one respect: all that is left of the English part of the final quire is *three* leaves (ff. 196–8), f. 199 being differently ruled and presumably as intrusive as f. 200; thus, only one leaf is lacking before f. 196, and the other four missing leaves of this quire come after f. 198: proof (were more needed) that a significant amount of this book's content no longer survives, and in particular after 'Block' IIIb.

209   On Bodley MS 718, see Kerff, *Der Quadripartitus*, pp. 20–4, 72–3; and for its script and influence on the pontificals, Dumville, *Liturgy*, pp. 82–6. On the Ghaerbald capitulary, see Brommer's edition; and on Ecgberht's Penitential, Frantzen, *Literature of Penance*, pp. 69–77.

210   See *Wulfstan Manuscript*, ed. Loyn, f. 127v.

211   Thus far Hohler, 'Some Service Books', n. 47, pp. 223–4, the broadside that first cleared a path through this textual thicket. Yet Hohler failed to follow the logic of his justified insistence that Nero's 'Ecgberht' rubric relates to the capitulary, not the '*Excerptiones*' as a whole: if this is so, there is no reason to see Nero as 'textually a later stage in the process' (*sc.* than Corpus 265); and, it might be added, if such disentanglement could be managed, some at least of Mr Hohler's scorn for the intellectual capacities of later Saxon churchmen is misplaced.

212   I give a breakdown of CCCC 265 content in 'Archbishop Wulfstan', table 9.

survival of a fragment (**VIIa**) in Corpus 265's 'status block'. Texts of the same sort also preface the *Excerptiones* in Nero, the next most 'evolved' collection. Again, Ghaerbald's capitulary, addressed as its current rubric said to priests, is logically preceded in Corpus 265 by chapters of the Irish Canon Collection devoted (as the rubric also declared) to bishops. The Corpus arrangement is not an unqualified success. There is a hiatus at p. 72, where several lines of red ink usher in 'Directions for Use of a Confessor' (**IVb**), the sole vernacular text in section a). There is a change in the manuscript's character about half way through. Texts are now more often quoted in full, or as sets of excerpts from one author at a time. It is as if the compiler had switched emphasis from what his authorities had to say on particular topics to those authorities in their own right. But as a considered review of canon law Corpus 265 compares well with its siblings. The same can be said of Nero A.i in comparison to its closest relative, Corpus 190. There is in fact an impression that the series is moving in a more systematic direction. Corpus 265 and Nero A.i are more purely legal, where law, homily and liturgy are jumbled together in Barlow, Rouen and Corpus 190. Copenhagen for its part concentrates on homily and liturgy. At the same time, Corpus 265 and Nero are sufficiently unlike in content and appearance to suggest that they may have had rather different objectives. Corpus 265 is more discursive, readier to appeal to its sources, and to that extent more of a work of learning. Nero's tightly structured set of canons goes straight into the subject of priestly behaviour with Ghaerbald's capitulary, whereas from the outset Corpus 265 has more canons on episcopal concerns.[213] It may be relevant that 265 is a more elegant book. Rubrics are clear even when cramped; initials exploit a range of colour, if only one at a time. The script is 'uncalligraphic', but luxuriates in the space at its disposal, where Nero gives the impression of using every rationed square centimetre. Nero is a book for carrying about. Corpus 265 is a book to admire.

The main point is that both Corpus 265 section a) and (*mutatis mutandis*) Nero A.i sections d)-e) can be seen *if taken as wholes* to be selections from the canons interspersed with pastoral and penitential texts. The corollary is that there is no longer any particular reason to believe in the independent existence of something called the 'Excerptiones Ecgberhti'. What Spelman and then Thorpe printed under this title was simply what they found between the pastoral and penitential sections of Nero A.i; the title itself ('Excerptiones (D.) Egberti Eboracensis Archiepiscopi e dictis et canonibus sanctorum patrum concinnatae') apparently deriving from the rubric that actually belonged, as has been seen, to Ghaerbald's 'iura'.[214] These Excerpts are not recorded, under that title or any other, outwith

---

213 Unparalleled and specifically episcopal canons in MS 265 are (Aronstam nos) i–ii, iv, x–xi (*Collection of Canons*, tr. Johnson, 1–2, 15, 73–4, and cf. 21–2, 71, 75). Canons in Nero but not 265 are (Thorpe nos) 22–8, 30, 35–6, 41–3, 52 (pt.), 54–5, 60, 62, 74, 77, 79, 82, 96, 100, 102–3, 108–11, (116–17, 119, 121, but cf. Corpus 265 'Block' V), 130, 135–40, 146–8, 150–1, 156, 158–62 (but cf. Corpus 265 'Block' VIIIe): on the whole, these do concern priests rather than bishops, and among them is (60) the Chalcedon canon on clerics conspiring *against* bishops.

214 *Concilia*, ed. Spelman, pp. 258–75; *Ancient Laws*, ed. Thorpe, pp. 326–42. Spelman and Thorpe incorporated as genuine *Excerptiones* the twelfth-century additions, '141–5', inserted into the blank space on Nero's ff. 148r – 149r (cf. table 4.2, and n. 229). I develop this argument in 'Archbishop Wulfstan'.

the manuscripts under discussion here.[215] One of their major sources, the Carolingian canon law handbook known as *Quadripartitus* happens to be the last and largest item in Bodley 718, the book that generated the very idea of 'Excerptiones Ecgberhti'.[216] Corpus 265 contains further longer selections from the same texts (*Hibernensis*, *Dionysiana*, Ansegisus, Theodulf) as it quarried for 'excerpts' so-called. If it is not quite the case that these collections take shape before the historian's eyes, they seemingly came into being only just before they become visible.[217]

That being so, 'Excerptiones Ecgberhti' is not the only term due for super-annuation. Mary Bateson, the one scholar who described these books as wholes, called Corpus 265 'a kind of theological commonplace-book specially intended for a bishop's use'. Never a felicitous phrase, it is now well past retirement age. Little of the content is in any sense theological. Nor is it a set of random jottings. Here and in Nero A.i, a serious effort is made to create groups of canons on successive topics. It is not a 'commonplace book' but an at least pupescent canon law collection. All that is lacking from what made the contemporary work of Burchard of Wörms a celebrated primer of ecclesiastical organization (chapter 6, pp. 456–7) are headings to bring out this element of system, and of course the infinitely richer range of Carolingian sources on which Burchard could draw. Yet in the phrase 'Archbishop Wulfstan's Commonplace book', there can be no quarrel with the first two words. Wulfstan regularly cited their content in homilies, laws and *Institutes of Polity*. His hand was at work on sources that contributed to them.[218] That the collection originated with him may be more than the evidence allows. It must not be forgotten that Corpus 265 itself is a book from after his time. But if it is right that Corpus 265, Nero and Copenhagen repre-sent evolution towards a more systematic arrangement of the materials, then it must be significant that two of these three contain his annotations. Much has already been said in this book, and a great deal more remains to be said, about Wulfstan's place in the history of Old English secular law. It seems that his

215   There is no textual trace of other MSS in Spelman. The most serious evidence for the prior or distinct existence of a text corresponding to the 'Excerptiones' is their apparent use by Ælfric in his 'Pastoral Letters' for Wulfstan: *Hirtenbriefe*, ed. Fehr, pp. xcvii–cx. Ælfric did use the Ghaerbald *capitula* in his first epistle (for Bishop Wulfsige of Sherborne). But in 'Archbishop Wulfstan', I argue that the relationship of the 'Excerpts' with his letters to Wulfstan was the other way about: Ælfric was their *source*; which posi-tion has (again independently) been reached by Professor Cross (with A. Hamer), 'Ælfric's letters and the *Excerptiones Ecgberhti*'.

216   A full-scale study of *Excerptiones* sources is forthcoming from the late Professor Cross and Dr Hamer. It may be noted for now (i) that there are close textual links between the *Excerptiones* and Bodley 718 (Kerff, *Quadripartitus*, pp. 21–2 (n. 32), 72–3 (n. 35)); but (ii) the Excerptiones sometimes give the source (true or false) of a canon as recorded in continental copies of *Quadripartitus* but not Bodley 718. In 'Archbishop Wulfstan' (and in chapter 13), I discuss the possible contribution of Bodleian MS Hatton 42.

217   There can thus be no role for Hucarius the Deacon, Dr Aronstam's hero, 'Latin Canonical Tradition', pp. 23–33, and 'Recovering Hucarius'; her evidence means merely that there was a MS of Hucarius' homilies to which 'Ecgberhtine' *Excerptiones* ('paucas constitutiones', so perhaps just Ghaerbald's *iura*) were prefixed; and given that there is no real reason to think that Bodley 718 originated at Exeter (below, n. 240), Hucarius' alleged Cornish origin is neither here nor there.

218   Ker, 'Handwriting', pp. 328–30 (on Hatton 42); what Wulfstan is seen to be doing is gloss the text of Ansegisus from the inevitably different readings of Corpus 265's text of the *Admonitio Generalis*.

importance to the law of the English Church was no less. No one between Theodore and Lanfranc came closer to codifying it.

Corpus 265 is undoubtedly a Worcester book. Added on its front flyleaf was a monastic profession to the 'lord bishop Wulfstan': not this time the great arch-bishop but his namesake and successor (St) Wulfstan II, as the date of its script shows.[219] If bishops between the two Wulfstans contributed to the book, the results may lie in the sections following b). Section c) contains Ælfric's version of the *Regularis Concordia* for his monks at Eynsham, expanded by items 'from the book of Amalarius the priest' (the *Liber Officialis*).[220] It may not have been long before parts of the 'Romano-German pontifical' as well as further selections from Amalarius were added to form section d).[221] The Romano-German pontifical especially seems to reflect the interests of Bishop Ealdred (chapter 3, pp. 130–1). At the same time, the 'Commonplace book' section of Corpus 190 also contains extracts of the *Concordia* supplemented by Amalarius and gener-ally echoing Ælfric's revision (**XIIIabc**). Ealdred and/or Wulfstan II could therefore have followed a Wulfstanian lead. More intriguing yet, among the last items in the relevant part of Barlow are the excommunication and penitential rituals of Corpus 265 section b).[222] Soon afterwards came excerpts from Carolingian law on tithes, probably mediated by Burchard of Wörms. Burchard was a central figure for the Barlow compiler but is not known to have been avail-able to the Anglo-Saxons. Could Burchard's passages have replaced another text on tithes that would have seemed less impressive to twelfth-century churchmen? Might IV Edgar then have been in the pristine collection, like the rituals that accompanied it in Corpus 265? It would follow that section b) was a near-integral part of the collection from the early stage that the Barlow manuscript reflects. Given Wulfstan's well-attested interest in Edgar's laws, it would be no surprise to find them quoted on the tender topic of tithe.[223]

One matter remains. IV Edgar is given in Latin as well as Old English. Wulfstan made digests in Latin as a basis for vernacular homilies. He turns out to have done so with at least one law-code (chapter 5, pp. 334–5). But this translation is unparalleled. A possible explanation of its presence is that it catered for the code's inclusion in a collection otherwise composed overwhelmingly of texts in Latin. The solitary other exception, 'Directions for a Confessor', shows several signs of being out of place (p. 217). Special steps may, then, have been taken for a special situation: a secular code was being enrolled in the learned law of the Church.

219   Ker, *Catalogue*, p. 94: it was at Worcester in the sixteenth century, when Joscelyn dismissed an (eleventh-century) amendment to Ælfric's views on transubstantiation as the work of 'quidam papista'!
220   'Ælfrici epistula ad monachos Egneshamnenses', ed. Nocent. For full discussion, see Hill, '"Regularis Concordia"', pp. 302–8.
221   Amalarius, *Eclogae*; the last page (268) of section c) shows signs of long exposure as the end of the book, but Ker was convinced (*Catalogue*, p. 94) that 'the liturgical texts on pp. 269–442 were probably here from the first (s. xi², xi/xii)'. I am grateful to Dr Drew Jones for discussion of this part of the MS.
222   Fehr, *Hirtenbriefe* Anh III 1–13. Cross, 'Newly Identified MS', pp. 65–7; Sauer, 'Zur Überlieferung', pp. 354–5 (nos 35–6).
223   Sauer, pp. 355 (no. 39), 370–2; cf. Whitelock, 'Archbishop Wulfstan', p. 32.

(ii) Cambridge, Corpus Christi College, MS 190

So much having been said of its kindred manuscripts, there is no need to dwell for long on Corpus MS 190.[224] Questions of provenance are easily disposed of. It was certainly at Exeter in the early-fourteenth century, and was presumably one of the Dean and Chapter's 'gifts' to Archbishop Parker.[225] It looks very much as if it was the 'Canon in Latin and Confessional in English' (an accurate enough description of the book's two parts) listed among the books that Bishop Leofric (1046–72) secured for his new cathedral.[226] An Exeter domicile is further established by the script of pieces later in the manuscript and of additions to section a).[227] But there is no proof of Exeter influence before these scribes were active, nor can it be assumed that the two parts of the manuscript (sections a) and b) -c) -d)) were united until then. The manuscript in fact has every appearance of falling into distinct halves, and needs to be treated as such (table 4.5, p. 222).

To return briefly, first, to section a)'s place in the 'Commonplace-book' tradition (Table 4.4). Its 's. xi¹' date is contemporary with Rouen and earlier than Corpus 265. It is 'almost certainly' in a Worcester hand.[228] The difficulty in analysing its content is that a crucial part is missing after p. 110. The lost quire(s) coincide with the point at which its selection of 'Excerptiones' (I i, essentially the version in Nero A.i) gets under way. The sole guide is the chapter list at the front of the whole book, and what this shows is baffling. A series of canonical texts that had begun on p. 94 seems to have continued well into the missing section, before reaching the prologues that the 'Excerptiones' have in Nero. But these were followed by twenty-five chapters that are patently *not* Nero/Thorpe excerpts. They do not even match the Nero/Thorpe Excerpts that make an appearance in MS 190 from p. 111. Only with 'chapter 26', a likely reference to Excerpt '113', does contact resume.[229] There is no easy answer to this riddle. But one possibility is that the Corpus 190 canons are the outcome of a wholesale revision of the material to which the chapter-list referred. This material may once upon a time have resembled the texts on pp. 94–110; those texts were indeed

---

224   It has the *siglum* 'O' for Liebermann (*Gesetze* I, p. xxxv) and Fehr, 'W' for the Homily editors, and 'X' for Aronstam; it is Ker, *Catalogue*, no. 45.

225   Ker, *Catalogue*, p. 73, and cf. p. 31.

226   A valuable edition of this list is Conner, *Anglo-Saxon Exeter*, App. V, pp. 226–35 (here [9], pp. 232–3); but see below, n. 240.

227   Drage, 'Bishop Leofric', pp. 156–7, 170–2, identifies three scribes where Ker appears to have seen just one (p. 73): her Scribe '5' did pp. 351–9, Scribe '14' did pp. 308–19, and Scribe '15', pp. 295–308. Of the hands in section a), her Scribes '2' (p. 151) and '10' (p. 163) added the canon law materials, ancient or updated, on pp. 130–1, 292–4; and the small, neat hand she ascribes to Leofric himself (pp. 139–41, 149–50) made notes on pp. 131, 247, 292.

228   Dumville, *English Caroline Script*, pp. 52 (n. 228), 55, Pl. III.

229   Bateson, 'Worcester Cathedral Book', pp. 716–20. The chapter-list contains (*after* what is evidently the prologue) the rubric 'Incipit capitula de sacerdotali iure Ecgberti archiepisopi': thus, the fatefully formative pattern of Nero, f. 127v (above, n. 210). A further clue to the closeness of the Nero/CCCC 190 relationship are the former's blank folios where extra canons were inserted in the twelfth century (table 4.2): at just this point in MS 190 (pp. 132–3, after *Exc. Can.* 140), there is a consanguinity diagram.

exploited for what became *Excerptiones*.[230] That would mean that Corpus 190 provides another glimpse of 'excerpts' at the manufacturing stage. At any rate, the position reflected in the chapter-list should predate the *Excerptiones* in their Nero/Thorpe form.

There is a definite tendency for pieces that appear among the excerpts proper in the Nero and Corpus 265/Rouen/Barlow collections to be somewhere else in Corpus 190. It has, for instance, a complete text of the 'Pseudo-Theodore' penitential, which was often excerpted (table 4.4: **IIa, IIIf**, etc.).[231] The sequence from pp. 94–110 includes passages from Atto of Vercelli on respect for Church property (**VIIIb**, more briefly quoted in Corpus 265 and Barlow), and one on the definition and grades of clergy that precedes the *Excerptiones* in Nero (**IXi/j**).[232] After its 'Excerpts' Corpus 190 becomes progressively liturgical, but continues to feature texts recycled elsewhere: for example, passages on clerical ranks from the 816 Council of Aachen and Hrabanus' *De Institutione Clericorum*, which reappear in slightly variant form in MS 265 and Barlow. Corpus 190's presentation of some of these texts seems anything but pristine. Its edited version of Ælfric's carefully crafted digest of the 816 Aachen decrees (omitting the all-important topic of bishops) hardly looks earlier than the comprehensive exposition in MS 265 (**IXh**).[233] Nor is its conflated Amalarius/*Regularis Concordia* sequence likely to antedate the lucid ordering of the first Rouen folios.[234] Yet the 'Ranks of Clergy' block (**IX**) is disordered in Barlow, which is probably prior to Corpus 265. The very presence of extended *liturgica* seems an early symptom, in that it is mirrored in Rouen but not Corpus 265. When Bethurum discovered 'Wulfstan's Commonplace book', she felt that Corpus 190 was its earliest phase because it linked to the homilies she knew best.[235] She was probably right, if not quite for that reason. It is not early as it stands. But it is a bundle of the ingredients that went to make up its relatives: the sort of book that might perhaps have been (hastily?) copied for use somewhere other than its Worcester birthplace.

The second part of the manuscript, the part to which its legal texts belong, poses different problems. Its structure is another complex one (table 4.5). Section

---

230 It is here, not in the series of 'excerpts' proper, that one finds nos 98–9; and given that nos 31–2 come out of sequence on p. 138, it is unlikely that 33 would have been found in the absent quires, whereas it is on p. 107. It is not suggested that revision was carried out in MS 190 itself: the confusion presumably goes back to the exemplar.

231 Thorpe printed it from here, *Ancient Laws*, pp. 277–306, in what is deplorably the sole 'edition' of a self-evidently important document for the late Old English Church. There is another apparently incomplete text in Brussels MS 8558–63 (Ker, *Catalogue* no. 10 (B); Frantzen, *Literature of Penance*, pp. 132–3; Dumville, *Liturgy*, p. 134, and *English Caroline Script*, pp. 51–2). Cf. Sauer, 'Zur Überlieferung', pp. 346–7 (n. 8) for a suggestion that what is usually supposed a Frankish text may actually be English.

232 Atto, *De Pressuris*, pp. v–xiii; Sauer, pp. 383–4.

233 On Ælfric's treatise and its handling in 'Commonplace book' MSS, see Cross and Morrish Tunberg, *Copenhagen Wulfstan*, pp. 15–16. There is no significance, however, in the fact that MS 190 cites all ten of the relevant Hrabanus chapters where MS 265 breaks off at ch. 7: all of it is in Barlow, so that it looks as if this part of MS 265 (which was followed by an eleven-line gap) was simply left unfinished.

234 Cross, 'Newly Identified Manuscript', pp. 65–7; Professor Cross notes that MS 190's exemplar has suffered another of its misfortunes with regard to p. 238.

235 See n. 156. The MS's last pieces reinforce the homiletic link: Adso's Antichrist letter ('Block' **IVg**) was a Wulfstan source (ch. 6, pp. 452–3), and cf. *Hom.*, pp. 339–40 for the *Liber Scintillarum*.

Table 4.5 Structure of Corpus 190, Pt. II

b. pp. 319–50, 365–420 (quires 23–4, 26–9): quire 29 (pp. 411–20) is a '6' with last leaf excised (probably blank); originally blank were pp. 319, 365, 418 ln 14–420. Ælfric *Briefe* II, III, Anh. I–II (pp. 320–50); *Conf. Ps.Ecgb.*; *Rule of Chrodegang* lxxxiii (Th, p. 361); *Conf. Ps.Ecgb.* ii (pp. 366–86); *Penit. Ps.Ecgb.* i–iv + caps. lxiii–lxviii (Th, pp. 385–9) (pp. 387a–418).

c. pp. 365, 418–20 (quires 26, 29): p. 420 lns 5–28 remain blank, p. 420 is very worn. Forms of confession and absolution (p. 365); *Mirc., Að* 1, *Að* 2, *Had.* (pp. 418–20).

d. pp. 295–319, 351–64 (quires 21–3, 25): quire 22 ruled for 27 lines, quire 25 for 25 (norm in this part of MS is 28); at first blank were pp. 359 ln 14 – 364. Ælfric *Brief* I (pp. 295–308); Ælfric, *Hom.* II xxxvi [Godden] (pp. 308–14); *Inst. Pol.* XXIV 1–52 (pp. 315–19); Fe, Anh. III 42 + OE *Hom.* 'S 29' [DOE] (cf. Pt I, pp. 247–9) (pp. 351–3); Wulfstan, *Hom.* App. I (OE) (cf. Fe, Anh. III 46, and this MS Pt I, pp.253–8) (pp. 353–9); [canons on excommunication, s. xi^ex (p. 360); *Invectivum in damnantes coniugia sacerdotum*, s. xi^ex (p. 361); *Excom.* III, s. xii^in (p. 364)]

b) comprises six quires, the last of which does look as if it came to round off the collection. Its date is s. xi^med, its origin unknown. It contains the vernacular versions of Ælfric's Pastoral Letters for Wulfstan, and then (in a fresh quire) two penitentials; to confound confusion, the scribe assigned the first penitential, and convention credits both, to Archbishop Ecgberht.[236] The diffusion and inter-relationship of these texts need not be probed here.[237] What matters is that their combination points almost as squarely at Wulfstan's Worcester as the content of section a). The only other manuscript with both Pastoral Letters for Wulfstan is a later-twelfth-century book that was in the West Midlands by the thirteenth. The first of them is otherwise in Corpus 201, the second in the important Worcester Wulfstan manuscript of s. xi^3/4, Bodleian MS Junius 121 (though sections of it reached Rochester and Canterbury). The only other manuscripts to unite the 'Ecgberhtine' penitentials were Junius 121 and a book that was at Worcester by the thirteenth century; in both they were combined with the 'Directions for use of a Confessor' encountered above in Corpus 201 and 265. Ælfric's letters *were*, the penitentials might well seem, translations of what was in section a).[238] One implication of section b)'s content is thus that a vernacular-ization process was already under way at Worcester. It can no longer be doubted

---

236   The trouble this time stems from Wilkins, whose *Concilia* I, pp. 113–44, printed both penitentials as five books entitled 'Poenitentiale Ecgberhti Archiepiscopi', so following the MS 190 rubric attributing the first to Ecgberht; it was Thorpe who divided the 'Confessional' (his reasonable translation of the rubric's 'Scrift Boc') from the four ensuing books, retaining the title 'Penitential of Ecgberht' for the latter: Frantzen, *Literature of Penance*, pp. 133–4.

237   For the Pastoral Letters, there is a lucid update by Clemoes, *Hirtenbriefe*, pp. cxxxix–cxliv. For the Penitentials, see the editions by Spindler, *Altenglische Bußbuch*, pp. 1–13, 126–32; and by Raith, *Altenglische Version des Halitgarschen Bubuches*, pp. iv–xx. See Frantzen, *Literature of Penance*, pp. 134–41, with Fowler (ed), 'Handbook', pp. 1–14, and suggestive remarks by Dumville, *English Caroline Script*, p. 52. I give only the baldest *précis* of their conclusions.

238   The 'Confessional' was not a translation of *Pseudo-Theodore*, but it both drew, and more important purported to draw, on *genuine* Theodore: *Altenglische Bußbuch*, pp. 19–23, 87–90.

that this was the intention when the book was augmented under Leofric's auspices, not by tacking new quires on to the end as in MS 265, but by interspersing them among those already there (whence Table 4.5, section d)). Ælfric's first pastoral letter (to Wulfsige of Sherborne) now joined the other two, along with his Homily celebrating the apostolic mission to preach – the motif rehearsed in Corpus 265's sketch-map. There is also a *Polity* (so vernacular) text on clerical ranks, and translations of two of Abbo's penitential sermons. The result was the harmonized single volume in Leofric's list. Latin 'Canon' was counterpointed by Old English 'Scriftboc'.

Section c) of the manuscript consists of forms of confession and absolution and three brief legal tracts, added to the quires that form section b). The former is in a hand of Exeter type and was probably inserted before the incorporation of section d).[239] Where and when the legal texts were added is less clear. But three points can be made. First, they are statements of rank with corresponding wergelds and oath-values from the collection that Corpus 201 gives in full (chapter 5, pp. 391–4); that 'Mercian' law is included but not 'Northumbrian' *may* suggest that Worcester interests still predominated. Second, the tract *Að* is divided by a large rubric into clauses on thegn and priest. This last is linked by a *smaller* rubric with a tariff of compensations *for the seven grades of holy orders*. The parallels with passages to the same effect in section a)'s *De Septem Gradibus* and in section d)'s *Polity* extract are unmissable. Inclusion of these tracts could therefore have been inspired by the spirit either of Worcester's original 'Canon', or of Exeter's elaborated 'Scriftboc'. Either way, the vernacularization of Canon Collection ingredients has been on-going. Third, another candidate for unifier of the volume besides Leofric is Lyfing, bishop of Crediton 1027–46, and in 1038–40 and again 1041–6 the bishop of Worcester too. He is a likely author of Cnut's second (1027) letter (chapter 5, pp. 348–9). He looks just the man to have raided Worcester's shelves for what could benefit his far south-western see.[240]

This section has gone in detail into books containing little secular law. Wulfstan would have denied the relevance of the distinction involved. He tirelessly laid down law 'for God and World'. The Church had its special duties,

239   The confessional forms were inserted before the *scriftboc* when there was ample room for them after the Abbo penitential homilies.
240   It will be clear that I reluctantly dissent from Professor Conner's valiant effort, *Anglo-Saxon Exeter*, pp. 1–47, 221–35, etc., to resurrect the Exeter library, usually thought, given Leofric's efforts, to have been dismembered by the Danish onslaught of 1003. It is of course persuasive to find three tenth-century MSS in a single script (among them Bodley 718), one of which was corrected in the hand of three other MSS, and four of which six are of Exeter provenance. But the weakness of such tightly knotted argumentation is that the failure of one strand attenuates the whole; in this case, one of the manuscripts has an inscription where erasure of the beneficiary's name shows that this *cannot* have been Exeter; and if the hand of the 'Exeter Book' itself was being used to produce books for other patrons to give to other clients, then positive reasons for regarding it as an Exeter hand seriously recede (for the possibility that the intended recipient was Buckfast, see Keynes, 'Cnut's Earls', pp. 67–9). Leofric's initiative is enough to account for so many Exeter provenances, even if one dismisses his account of the poverty of the library he found as the kind of 'worst-case scenario' to which enthused reformers were prone: Dumville, *Liturgy*, pp. 82–4. Professor Conner does not reckon with the feeble survival-rate of tenth-century Exeter charters (Chaplais, 'Authenticity of the Diplomas of Exeter', pp. 5–9), and hardly notices Crediton's possible part in the story. The case that Bodley 718 (or its exemplar) was within reach of those who made the excerpts in the certainly or probably Worcester MSS, Nero A.i, Corpus 265 and Corpus 190 seems to hold.

and so books of its own law. But laymen owed it both obedience and repentance. Lyfing and Ealdred, Wulfstan's successors at Worcester and men to whom it is rational to credit books of s. xi[1'] and s. xi[med'], apparently shared his profound conviction of the service that secular law could and must do for God.

6   Legal Encyclopaedias

With the sixth group of early English legal manuscripts, the frontier of the Norman Conquest is crossed, and one is at once in a new world. All the manuscripts in this group contain several lawcodes. That is not unprecedented. In addition, however, they contain *nothing but* laws. That is new. The same logic applies to this group as to the first, third, fourth and fifth. That a set of manuscripts behaves in much the same way argues that their disposition is not arbitrary. It meant something to more than one scribe. In the case of the 'encyclopaedia' group, there is scant evidence of the sort of authorial and/or scriptorial ties detectable within the *Gesta* series or the three sorts of 'Wulfstan manuscript'. Nevertheless, they have a strong family resemblance. It is a physiognomy that one is not surprised to find showing itself in the circumstances that the Conquest had created.

(i) BL, Cotton MS Nero A.i(A)

The 'encyclopaedias' or 'post-conquest' group begins with a book that is scarcely encyclopaedic and may not postdate 1066. But it does contain a sequence of codes, like later manuscripts in this series. And if its script is not certainly post-conquest, it is barely if at all older. It is thus a foretaste of the direction that law-books were taking by the twelfth century. However, the first question to ask is whether it does represent a new manuscript, or was merely grafted onto the earlier book that now follows it (above, p. 198).[241]

There is a paradox here: the more bizarre the juxtaposition of items in an early medieval manuscript (above, pp. 183–4), the more likely it is to go back a long way; whereas similarity of subject-matter, so far from being a compelling argument for early association, may actually be suspicious. Sir Robert Cotton liked to join manuscripts with related content; Nero A.i's laws may no more share a birthplace than Claudius A iii's pontificals. Homogeneous appearances can also mislead. Cotton Nero A.i is less obviously composite than Harley MS 55, but only because its pages are the same size throughout. Yet the binders used by Cotton or more recent librarians could cut an amalgam's ingredients down to a uniform size. Each half of Nero A.i has visibly been pared. Slight differences in the degree of mutilation suffered by their respective marginalia suggest that Part

---

241   Liebermann gave it the *siglum* 'G' (n. 147), the same as that of its second part; this judgement was perhaps affected by the fact that, while his date for Part 'A' was (roughly correctly) 'um 1070', he dated 'B' at least forty years too late 'um 1060–80'. 'A' is Ker, *Catalogue* no. 163 (and dated 's xi [med']), 'B' no. 164, with no hint of a recognized kinship between the two (cf. also *ibid.*, pp. xliv–xlv).

'A' was in fact smaller than Part 'B'.[242] The known behaviour of Tudor and Stuart antiquarians puts a heavy burden of proof on any case for the unity of a manuscript that is not visibly coherent. The burden in this instance has little chance of being sustained.[243]

To be fair, the two parts may have been welded before Cotton acquired them. Their foliation in a continuous sequence was probably carried out when they entered his library, and was evidently not in place when an index for both parts, with cross-references from one to the other, was added to the end of the second.[244] But further back than that one cannot go.[245] Talbot scattered marginalia throughout part 'B' while leaving 'A' unscathed. It is as good as certain that 'A' was known to Nowell and used in Lambarde's *Archaionomia* of 1568 (pp. 261–2), whereas if Lambarde ever came upon 'B' at all it was not before 1580.[246] Nor is there much to link the two in the Middle Ages. Alphabetical scribbles of the 'Amen dico vobis' variety are the only marginalia found in both. Were these by identical hands, they would at best establish that each part of the manuscript was by then in the same *scriptorium*. In fact they are in different hands and rather differing styles. More than one medieval *scriptorium* developed this habit.[247] Many of the more substantial 'B' marginalia relate to penance (above, pp. 198–9), and naturally cluster around its Latin texts, so there is no necessary significance in their absence from the wholly vernacular 'A'.[248] There might be something in the way that two different (unknown) 'magistri' were caught up in the history of each part.[249] Provided one is prepared to assign 'B' to Worcester not York, it *could* be relevant that an agreement dated 1315 to which

---

242   Compare Joscelyn's marginalia (below) on f. 10r, 16r, 44v and 116v: losses in the first three instances amount to a maximum of four letters, more normally to 2–3, but in the last case to 5–6. Talbot's marginalia in Part 'B' are set sufficiently far from the text as to suggest that he was exploiting a wide margin.

243   The best case for uniting the two is that of Professor Loyn, in his facsimile edition of the whole, *Wulfstan Manuscript*, pp. 32–44.

244   *Wulfstan Manuscript*, ed. Loyn, pp. 41–4.

245   Professor Loyn's regular references to an 'Elizabethan binding' appear to arise from his belief that Joscelyn was responsible for joining the two parts (cf. p. 32). Joscelyn did work hard on part 'A': Loyn, pp. 37–9, cf. Bately, 'John Joscelyn'; he also seems to have possessed 'B' by November 1580, to judge from a note by Francis Tate in BL Cotton Julius C ii, f. 52r, but he glossed it less heavily than 'A', and it made less of a contribution to his 'Dictionary': Loyn, pp. 40–1, Bately, pp. 438–9 (n. 23), 445–65; this in itself implies that he is unlikely to have actually bound the two together.

246   The note on f. 52r of Cotton MS Julius C ii (above), tracing a transcript of V Atr and Grið to a copy in Joscelyn's possession as of November 1580, is now known to be by Tate not Lambarde, though its mention of 'W. Lambert' presumably means that Lambarde had by then seen it. But had Lambarde known part 'B' in 1568, he would not have had to print his bastardized text of I As (below, p. 261). By contrast, 'A' did supply his text of II–III Eg : given Professor Loyn's well-merited authority, it must regrettably be stressed that it is most unlikely to be true that 'neither [Lambarde] nor Nowell shows any familiarity whatsoever with A' (p. 32) – as Ker already saw, *Catalogue*, p. li. The best account of this and most other 'Nero A' issues is that of Torkar, *Altenglische Übersetzung*, pp. 168–85.

247   Loyn, pp. 35–6 (and n. 1).

248   Loyn, pp. 34–5.

249   f.4r: 'magister daniel de ditone … scribit' (Ker, p. 211; Loyn, p. 34); f. 124: 'amico suo speciali socio precordial' Magistro Waltero de Driston' suus in omnibus Robertus corbet clericus salutem' (Ker, p. 214; Loyn, p. 35). Nobody with anything resembling these names seems to feature in Emden's *Biographical Registers*.

'the lord Archbishop Walter' was a party appears in the margin of 'A'; *prima facie*, this would place 'A' at Canterbury, but Walter Reynolds was bishop of Worcester before his elevation.[250] Yet, however suggestive any of this may be, it comes nowhere near the proof needed to outweigh the evidence that the two parts were not yet together in the mid-sixteenth century.

Aspects of the manuscript's content also argue against any early association of its two parts. 'A' contains the code of Cnut, followed by Edgar's Andover ('II–III') legislation and then by Alfred's *domboc*, which breaks off towards the end of the preface (Joscelyn supplying the rest from the Parker manuscript). The version of Cnut varies in several important ways from the common stock. Its wording is adjusted to reckon with Kentish law, especially the archbishop's *mundbryce*, a point taken on board by Wulfstan in his tract on sanctuary (*Grið*).[251] At least one passage in Alfred's preface smacks of Wulfstan glossing.[252] These could be signs that the manuscript was from a library exposed to his interventions, like Worcester or York. But the natural implication of the extra Cnut clauses is again that the volume is from Canterbury, where Wulfstan's influence was certainly felt.[253] In any case, the II–III Edgar text in 'A' is not of the interpolated type found in all Wulfstan manuscripts (pp. 188–9).[254] 'A' therefore departed from the version of the Andover code preferred in Wulfstan's *scriptoria* in details close to Wulfstan's heart. It can hardly have drawn on an exemplar from Worcester or York. 'B' very probably did originate at Worcester or York. Hence, 'A' and 'B' must have had different origins. They were not associated by design. Nothing before the late-sixteenth century suggests that they were associated by accident.

Part 'A' in fact poses the same additional problem as 'B'. It is not impossible that it constitutes two volumes in its own right. The thirty-eight-and-a-half folios devoted to Cnut's code were followed by a blank page and then by three more (themselves presumably blank) which have been cut out. Only after an inserted leaf, also blank, does the Edgar code begin with a fresh quire. There are other symptoms of an 'important break'.[255] The Edgar and Alfred codes are the work of a second scribe. The pages are still ruled for nineteen lines, but the written space is now 75–80 mm wide, where before it had been 70 mm. Cnut's laws have a wealth of initials, red, green, and sometimes 'boxed', as well as plain black. Later texts have only inauguratory initials, plus those in the Alfred rubric list (chapter 5, pp. 267–9); the former exploit a green pigment like that of some Cnut initials, but the latter use a different kind of oxidized red.[256] It may also be significant that the II–III Edgar text is close to that of *Quadripartitus* when there is no such relationship for the Cnut or Alfred codes (chapter 5, pp. 349–51). None of

---

250   See the transliterations of what may (or may not) be a continuous note on ff. 15v, 25v, 42r, by Ker, p. 211, and Loyn, p. 34. Professor Jeff Denton kindly tells me that in his view, 'tomam de 50' should be read as 'tomam de ho', i.e. Thomas of Hoo.

251   I Cn 3:2, II Cn 62, *Grið* 6, 11; see also chapter 5, pp. 394–5.

252   Af Int. 43.

253   As in BL, Cotton Tiberius A. iii: Ker, *Catalogue* 186 (19).

254   II Eg ('G²') 2:3, 5:1–3, III 8:1–3.

255   Loyn, p. 18; Ker, p. 211.

256   Compare, e.g., the red and green on ff. 47v–48r, or the silver/ green at f. 42r, with that at ff. 6v–7r, 13v–15r.

these considerations, however, quite amount to the all round case for separating some of the 'B' booklets. And against them is one decisive argument. Cnut's law on unjust judgement is in part verbally identical with Edgar's, each providing that a culprit lose his thegnhood 'unless he redeem it from the king so far as he is willing to allow him'. In both, the Nero scribe inserts '*eft* (again)', but at different places in the sentence. It is hard to see how this could happen had 'eft' not been entered as a gloss in the margin of both exemplars, and transferred thence to slightly variant points in the main text by each scribe. The two sections of part 'A' would then be from the same *scriptorium*.[257] That in turn implies that they were conjoined early in their history if not at the start.

Two other features of Nero 'A' deserve attention. One is that two anonymous legal statements were inserted between the rubrics and main text of Alfred's laws. *Romscot* is one of the briefest Anglo-Saxon 'codes'. It applies the sanctions of Ine's law on church scot to non-payment of 'Rome money', and was presumably formulated before Edgar introduced stiffer penalties for this.[258] A good guess is that someone entrusted with enforcement of Alfred's *domboc* both devised and inserted it into a convenient space between the code's rubrics and text, which position it then retained down the chain of transmission.[259] *Iudex* is a different matter. It is an elaborated tract on the unjust judge and is extant in two other traditions (chapter 5, pp. 382–3). But its central theme does expand on Alfred's prefatory discussion of the principle that one should judge as one wishes to be judged – the point picked out by the first of the *domboc* rubrics. One can envisage that a scribe (or 'judge') was prompted to reinforce what he took to be the main burden of Alfred's preface with a full treatment of the same topic.[260] Here, then, is further illustration of the tendency for minor texts to cluster around the major expositions of Anglo-Saxon law (above, pp. 175–6). The trend accelerates in the twelfth century.

The other notable Nero 'A' feature is the treatment of Cnut's code. While other early manuscripts show efforts to break up a code's uninterrupted prose by enlarging initials or inserting marks (pp. 189–90, 235), this one does something otherwise found only in the special case of Alfred–Ine: Cnut's laws are divided into paragraphs with their own initials, giving them some of the appearance of a modern edition.[261] If authorial, they are not encountered in other copies of this code. If scribal, scribe 2 ignored his colleague's lead. Whatever their origin, they testify to concern in legally expert quarters that English law have the segmented form of continental *leges* and capitularies (chapter 2, p. 50).

The strongest impression left by Nero 'A' is of a patchwork with its seams showing. Almost everything about its two sections diverges, save their (present) dimensions, their date and their unqualified legal focus. If Nero 'B' is a conflation

257 III Eg 3, II Cn 15:1; Torkar, *Altenglische Übersetzung*, p. 171.
258 *Gesetze* I, p. 474; cf. Ine 4, II Eg 4 – 4:3.
259 Note the gaps at the end of the rubrics in the Parker MS, f. 35r, and the Nowell transcript, f. 238r.
260 Torkar, pp. 171–4, a characteristically illuminating discussion.
261 Often, though *by no means always*, these clauses coincide with those of modern editors: e.g. there are new clauses where Liebermann gives unfragmented numerals (1, 10, not 1:1, 10:1, etc.), but also at I 2:1 (not 2), 3:2 (not 3), 4:2, 5:1, 5:2, 5:2b, 5:2d, 5:3, 11:1 (not 12), etc. This is more fully discussed in chapter 5, p. 350.

of two or more Wulfstanian clones, 'A' looks like a hybrid of ill-matched forebears. What it seems to reflect is dawning awareness that major statements of
Anglo-Saxon law should be supplemented by the codes that contributed to them:
Æthelred's laws aside, Edgar and Alfred-Ine are indeed Cnut's major sources.[262]
One reason for setting it on or just after the 1066 watershed when its script points
impartially to either slope of the ridge is that this awareness became more and
more widespread after the conquest. Furthermore, 'A' like 'B' is a strikingly small
book. The portability of 'B' may be a function of its homiletic message (above,
pp. 202–3). That of 'A' heralds the dimensions of Anglo-Norman law-books as
well as the generally reduced size of twelfth-century volumes. Nero 'A', it has
been supposed, was a book such as St Wulfstan would have wished to have.
Equally, it is the sort of book that ex-Bishop Æthelric (also ex-monk of Christ
Church Canterbury) might have taken in his cart to the great Penenden Heath
confrontation (p. 159, n. 150, chapter 14).[263] However any of that might be, it
is a type of collection that was much in demand by 1100.

(ii) Cambridge, Corpus Christi College, MS 383

The reign of Henry I was the most important period in the history of Old English
law from 1066 itself to the reign of Elizabeth. What was then done to preserve
and transmit its memorials in large measure determined what was known of it
for the next four and a half centuries. To a great extent, it determines what is
known of it still. A fair proportion of codes survive only in manuscripts from that
time. It was then that accounts of pre-conquest law that have deeply influenced
its understanding were written. One can reasonably speak of a sustained effort
to make the kingdom's jurisprudence accessible to new masters. Corpus
Cambridge 383 is perhaps the earliest of three collections from the first quarter
of the twelfth century which are fuller than any others, and which more than any
others look like attempts to bring as much Anglo-Saxon law as possible within
a single compass.[264]
   The Corpus package introduces students of Old English law-books to a new
class of complexities. It is no longer a matter of working out what laws were
doing in books largely devoted to other matters. Only legal materials are now

---

262   Not only, moreover, were the laws of Cnut the basic text to which post-conquest authorities (and
the 1065 rebels, chapter 3, pp. 129–33) appealed, but those of Edgar were the foundation of the 1018
agreement (*ibid.*), while Alfred's code was seen as the *fons et origo* of the Old English legislative tradition
(chapter 3, pp. 129–30). A note of warning, here as with Nero 'B', is that the MS is incomplete, and may
well have contained more laws (or indeed something else).
263   Loyn, *Wulfstan Manuscript*, p. 45; *English Lawsuits*, ed. van Caenegem, no. 5, p. 9. Yet this may
be the place to note that the 'Leges aliquot regum Saxonice' seen by Leland at Christchurch (Hants) (Ker,
p. xlvi) fits Nero A.i(A) better than other unplaced survivals.
264   The manuscript is given the *siglum* 'B' by Liebermann (*Gesetze* I, p. xix), and is no. 65 in Ker,
Catalogue. Discussion by other modern scholars has remained sparse, attention being diverted to
Quadripartitus and (still more) *Textus Roffensis* (below, pp. 236–44, 244–53). Unfortunately, there is not
the space to address all the manuscript's absorbing problems here; I hope to return to these in a proposed
facsimile edition, to be edited by Dr Mildred Budny, Professor Ray Page and myself. I am grateful to
Professor Page for the opportunity to examine it when unbound for conservation in 1991.

Table 4.6   Contents of Corpus 383
(in main hand unless otherwise specified)

(Quire "a")	II-III Eg (pp. "C"–"H" ln 13)
	– Hand of s xvi[2]
	– Flyleaves ("A"-"B") and pp. "I/J"–"S" of this preliminary quire are blank
Quire 1	*Blas.* (from 3 '… bringan ne mæge'), p. 1 (lns 1–6)
	Forf., p. 1 (lns 6–19)
	Hu., pp. 1 (ln 19) – 3 (ln 9)
	I Atr, pp. 3 (ln 10) – 5 (ln 20)
	AGu (B[2]), p. 6
	EGu, p. 7 (ln 1) – 10 (ln 24)
	II As (to 6 'his ætsacan …'), pp. 10 (ln 24) – 12 (ln 26)
	– Text in French, p. 5 lns 20–6, s xiii
Quire 2	Af–Ine (from Af 3 '… Oþres bisceopes'), pp. 13–26
	– Leaf missing after p. 22 (Af 41 'Be Bocland …' – 43 '… dagas to eastron')
Quire 3	Af-Ine (cont.), pp. 27–42 (ln 19)
	Blas. (to 3 'að forð– …'), p. 42 (lns 20–6)
	– 'Matildis bey soror magistri Roberti bey de Abbend …', p. 29 lower margin, s xiii
(Quire "4")	I Cn (to 17:1 '… on xiiii kl iuni. And …')
	– Hand of s xvi[2]
	– Text from I Cn 14:2 ('… mæsse dæg swa he beboden beo') is scored through
	– Last three leaves of this originally 10-leaf quire have been cut out
	– First 2 pp. blank and unnumbered, first written p. "44", the rest unnumbered
Quire 4	I–II Cn (from 14:2 '… mæsse dæge, swa he beboden beo'), pp. 43–58
	– Extensive Latin/French text in lower margin, pp. 48–52, s xii/xiii
Quire 5	I–II Cn (cont.), pp. 59–72 (ln 1)
	I–II Ew, pp. 72 (ln 9) – 74
Quire 6	I–II Ew (cont.), pp. 77–78 (ln 2)
	I–II Em, pp. 78 (ln 4) – 81 (ln 11)
	Swer., pp. 81 (ln 12) – 83 (ln 14)
	AGu (B[1]), pp. 83 (ln 17) – 84 (ln 23)
	Wif., pp. 84 (ln 23) – 86 (ln 4)
	Wer., pp. 86 (ln 5) – 87 (ln 6)
	Charm for recovery of stolen cattle, p. 87 (lns 6–20)
	– Text scored through in red ink
	Hit becwæð, pp. 87 (ln 21) – 88 (ln 16)
	II Atr (with 'Appendix', i.e. clauses 8 – 9:4), pp. 88 (ln 17) – 92
	– Misnumbering omits pp. nos 75–6
Quire 7	II Atr (cont.), p. 93 (to ln 2)
	Duns., pp. 93 (ln 3) – 95
	Rect., pp. 96–102 (ln 23)
	Ger., pp. 102 (ln 23) – 107 (ln 14)
	[St Paul's 'Shipmen' list, pp. 107 (ln 15) – 108 (ln 2), s xii[1]]
	[Truncated WSax genealogical regnal list, p. 108 (lns 3–26), s xii[1]]

involved. The problem becomes how and why these were put together. Table 4.6 should again assist enquiry. The first thing to emerge from it are the vicissitudes experienced by the manuscript. Quire 1 is out of place. It begins with the last half of the tract *Be Blaserum*, and should follow quire 3, which concludes with its first half. At least three quires have got lost, before current quire 2, after quire 1, and after quire 7. This appears to have been the situation by the time the manuscript came into the hands of Archbishop Parker's circle. The page-numbering quoted in table 4.6 is in Parker's typical red crayon, and the list of contents he put on the verso of the first flyleaf show that the book's contents were already in their current order.[265] The Parker group supplied a transcript of the missing part of I Cnut and also of II–III Edgar at the outset.[266] Before it reached Parker, the manuscript was annotated by Talbot.[267] Well before that, to judge from the item at the foot of p. 5, it had left the ecclesiastical community where it was in the early-twelfth century. That community can be identified from the most important addition to the volume: the list of shipmen in a near-contemporary hand on pp. 107–8. The estates in this list belonged at the time to St Paul's London. This collection, then, was either made at or soon procured by St Paul's.[268]

Can one have any idea of what is missing from the original compilation? Something may be guessed through arithmetical extrapolation from other manuscripts. Comparison of the Corpus Alfred–Ine with the contemporary copy in *Textus Roffensis* suggests that Alfred's preface and first three clauses would have

---

265   It is suggested that the manuscript may have been more complete when used by Nowell/Lambarde for *Archaionomia*: Dammery, 'Law-Code of King Alfred' I, pp. 60–1; Ker, *Catalogue*, p. 111; for doubts about the latter proposition see my 'Lambarde problem', p. 249 (152). In any case, the quire missing after current quire 1 was already absent when Nowell wrote 'Desunt nonnulla' in the margin of BL Add. MS 43703 (above, pp. 173–7) just where CCCC 383's text of II As breaks off.

266   Each copy was taken from what are now the two parts of Harley 55; see above n. 97 and below nn. 342–3 for the point that this was done at different times, noting further that Cnut's code has a title in Parker's hand where the Edgar title is in different script (and language), and that Edgar is paginated alphabetically, with a reference to it added at the top of the contents list, where the Cnut insertion is recorded there by adding '44' to the pre-existing '43', with '44' then entered on the first page of the transcript, the rest being left unpaginated (and the text of Cnut proper starting at '43' twelve pages later!). The Cnut transcript was perhaps *not* made with the Corpus 383 lacuna in mind: the extant text runs to I Cn 17:1, with at least three leaves then cut out, and a line through the text from 14:2 onwards; i.e. what was not needed to make good the missing text was deleted, and this copy might even once have been complete.

267   He was especially interested in the place-names of AGu and *Duns.* (pp. 6, 83, 93–5); his attention was also caught, like that of so many later scholars, by 'bocland' and 'folcland' (p. 73); and for no clear reason, he annotated I Em (pp. 78–9); see also next n.

268   Liebermann, 'Matrosenstellung'; his assertion that sixteenth-century marginal notes show that the book was then still at St Paul's presumably refers to the note that Caddington 'pertinet sco Paulo', but this is Talbot's work so no proof of continuing St Paul's ownership. The French texts on pp. 5, 48–52 are printed by James, *Catalogue of Corpus* II, pp. 230–1, and Wilkins, *Catalogue des manuscrits français*, pp. 100–1; I am indebted to my colleague Donald Whitton for the information that the one on p. 5 is an ornithological courtly love *esquisse*, somewhat in the *Owl/Nightingale* idiom. If the 'Master Robert of Abingdon' of p. 29 is actually Robert of Abingdon, brother of the sainted Archbishop Edmund, as is possible given the script's date though they had no known sister called Matilda (Emden, *Register Oxford* I, pp. 8–9; Lawrence, *Saint Edmund*, pp. 37–9, 106–10, 144–6; Dammery, 'Law-Code of King Alfred', p. 63), Robert perhaps acquired the manuscript through his contacts with the Langton family – Archbishop Stephen's brother, Simon, was in touch with St Paul's on legal issues: Holt, 'Origins of the Constitutional Tradition', pp. 16–17. If the MS did pass from its 'home' library to semi-academic hands, there is an interesting parallel with Nero A.i(A), above, n. 249.

taken 314 lines; which, at twenty-six lines to the page, is twelve pages and two lines.[269] In other words, a six-leaf quire like current quire 1 would have afforded the space for Corpus to have begun its Alfred–Ine text with its Mosaic preface. That it did not have an inaugural rubric-list will become clear later. It is of course possible that there were other preceding items in one or more preceding quires, but there is no particular reason to think so. The position with what is lost after current quire 1 is more complicated. *Textus Roffensis* comparison suggests that Corpus would have needed 183 lines to complete II Æthelstan.[270] The nearest equivalent for its text of Cnut (though not as like Corpus in either texts or layout as *Textus Roffensis*) is Harley 55(B), and this implies that the missing portion would have taken 189 lines.[271] The hypothetical combined total for Æthelstan and Cnut thus comes to 372 lines, or fourteen pages and eight lines. Clearly, then, an item or two is lost, but perhaps no more than a page and a half of text.[272]

Turning to the arrangement of what does survive, the most telling evidence comes from the texts following Alfred–Ine (pp. 42, 1). On the very next line begins the tract known as '*Be Blaserum*, About Arsonists' (here '*Be Morðslihtum*, secret(?) killers'). Its large initial and capitalized first words would seem to mark the start of a new text, except that numerous clauses in Alfred's law-book are introduced in just the same way.[273] Next is another short statement, '*Forfang*, Attachment [process]', whose first clause is marked by no break at all, while its second behaves like an average Alfred–Ine clause. These two texts relate to the legislation of Æthelstan and Æthelred (if anyone's), not Ine's or Alfred's (chapter 5, pp. 367–8, 369–70). They have been hooked onto Alfred–Ine in the same way as was the adultery clause in Otho B.xi (above, pp. 175–6). This must have happened in the Corpus exemplar. The first draft of *Quadripartitus*, the collection to be studied next, has the same feature (pp. 242–3). Nor is that the end of the story. After *Forfang* Corpus 383 launches into the Hundred Ordinance as if it too were part of the same text. In fact an eyeskip permits omission of the Ordinance rubric's last three words and the first of the opening clause: a blunder that could hardly have occurred had the text been at all clearly differentiated. Again, the pattern recurs in *Quadripartitus*, though here the tracts are not

269   The 826 lines of extant Af–Ine in CCCC 383 (with 52 lines on the missing leaf after p. 22) correspond to 724 in *TR*, which devoted 275 lines, excluding the rubric list, to what Corpus lacks; to cover this material, Corpus should thus have taken 275 x 826/724 lines, i.e. 314.

270   The extant II As in CCCC 383 takes 54 lines, compared to 45 in *TR*, where what Corpus lacks occupies 152 lines; to complete that code, Corpus should therefore have needed 152 x 54/45 = *c.* 183 lines.

271   Harley uses 966 lines for the part of I–II Cn preserved by CCCC 383 in 752 (not counting the I Cn 'epilogue', extant in Corpus alone), and 242 for what it has lost; the part not preserved by Corpus should therefore have filled 242 x 752/966 = 189.

272   It may be noted that if the Corpus text of II As concluded at clause 25, like that of Otho B.xi (above, pp. 176–8), it would have taken 170 lines, and could thus have been accommodated in an irregular fourteen-page quire. At any rate, a sixteen-page quire would not have left room for V As to have followed II As as in *TR* and Nowell's lost MS (below, p. 262): *TR* devotes 46 lines to it, meaning that Corpus would have needed 55, and the space left in an eight-leaf quire after accommodating the missing bits of II As and I Cn comes to 44 lines max. Also noteworthy, however, is that Corpus would have taken almost exactly 43 lines to provide a text of *Ordal*, which has strong links with Æthelstan's legislation (chapter 5, pp. 373–4).

273   E.g., moving back from the end of the code, Ine 63, 60, 54, 53, etc.; the introduction to Ine's code (p. 27) is much more prominent.

actually conflated. Aside from his own not inconsiderable limitations, the Corpus scribe fell victim to a transmission where the Alfred–Ine *domboc* led on to statements of the law on arson, murder and cattle-theft. His own shortcomings can, however, be squarely blamed for the next development: he ran *Hundred* into the first code of Æthelred (p. 3). This time he saw the error of his ways. The line where this happened was erased to make way for Æthelred's introduction, and room was found in the margin for the last few words of *Hundred*, together with a rubric and suitably enlarged initial for the royal code. His ability to correct himself, and the fact that the *Quadripartitus* editor here did much better, imply that some sort of (not instantly evident) break marked the transition in the exemplar. It is still safe to say that this exemplar had supplied copies of Alfred–Ine, *Be Blaserum, Forfang, Hundred* and I Æthelred in fairly undiscriminated succession.

Comparison between Corpus 383 and *Quadripartitus* and/or *Textus Roffensis*, the other two early-twelfth-century compilations of this type, shows that it contained further mini-collections where some of the work of assembly had already been done. There is, for instance, no obvious reason why two codes of Edmund, but not the third, should follow the two of Edward (pp. 72–81), omitting all those of Æthelstan that came between. Yet this arrangement persists throughout *Quadripartitus* and *Textus Roffensis*, suggesting strongly that it was found in the exemplar of each. In *Quadripartitus* as well as Corpus 383, these paired codes precede the tracts called *Swerian, Wifmannes Beweddung* and *Wergeld*; while in *Roffensis* as in Corpus, neighbouring items are a charm to recover stolen cattle and the formulary *Hit Becwæð*. Though it voices a dominant preoccupation of Anglo-Saxon law, the charm is not of course a legal text, and in Corpus 383 a red line is duly drawn through it, probably by the rubricator (p. 87).[274] The Corpus scribe is again caught working on auto-pilot. A pointer in the same direction is that a text of the Alfred–Guthrum treaty occurs in this part of the manuscript (pp. 83–4), though it had been copied in earlier.[275] A reasoned conclusion is that a mini-collection comprising the paired Edward and Edmund codes, Alfred–Guthrum, *Swerian, Wifmannes Beweddung, Wergeld*, Charm and *Hit Becwæð* reached all three twelfth-century editors. This group, it may be noted, is not unlike the mini-collection already encountered in Nero A.i(A).

Another possible group is made up of II Æthelred (an Anglo-Viking treaty), the code known as *Dunsæte* and perhaps the so-called *Rectitudines Singularum Personarum* (pp. 88–102/7). In Corpus and in *Quadripartitus* Æthelred's treaty has a seemingly irrelevant Appendix on the process of vouching to warranty, unsignalled by any clear break in the text.[276] The Appendix must have been unrecognizably buried in the treaty well back in its transmission. *Dunsæte* is the next item in both collections, though as an evidently distinct text. It was a treaty of sorts in its own right and concerned with cattle-theft, so its association with

---

274   This line is definitely *not* in Parker's red crayon.
275   Keynes, 'Royal Government and the written word', pp. 233–4. The complex problem of the relationship of the AGu and EGu texts to the detectable groups in this manuscript and the others is left for discussion of these texts in chapter 5 (p. 390).
276   In the 'M' MS of *Quadripartitus* (below, pp. 237–8), the Appendix is Chapter 'X' of the treaty, and in its 'Hk' relative, X–XI (with the break at editorial clause 9).

the foregoing is intelligible. What follows in Corpus 383 is *Rectitudines*, with, as a concluding section, an account of an estate reeve's duties headed 'Be Gesceadwisan Gerefan'. In *Quadripartitus*, *Rectitudines* comes later and lacks the *Gerefa* supplement. There should not then be any question of its having belonged with the rest in a hypothetical Corpus/*Quadripartitus urexemplar*. Yet the *Quadripartitus* author was evidently better able to rearrange his materials than the Corpus scribe, and could well have thought that *Rectitudines*, more clearly non-royal legislation than anything else he was handling, was appropriately relegated to the end of his pre-conquest series. He could also have decided to drop *Gerefa* as a text that more obviously than *Rectitudines* itself dealt with estate duties not legal rights, and/or one that would have taxed his capacities as a translator even further than anything else in Anglo-Saxon law.[277] But what positive reasons are there for supposing that so motley a set of texts as these were ever put together? The first is that aspects of its vocabulary link *Rectitudines* with Somerset, and further with a late Saxon survey of the manor of Tidenham on the Wye, which belonged to Bath Abbey till just before the Conquest.[278] The population group designated 'Dunsæte' were located on a river that was probably the Wye, and a case has been made for identifying their boundaries as those of the Deanery of Ross, which extended south to within half a dozen miles of Tidenham.[279] And at the time that Æthelred II negotiated his treaty with the Viking leadership (chapter 5, pp. 320–1, 326), the abbot of Bath was Ælfhere, who brought the king's seal to the 990 Berkshire lawsuit (chapter 3, pp. 151); such a member of inner government circles could have kept a copy of the treaty.[280] One might thus envisage that someone at Bath was prompted by the treaty's provision on cattle theft to add the clauses of some other code on vouching to warranty, and then another treaty text in the abbey's possession that also dealt with rustling between its parties. At a later stage, this set of texts was joined to tracts on estate customs. The argument has by now become far more tenuous than is warranted in a part of this book where speculation is meant to be rationed. What matters more than the hypothetical details is the evidence that otherwise unrelated texts were forming up in groups.

The bulk of the Corpus compilation was written by a single scribe at the turn of the eleventh and twelfth centuries. He has emerged so far as an assembler of preconstructed building-blocks. What can be said of the resulting edifice? A first point is that his mistakes were not confined to an inability to tell when one code ended and another began. His errors in Old English would shame the most recalcitrant of those still subjected to compulsory Anglo-Saxon.[281] Inconsistent word division reaches the point where one wonders whether the scribe was under

---

277   For this and what follows, see Harvey's fine study of 'Rectitudines Singularum Personarum and Gerefa', especially pp. 3–8.

278   S 1555.

279   Noble, *Offa's Dyke Reviewed*, pp. 14–18, with maps 2, 8–11. See also chapter 5, pp. 381–2.

280   For charters attested by Abbot Ælfhere, cf. Keynes, *Atlas of Attestations* LXI, LXVII (S 856 (985) – S 963 (1031)).

281   These issues will be discussed by Professor Page in the promised facsimile volume; see meanwhile his 'Gerefa', pp. 215–16.

the impression that 'Bege' was an Old English word.[282] There are wildly inconsistent spellings, renditions of 'king' ranging from 'kyning' through to 'cing', and not infrequently within a few lines of one another.[283] It is suggested that such orthographical eccentricities 'indicate that there were uncertainties of pronunciation, probably due to sound developments in the language'.[284] Some were shared by other twelfth-century manuscripts. But the profusion and variety of the Corpus scribe's errors raise a suspicion that, though he had heard the English language spoken, it was anything but his habitual means of expression.

The scribe's forest of blunders produced a corresponding outcrop of corrections, some by himself, many more by at least two other hands.[285] Some of these amendments were presumably supplied from the exemplar.[286] To say that a corrector who may have been the shipmen-list scribe had access to the exemplar(s) is of course to imply that the manuscript itself was written at St Paul's. Another type of correction has the effect of bringing Corpus into line with *variations* in other manuscripts, notably perceptible alterations in *Textus Roffensis* or changes made in one of the later editions of *Quadripartitus* (pp. 243, 249).[287] The implication here is that variant versions were reaching the compilers.[288] Yet another species of amendments are more accurately described as glosses. They represent alterations to the text that clarify its meaning or alter its legalistic purport. 'æþel' is inserted before 'borenran' in Alfred clause 11:5, where '*nobly* born' is indeed the meaning (and where *Textus Roffensis* inserts 'bett'); in the next clause, 'thirty shillings' is glossed as a 'half pound', which, on a Mercian reckoning of four pennies to a shilling (such as was used in an amendment to Ine 59), is in fact correct.[289] Supply of 'do' in Ine 28:1 represents an intelligent attempt to come to terms with an original that mangled '*oðierne* (escape)' as '*oðerna* (other)'. So one could go on. As testimony to the legal sophistication of the Corpus enterprise they do not come to much. But they are a useful corrective to the atmosphere of virtual indifference to content so far

---

282   As in the title of *Ger*. 'Bege sceadwisan gerefan' (p. 102); or 'Bege feohtum' (Ine 6, p. 28), etc. Cf. Af 5:4 'ærge yppednære' (p. 14), Af 19:3 'feor mung' (p. 17).
283   Af 7 'kyninges' 'cyninges' (p. 14), Ine 23 'cyng', Ine 23:1,2 'cyning' (p. 31), Ine 76:1 'kyninges, cinge' (p. 42), AGu Pr. 'cyng', 'cing' (p. 6), 'cyninc', 'cyning' (p. 83), I Em 3 'cyniges', 'cyninges' (p.78, line 21), I Atr Pr 'cining' (p. 3), I Atr 1:9a 'cyng' (p. 4), etc. Cf. the three spellings of Ine 59 'pening (penny)' (p. 39).
284   Quoting Professor Page's paper to the 1991 seminar on the MS.
285   These include those wrongly designated '16 Jh.' by Liebermann (Ker, *Catalogue*, p. 111), but his notices of them were far from exhaustive. I hope to return to this issue in the facsimile volume. Suffice it to say here that one correcting hand is small and neat, and possibly that of the rubricator, while another one (or two) writes in brown ink and in an angular mode with a notably scratchy quill: he may be identical with the scribe of the diagnostically St Paul's shipmen-list and the West Saxon genealogy.
286   They include passages where the original was distorted by eye-skip or other lapses of attention: e.g. p. 21: Af 35:5 (p. 69, n. 3); p. 24: Af 48 (p. 80, n. 3); p. 42: Ine 75 (p. 123, nn. 1–2); p. 10: II As 1 (p. 150, n. 2); p. 45: I Cn 22:1 (p. 302, n. 4).
287   E.g. p. 32: Ine 25:1 (p. 100, nn. *, 5), where *TR* erases its original to give 'man forstolen feoh æt ceapmen', and where a mixture of erasures and inserts produces the same text in Corpus; or p. 52: II Cn 18 (p. 320, n. 6), where the correction 'neod' parallels 'necesse' in later *Quadripartitus*.
288   Liebermann plausibly guessed, *Gesetze* III, p. 31 (7), that the Corpus exemplar had interlinear glosses: hence the scribe's failure to pick them up first time around.
289   Some other monetary interpretations were less felicitous: on p. 17, Af. 16, 'sixty shillings' was altered to 'forty', where the original read one (Liebermann, p. 58, n. 2)!

created by the main scribe's record. The correctors, or at any rate the source(s) they drew upon, showed some concern that their product make sense.

A further feature of their codex reinforces that lesson. A theme recurring ever since the third manuscript discussed in this chapter is attempts to divide continuous texts into clauses. The trend accelerates in Corpus. Alfred–Ine was in effect re-rerubricated. Brackets in the form of an inverted 'L' were inserted or entered marginally where the sense seemed to demand a new clause not provided by the original rubricator (chapter 5, pp. 267–8).[290] On top of that, *red ink* brackets were entered at other points and followed up with new rubrics not in the original preliminary list.[291] Above all, the rubrics in that list were redeployed, as in no other copy, into proximity with the clause itself. The pressure of space on most of these rubrics suggests that room was at first left only for chapter *numbers* (as in other manuscripts). The treatment of Alfred–Ine is of a piece with what looks like a policy about chapter divisions. In the case of II Æthelstan, the rubrics in *Textus Roffensis* imply that they were part of the original text, or at least central to its transmission. *Swerian* and *Rectitudines*, by contrast, lack rubrics in other versions, but space was left for them in Corpus – even if not invariably taken up.[292] When it came to Cnut's code, rubrics or brackets were supplied which are virtually certain not to have been inherited from any exemplar. There are none in either of the other extant versions, though the parcelization of the Nero A.i(A) text left so much room for them (pp. 227, 350). In Corpus itself clauses were at first designated only by coloured initials (sometimes in the middle of lines). Headings, when they appear, are even more clearly squeezed into the margin than with Alfred–Ine.[293] It follows from much of this that the rubrication is not likely to have been inserted by the original scribe. Chapter division was part of a process designed to make his work more user-friendly.

The seriousness of the Corpus enterprise is emphasized, finally, by its shape and themes. Like Nero A.i(A), it is a small book. Here too, exclusively legal texts are made portable. Its coverage of Anglo-Saxon lawmaking is less comprehensive than that of other twelfth-century collections, but is also more prosaic and matter-of-fact. Despite its cathedral provenance, there is no trace of the ecclesiastical interest evident in *Quadripartitus* or *Textus Roffensis*. If there is any dominant or recurrent *motif*, that is relations between peoples. It is responsible for *both* extant Old English versions of Alfred's treaty with Guthrum. One might admittedly think that a scribe with so little awareness of what he was doing

---

290   E.g. p. 14: Af 5:4, 5:5; p. 15: Af 9:2; p. 23: Af 43, between 'ymbrenwucum' and 'þeowum mannum' (where the result is syntactic nonsense); p. 25: Af 62:1, 67; p. 31: Ine 21:1; p. 32: Ine 25:1 (incorporating the n. 287 amendment), etc.

291   pp. 16–17: Af 13, 16; pp. 24–6: the Af injury tariff (where, however, new rubrics are not supplied); on p. 22, red initials are supplied with new rubrics for Af 38:2 (merely 'Eft, again') and 40.

292   p. 11: II As 2, with unused space on p. 12 for rubrics at 3, 4, 6 (for the II As rubrics see chapter 5, pp. 300); pp. 81–3: *Swer.* 2 – 9, 11, with space at 10; pp. 96–102: *Rect.* 2 – 19, with space at 4:4, 21 (see below, pp. 242–3 for *Quad.* rubrics here).

293   Red ink brackets are at p. 51: II Cn 14; p. 54: II Cn 24:3, 25a; p. 60: II Cn 44; pp. 64–5, II Cn 67, 68. Red ink brackets with new rubrics in margin are at p. 59, II Cn 39; p. 61, II Cn 46; pp. 62–5, II Cn 50, 51, 52, 52:1, 53, 56 – 66. There are new rubrics without marking brackets at e.g. I Cn 16, 18:1, 23, II Cn 4a, 5, 8, 13, 17:1, 19, 20, 21, 26 (a repeat of 21!), etc.

copied out the second text (which lacks a rubric) as part of the package that also contained the codes of Edward and Edmund, *Swerian* and the rest (above, pp. 231–2), without realizing that he had already done so seventy-seven pages earlier.[294] Yet it is something to have included Alfred-Guthrum at all, along with the sole vernacular text of II Æthelred, the other surviving Anglo-Viking treaty of the pre-conquest period. The relations of potentially hostile peoples were obviously topical in post-conquest conditions.[295] In addition, it has been shown that the sums payable as *Murdrum* fines under the Conqueror's scheme to insure the lives of his followers were based on that demanded for the slaying of Dane or Englishman under Alfred's treaty.[296] In the circumstances, it seems rather more than chance that the bishop of London when Corpus 383 was written was Maurice, ex-royal chaplain and ex-chancellor.[297] A man like Maurice should, to say no more, have been interested in a book like this.

Corpus 383 therefore adds up to an intriguing and conceivably instructive paradox. It was mainly the work of a scribe whose skills did not extend to accurate writing of the English language. It mattered more to copy out large quantities of pre-conquest law than to master the tongue in which it was expressed. Yet the book was probably written for, certainly kept in, a church whose bishop had been a central figure in the post-conquest regime. One of its chief concerns, Anglo-Danish relations, was of course a preoccupation of that regime. These contradictory indicators may in fact be sides of the same coin. Old English law was important enough to need copying by someone not competent to do so. One could argue that its preservation was urgent just *because* those who understood it were increasingly thin on the ground. The next collection shows that dedication to the accessibility of pre-conquest jurisprudence was shared by at least one other member of the new francophone ascendancy.

(iii) Quadripartitus

The second collection in the compilatory tradition that became established under Henry I was not in fact a manuscript at all. The work known as 'Quadripartitus' since Liebermann first isolated and scrutinized it was no less than a major editorial achievement.[298] It assembled the largest extant set of pre-conquest legal materials, and translated them into Latin. The results survive not in one

---

294   If so, a corrector realized the mistake and supplied readings from the fuller second text into the margins of the first, p. 6: Keynes, 'Royal government and the written word', pp. 233–4.

295   Richards, 'Manuscript Contexts', pp. 180–4.

296   Garnett, '"Franci et Angli"', pp. 125–7.

297   *RRAN* I, p. xvii; Barlow, *English Church 1066–1154*, pp. 64, 73.

298   Liebermann, *Quadripartitus*, the first of his titanic contributions to early English legal studies, and the first to see that what earlier scholars had reproduced as the 'Old [Latin] Version' was a lawbook in its own right, launched by the prefaces that he christened 'Dedicatio' and 'Argumentum' (see below). Liebermann unfortunately compounded the confusions surrounding this work in that he never edited it as such: his 1892 study referred to Schmid's edition for actual texts of all bar the prefaces and rubrics, and his *Gesetze*, like Schmid's, juxtaposed the Latin translations of the laws with their Old English originals (as if they were indeed a 'manuscript'), reserving prefaces and rubrics for their proper chronological place near the end of Vol. I (pp. 529–46). See chapter 1, p. 21.

manuscript but in several. Not content with putting together items from a variety of sources as the Corpus collector seems to have done, the *Quadripartitus* author (henceforth 'Q') revised his work in the light of alternative readings in freshly discovered copies. This clearly represents a different order of enterprise from the otherwise similar 'encyclopaedias' made at much the same time. It can hardly be treated in exactly the same way. For all that, *Quadripartitus* breathes the same spirit as the other books. In its primal forms, it will have resembled them. It is thus open to the same sort of questioning. What was at the compiler's disposal? How was it handled? What does this say about the sort of mentality that preserved legal evidence?

Unfortunately, *Quadripartitus* is even more overgrown by verdant complexity than other early law-books. Q's purpose seems to change as he went on. His product may not be fully reflected in any surviving rendition. All versions have been mutilated or otherwise tampered with. Not a native English speaker, he was unequal to all challenges posed by his originals. His Latin was beyond the grasp of any modern reader until recently. This tangle will, however, yield to laborious unravelling, providing at least an outline of what the whole exercise involved.[299] A first step is to summarize the manuscripts in which this equivalent to a 'manuscript' survives.

1   BL, Cotton MS Domitian viii, ff. 96r – 110v [Dm]; s. xii$^{2/4}$; ?West Midlands origin.

2   Manchester, John Rylands Library, MS Lat 420 [M]; s. xii^{med}; origin and provenance unknown until ? in Library of Sir Henry Sidney c.1580; later studied by Spelman.[300]

3   BL, Royal MS 11.B.ii, ff. 103r – 166v [R]; s. xii$^{3/4}$; provenance Worcester.[301]

4   BL, Additional MS 49366 [Hk]; s. xii$^{3/4}$; origin and provenance unknown until in hands of Archbishop Parker, thence in those of Sir Edward Coke and his descendants at Holkham Hall.

5   BL, Cotton MS Titus A.xxvii, ff. 89r – 174v [T]; s. xii/xiii; provenance St Augustine's Canterbury.[302]

6a   Manchester, John Rylands Library, Lat MS 155 (+ BL, Additional MS 14252) [Rs]; s. xiii^{in}; medieval provenance London Guildhall.[303]

6b   BL Cotton MS Claudius D.ii [K2]; s xiv^1; used by Andrew Horn when finalizing the texts in 6c, 6d; bequeathed by him to Guildhall.[304]

---

299   For all that follows, including more detailed exposition of much of the argument, see my '"*Quadripartitus*"' (e.g. origin of the title, pp. 115, 137 (pp. 84–5, 105); this was a joint enterprise with Richard Sharpe, and is followed by his pioneer translation of the 'Prefaces'.

300   Catalogued Taylor, *Supplementary Handlist*, pp. 13–14.

301   Catalogued Warner and Gilson, *Catalogue of Western MSS in Royal and King's Collections* I, pp. 343–4.

302   Described by Crick, *Historia Regum Britanniae: Summary Catalogue of the Manuscripts*, no. 95, pp. 156–8.

303   Catalogued James, *John Rylands Library*, pp. 265–70; described by Liebermann, 'Contemporary Manuscript of the "Leges Anglorum"': discovery of this MS twenty years after he had established the identity of the 'London Collection' (above, n. 67) brilliantly upheld the date for which he had earlier argued (against e.g. Stubbs).

304   Described and figuratively reassembled, along with 6a, 6c, 6d (after Tudor and Stuart antiquaries

6c   Cambridge, Corpus Christi College, MSS 70+258 [Co]; s xiv[1]; Horn's 'working copy', also given to Guildhall.

6d   Oxford, Oriel College, MS 46 [Or]; s xiv[1]; also probably Horn's work, also given to Guildhall.[305]

The last four of these manuscripts were copies of the 'London Collection' (above, p. 179), a large assemblage of legal texts from Ine to Henry II, drawing on *Quadripartitus* for the pre-twelfth-century period, which arranged its texts in chronological order and equipped them with historical commentary; its remarkable compound of constitutional defensiveness and imperialist assertion belongs to the history of John's reign.[306] Rs (6a) is a copy very close in date to the work itself, and even shows signs that the argument was still developing as it was being written; its copy of Glanvill was later hived off and augmented with pieces of more specific concern to Londoners. K2, Co and Or (6b-d) represent various adaptations of the 'Leges Anglorum' to the purposes of the London businessman and worthy Andrew Horn over a century later.[307] T (5), otherwise perhaps the latest manuscript, was also given a historical slant by the fourteenth century: *Quadripartitus* was slotted between Geoffrey of Monmouth and other pseudo-historical marvels, including 'Prester John's' letter to Emperor Manuel.[308] But its legal section, where *Quadripartitus* was supplemented by related matter, was apparently at first distinct. Its near-contemporary, Hk (4), the smallest of the set, was also supplemented by other legal texts. R (3) was added in its Worcester home to a collection of canon law materials, and also more incongruously accompanied by a list of the 'Seven Wonders of the World' and by poetry of Hildebert of Tours; this loss of legal focus is of a piece with its regular lapses of scribal concentration.[309] M (2) is another to provide *Quadripartitus* with a relevant appendix, the 1153 treaty whereby Stephen acknowledged his successor; it is a plain and compact volume, whose script is said to have 'notarial elements'.[310] Finally, Dm (1), the earliest of the series, is also the most important despite lacking all but its first two quires. This is because its scribes reproduce a variety of amendments to the text, evidently from the archetype. Words are added or

---

had again done their worst), by Ker, 'Liber Custumarum'; further penetrating discussion of this whole group by Catto, 'Andrew Horn'.

305   Further discussion and references for these MSS, including those for which no published description is available (but which were there elucidated by kind friends) in Wormald, '"*Quadripartitus*"', pp. 114–121 (pp. 83–90); here, I follow the logic of the datings suggested by Dr Michael Gullick (and Liebermann himself) in placing Hk before T. It should also be noted that large parts of Hk (including its extensive additions from Archbishop Parker and his circle) were copied by Nowell in what is now University of California MS 170/529, ff. 135v – 197v, with reference to another MS (probably M) as 'libro domini Sydney'.

306   Liebermann, *Über die Leges Anglorum*; Holt, 'Origins of the Constitutional Tradition', p. 13.

307   Liebermann, *Über die Leges Anglorum*, pp. 85–90, and 'A Contemporary Manuscript', pp. 743–4; Catto, 'Andrew Horn', pp. 372–80; Wormald, '"*Quadripartitus*"', pp. 119–21 (pp. 88–90); Rumble, 'The Manuscripts', pp. 47–51.

308   This collector's piece was also in the 'London Collection'; for its possible significance, see Hamilton, 'Prester John and the Three Kings of Cologne'.

309   Thirteenth-century Worcester 'business' letters are at the foot of ff. 55v (in the canonical section) and 128v – 129r. Hildebert is not, however, in the same hand as *Quadripartitus*.

310   The view of Dr Alex Rumble, who kindly advised me on the MS.

changed by adjacent or interlinear glosses, while underlinings or vertical lines in the margin designate deletions. Of all these books, only R and the copies of the London collection were in any way calligraphic. Most have an air of neat and sober practicality.

These witnesses to *Quadripartitus* are spread over the century after it was compiled. Each is textually corrupt enough to show that intermediary copics lie behind it. Most lines of transmission have developed their own idiosyncracies.[311] But the crucial point is that the various manuscripts catch the enterprise at different stages in its evolution. Table 4.7 shows how large a collection of codes and tracts from either side of the Conquest are represented. It can be seen at a glance that their deployment varies. The London collector's determination to observe chronology means that Ine's code comes before Alfred's for the first time since the earlier tenth century. R eccentricities extend to the omission of several items and displacement of others. T differs from M and Hk in its placing of III Edmund and of a whole block of texts from Alfred-Guthrum to *Wergeld*. Only M and Hk agree in all particulars: M's first two quires are lost, but the sixteenth-century table of contents on its flyleaf suggests that it omitted the prefaces and began with Cnut, just as did Hk (before the 'Argumentum' was inserted at the front in the sixteenth century).[312] Some of these changes could be explained by accidental shifting of quires during copying. But III Edmund's movement from a place after II–III Edgar to join Edmund's other two codes was surely deliberate; which argues that MHk represents a later stage in the collection's history than T.

Three lessons can in fact be drawn from the varied distribution of *Quadripartitus* contents in successive manuscripts. The first is how *little* attention seems to be paid to chronology at any stage before the London collection. Beginning the sequence with Cnut made good sense in terms of the author's purpose, stated in his 'Argumentum', and in his 'mini-preface' to the Cnut code.[313] Otherwise, though a rough approximation to chronology may be attempted, the primary determinant of an item's place is the one it had in the collection's source. So, Alfred comes before Æthelstan, he before Æthelred. But Edward the Elder's codes follow those of his eldest son, because they were apparently linked immovably with those of his younger son, Edmund. Edgar likewise comes after *his* son, because his codes had previously been tied up with one

---

311 Thus, R likes to dispense with preliminary lists of rubrics (and after Cnut to do without them altogether), whereas T has a tendency to join up chapters that other copies kept separate: Wormald '"*Quadripartitus*"', n. 41; M and Hk are very similar (see below), but M does not give chapter numbers in the text itself where Hk does. Liebermann provides details of textual deviance throughout his account of the MSS, *Quadripartitus*, pp. 58–72, as well as exhaustively in footnotes to the 'Quadripartitus' column in *Gesetze* I.

312 For possible implications of Hk's Parkerian copy of the 'Argumentum' 'e libro veteri ecclesiae Wigorniensis', see my '"*Quadripartitus*"', at nn. 10, 24–5.

313 The 'Argumentum' proclaims (ch. 27, tr. Sharpe, p. 167) that Henry I 'has given us back the law of King Edward', having previously explained (ch. 9, p. 164) how Edward himself 'guaranteed on oath that the laws of Cnut ... should continue in his time with unshaken firmness'. The rendition of Cnut's code begins with an expanded prologue describing its translation procedure, and continuing (in a sentence missing from the London collection version) 'there also follow laws of a number of kings in which whatever did not differ by comparison with that continued in force (*de quibus teneri liceat quicquid ista contemplatione non discrepat* (!))'.

Table 4.7 Contents of *Quadripartitus*

	Dm.	*M.*	*R.*	*Hk*	*T.*	*London*
I	Dedic.		Argum. 32	[Argum.]	Argum.	*Geographical*
	Argum.		I–II Cn	I–II Cn	I–II Cn	Ine
	I–II Cn	…Ine	Af–Ine	Af–Ine	Af–Ine	Blas.
	Af…	I–II As	I–II As	I–II As	I–II As	Forf.
		Episc.	Ord.	Episc.	Episc.	Hu.
		Norðl.	Episc.	Norðl.	Norðl.	*Historical*
		Mirc.	Norðl.	Mirc.	Mirc.	Af
		Að	Geþyn.	Að	Að	AGu
		Had.	Mirc.	Had.	Had.	App. AGu
		Blas.	Að	Blas.	Blas.	EGu
		Forf.	Had.	Forf.	Forf.	*Historical*
		Hu.	Blas.	Hu.	Hu.	I–II As.
		III–VI As	Forf.	III–VI As	III–VI As	Episc.
		Ord.	Hu.	Ord.	Ord.	Norðl.
		I/III Atr	III–VI As	I/III Atr	AGu	Mirc.
		Pax	I/III Atr	Pax	App. AGu	Að
		Wal.	Pax	Wal.	EGu	Had.
		IV Atr	EGu 9ff.	IV Atr	I–II Ew	III–VI As
		II Atr	Wal.	II Atr	I–II Em	Ord.
		Duns.	II Em	Duns.	Swer.	*Historical*
		VII Atr	Swer.	VII Atr	Wif.	I–II Cn.
		Iudex	Wif.	Iudex	Wer.	*Historical*
		II–III Eg	Wer.	II–III Eg	I/III Atr	
		AGu	III Atr	AGu	Pax	
		App. AGu	Pax	App. AGu	Wal.	
		EGu	Wal.	EGu	IV Atr	
		I–II Ew	IV Atr	I–II Ew	II Atr	
			II Atr			

I–III Em	Duns.	I–III Em	Duns.	*Wl Art.*
Swer.	Iudex	Swer.	VII Atr	*ECf*
Wif.		Wif.	Iudex	*Geneal. Duc. Norm.*
Wer.		Wer.	II–III Eg	*Historical*
			III Em	CHn cor
Wl lad	Rect.	Wl lad	Wl lad	*Hn Lond*
	Wl lad		*Wl Art.*	*Hn.*
Gebyn.		Gebyn.	Gebyn.	*etc. etc.*
Rect.		Rect.	Rect.	
II			Praef.	
CHn cor		CHn cor	CHn cor	
II 4–8:3, 18		II 4–8:3, 18	II 4–18	
Hn Com		Hn Com	Hn Com	
[*Tr. Winch.*]		[*Ps. Ulpian*]	[*Inst Cn*]	
		[*Leis Wl*]		
		[*ECf*]		
		[*Cons Cn*]		

Italics: not in original collection; [ ]: by other scribe(s).

of Æthelred's later decrees ('VII'). The large number of codes or tracts with no named royal sponsor seem to have the place they do because Q found them there. The best way to demonstrate this is to look forward to Table 4.9, where the contents of *Quadripartitus* are set out in parallel with those of Corpus 383 and *Textus Roffensis*.

It is at once evident that the London collection, like Corpus 383, made *Be Blaserum*, *Forfang* and the Hundred Ordinance a continuation of Alfred–Ine. The codes of Edward the Elder and Edmund are together in both collections, and also alongside the Alfred–Guthrum treaty and the tracts *Swerian*, *Wifmannes Beweddung* and *Wergeld*.[314] The Wulfstanian group, *Norðleoda Laga – Mircna Laga – Að – Hadbot* (above, pp. 208, 223) is integrated into Æthelstan's codes, along with *Episcopus*, another Wulfstan work.[315] The fact that *Pax*, *Walreaf* and (so-called) 'IV Æthelred' are treated as part of III Æthelred in T and numbered by MHk as further chapters of it suggests that they too may have appeared as constituents of a royal code in the *Quadripartitus* exemplar.[316] Corpus 383 demonstrates that royal legislation acquired 'tails' of originally unrelated but no longer distinguishable matter. The difference in *Quadripartitus* is that Q had better control over the disposal of his texts. The absence of the cattle charm and *Hit Becwæð* from the Edward–Edmund group is presumably because Q had a sharper eye than the St Paul's or even Rochester scribes for their irrelevance. Likewise, the removal of *Rectitudines* from the II Æthelred group could be because because its subject-matter was more obviously distinct than most 'private' pieces in the collection (above, pp. 232–3).[317] The impression still persists that *Quadripartitus*, like Corpus 383 and *Textus Roffensis*, was a collection made up of 'mini-collections'.

The second lesson of the *Quadripartitus* arrangements is that, as already suggested by the case of III Edmund, it was *deliberately* rearranged from one surviving version to the next. This reordering is only part of the evidence for conscious authorial revision. There is also the rubrication, which is one of the most pronounced traits of *Quadripartitus*. All versions give rubrics for the codes of Cnut and Æthelstan. Dm added rubrics for Alfred's Mosaic introduction. Hk moved the Ine rubrics to the front of the code to which they apply.[318] Also supplied at this point were reconsidered rubrics for the entire *domboc*, while other codes in the collection, elsewhere left as undifferentiated blocks of text, were now rubricated. This feature has an important rider. Had rubrics such as those of MHk been available to the London compiler, it is hard to see why they were ignored. Nor does it seem likely that a set of rubrics attached to Ine's code would have been transferred back to join those for the other parts of Alfred–Ine

314   See below, p. 249 for different handling of *Blas.* etc. by *TR*, and chapter 5, p. 390, for Corpus and *TR* treatment of EGu.

315   See my '"*Quadripartitus*"', pp. 124–5 (pp. 91, 94), for the numbering of these pieces as Æthelstan codes.

316   See further chapter 5, pp. 322–3, 371–2.

317   The transfer of *Geþyn.* away from the rest of its group (except in R) could also have arisen from the reflection that it does not *read* like royal legislation.

318   T also inserted the rubrics for Alfred's own laws before his code proper, leaving only those for the Mosaic preface at the head of the *domboc* as a whole.

in a single indigestible list like Dm's. The rubrics of I–II Cnut show signs of revision between London, R, Dm, T and MHk versions, and in that order.[319] It therefore seems that the London Collection, though preserved by the latest copies, drew on the author's earliest efforts; while MHk looks very like the nearest that surviving manuscripts offer to a final version, though M is the second oldest manuscript.

On top of that, Q changed his translations in successive versions. There are definite improvements in style and rendering of Old English technicalities. Dm, as has been seen, shows these amendments in the process of gestation. The results are as often as not incorporated in T and MHk.[320] But this sort of correction is less likely to occur in R, and less likely still in 'London'. There is thus reason to think that the order in which surviving recensions left the author's pen was (i) London, (ii) R, (iii) Dm, (iv) T, (v) MHk. Actually, things are not quite so straightforward (they seldom are with *Quadripartitus*). The author was given to second thoughts in his choice of the *mot* (or *phrase*) *juste*, nor did revision follow a consistent direction. This makes it difficult to imagine that each extant version is a fully worked-out edition. They look more like drafts: as if behind each extant copy lies a source resembling Dm, from which scribes made their own choice of amendments.[321] MHk may, however, be regarded as a considered edition: it alone is preserved in two manuscripts.[322] Overall, the evolutionary pattern remains recognizable enough: from London through R, Dm and T, to MHk.

The third conclusion to be drawn from *Quadripartitus* redeployments is that among the impulses encouraging revision was probably the discovery of new sources. There is no reason why *Blas.* and *Forf.* should have been moved from their erstwhile place after Alfred–Ine unless this was prompted by a manuscript which, unlike Corpus 383 or *Textus Roffensis*, did not put them there. How could Alfred–Ine rubrics appear in Dm, having apparently been unavailable at the 'London' stage, unless another manuscript had meanwhile brought the original Anglo-Saxon list to light? Half a dozen of the textual changes made as the collection evolved have an alternative manuscript reading as a likely explanation.[323] It is also likely that some codes that feature only in later recensions, notably those of Edgar, were unearthed in the course of further research on the author's part.

More will be said about *Quadripartitus* ends and means in the next two chapters (pp. 411–13, 465–73). It will emerge that the nature of the whole exercise changed more radically than is yet evident. The effort to amass texts developed into an ambitious if not wholly successful attempt to realize the 'Law of King Edward' as current practice. The question that remains for now is whether, given so much revision from one extant version to the next, they *can* all

---

319   Details in my '"*Quadripartitus*"', pp. 125–7 (pp. 94–6).
320   Details (plus further table) in '"*Quadripartitus*"', pp. 127–31 (pp. 96–100).
321   This was Liebermann's suggestion, *Quadripartitus*, pp. 64–5, and one that makes better sense of the evidence than in some of the other contexts where he also proposed it; for details of the verbal variations, see '"*Quadripartitus*"', pp. 131–2 (pp. 99–100).
322   It was also incorporated (arranged chronologically and with omissions) in the fourteenth-century chronicle once ascribed to John Brompton: Gransden, *Historical Writing* II, pp. 56–7, 359 (n. 103).
323   Examples in '"*Quadripartitus*"', p. 132 (pp. 100–1), n. 57.

be ascribed to a single author. The answer seems to be yes. Dm provides the proof. It alone preserves the eccentric and barely intelligible 'Dedicatio', which was perhaps out-of-date by the time the author's work was complete, and which no one but an author would have been likely to keep in a revised text. At the same time, a high proportion of the rubrics introduced at the (late) MHk stage are foreshadowed in Dm's margins.[324] Textual changes tend to exploit the same fairly distinctive vocabulary throughout. The only kind of different author credible in these circumstances would be so close a disciple of the first as to make little difference to the argument.

Discussion of Q's date and circumstances is another thing better left till attention is given to the rest of his work and its context. All that needs saying now is that there is a very marked change of tone between the bizarre 'Dedicatio', which is generally pessimistic and also hints at the notorious excesses of Rufus' court, and the exuberance of the 'Argumentum', or second preface, over what Henry I was offering. The project may therefore have got under way before 1100. There is certainly little to uphold a completion date as late as Liebermann's 1114: the only recognizable 'recent event' referred to is Henry's 1106 conquest of Normandy, and the latest texts in Part II are dated 1108.[325] But Liebermann was probably right that Q was from the West Saxon rather than Mercian or Danelaw 'legal province', perhaps more specifically from Hampshire.[326] Whatever its background, it is already clear why *Quadripartitus* would be the most important of the contributions made at this time to the perpetuation of the early English legal heritage. A serious attempt to transmit pre-conquest texts in a language which all who mattered might understand, it stood the best chance of being the collection that lasted. Last it did. Unlike any other 'manuscript' surveyed in this section, it was recopied: it met a demand. While vernacular manuscripts languished unread or worse over the centuries to come, *Quadripartitus* was consulted, by 'Bracton' and Fortescue among others. It is more than symbolically significant that one of the surviving copies belonged to Sir Edward Coke (chapter 1, p. 7).

(iv) Textus Roffensis

Textus Roffensis has nearly always been the most famous early English legal manuscript.[327] The fullest set of texts apart from *Quadripartitus*, it retained their original vernacular form as *Quadripartitus* did not, and it handled them less hamfistedly than Corpus 383, otherwise its nearest equivalent. It also included a

---

324   See '"*Quadripartitus*"', pp. 127 (97), n. 46, 134–5 (102).
325   Sharpe, 'Prefaces', pp. 150–1, 'Dedicatio' 10–27, 35, pp. 153–61, 'Argumentum' 16–28, pp. 165–8, Preface to 'Book II', pp. 169–72.
326   '"*Quadripartitus*"', p. 140 (p. 107), and n. 78.
327   Liebermann devotes four times as many lines to it (under the *siglum* 'H') than his next longest entry (for Lambarde) in his 'Verzeichnis', *Gesetze* I, pp. xxvi–xxviii; he also provided a full account in his 'Notes', a paper supplemented by A. A. Arnold. Both parts of the book were edited in facsimile by Sawyer, *Textus Roffensis*. There is also a detailed study by Richards, *Texts and their Traditions*, pp. 43–60. It is no. 373 in Ker, *Catalogue*.

larger body of works composed in Latin than *Quadripartitus*, among them an interesting series of ordeal rituals and a short selection of current canon law. For legal historians, its chief importance has been that it alone preserves the codes of the seventh-century Kentish kings. But it matters crucially for the study of Anglo-Saxon charters too, because the second part of the manuscript is a cartulary containing three dozen pre-conquest documents.[328]

The contents of this magnificent collection's first part are set out in table 4.8. The numbers to the left give the order of quires as the manuscript now stands; those in brackets will be explained in a moment. It can be seen that a hundred folios of broadly legal material, in which (except in quire 6), Old English and Latin are kept separate, are followed by two quires containing lists of Anglo-Saxon kings recorded genealogically, of popes, emperors and patriarchs, and of English bishops. The cartulary then begins on f. 119, and effectively concludes with a catalogue of the cathedral library on ff. 224–30; here too, pre-conquest texts, ordered chronologically, are kept distinct from the more haphazardly arranged post-1066 records that follow. By comparison with many manuscripts reviewed in this chapter, some aspects of *Textus Roffensis* are straightforward. All is the work of a single scribe, except for a few insertions in Part I and rather more in Part II.[329] He can be identified (though not named) as one of the main contributors to the build-up of Rochester's library in the early-twelfth century.[330] The manuscript's list of bishops was copied from a Canterbury exemplar that cannot be earlier than 20 October 1122 (below, pp. 249, 252). A colophon on the first folio says that it was made 'per' Bishop Ernulf, who died in 1124. If this is to be trusted (and, though the colophon is actually in an early-fourteenth hand, there is reason to do so), the book can be tied down to the single year, 1123–4. The colophon implies that the two parts were bound as one by the time it was written, since Rochester colophons were regularly entered on opening pages, and there is none at the start of Part II. The similarity of layout and ornamentation throughout both parts suggests that they were indeed conceived as a unity.

That said, the problems begin. The first concerns the book's overall structure. Each part has a series of quire signatures. Those in Part I have mostly been shorn off. But 'ii' is clearly legible on f. 73v, as is 'ix' on f. 47v. Almost as evident are 'i' and 'iii' on ff. 65v, 87v, also 'viii' on f. 95v where one would expect 'iiii' given f. 87v's 'iii'. Current quire 10 thus seems to have strayed into the part of the manuscript designated for Latin laws, and ought to precede current quire 5. But if quires 10 and 5 are 'signatured 'viii' and 'ix', there ought to be seven preceding quires, not the current four; it follows that when the quires were signatured, the Latin texts in quires 7–9 came first. On the other hand, the initial lettering for the Kentish laws on quire 1 is fairly spectacular (as is that at the outset of Alfred's law-book on f. 11) whereas f. 58r makes a poorish show as the opening page of so singular a book. It is true that *Instituta Cnuti* is headed 'Instituta de legibus regum Anglorum', as if more than Cnut's laws were involved, and what seems to

---

328   *Roch. Ch.* pp. xiii–xiv; Keynes, *Diplomas*, p. 10. Parallel discussion of the post-conquest records (study of which, however, has scarcely got under way): Brett, 'Forgery at Rochester'.
329   *Textus Roffensis*, ed. Sawyer, I, pp. 13–14, 16–18 (nos. 27, 41ab, 42, 45–6); II, pp. 14–15.
330   Ker, *English Manuscripts after the Norman Conquest*, p. 31.

Table 4.8   Contents of *Textus Roffensis*, Pt. I

1	(4)	Laws of Kentish kings, ff. 1r–6v (ln 23) Had., ff. 7r–7v (ln 10) West Saxon genealogical regnal list, ff. 7v (ln 12)–8v (ln 27) – f. 8r is 25 lines
2	(5)	Af-Ine, ff. 9r (ln 6)–18v – ff. 12–13 are inserted leaves; ff. 11/16 *may be* a replacement sheet
3	(6)	Af-Ine (cont.), ff. 19r–26v
4	(7)	Af-Ine (cont.), ff. 27r–31v (ln 20) Blas., Forf. 1, ff. 31v (ln 21)–32r (ln 8) Ord., ff. 32r (ln 10)–32v (ln 21) Wal., f. 32v (lns 22–4) II As, ff. 33r–37r (ln 6) V As, ff. 37r (ln 7)–38r (ln 5) IV As frag., f. 38r (lns 5–18) Pax, f. 38r (lns 20–4) Swer., ff. 38v–39v (ln 4) Að, f. 39v (lns 5–13) Mirc., f. 39v (lns 14–22) – f. 32 is an inserted leaf
5	(9)	EGu, ff. 40r–41v (ln 19) Wer., ff. 41v (ln 19)–42r (ln 21) I–II Ew, ff. 42r (ln 22)–44r (ln 22) I–II Em, ff. 44r (ln 22)–46r (ln 11) I Atr, ff 46r (ln 11)–47r (ln 23) Wl lad, ff. 47r (ln 23)–47v (ln 26) – Quire-signature 'ix' at foot of f. 47v
6	(10)	III Atr, ff. 48r–49v (ln 18) *Iudicia Dei* I–III, ff. 49v (ln 19)–57r (ln 21) Frag. record of *Cnut's grant of Sandwich* to Christ Church Canterbury, f. 57v (lns 2–12)
7	(1)	*Inst Cn*, ff. 58r–65v – Probable quire-signature 'i' at foot of f. 65v
8	(2)	*Inst Cn* (cont.), ff. 66r–73v – Quire-signature 'ii' at foot of f. 73v
9	(3)	*Inst Cn* (cont.), ff. 74r–80r (ln 19) *Wl Art.*, ff. 80r (ln 19)–81v (ln 14) *Exc. ex decr. pont.*, ff. 81v (ln 22)–87r (ln 19) – f. 85 is an inserted, and f. 87 an added, leaf – Probable quire-signature 'iii' at foot of f. 87v

Table 4.8   *(Continued)*

10	(8)	VI As, ff. 88r–93r (ln 16)
		Geþyn., ff. 93r (ln 16)–93v (ln 23)
		Norðl., ff. 93v (ln 23)–94r
		Wif., ff. 94v–95r (ln 9)
		Charm for recovery of cattle, f. 95r (lns 10–23)
		Hit becwæð., f. 95r (ln 23)–95v (ln 18)
		– Quire-signature 'viii' (probably rather than 'iiii') at foot of f. 95v
11	(11)	*CHn cor*, ff. 96r–97v (ln 25)
		Excom VIII, ff. 98r–99v (ln 15)
		Excom IX, ff. 99v (ln 16)–100r (ln 2)
		– Last three (?blank) leaves of quire excised
12	(12)	Anglo-Saxon royal genealogies, ff. 101r–104r
		Lists of popes, emperors, patriarchs, ff. 105r–108v
		– f. 106 is a replacement leaf of *c.* 1200
13	(13)	Lists of patriarchs (cont.), ff. 109r–110r
		Lists of Anglo-Saxon bishops, ff. 110v–116r
		Supplementary info. (e.g. liturgical innovations by popes), ff. 116v–117r

Note: Pieces in Latin are italicized

be this manuscript is labelled 'Institutiones Regum Anglorum' in Part II's library list. But the 'H' beginning *Instituta Cnuti* is a modest creation beside the superb historiated 'R' inaugurating the cartulary on f. 119. It does, then, look as though the Old English parts of the collection were originally envisaged as the first, even if the order was changed before the quires were signed.[331]

Another intriguing message from table 4.8 is that most quires are self-contained. Except where outsize pieces like the Alfred–Ine law-book or *Instituta Cnuti* demand more than one, each quire starts with a fresh text and ends with a completed item. Special efforts were made to achieve this. The last two pages of the West Saxon genealogical regnal list (ff.8rv) are of twenty-five and twenty-seven lines, and the script is noticeably sqeezed up. The last page of Wl lad (f. 47v) is another with twenty-five lines. In quires 4, 6 and 9, more leaves than the usual eight were furnished from the outset; and when it nevertheless looked as if the allotted space would not accommodate the intended content, extra leaves were supplied (ff. 12–13 in quire 2, f. 32 in quire 4, ff. 85, 87 in quire 9). An expedient with special significance for understanding the manuscript was the apparent use of shorter texts as 'space-fillers'. *Hadbot*, listing compensations for ranks of clergy, looks in place after Wihtræd's code, which covers the same ground (ff. 7rv). *Að* ('oath') is likewise a suitable follow-up to *Swerian* ('to swear') (ff. 38v – 39v). But its sequel, *Mircna Laga*, serves only to round off the

---

331   For this point and most of those that follow, see another of this chapter's 'companion pieces', my *'Laga Eadwardi'*.

quire.[332] The one-clause statements, *Walreaf* and *Pax*, occupy the last lines of ff. 32v and 38r. The *Roffensis* scribe seems carefully to have reordered his material, sometimes with the intention of bringing related items together, but also in order to preserve a 'quire integrity' that would facilitate access to the major codes.[333]

The importance of this space-filling technique is that it becomes possible to guess that redeployment has concealed the extent to which *Roffensis* incorporated some of the same mini-collections as formed the building-blocks of Corpus 383 and *Quadripartitus*. The contents of all three are tabulated for ease of reference (table 4.9). The obvious case is again the Edward-Edmund group. There must, as already argued, be a high probability that a group of texts consisting not only of the paired royal codes and of the same 'unofficial' statements but also of a cattle charm was available in roughly the same form to each of the three compilers. The next chapter will find a series of shared textual idiosyncrasies and few significant discrepancies (chapter 5, pp. 286–7, 308–9, 384, 385–6). Problems remain. *Wergeld* has become inextricably attached to Edward/ Guthrum in *Roffensis*, an unusual case of this manuscript reproducing its exemplar as automatically as Corpus often did. Alfred-Guthrum is not in *Roffensis*, though the opening of 'Edward-Guthrum' ('And this too is the decree that King Alfred and King Guthrum …') shows that it must have been somewhere in the background (cf. chapter 5, p . 390). I Æthelred is textually consistent throughout the three collections, but there is no sign in either of the other two of the intimate association that it has with *Hundred* in Corpus 383. Groups like this were apparently transmitted in such a way (loose leaves in a folder?) that they could be reshuffled as they passed from one handler to the next.

This being the position for the Edward-Edmund group, despite the fact that its content is distributed between two *Roffensis* quires, one may legitimately harbour the suspicion that other likely groupings have been broken up. The *Geþyncðu – Norðleoda Laga* series was previously encountered in Corpus 201 (p. 208). In *Quadripartitus*, it has got entwined (along with Wulfstan's *Episcopus*) in the sequence of Æthelstan codes, which in this collection, as will be seen (chapter 5, pp. 294–300) have a marked taste of Canterbury. Rochester's Æthelstan material is quite different: V Æthelstan supplements II, and 'IV' is appended as its continuation, geared for a bishop's rather than archbishop's use. *Roffensis* may thus have drawn on an episcopal library (presumably its own) for what it had of Æthelstan, while taking the 'Wulfstan group' from elsewhere. Similar possibilities are raised by *Pax* and *Walreaf*. In *Quadripartitus*, they and the set of London observances known as 'IV Æthelred' were treated as extensions of III Æthelred. Chapter 5 will again find reasons to think that *Pax* and *Walreaf* would have been appropriate companion pieces for III Æthelred, and that the latter's *Roffensis* text is linked with 'IV Æthelred' (pp. 322–3, 371–2).[334]

---

332   The conjunction could possibly have been in some way influenced by the fact that *Að* is entitled 'Be Mirciscan Aðe/Mercena Lage' in MSS CCCC 201, 190 (above, pp. 208, 223). But *Roffensis* makes this a text about oaths exclusively (reversing the order of the two clauses), and has no reference to Mercians of any sort.

333   Further details in my '*Laga Eadwardi*', pp. 248–50 (pp. 120–1).

334   See also further discussion in my '*Laga Eadwardi*', pp. 253–6, 259–60 (pp. 122–6, 129–30).

Rochester's codex, then, seems to have been constructed from a mixture of its own resources and material shared with *Quadripartitus* and Corpus 383. Special interest attaches to its treatment of Alfred–Ine. But before this is tackled, something must be said of another of its features, the corrections. Unlike the scribe of Corpus 383, this one adapted his spelling to the demands of twelfth-century phonology. But amendments of this type cease altogether from about f. 38, just the point when its old-fashioned letter-forms also disappear. The likeliest reason for this change is that after f. 38 the scribe updated his orthography and script as he went along, instead of leaving the job for the reading-over stage.[335] The Rochester scribe also made more changes than his Corpus counterpart to the very sense of his material, altering words and adding phrases. These amendments, *not* his original readings, bring his Alfred–Ine text into line with that of Corpus. Much the most important is the presence of *Be Blaserum* and *Forfang* 1 as sequels to Alfred's *domboc*. This is what convinced Liebermann that Corpus, *Quadripartitus* and *Roffensis* had a common source, 'hbq'. Yet it is possible to see even in the *Roffensis* facsimile that the ink of these pieces is darker and the lettering larger than in the immediately preceding text of Ine (f. 31v), or in that of II Æthelstan a folio beyond (f. 33r). Furthermore, the leaf on which they continue is one of the inserts (f. 32), and almost wholly devoid of the orthographical corrections that still occur in this bit of the manuscript, *except* on the certainly or probably inserted sheets (ff. 12–13, 11/16). As a last point, the relevant chapter in the rubric list ('CXXI', f. 11r) has detectably been written after and over the 'D' introducing Alfred. There is every sign, then, that these tracts were *subsequently* added by the scribe, and were not in the exemplar that he first transcribed. It is its corrected, not its primary, version of Alfred-Ine that *Roffensis* shares with Corpus and *Quadripartitus*. On the other hand, readings shared with *Quadripartitus* alone (or sometimes with Lawrence Nowell's lost codex, below, p. 262) are quite possibly part of a more general transmission; some may even be better witnesses to the 'original' than the Parker manuscript.[336]

Given that the corrected *Roffensis* Alfred–Ine is close to that of Corpus, and that the two have a common ancestor for the Edward-Edmund group, it is a logical deduction that the second Alfred–Ine recension reached Rochester from the same source: not St Paul's itself, because there are still too many differences between them for one to have borrowed directly from the other (or *vice versa*); but not improbably whoever supplied St Paul's. Rochester's collector seems to have gone in search of further material in something of the same manner as Q, if not to so far-reaching an effect. Can anything more be said of the repositories he exploited? Here, as with much else in Rochester's early-twelfth-century library, there is a likely debt to Canterbury. The evidence is best for the regnal and episcopal lists. They evidently shared an exemplar with those in the impressive 'wonder book', Cotton Tiberius B.v, known to have been written at Canterbury around the turn of the millennium.[337] This would explain how it is

335   *Textus Roffensis*, ed. Sawyer, pp. 13–14.
336   For other examples, see the discussion and table in my '*Laga Eadwardi*', pp. 256–9 (pp. 126–9), also Af 37:1, 65, 68, etc.
337   Dumville, 'Catalogue Texts', and 'Anglian Collection', pp. 26–8, 43–5.

Table 4.9 *TR* content compared with contemporary collections

TR	Corpus 383	Quadr. (MSS 6)	Quadr. (MS 5)	Other
Abt	Af-Ine	Ine	I-II Cn	
Hl	Blas.	Blas.	Af-Ine	
Wi	Forf. 1–3:2	Forf. 1–3:2	I-II As	Corpus 201
Had.	Hu	Hu	Episc.	Geþyn
Geneal. list	I Atr	Af	Norðl.	Norðl.
Af-Ine	AGu (2)	AGu	Mirc.	Mirc.
Blas.	EGu	App. AGu	Að	Að
Forf. 1	II As …	EGu	Had.	Had.
Ord.		I-II As	Blas.	(cf. Corpus 190)
Wal.	… I-II Cn	Episc.	Forf. 1–3:2	Mirc.
II As	I-II Ew	Norðl.	Hu.	Að
V As	I-II Em	Mirc.	III-VI As	Had.
IV As fr.	Swer.	Að	Ord.	
Pax	AGu	Had.	AGu	
Swer.	Wif.	III-VI As	App. AGu	
Að	Wer.	Ord.	EGu	
Mirc.	Charm	I-II Cn	I-II Ew	
VI As	Becw.		I-II Em	
Geþyn.	II Atr		Swer.	
Norðl.	Duns.		Wif.	
Wif.	Rect.		Wer.	
Charm	Ger.		I/III Atr	
Becw.	[St Paul's shipmen list; genealogical list]		Pax	
EGu			Wal.	
Wer.			IV Atr	
I-II Ew			II Atr	
I-II Em			Duns.	

		Rawlinson C 641
I Atr	VII Atr	Inst Cn
Wl lad	Iudex	CHn cor
III Atr	II–III Eg	Wl Art.
Iud. Dei	III Em	
[Cnut writ]	Wl lad	
Inst Cn	[Wl Art.]	
Wl Art.	Gebyn.	
Exc. Decr. Pont.	Rect.	
CHn cor	CHn cor	
Excom.	Hn com	
	[Inst Cn]	

Note: [ ] denotes inserted text.

that the scribe could bring the list of Canterbury archbishops right up-to-date with Archbishop Ralph's death on 20 October 1122, but dried up on his Rochester bishops in the 1050s and on other sees as far back as *c.* 1000. Canterbury is also as likely a source as any (though no more so) for the Edward-Edmund group, and for the *Roffensis* ordeal rituals.[338] But it has already been seen that a Canterbury source is almost ruled out for its texts of Æthelstan. For one set of texts, *Instituta Cnuti* and its sequels, a local origin is virtually certain. *Roffensis* is here closely related to Bodleian Rawlinson C 641, and among things on which they agree is that Bishop Gundulf of Rochester was a witness of Henry I's 1100 Charter. On the evidence of its many other copies, he was not. Liebermann guessed that Gundulf was a mistaken expansion of 'G', which in fact stood for Bishop Gerard of Hereford. The error would be natural at Rochester but hardly elsewhere. Rochester itself is also just as likely a source as Canterbury for the most celebrated *Roffensis* ingredient, its early Kentish codes. That Æthelberht should be quoted as offering protection to a *bishop's* property (chapter 2, pp. 97–8), with no mention of the archiepiscopal status consistently claimed by Canterbury after 679, would be less surprising in a Rochester book.[339] For the rest, the possibilities are wide. The essential point is that no more than Q was the Rochester compiler content to reproduce what appeared on his desk. His collection is researched as carefully as it is structured. Like *Quadripartitus*, it is not merely a collection but also an edition.

Further enlightenment on the nature and purpose of this edition, as of the other, must await chapter 6's account of the early-twelfth-century *Zeitgeist*. For now, it leaves a curiously mixed impression. It has rightly been called a work of scholarship.[340] If forensic uses could still be found for any vernacular collection in the 1120s, *Textus Roffensis* could have been used. A more imposing combination of laws and charters than any considered so far, it would have made an impressive weapon for a churchman seeking to defend the position of his English foundation against prowling Norman predators. It is certainly a 'bishop's book', and Ernulf's successor was among those present at the great Sandwich plea of 1127: a point that puts the incorporation into the manuscript of Cnut's Sandwich writ (f. 57v) in an interesting light. On the other hand, the book came to be called a 'Textus', like a copy of the Gospels, and apparently to be kept in the Church rather than the library. Part II's long register of often modest donations by no less modest local donors may have been made with a view to their liturgical commemoration. The royal sponsors of its charters and makers of its laws could be prayed for as guardians of the church's peace and prosperity, along with the rulers of Church and State in Christendom at large who made up the lists at the end of Part I. It may say something that though this volume is smaller (225–30 × 150–5 mm, admittedly after shearing) than any pre-conquest law-book except Nero A.i, it is bigger than any surviving collection of Anglo-Saxon law from after 1066, bar *Quadripartitus'* intentionally calligraphic R and Horn's presentation

338 Note Professor Dumville's views on the provenance of MSS listed in Liebermann's summary (*Gesetze* I, p. 401, *b*), *Liturgy*, pp. 66–95.
339 Cf. Wormald, '*Laga Eadwardi*', pp. 259–62 (pp. 129–32).
340 Southern, 'European Tradition of Historical Writing: 4', p. 253.

copies of the London collection (6b, 6d; it is much the same size as the earlier 'fair copy', 6a). If not Law as Holy Writ, like some Wulfstan books, it has its own solemnity. It is not, then, merely its measureless importance to the historian of early English law that gives the book something of a monumental air. More than any other legal manuscript, it was both memorial to the past and instrument of its adaptation in a new world.

7 Law as pamphlet? BL, Harley MS 55(B)

Not least among the surprises awaiting the student of early English law-books is that the manuscript which behaves most like a book of law might be expected to behave ends by posing the biggest mystery of all. The second part of Harley 55 is a straightforward copy of Cnut's code. Its text has lapses but no real anomalies. It is uncluttered by the company of seemingly irrelevant material. Its format made it easy to handle or indeed use. Yet its date is 's xii^med': up to a century after vernacular texts of Anglo-Saxon law should have been devalued by the demise of an English-speaking Establishment. Only when it is hard to see how it can have been of much use does an English legal manuscript survive in easily usable form.[341]

The first thing to be said about this manuscript is to reiterate that, though it is now bound up with another set of legally orientated pages, this is not likely to have been before Selden's time (above, pp. 185–6). The two layouts contrast in almost all imaginable ways. The Edgar code in part 'A' is sandwiched between a medical text and a statement of York property claims; Cnut stands on its own in part 'B'. 'B' is some two centimetres shorter and a bit narrower than part 'A'. Edgar's laws are in long lines on quite high-quality parchment, Cnut's in two columns on pages at once thick, crinkling and yellowish. On the other hand, Cnut's opening clause and initials are in red ink, where Edgar is solidly mono-chrome. It was suggested above that 'A' may consist of pages from a high-status and perhaps liturgical book. 'B' leaves no such impression. Nor does their sixteenth-century history suggest that they had been together long before their first recorded association in a letter to Selden. 'B' was transcribed by Nowell so used by Lambarde (below, p. 261). The special 'A' Edgar readings leave no trace in *Archaionomia*. Each part was used to supply *lacunae* in Corpus 383, but the transcripts were probably made at different times (above, pp. 229–30). Edgar's code has been divided into chapters by inserting square brackets and Arabic numerals. Something similar is done to Cnut's, partly it seems by Parker's circle, but much less consistently.[342] When glossing Nero A.i(A), Joscelyn had constant recourse to the Harley 'A' copy of Edgar, but was usually satisfied with Lambarde

341 Liebermann uses the *siglum* 'A' for the MS, as for its first part (see next n.); it is no. 226 in Ker's *Catalogue*, which provides the date quoted above.
342 '2' is changed to 3' in black ink (with L-shaped bracket) at I Cn 2:1; '3' with bracket is in black ink within I 3:2, at 'And þonne gyt læssan'; '10' in Parker's own red crayon at I 6:1, and '18' with red under-lining at I 16; then '19', '21', '22' in black ink with brackets or underlining at I 17, 18, 18:1; the only other numeral is '23' in a quite different hand opposite I 19:1, with a bracket scrawled across 'fadige'. The Edgar chapter numbers substituted for Lambarde's in the Joscelyn/(John) Parker copy of *Archaionomia* now in

readings for Cnut.[343] The first indisputable evidence of an 'A' and 'B' union is the titles each received in a hand of 's xvi^ex'.

It was presumably at this stage that both parts of the manuscript received their very singular ink foliation. On the second (recto) page of the Edgar code appears the number '2'. It is actually the fourth folio of the manuscript, counting from the start of its medical text; nor is it anywhere foreshadowed by a '1'. The first folio of Cnut's code is numbered '3' and is indeed the next, the sequence then running on to the last, numbered '11'. Someone apparently decided to number only those pages of the manuscript as a whole that contained lawcodes.[344] The pages of 'A' are actually loose leaves that must have been cut from some other book. 'B' by contrast is a self-contained quire.[345] It too could have been taken from another manuscript, but the last page is no more battered than the first (which has been torn and resewn, cf. p. 186). All pages look 'well-thumbed' (chapter 2, p. 58). In any event, 'B' had the potential to serve as a pamphlet in its own right. Of no other copy of an Anglo-Saxon law-code can this so confidently be said.

The text is arranged in two columns, like the earliest and most workmanlike of *Quadripartitus* copies (Dm.) and calligraphic specimens of the later-twelfth and early-fourteenth centuries (R., K2). Like the Corpus 383 version of Cnut's code, it is effectively in continuous prose. Fairly ornate red initials mark the opening of the preface and I Cnut as such. There are enlarged but undecorated initials at the outset of II Cnut, at clause 12 (as in the Corpus copy and some of *Quadripartitus*), and at clause 84.[346] Otherwise, clauses are mostly marked by no more than a splash of red highlighting.[347] The sole concession to the sort of sub-division carried out in Nero A.i(A) is intrusion of an inverted 'L' at some points of perhaps special significance.[348] Whether or not Harley 55(B) was a working text, no one can have been under any illusion that it was a presentation copy.

The text copied is essentially that of the twelfth-century 'vulgate' of Cnut's code (see chapter 5, pp. 350–1). Shared with the version known as the *Consiliatio Cnuti* is an extra prologue, making a doubtful claim (for the code's 1020/1 date) to Cnut's rule of Norway; this could conceivably be an 'official' later addition (chapter 5, pp. 348, 351).[349] Other links with *Quadripartitus* and *Instituta* or

---

Japan (Bately, 'John Joscelyn', pp. 442, 448–9) do correspond to those in Harley 55(A), so raising the possibility that the Parker circle was ultimately responsible for these too, but this must have been on a different occasion from their sporadic entries in 'B'.

343 *Wulfstan Manuscript*, ed. Loyn, pp. 37–8; Bately, 'John Joscelyn', p. 441 (and n. 43). However, 'A' needed to be cited for Edgar, as it did not contribute to Lambarde, whereas Lambarde's text of Cnut was already based indirectly on that of 'B' (below, p. 261).

344 These page-numbers are fairly clearly *not* the same as the chapter numbers entered in the margins of either Edgar or Cnut.

345 Or was once: the last leaf has been cut away, presumably because blank (like the column and a quarter when the text finished).

346 But not at II Cn 69, as with Corpus and *Quadripartitus* versions; see chapter 5, pp. 351–2, 361 for the possible significance of these divisions.

347 These again by no means coincide with Liebermann's main numerals (cf. n. 261); they are (e.g.) at: I 2:1, 2:3–5, 7:1 (also at 'ne on ælæten'), 7:2–3, 17:1–2 (also at 'And sancte'), but not at I 2, 7, 17.

348 I Cn 5, II 8, 12, 20. In addition, there is an exceptionally large initial with no bracket at II 6, 20:1.

349 The Corpus lacuna (above, p. 230) prevents one knowing whether it appeared there; it is not in *Instituta* or *Quadripartitus*.

Consiliatio Cnuti are seemingly random (chapter 5, pp. 349–51). Nor are there are any spectacular divergences. The Harley scribe's sins are not mortal. Lines are thrice omitted by scribal oversight.[350] Language is distorted by little more than the usual twelfth-century modernisms. There are cases of a 'ge-' prefix divorced from its parent word, such as to imply that the scribe was unsure what he was copying.[351] But other mistakes, while betraying a superficial reading of the exemplar – as when '*deore* (dearly)' emerges as '*deope* (deeply)', or '*freme* (repute)' as '*feorme* (sustenance)' – at least make sense; they are the sort born of over-familiarity with a language where Corpus blunders bespeak ignorance.[352] Harley scarcely ranks as a work of scholarly reconstruction like *Quadripartitus* or *Textus Roffensis*, but nor does it convey an impression of overstretched capacity. It is, as usual, ordinary.

Perhaps the best comment on the Harley manuscript is that there is ultimately so little to say about it. It poses few of the problems of the others. More than any extant manuscript from the Anglo-Saxon period, it *looks like* a book of law. If not pocket-sized, it would be convenient to carry. On the other hand, little can be said about the central problem that it does pose: it is from long after the Anglo-Saxon period. It leaves few clues to the motives or milieu of those responsible for it. It has no assigned provenance. One might suspect a link with the religious houses still producing vernacular books in the twelfth century, like Worcester or Rochester. But there is nothing to harden suspicion even as far as hypothesis. All that can be done is to face up to the evidence as it stands. If vernacular copies of Cnut's code were being made without any apparent frills or strain in the mid-twelfth century, then the day when Anglo-Saxon law was of exclusively antiquarian concern had not yet dawned.

8 Fragmentary or Lost Manuscripts

The last grouping of early English legal manuscripts comprises those that have little to teach about the context of legislative texts. That context has been subverted by the depredations of time. Two of the manuscripts in this group are extant as fragments. One was totally destroyed in the Cottonian fire, and has to be recreated (to the limited extent possible) from its description by Wanley. All that survives of the others is their ghosts, in the form of transcripts made in the mid-sixteenth or early-nineteenth century. The strange thing is that the patterns created by these sherds and shadows tend to repeat those detectable in more fully

---

350   I Cn 14:1, II 3, 26:1; these could of course be the fault of an exemplar, but it may be significant that the first occurs at a transition between columns, f. 6v.

351   E.g. f. 13r (col. 1, ln 9), II 76:1b 'ge-laðyan' – apparently a non-existent word in any case. However 'scepige' for 'sceawige', II 25, recurs (by a striking coincidence) in the Harley(A) text of III Eg 7 in exactly the same context, so that this misrepresentation of OE 'wynn' evidently did not result in nonsense (see Liebermann's suggestion, Gesetze II, p. 189), and may be from a distant exemplar.

352   II Cn 2:1, 16 (the first of these had happened in *Quadripartitus'* exemplar too). Similarly, 'borh' is misread as 'burg', II 58:2, though the scribe got it right in the two previous clauses. But Liebermann's reading of f. 13v (col. 1, ln 14), II Cn 84:4 'ealswa', does the scribe an injustice: 'ealra' is detectable as a correction under ultra-violet light.

preserved books. Recurrent patterns, as has been said before, have a way of underlining their own logic.

(i) Vatican, Codex Reginensis latina 946, f. 75v

The older of the two surviving fragments consists of a single (verso) page amongst a set of leaves bound in with a French historical miscellany of the early-fourteenth century, itself an item in the library that Queen Christina of Sweden bequeathed to the Pope.[353] The leaves have no noticeable or likely connection with the rest: the queen's binders could take the same liberties in organizing her collection as their English counterparts. These pages are larger than those of any other early legal manuscript except Nero E.i; which, it will be recalled (pp. 182–4), juxta-posed legal and liturgical texts, and had probably been bound into a sumptuous Bible. Size and quality of parchment alike suggest that they were end- or front-leaves from a 'de luxe service book' (cf. pp. 187–8). Added to them in the twelfth century was a record of the forms of obedience owed to the bishop of Avranches by the monasteries in his diocese, and by Avranches to Rouen. This would thus seem to have been an English Gospel-book, Psalter or Pontifical that was removed to Avranches on the morrow of the Conquest.

The inter-relationship of the 'Avranches leaves' is far from straightforward. The first and last as they stand (ff. 72, 76) are a bifolium, of which f. 72r and all of f. 76 are blank. The other three are half-sheets, with the Avranches entries on ff. 72v, 73rv and 74rv, and the Anglo-Saxon law on f. 75v.[354] Folio 75 has been badly damaged by damp and tearing down its outer margin, so must have been exposed to the elements as the others were not. Even with so much un-certain, one may hazard a guess at what has happened. In a hypothetical eight-leaf quire 'A' to 'H', the Anglo-Saxon law-code could have been entered on the inner bifolium ('D'v – 'E'r), and on ensuing pages at least as far as the penultimate recto ('G'r). When Avranches scribes added their customs on ff. 'A'v, 'B'rv and 'C'rv (current ff. 72v – 74v), they tore out three of the pages con-taminated by writing in an unknown tongue ('E', 'F' and 'G'), making 'B', 'C' and 'D' (ff. 73–5) into half-sheets but leaving the 'A'-'H' bifolium intact. 'D' was left in place with Old English on its verso, because its recto might have come in useful for continuations of the Avranches material (this was indeed expanded by later hands on ff. 73rv, 74r); it was subsequently seen to be surplus and moved out of the bifolium's protecting embrace to a place in the parent book where it was more easily harmed. It would follow from this hypothesis that the law-code beginning on f. 75v extended over more than four further pages (ff. 'E'rv, 'F'rv, and at least part of 'G'r), and may have gone on for up to six (covering all of 'G'rv).

---

353   The fragment is given the *siglum Vr* by Liebermann (*Gesetze* I, p. xlii), and is no. 392 in Ker, *Catalogue* (whence the opinions quoted on the original character of the volume and date of the script). I am grateful to Donald Bullough for advice on this manuscript.
354   More could doubtless be said about this situation if the Avranches material were properly edited, but it apparently remains unpublished.

The code thus preserved was Liebermann's discovery and he printed it as 'X Æthelred'. The script is dated 's. xi¹', so not a lot later than the presumable date of the law. The text itself consists of an elaborate prologue and three clauses in Wulfstan's style, introducing a decree 'that we wish to hold, just as we firmly declared at Enham'.[355] It will be suggested in chapter 5 (pp. 336–7) that it is another, conceivably the 'official', version of the code issued there in 1008 (above, pp. 191, 199). What may be noted here is that if 'X Æthelred' *were* a code of approximately the same length as 'V', it would have taken 90–100 more lines.[356] Intriguingly, the hypothesis on the fragment's background sketched above would require that the missing text occupy from eighty-one to 120 lines. However any of this may be, the Vatican fragment's importance is that it preserves Wulfstanian legislation in a manuscript not known to have been connected with him, and which seems to give law the same solemn setting as some of those discussed earlier.

(ii) BL, Burney MS 277, f. 42

The other fragment was from a much less grand book, and has been a lot more battered by its subsequent history.[357] It is a bifolium, whose leaves of 207 x 130 mm are larger only than those of Nero A.i among pre-1100 law-books, though nearer the average twelfth-century size. It was the central bifolium of a quire, thus preserving four continuous pages of text. Its initials are nothing special: Ine's first law has an enlarged one, in a mixture of red and black; of the rest, one is red and the others black, with two Gs rather perfunctorily ornamented. The first stage of its descent into destitution was that it was used for pen-trials before and during the thirteenth century. Since none are detectably later than this, it was presumably about then that the book was broken up, and the Burney bifolium became a wrapper.[358]

The fragment features part of the Alfred–Ine law-book, from the last few words of Ine's prologue to the end of Ine 23. The dialect involved has been called 'Kentish'. This is interesting even if the categorization is widened to 'south-eastern', in that the text is distinct in a couple of respects from that represented by Corpus 383 and *Textus Roffensis*.[359] As for the fragment's parent manuscript, comparison with *Textus Roffensis*, the only complete copy of Alfred–Ine of anywhere near the same date, suggests that the rest of the quire would not have been nearly enough to accommodate the remainder of the text, which is also most

---

355   X Atr. Pr – Pr.:3.

356   The twelve lines dedicated to V Atr ('G2') 1 – 1:2 in Nero A.i(B) correspond to seven in *Vr*; the rest takes another 161 lines; so in *Vr*, the equivalent number of lines would be 161 x 7/12 = 93.92.

357   It was given the *siglum* Bu. by Liebermann (*Gesetze* I, p. xx), and is no. 136 in Ker, *Catalogue*, where its script is dated 's xi²'.

358   Ker, p. 172, points out that the capital letter 'S' is visible on what became the wrapper's spine; there may also be a 'B'.

359   It lacks the additions to Ine 3:1–2 integral in Corpus and inserted into *TR*; and minor verbal discrepancies in Ine 6:3, 6:5, 8 and 21, along with the archaic dual 'twædne' in clause 23, distinguish it from pre-correction *TR* (though for possible overlaps with *TR*, see *Gesetze* III, p. 31 (8)).

unlikely to have begun at the outset of a quire.[360] If, then, the parent manuscript offered a full version of Alfred–Ine and had an even roughly regular quire structure, this was not a self-contained copy. Its content may have been as heterogeneous as that of many pre-conquest law-books. But it is worth pondering that it is nearest in date, size and general appearance to Nero A.i(A). It might not be too wild a guess that it was the same sort of book, and was perhaps made for the same sort of purpose.

(iii) BL, Cotton MS Otho A.x

The manuscript of an Æthelred code (*inter alia*) that was shelved by Cotton immediately above the Otho assemblage of Laws, Old English Bede and *Chronicle* (pp. 172–81) is more completely a 'closed book' than any other memorial of early English law.[361] It was apparently the last item in a volume containing Æthelweard's *Chronicle* and Paul the Deacon's *Historia Langobardorum*. The 1731 fire left eighteen charred pieces of the first ('s xi in')and one of the second ('s xii')but nothing at all of Æthelred's law. Those who saw it before its destruction imply that it was already a fragment: 'desunt reliqua' says Wanley, and Smith's 'solummodo duas paginas continet' seems to expect more.[362] Other evidence is contradictory: a note in the British Library 'Keeper's copy' of Smith says that it began on 'f. 194b', yet the total number of leaves in the manuscript is said to have been 152.[363] The prologue quoted by Wanley shows that the code was issued at Woodstock, yet the wording is not that of Æthelred's extant Woodstock code (I Æthelred), which is why Liebermann numbered it 'IX'. The style is Wulfstanian, and chapter V suggests (pp. 336–7) that it was probably an otherwise lost Æthelred code echoed in a Wulfstan homily and *perhaps* paralleled by the text known as 'VIII Æthelred'. But reconstructing an unknown text from a fragment in a lost book of which accounts are ambiguous is a matter not so much of doing a post-mortem on an arm and a leg, as of essaying an autopsy on an incubus.

Much the likeliest suggestion is Ker's: 'probably the two leaves in OE had nothing to do with the rest of Otho A x'. This chapter has more than once found Cotton and others adding superficially akin items to manuscripts with which they had no actual kinship (pp. 190–1, 206, 224–6). An Æthelred code might have seemed good company for Æthelweard's *Chronicle*, which was written in his reign.[364] But Cotton would hardly have removed it from a collection of other legal

---

360   The 100 lines of Bu correspond to 88 for the same passage in *TR*, which takes *c.* 256 more lines to the end of Ine's code; to finish the lawbook, Bu. should thus have needed 256 x 100/88 = 290+ lines, or (at 25 lines to the page) 11.75 pages. *TR* devotes 655 lines to the Af–Ine law-book down to where the fragment begins, implying that the latter would have used 655 x 100/88 = 744, or 29.75 pages.

361   As a wholly lost MS, it does not even qualify for a Liebermann *siglum* (cf. *Gesetze* I, p. 269), but it is no. 170 in Ker, *Catalogue*.

362   Smith, *Catalogus*, p. 67; Wanley, *Catalogus*, p. 232: the *explicit* quoted by Wanley, 'Uton ænne cyne Hlaford holdliche ... ' does indeed break off with no main verb.

363   Ker, p. 220; the figure of 152 is given by Wanley's hand in Bodleian, Add. MS D.82 (p. 67), as well as in the BL 'Keeper's Copy'.

texts (cf. pp. 182–4). The report that the code began on 'f. 194b' in a 152-leaf volume is no insuperable problem. The 'Keeper's Copy' says that the *Lombard History* began on 'f. 55', so there were ninety-eight leaves from here to the end. If this part of the book were at first numbered separately, *by page not folio* (i.e. on verso as well as recto), the number on the ante-penultimate page would indeed be '194'. The 'Keeper's Copy' annotator usually dealt in folios, and could have written 'f 194v' for 'p. 194'. The real difficulty is that a text described as having two pages is said to begin on a verso and to be imperfect.[365] This must mean either that it finished incomplete at or soon after the bottom of the next recto, in which case it was a *copy* of a fragment; or that it began at the foot of a verso and spread over both sides of the next leaf, in which case this leaf was not a stray from elsewhere. Yet to add an Anglo-Saxon law-code to the end of a text, which, on the evidence of its surviving fragment, was in a twelfth-century hand, would be unparalleled and inexplicable. A possible solution, remote but no more so than that, is that the Æthelred code was appended to Æthelweard's *Chronicle*, and that when Paul the Deacon was incorporated, the code plus Æthelweard's conclusion were clumsily shifted to the end of the book.[366] This would then be another case of the association of laws and *gesta*, like that in Cotton Otho B.xi at the same early-eleventh-century date.

(iv) Oxford, Bodleian Library, Vet. A.3 c.196

This is the classmark of a Bodleian copy of Whelock's edition of Lambarde's *Archaionomia*, whose distinction is that it bears witness to a lost manuscript of II–III Edgar. On the first page of its text of this code, its owner in 1811, Richard Taylor, records that he had seen what he describes as 'a parchment leaf in the possession of Mr Stevenson of Norwich, printer … pasted in the inside of the cover of a more recent MS'. That leaf has never been seen again. But Taylor entered its variant readings in the margin of the Lambarde/Whelock text. He also seems (though he does not say so) to have made the facsimile of it now attached to the inside of the back cover.[367]

---

364   For evidence that Æthelweard at least meant to continue into Æthelred's reign, see Barker, 'Cottonian Fragments'; to the contrary, *Chronicle of Æthelweard*, ed. Campbell, pp. xi–xii.

365   Ker presumably spoke of 'two leaves' when Smith specified 'duas paginas', because he saw that a text beginning on a verso must have *extended over* two leaves even if it did basically consist of two pages. There need anyway be no doubt that Smith, like Wanley, meant 'page' by 'pagina' and 'leaf' by 'folium': items 4 in Claudius A iv, 17 in Nero C ix, 16 in Nero D x, and 4 in Faustina A ii are all described as 'unica pagina', and are indeed of a single page or less; while no. 29 in Otho D viii appears to run from f. 231v to the top of f. 233v: in effect, the 'quattuor paginis' reported (p. 76).

366   This might *conceivably* explain how Savile's text contrived to omit the passage on Æthelred's reign which the surviving contents-list anticipated; but cf. Barker (as n. 364), p. 54.

367   The book belonged to Kenneth Sisam, who announced the transcript's existence in the 1953 re-edition of his Lambarde paper (below, n. 371) and whose daughter, Miss Celia Sisam, gave it to the Bodleian. It has otherwise been noted only by Ker, *Catalogue*, no. 411, and by Whitelock in her edition of II Edgar, *Councils and Synods*, pp. 95–102. Taylor's signed and dated note of his discovery is at the foot of p. 62; the facsimile is clearly in the same script as the variants on pp. 62–4, for which this note claims responsibility; and the note is likewise in the same hand as the translation begun and then abandoned on the facsimile's first facing verso.

All the signs are that Taylor took a lot of trouble to reproduce the appearance as well as the text of the original. He says that he 'endeavoured to imitate the characters (though) some trifling differences of spelling have been passed over'. The measure of his success is that Ker was able to identify the script of the lost exemplar as 's. xii', and Sisam (presumably going on language as well as script) to call it 'late-twelfth-century'.[368] The Norwich leaf therefore seems to be part of a manuscript roughly contemporary with the Harleian Cnut. It had probably suffered a certain amount of damage. Taylor left gaps, perhaps because the original could no longer be read; defects just before the text breaks off suggest that its bottom margin was stained or torn. But it may not have been anything special even in pristine condition. Space is left for an initial that Taylor should have supplied had there been one to copy. The most important feature of the facsimile for present purposes is that Taylor seems to reproduce line endings as he found them.[369] Since there are fifty-two lines in all, one can envisage an original with twenty-six long lines. The number of words per line is about the same as in *Textus Roffensis*. Such a text is unlikely to have been inserted in a *de luxe* book at so late a date. It might have come from one of the legal encyclopedias of the time, or it could have stood alone, like the Harleian Cnut. Here, in any case, is a further sign that interest in Anglo-Saxon vernacular legislation was still alive into Henry II's time.

That apart, the most significant thing about the Norwich leaf is that it furnishes a text of II–III Edgar which, like those in Nero A.i(A) and *Quadripartitus*, lack the variants of Wulfstan manuscripts (above, pp. 188–9, 226).[370] It does include 'eft' in the clause about an unjust reeve's royal pardon, the feature which in Nero A.i(A) looked like a scriptorial whim (p. 227). If this is not a coincidence that weakens conclusions drawn from the word's presence in Nero(A), it implies that Taylor's text was more akin to Nero's than otherwise appears. In any event, the main point stands: the survival of this fragment by the merest fluke provides more evidence of the circulation of Anglo-Saxon law's major monuments in divergent versions.

(v) The Lambarde problem

This review of legal manuscripts which are lost or nearly so can be brought to an appropriate conclusion by considering a manuscript (or manuscripts) that may be lost, but then again may not. Liebermann thought that Lambarde's

---

368   Professor Malcolm Godden kindly confirms that 'the first page (is) a very good ... imitation of a 12thC hand, a genuine attempt at a facsimile ... the word division ... is characteristic of late AS copying ... and the variations in the form of final s (are) a genuine feature of the period ... The underlying text seems in turn to be a very good 12th-century copy of an earlier OE text, showing a few linguistic features that are not correct late OE but generally looking perfectly acceptable as a copy of a 10thC original'.

369   In ln 4 of the first page, Taylor hyphenated 'teoþunga', but the spacing out of the last three words show that he could have fitted the whole word into the line; lns 7–9 by contrast are squeezed up.

370   Whitelock gives all the most significant textual variants for II Eg in her *Councils and Synods*, though one should note that 'blank until *nonan* (sic)', II Eg 5 (p. 101, n. ᵉ), may be another passage where the original had become illegible (it begins a line). Among III Eg variants from Nero A.i(A) are 1:2, 'eac for worulde aberendlic'; 3, 'oðrum **woh** gedeme'; others echo developments in Wulfstan texts: 'ealdum

Archaionomia, the *editio princeps* of Anglo-Saxon law, drew on some no longer extant manuscripts. But just before he died, his thesis ran into a devastating enfilade from Kenneth Sisam. Sisam proved that Lambarde's aberrant texts of two Æthelstan ordinances and three Wulfstan tracts were not lost medieval copies but 'translations of the Quadripartitus into Elizabethan Anglo-Saxon', and theorized that Nowell, Lambarde's friend and teacher, had provided these in transcripts that formed the raw material for his edition.[371] That was how Æthelstan came to offer the poor of his realm the unlikely solace of 'a leg of bacon and a ram'. Ker consequently declared that 'the manuscripts used for *Archaionomia* are not, as Liebermann thought, numerous and now largely missing, but few and extant'.[372] Yet Sisam had claimed only that his argument covered the few *Archaionomia* texts he discussed. It has not been established that it holds good for the remainder.[373]

There can be little doubt that for most it does. Within a decade, Robin Flower drew attention to some of the actual transcripts made by Nowell.[374] These included the copy of Cotton Otho B.xi discussed above (pp. 173–8), and also one of Cnut's code in Canterbury cathedral that shows every sign of being what Lambarde actually sent to his printers.[375] This last is essentially a transcript of Harley 55(B). The two crucial points are that it featured all the linguistic solecisms which characterize *Archaionomia* texts, and which are thereby shown to be products of Nowell's pen rather than lost textual traditions; and second that Nowell went on to smother the Harley text with interlinear or marginal emendations drawn from variants in Nero A.i(A) and Corpus 383, from translations of *Quadripartitus*, or from his own fertile mind.[376] Liebermann's *stemma* for Lambarde's text, postulating its access to Harley, Nero, Corpus and a lost vernacular sibling of *Quadripartitus*, was thus spot on, except that the lost manuscript, 'l', was Nowell's transcript.[377] Much the same can be said of Lambarde's texts of Edward's, Edmund's and Æthelred's laws, and of the Anglo-Scandinavian treaties. These were taken from Corpus 383, and every indication is that a similar publication process was involved, though no Nowell transcript survives.[378] For Edgar's laws there is a transcript, though Liebermann attributed

---

mynstrum' (i.e. plural), II 1:1; 'hlaford', II 3:1 (cf. III 7:1, also *Quad.* 'domino'); mistakes attributable to Taylor or his source may include II 2, 'þonne'; III 2:2, 'boc wyrðan'.

371 I As, As Alm, *Norðl.*, *Mirc.*, *Að*; Sisam, 'Authenticity of Texts in Lambard's *Archaionomia*'; cf. Liebermann's inadequate reply to the first (and gentler) of these onslaughts, 'Ist Lambards Text der Gesetze Æthelstans neuzeitliche Fälschung?'.

372 *Catalogue*, p. li; Ker went on to say what he thought they were.

373 This is too complex an issue to treat in full at a late stage of an already lengthy chapter, but I set out my views in detail (with a series of tables) in 'The Lambarde Problem: Eighty Years On'.

374 Flower, 'Laurence Nowell and the discovery of England'; the decisive factor was Lord Howard de Walden's 1934 bequest to the British Museum of the Nowell transcripts that were in Lambarde family ownership since his own time, and which are now Add. MSS 43703–10.

375 Canterbury Cathedral Lit. MS E.2, not in the Walden bequest, but Flower refers to it in n. 17; for some incomprehensible reason, it eluded Liebermann's notice, though he knew the Canterbury library well. See Dammery, 'Editing the Anglo-Saxon Laws', n. 11, and my 'The Lambarde Problem', p. 241 (pp. 143–4).

376 'The Lambarde problem', pp. 242–9 (pp. 144–52).

377 *Gesetze* III, p. 193 (10).

378 'The Lambarde problem', pp. 251–4 (pp. 154–7).

it to William Somner, its seventeenth-century owner, and thought that it too drew on one or more lost manuscripts.[379] It was in fact another Nowell editorial exercise, based on Nero A.i(A), and not what was printed by Lambarde but closely akin to it.[380]

For Æthelstan's Grately and Exeter codes ('II', 'V') and for the Alfred–Ine *domboc*, the story is both similar and crucially different. There are again extant Nowell transcripts: that of Cotton Otho B.xi, the one Liebermann labelled 'Somner', and a third which is a *de luxe* presentation of Alfred's laws only.[381] They too are part of the process that gave rise to Lambarde's texts rather than his immediate sources.[382] They show Nowell at work on the supply of accurate clause headings, which strongly suggests that Lambarde's chapters for those codes and most others were Nowell coinages, not survivals from Liebermann's putative 'mittelalterliche Zwischenstufe'. And yet it could be seen at an earlier stage of this chapter (pp. 176–7) that Nowell's Otho transcript must have had access to a second copy of Grately, which was his source for Exeter (and *Iudex*) too. That copy was clearly not *Textus Roffensis*, which offered the only other surviving vernacular text of Æthelstan's codes, but which (apart from anything else) does not contain *Iudex*. It *must* therefore have been a lost manuscript.[383] Now, there are a number of Alfred–Ine readings in the transcript's margins that are plausible enough but traceable to no known copy. One might think that they came from *Textus Roffensis*, were it not certain that the Rochester codex was unknown to Nowell.[384] The natural conclusion is that there was a lost manuscript of Alfred–Ine too, identifiable in the interests of intellectual economy with the Æthelstan-*Iudex* volume, and perhaps best envisaged as the same sort of highly vulnerable artefact as the loose leaves and 'pamphlet' that make up Harley 55. Liebermann's handling of legal manuscripts has often been found wanting in this chapter. It is good to conclude by noting that in the one area where he was challenged in his lifetime, he stands partially vindicated.

So rich and dense a body of material as the manuscripts of early English law cries out for distillation. Chapter 7 gathers together the implications of the evidence reviewed in Part II of this book. The briefest summary must suffice for now.

The first and most obvious point is the tenuousness of preservation. Five of the

---

379   *Gesetze* I, p. xl.

380   Canterbury, MS Lit. B.2: its Nowell authorship was the discovery of Carl Berkhout, currently the doyen of Nowell studies; cf. 'The Lambarde problem', pp. 254–5 (pp. 157–8).

381   BL, Printed Books, Henry Davis Collection 59: another Berkhout discovery.

382   For what follows, see 'The Lambarde problem', pp. 256–74 (pp. 158–77).

383   As Torkar strongly argues, *Altenglische Übersetzung*, pp. 86–128.

384   Af Int 41 'geclefs'; Af 12 'monig'; Af 34 'men up'; Af 42:7 'æwumborenre'; above all Af 22 , '7 fo to þæm wite'; cf. 'The Lambarde Problem', pp. 273–4 (pp. 176–7). Among numerous indications that Lambarde (*ergo* Nowell) did not know *TR* in 1568, the clearest are provided by his reactions to its discovery in his own annotated copies: Bodl. 4to L.5 Jur. Seld., ff. Biiiv, announces that he now knows III Atr 'Saxonice scriptas', as he would in *Roffensis*; f. 71r, notes the markedly different text of *Wer.* in 'Textu Roffensi', and enters the emendations arising; and in Huntington Library 30/B5 c.15142, f. Bjv, Lambarde says that he has 'at last' come across Æthelberht's code, to Bede's account of which his preface had referred. Cf. 'The Lambarde problem', p. 241 (p. 143), n. 15.

twenty books surveyed in this chapter survive in a battered state or not at all. In marked contrast to the continental position (chapter 2, pp. 58–70), no code is extant from the Anglo-Saxon era in a book whose primary concern was legal, apart from the few in books of ecclesiastical law. Old English laws come down to posterity only if inserted in books kept for religious or historical reasons, or if collected under the first Norman kings when the uncertainties of the time called for the assembly of the kingdom's legislative records. There is an analogy here with charters. Single-sheets are rare from nearly all archives because they were superseded by cartularies. There was likewise no need to keep individual copies of codes once they – or the files enfolding them – had been absorbed into collections (one of which was in Latin); though some single codes did survive, like some charters, if entered in holy books. It would be absurd to conclude that either laws or charters were available only as now extant.

Yet it would be wrong to disregard all lessons of law books as they stand. It is striking that a classification of books by type has turned out broadly chronological. Both 'Laws and *Gesta*' manuscripts are relatively early, and one is the earliest. 'Laws in Holy Books', which for the sake of argument may be taken to include 'Laws on Loose Leaves', are always pre-conquest. Some of them, and all cases of 'Law and Homily' or 'Law and Penance', were shaped by the initiatives of Archbishop Wulfstan. Assemblages of multiple codes in single volumes were driven by the determination of Anglo-Norman bibliographers to retain what they could of their legislative heritage. The chronological pattern reflects evolving conceptions of how law could shape the kingdom's destinies. More generally, few of these books have proved impossible to provenance. Indicators point strongly to bishops' libraries: Wulfstan's Worcester/York above all, Winchester, Exeter, London, Rochester, perhaps Canterbury. Only Corpus 201 is not from a cathedral, and it hardly needs saying that the New Minster's concerns are not easily separated from its episcopal neighbour's. As has been and will be repeatedly stressed throughout this book, bishops had lead parts on the stage of early English law. Wulfstan's role is highlighted by his distinctive style and indeed script. He was far from the only bishop to be legally active (cf. chapter 3, pp. 152–3, above, pp. 223, 228, 252). It was his namesake's (alleged) habit of nodding off when secular cases came up that was exceptional, which is why William of Malmesbury made it an aspect of his sanctity.[385] Law books from episcopal *scriptoria* uncover the attitudes of men who, in England as on the continent, were deeply engaged. Their duties extended beyond constructing a vision of society, to the actual alignment of social behaviour with the standards of civilization and the demands of God.

385 *William of Malmesbury, Gesta Pontificum* iv 140, p. 282.

CHAPTER 5

Legislation as Legal Text

The quest for the earliest English legal records now penetrates to what might seem its goal. This chapter discusses the extant legislative texts of the first kings of the English and their officials, from the time of Alfred until some seventy years after the Norman Conquest. Anonymous (i.e. apparently non-royal) decrees are considered as a group after those attributed to kings. Otherwise, the survey follows the chronological order of rulers, and what is rightly or wrongly perceived to be the sequence of their enactments.

A primary message of this chapter, however, is that 'law-codes' are themselves in one sense a contextual stratum. For it must be said at the outset that many, perhaps most, codes survive in forms which raise awkward questions about their applicability or relevance as they stand. The evidence of manuscripts is that law-codes were preserved before 1066 for reasons other than the strictly utilitarian. The evidence of lawsuits is that codes were not in fact cited in court records. Either type of evidence marches with the strange form that many extant law-codes take. Yet this is a problem that editors and commentators for the most part ignore. The codes appear throughout standard editions in neatly serried ranks, as self-contained and self-evident government pronouncements. The material is presented as if editors knew its nature and purpose better than the scribes who transmitted it. The methodological propriety of this approach is at least questionable. The intentions of law-makers cannot so easily be distinguished from the responses of their servants – least of all when these included the kingdom's leading bishops, one of whom, Wulfstan, was a major legislative authority in his own right. Even if the distinction could be made, the internal evidence of legal texts indicates the reactions to law-making in influential circles (chapter 4, pp. 162, 263). This is as significant as the reception revealed by the external evidence of law books, *placita* or narrative histories, and for the same reason. The preservers of law-codes were among those most intimately involved and corporately interested in the maintenance of law and order. Their treatment of the material deserves attention for its own sake. It may in any case be that apparent textual anomalies have a rationale after all. This chapter, therefore, examines the often unprepossessing pose in which later Anglo-Saxon legislation stands before the historian. It takes not intermittent but constant notice of what manuscript and textual evidence implies about attitudes to legal texts. Chapter 6 then investigates ways in which the eccentricities of that pose might perhaps be understood.

1   King Alfred's *Domboc*

King Alfred issued not one but two extant pieces of legislation. Most obviously there is his huge and stately *domboc*. Comprising an extended preface of Mosaic and apostolic law, the king's own decrees, and those attributed to his predecessor Ine (chapter 2, pp. 103–6), it occupies 108 pages of Liebermann's edition and is, at 8773 words, much the longest pre-conquest legal statement.[1] But there is also his succinct and extremely interesting legal agreement with the Danish King Guthrum/Æthelstan, the earliest even remotely diplomatic agreement in English history.[2] This section will begin and be very largely concerned with the *domboc*. But the Guthrum treaty will serve as an appendix that complements, because it in several ways contrasts with, the major text.

(i) The Domboc: transmission and structure

King Alfred's great law-book is better-preserved than any English legal statement before Henry I's Coronation Charter.[3] It survives, wholly or partly, in the following ten copies (listed in approximately chronological order):

'E'.	CCCC 173 (chapter 4, pp. 163–72);
'Ot'.	BL Cotton Otho B.xi (chapter 4, pp. 172–81);
'G'.	BL Cotton Nero A.i (A) (chapter 4, pp. 224–8);
'Bu'.	BL Burney MS 277 (chapter 4, pp. 257–8);
Inst. Cn.	*Instituta Cnuti* III 1–41, etc. (below, pp. 402–5);
'B'.	CCCC 383 (chapter 4, pp. 228–36);
'Q (Lond.)'.	*Quadripartitus* (London) (chapter 4, pp. 237–8, 240–3);
'Q (rev.)'.	*Quadripartitus* (revised) (chapter 4, pp. 237, 238–43);
'H'.	*Textus Roffensis* (chapter 4, pp. 244–53);
'Nw2'.	(probably) Nowell's lost MS (chapter 4, pp. 260–2).

Liebermann's stemmatic analysis of these textual witnesses was so vitiated by misconceptions about manuscript origins, major lost codices and so on that it would be pointless to reproduce here; while any attempted substitute would fall foul of a plethora of irresolvable uncertainties.[4] The essentials of the position are these: Liebermann thought that 'E' came from Canterbury (as by 1070 it did), and in recognizing that 'Ot' was its offshoot he could suppose the same of that

---

1   I am grateful to Dr Jürg Schwyter for this figure (from his own adjusted version of the *Toronto Electronic Corpus*); it includes not only Ine (2827 words) but also the rubrics (220 words) and indeed the chapter numbers; Alfred's Mosaic preface is 1967 and his own laws 3345, meaning that his personal input was 5312 words. The next longest text was the complete code of Cnut (I–II Cn), at 7196 words.
2   See below, pp. 285–6, for full reference and recent literature.
3   Liebermann's full account of the MSS and *stemma* (with inevitable stylized diagram) is in *Gesetze* III, pp. 31–2. The other codes even comparably preserved are II As (5 copies, below, pp. 291–5), II–III Eg (6, below, pp. 313–15), and I–II Cn (6, below, pp. 349–52)
4   Liebermann in fact ignored the textual implications of the *Instituta Cnuti* extracts – which are indeed too fragmentary to signify in the discussion that follows.

too. 'G' certainly has at least superficially Canterbury symptoms (chapter 4, pp. 225–6). There was also 'Bu' as an idiosyncratic 'Kentish' witness. Most crucial was the group to which Liebermann gave the family name 'hbq', in that he ignored any possible revision of *Quadripartitus* (chapter 4, pp. 242–3), and over-looked the evidence that the similarities of B and H arose from the *corrections*, not the basic text, of the latter (chapter 4, p. 249). The shared ancestry of hbq could thus be deduced from the common presence of the *Be Blaserum* appendix (chapter 4, pp. 231, 240–2); and given Rochester's known debt to Canterbury, it was easy to allot hbq a Canterbury ancestry too. Finally, Liebermann's knowl-edge of 'Nw2', so far as it went, was irreparably contaminated by his views on Lambarde and 'Somner' (chapter 4, pp. 260–2); but both had evident Kentish connections. Liebermann could thus reduce the whole prolific textual progeny of Alfred's *domboc* to the paternity of England's premier church. This was extremely important, because it enabled him to postulate an archetype that had both the independence and the impetus needed to account for the pronounced textual anomalies which, as will be seen in a moment, are found throughout the transmission of Alfred's law-book.

A preliminary comment on this thesis is that it does no service to medieval mentalities to rescue the credibility of legislating kings by making numbskulls of those who served them. If the scribes of the archbishop could perpetrate textual absurdities, why could not the clerks of the king's court? But in any case, the whole core of Liebermann's thesis has been eaten away by the palaeographical and textual burrowings of subsequent scholars. E and Ot represent not a Canterbury but a Court-Winchester nexus in the relevant 940–1010 period. G may be from Canterbury but could just as well be from elsewhere. Bu and B-Q-H are assuredly south-eastern, but H and Q (rev.) witness *different* textual traditions from that of B and Q (Lond.). There is some reason to connect Nowell's lost codex with Kent but equally good or better reasons not to.[5] All in all, it is impossible to say how many branches there are to the textual tree of Alfred's law-book; though one may perhaps think in terms of up to half a dozen.[6] What is clearly unwarranted is to trace all offshoots to a Canterbury root. The archetype beneath the blemishes of the entire tradition must be planted elsewhere. *Prima facie*, the only soil of comparable fertility is the royal court itself.

It is time to turn to the peculiarities that apparently called for Liebermann's stemmatic excuse. Alfred's law-book picked up appendages like burrs as it passed down the years, the *Be Blaserum* supplement being the obvious example

---

5   Torkar argues an early-ish date, plus 'Anglian' elements with 'great probability' and 'Kentish' with 'some', for the Æthelstan/*Iudex* components, *Altenglische Übersetzng*, pp. 111–21. The proposed Alfredian elements consist of isolated glosses, so it is impossible to suggest anything very constructive about them; but see next note.

6   E/Ot are clearly distinct, given their 'ceap/ceac' error (chapter 4., n. 40); G shows symptoms of indi-viduality (Af Int 21, 43), and likewise Bu (chapter 4, pp. 257–8). Accepting the kinship of B-Q(Lond.), little can be said about Q (rev.), H or Nw2, *except that* they are not the same as B-Q (Lond.) (or E/Ot). Bu is perhaps distinct from H as well as B-Q (Lond.) (chapter 4, n. 359), but there seems to be no way of knowing how different was H from Q (rev.) or Nw2; my 'Lambarde problem', pp. 273–4 (pp. 176–7). observes links between Nw2 and H, but these need to be digested as flavoured by Torkar's comments on Nowell's Æthelstan texts (see previous n.)

(chapter 4, pp. 175–6, cf. pp. 227, 242). But much more striking are idiosyncracies shared by all extant texts. The best way to bring these out is to note that it is *only* in Liebermann's great edition (and two other honourable exceptions) that one finds the *domboc* as actually transmitted. Every manuscript either opens with a list of 120 chapter rubrics, or uses these rubrics throughout the text. The first chapter covers the 'Golden Rule', that one should not judge others except as one would wish to be judged oneself, and relates to the last section of the Mosaic introduction. The ensuing 119 apply both to Alfred's laws and to Ine's. Alfred's own laws have forty-three, all but three clauses of his long injury-tariff being concentrated into the forty-third. Ine's prologue is chapter 44, and there are then another seventy-six clauses of his laws. It is in a sense unsurprising that this format should be hard to detect in any published edition.[7] It is undeniably odd. Apart from the fact that the Mosaic preface has, in Attenborough's words, 'no bearing on Anglo-Saxon law' (he omitted it), Ine's laws followed Alfred's, when chronologically they were prior. Worse, there were a significant number of cases where Alfred contradicted Ine. Ine, for example, set the '*burhbryce* (enclosure penetration)' of king and bishop at 120 shillings, that of an ealdorman at eighty, of a 'king's thegn' at sixty, and of a '*gesith*-born' man with land at thirty-five. With Alfred, 120 shillings applied to the king alone, the other figures being ninety for an archbishop, sixty for bishop or ealdorman, thirty for a 'twelve-hundred shilling man' (*gesith* with property?), fifteen for a 'six hundred man' (unlanded *gesith*?) and five for '*edorbryce* (fence-breach)' of a *ceorl*.[8] A bishop or ealdorman brandishing the *domboc* in front of an invader of his *burh* must have been sorely tempted to quote Ine instead of Alfred. That is why Schmid for one thought that the two codes were put together by a lesser mortal at a later stage.[9]

More anomalous yet is the text's division into 120 chapters. The numbering

---

7   Lambarde's *Archaionomia* (chapter 4, pp. 260–1), ff. 0v – 44r, printed the complete preface, but not the rubric list, and reorganized the text of Alfred's laws into forty numbered chapters with titles derived in part from the original rubrics and in part from his own and Nowell's efforts (chapter 4, p. 262); Ine's laws were made to precede Alfred's, and distributed in seventy-five numbered chapters, on the same lines as Alfred's. Wilkins (chapter 1, pp. 21–2), pp. 14–46, followed Lambarde in his Ine–Alfred order and in omitting the rubric list, but restored most of the primary Ine chapter divisions, together with nearly all the rubrics' original wording, thus arriving at the 76 chapters that form the basis of modern editions; this makes it all the less explicable that he retained the Lambarde rubric/chapters for Alfred, albeit dividing Alfred's preface into the 49 basic clauses of modern editions. Thorpe (chapter 1, p. 22), pp. 20–65, restored the Alfred–Ine order, though still ignoring the rubric-list, and retrieved the original wording and numbering of Alfred's rubrics, though numbering the injury list to give the 77 modern chapters. Schmid (chapter 1, p. 22), pp. 20–105, replaced Ine before Alfred, again omitted the rubric list, and gave the same divisions as Thorpe, except that he supplied most of the numbered sub-clauses in modern editions. Liebermann himself did print the rubric list/primary numbering, but retained Thorpe's chapter divisions and Schmid's subdivisions, adding a few of his own (e.g. in Alfred's injury tariff). Attenborough used Liebermann's chapter divisions, but again put Ine before Alfred, and omitted not only the rubric list/numbering but also almost all Alfred's preface. One 'honourable exception' was Turk's *Legal Code of Alfred the Great* (harshly handled at times by Liebermann) which reproduced the text as transmitted, relegating modern sub-divisions to the margin; the other is Richard Dammery's 1991 Cambridge doctoral thesis, from which I have learned much – *especially* where our views differ. But Alfred's *domboc* remains the *locus classicus* of the vulnerability of Anglo-Saxon legal studies to editorial buccaneering.

8   Ine 45, Af. 40; for these problems, see below, pp. 278–80.

9   Schmid, pp. xl–xli (in some ways more perceptive than Liebermann).

of Ine's prologue as chapter forty-four is not all that makes little sense. Chapter X, entitled '*Be bearneacnum wife ofslegenum* (on the slaying of a pregnant woman)', contained a law devoted to this subject, but then went on to the ratio of '*wite* (fine)' and '*angyld* (restitution)', that can hardly relate to killing the pregnant, and to a change in the fines for theft of gold, horses and bees, which certainly did not.[10] Chapter XXVII was indeed about the 'rape of under-age girls (*be ungewintredes wifmonnes nedhæmde*)', but was also about crimes committed by kinless men; chapter XXVIII was then labelled 'the killing of such a man', where the reference was of course to the kinless, not to the under-age girl of the previous chapter's title.[11] So it was with Ine. Chapter CIII, '*Be cuus horne* (on the cow's horn)', went logically with Cap CII on that of an ox; but it proceeded to cover the value of eye and tail of ox and cow alike, before also including the going rate of '*beregafol* (barley-rent)'. Cattle horns were among numerous cases when laws seeming to belong together nonetheless got chapters of their own: two-hundred, six-hundred and twelve-hundred shilling men slain by a 'gang (*hloð*)' were covered by chapters XXIV–XXVI, the last of which also provided for the gang's prosecution and punishment. Editorial repudiation of such rubrication is thus understandable. Judges were not assisted to find the 'food-rent' from ten hides by an arrangement that classified it with '*manbot* (compensation to a lord for his man's death)', under a rubric '*Be twyhyndum were* (on the two-hundred shilling wergeld)'.[12]

Yet one ought to be consistent here. Liebermann and others have accepted that Ine's code was an integral part of Alfred's original *domboc*. Decisive for Liebermann was a law in the second code of Alfred's successor, Edward the Elder:

> If anyone neglects [what had gone before] and breaks his oath and pledge (*his að 7 his wæd*), let him pay as the lawbook declares (*swa domboc tæce*) ... If anyone harbours him thereafter, let him pay as the lawbook says, and as he should that harbours a fugitive (*swa seo domboc sæcge, 7 se scyle ðe flyman feormige*).

The second of these provisions can be taken to refer to Ine's law on '*fliemanfeorm* (fugitive harbouring)', which is thus shown to belong to the single *domboc*.[13]' Other arguments can be brought to bear. Alfred without Ine would, for instance, be a code almost without coverage of theft, and as such unique in European legislation of the early Middle Ages.[14] It can hardly be imagined that a scribe wilfully replaced a text of Ine as revised by Alfred with one that was unrevised. To accept that Alfred needed Ine's code is therefore to grant that he tolerated its presence as it stood, contradictions and all. That the anomalous rubrication was likewise original was, however, denied by Liebermann with some heat; 'mistake-ridden,

---

10   Af 9 – 9:2; 'angyld' almost certainly relates to theft, like the 60-shilling fine to which the 30-shilling *angyld* is related (Ine 10, 43), though 60s is also the lowest possible wergeld payable, Ine 32.

11   Af 26 – 28.

12   Ine 58 – 59:1; Af 29 – 31:1; Ine 70 – 70:1, Ine Rb CXIIII.

13   I Ew 5 – 5:2; Ine 30; *Gesetze* III, pp. 30–1 (1); yet II Ew 5 pretty clearly refers to Af 1, whose ramifications can be shown to extend to theft (chapter 9); nor is it really the case, as suggested in *Gesetze* III, p. 39 (36), that II Ew 7 followed Ine 39, rather than Af 37 – 37:2 (below, pp. 274, 280). The first unambiguous citations of Ine as part of the *domboc*, therefore, are II Eg 3, 5, referring to Ine 4, 3.

14   One of the arguments originally put by Turk, pp. 42–7; cf. his earlier comment, p. 30: 'Our code has suffered in the past from a too zealous separation into parts'.

awkward and incomplete' was his view of what he credited to a 'clueless scribe'.[15] Yet the wording of Edward's supposed citation of Ine's law ('ðe flieman feormige') was actually closer to that of the rubric than to that of Ine's text.[16] The case for the originality of the rubrication is generally no better or worse than that for the Ine appendix. Above all, the manuscript authority for the rubrics is as good as for Ine's code, or the Mosaic preface for that matter. And if there was little logic in laws on different issues within the same chapter, there was not much in an Ine that contradicted Alfred, or even laws of Moses whose scale matched Alfred's own. It is rational, though difficult, to argue that an unoriginal archetype foisted both Ine and rubrics on the whole manuscript tradition. It is also rational (and conceivably not so difficult) to think both Alfredian. It is irrational to accept one but not the other on largely subjective grounds.[17]

Before leaving structural issues for now, one other feature of the *domboc* should be noted.[18] It would not have been easy for court authorities to find their way around Alfred's laws, even without the double-edged assistance of the rubrics. There has been at least one relatively persuasive attempt to find system of sorts in the decrees he formulated. His first dozen laws were linked by a concern with overlapping categories of breach of peace or protection. Special protections were also involved in the next laws on nuns, adultery and rape. Later, it is possible to see an underlying preoccupation with the rights and responsibilities of owners and trustees as regards animate or inanimate objects. In the last few clauses before the injury tariff, the law on leaving one ealdorman's jurisdiction for another's led to fighting before an ealdorman and in a ceorl's house, so to *burhbryce* (aggravated during Lent, which prompted a law on the extra

---

15   *Gesetze* III, p. 40; cf. his 'Über die Gesetze Ines', pp. 28–9.

16   Ine Rb 30; cf. Ine 30, 'Gif ... fliemanfeorme teo'.

17   Cf. the discussion by Dammery, 'Law-code of Alfred', pp. 175–206, 251–63, which reaches the opposite conclusion. It is (as he says) instructive to compare the problem of the chapter headings in the *Old English Bede* and *Orosius* (neither of them Alfredian, below, n. 30). Whitelock, 'List of Chapter Headings in the Old English Bede', shows that the vocabulary of this list is that of the translator himself, yet the relationship of list to text is such as to suggest that the former, as it stands, was not the translator's work. Bately's edition of *The Old English Orosius*, pp. xxxvii–xxxix, lxxxi–lxxxiii, finds that its list of chapter headings is 'unselective, mechanical and unhelpful', and unlikely to be the translator's own work. In the *domboc*, one might take 'forlegenum', Af Rb 10, as against 'hæme', Af 10, and likewise 'befæstað', Af Rb 20, as against 'oðfæste', Af 20, as evidence that the rubrics were by another author (Dammery, 'Law-code, pp. 192–3), though neither rubric usage is wholly unAlfredian (below, nn. 55, 58). It is clear enough in any case that the rubric list was made after the text was finished: see above on Cap XXVIII (Af Rb 28). But it is at least a striking coincidence that three different texts from the Alfredian circle have rubrics that raise the same sort of questions, and one whose effect may enhance the authority of each. And Alfred (or his immediate political and intellectual heirs, which is to say not much less) could have ordered the division of a text into a number of chapters that had its own inner meaning, (chapter 6, pp. 417–18), without performing the task in person.

18   As well as the structural point to follow, it is apposite to note apparent textual blemishes common to *all* MSS; cf. *Gesetze* III, pp. 32 (18), 64 (6). In Af 47, 71, 'VI' should be 'III' (one-third of 200, cf. *Quadripartitus*), the repetition of the error inclining one to blame authorial mathematics rather than scribal carelessness. In Ine 17:1, sense appears to require 'gedyrned' rather than 'gedyrneð' (cf. *Quadripartitus*); and it is at least likely that Ine 6:3–4, should read 'XXX', not 'CXX', likewise Ine 54:2 'XXIV', not 'XXXIV'. It is perhaps significant that the more serious errors come in Ine, and that those in Af are sufficiently minor to be no great matter if the collection's concern was less with legal detail than with overall effect (chapter 6, pp. 415–29).

penalty for spiritual crime in Lent), to bookland (once *ius ecclesiasticum*), to feud (with special reference to the restriction of violence at home), and to religious festivals. A common theme, as at the start, was the effect upon legal norms of exceptional circumstances of place, time or office.[19] 'As a whole', the argument concludes, 'the arrangement of the code corresponds to what would be expected of so talented a man as Alfred'. Yet the next sentence concedes that the confused parts look 'um so krasser'. Little can be done for the central part of the code beyond the counsel of despair that the manuscript tradition has become confused (though this possibility did occur to the scribe of *Textus Roffensis* or his exemplar(s), with the result that the order was partly rearranged).[20] Not even scribal quirks can explain why the later laws on 'privileged peaces' were not grouped with the earlier, or why fighting in the king's hall, before archbishop, bishop or ealdorman, and before an ealdorman at a meeting were covered (in modern numeration) by chapters seven, fifteen and thirty-eight respectively.[21] The sole principle of order, whether in parts of the code where common themes are detectable or in those where they are not, is thought-association. Alfred's laws on the ratio of fine to restitution and on fines for theft in general were tucked in between decrees on killing a pregnant woman and on adultery, because the first was suggested by the pregnancy law's reference to proportions, and the second in turn prompted by the first.[22] Most clauses were linked in this way; continuity was preserved, even if the overall result was that the code went round in circles. Nor is it accident that the only 'barbarian' code as disorganized as Alfred's was Ine's (chapter 2, pp. 104–5). Ine was of course his main legislative 'role-model' (below, pp. 279–80).

Chapter 2 showed that the behaviour of continental law books could be paradoxical to the point of perversity. It is no longer quite so alarming that Alfred's laws should be cheek-by-jowl with contradictory provisions by Ine, when the multiple manuscripts of *Lex Salica Karolina* proferred two penalties for the same crime, one nearly double the other, or when *capitularia legibus addenda* were aligned with the *Lex* they revised. Nonsensical rubrics might appear more conceivably authorial when Visigoths preferred to have twelve books of law than an even distribution of material between them. By modern, or even later medieval standards, it seems absurd that anyone could have tolerated, let alone initiated,

---

19   Korte, *Untersuchungen*, pp. 84–95 (cf. chapter 2, pp. 96, 102–3, 104–5).

20   Af 25 – 31:1 (col. H): H puts Af 25 – 25:1, on the rape of a ceorl's slave-girl, after the laws on gang-slaying (Af 29 – 31:1), and immediately before Af. 26, on the rape of the underage, accordingly renumbering the chapters in text and rubric-list. The reason why this sounds odd is that Lambarde did his own rearranging, moving the underage law to follow that on slave-girls, while Thorpe went further in putting 'kinless men' laws after those on rape and before those on gang-slaying. Since Schmid followed suit, Liebermann felt obliged to use this numbering, while restoring the order of most MSS; hence '29 – 31:1' precede '26 – 28'. Attenborough retained the MS order but renumbered on his own initiative; Whitelock, *EHD I*, p. 413, gives Attenborough's order and numbering, with that of Thorpe/Schmid/Liebermann in brackets. This near farcical confusion is a comment in itself on the arrangement of Alfred's laws as preserved.

21   Note too that Af 18 (lewd approaches to nuns) and 26 (under-age rape) actually cite 11, 11:2 (equivalent for laity/adult); and cf. the separation of Af. 42:1–2 (invulnerability of home/church in a feud, with cross-reference) from 5, 5:3 (sanctuary).

22   Korte, p. 89, exaggerates the pertinence of 9:1 to 9 by reading it as a reference to fine *and wergeld* (so picking up the variation of wergeld in 9), rather than fine and *angyld*: see above, n. 10.

a structure like that of the *domboc*. But if something similar occurred in comparable contexts, then perhaps early medieval standards themselves differed. To deny that Alfred transmitted the *domboc* as it stands assaults the evidence in the name of assumptions about what is plausible. But chapter 6 will argue that early medieval priorities may after all make sense of the transmitted arrangement.

(ii) The Domboc: language and style

Chapter 2 of this book discovered that, whatever historical instances and scholarly instincts urge otherwise, it is possible to detect a trend towards increasing stylistic complexity in post-Roman legislation generally and in that of the Anglo-Saxons specifically (pp. 95, 103–4). That trend will remain evident throughout the course of this chapter (e.g. pp. 288, 301–2, 309–10). From such a viewpoint, the pattern of Alfred's own laws is both interesting and surprising.[23]

> Laws phrased as comparatively simple 'if'-clauses or as straight valuations: 3 (a-b-c), 9:1–2, 10 (a-b-c), 11 – 11:5, 12, 15 (a-b), 16, 18:2–3, 23, 25–25:1, 29 – 31, 26, 35 – 35:6, 38:1–2, 39 – 39:2, 40 – 40:2, 44 – 76:   **96.**
>
> Laws with form of relative clause: 4:2, 5:5, 41, 42:   **4.**
>
> Laws admitting procedural complications in conditional clauses: 6:1, 7, 7:1, 17, 22, 32, 33:   **7.**
>
> Laws making commands or stating principles: 1, 5, 5:2, 34 (a-b-c), 42:5–7, 43 (a-b):   **11.**

This pattern brings Alfred nearer to Æthelberht than to Ine (chapter 2, pp. 95, 104); which is all the stranger in that the Mosaic laws forming his preface had many more relatives, statements of principle and (need it be said?) commandments.[24] Alfred offered three times as many 'simple' formulations as Ine, but fewer than quarter his number of relative constructions, two-thirds his total of statements of principle, and nowhere near so many clauses rendered complex by introduction of procedural detail.[25] Stylistic analysis thus suggests the conclusion

---

23   To what follows, compare the assessments of Beyerle, Daube, Korte and Schwyter (as chapter 2, nn. 70, 333, 351, etc.), and my '*Inter cetera bona ...*', pp. 969–77 (pp. 183–8). It is important to repeat here that (modern) editorial clause divisions have no manuscript/ textual basis whatsoever (above, n. 7). For the statistical purposes to be served here, laws of Alfred and Ine are defined as two-clause sentences with a main verb (which suffices for many subdivisions inserted by Schmid/Liebermann). For Ine, this increases the 121 clauses actually numbered in Liebermann's edition by sixteen (Ine 2, 4, 17, 22, 29, 30, 35, 35:1, 40, 46:1, 57, 59 (x 3, for consistency with 58), 60, 74:1 (x 3); cf. chapter 2, n. 361); the total for Alfred is 173, or 118 less the injury tariff: the 160 separately numbered clauses of Liebermann's edition are amplified from Af. 3 (x 3), 5, 10 (x 3), 15, 34 (x 3), 42:1, 42:3, 42:4 (x 3) and 43. (The table following here omits clauses not falling clearly into any of its categories).
24   Af Int 1 – 15, 17 – 19, 21, 25, 28, 29 – 48; for the layered structure of Mosaic law, see Kleinknecht and Gutbrod, *Law*, pp. 23–77.
25   Further to category three above: Af. 1:2–4,6–8, 2, 4:1–2, 5 (a-b), 5:1–4, 6:1, 7 – 7:1, 8 – 8:3, 11:4, 13 – 14, 17, 18:1, 19, 19:2, 21 – 22, 24, 31:1, 27 – 27:1, 28, 32 – 33, 34 (a-b-c), 36 – 36:2, 37, 38, 41–2, 41 – 42, 42:1 (a-b), 42:2, 42:3 (a-b), 42:4 (a-b-c), 77. Ine figures: '*Inter cetera bona ...*', p. 977 (p. 188).

that the content of Alfred's code was largely traditional. Such was at any rate the impression the king wished to give: he wrote in finishing his preface, 'I dared not presume to put in writing at all many of my own [laws], because it was unknown to me which of them would please those that were after us'.[26]

Alfred certainly could legislate in a 'developed' style. Here is his decree on sanctuary as applied to feud:

> Further we fix (*Eac we settað*) this peace for each church that a bishop has consecrated: if a man at feud (*fahmon*) reaches it running or riding, let no one pull him out for seven days. If, however, anyone does this (*Gif hit þonne hwa do*), then let him be liable for the king's protection-value (*mundbyrde*) and for the church's peace (*cirican friðes*), more, if he takes more from there (*mare, gif he ðær mare ofgefo*) – so long as he can live in spite of his hunger (*gif he for hungre libban mæge*), without himself fighting his way out (*buton he self utfeohte*).

The structural complexity of this law, its whole message governed by the hunger proviso, is obvious enough.[27] So is its self-consciously legislative tone, with something like an opening statement of intent. The law also features the only two ways in which Alfred's code looks forward to those of his tenth-century successors rather than back before Ine's days. One is the fact that it begins with a conjunctive adverb. This is true of seven other Alfred laws, but of just one of Ine's and none of Æthelberht's.[28] The other is that it contains cross-references to the rest of the code. 'Cirican friðes' is covered by clause 2:1, and 'cyninges mundbyrd' by clause 3. Depending on what one reckons a cross-reference, there were up to eleven such among Alfred's laws. One, in a clause on feud, was uniquely explicit: 'If he then reaches a church, then let it be according to the church's privilege, as we said above'; the reference is to the law just quoted in full. Ine's code had nothing comparable; the only prior cross references were two in Wihtræd's.[29] These features can fairly be seen as symptoms of more literate law-giving. They made the code behave more like a book.

The style of the *domboc* offers an opportunity seldom encountered in early medieval legislation, and only once otherwise among Anglo-Saxon codes. Alfred, of course, wrote other books. An age which has fragmented the oeuvre of St Paul and vindicated the cohesion of the *Iliad* has also established an Alfredian canon. Distinctive foibles of syntax and vocabulary show that the translations of Gregory the Great's *Pastoral Rule*, of Boethius' *Consolation of Philosophy*, of Augustine's *Soliloquies* and of the first fifty Psalms in the Paris Psalter were products of the same mind. The first two had a preface, the third an epilogue, declaring that this mind was King Alfred's. By the same token, further texts more

---

26   Af. 49:9.

27   Af 5; for the 'buton' qualifier, see pp. 301, 309, 316, 340, 354.

28   Af 4:2, 5, 5:4, 34, 36, 42, 42:4, 42:5; Ine 1:1; there are also simple conjunctions, 34 (b-c), 42:1, 42:7, 43 (b), against one apiece for Ine, 6:4, and Abt, 51 (d); cf. below, pp. 288, 302, 309, 340.

29   Af 42:2 (ref. as n. 27); Af. 2:1 (ref. Af 35, 35:6, 44 – 77), 5:5 (ref. 40:2), 6, (ref. 9:1), 6:1 (ref. 71), 18 (ref. 11 – 11:2), 23:2 (ref. 44 – 77), 26 (ref. 11:2–5), 32 (ref. 52), Af. 38 – 38:1 (ref. 15), 42:4 (c) (ref. 39 – 39:2, 44 – 77); and cf. n. 80 below; Wi. 2, 5. Note that conjunctions and cross-references, like relative clauses and statements of principle, are most prominent in the first few clauses and in those immediately preceding the injury tariff: it might be thought that this is where a legislator would be more likely to launch away from the shores of coralled tradition.

or less plausibly linked with the king's patronage were not his own work: the Old English *Orosius*, the 'core' *Anglo-Saxon Chronicle* and, as has long been seen, the Old English *Bede*.[30] Like most of the first but not the second set, the *domboc* actually claimed Alfred as author. It should be possible to test that claim by stylistic analysis.[31]

It is possible, but not easy. The Alfredian canon was first created to show what the king did *not* write. With so few texts to act as controls, one cannot *prove* royal authorship. The exercise is further handicapped by the small size of the sample. Most recognized Alfredian traits are represented by a statistically measurable preference for a particular lexical variant; nothing is gained by comparing a 1:1 with a 1:10 ratio when the former's quotient is two. Again, the legislative medium allows little room for the employment of some characteristics of Alfredian prose. His usual word for 'yet, however' was 'swaþeah' or 'þeahhwæþ(e)re', not 'hwæþ(e)re', which was used by the *Orosius*. In the laws, 'hwæðre' appeared three times and 'þeah' (in this sense) once; yet elegant conjunctive contributions to the flow of argument are out of place amidst the austerities of law-making.[32] A further problem is posed by the reticence that has already been found characteristic of Alfred's laws (pp. 271–2): his relatively low personal profile may have reduced the prominence of his style. Significantly, the passage where he describes his legislative activity had a concentration of 'Alfredisms' unmatched elsewhere in the *domboc*, and his favoured words and phrases were commoner in his preface than in the main body of his laws, where the problems tend to cluster.[33] Traditional legal vocabulary may have imposed restraints. Thus, the normal word for 'to fight' in Alfredian texts was 'winnan', which was rare in the *Chronicle*; 'gefeohtan', preferred by the *Chronicle* and second choice for the *Orosius*, was almost never used; while 'feohtan' was second preference for the Alfredian canon and the *Chronicle*, third for the *Orosius*. Alfred's laws preferred 'feohtan', five times resorted to 'gefeohtan', and never used 'winnan'. But this is understandable so soon as one notes that 'winnan' (whose connotations of 'struggle' were suited to heroic or homiletic idioms) never

---

30   This is above all the achievement of Professor Janet Bately: 'King Alfred and the Old English Orosius'; 'Compilation of the Anglo-Saxon Chronicle'; *Old English Orosius*, pp. lxxiii–lxxv; 'Lexical evidence for the authorship of the prose psalms' (the first of the series seeking to establish rather than disprove Alfredian authorship). There seems no reason to doubt that Alfred 'wrote' his books in the same sense as any other early medieval writer, regardless of whether he personally wielded a pen or dictated to a scribe (Clement, 'Production of the *Pastoral Care*', pp. 131–2; Bately, 'Question of Dictation'). Modern doubts appear to arise from a sense that he would have been 'too busy' to write himself. But we know nothing of an early medieval king's timetable; and faced with an enterprise as unique as Alfred's, we have no right to make assumptions about 'normal' production methods. Accordingly, the word 'write' is used henceforth without hesitation or embarrassment.

31   What follows of course depends overwhelmingly on Professor Bately's studies; it aims only to resolve her doubts as regards the laws, 'King Alfred', pp. 452–3. Like hers, my argument is based on the oldest extant MS, i.e. 'E' (chapter 4, pp. 163–72).

32   Af Int 16 (cf. Ine 72), Af 23:1, 37:1, 77; Bately, 'King Alfred', pp. 447, 458. Cf. *Alfred's Pastoral Care*, pp. 73 ln 7, 395 ln 19, 431 ln 26 ('hwæþ(e)re'), 47 ln 23, 117 ln 14, 151 ln 13, 175 ln 4, 267 ln 13, 305 ln 1 (þeahhwæþ(e)re).

33   Af Int 49:9–10: 'gegaderode', 'licodon/lician/licode', 'geþeahte', 'forðam', 'awðer ... oððe ... oððe', 'ðuhton', 'geeowde'; Bately, 'King Alfred', p. 452, and nn. 37, 39–41, 51–3, 56 below. It may also be noted that Alfredian traits tend to concentrate in laws with symptoms of a more 'developed' style (above, pp. 271–2).

appears in the Old English legislative corpus, whereas four of five Alfredian uses of 'gefeohtan' are scattered ramifications of Ine's law on fighting before the privileged.[34]

The remaining problems subdivide into non-Alfredian language that does appear and Alfredian features that do not. Foremost in the first category are words usually thought 'Mercian'. One of the king's most important laws concerns the abandonment of one lord for another in a different district. The word used for 'district', *boldgetæl*, otherwise appears only in the translation of Gregory's *Dialogues* by Bishop Wærferth of Worcester, and place-names formed with *bold-* are confined to the North and Midlands. The word has thus been cited as a remnant of the 'lost laws of Offa', whose influence on his own legislation Alfred admitted. But that hypothesis, whatever its other virtues, is redundant here. Alfred's law modified one of Ine where the word used had been *scir* (below, p. 280), and chapter 10 will propose that this word had acquired its modern sense of 'shire' since Ine's time. One can thus envisage Alfred casting about for a suitable alternative and being 'fed' *boldgetæl* by Wærferth, whose *Dialogues* are said to have been among his favourite reading.[35] Sisam could in any case observe that 'Alfred's literary language was peculiarly subject to Mercian influence'; as he also noted, the king would have encountered Mercian speech in bed as well as in his council chamber.[36] Other words more prominent in Alfred's laws than they might be on a strict reading of the Alfredian canon are *forþon/forþonðe* as opposed to *forþæm/am(þe)* ('because', 'therefore'); *besittan* rather than *behringan* or compounds of these words prefixed by *ymb* ('to besiege'); and *gesamnian* ('to gather'), *gylt* ('guilt', 'crime') and *gelician* ('to like'), as opposed to more typically Alfredian *gegaderian*, *scyld* and *lician*.[37] But these terms also appear to an exceptional degree in Alfred's *Gregory*, which has eccentricities of its own.[38] Forms of *forðon*, for example, outnumber those of *forþæm* by a factor of 7:5 in the first

34   Af 7, 15, 27, 38, 39 (note that Af Rb 7, 15 had 'feohte', 'feohtað'); Ine 6 – 6:4; Bately, 'Compilation', pp. 122–3, 'Lexical Evidence', p. 91. Af 17 used '*forfaran*, die', when Alfred normally used 'gefaran', but cf. Ine 38; likewise, 'sweltan' (Bately, 'Compilation', p. 121) appeared in Af Int 13 – 15, 25, 31 – 32 (all but once with 'deaðe' as object, for which see Ine 12, and cf. Abt 78); the word does appear in *Alfred's Pastoral Care*, pp. 93 ln 8 x 2, 403 ln 16, but not elsewhere in acknowledged Alfred works.

35   Af 37, cf. Ine 39; *Bischof Wærferths von Worcester Übersetzung*, ed. Hecht, pp. 45 ln 22, 229 ln 11, 293 ln 23 (on this text and its authorship see now Godden, 'Wærferth and King Alfred'). For the general argument, cf. *Councils and Synods* I, p. 18; and Campbell, 'Bede's Words for Places', pp. 48–9 (113–14), n. 19. A similar suggestion has been made as regards 'lefness' (Af 8, 20, laws concerning nuns, monks and their 'lords'), a word otherwise confined to the *Old English Bede* I, pp. 10 ln 7, 56 ln 21, 112 ln 6, 400 lns 8, 11, 418 ln 23; cf. Whitelock, 'Old English Bede', pp. 67–70; her objections to Archbishop Plegmund's authorship may be over-cautious. On the putative 'laws of Offa', see chapter 2, pp. 106–7, and my 'In Search of the Laws of Offa', p. 27 (pp. 203–4), with nn. 6–7.

36   Sisam, 'Authorship of the verse translation of Boethius's *Metra*', in his *Studies*, p. 294; cf. Bately, 'Lexical Evidence', pp. 78–9, n. 63. There is of course a considerable literature (and little consensus) on OE dialects; the most significant recent study is Weinisch, *Spezifisch anglisches Wortgut*, pp. 11–82.

37   'Forðon', etc.: Af Int 2, 3, 17, 20, 33, 46 (cf. Ine 43:1, 50, 57); 'forþam(ðe)': Af Int 3, 49:7,9 (cf. Ine 43); see Liggins, 'Authorship of the Old English Orosius', pp. 302–4; Bately, 'Lexical Evidence', p. 93, n. 156. 'Besittan': Af 42:1,3; Bately, 'Lexical Evidence', pp. 74, 87–8. 'Gesamnian': Af Int 49:3, Af 19 – 19:1 (cf Wi. Pr., Ine Pr. 'gesomnunge'). 'Gylt': Af Int 49:7, Af 5:4, 7:1 (cf. Ine 73). 'Gelician': Af Int 49:3. In general, Bately, 'King Alfred', pp. 443–4, 446, 452–3, and 'Lexical evidence', pp. 75, 87, 88 (n. 120), 93.

38   Cf. nn. 32, 34 above, and Bately, 'King Alfred', pp. 457–8, for other *Pastoral Care* abnormalities. (The translation of Exodus 21:33, on oxen falling into wells, is different in Af Int 22, and *Alfred's Pastoral*

book of the *Gregory*; whereas in Book II, *forþæm* etc. is over seven times more common; and in the remaining two-thirds of the work, *forþon* forms become quite scarce, *forþæm* and its variants being massively preponderant.[39] This trend seems more likely to reflect a development of authorial style than the influence of new scribes or different advisers; and in the laws' most personal passage, at the end of the preface, the preferred word is *forðam*.[40]

Similar considerations apply to typically Alfredian formulations that are missing. The Alfredian corpus liked to introduce 'oþþe ... oþþe (either ... or') phrases with preliminary 'awþer' or 'oþer twegea', whereas the *Orosius* always used an introductory 'oðer' with the main verb or with 'ðara (of these'). The most personal part of the preface to the laws duly had an *awþer* formulation, but in the first clause of the laws proper there was an 'oþþe ... oþþe' set up by 'to hwæðrum þissa'. At least the latter is not the Orosian construction; besides, Alfred's habitual choice is missing from the *Gregory*.[41] Similarly, Alfredian '*swa ilce* (likewise') was absent not only from the laws (though present in three of Ine's) but also from the *Gregory*, whose regular 'swa eac' parallels the laws' 'eac swa'.[42]

The difficulties of attributing the *domboc* to Alfred personally can thus be surmounted. They can also be set against all the positive indicators in its language: *adrifan*, 'to drive away', not *adræfan*;[43] *æghwelc*, 'each', rather than *ælc*, never *gehwelc*;[44] *(ge-)brengan*, 'to bring', not *bringan*;[45] *cigan*, 'to call', as well as *cleopian*;[46] *eardian*, 'to live';[47] *elles*, 'otherwise';[48] *fultumian*, 'to help', not *gefylstan*;[49] *gan*, 'to go', alongside *gangan*;[50] *(ge)eowian*, 'to show', not *oðiewan*;[51] *gegaderian*, 'to gather', as well as *gesamnian*;[52] *geþeaht(ere)*,

---

Care, p. 459; but Gregory's Latin, *Règle Pastorale*, iii 39, pp. 528–9, is paraphrasing rather than quoting the Vulgate, and the translation closely follows its source in each instance.)

39 'Forþon': *Alfred's Pastoral Care*, pp. 5 ln 1, 23 ln 10, 27 ln 8, 29 ln 4, 31 ln 12, 33 ln 6, 43 ln 21, 47 ln 8, 49 lns 11, 15, 53 ln 23, 57 ln 16, 67 ln 7, 71 ln 10, 73 ln 15 (total 15, with one in preface); 79 lns 9, 23, 81 ln 8, 83 ln 7, 87 ln 17, 89 ln 12; 93 lns 10, 18, 109 ln 19, 129 ln 4, 147 ln 13 (total 11); thirteen more in the rest of the book. 'Forþonþe': 25 lns 10, 15, 27 ln 2, 41 ln 12, 45 ln 4, 49 ln 24 (total 6); 109 ln 22; six in rest of book. 'Forþam/æm' occurs eleven times in chapters I – XI plus twice in the prefaces, another seventy-seven times chs XII – XXII, and innumerably (especially 'forþæm') thereafter. 'Forþam/æmþe' appears four times in chapters I – XI plus thrice in the prose preface, then ten times from chs XII – XXII and more than eighty times (especially 'forþæmþe') thereafter. (The preface was of course written last.)

40 Af Int 49:9 (x 2).

41 Af Int 49:9, Af. 1:1, cf. Af 42:7. Bately, 'Alfred', pp. 450–3.

42 Ine 76 – 76:2; Af. Int. 23, 49:7 (cf. Af. 42:4); Bately, 'King Alfred', pp. 448, 453, 458 (n. 200).

43 Af 16 (cf. Ine 40, 68); Bately, 'Lexical Evidence', p. 91.

44 Af Int 49:6, Af 1, 2:1, 5, 12, 29, 66:1 (cf. AGu 3); Af 12, 30 (cf. Ine 43:1, 46:2); Bately, 'King Alfred', p. 448, 452, 456.

45 Af Int 11, Af 34; Bately, 'King Alfred', pp. 446, 456.

46 Af Int 2; Af Int 34, 36, 48; Bately, 'Lexical Evidence', p. 89.

47 Af Int 35; Bately, 'Lexical Evidence', pp. 76, 87, 88 (n. 120). 'Wunian' was the normal legal term: *Gesetze* II, p. 251.

48 Af Int 34, Af 1:4 (cf. Ine 37); Bately, 'King Alfred', pp. 448, 451, 453, 455–6.

49 Af 42:3; Bately, 'King Alfred', pp. 445, 451, 453, 456; 'Lexical Evidence', p. 91.

50 Af 42:1,4, 71 (cf. Ine 42, 42:1, 46:1); Af Int 11 (cf. Ine 7:1, 20, 69); Bately, 'Lexical Evidence', pp. 76, 88.

51 Af Int 49:10; Bately, 'Lexical Evidence', p. 90.

52 Af Int 49:7,9; Af Int 49:3, Af 19 – 19:1. Cf. n. 37 above, and Bately, 'Lexical Evidence', pp. 87, 88 (n. 120).

'counsel(lor)', not *rædþeahtung/ere*;[53] *geo/giu*, 'long ago', not *ær/ealddagum*;[54] *hæman* (plus compounds), 'to have sexual intercourse', rather than *licgan* (plus compounds) in this sense;[55] *lician*, 'to please', rather than *gelician*;[56] *mildheortnes*, 'mercy', not *milts(ung)*;[57] *oðfæstan* (or *befæstan*), 'to entrust', not *betæcan*;[58] *scyld*, 'guilt', 'crime', also *scyldig*, *unscyldig*, rather than *gylt*, and never *ungyltig*;[59] *simle*, 'always', not *on symbel*;[60] *unriht*, 'injustice', not *unrihtwisnes*;[61] *unwillum*, 'unwillingly', not *unþances*'.[62] This catalogue clearly eclipses the problem cases previously reviewed. Though it is better evidence that the laws were not written by the *Orosius* or *Chronicle* authors than that they were written by Alfred, its cumulative effect is reinforced by three expressions found *only* in the laws and in Alfredian books. *Friþstow* ('place of refuge') also appears in the *Gregory*, *Boethius* and *Psalms*, though *gebeorh* is an adequate alternative in later laws (and *Psalms*).[63] For *geclysp* ('clamour') alternatives were plentiful, and its use was limited to Alfred's Mosaic preface and (twice) his *Gregory*.[64] Lastly, the cross-reference in Alfred's feud law quoted above uses the phrase 'swa we ær bufan cwædon'; it recurs in this form just twice in Anglo-Saxon literature, and one of these is in the *Gregory*.[65] Idiosyncratic vocabulary in what was of course a stock formula may be as telling as anything.

Scholars normally explain exceptional usage in other Alfredian texts in terms of particular features of the Latin originals, or the general effect of the sort of text the author aimed to render; but they sometimes invoke the influence of Alfred's assistants.[66] The first two considerations strongly apply to the *domboc*; so does adviser influence, vouched for by the preface of the laws as of the *Gregory*. A further solution, of which scholars tend to fight shy, is that vocabulary patterns were affected by the order in which Alfred's books were written. If (and it is a big 'if') there is anything in the fact that the clearest echoes of the laws, positive and negative, occur in the *Gregory*, it might be suggested

---

53   Af Int 49:9; Bately, 'King Alfred', p. 442, 452, 454.
54   Af Int 33, Af 9:2; Bately, 'King Alfred', pp. 447, 451, 452–3, 455, 456.
55   Af Rb 8, 25, 26, Af Int 12, 31, Af 10, 11:1–2, 18, 25, 26; Af Rb 10, Af Int 6, 49:5, Af 11:3, 18:1; Bately, 'King Alfred', pp. 442, 452, 455, 457 (Abt, likely inspiration for Alfred's laws on sexual matters (below, pp. 279, 281), used 'geligeð', 10, 14, 16, 31, 85).
56   Af Int 49:9–10. Cf. n. 37 above, and Bately, 'King Alfred', pp. 446, 452–3, 455, 457.
57   Af Int 49, 49:7; Bately, 'Lexical Evidence', p. 91; but note 'miltse', AGu. Pr.
58   Af Rb 20, Af Int 28, Af 17, 20. Cf. n. 17 above, and Bately, 'King Alfred', pp. 445, 451, 452–3, 455, 456.
59   Af Int 2, 17, 21, 25, 25:2, 45, Af 2, 4, 4:2 – 5 (cf. Ine 4 – 5, 6, 11, 28:1, 37); Af Int 49:7, Af 5:4, 7:1 (cf. Ine 73). Cf. n. 37 above, and Bately, 'Lexical Evidence', p. 93; 'gylt' remains the normal legal word for 'crime', so that the usage of Af Int 17, Af 2 and Ine 37 is distinctive: *Gesetze* II, pp. 107, 192.
60   Af 34 (cf. Ine 59:1); Bately, 'King Alfred', pp. 447, 451, etc.
61   Af Int 9, 41, 47; Bately, 'Lexical Evidence', pp. 73, 87.
62   Af Int 13; Bately, 'King Alfred', pp. 448, 451.
63   Af Int 13; *Alfred's Pastoral Care*, p. 167 ln 2; *Alfred's Boethius*, pp. 89 ln 11, 186 ln 16; *Liber Psalmorum*, 9:9, 17:1, 30:3; Bately, 'Lexical Evidence', pp. 82–3; for 'gebeor(g)h', see *Gesetze* II, p. 87.
64   Af Int 41; *Alfred's Pastoral Care*, p. 222 lns 9, 13. Bately, 'Lexical Evidence', pp. 80–1.
65   Af 42:2; *Alfred's Pastoral Care*, p. 341 ln 1; *Theodulfi Capitula in England*, ed. Sauer, p. 351 ln 18. Cf. Bately, 'King Alfred', p. 457. Wærferth's *Dialogues* used something like this formula over thirty times, but significantly never in precisely Laws/*Pastoral Care* form.
66   Bately, 'King Alfred', pp. 453 (n. 159), 458; 'Lexical Evidence', pp. 78–9; Clement, 'Production of the *Pastoral Care*', pp. 130, 133–6, 139–40; Frantzen, *King Alfred*, pp. 7–10.

that both were produced early in the king's career as a writer. This much can anyway be said: Alfred's authorship of his law-code may not be as securely attested as Archbishop Wulfstan's later contributions (chapter 4, pp. 188, 191; below, pp. 330, 365). But one can make about as good a case for it as for his authorship of the *Pastoral Care*.

(iii) The Domboc: contents

It is time to turn from the presentation of Alfred's laws to what they in fact say. Attention is concentrated here on the king's legislation in a strict sense, the laws for which he was answerable. The Mosaic preface and Ine appendix convey the underlying ideology of the *domboc*, so are deferred to chapter 6. The starting-point must be the famous passage at the end of the preface where the king describes his law-making. Alfred had just referred to 'synod-books (*senoðbec*)', in which 'compensations for many human misdeeds' were 'fixed' 'throughout the whole world and also throughout the English (*geond ealne middangeard ... 7 eac swa geond Angelcyn*)'. He continued:

> Then I, King Alfred, gathered these (*þas*) together and commanded to be written down many of those which our predecessors (*foregengan*) held, those which pleased me; and many of them that did not please me I rejected (*awearp*) with the counsel of my wise men, and ordered that they be observed in other ways. I dared not presume to put in writing at all many of my own, because it was unknown to me which of them would please those that were after us. But those that I found either in the time of Ine my kinsman, or of Offa king of the Mercians, or of Æthelberht, who first among the English received baptism, those that seemed most lawful, I gathered them herein, and left out (*forlet*) the others. Then I, Alfred, king of the West Saxons, showed these to all my wise men, and they then said that it pleased them all to observe them.[67]

This crucial text is not easily understood, and has arguably been misunderstood by most commentators. The first point to note is that it contained a *topos*. In his huge seventh 'Novella' (on the always topical subject of ecclesiastical property), the Emperor Justinian declared his intention to make a single law covering the subject, 'which would renew and emend all previous [laws], and add what was lacking and cut away what was superfluous (*quae priores omnes et renovet et emendet et quod deest adiciat et quod superfluum est abscidat*)'.[68] The theme was picked up by King Rothari in issuing his Lombard edict. Rothari aimed to correct the present law: 'quae priores omnes renovet et emendet, et quod deest adiciat et quod superfluum est abscidat'.[69] There is a fainter though still distinct echo in the Prologue to Charlemagne's *Admonitio Generalis* (which came to serve as a preface to Ansegisus):

---

67   Af. Int. 49:9–10.
68   *Corp. Iur. III, Novellae* vii Pr., p. 48. For what follows, see especially Dilcher, 'Gesetzgebung als Rechtserneuerung'. Wallace-Hadrill, *Early Germanic Kingship*, pp. 34–5, was the first to note the possible relevance of the theme for Alfred's preface.
69   *Ed. Ro.* Pr., pp. 1–2; cf. Zeumer, 'Zur Geschichte', pp. 428–30.

Let no one, I beg, think this pious Admonition presumptuous, in which we try to correct what was wrong, to cut away what was superfluous, and to constrain what is just (*errata corrigere, superflua absidere, recta coartare*) For we read in the Book of Kingdoms how holy Josiah tried to recall the kingdom given him by God to the worship of the true God by going about, correcting and admonishing.[70]

The themes of renewal and amendment, addition and subtraction, are here expressed with an added note of modesty, as they are by Alfred. That note was sounded more clearly still by Archbishop Hincmar: 'Everyone should so keep the good statutes of their predecessors in all things, as they would wish their own to be kept by their successors'.[71] *Topoi*, as has been said before in this book, are not to be disregarded altogether. They were used because they seemed to fit a context and can be important evidence for that context. Alfred was indeed traditional in legislative style. He probably respected his predecessors to the point of adding Ine's laws to his own. But *topoi* are also warnings to be cautious about the details of any claim they make. If there was a legislative model behind what Alfred said, there is a risk that it may not exactly reflect what he did.

Discussion of Alfred's relationship with his predecessors' legislation faces the initial difficulty that Ine's code, the major influence upon him, is transmitted only beside his own. How, then, can we be sure that the code he saw was the one included in the *domboc*? Did he not only change Ine's measures in his own laws but also, as Liebermann and others supposed, amend Ine's actual text? Happily, a relatively confident answer can be given to this critical question. As has been seen, Alfred contradicted Ine on several points. The *burhbryce* issue aside, there are differences in the sums levied for fighting before an ealdorman or felling another's trees; most crucially, where Ine called sixty shillings the 'full fine' with evident reference to theft, Alfred stipulated that 120 shillings was to be the fine for all thefts except abduction.[72] Readers of this book are more than once warned to be wary of appeals to logic when studying early medieval legislation. It nevertheless beggars belief that Alfred excised some Ine laws (for example on idolatry), to which he could have had no objection, yet left in place those that he had modified. In other words, the very fact that Alfred contradicted Ine shows that the subjoined text was itself untouched (which is not, as has been seen, chapter 2, pp. 104–5, to say that it was exactly what Ine had himself issued). The text Alfred worked from was what he (or conceivably a redacting *alter ego*) passed on.

What the king himself said was that he 'left out (*forlet*)' the laws of Ine, Offa and Æthelberht that he had not 'gathered (*gegaderode*)' into his own. Earlier in the passage, Alfred described how he 'rejected (*awearp*)' 'these' he and his counsellors disliked. Thorpe translated both 'awearp' and 'forlet' as 'rejected', so equating the two processes. Attenborough had 'rejected'/'annulled'. Liebermann, rendering 'forlet' as 'liess ich weg', i.e. 'omit', had no doubt that what Alfred said he had gathered and winnowed at the start of the clause were the English 'synod-books' of Ine, Offa and Æthelberht. But 'awearp' and 'for-

70   *Cap.* 22:Pr. = *Ans.* Pr., p. 442.
71   *Hinkmar, De Divortio* xii, p. 187. See chapter 6, pp. 423–5.
72   Af 15, 38, Ine 6:2; Af 12, Ine 43:1; Af 9:2, Ine 43 (and cf. Ine 7, 10, 46).

let' are not synonyms; the latter has a basic sense of 'leave', 'abandon' or 'neglect'.[73] And the 'þas' of Alfred's opening sentence could as well look back to 'synod-books' from all over the world, England included, as forward to the predecessors he was about to name.[74] Alfred himself separated the processes in the first and second halves of the clause by the word 'but (ac)'. This passage was thus saying two different things: on the one hand, he made (some) selections from the accepted legislation of Christendom; on the other, he gathered up some of his English predecessors' decrees and *left the rest alone*. Hence the treatment of Ine's laws.

However, less can be done for the passage's credibility in other respects. Alfred claimed to have 'gathered herein' those decrees of Ine, Offa and Æthelberht 'that seemed most just'. He did no such thing. Offa's and Æthelberht's codes were not 'gathered in' in the same sense as Ine's was.[75] Leaving aside the question of Offa's alleged code (chapter 2, pp. 106–7), no single law of Alfred's was an unaltered rehearsal of one of Æthelberht's or Ine's. Alfred's law on fights in a king's hall was much the same as Ine's, but for Alfred the offence included drawing a weapon, and he went on to envisage the offender's escape (a point obscured by modern clause division). His penalty of six shillings for fighting on a *ceorl*'s 'floor' was the same as Ine's, but this is one of several laws that went on to fix bigger sums for those with higher wergelds.[76] Similarly, Alfred levied £5 as *cyninges borg*, and his meaning is revealed by the fact that £5 was later payable for the royal *'mundbryce* (protection-breach)'. His law could thus be said to be 'gathered' from Æthelberht's on the same subject. Yet £5 is 240 West Saxon shillings or 1200 silver pence, where Æthelberht's fifty (golden) shillings would, at the likely rate of early-seventh-century exchange, have corresponded to 600 silver pence.[77] However 'influenced' by Æthelberht, Alfred doubled the price of royal 'protection'. Alfred was therefore professing a greater respect for precedent than he actually practised. It can be suggested that what he meant was roughly this: I made a collection of 'synod-books', and selected some for inclusion while rejecting what neither I nor my counsellors liked. *But* when I found precedents

---

73   This, in his *Pastoral Care* preface, p. 5 ln 24, Alfred said that past scholars did not translate books from Latin but 'hit forleton', on the assumption that knowledge of languages would keep pace with the growth of 'wisdom'; he of course meant not that they were *opposed* to translation but that they could not be bothered. The Toronto Microfiche Concordance lists 132 occurrences of 'forlætan' in *Alfred's Pastoral Care*, and for not one is 'omit' in the sense of 'reject' the appropriate translation (the nearest being, perhaps, pp. 73 ln 14, 222 ln 11); so also the *Boethius*, *Augustine* and *Psalms*. Liebermann's *Wörterbuch* (as Professor Stanley points out to me) proposed 'fallen lassen (discontinue)' for this passage, but I suspect that he was guided by his prior interpretation of the text.

74   Liebermann thought otherwise, *Gesetze* III, p. 50 *ad loc.*, on the engagingly circular argument, 'denn nicht jenen ganzen Stoff aller Synodbücher der Vergangenheit liess Ælfred abschrieben'! Turk, *Legal Code*, p. 39, was, for far from the only time, nearer the mark. But see also Stanley, 'On the Laws of King Alfred', pp. 211–12 (n. 2).

75   Palgrave's view, *Rise and Progress* I, p. 47, that Offa's laws were correspondingly present in Mercian MSS of the *domboc* should mean that Abt was substituted for Ine in Kent, which is not the case.

76   Af 7 – 7:1, Ine 6; Af 39 – 39:2, Ine 6:3; contrast *Gesetze* III, pp. 35–6 (28).

77   Af 3, Abt 8; for this monetary exchange-rate, see Grierson, 'Fonction sociale', pp. 350–5; with his 'Ford Lecturers' as mediated by Bullough, 'Anglo-Saxon Institutions', p. 650; and Grierson and Blackburn, *Medieval European Coinage*, pp. 157–8 (though cf. also Sawyer, *Roman Britain to Norman England*, p. 172).

set in the reigns of Ine, Offa or Æthelberht, I allowed myself to be influenced by those with the most potential and left the others alone. Whatever the king's exact meaning, the moral of the story so far is that what Alfred said he was doing matters less than what he can be seen to have done.

What, then, did Alfred actually do with Ine's laws? Up to forty, about one-third, of the items from (modern) clauses one to forty-three look like glosses to Ine. Some extended Ine's coverage, for example with reference to the kinless; others positively 'reformed' Ine's decrees (as on *burhbryce*); many seem to take up what a modern secretarial minute would call 'matters arising' (such as possible impediments to bringing a suit).[78] Of the two trends that stand out when comparing Alfred with his predecessor, the first is the rights of the Church. On the one hand, sanctuary was given a time-limit; on the other, its range was extended from the church itself to conventual buildings, theft from a church was additionally penalized, and sacramental confession of a hitherto undiscovered offence would halve the compensation due.[79] The second preeminent trend was the status and duties of lordship. Alfred enumerated the wergelds of the different ranks of West Saxon society five times as against Ine's once (near the end).[80] When comparing his and Ine's laws on changing lords (above, p. 274), one finds it now required that ealdormen be informed of the transaction; that the penalty for not doing so was paid not to the forsaken lord but to the king; that it was new lord, not new follower, who was obliged to pay; and, not least, that the sum payable was doubled.[81] The rights and obligations of lords were underwritten as a matter of policy. The general effect of these changes and others was to make West Saxon government look more Carolingian. Carolingian legislation both extended and restricted the purview of sanctuary; it emphasized the duty of standing by a lord and a lord's corresponding responsibilities; and the *leges* of Charlemagne's time put more emphasis on aristocratic wergelds than had Merovingian codes.[82] The implication is that Alfred may have meant just what he said when apparently claiming to have made selections from 'synod-books' 'throughout the whole world'; the 'foregengan' he acknowledged could perhaps in context be *any* (Christian) predecessors.

Once Alfred's approach to other Anglo-Saxon legislation is studied in the light of his perceived treatment of Ine, it falls into place. If what he meant by law-making 'in the time of ... Offa' is in any way represented by the legatine capitulary of 786, its influence upon him was restricted to his important treason law and another on the disinheritance of the children of nuns. Here too, the model was not so much reproduced as adapted: 'let no one conspire to kill a

78   See above, nn. 72, 76; add Af 22 compared to Ine 8 (or 13, 35:1, 75); Af 29 – 31:1/Ine 13:1 – 15:1 (gangs); Af. 34/Ine 25 (traders); Af 40/Ine 45 (*burhbryce*); Af. 43/Ine 3 – 3:2 (holidays, etc.); and next three notes.

79   Af 2 – 2:1, 5 – 5:4, 6 – 6:1; Ine 5 – 5:1, 6:1.

80   Af 10, 18:1–3, 29 – 31, 39 – 39:2, 40; Ine 70.

81   Af 37 – 37:2; Ine 39.

82   Sanctuary and Sacrilege: (e.g.) *Cap.* 20:8, 26:2–4, 39:3 (= *Ans.* i 134), 139:1 (= *Ans.* iv 13 = *Cap.* 193:1); lordship: *Cap.* 52:6, 64:9,17 (= *Ans.* iii 60, 63), 94:5,13, 204:iii (3), 262:13; aristocratic wergelds in ninth-century *leges*: *Lex Sax.* i, xvi, xx, *Lex Thur.* i, iv, vi, viii, xii, xvi, *Lex Fris.* i 1–5, 8, 13, 16, 19, ii 1–4, 6, 9, iii 1–2, ix 12. The nature of Carolingian influence on Anglo-Saxon legislation is more fully discussed in chapter 13 below.

king' became 'if anyone plots against the king's life ... [*or* his lord's life], he is liable for his life and all that he owns ... or to clear himself by the king's [lord's] wergeld'.[83] Even the kindred of child-bearing nuns get no compensation if the child is killed, though the father's kin retained its share.[84] Æthelberht's influence is most obviously evident in Alfred's inclusion of an injury tariff like his and nearly every other primary record of 'barbarian' law except (apparently) Ine's. Particularly striking is the fact that, having given 66 shillings 6 and one-third pence as compensation for loss of an eye, Alfred later explained that this is the value of eye, hand and foot alike. The equation was something of a commonplace in barbarian codes, and Charlemagne made it explicit in an Italian capitulary (chapter 2, p. 46 and n. 88); Æthelberht had specified fifty shillings for eye and foot, and that is also the rough total of payments due for thumb and four fingers (less nails). It was Alfred's return to the topic, in making a point that was visibly or by calculation one of Æthelberht's, which argues that the one was inspired by the other.[85] Other possible effects of Æthelberht's influence are that Alfred had much more to say than Ine about sexual offences, binding of freemen, a lender's liability for any blood spilt by the weapon loaned, and violence perpetrated at public meetings held by royal officials (especially as Alfred's laws on this issue took up a theme that had already in part been dealt with).[86]

None of this means that Alfred was revising the law of non-West Saxon peoples in an attempt to create a code for all Englishmen. There is no more evidence that Kentish law was changed by his intervention than that West Saxon law was aligned with Kentish.[87] Alfred legislated as 'Westseaxna cyning'. It was another sign of his anxiety not to seem innovative, given the grounds for dating the code late in his reign (below, p. 286, chapter 6, pp. 425–6), when he was otherwise called 'king of Anglo-Saxons'.[88] The best way to reconcile what Alfred seems to have done with what he claimed to owe Offa and Æthelberht is to suppose that when he found Mercian and Kentish laws with no counterpart in Ine, he wrote down his own laws on the topics concerned. It is unlikely that so 'traditionalist' a text thereby changed West Saxon law or anyone else's. With Offa and Æthelberht as with Ine, 'matters arising' strikes the right note.

Nevertheless, those elements in Alfred's own laws that were, in whatever

---

83   Af 4 – 4:2 (the square brackets in the text above merging these measures into one sentence); cf. *Alcuin, Epistolae* 3 (xii).
84   Af 8 – 8:3; cf. *Alcuin, Epistolae* 3 (xvi).
85   Af 47, 71; Abt 43, 54 – 54:5, 69; *Cap.* 98:5; cf. *Lex Sax.* xi, *Lex Thur.* xii – xv. The sum specified by Alfred represents 330 ⅓ silver pence as against Abt's (notional) 500–600; (Liebermann's supposed ratio of 2.5/1 WS/Kt. shillings (*Gesetze* III, p. 33 (23)) is now superseded by Grierson's research (as n. 77)).
86   Af 10 – 11:5, 18:1–3, 25 – 25:1, 26; Abt 10 – 11, 14, 16, 31, 82 – 85. Af 35 – 35:6; Abt 24. Af 19 – 19:3; Abt 18 – 20. Af 38 – 38:2 (cf. 15); Abt 1 ('mæðl frið') – 2 ('king's *leode*').
87   If the content of *Textus Roffensis* does not necessarily prove that Kentish law remained unchanged by Alfred's initiative, Wulfstan's tract on 'Church-peace (Grið)' (below, pp. 394–5) is more persuasive: *Grið* 6 – 8 equates the *mundbyrd* of king, archbishop and 'Christ's church' *on Cantwara lage* as in Wi 2, and rehearses the 'archbishop's (*sic*)' and king's compensation multiples as in Abt 1, 4; whereas Af 3 set the 'archbishop's *borh*' at £3, and the king's at £5. But the values in Af 3 do recur in the 'G' MS of Wulfstan's I Cn 3:2, II 62.
88   Af Int 49:10; *Alfred*, tr. Keynes and Lapidge, pp. 227–8.

manner of speaking, 'borrowed' from earlier English legislation account for only 75 per cent of the whole. About forty items remain. Some may have been prompted by the Mosaic laws excerpted in the preface. An obvious example is the decree on killing a pregnant woman.[89] A number of these laws, however, are characterized by concern with very specific, and (one would think) quite *recherché* circumstances. For example, the law on injuries caused by spears that attracted Maitland's notice means that there could be suspicion of intentional harm if a spear were pointed forwards and upwards, but none if it were over its carrier's shoulder. Yet why was Alfred's concern limited to negligence involving spears? Why not any weapon? Such laws are best understood as judgements on particular cases, included in the written code because they were recent or otherwise topical.[90] 'If a man be born dumb or deaf, so that he cannot deny or admit offences, let the father compensate his misdeeds'. Alfred's law has no real parallel in the legislation of barbarian Europe. One would not think the problem that rare. One might indeed think Alfred's measure rather obvious. But its inclusion is explained if there had been a notorious instance of refusal to take responsibility for a mute son.[91] Legislation of this type, then, was law-making in response to contingency such as typified Roman imperial edicts and several sub-Roman *leges* (and Ine); the primary (legal) meaning of the very word *dom* was 'judgement' (chapter 2, pp. 37, 42, 94–5, 102–5).

This leaves a residue of two dozen or so items among Alfred's laws that were legislation in the sense that they seem to establish new legal principles: the opening clauses on oath and pledge; the doubling of penalties for offences involving holy seasons or persons; the ratio of fines and compensation; payment of the sum of 120 shilings for all thefts except abduction; 'public slander (*folcleasung*)'; 'pledges sworn by God (*Godborg*)'; entailment of succession to bookland; feud; and public holidays.[92] Interestingly, they tend to be laws in the more 'developed' style, and ones without words untypical of Alfredian prose (above, pp. 271–2, 273–5). Yet even these may not be what they seem. The laws on offences aggravated by a religious dimension look like after-thoughts prompted by what had just been said rather than resonant statements of royal will. The bookland law most probably arose from Alfred's arrangements for his own estate, as described in his will.[93] The brutal penalty for *folcleasung*, loss of one's tongue, happens to be that of the *Theodosian Code*, hence of the 'Breviary of Alaric', and its topicality in the ninth century is shown by its appearance both in a forged decretal and in the writings of Hincmar.[94] More intriguing still, the obscure decree on *Godborg* finds its closest counterpart in Welsh law,

---

89   Af 9, Af Int 18; cf. (e.g.) Af 23 – 24, Af Int 21 on harm done to humans by animals.

90   Af 36 – 36:2. PM I, pp. 53–4 and n. *Gesetze* III, p. 58 *ad loc.* compared *Lex Fris.* Add. III 69 (pp. 96–7), by way of demonstrating that 'keineswegs ein bei Hofe damals wohl bekanntes Ereignis brauchte zu diesem Gesetz den Anlass zu geben'; but the parallel, which is not close inasmuch as the Frisian reference is to any kind of 'telum', shows only that such accidents were (unsurprisingly) common.

91   Af 14. Among laws so far attributed to the influence of other codes, some might equally be contingent legislation of this sort: Af 8 – 8:3, 19 – 19:3, 22. See also Af 16 (if not Af Int 24), Af 17 (if not Af Int. 35 – 36), Af 20 (if not Af Int 28).

92   Af 1 – 1:8, 5:5, 9:1–2, 18, 32, 33, 40:1–2, 41, 42 – 42:7, 43.

93   HaSD xi, p. 19. But cf. the comments of Keynes and Lapidge, *Alfred the Great*, p. 309.

94   Af 32; *Cod. Theod.* X x 2 (= *LRV* X v 1); 'Pseudo-Angrilamn' 44, ed. Hinschius, *Decretales pseudo-*

though the elaborate Mosaic ceremonies at the Temple door included in Alfred's preface could be an indirect influence.[95] Perhaps the idea of making such stipulations came from Moses, but their details were suggested by the relevant adviser.

One could of course say that all legislation is contingent in the sense of being stimulated by circumstance. For all that, a few of Alfred's laws bear the stamp of considered policy in areas known or reasonably guessed to have been among Alfred's preoccupations (if not *idées fixes*). His laws on feud perhaps came closest to legislation as Lombards, Carolingians or his own successors understood it. They form a careful scheme to defer violence and limit reprisal. But when the king decreed that 'one may fight beside one's lord without conflict if the lord is attacked ... In the same way, one may fight beside one's blood-kin except against one's lord: that we do not allow', he made the sole law to this effect in all the early medieval West. One can hardly help recalling the very same point being made by the Cynewulf-Cyneheard tale in the *Anglo-Saxon Chronicle*; nor the outrage voiced by Asser (going well beyond the *Chronicle* words) at the disloyalty of the Northumbrians in 866 or of the Franks in the 880s.[96] Alfred was brought up on 'Saxonica carmina', and they were educational media in his court-school. Does his loyalty obsession explain how his preface came to make the unique and bizarre claim that Christ ordered that one love one's lord as oneself?[97]

A rather different but no less important point is made by the king's more explicit treason legislation.[98] It was hinted in chapter 3 (pp. 137, 148) and will be argued at length in chapter 9 that Alfred's introductory laws on 'oath and pledge' hold the key to early English law and order. It needs to be said here that what these clauses established was not thereby *first* established. The duty to keep one's 'oath and pledge' was clearly something already in existence. Alfred aimed to tidy up particular problems that had arisen: disloyal oaths, those who could not be held to their obligations. The obscure final phrase described 'borgbryce' as if it were familiar. It is because these laws look so much like confirmations of established practice that they are usually thought to be about vague principles

---

isidorianae, p. 765; Hincmar, 'Opusculum LV capitulorum' xxiv, cols 377–8; cf. chapter 6,, pp. 423–6); though note also Af Int 40, 44.

95   Af 33, Af Int 11; see Ellis, *Welsh Tribal Law* II, p. 4; Binchy, 'Celtic Suretyship', pp. 362–3; the relevant passage is in *Welsh Medieval Law*, ed. and tr. Wade-Evans, pp. 85, 230, and *Law of Hywel Dda*, ed. and tr. Jenkins, pp. 78–9, 252. I owe this idea and these references to Dr Huw Pryce; being unable to read his own discussion, 'Duw yn lle mach', I am grateful for the following observations: the relevant Welsh law 'is almost certainly no later than the twelfth century', and 'the essential concept underlying *briduw* (lit. 'honour' or 'power' of God, i.e. taking of God as surety), is probably earlier than the twelfth century ... The parallels between Af. 33 and the Welsh rule ... are [not] sufficiently close to suggest direct influence of one upon the other ... On the other hand, Af. 33 is the closest parallel to the Welsh rule ... Given that *godborh* is otherwise unattested in Anglo-Saxon law, and given Alfred's connection with Wales *via* Asser, it may not be too fanciful to postulate that Alfred adapted a Welsh legal institution ... If there is any relationship between *briduw* and *godborh* ... it is more likely to be one of Welsh influence on English law ... Given that an analogous concept is found in early Irish law ... it is probable that legal recognition of divine suretyship is of Celtic rather than of Anglo-Saxon origin'.

96   Af 42:5–6, ASC 757A-E, pp. 46–50; *Asser* 27, 85, pp. 22–3, 71–2. White, 'Kinship and Lordship', sheds fresh light on this weary theme.

97   Af Int 49:7 ('he bebead þone hlaford lufian swa hine').

98   Af 1 – 1:8, 4 – 4:2.

of sound citizenship. Hence, if it can be shown that there is really no trace (in England) of the system that they evoke before Alfred's time, it must follow that he brought it into being *before issuing his code*. Putting the point another way, there was a law on oath and pledge in Alfred's *domboc*; but it was not inclusion in the *domboc* that made oath and pledge lawful. *Legislation*, commitment of law to writing, showed what the law was, whether in custom or as the result of royal adjudication or decree. It was not, at this stage, necessarily the same thing as *making law*.

A good indicator of the complexities of Alfred's *domboc* is that it has done so little for his lustrous modern reputation. In what is still the most satisfactory study of the king, Charles Plummer could only utter the *cri de coeur* quoted at the outset of this book's first chapter (p. 3, and cf. pp. 9, n. 30, 11, n. 39). Stenton's verdict is typical:

> Towards the end of his reign he issued a . . . lengthy code . . . There is no trace of any extraneous element in . . . his laws, which are, indeed, remarkably conservative . . . They include features protecting the weaker members of society against oppressions, limiting . . . bloodfeud, and emphasizing the duty of a man to his lord . . . But Alfred's code has a significance . . . independent of its subject-matter. In his preface Alfred gives himself no higher title than King of the West Saxons, and he names his kinsman Ine first among the three kings whose work had influenced his own. But the names of Offa and Æthelberht, which follow . . . imply that Alfred's code was intended to cover, not only Wessex, but Kent and English Mercia. It thus becomes important evidence of the new political unity forced upon the . . . English peoples by the struggle against the Danes.[99]

Sir Frank was his percipient self about Alfred's conservative tenor, even if one might wonder whether his characteristic interest in 'English unification' did not lead him to claim a wider application for Alfred's laws than they ever truly had. The objection is not so much to what Stenton or anyone else said as to what was left unsaid. Vast tracts of the *domboc* attract no notice at all, above all because they are not legislation of a sort that modern eyes easily recognize.

The real difficulty of Alfred's legislation is that it did so many different things at once. Major policy departures were mixed with reminders of custom that should have been familiar. Minutiae that could at best serve as legislation by 'leading case' (laws on spear-carrying tell officials what to do about other negligence) jostled with decrees on something as basic – and presumably far from uncommon – as violence in court. Kentish or Mercian law were not introduced to Wessex nor themselves reformed. They were complimented by imitation, the effect being heightened by their inclusion in a legislative tradition said to have extended what God gave Moses (chapter 6, pp. 421–7). The continental texts most like Alfred's are perhaps the *capitularia legibus addenda* of Charlemagne and Louis the Pious (chapter 2, pp. 47–8, 66–7). But these were not so firmly

---

99   Plummer, *Life and Times*, pp. 121–4; Stenton, *Anglo-Saxon England*, pp. 275–6. Other more or less unsatisfactory discussions include (T.) Hodgkin, *History of England*, pp. 299–305; Lees, *Alfred the Great*, pp. 207–23; (R.) Hodgkin, *History of the Anglo-Saxons* II, pp. 601–5. Liebermann's terse comment, *Gesetze* III, p. 38 (34), was 'nicht sie [the *domboc*] würde den Beinamen des Großen rechtfertigen'.

linked to the primary *lex* as were Alfred's laws to Ine's; in any case, Alfred was often the traditionalist, in style or substance, where Ine looked more the reformer (chapter 2, pp. 104–6). The ultimate impression left by the *domboc* is of discrepancy between legislative input and law-making effect. It was a huge exercise in 'gap-filling'. The law of the West Saxons must be written down or re-written so as to make the most comprehensive impression. Alfred's own laws do not explain why he was thought 'founder of English law' in Henry II's time. The fact that he issued his mighty *domboc* does.

(iv) The Guthrum Treaty

Before leaving Alfred for his heirs and successors, a little may be said of his agreement with his once inveterate enemy, Guthrum.[100] As hinted at the outset of this discussion, its brevity is by no means the only respect in which it contrasts with the *domboc*. For one thing, its textual tradition is less stable, despite its being so infinitely more manageable. There are two markedly variant texts in the one manuscript that preserves the vernacular version (chapter 4, pp. 231–3).[101] In general, the second text was 'depersonalized', most instances of 'we' being replaced by 'they'; that apart, the bounds of the two spheres of influence were viewed from a slightly different angle, and what one might otherwise have thought important riders on the value of goods in dispute between the two sides, the compensation due from parties that dare not 'clear' themselves, and the use of warrantors for all business involving men, horses or oxen, were omitted (perhaps by accident). Meanwhile, the *Quadripartitus* author encountered the text with an otherwise unknown appendix of selections from earlier-tenth-century royal codes (below, pp. 379–80). On top of that, the Rochester text of (pseudo-) 'Edward-Guthrum' was phrased as a continuation of Alfred's treaty, Alfred's, however, being overlooked (below, p. 390). This is a first indication of how complex the textual tradition of early English legislation could become; by which standards that of the *domboc* proper is the more strikingly uniform, oddities and all.

There are two other singular differences between Alfred's treaty and his main lawbook. One is that its style is very much that of the longer and more convoluted of Alfred's own laws, near the beginning and just before his injury tariff (above, pp. 271–2). Sentence structure was complex, 'clause 3' for example being (in one version) particularly elaborate. One clause in one version and two

100   Like II Atr, 'EGu' and *Duns* (below, pp. 320–1, 390–1, 380–1), AGu has been treated as part of the Old English legal corpus since at least the early-twelfth century, and is reproduced in all standard editions; much the best translation (if only of one version) is *EHD I* 34, though the dating needs reassessment in view of Dumville's argument (below, n. 105). Note that Carolingian tradition often included treaties between Charlemagne's descendants *Cap.* 204–7, 242–6, 254, 268, etc.; but *not* the agreements with Viking assailants recorded in *Annales de St Bertin*, pp. 4, 82–3, 85–6, 194–5, 247–8; *Annales Fuldenses*, pp. 39, 78–9, 108–9, etc.

101   Keynes, 'Royal Government and the Written Word', pp. 233–4; the differing texts are nicely revealed by Liebermann's use of bold type for variants in the second (which in the MS is actually the earlier).

in the other open with '*we cwædon*, we declared'.[102] This is the idiom above all of Edward the Elder, Æthelstan and Edmund (below, pp. 289, 303, 367, 378) though not of their successors. To that extent, the treaty looked forward where the *domboc* so often looked back. The other contrast with the *domboc* is in content. Alfred negotiated with Guthrum not as *Westseaxna cyning* but as leader of 'all the *witan* of the English people'. Having settled the boundaries and dealt, in a spirit of some mutual generosity, with compensation for killing Englishman or Dane (its words), it went on to demand that business transactions be properly witnessed, that fugitives, slave or free, be not taken in from one side by the other, and that traffic of any kind be guaranteed by the use of hostages.[103] These were in general not unlike the terms of Æthelred's treaty with Olaf and others a century later, or those hammered out on the Anglo-Welsh border. They also resembled what tenth-century kings became inclined to say about transactions in movable goods, above all cattle.[104] Here too the treaty was the more forward-looking of Alfred's laws. Yet it is as certain as anything on this dimly lit field can be that the treaty was the earlier text.[105] It must pre-date Guthrum's death in 890, perhaps by over a decade, whereas to judge from Asser's silence, the *domboc* was post-893 (chapter 3, pp. 120–1). The treaty is thus further evidence of the kind of legislation Alfred could issue when he chose. It follows that he chose *not* to do so in more than a small part of his *domboc*. The needs of that moment were not for the making of new law but the stating of old. Chapter 6 will suggest why.

2   The Codes of Edward the Elder

'King Edward commands all his reeves that you pronounce such just sentences as you know how to, as best for the administration of justice, and as it stands in the *domboc*.' The opening sentence of Edward the Elder's first code announced his concern not only that justice be done but that it adopt the programme laid down by Alfred's lawbook. Edward intended to maintain the momentum that his father had built up. His own codes helped to ensure that the tradition of Anglo-Saxon written law, finally revived at the end of the ninth century, would be maintained throughout the tenth. In the 135 years after 900 there were only thirteen when kings not known to have issued codes were on the throne.[106]

Examination of Edward's legislation, like Alfred's, should begin with its transmission. This contrasts starkly with the multiple branches of the Alfredian

---

102   AGu 5 ('B²' 2, 5 – the latter modified by substitution of third for first person, as above); cf. Af 42:5 (also 42), AGu Pr.

103   AGu 1, 2 – 3, 4 – 5.

104.   II Atr (below, pp. 321, 326), *Duns* (below, pp. 381–2); I Ew 1 – 1:5; II As 12, 13:1; II As 22 – 22:2; IV Eg 3 – 11, etc.

105   On the date of the treaty, I now follow Dumville's incisive discussion, 'The treaty of Alfred and Guthrum'; enlightenment on the key topic of the history of London in this period may now be had from Keynes, 'King Alfred and the Mercians'.

106   That is Eadred (946–55) and Eadwig (955–9). Note, however, that *Hundred* is *not* securely attributable to Edgar, and could have been issued by either of these kings (below, pp. 378–9).

stemma. Edward's two codes survive together in three copies: Corpus 383 ['B'], *Quadripartitus* (later editions) ['Q'], and *Textus Roffensis* ['H']. But chapter 4 argued (pp. 229, 232, 239–42, 246–8) that for Edward's and other codes these formed one closely related textual family. That proposition is not gainsaid by the few discrepancies there were. For Edward, the most interesting variations came in clause 1:5 of his first code:

> We also declared that if there is any false person (**H** *enig yfelra manna*/**B** *hwa gemearra manna*/**Q** *aliquis malorum*) who would put another's livestock in pledge by way of counter-charge, he then make it clear with an oath that he did it not as any trick but in full justice (**H** *fulryhte*/**B** *folcrihte*/**Q** *plena rectitudine*), without deceit or fraud. And he with whom it is attached is to do whichever he dare, establish title to it or warrant it.

B's 'folcrihte' does look better than H's 'fulryhte', even if the latter is supported by Q. But it also shows the preference for a more familiar word that is to be expected of this scribal *ingenu*.[107] Conversely, B's 'gemearra' is unique as an adjective and rare as a noun, but was also used by Alfred (and Wulfstan) with connotations of 'irrelevance', so would be not inappropriate for a litigant trying to launch a frivolous counter-suit.[108] This may thus be the original reading, with 'evil' offered as a concommitant gloss that was ultimately preferred by H and Q compilers (or their exemplar(s)). Neither these variations, therefore, nor any others outweigh the implications of Edward's codes' consistent membership of a single manuscript group.[109]

Two important consequences follow. First, the agreement of the three manuscript witnesses says nothing about the *quality* of the text they purvey. It will soon be clear that there can be startlingly substantial variations between extant versions of tenth-century legislation. That there were so few in Edward's case means only that a single branch of the tradition survived. Secondly, the two codes need not have been meant to go together. They are ill-matched in legislative tone. The first had no prologue and directly addressed the king's reeves, launching straight into what was required of them. The second instructed the *witan* assembled at Exeter in the general 'law and order' crisis before getting down to specifics.[110] It also covered a wider range of topics. In Carolingian terms, the second was more like a *capitulare legibus addendum*, whereas the first approximates to a *capitulare missorum* (chapter 2, pp. 47, 50). Yet the second code cited

---

107 I Ew 1:5; Liebermann, *Gesetze* III, p. 94 *ad loc.*, was tempted to credit Corpus with the original reading, at least to the extent that it was 'fullan folcrihte', as in *Swer.* 2; this would still correspond to the *Quadripartitus* Latin.

108 *Alfred's Pastoral Care*, p. 401 ln 20; *Can. Eg.* 16.

109 Cf. II Ew 7, **H** 'syllað leas' ('they give falsehood'?) for **B** 'sy laðleas'/**Q**. 'innocens erit': a reading that is not quite nonsense and a slip that one can imagine being made even by this relatively careful scribe. At II Ew Pr., on the other hand, **B** 'mid his witan' ('[?discussed] with his *witan*') looks like a typical Corpus simplification/slip for **H** 'myngode his wytan'/**Q**. 'admonuit omnes sapientes' ('instructed his wise men'). Yet more typical of the Corpus scribe is the (uncorrected) *saut du même à même* on 'folclande', I Ew 2. The strongest textual *similarities* within this group occur in Edmund's code and in *Becw.* (below, pp. 308–9, 384).

110 It typifies the perversity of editorial practice that the first clause of I Ew, containing legislative measures, is designated a 'prologue', but the generalities opening II Ew are numbered '1, 1:1'.

'what was written before', meaning the first.[111] It is a good guess that behind the extant copies lay a text where a royal official accepted the invitation to look from one to the other.

Edward's codes signalled a stylistic revolution; or, to be more precise, the full ripening of a legislative style whose first shoots can be detected in Alfred's laws and treaty.[112] The features detectable in the Guthrum treaty and in what look like Alfred's more 'personal' laws (above, pp. 271–2, 285–6) were now abundant. The conjunctive, 'eac' had been exploited eight times by Alfred. Every clause of Edward's first code bar three (over 75 per cent) opened, like the above-quoted text, with '7', 'eac' or 'swa'.[113] This may reflect the style of an address to reeves; the ratio fell to two out of seventeen in the more formal second code. Here, however, there were several cross-references, two to the *domboc*, one (as already noted) to the first code, and one to an earlier clause in the second.[114] Other stylistic features were common to both. Qualified conditional clauses were almost universal, whether in the form of the quoted text's relative clause, or at least in so far as specified consequences were multiple; the quoted text used a second relative clause to switch the subject to the defending party, whose options were coloured by the interjection, 'whichever he dare'. Moralistic vocabulary was not confined to prologues, as witness *'ful* (foulness)' and the first reference outside Alfred's preface to bribes.[115] Both codes were particularly rich in 'dependent directives', generalized statements of what should be done followed by specification of the consequences of not doing it. The provisions on urban commerce in the reeves' code started with a series of norms. Exeter's opening injunction was the resounding 'let no man deny another's rights'; and all but two of the substantial issues raised there were introduced in this way.[116] As the quoted sample shows, complexities of procedure were still a prime fount of elaborated syntax. But rhetoric was now having an impact that Alfred's discursive phrasing lacked. It was earlier suggested that even the intermittent fluency of his legislative prose made codes more like books. Chapter 4 also observed (pp. 189, 227, 235) that nearly all pre-conquest codes appear on the page as a continuous text. From 899 such presentation was matched by less staccato legal expression.[117]

To go with the new style was a new legislative terminology. To make law as an act of personal royal 'will' like Edward was something Ine and Alfred had taken care not to do. Each had at once associated their 'wise men' with their decisions, and the first person in their codes is usually plural, denoting not

---

111   II Ew 1:3, referring to I Ew 2:1.

112   For what follows, see once more Korte, *Untersuchungen*, and Schwyter, 'Syntax and Style'.

113   Exceptions: I Ew Pr. (2nd sentence), 1:4, 2:1. It must again be stressed that modern divisions are *not* an accurate guide to clauses as envisaged by the legislator: the 2nd and 3rd sentences of I Ew Pr, and the 2nd sentence of I Ew 1 are just as distinct as 1:1, 1:4, likewise the 2nd sentence of II Ew 8; total clauses may be reckoned as 13 (I Ew) and 17 (II Ew).

114   II Ew 5, 5:2, 1:3 (above, pp. 268–9, 287–8); II Ew 8.

115   II Ew 4.

116   I Ew 1; II Ew 1:2, 4 (three connected statements, leading into 5 – 5:2), 7, 8; exceptions: II Ew 3, 6.

117   A further symptom of syntactic development noted by Dr Schwyter, *Old English Legal Language*, pp. 79–81, is that mood-agreement of protasis and apodosis (subjunctive or indicative in both) is normal, as it was not in Alfred's laws, or at least in his injury list.

majesty but collective resolution.[118] But the 'willan' used by Edward at Exeter would be a law-making verb for the rest of the Old English series.[119] The 'we cwædon' formulation of the quoted passage had a briefer life-span, though perhaps the more notable for that. It first appeared as an introductory formula in Alfred's treaty and once in his laws (above, n. 102). Edward's reeves' code employed it five times, almost as often as not, though at Exeter it was reserved for its more usual function of cross-referencing.[120] The phrase need not imply that law-making was still in essence oral.[121] More pertinent is its place in a legislative vocabulary stretching from Alfred to Edmund: 'gearowe, ready', 'gelyfan, to trust', 'ungeligen, unimpeachable', 'wyrnan, to deny (legal rights)', even 'port, market'.[122] It will emerge that the abandonment of these words around the time of the *Hundred* Ordinance coincided with other changes of legislative style. This can hardly mean that a single group of law-makers was at work over two generations. What it may mean is that legal draftsmen were paying close attention to their predecessors, itself a point of some importance.

Edward's codes differed in scale and scope as well as tone. The first, directed at reeves in their judicial role, was limited to three problems of litigation. The demand that trading be done only in a 'port' ensured that disputes arising could be resolved by reliable witnesses, the 'port-reeve' among them. Litigants unable to raise their own oath-helpers would have them supplied 'from the same *geburhscipe*', an interesting term evoking the burghal concerns of Edward and his father. Next came laws on suits about land, among very few on this topic in the Anglo-Saxon series. Finally and in the same forensic frame, there was a law depriving proven perjurors of their right to compurgation. This litigatory theme was taken up at Exeter. Reeves failing to do justice were penalized with reference to the first code. But the following four laws concern aspects of theft: surety for those accused of it, cooperation in pursuing missing stock, sanctions on accomplices of rustlers, and those who have forfeited freedom through conviction for theft and abandonment by their kin. There was then a law about changing lords, before the code returned in conclusion to expectations of the reeve's justice.

The difference in form of address and range of content between the two codes heralds an inicipient bifurcation in law-making idiom that would become more and more visible. That being so, it must be stressed that they did not differ in any other way. Each built on themes covered by Alfred. Given that Edward inaugurated his legislation with an appeal to the *domboc*, this is no surprise.

---

118 Ine Pr., 1, 13:1; Af Int. 49:9–10, 1, 5, 5:5, 42, 42:5 (note the limitation of this form of address to Alfred's more 'developed' laws). Kentish law was invariably in the third person.
119 'Ic wille', I Ew 1, II 4, 8; cf. I As 1, 4, 5, V As 1:1 (Nw2), II Em 1:1, III Eg 1, 1:1, IV Eg 1:6, 2 – 3, 12, 13, 14:1, X Atr Pr.:2, Cn 1020 7, 10, II Cn 1, 69, 80, 82; cf. VI As 8:9, *Hu.* 7, V Atr 1, VI Atr 6, 41 – 42, VIIa Atr 1, VIII Atr 31:1, X Atr Pr.:3, I Cn 6, II Cn 20, 21 ('we'); VIII Atr 1 ('he').
120 I Ew 1:2,3,5, 2, 3, II 8; cf. Abt 71 'ealswa ... ys cwiden'; Af 42:2, etc. (above, p. 286); *Hu.* 4–5; *Blas.* 1; Ord. 3 (for implications, see below, pp. 367, 374, 378–9).
121 *Contra* my previous deduction, 'Lex Scripta', p. 123 (p. 23) and n. 107.
122 II Ew 4, V As Pr.:1, VI As 8:9; I Ew 1, 1:2, VI As 8:9, 12:3, II Em 5; I Ew 1, 1:2–3, II As 10, 12, V As 1:5; I Ew 2, 2:1, II Ew 1:2, II As 3, VI As 8:2, and EGu 5, II Cn 44 – 44:1; I Ew 1, 1:1, II As 12, 13:1, 14, VI As 10, and III Atr 7. Cf. 'oferhebban, neglect', II Ew 5, 8, V As Pr.:3, VI As 8:5; 'laðleas, unimpugned', II Ew 7, V As 1:1.

Alfred, himself building on Ine, demanded that traders register their escorts before a king's reeve with the witness of a 'folcgemot'.[123] One of Alfred's most important laws was about 'bookland', and it helps to explain what his son said about it (chapter 11).[124] The Exeter code was only superficially more innovatory. Ine had already exacted thirty shillings compensation for default of justice before a *scirman* or other *dema*, and required that expectations be met within seven days; it is a short step thence to what Edward demanded of his reeves, and one that could only be hastened by the stress of Alfred/ Moses on due justice.[125] It has already been implied (above, n. 13), and will be fully argued in chapter 9, that Exeter's laws on surety and theft were intimately linked with Alfred's 'oath and pledge'. Penal slaves and the obligations of their kin (if any) had also been covered by Ine.[126] Taking on another lord's man was the subject of decrees by both Ine and Alfred (above, pp. 274, 280).

The suggestion that English legislation from Edward the Elder onwards resembled Frankish capitularies was more than once made by Maitland.[127] There is a similar impression of laws meant to advance on selected fronts from the base established by an accepted *lex*. As in Francia, greater solemnity seems to attach to some law-giving sessions than to others, but this is not necessarily reflected in the number of copies preserved (chapter 2, pp. 49–50, 51–2). There is a distinct possibility (as again Maitland saw) that Edward and his successors were aware of Frankish example, not least in judges' answerability to *lex scripta*.[128] More will be said of that possibility later in this book. But Frankish precedents already confirm that, whatever the case with Alfred's *domboc*, there is nothing anomalous in this sort of law-making. The questions that do arise are where such revision left the kingdom's basic law, and why that basic law survives in many more copies than the revision.

3   The Legislation of Æthelstan

The codes standing in Æthelstan's name bring the Anglo-Saxon legislative tradition to the first of two climaxes. One sign of this is the knotted profusion of extant material. More laws were preserved for Æthelstan than for any other tenth-century king: officially six, actually seven.[129] Two incorporate two (or

---

123   Af 34, Ine 25.
124   Af 41.
125   Ine 8, Af Int 43, 46; discussion in chapter 10.
126   Ine 24 – 24:1, 74 – 74:2.
127   PM I, pp. 19–20; SE, pp. 97–8.
128   E.g. *Cap.* 22:63–4 (= *Ans.* i 60–1); *Cap.* 61:7 (= *Ans.* iii 53).
129   It must once and for all be said that the conventional numbering of Æthelstan's legislation is largely without rational basis, and that Liebermann himself used it only out of reluctance to disturb editorial convention. Current numbering originates with Schmid: he followed the Wilkins/Thorpe order in printing the Tithe and Charity ordinances as preliminary to 'II As' (Grately), but understood the manuscript position well enough to make tithes ('I As') a separate item, while keeping 'Charity' as Grately's first clause. That is why it lacks a serial number of its own in Liebermann. Schmid also followed Thorpe in defying the chronological sequence indicated by the texts themselves and printing the Faversham and Thunderfield

more) law-making sessions apiece. Another exists in an alternative if fragmentary variant. And this is to ignore two other pieces that have never been attributed to Æthelstan but are reasonably linked with his efforts (below, pp. 367–8, 373–4). The first necessary stage is to examine the transmission of these codes in all its complexity, bearing in mind that its complexity is a central part of the story.

(i) Transmission

As the accompanying table 5.1 is designed to show, Æthelstan's laws flowed from their sources in the royal councils to their estuary in the manuscripts printed since 1568 through three principal streams and several tributaries. The first stream is represented by Cotton Otho B.xi ['Ot']. As was recounted in chapter 4 (pp. 172–8), little more than cinders of this survive, but it had been transcribed by Laurence Nowell ['Nw1']. Fragments and transcript alike strongly suggest (chapter 4, pp. 176–8, 262) that it contained only Æthelstan's Grately code ('II'), and in a form earlier than other extant specimens. It had no rubrics such as appear in all other versions. There is reason to think that it lacked the final clause on perjury, which does look like an afterthought (below, pp. 307–8). Also missing was the clause ('24:1') banning Sunday trading, its absence logically connected with the deliberations at Thunderfield ('IV') that abrogated previous decisions about Sunday business.[130] The text of Grately in Corpus 383 ['B'] was perhaps intermediate between Ot's and the rest. On the one hand, it is unlikely to have been followed by 'V', the Exeter code, as it is in *Textus Roffensis* (chapter 4, p. 231).[131] On the other, it had rubrics or space for them, as Ot did not (pp. 294,

---

texts before Exeter's (though renumbering these 'III' – 'V' in place of Thorpe's 'II' – 'IV' to reflect his identification of 'I As'). Liebermann betrayed his impatience with this situation in that (unlike Attenborough) he printed V before III – IV, but he felt unable to change the intitulation. Few things better betray the enslavement of early English legal studies to traditional practice than continuing use of numeration for Æthelstan's laws that everyone since at least 1858 has known to be wrong.

130   II As 24:1, IV As 2, VI As 10. That probably *is* the right way to read this sequence of laws. The difficulties are a) that Ot would then in this respect represent a more *up-to-date* version than the others, and b) that there is no other evidence of Sunday trading being allowed after all: when Wulfstan resumed the Sabbatarian theme, EGu 7, V Atr 13:1, etc., he was unabashed by any notion that prohibition had previously been repealed. So it may be worth scouting an alternative possibility, that II As 24:1 in some way represents *innovation*. VI As 10 says that obedience was pledged to what had been enacted at Grately, Exeter, Faversham and Thunderfield, 'except for what was there previously struck out (*ofadone*, cf. Af 70:1, 74, Q. *exceptum*), that was Sunday trading, and that one might trade outside a port (*ceapian butan porte*, Q. *emi extra portum*) with full and trustworthy witness'; the summary IV As 2, preserved only in *Quadripartitus* Latin (below, pp. 295–6), says simply 'preter mercatum civitatis et diei dominice'. This *could* be taken to mean that it was Sunday trading that was subsequently 'struck out' (i.e. forbidden) and trade outside a port that was in certain circumstances allowed. II 12 does have a permissive rider, 'or else with the witness of the reeves at a *folcgemote*', which is missing from the outright prohibition of extra-market commerce in II 13:1 (this second clause being from a section of the Grately code that evidently does represent earlier dispositions, below, pp. 294, 299). In other words, Ot's text of II As was up-to-date enough to include the relaxation of the 'market' monopoly in cl. 12, but not sufficiently *au fait* to contain the Sunday prohibition of 24:1 (or the perjury clause, 26–26:1). Whatever the true position, it reflects as poorly on the distribution system of Æthelstan's laws as on their lucidity: below, pp. 299–300.

131   Note, chapter 4, *ibid.*, the indications that the Corpus text did not contain II 26 – 26:1 (or 24:1?).

Table 5.1 Transmission of Æthelstan's legislation

Nero A i (B)/ CCCC 201	CCCC 383	Otho B.xi/Nw1	Nw2	H(a)	Quad.	H(b)
I As (tithes) (1st person) – 4 rephrased?					I As (tithes) (1st person) As Alm (Charity) – 'secundum'	
	II As (Grately) (1st person) – No prologue . . . breaks off in clause 6 – Rubrics or rubric spaces	II As (Grately) (1st person) – No prologue – No epilogue – No 24:1, 26–26:1 – No rubrics or clause division	II As (Grately) (1st person) – No prologue – No epilogue – Has 24:1, 26–26:1 – Nowell inserts clause divisions V As (Exeter) (1st person) – refers to Grately – Has 'amnesty' clause at 3:1 – Nowell inserts clause divisions	II As (Grately) (1st person) – No prologue – No epilogue – Has 24:1, 26–26:1 – Rubrics or rubric spaces V As (Exeter) (1st person) – refers to Grately – No 'amnesty' clause – coloured initials in Pr.:1, etc. IV As 6 – 6:3 (Thunderfield) (1st person) – robber has 9 days *fyrst* if seeking king, church or *bishop*	II As (Grately) (1st person) – 'tertium' – Has epilogue – Has 24:1, 26–26:1 – Rubrics in all versions [*Episc* 'quartum' – cl 9 'quintum' – *Norðl* 'sextus' – *Mirc* 'vii de' – *Að* 'viii de' – *Had*] IV As (Thunderfield) (3rd person) – robber has 9 days 'de termino' if seeking king, church or *archbishop*	H(b)

– coloured initials
  at 6:2abc

– rubrics only in
  MHk texts
– refers to Exeter,
  Faversham,
  Thunderfield and
  Grately
V As (Exeter)
  (1st person)
– refers to Grately
– No 'amnesty'
  clause
– rubrics only in
  MHk texts
III As (Kent)
  (2nd person)
– refers to Grately,
  'the West'
– rubrics only in
  MHk texts

VI As (London)
  (1–10, 12 3rd
  person, 11 1st
  person)
– refers to Grately,
  Exeter,
  Thunderfield and
  Faversham; cl. 12
  refers to
  Whittlebury
– numbered clauses
  and/or ornate
  initials

VI As (London)
– Text as Quad.

– paragraphing
  with coloured
  initials for
  subdivisions

300). Its version of an extremely obscure and elliptical passage near the start of the code, on thieves who resist arrest, was closer to Ot than to *Roffensis*.[132]

The next main stream of transmission descends through *Textus Roffensis* ['H(a)'] and the lost manuscript ['Nw2'] with which Nowell eked out his transcript of Ot (chapter 4, pp. 176–8, 261–2). Here Grately was backed up by a record of the Christmas council at Exeter ('V'), where Æthelstan took further action in exasperation at how little had been achieved so far. These versions of Grately were paragraphed like that in B; room was left for rubrics in H even when they were not supplied, and Nw2 added marks of clause division to Nw1.[133] Grately's Sunday trading and perjury clauses appeared in both. Its law on thieves resisting arrest was simpler in H than in Ot or B.[134] The main difference between H and Nw2 is that Nw2 added a clause to the Exeter decree allowing theft to be compensated without further sanction 'until the Rogation Days'; it is obvious enough why this provisional measure should have vanished from other versions.[135] H for its part moved almost imperceptibly on to what 'we declared in the meeting at Thunderfield' ('IV'). Its text here corresponded to that of Q, the other extant Thunderfield record, except that nine days respite was given to thieves who sought out king, church or *bishop*, whereas Q confined nine days' cover to the king, church or *archbishop*, and allowed only three days for a bishop (as for an ealdorman or thegn).[136]

All versions of Grately so far discussed had two other anomalies. For one thing, they lacked prologue or epilogue. As a result, the code offered no indication of its authorship. It is most unusual for Anglo-Saxon law-codes to be unattributed, bar the special circumstances pertaining to Æthelberht and Æthelred (chapter 2, pp. 93–4, below, pp. 333–5).[137] Second, Grately seems to contain an earlier code within itself. Clauses '13:1' – '18' are classified 'secondly' to 'seventhly'. They mostly relate to affairs of the 'borough', like trade or minting: issues, that is, coming under the aegis of borough reeves, whose duty to witness large-scale transactions was stressed in the immediately preceding clause '12' (above, n. 130).

Much the deepest channel of Æthelstan legislation flows through *Quadri-*

---

132   II As 1:2–3, and cf. Whitelock's account and translation, *EHD I*, p. 417 (though noting that 'ær ðam oder æfter' is not, as she says, the Ot reading but that of 'Somner' (i.e. 'Nw3', chapter 4, pp. 261–2), and that 'æfter' is therefore very probably a marginal gloss introduced by Nowell from Q 'postea' (cf. my 'Lambarde problem', p. 260 (pp. 158–9), n. 60). Omission of 'ær ðam' by H and insertion of 'postea' by Q most likely represent (much-needed) clarifications of a meaning close to the one Whitelock gives. But one should also note that 'Oðer gif' in B is a correction over an erasure.

133   Actual rubrics in H are at II As 3, 4, 6, 6:2, 8, 9, 10, 10:1, with spaces at II 1:3, 2, 12, 13, 14:2, 15 – 17, 19 – 21, 23 – 24, 26; B rubrics are at II 1, 2, with spaces at 3 – 4, 6; Nw2 clause marks are at II 3:1, 4, 6, 7 – 10, 11 – 13, 14, 15 – 20, 21 – 22, 23, 24, 24:1, 25, 26, also at V As 2.

134   This could have been the case in Nw2 also, since Nowell did not necessarily register the deletions as he did the substitutions or additions of his second exemplar.

135   Hence Lambarde's version, as reproduced by Liebermann, *Gesetze* I, p. 168 ('Ld'). Other differences to note between H and Nw2 are at V As 1 'getruwian'/'gesteoran', and V 1:2 '7 he hine ungereccan ne mæge'; Nw2 each time corresponds to Q, so both could be H slips.

136   V As 6 – 6:3 (*Gesetze* I, p. 171); IV As 6:1–2c, p. 172; H's version also includes a clause on breach of sanctuary (6:2b).

137   But note that some 'unofficial' codes may be so regarded only because they have accidentally lost evidence of royal sponsorship: below, pp. 366–80.

partitus ('Q'), and is thus muddied by early-twelfth-century Latin. The sequence here began with the king's decrees that tithes be paid ('I') and that the poor be provided with food and clothing ('Alm'). Of the latter there is no Old English text, Lambarde's having been exposed as a Nowell coinage (chapter 4, pp. 261–2). The former, however, was also diverted into two Wulfstan manuscripts, where it must be suspected that the demands for soul-scot and plough-alms, which are not in Q, were Wulfstan's intrusions (below, pp. 309, 314–15). Both ordinances addressed the king's reeves, the Old English text of 'I' specifying 'the reeves in each borough'. Both adduced the counsel of Archbishop Wulfhelm. Hard upon 'Alm' followed the Q text of Grately. In the London version (chapter 4, pp. 237–42), it was 'tertium', 'Alm' being 'secundum'; in one copy of the final edition it is 'II Lib.', with 'I' and 'Alm' fused into a single text.[138] Q liked to group a king's laws together. But all editions went on to add a set of texts assembled and recast by Wulfstan; the London version numbered these 'quartum' to 'viii', while no other edition marked a clear break after Grately. They obviously did not belong to the Æthelstan corpus, and the compiler had no reason to put them there. He must have found them incorporated into it in his exemplar (below, pp. 391–4). Hence, he came upon 'Alm' and Grately in such proximity to 'I' as to resemble 'second' and 'third' items. For Q, then, Grately *did* in effect have a prologue and was consequently not anonymous.

The other notable features of the Q text of Grately are that it had rubrics in all editions, not merely in those where the compiler made a policy of inserting them (chapter 4, pp. 242–3); and that it had not only what amounted to a 'prologue' but an epilogue too. 'All this', it says, 'was decreed in the great synod at Grately, at which Archbishop Wulfhelm was present, and all the chief and wise men whom King Æthelstan could gather'.[139] It may or may not be significant that Æthelstan is not actually said to have been present himself. It surely is significant that Wulfhelm is once again singled out as a key participant in proceedings. The Q texts of Æthelstan's first three pronouncements have the air of something for which the archbishop had special responsibility.

Q put its other records of Æthelstan legislation after the Wulfstan tracts, but this time with enough of a hiatus to imply that they were discrete from the first set in his exemplar. They in fact form two blocks.[140] One comprises the codes usually numbered 'IV', 'V' and 'III', and ascribed respectively to Thunderfield, Exeter and a Kentish council at Faversham. The Thunderfield text opened:

> These are the judgements which the wise decreed at Exeter by the counsel of King Æthelstan, and again at Faversham, and a third time at Thunderfield, where all this

---

138   The copy in question is 'M' (chapter 4, p. 237, no. 2).

139   II As Epil. For Lambarde's Old English version as another of his translations from Q, see my 'Lambarde problem', p. 260 (p. 159).

140   Both MS Rs f. 27v and MS K2 f. 12v (cf. chapter 4, p. 237) have initials at the start of 'IV' As such as to suggest legislation by a new king, and there is an unusually prominent initial at MS R, f. 146r. The initials for 'VI' As in Rs, f. 30r, K2, f. 14r, and R, f. 147v, are like those inaugurating 'IV'. In all three MSS, the initials for 'V' and 'III' are not very different from those used within the text of 'VI'; but MSS MHk do give separate chapter-lists to 'IV' and 'V'–'III'.

was defined and at the same time confirmed. And this is first, that they observe all judgements which were laid down at Grately, except the borough market and Sunday ...

After annulling (or in some sense modifying, above, n. 130) Grately's provisions about trading in towns and on Sundays, 'IV' gave a digest of what Exeter proposed for those who defied the Grately decrees, and who illicitly changed lords (this itself elaborating a Grately law). But its wording was more like that used at Faversham.[141] Next came brutal measures against those of any sex or status who persisted in theft after this council. Included among them was a counterpart to the Thunderfield provisions on sanctuary found in H, but with an *arch*bishop's protection equated to a king's, and a bishop's reduced to the ealdorman's level.[142] The text concluded by repeating Exeter's condemnation of uncooperative reeves.[143] As preserved in Q, then, 'IV As' was not so much a code in its own right as a summary of resolutions at a series of assemblies, Thunderfield among them. Æthelstan was named only at the outset in connection with the Exeter council. Otherwise, he was simply 'the king', and always in the third person.

Such being the nature of 'IV' in Q, it was logically followed at once by the Exeter code (less 'amnesty' clause), and then by a record of the decisions of the '*sapientum* ... bishops, thegns, *comites et villani* of Kent', 'in council at Faversham'.[144] This remarkable document featured the king in the *second* person ('karissime' – 'leofost'?). It expressed appreciation of his arrangements 'for our peace and welfare' and announced what was being done in return 'with the help of those wise men whom you sent us'. Its clauses were studiously numbered 'first' to 'eighth'. Reference was made to the Tithe Ordinance, to the Grately 'scriptum pacis' and to 'what was declared in the West' (i.e. at Exeter).[145] Topics covered were on the whole the same as in 'IV'. But there was an 'amnesty' clause, this time extended to 'August' as opposed to Exeter's (May?) Rogation Days.[146] There was also a new departure in the clause on the responsibility 'to hold one's men in surety against theft'; this related only indirectly to the Grately and Exeter demands, but was strikingly paralleled in the text to be examined next.[147] Either Kentish bishop could have preserved this communication. But it is not extant in Rochester's codex, and in *Quadripartitus* it is linked with a version of 'IV' which put the archbishop where H had put a bishop. Canterbury, so again Wulfhelm, seems to be indicated.

The code conventionally known as 'VI Æthelstan' was the last of the series

---

141   V As Pr. – Pr.:3, III As 6, IV As 3 – 3:2 (III 6, 'adeo dives vel tante parentele'/IV 3 'adeo dives sit vel tante cognationis', a point merely implied at Exeter); II As 22 – 22:2, V As 1 – 1:1, III As 4 – 4:1, IV As 4 – 5 (V 1:1, a new decision about those unjustly accused by their lords, echoed in IV 5, which uses the word 'hlafordsocnam' as in III 4:1); these links would, one imagines, be clearer if 'III' and 'IV' were extant in their original form.
142   IV As 6 – 6:7 (*Gesetze* I, p. 172), and cf. n. 136.
143   II As 25 – 25:2, V As 1:2–4, IV 7.
144   III As Pr., 2, 3.
145   III As Pr. – 1:1, 5, 6, and cf. 7:3, 8.
146   III As 3, and cf. n. 141.
147   III As 7 – 7:2; cf. II As 2 – 3:2, V As 1:5 – 2, and below.

credited to him in Q, where it was perceptibly distinct from what went before.[148] There was also a vernacular text in *Textus Roffensis* ('H(b)', table 5.1). This, however, shared crucial errors with Q, whose readings are on the whole better.[149] H(b) was separated from the H(a) texts of 'II', 'V' and 'IV' by a set of 'quire-fillers' and inaugurated a quire of its own (chapter 4, pp. 245–8). It was textually much closer than H(a) to Q. Since Rochester's collection was built up from various sources, it could well have had a different exemplar for 'VI' than for 'II' – 'V' – 'IV'. One can easily forget that behind *Quadripartitus* was a vernacular compilation like Rochester's or St Paul's, which might in principle be a superior text. In this instance it is highly likely that H(b) is derivative from the source of Q, which thus becomes the primary witness.

The 'code' as it stands begins by sounding the same note as 'III' and 'IV':

This is the ordinance that the bishops and reeves who belong to London have declared and confirmed with pledges in our peace-guild (*mid weddum gefæstnod on urum friðgegyldum*), both nobles and ceorls, in addition to the judgements that were laid down at Grately and at Exeter and [again, Q *item*] at Thunderfield.

London's 'bishops and reeves ... *ge eorlisce ge ceorlisce*' were equivalent to Kent's 'bishops, thegns, *comites et villani*'. The invocation of 'Grately ... Exeter and [again] Thunderfield' recalls that of 'Exeter ... Faversham and ... third Thunderfield in 'IV'. The extraordinary account of London's 'peace-guild' that followed can be plausibly seen as a hugely amplified correlative of the Kentish undertaking to provide surety for dependents.[150] 'VI' was thus not composite in quite the same sense as 'IV', but it too was made up of diverse elements. Its 'first' and 'ninth' clauses are about the (savage) punishment of thieves in general. They could have drawn on the Thunderfield edicts that left traces in the two versions of 'IV'. More clear-cut is the implication of the concluding clauses:

Tenth, all the wise all together gave their pledge (*þa witan ealle sealdan heora wedd ealle togædere*) to the archbishop at Thunderfield, when Ælfheah Stybb and Brihtnoth, Odda's son, joined that meeting at the king's command (H *worde*/Q(Lond.) *verbo*/Q(rev.) *ore*), that every reeve take the pledge in his own shire, that they would all keep that peace as King Æthelstan and his wise men had ordained it first at Grately and again at Exeter and afterwards at Faversham and a fourth time at Thunderfield before the archbishop and all the bishops and his wise men nominated by the king himself who were present, that the judgements that were laid down at this meeting should be kept (*þæt man þas domas healdan sceoldan þe on þissum gemote gesette wæron*), except ...

Eleventh, Æthelstan commands his bishops and his ealdormen and all his reeves throughout all my dominion, that you so keep the peace as I and my wise men have ordained. If any of you neglects to do so, and will not obey me, and will not take the pledge from his dependents as I have ordered and as stands in our writings (*urum*

---

148 See n. 140 for the text's initial in editions of Q.
149 VI As 6:3 (**H(b)** 'oðseoce / **Q(Lond.)** 'neget' for ?'osceote', cf. **Q(rev.)** 'aufugiat'); 8:1 (**H(b)** 'XII'/Q 'duodecim'; one expects 'eleven', *EHD I*, p. 425, n. 3). For the overall textual position and the inferiority of H(b) readings, see *Gesetze* III, p. 114 (1).
150 VI As 2 – 8:9, III As 7 – 7:2; more obviously, the peace-guild reflects the Grately and Exeter laws about pursuit of cattle thieves and the generally uncooperative, II As 9, 20 – 20:8, V As 1:5 – 2.

gewritum), then let the reeve be without his office and without my friendship ...

Twelfth, the king now again speaks to his wise men at Whittlebury and orders it to be made known to the archbishop through Bishop Theodred that it seemed too cruel to him that a man should be killed so young or furthermore for so little as he had discovered was being done everywhere. He says ... that no man younger than fifteen should be killed unless he ... would not surrender ...

This passage was clearly not part of the peace-guild's constitution. If the pledge of the *witan* in clause 'ten' is that of the guild itself, on a par with Kent's *sapientes*, the clause can be read as a promise to deliver that constitution.[151] In clause 'eleven' the king speaks in the first person as he does not otherwise in this text until the end; this looks like a quotation of 'the king's word' specified in clause 'ten', that reeves take pledges in their shires.[152] Clause 'twelve' relates to another set of proceedings alotgether. If London's clauses were numbered from the outset, like Kent's, then someone artifically extended the numeration.[153]

The best understanding of the story these clauses tell may be this: Ælfheah and Brihtnoth brought instructions from the king to a council at Thunderfield under Archbishop Wulfhelm's presidency. The instructions were for reeves to take pledges that his peace be kept. The peace-guild was the responding pledge of the reeves (and bishops) of London.[154] Especially noteworthy is Wulfhelm's role. The pledge was given to him. He was present with other bishops and royal nominees when the Grately, Exeter and Faversham enactments were reiterated. It was also to him that Bishop Theodred brought fresh injunctions from the king's Whittlebury council modifying the severity of what had been decreed since Grately. 'VI Æthelstan' may thus be a compound of reports collected by Wulfhelm in fulfilment of royal orders.[155] Essentially, it is a *Quadripartitus* block made up of the peace-guild's rules, an account of its inception, and a later order restraining some of its rigour. It corresponded to the block combining the 'IV Æthelstan' summary with the Exeter and Kentish records on which it was partly

---

151   That the peace-guild text was not drafted until Thunderfield had dispersed is suggested by the phrase 'in addition to the laws (*to ecan þam domum*)' in the prologue (above). Note too that unlike VI As 10, VI 1 does not refer to Faversham: London responds to royal commands, but Kentish arrangements merely run parallel with theirs.

152   Any interpretation is obfuscated by the text's barely permeable syntax. I take 'þæt ælc gerefa name þæt wedd' ('10') as governed by 'þæs cinges worde', because (i) if it were governed by 'þa witan ealle sealdan heora wedd' at the start of the clause, the *witan* would be pledging that reeves take pledges, which seems excessively convoluted, and the *witan's* pledge can then be related to 'þæt man þas domas healdan sceolde' near the end of the clause, which otherwise lacks an antecedent; and because (ii) clause '11' shows that such a royal 'word' was indeed issued. There is punctuation after 'worde' in H(b), but not in Q(Lond.).

153   But if VI As 1 - 1:5 and 9 were distinct from the peace-guild's regulations, it was the editor of this block of texts who was responsible for the numbering throughout.

154   Such is not quite the understanding of Dr Keynes's acute discussion, 'Royal government and the written word', p. 240, but it is not clear that his is to be preferred. '10' does indeed refer to a 'general meeting of the king's councillors', but that need not mean that Ælfheah and Brihtnoth were 'summoned' to that council as 'local representatives, perhaps ... reeves of the borough of London', nor that '10' derives 'from their report back to the peace-guild'. The two men were listed royal councillors in the 930s (Keynes, *Atlas* XXXIX(1)), so it seems superfluous to make them local reeves rather than carriers of royal messages. That '10' derives from the *guild's* report to the *archbishop* is not only what it seems to say but also fits with '12' (below).

155   If so, the archbishop quoted the king's Whittlebury message directly at the end of VI As 12:3.

based, wherein Wulfhelm involvement may again be inferred. The difference is that this one passed over to Rochester.

This pile of slivers may now be glued into a possible model of Æthelstan's law-making and its transmission. The sequence in Q and the order of Kent's responses imply that the Tithe Ordinance ('I') came first. Wulfhelm was singled out among the bishops who initiated it. At some point, not necessarily at once, he and his colleagues prompted a similar measure about poor relief. The former later interested Archbishop Wulfstan, whereas the latter was not taken up by any other collection. 'I' addresses 'reeves in each borough'; it was accompanied by secular instructions directed to those in charge of business in a borough or its environs. In a council at Grately where Wulfhelm was among those attending (but where there is no *direct* evidence that the king was present), it was decided to expand these into a more substantial code.[156] The unfortunate effect was that 'II' was parted from its mooring alongside 'I' and cast anonymously adrift. It was preserved in truncated form at Winchester, London and Rochester. But at Canterbury Wulfhelm retained the bond with the Tithe and Charity Ordinances. At some stage it was decided to give Grately clauses, so it usually had rubrics too.

The king was not long content with the outcome of this effort. A new council at Exeter launched a campaign to tighten up observance of the 'peace'. This code was subjoined to Grately's, displacing its epilogue, at Rochester and the domicile of Nw2. It was also communicated to Wulfhelm, who was *not* said to have been at Exeter. He reacted by organizing a set of local initiatives in collaboration with councillors sent out by the king. Their work was consummated in a decidedly busy council at Thunderfield. Earlier law was recapitulated. Previous amnesties made way for steps of marked ferocity against all types of thief. The royal demand that reeves pledge their shires' compliance was met by organized pledges from London and doubtless elsewhere. Part of this council's minutes took the place of Exeter's amnesty provision at Rochester. Parts were summarized in a report, apparently kept by Wulfhelm, which was prefaced to the Exeter and Faversham texts that contributed to the Thunderfield proceedings. Wulfhelm also kept a record of London's initiative, itself pledged at Thunderfield, following this up by quoting the royal 'word' that had evoked it, and then with new orders toning down some of the campaign's excesses. A copy of this second record got to Rochester, though not necessarily before the 1120s.

This of course is only one possible reconstruction of how Æthelstan's legislation assumed its current form. Yet two points stay relatively fixed. One is Wulfhelm's role. In no other memorials of Anglo-Saxon law is a non-royal individual so prominent. Wulfstan himself was unmentioned in all decrees he composed except one version of one code (where he is first the junior archbishop, then enters his own name where the scribe had left a blank).[157] That Wulfhelm wrote his master's laws is beyond legitimate speculation. That he was behind the

---

156 Royal presence at Grately is not explicit in V As Pr., III As 2, 5, 7:3, IV As 2 or VI As 1:4, 12:1, though II As 25 uses the first person singular. VI As 10 adverts to what 'King Æthelstan and his wise men had ordained first at Grately and again at Exeter and afterwards at Faversham and a fourth time at Thunderfield', and the king was certainly at Exeter, but equally clearly he was not at Faversham or Thunderfield.

157 VI Atr (Lat) Pr., 40:2: see chapter 4, p. 191, and below, pp. 333–5. There are solitary references to

extant form of some texts is likely. That he was the chief agent of their preservation is probable.[158] The other nodal point is the discrepancy between the energy
with which king and councillors set about making law and the ineffiency of their
work's circulation. Winchester apparently had nothing to show for it except a
text of Grately less its prologue and Sunday and perjury laws. Rochester had a
headless Grately code and a mere fragment of Thunderfield to put beside
Exeter.[159] Only Wulfhelm's collection, presumably from Canterbury and pickled
in *Quadripartitus*, preserves anything like a full set; and here royal laws were
well-nigh submerged in locally produced materials. One has a sense that it may
have been as hard for judges as for modern scholars to ascertain the current law.
The hallmark of Æthelstan's law-making is the gulf dividing its exalted aspirations from his spasmodic impact.

(ii) Style

The style of Æthelstan's legislation represents an extension, indeed intensification, of trends set by his father's. Two provisos are that some of it is unavailable
in its original language, and that so heterogeneous a body of texts is *a priori*
unlikely to manifest the same style throughout. Nevertheless, the symptoms of a
more 'developed' style are omnipresent and on the rise.

Discussion must centre on the Grately code ('II'), the major 'official' statement
of the reign. Exeter ('V') may be taken with it, leaving 'I' and ostensibly non-royal
laws for separate consideration. The most striking thing about 'II' is its division
into clauses so early in its transmission as to suggest that this was an 'official'
feature. The actual rubrics are too inconsistent to have been provided at source,
but space was often enough left for them at the same points.[160] Moreover,
Grately's clause divisions on the whole make more sense of their content than
those of Alfred–Ine. Exceptions are laws on sacrilege and arson that were not
distinguished as they might have been, and one on a lord conniving in theft by
his slave which may have been marked off unwarrantably.[161] A legislator is thus
seen to construct clauses that go beyond intricate syntactic subordination to the
point of associating complete sentences.[162]

---

clerics in Wi Pr., Ine Pr. and I Em Pr., while IV Eg refers to an unnamed archbishop (1:4) and to the
ealdormen entrusted with distributing copies (15 – 15:1).
158   To this extent I stand by what I wrote in 'Uses of Literacy', p. 112, though regretting that I did not
then make my meaning clearer.
159   See Table 5.4 for Archbishop Wulfstan's knowledge of II As and perhaps IV As (in Canterbury
form?), but of no other Æthelstan code.
160   Cf n. 133; comparison suggests that clauses were intended at 2, 3, 4, 6, then wherever Liebermann
has a fresh integer (10, 13, not 10:1, 13:1, etc.). More problematic are 1:3 (space in H, but barely in B
and not in Nw2 or Q before MHk), 3:1 (Nw2, Q, not H, B), 5 (H?, not – *pace* Liebermann – B nor Nw2,
early Q), 6:2 (H and Q MHk), 14 (Nw2, Q, not – *pace* Liebermann – H), 14:2 (H, not Nw2, Q). Some
of these may be cases of scribal initiative or error: medieval scribes were as able to make their own decisions
on this matter as editors since Nowell/Lambarde (chapter 4, p. 262).
161   II As 5, 6:2, 3:1, and see previous n.
162   One effect of this is that H has small coloured initials, like those in Wulfstan MSS (chapter 4,
pp. 196–7, 202, 208), within the main clauses, usually at the points where modern editors make sub-

Not that the Grately and Exeter codes were other than syntactically elaborate. Good contrasting samples are these:[163]

> Incendiaries and those who avenge a thief are to be subject to the same penalty (*Đa blysieras ond þa ðe ðeof wrecen, beon þæs ilcan ryhtes wyrðe*).
>
> And we declared (*Ond we cwædon*) that he who should demand payment owed for a slain thief (*se ðe scyldunga bæde æt ofslagenum ðeofe*) is to come forward (*eode*) as one of three, two from the paternal kin and a third from the maternal, and they are to give the oath (*aþ syllen*) that they knew of no theft on the part of their kinsman for which crime he did not deserve to live; and they are afterwards to go as a party of twelve and incriminate him (*gescyldigen hine*), as it was declared before; and if the dead man's kin will not come thither on the due day (*to ðam andagan*), each who earlier sued (*ðe hit ær sprece*) is to pay 120 shillings.

Though chosen as extreme examples, these are faithful reflections of Grately/Exeter modes of expression. The second is not in fact the most exaggerated case of subordination.[164] The specific conditional was so submerged by more generic forms overall that 'Gif' became an unusual means of introducing new topics. Where it did occur, this was most often in order to usher in sub-clauses (whether or not reflected by modern editorial practice). In other words, its chief function was to bring forward contingencies other than a clause's main concern.[165] Relative clauses were now commoner than conditionals as overtures to the major themes, and not much less so in general.[166] A more popular strategy yet was to state a clause's central assumption, whether in the form of a straightforward order or of value-laden terms like 'incendiaries', before discussing action arising.[167] Value-laden terminology meant taking the nature of an offence for granted. Over a third of the occurrences of the word 'þeof' in Anglo-Saxon laws were in Æthelstan's codes, and another 21 per cent in Ine's, whose legislative 'mind-set' he thus revived.[168] It is one aspect of a more technicalized vocabulary; another being words like 'gescyldigan' in the second quoted sample, so rare that its sense is uncertain. If it still seems to beg some legal-historical questions to call

---

divisions. But they do not occur in B or Q, so are unlikely to be archetypal. Similarly, the rubrics supplied by Q MHk for I and III – V As (chapter 4, pp. 242–3), and H's internal initials in V – IV are probably scribal (though NB the Nw2 clause-mark at V As 2).

163   II As 6:2, 11 (ignoring textual variants in Ot, Nw2).

164   See, e.g., II As 3, 7, 8, 9; V 1:1; and more regular use of 'butan' as a qualifier sometimes envisaging an accused's repentance: II As 18, 20:6,8, 21, 23:2, 26; V Pr.:1,3. Cf. I Ew 2:1, and below, pp. 309, 316, 340, 354; with Schwyter, 'Syntax and Style', pp. 202–204.

165   Further to II 11 ('7 gif ðæs deadan mægas'): see II 1:1–5, 2:1, 3:1 ('gif he hit oftor do'), 6:1, 10 ('Gif he hit hwa do'), 14:1 (also '7 gif hit þonne tyhtle sy', and 'gif he on þam ordale'), 15 ('7 gif he hit do'), 20:1–2,5–8, 22:1, 23:1, 26:1; V Pr.:2, 1:1,2 ('gif hit man him ongerecce'), 1:4, 2 ('gif he ne mæge'). New topics are conditionally introduced only at II 8, 17, 20, 21, 23, 25.

166   Further to II As 11: II 6:3, 9 (and NB 'se þe hit him geagnian wille'), 20:4, 24, 25:2, 26, V Pr.:3, plus 'post-nominal relatives' at II 3, 3:1, 7, V 1:2. Cf. also 'swilc/swylc' at II 3:2, V 1:2,3.

167   Further to II As 6:2: II 2, 4, 5, 6, 10, 12, 14, 15, 19, 20:3, 22, 23:2, 24:1, 26:1; V Pr.:1, 1:1 ('forðy þe ic an'), 1:5, 3.

168   Schwyter, *Old English Legal Language*, pp. 43 (fig. 3a), 48–9, 111–32; and for possible implications, Daube, *Roman Law*, pp. 2–63.

these 'more advanced modes' or tokens of innovation, they do at least reveal new willingness to think in legal categories.[169]

The trend towards continuous prose was also sustained. Most clauses began with conjunctives of a sort, even when that cut across the paragraphing also provided.[170] Cross-referencing was standard; the first sample is meaningless without it. References stretched, like Edward's, to the *domboc*.[171] Earlier Æthelstan codes were habitually cited.[172] Targeting of morally obnoxious categories showed a propensity to rhetorical embellishment that was more marked at Exeter. The exasperation expressed there by Æthelstan went beyond his father's comparatively cool reaction (in the same town, oddly enough). Justification of what might seem extreme measures betrayed a legislative self-consciousness not hitherto seen in Anglo-Saxon law, which became more and more pronounced over subsequent reigns.

Its clearest manifestation in Æthelstan's codes was the Tithe Ordinance. Caution is advised here. Its vernacular text is confined to Wulfstan manuscripts, and the archbishop may have touched up its content (above, p. 295). At least one phrase has a Wulfstanian *timbre*.[173] Yet *Quadripartitus* alone shows that the text was couched in homiletic vein. One sentiment, somehow dropped from the vernacular version, reads like the proem of an Anglo-Saxon charter – at a time when charters touched new heights of loquaciousness in this very respect.[174] The Ordinance may therefore be taken at near its face value. Its import is then twofold. First, it had a restricted address, like I Edward (above, pp. 287, 289). Æthelstan too used first person singular and second person plural.[175] This time, just one topic was covered. Second, law was now for the first time (the special case of Alfred's preface aside) made on grounds of vigorously phrased religious principle. Æthelstan laid bare the ideological foundations underpinning the development of English law since Alfred:

Now you [*sc.* the reeves] are to hear, says the king, what I grant to God and what

---

169   Daube, *Forms of Roman Legislation*, pp. 6, 24. Further evidence of heightened stylistic sophistication is consistent agreement of verbal mood between protasis and apodasis: cf. n. 117 above.

170   Exceptions (allowing that scribes were prone to drop conjunctives, precisely because of clause-divisions): II 13:1, 14, 15 – 18 (NB that this is Grately's 'code within a code', where numerals serve something of the same purpose), 20, 21, 23, 25.

171   II As 5; II 4 is an echo of Af 4:2, and II 12 of I Ew 1.

172   See sub-section 3(i) above. This may be what is involved in II As 11, since 'swa hit ær gecweden wæs' does not obviously refer to anything earlier in this code; cf. II 23:2 for another unanchored cross-reference. There may have been measures along these lines in the code of which II 13 – 18 are the remnants; alternatively, the references may be to lost codes or indeed to laws that were never written down (chapter 3, pp. 126–8).

173   'Se þe þonne nelle, þolige þare are oðde eft to rihte gecirre', 'ar' and 'gecirran' in these senses being almost exclusive to Wulfstan codes, and the whole phrase being absent from *Quadripartitus*. Note also I As 2, a quotation of Exod. 22:29 naturally favoured by Wulfstan, where *Quadripartitus* quotes Matt. 25:29 – not so much more obviously pertinent that Q is likely to have substituted it.

174   I As 4: 'Hortatur nos sermo divinus eterna cum terrenis, celestia cum caducis promereri'. Cf. the sentiments (more fulsomely articulated because couched in the Latin of the early-tenth, not the early-twelfth, century) of the 'Flebilia fortiter detestanda' and 'Fortuna fallentis saeculi' proems used by the charter draftsman 'Æthelstan A' (respectively S 412–13, 416–19, 422, etc. dated March 931 – January 933, and S 425, 407, 426, 434, etc., dated May 934 – Christmas 935). See chapter 6, pp. 432, 439–40.

175   I As Pr., 4, and cf. As Alm Pr., 1.

you should perform on pain of disobedience (*oferhyrnysse*) to me; and arrange that you grant me my own . . . And you are to guard both yourselves and those whom you should admonish against the anger of God and against disobedience to me (7 *beorgað ægþer ge eow ge ðam þe ge myngian scylan wið Godes yrre 7 wið mine oferhyrnesse*).[176]

The remaining legislation standing in Æthelstan's name cannot be considered royal law in the same sense as 'I', 'II' or 'V'. It is therefore interesting that the same proclivities appear. Verbally numbered clauses, as in Grately's code 'within a code', were offered by the letter expressing the Kentish authorites' enthusiastic compliance. It and the Thunderfield summary ('IV') used relative clauses, conjunctions and cross-references much as 'II' and 'V' did.[177] Each resorts to thumping statements of principle.[178] Thunderfield's theft clause is a remarkable illustration of syntactic intricacy, in that the main point, that there is no safety for thieves, was followed by a review of all possible variations in the status of thieves or the process used to convict – all with the same dire consequence.[179] But it is the phenomenal manifesto of the London peace-guild that showed Æthelstanian legislation at its most evolved. Its stylistic traits deserve more detailed study than there is scope for here. Suffice it to say that its 'eighth' clause occupied seventy-four lines in *Textus Roffensis*, where it was unsurprisingly given fifteen subdivisions.[180] If exceptional in length, it was typical of the rest in the fact that it was numbered, like 'III' and the central part of 'II'; in its labyrinthine sentence structure; in the way that relative clauses characterized group-activity; and in a communal rhetoric again reminiscent of its Kentish counterpart. There were explicit cross-references (one even to 'urum gewritum').[181]

It is almost impossible to be sure how far the London document stands apart from the main line of Æthelstan law-making. What would otherwise have furnished the best comparison, the Faversham record, survives only in Latin. But basic vocabulary may provide some clues. Æthelstan codes shared the linguistic range of early tenth-century legislation, as witness the ubiquitous 'we cwædon' formula. The peace-guild regulations had it too.[182] Nonetheless, the parts of the text sharing the most words and phrases with the rest of the king's corpus are the early and final clauses: just those likeliest to have been drafted by someone other than a member or agent of the guild. Examples are '*utniman*, take out', '*geswican*,

---

176   I As 5, citing the (earlier) Nero text.
177   Of the main (i.e. textually numbered) clauses in III As, only cl. 6 uses 'si'; all main clauses of IV As begin with 'et', but only cll. 3, 7 begin 'et si quis').
178   III As 4 – 4:1 (with nothing substantial to follow); IV As 6.
179   IV As 6; note too the explanatory gloss, 'id est si verbum non dixerit ut adsaca sit', though this may be later (*Gesetze* I *ad loc.*).
180   VI As 8:1–9.
181   VI As 8:5; cf 3 ('þæt we on urum gerædnessum gecweden habbað'); or the mention of 'disobedience (*oferhyrnesse*) to us' (7), which may indicate the 30 pence penalty laid down before for witholding dues (3, 8:5). Cll. 1 – 1:5, 9 are disregarded in this review, as they may belong not to the guild regulations but to more general Thunderfield legislation (above, pp. 297–8, and below).
182   See above, p. 289; II As 2, 4 – 6, 7 – 8, 11 – 12, 19, (23:2), (IV As(H) 6:2c), VI As 2, 6:3, 7 (and NB *Blas.* 1, *Ord.* 3, below, pp. 367–8, 373–4); cf. also I As 1, 3, 5, II 14:1, 25, V Pr., 1:3, VI 1, 1:4, 3, 6:4, 8:5,8, 12:1,3.

desist', and '*on þa/þæt (ilce) gerad (. . .) þe/þæt*, on the understanding that'.[183] By contrast, there are perhaps three peace-guild usages that are suggestively shared with more explicitly royal texts ('*manung*, district', '*spor*, track', and '*ofereacan*, surplus'), against at least two ('*æsce*, pursuit', '*teona*, damages?'), that might have been but were not.[184] The balance of indications makes the peace-guild regulations marginally more likely to be an independent product.

It can fairly be said, then, that the quantity and variety of law made under Æthelstan was matched by its stylistic sophistication. There is ample evidence of a will and an ability to put the resources of vernacular prose at the government's disposal; to make it a vessel worthy of its solemn cargo. The implications go beyond the merely legal sphere. The current tendency to credit the bulk of early vernacular prose to Alfred's court leaves a vacuum between his 'Renaissance' and that of the tenth-century reformers which is hardly filled by the jejune annals of the *Chronicles*. The laws made by his grandson's regime are a good measure of the effects of Alfredian education on the capacity to express ideas in layman's language.[185]

(iii) Content

It would be surprising if the content of Æthelstan's legislation did not reflect its enhanced ambitions and upgraded techniques. So it does. For which reason, note should first be taken of an area where advance is not apparent. One can no more say of his laws than of Alfred's (pp. 269–70) that they were arranged in any very logical pattern. The Grately code is the only one long enough to pose problems of arrangement. They were not successfully solved. The text launched straight into laws against theft, flagrant or otherwise, before moving on from harbouring thieves to the appointment of lords for 'those from whom no justice is to be had', then to lords or royal officials who were accessories to theft. This in turn prompted rehearsal of Alfred's law on treachery to lords; the next item, on breaking into churches, may have been suggested by the fact that it was also Alfred's next topic.[186] After that came laws on witchcraft, arson and avenging a thief; if sorcery was linked with sacrilege, vengeance for thieves would have gone more logically with the earlier laws on succouring them. The sequence after the apparently inserted burghal clauses looks more arbitrary still. Punishment of slaves (presumably, not explicitly, thieves) made way for detailed dispositions on defiance of – previously defined – surety provisions, then a procedural item on the ordeal, then a law against illicitly swapping lords, then detailed treatment of

---

183   (II As 6:1), VI 1:4, 9, 12:2; II As 1:3, 6:1, 20:4, V Pr.:1, VI 1:4, 12:2 ('geswican' was much favoured by Wulfstan, but is otherwise found only in Af 22, I Ew 2:1, I Atr 1:5); I As 4, 5, II 8, V Pr.:1, VI 9.
184   V As 1:5, VI 8:2,4; V As 2, VI 4, 8:4,7–8; VI As 1:1, 6:1,3; VI As 2, 5, 6:4, 7, 8:8; VI As 7, 8:3; it may be significant that *Duns.* uses both 'spor' (1) and 'æsc' (1:1): below, pp. 381–2.
185   The Æthelstan laws are thus a vernacular counterpart to the literary achievement of his Latin charters, and to the square minuscule in which they were written (chapter 4, pp. 166–70, above, n 174; see also Bullough, 'Educational Tradition', pp. 466–73). The collocation is of course hugely significant: chapter 6, pp. 439–40, 444–8.
186   II As 4 – 5; Af 4:2 – 5.

ordeals. A law on witnessed purchase of livestock might have been grouped with either of two previous orders to the same effect; this time, its rider was the ban on Sunday trading.[187] The impact of a wholly logical conclusion, punishing disobedience to whatever the code commanded, was dissipated by the law on perjury that follows in all texts but one.

It is not that this arrangement is absolutely devoid of rhyme or reason. Rather, there is little evidence of the sense of *system* that was displayed in Æthelberht's code but had since vanished. As with Alfred, the sole operative principle is thought-association: the similarity of penalties for witchcraft, arson and avenging thieves was what connected these clauses, as the text said. Even this principle seems to break down towards the end of Grately, where the impression left is like Ine's (chapter 2, pp. 104–5): one of matters brought to a legislator's attention, perhaps by those with responsibility for administering the law. The perjury afterthought can be explained this way, as will soon appear. As for the later codes, the Faversham record addressed change of lords ahead of overmighty kins, so reversing the Exeter code's order (which, however, was retained by the Thunderfield summary). Laws about thieves were disposed at either end of London's peace-guild rules. If clause divisions made it easier for judges to find a relevant decree among the king's many pronouncements, the marshalling of clauses did not.

The dominant issues in Æthelstan's legislation can be gathered from all that has by now been said. Apart from the Exeter instruction that fifty psalms be sung for the king and for his adjutants in every minster each Friday, clerical interests were not evinced after the seemingly early ordinances on tithes and charity. From 'II' onwards, the main preoccupation was theft. By the end of the series it had become almost an obsession. Æthelstan carried on where his father left off in demanding sureties against theft, in enlisting the resources of lordship to enforce rather than to obstruct justice, and in requiring supervised sale or purchase.[188] He was also increasingly blunt about penalties. His war on thieves will be pivotal to the thesis of chapter 9. The point to note here is that it fell into two phases. The first stage was to demand that thieves caught in the act be killed, and to enforce the (?Alfredian) penalty of 120 shillings on those convicted by due process; Ine had merely forbidden vendetta for thieves killed *in flagrante*, and his penalty for others seems to have been 60 shillings.[189] But as the prologue to the Exeter code admitted, little was achieved by these measures: the 'oaths and pledges' given at Grately were all broken. The king reacted with a time-limited amnesty, followed up by a sharp increase in severity. All thieves, howsoever convicted, were now to be executed; those who harboured or supported them were to be killed as accessories.[190] Even the royal change of heart which finally raised the age of liability to execution from twelve to fifteen would not save second offenders aged twelve.[191] At the same time, steps were taken to ensure better observation of the 'pledges' made at Grately and subsequently broken.

---

187 II As 24 – 24:1; 9 – 10; 12, 13:1.
188 II As 1:3, 2 – 3:2, 7 – 8, 10 – 10:1, 12, 13:1, 22 – 22:2, 24.
189 II As 1 – 1:5; Af 9:2; Ine 7, 10, 35, 43, 46.
190 V As Pr.; V As 3:1, III As 3; IV As 6, 6:3, VI 1:1–3.
191 VI As 12:1–2.

Local response was now organized. The men of Kent wrote offering their co-operation. Londoners were mustered in a peace-guild, whose pledge extended to detailed implementation of what Grately had outlined for pursuit of delinquents.[192] Neither Kent nor London need have been alone in this; it certainly was not intended that they be. Though nothing shows that these new expedients had any more success than the old, it was perhaps a mark of growing legislative maturity that a ruler used writing both to admit and to respond to failure.

Two other aspects of the laws made by and on behalf of Æthelstan reinforce the point. One is the acknowledged influence of an external source. Alfred began by translating Mosaic and Apostolic law. His grandson incorporated quotations from Old and New Testaments into his Tithe Ordinance.[193] A further citation followed: 'It is for us to ponder how terribly it is said in books: If we will not pay our tenths, that God will take away from us the nine parts when we least expect it, and we shall have the sin to reckon with too'.[194] The book in question ought to be identifiable. Liebermann referenced the 786 'capitulary'. It is an attractive possibility, given its likely influence on Alfred's code and certain use by the 'Constitutions' of Archbishop Oda a decade or two later.[195] But the point about the loss of nine parts more nearly echoed a sermon attributed to St Augustine and was closely based on one of Caesarius of Arles. This text was quoted alongside the relevant Mosaic extract by the tract 'De Decimis', which was incorporated into some manuscripts of the the 'B' version of the Irish Canon Collection. One copy of that collection was probably in England by this time, and is a likely source of other Oda Constitutions.[196] Æthelstan may have had models from further afield (as befitted the most cosmopolitan of early English kings). The demand that the hand of an erring moneyer be struck off and put up above his shop might seem an obvious if grisly application of homoeopathic justice. But it may also be relevant that the penalty was widespread for coining throughout the sub-Byzantine world, passing from either the Visigoths or the Lombards to the Franks, who enshrined it in the capitulary collection of Ansegisus.[197] The odds that Carolingian example was at work are shortened by the fact that Æthelstan was the first English king to legislate at length on ordeals, and there is a clear connection between Frankish and English ordeal liturgies (chapter 8).[198]

There is, secondly, a connection between Æthelstan's laws and charters. This, as became clear in chapter 3, is unusual. But part of the evidence for a new approach to crime in the Old English kingdom is the salience of forfeiture from Alfred's time. So it may not be chance that it was in the reign of a king who was

---

192   III As 7 – 7:3; VI As 2 – 8:9, and cf. II As 20 – 20:8.
193   I As 2; cf. above, n. 173.
194   I As 3.
195   *Gesetze* III, pp. 97–8, n. 2 *ad loc.*; *Alcuin, Epistolae* 3 (xvii); '"Constitutions" of Archbishop Oda' x.
196   Caesarius, Sermo xxxiii, I, p. 144–5; cf. Kottje, *Studien zum Einfluß*, pp. 62–6, and fuller discussion (e.g. of Bodleian MS Hatton 42) in chapter 13.
197   II As 14:1; *Leg. Vis.* VII vi 2, Ed. Ro. 242, *Cap.* 139:19 (= *Ans.* iv 31 = *Cap.* 273:16). For this connection, see Lopez, 'Byzantine Law in the seventh century', pp. 449–54, and Campbell, 'Observations on English Government', p. 45 (160–1).
198   II As 23 – 23:2 (and cf. *Ord.*, below, pp. 373–4).

so set on capital punishment for theft that there occurs the earliest charter describing the execution as well as forfeiture of thieves.[199] That apart, an interesting group of grants dated from Christmas Eve 932 to late January 933 commissioned the feeding of the poor and regular psalm-singing for the king, as in the Charity Ordinance and Exeter code respectively. Whether laws occasioned charters or *vice versa*, the worlds of law and charter had met, as they rarely do in the Old English era.[200]

But there is a yet more striking instance of such contact in the case of a certain Ælfred. According to a narrative that William of Malmesbury claimed to have found among Æthelstan's grants to his abbey, Ælfred plotted to blind the king at Winchester when his father died, and fled to Rome when his plot was discovered. There he swore his innocence before Pope John, only to collapse and be borne off to die three days later in the *Schola Anglorum*. On being consulted by the Pope as to whether he should be buried 'with other Christians', the magnates of the realm and Ælfred's kin begged that he should, but his whole property was forfeit (and granted to Malmesbury among other places). This decidedly tall story occurs only in William's histories and in bogus charters based upon them.[201] It would not be worth another moment's notice, did it not harmonize in an arresting way with the last clause of the Grately code. In what looks like an appendix simply because it follows a clause on obedience to the code as a whole, not to mention its absence from the Ot text (above, pp. 177, 291), those who swore false oaths were to be denied Christian burial – whereas Edward the Elder had merely denied perjurers any future oath-worthiness (above, p. 289). Æthelstan did face a serious conspiracy around 933, if not at his accession.[202] He was not popular at Winchester, or not at his father's New Minster family shrine, with which a thegn named Ælfred had dealings. Where there had been two (or even three) Ælfred *ministri* in the witness-lists of the king's early charters, there was just one in the 930s till 944.[203] Thus, however fictionalized the story told by

199   LS 31, S 443. The charter, from the Old Minster cartulary, is also extant as a single sheet, but cannot be authentic as it stands: it is dated to the A.D. year of *Brunanburh*, given as 938, the 'corrected' date in the Parker MS of the *Chronicle* (*Anglo-Saxon Chronicle MS A*, pp. xcviii–xcix, 70). The forfeiture is supposed to have occurred not in Æthelstan's reign but in that of Æthelheard two centuries before, as another forgery 'confirms', S 254; but there is no mention of the thieves' execution in the Æthelheard text.
200   S 419, 422, 423 (spurious but founded on a genuine text); S 418, 379 (again an adaptation of an authentic text): there was certainly no immediate connection, given that these grants were issued from places in Wiltshire, and V As locates the king at Exeter 'to middanwintre'. On this question see Keynes, 'Royal government and the written word', pp. 236–8, and his paper on 'Æthelstan "A"', with further discussion in chapter 6, p. 439.
201   LS 31; *William of Malmesbury, Gesta Regum* ii 136, I, p. 153; *Gesta Pontificum* v 250, pp. 401–3 = S 436. William's charter appears to be based on a combination of S 434 (or its authentic exemplar) with S 415, 435 (themselves spurious). The verbally almost identical story in the Bath forgery, S 414, could presumably have been taken from William, but it needs to be explained how the forgery equates with S 415, not William's text. Given that William quoted different bits of the 'charter' in his two books, it may be wrong to charge him with its fabrication, as did Stevenson and Birch.
202   As powerfully hinted by Folcuin's *Gesta abbatum* 107, p. 629 (trans. *EHD I* 26, pp. 346–7); cf. Stenton, *Anglo-Saxon England*, pp. 355–6. Incidentally, Pope John X reigned 914–28 and John XI 931–5.
203   *Liber Vitae of New Minster*, ed. Keynes, pp. 19–22; S 418 (one of the charters discussed in n. 200), 1417, 1509; Keynes, *Atlas of Attestations*, XXXIX(1), XL, XLIII(1–2).

William and his charter sources, Grately's perjury clause may suggest that something along these lines really happened.

All in all, Æthelstan's law-making confronts the commentator with another of early English law's paradoxes. Nearly everything about it betokened accelerated effort. Codes were disseminated as a matter of policy and practice. Law was reformed, first in a more stringent direction, then in one of (relative) leniency. Local implementation was articulated in writing. Steps were taken to see that written law was easier to use. Law was expressed in increasingly confident, if by no means always limpid, prose. Its vocabulary was growing more technical. There were signs of closer attention to the example of august legislative models. There was closer correlation than there would be again till the later-twelfth century between royal law and charter evidence for its implementation. The pulsing heart of all this was an ideology finding new legislative expression in what the king said about his rights and God's.

Yet this section began with a wearisome disentanglement of textual knots. By the early-twelfth century, perhaps even a hundred years before, Canterbury may have been the one place where a full conspectus of Æthelstan's second-phase legislation was available, and then already in somewhat garbled form. Elsewhere, it apparently remained easier to ascertain the compensation for removing a West Saxon's little finger-nail, than what the king of Wessex expected by way of local law-enforcement. The legislative activity of Æthelstan's reign has rightly been dubbed 'feverish'. The king's officials were bombarded with his ideas. They were so infected by his enthusiasm that their answering bustle has left marks in the evidence which would not be replicated for more than two centuries. But the extant results are, frankly, a mess. Part III of this book will supply copious evidence for the efficacy of tenth-century government. That evidence is not matched by the condition of its legal memorials. It is as if the regime's very energy pushed the system beyond the limits of what it could sustain. Above all, one would expect the momentum manifested by Æthelstan's laws to be carried forward into later reigns. It was not. Continuity was maintained but at a slower pace. By the time legislative output picked up again, it was in a different spirit and in pursuit of a remodelled design.

4   Edmund's Codes

Three codes survive in the name of Æthelstan's brother Edmund. There need for once be no quibble with either the total in modern editions or its sequence.[204] The overall picture is also somewhat clearer than for Æthelstan, and will permit brisker treatment.

Most of Edmund's legislation was transmitted alongside that of Edward the Elder. Codes 'I' and 'II' form a pair in *Textus Roffensis* ('H'), Corpus 383 ('B') and *Quadripartitus* ('Q'), immediately following Edward's in each instance (chapter 4, pp. 229, 232, 239–42, 246–8). The inference is that they had a

---

204   But for a problem about II Em 7 and *Wer.*, see below, pp. 311, 374–8.

common ancestor. Confirmation comes from two egregious errors shared by all three.[205] But for Edmund there are two twists to the story. In the first place, 'I' survives outwith this tradition, by courtesy of Wulfstan manuscripts.[206] As with Æthelstan's Tithe edict (above, p. 302), there must be a suspicion that the archbishop adjusted the text. 'Ælmesfeoh' (H/B/Q) becomes 'Romfeoh 7 sulhælmessan' in his Corpus 201 ('D'). 'Peter's Pence' and 'plough-alms' are not otherwise attested before Edgar's campaign on Church dues; and even there, Wulfstan could well have intruded plough-alms (above, p. 295, below, pp. 314–15).[207] 'Almswealth' was a perfectly good designation for what Æthelstan commissioned under the terms of his Charity Ordinance, so an appropriate triplet for the tithes and church-scot that Edmund was calling for. The other twist is that there was a third Edmund code, issued at Colyton (Devon), and recorded only in *Quadripartitus*. Although Q was able to enrol it beside the other two in his final edition, it followed 'II–III Edgar' in what was almost certainly an earlier draft (chapter 4, pp. 239–43). Its transmission was clearly quite distinct from that of the first pair.

Stylistically, all three codes reflect the trends that were becoming established under Edward and Æthelstan. There seem to have been no clause divisions, but the brevity of the texts did not warrant any.[208] The first code three times introduced issues with a directive of intent, twice with a relative clause, and once with a conditional; one clause began with a conjunctive. In the second, an emotionally charged prologue led straight into five interrelated 'Gyf' clauses, and was followed by five declarations of will, one initiated by '7' and three by 'eac'; the fifth, which had no conjunctive, was subdivided into stages of action, each marked by 'Ðonne'. The Colyton laws were linked by conjunctions throughout; all its clauses were declaratory statements, except one opening 'Et dictum est de servis: si qui … '; only two of these went on to use conditional clauses for the eventualities evisaged, while four used relatives. Syntactical complexity was generally pitched at the same level as in Æthelstan's laws.[209] If such

---

205 II Em 7, **H/B** 'æfter folcrihtes laga (according to the law of custom', cf. **Q** 'iuxta rectam populi lagam') for 'æfter folcrihte slaga (according to custom, the killer)'; II Em 4, **H/B** 'wið þam ægðe(r)' (?!, understandably left untranslated by **Q**); cf. above, p. 287, below, pp. 384–6. On the other hand, there seems no reason to think II Em 4, (**Q**) 'eum qui sanguinem fundet humanum' any more than a translator's gloss, presumably following the lead of I Em 3; and I Em 3, **H/Q** 'ansyne'/'conspectu regis' as against **D/B** 'cyninges neawiste' seems to be another case of the slightly closer textual affinity of H and Q than of B and Q: chapter 4, pp. 248–9, below, pp. 385–6.

206 See chapter 4, pp. 198–203, 204–10. All but the first seven lines of the text of I Em are missing in Nero A i ('G') because of loss of the quire's central bifolium, but there is no question of any more than I Em and the opening sections of II–III Eg having been included here: G covers III Eg from the point where its text resumes after the missing bifolium in 50 lines, where D needs 31; D has 18 lines of I Em from the beginning of G's lacuna, and 43 of II–III Eg before G resumes; G's missing text should thus have occupied 61 x 50/31 = 98.4 lines; the missing bifolium would have yielded 96.

207 I Em 2. Cf. the Wulfstanian 'georne', I Em Pr., **G**, and 'þe geornor', I Em 6, **D**.

208 The rubrics in Q (MHk) must be its usual final edition exercise (chapter 4, pp. 242–3); H has coloured mid-line initials, but these are probably scribal (above, p. 301), and there is nothing to correspond in B, beyond admittedly quite prominent initials at II Em 2, 7 (on the latter, see below); D's colour-washed initials should also be scriptorial (chapter 4, pp. 202, 208).

209 I Em 1, 4, 6 (and ?III 2) have 'buton' provisos, giving scope for repentance or amendment: cf. above, nn. 27, 164, and below on I–II Cn.

are indeed criteria of a developed legislative tradition, then Edmund's laws meet them triumphantly.[210] His lawmaking vocabulary was still essentially that of his predecessors (above, pp. 288–9, 303–4).[211] At the same time, it witnessed the debut of technical terms with a long afterlife: *mundbrice*, *hamsocn* and *forsteal*, three of the 'pleas of the crown'; and probably *tihtbysig*, the notoriously suspect.[212] These words voiced a rising sense of the peace of the realm, of its royal sponsor and of its inveterate enemies, as the springs of legislative action.

That said, the three codes also exhibited pronounced differences. The first opened by describing the summons of a council, like Edward's and Æthelstan's Exeter codes; as often in Æthelstan's laws, the emphasis was on the presence of bishops, and Archbishops Oda and Wulfstan (I) were named. Its concerns were clerical celibacy and adultery, church dues and alms, and restoration of church buildings (the king being adjured to intervene, as if he were not directly involved in the deliberations). Bloodshed, perjury and sorcery were stigmatized as well, but even they were punished by the Church's sanctions of excommunication and denial of consecrated burial. The only secular penalties were exclusion from the royal presence for bloodletting and forfeiture of worldly goods for unchastity. These look like essentially synodical proceedings, as Liebermann said. One might almost have expected to find them in Latin. It is possible that in a sense one does. The code's terms were in general very close to the 'Constitutions' of Archbishop Oda, one of the two prelates singled out as present at the council. The Constitutions dwelt on the duty of episcopal visitation and the need for good clerical example with special stress on sexual purity, on mutual love and peace among Christians, on 'magical illusion' and on tithes.[213] Some topics were covered here but not by the code.[214] Nonetheless, I Edmund could be described as an attempt to put the impetus of vernacular law behind the principles expounded by Oda. Right behind Oda's text lay the *Capitulare* of the papal legates in 786. When the London council threatened uncelibate clerics with loss of earthly property and Christian burial, 'as it says in the canon', the reference is probably to the legatine decree.[215]

Edmund's second code cannot be seen as a secular counterpart to the ecclesiastical matter of his first, as with the double codes of Edgar and Cnut (below, pp. 313–16, 355–61). The repetition in 'II' of the ban in 'I' on a homicide's access to the king would then have been pointless. The object of 'II' was to work out

---

210   Note also the internal cross-references, I Em 4 ('þæt ilce we cwædon be … '), II Em 2 ('ðe hit her beforan cwæð'), III Em 6 ('que supra dicta sunt').
211   Note the graphic use of (mainly poetic) '(ge-/un-)fah*, at enmity with [sc. the king]', II As 20:7, II Em 1:1,3.
212   II Em 6, III Em 6, III Em 7 ('infamati et accusationibus ingravati', Q III Eg 7 translating 'tihtbysig' 'accusationibus infamatus').
213   '"Constitutions" of Oda' ii – vii, viii, ix, x; the link was noted by Liebermann, *Gesetze* III, p. 124 (9). See also his *National Assembly*, pp. 15–17; Darlington, 'Ecclesiastical Reform', pp. 386, 415–16; and Lawson, 'Archbishop Wulfstan', p. 569.
214   Observance of fasts, feasts and Sundays, '"Constitutions"' ix.
215   *Alcuin, Epistolae* 3 (xv – xvi), ln 33 'sicut in canone'. See above, p. 306, and my 'In Search of Offa's "Law-code"', pp. 38–40 (pp. 215–17); the capitulary's logic points to disinheritance on top of excommunication (hence no christian burial); Liebermann's anxiety, *Gesetze* III, p. 125 *ad loc.*, was misplaced. See also my 'Giving God and King their Due', pp. 554–6 (pp. 334–6).

the inference of the London council's precepts on the particular question of bloodfeud. Charlemagne, in a text which could by then have been accessible to English law-makers, saw what Christian 'peace and unanimity' implied for vendetta; in principle at least, he prohibited feud outright.[216] Edmund now followed suit. The result was another code in the style of Edward's mandate to his reeves or Æthelstan's Ordinances (above, pp. 287, 289, 302). Its subject-matter was restricted and its tone personalized: it began and ended in the first person plural, the dominant voice of the London council, but was otherwise inclined to the singular.[217] The main difference was that it apostraphized 'all people in his realm, young and old':

> King Edmund announces (*cyð*) to all … that … I have been deliberating with the advice of my wise men … how I might most exalt Christianity. First then it seemed to us (*ðuhte us*) most necessary that we should most firmly keep between us our peaceableness and harmony (*gesibsumnesse 7 geðwærnesse*) throughout all my dominion. I and all of us are greatly distressed (*Me eleð swyðe 7 us eallum*) by the unlawful and manifold fights (*gefeoht*) that there are between us. We therefore declared … Also I thank God and you all, who have well supported me, for the peace from thefts that we now have, and I therefore trust you (*gelyfe ic to eow*) that you are willing to support this, so much the better as the need is the greater for us all that it be kept.

This legislative idiom will recur in Edgar's 'fourth' code, and in Cnut's letters from abroad. It begins to look as though Anglo-Saxon kings were evolving a less formal legislative technique that would come into its own after 1066 (below, pp. 318–19, 347–8). There was, however, a marked change of manner in the code's final clauses. The topic reverted to feud after having switched to other matters. The first person vanished. There is an unusually prominent initial in B and perhaps in H too. In twelfth-century collections these are often signs of the partially suppressed opening of a new text. In addition, the conclusion of 'II' was verbally very like an apparently 'unofficial' tract called *Wergeld*. It could be that an originally unconnected piece on a related theme has got tacked on to Edmund's decree (below, pp. 374–8). The unanimity of the transmission is no disproof. The three copies are not independent witnesses.

The Colyton code was something else again. Its subject-matter was largely traditional. Even its first and most memorable item, on the oath of loyalty and good behaviour to be sworn by all, seems in part a verbal quotation from the prologue of Edward's Exeter code. The rest retrod ground covered by Edward and Æthelstan: changing lords, trade before witnesses, readiness to track stolen cattle, pursuit of the incorrigible (though thieves were more explicitly targeted), providing surety for one's men. The only clause without apparent precedent was on the punishment of gangs of servile thieves; its gruesomeness recalls the spirit

---

216   *Cap.* 22:62, 66–7 (= *Ans.* i 59, 63, iii 89); for its accessibility in tenth-century England, see chapter 4, pp. 217–18, chapter 13. The 786 *capitulare* and Oda's "Constitutions" stressed Christian concord without drawing so drastic a conclusion.

217   Cf., further to the passage quoted below, II Em 1:1, 2, 3, 4; I Em 2, 4, 5 (I Em 1, 'hi budon' is only in Wulfstan's D).

of Æthelstan's Thunderfield edicts.[218] On the other hand, the form of Colyton marked the inauguration of new traits. The prologue was not at all personalized, as had been habitual in one way or another since Alfred (indeed Ine). Instead there was the relatively flat announcement, 'This is the ordinance (*institutio*) which King Edmund and his bishops with his wise men decreed at Colyton about the peace and the making of oaths'. All his instructions bar one were couched in the third person.[219] One might be inclined to think this the same sort of semi-official record as 'IV Æthelstan'. Yet prefatory detachment and third person became standard under Edgar and Æthelred.[220] In particular, 'gerædnes', the word that probably underlay 'institutio', and that had hitherto appeared only in the finale of 'II Æthelstan' and twice in the London peace-guild, was henceforth the conventional term for a law-code.[221]

The codes of Edmund are, then, an object-lesson in the variety of Anglo-Saxon legal texts. But more important is what they have in common. Most striking is a heightened rhetorical tone which spilt over from forms of address into legal ideas. A 'manslaga' was shut off from the king's company, and eventually from God's. Æthelberht had once demanded doubled compensation for offences committed before the king. It was now an affront to the royal personage to kill anywhere. For Ine and Alfred, it was a potentially capital crime to draw a weapon in the king's hall. The same penalty now threatened those infringing the royal *mund* wheresoever, or attacking anyone in his home.[222] To feud with pursuers of thieves was to be the enemy of the king and of his friends; to be loyal was to love what the king loved, to shun what he shunned.[223] Empowering these principles was a strengthening ideological current. It had become easier to mortally offend the king. He personified good order. He answered for it to God. The peace is the king's.

English royal lawgiving had come a fair distance in the half century since Alfred's *domboc*. Whether or not judgement was in fact 'as it stands in the lawbook', the king's law was being laid down in robust prose, and could claim to meet the needs of king, people – and God. Yet Edmund's laws have the character of appendices to his brother's. Perhaps he thought that his family had reached their goal of a secure peace. He said as much in an arresting departure from his predecessors' abiding anxiety. He soon discovered his error. A king who shut his doors to those with Christian blood on their hands, and felicitated his people on their freedom from theft, was stabbed to death in one of his royal halls by 'a most wicked robber'.[224]

---

218   III Em 4; for other clauses, note Liebermann's marginalia.
219   III Em 2, 4, 6; the exception is 3, 'Et nolo'.
220   See below, pp. 315, 324. Is it coincidence that the final year of Edmund's reign saw the advent of a new charter-style, which persisted over the next quarter-century, and was marked by the lack of a proem?: Keynes, '"Dunstan B" charters', p. 180.
221   II As 25:2, VI As Pr., 3; cf. *Gesetze* II, p. 96, *s.v.* In the majority of cases, the Q translation was 'institutio'.
222   I Em 3, II 4, 6; Abt 3; Hl 11 – 12; Ine 6, Af 7.
223   III Em 2, 1; the first echoes II As 20:7, the second II Ew 1.
224   *JW.* pp. 398–9.

5   The Laws of Edgar

After a pause of (at least) thirteen years, the Old English legislative tradition was resumed by Edgar: the king who was above all renowned for his strong peace (chapter 3, p. 136), and the very uneventfulness of whose rule vindicated this image in Stenton's eyes.[225] It is surprising, therefore, that only four codes were ever ascribed to Edgar, and that this number should in fact be reduced to two. To give the name 'I Edgar' to the 'Hundred Ordinance' turns a possibility into an assumption (below, pp. 378–9). 'II' and 'III' Edgar are the ecclesiastical and secular parts of a single code. 'IV Edgar' was thus his second (but cf. pp. 125–6, 321, 370). These two codes are more radically different documents than Edward's pair, Edmund's three, or even Æthelstan's seven. They not only differ in style and scope but also have completely independent transmissions. It is better this time to give each text its own subsection.

(i) The Andover Code ('II–III' Edgar)

The major legislative statement of Edgar's reign was issued at Andover; though it does not say so itself, the next code cites one of its measures as 'what my wise men decreed at Andover'.[226] It survives, in whole or part, in six manuscripts or the equivalent, making it the best attested legal text of the Anglo-Saxon era other than the Alfred–Ine law-book (see n. 3). Furthermore, these witnesses include only one of the early-twelfth-century collections that normally dominate the diffusion of early English law. On closer inspection, the six lines of descent form two, or more probably three, groups.

The best evidence on this came up in chapter 4. 'III Edgar' and 'II Cnut' had in effect verbally identical provisions on unjust judges, but the Nero A.i(A) copy ('G') each time inserted the word '*eft*, again' at slightly different points (p. 227). The early-nineteenth-century transcript of a leaf of Edgar's code that had turned up in a Norwich bookseller also had this insertion (pp. 259–60). The transcript was free enough of G's more heinous mistakes to rule out a direct relationship; but it would push coincidence to the limit of credibility to deny that they shared a recent ancestor. The next clause of III Edgar was about defamation, and the manuscripts differ as to whether it was a victim's 'property or life (*feo oððe feore*)', or 'property or interest/advantage (*feo oððe freme*)' that was at stake (pp. 188–9). The former reading was that of G and the Norwich leaf, the latter that of Wulfstan's manuscripts (in one of which ' freme' was an interlinear substitution). Q's 'vita vel commodo' suggests that its vernacular original read 'freme'. The signs are that the phrase was causing a muddle, but that 'freme' is probably the better reading.[227] The effect is again to align the Norwich leaf with G. The

---

225   *Anglo-Saxon England*, p. 368.
226   IV Eg 1:4.
227   Among other considerations bringing more or less weight to bear on the balance of probabilities are these: (i) III Eg 4 is again repeated by II Cn 16, where the phrase (also Wulfstan's own) is 'feo oððe

evidence is insufficient to locate Q itself in either of these textual traditions: it omits the tell-tale phrase about the unjust judge. But it may be *à propos* that it at first grouped the Andover code with Æthelred's penitential decree ('VII'), with *Iudex*, the tract on the good judge, and with Edmund's Colyton code (chapter 4, table 4.7, MS T), and that its text of *Iudex* affiliated with G's rather than Nw2's (below, pp. 382–3). In other words it was with G on judges and with Wulfstan manuscripts on false accusations; and may thus be regarded as independent of either.

In the 'Wulfstan' manuscripts, however, the archbishop's interventions were by no means confined to the restoration of good readings. In both 'II' and 'III' there were whole new clauses. Instructions on plough-alms appeared beside the demand for church-scot, and on Friday fasts, soul-scot and sanctuary beside the orders to observe Sundays and fasts in general. In the final clause, there were to be standardized weights as well as measures, London joined Winchester as an authoritative benchmark, and it was underpricing rather than overcharging that was penalized.[228] These were important alterations in law. Liebermann was prepared to countenance their 'official' status, though he did consider interference by a 'clerical scribe'.[229] The discovery since his time of Archbishop Wulfstan's massive role in the composition and transmission of later Anglo-Saxon law puts the matter in a new light. His likely part in changing the text of Æthelstan's and Edmund's laws to increase the range of Church revenues was noted above. The passages in II Edgar were otherwise first found in Æthelred's Enham code, Wulfstan's authorship of which is certain (below, pp. 332–5, 339). They recurred, very similarly phrased, in other Wulfstan codes and also homilies.[230] Even were nothing known of Wulfstan, there might well be occasion for surmise in the intrusion of these laws, and of comparable I Æthelstan and I Edmund variations, into manuscripts where the next laws to make these demands also appeared, and in one of which the hand seen at work on the Andover code was also active. Since sentiment, style and script alike are known to be Wulfstan's, further argument is otiose. The archbishop held out Edgar (along with Æthelstan and Edmund) as examples of legislators who 'kept God's law and paid God's tribute (*gafel*)'.[231] It seems that when having Edgar's laws copied, he

---

freme'; (ii) here and in *Rect.* 10:1 Q translates 'fremu' as 'commodum', whereas it usually (and sometimes wrongly) gives 'feoh' a monetary sense (Ine 35:1, V As 1:5, VI As 2, EGu 12/II Cn 40); and when in Hn 34:7 the same translator (below, p. 412) made the same point, he wrote 'vita vel honoris' as if aware that interest was at stake; (iii) though *Inst. Cn.* has 'pecuniam aut vitam' at its equivalents for II Cn 16 *and* 40, the more accurate *Cons. Cn.* has 'censu aut commodo' (exactly 'feo oððe freme') in the first instance and 'substantia aut vita' (precisely 'feo oððe feore') in the second; (iv) 'feo oððe feore' is an alliterative doublet such as one might have expected Edgar to have used, but equally a scribe to have substituted: cf. Liebermann's note, *Gesetze* III, p. 136, *ad loc.*; (v) the savage penalty (loss of tongue) may point to life-threatening traducement (cf. *LR V* X v 1), but Af 32 decreed the same for 'folcleasunge', which Whitelock renders 'public slander', *EHD I*, p. 413; (vi) 'freme' is on the whole the *lectio difficilior*, and was duly mangled as 'feorme' in II Cn 16, MS 'A'.

228 II Eg 2:3, 5:1–3, III Eg 8:1–3; the Friday provision, II 5:1 is only in Harley 55(A).
229 *Gesetze* III, pp. 134 (3), 135 *ad loc.*
230 V Atr 11:1, 12:1, 17; VI Atr 16, 21, 24; Cn 1018 13:1,7, 14:7; I Cn, 13:1, 16a; *HomN*, pp. 116–17, etc.
231 VIII Atr 43.

expected Cnut's laws to be read back into them. He not only drafted royal laws; he amended those already made.

The Andover code's legislative style is essentially the one that may be detected beneath Colyton's Latin, but there are also new directions. II–III Edgar is a *geatdnes*. The prologue has rather less rhetorical embellishment than Ine's. There is one cross-reference to 'what we have declared'; 'ic wille' occurs twice.[232] Otherwise, the lawmaker is third person singular, and in contexts where earlier kings had spoken personally.[233] Andover was probably not divided into clauses, except in Wulfstan's *scriptoria* (cf. chapter 4, pp. 189–90, below, pp. 341, 350). Nevertheless, almost all its provisions are recognizably distinct and consistently structured.[234] Each begins with a directive: 'let every hearth-penny be paid by St Peter's day'. Each time, the foreseen implications, most obviously non-compliance, are then covered in subordinated clauses introduced by relatives, conditionals or adverbial phrases, and usually also by 'and': 'and he who has not rendered it by the due day ... and if he would not pay again ... on the third occasion '.[235] The most remarkable example of this pattern is the opening of the code's secular section:

> Namely, then, [first], that I will that every man, whether poor or rich, is to be entitled to the customary law (*ælc man sy folcrihtes wyrðe, ge earm ge eadig*), and let one judge just judgements for him. And let there be such remission in the atonement as may be warrantable before God and acceptable to the world (7 *sy on þære bote swylc forgifnes swylce hit for Gode gebeorglic sy 7 for worulde aberendlic*). And let no one seek the king in any suit unless he may not be entitled to justice or cannot obtain it at home (7 *ne gesece nan man þone cyng for nanre spræce, butan he æt ham rihtes wyrðe beon ne mote oððe riht abiddan ne mæge*). If that justice be too severe, let him then seek alleviation from the king. And for no amendable crime (*botwyrðum gylte*) is one to forfeit more than one's wergeld. And the judge who adjudicates wrongly on another [party] (7 *se dema se ðe oðrum on woh gedeme*) is to pay the king 120 shillings as compensation, unless he dare declare on oath that he did not know how to do it more justly, and let him always suffer loss of his thegnhood, unless he redeem it [again] from the king, as he is willing to allow him. And let the bishop of the shire exact the compensation on the king's behalf. And he who wishes to accuse another wrongly, so that he is worse off in either property or interest [life], if the other can then prove false what he was charged with, let him be liable for his tongue, unless he pay for himself with his wergeld.

This amounts almost to a title with sub-clauses in the Visigothic or Roman manner. The three main points are made first: just judgement, apposite punishment, restraint on resort to the king. Matters arising then come in reverse order: invocation of the king if penalties are too steep; particular limits on fines; false

---

232 II Eg 3:1, III Eg 1, 1:1. There are also cross-references to the *domboc* (above, n. 13).
233 Compare III Eg 2 with II Em 4, III 3 with II Ew 5:1, III 8 with II Em Pr.:1; and the code's forfeiture clauses (II 4:1–3, III 7:1) with, e.g., II Ew 7, I As 5, II 25, 25:2.
234 The usual proviso is that modern editorial clause-divisions must be ignored. I detect changes of subject sufficiently pronounced to imply hypothetical fresh 'clauses' at II 1:1, 2:2, 3, 4, 5, III 1:1, 5, 6, 7, 8. Whether or not this has the effect of making the following argument circular, it remains true that the code follows a broadly similar pattern in the successive points it makes.
235 II Eg 4 – 4:3.

judgement, followed by false accusation. These are raised *via* an 'if'-clause, another directive, and two relatives (of which one is post-nominal); conjunctions appear each time, except at the switch from substantive statements to subsidiary issues. The paradoxical effect of this structure was to simplify the syntax. Edgar was more likely than his predecessors to link topics by coordination of outright statements.[236] Anglo-Saxon legislative prose had moved from contingency followed by remedy through directive followed by contingency towards un-encumbered directive. The way was clearing for Wulfstan's moralizations.[237]

The content of the Andover code was both rational and rationed. Matching laws for Church and Society was a Carolingian ploy.[238] Edgar dealt in turn with a few of the main themes ventilated by recent predecessors. On nearly all, he had new proposals to offer. Church taxation had been backed by (heavy) sanctions as early as Ine's time. But neither Æthelstan nor Edmund buttressed their orders to pay tithes with explicit punishments.[239] Edgar incorporated 'Rome-money' into the range of dues, said who was to receive them, and decreed penalties for non-payment; these included materialization of Æthelstan's warning that witholders of tenth parts risked losing the other nine.[240] Ine's order for Sunday observance was cited with a notably wider definition of the timespan involved, and with an extra demand for prescribed fasts.[241] Edgar's secular laws were dominated by the topics of judicial organization and surety against theft. He brought together what Edward, Æthelstan and the 'Hundred Ordinance' said about judicial time-tabling, corrupt officials, and precipitate resort to the king, in the comprehensive justicial statute quoted above, going on to provide for meet-ings of the Borough and Shire courts parallel with the Hundred's.[242] The overall effect was to make English justice look yet more Carolingian.[243] The efforts of earlier tenth-century legislators to organize surety against anti-social behaviour, chiefly theft, tended to revolve around the role of kins or lords. Edgar was the first to stipulate what amounted to neighbourhood sureties; before at once (and the context matters, as chapter 9 will show) recapitulating and refining Æthelstan's laws on the dragooning of society's bad risks.[244] Lastly, he reinforced Æthelstan's demand for a single currency throughout his realm with uniform measures and a fixed price for wool.[245]

---

236   At the same time, the sub-clause on the unjust judge (above), with its two 'butan' provisos (cf. above, n. 209, etc.), shows how tortuous Edgar's phraseology could be.
237   See Schwyter, 'Syntax and Style', pp. 211–16, with fig. 5, for a growing divorce between 'dependent directives' and directives with dependent 'if – then'; but note too II Atr App. (below, pp. 325–6).
238   Starting with *Cap.* 43 – 44, and enshrined by Ansegisus (chapter 2, pp. 52–3, 107).
239   Ine 4 (cf. *Romscot*, below, pp. 368–9); I As (though NB cl. 5); I Em 2.
240   II Eg 3:1, I As 3.
241   II Eg 5, Ine 3 – 3:2; cf. the slightly more restrained Wi 9; also *Cap.* 22:15 (= *Ans.* i 15); see also chapter 8.
242   III Eg 1:1 – 4, 5 – 5:2; I Ew Pr., 2 – 2:1, II 1:2 – 2, 8; II As 3, 25, V 1:2–4, III 7:3, IV 7, VI 11; III Em 7:2; *Hu.* 1, 7 – 7:1
243   Cf., e.g., *Cap.* 39:4, 61:7,11, 64:1 (= *Ans.* iii 27, 53, 56, 59); see above, pp. 280, 290, 306, and chapter 13.
244   III Eg 6 – 7:3; II Ew 3 – 3:2; II As 2 – 2:1, III 7 – 7:2, III Em 7 – 7:1.
245   III Eg 8 – 8:2; II As 14.

So far as it went, the Andover code was impressive legislation. As a coherent response to perceived issues it was the most thoughtfully crafted Anglo-Saxon law-making to date. The extent of its propagation matched the quality of its composition. The outstanding problem is why it went only so far. This English king might have been expected to make laws about monastic observance, as Carolingians had. Neither at Andover nor elsewhere is he known to have done so.[246] When assessing the place of written legislation in the making of early medieval law, silences can be as revealing as utterances.

(ii) The Wihtbordesstan Code ('IV' Edgar)

Edgar's 'fourth' (i.e. second) legal pronouncement was promulgated at the unidentified location of *Wihtbordesstan*, apparently in the aftermath of a wide-spread pestilence.[247] Unlike the Andover code, it survives in a mere two manuscripts (though one offers versions in Latin as well as Old English, chapter 4, pp. 182–5, 211–19). Each manuscript is very probably from Worcester. In effect, they represent no more than a single line of transmission.[248] This may be the most restricted distribution of any Anglo-Saxon royal code, other than those of early Kent and the few extant only in *Quadripartitus*. So limited a circulation is embarrassingly at variance with the fact that the *Wihtbordesstan* code is also the only one that provides for its own multiple copying: 'And many documents (*gewrita*) are to be made about this, and to be sent both to Ealdorman Ælfhere and to Ealdorman Æthelwine, and by them in all directions, that this measure be made known to both poor and rich'. Edgar also called on the support of Earl Oslac and 'all the *here*' in his ealdormanry. It thus becomes clear that the text as it stands was directed at the Danelaw, in various parts of which Oslac, Ælfhere and Æthelwine held office.[249] Its failure to leave much trace of the dissemination demanded can then be explained by the poor preservation of Danelaw archives, notably the York cathedral library. Archbishop Oswald, who doubled as Bishop of Worcester like four of his successors (chapter 4, pp. 184–5), could be indirectly responsible for the extant copies.[250]

The *Wihtbordesstan* code was similar to Andover's in its style, but with two

---

246   Yet in one sense he did: *Reg. Conc.* Pr. opens with a royal *intitulatio*, and 69 ('Epilogue') conveys royal instructions. Cf. most obviously *Cap.* 170, with Mordek, *Bibliotheca*, pp. 1098–9.

247   IV Eg Pr. refers to a 'færcwealm' (for the dating implications, see chapter 6, pp. 441–2); the reference to *Wihtbordesstan* is only in 1:4, but editorial clauses mislead as usual: despite 'Ðæt is þonne ærest (1), 1:4 is really the end of a very extended prologue.

248   Their textual kinship was asserted by Liebermann, *Gesetze* III, p. 138 (3–4), who went on to make heavy weather of what discrepancies there are. Allowing the odd trivial slip in Nero E.i ('F'), and that CCCC 265 ('C') may have been as careless in executing OE as Latin, provides adequate explanations of all variants he listed. Latin and OE texts in C also share a diagnostic error (11, 'frige að'/'iusiurandi sacramento'(!)); and if one accepts this scribe's failings, there is no evidence that he had a better exemplar for his Latin than for his Old English. One might speculate that C's texts were taken from F, though a sister MS at Worcester remains a more likely source.

249   IV Eg 15 – 15:1; for the chronological implications, see chapter 6, p. 442.

250   There remains the problem of the disappearance of the equivalent decree for 'English England'; for possible traces, see chapter 3, pp. 125–8, and below, pp. 321, 370.

crucial differences. It was in (somewhat unequal) ecclesiastical and secular halves. The drawn-out prologue pondered the ways of God as judge and governor, concluding that He can be expected to act much like any other landlord confronted with tenants witholding their rent. The tenants' behaviour was reviewed in 'if/ then' clauses. Reeves were consequently ordered to enforce tithe-payment (with reference back to Andover). Another conditional clause covered persistent non-payers. The secular part opened with generalities about the 'rights (*gerihta*)' of subjects and king, the Danes' entitlement to decide their own 'woruldgerihta', and the application to Englishmen of whatever king and witan laid down. It was then explained that one provision applied to all, namely the organization of sworn witnesses to supervise buying and selling in every borough and 'wapentake'. Each of these points were expressed as directives, the last (dictating the oath to be sworn by witnesses) itself of some intricacy.[251] Contingencies were then covered in a relative clause and five complex 'if'-clauses. The topics addressed at *Wihtbordesstan* were thus handled much as the main issues at Andover had been, but more wordily. Wordiness was the first main difference between the two. IV Edgar was rhetorical as no previous Anglo-Saxon laws had been:

> Nevertheless, this measure is to be common to the whole people, whether Englishmen or Danes or Britons, in every part of my dominion, so that poor and rich may possess what they rightly acquire (*earm 7 eadig mote agan þæt hy mid rihte gestrynað*), and a thief should not know where to dispose of stolen goods ... and let them be so guarded against in their own despite that too many of them do not get away.[252]

The sternness of these sentiments is at odds with the little said of punishment. Delinquent reeves lost property and royal favour; those failing to declare purchases lost them; unsupported claims of legitimate purchase entailed death and forfeiture.[253] That was all. The precision over sanctions characteristic of earlier codes was swallowed up in a level of official indignation not articulated before.

The other difference between Edgar's earlier and later laws is that the one was as personal as the other was detached. After an initial account of the reflections of king and council in the third person, Edgar never afterwards appeared except as 'ic' and 'min'.

> Further, I will that God's dues prevail everywhere alike in my dominion ... And I and my thegns will oblige our priests ... I will that secular rights be in force among the entire people as well as they can be devised, to the satisfaction of God, and for my full kingship ... And ... I am to have the rights of my kingship (*mines cynescipes gerihta*) as my father had, and my thegns are to have their dignity in my time as they had in my father's ... Let that apply among the English which I and my wise men have added to the judgements of my ancestors ... Namely, then, I will that ... Further, I will that such good laws be in force among the Danes as they best prefer, and I have always granted them (this), and will grant (it) as long as my life endures,

251   IV Eg 6:1.
252   IV Eg 2:2.
253   IV Eg 1:5, 9, 11.

for your obedience which you have ever manifested to me ... I therefore will that what you have preferred for the betterment of the peace, with great wisdom and in a way very pleasing to me, shall ever be kept among you ... I am to be a true lord to you while my life endures, and am very pleased with you because you are so eager for peace.[254]

So intimate if minatory a tone represented considerable development from the otherwise comparable addresses of Edward, Æthelstan and Edmund (above, pp. 289, 302, 311). Nothing else in Old English law is quite like it, except Cnut's letters to England of 1020 and 1027 (below, pp. 347–9). Those letters used writ formulae at their outset. The *Wihtbordesstan* code begins with the words, 'Her is geswutelod on þissum gewrite', like a documentary memo-randum.[255] Cnut's letters too sought contact with a political community at a distance. They offered the same mix of promises, assurances and demands as Edgar, as self-justifying governments of any time.[256] If it is not yet possible to speak of post-conquest-style law-making by writ, *Wihtbordesstan* marked another stage in the evolution of a more informal, and at the same time more flamboyant, legislative mode.

It is worth adding that, to judge from its vocabulary, IV Edgar may not have had different draftsmen from II–III. Both used '*leodscipe*, people' and '*anweald*, dominion'; the first appeared only twice more in the Anglo-Saxon legal corpus, and the second was otherwise confined to laws of Æthelstan and Edmund.[257] The 'earm'/'eadig' pairing occurred in II–III and repeatedly in IV, but otherwise less than might be expected.[258] Another word surprisingly confined to these codes (and ordeal rituals) was 'forgifnes'.[259] Granted that the *Wihtbordesstan* code was the first that used Scandinavian terminology to any marked degree (including the very word 'lagu'), there was enough overlap to suggest the same agencies at work in each of Edgar's codes. If 'it is tempting to connect (*Wihtbordesstan*) with one of the great churchmen who surrounded King Edgar', then they were arguably involved in his law-making from the outset.[260]

Notwithstanding its emphatic language, IV Edgar had a restricted remit, like its equivalents under Æthelstan and Edmund. The first part was concerned with tithes where Andover covered all church dues. The second ramified earlier laws on supervised trade and the activity of local courts; the ultimate concern was, as usual, theft. But there was a clarity of detail in the regularization of cattle-trading

---

254   IV Eg 1:6, 1:8, 2 – 2a, 2:1a, 3, 12, 14:1, 16.
255   RoAsCh XXXVII, XXXVIII, etc.: this sequence begins around Edgar's time.
256   A shrewd appreciation of the place of IV Eg in this tradition is Lund, 'King Edgar and the Danelaw'.
257   II Eg Pr., IV Eg Pr., 2, 2:1a–2, 12:1, II Atr 1, X Atr Pr.; III Eg 8, IV Eg Pr., 1:6, 2:2, II As 14, VI As 11, II Em Pr., Pr.:1.
258   III Eg 1:1, IV Eg 1:4, 2, 2:2, 15:1; VI Atr 8:1 = II Cn 1:1.
259   III Eg 1:2, IV Eg 1:1, 1:5, 9.
260   *EHD I*, p. 434; cf. Whitelock, 'Account of King Edgar's Establishment of Monasteries'; Æthelwold's usage is not much like *Wihtbordesstan's* (though NB 'mynegung', IV Eg 1:3, 6, 'anweald', as n. 330, 'fyrþrige', IV Eg 15:1); but the idea that God reacts like an earthly landlord is similar to Æthelwold's argument in 'Account' and two charters (S 745, 782) that God's property is not jeopardized when criminous clerics are liable to forfeiture (Whitelock, pp. 130–3).

that was largely absent from what had gone before, and which otherwise appeared only in the Appendix to 'II Æthelred' (itself not improbably a fragment of a lost Edgar code, below, pp. 321, 370). Nor should the rift between rhetoric and substance qualify the point that this was the clearest statement yet of the ideological charge that drove tenth-century law-making: 'A calamity of this kind was earned by sins and by disobedience to God's commands'. Here, then, is more paradox. IV Edgar shows what Anglo-Saxon legislation could aim to do. Its directions for publication are especially noteworthy and sound another Carolingian note (chapter 2, pp. 51–2). Yet these orders were both unparalleled and apparently ill-observed. Chapter 6 will raise the possibility that the code was issued in the most solemn circumstances (pp. 442, 448). That may partly account for its portentous manner. But expectations thus aroused could not be sustained with any consistency by Edgar's regime or its successors.

6   The Early Legislation of Æthelred

The supposed 'ten codes' of Æthelred are the clearest lesson in the diversity of Anglo-Saxon legislation and of the problems this poses.[261] Liebermann actually printed twelve texts. He reached his figure of ten by giving the same number to the Latin and Old English versions of 'VI' and 'VII' but not to the no less obviously interrelated 'V' and 'VI', and by ignoring a distinct possibility that 'X' was a fragment of another product of the session that gave rise to 'V' and 'VI'. He otherwise reproduced texts as he found them, though aware that 'II' was composite, and that 'IV' may contain as many as three elements, none demonstrably of Æthelred's time.[262] The position is like that created by Æthelstan's laws. It must be approached with the same assiduous regard to what the manuscripts reveal about the sources of confusion. But the first four 'codes' contrast more absolutely with the other six (or so) than do Andover and *Wihtbordesstan*. Earlier and later groups demand sections to themselves.

(i) Texts and transmission

The texts dubbed 'I – IV Æthelred' were preserved solely in the twelfth-century encyclopaedias. That is about where the similarities end. Taking the most straightforward case first (it may even be the earliest), 'II' is extant in Corpus 383

---

261   I discussed the legislation of Æthelred at length in 'Æthelred the Lawmaker'; reference to that paper is made below for points where I have not greatly altered my view in two decades.
262   Liebermann was as ever the self-sentenced captive of earlier editors. Lambarde printed 'I' and 'II' from Corpus 383, and so set the fashion for taking the 'Appendix' (8 – 9:4) as part of the latter; Wilkins added 'V', 'VIII', 'III' and 'VI', in that order, and also included *Grið* as an addition to 'V'. Thorpe and Schmid (first edition) introduced 'IV' and were thus responsible for the numbering 'I' – 'IV'; they also perpetuated the designation of 'V' and 'VI' as separate items, though Schmid relegated *Grið* to his appendices and Thorpe made it 'VII', with 'VII' itself (Latin only) and 'VIII' as his 'VIII' and 'IX'. Schmid's second edition added the Latin text of 'VI', and the Old English of 'VII', so producing the sequence 'I' – 'VIII' that has been followed ever since; it only remained for Liebermann to add the fragments 'IX' and 'X'.

('B') and *Quadripartitus* ('Q').[263] In both it was so tightly welded to an unrelated 'Appendix' that no scribe spotted the join. Also in both *Dunsæte* came next, though as a visibly separate item; there is a case that both derived this set of documents from the same 'mini-collection', perhaps made at Bath in Æthelred's time (chapter 4, pp. 232–3, below, p. 388).[264] However that may be, it was clearly an agency other than central government that added the Appendix. The main body of 'II' is the king's 994 treaty with Viking leaders.[265] Like Alfred's Guthrum treaty (above, pp. 285–6), it is close enough to what Anglo-Saxons understood by a law-code for there to be no puzzle about its presence in legal collections. It was presumably its clause about charges of homicide and cattle-theft that led someone to add the sophisticated review of procedure in cases of stolen movables that forms the Appendix.[266] This looks like part of a text whose 'official' status is suggested by the phrase 'Then the wise decreed'.[267] In phraseology and content it is most like *Forfang*, another anonymous but perhaps 'official' fragment. Its nearest equivalent otherwise is the *Wihtbordesstan* section on livestock transactions. Appendix and *Forfang* may be parts of a code for 'English England' parallel with 'IV Edgar' (below, pp. 369–70).[268] But the Appendix may reasonably be discussed alongside Æthelred laws. It must be roughly contemporary with them.

'I' Æthelred has a different history in most respects. It called itself a decree issued at Woodstock 'according to English law (*æfter Engla lage*)'. It is in each twelfth-century collection ('H', 'B', 'Q'), and in ways that raise unusual possibilities about its route thither. There are no significant variants in any copy; they share two apparent defects.[269] But unlike the Edward and Edmund codes (pp. 286–7, 308–9), they have diverse manuscript contexts. The Woodstock code evidently reached B in such close association with *Hundred, Be Blaserum-Forfang* and Alfred–Ine that he began by taking them all as the same text (chapter 4, pp. 231–2). The Alfred–Ine/ *Blas./Forf./Hu.* group was also available to the Q compiler, but by his later drafts he knew that the last three were no part of the *domboc* and moved them elsewhere (chapter 4, Table 4.7). He may have found 'I Æthelred' in this group and, following his usual practice, put it next to Æthelred's Wantage (or 'third') code; or he may have found it paired with 'III' already. It will soon emerge that this association would be logical. In any event,

263   'I' has always preceded 'II' simply because it does so in B (see n. 262); for dates, see nn. 265, 297–8, and chapter 6, pp. 442–4.
264   As Liebermann of course recognized, *Gesetze* III, p. 149 (1); B and Q texts of *Duns.* share diagnostic errors, see n. 523.
265   For the date, with text and translation, see Keynes, 'Historical Context of the Battle of Maldon', pp. 103–7; an important discussion of the transaction, featuring similarities with ninth-century 'treaties', is Lund, 'Peace and Non-peace in the Viking Age'.
266   II Atr 7 – 7:1.
267   II Atr 9.
268   *Forf.*, 2, 3. As II Atr App. *is* a fragment, it is hard to know how much to make of Liebermann's argument, *Gesetze* III, p. 155 (3), that it makes no mention of the arrangements in I Atr 3, III Atr 6:1.
269   I Atr 1:2, 1:5 (II Cn 30:1,3b has phrases one might expect to find there too): *Gesetze* III, p. 146 (1); but note that there is also a difference between I Atr 1:7 and II Cn 30:6 ('þam cincge … oððe þam þe … ') to which Liebermann attaches no significance: it is not inconceivable that I Atr had these (very minor) defects from the outset, and that Cnut remedied them. H, B and Q variants (Liebermann, *loc. cit.*) could obviously be slips by their own scribes.

the version in H must have had a different prehistory. *Hundred* did not appear here at all. *Be Blaserum* and *Forfang* were added to Alfred–Ine only at the correction stage (chapter 4, p. 249, below, pp. 368, 370, 379); since the scribe added a leaf to do this, he would have had ample room for *Hundred*, and nothing in his record implies that he would have omitted it deliberately. And if he had found Woodstock and Wantage together (as in Q), he would have had no reason to interpose the Conqueror's Exculpation decree between them (chapter 4, Table 4.8).[270] Either, therefore, he found 'I Æthelred' where he put it, in the Edward–Edmund group (table 4.9), or it had no particular prior association, and he slotted it into a convenient space (chapter 4, pp. 247–8). Either way, this is a rare case of a largely homogeneous text with two or even three substantially independent transmissions. For that reason alone, the three texts may not be far from the archetype.

The cases of 'III' and 'IV Æthelred' are different again. 'III' is a code promulgated at Wantage with particular reference to the Danelaw Five Boroughs: its Scandinavian quality is notorious.[271] 'IV' is a code (or codes) with London relevance. The grounds for taking them together emerge from table 5.2. The text that has gone by the name 'IV Æthelred' since 1840 exists only in later editions of Q (chapter 4, pp. 239–43). As table 5.2 shows, it there constituted the last five clauses of 'III'.[272] So far as Q was concerned, the one-sentence tracts *Pax* and *Walreaf* were also parts of the Wantage code; it will later be seen that they would have fitted very well there (below, pp. 371–2). But 'IV Æthelred' itself is clearly hybrid. Its first dozen sentences were succint port and city of London regulations. The next half dozen were more discursive rules on paying tolls and keeping town peace, and their concluding phrase, 'if the king concede that to us', shows that it was townsmen who were making them. After that came a detailed set of laws on coinage and weights, where first person pronouns designated king and/or council. These would have applied not only to London but to any borough with a mint, the 'Five Boroughs' included.[273] They could have been interpolated into a collection of materials whose common denominator was that they concerned borough government. In *Quadripartitus*, then, the Wantage code came equipped with a set of barely distinct codicils.

Yet there are also signs that the Wantage code was composite. One is that it had a rather motley structure by comparison with 'I'; after its opening clauses it

---

270   Wl lad is squeezed into the end of a quire, with III Atr commencing a fresh one. Rochester's compiler liked to achieve this effect (chapter 4, pp. 247–8), but the parallel with Æthelstan's codes (above, p. 297) suggests that I and III Atr reached him from different sources.

271   On the Scandinavian language and legal ideas of this code, see subsections (ii) and (iii) respectively; a general solution to its many problems is offered at pp. 328–9.

272   There are hints that Q recognized the distinct identity of *Pax* and (at least some of) 'IV Atr' in the rubrics that these both had in MS R (see table); but at the start of 'III' R had 'Institutiones Æþelredi regis' with an enlarged initial; and MS T has only an enlarged initial at IV 1 in a text otherwise continuous from the fresh line on which 'III' begins. It should be added that the actual *numbering* of MHk rubrics is too inconsistent to be original; and that Hk, which alone puts chapter numbers in the text (chapter 4, n. 311), makes IV Atr 2:10 'XXII', with subsequent chapters numbered 'XXIII' – 'XXV', and brackets at 4:1, 6, 7, 8, etc.

273   The rubric 'Item rex Lundonie' in Q's MS R, and MHk's 'XX De Institutis Lundonie', need not apply to more than IV Atr 1 – 4:2.

Table 5.2   Transmissions of 'III' and 'IV Æthelred'

Q (MHk)	H
'Institutiones Ethelredi regis'	III Atr 1 – 13:4
III Atr 1 – 13:4: 'I' – 'XV', etc.	
III Atr 15: 'XVI, Qui robariam indicaverit'	III Atr 14
III Atr 14: 'XVII, De eius herede qui sine calumpnia vixerit'	III Atr 15
Pax [R: 'De pace in curia regis']: 'XVIII,	
Quam procul a porta pax regis esse debeat'	
Wal.: 'XIX, De wealref'	
IV Atr 1 [R 'Item rex Lundonie']: 'XX, De	
Institutis Lundonie, et primum . . .	
IV Atr 2–2:12: 'XXI, De teloneo dando	
ad Bilingesgate'	
IV Atr 3–3:3: 'XXII, De teloneo retento'	
IV Atr 4–4:2: 'XXIII, De hamsocna vel	
in porto vel in via regia'	
IV Atr 5–9, 'XXIV, De falsariis et eis consentientibus'	III Atr 16 = 'IV Atr 5:4'
	Wal. (f. 32v)
	Pax (f. 38r)

appears to consist of *ad hoc* responses on miscellaneous issues (see next sub-section). Another is that its vernacular version (H) reverses the order of two of its last three clauses, while the third is in effect the same as a provision in 'IV Æthelred'.[274] Each version, that is to say, had accumulated a series of similar but diversely ordered supplements. If these were even dimly detectable in H's raw material, it would accord with its usual practice that *Pax* and *Walreaf* were hived off elsewhere as 'space-fillers' (chapter 4, pp. 247–8). The scenario for 'III Æthelred' and its additions may thus resemble the one suggested for Æthelstan's later legislation. Though H and Q presentations are not so closely related in this instance, Q may reasonably be considered primary. 'III Æthelred' looks like the same sort of semi-detached summary as 'IV Æthelstan'. Here too, and in contrast with Æthelred's Woodstock or (presumed) monetary laws, there was not even a hint of the royal first person. Like 'Thunderfield', Wantage drew satellites into its orbit. One was what is called 'IV Æthelred'. It seems, like 'VI Æthelstan', to be a blend of royal and local directions. In each reign, the initiative came not from the king but from one of his servants.

---

274   A further link between Q and H versions is that they share a possible textual flaw in III Atr 1:2 ('þær'/'ubi' for 'þæt' (*Gesetze* III, p. 156 (1); cf. Whitelock, *EHD I*, p. 439, 'that which'); but Professor Stanley tells me that he would find 'þær' acceptable OE.

(ii) Structure, style and language

As the Æthelstan analogy leads one to expect, Æthelred's early 'codes' exhibit a variety of legislative idioms. Here too, it is best to begin with what looks like the central document, and then compare the rest. The obvious candidate is the Woodstock code, with its widespread and relatively uncontaminated circulation. Its prologue followed the same pared down lines as Edgar's Andover code. This too was a '*gerædnys* (decree)' that king and wise men '*geræddon*'. Like Andover, it was third-person legislation, except that the final clause referred back to 'the declaration of us all' in penalizing failure to implement it.[275] In structure too it resembled Andover, but with intriguing developments.[276]

A. That is, that every free man have trustworthy surety (*getreowne borh*) that the surety hold him to all justice if he be charged (*betyhtlad wurðe*).

(i) a) If then he be charge-laden (*tyhtbysig*), let him go to the threefold ordeal.

b) If his lord say that neither oath nor ordeal failed for him since there was a meeting at *Bromdune*, let his lord take for him two trustworthy thegns within the hundred and swear that the oath never failed for him nor did he pay thief-payment (*þeofgyld*) – unless he have a reeve who is entitled to do this.

c) If then the oath be forthcoming, let the man who is there charged then choose whichever he will, either the single ordeal or the oath worth a pound within the three hundreds, [for a suit of] over thirty pence.

d) If then they dare not give the oath, let him go to the threefold ordeal.

(ii) a) If then he be found guilty (*ful*), on the first occasion let him compensate the accuser twofold and the lord with his wergeld, and let trustworthy sureties be appointed that he afterwards desist from all wrongdoing.

b) And on the second occasion, let there be no other compensation there but his head.

(iii) a) If then he escape and avoid the ordeal, let the surety pay the accuser the value of his goods (*ceapgyld*) and his wergeld to the lord who is entitled to his fine (*þe his wites wyrðe sy*).

b) And if one accuse the lord that it was by his counsel that he escaped and had committed wrong, let him take five thegns and be himself the sixth and clear himself of that.

c) And if the clearance be forthcoming, let him be entitled to the wergeld.

d) And if it be not forthcoming, let the king take the wergeld, and let the thief be outlaw against the whole people.

B. Let every lord have his householdmen in his own surety.

a) If however he be accused and he escape, let the lord pay the man's wergeld to the king.

---

275   I Atr 4:3.
276   I Atr 1 – 2:1 (orthography and punctuation largely as in H).

b)   And if one accuse the lord that it was by his counsel that he escaped, let him clear himself with five thegns and be himself the sixth.

c)   And if the clearance fail, let him pay the king his wergeld, and let the man be outlaw.

C.   And let the king be entitled to all the fines which men who have bookland pay, and let no one compound for any charge (*7 ne bete nan man for nanre tyhtlan*) unless it be with the knowledge of the king's reeve.

D.   a)   And if a slave be found guilty at the ordeal, let one brand him on the first occasion.

b)   And on the second occasion, let there be no other compensation there but his head.

At 380 words, this is one of the bulkiest single-issue laws in the Anglo-Saxon corpus. Its affinities lie with the secular part of the *Wihtbordesstan* code, and with the Appendix of the 994 treaty. The pattern fixed at Andover had been elaborated. There were statements of principle at the points marked A, B and C in the above quotation.[277] A series of imaginable deviations from the prescribed norm was then reviewed. Æthelred had only conditional clauses for these, but smoothed the flow of the prose by qualifying 'Gif' with 'þonne'. What took the place of earlier refinements of the 'if . . . then' template was a high level of verbal repetition. Contingency (i) was the liability of the *tyhtbysig* to the threefold ordeal, and the way his lord could help him to evade this. Contingency (ii) was successive failure at the threefold ordeal. Contingency (iii) related to the thief's escape, and where this left his surety and lord: (iii) a) echoed (ii) a), and (iii) c) partly repeated (i) c). Principle B then ushered in a survey of the same set of possibilities from its viewpoint: B a) covered the same ground as A (iii) a), B b) as A (iii) b), and B c) as A (iii) d). After a gloss on the king's entitlements (C), D a) and b) returned to the theme and some of the wording of A (ii) a) and b). Word for word iteration might characterize oral records. But there was nothing formulaic about this passage. It aimed to train the same line of thought on all forseeable cases. In a word, it was 'legalese'.

Not that the Woodstock code achieved a completely consistent structure. D would be better placed within the parameters of A, or perhaps B. Æthelred returned to the issue of those viewed with general suspicion after another clause taking up Edgar's *Wihtbordesstan* point about surety and witness in business dealings. Still, there was a logic about all this that commands respect. English legislation had seldom before been so thoroughly planned.[278] The same, so far as one can see, goes for the 'II Æthelred' Appendix, which may not be an Æthelred product, and to the coinage laws in 'IV Æthelred', which probably are.[279] In the Appendix, a point of principle, that vouching cases be heard where goods were first sought, was lengthily glossed to the effect that accepted practice was thereby changed, then followed by another statement on the need for witness good

277   Clause-markers given here are designed to facilitate perception of the code's structure; they do not of course correspond to those of modern editors (as misleading as ever), nor to those of any MS.

278   Cf. Liebermann's comments, *Gesetze* III, p. 146 (8), which perhaps overlook the extent of *deliberate* reiteration.

279   Note that Richardson and Sayles, *Law and Legislation*, pp. 25–6, award these decrees higher marks than any other.

enough to settle cases even when one party was dead, or to uphold any title: eventualities also covered by 'if' clauses.[280] This text was prone too to legalistic remarks: 'he should toil more in whose hands lay the unjust gain, less he who claim there justly'; 'for title is nearer him that has than him who claims'.[281] The later part of 'IV' was as exhaustive a review of monetary affairs as was Woodstock's of criminal surety. A series of depositions in a curious mix of first and third person were foundations for sanctions against the aberrant. Three different types of fraudster come into the same category and are to be punished accordingly; those who establish that they innocently brought forged or defective coin to market are, in what is almost a flash of wit, to pay for their carelessness by trading it in for decent money at what would presumably be highly unfavourable rates of exchange.[282] It is hard not to be impressed by the panache with which draftsmen were by now handling legal material. It may be linked with the readiness of Æthelred's charters to expatiate on criminality (chapter 3, pp. 149–50).

It also sets off the quality of the other two texts in question. The treaty was a cruder document than those discussed so far. It opened with the usual antiphony of generality and circumstance: 'And every trading ship which enters an estuary is to have peace, though it be a ship not covered by the peace (*unfriðscyp*), provided it be not driven ashore; and though it be driven ashore and it take refuge in any borough covered by the peace (*friðbyrig*) ... then the men and what they bring with them are to have peace ... If a man of King Æthelred covered by the peace (*Æðelredes cynges friðmann*) come to land not so covered (*unfriðland*) ...'[283] However, from that point to the end (except for three of the last five clauses), the text dealt only in conditional formulations, nearly always 'left-branching' if also 'multilayered'. The style was a throwback to that of two generations before.[284] And there were also Scandinavianisms that do not appear in Æthelred's other early laws, Wantage excepted.[285]

The Wantage code has been seen from the time of *Quadripartitus* as a 'pair' for Woodstock. There are good reasons for this. But it is first necessary to stress the contrasts between them. Wantage dealt with a much wider range of issues than Woodstock, but much more tersely. There were just six clauses on the 'tihtbysig' and his lord. Reference was made to the meeting at *Bromdune*, but coverage of the whole was comparatively abrupt.[286] Three more clauses briefly

---

280   Editorial clausing is more unhelpful than ever: the main breaks should be at '8' (or before), '8:4', '9:1', and perhaps '9:4'.
281   II Atr. 9, 9:4; the second remark has an interesting resonance.
282   IV Atr 5 – 5:1, 7:2. Cross-reference was especially abundant in this code, where in I Atr it was rationed to a single rather elegant specimen in the concluding phrase (above, n. 275).
283   II Atr 2 – 3:1; translation from Keynes, 'Historical Context', with slight changes in the direction of verbal consistency.
284   Exceptions: II Atr 6:1–2, 7:2 (this effectively an appendix); cf. Schwyter, 'Syntax and Style', pp. 193–8.
285   E.g. 'ðræl', II Atr 5:1, contrasted with 'þeowman', I Atr 2, etc. The rare or unique compounds of 'frið' are accounted for by the text's unusual subject: see Fell, '*Unfrið*: an approach to a definition', pp. 96–8.
286   III Atr 3:2 – 4:2; for this and much of what follows, see my 'Æthelred', pp. 61–2; also chapter 9 for contrasting ways in which 'I' and 'III' handle prosecution of the *tihtbysig*.

resumed the monetary theme of 'IV Æthelred', and apparently cited one of its laws, which is the chief reason for attributing them to this reign.[287] Woodstock's law on having stock without surety made a fleeting (and somewhat altered) appearance.[288] Otherwise, the code concerned the cost of infringing the peace ('grið') at various levels, the validity of 'gewitnes', conduct of ordeals, clearance of the condemned thief, and so on, through a string of ever more isolated if not trivial matters: guarantees on a slaughtered ox, fugitives, jurisdiction over kings' thegns, arbitration, security of tenure, daylight robbery. There was a more pronounced tendency than at Woodstock to return to topics addressed before: the clauses about ordeals and clearing a thief could precede that on live-stock surety, which might accompany those on slaughter of oxen; the late clause on unchallenged tenure belonged with that on valid title. Most obviously, the provision for 'majority voting' among the twelve thegns was a long way out of place.[289] This interwoven pattern is all the more notable in that it was *not* linked by cross-references. The opening clauses were repetitive ('and that *grið* which [X] give/is given'), but in a way that recalled Æthelberht, not Woodstock. Or again:

> And let each accuser have a choice, whichever he will, whether water or iron. And each vouching and each ordeal is to be in the king's borough. And if he flee from the ordeal, let the surety pay for him with his wergeld.[290]

The change of subject heralded by no more than an ungoverned pronoun is reminiscent of Ine.

The outstanding peculiarity of the Wantage code is of course its Scandinavian vocabulary.[291] The point needs no labouring. Forms of 'lagu' appear four times. Previous appearances were in a clause of Æthelstan's Tithe Ordinance where interpolation by Wulfstan is probable, and in Edgar's *Wihtbordesstan* code, when the king singled out laws preferred by the Danes.[292] 'Grið' appears where earlier codes, Æthelred's included, spoke of 'frið'.[293] These are acknowledged Scandinavianisms. The trio 'landcop ... lahcop 7 witword', and the pair 'sac/sacleas' seem likely to be Scandinavian in origin.[294] Any one of these words and phrases might be put down to creeping Danish influence on the speech of the tenth-century elite. Several occur in Wulfstan's works. But so dense a combination must reflect the usage of the Five Boroughs to which the code was apparently directed. Along with a transmission mediated by local government action go strong indications that its language was a locality's.

---

287   III Atr 8 – 8:2, IV Atr 5 – 5:2; III Atr 16, IV 5:4.
288   III Atr 5, I 3 – 3:1.
289   Cf. *Gesetze* III, p. 157 (9). On the significance of the 'Twelve Thegns', see chapter 1, pp. 7–8, 17–18, chapter 9, section 3.
290   III Atr 6 – 6:2.
291   *Gesetze* III, p. 156 (3). The fullest recent survey is Neff, 'Scandinavian Elements', especially pp. 287–93.
292   III Atr Pr., 3:3, 8:2, 13:3; I As 2 ('Godes lage', a most Wulfstanian phrase, linked with a Wulfstanian Biblical axiom, above, n. 173); IV Eg 2:1, 12, 13:1. But 'utlah' is already in *Hu.* 3:1.
293   Fell, *'Unfrið'*, pp. 86–91.
294   III Atr 3, 3:1. The primary Old English sense of 'sacu' is 'dispute' (as in the standard jurisdictional formula, chapter 10); but here the adjective 'sac' apparently means 'guilty'.

(iii) Legal policy

The most striking feature of Æthelred's pre-Wulfstan laws is that their themes were as resolutely secular as Wulfstan's were overwhelmingly ecclesiastical. Wantage apart, their purview was in fact relatively restricted. Woodstock was very largely concerned with criminal surety. Where Edgar had stressed the role of community sureties, and previous kings had dwelt on kindreds or lords, Æthelred now sought to integrate the activity of lord and neigbourhood. The result was the bi-polar configuration of district and household sureties which passed down to Cnut and post-conquest commentators (chapter 9). The other major point addressed by Æthelred's early legislation was coinage. The truncated set of laws in 'IV' are the most sophisticated discussion of the subject in the Anglo-Saxon corpus. There is again a general resemblance to what Carolingians were aiming at by the later-ninth century.[295] 'I' and 'III' both refer to a previous meeting at *Bromdune*, in a way suggesting that it too had promulgated legislation. Wantage also appears to cite one of the coinage laws in 'IV', so it is possible that these were among the *Bromdune* decrees (the 'II Æthelred Appendix' might even have come from this source).[296] Just as plausibly, either or both (or neither) could have originated in a council of Pentecost 993 at Winchester, which the king invited to discuss 'whatever was worthy of the heavenly Creator, whatever was suited to the salvation of my soul ... and whatever was timely for all the people of the English'.[297]

Another Æthelred charter described a gathering of the regime's great and good at Wantage in 997, 'for the reform of matters of various sorts'.[298] One is naturally tempted to connect this meeting with the issue of the 'Wantage Code'. But if so, the question of just what this code was doing must finally be confronted squarely. The difficulty of the question is reflected in the diametrically opposed solutions it received from Sir Frank Stenton and Messrs Richardson and Sayles.[299] A first point must be that much of the wording of the prologue was virtually the same as Woodstock's, apart from the change of *venue*, and replacement of 'gerædnys' by 'laga'; and though the Wantage prologue said nothing about 'Danish law', the fact that Woodstock is 'æfter Engla lage' (the first such expression in Anglo-Saxon law) certainly implies that it meant to.[300] Nor can it be disputed that parts of 'III Æthelred' gave 'I' and 'IV' a harsher application. The

---

295   The great statement of Carolingian currency law is the Edict of Pîtres, *Cap.* 273:8–24 (chapter 2, pp. 50–1), which can hardly have been accessible to Anglo-Saxons, but some of it was based on material garnered in *Ans.* ii 18, iii 13, iv 30–1 (chapter 13).

296   I Atr 1:2, III Atr 4, III Atr 8, IV Atr 5 – 5:2 (not to forget II As 14). Cf. my 'Æthelred', pp. 62–3 – but it no longer seems so likely as it did in 1978 that the IV Atr coinage laws can be tied to a particular moment in the later Anglo-Saxon monetary cycle.

297   S 876. This charter marked a major turning-point in the reign: Keynes, *Diplomas*, pp. 183–93, etc., and chapter 6, pp. 442–4.

298   S 891; Keynes, *Diplomas*, pp. 196–7; chapter 6, p. 443.

299   Stenton, *Anglo-Saxon England*, p. 508; Richardson and Sayles, p. 25; the contradiction is neatly exposed and exploited by Neff, 'Scandinavian Elements', pp. 285, 310–11.

300   Cf. Wulfstan's pairing, within no more than two decades, of 'Ængla lage' and 'Dena lage', VI Atr 37; or II Cn 15:1–3, 62, 65.

tihtbysig went to the threefold ordeal or paid four times over, reduced to three times if his lord intervened; Woodstock arrangements were for double restitution, even after conviction by threefold ordeal, and, unlike Wantage, afforded the guilty a second chance. 'IV' consigned forgers to 'full ordeal', but ordered death only for coiners in the woods or importers of defective coin; under 'III', guilt at the ordeal was capital.[301] These points are not easily reconciled with a view that the code was giving the royal blessing to regional custom.[302] Yet it is equally hard to deny that regional, and probably Scandinavian, custom has left its mark on it. Discounting the entire debate about the Scandinavian origin of the 'twelve thegns', and making every allowance for the fact that Scandinavian evidence is invariably late and not impossibly influenced by Danelaw practice, there remain aspects of 'III Æthelred' that are unlike anything in English law since the seventh century, and which happen to be couched in Scandinavian terminology. That one should *buy* law is, for instance, an idea not unknown in the far North.[303]

A resolution of the riddle may be to hand in what was previously suggested about the transmission and structure of the Wantage code. The crux is the dichotomy between objective and execution. Æthelred evidently scheduled a vigorous enforcement of his will in (what was not yet called) the Danelaw. This decision was taken at Wantage in the heart of Wessex, perhaps soon after the session at Woodstock, to which it was the intended counterpart. What Æthelstan did at and after his Exeter council was not dissimilar. Implementation was entrusted to the king's representatives in the area; it was just then that Sigeferth became the first bishop in Lindsey since the Danish conquest.[304] The upshot, as in Archbishop Wulfhelm's time, was the emergence of a text where royal resolutions were fused with local measures and practices. Under Æthelstan, the response was explicitly regional. Under Æthelred, provincial initiative was implicit in unmetropolitan language and less professional presentation. Danish custom was the incidental, not the intended, beneficiary.

Parallels with Æthelstan have recurred more than once in these pages. They may not be fortuitous. Close examination reveals quite an intense level of legislative action in Æthelred's first quarter century. Up to half a dozen sessions are somehow signalled, though only one code came through in anything like the form with which it left the king's council. The educational impetus of the 'Tenth-Century Reformation' may have advanced legal writing in the generation after Edgar, as Alfred's work did under his immediate descendants.[305] Archival

301 I Atr 1:4–6; III Atr 3:4 – 4:1, 8; IV Atr 5 – 5:4, 7 – 7:1.
302 As powerfully argued by Lund, 'King Edgar and the Danelaw', pp. 193–4. Note too the implications of the Domesday evidence marshalled by Maitland, 'Criminal Liability of the Hundred', *CP* I, pp. 230–46 one of his earliest and most brilliant papers.
303 III Atr 3 ('lahcop', a formulation like 'lahslit', below, p. 396), 3:3, 8:2 (what is contemplated for the accused moneyer does not look like monetary redemption of crime); cf. Neff, pp. 290–1.
304 Keynes, *Atlas of Attestations* LXa(2)–LXb(1) (S 878, 891, 899, 904, 906) (996–1004); S 891 is the Wantage 'reform council'.
305 Here, then, would be a further dimension to the development identified by Professor Gneuss's celebrated paper, 'The Origin of Standard Old English'; cf. Hofstetter, 'Winchester and the standardization of Old English vocabulary'. But this would be a matter merely of general encouragement: there is too little overlap between the vocabulary isolated for Æthelwold's disciples and the corpus of laws; and Wulfstan was not a product of Æthelwoldian education.

recording remained less sophisticated. But the Anglo-Saxon legislative tradition was in any case about to be given a new articulacy and a fresh direction.

7 Æthelred's Later Codes

The last phase of Old English law extends from the closing years of Æthelred's reign to the first decade of Cnut's. More than any other part of the corpus, it has been profoundly transformed since Liebermann's day by research and rethinking. It is now beyond question that a very large part of it was written by Archbishop Wulfstan of York and Worcester, to whom Liebermann gave barely a walk-on part. But by no means all the implications of Wulfstan's activity have yet been worked out. This section and the next subject his work to the same kind of scrutiny as was devoted to his predecessors. What that means above all is that the message of the manuscripts studied in chapter 4 must remain basic.

(i) Wulfstan's books

Transmission of Æthelred's later codes flows in three currents. All three texts of 'V', one recension of 'VII' and both versions of 'VIII' survive in Cotton Nero A.i(B) ('G') and/or Corpus Cambridge 201 ('D'). Chapter 4 established that the relevant part of each of these books were collections of Wulfstan homilies, laws and other prescriptive works; the first (which probably comprises two such collections) is annotated by the archbishop's own hand. Both the Latin and Old English forms of what goes under the name 'VI Æthelred' stand side-by-side on preliminary leaves of the triple pontifical in Cotton Claudius A.iii ('K'); here too Wulfstan's hand has been at work. The third channel has no evident link with Wulfstan: the other recension of 'VII' is in Q; the fragment numbered 'IX' was a lost leaf in the incinerated Cotton Otho A.x; and 'X', also a fragment, is among leaves which look as if they came from a de luxe volume. This is to say that, with one exception, all intact texts of Æthelred's later codes are extant only in manuscripts under Wulfstan's direct or indirect influence. To begin with the exception will supply a thread to follow when exploring the rest of the maze created by his tireless activity.

'VII' was preceded in *Quadripartitus* by the 994 treaty-plus-Appendix and *Dunsæte*, and followed by *Iudex*, II–III Edgar and (probably) III Edmund (Table 4.7). There is no sign that it had any earlier association with the treaty texts. But it could well have been part of the same group as *Iudex* and Edgar's code: the Q compiler would have had no other reason to put them together.[306] This is important, because the Q text of II–III Edgar lacks the Wulfstan interpolations (above, pp. 226, 314); it cannot, then, have come from a Wulfstanian stable, so

---

306 This group was available to Q by the time the archetype of the R MS was compiled (chapter 4, pp. 239–43); but see my '"Quadripartitus"', pp. 132–3 (100–1), for evidence that it was not accessible at the stage represented by 'Lond.'

'VII Æthelred' probably did not. Nevertheless, shining through the frosted glass of the *Quadripartitus* Latin are many marks of Wulfstan composition. Compare the first clause with phrases from 'V' and 'VI':

Inprimis ut unus Deus super omnia diligatur et honoretur, et ut omnes regi suo pareant, sicut antecessores sui melius fecerunt, et cum eo pariter defendant regnum suum.	Ðæt is þonne ærest, þæt we ealle ænne God lufian 7 7 weorðian ... ... 7 utan ænne cynehlaford holdlice healdan 7 lif 7 land samod ealle werian.[307]

Wulfstanisms seem to be indicated by phrases such as 'sicut in diebus antecessorum nostrorum stetit quando melius stetit' ('swa swa þa heoldon þa þe betst heoldan').[308] The remedies ordained for military failure included a halt to the sale of people overseas; traffic in Christian souls was one of the archbishop's constant anxieties.[309]

There are three extant vernacular versions of what is to every appearance the same set of measures. The one Liebermann printed (from D) corresponded so closely with the Q text as to leave their connection in little doubt. But there were also differences.[310] Successive clauses on church dues, enslavement, banditry and justice in general were omitted.[311] The order of others was changed, so that specification of a fast for the whole people on the Monday, Tuesday and Wednesday before Michaelmas preceded the dispositions for penance and charity, which were themselves rearranged.[312] But the most interesting variation was in the prologue. That of the Q recension is 'Hoc instituerunt Æþelredus rex et sapientes eius apud Badam (Bath)'. This is not at all far from 'Ðis is seo gerædnys ðe Æþelred cyning 7 his witan geræddon æt Wudestoce'.[313] The Old English was simply headed 'This is what was decreed when the great army came to the country'. Instead of a place or king's name, there was a phrase which gives scholars the date 1009, and gave a contemporary audience an explanation of the emergency regulations laid down.[314] The vernacular text acquired more general application inasmuch as it was no longer what a ruler did in a recollected spatial context, and became what was agreed in a predicament that must at all costs not

---

307   VII Atr 1, V Atr 1, 35.

308   VII Atr 4, V Atr 15; compare too VII Atr 7:1, 'Et omnibus annis deinceps reddantur Dei rectitudines in omnibus rebus ...', with V Atr 11, '7 gelæste man Godes gerihta georne æghwylce geare'.

309   VII Atr 5; cf. V Atr 2, VI Atr 9, etc.

310   The differences are easily perceived through Liebermann's use of reduced print-size and marginal references.

311   VII Atr 4 – 6:3.

312   VIIa Atr 1 – 5. The penalty for a thegn's non-compliance with the fast was reduced from 120 shillings (VII 2:4) to 30 (VIIa 3); either could be textual corruptions, yet 'XXX' is supported by *HomN* XXXV (below), while 'CXX' is not only appropriate as a payment to the king (chapter 9), but also the *lectio difficilior* given the immediately preceding stipulation of 'XXX p'; this may therefore be a deliberate alteration by Wulfstan. Liebermann was surely right that the Q sequence is prior: *Gesetze* III, p. 178 (1).

313   VII Atr Pr., I Atr Pr.

314   Further to Whitelock's comment on the date (*EHD I*, p. 447), the Monday to Wednesday fast (VII Atr 2:3a, VIIa 1) makes most sense if Michaelmas fell on Thursday, and 1009 was the only year between 998 and 1015 when it did so; cf. Keynes, *Diplomas*, p. 217, n. 224.

recur. It was no longer the law of a king who was thoroughly discredited by the time the collection in Corpus 201 was put together.[315]

The other Old English versions are in D and in Cotton Tiberius A iii, which is not a Wulfstan book but one with considerable Wulfstan input. Here the process of generalization went further. Both opened 'if it happen that the people experience profound misfortune, army or famine, fire or slaughter, crop-failure or tempest, murrain or pestilence'.[316] Reference was made to David and Nineveh. The three days fast was untied from any point in the calendar. Alternatives to penny payments might be 'as wise men then decreed for the emergency'. Penalties for breach of obligations would be 'as wise men of the shire decide'.[317] What had begun as royal law was converted into a renewable cycle of reactions to disaster.[318] On the one occasion, therefore, when the text of an Æthelred code given by Wulfstan's books can be checked against an independent transmission, it emerges that it was very substantially altered. This discovery has serious implications for the codes where there is no such test.

The most important of these, and much the most discussed are those covered by the labels 'V' and 'VI' Æthelred. According to one of three vernacular versions of 'V', the laws in question were promulgated in 1008. The prologue to the Latin recension of 'VI' says that the council responsible met at Enham, and its final clause records that the results were committed to writing by Wulfstan (chapter 4, pp. 191–2). The 'V' texts all come from what might be epitomized as 'Wulfstan Pastoral Handbooks': two are in different, probably once distinct, parts of G, and the third in D (cf. tables 4.2–3). The variations between them are not as great as those distinguishing 'V' from VI', or the Q and vernacular recensions of 'VII'. But they are not negligible. The differences of the two G texts were reviewed in chapter 4 (p. 199). A pledge of loyalty to 'one Christianity under one kingdom' was exchanged for a more obviously homiletic message of sincere repentance and eager atonement; the prose was intensified by a 'huru' and a 'georne'; there was a change of substance too, in that instead of forfeiting life and property, deserters had the option of buying life with wergeld.[319] Critically, the extras included some in the Wulfstan hand: ship service was to be furnished

---

315   See chapter 4, pp. 207–8: CCCC 201 contains Cnut's law of 1018, as well as material that probably postdates Wulfstan himself.

316   *HomN* XXXV, pp. 169–70, XXXVI, p. 172.

317   *ibid.*, pp. 170, 171–2, 172–3, 173–4: XXXV provides the option of the 30 pence/30 shilling fine, as in VIIa Atr, while XXXVI leaves punishment to the discretion of the 'shire-bishop'.

318   The one substantial account of this material since Liebermann's notes is Jost's *Wulfstanstudien*, pp. 211–16. He concluded that Napier XXXIX (i.e. VIIa Atr) was authentic Wulfstan work, but that XXXV, XXXVI had been touched up by later hands, and that the latter part of XXXVI was an addition; Wilcox dissents, at least as regards XXXV, 'Dissemination of Wulfstan's Homilies', pp. 200–1. Jost also thought that XXXIX/VIIa Atr was formally promulgated by the archbishop in his diocese, and followed Liebermann in speculating that the variant content of XXXV/XXXVI derived from the decree of a diocesan synod (whence 'scire witan', 'scirbisceop'). This may be right; but there is no *direct* evidence that Wulfstan did any more at any stage than redraft what he had originally penned as a royal code: the decisions of bishop and shire court are envisaged in the *subjunctive*, not cited in the preterite ('deman'/'geceosan').

319   V Atr 1, 11:1, 14:1 (these and other differences are easily spotted thanks to Liebermann's use of bold type); V Atr 28; but '7 ymbe bricbota' (V 26:1) is probably just an uncorrupted reading.

soon after Easter each year 'if it is decreed' – which suggests that times had changed to the extent that this was no longer necessary every year.[320]

The D copy of 'V' took a similar road. Except at the outset, it tended to follow G[2], but it also had its own variations.[321] At the end of the code were inserted chapters from the *Institutes of Polity* that are in part verbally identical with the last phrases of the 1014 'Sermo Lupi'.[322] There could be no clearer revelation of reluctance – or inability – to distinguish the status of law-code and homily. A set of abuses, some prevalent 'in the West' or 'in the North', were intruded between vague demands that every illegality be brought to an end.[323] Most important of all is something each version of 'V' has in common: anonymity. The prologue always described it as a decree made by 'the king of the English and wise men whether clerical or lay'. Most early laws were introduced as 'decrees of our lord and his wise men', or in G[2]'s case merely as 'decrees of the wise'. Though the inscription of the first G redaction was 'In nomine Domini, anno dominicae incarnationis MVIII', the second was headed 'Be Angolwitena gerednessa', not at all unlike a homily or a section of *Polity*; D simply had 'In Nomine Domini'. This is precisely the same retreat from the particular towards the general as was encountered with the Bath edict. The one concession to time and place, the date given to one Nero text was, as it happens, reflected in the definitive Wulfstan homily of 1014, which was dated in its Corpus, Nero and Hatton copies. The conclusion to be drawn is inescapable. Behind the emergence of the earliest extant version of 'V' lies an evolutionary process like that which can be witnessed in the extant versions themselves. Nor can the earliest be identified with confidence: the dated copies of the 1014 sermon are the later ones.[324]

The position as regards the Latin and Old English recensions of 'VI' is rather different but best approached from the same direction.[325] Both texts are in a pontifical which is not likely to have remained Wulfstan's current service-book for long after 1002 (chapter 4, pp. 192–4). Neither recurs anywhere else. The Latin was written on blank early leaves of the pontifical, the Old English on pages that were possibly inserted to take it. The last clause of the Latin may have been penned a little after the rest, and there is no compelling reason to think that Latin and Old English were drafted at the same time (chapter 4, pp. 191–2). Their most important common feature is that the order of their clauses differs from that of the various versions of 'V': for instance, the admonitions on regular life for monks and canons and on chastity of clergy preceded the laws on justice.[326]

---

320 V Atr 27; Ker, 'Handwriting of Archbishop Wulfstan', p. 323.

321 V Atr 28, 34, 35:1; 11:1 is obviously a textual slip, 26:1 is a typical intensification, but omission of 28:1 and alteration to 30 may be further changes of substance.

322 V Atr 33:1 (p. 245, n. 4); *Inst. Pol.* II 223–36; *Sermo Lupi*, ed. Whitelock, lns 201–11.

323 V Atr 32 – 33; V Atr 32 in D is phrased so as to emphasize that 'ure hlaford' has ordered an end to such abuses, where the G texts merely demand that they cease. The fact that the latter then at once repeat the same point in more or less the same words, V Atr 33, cf. 32:5, suggests that they have been contaminated by the interpolation, though omitting D's details; this is a good case-study in the impossibility of deciding which V Atr version is the more 'original'.

324 Godden, 'Apocalypse and Invasion', pp. 143–52.

325 What follows represents a different path towards essentially the same conclusion as I reached in 'Æthelred the Lawmaker', pp. 50–5.

326 VI Atr 2 – 5:4, 8 – 10:1, noting Liebermann's marginal references to V.

Among other features shared by the 'VI' texts against 'V' are that they amplified the rejection of 'heathendom' with details about pagan practices; that they included provision for Church-scot; that they did not command celebration of the feast of the king's martyred brother Edward; and that they elaborated on naval preparations.[327] For the rest, discrepancies between the two texts of 'VI' are at least as marked as similarities. The Latin text identified the synod responsible for all these decrees.[328] It quoted its sources, most but not all Biblical.[329] At the end came the important clause wherein 'Archbishop [Wulfstan] of York', speaking in the first person, says that he has written down 'what King [Æthelred] decreed and what magnates promised faithfully to observe'; 'N' was entered in place of the king's and archbishop's names, and it was Wulfstan's hand that filled in the blanks.[330] The Old English 'VI Æthelred' had none of this. Much of it is neither in its Latin equivalent nor in 'V'. It alone added the gloss on priests with two or more wives (though this reappeared in an important Wulfstan homily).[331] It expanded on heathen usage, on appropriately merciful punishments, on the prohibited decrees of marriage and on fidelity to a single wife, on what was to be eschewed during feasts and fasts, and on improvement of the peace and standardization of coin, weights and measures. Above all, it added a set of clauses summarizing some of its main themes, followed by a thoughtful discussion of the theory and practice of punishment. Almost all these additions recurred in codes later drafted by Wulfstan for Cnut.[332] This text also lined up with the second G statement of 'V' in nearly every way that it varied from the first.[333] The legislative formula was again 'witena geraednes is', the title 'Be witena geraednessan'.

The implication is once again clear: the 'VI Æthelred' texts were part of the process that produced the various versions of 'V'. The difference is that they (and especially the Old English) had moved much further, and in a direction that aligned them with laws and homilies of later date. This being so, the additional possibility arises that they were *part of the process that produced the later laws*; in sum, that they were drafts. So much is after all the force of the Latin's blanks in place of a king's name. It may also be implied by the very existence of a Latin text. In this respect, 'VI Æthelred' is in exactly the position of some Wulfstan

---

327   VI Atr 6 – 7, 18:1, 23:1 (Liebermann's 'D' text is Cn 1018, below, pp. 346–7), 33 – 34; see also 23, 35, 39.

328   VI Atr (lat.) Pr. ff.

329   VI Atr (lat) 1:3, 2 (note also reference to St Benedict), 3 (also an echo of the *Rule*), 9 – 12, 15 – 15:2, 28:2, etc. (see below, p. 335, and Jost 'Das Gesetz von Eanham (V. VI Æthelred)', *Wulfstanstudien*, pp. 22–9.

330   VI Atr 40:2; in 40, the blank after 'rex' was not filled in.

331   VI Atr 5:2; *HomN*, p. 269.

332   VI Atr 7, Cn 1018 7, 9, II Cn 4a, 6, *HomN* LX, pp. 309–10; VI Atr 10:2–3, Cn 1018 4 – 4:1, II Cn 2a; VI Atr 12 – 12:2, Cn 1018 12 – 12:4, I Cn 7 – 7:1, 7:3, *HomN* L, p. 271, LIX, p. 308; VI Atr 22:1 ('huntaðfara'), Cn 1018 14:1, I Cn 15 – 15:1; VI Atr 25 ('wifunga', *HomN* XXIII, p. 117, added to margin of one MS); VI Atr 32 – 32:2, Cn 1018 20:1 – 21, II Cn 8, 9, *HomN* L, pp. 271–2; VI Atr 41, Cn 1018 11:1, 11, I Cn 6:1, 6a; VI Atr 42 – 49, Cn 1018 28 – 36, *HomN* LIX, pp. 308–9; VI Atr 52 – 53, II Cn 38:1, 68:1–3. Cf.also VI Atr 50, *Northu*.46, 66 (with the proviso below, pp. 396–7).

333   VI Atr 1, V 1 (incitement to amendment of life); VI 16, V 11:1; VI 22:3, V 14:1; VI 28:3, V 25. The G² option of buying off death for desertion, V 28, squares with VI Atr 35, loss of property alone.

homilies.[334] They too were accompanied by Latin arrangements of the matter intended for vernacular exposition. For that reason, they also quoted sources. On analogy with the homilies that are so often phrased like Wulfstan's laws, and that are peas in the same manuscript pod, drafting of Latin prolegomena is just what one might expect Wulfstan to do. This hypothesis does not cover every facet of the Enham crux. Given Wulfstan's working method, it is unlikely that any solution could. There is, for example, no certainty about which legislation Wulfstan had in mind when making these drafts. The Latin is close enough to 'V' for it to have underlain the Enham session itself.[335] If not, it may have been adapted from one made for Enham, to which it as yet had relatively little to add. The Wulfstan works most like the Old English 'VI' were the Oxford code of 1018 and the arguably associated homily 'L'.[336] Curiously, the two main divergences, that the 1018 code did not number Church-scot among Church dues, and that it did include the feast of Edward the Martyr, are ways in which 'V' differed from 'VI'.[337] It looks as if Wulfstan for some reason returned to the 1008 pronouncements ten years later, largely ignoring what he had meanwhile said in 1014 (below, pp. 336, 340–1). In any case, the central message of the Enham output stands. To one degree or other, and for one reason or another, everything that is extant has been, *or is being,* adapted. The original lies submerged beneath the tides of its author's further enterprises.[338]

---

334 *Hom.* I, VIII, X, XVI, and pp. 29, 31, 33. There are also extensive Latin preambles, quoting their Biblical (or in one case Ælfrician) foundation in II, IX and XIX, cf. pp. 286, 321, 354. The relationship of Latin and Old English homiletic texts was first worked out in Jost's classic, 'Einige Wulfstantexte', especially pp. 267–71, 277–88, 301–9; but, despite the strong similarity of the arguments used in his *Wulfstanstudien* paper (above, n. 329), he did not see its relevance for V/VI Æthelred.

335 Cf. Lawson, 'Archbishop Wulfstan', pp. 573–4. The similar ordering of the two 'VI Atr' texts could be explained by their appearance in the same MS; but it can be said that the VI Atr transfer of the section on clerical morals (above, n. 326) creates a semi-anomalous gulf between this and lay morality, implying that even the Latin 'VI' is likely to be later than (original) 'V'.

336 *HomN* L, pp. 266–74; Jost, *Wulfstanstudien*, pp. 249–61 (where it is suggested that 'L' is a homily preached to the *witan*, but not by Wulfstan himself); Kennedy, 'Cnut's code of 1018', pp. 62–6.

337 V Atr 11:1, 16, VI Atr 18:1, 23:1, Cn 1018 13:4–5, 14:6. It should be noted that Church-scot is also omitted by EGu, another early Wulfstan text (below, pp. 389–91); as the most ancient of the relevant levies, it may at times have been taken for granted by Wulfstan. On the feast of Edward the Martyr, see below, pp. 343–4.

338 My conclusion therefore differs from the theory made standard by Kenneth Sisam, *Studies*, pp. 278–87, endorsed as it was by Whitelock (*EHD I*, p. 442, *Councils and Synods* I, pp. 341–3). It is not easy to withstand such a weight of authority. Nevertheless, Sisam's solution, that V best represents the established text, and that the two recensions of VI are authorized adaptations, respectively for senior and parish clergy, in Wulfstan's province of York, hardly accounts for all the variations between V and VI Atr or between the different varieties of either. If Gregorian Ember Day practice was in 1008 more acceptable to North than South, this does not explain why it was enjoined on Danes and English in Cn 1018 14:5; penalties for desertion in V are varied depending on the king's presence or absence, and it is the lighter penalty levied in the king's absence, which one would think likelier in the North, that VI omitted; restraint as to penalties in general (e.g. VI 35 – 36) is hardly evident in III Atr, definitely targeted at the Danelaw (cf. here my 'Æthelred', pp. 54–5); as Whitelock noted (*Councils*, p. 342), the preoccupation of VI Atr, especially its Latin, with monastic orders was hardly appropriate for the northern province; finally, Sisam fails so much as to mention the major additions to VI Atr OE, nor their relationship to Cn 1018 (whose nature was only being clarified by Whitelock while he wrote, p. 278, n. 3) and to I–II Cn. None of the differences highlighted by Sisam are not equally or better explained by the proposition that VI Atr (especially the OE) is simply closer in time to later Wulfstan materials than most of what underlies the 'V' texts. Wulfstan's deepening experience of Danelaw conditions was an influence on his evolving line, but

So much having been said about the legislation of 1008 and 1009, the rest of what Wulfstan composed on Æthelred's behalf falls into place. 'VIII' exists in two recensions, one in G and the other in D. Each is anonymous, 'what the king of the English composed (*gedihte*) with the advice of his councillors'. The D version was dated 1014; that in G was merely headed 'Be cyricgriðe. In nomine Domini'. The two were close for as long as both were extant. When they differed, G's corresponded to the reading in Cnut's code.[339] This may mean that it is more accurate, but also that it is more up-to-date. The chief disparity is that G stopped when it had finished with the subject of sanctuary (as its title implies). The manuscript then has a short, and now often illegible, statement of the particular 'grið' of sundry northern churches, before the quire breaks off. One cannot therefore tell whether the G copy continued after this interruption, or with what further differences.[340] If not an exact counterpart to the variegation of the Enham texts, this is another example of the archbishop's readiness to adjust legislation to current preoccupations. Indeed, both copies of the 1014 code virtually declared their second-hand status: 'This is *one of* the decrees (*an ðæra geædnessa*) that the king composed'. The very largely ecclesiastical constituents of the code as it survives were evidently singled out by Wulfstan or his scribe, and for obvious reasons. One can compare the treatment of the Bath edict, or even the same manuscripts' handling of Æthelstan's and Edmund's codes.

The texts added by Liebermann to the corpus under the labels 'IX' and 'X Æthelred' are the detritus respectively of the Cottonian fire and (at a guess) of pruning by Avranches librarians with no knowledge of Old English (chapter 4, pp. 256–7, 258–9). Liebermann regarded them as distinct items because their content differed from any other surviving Æthelred law. Yet they consist in the first case of a code's beginning and end (as reported by Wanley), and in the second of a beginning alone. The realization that if all that were left of any of the pieces discussed so far were their beginning and end, the two versions of Bath and four of the five recensions of Enham would likewise have been reckoned as separate codes should give pause. 'X' is an especially problematic case. It opened as follows:

One is Eternal God, Ruler and Creator of all Creation; and in reverence for His Name, I King Æthelred considered first how I could always most surely exalt Christianity and just kingship, and how I could decree most profitably for myself before both God and the world, and most justly lay down as law for all my people those things that we must keep necessarily (*eallum minum leodscype rihtlicast lagian þa þing to þearfe þe we scylan healdan*). It has often and frequently preoccupied my

---

not the only one nor necessarily the most pressing. Sisam's solution was conditioned by assumptions about the nature of law-codes, and by still only emergent perceptions of Wulfstanian activity; it is now obvious that the latter have a serious bearing on the former. I can perhaps add a) that my conclusion substantially accords with that of Jost (*Wulfstanstudien*, p. 44), a Wulfstan scholar of no less repute than Sisam; b) that Whitelock's main objection ('surely Wulfstan would not have gone to such trouble unless he at least hoped to bring forward this improved version [VI] on some other occasion', *Councils*, p. 341) is met by my proposal that Wulfstan *was* in fact thinking of 'some other occasion'.
339   VIII Atr 3, 4, 5:1, I Cn 2:5, 3, 3:2; the exception is 'geteald', VIII 2:1, which is not repeated in any other work.
340   *Nor. grið*, f. 96v. Dammery, 'Editing the Anglo-Saxon Laws', pp. 256–9 (and fig. 9) valuably establishes that G treated it as a chapter of VIII Atr. (I am grateful to Dr Dammery for showing me an unpublished paper in which he expands on other aspects of VIII Atr.)

mind that divine teachings and wise secular laws further Christianity and enhance kingship, profit the people and command respect, bring about peace and settlements, terminate disputes and improve all public behaviour (*þeode þeawas ealle gebetað*) ... And this is the decree that we desire to observe, as we firmly declared it at Enham (*þis is seo gerædnes þe we willað healdan swa swa we æt Eanham fæste gecwædon*).

This remarkable prologue is again Wulfstan's work.[341] It is unlike anything in Anglo-Saxon law since Edmund's second code and Edgar's 'fourth'. The first sentence resembles nothing so much as the invocation of a diploma, a device unparalleled in pre-conquest law-making.[342] The most intriguing point otherwise is the mention of Enham. Had this been a reference *back* to the assembly of 1008, then analogy with earlier formulations of that type would argue that the place of the current meeting should have been identified too.[343] Since it was not, the implication may be that 'X Æthelred' too was issued from Enham. And since the text's next three clauses are word for word the same as the G² copy of 'V Æthelred' (verbally closer than any two out of the three established texts of this code), there must be a serious possibility that 'X' is a fragment of another version of the 1008 decrees. Putting the evidence of its sonorous prologue beside the point that the book from which it came is not known (though not known not) to have been one of Wulfstan's, this may be the nearest one gets to an *official* text. Much the same arguments apply to 'IX'. It is said, in terms very like those of 'I', to have been decreed at Woodstock. That eliminates 'V' – 'VII' as possible alternative versions, but not 'VIII'. The first of the two other clauses quoted by Wanley is unlike any in the Wulfstan series; the second is almost the same as the finale of 'V'. These indications mean little. All one can say is that, had 'IX' been a fuller and more official statement of what survives as 'VIII', it could still have differed as much from 'VIII' as its residue does.[344]

The lessons to be learned from the Æthelred codes preserved by Wulfstan are patent and at first sight disheartening. Apart from the Q recension of the Bath decree (when twelfth-century Latin brings down its own barrier), and perhaps 'IX' and 'X', themselves no more than debris, their original or official form (if any) is out of reach. Convictions that one or other Enham version must be at least roughly 'what the *witan* decreed', and that variants also have some sort of

341   As Liebermann notes (*Gesetze* I, p. 269, n. ** – though Ker, *Catalogue* 392 is reticent), the scribe added to the margin opposite Pr.:3 an apparent invocation of the inspiration of Æthelred's father, Edgar; this is itself a Wulfstanian feature: below, pp. 355, 362.

342   E.g. (in chronological order, as established by Keynes, *Diplomas*, pp. 249–66) S 942, 891, 937, 899, 903, 911, 919, 920, 921, 928; there is even a slight cluster in the years around 1008.

343   VI As 12 ('nu eft æt Witlanbyrig ... swa hit æt Greatanlea'); IV Eg 1:4 ('þe æt Andeferan 7 nu eft æt Wihtbordesstan'). It is only proper to note Whitelock's reservations, *Councils*, p. 340, n. 2, about this thesis as proposed in my 'Æthelred', p. 53.

344   Room needs to be found (probably in Æthelred's reign, though perhaps in Cnut's) for *HomN* LI, which Jost, *Wulfstanstudien*, pp. 104–9, persuasively describes as a 'Gesetzesantrag' (i.e. address to a law-making assembly). It does overlap in suggestive ways with VIII Atr 26, 44, and also with V 35 and IX Expl.; in addition, it seems to refer to secular law on 'bootless' crimes, not otherwise encountered before II Cn 64. If one were to suppose that 'VIII' once had a secular counterpart which later contributed to II Cn (below, p. 361), then *HomN* LI could have been preached in 1014, and IX could indeed be a fragment of it. Equally, the sermon could have been preached to whichever council at whatever time issued an entirely separate IX (or X, or indeed a code of which no other trace remains).

Table 5.3 Wulfstan's injunctions on Church Dues compared

Hom XIII lns 70–6	Canons of Edgar (I) 54	Edward/Guthrum 5:1–6:4	V Æthelred 11–12:2
[Let us (*Uton*) . . .] and share out and discharge to God with a happy heart (*bliðum mode*) the dues that belong to him, namely the tenth of all the goods that He has allowed us in this transitory life, and our first yield of what springs up and grows (*frumgripan gangendes 7 weaxendes*), and so we deserve with that little much more that is needful for ourselves (*7 gearnian us mid þam lytlan mycle mare us sylfum to þearfe*). Then it must in addition (*þærtoeacan*) be understood too that we also humbly discharge everything in yearly dues that our ancestors once commanded for God; namely plough-alms and Rome-pennies and church-scots and light-scots. And he who does that which I am speaking about, he does much that is needful for himself (*7 se ðe þæt deð þæt ic ymbe spece he deð him sylfum mycle ðearfe*).	And we instruct that priests remind the people (*7 we lærað þæt preostas folc mynegian*) of what they must do for God by way of dues, in tithes and in other things: first, plough-alms 15 days after Easter, and the tithe of the young by Pentecost, and fruits of the earth by All Saints, and Rome-money by St Peter's Day, and Church-scot by Martinmas.	And let all God's dues be eagerly forwarded for (hope of) God's mercy and of the fines which wise men have laid down (*7 ealle Godes gerihte forðige man georne be Godes mildse 7 be þam witan ðe witan tolædan*). If anyone withold tithes, let him pay *lahslit* among the Danes, a fine among the English (*Gif hwa teoþunge forhealde, gylde lahslit mid Denum, wite mid Englum*). If anyone withold Rome-money, let him pay *lahslit* among the Danes, a fine among the English. If anyone do not discharge light-scot, let him pay *lahslit* among the Danes, a fine among the English. If anyone do not give plough-alms, let him pay *lahslit* among the Danes, a fine among the English. If anyone refuse any divine dues (*ænigra godcundra gerihta forwyrne*), let him pay *lahslit* among the Danes, a fine among the English.	And let God's dues be eagerly discharged every year. Namely, plough-alms 15 days after Easter, and the tithe of the young by Pentecost, and fruits of the earth by All Saints, and Rome-money by St Peter's day, and light-scot three times a year. And it is most proper that soul-scot be discharged at the open grave (*þæt man symle geleste æt openum græfe*). And if any corpse lie elsewhere, outside the correct parish (*riht-scriftscire*), let soul-scot nevertheless be discharged at the minster to which it belonged. And let God's dues be eagerly furthered as is needful (*7 ealle Godes gerihta forðige man georne, ealswa hit þearf is*).

licensed status, depend upon a view of written law that should be the outcome of argument, not its premiss. That view has of course been reinforced by the fact that one set of Wulfstan texts has been printed as 'laws', with running titles to that effect, and clauses that make a legislative impression; while another set are edited as 'Homilies' in continuous prose, the standard edition of which deliberately avoids whatever most resembles laws. It badly needs replacement by a perspective drawn from the books where both types of work survive. There was no distinction there between clauses allotted to 'law' or 'homily'. Headings were in the same style, and were sometimes similarly worded. Wulfstan's scribes took their cue from the archbishop's conception that 'law' and 'homily' ran side by side towards the same goal. Wulfstan's activity can be regarded as exceptional.[345] All that is clearly exceptional is a style so easily identified in so much else, and manuscripts so contemporary as to bear his own hand. It might be unsound to see him as the aberration, and codes with far more attenuated and twisted skeins of transmission as the norm. Previous discussion has thrown out hints that other royal pronouncements may have been manhandled in a not dissimilar way. Wulfstan stands out not in his remoulding of the king's law but in the cogency with which he reshaped it.

(ii) Style and genre

Much has been written by great scholars about Wulfstan's modes of expression. Much will be said in the next chapter about his ideas. The next two subsections of this chapter can therefore be briefer than the last. There is, to repeat, no doubt that Wulfstan was the author, in all accepted senses of that word, of the codes discussed here.[346] Inasmuch as it looks as if whatever he composed for Æthelred he then recast in semi-homiletic form, this is no surprise. It makes it profitable to compare his homiletic and legislative styles. table 5.3 shows that Wulfstan did see a distinction between a 'gerædnes' and a 'larspell'. He had a different style of address for each, laws being less fluent and more abrupt. The homily, which in Corpus 201 had a preamble implying that it was by way of being an encyclical, expatiated on the logic of repaying to God something of what he has bestowed on creation, and on the further blessings to be expected in return.[347] But it contained an implicit legal element in the reference to the commands of 'our ancestors'.[348] Besides, the real contrast in tone and technique lies between Enham's code and the 'Peace of Edward and Guthrum', which was probably one of Wulfstan's two first, pre-Enham, legislative pieces (below, pp. 389–91).

345   Keynes, 'Royal Government and the written word', pp. 242–3.
346   Liebermann (no friend to Wulfstan's claims, 'Wulfstan und Cnut') was ready to countenance his role at Enham, *Gesetze* III, p. 168 (7), though he apparently preferred to see him as the author of the Latin version; he also thought that he directly or indirectly 'influenced' VIII Atr (p. 182 (10)) but had nothing to say of VII. On the archbishop's authorship of V – VIII Atr, the decisive authority was Jost's *Wulfstanstudien*, pp. 13–44, 104–9, 211–16, etc.
347   Bethurum, *Hom.*, p. 339, calls it 'Wulfstan's Pastoral Letter'.
348   The reference may be disingenuous, in so far as plough-alms was probably added by Wulfstan himself to earlier codes (above, pp. 295, 314), and light-scot was not enjoined by any king before Æthelred.

Edward-Guthrum was here as blunt and unadorned, as frankly formulaic, a legal statement as any since Æthelberht. In the Enham code, the homiletic style has reacted with the legislative, and the resulting precipitate has as much of the colouring of one as of the other. In particular, Enham had no sanctions, like the homily but unlike the pseudo-treaty. Its manner is most like Wulfstan's 'Canons of Edgar', probably a code for the priests of his diocese.[349]

How did this new style of legal drafting affect the trends of the post-Alfredian period? Its main effect was to simplify syntactical structure. Wulfstan's sentences were not complicated. When lengthy, they were strung together by coordinating conjunctions.[350] At this stage he still made sparing use of exceptions introduced by 'butan'.[351] His was the language of the preacher, not the lawyer. The overwhelming majority of clauses in the Enham codes are non-dependent directives. Thus, payment of church dues was simply encouraged in the subjunctive, with an extra mention of what was 'most proper (*rihtast*)'. The 'if'-clause here was one of just three in the first forty-six (editorial) clauses of 'V Æthelred', to compare with five relatives.[352] Subordinated clauses largely ceased to be any part of the structure of codes; they were used as and when homiletic argument required. Towards the end of the Enham regulations, however, when Wulfstan moved onto the sort of substantive issues that his predecessors made law about, 'gif' is more in evidence.[353] This looked forward to the 1014 code, where his repertoire was more ambitious, hence also more traditional. This code's structure is reminiscent of the Andover code. It can hardly be coincidence that Andover was cited and quoted *verbatim*, a most unusual departure for early English legislation.[354] As before, the objective was stated first, followed by contingencies phrased as conditional or occasionally relative clauses of some complexity.[355] 'Butan' qualifications were more frequent.[356] The listed compensations for churches of variable rank in one way recall the earliest Kentish law (which Wulfstan by then knew), though it was explained too that the sums in question are the corresponding royal fines.[357] The contrast between 1008 and

---

349   I have elsewhere attempted to establish a chronology which puts most of the homilies printed by Bethurum, plus EGu and *Can. Eg.*, before 1008, in Biggs *et al.* (eds), *Sources of Anglo-Saxon Literary Culture*: the argument depends in part on the comparative reticence of their claims for Church dues.

350   E.g. V Atr 1 – 1:2, 2 (VI 9), 6 – 6:1 (VI 3:1–2), 9 – 9:2 (VI 5:1,3–4), 22 – 22:2 (VI 27 – 27:1); note that the conjunction can now be '*ac*, but', V Atr 3:1 (VI 10:1), 26 (VI 30), VI 5:2, 10:2. It must as ever be borne in mind that 'clauses' are mostly modern editorial constructs; but see below.

351   V Atr 17 (VI 24), 29 (VI 36), VI 7, 22:3; the last two could be seen as further signs of VI Atr's more 'evolved' stature. For 'butan' see above, nn. 27, 164, 209, and below on I–II Cn.

352   V Atr 6:1 (VI 3:2), 12:1 (VI 21), 20 (VI 25:2); V Atr 5 (VI 3), 6 (VI 3:1), 9:1–2 (VI 5:3–4), 21 (VI 26).

353   V Atr 28 (VI 35), 29 (VI 36), 30 (x 2, VI 37), 31 – 31:1 (VI 38), VI 39, 51, 52:1; and note 'se þe', V Atr 28:1, VI 50.

354   VIII Atr 7 – 8.

355   VIII Atr 1 – 5:2, where the circumstances in which compensation may be allowed were carefully itemized, and the shares of king and Church justified in principle; 6 – 15, where a very elaborate introduction featuring the Edgar quotation ushers in a restatement of dues decreed at Enham, but with infringements envisaged *via* two relative clauses and a conditional clause; 18 – 29, a very full review largely phrased in conditional clauses, of the legal status of priests; 39 – 42, as compared with V 23 – 25 (VI 28:1–3).

356   VIII Atr 1:1, 22, 27, 33, 40, 41; this is already much closer to the archbishop's usage under Cnut.

357   VIII Atr 5:1, Abt 1, Wi 2; see on *Grið* below, pp. 394–5.

1014 is important. It is part of the evidence that Wulfstan was moving from a basically homiletic mode to one with a more evenly balanced blend of the conventions of preaching and law-making.

One of the most interesting features of Wulfstan's presentation is its use of clauses. Normally of course, divisions appearing in manuscripts merely reveal scribal practice. Only the near-unanimity of the transmission argues that the clauses of Alfred's law-book and the Grately code could be authorial. But Wulfstan's work is extant in contemporary manuscripts that may thus show something of his own attitude. Chapter 4 found evidence of a desire in his *scriptorium* to break up the continuous prose of the Andover code (pp. 189–90). The manuscript of VI Æthelred used paragraphs, introduced clauses with the letter 'k' (*kapitulum?*), and highlighted initials in each text.[358] The results are not entirely satisfactory. The Latin was wayward in paragraphing and distributing 'k'; the Old English was less erratic with 'k', but soon lost interest in paragraphs.[359] Yet leaving a margin for scribal negligence, it does look as if 'k', whether or not matched by paragraphs, was meant to mark major changes of subject in both versions; while highlighted initials were to designate subdivisions of the topic concerned.[360] This fits quite well with the G texts of 'V'. These lacked paragraphs as such (especially the second), but they did have a roughly consistent set of initials.[361] Yet the central point is one that has already been stressed more than once. Laws and homilies are treated in essentially the same way. Minor initials broke the ceaseless flow of the text, whether from the mouth of the preacher or from that of an adjudicating official (supposing these to be separate personages). To adapt one of the late-twentieth century's uglier coinages, homily and law-code were wrapped into eleventh-century equivalents of the 'sound-bite'.

(iii) Content and objectives

The subject-matter of Wulfstan's codes for Æthelred could be predicted from what has been said about their context and idiom. Its emphasis was massively ecclesiastical. Even the early clauses of 'V', pertaining to the quality of justice,

---

358 Liebermann's marking of 'k' in both texts is inexplicably erratic. Their distribution is as follows: *lat.*: 1:1, 2, 3, 4, 5, 6, 7, 8:2, 9, 10, 11, 13, 16, 18, 18:1, 20, 22 – 22:3, 23, 24, 25, 26, 27, 28, 28:1, 32, 32:1, 32:3, 33, 35, 36, 37, 38, 39; OE: 1, 2, 3, 4, 5, 6, 7, 8, 9, 10, 13, 16, 18, 19, 20, 22, 22:2, 23, 24, 25, 26, 27, 28, 31, 33, 35, 36, 37, 38, 39, 40, 41.

359 It almost forgot about paragraphs as early as cl. 5 (end of f. 35v): '7 ealle Godes þeowas' was first written immediately after 'se þe þæt nelle', then erased; there ought also to be a para. at 6. Otherwise, it missed the 'k' one would expect at 8:2 and inserted one unexpectedly at 19. The Latin was off-line on paras at (e.g.) 11, 16, 32:3, and on 'k' at 1:1, 8, 18:1, 22:3, 27:1, 40, etc.

360 lat. had more such initials earlier on, but oddly omitted them at 12, 15, 15:2, 17; only the absence of an initial at 5:3 is really odd in the OE. Note that (*pace* Liebermann), there were nothing but initials in the Appendix unique to the OE.

361 Neither copy has initials at Liebermann's clauses 1:2, 3:1, 4:1, 6:1, 9:1–2, 12:2, 21:1, 22:1–2, 28:1, 31:1, 33:1, and the second lacks them at 16 (see below, n. 371), 19, 20; the first has initials at: 1 ('7 þæt we habbað') 1:1 ('7 þæt man læte'), the second at 4:1 ('Biscopas'), and both insert them in 11:1 at '7 Romfeoh', and at '7 leoht-scot'. Allowing that there is no distinction between major and minor sections (which are not consistent in modern editions), one could say that Wulfstan's scribes did better than nineteenth-century editors.

were couched in terms of Christian ethics: 'Christian men are not to be condemned to death for altogether too little; but otherwise one is to devise lenient punishments for the people's benefit, and not ruin for little God's handiwork and his own merchandise, that he so dearly bought'.[362] By 1014, Wulfstan's anxiety was that there was a growing distinction between penalties which had once been 'common to Christ and king'. The sense is probably that offences against the Church were no longer sufficiently regarded as punishable crimes.[363] The security of Church and clergy was the main concern of the 1014 code, where its implications for the involvement of clerics in disputes were spelled out in legalistic detail.[364] But the understanding was that clerics earned their privileges by maintaining a suitable lifestyle. What was stated as principle at Enham, and with particular attention to chastity, became in 1014 a review of all species of criminous clericalism, and the principle was then restated with renewed vigour: 'If an altar-thegn order his own life correctly in line with the teachings of books, let him then be entitled to full thegnly status and dignity, both in life and in the grave. And if he misorder his life, let his dignity diminish in proportion to what he does. Let him know if he will that neither business with a woman nor with worldly strife befits him if he will obey God correctly and keep God's laws'.[365]

The obligations of the laity itemized at Enham also entailed due sexual purity, and refraining from a catalogue of enormities such as Wulfstan loved to deploy in his homilies.[366] These horrendous sins and/or crimes (Wulfstan was effectively blind to the distinction) naturally included heathen practices, though they were detailed only in 'VI'.[367] More particularly, the list of dues payable to the Church was very considerably expanded by comparison with the demands of earlier kings. The likelihood that 'light-scot', 'soul-scot' and probably plough-alms represent innovations is strengthened by their absence from what are probably earlier pronouncements by Wulfstan.[368] By 1014, the mere expectations of 1008 were reinforced by sanctions, though as yet nothing more serious than what was decreed by Edgar, and by Ine long before.[369] On top of what God's people were

---

362 V Atr 3 – 3:1.
363 VIII Atr 36 – 39. Whitelock (*EHD I*, p. 451, and *Councils*, p. 400) translates 38, 'And þa man getwæmde þæt wæs gemæne Criste 7 cynincge on worldlicre steore', 'And then was separated what [before] had been divided between Christ and the king in secular penalties'. Cf. Vollrath, *Synoden Englands*, pp. 328–38.
364 VIII Atr 18 – 25; cf. V Atr 10:1–2 (VI 13 – 15:1).
365 VIII Atr 28, and 26 – 27:1, 29 – 30; cf. V Atr 9 – 9:2 (VI 5:1–4, with new matter).
366 V Atr 10, VI 11 – 12:2 (most of this not in V, nor VI lat.), V 23 – 25, VI 28 – 30 (again expanded); cf., e.g., *Sermo Lupi* lns 161–5, or *HomN* L, p. 266, LIX, pp. 309–10 (these representing amplification of more modest lists in *Hom* VII lns 128–33, Xa lns 11–16, VIIIc lns 160–4, XIII lines 93–5.
367 VI Atr 7 (cf. lat.). It may be that Wulfstan's growing preoccupation with the issue reflected his experience of his archdiocese (cf. my 'Æthelred', pp. 54–5); it was a preoccupation that led him to give an even fuller treatment in Cn 1018 7 – 10, II Cn 4a – 7:1.
368 See table 5.3 for *Hom.* XIII, *Can. Eg.*, EGu, V Atr on these matters; also VI Atr 16 – 21:1. My argument (*contra* Bethurum, p. 341) in Biggs *et al.* (eds), *Sources of Anglo-Saxon Literary Culture* is that it is scarcely probable that the archbishop would have omitted from his 'Pastoral Letter' or Canons for his diocese the dues of soul-scot and light-scot if these were already made compulsory by his legal dratsmanship (in later versions of 'Pastoral Letter' and *Can. Eg.*, he did not). See above, pp. 295, 309, 314–15 for the probability that the alleged statements of Æthelstan, Edmund and Edgar in this regard were Wulfstan insertions. See also chapter 8.
369 VIII Atr 6 – 15; II Eg 3 – 4:3, Ine 4.

now expected to pay for the attentions of His servants, the cycle of festivals and fasts was expanded. The rituals commissioned in 1009 were expressly a set of one-off measures for (optimistically) a uniquely dire emergency. But regular Friday fasts were now added to Sunday observance. Vigils and feasts of the Virgin and of all apostles augmented the holidays allowed by Alfred. Trade, legal business, and other kinds of secular distraction were banned at holy times.[370] All this will be more fully analysed in chapter 8. But one stipulated Saint's Day poses problems that must be faced now: 'And for St Edward's mass-day the *witan* have decided that it be celebrated throughout all England on 18th March'. The difficulty is that the law is in all copies of 'V' but in neither text of 'VI'. It is not easy to see how it came to be omitted from 'VI' if it had appeared in the original version of 'V', on which 'VI' was so obviously based. Nearly fifty years ago, Kenneth Sisam pointed out that its formulation implies its interpolation at a later date. His view gains force from what was said above about the character of the 'V' recension.[371] The cult of Edward the Martyr was undoubtedly established by 1008, and had even penetrated the royal family. Yet it is odd that Wulfstan should not have recognized it in his 1014 sermon, had he by then helped to decree its observance.[372] Enham apart, Æthelred's view is best attested by evidence from

370 V Atr 12:3 – 20, VI 22–25:2 (where additions include hunting among prohibited Sunday activities, weddings among those ruled out in holy seasons, and Ember Days – though for these cf. Af 43).

371 Sisam, *Studies*, pp. 280–1, and my 'Æthelred', pp. 53–4; it could be relevant that the text of V Atr 16 is followed on f. 91r by the nearest this MS ever gets to a paragraph break. If, as argued by Whitelock, *Councils*, p. 353, the omission is another of VI's 'Danelaw' concessions, Cnut did not worry: 1018 14:6, I Cn 17:1.

372 *Sermo Lupi* lines 78–9. 'Vita S. Oswaldi', pp. 451–2 (where miracles are known to Archbishop Ælfric, d. 1005); the Will of Æthelstan, WhW XX, pp. 58–9. Dr Keynes and Dr Paul Hayward persuade me that serious efforts were at any rate made to interest Æthelred in his brother's cult.

373 Keynes, *Diplomas*, pp. 169–71, and Ridyard, *Royal Saints*, pp. 154–67. The evidence of Goscelin's *Passio* (*Edward King and Martyr*, ed. Fell) obviously came from what he was told by the Shaftesbury nuns. Æthelred's 1001 charter, S 899, is more substantial evidence, but one should at least consider the possibility that the ladies interpolated the relevant clauses. The charter is closely parallel to S 904, for Wherwell (1002) (Keynes, *Diplomas*, pp. 104–7), and this allows an instructive comparison of formulations:

S 899: **quoddam Christo [& sancto** suo germano scilicet meo Edwardo quem proprio cruore perfusum per multiplicia virtutum signa ipse dominus nostris mirificare dignatus est temporibus] **cum** adiacente undique **villa humili devocione** **offero cenobium quod vulgariter** et Bradeforda cognominatur ... ... quatenus adversus barbarorum insidias ipsa religiosa congregacio [cum beati martiris ceterorumque sanctorum reliquiis] ibidem Deo **serviendi** impenetrabile optineat confugium ... **Ego Æthelredus Rex** hanc largitatem **Christo** [sanctoque martiri Edwardo] humili **optuli devocione**	S 904: **quoddam** nobile **coenobium** **cum villa** circumquaque sibi connexa, **Christo sanctisque** omnibus **humillima offero** **devotione quod vulgares** suapte a vicinitate fontis æt Werewelle appellare consueverunt ... ... ad adminiculum victus et vestitus sanctimonialium in praenotato monasterio Christo sedulo **servientium** famulatu ... **Ego Æðelred rex** Anglorum hoc **munus Christo devote offerens**

One's reaction to this position will depend upon how clumsy one thinks that Æthelred's charter draftsmen could be; but it can hardly be denied that the Latin of S 899 reads more smoothly, and very much more

the cult centre of Shaftesbury.[373] The honest answer to the puzzle is 'non liquet'. But 'V Æthelred' should not count as proof that the king promoted his brother's sanctity.

Even as preserved by Wulfstan, the content of Æthelred's later legislation is not exclusively ecclesiastical. Later clauses of Enham offer a hint of what might have been in a hypothetical secular counterpart to 'VIII'. They restated the law of treason, reopened the question of military desertion, which had not been aired since Ine's day, and made the first legislative statement of the obligation to maintain bridges and fortifications that had been standard in royal charters since the time of Offa. Demands for military service also now extended to provision for ships.[374] These measures seem only too apt a comment on conditions in the later part of Æthelred's reign. But the king's impressive monetary record was reflected in a reissue of (Wulfstan version of) Edgar's law on coin, weights and measures.[375] There were also distinct echoes of Edmund's codes in the laws on those forbidden to come near the king and on 'forsteal'.[376] One of Wulfstan's most striking traits was his consciousness of previous English lawgiving; in 1014, he singled out the example of Æthelstan, Edmund and Edgar, though admittedly with what they said about 'God's tribute' mainly in mind.[377] Other, more distant and grandiloquent influences were also at work upon him. The influence of Carolingian legislation, of which there have hitherto only been hints, now becomes certain, for example on the distribution of tithes.[378] It is no surprise that Wulfstan should cite the Carolingians. His books included (annotated) texts of Ansegisus' capitulary collection, of the *capitula* of Bishops Theodulf and Radulf, and of part of the *Admonitio Generalis* itself (chapter 4, pp. 213–18). There is also a chance that Wulfstan was aware of more recent models. His laws on overseas sale of Christians parallel the same prohibition made two years before by the Emperor Henry II.[379]

The conclusion to this sub-section needs to resume the question that dominated the first. How far were the texts that Wulfstan bequeathed to posterity his own (mis)representation of what had really been decreed? This obviously happened up to a point. 'VIII Æthelred' called itself part of a whole. If there were no *Quadripartitus* text of 'VII Æthelred', knowledge of the law made at Bath would be neither complete nor exact. Yet 'VII', to repeat, is a case of an unmistakably Wulfstanian code in non-Wulfstanian transmission. Had it been

---

like that of S 904, if the square-bracketed clauses are cut; I find nothing so elephantine in Anglo-Saxon diplomatic from 928 to 1066, though there are echoes of various kinds in S 866, 885, 888, 893, 926, 956, 1015 and 1028; and it may perhaps be suggested that the original had some such phrase as 'Christo et sanctae suae genetrici' at the start (cf. S 850, also S 866 for Glastonbury), with appropriate variants in the second and third cases. But it should be noted that Dr Kelly, *Shaft. Ch.* 29 does not share my suspicions.

374   V Atr 26:1 – 30 (VI 31 – 37, 34 on damage to ships is new); cf. Ine 51, Af 4 – 4:1; Brooks, 'Development of military obligations'.

375   VI Atr 32:1–2 (only residually in V Atr 26:1, however); III Eg 8 – 8:1 (and above, p. 314).

376   V Atr 29 and especially VI 36, V Atr 31 – 31:1 (VI 38); I Em 3, II Em 4, III Em 6.

377   VIII Atr 43.

378   VIII Atr 6: *Cap.* 36:7; *Capitula Episcoporum*, ed. Brommer, I, pp. 17–18; *Exc. Can.* 5. Once again, detailed study is better deferred to chapters 8, 13. There is a fairly full account in my 'Æthelred', pp. 70–3.

379   Lawson, 'Archbishop Wulfstan', pp. 566, 575 (noting inspiration closer to home from the 'Penitential of Pseudo-Ecgberht' iv 21, *Altenglische Version des Halitgarschen Bußbuches*, p. 57).

extant in a known Wulfstan book, one would have suspected characteristically sacerdotal distortion of presumably more realistic responses to invasion. But in 1009 at least, he would seem to have been able to dominate the *witan* as completely as he did his *scriptoria*. Wulfstan's later laws and homilies on church dues show that he was eminently capable of demanding heavy penalties for breach of church privilege when he acquired the urge to do so. In two of its three manuscripts, the homily that Napier prints as 'XXIII' is in fact an extension of the 'Pastoral Letter' (table 5.3). One copy included a version of the sanctions in Napier LXI. 'LXI' itself is one of the three adjoining Cnut's 1020 letter in the York Gospels, where Wulfstan himself amended it so as to reflect his 1014 mildening of Edgar's penalties for witholding 'Rome-money'.[380] Had the king's laws at Enham been more concrete than they were, therefore, Wulfstan would have had no reason to obscure the fact. From 1014 at the latest, he did not. Thus, the contrast is not between law and homily, nor between Wulfstanian and conceivably non-Wulfstanian statements of royal law. It is a contrast between an early Wulfstan, still feeling his way from pulpit to council chamber, and a later archbishop with the full confidence to put governmental power behind the needs of God's Church and people.[381] What has been happening is something much more interesting and instructive than the concealment of realistic approaches to crisis behind an other-worldly prelate's phrenetic moralizations. The germinating Mosaic and Carolingian ideology of earlier legislation was now yielding its full harvest. Law designed to repress sin and crime was increasingly fused with a pastoral tradition striving for moral and spiritual rearmament. That pattern would become abundantly evident under Cnut, and will be fully drawn out in chapter 6 (pp. 462–4). To sum up for now, Wulfstan treated his laws as current homilies, because he had come to think homiletic legislation the best way to achieve the purposes for which Anglo-Saxon legislation had always been intended.

8   The Laws of Cnut

The great code of Cnut was issued from Winchester at Christmas 1020 or 1021.[382] It was the fullest single record of Anglo-Saxon law.[383] For that reason, and because it was also in effect the last, it had most influence on perceptions of pre-conquest law after 1066. But it was in fact neither Cnut's first legal pronouncement nor even his last. Attention must go first to his code of some two years previously, and to the letters he sent the English in 1020 and 1027.

---

380   Ker, *Catalogue* 49:11, 186:19(f) (the one with the gloss to which the text above refers); also 68:2, 10. See also chapter 4, above, pp. 196–7, and Keynes, 'Additions in Old English', pp. 94–5.

381   If some of Wulfstan's homilies were preached before lawmaking sessions (above, nn. 336, 344, Lawson 'Archbishop Wulfstan, pp. 576–9), this can only have brought law and homily yet closer together.

382   I Cn Pr. Wulfstan's authorship means that it must pre-date May 1023 (see n. 391), and Cnut himself was in Scandinavia in the winter of 1022/3 (Lawson, *Cnut*, pp. 89–95); earlier dates are precluded by the 1020 letter's reference not to the Winchester but to the Oxford code (below). The point needs making now, as it bears on the code's relationship to other Wulfstan works: below, pp. 364–5.

383   The word-count is 7196 (see n. 1).

(i) Preliminaries – and postscript: 1018, 1020, 1027

All the *Anglo-Saxon Chronicles* for 1018 report that the Danes and the English 'reached agreement (*wurdon sammæle*) at Oxford'. The one in Cotton Tiberius B.iv adds 'according to Edgar's law'. As was established at length in chapter 3 (pp. 129–33), a record of the meeting survives in Corpus Cambridge 201 ('D'). It can scarcely be chance that this text refers both to an Anglo-Danish peace and to Edgar's law, while Cnut's 1020 letter defers to Edgar's law as sworn at Oxford: each has two different elements of the three contained by the annal.[384] Everything suggests that the D *gerædnes* is a record of what was either submitted to or decided by the 1018 Oxford assembly.

The record is in a Wulfstan book (chapter 4, pp. 206–10). It was also beyond dispute Wulfstan's work.[385] What Wulfstan presented was a version of the Enham code of 1008, which was verbally close to the text called 'VI Æthelred', but with an order and some details of content nearer to those of 'V', and closer still to the sequence of Cnut's main code.[386] The 1018 code also omitted most secular dispositions from ten years before.[387] They were replaced by a single contribution from Edgar, which concerned judicial integrity, and which was followed by a new list of the fines appropriate to the different ranks of those affronted by any injustice.[388] The code concluded with an near-exact reproduction of the first part of the 'VI Æthelred Appendix'.[389] The ineluctible inference from all this is that the 1018 code represents a provisional statement of the aspects of the previous regime that the archbishop considered fundamental (those, that is to say, which directly affected its relationship with God), while foreshadowing the infinitely fuller promulgation that these and everything else would be given a couple of years later.[390] The relevance of 'Edgar's law' was not so much (yet) what that king

384   ASC 1018D (+ CE), pp. 154–5; Cn 1018 Pr. – 1; Cn 1020 13; the possibility that any of these sources drew on the others (Lawson, *Cnut*, p. 53) hardly weakens the link between them.
385   As definitively established by Whitelock, 'Wulfstan and the Laws of Cnut', and (in reply to Jost, 'Cnut und Wulfstan', *Wulfstanstudien*, pp. 73–103) 'Wulfstan's Authorship of Cnut's Laws'. Her case was well summarized and slightly corrected by Kennedy's edition, 'Cnut's law code of 1018', and there is no point in going over the ground again here.
386   As can be clearly seen from Kennedy's Table, p. 59 (superseding Whitelock, 'Wulfstan and the laws of Cnut', pp. 434–5). But one should add that Cn 1018 11:3 is more like V Atr 10 than VI Atr 11 (and yet more like I Cn 6:3), while Cn 1018 13 – 14 follows V Atr 11 – 12:3, especially 'G²'/'D', rather than VI Atr 16 – 22.
387   A minor but telling detail is that VI Atr 32:3, '7 fyrdunga eac [7 scypfyrdungan, **not in** V 26:1] ealswa, a þonne neod sy swa swa man geræde for gemænlicre neode', becomes Cn 1018 23, 'And fyrdunga eac swa a þonne þearf sy for gemænlicre neode'.
388   Cn 1018 25 – 27; III Eg 3 (and cf., again, II Cn 15:1,2–3).
389   Cn 1018 28 – 36, VI Atr App. 42 – 49; the passage is also almost verbally identical with *HomN* LIX, pp. 308–9. Given the archbishop's work habits, it is impossible to decide which of these is earlier than the others (*HomN* LIX is thinner than VI Atr App. 42 – 42:1/Cn 1018 28, and lines up with VI Atr App. 42:1 on 'anrædlice' and 'geornlice', but it also shares '7 þæt he … his Drihten' with Cn 1018 28); it is at any rate likely that, like VI Atr itself, *HomN* LIX was connected with the drafting of Cn 1018: above, p. 335.
390   It is not certain that Cn 1018 1:1, 'they declared that they would consider further at leisure (*on æmtan*) the needs of the people with God's help as best they could' anticipates the deliberations that produced I–II Cn. If it does, the rest of 1018, beginning 'Nu wille we swutelian' must cover what Wulfstan thought urgent.

had actually decreed. Instead, it stood for a time of prosperity and harmony which both parties in 1018 could recall positively. It signalled resumption of normal business so far as possible. But one further point is raised by what was argued in the previous section. Cnut's Winchester code was not included in any known Wulfstan book. That of Oxford was; and in a collection almost certainly assembled when the main code was available. It seems that this sort of text, though remote from the presumptively most pressing legal issues, was better suited for circulation in Wulfstan's pastoral handbooks.

The earlier of Cnut's letter-proclamations survives only in the York Gospels. It was evidently added at much the same time as three Wulfstan homilies annotated in his hand (chapter 4, pp. 196–7). The style of the later part of the letter has strong Wulfstan echoes. A date for it before Wulfstan's death on 28 May 1023 is therefore certain.[391] It was particularly addressed to Earl Thorkell, and the likelihood is that it was sent from Denmark in the winter of 1019/20 or soon afterwards, when Thorkell was regent in England.[392] These details are important, precisely because the letter as it stands seems to have been subjected to Wulfstan's intervention. Apart from the evidence of his style, the concluding section rounds up all the archbishop's usual suspects: breakers of oaths and pledges, 'kinslayers and secret slayers and perjurors and witches and valkyries and adulterers and incest', and married nuns.[393] The letter therefore seems to have been written in a context where Wulfstan's influence was not exerted, and expanded to suit his preoccupations.[394] Cnut's letter proper perhaps finished on the note that 'all had decided and sworn at Oxford to observe Edgar's law'.

The letter opens, 'King Cnut greets his archbishops and his diocesan bishops and Earl Thorkell and all his earls and all his people, twelve-hundred men and two-hundred men, clerical and lay, in England, with friendship (*Cnut cyning gret his arcebiscopas ... 7 ealne his þeodscype twelfhynde 7 twyhynde ... on Englalande freondlice*)'. The friendly greeting is no more than would be expected in any letter. But the scope of the address, to the leading officials of Church and State, then to any (free) subject of higher or lower degree, does have a definite flavour of the more stereotyped writ.[395] It thereby ties in with the fact that Edgar's *Wihtbordesstan* code called itself a 'gewrit', and contributes to the impression

391 Wulfstan's *obit* is recorded in *Liber Eliensis* ii 87, p. 157.
392 Cf. Lawson, *Cnut*, pp. 89–91; Keynes, 'Cnut's Earls', pp. 54–7, 82–4; Whitelock, *Councils*, p. 435.
393 Cn 1020 14 – 17 (and note 18 on Sunday observance); as pointed out by Whitelock (*Councils*, p. 440, n. 1), 'wælcyrian' also crop up in later versions of *Sermo Lupi*, lns 166–73). The phrasing of 16 – 18 also echoes *HomN* L, pp. 271, lns 21–7, 272, lns 13–16 (cf. XXIII, p. 117), and is closer to I Cn 14:2 – 16 than to anything earlier.
394 Keynes, 'Additions in Old English', pp. 95–6; Kennedy, Cnut's law code', pp. 62–4. This was the only respect in which Jost's 1950 critique led Whitelock to modify her position on Wulfstan's activity ('Wulfstan's authorship', pp. 83–4). All the same, his ideas and phraseology are not without effect on the first part of the letter: note '*adwæsce* (quench)', Cn 1020 10, as otherwise used in *Can. Eg.* 16; also Cn 1020 8 ('Godes gerihta'), 9 ('swa dyrstig sy, gehadod oððe læwede ... betan 7 geswican æfter minra biscopa tæcinga'). It would be no great surprise if Wulfstanisms were ringing in the ears of all royal advisers by 1020.
395 HaWr, pp. 17, 24–8, 41–57, referring to Stevenson, 'Yorkshire Surveys', pp. 3–8, where this point was first made. For these purposes, it makes no difference if, as argued by Chaplais, 'Anglo-Saxon Chancery', pp. 173–4, Cnut's message drew on the conventions of oral address, since the link with government business holds good anyway.

that kings of England were developing more informal channels of communication with their subjects than solemn law-giving: channels which were the only way that post-conquest kings are known to have made law at all (above, pp. 289, 302, 311, 319, below, pp. 400–2). Cnut's letter did the same sort of thing as Edgar's code, promising good lordship in return for obedience. Good lordship in this case entailed an assurance that the king had removed the threat that events in Denmark seemed to pose; instead, 'help and deliverance' could be counted on from that quarter – though whether, given its recent staggering price, this was such good news for Englishmen, may be doubted.[396] What the king wished in return was that 'ealdormen help the bishops as regards God's dues and my kingship and the needs of all the people', that defiance of God's law and 'kingship or secular justice' be punished with death or exile, that just judgements be observed (to the satisfaction of local bishops), and that harbourers of thieves be punished like thieves themselves. This programme, interestingly, was rather closer to that of Edgar's Andover code than was the 1018 text, with its professed adherence to 'Edgar's law'.[397] It may be that Cnut and councillors other than Wulfstan were taking the Edgar model as seriously as did the archbishop himself.

Cnut's second encyclical was transmitted by the twelfth-century historians John of Worcester and William of Malmesbury, so only in Latin translation.[398] John specifically mentioned Abbot Lyfing of Tavistock among 'other messengers' as the agent of the letter's delivery. Lyfing was, as he says, soon to be Bishop of Crediton, and would eventually be Bishop of Worcester too. In recording his death, the D *Chronicle* (with Worcester connections) calls him 'the eloquent bishop'. He was credited in chapter 4 (p. 223) with a possible role in editing memorials of Archbishop Wulfstan for the benefit of his south-western diocese. It is no outrageous speculation that he was not merely the carrier of the letter but also its author.[399] The evidence that he was still an abbot at the time confirms that the letter is to be dated 1027, soon after Cnut attended the imperial coronation of Conrad II, to which it (obliquely) refers, and not to 1031, the date John actually gives.[400] *Mutatis mutandis*, the 1027 letter was like its predecessor. It opened by greeting archbishops, bishops and 'primates', and the whole English people, 'noble and plebeian', though this time, the archbishops were named, and the king's title proclaimed his rule of England, Denmark, Norway and part of Sweden. Later, it addressed itself to 'vicecomitibus et prepositis', who were presumably 'scirgerefan 7 gerefan' in the Old English original.[401] The letter's voice was consistently first person singular. The good lordship proffered encompassed the prayers for his kingdoms and peoples that Cnut had put to St Peter; with the less ethereal benefits of a lightening of tolls and barriers through

396   Cn 1020 4 – 6; cf. Lawson, '"Those Stories Look True"', pp. 395–400.
397   Note also an echo of IV Eg 16 in Cn 1020 2.
398   *JW* II, pp. 512–19; *William of Malmesbury, Gesta Regum* ii 183, I, pp. 221–4. It is not certain that William took his text of the letter from John, but he adds nothing to John's account, and there is little doubt that he was as reliant as John on Worcester archives: Brett, 'John of Worcester', pp. 113–17. This matters: see below.
399   ASC 1047D, p. 165. So also Lawson, *Cnut*, p. 64.
400   Whitelock, *Councils*, p. 507; Lawson, *Cnut*, pp. 102–4.
401   Cn 1027 Inscr., 12.

which Englishmen and Danes were obliged to pass *en route* to Rome, and the lifting of the sums paid by archbishops for their *pallia*.[402] He again promised security from Scandinavia, ordering in return that justice be mercifully and impartially applied, and that all God's dues be levied under established legal sanctions. But an ominous departure from previous norms was that deviation from justice would be inspired neither by 'royal favour', nor by hopes of enhanced royal revenue.[403] In other words, the king's side of the bargain was now that he would rein in excesses by his officials. It was a note that had already been loudly sounded in Cnut's code itself.

(ii) I–II Cnut: memorials

It will soon be evident that Cnut's code was just what the word conventionally means: a codification of mostly pre-existent law. Like Alfred's law-book, of which the same is conspicuously true, it was textually quite stable across the range of its extant memorials. That range was fairly wide. There are three Old English texts, none visibly close kin to any other; and besides the Latin translation in *Quadripartitus*, there are two other post-conquest Latin adaptations, neither so free that it is not also a textual witness (chapter 4, pp. 224–8, 228–44, 253–5; below, pp. 402–6). However, extraneous elements accrued even to Alfred's *domboc* (above, pp. 175–6, 227, 231–2). There were also differences of detail between versions of Cnut's code. Above all, the text in the earliest, Cotton Nero A.i(A) ('G'), differed significantly from those circulating in the twelfth century.

For one thing, it had textual variants in at least twenty clauses. This is not a lot out of a total of over three hundred; nor are they all of much substance.[404] Yet it is a matter of some interest that G should twice go out of its way to note Kentish variations, in the archbishop's favour.[405] One's initial reaction, that this must be a book with a Kentish origin or ancestry, could well be right. On the other hand, both departures from the norm were implicit in what the tract *Grið* said about the privileges of the Kentish church; and *Grið* was another work by Wulfstan, author of Cnut's code itself.[406] Some other changes have a *prima facie* look of Wulfstan glosses.[407] Others still are the kind of change any scribe might

---

402 Cn 1027 2 – 4, 6 – 8.
403 Cn 1027 11 – 17.
404 Examples (a comprehensive list could not easily be delimited): I Cn 2, 3:2, 19, 22:4–5; II Cn 2a, 12, 17, 19:2, 20, 22, 37, 38, 38:2, 40, 62, 63, 68, 75, 79 (but I Cn 19, II 17, 22 are variants which emerge only in their erasure and replacement by a 'normal' reading in the sixteenth century, so that nothing more can be said of them). In addition, I Cn 3:1, 17:1, II Pr., 8, 47, 51:1 may be scribal error, but I 3:1, II 47 are echoed by Q (Lond). For what is meant by 'clause' in this code, see below: the 305 total (I: 91, II: 214) comes from adding up Liebermann's clauses and sub-clauses.
405 I Cn 3:2, II Cn 62. See chapter 4, pp. 225–6, for other angles on the Wulfstan/Canterbury provenance of this manuscript (there inclining to Canterbury's case rather than Wulfstan's).
406 There is no more need to argue Wulfstan's authorship of I–II Cn than of all other codes discussed in the foregoing pages: it becomes ever more obvious in the discussion to follow. The fundamental groundwork is the papers of Whitelock and Kennedy, above, n. 385.
407 I Cn 2 *could* be Wulfstan, though otherwise unattested in this context; I 22:4–5 is in one aspect

make for clarity's sake.[408] A residue comprises points of possible legal significance that are not instantly attributable to Wulfstan's convictions: they included a rider that a previous owner 'would not or could not' discharge the obligations on a property successfully 'defended' by its current owner.[409] Overall, it seems most unlikely that these were elements of the original text that every other version contrived to drop. Almost all look like additions. Several look distinctly authorial: if not Wulfstanian in character, then arguably official. It follows that this is a further case of the archbishop's altering a current code. But this time it was not done to convert the code into a homily, nor necessarily on Wulfstan's initiative alone.

The G copy's other singularity was already observed in chapter 4 (p. 227). It was divided throughout into paragraphs. These are barely an improvement on those of modern editors. Their effect in the opening section is that the topic of grið first appears as a part of the introductory statement on love of God and loyalty to the king; that there is a new chapter for offences within church walls, their punishment having already been announced in the previous one; that the various grades of church have a chapter of their own, after the point that there are different ranks of churches had been made in a clause ostensibly devoted to non-fatal assaults; that part of Wulfstan's homiletic comment on angelic hovering over sacramental acts has a clause to itself, the value of the priest's role in performing these having been addressed in the one before; and so on.[410] Little of this suggests authorial initiative. It will soon be clear that nothing so elaborate underlies twelfth-century copies. Nor, however, is there any sign that they were the product of the scriptorium where G originated: nothing comparable was done for the volume's other texts (chapter 4, p. 227). Wulfstan or his scribes evidently did believe in chapters. The paragraphing of Cnut's code could have been an aspect of the same (?semi-)official revision as produced the main textual changes.

The twelfth-century witnesses to Cnut's code are idiosyncratic enough to imply their essential independence, yet sufficiently similar to show that a fundamentally homogeneous text was circulating by then. Comparing the Latin Q, Instituta

---

slightly closer to Can. Eg. 22; II Cn 2a is the sort of gloss often supplied by Wulfstan (e.g. Inst. Pol. I 17, 19–23); II Cn 38 'fæstentidan' is confirmed by 'Conf.' III, p. 19, and the drift of the archbishop's ideas on such matters (I Cn 17, etc.); II 38:2 'boctæcing' is upheld by Can. Eg. 68b.

408   II 12, II 19:2, II 20 ('afylle', a possibly unclear reading, albeit one whose authenticity is upheld by Q (Lond.) and by Inst. Cn, Cons. Cn, and in any event a Wulfstan word); II 37 (explaining 'landrica'), II 40, II 68 ('nime' a simpler alternative for the perhaps over-elaborate 'lese'). II Cn 75 is a case where G (and Cons. Cn) have the less simple reading.

409   II Cn 79 (cf. Lawson, 'Collection of Danegeld and Heregeld', pp. 723–4, and chapter 9: Wulfstan confronted something like this issue elsewhere: V Atr 32:3 ('D')). Cf. also II Cn 63, 'oððe wið þone þe his socne age', as in II 37 (previous n.).

410   G's breaks are at I Cn 2:1, 2:3, 2:4, 3, 3:2, 4, 4:2, and then (as regards charges against clerics) at 5, 5:1, 5:2, 5:2b, 5:2d, 5:3; a better set might have been 2, 2:2, 3a, 4, 5, 5:2a, 5:2b, 5:2d, 5:3. Later clauses that make more sense than Liebermann's include I 6:3 (general ban on illicit sexuality), not 7 (degrees of prohibited kindred); I 14:1 (start of laws on feasts and fasts). There is justification for the paragraphs at II 15:1, 15:2, less so at 15:1a, 15:3; II 21 is not a new clause and hardly deserves to be (cf. chapter 9), but 20 ought to have had one; II 28 introduces a new subject, and the break comes instead at 28:1; also understandable is the lack of a break at II 55, but scarcely the presence of one at 58:2; etc. Cases where the MS looks more illogical than modern editions include I 11:1, not 12; II 8:1–2, not 10, 11; II 17:1, not 18; and II 22:1, 22:2, not 22, 23, 24.

Cnuti and *Consiliatio Cnuti* with the vernacular Corpus Cambridge 383 ('B') and BL Harley 55 ('A') (chapter 4, pp. 228–36, 253–5) reveals few oddities specific to one copy or shared by all. The most important came at the start. 'A' had a preface which is neither in Q nor G (it is absent from B too, if only because the whole of the first part of the code is lost). Something very similar, however, was clearly available to the *Consiliatio*; it *might* therefore be original. Its most significant element was Cnut's claim to be king of the Norwegians, which was also in the 1027 letter's greeting formula; the point here is not whether or when Cnut was in any real sense ruler of Norway, but when he wished it to be thought that he was, which could have been from early in his reign.[411] It is at any rate not impossible that the preface was 'officially' added some time after the code's promulgation.

Thereafter, the pattern of textual variants can only be called random. Nine of G's eccentricities turn up in other copies.[412] Three are in the *Consiliatio*, two in *Instituta Cnuti*, two in first edition Q, and one in its revised edition.[413] There are lapses more or less in the character of individual manuscripts (chapter 4, pp. 253–5, 254–5).[414] Otherwise, there are in effect indiscriminate alliances between G, B, and/or A on the one hand and any one Latin text on the other.[415] These *minutiae* matter, however deplorably, because it is practically impossible to force them into a *stemma*. Liebermann did his manful best, and his attempt of course merits respect.[416] But it depends on one of his imagined multiglossed archetypes, and it would be easier to believe in these, had anything much like one survived.[417] The only viable alternative is that the code circulated with enough velocity in the century after 1020 to attract almost any available variant, like (to stretch a point) texts of the liturgy or the Bible. It is best to speak of a 'post-conquest vulgate' of Cnut's code.

There is little evidence that this 'vulgate' was ever divided systematically into clauses, surprising though that seems for so gigantic a text. Q's rubrics look like the compiler's own work (chapter 4, p. 235). B and A have coloured initials at

---

411   The claim to Norway had no very sound factual basis when made in the 1027 letter. Cnut's charters are unhelpful, since he is rarely more than 'rex Anglorum', etc. (if also 'ceterarum gentium persistentium', etc., this ancient formula having new relevance); exceptions are the doubtful S 976 ('totius Angliae regni et Danorum'), and the ludicrous S 965 (echoing the 1027 letter in its reference to part of Sweden). Cf. Sawyer, 'Cnut's Scandinavian empire', pp. 18–19.

412   Liebermann's analysis (*Gesetze* III, pp. 192–3 (3–10)) is flawed by his faith in a lost Lambarde 'master-copy' (chapter 4, pp. 260–2); for this and more obvious reasons (above, n. 404), I discount his variants α), β), ε), but add I 2, 3:1, II 12, 22:4.

413   II Cn 19:2, 68, 75; I 2, II 12; I 3:1, II 47; II 20.

414   Liebermann, in an uncharacteristic lapse, wrongly implies that II Cn 77:1 is missing from B.

415   E.g., I Cn 12, G/A in error against latin texts (B defective); II 32, B/A in error against G/latin; I Ep., B/*Cons.* against G/A/ other latin; I 26, B/Q(Lond) against the rest; I Cn 7:3, II 5:1, A/Q(Lond) against the rest; II 2:1, 68:1a, ? I 14:1, A/Q; I 4:1, II 3, A/*Inst.* (note that H *Inst.* is itself corrected in the first case); II 26, A/*Inst./Cons.*; II 75, A/Q/B uncor., against G/*Cons./*B cor.

416   He detected three groups, G/*Inst.*, B/*Cons.* and A/Q. But he badly needed his glossed archetype to account for ways in which G readings show up in *Cons.* (p. 192 (3)); and his argument anyway fails to account for I 12, I 26, II 32 or II 75 (in the last case, he thought the B correction sixteenth-century); he also largely ignored the correction factor in Q, and overlooked I 4:1, II 3, 26.

417   The vast majority of B emendations arose from its scribe's deficiencies (chapter 4, above, pp. 233–5); but this MS's exemplar would be the best instance of a possibly glossed master-text.

(mostly) relevant points. Yet the rubrics and most other species of text-break in B were undoubtedly later additions, and little was done along those lines in A (chapter 4, nn. 346–8). At the same time, all manuscripts have outsize initials at particular points, notably when introducing the 'king's rights' (II 12), and the promise of specific 'alleviations' (II 69).[418] These coincide with what look like important departures in the text. In B, the break at II 69 is followed by an unprecedented run of paragraphs. It is hard to see why the scribe should have done this without encouragement from his exemplar; and would the exemplar have broken so notably from scribal habit without some sort of lead from the original text (see below, pp. 361–2)?

There is an intriguing postscript to this account. Both the *Instituta* and the *Consiliatio* were post-conquest recreations of Anglo-Saxon law based on trans-lations of Cnut's code (below, pp. 404–6). But Book III of the *Instituta* ranged beyond Cnut to add information about ranks and royal rights, which drew extensively on the collection of status-tracts assembled by Wulfstan.[419] The *Consiliatio* stayed closer to Cnut, but also included clauses from 'VIII Æthelred' about abbots not being bothered with worldly business, and the concluding exhortations to love God, obey His law, honour Christianity, abjure hea-thenism, and keep faith to king and friends.[420] This too was a Wulfstan text, confined as things now stand to Wulfstan manuscripts, and the principles in question had not been voiced in as many words earlier in Cnut's code. It is of course possible, even likely, that these supplementary items were unearthed elsewhere by post-conquest compilers, and incorporated because of their obvi-ous relevance. But, after all that has by now been seen of the handling of royal law by Wulfstan's *scriptoria*, one can entertain the possibility that he or an *amanuensis* tacked them on, or associated them intimately enough to make them available alongside Cnut's code to two post-1066 translators. The end-product would after all be a more complete picture of the law as Wulfstan's circle envisaged it.

(iii) Wulfstan's mature legislative style

The key to the understanding of what was decreed at Winchester is that it was largely a compound of earlier legislation. This is fully discussed in sub-section (iv). But a preliminary glance at table 5.4 instantly explains why the code is in such a curious mix of styles. When Alfred's *domboc* was quoted on the conse-quences of impairing the king's special *ambience*, the result duly had the

---

418   Q has them at II 69 in all editions (least marked in 'Hk'), and at II 12 in all bar Lond. and R; B has new paragraphs at II 12, 69 (otherwise previously only at II Pr., 68:3); A has a significant break at II 12, not at II 69, but at II 83 as well as at II 8, 20, 84 (chapter 4, p. 254). There are hints of something similar in H *Inst. Cn* at II 12, 69, and in *Cons. Cn* at 69, 82 (below, n. 658). For possible reasons behind all this, see below, pp. 361–2.

419   *Inst. Cn* III 42 – 45:3, 56 – 57, 60 – 63:1.

420   *Gesetze* I, pp. 267–8.

simplicity of so many Alfredian laws.[421] But the position is a little more complicated than that. Alfred's law was not so much quoted as paraphrased in a comparable idiom. Nearly all laws in this part of the code had the manner of earlier phases of Anglo-Saxon legislation, but relatively few were visibly quoted from previous models.[422] The next sub-section explores the possibility that some or all of them were taken from codes that are now lost. However, the immediately preceding laws concerned marriage and its infringements. Most of them were expressed in the clipped 'if ... then' style of codes before 899. Yet two at least partook of Wulfstan's homiletic mode.[423] The topic of illicit sexuality was right at the top of his agenda, but had seemingly interested no other law-maker since Alfred.[424] The one text detectably quoted was the 'Handbook for a Confessor', which, if not a work by Wulfstan, was certainly accessible to him.[425] Indeed, the introduction of the theme of '*æwbryce* (adultery)' directly after '*hadbryce* (violation of holy orders)' recalls a typical pairing in the archbishop's 'outrage catalogues'.[426] It here looks as if Wulfstan were deliberately drafting laws in a less high-flown and more traditional parlance. He would in fact have been reverting to the language he had used throughout his 'Peace of Edward and Guthrum' and it so happens that passages from this tract had directly or indirectly inspired most of the clauses in the foregoing 'hadbryce' section.[427] Straightforward offences demanded simple formulations, just as eloquence was required for matters of principle.

Wulfstan was certainly ready to adopt a more clearly homiletic approach in Cnut's code than in 1008 or 1014 or even 1018. Here, as in Æthelred's later laws, the first person plural was preferred, except once when quoting Edgar and in a distinct passage to be considered shortly. Its sense was surely more congregational than majestic: '*we lærað* (we instruct)' was not much less regular than 'we wyllað'.[428] As well as laws, Wulfstan now recycled extracts from his *Institutes of Polity* or later Homilies – or even from earlier series – to round off more direct injunctions. The last nineteen clauses of the first, ecclesiastical, part distilled what was said in a late addition to the 'Pastoral Letter', in one of the York Gospels tracts, in homilies probably of late Æthelred/early Cnut vintage, and also in *Grið*, in the *Canons of Edgar* (supplemented by a passage from an early 'catechetical' homily) and in all editions of *Institutes of Polity*.[429] The effect was to stress the need for political loyalty, for the living of a Christian life based

421   II Cn 58 – 58:2, Af 3. Likewise, II 57, 59: rephrased Af 4 – 4:2, 7 respectively.
422   A virtual quotation is II Cn 55/Wi 4 (note B's unease with early Kentish syntax).
423   II Cn 50:1: 'Yfel æwbryce byð þæt eawfæst man mid æmtige forlicge 7 mycele wyrse wið oðres æwe oððe wið gehadode'; II 51:1: 'Ne byð na gelic ðæt man wið swustor gehæme 7 hit wære feor sib'.
424   II Cn 50 – 55; the only (partial) post-Alfredian precedent is I Em 4, a text available to Wulfstan (above, p. 309).
425   'Conf.', p. 22 lns 179–81; see chapter 4, pp. 205, 222.
426   E.g. *Sermo Lupi* ln 142.
427   See above, Table 5.3; II Cn 43 – 48:3 (cf. table 5.4). As regards II Cn 58 – 58:2 above, note that the form of the equivalent law in *Grið* 11 is in some ways closer to Alfred's original.
428   Cf. I Cn 6, 6:1, 7, 17, 18, 21, 22, 23, 24, 25, II 2; and note 'uton' (I 2?, 18:1, 20, II 8, 68, 84:3): not exactly the voice of royal command. Exceptions: II Cn 1 (III Eg 1).
429   I Cn 20 – 26:4; for parallels in other *Wulfstaniana*, see table 5.4. Against the possibility that such echoes resulted from quotation of Cnut's code by Wulfstan's late works, see below, pp. 364–5.

on prayer, continence and fear of the Last Judgement, and for acceptance of episcopal responsibility by all concerned. Wulfstan was also ready to introduce complexity into his sources. The conjunction 'butan' appears at least twenty-six times, half of which were interjections in known sources.[430] Some expressed what has been called his 'soul-saving agenda'; more reflected attempts to get to grips with less than simple issues. Cnut's laws on warranty were as elaborate as anything in Æthelstan's or Æthelred's early legislation.[431] The code's conclusion is a good illustration of his mature method. First came three clauses following the model of Æthelstan's summary punishing disobedience to the Grately code. But except for one phrase, the Cnut wording was entirely new: third person replaced first, payment of wergeld was the penalty for first, not second, offence, with a *doubled* wergeld second time around.[432] Wulfstan then launched into a homiletic *exordium* that was word-for-word the same as one of the supplements to *Institutes of Polity*, and which again underlined the centrality of obedience to the king and the role of spiritual teachers.[433] Last of all was a benediction. Compulsion and exhortation combined to emphasize the necessity of discipline in a Christian society.

The results of Wulfstan's patchwork approach are not as uneven as they might have been. This master of congregations knew how to maintain the flow of exposition. There is more than a trace of system in the code's structure. The ecclesiastical part opened with the Church's 'peace', meaning the security of its buildings and charges against its personnel. This led on to the standards, above all of sexual purity, expected of the clergy, and so to the sanctity of marriage. There was then a long series of laws on Church dues, feasts and fasts, followed by clauses on regular penance and communion, and thereafter by an extended homiletic conclusion. The secular part of the code began with the principles of justice, then proceeded to heathen practices (a problem of ecclesiastical concern, but one to which laymen were of course more exposed). Laws on sound money with a homiletic mini-summary introduced a long sequence on judicial organization, prefaced by an account of the 'king's rights'. Coverage of this subject extended to trustworthiness, which led into prosecution of notorious suspects and perjury. Attention then reverted to the Church's status, but with the focus on crimes committed by or against men in orders, and aggravated defiance of the Church's demands: manual work on a festival, violence or sexual intercourse during Lent, forcible resistance to Church dues; matters seen from the angle of behaviour to which the laity was especially prone. Similarly, the following section on sexual offences covered the same ground as Part I, but with reference to the sanctions prescribed rather than the principles at stake. After that were laws on major crimes, extending to the duties of fortification and military service. That section ended with a sophisticated review of circumstances bearing on

430   I Cn 2:2–3, 15, 16:1, 26:1, II 4a, 4:1–2, 12, 13:2, 15, 15:1a, 18, 23, 24, 30, 39, 41:2, 45, 57, 59, 69:1, 73:2,4, 74, 76:1, 82. See Schwyter, 'Syntax and Style', pp. 202–204 and fig. 2 (Dr Schwyter also notes, p. 199, the preponderance of 'early' style in parts of the code).
431   II Cn 24 – 24:3; cf., e.g., II 75 – 75:1.
432   II Cn 83 – 83:2; II As 25:2.
433   II Cn 84 – 84:4b: see Table 5.4.

sentences, such as the difference between intentional and unintentional misdeeds. There was then a series of 'alleviations'; before the whole code finished
as related above.

Yet the logic of all this can be overstated.[434] The code tended to retain the shape
of its sources. The arrangement of the early sections of Part II seems to be determined by that of the 1018 code, though its laws on sexual standards and Church
dues were hived off into Part I.[435] That is why burghal and military obligations
came up in clause '10', and penalties for their neglect as far away as clause '65'.
It accounts too for the mini-homily that followed. The fact that the Oxford code
went on to incur its only real debt to 'Edgar's law' by quoting Andover on injustice and adding a new set of fines for offenders under English and Danish law,
may have sparked off the review of 'king's rights' in the various jurisdictions from
clause '12' onwards, plus the whole ensuing section on justice, itself an expansion of Edgar's measures (see table 5.4). The consequence was that theft was dealt
with long before the section on other serious crime. The review of mitigating
circumstance concluding that section was separated by most of the length of Part
II from its inaugural laws on judicial mercy, because they corresponded to the
'VI Æthelred' appendix whereas due regard for God's love of his creatures was
commended at the very outset of the Enham code. The final impression is that
Wulfstan gave much thought to the deployment of the blocks of material with
which he was working; it counts for something that blatant repetition was rare.
But he did not often sacrifice the integrity of those blocks to rigorous legal logic.
The result was, if not an adequate work of reference, then at least a book that
the kingdom's servants could read right through, and with profit.

(iv) Content and context

Cnut began his law-making by harking back to the prototype of Edgar. His own
massive code was above all a tribute to the legislative achievement of kings since
Alfred. Almost all their major interests were reflected. Much of their work was
quoted. For his own part, Wulfstan decanted most of the ideas that had been
fomenting over the previous dozen years in his earlier codes and tracts, homilies
and *Institutes of Polity*. A table of Cnut's sources makes this clearer than any
amount of verbal statement (table 5.4). Thus, of the 305 'clauses' (as edited by
Liebermann), nearly 75 per cent derived directly or indirectly from one or more
earlier models. Over half were outright quotations of previous texts, though
forty-six of these were from the code Wulfstan had drafted for Cnut only two or
three years before, and another forty-five were from his other writings.
Unsurprisingly, his codes for Æthelred predominated among pre-1016 laws, and
the more recent were the more likely to be quoted verbally. But similar respect
was shown for Edgar's Andover laws, a well-known lode-star of the archbishop's,
and also for Æthelred's Woodstock code, which had not previously attracted his

---

434   The degree of planning in Cnut's code is emphasized, though in less detail (other than an illuminating breakdown of the 'alleviation' clauses), by Korte, *Untersuchungen*, pp. 95–101.
435   See Kennedy's table, 'Cnut's law code of 1018', p. 59.

Table 5.4 I–II Cnut, analysis of sources[436]

I Pr.	(HomN)	Cn 1018	II Can Eg	(HomN L)	VIII Atr	Grið	Pol./Had.	VI Atr	EGu	II Eg. Pr
1		Cn 1018 1		(HomN L)				VI Atr 1–1:1		
2		Cn 1018 2,						VI Atr 42:3		
2:1		Cn 1018 2:1		(HomN L)		**Grið 31:2, 1**	Pol. I 101,	VI Atr 13		
2:2		Cn 1018 2:2			**VIII Atr 1:1–5:1**	**Grið 2,**	Pol. I 100,	VI Atr 14,	EGu 1	
2:3–3:2							Had. 1:1, 1:3			
4										
4:1–3										
5			**II Can Eg 68e**		**VIII Atr 19**					
5a–5:2b			**II Can Eg 68e-i**		**VIII Atr 19:1–23**					
5:2c			**II Can Eg 68i**		**VIII Atr 24**					
5:2d–5:4					**VIII Atr 25 – 27:1**					
6–6a		**Cn 1018 11**		(HomN L)				**VI Atr 2:1–2, 41**		
6:1–2a		**Cn 1018 11:1–2**						VI Atr 5–5:1, 5:3		
6:3		Cn 1018 11:3						VI Atr 11		
7–7:3	(HomN LIX)	Cn 1018 12–12:4						VI Atr 12–12:2		
8–8:1		Cn 1018 13 – 13:3						**VI Atr 16–17**		
8:2		Cn 1018 13:4		(HomN L)	VIII Atr 7–8			VI Atr 18		**II Eg 3:1**
9										
9:1	(HomN LXI)				VIII Atr 10:1			**VI Atr 18:1**		
10										
10:1	(HomN LXI)				VIII Atr 11:1					
11–11:2										**II Eg 2–2:2**
12	(HomN XXIII, LXI)	Cn 1018 13:5 (II Can Eg 54			VIII Atr 12:1,			VI Atr 19)		
13		**Cn 1018 13:6**			**VIII Atr 13,**			**VI Atr 20**		
13:1		**Cn 1018 13:7**						**VI Atr 21**		
14–14:1		**Cn 1018 14–14:1**		**(Hom N L)**				**VI Atr 21:1–22**		**II Eg 5**
14:2	(Cn 1020 18, HomN XXIII)			**(Hom N L)**						
15–15:1		**Cn 1018:14:1**						VI Atr 22:1		
16										
16a		Cn 1018 14:2–3						VI Atr 22:2–3, 24		**II Eg 5:1**

17	Cn 1018 15			VI Atr 25,	EGu 9 (Can.Eg. 24)
17:1	Cn 1018 14:6			V Atr 16	
17:2–3	Cn 1018 15:1–2			**VI Atr 25:1–2**	
18a–18b					(Hom XIII)
18:1	Cn 1018 1:3			VI Atr 1	
18:2				VI Atr 49	
19	Cn 1018 17–17:1			VI Atr 27–27:1	Af 1
19:1–2	Cn 1018 18–19			**VI Atr 28–28:1**	
19:3	Cn 1018 19			VI Atr 30	
20–20:2	(HomN XXIV)				
21	(HomN LIX)				
22, 22:5–6	(HomN LIX)			VI Atr 42:2	Can Eg 22
22:1–4					(Hom VII)
23–24	(HomN LIX)				
26, 26:4			(Hom XVII)		
26:1–3			Grið 19:1 – 20 Pol I 43, 51		
			(Hom XVIb) Pol I 47–50		
II Pr.					
1	Cn 1018 3			VI Atr 8	III Eg Pr
1:1	Cn 1018 3:1			VI Atr 8:1,	III Eg 1:1
2	Cn 1018 4			VI Atr 10:2	
2a	**Cn 1018 4:1**			**VI Atr 10:3**	
2:1	Cn 1018 5			**VI Atr 10–10:1**	
3	Cn 1018 6			VI Atr 9	
4	Cn 1018 7		VIII Atr 40		
4a	Cn 1018 7			**VI Atr 7** EGu 11	(Hom VII, etc.)
4:1	Cn 1018 8		VIII Atr 41 – 42		
4:2	Cn 1018 8:1				
5–5:1			(Hom XII)		
6–7	(Cn 1020 15, HomN LX) **Cn 1018 9–10**	(HomN L)	(Hom XX)		(Can Eg 16)
7:1	**Cn 1018 10:1**	**(HomN L)**	VIII Atr 40		(Hom VII, etc.)
8	Cn 1018 20–20:2	(HomN L)		VI Atr 31–32:1	III Eg 8

Table 5.4 *(Continued)*

8:1			IV Atr 5:3 ⎫ II As 14:1 ⎬ IV Atr 7:3 ⎭
8:2		VI Atr 32:2	
9	Cn 1018 21	VI Atr 32:3	
10	Cn 1018 22–23	VI Atr 40–40:1	
11–11:1	Cn 1018 24	(HomN L)	I Atr 1:14
13:1			(II As 20:8)
13:2			(II Ew 5:2)
15a			III Eg 3
15:1	Cn 1018 25		
15:2–3	Cn 1018 26–27		
16			**III Eg 4**
17			III Eg 2
17:1–18			III Eg 5–5:1
18:1			**III Eg 5:2**
20a			III Eg 6
22			I Atr 1–1:2
23			(I Ew 1:2)
23:1			(Swer. 8)
25–26			**III Eg 7–7:3**
26:1			(IV As 6:2c)
28–28:1			II As 22, 22:2
29			(IV As 6:3)
30			I Atr 1:1
30:1–3			**I Atr 1:2–4**
30:3b–4			I Atr 1:5–6
30:6			I Atr 1:7
30:7–31			I Atr 1:8–10
31:1–2			I Atr 1:11–13
32–32:1			I Atr 2–2:1
33–33:2			I Atr 4–4:3

36–36:1				(II As 26)
38				
38:1			VI Atr 52	**Conf. III**
38:2			VI Atr 52	**Conf. III**
40		**VIII Atr 33**	Geþyn 8	**EGu 12**
40:1		**VIII Atr 34**		**EGu 12**
40:2		VIII Atr 35		
41		**VIII Atr 26**		
41:1		VIII Atr 27:1		
42		VIII Atr 33–34		
43–44				EGu 4:2–5
45				EGu 9:1
45:1–46				EGu 7–8 ⎡Ine 3–3:2 ⎣Wi 11
46:2				**EGu 8**
47				Af 5:5,40:1
48–48:3				EGu 6:4–7
54:1				Conf. IV
55				
57			VI Atr 37	**Wi 4**
58–58:2		Grið 11		Af 4:2
59				Af 3
60				Af 7 (Abt 18,24)
62–62:1		VIII Atr 42		IV Atr 4–4:1
66–66:1			VI Atr 52–53,	Conf. III
68:1–3	(Hom N L)			(III Atr 14)
72–72:1			**VI Atr 26:1**	
73	Cn 1018 16:1			
76–76:1b	(Hom XX)			
76:2				Ine 57
81				(III Atr 3)
82				(III Atr 1–1:2)

Table 5.4 *(Continued)*

83–83:2	II As 25:2
84–84:4b	Pol. XXXVI 146–53
84:5	Pol. XXXVI 154

In summary form, the debts of Cnut's code are as follows:

	Verbally quoted	Modified	Possible Influence
Æthelberht			1
Wihtred	1	1	
Ine		8	
Alfred		7	
I–II Edward			2
II Æthelstan		6	2
IV Æthelstan			2
II–III Edgar	12	10	
I Æthelred	16	6	
III Æthelred			4
IV Æthelred		4	
V/VI Æthelred	21	35	1
VIII Æthelred	20	13	
Cnut 1018	46	11	
Cn 1020			2
Wulfstan, tracts	15	15	4
Polity	14	3	
homilies	16	14	6
Other codes, etc.	2	2	1
TOTALS	163	135	25

Unattributable: 82

436   Entries in bold indicate (virtually) verbal quotation of the source, and brackets an indirect or uncertain relationship: parallels in homilies are invariably in brackets because, even where wordings are identical, it is impossible to be sure about the priority of one or other. That aside, texts have, so far as manageable, been arranged in chronological sequence, those nearest in time to the Winchester code leftwards. However, the chronology of Wulfstan's works is extremely hard to establish: for the effort of mine on which the above is based, see above, n. 368. In the summary table, the clauses counted are those of Cnut's code, not those of its sources. There are of course grey areas, especially between the 'possible influence' and 'unattributable' categories, so that the figures should not be seen as exact.

notice; like Andover, it was excerpted virtually in full.[437] Of legislation prior to his lifetime, Æthelstan's Grately code and the Alfred–Ine *domboc* were quarried for topics not fully addressed since, and Wulfstan was prepared to look as far back as as Wihtræd, even Æthelberht.[438]

At the same time, over a quarter of the code, and more than a third of its secular part, had no identifiable source. That there is no extant source does not guarantee that none ever existed. Were Æthelred's legislation not preserved in books closely connected with Wulfstan, there would be no indication (other than William of Malmesbury's expert eye) of how much Cnut owed to them (chapter 3, pp. 137–8). Lost codes, or lost parts of what is only fragmentarily extant, could lie behind much of what seems to be new. The laws on 'the king's rights' and on grave crimes feature *hamsocn*, an outrage that had not figured in acknowledged royal legislation since Edmund. It so happens, however, that it does crop up in one of the less ostensibly 'official' parts of 'IV Æthelred'; while Wulfstan had made a mention of *forsteal*, another 'king's plea', at Enham, and had preached to an apparently lawmaking assembly, almost certainly *not* the one that met at Winchester in 1020/1, about crimes so serious as to be 'unamendable (*botleas*)'.[439] Either or both the relevant sections of Cnut's code could be exploiting a fuller text of what went to make up 'IV Æthelred', and/or (say) those secular decrees of 1014 discarded from VIII Æthelred. Yet it has already been shown that the fresh departure of laws punishing sexual abuses most probably represent *in situ* additions by Wulfstan (above, p. 353). More will be discovered to the same effect by the end of this section.

Notice should meanwhile be taken of a part of the code that is very likely to embody a lost text. The thirty-eight 'clauses' beginning, 'this is the alleviation (*lihting*) whereby I wish to secure the whole people against what has hitherto oppressed them altogether too much' were marked off in various ways. They were inaugurated by an exceptional initial in most copies (above, p. 352). In the 'B' manuscript, not known for its scribe's constructive initiatives (above, p. 352, chapter 4, pp. 233–5,) the whole section was divided into clauses as the rest of the code was not. The first person singular was used in clauses '69 – 69:1' and six more times in the ensuing clauses, as otherwise only when the preface of Part II quoted Edgar.[440] 'Clause 69:1' itself began 'that, then, is first', just as if it were introductory. It is surely pertinent that a third of the code's unattributable clauses came from this part. Finally, there was a notable change of legislative tone at this point. The emphasis was no longer on what the subject should do for authority

---

437 The ignored clauses are I Atr 3 – 3:1; their subject is covered by II Cn 23 – 24, itself based on ?I Ew 1:2, II As 10, 12, ?III Em 5.

438 Wulfstan's interest in these codes is evident in *Grið* 6 – 8 (below, pp. 394–5); and though Liebermann adduces only Af 35 as an influence on II Cn 60, the association of weapons loaned to mischievous purpose with tying someone up is hardly less reminiscent of Abt 18 – 19, 24. In addition, *HomN* XXIV (p. 120 lns 8ff., an extension of *Hom.* XIII), is clearly based on Ine 2; see also below, n. 611.

439 II Cn 12, 62; II Em 6; IV Atr 4 – 4:1; V Atr 31 (VI 38); *HomN* LI, p. 274; and cf. II Cn 64.

440 II Cn 75, 76:3, 80, 82, 84 ('ic'), 80:1 ('ic', 'minne'); II Cn Pr. 1. 'Cl. 84' opens the code's concluding passage, 'Nu bidde ic georne', as against its *Polity* original's 'Nu lære we georne' (p. 259); but cf. the change of pronoun compared with the Æthelstan source in II 83 (above, n. 432), also the behaviour of *Cons. Cn* as against the Harley MS (above, n. 418, below, n. 658); this is why I prefer (unlike Dr Stafford, see next n.) to see these clauses as a summary of the code overall, not merely of this part of it.

but on what authority could do for its subjects. Its spirit was more like that of Cnut's 1020 or 1027 letters (or Edgar's *Wihtbordesstan* code) than the general run of early English law-making. Clearly, then, these clauses stand in some sense apart from all the others. It has been strongly argued that they constitute the original 'Coronation Charter' of Cnut; or (as is not an exclusive alternative) a residue of undertakings given by Æthelred when he returned to power in 1014, promising 'to be a gracious lord to [his people] and reform all the things which they hated': they might thus have corresponded to whatever Wulfstan's scribes jettisoned from 'VIII Æthelred' of that year.[441] There is something of a match between this section's content and that of the great charters from 1100 to 1215.[442] Cnut's regime began with legislative reconciliation. Incorporating the 'lihting' into his main code carried that programme forward.

Thus far, the Winchester code's sources. Table 5.4 also gives an overview of Wulfstan's codificatory strategy. The inspiration of Edgar's law had been acknowledged in 1018 and 1020. A first step was therefore to divide the code into ecclesiastical and secular components, like Andover. Thereafter the frame-work of the 1018 text was adopted so far as was compatible with the 'Church/State' divide.[443] None of it is omitted, apart from its exhortatory and often repetitive conclusion. But the Oxford code, as established above, was for some reason almost exclusively dependent on the Enham decrees. What Wulfstan now did was to slot into appropriate places the material from 1014 and Andover which gave the hard edge of sanctions to the more shapeless expostulations of 1008/1018. The 'Church's peace' was protected by compensations, its clergy by formal procedure, its dues by fines. Edgar's laws were quoted on the cost of not paying tithe, as they had been in 1014, and on the proper recipients of the revenues accruing.[444] Laws of 1014 that seemed more applicable to laymen were assigned, along with Edgar's own secular unit, to Part II. They were backed up by appropriate selections from Wulfstan's 'Peace of Edward and Guthrum', and by a near-complete text of I Æthelred.

But Andover's restricted range, and the relatively little that Wulfstan had yet said about secular matters (so far as is known), meant that II Cnut required an altogether fresher approach. There were a lot more passages with no evident source. Quotations were less likely to be verbal. The handling of Edgar's laws on courts was characteristic. His opening injunctions on justice were placed, as

---

441   Stafford, 'Laws of Cnut and Anglo-Saxon royal promises', pp. 176–82. As she says, the 'heriot' clauses, II Cn 70 – 71:5, central to the 'alleviation', suit circumstances late in Æthelred's reign, for reasons given by Brooks, 'Arms, Status and Warfare', pp. 89–90.

442   To add to the parallels offered by Stafford, pp. 178–9, 189–90, is a possible correspondence between II Cn 69:1, 'I command all my reeves that they provide for me lawfully from my own property, and sustain me from it, and that no one need supply anything to them for sustenance unless he himself wish'; and the principle underlying Magna Carta clause 25 (Holt, *Magna Carta*, pp. 336–7). It is no insuperable objection that II 75 – 76:3 raise seemingly marginal cases of a subject's vulnerability to overzealous justice (Lawson, 'Archbishop Wulfstan', p. 581, n. 6); inequitable prosecution by hyperactive royal reeves is well-attested at this period (V Atr ['D'] 32:4, *Sermo Lupi* lns 36–52); and Magna Carta has its own *minutiae*.

443   The exceptions are I Cn 18:1/Cn 1018 1:3, II Cn 73/Cn 1018 16 – 16:1; the first of which is the sort of admonitory theme that might be relocated anywhere, while the second is important evidence that Wulfstan envisaged the 'lihting' as an integral part of the code.

444   I Cn 8:2, 11 – 11:2: see table 5.4.

mediated by the Enham and Oxford codes, at the head of Part II. When Wulfstan had finished most of what Enham/Oxford had to offer, and had added in the clauses on the 'king's rights', the few laws of Edgar that did inspire the 1018 draft were recycled, but amplified by further Andover clauses in an arguably more logical order.[445] Gaps left by Edgar were filled by ordering that a triple summons in the hundred should precede recourse to the shire, and allowing licensed self-help if that too failed.[446] On the evidence of the Ely *libellus*, it was not this procedure that was new but its endorsement in royal law (chapter 3, pp. 155–6). Edgar had gone on to demand surety for all in general terms; Cnut had a detailed statement about membership of hundred and tithing, and the oath which (as argued in chapter 9) was integral to it. After the section on surety and obstructive lords, which blended I Æthelred with decrees more loosely based on those of earlier kings, Wulfstan had less guidance from accepted authorities. That did not stop him adding laws on sex and crime, and on equitable ways of curbing each. There was a drive towards comprehensiveness, towards provision for the gamut of human failings.

So where did this second climax in the story of Old English legislation leave the condition of early English law? Most obviously, the English Church was buttressed by a remarkably full system of legal support. There was corresponding reinforcement for the morality of a Christian society. Something like a complete judicial structure was in place, even if less was said than might have been about appeals to its royal fountainhead, or about the full configuration of surety (chapter 10, chapter 9). The preoccupation of earlier kings with theft and its ramifications was now matched by laws on other grave offences, varieties of adultery among them. Other features of interest include awareness of the government's own illegalities; of motive and exentuating circumstance (notoriously foreign to 'primitive' law-giving); and once more of Carolingian example. To single out only the last: Cnut had a law like one of Charlemagne's that not only demanded death for deserters from a campaign, but insisted too that possessors of privileged property (English bookland, Frankish 'beneficium principis') forfeit it to the king. Perjury had been addressed by several of Cnut's forerunners. Now, for the first time, penalties were to include loss of the hand that by implication had touched the relics thus traduced; and such had been the Carolingian sanction since 779.[447]

Yet Cnut's laws were not a complete codification of pre-existing law. The most surprising absentee is anything about restraint of feud (above, pp. 283, 311–12). Cnut did say that perpetrators of 'mord' were to be handed over to their victim's kin, their own kin being obviously unable to help. But whatever 'mord' meant, it was not 'normal' homicide (chapter 9). Edmund's second code is generally conspicuous for its lack of effect. One might question that Wulfstan even knew it, except that it was apparently meant to supplement the London synod, which

---

445   II Cn 15:1 – 18:1, and see table 5.4; II 15:1a is a 'Danelaw rider' of the sort which Wulfstan now often sought to include, and which fitted the context of laws on variable 'king's rights'.
446   II Cn 19 – 19:2.
447   II Cn 77 – 77:1, *Cap.* 74:4–5 (= *Ans.* iii 70–1); II Cn 36, *Cap.* 20:10, 44:11 (= *Ans.* iii 10), 52:4, 139:10 (= *Ans.* iv 22), 273:9 (citing *Ans.* iii 10). See chapter 13.

he did include in his collections (above, pp. 309, 311).[448] More to the point, he did countenance some of the fundamentals of feud. In laws of 1014 that were assumed bodily into Cnut's code, he required that the kin of a cleric charged with homicide 'may (*moton*) bear the feud with him or compensate for it'; while the 'cloistered monk' should neither receive nor pay 'feud-money', in that 'he departs from his kin-law when he submits to rule-law' – the implication being that clerics not subject to 'regollage' *were* liable to 'mæglage'.[449] *Mæglage* would then apply *a fortiori* to laymen, though this was in apparent contradiction of Edmund's concession that kinsmen could opt out of bloodfeud liabilities (chapter 9). Even had Wulfstan not taken this line, he might have needed more than his formidable rhetorical powers to persuade his new royal master amid his Scandinavian entourage of the illegitimacy of kin-vengeance. Other silences may be inherent in the nature of the record. Maitland was plunged into his deepest error by supposing that Cnut's list encompassed all the 'pleas of the crown'. In fact, it isolated only those pleas that might potentially be alienated to favoured benefi-ciaries, not the larger and more important number that might *not* (chapter 10).[450] Even if Wulfstan and Cnut aimed for something like a plenary digest of Englishmen's obligations under the law, their efforts were limited by the tendency of 'barbarian' law to pick out points of contention (chapter 2, p. 105).

As for the code's place in the sequence of Wulfstan's writings, table 5.4 may be allowed to speak for itself. It is of course not impossible that those of Cnut's laws that seem least Wulfstanian were contributed by fellow-members of the king's council. But even the 'alleviatory' clauses, of which this looks most likely, were introduced by the unmissable Wulfstanism 'ealles to swyðe'.[451] Because nothing is (yet) known to be from Wulfstan's pen that is not more or less overtly ecclesiastical in interest, it remains uncertain whether he can be credited with Cnut's most resolutely secular decrees. One thing does seem sure. The framework of the code was set by Andover and Oxford. Wulfstan certainly wrote all the second, and did so explicitly in Edgar's name. The beginning and end of the Winchester code's two parts rehearsed other works by the archbishop. The vision thereby encapsulated is securely his.

Nor is there much doubt that this was among the last of his writings. The editor of his homilies, who was confident that these could be set apart from his legisla-tive output (chapter 4, p. 196), also thought that they followed leads given by 'the Witan'.[452] Yet it is barely imaginable that *every* echo of Cnut's code in his homilies or *Institutes of Polity* was sounded after its promulgation a mere twenty-nine (or just as probably seventeen) months before his death.[453] It was argued in

448   Nonetheless, it is curious that Wulfstan never positively echoes any of the laws making up the 'Edward/Edmund' group (above, pp. 232, 242, 248), except I Em and his own EGu.

449   I Cn 5:2b-d, VIII Atr 23 – 25; Wulfstan may have taken his inspiration here from the 'Dialogue of Ecgberht' his distinguished predecessor at York (*Councils*, ed. Haddan and Stubbs, pp. 408–9), as this very passage appears in his 'Canon Collection' (table 4.4).

450   II Cn 12 – 15.

451   II Cn 69.

452   *Hom.*, pp. 341, 36–9, etc. For my attempt at a detailed reconstruction of Wulfstanian chronology, see above, n. 368; apart from the specific question of ecclesiastical privilege, my main argument is that he was a great deal more prone to expand and elaborate his views than to prune or condense them.

453   The strongest candidate for composition at the very close of Wulfstan's life is the final edition of

the previous section that homily and law tended to merge into each other as Wulfstan's work went on, and as much because homilies came to make legal demands as because laws gave voice to homiletic admonition. Table 5.4 creates an irresistible impression that Wulfstan here brought together into the most solemn and binding possible form every concern that had risen to the top of his mind and nib of his pen over his previous dozen years of pondering the destinies of English society under God. That is why more reference was made to his homilies as well as to his unofficial tracts and *Polity*. The question whether the code gives an entirely idealized impression of Cnut's regime can therefore be rephrased.[454] However defective as a picture of legal and political reality, it consummated Wulfstan's campaign to organize the sort of society he was sure that the English kingdom had to be. Having started out in 1008 and 1009 with a reaction to gathering crisis that hardly advanced on his pulpit response to the prospect of a millennial Apocalypse (chapter 6, pp. 451–3), he came to recognize in the potentially radical disruption of 1016 the possibility of a fresh start upon old foundations. His code for Cnut was thus a blend of law as Anglo-Saxons now understood it with techniques of persuasion that had took an increasingly legal form in his later work. Whether or not he had contrived a real code of early English law, he had certainly codified his own ideas.

'If [Cnut] is not the greatest legislator of the eleventh century, we must go as far as Barcelona to find his peer'.[455] As so often with this master of irony, one cannot know how much of a smile was playing around Maitland's eyes as he issued his verdict. Actually, it now seems certain that Catalonia's *Usatges* were essentially the creation of twelfth-century rulers, and they drew on deeply-laid traditions of Iberian *Lex Scripta* that were half a world away from the context in which English law-makers had to work.[456] In any event, the Winchester code does deserve to rank among the most sophisticated legislative statements of post-Roman Europe. It certainly merits more attention than it has often had from historians.[457] One lead to follow is its importance for those who sought to piece together a law for England in the aftermath of the blast of 1066. For Northumbria's rebels the year before, it possessed the significance that Edgar's law had had after the Danish conquest (chapter 3, pp. 131–3). It dominated every essay in legislative reconstruction over the century that ensued.[458] Yet it is the end of a story as much as the beginning of a new one. After Cnut came a complete break. In eleventh-century England, as four hundred years before, or for that matter in Merovingian and Carolingian Francia, the legislative flow petered out. That Cnut and Wulfstan did their work too well can only be part of the expla-

---

Polity in Bodl. Junius 121, in that it is uncertain that the collection in this MS was assembled by the arch-bishop himself: ed. Jost, pp. 16–34.

454   Cf. Lawson, 'Archbishop Wulfstan', e.g. p. 580.

455   PM I, p. 20.

456   See now the long and judicious introduction by Kagay to his 1994 translation, especially the historiographical review, pp. 51–7.

457   Among warmer assessments was that of Freeman, *Norman Conquest* I, pp. 434–6 – even if his heartiest approval went to the law allowing 'every man to hunt on his own land'.

458   On all this, see Hudson, 'Administration, Family and Perceptions of the Past: Appendix', pp. 94–8; also O'Brien, 'Propaganda, Forgery and the Orality of English Law', and chapter 14.

nation. It was not because Justinian's *Corpus Iuris* achieved what he intended that it found so few imitators during Byzantium's next two centuries (chapter 2, p. 36). Cnut's was almost all that a sub-Roman code could be. But codifying the law did not necessarily fill the bill of those who had to live and enforce it.

9   Anonymous Codes

Cnut's code set a seal on Old English royal legislation. But it may surprise those who have only a nodding acquaintance with Anglo-Saxon law that 20 per cent of the published corpus comprises anonymous, so at first sight unofficial, materials.[459] Except when masquerading as royal law, they have seldom been edited and even less often translated; nor is their nature well understood. Before examining them piecemeal, something should be said of their common characteristics.

Anonymity is by no means alone among these. In several cases, it could indeed be a coincidental side-effect of their conditions of survival. Only the preservation of its Latin version secured 'official' status for V/VI Æthelred (above, pp. 333–4). Conversely, it is merely a compound of codicological chance and editorial caprice that has bestowed the mask of 'officialdom' on *Hundred* or the early clauses of 'IV Æthelred'. Another way of making the point is to say that copiers of these texts often did not intend that they be seen as distinct, let alone anonymous. They were passed down in collections of mostly royal law. Their most important shared feature is in fact the narrowness of their transmission; by which is meant not so much that 'Anonymous' codes are extant in few manuscripts, as that they rarely appear in more than one textual family. Not only does that tend to confirm their 'unofficial' origin.[460] It also ensures that nothing is on hand to counterbalance an anonymity that might derive from scribal quirks. The following analysis thus begins with short and/or fragmentary texts that look most likely to have been conceived as elements in an 'official' record. It then moves through articles of which this may or may not be true, and it finishes with tracts that leave the strongest sense of being self-contained. Within these categories, the order adopted is chronological so far as that is ascertainable; when it is not, arrangement is determined by linkage in manuscript presentation or in subject-matter.[461]

---

459   Nearly 10,000 out of about 48,000 words: once again using Dr Schwyter's word-counts (see n. 1), and including among 'anonymous'/ 'unofficial' texts EGu, *Hu.*, IV Atr 1 – 4:2 (see below), but not the bulky ordeal or excommunication rituals (*Gesetze* I, pp. 401–41), nor *Can. Eg.* or 'Episcopus' (see nn. 579, 584 below).
460   Royal codes with narrow transmissions tend to belong to the more 'informal' category tentatively isolated above (e.g. IV Eg).
461   Liebermann's order was sometimes taken from Schmid but mostly based on chronology as he perceived it; his view depended heavily on the elusive criteria of philology, and has of course been seriously vitiated by the discovery of Wulfstan's overwhelming presence in 'official' and 'unofficial' classes alike. However, for the usual reasons, I retain Liebermann's titles, abbreviations and textual divisions. Inverted commas around 'official' and 'unofficial' should henceforth be taken as read.

(i) Be Blaserum

It may help to fix perspectives to quote what is quite possibly the earliest anonymous text in full:[462]

> We declared about incendiaries and underhand killings that the oath be deepened threefold and the ordeal-iron enlarged to a weight of three pounds. And the person charged is to go himself to the ordeal, and the accuser to have a choice between water-ordeal and iron-ordeal, whichever he prefer. If he cannot produce the oath and so be guilty (*ful*), let it be in the judgement of the most senior men that belong to the borough whether he have life or not.

The best way to reckon with this text is to say that, had it cropped up in the midst of Æthelstan's Grately code, it would not look a whit out of place.[463] 'We cwædon' is normal as an introductory phrase for Grately, but hardly occurs beyond the span of time between Alfred's Guthrum treaty and Edmund's code on bloodfeud (above, pp. 289, 303). The derogatory word 'ful' for guilty was another coinage that was common under Æthelstan, but then dropped out, though revived early in Æthelred's series.[464] Especially interesting, the '*yldeste men* that belong to the borough' recur in the Grately code.[465] Besides, the very topics of underhand killing and arson were covered in successive Grately laws, and just when verbal parallels to *Be Blaserum* were closest.[466] This was also where Æthelstan showed special interest in the triple oath/ordeal: it too was a theme not revived (*Hundred* aside) until the early Æthelred codes, which is where one otherwise hears of an accuser's choice of water and iron ordeals.[467] Yet Æthelstan did *not* leave it to the discretion of 'senior men that belong to the borough' whether those convicted by due process 'have life or not'. Those who failed a triple ordeal against charges of 'morþ' or arson were to be imprisoned for 120 days, then redeemed by their kin, giving surety that they would in future desist, and those unable even to attempt denial were to be executed outright.[468] *Be Blaserum* can hardly, then, be a fragment of Grately itself. The most economical

---

462   This is one of the few translated texts: I follow the *Laws* (At) rendition, though with more changes than needed when taking a lead from *EHD I*. For reasons discussed in chapter 9, I do not translate 'morþslyht' as 'secret killing', but seek to retain an element of the furtiveness that must have been involved in killings out of reach of immediate reprisal.

463   This was acknowledged by Liebermann, who also made most of the points that follow, *Gesetze* III, p. 228 (3–5); Thorpe, *Ancient Laws*, p. 95, already reached this conclusion, to the extent of printing it as V (his 'IV') As 6 (p. 95).

464   II Ew 4, II As 4, 5, 6:1, 7, 14:1, 19, VI As 1:1–2,4, 9; I Atr 1:5, 2, 4 (echoed by II Cn 30:3b,4, 32, 33), III Atr 4:1, 7:1, 8. Note that except when quoting I Atr, Wulfstan uses the word to rather different effect, EGu 11, VI Atr 28:2, I Cn 24.

465   II As 20:1,4; though again otherwise (more or less) in the famous III Atr 3:1.

466   II As 6, 6:2.

467   II As 4, 5, 6:1, (7), note also II 23:1 ('ysenordal'); *Hu*. 9; I Atr 1:1,4/II Cn 30:1,3,3a, III Atr 3:4, 6, 7; this theme did interest Wulfstan too, though he usually preferred to speak of 'suit (*sp(r)æce*)' and 'clearance (*lad*)', and his targets tend to differ: VIII Atr 19 – 21/I Cn 5 – 5:2, VIII Atr 27:1/II Cn 41:1; V Atr 30/VI 37/II Cn 8:2, etc.

468   II As 6 – 6:2 (accepting that 'þæs ilcan ryhtes' of 6:2 means that incendiaries are covered by the terms of 6:1).

hypothesis would be that 'those who belong to the borough', who were elsewhere in the code instructed on handling the lawless, were here reformulating its commands at ground level.

The manuscript context of this piece is best discussed after reviewing those with which it is most intimately associated (below, pp. 369–70, 378–9). But it can be said now that in three of its four textual witnesses it followed immediately upon the Alfred–Ine *domboc*, and that in all four, it is at once followed in turn by *Forfang*. Now, the associations of *Forfang* are largely with laws best dated to the late Edgar/early Æthelred period (below, pp. 369–70). The *Forfang* coupling therefore recalls the similarities between *Be Blaserum* and the Woodstock and Wantage codes. An alternative to the hypothetical role of officials seeking to implement Grately would be servants of Æthelred adapting its message to their own purposes. What each hypothesis has in common is local initiative rather than central guidance. It is not easy to imagine what else could have spawned something so pertinent yet so mundane.

(ii) Romscot

This is a tract of just twenty-four words which commanded payment of 'Rome money' before noon on St Peter's Day after midsummer.[469] Disobedience entailed a sixty shilling fine and twelvefold multiplication of the sum due. The piece's genesis is easily reconstructed. The sixty shilling/twelvefold restitution penalty was demanded by Ine for non-payment of Church-scot, and his law was verbally quoted here.[470] The piece was inserted between the rubrics and text of Alfred–Ine in the post-1050 part of Cotton Nero A.i (chapter 4, p. 227). An adaptation of Ine's Church-scot law to 'Rome-money' must have been made in the margin, then given a more prominent position by the Nero scribe or his exemplar. Now, Edgar, the first king known for sure to have legislated on this point (above, pp. 309, 316), stipulated a much stiffer penalty for non-compliance: the fine was doubled, restitution multiplied by thirty not twelve, and guilty parties had to get the money to Rome themselves; sanctions were raised afresh for repeated offences, culminating in total forfeiture.[471] An author for *Romscot* who wrote after Edgar's time, and who ignored something so much better suited to his purpose, must have inhabited a singularly well-fortified ivory tower. The logical deduction is that the tract predates 959.[472] At all events, the role of private enterprise seems certain.

---

469   Liebermann translates 'ær undern' as 'vor mittag'; 9 a.m. seems another possibility, Bosworth/ Toller *s.v.*

470   Ine 4: ' ... sin agifene be sce ... LX scill. 7 be XIIfealdum agife þone ... '. The coinage 'Romscot' may itself be inspired by Ine, in that it is not otherwise attested before 1066, being confined to *Inst. Cn* I 9, to a late text of Hn 11:3 and to ECf retr. 10 (the 'Rompenincg' of *Romscot* 2 recurs in *Northu* 57:1, and Andrew Horn's *Quadripartitus* MS (chapter 4, pp. 237–8) of II Eg 4). Normal preconquest (i.e. Wulfstan) usage was 'Romfeoh': Liebermann, *Gesetze* II, p. 187.

471   II Eg 4:1–3 (payment of 'thirty pence' would mean multiplication by thirty if the sum originally due was one penny, as it certainly was later). Wulfstan allowed restitution to be made to Rome without going in person (VIII Atr 10:1, *HomN* LXI, p. 311, cf. Keynes, 'Additions in Old English', nn. 168, 176); in I Cn 9:1, it goes no further than the bishop (cf. *HomN* XXIII, p. 116).

472   The one feasible alternative would be composition long after Edgar's time, in fact after the Conquest.

Peter's Pence may have been been obligatory enough before Edgar formally decreed it for an equation with Church-scot to occur to a government servant or his *amanuensis*. But a royal pronouncement on the point is unlikely to have occupied so marginal a place in the record as this.

(iii) Forfang (and 'II Æthelred 8 – 9:4')

Forfang, a slightly longer text than the two considered so far, concerns rewards for retrieving stolen property, probably through the formal process of 'attachment'.[473] The opening clause, as Liebermann came to acknowledge after printing it as '1', is merely a summary of what follows.[474] The gist is that 'wise men have ordained (*witan habbað geræedd*)' that the reward is to be fifteen pence, whether for men (i.e. runaways) or horses, throughout the whole land, regardless of the number of shires traversed in the search. It had once been the case that rewards were proportionate to the distances involved, and paid at the rate of one penny for every shilling's worth of goods stolen, but it was now thought unfair to burden the 'small man' with the cost of an excessive reward as well as extended travel. Pursuit of stolen goods worried most early English law-makers, but few of them cast much light on rewards. Still, a hard look between the lines of Æthelstan's peace-guild rules implies that rewards were aligned with values, and a one penny/one shilling ratio would there yield a reward of over fifteen pence.[475] In other words, the policy decreed by *Forfang* was not that of Æthelstan's reign. As it happens, changes with much the same motives were under way in the 'II Æthelred Appendix' (above, pp. 321, 325–6): once upon a time (the phrase is 'Hwilon stod', as in *Forfang*), vouchings to warranty would be switched, after a triple summons at the home of an aggrieved party, to that of the person vouched. But 'geræddan witan' (as in *Forfang*) that it would be fairer to keep the entire hearing wherever the attachment began, since weaker brethren should not face the trouble of distant travel.[476] The tract's concern, that in an owner's interests rewards do not vary with the number of shires involved, fits nicely with the Appendix's extension of a suitor's time-limit by a week for every shire between him and his opponent.[477] A number of

---

That proposition is supported by aspects of its language, even including the very word 'Romscot' (see n. 470; it was linguistic considerations that led Liebermann to locate it among the latest of his corpus: *Gesetze* III, p. 267). But it is palaeographically improbable; cf. Torkar, *Altenglische Übersetzung*, pp. 183–5. Loyn, 'Peter's Pence', p. 241 is 'tempted to associate this curious interpolation' with the ups and downs of Anglo-papal relations under the Conqueror, but has no more to say of it in his illuminating discussion.

473 Bosworth/Toller, *s.v.*, translate the tract almost in full. Cf. *Leis Wl* 5, and S 1041 (an Osbert de Clare forgery for Westminster).

474 *Gesetze* III, pp. 228–9 (6): a handsome retraction.

475 VI As 3 – 8:8, especially 6:1–3, 7: sums are mostly 'ceapgild' (compensations for loss), horse and slave being reckoned at 'half a pound' (120 pence, or 30 (London, Mercian) or 24 (W. Saxon) shillings); rewards depending on costs incurred are envisaged in VI 7.

476 II Atr 9; Liebermann naturally spotted these parallels, *Gesetze* III, p. 228 (5), but he did not press their significance.

477 *Forf.* 2, II Atr 8:3.

Forfang words recur in the Appendix, and also in Edgar's *Wihtbordesstan* code, but nowhere else in Anglo-Saxon law.[478] The implication of all this is that *Forfang* was part of the movement that produced the Appendix, perhaps indeed of the same text.

A further possibility then arises. Almost everything about the phrasing and structure of the II Æthelred Appendix is redolent of royal law. Its tendency to proffer philosophical observations on the justice of what is decreed, was marked in *Forfang*, and already in 'IV Edgar'.[479] There must be a case that Appendix and *Forfang* came from an official code of early in Æthelred's time or late in Edgar's. In fact, the subject matter of both was close to that of the secular clauses in the *Wihtbordesstan* code, and this did mention more detailed measures taken for English England, even hinting that they included rewards for those helping to nail crime.[480] Notwithstanding the hope of banishing mistier speculations to other parts of this book, it may be time to face the possibility that the Appendix and *Forfang* were both sherds of the lost English counterpart to 'IV Edgar', one ghastly outcome of which was perhaps exposed by Lantfred's *Miracula* of St Swithun (chapter 3, pp. 125–7). That said, the point for present purposes is that both are fragments: they have been carved out of a larger body by a hand that can hardly have belonged to the larger's body's progenitor.

The transmission of *Forfang*, like that of the intimately related *Be Blaserum* is best investigated when looking at *Hundred*, the third member of this textual trio. But it is relevant here that 'H' broke off after the first (summary) clause. Since it is not a bit likely that Rochester's scribe would have omitted the rest of *Forfang* or *Hundred*, the exemplar which persuaded him that *Be Blaserum* and *Forfang* pertained to Alfred's law-book (chapter 4, p. 249) must already have been truncated. A possible model of this text's prehistory is thus that its 'clause 1' summary was made when it was first lifted from its parent source, presumably when it and the other texts were added to the *domboc*. One of the resulting Alfred-Ine manuscripts then dispensed, deliberately or otherwise, with all of *Forfang* except its introduction, and the ensuing *Hundred*. That manuscript was what reached the Rochester scribe.

478   Particularly striking is 'standan' meaning 'to be valid [law]', *Forf.* 3, II Atr 9, with IV Eg 1:6, 2, 2:1–1a, 12, 15, though this is also Wulfstan usage in II Cn 34, 62, 65, *Grið* 4, 9, 13 (and further in *Rect.* 2, 3, 4:4, 6, 6:1, which may be significant in the light of the argument about the II Atr – Rect. mini-collection's origins, chapter 4, pp. 232–3). See also *Forf.* 2 'swince', II Atr 9, 9:1 'swencte', 'swunce', 'swence'; *Forf.* 3:1, IV Eg 14 'ahret' (from 'ahreddan', a word limited in a specialized legal sense to LS 25); and the in this context unusual uses of 'smalon' (*Forf.* 1, IV Eg 5), and 'æfre' (*Forf.* 1, II Atr 8:4, 9). A notable common feature of Appendix and IV Eg is '*cennan*, bring forth, declare' (IV Eg 10, 11, II Atr 8, 8:2,3, 9, 9:2,4): though suited to a number of possible contexts, the only other Anglo-Saxon legislator to use it was Wi 17, 22.

479   *Forf.* 2, 3:2; IV Eg 1:1–3, 2:2; earlier self-justifications (e.g. above, pp. 287, 302) tended to go no further than the needs of the 'peace', and Wulfstan's edificatory rationalisations are of a different species, though perhaps of the same *genus*.

480   IV Eg 2:1a, 14.

(iv) 'IV Æthelred 1 – 4:2'

'IV Æthelred' as it stands began by stating that Aldersgate and Cripplegate were (past tense) in the charge of guards. It then listed the rules governing the payment of toll at Billingsgate, while 'a merchant who came to the bridge with a boatload of fish gave a halfpenny [obol!] in toll, and for a larger ship a penny'. Special arrangements were on offer to dealers from itemized parts of northern Europe; notably 'emperor's men', who 'were worthy of the same good laws as ourselves', though not of whatever might give them a market advantage.[481] The past tense was retained throughout. Then came four clauses about procedure to be followed in charges of withholding toll, couched as subjunctive conditionals; and thereafter a pronouncement ('diximus') about the offences 'inside the port' of *hamsocn*, assault on the 'king's road', or resorting to arms before seeking justice more formally. Serious as these infringements of the king's peace were, the last clause of the section observes that 'if [the offender] care for the friendship of the port itself, let him pay us thirty shillings compensation [the 'hundred fine', chapter 10] if the king allow it to us'.[482]

The well-honed vision of Richardson and Sayles detected here something uncommonly like the borough customs that tend to precede the 'terra regis' in Domesday Book surveys of individual counties: 'it shows the king directing an enquiry … very much like the enquiries held by the Domesday commissioners … If chance were to bring [the missing London part of Domesday] to light, we should not be surprised to find there entries such as these replies'.[483] Among points of resemblance is the way that its accounts of revenue from renders are rounded off by a review of the profits to the king and others from particular pleas.[484] Even if the parallel be rejected, there is no disputing that the voice in these clauses was that of London's citzens, whose share of judicial profits depended on royal favour. This case therefore seems unusually clear-cut. A statement of current London customs was harnessed to royal mintage laws whose relevance to urban government is obvious. It could have been done by officials in London itself; or (above, pp. 322–3) by someone whose responsibility for borough administration extended as far as the Danish Midlands. It can hardly have been central government work.

(v) Pax, Walreaf

Like the 'IV Æthelred' *ensemble*, the mini-codes *Pax* and *Walreaf* were treated as extensions of 'III Æthelred' by *Quadripartitus*. They can reasonably be taken

---

481   IV Atr 1, 2, 2:4,8–10.
482   IV Atr 4 – 4:2.
483   Richardson and Sayles, *Law and Legislation*, p. 28; cf. Campbell, 'Observations on English Government', p. 50 (166).
484   E.g. *DB* i 1ab, *Kent* D:1–5, 12–24 (Dover); i 172a, *Worcestershire* C:1–2, 4–5; i 238a, *Warwickshire* B:3–6; cf. chapter 12.

as a pair. It may have been nothing more than the codicological priorities of *Textus Roffensis* that ever split them up (chapter 4, pp. 247–8). *Pax* fixed the limit of the king's 'griŏ' from the 'gatehouse (*burhgeate*)' where he was seated, down to the smallest 'shaftment' and barley-grain.[485] *Walreaf* defined corpse-robbery as the act of a '*niŏing* (outlaw)', to be refuted by an oath of forty-eight 'thegns'. 'Griŏ' and 'niŏing' are each Scandinavianisms of the type that litter the text of III Æthelred (above, pp. 327–9). The Wantage code's early clauses were about fines for breach of the peace of the king and of other parties. Exact delimitation of royal peace was a long-term concern in northern England.[486] And if nothing in the archaeological record implies that grave-robbers were a particular curse of Danelaw life, the Wantage demand that accusations of feeding a man who 'has broken our lord's peace' be cleared with 'three twelves' match the *Walreaf* stipulation that this outlaw's deed be answered with an oath of forty-eight.[487] In short, *Pax* and *Walreaf* were anything but out of place in the III Æthelred context where *Quadripartitus* put them. They could well have been added on to the text which the king's agents took northwards with them from his Wantage Council. It will be recalled that several clauses in the supposedly main body of the Wantage code itself give exactly this impression of *addenda* (above, pp. 326–7).

(vi) Ymb Æwbricas

The last of the texts in the class of those most likely to have been conceived as supplements to official legislation came to light only in Nowell's transcript of Cotton Otho B.xi (chapter 4, pp. 175–6). It was thus unknown to Liebermann and has never been translated. It too should therefore be quoted *in extenso*:[488]

> And on your question about adulterers, whether with nuns or lay women, the forfeited woman and man (*wæpned*) go respectively to the bishopric with her third, and to the lord – whether it be bookland or folkland, whether of the king himself or of any man (*sie swa bocland swa folcland swaþer hit sie cyninges selfes ge ælces monnes*) – he goes with his two parts (*mid his twæde*) to his lord if he has wicked intercourse, and they are both forfeit.

This brief but valuable text was evidently added on to the 'Ot' copy of the Alfred–Ine law-book. The scribe's concern to make it part of the *domboc* is reflected in Nowell's failure to mark a break between it and what had gone before (or Wanley's to notice it at all). As there is no sign of it in the 'Parker' manuscript from which Ot was taken (chapter 4, pp. 174–5), it must have been added by the scribe at about the time he penned Alfred–Ine. Yet the text can

---

485　For 'scæftamunda' as a linear measurement, cf. Bosworth/Toller *s.v.* 'sceaft', Liebermann, 'Sachglossar', *Gesetze* II, p. 491 (12).
486　Cf. *English Lawsuits*, ed. van Caenegem, 172, and the Ripon and Beverley forgeries, S 451, 456–7.
487　III Atr 13. Moreover, might the Wantage provision that corpses of executed thieves could be 'taken up' [*sc.* from unconsecrated ground] if subsequently cleared by their kinsmen (III 7 – 7:1), conceivably have been construed as a licence for unwarranted interference with interments? See further chapter 9.
488　It was printed by Flower, 'Text of the Burghal Hidage', p. 62.

hardly have originated there. It is obviously a fragment from a letter or treatise, confronting a recipient's doubts about more topics than illicit sex.[489] One linguistic feature, '*twæde*, two-thirds', suggests that the piece was composed some while before it was entered in the manuscript.[490] On the other hand, fornication surfaced as a particularly 'live' issue for Anglo-Saxon law-makers at just the time when the passage was copied out. It was prominent in the laws that Wulfstan drafted, and the closest to an echo of *Ymb Æwbricas* is in his 'Peace of Edward and Guthrum'.[491] Prosecutions for sexual malfeasance (by women, naturally) were also the order of that day.[492] Perhaps the best reconstruction is that the excerpt was made at the manuscript's early-eleventh-century date, but the work from which it was taken was written two or three generations before, say at the time when such offences were stigmatized by Edmund's London council.[493] If the sanctions it stipulated were already established norms, penalties for fornication had somehow developed beyond the point where Alfred left them, but without becoming widely enough known to raise no questions. They finally appeared in an official record on the initiative of a scribe or his judicially involved director. They were never part of any surviving formal legislation.

(vii) Ordal

Ordal is the first of three texts of which it is impossible to say whether they are excerpts of official legislation, amplifications of a current code by someone active in law enforcement, or independent treatises by a person with such experience. It was a detailed account of the administration of the ordeals of hot water and hot iron. It was preserved in textually related versions by 'H' and Q.[494] The former put it in the space between the end of *Forfang* and the start of the Grately code at the top of the next leaf (chapter 4, pp. 246, 249). In the latter, it was usually at the end of the Æthelstan section; however, the R manuscript slotted it in right after Grately's law on the conduct of ordeals.[495] These associations may not be fortuitous. The Grately code gave the first and fullest official statement on ordeal procedure in the Anglo-Saxon corpus.[496]

---

489 A possible parallel is Ælfric's Pastoral Letter II 154–6 (*Councils*, ed. Whitelock, 46, pp. 290–1) but it was not phrased in quite this way, addressed as it was to priests (plural). A closer parallel is the anonymous 'Brother Edward' letter (chapter 4, n. 73).

490 As pointed out to me by Professor Torkar: the form appears in Ine 23, in 'Bald's Leechbook' (chapter 4, p. 178), and in S 1437, a doubtfully contemporary but probably early vernacular record of a dispute in 825 (LS15). (I am also grateful to Professor Godden for advice about this.)

491 EGu 4; cf. V Atr 10 (VI 11 – 12:2), Cn 1018 11:3 – 12:4, I Cn 6:3 – 7:3, II 50 – 55; and chapter 8.

492 LS 68, 70, 73; also 78 (a later charge, and levelled at a man).

493 I Em 4.

494 They have a shared textual flaw in *Ord.* 1b (*Gesetze* III, p. 226 (1)); Liebermann's whole analysis is much to the point.

495 It is interesting that the Q/H relationship here, with Q the superior text, reflects the pattern of 'VI Æthelstan' (above, pp. 296–7). Note too (chapter 4, n. 272), the possibility that *Ord.* once followed II As in B.

496 II As 23 – 23:2; like *Blas.*, *Ord.* was translated in an appendix to *Laws* (At); but in taking his text solely from H, he omitted *Ord.* 5 – 5:1.

Ordal was on the whole more specific about the ordeal ritual itself: only he who was to take an ordeal and the priest (with whom, according to Æthelstan, he had spent the previous three days) were to enter the church after the fire has been lit; the distance that a hot iron must be carried was specified; in hot water ordeals, the hand was to be plunged in to the depth of wrist or elbow, depending on whether the ordeal was 'single' or 'triple'; supporters of defendant and plaintiff who attend the ordeal in equal numbers should themselves have fasted and abstained from their wives, and so on; finally, the king's 120 shilling 'disobedience fine' was payable were any rules broken. On the one hand, then, *Ordal* was a vernacular version of the rubrics which accompany Latin ordeal liturgies, and which were not otherwise translated (as the prayers themselves in the 'Durham Ritual' were).[497] On the other, and more particularly, it filled gaps left by Grately itself: only the point that three days were allowed for an accused's hand to heal was common to both.

The text reads like an excerpt: it begins 'And', as *Ymb Æwbricas* opens '7'. It also shares phrases with Æthelstan's ordeal laws: 'Godes bebode 7 ðæs arcebiscopes', 'on ægðre [naþre] healfe', 'beo ðæt ordal forad'.[498] The vocabulary is of Æthelstan's period.[499] The evidence is thus comptatible with either of two propositions: a later session of the Grately council added details not fully integrated even into the Wulfhelm collection that seems to underlie the Q assemblage (above, pp. 294–300); or an ordeal administrator wrote an extended gloss on Æthelstan's law, which he deliberately modelled on the style of the original, and which he intended for consultation alongside it. If an imitative gloss, it need not have been composed near the time of Grately; unlike *Be Blaserum*, it has one post-950 symptom in the word 'lage'.[500] The most that one can sensibly say is that *Ordal* seemed an apposite commentary on the conduct of ordeals to someone who knew what he was talking about.

(viii) Wergeld

Wergeld is the first among the anonymous codes so far reviewed to come from the Edward-Edmund group common to 'B', 'H' and Q.[501] It followed *Wifmannes Beweddung* in B and Q, but in H it was so fully integrated into 'Edward and Guthrum' that the transition was missed by a scribe who was usually sensitive to the end of one text and the beginning of another (chapter 4, pp. 247–8). In content, its associations lie as clearly with Edmund's bloodfeud edict as do those of *Be Blaserum* or *Ordal* with II Æthelstan. The best way to bring this out is to

---

497   *Durham Collectar*, ed. Correa, pp. 216–18, 225–7; *Durham Ritual*, ed. Brown, pp. 15, 37–9; *Gesetze* I, pp. 409–12, 413–15; also Dumville, *Liturgy*, pp. 129–30; and more detailed discussion in chapter 8.
498   *Ord.* 1, 4, 6, II As 23:2; 'on twa healfa' is also in VI As 8:3.
499   E.g. 'gemetan = measure off', *Ord.* 1a, I As Pr.; even 'ful', *Ord.* 5:2 and see n. 464 above.
500   *Ord.* 6.
501   See Liebermann's comments, *Gesetze* III, p. 231 (1, 4).

Table 5.5   II Edmund and *Wergeld* compared

II Em 1, 7–7:3	Wergeld
	Twelfhyndes mannes wer is twelf hund scyllinga. Twyhyndes mannes wer is twa hund scill'.
Gif hwa heononforð ænigne man ofslea ðæt he wege sylf ða fæhþe butan he hy mid freonda fylste binnan twelf monðum forgylde be	*Gif man ofslægen weorðe,*
fullan were swa boren swa he sy ... Witan scylan fæhðe sectan.	*gylde hine man swa he geboren sy.*
Ærest æfter folcrihte slaga sceal his forspecan on hand syllan 7 se forspeca magum þæt se slaga wylle	*7 riht is ðæt se slaga*
betan wið mæge. Ðonne syððan gebyreð þæt man sylle ðæs slagan forspecan on hand ðæt se slaga mote mid griðe nyr 7 sylf wæres weddian. Ðonne he ðæs beweddod	*siððan*
hæbbe ðonne finde he ðærto wærborh.	*he weres beweddod hæbbe finde ðærto wærborh be þam ðe ðærto gebyrige, ðæt is æt twelfhyndum were gebyriað twelf men to werborge, VIII fæderenmægðe 7 IIII medrenmægðe.*
Ðonne ðæt gedon sy ðonne rære man cyninges munde.	*Ðonne ðæt gedon sy ðonne rære man cyninges munde, ðæt is ðæt hy ealle gemænum handum of ægðere mægðe on anum wæpne ðam semende syllan þæt cyninges mund stande.*
Of ðæm dæge on XXI nihton gylde man healsfang,	*Of ðam dæge on XXI nihtan gylde man CXX scll' to healsfang æt twelfhyndum were. Healsfang gebyreð bearnum broðrum 7 fæderan, ne gebyreð nanum mæge þæt feoh bute ðam ðe sy binnan cneowe. Of ðam dæge ðe ðæt healsfang agolden sy on*
ðæs on XXI niht manbote,	*XXI nihtan gylde man ða manbote, ðæs on XXI nihtan þæt fyhtewite,*
ðæs on XXI niht ðæs weres ðæt frumgyld.	*ðæs on XXI nihtan ðæs weres ðæt frumgyld, 7 swa forð þæt fulgolden sy on ðam fyrste ðe witan geræden. Siððan man mot mid lufe ofgan gif man wille fulle freondrædne habban. Eal man sceal æt cyrliscum were be þære mæðe don ðe him to gebyreð swa we be twelfhyndum tealdan.*

Table 5.5   *(continued)*

II Em 1, 7–7:3	*Wergeld*
	A twelve-hundred man's wergeld is 1200 shillings, a two-hundred man's wergeld is 200 shillings.
If henceforth anyone **kill** a man he should himself bear the weight of the feud, unless with his friends' help he **pay** for it inside twelve months with the full wergeld, **to whatever station he be born** … Wise men should settle feuds. First, according to **the law** of custom, **the killer** should give a pledge to his advocate, and the advocate to his kinsmen, that the killer be willing to compensate the kin. Then **after**wards it is fitting that a pledge be given to the killer's advocate that the killer may approach in security and himself pledge **the wergeld**. When **he has pledged** that, then **he should find wergeld-surety for it.**	If someone is **killed** let him be **paid** for, **to whatever station he be born.** It is **the law** that **the killer**, **after** he has pledged the wergeld, should find wergeld-surety for it: that is for a twelve hundred shilling wergeld, twelve men are appropriate as wergeld surety, eight from the paternal kin and four from the maternal.
When that is done, the king's *mund* **is to be established;**	**When that is done, the king's** *mund* **is to be established,** that is that all from either kin give a common pledge on a single weapon to the arbitrator that the king's *mund* will stand.
twenty-one days from that day let one pay *healsfang*;	**Twenty-one days from that day, let one pay** *healsfang* of 120 shillings for a twelve-hundred shilling wergeld: *healsfang* is due to the children, brothers and fathers; that money is not due to any kin except those within the knee. From the day when *healsfang* is to be paid,
then **within twenty-one days** *manbot* **is to be paid;**	**within twenty-one days,** *manbot* **is to be paid;** then within twenty-one days the fighting-fine;

Table 5.5 *(continued)*

II Em 1, 7–7:3	Wergeld
then within twenty-one days the first instalment of the wergeld.	then within twenty-one days the first instalment of the wergeld; and so on, until full payment is made within the time-limit that wise men have ordained. Afterwards, one may depart with love, if one wish to have full friendship. With a ceorl's wergeld, everyone shall proceed along the lines proper for him, as we reckoned for twelve-hundredmen.

set out their texts in parallel columns (Table 5.5).[502] Like *Ordal*, the tract discussed a topic addressed by royal legislation, covering angles it had left unexplored: it was on payment procedure, not pledging or kin-involvement, that detail was supplied. There can here be really no question at all of the connection between code and tract. It is not just that the same words, indeed phrases, feature in each; as near as makes no difference, they recur in the same order. Nor can there be much doubt that the tract was unofficial.[503] To all appearances, *Wergeld* aimed to fill gaps in Edmund's laws by spelling out how killings should be paid for. Yet that story has an unexpected complication. As already observed (pp. 310–11), the last clauses of II Edmund, those most directly comparable with *Wergeld*, show signs of being out of place. It was hardly logical to return to the topic of feud after a clause thanking his subjects for the peace they were upholding, and another on *mundbrice* and *hamsocn*. The law-making person changed, outsize initials appear in the manuscripts, and there was perhaps a shift of emphasis from the exemption that kins were allowed in the early clauses to an account of their rights and duties. Might it then be that *both* texts (from 'Wise men should settle feuds' in the one case, and from the top in the other) were different versions of a tract that built out from the nucleus of what Edmund said, one getting locked onto the king's words, while the other floated in their orbit? In one respect *Wergeld* offered a better reading: table 5.5 shows how the scribe of the Edward-Edmund group exemplar could by *saut du même à même* have omitted *fihtwite*; the line included in *Wergeld* was more than likely part of the pristine text, official or not.[504] *Wergeld* comes out of all this looking like an unofficial treatise inspired by royal legislation. But it could be that, in a reversal of

502 The Anglo-Saxon original is given first as the argument hinges on verbal similarities; the translation that follows is based upon *EHD I* in the usual way for II Em, and is my own for *Wergeld* (for which there is a published translation, though with the usual drawbacks, in Thorpe, *Ancient Laws*, p. 75).
503 One might nonetheless note that 'witan geræden' (*Wer.* 6) was taken by Liebermann as evidence of an official tone in II Atr App. 9 and *Forf.* 2, *Gesetze* III, pp. 154 (2), 228 (4).
504 A fighting-fine had been an acknowledged element in the process since Alfred's time, Af 42:4, if not Ine's, Ine 6:3–4.

usual patterns, one version got incorporated into official legislation, to the satisfaction not merely of medieval scribes but of modern editors too.

(ix) Hundred

The *Hundred Ordinance* tells a tale differing in many ways from that of other texts in this section. It is far better known than almost all the rest. It was once canonized as 'I Edgar'.[505] As a chronological marker, this may be about right, though it has no better foundation than that Edgar's brother and junior uncle have no accredited legislation.[506] *Hundred* also differs from *Ordal* or *Wergeld* in that there is nothing extant for it to gloss, despite hints that it was affected by laws of Edward the Elder and Edmund.[507] Its rubric described it as 'the ordinance how one should hold the hundred'. If original, and something along these lines seems required by the wording of the first clause ('That they assemble ... '), then this cannot be a royal code. But it could have been excerpted from one by someone who himself supplied the rubric. The law-making voice was in part first person plural. Two clauses were initiated by 'we cwædon'; one expresses what 'we wyllað'.[508] But the London peace-guild spoke in similar terms: an analogy which implies that *Hundred* could have been drafted for, or by, any single hundred. It was about the hundred's duty to assemble every four weeks; to pursue stolen goods, prosecuting those who refuse to participate in the adventure, and liaising with next-door hundreds; to witness trading in cattle; and to follow accepted routines in suits that came before it. The affinities of these instructions are clear enough. There were very similar provisions in what Æthelstan decreed at Grately, and Edmund at Colyton.[509] Furthermore, Edmund was actually named, which makes this much the most datable of anonymous items: when else would Edmund's laws on thieves be singled out except during or soon after his reign?[510] Official or no, then, the Hundred Ordinance can best be seen as part of a heavily encouraged trend towards organization of local peace initiatives.

---

505   Schmid, *Gesetze*, pp. xlviii, 182; Thorpe, *Ancient Laws*, p. 109: this 'is undoubtedly the set of dooms alluded to at p. 85, n. *a*'; i.e. the Anglo-Saxon original of what 'Bromton' (*ergo* the final edition of *Quadripartitus*) had included after *Blas./Forf.* in the midst of Æthelstan's laws, and actually described as an Æthelstan law; it thus seems to have been Thorpe's decision to make this 'I Edgar', though it is not at all clear what can be meant (p. 110, n. *a*) by 'its place in the MS at the beginning of Edgar's Laws', as there is no such MS. Liebermann himself, *Gesetze* III, pp. 130–1 (2), has one good argument (IV Eg 3:1 – 6 envisages organized panels playing the role given by *Hu.* 4 to the head of the hundred), and some not so good (alleged references to it by III Eg 5, 7:1), that *Hu.* precedes mainline Edgar; he finds 'nothing against' the view of Thorpe, Schmid, and also Kemble (*Saxons in England* 'II' [*recte* I], p. 514) that the text is one of Edgar, but also no compelling argument in favour; and he was evidently hesitant about the 'I Eadgar' label, preferring the abbreviation '*Hu.*' from the outset.
506   Cf. Whitelock, *EHD I*, p. 429, an unusually extended introduction, of exemplary insight and prudence.
507   *Gesetze* III, p. 131 (5)): II Ew 8, III Em 2; III Eg 5 may refer to the more formal source of the extant Ordinance.
508   *Hu.* 4, 5, 7.
509   II As 20, III Em 2, 6; see also sub-sections (x), (xi) below.
510   *Hu.* 2; III Em 2, 4; Professor Whitelock, *EHD I*, p. 429, missed the reference, perhaps because she was looking for a more precise echo than is permitted by Colyton's preservation only in Q's Latin.

Perhaps the best argument for its official status is the striking affinity with earlier Frankish legislation to the same effect.[511] Yet the borrowing could be by an informed cleric.

The difficulty of deciding these issues is, as ever with nameless texts, the restricted range of transmission involved. The fame of the Hundred Ordinance should not obscure the point that it appears in just one context: as a sequel to the full text of *Forfang*, hence also to *Be Blaserum*, and thus as a further extension of Alfred–Ine in B and Q (above, pp. 231–2, 240–2). The sequence also forms an appendix to the curious post-1066 version of Cnut's code known as *Consiliatio Cnuti* (below, pp. 405–6). It is now time to hazard a guess about how this transmission came about. *Be Blaserum* put the fate of arsonists and underhand killers in the hands of 'those who belong to the borough'. But 'those who belong to the borough' were the Hundred in an as yet indistinct guise. Æthelstan's laws on how these people were to pursue those who thrice absented themselves from a 'gemot', and take half the goods of the contumacious party, are to all intents and purposes the same as the provisions of *Hundred*.[512] What is more, the rewards fixed by *Forfang* were for assistance in the search for stolen goods that was among Hundred duties under its Ordinance. The common factor in *Be Blaserum*, *Forfang* and *Hundred* is action by those locally entrusted with law enforcement and its rewards. It is a fair enough deduction that the set was put together for (and/or by) one such body; it would have been suitably enough appended to the *domboc*, given Edward the Elder's insistence that this be the reeve's working tool (above, pp. 286, 289). A last and perhaps decisive point is that *Hundred* was itself composite. The final clauses, on the use of cow's bell, dog's collar and blast-horn in evidence, and on the weight of the iron in a threefold ordeal, had a barely tangential connection with what went before, which had already sounded a concluding note. But the point about the threefold ordeal repeated a basic concern of *Be Blaserum*.[513] This trio of supplements can thus reasonably be seen as evidence of written law in action. As for their appendage to *Consiliatio Cnuti*, it is possible that they were transferred to Cnut's code some time in the prehistory of the version translated by this author. But it is likelier that he added them to Cnut on his own initiative. Cnut had not said enough about arson, rewards for tracing stolen goods, or even Hundreds; though one of his Edgar-derived clauses positively invited exposition on the latter.[514]

(x) The 'Alfred–Guthrum Appendix'

If *Hundred* is the best-known anonymous code, the next one is perhaps the least familiar, and one of the oddest of all.[515] In the 'London' edition of

---

511   Especially *Pact.* xcii–xciii, *Dec. Ch.* iii 5; see chapter 13.
512   II As 20 – 20:4; *Hu.* 2 – 3:1.
513   *Hu.* 8 – 9 (cf. 7:1); *Blas.* 1.
514   II Cn 17 – 17:1; cf. III Eg 2, 5.
515   Schmid appears to have discovered this collection, and followed his source, 'Bromton', in calling it 'Pseudo-leges Aluredi regis et Godrini Daci regis EstAngliae', *Gesetze*, p. 424.

Quadripartitus, this set of clauses led straight on from the Alfred–Guthrum treaty. Q must, then, have originally found them as a sequel to it. In later versions, perhaps having discovered their distinct identity from another copy of the treaty, he gave them an initial like that of the alleged 'Peace of Edward and Guthrum', and ultimately even their own rubrics.[516] The 'Alfred–Guthrum Appendix' was a digest of existing legislation about thieves, their accomplices and the complicity of their lords, mostly from Ine's code, but also from Alfred's, Edward's at Exeter, Æthelstan's at Grately and Edmund's at Colyton. As it survived only in *Quadripartitus* Latin, one cannot be sure that the Old English original quoted these sources in their own words; Q did not always translate identical vernacular passages in the same way.[517] There may thus be no significance in the plural 'shiremen or other judges' replacing Ine's singular. Possibly more telling are cases where the source was shortened, with the effect of harshening the measure involved: when a thief was avenged, it was no longer necessary for there to be fatal results (as Æthelstan decreed) for an avenger to become a king's enemy.[518] This exercise acquires extra relevance *as a sequel to Alfred–Guthrum* from Edward the Elder's insistence that 'he who defends, countenances or nourishes foulness (*ful*)' should be dealt with according to the *domboc* if within his own kingdom, but 'by what the peace-documents (*friðgewritu*) say if in the East or North' (i.e. in one of the Anglo-Danish kingdoms yet to be ingested by Wessex).[519] But the Alfred–Guthrum treaty says next to nothing about this matter, and the 'Peace of Edward and Guthrum' (by Wulfstan, pp. 389–90) had another agenda.[520] Could this singular text then have been drafted by someone who spotted the gap left by what Edward expected of his treaties? Not to be overlooked is its remarkable colophon:

> Consider, then, you who are mine, how unfitting it seems if I have the name of king and not the power to go with it, or what respect a follower shows his lord if he does not in general accord him the appropriate competency.

This striking echo of the principle that royal power and royal office go together, whereby the Carolingians justified their 750/1 *coup*, has a tone like the proclamations conveying the pleasure or displeasure of Edward, Æthelstan and Edmund at the state of their 'peace'. The possibilities are that the compiler knew the *topos* and thought it a suitable coda; or that this is an official text that lost its prologue, like Grately: a mid-tenth-century king (Eadred, Edgar) could have tried to extend the ramifications of English law northwards, as he made his power felt.[521] In either case, the extant text came from somewhere in the government apparatus, not from its apex.

---

516   Liebermann, *Leges Anglorum s. xiii*, p. v (10ab), and his *Quadripartitus*, pp. 130–1.

517   Where II Cn 25 – 26 and III Eg 7 – 7:3 used as near as makes no difference the same vernacular vocabulary, Q produced the following variants: 'subterfugerit'/'declinaverit', 'plegios'/'fideiussores', 'sicut alterutrum'/'quibus modis', 'solvatur'/'reddatur', 'solvat'/ 'emendet'; 'tractavit'/'cogitaverit'; and 'adquirant'/'perquirat' (III Eg 7:3 'hi' having apparently been misread as 'he').

518   App. AGu 1, Ine 8; App AGu 2:1, II As 20:7.

519   II Ew 4 – 5:2; cf. chapter 6, pp. 438–9.

520   App. AGu quotes no source later than III Em (not, for instance, even the very pertinent laws of I Atr on lords and men, one of its main themes), arguing that it was drafted before Wulfstan's time.

521   Such was Liebermann's suggestion, *Gesetze* III, p. 233 (6).

(xi) Dunsæte

After these dozen or so conceivably official texts come another series more clearly unofficial in their origins and coherent in their own terms. The first is one of the more celebrated of the anonymous set, one of the few already printed by Lambarde.[522] It was part of the group that coalesced around Æthelred's 994 treaty, a process whose possible outlines were sketched in chapter 4 (pp. 232–3).[523] The main point is its persistent connection with the 'II Æthelred Appendix', which shared its concern with cattle-rustling. It called itself a 'gerædnes' of 'Angelcynnes witan 7 Wealhðeode', and its conceptual affinity was thus with the Alfred–Guthrum Treaty.[524] One can see why it might interest a reader of Æthelred's 'friðmal' with Olaf. Yet it applied to a corner of the Anglo-Welsh border so remote that it escaped notice by the 'Tribal Hidage' before and by Domesday Book afterwards, and has defied convincing location ever since.[525] Consensus now fastens on the mixed Anglo-Welsh population and customs of Archenfield, south-west of Hereford. The river separating the two parties to the agreement would then be the Wye, or perhaps the Wye-Monnow-Dore.[526]

Two counterpointed themes need to be harmonized in approaches to Dunsæte. On the one hand, it was a treaty at the most local of levels between two inter-locked political communities. Some of its allowances for regional custom lasted well beyond 1066.[527] At the same time, its central concerns, cattle-tracking, forensic procedures, inter-community killing, valuing of livestock, vouching to warranty, were detectably those of the movement that produced Æthelstan's peace-guild and the Hundred Ordinance. Its style, an uneven mix of conditional and relative clauses with snappy orders, was crude by peace-guild standards. The only echo of current legislation after Edmund was the panel of twelve 'lahmen', their property forfeit for false judgement, which resembles the system set up under Edgar's Wihtbordesstan code; yet this could easily be an interpolation, made when the text was added to the collection that began with II Æthelred.[528]

---

522 Lambarde's charmingly misconceived title (presumably derived from Nowell's toponymic ingenuity, though cf. Gesetze III, p. 217 ad loc.) was Senatusconsultum de Monticolis Walliae. The word is not in fact likely to arise from a place whose name began with the Welsh element Dun- ([hill] fort)', like otherwise geographically apposite Dinedor; cf. Noble, Offa's Dyke, pp. 16–18; Lewis, 'An Introduction' (The Herefordshire Domesday), pp. 6–7; Gelling, West Midlands, pp. 112–19. Wilkins, pp. 125–6, gave it the same title (and chronological place) as Lambarde; its current title derives from Thorpe, Ancient Laws, pp. 150–2; cf. Schmid (1858), pp. 358–63.
523 To be added is that B and Q share diagnostic textual errors at Duns. 1:2, and in the displacement of the goat's value, 7:1.
524 At least one significant verbal link, Duns. 6/AGu 5, was noted by Liebermann, Gesetze III, pp. 215–16 (6); it might be added that Duns. 9:1 makes a stipulation about 'hostages for peace (frið-gislas)', which compares with AGu 5 (B): neither word nor principle occurs in any other Anglo-Saxon legal text.
525 The most persuasive (though duly hesitant) discussion is that of Gelling, West Midlands.
526 'Stream(e)', Duns. 8, 8:3; its 'banks (stæðe)', Duns. 1, 1:2, 2, 2:2, 6; cf. Gelling, fig. 46.
527 Gesetze III, p. 216 (8) – though not all of Liebermann's points remain fully persuasive.
528 Duns. 3:2–3, IV Eg 5 – 6:1.

If one asks when an agreement of this type is most likely to have been entrenched either side of the River Wye, the common-sense reply is Æthelstan's over-powering negotiations with the 'North Welsh' at Hereford c.930. Besides levying a stupefying tribute (recalling the 'gafol and gislas' claimed in the text to be owed by the 'Wentsæte ... into Westsexan'), he was said to have fixed the Anglo-Welsh frontier on the Wye.[529] In that case, Dunsæte comes close to official status. Yet its last clause asked that 'the Dunsæte too have peace-hostages, if the king will grant it to them' (compare London, above, sub-section (iv)); the objective presumably being to make them as secure as the West Saxons against 'Wentsæte' action.[530] Putting these points together, Dunsæte looks most like a (very) local example of the sort of initiative so strongly encouraged by Æthelstan's government and its successors.

(xii) Iudex

The next text to consider is among very few anonymous pieces with more than one line of transmission.[531] Iudex was in the lost codex used by Nowell to fill out his copy of Cotton Otho B.xi ('Nw2', chapter 4, pp. 261–2), where it accompanied Æthelstan's Grately and Exeter laws. In Nero A.i(A) ('G'), it was inserted alongside Romscot between capitula and text of the Alfred–Ine law-book (chapter 4, p. 227). Finally, Q put it in the group that also contained VII Æthelred and II–III Edgar (table 4.7). Textually, G and Q were related but not directly, while Nw2 had a more remote ancestry.[532] Clearly, then, Iudex was available to more than one Anglo-Saxon legal compiler. The down-side is that it did not even pretend to be a statement of current law. It was a short treatise on judicial morals. If its relevance is thus far obvious, its applicability is open to question. It was in fact a translation of chapter 20, 'De iudicibus', from the treatise 'On Virtues and Vices' that Alcuin addressed to the Carolingian grandee, Count Guy of Brittany.[533] Alcuin's major concern was judicial bias and corruption, and on the two occasions when the translator elaborated upon his original, it was to underline the evils of excessive respect for the rank of suitor or accused.[534] Alcuin's work was widely known in later Saxon England.[535] The value of its section on

---

529   Duns. 9; William of Malmesbury, Gesta Regum ii 134, I, p. 148. This means agreeing that William had a reliable source for Æthelstan's gesta; a new paper by Michael Wood strongly argues that one should, for all the authority of Professor Lapidge, 'Some Latin poems', pp. 62–71.

530   Duns. 9:1 (cf. 9).

531   It is also the only legal text other than the works of Wulfstan to have been given a major post-Liebermann study: Torkar, Altenglische Übersetzung; as might be anticipated from the debts already incurred by this book to Professor Torkar's work (e.g. chapter 4, pp. 172–8), my account depends heavily on his, which should be consulted for all points of substance.

532   Torkar, pp. 195–6, and stemma on p. 193.

533   The text is available in PL CI, cols 628–9; but Professor Torkar reedits it from mainly English witnesses as part of his edition, pp. 248–55. Professor Paul Szarmach plans a new edition.

534   Torkar conclusively shows, pp. 197–8, that these passages are the translator's work, and deploy his distinctive vocabulary.

535   There is a translation of the first sixteen chapters, another of the concluding section on the principal vices in the 'Vercelli Book', and translations for a presumably monastic audience of the chapters on

judges evidently struck a legally minded translator, just as that of other sections appealed to other writers for their own reasons. It stands on its own: there is no sign that it was translated as part of a more widely conceived enterprise.[536] Hence, the message of *Iudex* cuts both ways. It would be absurd to take it as reflecting the Anglo-Saxon (or Carolingian) judicial system. Yet its composition, and still more its dissemination, argues that mirrors of judicial behaviour were thought to bear on the administration of law in the pre-conquest period.

The date of the treatise is as elusive as that of nearly every text in this section. Its appearance in Nw2 beside Æthelstan codes could be significant, given that king's abiding interest in the topic. But the main likenesses are with III Edgar, which said more about judicial misbehaviour than any laws since the immediately post-Alfredian period, and whose comments differed from those Wulfstan circulated.[537] There is therefore a case for putting its composition early in Edgar's time, perhaps as part of the process that generated Andover; so much is also hinted by the manuscript associations of the G and Q copies (chapter 4, pp. 226–7, 240–3). The usual sort of outcome of independent, even in effect private, enterprise, *Iudex* still had impetus enough to ensure an unusually wide circulation.

(xiii) Swerian

Swerian is the first of three texts which were closely associated in the 'Edward-Edmund' group (chapter 4, pp. 232, 242). In B and Q, it directly followed II Edmund.[538] In H, it followed *Pax* and was itself followed by *Að*; *Pax* probably, *Að* almost certainly, were moved to their present places from other groups (chapter 4, pp. 242, 248, 250–1), and the same could in principle have happened with *Swerian*.[539] The piece consists of oath formulae for a variety of legal encounters, opening with one of loyalty to lords, ranging through four for accuser and defender in warranty suits, two more straightforward matching oaths of accusation and clearance along with one for oathhelpers, and finishing with four oaths about the quality of goods and payment for them. Sandwiched among these is one of a witness to transactions: 'In the name of Almighty God, as I here stand for N. in true witness, unsolicited and unbought, so I saw with my own eyes and

---

conversion of life and good works in Canterbury's Cotton Tiberius A.iii (Förster, 'Altenglische Predigtsquellen'); it was drawn upon by three other homilies, by Ælfric, and less certainly by an item in the Wulfstan *ensemble*, Corpus Cambridge 201; see Torkar, pp. 223–5; and Szarmach, in Biggs, Hill and Szarmach, eds, *Sources*, pp. 20–1.

536   It is, however, revealing that this same chapter was excerpted from an Old Norse translation of the whole in Icelandic legal MSS: Wallach, *Alcuin and Charlemagne*, pp. 247–51; Torkar, pp. 15–22, 35–6.

537   III Eg 1:1 – 3; cf. Af Int. 40 – 46, 49:5–6, I Ew Pr., 2 – 2:1, II Ew 1:2 – 2, 8; II As 3:2, 25 – 25:1, V As 1:2–5, VI As 11.

538   This correlation was conceivably affected by the similarity of its opening to that of III Edmund; the piece's general rubric is only in Q, so nothing in the original will have obstructed the access of a scribal eye to the first formula, resembling III Em 1.

539   Liebermann in effect allows for an 'hbq' archetype, *Gesetze* III, p. 233 (1): the corruptions of H and B could spring from deficiencies of either their scribes or exemplars, while 3, Q 'vel facinus' may as well be a compiler's gloss as part of a better text.

heard with my own ears that which I declare on his behalf'.[540]

An assortment of oath formulae is likely to have a whole variety of dates. Some may indeed go back a long way. Expressions like 'butan bræde 7 biswice', 'ge dæde ge dihtes', or 'ful ne facn, ne wac ne wom' were meat and drink to the long-established 'oral-formulaic' school of interpretation in Anglo-Saxon poetry.[541] Most of the transactions covered by *Swerian* formulae were at least as old as seventh-century laws.[542] But the date of the collection *as a whole* cannot of course be earlier than the latest formula it contains. The relevant ones here are those of loyalty and witnessing. In so far as the former is modelled on that of loyalty to the king (which is not certain), it ought to post-date Alfred (above, pp. 283–4, chapter 9). One would anyway think that the oath dates to a time when so much was made of lordship by legislators from Edward the Elder onwards.[543] The witness's oath is more suggestive still. The exact words, 'eagum oferseah 7 earum oferhyrde', recurred in Cnut's laws about warranty, which probably reflected the process laid down by Edgar at *Wihtbordesstan* (above, pp. 319–20).[544] Witness had always been central to English legal procedure.[545] But the presence of this particular formula at a point where it seems to interrupt the collection's line of thought may reflect pressure from the top: in the early-tenth century, or when Edgar organized semi-professional witness panels. It is at least a reasonable guess that making a group of these formulae was prompted by the amount of written law put into currency about the processes involved from 900 onwards.

(xiv) Hit Becwæð

In both its H and B copies, *Hit Becwæð* came after a charm for recovery of stolen cattle. If it is not exactly a shock to find the charm in this connection, it is odd enough to indicate shared ancestry. The absence of both from Q is another sign of that compiler's not always undiscriminating eye; and H and B shared one corruption which is strong evidence of a common progenitor.[546] *Becwæð* is a more expansive formula than any of the *Swerian* items.[547] It should be possible to convey its meaning without sacrifice of its cadence:

---

540   *Swer.* 8.
541   *Swer.* 2, 5, 9; see Clemoes, *Interactions of Thought and Language*, pp. 159, 163; cf. also Liebermann, 'pangermanisch', *Gesetze* III, p. 234 (5). But note the reservations of Stanley, 'On the Laws of King Alfred', pp. 216–21.
542   E.g. Hl 7, 16 – 16:3, Ine 25:1, 35:1, 46 – 46:2, 53 – 53:1, 56, 75, cf. also *Duns.* 6:2.
543   Liebermann's verbal parallels, *Gesetze* III, p. 234 (6), are for the most part optimistic; but there is no doubt about *Swer.* 1/II Ew 1:1/III Em 1.
544   II Cn 23:1, IV Eg 6:1 ('þæt he geseah oððe gehyrde').
545   Wormald, 'Charters, Law', pp. 160–1 (pp. 300–1); Kelly, 'Anglo-Saxon Lay Society and the Written Word', pp. 50–1.
546   *Becwæð* 3:1.
547   It was treated as a sequel of *Swer.* by Price/Thorpe, *Ancient Laws*, p. 78 (though not by Schmid (1858), pp. 408–9), honoured with metrical reproduction by nineteenth-century scholars, e.g. Cockayne, *Leechdoms* III, p. 286; and it prompted an extravagant rendition even by Thorpe's standards. My own translation mostly follows suggestions by Professor Stanley.

That he bequeathed and [thereafter] died (*Hit becwæð 7 becwæl*): he who owned it in full customary law, just as his ancestors lawfully acquired it with their property and person (*swa swa hit his yldran mid feo 7 mid feore rihte begeatan*), and left and made over to the keeping of him to whom they had good cause to grant it (*to gewealde ðe hy wel uðan*). And as he gave it who had the power to give, without fraud or prohibition, so I have it. And I wish to own as my own property what I have, and never to devise to you [anything], plot or ploughland, turf or toft, furrow or footmark, land or meadow, fresh water or marshland, brushwood land or clearing, wood or field, land or shore, wood or water; except that it may last as long as I live. For there is no man alive who ever heard that it was claimed or craved in hundred or any other meeting, in market-place or church-congregation as long as he lived: uncontested he was in life, let him be so in his grave as he has every reason (*mote*). Do as I instruct: you stay with yours and leave me with mine: I do not grudge what is yours, lathe or land, sake or soke; you have no need for mine, nor do I devise you anything.

This is a formula, therefore, for emphasizing an owner's freedom to do as he wished with a property, and to hold it for his lifetime. It is the position inherent in the whole principle of bookland, though the sort of usufruct that is hinted at here only became prominent in the evidence from the ninth century (chapter 11). There are a number of Norse loanwords (even if *Becwæð* twists the Nordic formula 'land 7 lað' into 'ne læðes ne landes', conceivably under Kentish influence); and perhaps just enough common ground with *Swerian* to suggest a link between the two.[548] A date in rough conjunction with the tensions over property disposal that inspired laws by Æthelred and Cnut is compatible with what other evidence there is.[549]

(xv) Wifmannes Beweddung

Wifmannes Beweddung followed *Swerian* in Q, and also, after the free-moving Alfred-Guthrum treaty, in B; it preceded the cattle-charm and *Hit Becwæð* in H, and (barring *Wergeld*, another roving item) in B. The presence of this formulary near the others begins to give the impression of a pattern.[550] Textual evidence indicated to Liebermann that B and Q were closer akin than was either to H. This may be right, as it often is, but Liebermann sometimes adopted the worm's perspective on a molehill: that Q read 'pecuniam' does not mean that it found

---

548   *Swer.* 3:1/*Becwæð* 1, *Swer.* 3:3/*Becwæð* 2; *Gesetze* III, p. 236 (2)
549   III Atr 14, II Cn 72 (it could, however, be noted that their formulaic 'sæt uncwydd 7 unbecrafod' does *not* (quite) recur here). The phrases 'unbecwedene 7 unforbodene' and 'swa þa land geagnian derr swa him se sealde þe to syllene ahte' (cf. *Becwæð* 2) recur at the end of S 1447 (*c.*968); 'unforbod(e)an 7 unbesacan' (twice), and 'fulriht þæt land ahte þa se geanwyrde wæs þe him land sealde' (cf. *Becwæð* 1 – 2) in S 1460 (*c.*1020). For the overall situation, see chapter 11; but it should be said now that Liebermann (*Gesetze* III, p. 236 (4)) was surely wrong to think that this formulary excluded bookland, nor is it clear that there are three separate transactions.
550   In R and T MSS of *Quadripartitus*, it has an initial, but is treated as essentially a continuation of *Swerian*, and 'MHk' make it (and *Wergeld*) actual *Swerian* chapters; which is what induced 'Bromton', who had spotted the relevance of *Swer.* 1 to III Em 1, to say that it was 'tempore regis Edmundi'; which in turn explains its following III Em in Thorpe, *Ancient Laws*, pp. 108–9.

B's 'orfes' rather than H's 'yrfes' in its exemplar, given that it frequently rendered 'ierfe' by 'pecunia'.[551] Meanwhile, there is a hint of a defective archetype for all three versions.[552]

Wifmannes Beweddung is not actually a formulary in the same sense as the other two: it is about what one does rather than says. The would-be bridegroom must promise his beloved's advocates that he would maintain her as a man should 'æfter Godes rihte', pledge remuneration to those who had brought her up, and announce what he was giving her to keep should she outlive him. This is all warranted by sureties. She was then entitled to 'half the property (*yrfes*)', or all of it if they had a child, though not if she then remarry. Her kin should then arrange her betrothal, its sponsor ('se ðe ðæs weddes waldend sy') receiving security for it. If she were taken 'into another thegn's land', her kin might still assist her to pay compensations to which she was liable. When the ceremony occurred, a priest was to be present, 'who should arrange their union with God's blessing in all prosperity'; and it must be certain that they were not so closely related that they would later have to be split up. There is much here of exceptional interest for historians of marriage, not least the prominence of the priest.[553] Its relevance for a legal collection of this date is obvious enough. Marital property fired more than one heated late Saxon lawsuit. There may be a connection too between its final clause and efforts by the likes of Wulfstan to outlaw consanguineous unions. The two extant Old English marital agreements also focus on the property bequests involved: the one involving Wulfstan himself appearing to distinguish between lands secured for the short or medium term and an estate that remained the bride's to do with as she wished.[554] The upshot seems to be that free disposition was allowed for what was freely acquired; that should be the sense of 'yrfes' in the clause about a betrothed's entitlement. The date to which all this points is Wulfstan's era (that of the *Ymb Æwbricas* excerpt). The tract shares the phrase 'æfter Godes rihte 7 æfter woruldgerysnum' with *Swerian*, and has another clutch of possibly Scandinavian loans.[555] There may be a link between the bride's retention of 'yrf' if she remain a widow and Cnut's law on forfeiture of morning-gift for precipitate remarriage; just as a Cnut law may link up with *Becwæð*.[556] It makes sense to guess that it was written or assembled by the same hand as *Swerian* and *Becwæð*; or perhaps better, that it and *Becwæð* were added to the

---

551   AGu 5, Af 1:4, 8:1, Ine 6, 53:1, V As Pr.:1, VI As 1:1, 7, *Duns.* 1:1 (where both 'yrfe' and 'orfes' are translated this way); which is to say that H, B and Q, not to mention the battalions of modern scholarship, were unclear about distinctions between cattle and property: see chapter 11.

552   *Wif.* 9: plural after 'man'.

553   Cf. Brooke, *Medieval Idea of Marriage*, pp. 126, 258–86; and Wallace-Hadrill, *The Frankish Church*, pp. 403–11. There are already blessings for conjugal rites (including blessing the bed) in English pontificals from either side of AD 1000: *Two Anglo-Saxon Pontificals*, ed. Banting, pp. 133–4, 140; also *Claudius Pontificals*, ed. Turner, p. 72–3.

554   *EHD* I 50, 128 and 130 are translations of all three documents; cf. also Whitelock's edition and discussion of *Wif.* in *Councils*, pp. 427–31; but it need not follow (and seems unlikely given the kind of property settlement envisaged) that this is a union of ceorls subject to a lord: see chapter 11.

555   *Gesetze* III, p. 241 (1). Symptoms of more archaic speech are again such as might be expected in any formulaic transaction.

556   *Wif.* 4, II Cn 73 – 73:2.

Swerian series by him. In either case, the same purpose was served: this was a handbook on procedures that responsible local officials could expect to oversee.

(xvi) Rectitudines Singularum Personarum, Gerefa

Along with the Hundred Ordinance, these are probably the best-known of the apparently unofficial legal tracts. Yet they are barely legal documents at all. This is not to beg the question of what a society like pre-conquest England did or did not consider law. The title, 'Rights/Duties of Individuals' was only that of the last *Quadripartitus* edition, but the text's chapter-headings began with 'Ðegenes Lagu', then thrice specified the 'riht' or 'gerihte' of other ranks before settling down to the titles of estate officers.[557] The last set of clauses were musings on the multiplicty of 'landlaga' or 'folcgerihtu', and the need to learn them all if one wished to retain respect on the estate. The sequel (in the vernacular version only) was a tract headed 'About the discriminating reeve', which announced at once that 'se scadwis gerefa' should know both a lord's 'landriht' and *'folces gerihtu, as wise men ordained it in olden days'* – though it is not long before it too got down to more explicitly rustic matters.[558] All of which helps to explain why the scribe of B (or his exemplar) put these texts into his book, and why Q did the same with the first of them. It may, however, be wrong to assume from its presence in legal collections that an Anglo-Saxon text like this would have had the force it might have enjoyed in later times, when it could have been enforced by a manorial court.[559]

A superb study by Professor Paul Harvey now convincingly argues that, for one thing, these were two distinct and differently motivated pieces; and, for another, the original motivation of neither was in any normal sense legal.[560] *Gerefa* was essentially a literary work, perhaps added to *Rectitudines* out of a sense that it complemented it. The man who combined the two made a number of discursive interpolations in *Rectitudines*, such as those already mentioned on the variety of estate customs, and on *post obit* arrangements for some classes of worker: 'he who administers the shire should take care (*hede se ðe scire healde*)' – exactly this phrase recurs early on in *Gerefa* – 'that he always know what the ancient tradition of the land (*ealdlandræden*) is, and what the custom of the people (*ðeode ðeaw*)'.[561] The same mind could well have introduced the first *Rectitudines* clause

557 'Rectitudines singularum personarum' is in MHk (which also, as Liebermann notes, *Gesetze* I, p. 444, n. 2 *ad loc.*, uses 'singularum personarum' for *Norðl.*). MS R has 'De Dignitate Hominum', while T omits an inscription, and the London Collection ignores the text altogether. Chapter headings may not be original in that they are seldom the same in B and Q; but Q MSS have quite a consistent pattern of prominent initials, and B usually left space for headings.
558 *Rect.* 21, 21:4; *Ger.* 1.
559 Cf. Dyer, 'St Oswald and 10,000 West Midland Peasants', p. 185. Such reservations may explain why these texts were ignored by Nowell/ Lambarde, who knew the Corpus MS well (chapter 4, p. 261), and first surfaced as a result of Sir Henry Ellis's Domesday studies: Harvey (as next n.), pp. 2–4. Modern English translations include *EHD II*, 172 (*Rect.*) and (both) Swanton, *Anglo-Saxon Prose*, pp. 21–7.
560 Harvey, 'Rectitudines Singularum Personarum and Gerefa'.
561 *Rect.* 4:4–6, 5:4, 6:3, 21 – 21:5; 4:3c, 5:5, 6:4; *Ger.* 2.

on the 'Thegn's law': apart from the fact that 'lagu' made its sole appearance in either text at this point, it was out of kilter with the tone or substance of the rest.[562] But *Rectitudines* was basically about estate management; what legal content it had (in the sense applicable to other texts described here) was introduced when an interpolator recognized its potential for a different genre.

Accepting Professor Harvey's case thus far (and it is hard to see how it can be rebutted), the remaining issues are the question of why, if these pieces were joined early in their history, they had divergent manuscript stories; and whether the interpolator's activity marked another appearance for the ebullient Archbishop Wulfstan. As was observed in chapter 4 (pp. 232–3), as well as earlier in this chapter (pp. 320–1), the two pieces followed *Dunsæte* in B, and could have done so in Q's exemplar, since he would have had good reason both to move *Rectitudines* to the end of his series and to omit *Gerefa*. *Rectitudines* made arrangements for an estate remarkably like those applied at Bath's manor of Tidenham, in close proximity to the area covered by *Dunsæte*. In any case, there is a critical because minor textual error common to B and Q versions.[563] There need, then, be only the slightest hesitation in accepting that *Rectitudines* and *Gerefa* reached their twelfth-century memorialists together.[564] This textual history would be seriously complicated if Wulfstan had to be fitted into it somewhere (for example by identifying him with the interpolating editor). That he should be was argued by Dorothy Bethurum, one of three main architects of his now colossal presence on the Anglo-Saxon scene. Her case has not met with the acclaim given to most of her achievement; nor, in the last resort, did it deserve to.[565] *Rectitudines* differed in tone, vocabulary and message from the corpus of the archbishop's accepted writings. It was not the customary archiepiscopal voice that said, 'this country custom is in force in some places; in some places it is, as I said before, heavier, in some … lighter, for all country ways are not alike (*forðam ealle landsida ne syn gelice*)'; Wulfstan made that sort of point, but with quite different emphasis and rhythm.[566] He employed 'gescead' and 'gesceadlice', but never (unlike King Alfred or the 'Handbook for a Confessor', works he knew) '(ge-)sceadwis'.[567] Wulfstan did actually write a piece on reeves, in the second

---

562 *Rect.* 1; Harvey, pp. 13, 16–17.

563 *Rect.* 4:1, Liebermann, *Gesetze* I, p. 446, n. *c.*; the rest of his arguments (III, p. 244 (1)) are not so telling, and in particular there seems no reason to tie these texts to *Swer.* and the rest, given that they do not appear in H.

564 Professor Page's discussion, '*Gerefa*, problems of meaning', pp. 212–14, overlooks the *prima facie* textual indication that B and Q had the same source for that part of their collections, with its corollary that *Ger.* was omitted from Q as a matter of policy; he does not specify what 'good philological, historical and archaeologicial reasons' there are 'for treating *Gerefa* as a distinct text', p. 214.

565 Bethurum, 'Episcopal Magnificence'; her case is accepted only with very evident hesitation by Professor Harvey (and though Professor Dyer is more enthusiastic, 'St Oswald', pp. 183–5, he notes a difference between *Rect.* and Worcester arrangements). This is not the place for detailed polemic against a great Wulfstan scholar; I set out my full case for or against Wulfstan's authorship of the remaining texts in this sub-section in an Appendix to 'Archbishop Wulfstan and the Holiness of Society' (pp. 247–51).

566 *Rect.* 4:4; cf. 'ne synd ealle cyricean na gelicra mæðe woruldlice wursðcipes wyrðe', I Cn 3:1 (from VIII Atr 5); 'forþamþe se maga 7 se unmaga ne beo na gelice', VI Atr 52, etc. Nor indeed did he at all often use the first person, even on behalf of kings: cf. above, pp. 361–2, on Cnut's *lihting* clauses.

567 *Ger.* 1.

edition of *Institutes of Polity*. The Polity passage was about how reeves should be 'shepherds' of their people, but were in fact 'robbers'. The idea of a 'manna hyrde' occurred just once in *Gerefa*, and then he was expected to be '*gemetfæstan*, frugal': not on the Polity list of good qualities; and so far from showing concern that a reeve might abuse his office at people's expense, *Gerefa* was anxious lest people exploit him to his lord's disadvantage.[568]

To return, then, to Professor Harvey's case: *Rectitudines* was a manual of estate administration, quite probably put together at Bath abbey, and in any case implemented on one Bath property. *Gerefa* was a literary work with a possibly Roman inspiration, and of the *Colloquy* type popular at the time. The two were joined by a reviser with a special interest in 'landlaga' and 'folc(es) gerihta'; he may have been guided by ideas that Wulfstan was expressing, but he is likelier to have been a colleague of Wulfstan, perhaps trained to think like him, than anything closer.[569] What he thus created was rather like Wulfstan's *Geþyncðu* (below, pp. 393–4): a work in the genre of 'estates literature' rather than estate management. That was what induced someone to add the paired works to a legal collection, just as the similarity of *Rectitudines* and *Geþyncðu* persuaded Q to put them together at the end of most of his editions. But neither parts nor whole are legal works as such. They have little legal content. Nor did this blueprint for an early manor say anything whatsoever about a manorial court (chapter 10).

(xvii) 'Peace of Edward and Guthrum'

'And this too is the ordinance that King Alfred and King Guthrum, and again King Edward and King Guthrum, decided and declared, when the English and Danes resorted unreservedly to peace and friendship; and the wise men who came afterwards also often and regularly renewed the same and supplemented it to good effect'.[570] From 1568 until 1941, no one seems to have doubted that this text was just what it claimed to be.[571] But a masterly paper by Dorothy Whitelock then showed that it was a work by Archbishop Wulfstan, and in effect launched the Wulfstan revolution.[572] All the arguments that were to be so decisive over the next forty years were already there. Chiefly, there was the extent of overlap in vocabulary and in subject-matter with Enham, a code of known

---

568   *Ger.* 18:2; *Inst. Pol.* II 94–101.
569   As to dating, Liebermann was confident that the philological evidence indicated either side of 1000, *Gesetze* III, pp. 244–5 (2–4); and cf. Harvey, pp. 17–19, against *a priori* assumptions on the 'manorial' conditions here depicted. As to law itself, the stress in *Rect.* 1 on a thegn's triple duty of 'fyrdfæreld 7 burhbote 7 brycgeweorc' recalls the decree drafted by Wulfstan drafted at Enham, VI Atr 32:3, etc. (though, again, *not* its language)
570   EGu Pr.; translation here and henceforth is based on that of Whitelock, *Councils* I, pp. 302–12.
571   Thorpe, *Ancient Laws*, p. 71, Schmid (1858), p. xlii, with a solution to the *crux* that Edward the Elder and Guthrum were not contemporaries that Liebermann knew would not do, *Gesetze* III, p. 88 (7); Liebermann himself was not prepared to jettison a (late) Edwardian date for the core, while accepting that it had supplements that might date as late as Æthelred's time, pp. 88–9 (8–14).
572   Whitelock, 'Wulfstan and the so-called Laws of Edward and Guthrum'; the arguments as regards Æthelred were, however, anticipated in her first (1939) edition of the *Sermo Lupi*, p. 15.

Wulfstan authorship, or with laws found in Wulfstan manuscripts.[573] The code contained institutions and ideas not known to have been current until he was at work, including an assortment of church dues, and a preoccupation with heathenism.

Textually, the 'Edward–Guthrum' situation is puzzling. H and B are as closely related as they are for any other text in what is by now familiar as the 'Edward–Edmund dossier'. Both phrased their opening clause as quoted above, with the clear implication that the text was meant to follow Alfred–Guthrum. Yet B made it a sequel to its first Alfred–Guthrum text, which is the one that *differed* from Q's, as its second text, in amongst the H-B-Q dossier pieces, did not. The scribe may have chosen to move 'Edward–Guthrum' into alignment with his first Alfred–Guthrum text, and repeated Alfred–Guthrum later out of carelessness, or because he thought the second text had enough extra matter to justify it (chapter 4, pp. 235–6). Meanwhile, H followed 'Edward–Guthrum' by *Wergeld* with no break, as if the two had become inextricably entwined, and it had no copy of Alfred–Guthrum at all. H's copy of the dossier, evidently disordered in that *Wergeld* came so hard on 'Edward–Guthrum', may just have lost Alfred–Guthrum, to which its rubric for 'Edward–Guthrum' ('these are the decrees that King Alfred and King Guthrum selected') should have applied; there was obvious scope for a *saut du même à même* in the transmission. Q for its part simply called its text the 'consilium' devised by Alfred and Guthrum, with no reference either to Edward or a repeated Guthrum. Here too, it was separated by the 'Appendix' (above, pp. 379–80) from Alfred–Guthrum, to which it was otherwise so obviously a sequel. A possibility is that Q's original copy made a sequence of 'Alfred–Guthrum'/(undistinguished) 'Appendix'/'Edward–Guthrum'; and that when he came upon a dossier-type collection (the 'London Collection' having no Edward–Edmund laws at all), he thus discovered that the 'Appendix' was a distinct work and was induced to supply an initial and rubrics for it as well as the others.

There is no very satisfactory solution to this set of problems. But the key fact is that 'Edward–Guthrum' was carefully fostered as a sequel to Alfred–Guthrum. The pattern seems likely to go back to the author: to Wulfstan himself. The last part of the prologue shows what Wulfstan was trying to do:

> They [the 'wise men'] fixed secular punishments also, out of the knowledge that otherwise they would not be able to restrain many people, nor would many people otherwise submit to godly amendment as they should; and they fixed secular amendments that were common to Christ and the king wherever anyone would not rightly and on the bishops' instruction submit to godly amendment.

Wulfstan said this sort of thing in other contexts.[574] In particular, he said it in *Hadbot* and *Grið*, the latter probably drawing upon the former (below, pp. 394–5).[575] *Grið* had several references to offences covered by 'Edward–

---

573   Wulfstanian vocabulary in this text is analysed as the standard for other works attributed to the archbishop in the Appendix to my 'Archbishop Wulfstan' (see n. 565).
574   EGu Pr.:2; cf. VIII Atr 36–8, with n. 363 above on its meaning.
575   *Had.* 11, *Grið* 24 – 25.

Guthrum'. One said that whoever killed someone within church walls, 'is liable for his life according to North English Law'; and, also 'according to North English Law', killing someone within a church precinct cost 120 shillings, or thirty if he survived. These claims for northern conditions of course have no documentary basis, unlike the references to 'Kentish' or '(South) English law' on similar themes.[576] But the question of the Church's security from attack was precisely the concern of 'Edward–Guthrum's' first clause, and is probably behind a pair of clauses about assaults on clergy later on.[577] Bearing in mind that at least one other person sought to make good the defects of Edward's northern and eastern 'peace-documents' with what became the 'Alfred–Guthrum Appendix' (above, pp. 379–80), it is possible to see the new archbishop aiming to create a more satisfactory situation for the northern province, in the name of those who first codified the relationships between native and newcomer. This, then, was essentially a 'forgery'. It is revealing in more ways than one that security for the Church, vested by Carolingian scholars in a mighty series of bogus papal decretals, could be sought by an English archbishop from a fictitious agreement between kings. But it was early days yet; Wulfstan would soon spell things out more fully in official and unofficial legislation. A comparatively 'primitive' stage is also evident in his 'Edward–Guthrum' style. Most of it was in easy 'gif' constructions; the exceptions were one 'se þe' and one mandate.[578] Wulfstan had not yet integrated the 'gif' style with the 'we læraδ þæt'/'riht is þæt' he used in his 'Canons of Edgar'. With the possible exception of this last, the 'Peace of Edward and Guthrum' must be his first extant exercise in legal formulation.[579]

(xviii) Wulfstan's compilation on status: the Geþyncδu group

The next set of Wulfstanian 'private' texts have more complex ramifications. They form a group, and were clearly meant to, but it is a group with an amoebic tendency to divide and multiply. The compilation falls into two textual classes. One comprises copies in Wulfstan manuscripts (which, so far as can be ascertained, was the version used by the author of *Instituta Cnuti* too, below, pp. 404–5).[580] Corpus 201 ('D') contains the whole set in what was probably the intended order: *Geþyncδu*, *Norδleoda laga*, *Mircna Laga*, *Aδ* and *Hadbot*. Corpus 190 ('O') has only the last three, perhaps because this originally

---

576   *Griδ* 13 – 14, 1 – 6.
577   EGu 1, 6:4–5.
578   EGu 9, 4; EGu 11 – 12 are, however, decidedly involved conditional clauses.
579   On the 'Canons', to which Schmid and Liebermann were not prepared to give legislative status (unlike Thorpe, *Ancient Laws*, pp. 395–402), see *Can. Eg.*, ed. Fowler, which prints both main versions in full (unlike Whitelock, Councils I, pp. 313–38, who yet offers scholarly comment and translation). The *Canons* arguably *should* be considered here in their own right. But the fact that they 'instruct' exclusively, with no kind of specified sanction, affords an excuse to save on already overextended space. The name of Edgar (first edition rubric, p. 2) and Dunstan (second edition, 68c) may imply attempts to (re)create suitable standards for the clergy of Wulfstan's dioceses, parallel to what EGu did for northern society.
580   D and *Inst. Cn* both finish *Geþyn.* 7 with no mention of debarment from clerical office for an offence: cf. *EHD I*, p. 469, n. 2.

Worcester book chose to concentrate on matters Mercian and clerical (chapter 4, p. 223). The most notable common feature of these two copies is that the first clause of *Að*, 'On the Mercian Oath', was separated from the second, which was initiated by a more prominent rubric, 'On the oath of Ordained Men, and on Compensation for Orders', and which ran continuously into *Hadbot*, the text on compensation for the Ordained. This arrangement may retain a trace of the process whereby the group came into being (below).[581] The other textual family is formed by H and Q. Some shared sloppinesses confirm their common ancestry.[582] But their main feature is that *Norðleoda Laga* was a set of wergelds payable not by Northerners but 'by customary law among the English': an amendment to be expected of southern manuscripts. Here, *Að* was a coherent text, independent of *Hadbot* (though H reversed the order of *Að* clauses, so as to give a priest's oath prominence over a thegn's). H scattered the group throughout spare spaces of the codex as was its normal form. Q treated most of the '*Geþyncðu* group' as if part of the Æthelstan corpus, and there are reasons for thinking that he got his Æthelstan section from Canterbury (above, pp. 294–300).[583] One could thus suppose that the relationship between Q and H texts arose from the Canterbury-Rochester contact that produced the Rochester version of 'VI Æthelstan'. Awkwardly, however, the intra-Æthelstan group in Q was prefaced by *Episcopus*, another clearly Wulfstan piece intelligible as an intruder on the group, which in fact had nothing to do with it.[584] It may have passed to Rochester with the rest and been omitted by H because he had much more substantial and up-to-date things to offer about bishops. Thus, the overall picture is of a collection whose basis is found in Wulfstan-influenced manuscripts, and which travelled escorted by another Wulfstan text to Canterbury and probably on to Rochester.[585]

The core of this group was made up of the first half of *Norðleoda Laga*, *Mircna Laga* and probably the first clause only of *Að*. It was a crude yet clear statement of the wergelds of the various classes from king downwards in Northumbrian

---

581   The D/O arrangement is the one reproduced by Whitelock in her helpful translation, *EHD I* 51, cf. p. 470, n. 4.

582   E.g. *Norðl.* 7 ('CCXX'), *Mirc.* 3 (gap), *Had.* 11 (omitted).

583   For reasons given in chapter 4 (p. 242, also above p. 388.) Q in most editions transferred *Geþyn.* to the end of Book I, and the same motives may have induced *Inst. Cn* to put it at the end of its Book III (there is no conclusive evidence of shared textual ancestry, though *Inst. Cn* III 60 (*Geþyn.* 1) is 'pan-English').

584   *Episc.* (now re-edited and translated by Whitelock, *Councils*, pp. 417–22) is clearly meant to supplement 'vi' in the final (Junius 121) version of *Polity* II 58 – 76; that section is headed 'Item de Episcopis', *Episc.* itself begins 'Item', and *Polity* continues with another 'Item' at II 77. Whether (as denied by Jost, pp. 23–4, as well as Liebermann, *Gesetze* III, p. 270 (6)) it was written for inclusion in *Polity* is hard to say, and not the point. The question is whether its message and purpose was better perceived by the Junius 121 scribe at Worcester in 's xi (3rd quarter)' than by whoever prefaced it to the '*Geþyncðu* group', so ensuring that it ended up in Q. It is because it did end up there that it was treated as a 'legal source' by Liebermann, and its inclusion alongside the *Geþyncðu* texts is explicable in terms of its clauses 3 – 6, 9 – 12 and esp. 4 – 5, which cover a bishop's judicial role; but Worcester's assessment of its one-time bishop's intentions deserves respect, and Junius 121 contains no other even putatively legal texts.

585   To be added is that *Geþyn.* 3 is an instance of H self-correction; Q's problem with *Norðl.* 10 is an example of its own ability to correct its early confusions, while its text of *Norðl.* 8 ('LX et decem') could also be a correction of a mistaken exemplar.

and Mercian society, concluding with the oath-values of the the Mercian thegn and ceorl: 'little more than a valuation roll of society', to cite a brusque comment on the possibly related text known as the *Leges inter Brettos et Scottos*.[586] There is no hint that its composition owed anything to Wulfstan. The mention of a wergeld for the classes of *hold* and 'high-reeve' must mean that, as it stands, it postdated the Scandinavian invasions. Otherwise, it looks decidedly old-fashioned: after the 880s there was no longer a Mercian king to need a wergeld, nor after 952 a Northumbrian; and the royal wergeld had dropped out of main-line Anglo-Saxon law by 1020.[587] Wulfstan made this text the nucleus of something more sophisticated. His first move was the obvious one. Clauses were intruded into *Norðleoda Laga* equating the wergeld of priest and thegn, and into *Að* making the same point about their oaths; the archbishop stressed this principle from Enham onwards.[588] Mention in the new *Að* clause of the 'seven orders' of clergy led into (and in the Corpus family of texts, directly into) a longer review of compensations for clergy where the sum due went up by £1 for each rank in the hierarchy. It was suggested in chapter 4 (pp. 222–3) that this text was written, and in Corpus MS 190 actually reproduced, as an echo of the acknowledged manuals of clerical orders, made available by Hrabanus Maurus and others. The tract was then rounded off with a sentiment that is becoming familiar: the wise men of the world who added secular punishments to 'godly just laws' for the protection of God's house and servants were indeed wise. Wulfstan's vocabulary was by this stage as prominent as his ideas.[589]

Wulfstan also did something less predictable and more interesting with the core text. It was now preceded by 'About Ranks (*Be ... geþinðum (...)*', which is a tract on change of status.[590] The opening clause sounded a note of nostalgia for good times gone: 'Once it was that people and the law (*leod 7 lagu*) went by ranks, and the people's wise men (*þeodwitan*) were entitled to respect, each according to his station, whether earl or ceorl, thegn or prince'.[591] What followed are among the best-known lines in Anglo-Saxon law: ways in which a ceorl (or trader, or scholar) could so 'prosper (*geþeah*)' as to become a thegn, and a thegn an earl. The qualification for thegnhood was five hides of land, but seat and service in the king's hall was also mentioned, and for thegns aiming to improve themselves the element of royal office is more prominent; while traders must thrice cross the sea to be reckoned thegns, and scholars attaining orders must (of

---

586   *Norðl.* 1 – 6 (omitting 5: below), *Mirc.*, *Að* 1; Duncan, revision of Dickinson, *Scotland from the Earliest Times*, p. 51; for links between *Leges* and *Norðl.*, Chadwick, *Studies*, pp. 25, 104, etc.

587   II Cn 57, as against Af 4:1; the transition from V Atr 30 to VI 37 almost seems to trace the process of evaporation. One might also note the archaic 'þrymsa' unit in which wergelds are reckoned: on developments in Northumbrian numismatics, see the papers in Metcalf, *Coinage in Ninth-Century Northumbria*.

588   *Norðl.* 5, *Að* 2; V Atr 9:1 (VI 5:3), VIII Atr 28, Cn 1018 11:2, I Cn 6:2a, etc.

589   The case so far was established in Bethurum's seminal article on this group of texts, 'Six anonymous Old English Codes'.

590   The tract's title in D is 'Be wergeldum 7 be geðinðum', in H 'Be leode geþinðum 7 lage', and in Q 'De veteri consuetudine promotionum': I therefore concentrate, like the label in current use, on the element of rank, 'geþyncðu', common to all three.

591   *Geþyn.* 1; the text in H and Q, 'once it was *in English law* that ... ' simply reflects their urge to generalize (above, n. 583).

course) remain chaste. Inserted *Norðleoda Laga* clauses applied these principles
locally: Welsh who prospered to the extent of holding one hide and paying the
king's *gafol* had 120s wergeld, and so on; the son and grandson of a ceorl who
attained a thegn's wergeld might make high birth (*gesiðcund*) permanent by
holding on to their five hides; but 'if he prosper so that he have a helmet and mail-
coat and gold-adorned sword but have not the land, he is a ceorl nonetheless'.
Not the least arresting implication of this is that the author looked up Ine's law
on 'Welsh' status for guidance in a northern society with a still significant British
ingredient.[592] It has been questioned whether Wulfstan wrote all this extra
material *de novo*, or merely recast an existing text.[593] Hesitation is surely unwarranted. If all he did was revise, why is there no sign of his doing the same to
the core text? The logic of the point that *Geþyncðu* is in his style while the core
is not is that he wrote one but not the other. *Geþyncðu* principles comfortably
fit his patterns of thought. His *Institutes of Polity* was a study of the functioning
of a Christian society, with all in their proper place; and among the symptoms of
social distintegration in 1014 was that slaves became Vikings and acquired the
wergeld of a thegn, while thegns were enslaved with no wergeld payable for
them.[594] A society where social ranks were disregarded was one where no other
good could be taken for granted. *Geþyncðu* sought to restore past proprieties, as
orthodox legislation targeted other social ills. It was one more stage in the evolution of Wulfstan's programme (see chapter 6, pp. 457–62).

(xix) Grið, Nor grið

The last clause of *Geþyncðu* returned yet again to the point that injuries to clerics
were once corrected by bishop and king. This is the cue for a final work of
Wulfstan that gave this theme more attention than all the rest. *Grið* has a different
manuscript context from the status compilation, although it was perhaps associated with it in the source of *Instituta Cnuti*.[595] It is only in Cotton Nero MS A.i(B),
where it preceded a set of clauses from Æthelred's 1014 code, itself headed 'Be
cyricgriðe' (above, pp. 203, 336). The text began and ended by proclaiming the
supreme value of God's protection (*grið*), in words taken up by Cnut's code.[596]
It then echoed Wulfstan's habitual lament for a lost past when churches and holy
orders were respected, before launching into a carefully researched account of
the Church's legal privileges according to 'South English' law, meaning the codes
of Kentish kings, Alfred–Ine and Æthelstan.[597] One is reminded of the knowledge

---

592   *Norðl.* 7 – 9, 11 – 12, 10; cf. Ine 32 (and 23:3 for the factor of the king's 'gafol').
593   Bethurum, 'Six codes', pp. 457–8: she actually goes on to make a very strong case for his outright
authorship.
594   *Sermo Lupi* 104–8, 120–1.
595   *Inst. Cn* III 56 – 56:2; cf. above, nn. 580, 583, and below, p. 404.
596   *Grið* 1 – 2, 31:1, Cn 1018 2:1–2, I Cn 2:1–2; the fact that the Cnut order is *Grið* 31:1, 1, 2 would
alone imply that *Grið* was the earlier. It is the greatest pity that this important tract has been translated
only by Thorpe, *Ancient Laws*, pp. 141–4 (as 'VII Atr').
597   *Grið* 4 – 12, and cf. Liebermann's marginal allocations; there seems little doubt of the influence of
something like IV As: note that it is the *Canterbury* (i.e. archiepiscopal) version of sanctuary rights that

of earlier codes Wulfstan showed by 1014 as compared to 1008. There were then clauses on offences against the Church under 'North English' law. Since one described as 'North English law' the death penalty for killing within church walls made generally mandatory by VIII Æthelred and Cnut, Grið must have been drafted before 1014.[598] But it marked an advance on anything offered in this sphere by 'Edward-Guthrum'.

The rest of the text adopted the tone of *Hadbot*, *Geþyncðu* and the *Institutes of Polity* about the principles at stake. A passage on 'Bishops as Beadles' was adapted from what appears to be its original form in *Polity*.[599] Another passage, only superficially at odds with the message of *Geþyncðu*, described how God raised thrall to thegn, ceorl to eorl, chorister to priest, scribe to bishop, and indeed made a great king of a shepherd and a bishop of a fisherman: the point was that the great of the world had no excuse for defying their spiritual superiors just because they were social inferiors.[600] The code ended with yet another reflection on the wisdom of former law-makers in protecting churches and clergy, which extended, so was presumably a bit later than, the *Hadbot* version; and with a meditation on the blessings imparted by a godly ministry.[601] There is of course no doubt that this piece is by Wulfstan. It affords one more glimpse of the way that his ideas developed along quasi-legal lines as he built up to his 1014 sermon and laws. That 'God's servants' were treated worse than pagans would dare treat the servants of their false gods was among the evils of that increasingly grim time.[602]

Meanwhile, the manuscript that reproduced *Grið* as a prelude to VIII Æthelred contained a short but intriguing text that supplemented or interrupted it.[603] The piece Liebermann called *Nor. grið* described the sanctuaries of the churches of St Peter's York, St Wilfrid's Ripon and St John's Beverley, while referring more vaguely to lesser sums payable to other churches according to rank; women and weapons were banned from the church; church protection was sanctioned throughout the realm. Obviously, this was a local application of Wulfstan principles. It gave northern sanctuaries a ranking like that VIII Æthelred assigned to southern churches. Whether it was Wulfstan's work, it is too brief (and now illegible) to say. If not, it was by someone who had learned from him. It thus serves to bring in a last and more substantial text where that is a central problem.

Wulfstan gives, just as he quotes Abt 1 for the rights of an *arch*bishop, where the extant Rochester text referred only to a *bishop*.

598   *Grið* 13; cf. VIII Atr 1:1, I Cn 2:3.

599   *Grið* 19 – 20, *Inst. Pol.* II 42 (cf. I 41–51/II 58–68); it was also combined with nearby *Polity* passages to supply the conclusion to the ecclesiastical part of Cnut's code, I Cn 26 – 26:4; note the discussion by Bethurum, *Hom.*, pp. 351–2, who points out that a less 'logical' form than *Polity* occurs in *Hom.* XVII, a text not itself likely to date before 1014.

600   *Grið* 21 – 23:1; they represent the text 'Be Sacerdan' in CCCC 201, edited by Jost, *Inst. Pol.* 'D, p. 130, 135–41' (pp. 256–8).

601   *Grið* 24 – 31.

602   *Sermo Lupi* 31–6.

603   See above, n. 340, for the only discussion that this interesting little piece has received since Liebermann. Dr Dammery gives reasons to think that it was intended to be part of VIII Atr in MS 'G' and shows that *Nor. grið* 3 on women and weapons cites *Can. Eg.* 44, 46.

(xx) The Northumbrian Priests' Law

The final anonymous text was second in Liebermann's series, but may in fact be the only one to post-date 1023.[604] There is no problem about its text. The sole copy is in the Corpus 201 collection of Wulfstan laws and homilies (but not, quite, his alone) (chapter 4, pp. 207–8). It is quite a lengthy code in two distinguishable parts. The first two-thirds ('1' – '45') concerned offences committed against priests or churches, or committed by priests against secular and ecclesiastical law. The majority of clauses begin 'Gif preost', and a high proportion follow the condition with no more than 'let him pay 12 ores', or 'let him compensate that'.[605] This part of the code was heavily based on the 'Canons of Edgar', but there was some use of 'Edward–Guthrum', Enham, 1014 and Cnut.[606] The second part ('46' – '67:1') was more discursive, and was about the behaviour of northern society. There was greater syntactic variety and elaboration.[607] The sources were diversified. As well as (more) 'Edward–Guthrum', Æthelred and Cnut, the Wantage code was quoted. There was also sophisticated legislation punishing successive classes for heathen practices, non-observance of Sundays, festivals and fasts, or witholding church dues, by payment of Danelaw 'lahslit' (the sums for once itemized) to Christ, king or 'landrica'.[608] Only the last section on sexual offences was more rhetorical.

Wulfstan's influence on this code is obvious enough. Not only was a great deal quoted from texts he wrote; some of his mannerisms are evident in what is not known to be quotation. No less clearly, considerable tracts of the Northumbrian Priests' Law neither quote the archbishop nor read like him.[609] This, then, would be at best a case (like the core of the *Geþyncðu* group) where Wulfstan built upon pre-existent foundations. But the laws of northern Christianity were quite another matter from the wergelds of Northumbrian society. Wulfstan had no reason to elaborate the latter other than in the ways that he can be seen to have done. Almost every item in the Northumbrian Priests' Law, by contrast, was on topics dear to his heart. Yet his influence is as sparse when he was not quoted as it is intense when he was. Wulfstan's condemnation of heathen practices in Cnut's

---

604   Liebermann was (as usual) following Schmid, for whom this was 'Anhang II', but who did not in fact (1858, pp. lxii-lxiii) commit himself to an early date: as he pointed out, the text was ascribed by Spelman, *Concilia* I, p. 502, to Archbishop Oswald's time on the basis of its preceding II–III Eg in the MS, and of its matching his known interests. Thorpe was also-noncommittal, *Ancient Laws*, pp. 416–21, but put it between *Can. Eg.* and *Polity*; for Liebermann's own views, see *Gesetze* III pp. 220–1, esp. (7). As well as her *EHD I* translation, pp. 471–6, Whitelock gives updated text and translation with short commentary in *Councils*, pp. 449–68.
605   Exceptions: *Northu.* 2 ('Godes forbode we forbeodað ... '), 2:2 ('gilde se þe ... '), 2:3 ('7 ælc preost finde ... '), 3 ('And gif hwilc preost ... '), 10 ('æghwilc cild sy ... '), 10:1 ('7 gif hæþen cild ... '), 19 – 24 (all 'gif man', about what is done to church or priest); only 2:2, 3, 10:1 are at all syntactically elaborate.
606   See Liebermann's marginalia, also fnn. in Whitelock, *Councils*.
607   More straightforward 'Gif' clauses are confined to *Northu.* 46, 49 – 50, 66; cf., among clauses not quoted verbally from already extant sources, the elaborated *Northu.* 56 ('Se þe ... '), also 57:1-2, 67:1 ('7 we willað þæt ... '), 65 ('Ac healde gehwa ... ').
608   *Northu.* 48 – 54:1, 55 – 57, 57:1 – 60.
609   Points of vocabulary (for and against Wulfstan authorship) are reserved for technical discussion in the appendix to my 'Archbishop Wulfstan', discussion here being confined to points of substance.

code revelled in rhythmic variation, as he reviewed varieties of paganism in a flourish of style and scholarship. Variation in the Priests' Law came from a lawyerly concern to cover all angles, from thorough and ponderous pursuit of the aim to fine every heathen observance heavily.[610] Had Wulfstan encountered the Priests' Law on heathenism as it now stands, it would have been utterly out of his character to have left it unmarked. Differences with Wulfstan's known *oeuvre* extended to content as well as presentation. One clause of the Priests' Law was satisfied with prohibiting priests from *changing* wives. This, if Wulfstan's work, would be the only time he countenanced clerical marriage in any way.[611] One could argue that he was prepared to make concessions to his backward northern diocese; and were there other compelling evidence of his authorship, one would have to. As other evidence is weak, that is flimsy ground on which to base so huge a deviation from his cherished principles. All this being so, the natural conclusion is that the Priest's Law was influenced by Wulfstan but was not from his own desk. It was written by someone who knew his ideas and idioms well, without always subscribing to them.[612] The obvious candidate would be one of his two successors as archbishop.[613] The aim was perhaps to combine and update the 'Canons of Edgar' and 'Peace of Edward and Guthrum', the texts in which Wulfstan regulated northern Church and society respectively.

Quite enough has by now been said about the class of anonymous legal texts. But one may linger for a moment longer over the way that conclusions on the Northumbrian Priests' Law match those of the section on Cnut. It is not a lot easier to find evidence of unofficial than of official texts after 1023. There could be circularity in this argument. More royal codes survive from the Æthelstan-Æthelred period, so there is more to tie unsponsored documents onto. Yet the lack of any very obvious effect exercised by the huge and articulate code of Cnut is suggestive. Only the three formularies even seem to echo it; since they *are* formularies, they may just as well be quoted by Cnut as *vice versa*. Thus, if surface appearances mean anything, the corpus of Anglo-Saxon legislation was near closure by the end of the first quarter of the eleventh century.

---

610   II Cn 4a, 5:1; *Northu.* 48. Similar contrasts could be drawn between *Northu.* 24 (killing a priest) and already oft-cited Wulfstan laws; or 55 – 56 (Sundays, on the eve of which one may travel six miles out of York in disturbed times), with Enham or Cnut texts.

611   *Northu.* 35; compare (e.g.) VI Atr 5:1–2 (a code supposedly aimed at the Danelaw, above, n. 338), where it is an aggravation of an already serious offence that priests have more than one wife (and for doubts about the 'backwardness' of the northern province in this respect, see chapter 4, n. 165). A comparable case is *Northu.* 10 – 10:1, which allowed nine days to baptize an infant, whereas Ine 2 – 2:1, *HomN* XXIV, p. 120 and (probably) the first edition of *Can. Eg.* 15 allowed 30 days (II *Can. Eg.* altering this to 7, whence the textual corruption of the first edition to '37'?); whatever the explanation for the II Can Eg. position, is Wulfstan likely to have let the *Northu.* nine days stand?

612   Note that Corpus 201 contains homilies in the Wulfstan idiom but not his work (chapter 4, n. 181). Jost saw off the sort of slavish 'Wulfstan-imitator' Liebermann had to envisage in order to evade the implications of Wulfstanian style in so many laws ('Gab es Wulfstannachahmer', *Wulfstanstudien*, pp. 110–82); but to suppose that so forceful a writer and personality was without devoted disciples verges on the unreal.

613   A small clue may be the 'festermen' – not a word in Wulfstan's legal vocabulary – of *Northu.* 2:3; the York Gospels contain a long list of (Archbishop?) Ælfric's 'festermen', and for the possibility of his connection with the 'Wulfstan' part of CCCC 201, see chapter 4, n. 190; at the same time, the word was favoured by early Peterborough documents, and Ælfric's successor, Cynesige, apparently came from there; cf. Keynes, 'Additions in Old English', pp. 98–9.

10   Legislative Fact and Fiction after 1066

After a gap of a generation and a half (so far as extant evidence goes), the English legislative tradition resumed on the morrow of the Norman Conquest. But the balance of *genres* involved was quite different. The flow of anything that can be called official law-making never rose above a trickle for the next hundred years. That of unofficial treatises soon became something like a flood, carrying with it an infinitely wider and more substantial mass of matter than the pre-conquest texts that have just been examined. The logical *terminus* of this book is 1066. But a review of early English law-giving ought to conclude with a glance at what came afterwards. For one thing, the law that was written down under the earliest Norman kings complements the several major manuscripts of Anglo-Saxon law that were made then. Together with the historians discussed in chapter 3, they make up the evidence for the change of cultural climate that transformed the world of law in the twelfth century, so setting the scene for the 'Angevin Revolution': a metamorphosis in the English (and European) intellect that will be assessed in the last part of chapter 6. Then again, the account of the pre-conquest legal regime to come in Part III will be followed by a speculative exploration of its implications for received views of the Angevin record. The legal texts of the post-conquest period are the thin and tangled threads that link together the two panels of the tapestry.[614]

(i) The Writs of William I and Henry I

Within months, perhaps weeks, of his Coronation, William the Conqueror issued his 'London Charter'.[615] This is, as it happens, the only legislative enactment of the early medieval West to be extant in original form: as a writ, complete with seal, which has been kept by the appreciative London authorities ever since.[616] Whether it merits the name of legislation is open to question.[617] But it was in writ-form: 'William greets Bishop William and Portreeve Gosfrith and all the citizens (*burhwaru*) within London, French and English, with friendship'; and despite its more localized address, this recalls Cnut's proclamations of reassurance in 1020 and 1027. They in turn relate to the sort of document represented by Edgar's *Wihtbordesstan* code, personal in tone and balancing prescription by concession

---

614   This survey will be more summary and superficial than what has gone before. This chapter is long enough already, and the researches of Dr Bruce O'Brien are transforming the subject; I am most grateful to him for allowing me to refer to his work where appropriate; and to both him and Dr George Garnett for comments on this section.

615   The key dating evidence is the statement in *Gesta Guillelmi* ii 33 (cf. chapter 3, n. 41), that William benefitted London 'after his coronation'; see also *RRAN* i 15, with identification (after Round) of 'Gosfregð' as Geoffrey de Mandeville I (cf. Green, *English Sheriffs*, p. 56, with suggestion that Geoffrey may have doubled from the outset as Sheriff of Middlesex).

616   *Facsimiles of Royal Writs* (ed. Bishop and Chaplais) 15, Pl. XIV.

617   Not by austere Richardson and Sayles canons; but other pieces failing their test are not so easily dismissed (above, pp. 344–5).

(above, pp. 347–8). Furthermore, this writ fixes the central theme of post-conquest legislation: 'you shall be worthy of all those laws that yet were in the time of King Edward; and ... every child shall be his father's heir after his father's time, and I will not endure that any man inflict any wrong on you'. Perhaps the Londoners were not the only ones to receive such solace in the regime's early years.

Comparable in form was William's decree on Church courts. It too opened with a writ greeting. It survives not as an original, but in cartulary-copies of the versions sent to the dioceses of London (sheriffs of Essex, Hertfordshire, Middlesex), and Lincoln ('earls, sheriffs and all French and English ... in the bishopric of Remigius'). Only a Latin text is extant, but the London copy says that an English one was provided. The writ must post-date Lanfranc's arrival in 1070, so Old English texts were evidently supplied after the 1070 terminus usually assigned to them. Its essence was that 'a case pertaining to the rule of souls is not to be brought to the judgement of secular persons'. Even this may not be so much of a break with Anglo-Saxon attitudes to 'Church-State' relations as traditionally supposed.[618] A third writ is known to Anglophones as the 'Regulations concerning exculpation'. Its title in its Old English version was 'King William's *Asetnysse*', that of the Latin in *Quadripartitus* was 'Institutio regis Willelmi'. This is interesting: 'asetnysse' is the exact etymological equivalent of 'Assize', while 'institutio' was the usual *Quadripartitus* translation for Anglo-Saxon 'geræudnes' (above, pp. 312, 315, 328). These titles seem to promise something wider in scope than William's other ordinances. The writ was indeed generally addressed in all versions. But it was a writ nonetheless: 'gret ealle þa þe ðys gewrit to cymð ofer eall Englalond freondlice 7 beot 7 eac cyð eallum mannum ofer eall Angelcynn to healdenne'.[619] Communication from king to people now took this form, whether its burden was mandatory or promissory; the difference from the pre-conquest position was that no other legislative form was used. Most of William's *Asetnysse* was about suits brought by Englishmen against Frenchmen, so that its vernacular language may reflect its main intended audience rather than an early date.[620] Its style was as traditional as its language, consisting almost entirely of shortish 'gif' clauses. In fact, only its content, whose chief objective was to introduce the English to the unfamiliar challenges of Trial by Battle, in any way foreshadowed a new dispensation.

618 Wl ep., esp. 2; cf. Morris, 'William I and the Church Courts', with reference to the ideas in *Episc.* (above, n. 584, and chapter 8). A new edition using a full range of MSS (so showing that the 'London' copy reached Durham and Canterbury cartularies) is Brett, *Councils* II, pp. 620–4.
619 The textual position for Wl lad is unusual: it does not survive as an archive/cartulary copy, but is the only William pronouncement to enter the early-twelfth-century legal 'encyclopaedias': in *Textus Roffensis* ('H'), it is squeezed between 'I' and 'III Atr', and might have been associated with either (less probably with neither); Q puts it in chronological place at the end of Book I (though before the 'estates literature', *Geþyn.* and *Rect.*). There is no evidence for or against a H/Q textual link; but three MSS of *William of Malmesbury, Gesta Regum* (Liebermann's Cs, He and Ht) insert a Q text of Wl lad, plus *Quadr.* II 1–10 near the end of William I's reign (II, pp. 348–9); and two of these three MSS are from Rochester.
620 Liebermann assumed that there must have been a Latin as well as Old English original, *Gesetze* III, pp. 271–2 (1), but this remains no more than an assumption. Cf. the important reassessment of the measure as a whole by Garnett, '"Franci et Angli"', pp. 130–4.

This is all that can be said for the moment about the Conqueror's legislation. Meanwhile, after an apparent lull under Rufus, there was a new eddy of activity under Henry I. The first item was the *succès fou* of early English law-giving, Henry I's Coronation Charter. It subsists in a quite remarkable number of copies and references. According to Richard of Hexham, who reproduced it in full (the first complete quotation of a royal proclamation in a historical work, other than the Worcester *Chronicle's* text of Cnut's 1027 letter), there was a copy in the Exchequer. If this was not becoming a *topos*, under the inspiration of Domesday Book's burgeoning repute, it is odd that the thirteenth-century 'Red Book of the Exchequer' took its text from the copy that reached Worcestershire, and was presumably from the priory archive, as it also did for the next two pieces to be discussed. Other than the Worcestershire copy, and the text of the one for Hertfordshire in the St Alban's Chroniclers, there was a whole series bearing a general address. They included one in *Textus Roffensis* and its sister manuscript, Bodleian Rawlinson C.641, where the presence of Bishop Gundulf among the witnesses shows that the parent copy was from Rochester itself (chapter 4, pp. 251–2). Another set of copies can be traced to Westminster, its descendants reaching the Canterbury cartulary and the Register of the Bishops of Glasgow.[621] As well as this minimum of four localized traditions, and the full text quoted by Richard, there was a string of Chronicle summaries reaching as far as Saint Denis.[622] Once again, the Coronation Charter may also have been issued in Old English; it deserves emphasis that all four legislative acts so far discussed, covering a whole generation since 1066, turn out to have had at least an Old English recension.[623] However much it was affected by its importance as a spur to the enterprise of 1215, the Charter leaves an impression of unprecedented impact. Nor is this entirely attributable to the new richness of the historiographical traditions available: the 'Anglo-Saxon' and Worcester *Chronicles* were already 'live' in Cnut's time, yet the latter noted only the second of his letters, the former neither.[624]

The Charter was nevertheless a continuation of an old tradition as much as the beginning of a new one. It opened 'Sciatis me', like the rapidly multiplying series of conventional royal writs, and unlike the 'ic cyð eow' (Latinized as 'notifico vobis') of its preconquest equivalents.[625] But its personalized address was, to repeat, that of a not always distinct style of Anglo-Saxon law-making. In particular, it featured in the part of Cnut's code which seems to offer his subjects

---

621   On all this, *RRAN* ii 488, noting (i) that this misses the crucial point that Bishop Gundulf is *substituted* for Bishop Gerard in H and Rawl. C.641, (ii) that the second 'Red Book' copy comes from the Q series, and (iii) that (oddly enough) the 'London Collection' took its text from Westminster rather than what was available in Q. There is a thoughtful survey by Brett in *Councils* II, pp. 652–5.

622   *Historia Ricardi Hagustaldensis*, pp. 142–4; ASC 1100E, p. 236; *Eadmer, Historia Novorum*, p. 119; *JW* II, p. 47; *William of Malmesbury, Gesta Regum* v 393, II, p. 470; *Henry of Huntingdon* vii 22, pp. 448–9; *Ordericus* x 16, V, pp. 296–7; *Chronica Roberti de Torigneio*, p. 81; *Suger, Vie de Louis VI*, pp. 98–101.

623   Holt, 'Origins of the Constitutional Tradition', pp. 15–16.

624   A possible explanation for the complexity of the MS tradition is that the Charter was reissued by the government itself: see *RRAN* ii 531, together with the paper by L. Riess (cited ii 488), though the latter's attempt to reconstruct its contents has not found favour.

625   Cn 1020 Pr, 1027 1; cf. I As Pr, As Alm Pr., V As Pr., II Em Pr.

redress of grievances. The Charter's 'praecipio', 'defendo', 'condono', 'concedo' and 'reddo' compare with Cnut's 'ic bebeode', 'ic læte riht', 'ic forbeode' and 'ic wylle'.[626] Its interchange of 'si quis' and mandate formulations also paralleled the technique of Cnut's supposed charter.[627] As for subject-matter, its abiding message, like that of William's London charter, was the persistence of the 'Law of King Edward'.[628] But it also made the same sort of promises about the same sort of abuses as had Cnut in the 'alleviatory' part of his code. There was no such detail on 'reliefs' as Cnut had gone into over 'heriots'. There were clauses about minting and about debts to the king, murder-fines and military service. But there was as much overlap as contrast. Not only were relief and heriot at least counterparts; both texts were concerned with the position of widows, if not necessarily in quite the same way; both had clauses about the limits of royal forest.[629] Above all, each has the air of a political gesture that drew its effect from the extent of governmental abuse available for remission. Rufus had not been the first to overheat the engine of the English state.

There are three more ostensibly legislative texts of Henry I. His London Charter, from very late in the reign, was a detailed and locally directed equivalent of the 1100 manifesto. The rights it granted were much more specific than those conveyed by William's far shorter concession.[630] It was really, therefore, a Borough Charter, of admittedly exceptional interest, and no more is said of it here. The other texts were the regulations of 1100 about coinage, and of 1108 about county and hundred courts. The surviving Exchequer text of both once more came from the version sent to Worcestershire, though there was also a copy of the second in Book II of *Quadripartitus*.[631] They again make the point that legislative procedure was still by writ, witnessed and presumably once sealed. It is a reasonable assumption that copies went to all shires; but it is odd that Henry's sprouting Exchequer seems not to have kept its own.[632] In style and content, Henry's writs signalled departures from early Anglo-Norman pronouncements. That on coinage consisted of three commands ('I will and command', 'I forbid', most strikingly 'let no one dare'); 'if' clauses were subordinated to these. 'Counties and Hundreds' had 'I allow and command' and 'I will and command',

---

626   CHn cor. 4:2, 12, 5, 6, 6:1, 9, 7, 11, 13; II Cn 69:1, 75, 76:3, 80, 82. Cf. I Ew 1, II Ew 4, 8, I As 4, 5, V As Pr.:1, VI As 11, II Em Pr.:2, 3 – 5, III Eg 1:1 (whence II Cn 1), IV Eg 1:5,6,8, 2 – 3, 12, 13, 14:1, 16.

627   The ratio in CHn cor. of 'si quis' to outright command or concession is 13:10, with half a dozen of intermediate character and one relative clause.

628   CHn cor 5, 9, 13, and cf. 1:2, 8.

629   CHn cor 3:2 – 4, II Cn 74; CHn cor 10, II Cn 80 – 80:1; cf. Stafford's seminal discussion, above, nn. 440–2.

630   Like Wl Lond, Hn Lond survives only in a London context, though not as an original but in the early-thirteenth-century 'London Collection': this context would raise a *prima facie* suspicion of tampering, were there any other reason to doubt its authenticity: Hollister, 'London's first Charter of Liberties'.

631   In this case, the text was added to the 'London Collection', when it was reworked by Andrew Horn, from Q's original in MS T (chapter 4, n. 307), but it was later incorporated in MS K2 from the Exchequer text: Liebermann, *Gesetze* I, p. 524, n. *a*.

632   For this and all that has gone before on writ legislation (pp. 289, 302, 311, 319, 347–8), note the important observation by Campbell, 'Significance of the Anglo-Norman State', p. 124 (178), n. 34; now elaborated in his 'Late Anglo-Saxon State', pp. 58–9.

punctuated by 'I do not wish' and by three 'if' clauses. Apart from the personal tone appropriate to writs, this was more like the style of main-line Anglo-Saxon legislation; and thus foreshadowed Henry II's Assizes, where a smattering of 'Si quis', and 'Et qui' was steadily overlaid by subjunctives and by repetitions of 'the king commands/forbids that ... ' (chapter 14). The third person was re-entering royal law-making. The coinage writ explicitly, 'Counties and Hundreds' more hesitantly, were mandates, not concessions. In 'Counties and Hundreds', it was the king's interest as much as the subject's that was protected against judicial abuses by lords.[633] A medium designed for communication between throne and people, which was of its political nature two-way, and which in some political contexts could be almost exclusively concessionary, was steadily being adapted to the purpose of implementing government will.

More will be said in Part IV about the curious disparity between 'edicts' of Henry I that were described by narrative sources but do not survive, and decrees that are extant but were not noticed by chroniclers (chapter 14). What even this brief account of post-conquest legislation makes quite clear is that Anglo-Norman government was beginning to find means of imposing its legislative designs that in some ways looked forward to the later-twelfth century, and in not always different ways back to the Anglo-Saxon period. There was a harsh continuum to the exercise of power, even as there was variety verging on inconsistency in its expression.

(ii) Collections for conquerors: William and Cnut

Examination of apparently unauthorized legal literature after 1066 can begin with a text whose place between official and unofficial poles is even harder to fix than is that of some of the material in section 9. The 'Ten Articles' was Robertson's title for what Liebermann merely called *Willelmi Articuli (X)*. It has no medieval basis whatsoever.[634] But the work's title is the least of its difficulties. For this, as for every text considered henceforward, the manuscript tradition was seriously complicated by the activity of later-twelfth-century compilers. It is best to ignore their efforts so far as possible, and concentrate on what can be said about transmission in the first half of the twelfth century. In this case, it is of some importance that the earliest copy, in *Textus Roffensis*, put the 'Articles' just after the *Instituta Cnuti* (above, pp. 250–2, below, pp. 404–5).[635] The one version of *Quadripartitus* that included the 'Articles' at all also had the *Instituta*, more obviously intruded than the 'Articles' because by a different hand, yet perhaps a

---

633   Hn com 2, 3 – 3:2, 4.
634   In practice, Liebermann usually refers to the text by the first words of its inscription in the bulk of its medieval witnesses, '*Hic intimatur* quid Willelmus rex Anglorum cum principibus suis constituit post conquisitionem Anglie'; Douglas's title, 'Laws of William the Conqueror', *EHD II*, p. 431, is inexcusably unwarranted, except in so far as inspired by Stubbs' 'Statutes of William the Conqueror', *Select Charters*, pp. 98–9. For that matter, neither *Textus Roffensis* nor any other MS arranges the text in ten paragraphs.
635   In the very closely related Rawlinson C.641, it follows *Inst. Cn* and C Hn cor. (In '*Laga Eadwardi*', n. 38, I give my reason for thinking that H and Rl depend in this respect on a shared exemplar, rather than that Rl is H's descendant; Dr O' Brien, however, takes the other view.)

part of the same interpolatory process, and from the same source.[636] Further, the *Instituta* were nearly always associated with the form in which the 'Articles' were almost invariably preserved from the later-twelfth century, namely as the first ingredient of the so-called *Tripartita* (the other parts being a version of the 'Leges Eadwardi Confessoris' (below, pp. 409–11) and the genealogy of the Norman ducal house).[637] William's 'Articles' and Cnut's 'Institutes' thus had a very similar history from early on.[638]

The 'Articles' were hardly a legislative act of the Conqueror's in the same sense as those examined so far. The introductory rubric, 'Here is intimated what King William decreed with his chief men after the Conquest of England' was obviously the compiler's work. No less eloquent of 'private' origins was the tell-tale gloss, 'quod dicitur ceapgild' on the second (not the first) occurrence of the phrase 'quod calumniatum est'.[639] Then, between the fourth and fifth articles came a report that 'this decree was laid down at Gloucester'.[640] News of a place of issue hardly belongs in the middle of a code; but it could have been attached to a legislative writ, even as Henry's charters signed off by recording their issue at Westminster or Reading. Such evidence suggests that the Articles were a set of separate enactments.[641] For one this is certain: Article 6, on Exculpation, was clearly lifted (if not with total accuracy) from the independently extant text.[642] There could have been pronouncements of this sort on the oath (art. 2) with its relevance to the famous Salisbury episode, *murdrum* (art. 3), frankpledge (art. 8), and the rest, which were gathered in to one collection by a third party.[643]

636   *Gesetze* III, p. 277 (1); Wormald,'"*Quadripartitus*"', pp. 117 (p. 86) 122–3 (pp. 91–5) (and n. 34).
637   *Gesetze*, as previous n.. Both *Inst. Cn* and *Tripartita* were interpolated into MSS of Henry of Huntingdon's *Historia Anglorum*; the only noteworthy deviations from the pattern are the Cambridge MS of the *Tripartita* in French translation, and the London Collection; *Inst. Cn* may even have featured in the sources used by Roger of Howden and 'Bracton'. Liebermann's *stemma, ibid.*, needs to be reconciled with that for *Inst. Cn*, p. 330, a task well beyond the scope of these remarks. But it can at least be seen that all but one MS of *Inst. Cn* (Bodleian MS Digby 13) also contains the 'Articles' in earlier or *Tripartita* form; and to make sense of it all, it is only necessary to suppose that Digby 13 and the interpolator to HHunt shared a version of *Inst. Cn* terminating at III 44, and that the mutilated Digby MS lost *Tripartita*: in that case, Wl art. can move back to the Archetype stage; and the combination *Inst. Cn* + Wl art. occurs in all four families, 'hrl', 'T', 'Cb' and (Digby +) 'IpHunt'.
638   Liebermann did effectively concede this, 'On the Instituta Cnuti', p. 106, which makes his *Inst. Cn stemma* less comprehensible.
639   Wl. art. 8a, 8:3; *Gesetze* III, p. 279 (6).
640   Wl art. 4. Cf. 6, 'Decretum est etiam ibi', which seems no less clearly compiler's work (but it is not certain that 'ibi' means Gloucester, or that 4 – 6 were all parts of the same enactment: 6 is essentially the same as Wl lad (see below), and the latter makes no reference to Gloucester).
641   Less conclusive evidence to the same effect is the miscellany of legislative forms: 'statuimus' 2, 'volo' 3 (NB 'persolvere mihi' here, as against 2 'Willelmo regi fideles esse'), 'Decretum est' 6, 'antecessores nostri' 8, 'Prohibeo' 9, etc.; such variety exceeds that of even the most heterogeneous pre-conquest legal statements.
642   Garnett, '"Franci et Angli"', pp. 132–3, for one difference between the two, and a willingness to accept that the Wl lad of H and Q is not necessarily the best text.
643   See further discussion in chapters 9 and 14. It can, however, be said here that the Richardson and Sayles polemic about 2, *Law and Legislation*, p. 101, is misconceived: an oath to defend the king's lands and honour against his enemies is by no means wildly at odds with Af 1, 4, III Em 1, or their Carolingian prototypes; while 'foedere et sacramento' might well seem a rendition of 'að ond wedd'.

Another piece must now come into play. Not only did 'Articles' and *Instituta* have much the same manuscript history. The text of one also seems to influence the other.[644] The echoes were rarely verbal, but the resemblances were close enough as a series to be conclusive. Chapter 14 will return to the nice problem thus created over one of the Conqueror's best-known legal initiatives, his substitution of various mutilations for capital punishment.[645] It is at least clear that understanding the 'Articles' calls for a grasp of the nature of the *Instituta* too. In essence this was simply a translation of Cnut's code. The translation was, however, a good deal freer than that of *Quadripartitus*. This was not just a matter of the sort of misunderstanding that led a Francophone translator, too trusting in his dictionaries, to envisage compensation for wounded roast loin.[646] Cnut's provisions were adapted to post-1066 conditions: monetary reckoning was in twelve-pence shillings; the surely French interval of a 'year and a day' made an appearance. There was circumlocutory explanation for the benefit of those unfamiliar with native ways and technicalities.[647] The same sort of realistic purpose was served by leaving out Wulfstan's more flowery homiletic excursions, not to mention passages whose meaning was irretrievable.[648] But the *Instituta* did not draw on Cnut's code alone. Efforts were made to fill it out with material from elsewhere.[649] Book III consisted largely of excerpts from Alfred–Ine (the former contributing his injury tariff, the latter providing equivalent values for oxen and cows) or the '*Geþyncðu* group' and *Grið*. Other passages have no known source. Ten clauses were headed, 'such are the customs of kings among the English', meaning the judicial perquisites kings can expect; another, slightly later, follows an *Episcopus*-like sentence on the bishop's role with a list of some of his legal profits. It is suggested that these are a digest of a set of Domesday *brevia* such as fronted returns from individual shires. But something of the sort was encountered well back in the Anglo-Saxon period (p. 371); and three clauses are reminiscent of Wulfstan's oft-quoted principle on the division of fines for breach of church-peace; thus, the guiding sentiments could have come from the *Geþyncðu* group itself.[650]

The *Instituta* is usually dated to Henry I's reign, the same by extension then

---

644   *Gesetze* III, pp. 277–8 (2): As *Inst. Cn* is beyond question based on I–II Cn itself, influence must flow from that to Wl art.
645   Wl art. 10, cf. *Inst. Cn* II 2:1, 30:4–5 (though here there is no mention of testicles).
646   *Inst. Cn* III 31 'assatura renum', from Af 67 'lendenbræde': Liebermann, 'On the Instituta', p. 84.
647   II 33:2, 31:1; cf. I 3:2, 8 'mundam regis … secundum … legem Danorum', as in *DB* for Danelaw areas; I 5:3, 'liberalitate … quod Angli dicunt þegenscipe'; I 8:2, the lord 'in capite'; II Cn 22:1, 24:2, 49, good examples of explanatory glosses.
648   I Cn 23 – 26:4, II Cn 11 – 11:1 (with 10 on bridgework and the rest also omitted because covered in II 65?), II 67 – 68:3, II 84 – 84:6; omission of II 61:1 on 'samwyrce' (which baffled Q too) and II 81 on 'drincelean' were perhaps prompted by ignorance.
649   Af 20 was inserted after I Cn 5:2d, clearly enough prompted by its content; II Eg 4:1–3 on nonpayment of Peter's Pence replaced the milder Cnut penalty, I 9:1; Cnut's clauses on tithe-distribution, I 11 – 11:1, follow I 12 on light-scot, with the fuller II Eg 1:1 then substituted for I Cn 11:2; after II Cn 12 – 15:1a on payment of 'lahslit' came clauses drawing on the same pool of ideas as *Northu.* 51 – 53; finally, Af 15 – 17 and 38 – 39:2 came in after II Cn 58 – 59, which were themselves based on nearly related Alfred matter. The translator seems to know what sources Cnut had used.
650   *Inst. Cn* III 45:4 – 55, 58; O'Brien, forthcoming; cf.,e.g., VIII Atr 36 – 38, EGu Pr.:2, and especially *Grið* 6, 8, 24, etc.

applying to the 'Articles'. An earlier date could hold good for individual Articles, without this affecting the date of the collection overall.[651] It is the more important, therefore, that every argument for a Henrician date deployed by Liebermann is specious. Each of its four references to 'old times' were simple echoes of Wulfstanian sentiment, and one came straight out of *Geþyncðu*.[652] The best argument otherwise is a doubtful conclusion from a clause about episcopal jurisdiction, which would anyway take one no later than 1072, and an accurate rendition of the word 'Æþeling', supposedly possible only in the time of the doomed Prince William (1103–20). That being so, there is no reason why *Instituta* and 'Articles' should not have been produced in the combination that convergent evidence suggests they were, late in the Conqueror's own reign. The project of an updated guide to Old English law based on Cnut, and followed by a set of amendments introduced by the current regime, at once recalls a much more famous one with just the same form and objectives, which was carried through under Henry I, and to which attention will be given shortly. The interest of William's government in that of Cnut probably affected the content of one early-twelfth-century legal 'encyclopaedia' (chapter 4, pp. 235–6). All this is good news for the authenticity of the individual 'Articles'. It is even more important as a considered judgement on the relevance of Old English law, as codified by one conqueror, to what was enacted by another.

A further text explicitly asserted the on-going value of Cnut's code for the conquered realm. In some ways like the *Instituta*, it is in others a total contrast, and in any case an extraordinary product that deserves to be better-known by historians of post-conquest culture.[653] The *Consiliatio Cnuti* is very ill-served by manuscripts. Only one is complete, and that much the latest. Here, the *Consiliatio* led into the 'Laws of Edward the Confessor' (as the 'Articles' did in *Tripartita*), and its title is actually that of the 'Leges Edwardi' (below, pp. 409–11). For the rest, the compiler of a manuscript which later belonged to Colbert and is now in Paris substituted its prologue and first two chapters for those of the *Instituta*, and added its two last chapters and a list of rubrics to what is still essentially a text of the *Instituta*.[654] There was also an apparently random selection of clauses added to the Holkham copy of 'Leis Willelme' and 'Leges Edwardi Confessoris', themselves a supplement to the text of *Quadripartitus*.[655] The *Consiliatio* was a translation of Cnut's code, followed, for reasons guessed at in previous sections of this chapter, by a few clauses from Æthelred's 1014 code and by the *Be Blaserum/Forfang/Hundred* trio (above, pp. 352, 379). But it is not at all the same sort of translation as the *Instituta*.[656]

---

651 Cf. Garnett, '"Franci et Angli"', pp. 116–19, 129 (the reference to 'Conquisitio Angliae' as an early feature is especially telling if valid, since the phrase comes from the collection's title).
652 *Inst. Cn* III 51, 53, 57, and especially 60, to which cf. *Geþyn*. 1. That there is change in content and textual history at III 45 (above, n. 637), *Gesetze* III, pp. 330–1 (4), is a more serious point, but its chronological significance (if any) remains unclear.
653 Its interest is justly emphasized and sensitively assessed in O' Brien's forthcoming edition of post-conquest legal texts, to which my account is much indebted.
654 See the full account by Liebermann, *Consiliatio Cnuti* (Halle, 1893), pp. xv–xviii.
655 Liebermann, *Cons. Cn*, pp. xviii–xix: he can see no logic in the selection made.
656 The contrasting nature of the two translations is easily grasped by comparing the distribution of

There was little legal updating. New material was usually a matter of stylistic elegance.[657] Few alterations were on issues of substance.[658] The one notable item was a seemingly new law on tithings inserted just before what Cnut said about obligatory enrolment in them.[659] There were misunderstandings, as when '*æwbryce* (adultery)' was all too easily misread as '*æbryce*' ('*legis transgressio*'). But it was not ignorance of Anglo-Saxon language that the author was guilty of, so much as indifference to Old English law, at least compared to the value he attached to good Latin. The fact that Cnut's code was given in full is another symptom of the failure to update. This is not so much a work of law as a literary 'crib'.

The key to the whole exercise probably lies in its prologue:

> Since in the time of the ancients, as we learn from the authority of our elders, England was given over to the rule of many kings, individual kings presiding over particular provinces, there was a diversity of legal custom, which remained diverse in diverse provinces as they came under fewer rulers or one ... whence also popular customs remain and endure unchanged down to the present day. But when it happened that the most just king Cnut acquired the whole of England, he decreed with reasoned deliberation that the whole kingdom of England would be ruled by one law, just as it was by one king. ... He with common consent attempted, so far as human reason was able, to fix firmly what was just, to amend what was partly askew, and to abolish and entirely remove what altogether departed from the path of justice ...

The author's point, then, was that England had a single law, and that it was in place before 1066. It went along with an elegant variation on the 'adding, correcting, subtracting' theme, which was found in Alfred's code and which the *Quadripartitus* collector also picked up somehow.[660] Just as that theme went back to Justinian, so uniformity was a Roman legislative ideal *par excellence*. Along with classicizing language, the *Consiliatio* espoused Roman legal standards. This is what might have emerged, had William of Malmesbury decided to translate Cnut's laws. It was an intellectual's, not a lawyer's exercise: not an attempt to write live law, but to set a Roman example to which law-making kings of the English should aspire.

---

bold type and spaced lettering in the two relevant columns of Liebermann's *Gesetze*; new matter is in bold, and mistakes or deliberately changed meanings in spaced letters (though his 1893 edition of *Cons. Cn* did it the opposite way).

657   E.g. I 7: 'his mæges lafe', accurately enough translated by *Inst. Cn*, becomes 'alienam cum qua ... carnaliter conversatus est'.

658   I 8:2 (gratuitous reference to bishops as lords), II 30:6 (specification that a fugitive was 'sub fideius-sione'), II 69, 82 (rubrics that may be further evidence of the distinctive nature of this bit of the code, above, pp. 361–2), II 73:1 (gloss on 'socn').

659   *Cons. Cn* II 19:2a, *Gesetze* I, pp. 618–19; the explanation of 'foreoath' at II Cn 22:1b may be an example of the same tendency.

660   *Af* Int 49:9; *Quad.* 'Dedicatio' 38, tr. Sharpe, p. 162; Dilcher, 'Gesetzgebung als Rechtserneuerung'.

(iii) Current law in the name of Kings: William, 'Edward', Henry I

This chapter draws to its close with a glance at three texts which have at one time or another, and for reasons good and bad, attracted more attention than all the others so far discussed. One in particular, the so-called 'Leges Henrici Primi', is so familiar and influential that it is here left until last. It was probably in fact the earliest of the three, and was the work of the *Quadripartitus* compiler, who has put in regular appearances all through this chapter and the latter part of the last; in the final section of chapter 6, he will set the tone for the intellectual movement represented by twelfth-century texts. But because the *Leges Henrici Primi* has been studied in isolation from near-contemporary works, its place in a cultural climate has seldom been appreciated.

All three works were attempts to describe the law of England as currently experienced. They each did so in the name of kings. But there was no serious attempt to represent them as laws that kings had issued, in the sense that this was true of Cnut's code and its translations. None of them, therefore, is sensibly described as a 'forgery'. The proportion of truth to untruth in each varies (so far as this can be checked) in degree rather than kind.[661] The first to be discussed here, the tract known as 'Leis Willelme' was thought worthy to be in the standard collection of early English laws, like the 'Articles' but unlike anything else in this section. A specialized monograph has emerged recently. So has an exceptionally vituperative assault by Richardson and Sayles.[662] Difficulties stretch beyond the usual questions of textual descent and provenance to the language in which it was first written.

There are in effect three manuscripts of *Leis Willelme*: two in French and one in Latin.[663] The earlier French copy was added to the Holkham manuscript of *Quadripartitus*; it breaks off just over half way through, then launches into *Leges Edwardi Confessoris*.[664] The date of this manuscript may be more than half a century older than Liebermann's 'um 1230' (chapter 4, pp. 237–8). The Latin text comes from a thirteenth-century *portmanteau* lawbook, where it accompanied Glanvill, *Leges Edwardi Confessoris*, Henry I's Coronation Charter, further legal and historical/geographical texts, *Instituta Cnuti* and the

---

661 They thus contrast with 'Pseudo-Cnut De Foresta' (*Gesetze* I, pp. 620–6, separately edited and discussed by Liebermann (Halle, 1894)). This professes, as the others do *not*, to be laws issued by the king in person ('quas ego Canutus rex, cum consilio primariorum hominum meorum de foresta condo et facio', Pr; 'Attamen dico vobis', 13:1). It was of course no such thing, and may, therefore, reasonably be called a 'forgery'. It survives only in early-modern copies (none much if at all earlier than Holinshed's *Chronicle*), but perhaps goes back to Angevin times. Interesting and even important it may be, but only in the most residual sense part of the story told in this book.

662 Liebermann, 'Über die Leis Willelme'; *Laws* (Ro) (but '(So-called) Laws of William I'), pp. 252–75; Wuest, *Die 'Leis Willelme'*; Richardson and Sayles, *Law and Legislation*, pp. 121–3, 170–5.

663 To be precise, the second French copy, from the 'Chronicle of Pseudo-Ingulf' is only known through two independent early modern printings; while the Latin text is in two MSS, one of which is a badly burnt copy (by Nowell) of the other: *Gesetze* III, pp. 283–4 (1–4).

664 Precision may again be desired: the Hk MS (BL Add. MS 49366) breaks off at Leis Wl 20:3a (p. 506), but 20 – 20:3a, on reliefs, were relocated (to judge from the 'Ingulf' and Latin versions – which are, however, closely related) after 28:2: i.e. the break comes at 29 (p. 512).

first and third parts of *Tripartita*.[665] Now, the second French text and the Latin version share a pair of corruptions, and the Holkham copy offers a correct reading for the first (for the second, it is unfortunately unavailable). This can only mean that the extant Latin version and the second French text had a common ancestor; and this ancestor must have been in French, since the Holkham reading is correct. The work may have begun its life in Latin, but the extant Latin text cannot be a witness to it, and there is no direct evidence of its existence.[666] The chief argument for the Latin's originality is that it quoted the Roman law sources underlying its second part with an accuracy that could hardly have been achieved by retranslation from the French.[667] Liebermann conceded that the French text perhaps started out with its Latin sources supplied as glosses, so that these could in due course be exploited by the Latin translator. But the second and third sections, where alone there is serious question of access to Latin sources, may actually have been additions to an original terminating roughly where Holkham breaks off. If the translator was using a secondary French text, he could have drawn directly on Latin material, and there is no need to envisage a glossed original.[668] There is anyway no option but to accept that a law-book was being written in French by the mid-twelfth century. This is no more surprising than that a 'History of the English' in French verse should emerge at the same time.[669]

Structurally, *Leis Willelme* falls clearly into three parts. The first and much the most important, all that the Holkham manuscript preserved, was a review of 'the laws and the customs that King William granted to the people of England after the conquest of the land, those same that his cousin, King Edward, held before him'.[670] This looks like an evocation of the introduction to the 'Articles'. More clearly, it breathed the spirit of all other essays in recreat-

---

665   A radical recently-published view of the Holkham MS would have it 'mid-twelfth-century': Short, 'Patrons and Polyglots', p. 243, citing Woledge (and himself), 'Liste provisoire', p. 6. I was regrettably unaware of this trenchant opinion when writing '"*Quadripartitus*"', p. 118 (pp. 87–8); yet I doubt whether my expert palaeographical advisers on that occasion, much as they favoured dates earlier than Liebermann's, would have gone as far back as 1150 for this part of the MS, especially since it is fairly clearly an addition to the MS; a date of *c*.1175 seems safest. This does not affect the case for the priority of the French version over the Latin; but the medieval MS of the latter, BL. Harley 746 (Liebermann's S, *Gesetze* I, p. xxxix), is (as Dr O'Brien informs me) C13th at its core, with early-fourteenth-century additions.

666   Leis Wl 10:1, 47:3; the Richardson and Sayles polemic does not seem to confront this point; nor did Liebermann make as much of it as he might have, presumably because he thought it obvious, and that he had established the priority of the French on other grounds, *Gesetze* III, p. 284 (6). Cf. Wüest, *Leis Willelme*, pp. 8–11.

667   Richardson and Sayles, pp. 121–2, with particular reference to Leis Wl 37.

668   *Gesetze* III, pp. 283–4 (2, 4a). Liebermann was sure that the second and third parts were by the same author as the first ('laut identischer Sprache'), but this does not affect the case that the first had an independent transmission, and that the Latin 'Rudimenta' circulated only in the context that gave rise to the Latin translation: III, p. 284 (10). Note that the Richardson & Sayles argument in their 'Addendum', pp. 176–9, for the author's access to the Latin original of *Instituta Cnuti*, relates only to the work's *third* section; and their three columns show conclusively that where Leis Wl agrees with *Inst. Cn* or Q, the latter agree with each other – for the simple reason that these were the obvious, current, translations.

669   To Short, 'Patrons and Polyglots', pp. 243–5, add Gillingham, 'Kingship, Chivalry and Love' (chapter 3, p. 141).

670   Leis Wl Pr.

ing the 'Laws of King Edward'. Otherwise, the 'Articles' seem to influence only the clauses on *murdrum* and perhaps frankpledge.[671] There were also passages loosely based on Cnut's laws about the peace of Church and king and about heriots, interspersed with Alfred's injury-list and laws against assaults on women.[672] Overlaps with *Leges Edwardi Confessoris* included Peter's Pence and the peace of the four great roads.[673] But the parts on procedure against theft and homicide have no known source. There is no saying what in the way of research, memory or experience lay behind the statement that the thegn's wergeld is £20 in Mercia and £25 in Wessex (1200 shillings either way); but it seems unlikely that experience of the payment of a thegn's wergeld was easily come by in mid-twelfth-century Mercia, where the work probably originated.[674] The second section was the one containing Roman law, a jumble of clauses on adultery, inheritance, poisoning and shipwreck. Roman jurisprudence at so crude and superficial a level is no more an indication of late date than writing in French.[675] The third section is based on Cnut's code, particularly its laws on judicial administration. The *Instituta* was probably the mediatory source, as *Instituta* and 'Articles' tend to go together.[676] The main conclusion to be drawn about *Leis Willelme* is perhaps this: what impressions one might otherwise derive from it as to the relevance of Anglo-Saxon law to twelfth-century practice are offset by its deference to Roman laws that are most unlikely to have come into court-room cognizance. For all that it was written in French, it is an intellectual's exercise.

The second work considered here was once the most respected of all but has long been the most derided.[677] What made the *Leges Edwardi Confessoris* precious for Sir Edward Coke is what has earned it contumely since its exposure by a Tory historian in 1685 (chapter 1, p. 8): the infamous opening account of how, four years into his reign, William the Conqueror empanelled juries of twelve from each shire who swore to declare the law.[678] No such episode ever occurred. The story is at best a garbled reminiscence of the 1086 proceedings, such as led Richard fitz Nigel to connect the Domesday survey with the king's codification of English law in Mercian, Danish and West Saxon divisions. Yet fitz Nigel's veracity as a commentator on the Exchequer (or even Domesday) has not been discredited by his misconceptions about 1086. It is not clear that the *Leges Edwardi* author deserves worse. Nor is his story of the 1070 deliberations neces-

---

671   Leis Wl 22, 20:3a/25; though the former allows eight days' grace against Wl art. 3's five (and Hn 91:1's seven); cf. also Leis Wl 21 – 21:5, Wl art. 5 on witnessing and attachment of livestock.

672   Leis Wl 1 – 1:1, 20 – 20:3, 10 – 11:2, 19 – 19:1, 18 – 18:1.

673   Leis Wl 17 – 17:3, 26.

674   Leis Wl 8; for the text's (south-east?) Mercian origin, see *Gesetze* III, p. 284 (8).

675   Richardson and Sayles, pp. 122, 78–85. It is possibly relevant that in the Holkham MS Leis Wl is accompanied by 'Pseudo-Ulpian' maxims from a different but related hand.

676   Leis Wl 41 – 41:1 (on overseas sale of Christians) and 40 (on capital punishment) are (in all copies bar Nowell's, which is what has distorted the numbering) in the order of the 'Articles' (9, 10), not that of Cnut (II 3 – 3:1, 2:1).

677   This text has been the particular object of Dr Bruce O'Brien's researches, shortly to be published as an edition, translation and study under the title *God's Peace and King's Peace*.

678   ECf Pr. – Pr.:1; the story is rounded off at 34 – 34:1a (where the work concludes in one set of manuscripts, see below).

sarily so much more fictional than the Horstead council at which, according to the 'argumentum' of *Quadripartitus*, the incoming Edward the Confessor promised the bishop of Winchester, Earl Godwine, and 'the thegns of all England' to secure the continuance of Cnut's laws.[679] The authority of *Quadripartitus* is unaffected by this assertion. So it should be for *Leges Edwardi*. Its own title was in any case not that which it has had since the seventeenth century. One class of manuscripts of its earliest recension calls it 'Tract about the laws and customs of England as declared in the time of King William the Great'. Its prologue was one more way of saying what all these tracts say and William said himself: that the law he proposed to enforce was what he inherited from his predecessor.[680]

Leges Edwardi survives in a prodigious wealth of manuscripts. Broadly speaking, these fall into four classes. The first two are of the text as it left its original author's pen. The difference between them is that one concluded with William prevailed upon to allow 'Edward's law' to stand (despite his own sense that the laws of Norway, from which his Norman followers derived, were superior to those of the British, English and Picts); while the other had an epilogue on the history of the 'laws of Edward', then extra clauses on suits for the post-humous pardon of thieves, usury, and witnessed sales of goods. This extension could have been omitted by the archetype of the first manuscript group from the author's original draft, or added in an authorial second edition.[681] The third and fourth classes comprise copies of the text included respectively in *Tripartita* and the 'London Collection'. Both involved revision by other hands, and the latter some spectacular interpolations. The first class of manuscripts tends to associate the work with Glanvill. Nearly all the others are collections of English law which contain other texts too.[682] It is highly likely that the extent of its circulation reflects an impression that it had summarized the pre-conquest heritage for the benefit of later ages.

That it by no means did. Compared with anything else reviewed here, it showed very little knowledge of Anglo-Saxon legal texts: they were never quoted and seldom echoed. That does not make *Leges Edwardi* the fruit of ignorance or fantasy. It might be thought (with *Leges Henrici*, it usually is thought) that what did not come from reading is likely to derive from experience. The author liked

679   *Richard fitz Nigel, Dialogue* xv – xvi, pp. 62–3; Sharpe, 'Prefaces of "Quadripartitus"', p. 164.

680   *Gesetze* I, p. 627, n. *b*); cf. the 'retractatio' title, 'leges Edwardi regis quas Willelmus postea confirmavit'. O' Brien suggests that the Leges author was aware of the *topoi* applicable in this context, and of a strikingly similar account of Saxon 'constitutional' arrangements in 'Vita Lebuini', p. 793.

681   O'Brien observes no stylistic change at ECf 34:1b; hence (as against Richardson and Sayles, p. 48), there can be no question of interpolation by another hand. His improved readings supersede Liebermann's *stemma* (*Gesetze* III, p. 340), and dictate what follows.

682   Paris BN Lat 4771 (Liebermann's Cb), *Inst. Cn* amplified by *Cons. Cn* Pr., etc.; BL. Harley 1704 (Liebermann's Hr), the main *Cons. Cn* witness (above, n. 654); BL. Harley 746 (Liebermann's S), Latin Leis Wl; BL. Add. 49366 (Liebermann's Hk), the 'Holkham' MS of Q, Leis Wl, etc. (n. 665); Bodl. Rawlinson C.641 (Liebermann's Rl), ECf added to *Inst. Cn*, Wl Art, CHn cor (n. 635), and followed by Magna Carta.

683   Cf. the English 'technical terms' at 6:2a, 12, 12:3, 12:6 (a 'proverb'), 20, 20:3, 23:1 (also proverbial), 26:2, 28, 30:4 31:1, 35:1c-e, 36:5; Liebermann, *Über die Leges Edwardi*, pp. 18–19, 25–32. At 32 – 32:3, the author declared reasonably enough that the English office of 'reeve' was 'for us a prefecture', but imprudently went on to make a semantic connection with OE 'grið'.

to flaunt his etymological skills, and they not infrequently betrayed him.[683] In this too, he was typical of legal writers in his time; *Quadripartitus* and *Instituta Cnuti* were often defeated by the texts before them. In tone and content, *Leges Edwardi* was most like the first part of *Leis Willelme*. The chief differences were that it was interested in Danelaw idiosyncracies but not in those of Mercia, and that, though it knew nothing of Roman law, its approach was in other ways more intellectual. There was a more serious attempt at systematic exposition; the work can be read as a balance of the peace due to the Church as underwritten by a king, against the peace enforced by kings as endorsed (*via* the judgement on the Merovingians ascribed wrongly to a Pope John) by the Church.[684] Above all, there was the *penchant* for historical digressions, usually (perhaps not always) misconceived. These included the epilogue's ridiculous account of how Edward revived the laws of Edgar that Cnut and his sons neglected. There seems to be an interest in the family of Edgar Ætheling, which prompted a reference to the later tenure of his sister Christina's lands by Ralph de Limesey. The usual deduction is that the author was linked with the de Limesey family, perhaps a Coventry cleric under the episcopate of Ralph's brother Robert (1102–17).[685] That he was a bad historian need not mean that he was a fraud or even a bad lawyer. Lawyers are often bad historians, as no one knew better than Maitland. Had he not decked out his text with its historical *persiflage* and settled for a prologue like that of *Leis Willelme*, his work might have been assessed like the *Leis*: scholars would be puzzled, intrigued, but not necessarily dismissive. That could be right. Justice in Henry I's England is not so well illuminated that one authority can confidently be preferred to another.

Attention may turn finally to the work that customarily sets the scene of Henrician justice: the *Leges* that go under Henry I's name; the text that has had more effect on views of English law before Henry II than any other. The chief function of *Leges Henrici Primi* for Maitland and lesser lights has been to offset the startling 'progress' made by English law between its time and Glanvill's. Its status as evidence is high, even as its lack of accomplishment is scorned. Both estimates may be wrong. Its status may arise from the initial impression that it stands in the name of the king under whom it was composed, as *Instituta*, *Leis* and *Leges Edwardi* do not. Yet the title 'De libertate ecclesie et tocius Angliae observanda leges Henrici' merely echoed its first rubric, which clearly related in turn to the Coronation Charter at its outset. Even if it was the author's title, designed for the work as a whole, it still said no more than the work's *prooemium*, which repeated the last clause of the preface to *Quadripartitus* Book II, and which took up that preface's theme, that Henry was building on the work of predecessors collected in Book I.[686] The writer therefore said and did no more

---

684   ECf 17:1; Korte, *Untersuchungen*, pp. 116–19; but Dr Korte is somewhat generous to the 'logic' of the digression on baronial 'curiae', 9:1–3.

685   ECf 35 – 35:2; Liebermann, *Über die Leges*, pp. 10–21. Granted that the author knew of Ralph de Limesey's succession to Christina's lands, and so had some knowledge of Oxfordshire and/or Warwickshire where they were located (*DB* i 159b, *Oxfordshire* 54; i 244b, *Warwickshire* 42), it still seems legitimate to emphasize that his *interest* was in the progeny of Edward the Exile, and that this probably had some relevance to his high opinion of the truly English royal line and relatively low view of the Danish kings.

than what all his counterparts had said and done to link old law and new. He just found a less traditionalist way of expressing his aim.

Medieval bibliographers were less interested in the Laws of 'Henry' than modern scholars, just as they were more impressed by those of 'Edward'. There are two classes of manuscript, neither numerous. One is formed by the Exchequer 'Red Book' and a slightly later derivative, the other by the 'London Collection', which (for these purposes) has three lost offshoots, and the earliest copy of which was in some way affected by the Exchequer group.[687] Neither class makes *Leges Henrici* a sequel to *Quadripartitus*. Yet the 'Red Book's' inclusion of the *Leges* as late as *c*.1225 is surprising enough; it is scarcely odd that it disdained to reproduce the bulk of translated Anglo-Saxon law-codes as well. The 'London collector' did in a sense put them in sequence, but his historical outlook led him to interpose the *Tripartita* between them.[688] It remains more than probable that *Leges* and *Quadripartitus* were by the same author. Each tended to espouse the same readings and to be defeated by the same technicalities. The *Quadripartitus* 'Argumentum' announced a plan for four books, of which the third was to concern procedure and the fourth theft. However, alongside this passage, and perhaps intended to replace it, was one speaking only of two books. The 'Argumentum' declared that Henry 'not only has ... given us back the law of King Edward ... but strengthened as it was by the improvements introduced by his blessed father, he has improved it with his own laws'. Book II's preface said that 'our most blessed lord and king does not cease to enhance with daily praises the improvement of King William in the English laws. Hence, this book which I launched with a reproach of our own time, I have provided with a beginning but no conclusion'. *Quadripartitus* has a gloomy 'Dedicatio' and is indeed unfinished in that it lacks Books III and IV; while the *prooemium* of *Leges Henrici* repeats the panegyrical paragraph that in *Quadripartitus* Book II's preface followed the praise of Henry's legislation. This author's thought-processes can be as unfathomable as his Latin, but the connection seems clear. It looks very much as if he jettisoned his four book "Quadripartitus" project, because a work like *Leges Henrici* would be a more fitting tribute to Henry I's sustained legislative output. It was, for all that, a continuation of *Quadripartitus*.[689]

The content of *Leges Henrici* will be assessed, together with that of works of similar complexion, in Parts III and IV of this book. The last part of the next

---

686   *Leges Henrici*, ed. Downer, pp. 7, 72–3. Professor Downer was surer than Liebermann of the relevance of the *Inscriptio*, but offered no stronger argument than that it *could* have covered the entire work; 'primi' at least cannot be original.

687   See Downer's reassessment, pp. 45–73, of Liebermnn, *Über das englische Rechtsbuch Leges Henrici*, pp. 7–16, and *Gesetze* III, pp. 312–13 (1–2). My own comments, '"Quadripartitus"', p. 121 (pp. 89–90), and n. 31, doubtless verged on the brash, but it still seems right to insist that the relationship of these MSS can only be fully grasped when attention is given to their handling of *all* texts involved.

688   See Table 4.7; since Henry's 'London Charter' does not constitute chapter 2 in the Exchequer text, the likelihood is that it was a further insertion by the 'London Collector', prompted by his local rather than historical agenda. However, later editions of *Quadripartitus* (chapter 4, pp. 237–9) did not circulate with *Leges Henrici* attatched.

689   See the translations of 'Argumentum' 27, 30–2, and 'preface to King Henry's improvements in the laws' 12–14, by Sharpe, 'Prefaces of "Quadripartitus"', pp. 167–8, 171–2; and my discussion of their meaning, '"Quadripartitus"', pp. 137–8 (pp. 105–6).

chapter will be devoted to its conception of law and legal culture. All that is called for here is appreciation of its behaviour as a text. Of the utmost moment is that it was written by someone who had unambiguously committed himself to the relevance of pre-conquest law by rendering the largest known collection of it into serviceable language. Of some 950 clauses into which it is parcelled by modern editors, about a third consist of quotations from material already deployed in *Quadripartitus*.[690] In so far as he was dependent on texts, he was likely to over-state their applicability.[691] But when not following the lead of his sources, he must some of the time have been drawing on personal knowledge of the law's operations. He hoped that his work might profit 'professioni nostrae', though he was not sure that it would, and held a low opinion of some 'professores'.[692] It is therefore important that, though even more concerned than *Leges Edwardi* with baronial jurisdiction (his work was described by Maitland as a 'treatise on soke'), *Leges Henrici* was at pains to stress the over-reaching arm of royal justice.[693] And although Maitland constructed a scintillating *tableau* of juristic confusion by taking the *Leges* at face value, a modern scholar, starting from records of litigation itself, comments dryly that 'there is little sign that contemporaries were confused'.[694] The crucial question is how much of the *Leges* was taken from conduct of legal practice, how much from knowledge of texts, and how far practice was dictated by knowledge of texts. It is a question that remains unanswerable from the *Leges* alone.

The *Leges Henrici* was intellectually systematic to a degree quite eclipsing its counterparts. It was much the longest legal work from the pre-Angevin period: perhaps half as long again as the Alfred–Ine *domboc* or code of Cnut. Its bulk arose mainly from its aspirations to comprehensiveness. Gaps in the pre-conquest record were plugged. 'Pleas of the Crown' were given in full, as they were not by Cnut (above, p. 364).[695] There was a sustained attempt at systematic arrangement.[696] There were essays in rationalization. The 'leading case' judgements of earlier codes were now generalized: Alfred's law on clumsy spear-carriers (above, p. 282) was prefaced: 'In ... legal proceedings of this kind consideration must be given to the manner of carrying or laying down weapons (armorum)' – not just spears – 'the place in which they were laid down, the person who laid them there, what happened, and how it happened'.[697] *Leges Henrici* is well-known for such

690   These are easily enough spotted through Liebermann's use of small print.
691   Note the acute judgement of Hudson, 'Maitland and Anglo-Norman Law', p. 45: 'He drew on books, and he drew on personal experience. However, when written sources and personal experience clashed, his inclination was always to go by the book'.
692   Hn 8:7, *Quad*. 'Dedicatio' 24, 38 (Sharpe, 'Prefaces', pp. 160, 162); cf. the use of the first person in Hn 28:5, 45:5, 61:2, and especially 63:4. Maitland would much rather that he had not been a practitioner: *CP* III, pp. 470–1.
693   Soke: Maitland, *DBB*, p. 80; e.g. Hn 20 – 23, 25 – 33, 41, 46, 50, 57, 61, etc. Royal justice: e.g. Hn 6:2–2a: above the 'trina partitio' of Wessex, Mercia and Danelaw stands the 'tremendum regie maiestatis ... imperium'; cf. Loyn, 'De Iure Domini Regis, and chapters 6 (pp. 466, 474), 10.
694   PM I, pp. 105–7; Hudson, 'Maitland', p. 41.
695   Hn 10 – 10:1.
696   See the sympathetic treatment of Korte, *Untersuchungen*, pp. 119–30; one symptom of the new cultural climate is that Dr Korte's case now carries more conviction than for Alfred's code or Cnut's.
697   Hn 88:2; Af 36 – 36:2.

principles as 'who unknowingly offends will knowingly amend'.[698] Legal proverbs went down well with the *Leges Edwardi* too. They were notably, perhaps surprisingly, scarce in early records.

But the main mark of an intellectualizing approach is the influence of the early-twelfth century's mounting interest in academic jurisprudence. Over 10 per cent of *Leges* clauses were from sources with little or nothing to do with English law. Isidore was on hand to tell a reader which teeth are which (à *propos* Alfred's injury tariff), and that men have more than women.[699] The author had access to Pseudo-Isidore material from a canon collection other than Lanfranc's and to Ivo of Chartres (chapter 6, pp. 470–3). There was even room for Frankish codes and Carolingian capitularies. The results could be bizarre. What ought to be precious evidence of early English inheritance law (in a chapter headed 'Consuetudo Westsexe') was lifted almost word for word from *Lex Ribuaria*, five centuries before.[700] It goes without saying that these clauses owed their presence to something other than a wish to describe English law as it currently functioned. They were there because they contributed to the work's coherence as an intellectual exposition. That the chief impression left upon commentators should be one of muddle is not – certainly not primarily – testimony to its author's stupidity or the confusion of the times, but to the dreadful difficulties of accommodating law as known in the English kingdom to the disciplines of the new law-schools. By comparison with other English works of the age, the only comparison that carries weight, what stands out is the courage, even the success, of the enterprise.

The *resumé* of implications for which this chapter cries out even more than the last can be focused around a question that has cropped up throughout. What reason is there to think that the pre-conquest legislative tradition ran to many codes that are now lost? There is no doubt that this could easily have happened. Some texts studied in section 9 were fragments of lost wholes. Among ostensibly royal codes in earlier sections were composites of *déraciné* elements. The sheer fragility of the transmission of early English legal texts, a message of chapter 4, has been demonstrated from a different angle in this one. Alfred–Ine, II and V Æthelstan, II–III Edgar, I Æthelred, I–II Cnut, Alfred–Guthrum (and, oddly enough, its pseudo-Edward supplement), *Judex* and Wulfstan's status-tracts descend in more than single transmissions. The majority of texts do not, and among these are all the codes of Edward the Elder and Edmund, and the later output of Æthelstan, Edgar and Æthelred. When so much depends on preservation of texts by early-twelfth-century legal 'encyclopaedias', it is obvious that many laws may have been less fortunate. A hesitant proposition of this chapter is that early English kings were moving towards the creation of a less formal style of precept, further advanced by post-conquest law-makers. Among its features was less robust circulation than for more solemn edicts. It follows that there could have been very many more law-codes of that type, from either side of 1066. This

---

698   Hn 88:6a; cf., e.g., 'Pactum enim legem vincit et amor iudicium', Hn 49:5a.
699   Hn 93:6–6a.
700   Hn 70:18,20–20b, *Lex Rib.* lxxxiv, lvii (but with interesting amendments in the first).

is not to mention more direct evidence of losses: even if the fierce Edgar law on theft described by Lantfred survives in the fragments of the 'II Æthelred Appendix' and *Forfang*, the rest of it is gone beyond recall; so also Æthelred's 'Bromdun' laws that were benchmarks for the decrees of Woodstock and Wantage, whether or not their residue is the last part of 'IV Æthelred'.

Yet the early-twelfth-century record can be read another way. There is no doubt at all of the seriousness of the effort to retrieve the pre-conquest legacy. But however hard they looked, however much they revised, people still seemed to come up with the same laws. Isolated texts in post-conquest copies were the already familiar II–III Edgar or I–II Cnut. This chapter has surveyed some sixty-five texts, fifty-four from before 1066; the last chapter examined about twenty legal manuscripts. Were it a question of the chance survival of a fraction of the material once in circulation, the ratio should surely be wider than three codes for every one volume? It is one thing to say, as often is said, that vernacular writs and charters had little prospect of preservation in post-conquest repositories, hence that the Anglo-Saxon administrative achievement may be drastically under-documented. The same conspicuously does not go for laws. If, then, a wealth of written law failed to reach post-conquest compilers, that must be because it was not carefully enough kept nearer its own time. This is of a piece with an evident degree of indifference to the status of written legal records. The more formally promulgated 'gerædnessa' of king and *witan* may have the richest lines of descent, but more simply executive texts circulated beside them, regardless of their ostensibly lesser status. Codes were revised, not always by official agencies. The works in section 9 are most important evidence of how seriously written law was taken at ground level. But they also show that codified law was not sacred. Resort to script was widespread, sometimes startling. But there was nothing privileged about it. If the law of the pre-conquest kingdom was made only in writing and only by writing, scribes were remarkably cavalier in reporting it, and were frankly *blasé* about its preservation.

CHAPTER 6

Legislation as Literature

The last chapter found that the legislative materials of the first kings of the English do not always, or even regularly, behave as legal texts might be expected to. At least as they survive, their arrangement can be illogical, their style either quaintly elementary or ponderously rhetorical, their form inconsistent, their content a baffling mix of the unhelpfully specific and the ineffectually general. Much of the material is intelligible as statute law in a modern sense. The puzzle is that much is not. Earlier chapters showed that all pre-conquest manuscripts of legal texts were made and kept for other than legal reasons; and that, until the twelfth century brought new stimuli to bear, written law appears in historical narratives (if at all) as an ideal cherished by rulers in pursuit of a Hebraic or Roman image, and by peoples in defence of their traditions. In the late Roman empire legislation took a self-consciously literary form, as a consequence of the rhetorical training that was the Quaestor's qualification for office (chapter 2, pp. 36–8). Law and literature were never wholly disentangled in the sub-Roman West. Is it therefore possible to explain the behaviour of English codes, perhaps even their very existence, in literary and ideological terms?

1 King Alfred and the Mosaic Tradition

The extant form of Alfred's *domboc* looks harder to reconcile with judicial needs than almost any early medieval legislation. Yet its official status is clearer than that of 'chancery' texts of *Lex Salica* (chapter 2, pp. 41–2). Its language was that not of a royal writing-office but of a king in person (chapter 5, pp. 272–7). Alfred wrote other books. It is *a priori* plausible that his law-book should be understandable as a literary exercise, whatever its viability as a legal tool.[1] Some of the structural anomalies that led Liebermann and others to invoke scribal poltergeists of exceptional power and malignity respond perfectly well to literary analysis. The appendage of Ine's partly superseded code would be no problem if

---

1 The pioneer of this approach was the admirable Turk, *Legal Code of Alfred*; cf. p. v: 'the nature of this work rendered desirable its consideration from a literary point of view'. A commendable feature of Frantzen, *King Alfred* is that the lawbook is treated as one of the king's five literary works, with a chapter to itself, pp. 11–21.

Alfred's concern was less with legal consistency than with legislative continuity. He may not have meant the war-making and law-giving past of West Saxon kings to be juxtaposed, as in two of the earliest *domboc* manuscripts they were (chapter 4, pp. 163–82). But he could reasonably sense that his subjects needed reminding of their history as a people of written, of civilized, law, when their very political survival had been at risk.[2] Having acknowledged the influence of the laws of Æthelberht and Offa upon his own (above, pp. 277–80), it was natural to make his regard for West Saxon tradition clearer yet. When the Carolingians reissued *Lex Salica* soon after their *coup*, they changed little beyond recasting its sixty-five titles into 100, and replacing the prologue with one that stridently celebrated the Franks as a people and their *Merovingian* kings. Early medieval peoples located their identity in their ancient written laws. Only in Visigothic Spain was old law systematically traded in for new (chapter 2, pp. 38–41, 44–5, 49).

Frankish and Visigothic parallels show that the number of chapters in a code could matter more than the logical deployment of material (chapter 5, pp. 270–1). Alfred's 120 chapters (chapter 5, pp. 267–9) were more peculiar than most such deployments. But they also had a clearer rationale. In the number-symbolism displayed with such tireless ingenuity by early medieval exegetes, 120 stood for law, and more especially the relationship between Mosaic law and the new dispensation. When commenting on the 120 who assembled to elect a replacement for Judas in the first chapter of Acts, Bede observed that 'it was right that the preachers of new grace should designate in their number the sacrament that the *legislator* showed in his years'. The legislator was of course Moses, who died at that age.[3] Bede made the same point in his *De Templo Salomonis*, a work which one might guess to have had special resonance for Alfred. Construction of the Temple began 480 years after the exodus from Egypt:

> Four times 120 make 480; four fits aptly with evangelical perfection because of the number of evangelists, 120 with legal teaching (*doctrinae legali*) because so many were the years of the *legislator*, in which number the primitive Church received the grace of the Holy Spirit.

It was evidently believed that the same number had gathered at Pentecost as earlier met to elect Mathias. There was further symbolism in the fact that Moses had brought down his law fifty days after sacrificing a lamb, and fifty days likewise passed between the sacrifice of Calvary and the descent of the Holy Spirit.[4] Bede's views were found in Isidore earlier who was echoed by Hrabanus later.[5] The 'Moysaica aetas' was something of a commonplace. Now, the *domboc* not

---

2   The reassuring function of Alfredian literature was stressed in Wallace-Hadrill's seminal 'Franks and the English in the Ninth Century', pp. 216–17 (pp. 213–14).
3   Deuteronomy 34:7 (cf. 31:2); Acts 1:15. *Bedae Expositio Actuum*, p. 11; Bede also noted that there are fifteen 'Gradual' Psalms (i.e. nos 120–134, Vulgate 119–33), and that the sum of numbers one to fifteen is 120, a figure 'qui propter utriusque legum perfectionem in psalterio mystice continetur'.
4   *Bedae Libri De Templo*, p. 157; *Bedae Expositio Actuum*, pp. 14–15. Cf. Alcuin, ' Enchiridion', cols 572–3, 619.
5   Isidore, 'Quaestiones in Exodum' xxviii 1, col. 300 (cf. his 'Liber Numerorum qui in sanctis scripturis occurrunt' xxv, col. 199); Hrabanus, 'Commentarium in Exodus' ii 11, cols 91–2.

only began with prolonged excerpts from Mosaic law, but went on to describe how its stringency was modified by the early Church meeting in council at Jerusalem. The first chapter number came precisely when Alfred finished reporting the events of Scripture, and began his account of subsequent Christian legislation, culminating in his own. Biblical law for which 120 was multiply symbolic, was followed by post-biblical, more especially West Saxon, law in 120 chapters. One can see why an interpolating scribe might have wished to rearrange Alfred's law-book along these lines. One can also see why Alfred might have wished to do so himself (cf. chapter 5, n. 17).

Either way, the chaptering of the *domboc* directs attention to a problematic feature for which only Alfred can have been responsible. The Mosaic preface occupies over a fifth of the total book (chapter 5, n. 1). This is a far higher proportion than is given to prefatory material in any other early medieval law text. Largely ignored by translators since 1840, as having 'no bearing on Anglo-Saxon law', it was set aside in chapter 5 for similar reasons. But any assessment of Alfred's law-making should of course take in so outsize an overture. It may set the key of the whole enterprise.

As with Alfred's other books, his treatment of Moses must be studied with reference to the intellectual climate of his time. When noting deviations from the Latin original, one must look out for variants in the several families of early medieval Vulgate texts. When the translation seems to convey Alfred's own ideas, they can helpfully be compared with the views of other ninth-century writers.[6] For Alfred was far from the only early medieval legislator to ponder the relevance of Mosaic law for the Christian era. A *Collatio legum Romanarum et Mosaicarum*, compiled sometime in late Antiquity, aligned excerpts from the Pentateuch with passages of Roman law, mostly from legal textbooks of the period, but sometimes from imperial decrees, like Diocletian's Edict against the Manichees (for which it is the sole source).[7] Some manuscripts of the *Ecloga*, law-book of the Iconoclast emperors (chapter 2, n. 31), have an appendix of selections from Mosaic law.[8] The collection of Roman and Carolingian imperial legislation made by 'Benedict the Deacon' (chapter 2, n. 152) contains not only bogus decrees in the tradition of ninth-century Carolingian forgery but also (in its words) 'certain *capitula* excerpted *ex lege divina* ... that all may not be unaware that ... *capitula* [of the emperors] agree with divine laws and canonical rules'.[9] Moses stood at the head of the potted legal history in Isidore's *Etymologiae*, hence at the forefront of the Bavarian *Lex* (chapter 2, pp. 43–4); the arrangement of that code's titles duly followed a Decalogue format – as did the core section of Charlemagne's *Admonitio Generalis* (chapter 2, pp. 50–1).

---

6   Cf. Bately, 'Literary Prose of King Alfred's Reign': the approach exemplified by Otten, *König Alfreds Boethius*, by Frantzen, *King Alfred*, and by the essays of Professors Gatch and Bolton in Szarmach (ed.), *Studies in Earlier Old English Prose*, pp. 17–45, 153–68.
7   *Mosaicarum et Romanarum Legum Collatio*, ed. Mommsen; trans. Hyamson, *Mosaicarum et Romanarum Legum Collectio*.
8   *Ecloga*, ed. Montferratus, pp. 79–97, trans. Freshfield, pp. 142–4 (unfortunately, only a list of excerpts). Cf. 'Appendix Eclogae' and 'Nomos Mosaïkos', ed. Burgmann and Troianos; and Pieler, 'Byzantinische Rechtsliteratur', pp. 438–42.
9   *Benedicti Capitularia* Pr., ii 1–55, pp. 40, 75–6.

Finally, there is an important, though still unedited, Irish collection, the *Liber ex lege Moysi*, which circulated in manuscripts of Irish canon law, and is thus associated in one Breton MS with a text of *Lex Salica*. At least one copy reached England in the later Anglo-Saxon period. Part of what has been called 'les tendances bibliques du Droit canonique Irlandais', it has more than once been seen as a possible influence on Alfred.[10]

Alfred translated the best part of chapters 20 to 22 of Exodus, and the first third of chapter 23. The Decalogue itself led on to the Mosaic law on slavery, murder and injury, death caused by and to cattle, breaking and entering, damage to property by cattle or fire, loans, seduced virgins, sorcery, bestial intercourse, pagan sacrifice, obligations to society's weaker elements, first fruits, justice and equity. He translated the text less freely than he did Boethius or Augustine, but kept less close to the original than in his rendition of the first fifty Psalms, or even his *Pastoral Rule*.[11] An illustration of the possibilities is his text of Exodus 22:1f:

> If anyone steal another's ox and kill or sell it, let him give two in return, and four sheep in return for one. If he do not have anything to give, let him be sold himself in return for the stock. If a thief break into a man's house at night, and be killed there, let him not be guilty of any homicide. If he does this after sunrise, he is guilty of homicide, and he is then to die himself unless it were done in as an act of necessity (*buton he nieddæda wære*). If what he stole is found with him alive (*mid him cwicum*), let him compensate for it twofold.[12]

In the mainstream Vulgate text, the sentence about those with nothing to give followed the provision about killing burglars, where it must be admitted that it makes less sense. The *Liber ex lege Moysi* went along with Alfred on this point, raising the possibility that both used an insular text with this variant.[13] On the other hand, at least one Alfredian deviation is likely to arise from mistranslation. The implication of the final sentence is that the thief's life is in question, when the Vulgate has 'si inventum fuerit apud eum quod furatus est vivens', showing that the stolen stock is what was meant. Alfred's Vulgate text conceivably read 'viventem', but the *Liber ex lege* gives 'vivens'. And the omission of sheep at the start of the clause, when reference is then made to compensation for them as well as oxen, is surely mere carelessness. But the most intriguing problem is Alfred's inclusion of references to night-time and self-defence in the clause about burglary, which are not in the Vulgate at all. They could be spontaneous glosses by Alfred,

---

10   Fournier, 'Le Liber ex Lege Moysi', p. 230; Kottje, *Studien zum Einfluß des alten Testamentes*, pp. 11–43 (where an edition is promised at p. 12, n. 4); Ó'Corráin, Breatnach and Breen, 'Laws of the Irish', pp. 394–412 (an important general discussion of the influence of Mosaic law on secular and ecclesiastical Irish law); Treschow, 'Prologue to Alfred's Law Code'. The Breton MS of the 'Liber ex lege' is Paris, BN lat. 3182 (*Bibliothèque Nationale, Catalogue Général* IV, pp. 304–17); the MSS from England are Corpus Christi Cambridge 279, pp. 106–60, and BL, Cotton Otho E.xiii, ff. 3v–11r (Gneuss, 'Preliminary list' nos 81, 361).

11   Bately, 'Literary Prose', pp. 14–15; Frantzen, *King Alfred*, pp. 29–31. His omission of the second commandment on images has attracted notice since Lambarde's day; cf. Liebermann, *Gesetze* III, p. 37 (32); but Howlett, *British Books in Biblical Style*, pp. 357–8, notes that Exodus 20:23 is translated in Af Int 10.

12   Af Int 24 – 25.

13   CCCC 279, p. 113; Otho E xiii, f. 5r.

deduced from the context and from West Saxon practice.[14] It happens, however, that both are found in the afore-mentioned *Collatio*. Its clause on theft began with the Twelve Tables on nocturnal thieves killed when daring to defend themselves. 'Know, jurisconsults', it continued, 'that Moses decreed this first', and the Exodus verses then followed, with 'nocte' inserted.[15] One would certainly put this parallel down to coincidence, were it not that the *Collatio* was known to Archbishop Hincmar of Rheims; and Hincmarian themes will shortly be found pervading the whole argument of the preface (pp. 423–6).

As in other Alfredian works, then, not all idiosyncrasies are instances of the infiltration of the king's ideas. But as in the rest of the corpus, there is some of the (to historians) precious freedom with which Alfred approached his task. Shortly after his burglary section comes this:

> If anyone entrust property to his friend, if he steal it himself, let him compensate twofold. If he do not know who stole it, let him clear himself that he played no guilty part there. If, however. it were livestock, and he say that an army (*here*) took it or that it died naturally (*hit self acwæle*), and he have witness, he does not need to pay for it. If, however, he have no witness, and the other do not trust him, then let him swear.[16]

There are a number of marked differences between the Old English and the Latin original. Alfred began with a mistranslation: the Vulgate was quite clear that the entrusted object was stolen *from*, not *by*, the trustee; but its 'invenitur fur' was taken to mean that the trustee was 'found a thief', not that 'the thief was discovered'. The next Vulgate phrase was omitted: it had one of the embarrassing references to the 'gods (*deos*)' that repeatedly troubled Alfred.[17] The Latin went on to list a variety of possible stolen goods, among them an ass, but Alfred restricted himself to 'cucu feoh'; as Liebermann pointed out, the Old English word for ass ('esol') is very rare, and the animal itself was probably scarce in pre-conquest England.[18] The following remarks on the presence or absence of witness were an extensive gloss on an original where there must be an oath if 'nobody saw' the object's death or capture. Finally, the fact that capture by a 'here' was put first among an entrusted beast's misfortunes, where in the Latin it came after death and disease, has obvious relevance to recent West Saxon experience, and a close equivalent in Alfred's *Boethius*.[19]

---

14   Cf. Af 5, 42:4.
15   'Collatio' VII i 1–2, and the following excerpts from *Pauli Sententiae* and Ulpian, pp. 161–3. It may be noted that 'Collatio' XI i 1, p. 173, like Af Int 24, takes sale of the thief without means to compensate alongside theft of cattle (Exodus 22:4), not burglary as in the main Vulgate text. For Hincmar's knowledge of this work, first spotted by the remarkable Savigny, *Geschichte* II, pp. 280–3, see *Hinkmar, De Divortio* xii, p. 184–5 (cf. p. 178?); discussed by Dirksen, 'Über die Collatio', pp. 136–40, and by Devisse, *Hincmar et la Loi*, p. 27.
16   Af Int 28, Exodus 22:7–11, etc.
17   'Ad deos'; cf. Af Int 11, 37; Exodus 21:6, 22:28, 'diis'. It appears that the original meaning was 'judges'.
18   Liebermann, 'King Alfred and Mosaic Law', p. 31; Alfred likewise dropped the 'asinus' of Exodus 21:33/Af Int 22, though retaining it when translating Gregory's paraphrase of the passage: *Alfred's Pastoral Care*, p. 459; cf. chapter 5, n. 38.
19   *Alfred's Boethius*, p. 34: 'ne geherde non mon þa get nanne sciphere' – translating the original's '*classica*, trumpet signals' (*Boethius, Consolation of Philosophy* ii 5, pp. 208–9) as if relating to '*classis*, fleet'!

Alfred was therefore willing to adapt Holy Writ itself if he thus conveyed a clearer message to his audience. Unlike the late Roman or Byzantine collections, he did not rearrange the Mosaic Law by topic. But his was much more a selection than the *Liber ex lege Moysi*, which includes substantial tracts of the rest of the Pentateuch, including Jewish food taboos, and Deuteronomy's formidable list of curses.[20] He even omitted some of Exodus' more *recherché* passages, like that on the sabbatical year (which is in the *Liber ex lege*). His attitude was also more adaptive than that of 'Benedict the Deacon': he evidently could not accept the Mosaic 'you must not take pity on the pauper in a lawsuit', and left it out; but when he came to 'non declinabis in iudicio pauperis', he expanded the phrase:

> Judge very impartially (*emne*). Do not judge one judgement for the wealthy, another for the poor; nor are you to judge one for the dearer and another for the more hateful.[21]

No one today can fail to notice the general resemblance between the Mosaic law and the *Volksrechte* of early medieval Europe. Presumably no one could then. It was suggested in chapter 5 (p. 282) that one or two of Alfred's own clauses were directly inspired by items in his preface. The overall effect of his adjustments to Moses was to strengthen the resemblance. Not every irrelevance was ironed out. There was still talk of strangers in the land of Egypt. But shekels became shillings and Hebrews Christians; they remained shekels and Hebrews (though glossed in the former instance) in the *Liber ex lege*.[22] The Mosaic mirror in which West Saxons could anyway glimpse their own customs was polished so as to make the image unmistakable.

So what was achieved by the comparison thus invited? A first step towards answering this question is to quote the whole passage in which Alfred made the transition from one law to the other:

> These are the laws that God Almighty spoke himself to Moses, and commanded him to keep; and when the only begotten son of the Lord our God, that is the Saviour Christ, came into the world, he said that he came not to break these commandments nor to countermand them, but to extend them with everything good, and he taught mercy and humility. Then, after his passion, before his apostles set out to teach throughout all the earth, and when they were still together, they converted many heathen peoples to God. When they were all assembled, they sent messengers to Antioch and to Syria, to teach Christ's law (*æ*). When they perceived that these were not prospering, they sent an epistle to them. This is then the epistle that the apostles all sent to Antioch and to Syria and to Cilicia, who were just converted from heathen peoples to Christ: 'The Apostles and the elder brethren wish you health; and we inform you that we have heard that some of our fellows have come to you with our message and ordered you to keep more difficult customs than we ordered them, and have confused you too much with manifold orders, and have misled your souls more than they led you aright. Then

---

20   CCCC 279, pp. 122–3, 146–8 Leviticus 7:19–27, 11:35–6, Deuteronomy 27:15–26. The contrasts between Alfredian and Irish treatments is stressed by Lares, *Bible et Civilisation Anglaise*, pp. 119–28.
21   Af Int 43, Exodus 23:6. Benedict fails to quote either passage.
22   Af Int 33, 21, 11; CCCC 279, pp. 112, 108.

we assembled on that matter, and it pleased us all that we send Paul and Barnabas, men who long to give their souls for the Lord's name. With them we send Judas and Silas ... It seemed right to the Holy Spirit and to us that we should not put any burden on you beyond what is necessary for you to keep: that is, then, that you desist from worshipping idols, nor taste blood nor what is strangled, and avoid illicit sexual intercourse; and whatever you wish that other men should not do to you, you should not do that to other men'.

I. This one law can one remember, that he judges each man aright; he needs no other lawbooks (*ne ðearf he nanra domboca operra*). Let him remember to adjudge to no man what he would not be adjudged to him, were judgement sought over him. Afterwards, when it happened that many peoples received the faith of Christ, then were assembled throughout the whole world, as also throughout the English (*Angelcynn*) after they received the faith of Christ, many synods of holy bishops and other celebrated wise men. They then determined, for the mercy that Christ taught, that for almost every misdeed, lords of the world (*weoruldhlafordas*) might with their leave receive without sin at the first offence compensation in money (*fiohbote*), which they then fixed; save that for betraying one's lord they dared not declare any mercy, since God Almighty adjudged none to him who scorned him, nor did Christ, son of God, adjudge any to him who gave him over to death, and he ordered that one love one's lord as oneself. They then in many synods fixed compensations for many human misdeeds, and they wrote them in many synod-books, here one law, there another. Then I, King Alfred, gathered these (*þas*) together, and commanded to be written down many of those which our predecessors held ... [23]

Liebermann thought that Alfred's aim was, 'through a *Humanitätsideal*, first to raise the consciousness of his judges, and ultimately the *Rechtskultur* of the nation'.[24] If this was indeed Alfred's idea it had Carolingian precedent. Theodulf's 'Comparison of Ancient and Modern Law' declared that, 'while the precepts of early time were severe, those applied in our own times are more cruel'. Multiple restitution in the Mosaic law on cattle-theft was unfavourably compared with the executions and mutilations, scourgings and gulps of molten lead prescribed in contemporary usage (Theodulf was evidently thinking of Roman law, or possibly of his native Visigothic code). 'For shedding the blood of a pig, the head is nowadays given, human blood is poured out for cattle. I do not know whether these are laws or rage instead (*nescio sint leges an mage sitque furor*)'.[25] Yet Alfred's message was clearly different. It was *not* Moses who infused mildness into legislation, but Christ and his Church who infused it into Moses. Alfred did think that Christian synods had tempered the ferocity of primitive law by laying down money-compensations for first offences; the *Orosius* translator had a somewhat similar idea.[26] But he did not need three chapters of (in parts

---

23   Af Int 49 – 49:9. For translation of what follows, and for the probable sense of 'þas', see chapter 5, pp. 277–9, and nn. 73–4.

24   *Gesetze* III, p. 36 (30): 'Die Witan ... waren für eine orientalische Rechtsreform viel zu konservativ'.

25   'Theodulfi Carmen xxix', ed. Dümmler, *Poetae* I, pp. 517–19, lns 5–6, 25–32, 46–8.

26   *Old English Orosius* i 12, p. 34: 'Nu cyningas 7 caseras, þeah þe hwa wið hiora willan gegylte, hie ðeah for Godes lufan be ðæs gyltes mæþe forgifnesse doð'; the Latin original, *Orosius, Historiarum libri VII* I xx 6, argued that pre-christian tyrants tortured the innocent, whereas christian emperors, among the first to be converted, did not punish the crimes of the tyrants they crushed (a decidedly questionable account of later Roman imperial practice).

ferocious) Mosaic law to make the point that judicial mercy was a by-product of conversion.

What the Exodus excerpts did was to show that Christian law was rooted in the Divine Law given to Moses. From those roots it had grown organically under God's care, but it was still recognizably the same plant. Alfred's account of the history of Christian law-giving had its own echoes in the ninth-century world at large. The Apostolic Church at Jerusalem was the perceived prototype of Carolingian bishops in council.[27] 'Do to no one what you would not want done to you', the 'Golden Rule' on which Alfred laid such stress, was probably to be found in his original; it concludes the apostolic letter in 'western' Vulgate texts, including the Book of Armagh.[28] But it also struck a chord for the compilers of the Pseudo-Isidore Decretals. Early in their supplement to the much more ancient, if equally bogus, 'Epistle of Clement', they cited Christ's two great commandments, then continued: 'Hence is found written in the Old Testament: "What you would not have done to you, you are not to do to another". And the Lord said: "Everything that you wish that men do to you, you are to do likewise to them". Of the two commandments, malice is curbed by the one, and good will spread by the other'.[29] The collocation of the Golden Rule in old and new versions with the two 'great commandments', the second of which was so spectacularly distorted by Alfred in the cause of lordship, is noteworthy.

But it was the prolific writings of Archbishop Hincmar of Rheims, the most learned and penetrating legal mind of the early medieval West, that came closest to the views expounded and implicit in Alfred's preface.[30] Hincmar's idea of law is nowhere set out as a coherent thesis. It must be reconstructed from scattered, if reiterated, observations in polemics with varied objectives. Like everyone else for half a millennium either side of him, he started from the immutable law that was the word of God in Scripture: 'Let those with such views defend themselves as much as they wish, whether through the *leges* of the world, if there are any, or through human customs. Yet if they are Christians, they should know that they are to be judged in the Day of Judgement not by Roman nor by Salic nor by Burgundian (*Gundobadis*), but by divine and apostolic laws'. Again: 'The words of the Decalogue were written by the finger of God. He decreed that that law was to be valid in perpetuity, which he wrote with his finger, that is his Spirit'.[31] That proposition could not, of course, be challenged.

27   Wallace-Hadrill, '*Via Regia*', p. 32 (191).

28   *Novum Testamentum Latine* III (i), pp. 139–40. Turk, *Legal Code*, pp. 37–8, was the first to draw attention to this point; Liebermann was well aware of it (*Gesetze* III, p. 48, *ad. loc.*), though preferring to cite the rule in positive form, from Matthew 7:12, in his texts volume. For discussion of the history of the principle, which appears to originate in Hellentistic Jewry, see Dihle, *Goldene Regel*, pp. 80–112; and for its regular appearance in Augustine's works, la Bonnardière, 'En marge de la "Biblia Augustiniana"'.

29   'Epistola Clementis' xxii–xxiii, *Decretales pseudo-isidorianae*, ed. Hinschius, pp. 37–8. The doubled Golden Rule also appears in Theodulf, 'Erstes Kapitular' i 14, 'Zweites Kapitular' i 8.

30   For what follows see above all Devisse, *Hincmar et la Loi*, pp. 72–92, and *Hincmar Archevêque* I, pp. 549–64: the latter discussion is more *nuancée*, but the former is important for Hincmar's range of legal references and their MS sources. See also Wallace-Hadrill, '*Via Regia*', pp. 35–8 (193–6); and *Frankish Church*, pp. 294–303; with Nelson, 'Kingship, Law and Liturgy', pp. 254–8 (146–9).

31   *Hinkmar, De Divortio* v, p. 145; cf. the much better-known pronouncement of Archbishop Agobard of Lyons (chapter 2, n. 99); *De Divortio* xii, p. 188.

But since society visibly lived by other laws, a great variety of them known to Hincmar, these had to be fitted into the overall scheme. Hincmar argued, adapting St Paul's Epistle to the Romans, that there had been three different ages of law. The first was that of the law of nature, before the Law, the time of the Patriarchs; the second, that of the Law itself, from Moses onwards, 'suiting the hardness of the people'; and the third, the law of the Gospel, 'coming after in time, but before in grace (*tempore posterior sed gratia prior*)'. Christ had come to fulfil the law and the prophets, but had also brought release from bondage to the letter of the law.[32] Over time, the apostles and their successors had continued to propagate the law of evangelical grace:

> For, as we read in the Acts of the Apostles, the faithful did not at first discard the ceremonies of the law when they received the sacraments of the Gospel; and when the question arose whether the faithful among the gentiles should observe the ceremonies of the law, they received from the Apostles only three *capitula* to be kept.

Hincmar then gave a long account of subsequent conciliar and papal legislation, as dictated by contingent circumstances.[33] As for the Franks, the agent of grace was Hincmar's patron, St Remi: 'As Moses was constituted by the Lord *legislator* for the old people, so also blessed Remigius was *evangelicae gratiae lator* for the next people'.[34]

The Though Hincmar's position was well thought-out, there was as yet nothing very novel in it. His distinctive perception lay in the role he allotted secular legislation. Mankind was able neither to live by God's law nor to respond to God's grace. The laws of kings and emperors existed, adapting St Paul, 'because of transgressions'.[35] Hincmar made three further points about them. First, they can and must respond flexibly to society's needs. There was much in the Old and New Testaments as well as in papal decrees that seemed contradictory because adjusted to the nature of the case.[36] Second, it was everyone's business to know the law: ignorance was no excuse. In this connection, Hincmar quoted not only Celestine's decretal on the necessity that priests know their canons, but also 'legibus sacris', i.e. the Theodosian code: 'When it says, "no one should be ignorant of the laws, or despise what has been decreed", no one in any worldly station is excepted ... For kings and ministers of a republic have laws, by which they ought to rule the inhabitants of each territory; they have the *capitula* of christian kings their predecessors, which they promulgated to be held lawfully with the general consent of their faithful men'.[37] The association of canon, Roman and Frankish law in this passage is unique for the ninth century. Third, human law must therefore be written down: 'The makers of laws made and make laws not

---

32   Hincmar, 'Opusculum LV capitulorum' xx, col. 354, cf. xxv, col. 387; 'Explanatio in Ferculum Salomonis' col. 819.
33   'Opusculum' xx, cols 354–5, and cf. xxiv, col. 376; De Divortio Anh. iii, pp. 239–40 (referring to the 120 assembled at Pentecost).
34   Hincmar, 'Vita Sancti Remigii' xxxvii, cols 1159–60.
35   De Divortio xii, p. 188; 'Opusculum' xxv, col. 385; 'Libellus Expostulationis', PL CXXVI, col. 622.
36   'Opusculum' xxv, cols 385–91, and cf. Hinkmar, 'Kapitular' II 21, pp. 52–3.
37   *Hinkmar, De Ordine Palatii* iii, pp. 46–9; 'Ad Episcopos' xiii, col. 1015.

by the bare word but in writing, confirmed ... by signature (*subscriptione*)'.[38] It is probable that Hincmar personally drafted some of Charles the Bald's legislation, and almost certain that he was responsible for preserving much of it (chapter 2, nn. 101–2, 153–7). His commitment to written law was deeper, or at any rate clearer, than that of any other ninth-century north European.

It is evident that Hincmar and Alfred had the same conception of the structure of human legal history. Both saw Mosaic law as basic. For both, Christ's Advent and the Holy Spirit's descent on the Apostles and their successors preserved the essential continuity of God's legal revelation, by modifying and complementing its details. The role of written royal law, asserted by Hincmar, was put into effect by Alfred. Alfred's code demonstrably met the archbishop's criterion that man's law should so far as possible resemble God's. One of its baffling features, the retention of superseded items, finds an explanation in the tension between Hincmar's awareness that human law was flexible, and his expressed opinion, actually echoed by Alfred, that kings were bound by what their predecessors decreed (chapter 5, pp. 271–2, 278). A last point is that Hincmar too pondered the contrast between pagan custom and christian mercy:

> If anything arises which ... is punished by custom of the gentiles more cruelly than christian right or holy authority would rightly allow, let this be brought to the notice of the king, that he, together with those who know both laws and fear the statutes of God more than those of human laws, may so decree that both are observed where they can be, and, if not, the law of the world might rightly be suppressed, the justice of God preserved.[39]

It may now be recalled that Hincmar seems to have known the *Collatio* of Roman and Mosaic law, which at one point Alfred appears to follow. The *domboc* could almost be seen as a primer of Hincmarian principles.

Can this be coincidence? No doubt it can. Yet there is a good reason to suspect a connection. When Hincmar's successor, Archbishop Fulk, sent Grimbald to Alfred, he wrote as follows:

> Augustine, the first bishop of your people, sent to you by your apostle, blessed Gregory, neither could demonstrate in brief all the decrees of the Apostolic ordinances, nor wished suddenly to burden an ignorant and barbarous people with new and unknown laws ... And just as Peter and James ... with Barnabas and Paul and the other assembled elders, did not wish to burden the primitive Church, flocking from the pagans to the faith of Christ, with a heavier load, other than ordering them to "abstain from sacrificed things, from fornication, from strangled things and from blood", so we know that it was done at first with you ... But as time passed, and the Christian religion grew, the holy Church had no wish or right to be content with these things ... Hence councils were assembled not only from neighbouring cities and provinces but also from areas across the sea; hence synodal decrees (*synodalia decreta*) were often issued ...

38 Hincmar, 'Epistola xv, ad Carolum regem', *PL* CXXVI, col. 98. Cf. Schmitz, 'Wucher in Laon', for an example of Hincmar using capitularies to enforce the Biblical and canonical ban on usury, with Siems, *Handel und Wucher*, pp. 791–6; for its possible relevance to the influence of ninth-century Franks on tenth-century English, see chapter 9, chapter 13.

39 *De Ordine Palatii* v, pp. 70–3. Liebermann spotted this, *Gesetze* III, p. 36 (30), following von Amira, *Germanisches Recht* I, p. 48.

Fulk went on to see God's hand in the fact that Alfred had now sought further enlightenment from the see of Remigius, who had brought the Franks to Christ.[40] The echoes of Hincmar's ideas in Fulk's letter are clear and unsurprising. Scarcely less clear, though sometimes doubted, is Fulk's influence on Alfred's preface. Here is the restraint advised by the Council of Jerusalem, here too the subsequent series of Christian councils and synodal decrees throughout the world. Fulk thus serves as a bridge between Hincmarian theory and Alfredian practice. If this is true of the letter, it may be true also of the scholar whose credentials it supplied. Grimbald has been cast in many roles by historians of the Alfredian 'Renaissance'. Chapter 4 (p. 181) compared the format of two early copies of Alfred's *domboc* with that of a volume which Grimbald could have seen at Rheims. Further overlaps between Alfred's ideas and those of the school of Rheims will be suggested later in this chapter (pp. 460–1). Does it really overload the current of hypothesis to see Grimbald as the link between the singular structure of the *domboc* and the complex ideology of the foremost legal scholar of the era?[41]

At the very least, Hincmar's theories give Alfred's preface an intellectual context. It becomes possible to see why a ninth-century ruler should have produced such a thing. In this light, Alfred's lawbook was above all an ideological statement. He gave Mosaic law more prominence and more sophisticated handling than any other early medieval legislator. He thereby showed that West Saxon law – and implicitly Mercian and Kentish law too – belonged from the outset to the history of divine legislation for humanity. The emergent kingdom of the English was thus invited, even obliged, to live as a new Chosen People. 'The only object of this introduction was to acquaint his subjects with what Alfred regarded as a piece of model legislation'. Stenton's judgement on the preface (cf. chapter 5, p. 284) was nearer the mark than Liebermann's. But 'only' understates the urgency of the example. Alfred must have known the magnificent Deuteronomy verses where Moses commended his law to Israel:

> And now, O Israel, hear the commandments and judgements which I teach thee, that doing them thou mayst live, and entering mayst possess the land which the Lord the God of your fathers will give you ... For this is your wisdom and understanding (*sapientia et intellectus*) in the sight of the nations, that hearing all these precepts

---

40   *Councils and Synods* I, pp. 6–12; also translated in *Alfred*, ed. Keynes and Lapidge, pp. 182–6. Unnecessarily heavy weather has been made of this letter since Grierson's classic article of 1940 showed that unless it were genuine, there would have been no way of suspecting Grimbald's background at Rheims to which it so clearly testifies: see now Nelson, 'Fulk's letter to Alfred'. Nor is there any need to take Fulk's words as indicating that Grimbald was not part of his Rheims entourage; Fulk says that he had wished to see Grimbald achieve 'pontificale honore' in Francia, and be in *that* sense 'ministerii nostri consortem', so that 'quem habebamus filium fidelem' *should* mean that Grimbald was on his staff before departing for England. It was very much Fulk's point that St Remigius was bringing improved observance to England, and St Bertin's, though bound in confraternity with Rheims, was of course not in its diocese. There is thus a strong implication that Grimbald was already a Rheims man; and Whitelock, *Councils* I, p. 16, was surely justified in her reluctance to share Liebermann's hesitation as to the letter's influence on Alfred's preface.
41   *Gesetze* III, p. 34 (23): 'Die Veranlassung zur Kodifikation kann ihm fränkisches Beispiel gegeben haben' – though Liebermann went on to argue against this!

they may say, "Behold, a wise and understanding people, a great nation (*gens magna*)".[42]

The *domboc* could play just that role. It proclaimed the destiny of a kingdom that had survived God-given punishment, and might now enter its inheritance. If this was Alfred's point, it may have mattered less that his laws, seen as *laws*, were miscellaneous in content and erratic in arrangement. The objective would have been to get *any* West Saxon law into writing. Some of the blemishes for which modern minds have sought scribal scapegoats might not even have been noticed. Others, like the 120 chapters, would have enhanced the effect. Whether recited or read, by king, bishop or newly literate ealdorman, the law-book aimed for an overall impact on the collective consciousness by juxtaposing familiar customs, judgements and decrees with perceptibly similar laws of God. The whole was more important than the sum of its parts.

The argument thus returns to the point where it began, three chapters ago (pp. 121–4). A lawbook designed more for symbolic impact than for practical direction leaves no problem in the impression which Asser created by his silence, that it came after the king's campaign to educate his officials was well under way. Asser had Alfred demanding that his judges acquire *sapientia*, by which he appears to have meant the Wisdom of Solomon. Alfred's own conception of 'wisdom' has been much debated. Historians who have felt the need to stress its pragmatic quality are of course right, in so far as Alfred fought and thought in an everyday world.[43] But it is instructive to recall the way that attempts to divorce the king's warrior and intellectual values have affected views of Asser's authenticity.[44] The implied polarity of muddy burghal trenches with the gold and (appropriately) ivory *décor* of Boethius' study would have made no sense to a ninth-century mind. Alfred's *wisdom* was indeed not quite that of Boethius; but it was closer to the world of government only in so far as it was Solomonic. In Alfred's *Boethius*, 'Wisdom', replacing the Latin's 'Philosophia' as interlocutor, concludes her discourse on the perils of power with a sentiment that is not in the original but might come straight out of the Book of Kings: 'Therefore learn wisdom, and when you have learnt it, do not scorn it. Then I tell you without any doubt that you may through that achieve power, though you do not desire it'.[45] The Psalter, with its reiterated praise of God's Law, was a constant reminder of the interfaces of literacy, wisdom and justice. In Alfred's personal (if not wholly original) introductions to the first fifty psalms, 'justice (*rihtwisnes*)', 'trust (*treowa*)' and *wisdom* stand and fall together. The translation of Psalm 36

---

42   Deuteronomy 4:1,6.

43   Shippey, 'Wealth and Wisdom', pp. 353–4; Frantzen, *King Alfred*, p. 88; Nelson, 'Wealth and Wisdom', and 'Political Ideas of Alfred'; Otten, *König Alfreds Boethius*, stresses both his positive assessment of kingship and his spiritual perception of wisdom, pp. 86–118. Similar views to what follows are Bately 'Literary Prose', pp. 7–10, and Szarmach, 'Meaning of Alfred's *Preface*' (an important paper that might have made more use of evidence from the *Pastoral Care* itself).

44   The key sentence of Galbraith, 'Who wrote Asser?' is at the start of the final paragraph: 'It is a matter of some importance to have rescued Alfred from the charge of having been a *malade imaginaire*, and to see him again as the simple great-hearted warrior he was'.

45   *Alfred's Boethius* xvi, p. 35.

faithfully followed the original quoted in chapter 3 (p. 122): 'The mouth of the just man examines wisdom, his tongue speaks just judgements. The Law (*æ*) of his God is in his heart'.[46] But the most relevant of Alfred's works for understanding his laws is the one, perhaps written at much the same time, whose preface so memorably charts the decline of 'wisdom' among the English, with its consequent 'punishments in this world'.

The *Liber Regulae Pastoralis* was of course a book for bishops. But Gregory perceptibly blurred the boundaries of spiritual and secular government. He made copious use of examples from the world of the leaders, judges and kings of Israel. The books ascribed to Solomon were quoted as often as the Gospels, and more often than any other 'single' writer except St Paul. Words denoting priesthood were much less common than the adaptable vocabulary of rule, 'rector' and 'regere'. The frequent references to judgement deployed courtroom imagery to the point that one can forget that it is judgement of souls which is at issue. It is thus unsurprising that the book became a primer of early medieval government in general; or that, in what is the most 'literal' of Alfred's translations, 'the bishop's office and the king's come rather closer together'.[47] Gregory's 'rector' was sometimes rendered '*lareow* (teacher)', but 'reccere' also appeared where the original did not demand it. 'Praelati' and 'subditi' became 'ealdormen' and 'hieremenn'. Ezechiel personified a 'praepositus (man of authority)' for Gregory, and – in a significantly literal translation – a 'scirman' for Alfred.[48] It is thus significant that there was nothing very 'worldly' in what Alfred's Gregory says about law and wisdom. Alfred carefully removed the ambiguity in Gregory's resonant Pauline paradox:

> Those who know and love the tricks of this world (*ðisse worulde lotwrencas cunnan 7 ða lufigeað* – Latin: *sapientes huius saeculi*) are to be admonished in one way, the simple in another ... The cunning (*lytegan*, Latin *sapientes*) are to be admonished to scorn what they know ... With the cunning, we should work very hard that they abandon the *wisdom* that seems to themselves to be *wisdom*, and take to the *wisdom* of God that seems to them stupid (Latin: *ut sapientius stulti fiant, stultam sapientiam deserant, sapientem Dei stultitiam discant*).[49]

It is one of many occasions when the translation sacrificed elegance for clarity. Alfred might not have endorsed his modern admirers' insistence that his *wisdom* was firmly anchored in this world. His works were shot through with an intense sense of the duty to serve, derived from Gregory himself. That duty could not be performed by turning one's back on God's creatures. But to cherish the good

---

46   *Liber Psalmorum* xi: Pr., xiii: Pr., xxxvi: 30; cf. also Ps. 18:2, 48:3, 50:7; and for the sources of the introductions, O'Neill, 'The Old English Introductions to the Prose Psalms of the Paris Psalter'. For 'wisdom' in *Alfred's Augustine*, see pp. 56 lns 6–9, 62 lns 4–10, 74 lns 14–18, 75 ln 16 – 76 ln 24, 84 ln 21 – 85 ln 7; only the first and fourth passages have any real Latin equivalent.

47   Wallace-Hadrill, *Early Germanic Kingship*, p. 143.

48   'Rector'/'lareow': e.g. xiv, p. 81, xviii, p. 127 (heading; text has 'reccere'), xxi, p. 163; 'reccere' without Latin warrant: e.g. xviii, p. 131; 'praelati'/'ealdormen': xxviii, p. 189; 'subditi'/'hieremenn': x, p. 63, xvii, p. 125; 'praepositus'/'scirman': xxi, p. 153. Cf. also, e.g., 'folgoðes 7 ealdordomes', translating 'praedicationis officium'(!): vii, p. 47.

49   *Alfred's Pastoral Care* xxx, p. 203; the nearest that Alfred comes to commending 'wisdom' in a worldly sense is perhaps in chapter xx, p. 149 ln 16 (translating 'consilium').

things of life for their own sake, to desire them as Solomon had not, was itself a betrayal of duty that their Creator would not forgive.

One Carolingian council put 'mundanae leges' in the same category for counts and judges as was the *Pastoral Rule* for bishops and the *Rule of St Benedict* for monks.[50] Alfred may have had some such parallelism in mind when compiling his *domboc*. Its structure would then make excellent sense. The king's translations repeatedly categorized Holy Writ as 'The Law (*seo æ*)'.[51] In the *domboc*, God's Law duly set the tone for all that followed. But Professor Whitelock suggested that the 'Saxon books' from which his judges were to derive 'sapientia' 'could have been the Alfredian translations, especially that of the *Cura Pastoralis*'.[52] Considering how often Alfred applied its principles to 'ealdormen' and *scirmen*, this seems eminently likely. In any case, *Pastoral Rule* and *domboc* alike directed attention to the same ultimate source both of Wisdom and of The Law in Scripture. Whatever practical guidance judges received from a written code, it was the Bible that would teach them how to be judges.

How would this interpretation of the law-book's function affect assessment of its legal contents? This is a matter for chapter 7, where the corpus of Old English legislation can be viewed in the round. But it can be said now that one need not hesitate to take it as evidence of West Saxon law as actually experienced. The *domboc* could only convey its ideological message if its audience was familiar with what followed the preface. For the same reason, this could not be too innovative (chapter 5, pp. 271–2). What may be affected is one's view of the law-making process. Alfred's code need no longer be understood as a primarily legislative instrument. It neither *made* nor codified law (chapter 5, pp. 280–4). Instead, it said something of immense symbolic moment about the law of Wessex. That Alfred had an unrivalled grasp of the material necessities of government brooks no denial. The fact remains that he was also a ninth-century intellectual. He would not otherwise be the only early medieval king who wrote books about his job. It is therefore neither incongruous nor improbable that his priorities in compiling his lawbook should be literary and ideological: that he himself gave it the form that has descended to posterity. The chief objection is the modern instinct that he should not have done. So a final point is this. If Alfred's view of *written* law seems almost frivolous to more fully literate cultures, his view of law itself could hardly have been more serious. His sustained comparison of English law with what God gave Moses implied dramatic new ambitions for his people. Crime could now be perceived as an outrage against God, punishment as the expression of His anger. Much of the rest of this book argues that that is just what happened. The paradox of Alfred's *domboc* is that this deeply traditionalist text marks the point when law became the aggressive weapon of a new state.

---

50   Concilium Moguntinense (813): Pr., *Concil.* I, pp. 259–60.
51   E.g. *Alfred's Pastoral Care* v, p. 43 lns 17–18: the passage is evidence that, for Alfred anyway, the difference between 'dom' and 'æ' was functional rather than conceptual. Cf., e.g. i, p. 27, xiv, p. 81, xv, p. 91, xvi, p. 105, xxii, p. 169, xxxiii, p. 219, xlviii, p. 365, l, p. 391, li, p. 395, lxiii, p. 459.
52   *Councils*, p. 16. But cf. also Nelson, 'Wealth and Wisdom', p. 44.

2   From Alfred to Wulfstan: Intimations of Christian Empire

The extant laws of the century after 899 do not pose the same problems of content and presentation as does Alfred's *domboc*, or as do those penned by Archbishop Wulfstan. To all appearances, they are cogent records of what kings wished to happen. They raise few doubts about the compatibility of what the king commanded with the way in which he commanded it. Even the less official-seeming texts look like earnest attempts to realize the will of rulers. Yet the codes from Edward the Elder to Æthelred II (phase I) are not without their own oddities. One that cropped up throughout chapter 5 is the patchiness of the record. Law-making occurred in spurts that were not sustained. Edmund's younger brother and elder son apparently made no laws. Edgar made strangely few. If steam began to pick up again before Wulfstan took over the controls, it gave out altogether at his death. The simple solution to this riddle, that there were once many more codes, actually does no more than reformulate it. For these cannot have been lost through want of interest in preserving them during and after the period of the Norman Conquest. The commitment to Old English law shown by the compilers of *Quadripartitus*, *Textus Roffensis* or the Cnut renditions was such that any text which was at all accessible by their time had a good chance of being copied (chapter 5, pp. 414–15). Granted that Anglo-Saxon law may increasingly have been issued in less formal 'executive' style (pp. 347–8), how was it that Oswald of York/Worcester seems to have retained a copy of the Danelaw's version of 'IV Edgar' (chapter 4, pp. 184–5), when its equivalent for English England slipped through the grasp of Dunstan's Canterbury or Æthelwold's Winchester (whose contemporary hagiographer may in fact refer to it) – and this a law that took steps for its multiple transmission without parallel in the Old English series (chapter 3, pp. 125–8, chapter 5, pp. 369–70)? Why was the full range of Æthelstan's output reflected only by the archives of the archbishop who was so centrally involved in its production (chapter 5, pp. 299–300)? The pattern persisted long after 1066, when Henry I's post-coronation legislation survives by a hair's breadth or not at all (chapter 5, pp. 401–2) – and even Henry II's depended heavily for its preservation on a Justice of the Forest who happened to have been a major historian (chapter 14). There was a hit-and-miss quality about the engagement of law-maker and audience, an absence of resonance, which sits oddly with all the work put into law-giving. It insinuates a concern to cut a legislative dash that did not always impress those it was meant to.

For laws, orders that were by definition of universal and long-term relevance, it is not enough (as for the ephemeral administrative fiat it might be) to blame the failings of scribes and archivists. One must ask what their negligence says about attitudes to written law. Chapter 2's examination of the Carolingian programme raised the possibility that it expressed aspirations in ruling circles that had no real prospect of being fulfilled, because they asked more of their subjects and indeed servants than either was able to attain. It is not that kings and churchmen were other than deeply serious when they proclaimed the need for their people to live by the written laws that they made; more that a commitment to written law generated by elite identification with the 'civilized' standards of

Table 6.1   Times and places of royal legislative sessions[53]

	Place	Year	Time of Year
I Ew	–	–	–
II Ew	**Exeter**	–	–
I As	–	–	–
As Alm	–	–	–
II As	Grately	–	–
V As	**Exeter**	–	Christmas
IV As	(*Thunderfield*)	–	–
VI As 12	Whittlebury	–	–
I Em	**London**	–	Easter
II Em	–	–	–
III Em	*Colyton*	–	–
II–III Eg	*Andover*	–	–
IV Eg	'Wihtbordesstan'	–	–
IV Atr 5–9:3	? = 'Bromdun'	[or ? = S 876]	–
S 876	**Winchester**/*Gillingham*	993	Pentecost/17 July
I Atr	*Woodstock*	–	–
III Atr	*Wantage*	[? = S 891]	–
S 891	*Calne*/*Wantage*	997	Easter/'a few days later'
V/VI(?+ X) Atr	*King's Enham*	1008	Pentecost
VII Atr	**Bath**	1009	–
VIII Atr	–	1014 [?? = IX Atr]	–
IX Atr	*Woodstock*	[?? = VIII Atr]	–
Cn 1018	**Oxford**	(1018)	–
I–II Cn	**Winchester**	(1020/1021)	Christmas

Rome and the Bible came up against the inertia of a society with other priorities than its own wholesale reform as a Christian commonwealth, and whose conception of its *lex scripta* (if any) was well enough met by the ancient texts that had long served as talismans of ethnic identity (chapter 2, pp. 44–5, 49–51). To speak in such a context of law-codes as 'literature' is not to imply that they were exercises in creative imagination; but rather, that law-making in writing was a better expression of an image of society than of practical remedies for its discontents. Might this model hold good too for the new English kingdom, in so many ways the avatar of the Carolingian? Are there any indications that legislation (*written* law-making) arose from an ideological compulsion, rather than a sense of the need for black-and-white guidance of ruled by ruler? If so, the unevenness of the legislative record – not to mention its failure to feature in more

53   The argument thus extends for present purposes to cover Wulfstan's period, though the rather different considerations arising from his output are more fully addressed in section 3. In the 'Place' column of this and the following table, significant administrative centres (e.g. possessing a mint) are in bold, while estates guessed from other evidence to have been royal vills are in italics: Sawyer, 'The Royal *Tun*'. For the possibility that *Bromdun* (I Atr 1:2, III Atr 4), otherwise unlocated in time or place, corresponds to IV Atr 5 – 9:3, or alternatively that the latter corresponds to S 876, see below. Dates are given in the 'year' column' of table 6.1 only when indicated by MS or other strong evidence; for estimated dates of law-codes, see below.

Table 6.2   Times and places of other major royal councils[54]

Place	Year	Time of Year	Source
Winchester	900	–	S 359, 1284
Axminster	901	–	S 364
Southampton	901	–	S 368
Milton (Kt)	903	–	S 369
Southampton	903	–	S 372–4, 1286
?*Bickleigh* (De)	904	–	S 372–4, 1286
Warminster	900x24	–	S 1445
(*Kingston*)	925	4 Sept.	S 394, ASC 924
Abingdon	926	??Easter	GR i 135, (?S 1208)
Exeter	928	Easter	S 399, 400
Lyminster (Sx)	930	5 Apr.	S 403
Chippenham	930	29 Apr.	S 405
Colchester	931	23 Mar.	S 412
King's Worthy (Ha)	931	20 Jun.	S 413
E. Wellow (Ha)	931	15 July	S 1604
Kingston	931	6 Oct.	S 450
Lifton (De)	931	12 Nov.	S 416
Milton (Kt)	932	30 Aug.	S 417
Exeter	932	9 Nov.	S* 418a
Amesbury	932	Christmas	S 418–19
Wilton	933	11 Jan.	S 379
Chippenham	933	26 Jan.	S 422–3
Kingston	933	16 Dec.	S 420
Dorchester	933/934	Easter	S 391
Winchester	934	Pentecost	S 425
Nottingham	934	7 Jun.	S 407
Buckingham	934	12 Sept.	S 426
Frome (So)	934	16 Dec.	S 427
Cirencester	935	–	S 1792
Dorchester	(935)	21 Dec.	S 434–6
York	936	–	(*EHD I* 24, 936)
Hamsey (Sx)	925x39	–	S 1211
Colchester	940	–	S 472
Chippenham	940	–	S 473

54   Gratefully following the table in Keynes, *Diplomas of Æthelred*, Appendix 2, pp. 269–73, and cf. Biddle, 'Seasonal Festivals', pp. 56–9, 69–72; but adding meetings for which calendar-dates alone are known, and omitting those recorded in blatantly bogus charters (twelfth-century forgers were well able to invent councils at by then familiar times and places: S 731, 783, 894, 965, 1011, 1041, 1043, 1294; and cf. Keynes, '"Dunstan B" charters', pp. 175–7 for S 571, 670 and 'Glastonbury'). Coronation assemblies are also excluded unless they issued charters. As in table 6.1, bold and italic print is used respectively for 'towns' and royal vills, with what may be thought operative rather than secularized abbeys capitalized (see below, n. 64, for Canterbury etc. as towns, not churches). The periods of 'Æthelstan A' (see next n.) and of the (by Anglo-Saxon norms) garrulous annals of Edward the Confessor's last fifteen years are marked off, in that they provide an untypical level of detail.

Table 6.2   *(continued)*

Place	Year	Time of Year	Source
Cheddar	940/941	24 July	S 511
WINCHCOMBE	942	–	S 479
–	945	Palm Sunday	S 505
Kirtlington (Ox)	939x45	–	S* 1810d
Kingston	946	(16 Aug.)	S 520, JW 946
?*Gadshill* (Kt)	948	–	S 537
Somerton	949	Easter	S 549
ABINGDON	950	–	S* 552a
–	956	13 Feb.	S 607
Cheddar	956	29 Nov.	S 611
Cirencester	956	–	S 633
Edington (Wi)	957	9 May	S 646
Penkridge (St)	958	–	S 667
–	959	17 May	S 658
Bradford (Wi)	c. 959	–	Vit. S. Dunst. 25
Cheddar	968	Easter	S 806
Woolmer (Ha)	970	Easter	S 776, 779
?*Woodyates* (Do)	?970	?10 Aug.	[see n. 66]
London	973	–	S 1328
GLASTONBURY	975	–	S 802
London	963x75	–	S 1457
Puddletown	976	–	S 830
Kirtlington (Ox)	977	'after Easter'	ASC 977, JW 977
Calne	977	–	ASC 977, JW 977
Amesbury	977	–	JW 977
Andover	980	–	Narr. de S. Sw., p. 67
London	977x84	–	Lib. El. ii 11
Cirencester	985	–	S 896, 937
–	988	23 Mar.	S 873
–	988	16 Apr.	S 869
London	(pre next one)	–	S 877
London	988x90	–	S 877
Amesbury	995	Easter	ASC 'F' 995
–	997	25 July	S 890
–	998	Easter	S 893
Cookham	995x9	–	S 939
Canterbury	1002	11 July	S 905
Headington (Ox)	1004	7 Dec.	S 909
'Berchore'	1007	–	S 915
London	1012	Easter	ASC 1012
–	?1012	June/July	S 927
–	1013	18–20 Apr.	S* 931ab
Oxford	1015	–	ASC 1015
–	1019	Easter	S 956
Cirencester	1020	Easter	ASC 1020
–	1022	23 Jun.	S 958

Table 6.2 *(continued)*

Place	Year	Time of Year	Source
London	1023	8 Jun.	ASC 'D' 1023
London	1020x23	–	S 1463
Kingston	1032	Pentecost	S 1465
Canterbury	1032	–	S 993
Sutton Courtenay (Bk)	1042	–	S 1471
Canterbury	*c.*1045	–	S 1471
Winchester	1049	–	S 1018
London	1050	(mid-Lent)	ASC 'C' 1050/'E' 1047
Exeter	1050	–	S 1021
Gloucester	1051	–	ASC '1052' etc.
London	1051	late Sept.	ASC '1052' etc.
London	1052	–	ASC 'E' '1048'
Lincoln	1053x5	–	S 1478
London	1055	(mid-Lent)	ASC 'E' 1055
Windsor	1065	24 May	S 1042
Britford (Wi)	1065	–	*Vit. Edw. Reg.*, p. 52
Northampton/Oxford	1065	28 Oct.	ASC 1065
Westminster	1065–6	Christmas	ASC 1065/6 etc.
Westminster	1066	Easter	ASC 'C'/'D' 1066

than the odd narrative or in any report of actual legal process – may become easier to understand. At this stage of the argument, it must be emphasized, it is not argued that this (or any other) can be *the* answer to the problems of legislative materials. The quest is for any pattern that matches the shape of the evidence.

The angle of approach to the problem adopted here is through more attention than chapter 5 gave to the place and time of recorded law-making sessions. The more important codes were issued by assemblies of the king and his *witan*. Whatever the 'constitutional' significance of these meetings, they were certainly gatherings of the cream of the political nation. Can anything be learned of what they did and why from where they met and when? Table 6.1 lists legislative sessions after 899, and table 6.2 other assemblies whose location and/or date is known.

The first point to make about the information provided (or hazarded) here is how little can be known for sure. Just two codes are both located and dated. Only for the central seven years of Æthelstan's reign does the remarkable activity of the draftsman known as 'Æthelstan A' permit what is never otherwise possible in Anglo-Saxon history: the outlines of a royal itinerary such as is the stock-in-trade of continental or post-conquest historians.[55] Although the charters of Edward the Elder tended to continue his dynasty's (if not his

---

55   The existence – and designation – of 'Æthelstan A' was established by Drögereit, 'Gab es eine angel

father's) ninth-century habit of naming their place of issue, the shining example of 'Æthelstan A' was followed by fewer than fifty documents in the 130 years after he laid down his pen.[56] For all that, some patterns may be glimpsed in the evidential half-light.

Attention should go first to the aspect on which the material is least uninformative: the places at which assemblies were held. It is clear from tables 6.1–2 in combination that Anglo-Saxon councils which made law were part of the same mobile government machine as those that attested grants of property and privilege.[57] There is an important difference in this connection between the position before 1066 and that which had developed by the early-twelfth century. Old English diplomas tend to have long lists of witnesses, especially from Æthelstan's time, both because their form originated in witnessed late Roman private deeds, and because, as their formulae so often stressed, the consent of the Establishment was integral to their validity.[58] As 'writ-form' steadily took hold after the Conquest, witnessing was increasingly limited to one or a few members of the administration.[59] On the other hand, Anglo-Norman writs usually give a place of issue where Anglo-Saxon writs do not.[60] It can therefore *look* as if there was a distinction between law-making assemblies and more routine government business in the twelfth century which is not apparent before.[61]

An interesting clause of Wulfstan's 'eighth' code of Æthelred laments that,

---

sächsische Königskanzlei?', pp. 361–9; a further refinement was introduced by Chaplais, 'Origin and Authenticity of the Royal Anglo-Saxon Diploma', pp. 59–60. But Dr Chaplais' case is modified in turn by a most important forthcoming study of Dr Simon Keynes, which he has kindly shown me.

56   Of located charters, six are 'alliterative' (below, n. 81): S 472–3, 479, 520, 549, 633. Earlier Wessex placings (minus likely forgeries): S 1245, 1169, 245, 253, 256–7, 261, 267, 272/3, 275/6, 277, 283, 288, 290, 292, 298, 300/11, 1274, 329, 333, 334/342, 335–6, 340, 345, 1507, 1445 (cf. Keynes, 'West Saxon Charters of Æthelwulf'); other kingdoms (omitting synod records etc.): S 8, 10, 20, 23–4, 27–8, 34–6, 157, 40, 161, 170, 1264, 177, 186–7, 1266–7, 286–7, 293, 296–7, 1194, 330–2, 338a, 350, 1628 (Kent); S 1165, 235 ('Earconwald group'); S 1184 (Sussex); S 91–2, 109, 114, 116, 120, 123, 125, 128, 131, 144, 148, 152, 154–5, 163–4, 172, 178, 188, 192–9, 1273, 206–8, 210, 219–21, 1441, 225, 1446 (Mercia). See also n. 108.

57   Liebermann, *National Assembly*, pp. 13–15, 23–7, 43–5, 67–75 (but the list, pp. 45–7, is outdated: cf. nn. 54, 56).

58   Chaplais, 'Origin and Authenticity', pp. 49–50; *id.*, 'Some Early Anglo-Saxon Charters on Single Sheets', pp. 318–31; Wormald, *Bede and the Conversion of England*, pp. 11–19.

59   For the complexities of the change from diploma to writ either side of 1066, see Keynes, *Diplomas of Æthelred*, pp. 140–5, and 'Regenbald', pp. 217–21; cf. Liebermann, *National Assembly*, pp. 17–18.

60   HaWr, pp. 72–3 (applying to datings rather than placings, but ruling out the authenticity of the two writs, nos 61–2, which gave places of issue too – though cf. the anomalous no. 26, pp. 181–2). The first post-1066 writ (of Old English type) with place of issue appears to be *RRAN* i 63, the famous writ commanding the military service of Abbot Æthelwig of Evesham (for its likely 1068/9 date, see Gillingham, 'Introduction of Knight Service', pp. 57–8); and thereafter *RRAN* i ?47, ?58 (1070x1), 143 (1080x1), 243 (n.d.); locations evidently only become established late in Rufus' reign, and calendar dates (the major religious festivals aside) remain rare.

61   For post-conquest itineraries, see *RRAN* i, pp. xxi–xxii (to be totally overhauled in the forthcoming re-edition by Professor David Bates); *RRAN* ii, pp. xxix–xxxi; *RRAN* iii, pp. xxxix–xliv; with Barlow, *William Rufus*, pp. 449–52. The distinction made in the text is of course blurred by the use of writ-form for legislative purposes: cf. C Hn cor 'Dat.', Hn mon. 'Test', Hn com. 'Test'; but some Henrician Assizes again stress their conciliar aspect: *Select Charters*, ed. Stubbs, pp. 170, 186.

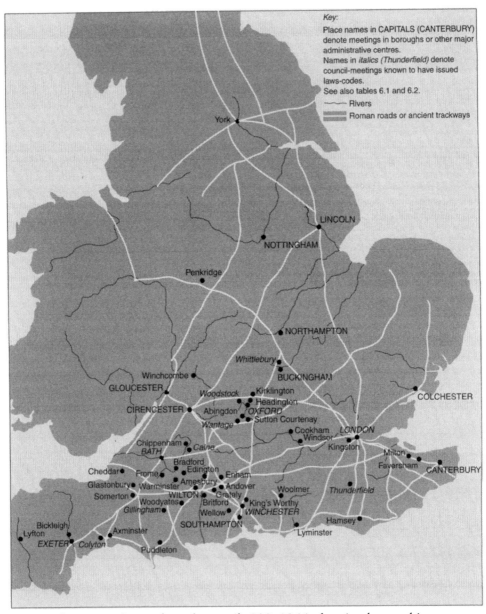

Map of meeting-places of royal councils 900–1066, showing law-making councils

though there used to be assemblies in 'well-known places (*namcuðan stowan*), after Edgar's lifetime, the laws of Christ declined and the laws of the king diminished'.[62] The implication is that by Wulfstan's time, councils held in certain places could almost be expected to make laws. Of places where laws were made (table 6.1), seven were towns or at least major administrative centres, while there were ten known, and four possible, royal vills.[63] In the early-Edward and 'Æthelstan A' periods, when specified locations were common, charter-issuing assemblies were held fourteen times in a *burh* or the like, and fifteen times in known or likely vills. From 935 till the end of the tenth century, there were nine meetings in a *burh*, as against eighteen in vills (with three in monasteries); in the eleventh century there were seventeen in a *burh* and seven in a vill.[64] These figures point strikingly to the increased urbanization of Anglo-Saxon political life in the eleventh century (and to the rapid rise of London's role from 957), but do not suggest much difference between places hosting assemblies that made laws and those that did not.

One reason for choosing places like Exeter, London and Winchester on the one hand, or Andover, Woodstock and Wantage on the other, for councils of either type is that both meant accommodating a large number of people. Because only one 'palace' of the period has ever been excavated, there can as yet be little idea of how this was managed, or whether it could be better managed in some places than others.[65] One clue to the realities of the situation may be the colophon in the 'Durham Ritual', where Aldred, provost of Chester-le-Street, described himself as making additions to a Collectar for his Bishop, 'south of Woodyates at Oakley ... on St Lawrence Day, a Wednesday [10 August 970], in his tent'. Woodyates (Dorset) was an established royal vill; given the presence there of a Bishop of Chester-le-Street, Edgar may well have been carrying on the sort of business that had occupied his council at Woolmer that Easter (table 6.2).[66] That a northern bishop should have been camping nearby suggests that only the very greatest in the land would have had more permanent quarters. Conciliar bed and board may not, however, have been the only consideration. Favoured stopping-points on post-conquest itineraries testify to the royal passion for the chase, and by no means all were on arterial routes. Among those places, only Woodstock

---

62 VIII Atr 37; there may be an echo here of a formula in synodical documents of two centuries before and kept at Worcester: e.g. S 1430 (789), 1437 (825), and Wormald, 'Lawsuits', p. 274 (p. 278).

63 Sawyer, 'Royal *Tun*', pp. 290–9; Professor Sawyer omits Whittlebury, but its claims seem just as good as those of *Bromdun*, Enham, Grately or *Wihtbordesstan*, which are identified only as locations of single legislative sessions: it does not appear in *DB*, but there was a fair concentration of royal land in the neighbourhood.

64 Cf. Sawyer, 'Royal *Tun*', p. 277, and Biddle (ed.), *Winchester in the Early Middle Ages*, pp. 289–92, 465–7. Neither at Canterbury, Winchester nor London does the evidence imply a Carolingian-style arrangement, whereby 'the ruler, on a visit to a *civitas* no longer necessarily resides in a *palatinum intramuraneum*, but in a monastery outside the walls, where the ruler from now on has ... a *domus* or *palatium* of his own': Brühl, 'The Town as a Political Centre', pp. 426–7; nor, however, is it sufficient to exclude this at Canterbury, while Edward the Confessor's Westminster, treated in table 6.2 as a royal vill, certainly evokes the continental pattern. If, as is likely, the pre-conquest royal residence at Oxford was on the site of its Angevin successor, it was some hundred metres outside the wall.

65 Rahtz, *Saxon and Medieval Palaces at Cheddar*.

66 *The Durham Ritual*, ed. Brown, pp. 23–4, f. 84r. For an earlier Woodyates meeting, cf. S 334/342 (869x70). Bishop Ælfsige's *only* recorded presence at Edgar's court is in S 781, sometime in 970.

was used for councils before 1066; and only Cheddar is otherwise known to have been treasured as a hunting-lodge.[67] What seems to have mattered most in selecting pre-conquest meeting-places was accessibility. Grately, Andover and King's Enham stood close together on or by the Roman road from London to Old Sarum, Dorchester and Exeter, and near where it was crossed by the roads to Winchester from Gloucester or Oxford; while Wantage was just off the Ridgeway; and even Colyton was not far from the Axminster-Exeter road. Most *rendez-vous* of non-legislative assemblies were similarly located; those a bit further from beaten tracks, like Kingston, Cookham, Chippenham and Bradford, were on important rivers.[68] It seems unlikely that this pattern is fortuitous. Whether dispensing patronage or making law, king and council met wherever was convenient for both.

The more pressing question of whether there was anything distinctive about the personnel of law-making assemblies is not possible to answer. The only times when a charter's listed witnesses even might have discussed legislation too were those at Lyfton in November 931 and Frome in December 934, or at Winchester/Gillingham in 993 and at Wantage in 997.[69] Outsize witness-lists were an 'Æthelstan A' speciality in any case; the 993 list was certainly exceptional, but more for its number of abbots, presumably connected with its dominant monastic theme, than for any other feature; and while the Wantage list does have an unusual number of 'ministri', it was not the largest of the reign.[70] Most lists survive in cartulary copies that were prone to distortion or abbreviation; Glastonbury's cartularist scythed down his witness-lists, so for instance grievously mutilating a possible record of Æthelstan's Whittlebury assembly (below, p. 440). There are altogether too many variables in the making and survival of witness-lists for them to serve as a set of conciliar *sederunts*.[71]

Rather more progress may perhaps be made with the years in which laws were issued – though paradoxically if so, since not one code was formally dated (chapter 5, pp. 330, 333). Starting with Edward the Elder, his second code ordered that harbourers of fugitives must 'amend as the *domboc* says', except that 'in the east or north', they might do so according to the 'peace-writings (*friðgewritu*)'. Liebermann took the latter to mean Edward's northern settlement of 920. But this was to ignore its reference to 'the east'; and once Edward's army had stormed through East Anglia and the East Midlands in 916/17, their 'peace-

---

67   From the famous tale in the 'B' *Vita Dunstani*, c. 14, pp. 23–5. But the Anglo-Saxon royal forest is poorly recorded: cf. Wickham, 'European Forests in the Early Middle Ages', pp. 485, 502–9.

68   The accompanying Map is based on the Ordnance Survey, *Britain before the Norman Conquest* (cf. n.80 below for Whittlebury). An unusually isolated case is Edington, where Eadwig's council met on 9 May 957 (S 646); 9 May was 'in the seventh week after Easter', 878: was the anniversary of Alfred's decisive victory being celebrated – as further implied by the charter's arresting and unique proem, 'Divina gratia largiente, et originali prosapia antecessorum meorum'?

69   S 416, 427 (see below, p. 439); S 876, 891 (table 6.1).

70   Keynes, *Diplomas of Æthelred*, pp. 95–104; and see below, pp. 442–3; there are as many *ministri* in S 862, 867, 906 as in S 891, with many more in S 911, the Eynsham foundation charter.

71   A responsible (if more optimistic) assessment is Keynes, *Diplomas of Æthelred*, pp. 130–4, 154–62; Liebermann, *National Assembly*, pp. 28–42, was not much worried by methodological problems.

writings' would not have been worth the parchment they were written on. Their only current law would thenceforward be Edward's own.[72] If Edward's second code therefore pre-dated 916, his first must have been long enough before that for the displeasure at the state of the general 'peace' he voiced in the second's prologue to have taken shape in his mind.[73] One might speculate that Edward's very *domboc*-conscious codes were both issued in the earlier years of his reign, and were themselves a response to his father's massive effort; whereas his final decade, dominated by the most effective campaigning in early English history, were as lacking in legislation as in that other medium of government articulacy, charters.[74]

The case of Æthelstan's codes is more complicated but also more instructive. The only internal indicators of chronology are that 'I' and 'II' (probably in that order) must precede 'V', 'III', 'IV', 'VI' and 'VI:12' (definitely in *that* order). However, external evidence is to hand in the itinerary deducible from the charters of 'Æthelstan A'. A glance at table 6.2 will show that, if 'V Æthelstan' was issued from Exeter at Christmas, then it was not issued in 932; nor, unless the king's court moved rapidly westward in midwinter, are 933 or 935 likely dates.[75] Since the king must have had time to grow disenchanted with his earlier measures (chapter 5, pp. 299, 305) and since room must be made too for the second thoughts behind the reduction of Exeter's severity which he urged from Whittlebury (pp. 298, 305), there are *a priori* arguments in favour of the relatively central dates 930, 931 or 934. Æthelstan was in fact within reach of an Exeter Christmas in November 931 and perhaps December 934.[76]

Two other things then come into the reckoning. First, the Grately code ('II') contains a set of laws on coinage unique among the Anglo-Saxon series in its concern to establish the exact number of moneyers per mint. The evidence of this

---

72   II Ew 5:2; ASC 917A, pp. 101–3; *Gesetze* III, p. 93 (2). Decisive evidence that Edward demanded outright surrender from the lands he attacked, on pain of total forfeiture, is *Lib. Æth.* 35/*Lib. El.* ii 25, pp. 98–9. The 'friðgewritu' Edward had in mind were most likely represented by AGu itself; this does not explicitly cover fugitives, but was amended in that direction in the earlier-tenth century (chapter 5, pp. 379–80).

73   II Ew Pr. – Pr.:1.

74   The charter hiatus is thoughtfully probed by Dumville, 'Æthelstan, first king of England', pp. 151–3.

75   For the probability that the forged Malmesbury charters S 434–6 (chapter 5, p. 307) draw on a genuine witness-list of 935, see Keynes's forthcoming paper, as n. 55.

76   See chapter 5, p. 307 for the point that V As 3, ordering psalm-singing for the king *each Friday* cannot be intimately connected to the provision for the singing of fifty psalms with that intention *daily or every Feast of All Saints* in charters dated Christmas 932 or late January 933; though nothing excludes a date about then for As Alm, reflecting the stipulation for almsgiving in the same group of charters. It may also be noted that, though V As is one of few codes at whose issue Æthelstan was definitely present, the same may not go for Archbishop Wulfhelm (chapter 5, p. 299), yet he did attend the November 931 and December 934 assemblies (S 416, 427). Another consideration is the possible connection (either way) between V As 3 and the liturgical cycles organized in 932 by the German king Henry the Fowler: Althoff, *Amicitiae und Pacta*, pp. 75–81; Barrow, 'Chronology of Forgery Production at Worcester'; given Professor Alfthoff's case for an association of the cycles with 'Burgenbau' and its rituals, VI As 8:6 may seem more germane than V As 3. Finally, if there *is* anything in the Alfred story (chapter 5, pp. 307–8), that might imply a 934 date for Exeter, since the perjury clause was added to II As rather than incorporated in V As, etc.

clause is not in fact as straightforward as it looks.[77] Æthelstan's monetary system mostly harked back to his father's.[78] But it is still reasonable to link a law itemizing mints with the fact that Æthelstan's coins were 'mint-signed' as a matter of course, where his predecessors' were not. This feature appeared not on his earliest coin series, but on those of 'cross-type', which were the first to bear the title 'Rex totius Britanniae', and also the first to be issued at York.[79] A mint-signed coinage should thus post-date the king's overrunning of Northumbria in 927. But the coinage clause is one of a series incorporated into Grately (chapter 5, p. 294); if it is indeed to be associated with the regularization of 'mint-signatures', Grately itself can hardly date before 928. The second point is that Whittlebury, where the king announced his change of heart about the most youthful and petty thieves, lay just south of Watling St, on the Roman road from Towcester down to the Goring Gap and ultimately Winchester. A royal council meeting there ought to be connected with one of the king's journeys north. It is not as if Æthelstan's movements were so well-charted, even during the *floruit* of 'Æthelstan A', that a northern progress can be ruled out between 927 and 934. Still, the first hint of one is the king's presence at Nottingham and then Buckingham (off the afore-mentioned road) in the latter year (table 6.2).[80] Northward moves are then attested in non-diplomatic sources for 936 and, on traditional assumptions about the site of *Brunanburh*, 937. It may not be over-bold to connect the Whittlebury session with 934 or 936x7, depending whether the Exeter Christmas were in 930x1 or 934. The effect, through a *not* entirely circular argument, is to identify the period of Æthelstan's law-making largely or even totally with that of 'Æthelstan A': the king's most self-consciously 'imperial' phase.[81]

The position regarding Edmund's codes is rather simpler. The edict on feud ('II') took its lead from a Council of London ('I') presided over by Archbishops

---

77 Blackburn, 'Mints, Burhs and the Grately Code'. Only mints intended to have more than one moneyer are itemized, but it is unclear why the list should be limited to southern Wessex plus Kent: Bath was established as a mint by Edward and seems to have had two moneyers under Æthelstan; nor is it obvious why provision should be made for moneyers of the archbishop, the bishop of Rochester and the 'abbot' (presumably of St Augustine's), when Wulfhelm was actually the first archbishop *not* to have his own coinage, the last bishop of Rochester known to have issued coins died in the 840s, and the Abbot of St Augustine's is never known to have done so. However, Dr Blackburn's solution, that the relevant clause was originally no more than an administrative memorandum later interpolated into the lawcode, has to reckon with the near-unanimity in this respect of a code otherwise prone to go separate ways (chapter 5, pp. 291–5).
78 Blunt, Stewart and Lyon, *Coinage in Tenth-Century England*, pp. 46–55; Blackburn, 'Mints, Burhs', pp. 164–5 and Table 3.
79 Blunt, 'Coinage of Æthelstan', pp. 40–1, 45–51, 55–8. Cf. the arguments of Liebermann, *Gesetze* III, pp. 100–1 (9).
80 Wulfhelm was certainly not present at Whittlebury (VI As 12:1, chapter 5, pp. 298–9); but it is impossible to say whether he was at Buckingham in September 934 (S 426), because this charter is one of the Glastonbury series with a severely truncated witness-list.
81 A supporting point is that 'Æthelstan A' was the one draftsman other than that of the 'alliterative charters' (*Burt. Ch.*, pp. xlvii–xlix; Walker, 'A Context for "Brunanburh"?', pp. 27–9) to specify the presence in witness-lists of 'kinglets' from the rest of the British Isles: Keynes (as n. 55); Loyn, 'Wales and England'. Note too that there is no diminution in the grandiloquence of the king's later charter-titles (below), but there is less assertiveness in what may be his later coins: Blunt, Coinage of Æthelstan', pp. 48, 56–7.

Oda of Canterbury and Wulfstan I of York.[82] Oda assumed office in 941; Wulfstan appeared in Edmund's (quite prolific) charters only in 942 and 944–6. Northern chronology in the critical decade and a half after Æthelstan's death is inextricably tangled.[83] But it seems fair to link Wulfstan's presence at Edmund's court with times of southern ascendancy over Northumbria: following the 'Redemption of the Five Boroughs' in 942, and Edmund's takeover of Northumbria itself in 944 or 945.[84] Now, the London Council met at Easter; and since it is unlikely that either of Edmund's northern campaigns occurred before April, the council's date is in effect pushed to 945–6, or 946 if 945 be preferred for the absorption of Northumbria. Yet the king was assassinated in late May 946; Easter was as early as March 22nd that year, but this still leaves little time for Edmund to have drafted his laws on blood-feud before his gratitude for the prevailing peace was revealed as so ironic. Either, therefore, Edmund's expulsion of his Scandinavian rivals was in 944, or his legislation was packed into the last months of his life.[85] Either way, it too coincides with its author's most 'imperial' period.[86]

Edgar's earlier (Andover) code is devoid of chronological indicators, internal or external.[87] Its dating depends on one's view of the subsequent *Wihtbordesstan* edict, where indicators are several but contradictory. The usual argument connects Edgar's reference to a 'pestilence (*færcwealme*) which greatly oppressed and reduced his people throughout his dominion', and which suggested to the king that God's anger needed soothing by readier payment of tithes, with a 'Parker' *Chronicle* mention of 'a very great mortality (*man cwealm)*' in 962.[88] Good argument as this is, it involves the assumption that a plague recorded by Winchester's *Chronicle* but not by other versions, could not have recurred over the next thirteen years without being noted by any of them. A further factor is that responsibility for disseminating the decree was given to

---

82   Nothing can be said about the date of 'III Em'; this may well follow 'I/II', because it anticipates trends in Edgar's legislation (chapter 5, pp. 311–12); but 'I' and 'II' are themselves eccentric enough in genre for it to be possible that the style reflected by 'III' was established earlier.

83   See (e.g.) Smyth, *Scandinavian York and Dublin* II, pp. 107–25, whom I mostly follow here. But compare the comments of Sawyer, 'Last Scandinavian Kings of York'; and I have learnt much from discussion with Marios Costambeys, who is preparing a paper on the topic.

84   Wulfstan's political record is assessed by Whitelock, 'Dealings of the Kings of England', pp. 71–3; cf. Sawyer, as n. 83, who notes that Wulfstan attended Eadred 946–50, when Olaf Sihtricsson probably ruled Northumbria, suggesting that Eadred could accept Olaf's northern rule as Edmund in the end could not.

85   Smyth, *Scandinavian York and Dublin*, pp. 113–14, 119, at first prefers 945 for Edmund's Northumbrian initiative, but later allows for the possibility of 944; Wulfstan's movements (if this is not a circular argument) favour 944. Liebermann, *Gesetze* III, p. 124 (6) inclined towards similar views of I Em's dating, on not dissimilar arguments. Note the implications of S 505 (table 6.2), a council on Palm Sunday 945 with a fuller than usual bench of bishops; also of Councils (ed. Whitelock) no. 19, a 'Pastoral Epistle' by Archbishop Oda which uses notably imperialistic language in Edmund's name.

86   Thus, his Strathclyde campaign (supported by the King of Dyfed) and settlement with Malcolm of Scotland: ASC 945, pp. 110–11, Smyth, *Scandinavian York and Dublin*, pp. 112–13. A partially garbled 'alliterative' charter (above, n. 81), in principle datable to any year in Edmund's reign but *perhaps* late, was witnessed by Hywel Dda (S 1497, 1810d), whereas Edmund's other alliterative charters are of 940 and 942 (S 472–3, 479, 484, 1606), and lack such subscriptions.

87   But one *might* take the failure of II–III Eg to refer to monks or monasteries (chapter 5, pp. 316–17; cf. II Eg 1 – 3:1 with IV Eg 1:7) as indicating a date before Æthelwold's reform gathered impetus.

88   IV Eg Pr.; ASC (A) 962, p. 114; *Gesetze* III, p. 138 (7); *EHD I*, p. 434.

Earl Oslac, and to Ealdormen Ælfhere and Æthelwine. Æthelwine joined Ælfhere among the ealdormen in 962 itself.[89] But Oslac's promotion to a Northumbrian ealdormanry was dated 966 by the 'northern' *Anglo-Saxon Chronicles*, which is already late in the day for action designed to remedy a 962 pestilence.[90] The evidence otherwise points to a date after 970: Oslac, Ælfhere and Æthelwine were singled out because IV Edgar was scheduled for the Danelaw (chapter 4, pp. 184–5, chapter 5, p. 317), and they were the ealdormen in charge of it; but at any date before 970, Æthelstan *Rota* should arguably have been included among them.[91] On top of that stands the inference from what chapter 3 and 5 proposed (pp. 125–7, 369–70) about the lost equivalent to this code for 'English England'. If it corresponded to the fierce *lex*, one of whose victims was restored to his full faculties by St Swithun, then English and Danelaw versions alike ought to post-date the saint's 971 *translatio*, which was the spur to all the *miracula* that Lantfred reported. Finally, there is the unparalleled 'imperialism' of the code itself, with its application to 'Englishmen, Danes and Britons in every part of my dominion', or to 'all of us together who live in these islands'. The code therewith echoed the increasingly hegemonial tone of Edgar's later charters, as well as the celebrated Bath coronation at Pentecost 973.[92] Thus, even if 'IV Edgar' did not date to the 970s, as seems cumulatively probable, it had unmistakably imperial overtones in its own right.[93]

Finally, there is the dating of Æthelred's pre-Wulfstan codes. Two charters of the 990s refer to royal councils which took decisions about the problems of the

---

89   IV Eg 15 – 15:1; Williams, *'Princeps Merciorum gentis'*, pp. 155–60; Hart, 'Athelstan "Half-king"' (revised), pp. 591–2, 601–4.

90   ASC 966DE, p. 119. Whitelock, 'Dealings of the Kings of England', p. 78, upheld the *Chronicle* date, despite charter evidence against it; not so Dr Keynes, 'Additions in Old English', pp. 86–7. Yet of the three 963 charters where Oslac appears, he is beneficiary of one (S 712, 'venerabili … nomine'), 'dominus' in another (S* 712a, the recently discovered Ballidon charter: Brooks *et al.*, 'A New Charter of King Edgar', pp. 140–2), and 'dux' only in the third (S 716), which, as a York charter, may have been retrospectively influenced by his later status; while the three Abingdon charters of 965 in which he has this title (S 732–4) are, as Whitelock pointed out, identically formulated and could share a dating error. There was an Oslac 'minister' in S 738, a 'single-sheet' charter of 966, though its implications are somewhat undermined by the appearance of another such in S 779 (970).

91   Hart, 'Æthelstan "Half-King"', p. 591, n. 92; and for Æthelstan *Rota*, *ibid.*, pp. 582–3, n. 54: one's assessment will depend on *how* 'south-eastern Mercian' one considers Æthelstan *Rota*'s ealdormanry to have been; that it was at least Mercian is clear from his alignment under Edgar 958–9 (S 674–9).

92   IV Eg 2:2, 14:2; (e.g.) S 751 (967/973x5), 775 (970, 'imperator augustus'!), 782 (971), 795 (974); Nelson, 'Inauguration rituals', pp. 69–70. This is not to say that the code must have been bound up with the coronation itself. But it may be worth comparing the position considered next, where Æthelred's court twice adjourned from a council on a great festival to a session elsewhere that took appropriate steps. *Wihtbordesstan* is a lost place-name; but 'Wihtbord's stone' was presumably named from a person of repute, and while the name was rare, one Wihtb(r)ord that comes to mind was the 'minister (*dux?*)' of Alfred and Edward the Elder, who was granted Fovant in Wiltshire (S 364), who took part in the Helmstan affair, centred in the next-door hundred (S 1445, chapter 3, pp. 144–8), and who witnessed several other charters (S 359, 368–9, 374, 1286, 375); a stone named from him need not, then, have been more than twenty miles from Bath. (The one other Wihtbrord listed by Searle, *Onomasticon*, p. 493, was a Kentish witness of the mid-eighth century (S 30–1).)

93   It is worth adding, despite the drift of the foregoing paragraph, that an 'imperial' tone might not have been inappropriate in 963, when Edgar was the first English king for a generation known to have held court at York, and with a decidedly large council, Keynes, 'Additions in Old English', p. 87.

kingdom in general, as well as rescinding moves that the king had made in his 'youth' against the abbeys of Abingdon and the Old Minster.[94] The first met in Winchester at Pentecost 993 and decreed 'condigna instituta', and the decision that most concerned the charter was then confirmed six weeks later at Gillingham (Dorset).[95] The second gathered at Calne over Easter 997; then, 'a few days later the whole army, a crowd of bishops, abbots, ealdormen, magnates and quite a number of nobles' was summoned to Wantage 'for the reform of matters of various sorts', the relevant charter being among its outcomes. The formulae of debate and correction used by the 993 and 997 charters are almost unparalleled in later Anglo-Saxon diplomatic, but are typical of the synodical legislation of the eighth/ninth century, when judgements in favour of particular churches were likewise coupled with those of more general moment to Church and society.[96] The language of these records was therefore wholly apposite for sessions that also made laws. Since Kemble's time, the 997 council has been recognized as the probable setting for 'III Æthelred', the royal core of which was issued at Wantage.[97] But if so, what was produced by the 993 assembly at Winchester/Gillingham? An answer would be to elide it with the meeting at an unidentified 'Bromdun' to which 'I' and 'III Æthelred' refer. But another set of laws seems to precede the Wantage code: the coinage clauses incorporated into 'IV Æthelred' (chapter 5, pp. 322, 328). If these were not part of the 'Bromdun' proceedings, they could have been promulgated by the 993 council(s).[98] In any event, there is reason to think that the mid–990s saw Æthelred's early codes emerge in a fairly concentrated burst. This could well have been inaugurated by the 993 council itself, which ushered in an important new phase of the king's reign, dominated by the disciples of the previous generation's monastic reform movement, and aiming at the restoration of the Edgarian regime. It may be relevant that the charters of this period are those most liable to elaborate on the

94   S 876, 891 (cf. chapter 5, p. 328).
95   Cf. Sawyer 'Royal *Tun*', p. 294: the Dorset Gillingham was royal land in 1086, while the Kentish one was held by the Archbishop and Odo of Bayeux: *DB* i 3c, 8bc (*Kent* 2:12, 5:88).
96   E.g. Conc. Hertf., 672 (*Hist. Eccl.* iv 5, pp. 348–53): 'tractaturos de necessariis ecclesiae negotiis ... in commune tractemus ... in commune tractatis ac definitis'; Conc. Clovesho, 747 (*Councils and Ecclesiastical Documents*, ed. Haddan and Stubbs, III, p. 362): 'de ... statu Christianae religionis, et concordia pacis tractanda confirmandaque pariter consederunt'; Conc. Clovesho, 803 (S* 1431–1431b – the only case where general decisions and specific judgements are both recorded): 'de necessariis et pluribus universae ecclesiae statutis congregarentur'; Conc. Chelsea, 816 (Haddan and Stubbs, III, p. 579): 'tractantes de necessariis et utilitatibus ecclesiarum'; Conc. Bapchild, '696x716' (S 22): 'pariter tractantes ancxie examinantes de statu ecclesiarum'; Conc. Clovesho, '742' (S 90 – for the forgery in the 810s or '20s of this and the previous text, see Brooks, *Early History of the Church of Canterbury*, pp. 191–7): 'necessaria ... examinantes de statu totius christianitatis ... '; Conc. Clovesho, 825 (S* 1436): 'ecclesiarum Dei utilitatem et necessitatem tractantes et scrutantes ... seu etiam generositatem stabilitatemque regni terrestris ... querentes'. For the origin of these protocols in papal conciliar procedure (and ultimately that of the Roman senate), see Cubitt, *Anglo-Saxon Church Councils*, pp. 77–87.
97   *Gesetze* III, p. 156 (2).
98   I Atr 1:2, III Atr 4. My proposition in 'Athelred the Lawmaker', pp. 62–3, that the IV Atr coinage laws may have been issued c. 984 (?at *Bromdun*) looks numismatically less plausible than it did then: cf. Dolley, 'Introduction to the Coinage of Æthelræd II', pp. 120–2, and Stewart, 'Coinage and Recoinage after Edgar's Reform', pp. 471–4.

illegalities putting the granted land at the king's disposal (chapter 3, pp. 148–50, chapter 5, p. 326).[99]

What is tentatively suggested, then, is that the legislative impulse of the Old English kingdom waxed and waned with its imperial consciousness. If Edward the Elder's codes are seen as an extension of Alfred's, which they both appear and in a sense professed to be, the impetus then subsided for up two decades, before resuming with unprecedented force at the very time when Æthelstan acquired a status never before paralleled, along with a spokesman fully capable of expressing it in his charters. It is much to the point that the penalty he decreed for coiners was the one established by Byzantine and Frankish imperial law (chapter 5, p. 306). Edmund's laws represented a fuller working out of some of his brother's themes, and signalled the final recovery of his hegemony. The hiatus that ensued coincided with a time of renewed tentativeness in West Saxon ambitions: Eadred was content for three years to be the overlord of an Ivarson king in Northumbria, and only drew the line at Eric Bloodaxe (above, pp. 440–1). For two years (957–9), it was even possible to contemplate repartition of the kingdom along the Thames. With Edgar came a revived imperial vision and a return to written law, especially perhaps as the vision intensified in the 970s. Æthelred's early years saw a reaction against Edgar's policies that may have embraced a retreat in law-making too. But legislation resumed with the restoration to power of those most influenced by his father's ideologists (not least his mother).[100] As for Cnut's laws, of which nothing has been said here, they fit the pattern well: there was a preliminary sketch as the regime was established, in 1018, and a vast statement after 1020, when Cnut became an emperor on a scale that dwarfed the aspirations of his predecessors.

That the first kings of the English laid claim to an imperial status is quite clear, even if its precise political implications are not. Kings from Æthelstan onwards repeatedly asserted in their charters that they ruled an empire.[101] The word 'imperator' was on the whole avoided in authentic documents, except by the notably assertive 'alliterative' series.[102] But in his Lifton charter of 931 Æthelstan was 'king of the English, raised by the right hand of the Almighty to the throne of the whole of Britain'; with the replacement of 'Æthelstan A', he became 'Basileus of all Albion'; and by the end of his reign he was 'Basileus of all the peoples living around about'.[103] Titles of this type were used many dozens of

---

99   Keynes, *Diplomas of Æthelred*, pp. 95–104; 993 saw the appointment as Northumbrian *dux* of Ælfhelm, brother of the monastic founder Wulfric Spot, whose north-east Mercian family may have had much to do with the implementation of the Wantage code as now extant (Whitelock, 'Dealings of the Kings of England', pp. 80–1).

100   For the implications of Ælfthryth's return to prominence, see Keynes, *Diplomas of Æthelred*, pp. 176–7, 187–9; Nelson, 'Second English *Ordo*', pp. 372–4; and Yorke, 'Æthelwold and the politics of the Tenth Century', pp. 81–8.

101   The subject has been much discussed in the thirty years since Eric John's path-breaking paper (in the teeth of then current wisdom), 'Orbis Britanniae', pp. 49–60; see now Kleinschmidt, 'Die Titulaturen englischer Könige', modifying his earlier *Untersuchungen über das englische Königtum*, pp. 33–105; and Campbell, 'United Kingdom of England', pp. 38–9. I also owe much to a convenient summary by Kelly, *Royal Styles in Anglo-Saxon Diplomas*.

102   So S 392, 548–50, 569, 572, 633 (S 406 is bogus); see above, n. 81, and for Edgar's use of 'imperator' in 970, n. 92.

times and with a wealth of variations, by all his successors till 1066. There was even talk of being 'crowned by the imperial diadem of the Anglo-Saxons', or of 'wielding the sceptre of the whole island of Albion'.[104] 'Albion' was undoubtedly a synonym for Britain rather than England (in so far as Englishmen could even then tell the difference); and 'Basileus' should surely be seen not as a characteristic hermeneutic Grecism, but as the known title of the heirs of Rome on the Bosphorus. Constant pretensions to rule over a variety of peoples (never mind their kings' presence at the English royal court, a regular *motif* of German imperialism) is proof that a hegemonial pose was consciously cultivated. For Anglo-Saxons, as for all barbarians, the definitive exponents of empire were the Romans. But there was also a model much nearer to hand. One of this book's persistent themes is the pervasive effect of Carolingian example on the makers of the English state and its law. The revised coronation ritual discussed below built Hincmarian extensions on an insular core. It is barely conceivable that Æthelstan was unaware of the symbolism of his receipt of Charlemagne's cherished relics.[105] The pursuit of monastic uniformity shows English sensitivity to one dimension of Christian Empire.[106] And Anglo-Saxons should have been aware of how Carolingian law-making was given new momentum by acquisition of an imperial role. Einhard unforgettably linked the taking of an 'imperial name' with the repair of deficiencies in the laws of one's own people and with the giving of written law to subject peoples. The English did not (so far as is known) 'give law' to the Welsh or Scots. But they were emperors in their own island. Legislation was an expression of their standing. Did they learn that from Einhard?[107]

If there is some significance in the particular years when early English kings made law, the same is at least equally arguable for the times of year when they did so. The information available for laws and charters alike is once again maddeningly deficient.[108] It may, however, suffice to show that special efforts to convene the great men of the kingdom on the major feasts of Christmas, Easter and Pentecost began under Cenwulf in Mercia and Ecgberht in Wessex, but not before.[109] After 900, at least four assemblies are on record as meeting at

---

103   S 416; S 429–31, 437, 441.

104   S 590, 598.

105   Leyser, *Rule and Conflict*, p. 88; with his 'Ottonians and Wessex', pp. 73–4, 82–3, 96–7; Wood, 'Making of King Æthelstan's Empire', pp. 266–7 (amplified as in the paper cited, n. 107).

106   Wormald, 'Æthelwold', pp. 31–2.

107   Einhard, *Vita Karoli* 29, p. 33. Michael Wood's forthcoming paper on William of Malmesbury's source for Æthelstan (chapter 5, n. 529) gives strong grounds for believing Einhard to have been known in tenth-century England.

108   Liebermann, *National Assembly*, pp. 48–50, 52 (with other lists, p. 49, nn.12–16, albeit neither accurate nor discriminating enough as to period). It is one of the perversities of Anglo-Saxon diplomatic that a higher proportion of pre-871 charters (especially the earliest and any from Kent) give a calendar date – or at least month – than those after 'Æthelstan A' ceased operations. Known cases (cf. n. 56) are: S 7–10, 12–13, 15–20, 1180, 23, 26–8, 156, **157**(E), 40, **163**(E), 168, 170, **187**(P), 188, 1266–7, 286, 286a, 293, 296, 1194 (Kent); S 1165, 1171, 1248, 65 ('Earconwald group'); S 51, 1167–8, 56 (Hwicce, etc.); S 86–8, 91, 95, 108, 116, **120**(C), **172**(C), **192**(E), **193–6**(C), **198**(C), **208**(E), 210, 225 (Mercia); S 1245, 1249, 1169, 1170, 238–40, 245, 248, 255, 1410, 257, **272–3**(C), **277**(C), **290**(C), 294–294b, **298**(C), **302/11**(E), 333(C, E), 347, 352 (Wessex).

109   They are marked in bold (+ C, E, P) in n. 108. So the earliest for Mercia is S 120 (780) or 163 (808), and for Wessex S 272–3 (825).

Christmas, thirteen at Easter and four at Pentecost (tables 6.1–2). Is this enough to suggest that the Anglo-Saxons staged festal 'crown-wearings', like those that William the Conqueror's Anglo-Saxon Chronicler made famous?[110] Knowledge of William's ceremonies depends on the more prolific evidence for his reign (not least the Chronicler's own very evident interest in the topic); it may not be as certain as scholars have often thought that they were a new departure, a token of a new ascendancy. After all, the simplest explanation for the interest in festival court-holding that appears in English charters in the first quarter of the ninth century is that it reflects the Carolingian preoccupation so evident in the Frankish Annals.[111] Moreover, it was from just that time that the earliest extant English king-making liturgy is likely to date.[112] If royal ceremonial was indeed established in the ninth century, is it conceivable that it was discontinued in the tenth?

The relevance of this is that the great feasts of the Church were associated with four of the extant twenty-two codes from 899 to 1022; or a quarter if the transactions recorded by the 990s charters are regarded as in some sense legislative; and nearly a third, if starting (as may be appropriate, for reasons that will appear) with the Grately code (table 6.1). The proportion is not so unlike that of other dated councils: four out of twenty dated 'Æthelstan A' occasions were at festivals, and eleven out of thirty-five recorded by less thorough charter draftsmen or narratives (table 6.2). The difference is that there are from twelve to eighteen codes (depending how many are conflated) for which no calendar date is given, but several hundred undated charters. In other words, the number of law-codes issued by councils on days when kings might wear their crown may be statistically significant.

What is more, coronation liturgy shows why it could be. It is now known that the earliest English royal inauguration ritual goes back at least to the era when Christmas and Easter courts are first attested.[113] It has been still more strongly

110   ASC 1087E, pp. 219–20 (and cf. 1067D, 1069D, pp. 202, 204, 1085–6E, p. 216); *RRAN* i (as n. 61); Biddle, 'Seasonal Festivals and residence', pp. 64–8; Bates, *William the Conqueror*, pp. 112–13; Cowdrey, 'Anglo-Norman *Laudes Regiae*', pp. 50–5 (though on the *Laudes Regiae* themselves, cf. Lapidge, 'Ealdred of York and MS. Cotton Vitellius E.xii', pp. 15–18). The Richardson and Sayles arguments for pre-1066 crown-wearing, *Governance of Medieval England*, pp. 405–12, are over-dependent on late evidence (and ignore the above considerations), but good use is made, e.g. at p. 406, of Byrhtferth's 'Vita S. Oswaldi' pp. 425, 436; and one might reasonably think William of Malmesbury's assertion that crown-wearings were an innovation by the Conqueror (*Vita S. Wulfstani* ii 12, p. 34) late evidence derived from the *Chronicle*. In so far as Norman practice borrowed from French (as orthodox opinion holds), French crown-wearings are themselves known only from late-eleventh century enrichment of the evidence; and even in the *Reich*, knowledge of crown-wearing depends on the availability of good quality narratives (Klewitz as next n.). The topic has been reopened by Hare's 'Kings, crowns and festivals', which I am much obliged to him for showing me before publication.
111   *Annales Regni Francorum*, pp. 16–127, 165–7, 178; *Annales de Saint-Bertin*, pp. 8–17, 35–43, 66, 87–95, 116–245; *Annales Fuldenses*, pp. 29–30, 43, 48, 71, 75–8, 82–3, 92–4, 109, 113–21, 123–4, 127, 130, 135: some were certainly festal crown-wearings (Brühl, below). On Ottonian and Salian crown-wearings, see Leyser, *Rule and Conflict*, pp. 90, 99–100, 105; the main continental discussions are Klewitz, 'Festkrönungen'; Brühl, 'Fränkischer Krönungsbrauch', and 'Kronen und Krönungsbrauch'; Jäschke, 'Frühmittelalterliche Festkrönungen?'.
112   See next n. A feature of mid-ninth-century charters in Mercia and Wessex (showing that neither is anachronistic) is that they make provisions anticipating Æthelstan (above, n. 76), for liturgical celebration of king, courtiers and people: S 193, 215, 303–5, 307–8.

argued that the 'Second *Ordo*', where actual crowning appears for the first time, was devised in the first quarter of the tenth century and only revised for Edgar, long supposed its original honorand.[114] These inauguration rituals resounded with the rhetoric of justice. The first words of the first *Ordo*'s opening antiphon were 'Thou art just, O Lord and have the right (*Iustus es domine et rectum*)'. The prayer immediately preceding the king's unction asked that 'in his days, let there be equity and justice for all, aid to friends, obstruction to enemies, solace for the humble, reproof for the rich, doctrine for the poor, piety and calm for pilgrims, peace and security for his own people in their fatherland'. The Postcommunion of the associated mass prayed that 'God, who hath prepared christian empire for the preaching of the Gospel of the eternal kingdom, hold out the heavenly arms of justice to thy servants, now our rulers, that the peace of the Church be disturbed by no storm of wars'. Finally, the 'three precepts declared to the people by the newly ordained king' were ' ... that the Church of God and all Christian people have true peace for all time ... that robberies and every injustice be forbidden to all ranks, and ... that he offer equity and mercy in all judgements'.[115]

In the second *Ordo*, the introduction of the crown was accompanied by a petition that 'God crown you with the crown of glory, the honour of justice and the duty of bravery'; bequest of the sceptre by the admonition that 'you protect the christian people committed to you by God from the wicked with royal courage, that you correct the wicked, give peace to the just, and lend your aid that they can keep to the just path'.[116] In the revised version, used from Edgar's time, the triple mandate, instructions from king to people which spelled out the implications of the preceding ceremony, became a threefold oath in much the same words, but which was a *prelude and condition* of the ritual to follow.[117] Two manuscripts preserve a vernacular text of this oath, attributing it to Dunstan and saying that 'it was administered to our lord at Kingston on the day that he was consecrated to kingship'; a king consecrated by Dunstan at Kingston, and

113   Nelson, 'Earliest Surviving Royal *Ordo*'; and, for a suggestion of my own, Campbell (ed.), *The Anglo-Saxons*, p. 140.
114   Hohler, 'Some Service Books', pp. 67–9, followed (and slightly modified) by Nelson, 'Second English *Ordo*'. I am rather less persuaded than Professor Nelson that the *Ordo* was devised for Edward rather than Æthelstan: the latter's succession on a 'Mercian ticket', in the aftermath of Edward's vigorous suppression of Mercian (semi-)independence perhaps makes best sense of the liturgy's stress on both these 'peoples', and it should be remembered that Æthelstan was consecrated in September 925, thirteen months after Ælfweard's death removed any serious question of a partition of the kingdoms (Nelson, p. 366). The adaptation of the rite by insertion of 'Northumbrians' after 'Saxons and Mercians' is appropriate for a king who was to add rule of the former to the latter in 927, and 'Albionis totius' is also better suited to Æthelstan than his father (Nelson, p. 364). As for the inclusion of a rite for the Queen (Nelson, pp. 366–7), this could just as well be another addition to the base-text, like the Northumbrians and 'Albion', in which case it could have been revised for the returning Louis IV in 936 (the obvious candidate for its exporter to France: Hohler, as above, Nelson, pp. 367–9) and/or Edmund, the heir apparent. Much of this (and what follows) is strongly argued by Michael Wood in his forthcoming paper (n. 107).
115   'Egbert Pontifical', *Two Anglo-Saxon Pontificals*, ed. Banting, pp. 109–13, which may or may not be an elaboration of the 'Leofric Missal' text: Nelson, 'Earliest Surviving Royal *Ordo*', pp. 353–9.
116   The composite version of the 'A' text (with an exclusively French circulation): Ward, 'Early Version of the Anglo-Saxon Coronation Ceremony', p. 355.
117   The earliest version seems to be that in *The Benedictional of Archbishop Robert*, pp. 140–8 (at p. 140); see Nelson, 'Second English *Ordo*', pp. 369–72.

still reigning at the time of writing, can only have been Æthelred.[118] It was accompanied by a homily, whose origins lay in Pseudo-Cyprian, and which may correspond to that said by two of the *Chronicles* to have been preached to Edward the Confessor in 1043: 'the duty of a consecrated king is that he judge no man falsely, and that he defend and protect widows and orphans and strangers, and forbid thefts, and amend illicit intercourse, and annul and totally forbid incestuous relationships, and eliminate witches and enchanters, and expel from the land kin-slayers and perjurers, and feed the needy with alms, and have old, wise and sober men as his counsellors …'.[119] On the continent, and in England after 1066, crown-wearings were heavily liturgical occasions, when the king was solemnly revested in church with regalia and robes before processing to a second church, where he was enthroned for a special mass when the *Laudes Regiae* were sung.[120] Apart from the *Laudes*, there is no record of the liturgy used, but it is scarcely an adventurous guess that elements of the original coronation prayers were recycled. The particular dates when V Æthelstan, I Edmund, V/VI Æthelred or I–II Cnut were issued could, then, have been times when kings had been reminded, in the most compelling way possible, of their obligation to be just, severe and merciful.

Much of the foregoing argument is of course highly tenuous. It is built on a framework of hints. The ideology of kingship between Alfred and Wulfstan cannot be elicited from anything but hints. That is not to say that there was no such ideology, or that the hints should not be taken. The facts are at least consonant with a theory that kings and their advisers were most likely to make written law when exposed to ideological stimulation. Law-making councils can be given contexts when the course of a king's reign, or the festal cycle of the Church and of his court, most emphasized his majesty. Even if the argument about crown-wearings be rejected, it still remains the case that turning-points in tenth-century legislative history came in the reigns of Æthelstan and Edgar when the coronation ceremony was being remodelled, with a final flurry in the 990s when those who orchestrated the 973 spectacular retrieved their positions of influence. Æthelstan, moreover, was the first English king to appear crowned on his coins.[121]

---

118   This is the text printed by Liebermann, *Gesetze* I, pp. 214–17 (and cf. *Gesetze* III, p. 144). For the MSS, see Ker, *Catalogue* 144, 213, and Drage, 'Bishop Leofric', pp. 359–61, 364–5. Given their respective dates as assigned by Ker and Drage, Cotton Vitellius A.vii can hardly have been copied from Cotton Cleopatra B.xiii, as Liebermann supposed, but since Cleopatra is an Exeter MS, and Vitellius found its way to Exeter, the relationship may well be the other way around. Since, moreover, Vitellius was originally a Ramsey MS (Dumville, *Liturgy*, p. 79), and in the light of Byrhtferth's wellknown interest in coronations (Lapidge, 'Byrhtferth of Ramsey and the early sections of the *Historia Regum*', p. 108), it might – at the risk of fathering further unwarranted progeny on Byrhtferth – be worth pondering his possible role in the oath's translation.

119   The homily was printed (with the oath) by Stubbs, *Memorials of St Dunstan*, pp. 355–7; cf. ASC ('C', 'E') 1043, pp. 162–3; and for its source (which is very close), the section on the 'Rex Iniquus', in *Pseudo-Cyprian*, ed. Hellmann, pp. 51–53. Cf. my 'Æthelred the Lawmaker', pp. 74–5. The idiom, though not the language, is already that of Wulfstan.

120   Klewitz, 'Festkrönungen', pp. 50–65, 70–5, 84; Brühl, 'Kronen und Krönungsbrauch', pp. 9, 13; Hare, 'Kings, crowns and festivals' discusses possible variations in English procedure.

121   Blunt, 'Coinage of Æthelstan', pp. 47–8; cf. the splendid reproduction in Campbell (ed.), *Anglo-Saxons*, p. 130, no. 9.

The association was not automatic. Coronation liturgy had been used for up to a century before Alfred's law-book. There were many tenth- and eleventh-century Christmases, Easters and Pentecosts with no legislation. English kings continued to legislate after Henry I wound down crown-wearing ceremonial as an economy measure.[122] Much of the tenth-century coronation liturgy is still in use, without its influence being writ large in the conduct of Her Majesty's Government. But what has been sought here is an explanation of the intermittency of tenth-century legislation, and of its uneven reception among those it addressed. The pressures of ideology are inherently more likely to have been intermittent than those of social disorder. To interpret legislation in this way is by no means to question the whole-heartedness of the commitment to the programme it articulated. Nothing suggests that the 'on-off' incidence of written law was matched by any wavering in the rigour with which that programme was applied (chapter 9). Which is exactly why it seems necessary to find a reason other than recurrent social crisis why laws were issued at some times but not others. Law-codes may plausibly be put down to the same inspiration as that which prompted so much harping on the royal duty to do justice. The law made did in fact reflect what their coronation told kings was their job. Thieves, sexual miscreants and for that matter witches were threatened and were punished. To make the connection is only to suggest that kings were no less (if also no more) affected by their ideological syllabus than are democratic politicians by their election manifestos.

There is a final reason why idealized perceptions may hold the key to patterns of legislation throughout the tenth century. That would explain, as little else can, what happened next: the appearance of codes that are often indistinguishable from homilies, because they were composed and usually transmitted by a master sermonizer.

3   Archbishop Wulfstan and the Law of God

Between the likely date of Æthelred's Wantage code and his next datable extant legislation, over a decade supervened. There had been several such intervals before. What was different this time was the startling transformation which then came over the character of the king's law. Compare:

> If there be any man that is untrustworthy for the whole people, let the king's reeve go and bring him under surety that one may lead him to justice with those who accused him. If, however, he has no surety, let him be slain and lie in filth;

with:

> And let each Christian do as is necessary for him. Let him make a habit of frequent confession … and let everyone also prepare himself often and frequently to go to communion. And let him order word and deed justly and carefully keep his oath and pledge. And let one eagerly eject from the country all injustice;

---

122   Green, *Government of England under Henry I*, pp. 20–1; cf. Biddle, 'Seasonal Festivals', p. 57, and Hare, 'Kings, Crowns and Festivals'; the last known Christmas legislation was Henry's writ on coinage of 1100 (chapter 5, p. 401).

or:

> And let every moneyer whom one accuses of striking false coin since it was forbidden go to the threefold ordeal; if he be guilty, let him be slain;

with:

> And let one very much shun deceitful deeds and loathsome abuses, that is false weights and wrong measures ... and let one be eager for the improvement of the peace and for the improvement of money everywhere in the land.

These pairings juxtapose Æthelred's laws from Enham with those from Woodstock and Wantage.[123] The subject of each pair was essentially the same. But they struck radically different notes. Largely or wholly secular codes, with an increasingly coherent structure and sinuous syntax, had been replaced by a ramble through the principles of a Christian life, whose cadences were as homiletic as its sanctions were few. It is as though the Brandenburg concertos had been reorchestrated by Bruckner. A council of the next year at Bath apparently considered organized penance *en masse* the most efficacious response to the 'great army' that had just landed. The code that followed in 1014 was not so devoid of penalty, but was yet more concentratedly ecclesiastical in content. The 1008 legislation was echoed all over again as Cnut secured his position at Oxford in 1018. Even his great Winchester code of 1020 or 1021, which was far from lacking in secular interest or terrestrial punishment, was also shot through with edifying sentiment. How is so marked a change of tone to be understood?

At one time, the descent into 'pseudo-legislation' was seen as another symptom of the degeneration of public affairs as Æthelred's regime drew to its disastrous close.[124] It is now recognized that the decisive factor was not a defeated government's despair but merely a change in the identity of its spokesman. (Something comparable happened to the voice of Roman imperial government early in the fourth century, with similar results for assessment of its competence; though historians have had no such criticisms of Charlemagne's switch to homiletic vein in the *Admonitio Generalis* of 789). Archbishop Wulfstan had brought to the language of law-making the sermonizing approach that was already his acknowledged speciality. To know that may not, however, be enough. Earlier chapters discovered that the manuscripts preserving the bulk of Æthelred's laws jumbled up law and homily, and that Wulfstan probably rewrote their versions of the former in the mode of the latter (chapter 4, pp. 195–208, chapter 5, pp. 330–45). But the one code to survive in a clearly non-Wulfstanian context was no less clearly his work; and that was the one that prescribed the decidedly 'otherworldly' remedy of mass penitence for the body politic's distempers. Hence, the archbishop's books cannot entirely misrepresent what was decreed by his king and fellow-councillors. King and councillors must up to a point have shared his approach. It becomes necessary to ask why. The evidence will not allow a direct answer to that question. The mind of Old English authority is translucent only when it is Alfred's. The best one can hope is that Wulfstan was a trusted enough

---

123   I Atr 4 – 4:1, V Atr 22 – 23; III Atr 8, V Atr 24, 26:1.
124   Richardson and Sayles, *Law and Legislation*, pp. 26–7; or even so acute a commentator as Stenton, *Anglo-Saxon England*, pp. 409–10.

servant of government (and no one except an emphatically Establishment figure would be given the northern archbishopric) for his own intellectual odyssey to shed some light on *élite* mentalities in general.

Wulfstan was first distinctly heard of when bishop of London (996–1002). A letter addressed to him in that capacity declined, for lack of the necessary time or competence, his request to render 'into Latin letters' a set of 'obscurities (*archana*)'; and goes on to contrast its author's own lack of skills with 'the most mellifluous sagacity of your eloquence ... the honeyed resonance of your tongue'. An attractive possibility, long ago spotted by Whitelock, is that Wulfstan established his reputation for eloquence with those extant homilies which evoke a searing vision of the reign of Antichrist, under the stimulus perhaps of the imminent millennium itself.[125] It is anyway likely enough that these homilies were among his earliest, and they hold important clues to the source of his anxiety. 'Just as the flood came once because of sin, so too because of sin will come fire upon mankind ... Then there will, as books say, be more grief and oppression than there ever was before ... when Antichrist rages and terrorizes the whole world ... It is clear and plain ... that we ... keep true faith among ourselves too weakly as regards God and the world. Therefore ... foreigners and people from overseas greatly harass us, just as Christ clearly said ... Nations shall rise up, he said, and become opposed and fiercely contend ... among themselves, because of the injustice that will be too widespread among men on earth. Beloved men ... our misdeeds constantly accuse us, in that we will not keep God's law as we should, nor ... pay our tithes as is incumbent on us, nor give out alms as we need ... That is why many created things ... harass us, as it is written: the world will contend ... against the proud who heed not God ... The earth contends with us when it denies earthly produce and brings forth too many weeds.'[126] What seems the climax of this series of homilies develops the specifically millenarian theme, and deserves fuller quotation:

> It is written and was long ago prophesied, 'after a thousand years will Satan be unbound'. A thousand years and more is now gone since Christ was among men in a human family, and Satan's bonds are now indeed slipped, and Antichrist's time is now close at hand ... There was often before manifold oppression, yet never like that which is to come after this. For it was often the case before that God's saints openly worked many wonders through God's power among those that suffered oppression ... But it will not be so in Antichrist's time. Holy men will not then be able to work any signs openly at that time, but must suffer everything that is done to them. Nor will God then be willing to declare his power nor his wonders himself for a while, as he often did before, but he will for a time let the devil Antichrist rave and rage, with those who follow him ... There is no man alive who can ... describe how evil it will be in that devilish time. A brother will not then support another for a time, nor a father his child, nor a child its own father, nor kinsman a kinsman any more than a stranger. And peoples will contend and dispute among themselves. There will also break out far and wide dispute and damage, envy and enmity and

---

125   The letter (in BL, Cotton Vespasian A.xiv) is *Hom.* Appendix II, pp. 376–7; discussed by Whitelock, 'Archbishop Wulfstan', pp. 28, 39–40; but her 'Note on the Career of Wulfstan', pp. 463–4, unlike her paper of 1942, rightly understands 'litteris Latinis commendare' as 'translate *into* Latin': cf. below, n. 141.
126   *Hom.* III lns 7–41.

rapine of robbers, hostility and hunger, burning and bloodshed and distressing disturbances, disease and death, and many misfortunes ... And it would destroy everything if God were not the more swiftly to shorten the Arch Enemy's lifetime with his power. But in support of those who are his chosen and whom he has been willing to maintain and help, he will crush the Arch-fiend, and sink him thenceforth in the depths of Hell with the whole gang that followed him ... Then will God's judgement be justly determined; and then certainly those who now love God and follow God's laws, and eagerly listen to God's teaching and keep it well, and continue resolutely in true belief until their end, will have eternal reward in heavenly delight with God Himself ... and with his saints for ever after ... [127]

That the end of the first millennium occasioned some agitation should not surprise a world making a rather more worldly fuss over the end of the second. But there is more to Wulfstan's position than that.

In the first place, apocalyptic anxiety was indeed 'in the air'. The quoted sermon elaborated Ælfric's account of Antichrist's impending advent in the preface to his First Series of Catholic Homilies, ten years before. Like Ælfric and probably through Ælfric, Wulfstan had come to know the *Tractatus de Antichristo* by Adso of Montier-en-Der. This short tract achieved a spectacular vogue. The copy in the Worcester/Exeter Corpus 190 is among the earliest, and stands at the head of an English family that is one of the two best witnesses to the original text.[128] Two other Wulfstan manuscripts contain a translation of most of Adso (with Biblical interpolations), which was not Wulfstan's work but was framed by passages from his homilies. These manuscripts also contain adaptations of a further homily on Judgement Day, whose oldest form is in the Vercelli Book.[129] When compared with these other treatments, Wulfstan's stand out for his sensitivity to contemporary events and to whatever could be given legal colouring.[130] Scandinavian depredation came to Ælfric's mind as an instance of 'Nation against Nation'; eschatological literature often noted the onset of

---

127   *Hom.* V lns 42–7, 57–66, 97–119; my translation is indebted, like much of the argument of this section, to Godden's important paper, 'Apocalypse and Invasion' (p. 143).

128   See chapter 4, pp. 221, n. 235. On Adso and the multifarious transmission of the *Tractatus*, see *Adso*, ed. Verhelst, pp. v–ix, etc., with, at pp. 20–30, the original available to Wulfstan; but there appears to be some confusion, e.g. at pp. 157–8, over the second English 'Anselmian' family of MSS: Cotton MS Vespasian D.ii is a book with 'Wulfstan connections' of 's xii²/⁴' (Cross, 'Wulfstan's *De Anticristo*', pp. 206, 216–17). The *Tractatus* is best-known (then, perhaps, as now) for its prediction that Antichrist will not come as long as 'reges Francorum' hold the 'Romanum imperium' as they should, and for its reference to a prophecy that 'unus ex regibus Francorum' will finally hold the Roman empire 'ex integro' (p. 26 lns 112–20); since the work was addressed to Otto the Great's sister, Gerberga, there may be a connection with Italian politics in the 950s and even the ideological fervour of the 990s: below, n. 136.

129   *HomN* XL, XLII; see Wilcox, 'Napier's "Wulfstan" Homilies XL and XLII: two anonymous works from Winchester?', with his 'Dissemination of Wulfstan Homilies', pp. 206–7; also Jost, *Wulfstanstudien*, pp. 218–21. Wilcox makes the arresting point that his translator has 'Bethsaida and Chorazin' in Adso's order (p. 24 lns 49–51), so implying his access to Adso's original, where Corpus 190 and other English MSS restore the Matthew 11:21 sequence; but his case that *HomN* XL/XLII were written at Winchester should be compared with the argument (chapter 4, pp. 208–10) that the New Minster acquired its *Wulfstaniana* corpus (including texts not by Wulfstan) from York; and Bodleian MS Hatton 114, featuring both Napier XL and XLII, is a Worcester book. For the Vercelli homily, see *Vercelli Homilies*, ed. Scragg, II, pp. 48–69, XXI, pp. 347–65.

130   Other Wulfstan homilies on the same theme are *Hom.* Ia-b (Latin notes on Adso and Scripture, with vernacular exposition), II, IV, VI lns 196–213, VII lns 104–58, IX lns 107–50, and of course XX (see

famine and plague, those other apocalyptic riders. But fraying of kindred ties was a variation of Wulfstan's own on the Gospel theme of mounting lawlessness and mutual hatred. Adso had lamented in another work the violation by 'tyrants' of rights and 'statutes'.[131] Neither he nor Ælfric nor the Vercelli homilist saw witheld tithes as a signal that Antichrist was on the march. Wulfstan, however, had already anticipated that central Enham preoccupation in preparing his congregations to meet their Doom.

An important part of his argument in these early homilies was that Antichrist will at first be irresistible: 'God ... will for a time let the devil Antichrist rave and rage'. Only in the end will He come to the aid of 'those who are his chosen'. They for their part must have retained their identity in that 'they love God and follow God's laws and eagerly listen to [his] teaching'. This is not a way to ward off Antichrist's assault, but a means of defining those who will come through the trial, and so profit from the Archangelic *revanche*. For that reason, reassertion of divine precepts was now so urgent that worldly punishment was barely relevant. It may already be too late to do much else. The Old Enemy had returned with impunity. Famine stalked the land. If this is how Wulfstan was thinking, there is no need to look any further for what inspired the Enham decrees and the Bath penitential edict. Even their more secular-looking provisions, the stress on fidelity 'under one king', viable weights and measures, unsullied coinage, adequate military and naval service, and loyalty to the king's person, address the 'lack of true faith among ourselves' picked out by Wulfstan's millenarian sermons.[132] One need only imagine that he imparted his sense of crisis to his fellow *witan*. Judging by the evidence for other responses to the 1008/9 emergency, his fellow-councillors were not so convinced of the irrelevance of more worldly solutions.[133] Yet there is also evidence that his approach was generally shared in the remarkable *Agnus Dei* coinage struck at just this time. The Lamb was not only a symbol of peace but also the ultimate apocalyptic emblem.[134]

Professional historians have understandably been chary of over-stressing millenarian expectations around the year 1000. Apart from their reluctance to reinforce notions of 'Dark Age' credulity, they know that attaching a date to the Second Coming was never doctrinally orthodox. But Wulfstan shows that the passing of a thousand years since the Incarnation had indeed thickened the atmosphere. However it was allegorized, the Book of Revelation explicitly

---

below); cf. too the Wulfstan-influenced *HomN* XXIX, pp. 136 ln 28 – 140 ln 2. On Ælfric's treatment, see Godden, 'Apocalypse and Invasion', pp. 132–42. I have learned from the doctoral research of Will Prideaux-Collins, who has independently reached similar conclusions about the relevance of Wulfstan's millenarianism for his reform programme; and see below, n. 138.

131   See Bisson, '"Feudal Revolution"', p. 10 and n. 11.

132   V Atr 1, 24, 26:1 – 30; cf. VI Atr (lat) 1:1, 28:2, 32:1 – 37.

133   ASC 1008–9, p. 138.

134   Dolley, 'The nummular brooch from Sulgrave', who is critical of the older view of an apocalyptic context, but chiefly because of his determination to date the series 1009 rather than 1000, and who does argue for a Wulfstan connection (the *cross-carrying* Lamb is of course particularly apocalyptic). Lawson, 'Archbishop Wulfstan', pp. 575–7, notes both the relevance of the Dove on the coinage's reverse to Pentecost when the code was issued, and also the singular fact that 'Enham' seems to mean 'place where lambs are bred'.

forecast the thousand-year reign of the martyrs between the 'first resurrection' and the escape of Satan.[135] Sharp detective-work has established the high probability that a sensational series of apocalyptic illustrated volumes from the library of Emperor Otto III were partly inspired by the millennium; their message, like Wulfstan's, was the need to prepare the Church for its great crisis.[136] A better-known parallel to the English legislation is the contemporary movement for a 'Peace of God' in south and central France.[137] It too aimed to shield churches and unarmed clerics from attack, and demanded the integrity and celibacy of clergy, observance of Sunday rest and Friday fast, and an end to 'incantation'. The French movement is usually (if no longer unanimously) explained as a response to mounting disorder and the atrophy of trusted peace-keeping machinery, rather than anything more dauntingly terminal.[138] Yet the rampages of castellans could surely foster the same sequence of thought in French churchmen as did those of Danish armies in Ælfric or Wulfstan. For French and English alike, unrest was attended by a rising tide of famine, with an especially severe outbreak in 1005.[139] The coincidence of the Peace Movement's date and priorities with Wulfstan's codes may imply that the one was millennium-minded like the other. There would be no knowing what fears underlay the Enham and Bath legislation, if further works by its leading architect did not happen to survive. As it is, the writers who chiefly recorded the Peace Movement, Ralph Glaber and Ademar of Chabannes, were also the most eloquent witnesses to deteriorating conditions of life and mounting eschatological neurosis.[140]

135   Revelation 20:3–10.
136   Mayr-Harting, *Ottonian Book Illumination*, II, pp. 11–55, especially pp. 45–8.
137   The parallels are noted by Campbell, 'England, France, Flanders and Germany', p. 257 (194), and Lawson, 'Archbishop Wulfstan', pp. 566, 575.
138   One of the hazards of this topic is the difficulty of achieving a conspectus of relevant texts. One set of (problematic) canons (Anse, ?994), is in Mansi, *Conciliorum ... Collectio*, XIX, cols 99–102, and another (Charroux, 989) is *ibid.*, cols 89–90, and translated by Head, in Head and Landes (as below), pp. 327–8; an exhaustively scholarly account of the movement and its materials is Hoffmann, *Gottesfriede und Treuga Dei*, especially chapters II–IV. The first modern English assessment was Cowdrey, 'Peace and Truce of God', but there is now an illuminating collection of studies (with documentary appendices) in Head and Landes (eds), *The Peace of God*: here Paxton, 'History, Historians and the Peace of God', pp. 27–8, draws attention to millenarian interpretations in an earlier phase of the movement's historiography, and Callahan, 'Peace of God and the Cult of Saints', pp. 170–2, takes some notice of apocalyptic expectations, as does Professor Landes himself, pp. 188–90, 201. On rampant disorder as causal factor, see now Bisson, '"Feudal Revolution"', pp. 14–28, though also the 'revisionism' he combats (e.g. the 'Debate' inspired by his paper, and Goetz, 'Protection of the Church, Defense of the Law and Reform', in Head and Landes, pp. 259–79). The Peace Movement's place in a wider social context is analysed by Poly and Bournazel, *Feudal Transformation*, pp. 151–62 (especially the maps, pp. 158–9); and more briefly (with texts) by Duby, *L'An Mil*, pp. 168–74. Neither Duby nor Focillon, *The Year 1000*, pp. 53–72, make anything of English evidence, whose possibilities have hardly been noticed by continental historiography; though something may perhaps be expected from publication of the 1996 Boston conference on 'The Apocalyptic Year 1000' (?Oxford), where there were significant contributions by Godden, 'The Millennium, Time and History for the Anglo-Saxons', and Prideaux-Collins, '"Satan's Bounds are extremely loose". Apocalyptic Expectation in Anglo-Saxon England during the Millennial Era', which their authors kindly showed me.
139   Leyser, 'Tenth-Century Condition', pp. 1–3; ASC 1005, p. 136.
140   *Glaber, Five Books of Histories*, ed. France *et al.*, II vi (10–12), xii (23), III iii–iv (9–13), ix (40), IV i (1), iv–vi (9–21), V i (15, 18); *Adémar, Chronique*, ed. Chavanon, iii 35 (tr. Landes, *Peace of God*, pp. 329–30), 46–7, 52, 58–9, 69. It may be noted that the same sources make several references to

The reason for the strange turn taken by English law-making in the early years of the second millennium was therefore that its prime mover did not think that it had many years to run. Wulfstan drew reasoned conclusions from the torments which God was allowing to befall the kingdom that Alfred and his heirs had tried to build in His name. The legislation with which that kingdom had hitherto been upheld was now failing to satisfy its Maker. So Wulfstan focused on the people's basic character, its moral frailties, in much the same accents as he had previously used to such stirring effect. Whether divine anger was all there was to fear, or something yet more terrifying was afoot, the proper response was to fortify the Church militant. Prayer, penance and payment of alms (not to forget tithes), might manage what conventionally secular measures could not.

Wulfstan's sense of the Church's needs must have been intensified in the years before 1008 by the discoveries in Canon law to which, as proposed in chapter 4 (pp. 217–18), he was led by Ælfric. The upshot of that earlier argument was that the so-called *Excerptiones Ecgberhti* was Wulfstan's response to Ælfric's *Pastoral Letters*, a response that Ælfric facilitated by making available the sources he had himself exploited. If the *Excerptiones* gave Wulfstan a taste for legislative action, that would also have helped to recommend him for his role at Enham.[141] At any rate, the influence of the *Excerptiones* (or their sources) on the 1008 legislation is patent (chapter 8, chapter 13). The prohibition on sale of an 'innocent Christian' into the hands of unbelievers, the first item of substance in the 'V Æthelred' version, was lifted straight from one of the *Excerptiones*, which is why the Latin text in 'VI Æthelred' referred to Jews as well as pagans.[142] But Enham's debt to the 'Excerpts' transcends verbal borrowing. Almost all its topics till it gets to such current business as coinage and 'triple obligation' are those of *Excerptiones*. The 1008 decrees (as extant) appear to derive what coherence they have from a wish to cover every issue in Wulfstan's 'Canon collection' that bore in any way on society at large (the relevance of clerical celibacy for laymen being that the laity was likely to supply the female accessory to any infringement). The only major *Excerptiones* subject not addressed was penance, and this was the central concern of the Bath legislation in the next year.[143] Ælfric

---

organized relic processions as a panacea for the evils of the time, which may perhaps be compared with what was prescribed by Æthelred and Wulfstan in 1009: *Glaber* III vi (19) IV iii (8) v (14); *Adémar* iii 35, 40, 49, 56, 57.

141   The (probably) first Wulfstan works to exploit *Exc. Can.* were EGu and *Can. Eg.*: see chapter 5, pp. 390–1, and n. 579. As regards the negative view of Wulfstan's Latinity deduced by Hohler (see chapter 4, n. 211) from the fact that Ælfric complied with a request to translate his Latin draft (Fehr, *Hirtenbriefe*, p. 68, Whitelock, *Councils*, p. 260): if Wulfstan commissioned a translation *into* Latin when still bishop of London (above, n. 125), the language can have held few terrors for him; but it would be perfectly good sense (as well as good manners) to make such a request of one whose canonical expertise he clearly regarded as superior to his own (Fehr, *Hirtenbriefe* '2a', pp. 222–7; Whitelock, *Councils*, pp. 242–55; and for the dating of the correspondence, Clemoes, supplement to Fehr, *Hirtenbriefe*, p. cxlv).

142   V Atr 2, VI lat 9, as noted by Jost, *Wulfstanstudien*, p. 24. The principle but not wording is found in sources contributing to the 'Commonplace book'/'Canon Collection' (table 4.4): *Bußordnungen*, ed. Wasserschleben, pp. 369, 374–5, 476; Pelteret, *Slavery in Early Medieval England*, p. 91; and see also chapter 5, pp. 341–4, 363–4.

143   VII Atr 1:1 – 2:5 (VIIa 1 – 2:3, 4 – 5); cf., e.g., *Penit. Ps.Th.* li, p. 306, Fehr, *Hirtenbriefe*, Anhang III 41–6.

launched the first of his two Letters for Wulfstan with an account of the three stages of legal time: that of the patriarchs, 'before the Law'; that of the prophets 'under the Law'; and that of Christians, since the Incarnation, 'under Grace'. Before the Law, men lived with 'carnal' knowledge; under it, they continued to live carnally, though the Law prohibited and punished sins. But Christ brought chastity as well as the Faith, intending it to be observed by all his true servants, male and female. The aftermath of His coming was, as He said himself, that the Kingdom of Heaven was attacked by violent men. Its citizens should therefore care nothing for what was done to their bodies, and fortify their souls by gird-ing their loins, that they win rest rather than punishment in eternity.[144] Ælfric's analysis was like Hincmar's, but replaced his provision for earthly laws with the principles of the Apostolic Life. Thus, where Alfred responded to the Hincmarian thesis by legislating for his people as Moses had (above, pp. 423–7), Wulfstan's response to Ælfric's ideal was an uncompromising exposition of the fundamentals of Grace. A People of God answers persecution with spotlessness.

Wulfstan's reaction to his canonical heritage can usefully be compared with that of two of his continental contemporaries, one West and the other East Frankish. Abbo of Fleury dedicated his Canon collection to Kings Hugh and Robert in the early 990s. After remarking the way that God had rescued them from 'initial misfortunes' at the hands of 'external peoples' and their leading subjects, he invited them to recall the good kings their predecessors, and 'just judgements'; for which purpose he offered a selection from 'books of canons or laws', which treated 'the essence of your job ... the way that the magnates of the kingdom should keep faith with you, [and] the protection of the monastic order'.[145] Within a generation, a far bigger and more influential collection was made by Bishop Burchard of Wörms. It was addressed to the provost of his cathedral, and meant to make the bulk of canon law and penitential discipline, neglected through its 'dissonance', more accessible to those now being educated than it had been to his coadjutors and predecessors.[146] Neither collection resembled the English in other than predictable respects. Abbo's was a quite brief though sophisticated review, specializing in the law of Church property. Burchard's was vast, running to 1785 chapters, and altogether more compre-hensive as well as more clearly laid out than Wulfstan's. Continental collections could exploit far more of the Carolingian tradition than could English.[147] Still, Abbo made a point of sworn loyalty to kings, as Wulfstan did. Burchard for his part accompanied his *Decretum* with a succinct statement of the 'Lex Familiae' of the Church of Wörms.[148] It was designed to end oppressive judgements

---

144   Combining the message of the Latin letter ('Brief 2'), Fehr, *Hirtenbriefe* 4–8, 10–15, 21–36, pp. 35–40, with that of its vernacular adaptation ('II'), Whitelock, *Councils* 8a–12, 14–34, pp. 262–9.
145   Abbo, 'Collectio Canonum' Pr., cols 473–4.
146   Burchard, 'Decretorum Libri' (prooemia), cols 499–500 (for this as Burchard's authentic preface, rather than that printed as such, see Fuhrmann, 'Zum Vorwort des Dekrets Bischof Burchards').
147   Fournier and Le Bras, *Histoire des Collections Canoniques* I, pp. 324–30, 371–7. Comparison of Burchard's sources (laid out superbly by Hoffmann and Pokorny, *Dekret des Bischofs Burchard*, pp. 165–274), with those of the *Excerptiones* shows that the main difference lies in access to Pseudo-Isidore; while Abbo could call on Roman law as well as a much fuller set of Carolingian capitularies than Wulfstan's.

enforced on 'the weaker' by those with a command of 'diversas leges', and some of its clauses covered the violence of 'servi ecclesiae' over the previous thirty-five years.

What all three canonists had in common was a concern to bring order to the accumulated law of the Church, and to assert its relevance to a society they felt to be threatened. The world had all too clearly failed to achieve the level of peace and order that Carolingian regimes strove to establish. It was time to go back to first principles. Carolingian capitularies and secular *leges* ceased to be copied in most parts of the continent. Collections of Canon Law assumed ever more systematic forms.[149] This development is paralleled by the way that Wulfstan for the moment lost sight of the kind of law that English kings had been laying down since Alfred, and sought instead to give that of the Church the widest possible application. One contrast between him and his contemporaries was that he could do so in the name of a king who still aspired to dictate to his kingdom as a whole. Another was that the vitality of royal legislation over the previous century enabled him to return to what it offered in the laws that he began to draft from then onwards.

The 1014 code, though extant only in Wulfstan manuscripts, and probably only in part, was less other-worldly than those of 1008 or 1009, in that penalties were now spelled out. Instead of, 'Let one eagerly keep the Sunday feast as befits it; and let one eagerly desist from markets and meetings on that holy day', there was: 'And let one eagerly forbid Sunday markets by the full secular fine (*be fullan worldwite*)'.[150] There was new emphasis on the specifically royal duty to protect the otherwise defenceless. This introduced a theme that became one of Wulfstan's signature *motifs*: once upon a time, secular law-making upheld 'godly rights (*godcundan rihtlagan*)', with the compensations arising shared by 'Christ and king'; but a distinction was today made between the sanctions appropriate to each (chapter 5, pp. 342, 390–1, 395).[151] Part of the context of the 1014 legislation was Wulfstan's deepening research into what earlier laws had actually said. The code quoted Edgar's sanction against witholders of tithe *in extenso*: a near-unique departure in early English law-giving.[152] Where 'Edward-Guthrum' referred vaguely to 'worldly compensations' fixed by earlier *witan*, *Grið* cited the 'south English law' of Ine, Alfred and Æthelstan, and the 'Kentish law' of Wihtræd and Æthelberht (chapter 5, pp. 389–90, 394–5). Ine's clauses on Welshmen were used as a way of extending the 'North-people's law' to Northumbria's British population (chapter 5, pp. 393–4).

Wulfstan's interest in Welshmen's ranking brings out another concern of the central phase of his career. For the proper ordering of society was the main theme of the '*Geþyncðu* group'. One might only move from ceorl to thegn by

148   Abbo, 'Collectio Canonum' iv, cols 478–9; Burchard, 'Lex Familiae Wormatiensis', ed. Weiland. Cf. Theuerkauf, 'Burchard von Wörms'.
149   Fournier and Le Bras, I, pp. 421–56; see chapter 2, pp. 69, 92.
150   VIII Atr 17, V Atr 13 – 13:1; a similar development may be found in Wulfstan's later homilies 'proper' (chapter 5, pp. 344–5).
151   VIII Atr 32–8.
152   VIII Atr 7 – 8.

meeting the requisite criteria; but among the symptoms of disturbance in the cosmos was lack of respect for these criteria. It was probably at just this time that Wulfstan essayed a more ambitious account of a Christian society's structure. The 'Institutes of Polity, Civil and Ecclesiastical' is a nineteenth-century characterization of a work whose manuscripts gave titles only for its sections, but which nonetheless has a more or less evident coherence.[153] Its first version reviewed the duty of society's main elements, from the king (his designated role amplified by discussions of 'kingship' and the 'throne') through bishops, earls, priests and others in holy orders, to laity and widows, concluding with a survey of the Church and of the Christian commonwealth in general.[154] The emphasis was throughout on what is due to God: obedience to His law, episcopal and sacerdotal preaching and example, protection of the poor and of churches and their ministers, monastic unworldliness, the celibacy of clergy and the chastity of laymen – most of which stipulations went along with complaints of their neglect. But the responsibilities of kings and earls also extended to the promotion of justice, and the punishment of 'robbers and plunderers and despoilers of the world's goods', 'thieves and those who prey on the people'.[155]

Kingship was said to rest on eight columns, seven qualities and three pillars. The eight and seven came from Sedulius Scottus and the Irish Canons. The columns were the cardinal virtues; the qualities included Fear of God, care for poor and Church, and justice for friend or stranger.[156] The three pillars were another matter:

> One is *oratores*, and the second is *laboratores*, and the third is *bellatores*. *Oratores* are prayer-men who should serve God and earnestly intercede for the whole people ... *Laboratores* are work-men who should produce the wherewithal for the whole people to live. *Bellatores* are warriors who should defend the land valiantly with weapons ... And should any of them collapse, then the throne will tumble down, and that will be utter disaster for the people. But let them be eagerly ... strengthened ... with God's wise laws, and that will be of lasting profit for the people. For what I say is true: should ... bad law be promoted anywhere in the land, or vices anywhere prevail, that will come as utter disaster for the people. But let one do as is needful: put down injustice and exalt the justice of God.[157]

---

153 The standard edition and only critical account of this, one of the most regrettably under-researched items in the Old English canon, is that of Jost, whose analysis and numbering I generally follow here; there is a modern English translation of what amounts to the second and 'final' version in Swanton's *Anglo-Saxon Prose*, pp. 125–38. For the 1008x14 dating of the first edition, see my arguments (mostly based on evolving ecclesiology from V Atr 10:1–2, to *Inst. Pol.* I 100–1, to *Grið* 1 – 2, 31:1, the latter in turn predating VIII Atr), 'LAWS', in Biggs *et al.* (eds) *Sources*.

154 This earliest version is in CCCC MS 201, pp. 87–93; Cotton Nero A.i, ff. 70r – 76v, 97r – 98v is an expanded equivalent, and ff. 99r – 105v, 109rv, 120r have passages like the second fuller version; this is in Bodleian MS Junius 121, ff. 9r – 59r, but an additional complexity is that it in part corresponds to (and is even extended by) what is in CCCC 201, pp. 40–2, 51, 108–11, 130 (above, tables 4.2–3).

155 *Inst. Pol.* I 7 (only the Nero version, but cf. I 5), I 60.

156 *Inst. Pol.* I 16–23; *Sedulius, Liber de Rectoribus Christianis* x, pp. 49–50; *Irische Kanonessammlung* xxv 15, p. 81; these texts were in Wulfstan's 'Canon Collection', CCCC 265, pp. 148–9, Barlow 37, f. 35v. See also *Ælfric's Catholic Homilies* II xix, pp. 183–4.

157 *Inst. Pol.* I 24–34.

Wulfstan's source here was Ælfric (and conceivably King Alfred).[158] More to the point, Ælfric and Wulfstan were both thereby aligned with near-exact European contemporaries who helped to make this triple ordering of society an enduring foundation of the *Ancien Régime*.[159]

What have come to be seen as the classical statements of the theme were made in the 1020s (or thereabouts) by two bishops who were closely related members of one of the greatest families in northern Europe. That of Gerard of Cambrai survives in a report of a speech he is said to have made at a council deliberating a 'letter from heaven' that had prohibited the bearing of arms even to avenge bloodshed or recover stolen goods, had proposed that fasts on Wednesday and Friday would suffice to purge any sin, and had envisaged an oath to these ends, refusal of which would entail excommunication. Gerard was having none of such radicalism. He 'showed that the human race was from the beginning divided threefold, *in oratoribus, agricultoribus, pugnatoribus*, and that each of these should support the other right and left'. Among justifications of military action was that priests girded kings with a sword: 'thus kings, instructed by holy fathers, decree firm laws, so that the Church or anyone else might recover goods unjustly lost ... No one is obliged to pardon a killing *absque placatione*'. Gerard argued that there would be no inequality except by God's will; good order would return if all accepted their place and kings performed their allotted role.[160] The other statement is the core of the '*Carmen* for King Robert' by Adalbero of Laon, a literary *tour de force* that was perhaps also a valedictory testament. This opened with a sparkling image of the world turned upside down: peasants bear jewel-encrusted crowns, warriors (called 'guardians of law') wear cowls, naked bishops follow the plough, singing the primordial song of Adam (a variant, presumably, on 'Who was then the Gentleman?'). It then launched into a vivid burlesque of the Cluniacs, so soaked in the military ethos that they take on invading Saracens near Tours in a clear echo of Charles Martel's immortal victory, and are, unlike Charles, worsted. Against this chaos model Adalbero invoked two laws: the divine, adapted by the Church from Moses, whereby all are equal; and the human, imposing the twin conditions of those who rule, 'warriors, protectors of the Churches, defenders of the crowd', and those who obey, 'the *divisio* of serfs'. 'God's house is thus not one but triple; *nunc orant, alii pugnant aliique laborant*.'

---

158 Ælfric's fullest exposition and the one closest to Wulfstan's was his (post-1005) 'Treatise on the Old and New Testament', pp. 71–2 lns 1207–19; his earlier statements were *Lives of Saints* XXV (The Maccabees), II, pp. 120–3 lns 812–22, and *Hirtenbriefe* '2a' xiv, p. 225 – where he guesses that Wulfstan will already be aware of the schema (the fourth such passage sometimes attributed to Ælfric, *Political Songs*, ed. Wright, pp. 363–5, is a ghost: so far from being a 'political song' or by Ælfric, it is the relevant chapter of Wulfstan's *Institutes of Polity*!). Cf. *Alfred's Boethius* xvii, p. 40: like Alfred, Wulfstan put those who pray first, whereas Ælfric did so only in his first account's sectional title; and Wulfstan's translations of the Latin terms were twice the same as Alfred's, where Ælfric paraphrased: Powell, 'The "Three Orders"', p. 120.

159 See pre-eminently Duby, *Les trois ordres* (references here are to the English translation). More has been written on this theme since the late 1970s than can be cited (or read); Duby, Powell and those in nn. 161, 164 apart, I have learned most from Brown, 'Georges Duby and the Three Orders', Constable, 'Orders of Society', Leyser, 'Early Medieval Canon Law', Murray, *Reason and Society* (pp. 81–101), and Oexle, 'Functionale Dreiteilung', and '"Wirklichkeit" und "Wissen"'.

160 *Gesta Pontificum Cameracensium* 52, pp. 485–6.

The trio is indissoluble because interdependent. 'So long as this *lex* prevailed, the world was at peace; now the *leges* have decayed, all peace is fled.' It is for the king to restore the balance. Law must be reconstituted by councils of those trained in it, who understand 'rewards and punishments'.[161]

There were differences between these views and those of Ælfric and Wulfstan. There was no millenarianism in Gerard and Adalbero, who were hostile to its manifestation in the principles and practices of the Peace Movement.[162] But English and French writers all stressed each order's function, their mutual dependence, and, as an associated principle, the need to purify the Church through observance of its law. Both assumed an 'isonomy between human and angelic society'.[163] Here, then, as with Alfred and Hincmar's theories, is a coincidence in timing and concept between the two sides of the Channel that was close enough to seem more than coincidence. The difference this time is that the English instances look chronologically prior, and that there is no obvious conduit of transmission. The first recognizable expression of the idea, from late-ninth-century Auxerre, was undoubtedly taken up by the Cluniacs at the turn of the tenth and eleventh centuries.[164] But that is not a plausible inspiration for Gerard or Adalbero; while the English testimonies lack the monastic imprint which Abbo gave the notion at Fleury, and which one might have looked for, especially in Ælfric, if that were their source.[165] More likely is that Auxerre's theory found its way to the school of Rheims, where Adalbero and Gerard were to be educated, and whence, again through Grimbald's agency, it could be transmitted to Alfred.[166] Thereafter, the English tradition would be self-contained, Ælfric and Wulfstan each adapting it to his own ends. It might indeed be wisest to take at face value the fact that the

---

161   *Adalbéron de Laon, Poème au Roi Robert* lns 33–42, 76–168, 227–43, 275–302, 360–76. King Robert then undertakes that the '*status ecclesiae* will hold *sua iura*, the *res puplica* will have written laws and no others, Basil and Benedict will have their own *regna* ... bishops will not celebrate rurally ... while our *ordo* does not presume to abandon its justicial rule': lines 410–17.

162   Duby, *Three Orders*, pp. 24–5, 28–9, 53–5; *Gest. Pontif. Camerac*. 27, p. 474 (a previous statement of Gerard's case, in response to a proposal by his fellow-bishops at the 1023 Council of Compiègne to adopt a 'peace-oath' like that of the Burgundian bishops in 1016); *Adalbéron* lns 41–2, 414–15 ('nudi pontifices', and their 'ruralia', as above), and cf. Carozzi's Introduction', pp. cviii-cxv, cxxxix.

163   For ecclesiastical purification in Ælfric and Wulfstan, see above, pp. 455–6; for Gerard, Duby, *Three Orders*, pp. 31–4; and for Adalbero, Duby, pp. 48–50, with *Adalbéron*, pp. cii-cv and lns 202–73; for 'isonomy', Duby, p. 128 (French edn, pp. 160–1).

164   The Carolingian dimension was noted by Duby, *Three Orders*, p. 109, but its importance was only established by Ortigues, 'L' Élaboration de la théorie des trois ordres', and (showing this topic's odd tendency for enlightenment to strike scholars near-simultaneously) by Iogna-Prat, 'Le "Baptême" du Schéma des Trois Ordres'; cf. his study of the genesis of the Maiolus cult, *Agni Immaculati* (especially pp. 341–5, and the relevant part of the Maiolus *sermo*, p. 300 lns 321–9).

165   Abbo, 'Liber Apologeticus', cols 463–4, with Duby, *Three Orders*, pp. 87–92; and for his influence on Ælfric (which could be further illustrated), see John, 'World of Abbot Ælfric'. The absence of a monastic element in Ælfric's version of the scheme is surprising enough as it is; especially as his use of the image of the Virgins of the Apocalypse (Brief '2' 25–7, Fehr, *Hirtenbriefe*, p. 38), and his reading of the Roman sack of Jerusalem as revenge for the deaths of Christ and of the early martyrs ('Treatise on the Old and New Testaments', pp. 73–4 lns 1236–56) are not unlike those in the Maiolus dossier: Iogna-Prat, *Agni Immaculati*, pp. 344, 358–9.

166   For a highly suggestive review of the possibilities, see Nelson, 'Political Ideas of Alfred', pp. 142–3.

Gerard/Adalbero schema found little resonance in Francia for 150 years (Adalbero's poem exists only in a manuscript supervised by himself); whereas the idea had a fairly continuous vogue in England until its currency in Henry II's circle reintroduced it to the French world. England's role in the making of estate theory, a key postulate of pre-modern European society, may, wondrous to relate, have been second only to Auxerre's.[167]

Even so, the coincidence remains. There should be a reason why English and continental writers highlighted the same principle at the same time. The early medieval West was awash with systems of ordering. But the standard categories were ecclesiastical and secular, and it was the former that was more often sub-divided into active and contemplative, continent and virginal, or whatever. So why was it this time the laity that was classified; and why into warriors and workers rather than rulers and ruled? The attention so far lavished on this problem has yet to take note that one adherent of the 'three orders' elsewhere clarified the source of his anxiety. Wulfstan's *Geþyncðu* opened with the explicit complaint that social rank was not maintained as it had been; its account of the way that the criteria for social climbing worked is in the *past* tense. He leaves no doubt about where the new pressures were coming from. Commercial wealth was as acceptable a qualification for thegnhood as royal service or scholarship (if buttressed by chastity). It was those with the equipment to make formidable warriors, but without the required five-hide property qualification, who were sternly denied thegnly status (chapter 5, pp. 393–4). His point had the more force for the fact that throughout much of England five hides was the expected holding of a fully kitted-out soldier.[168] The implication is that the new premium on war-like skills fostered by renewed Scandinavian assaults was enabling adventurers to penetrate the ranks of officially classified warriors. Which, again, is what Wulfstan elsewhere said. The *Sermon of the Wolf* denounced 'slaves' who acquired a thegn's wergeld by going Viking and compounded the enormity by enslaving their former masters (chapter 5, p. 394). The English position was not, then, so unlike that pictured by Duby and others on the continent.[169] The ranks of accredited nobility, whose salient quality was its military aptitude, needed guarding from upstarts whose *sole* quality was military. The difference in England was that there was a legal class marked out both by freedom and by the status of 'ceorl' rather than noble: a reservoir, as it were, of *parvenus* whose outflow was supposedly regulated by law. That they should do their military duties was right and proper. That they should become military specialists and so advance their social standing was not. It was just the sort of situation that might

---

167   Up to a point, therefore, I agree with Powell, '"Three Orders"', pp. 129–32, and cf. Brown, 'Georges Duby and the Three Orders', pp. 55–6. Duby does seem strangely unembarrassed by his own evidence of a century-and-a-half's silence south of the Channel, pp. 169–268, followed by revival 'around Henry Plantagenet' (repeatedly identified as 'French'), after some earlier-twelfth-century English 'sightings', pp. 271–92: the English part in the story is not obscured, but it is given no more than 'walk-on' status.

168   Cf. Abels, *Lordship and Military Obligation*, chapter 5, critically reviewing this principle's general applicability, but not denying that the amount of military service 'was … determined by the cadastral assessment charged against [one's] property'.

169   Duby, *Three Orders*, pp. 59, 98–9, 153, 157–8, 189–90; Murray, *Reason and Society*, pp. 96–8; Oexle, 'Funktionale Dreiteilung', pp. 46–8; Leyser, 'Early Medieval Canon Law', p. 552 (pp. 54–5).

be expected to focus a social moralist's gaze on the borderline between warrior and worker.[170]

Regardless of what was being 'transformed' or why, it is hardly controversial that the evidence from the early decades of the eleventh century gives off an aroma of revolutionary times.[171] Against this atmosphere, three high-born and conservative prelates set their convictions. All thought an ordered society inseparable from a just and lawful society. Wulfstan did so, unlike Adalbero and Gerard, as the foremost counsellor of a polity whose structures were well enough knit to be reactivated.[172] That became the goal of the third phase of his career. In the short term, things went from bad to worse. The first version of the definitive *Sermo Lupi* was as unstinted in its apocalyptic imagery as his earliest homilies. Wulfstan rained his verbal brimstone on the same desert of treachery and oppression as before, with betrayal of successive kings thrown in.[173] The second edition injected a ramified catalogue of Scandinavian atrocities, aggravated by the upending of social proprieties.[174] The awareness of specifically legal outrages was thus stronger in 1014 than in the millenarian series proper. Reinforcing it was an impression that Scandinavians were as much the agents of God's wrath at these affronts to His law as they were heralds of Antichrist. In the final version, a famously seminal passage makes that argument crystalline:

> There was a councillor (*þeodwita*) in the times of the Britons, called Gildas. He wrote about their misdeeds, how with their sins they so excessively angered God that finally he let the army (*here*) of the English conquer their land and utterly destroy the British Establishment (*Britta dugeþe*). That happened, so he said, through robbery by the powerful, and greed for ill-gotten gains, through lawlessness of the people and unjust judgements ... Let us do as is needful, be warned by such events ... and eagerly come to terms with God.[175]

The authority cited might be Gildas. But the argument was Alcuin's, and its premises were of course those of Bede's *Ecclesiastical History*, charter of the *Gens Anglorum*. The logic of Bede's book was that the English had acquired their land through the sins of the Britons, and could as easily lose them on the same grounds to another pagan people.[176] The English had a Covenant, like Israel's. The corpus of Wulfstan's homilies contains a number of meditations on Old Testament history, with its possible lessons for that of the English. One which

---

170   One might add a) that Alfred's laws were distinguished from Ine's by his extra concern with the 1200-men/200-men distinction (chapter 5, p. 280); and b) that few social situations can have been more likely to keep a warrior-worker distinction alive (or disturb the dreams of monarchs) than that which prevailed in England after 1066. Those who see 'paradox' in the absence of an English soldier-peasant distinction, or who impugn Duby's analysis on the grounds of the stability of English power structures, miss the point.

171   See above, n. 138, especially the *PP* 'Debate'; and further, the brilliant evocations of Moore, 'Family, Community and Cult', especially pp. 49–60 (with his 'Postscript' to Head and Landes, *Peace of God*), and of Leyser, 'On the Eve of the First European Revolution'.

172   Cf. Murray, *Reason and Society*, pp. 95–6.

173   *Hom.* XX (BH) lns 32–85; Godden 'Apocalypse', pp. 143–7.

174   *Hom.* XX (C) lns 97–126; Godden, pp.148–50.

175   *Hom.* XX (EI) lns 176–90; Godden, pp. 150–6.

176   As I have argued in '*Engla Lond*', pp. 13–16 (pp. 373–8). The Alcuin letter is in Cotton Vespasian A.xiv, f. 146r (Chase, *Letter Books*, p. 74).

may be closely linked with the 'Wolf's Sermon' warned that, for turning their hearts from God, they 'will be given into the power of enemies ... [who] will lay waste the land and burn the cities'.[177] In 1014 itself the blunt logic of the Covenant thesis was made plain.

The Anglo-Saxon legislative tradition recommenced with Alfred's compelling invitation to compare English law with the articles of God's Covenant with Israel. Much of the law issued in the tenth century is understandable as the English attempt to abide by its side of its bargain. To punish what God had condemned was the condition of His favour. The more that Wulfstan came to interpret the experience of his lifetime in terms of the Divine relationship with Israel, the more natural it was to reassert and elaborate the law made by earlier kings. A sermon probably linked with a law-making council, perhaps that of 1018, quotes the *Institutes of Polity* on the 'Three Orders' as pillars of the throne, but adds 'woroldlage' to 'Godes lage'.[178] It was in this period that collections of legal, homiletic and *Polity* texts like Cotton Nero A.i were made (table 4.2). They form a programme for a regenerated Christian people.

It is thus that Wulfstan's life's work culminated in Cnut's Winchester code. Not only is this plausibly regarded as one of his very last compositions; it also brought into a single compass all the ideas about the regimentation of a people of God that he had been developing since 1014 and before (chapter 5, pp. 356–65). His earliest work for the new regime, the heads of proposals at the 1018 Oxford council, reverted to the approach of 1008. The fundamentals of a Christian Commonwealth came first. But by the time that Cnut returned from Denmark with his assurances that English troubles from that quarter were over, it was possible to contemplate what amounted to a restatement and refinement of the tenth century's legal principles: the relaying of the legal foundations on which the kingdom of the English had been built, as the condition of its renewal under fresh management. The doctrines of 1008/1018 were now underpinned by the sanctions of 1014. 'Edgar's Law', as invoked at Oxford, duly provided the framework, and was cited almost in full, as were salient points from the laws of Alfred, Æthelstan, Æthelred, even seventh-century kings. Gaps left by Wulfstan's predecessors were filled as necessary. All was ornamented by suitably empurpled

---

177   *Hom.* VI (based on Ælfric's digest of Divine and human history), XI (bilingual excerpts from the visions of Isaiah and Jeremiah about Jerusalem, with much to say of vice and crime), XIX (also preceded by a *catena* of Latin quotations from Leviticus, the passage quoted above at lns 59–68): Godden, pp. 154–6. As Bethurum noted, pp. 297–8, the passage in VI on the Babylonian captivity (lns 115–22) is foreshadowed by an excerpt in CCCC MS 190, pp. 139–40, from *Abbo [of Saint Germain] Predigten 6*, pp. 94–9, which is then followed by extracts from Alcuin, the Gildas text included; Abbo, pp. 97–8, had drawn his own parallel between the disasters befalling 'Britannia' in the ninth century and Jewish history, warning 'Francia' to 'guard itself'.

178   *HomN* L, p. 267 lns 92–4; an addition that found its way into the final edition of *Inst. Pol.* (II 38). The chief features of this revised and expanded edition, perhaps unfinished or anyway unsorted by the time of Wulfstan's death, were a preliminary account of the 'heavenly king' as an epitome for earthly government (so a further instance of Heaven–earth 'isonomy'), a chapter on reeves and their oppressions to accompany that on earls, and above all a much amplified discussion of episcopal activity, stressing their role as 'councillors (*þeodwitan*)': *Inst. Pol.* II 1–3, 94–101, 77–84, 41–57, 154–69. So, just as Bede thought Gildas a 'historicus' like himself (*Hist. Eccl.* i 22, pp. 68–9), so Wulfstan thought him a 'þeodwita' like *him*self – and each insufficiently respected: *Geþyn.* 1.

passages from his *Institutes of Polity* and from his homilies. Theories of equitable justice were taken from a Confessor's Handbook that was not his work, but which he enlarged upon (table 5.4). So might God, pending His final Judgement, be expected to restore the favour He had justly withdrawn in 1013–16. The English could learn their lesson, as the Britons had not. Within fifty years, it became only too clear that they had done no such thing. Yet Cnut's code was on hand to form the basis of another conquering regime: a purpose that it duly served.

The approach to Wulfstan's legislation adopted here has two main messages. First, it is possible and may be advisable to view his work from a unitary perspective. His manuscripts imply that his laws, homilies and *Institutes* had a common aim. They brought together complementary means of realizing it. He changed his legislative technique as he altered his estimate of the destiny of the people he addressed: from the fundamentals appropriate for a society on the verge of terminal dissolution, to the details required by a kingdom given the chance to refashion itself. Wulfstan's conceptual development thus paralleled the trajectory of that kingdom, as it experienced the first of its two eleventh-century traumas. The impression that all was lost, to Sveinn if not to Antichrist, led Æthelred to take flight, as his great-great-grandfather so conspicuously had not. The new beginning which Æthelred promised in 1014, and which his kingdom's resilience permitted, was in the event fulfilled by the rule of a conqueror. Its future under a second conqueror would rest for a century after 1066 on the code Wulfstan drafted for the first.

The second message is the gain in understanding from aligning the English and continental experiences. The canonical enterprises of Abbo, Burchard and Wulfstan illuminate each other. Wulfstan's writings suggest that there may after all be some connection between millennial fears and the stipulations of the Peace of God, between the theory of Three Orders and the rise of men whose military skills were their sole distinction. It matters for Europe's as well as England's history that apocalyptic foreboding and social upheaval alike could be confronted by a leading figure in a governmental system that was still viable, and in ways that contributed to its survival. Wulfstan's code for Cnut emerges as a model of what could be done by law-making in the Carolingian idiom: the application to human society of the mandates of Heaven.

Eschatological moralist, codifier of canons, social idealist, engineer of a reformed regime: Wulfstan was all of these things, not just successively but to an extent concurrently. What suffused his whole *oeuvre* like a powerful dye was his conception of the 'Law of God'. Revealed primarily by Scripture but by Church authority too, it meant adoption of the complete Mosaic programme, hence justice for the socially helpless as well as prohibition of paganism and robbery. It required acceptance of Pauline sexual ideals, in that chastity was absolutely incumbent on priests, and restrained indulgence prescribed for laymen. It meant honouring of Christian festivals and (especially) fasts, due provision for the poor, and regard for God's handiwork in limited use of capital penalties. It demanded acquiescence in the social order ordained by God, so that each class must fulfil its assigned role in society. Nations were rewarded or punished as a whole to the extent that they met these standards or failed to. Enforcement was thus a pressing

$\downarrow$

priority, above all for bishops, but also for kings and secular officials. Wulfstan anticipated Gregorian themes in the urgency of his assault on clerical unchastity and in his consciousness of the exalted responsibility of churchmen. But he was *par excellence* a Carolingian ideologue in his integrated view of a holy people whose kings and bishops worked together to realize the kingdom of God. A century and a quarter after the fragmentation of the Carolingian ideal in its Frankish homeland, it was given its most consummate expression by one of the architects of a more enduring 'empire': the English state itself.

4   The Laws of England: the mind of the *Quadripartitus* author

The century after 1066 saw very little royal legislation. It was marked by other ways of recording the law: collections of Old English originals; translations, whether or not supplemented; and surveys of what was represented as current law on a more or less comprehensive range of topics (chapter 4, pp. 228–53; chapter 5, pp. 402–14). The man who compiled *Quadripartitus* also composed the *Leges Henrici*. The former was a collection as well as a translation, so he was active in all three fields characteristic of the age. He was more prolific than his counterparts, but fully representative of their mentality. He may stand a type for them all. His work, like that of Alfred, Wulfstan or the law-makers between, needs to be explained, not taken for granted. Arguably more so. It has had more influence than Anglo-Saxon legislators on the way that Old English law has been perceived ever since. Not only was *Quadripartitus* the exclusive means of access to it from Angevin to Tudor times; Maitland took more notice of the *Leges Henrici* than of any one other text, or indeed of the Anglo-Saxon corpus as a whole. What drove this author to write what he did?[179]

His programme had features not found (or less often found) before the Conquest. It was antiquarian in its concern with all available material, regardless of date. *Quadripartitus* opened with Cnut's code, the staple of written law till the mid-twelfth century. It then proceeded to add codes of earlier kings, because (so its author thought) 'whatever did not differ by comparison with that continued in force' (chapter 4, n. 313). He backed up this conviction to the extent that about one-third of his *Leges Henrici*, allegedly contemporary law, comprised excerpts from *Quadripartitus*. They extend to Alfred's tariff of compensations for personal injury and to Ine's laws on 'manbot' for slain dependents (or godsons).[180] His view of what was currently applicable was widely shared. Alfred's *domboc* was a core text for the other twelfth-century 'Encyclopedias' too (tables 4.6, 4.8). *Instituta Cnuti* and *Leis Willelme* also offered the substance of Alfred's injury list.[181] Only the so-called *Leges Edwardi Confessoris*

179   On Maitland and the *Leges Henrici*, see my 'Maitland and Anglo-Saxon Law', and 'Frederic William Maitland', with Hudson, 'Maitland and Anglo-Norman Law'. Like its counterpart in chapter 5, this section is merely a preliminary and provisional sketch. The mental world of the Anglo-Norman lawbooks demands (and thanks to Dr O'Brien is at last beginning to receive) a lot of further research from others much better qualified to undertake it.

180   Hn 93; 69:2, 75:5a, 79 – 79:1c, 88:20.

181   *Inst. Cn* III 9 – 39; Leis Wl 10:1, 11 – 11:2.

was – ironically, given the name and fame it acquired – unware of ancient laws. These authors made a point of the linkage of old law and new. *Leges Henrici* was *Quadripartitus'* sequel; the 'Articles of William' was probably a supplement to *Instituta Cnuti* (chapter 5, pp. 404–5). Each presupposed that the law of Norman kings flowed directly from their predecessors'. The 'Law of King Edward' was legal fact as well as political symbol. Yet all that is actually proved by this respect for the past is its espousal by these writers. It does not follow that English law remained rooted in the remoter past. Before accepting that the Norman regime itself subscribed to their antiquarianism, one should explore the possibility that its stimulus was intellectual as much as practical.

Other features of their programme do suggest that it was driven by what was mentally satisfying rather than judicially demanded. It aspired to completeness in covering topics that pre-conquest texts ignored. *Instituta Cnuti* and *Leges Henrici* offered much fuller lists of royal judicial perquisites. *Consiliatio Cnuti* and *Leges Henrici* dilated on Frankpledge. *Leis Willelme*, *Leges Edwardi* and *Leges Henrici* took a quite new interest in the law of the king's highways.[182] None of this need in any way mean that they were describing Norman legal innovations. That the *Leges Henrici* account of inheritance law was without precedent was hardly because the English had none before. Nor is it likely that it took that account from *Lex Ribuaria* because the author thought that English (or even Norman) custom resembled Frankish. Much more probable is that he filled a gap in his evidence with the most suitable matter to hand.[183] French experience may also have made a more general contribution to these texts. They were more interested than Anglo-Saxon codes in bringing out regional diversity (except for *Consiliatio Cnuti*, which had the opposite concern, chapter 5, pp. 405–6). All stressed what *Leges Henrici* called 'the awesome sway of royal majesty'.[184] They reflected the variety of customs rather than specializing in any one (chapter 5, pp. 408–9, 411, 413); their particular background might focus their gaze but did not blinker their vision. Nevertheless, *Leges Henrici* made a formative declaration of English law's division into three provinces.[185] Twelfth-century lawbooks said more of Mercian or Danelaw idiosyncracies than any official record. It could be that customary variation was given more attention because it was what commentators from a French *milieu* expected to find. That is not to say that the reported discrepancies were illusory. But they may have been more visible to French than English eyes.[186]

A third novelty in the Anglo-Norman *leges* is their attempt to produce an

---

182   *Inst. Cn* III 45:4 – 52, Hn 10 – 19:3; *Cons. Cn* II 19:2a-d, Hn 8 – 8:6; Leis Wl 26, ECf 12 – 12d, Hn 80:2–5a. Cf. chapter 3, pp. 140–1.

183   Hn 70:18–22a (incorporating Af 41 on bookland).

184   Hn 6:2a. Cf. the *Quadripartitus* 'Argumentum' and 'Preface to Book II', trans. Sharpe, pp. 165–72.

185   Hn 9:10.

186   See (e.g.) Yver, 'Les caractères originaux du groupe de Coûtumes de l' Ouest de la France', and 'Les deux groupes de Coûtumes de Nord'; and cf. the comments of Hyams, 'Common Law and the French Connection', especially pp. 78–82. The actual statements of French (or German) regional custom are up to a century or more later than the Anglo-Norman law-books. For discussion of how far English law was in fact localized, see chapter 12; and for the possibility that these writers' ideas on 'soke' were conditioned by service to a 'private' lordship rather than the king, see chapter 11.

impression of system that is conspicuously absent from most of what was previously put on record. Two of the three works with a free hand to structure their law-books (in that they were not translating a pre-existent text) did so. *Leges Edwardi* covered the prerogatives of Church and king in turn, then institutions trusted to preserve them. The linking passages are stylishly enough executed to suggest a more sophisticated process than thought-association.[187] *Leges Henrici* also set itself a scheme, even if it proceeded to execute it with somewhat Hibernian logic.[188] Introductory sections on the nature of legal proceedings and legal institutions led into a more or less progressive survey of how the latter handled the former. Courts and their treatment of particular suits ushered in a long central section on procedure, interspersed with further accounts of a variety of pleas. Last came a classification of cases in terms of the parties involved and the remedies available. The scope for digression and repetition offered by this scheme was amply indulged. But it has been persuasively interpreted as an attempt to impose the intellectual patterning of the new schools on a field not hitherto subjected to it.[189] Especially revealing is what has naturally attracted least notice from legal historians: the prefatory treatment of the 'Conduct and Definition of Cases'.[190] Among its sources was Isidore's *Etymologiae* on the nature of pleading. This was in fact from Isidore's Book II on 'The Art of Rhetoric': in other words, from his inaugural section on the Seven Liberal Arts (even if a chapter on law was included in deference to the centrality of the courtroom for Antiquity's orators).[191] The point was that law was susceptible to categorization by 'divisio', like any field of thought. It was the normal objective of eleventh-century schools.[192]

Finally, the *Leges Henrici* author liked to generalize about the theory and practice of law, and some of his *dicta* have acquired notoriety as indices of his limitations and/or those of the system he epitomized. Among the moralistic platitudes on the nature of justice that are recurrent in early medieval 'mirror' literature were comments of jurisprudential quality. 'The conduct of cases varies with the circumstances of place, time, persons and means of accusation'; 'witness is not needed as to what did not occur, but as to what an accused claims did occur'; ' agreement overcomes law and love judgement'; 'there is a difference in charging those of ill-repute, those caught in the act and those who are accessory'; and most notorious of all, 'who unknowingly offends will knowingly amend'.[193]

---

187 ECf 11 – 11:3, 19 – 19:2; see chapter 5, p. 411, following Korte, *Untersuchungen*, pp. 116–19, and more detailed analysis by O'Brien, *God's Peace*, pp. 63–102.
188 PM I, pp. 100–1; Downer, *Leges Henrici*, pp. 10–11.
189 Korte, *Untersuchungen*, pp. 119–30.
190 Hn 3 – 5. 'De Causarum Pertractatione et Diffinitione' fairly clearly covers not just 3 but 4, 'De Generibus Causarum', and 5, 'De Causarum Proprietatibus'. Much the same passages were quoted by this author in the 'Dedicatio' of *Quadripartitus* 29–31, Sharpe, pp. 160–1.
191 Isidore, ... *Etymologiarum* ... *Libri*, ed. Lindsay, II iv 1–2, v 2, vii – viii, x, xvi 1, xvii 1, xix 1, xx 2, xxi 1; the *Leges* did slip into II x (on law) a quote from V iv 1, the book mainly about law, changing Isidoran 'Ius naturale aut civile aut gentium' into 'aut naturale cognatorum aut morale extraneorum aut legale civium'. Fontaine, *Isidore de Seville* I, pp. 233–94, especially pp. 259–61.
192 Southern, *Making of the Middle Ages*, pp. 171–7; cf. Gibson, *Lanfranc of Bec,* pp. 47–50, 61–2.
193 Hn 9:7, 48:9, 49:5a, 61:18c, 88:6a.

Such observations were neither profound nor original. But they did convey a new sense that it should be possible to tease principles out of legal administration. Here too law began to acquire the rudiments of an intellectual discipline.

In the overall context of sub-Roman legal history these were not new departures. Lombard and Frankish law were each in different ways intensely aware of their past (chapter 2, pp. 39, 44–5). Comprehensiveness was the general goal of south European codes (chapter 2, pp. 39, 42). Systematization was attempted by Lupus in ninth-century Francia (chapter 2, pp. 33–5). Most relevantly perhaps, some of the best evidence of what passed for legal education in the Carolingian empire is afforded by manuscripts which juxtaposed legal texts with apposite sections of Isidore (albeit his books on Law and Kinship rather than Rhetoric).[194] Such precedents notwithstanding, there should be a reason why it now apparently mattered more to give the completest and most systematic account of English law. The clue may lie, as it did for earlier sections of this chapter, in what other parts of contemporary Europe were thinking and doing about law.

The first of two areas which could have lessons for the study of English developments is northern Italy.[195] More than anywhere else in the sub-Roman West except the Iberian peninsula, the Lombard kingdom had retained a culture of written law, reflected in its legislation, legal manuscripts and conduct of cases (chapter 2, pp. 67–9, 86–90). Ninth-century efforts to bring order of a sort to the accumulating mass of mandates (chapter 2, pp. 33, 67–8) culminated late in the tenth century with the production of the *Liber legis Langobardorum* (or, more probably, of an interrelated series of such collections).[196] This gave an encyclopaedic format to the law made by Italy's kings from Rothari to Otto the Great and beyond. Chapters of Carolingian capitularies irrelevant to Italy were omitted.[197] In the course of the eleventh century this was provided with at least two important commentaries. One was that ascribed to Walcausus by verses found in all copies.[198] It took the form of a courtroom dialogue between 'Peter' and 'Martin' in which the possible applications of each law were worked out. These hypothetical proceedings were close enough to real life for the language to switch at one point to proto-Italian. Italy's lawyers had graduated (or, given Roman models, reverted) to that staple of juristic literature, the imagined lawsuit.

---

194   E.g. (in chronological order) Vatican cod. Reg. lat. 846, Paris BN MS lat. 9653, 18237, Vatican cod. Reg. lat. 1050, Leiden MS Voss. lat. Q 119, Paris BN MS lat. 4409, and the 'Legal Treatise' in Paris BN MSS lat. 4995, 10758, 4760, 4628A, and 4626; cf. also Vatican cod. Reg. lat. 1128. See Riché, *Enseignement du Droit*, pp. 16–17.

195   For what follows, see especially the distillation and substantial revision of long-established scholarly positions by Radding, *Origins of Medieval Jurisprudence*; with its further ramifications in his 'Vatican Latin 1406', especially pp. 529–51; and his '"Petre te appellat Martinus." Eleventh-century Judicial Procedure as seen in the Glosses of Walcausus'; see also n. 210 below. (It should be added that Radding's critique of earlier studies as over-polemical has itself been found polemical by others).

196   Edited (in distracting conflation with the 'Gualcosina' and 'Expositio' (see below) by Boretius, *Liber Legis Langobardorum*: one of the problems of this important subject is the lack of anything like an adequate edition (or even any edition) of some primary memorials.

197   *Liber Papiensis*, pp. liii-lxxv; Radding, *Origins*, pp. 78–84. See also Leicht, *Storia del Diritto italiano*, pp. 81–106; with Wickham, 'Lawyer's Time', especially pp. 66–71.

198   *Liber Papiensis*, pp. lviii-lx, lxxv-lxxxiv (with table of glossed laws, pp. lxxvi–lxxvii); Radding, *Origins*, pp. 116–25, and '"Petre te appellat Martinus"', pp. 845–52.

The other commentary, in a single manuscript, was a set of 'Expositiones': again, one for each of the majority of laws in the Lombard corpus.[199] Each of these commentaries took the major step of incorporating annotations into the body of the manuscript, following the text being discussed: laws had become pegs on which to hang the analysis that was the author's main concern. Both, moreover, had debts and links of various kinds to Roman law.[200] Finally and from much the same time, there was the *Lombarda*.[201] This was a consummation of the trends represented by earlier exercises. Where Walcausus' courtroom staging regularly cross-referred from one law to another, as lawyers would, and the *Expositiones* were recast in thematic order, the *Lombarda* set out law and commentary in a systematically topical way. Barbarian law could now be presented in the style of the increasingly familiar and admired Roman monuments.

This story has an English relevance, as was implicitly recognized by Maitland.[202] It is a matter of contrasts as much as similarities. A turning-point in recent scholarship has been the demonstration that the rediscovery of Roman law was not cause but effect of a growing sophistication in Italian legal analysis. Advances in Lombard jurisprudence encouraged and facilitated a renewed approach to a Roman law which was never entirely lost in Italy (chapter 2, pp. 36, 69).[203] Italian developments represent the response of an increasingly self-confident *élite* of accredited legal experts, the 'judges' of the Pavia palace and their counterparts in other Italian cities, to their own long-established corpus of legal knowledge. They set about giving past enactments a theoretical dimension which made them adaptable to contingencies unforeseen by the original law-makers. Before long men of a similar cast of mind turned their skills on the 'law of the fief', producing in the *Libri Feudorum* a body of law for relationships never previously subjected to legal formulation.[204] In so far as they wanted to know how law could be applied in particular cases, their focus was procedural, and perhaps, to that extent at least, affected by the Roman preoccupation with *actiones*.[205] In this respect, and in their 'ability to think abstractly and in terms of legal categories', they are comparable with the *Quadripartitus/Leges Henrici* author. Another important parallel is that this new Italian expertise retained deep respect for its entire inheritance. 'Peter and Martin', the *Expositiones* commentator, even the *Lombarda*, did what they could with Rothari's huge catalogue of compensations for wounding freeman, 'aldius' or slave: a list that had still less to do with social

199   *Liber Papiensis*, pp. lxxxiv–xc; Radding, *Origins*, pp. 125–39, and cf. pp. 94–112.
200   *Liber Papiensis*, pp. lxxxviii–lxxxix; Radding, *Origins*, pp. 136–42 (and cf. pp. 84–6 for the earlier *Quaestiones ac Monita*, Roman maxims inserted on blank pages of a *Liber Legis* MS); Radding '"Petre te appellat Martinus"', pp. 838–40.
201   This evidently remarkable text has not attracted the same attention as the others, and has not been printed since 1613, though it is tabulated following *Liber Papiensis*, pp. 607–40, with a review of MSS by Bluhme, pp. xcviii–cxi; cf. also Radding, *Origins*, pp. 127, 175–6.
202   PM I, pp. 22–4, 77–8, 108, 116–18, 134.
203   The central (and thus far wholly convincing) lesson of Professor Radding's studies.
204   See Reynolds, *Fiefs and Vassals*, pp. 215–18: Ariprandus commented both on the earliest *Libri* treatises and on the *Lombarda*. The *Libri* are currently the subject of a fresh study by Dr Magnus Ryan, to whom I am indebted for much enlightenment.
205   Radding, *Origins*, pp. 167–9, and cf. pp. 136–8.

(as opposed to jural) reality in the Italy of 1100 than Alfred's in contemporary England.[206]

However, if the priorities of the *Quadripartitus/Leges Henrici* enterprise were in these ways similar to those of legal specialists a thousand miles to the south, the end-product was very different. The English scheme has an engaging amateurishness that would have reduced Italian experts to gales of laughter – as some English forgeries of the period actually did.[207] The Italian materials would alone argue the existence of a vigorous legal profession. *Leges Henrici* and its ilk are confirmation that there was none in England. Whatever the author meant by his references to 'professio nostra' (chapter 5, p. 413), it cannot have been that.[208] Nor was there in England the sort of corpus of native, let alone Roman, law that could stimulate or allow a cadre of professionals to emerge. The English impetus came, as implied by the preference for Book II over Book V of Isidore, from the Arts as much as law itself. The *Quadripartitus* author's impermeably turgid Latin paradoxically reveals that it was here that his skills lay. Like so many alert minds in the post-millennium West, his was swept away by the allurements of categorical analysis.

To say that is not, oddly enough, to exclude absolutely the possibility of an Anglo-Italian link. That Lanfranc, probably if not certainly a pre-Walcausian commentator on Lombard law, brought a juristic training to the development of English law is a suspicion which is hard to slough off, however sparsely it is supported by concrete evidence. His extant works are as marked by mastery of the *Artes*, dialectic above all, as they are unmarked by any specifically legal echo.[209] But by that token his primacy can hardly have failed to boost the study of the *Artes* in his new province. What is more, his textual command may have drawn on devices patented in the Italian schools, and on authorities better known there than in the North where he made his home. An approach to the Arts which perhaps owed something to lawyerly modes of thought may have encouraged an Arts-based approach to law.[210] If, then, there was a connection between the Pavia schools and the English law-books, the common ground resided in a similarly academic concern with the conversion of law into an intellectual discipline – with no diminution of respect for the monuments of an increasingly superannuated past.

Although not even the Italian evidence suggests that Roman law was in itself a sufficient spur to legal advance, the whole history of the eleventh- and twelfth-

---

206   *Liber Papiensis*, pp. 305–10; *Lombarda*, pp. 609–10.
207   *Hugh the Chanter, History of the Church of York* (ed. Johnson, Brett *et al.*), pp. 192–5.
208   Brand, *Origins of the English Legal Profession*, chapter 1.
209   Southern, 'Lanfranc of Bec and Berengar of Tours'; Gibson, *Lanfranc*, pp. 44–61, 81–91.
210   Radding, 'Vatican Latin 1406', pp. 535–6, 540–5; and his 'Geography of Learning in Early Eleventh-Century Europe', pp. 154–61. It is anyway evidently a mistake to make too much of North-South or Arts-Law divisions: Professor Radding prefers to ascribe the development of a lawyerly 'mind-set' in Italy to the dispersal and loss of monopoly experienced by Pavian judicial expertise after 950 (without making it entirely clear why the response should then have taken the intellectual form it did); but he is prepared to agree that it was influenced by 'the increase in the level of intellectual activity in general', *Origins*, p. 89, and that there may have been a role for Boethian and Parisian logic, p. 171. The *exordium* of the *Expositiones* was couched, like that of *Leges Henrici*, in the terms of the *Artes*: *Liber Papiensis*, pp. 290–1: Radding, *Origins*, p. 129.

century West suggests that study of any one area of law would tend to run alongside development in others. So slight a symptom as the Roman law in *Leis Willelme* (chapter 5, pp. 408–9) may illustrate the outcome of an encounter with the likes of Master Vacarius.[211] But the English were more obviously aware of the rise of the second great system of Learned Law, that of the Church. There is this time no question about Lanfranc's part in the story: his pseudo-Isidorian canon-collection provided one ingredient of *Textus Roffensis*.[212] However, he was far from being that story's sole protagonist. *Leges Henrici* was beholden to a collection of False Decretals which was not Lanfranc's.[213] After quoting Isidore, its introduction borrowed its next set of clauses from the *Panormia* and *Decretum* of Ivo of Chartres.[214] An altogether greater canonist than Lanfranc was at hand.

Ivo of Chartres produced an immense digest of ecclesiastical law, possibly over an astonishingly short and crowded period in the mid–1090s, but more probably in stages over two decades until his death in 1116.[215] A first version of a historically arranged anthology, known as 'Tripartita A', was followed by a *Decretum*, which more than doubled the size of Burchard's already massive work of the same name by adding texts from 'Tripartita A' and other recent compilations. The *Decretum* was then abbreviated twice over: in 'Tripartita B', which usually accompanies 'A' and evidently acted as its systematically organized version; and in the *Panormia*, the most widely distributed and studied of all pre-Gratianic collections. There is no reason to challenge the apparently obvious conclusion that what had stimulated this new level of interest in canon law was the 'Gregorian revolution', and the further research it had promoted. Ivo's collections were among a whole series produced in the

---

211   On Vacarius' alleged influence, see Southern, 'Master Vacarius'; I do not of course wish to imply that Vacarius was the actual source of the somewhat bizarre Leis Wl selections from the *Digest*: merely that his is the sort of career that may, at one or more removes, account for the appearance of Civilian materials in English contexts.

212   The classic demonstration is Brooke, *English Church and the Papacy*, pp. 57–83 (and pp. 84–99, though here at least subject to revision from on-going work by Martin Brett, e.g. 'Collectio Lanfranci', and see also below, n. 214). The TR extracts (almost all from Lanfranc's collection: Brett, 'Collectio Lanfranci', p. 162) are at ff. 81v – 87r; they are listed by Liebermann, 'De accusatoribus aus Pseudo-Isidor'.

213   Hn 5:2a,5a,9a,11–13a,17a,22–26,27a, 28:1,5, 29:1a, 31:6,7ab, 32:1a, 49:3bd,4ab, 57:3: variously from *Decretales pseudo-isidorianae*, pp. 73, 84, 126, 131–2, 166, 167–8, 237, 316, 419, 485, 489, 562–3, 759, 761–8; Lanfranc collection lacks the texts in Hn 5:26, 31:7a and 49:4a: cf. Brett, 'Collectio Lanfranci', p. 170, n. 51.

214   Hn 5:1–35 (their main concern was much the same as that of the TR excerpts, charges against clergy). The major sources, as designated by Liebermann and in part corrected by Downer's commentary, pp. 307–13, are Ivo's *Panormia* iv 44, 49–50, 64–5, 69, 74–5, 80–2, 86, 95, 97, 100, 102, 109, 118, 120, 132, viii 86, 106–7, 109–10, 111–13, 116–17, 123; there are also citations of his *Decretum* v 260, vi 313, 317, 331; and *Panormia* iv 103–4 reappears at Hn 28:4 and 49:3b, iv 109 at 33:5, ?iv 82 at 34:3, and *Decretum* iv 41 at 68:4. It should be stressed here, and with reference to what follows, that these and other citations must be taken as provisional, given the highly fluid state of pre-Gratianic canonical studies, especially as regards Ivo and his sources: Brett, 'Urban II', and 'Sources and influence of Paris Arsenal MS 713''. I am most grateful for Dr Brett's skilled and courageous sapper-work throughout this field.

215   The intense burst theory is that of Fournier, who distilled his own foundational researches in *idem* and Le Bras, *Histoire des Collections Canoniques* II, pp. 55–114; an evolutionary view seems to be preferred by modern scholarship, e.g. Brett, 'Urban II'. The only modern monograph on Ivo is Sprandel, *Ivo von Chartres* – pp. 52–85 for an account of the legal collections; for an up-to-date summary with bibliography, see Landau, 'Ivo von Chartres'.

post-1070 generation (and were not as supportive of papal claims as some of the others).[216] But they were much the most important for the English.

Ivo had perhaps been Lanfranc's pupil at Bec, and he corresponded with a number of Bec alumni and other English prelates.[217] There were English copies of each of Ivo's canon collections, from (at the latest) the mid-twelfth century.[218] Rochester's library had a set of his letters by the early 1120s, later joined by a 'Collectiones ecclesiasticarum regularum domini ivonis carnotensis'.[219] Since the evidence of this is the catalogue included in *Textus Roffensis* itself, it is of special interest in the present context. A fourteenth-century colophon credited Bishop Ernulf with having organized the *Textus* (chapter 4, pp. 245, 252). The assertion is borne out not just by the evidence that it was compiled soon after 1122, Ernulf dying in 1124, but by the fact too that its scribe also copied a tract by Augustine that was the chief source of 'De incestis coniugiis', one of Ernulf's few extant works.[220] Ernulf, another Bec pupil, was apparently known to Ivo.[221] It has been strongly argued that his 'De Incestis' implements principles in the study of law that Ivo set out in a famous 'prologue' found at the head of copies of the *Tripartita*, *Decretum* and *Panormia* alike. It is a question of applying argument ('ratio') to the law. The approach, that is to say, is dialectical. Compare Ivo:

> So some commands and prohibitions are flexible (*mobiles*), some binding (*immobiles*). The binding commands are those that the eternal law has decreed ... But the flexible are those that the eternal law did not decree, but the hard work of posterity devised by reason of utility, not primarily to obtain salvation but to make it more secure.

with Ernulf:

> What is commanded is not allowed not to be done; what is permitted is allowed not to be done ... When command intrudes, permission will cease. For command overcomes permission.[222]

Divine law is at the root of all and the best guide to what is applicable in any one context. But other types of law have other functions; and one is able to work out which is which. It can no longer be regarded as certain that Ivo's prologue was

---

216 Fournier and Le Bras, *Histoire des Collections* II, pp. 4–54, 127–92, 235–47; cf. more modern views on some of these works, in Brett, 'Urban II', and 'Paris Arsenal MS'; also Gilchrist, 'Collection in Four Books and Collection in Seventy-four Titles' (with a particularly suggestive postscript), and Hartmann, 'Kanonessammlung der Handschrift Vallicelliana B.89'.

217 See the important paper by Barker, 'Ivo of Chartres and the Anglo-Norman Cultural Tradition'.

218 Brett, 'Collectio Lanfranci', pp. 158–9, 163–5; Barker, Ivo of Chartres', p. 26; Landau, 'Das Dekret des Ivo von Chartres', pp. 9–10, 23–4; Brooke, *English Church and the Papacy*, pp. 244–5, with Cramer (as n. 223), n. 59.

219 *Textus Roffensis*, ed. Sawyer II, ff. 227r, 230r; cf. Richards, *Texts and their Traditions*, pp. 28 (no. 44), 32 (no. 98), noting too p. 29 (nos 56–7), 'Canones et decreta pontificum' and 'Exceptiones de eiusdem'.

220 See my 'Laga Eadwardi', pp. 260, 264–5 (pp. 130–1, 135–6).

221 Ivo, 'Epistolae' LXXVIII, col. 100: evaluated by Barker, 'Ivo of Chartres', pp. 21–2; the manuscript contexts of Ernulf's 'De Incestis' (Cramer, as n. 223, n. 2) are also suggestive.

222 Ivo 'Prologus', col. 50A; Ernulf, 'De Incestis Coniugiis', col. 1472A. The creative influence of Ivo's Prologue more generally is described by Brassington, '*Nachleben* of Ivo of Chartres'.

in existence as early as 1098, the *terminus ante* for Ernulf's piece.[223] If, however, one may envisage a community of interest stretching back into the youth of both men, then it is distinctly possible that they shared an agenda: that Ivo was making his developing ideas available to like-minded contemporaries with similar training. Among these ideas was the utility of the particular type of law that was secular legislation. Ivo's canon collection contains a far fuller selection of imperial and royal law than any to date (apart from Benedict the Deacon's forged capitularies). If Ivo influenced Ernulf, the value of human law-giving is one of the lessons he would have taught.[224]

For the *Quadripartitus/Leges Henrici* author, the evidence is yet more elusive but no less tempting. Of the two features of his personal profile that can be delineated with some confidence, the first is that he regarded England as his mother-country though his mother-tongue was not English. His identification with Henry I's Norman triumph was total. He is among the earliest evidence there is for the 'Anglicization' of the new Francophone ascendancy.[225] Secondly, a short file of letters making up the core of *Quadripartitus* Book II shows that the author had some sort of association with Archbishop Gerard of York (1100–8).[226] Liebermann and others were thereby incited into implausible theories about his alleged anti-papal position on Investitures and links with the famous polemics of the 'York (*recte* Norman) Anonymous'. But this may be an example of a wrong turning that leads in the right general direction. One thing shared by the 'Norman Anonymous', the *Quadripartitus* author and (possibly) Gerard of York was a connection of sorts with Ivo of Chartres. Ivo's views on metropolitan rights were probably as congenial to Gerard's *Quadripartitus* admirer as at York itself. He seems to have seen the Conqueror's as a model régime.[227] The *Quadripartitus/Leges Henrici* author's intellectual profile begins to look not unlike Ernulf's. The conclusion indicated is that behind some, perhaps most, early-twelfth-century law-books was a scholarly fraternity whose roots lay in what can be termed the Neustrian schools (so neatly evading the question of the exact parts played by Lanfranc or Ivo in its formation). Its scions were distributed through the cathedrals and episcopal households of the Anglo-Norman realm. Among its convictions were developing ideas of what could and should be done with law.

---

223 See the perceptive discussion of Cramer, 'Ernulf of Rochester'. In '*Laga Eadwardi*', I made more of the influence Ivo's 'Prologue' on Ernulf than Dr Brett advises me was wise. But Dr Cramer made no such claim, and his case works as well on the presumption sketched above.

224 Ivo, 'Prologus', cols. 47B, 58C–60A; see my '*Laga Eadwardi*', p. 265 (pp. 135–6). Cf. Gaudemet, 'L' Apport du Droit Romain', pp. 181–2; and Sprandel, *Ivo von Chartres*, p. 67.

225 'Argumentum' 16–21, Sharpe, 'Prefaces of "Quadripartitus"', pp. 165–6; cf. my '"*Quadripartitus*"', pp. 139–40 (pp. 106–8); and for what follows, pp. 140–2 (pp. 108–9).

226 Liebermann, *Quadripartitus* II 4 – 18; only Henry I's letters to the Pope, the account of Gerard's appointment and activity during Anselm's first exile, and the London and Westminster councils (II 4 – 8:3, 18) survive in the final (MHk) edition (the author's resentment at Gerard's treatment by the canons of York (17:4) showing that, whatever his connection with the archbishop, he was not one of them). For what little is known of Gerard, see Barlow, *English Church, 1066–1154*, p. 72; also next n.

227 Williams, *Norman Anonymous*, pp. 55–9; *Hugh the Chanter*, p. 25; and cf. some extremely suggestive paragraphs by Dr Barker, 'Ivo of Chartres', pp. 16, 30–2; note too (*ibid.*, p. 19) that Ivo was close to Gerard's predecessor and successor at York.

It is no very controversial proposition that the twelfth century saw a deep shift in European legal consciousness: the steady displacement of notions that had prevailed since the eclipse of Roman jurisprudence; the slow birth of something like modern ideas of law; and, as one symptom of all this, escalating confidence in the handling of legal texts.[228] What is not so often appreciated is that the English stage of this process got under way not in the second half of the century but in the first. The point has been obscured by the awful difficulty of the enterprise on which the Anglo-Norman law-books were engaged. The profound, almost shocking, contrast between their achievement and that of the Italian lawyers or Ivo arose not from a relative want of ambition or intelligence, but from the fact that they had so much less to work with. The ruling class that had known how the pre-conquest system worked had been destroyed. Post-conquest experts were left with little more than the written guides which are all that modern historians have. The result is a muddle, naturally; and one that gives the modern historian no better an idea of how much of the venerated old law was actually still in operation than post-conquest experts may have entertained themselves. In the end, it was simpler for the 'Glanvill' generation to pretend (and so convince modern historians) that there was no inheritance from the past: that what was needed was a clean-looking sheet.

What the Anglo-Norman lawyers did for 'the awesome sway of royal majesty' was nonetheless vastly important. Their image of the king exercising a directional power over English justice that was already centuries old left Henry II and his subjects in little doubt of either his powers or his responsibilities. The argument of the last few pages has tended to uphold the proposition that, however urgently practical the motives of those who made the St Paul's law-collection (chapter 4, pp. 235–6), the inspiration of the Rochester and *Leges Henrici* compilers might be better described as cultural. But this is in the end a false antithesis. A key characteristic of the English kingdom from the time of its Alfredian foundation was the extent to which its intellectual community was at the monarchy's disposal. This was not a ligature that the Norman kings or (most of) their spiritual advisers proposed to release. Among their first foundations was the cathedral community of Salisbury. Canons (like the St Paul's *familia*), and so spared a *Rule*'s binding obligation to forgo all worldly ties, the Salisbury clergy were remarkable both for a prodigious output of scholarly volumes and for evident involvement in the making of Domesday Book.[229] Their bishop from 1102 to 1139 was Roger, post-conquest kingship's ultimate henchman. His nephew was patron of a historian of 'the English', and perhaps the sponsor of a glossary of Old English legal terms; it is unlikely, to paraphrase James Campbell, that his interest in Anglo-Saxon law was nostalgic or academic.[230]

---

228 Kröschell, 'Recht und Rechtsbegriff in 12ten Jahrhundert' is a classic exposition among many. See also Kuttner, 'Revival of Jurisprudence'; and, for valuable *nuances*, Reynolds, *Kingdoms and Communities*, pp. 12–66 (and 'Introduction to 2nd Edition', pp. lvi-lxii). The latest Italian discussion (of many) is Cortese, *Rinascimento Giuridico Medievale*.
229 Webber, *Scribes and Scholars at Salisbury*; with her 'Salisbury and the Exon Domesday'.
230 Campbell, 'Some Twelfth-Century Views', p. 133 (p. 211); cf. my '"*Quadripartitus*"', p. 145 (p. 112).

There is a case that English universities were slow to form just because so many scholars were corraled by government.[231] The English *studium* was the king's court; in the field of law, it in a sense always would be. Those (by and large) good servants of the king, the bishops, would have been surprised and hurt to be told that study of canon law was at odds with their loyalty. Angevin action in due course spawned intellectual antibodies. But before that lay well over a century's dominance of the realm of the mind by royal patronage. Into that era fell the Anglo-Norman law-books. It is a nice reminiscence of tenth-century Winchester, and surely has more than symbolic meaning, that *Quadripartitus* and William of Malmesbury's *Gesta Regum* should alike seek the blessing of Queen Edith/Mathilda.[232]

'The Lord said not, "I am Custom" but "I am the Truth"'. The epigram ascribed to Gregory VII or Urban II (and recorded only by Ivo) was a dialogue-stopper.[233] As the Hohenstaufen confronted the Church's ever better articulated law, their one resort was its Justinianic rival. Roman lawyers already served some such purpose for the Emperors Henry IV and V.[234] 'Glanvill' could cite Justinian too (chapter 3, p. 129). But his text and all that followed his lead expounded a law that was both royal and English, and which made the king master of his subjects' behaviour. Becket's Truth was counterpointed by more than Custom. Only two years separated Clarendon's 'Constitutions' from its 'Assize'. The achievement of the *Quadripartitus* author and his peers was to stand by a tradition that might be unclear but was undeniably well-founded. To that extent their work, so often used to offset the single-mindedness and clarity of 'Glanvill', was a *sine qua non* of what he accomplished.

The next chapter will draw overall conclusions for Parts I and II. But three things need emphasis in a codicil to this one. First, it is not maintained that the literary or ideological motifs adumbrated here are the sole possible explanation for the forms taken by manuscripts or texts. The point for now is merely that they *can* explain them. Second, and that notwithstanding, there is a correlation between chapter 4, which found that no pre-1066 manuscript was exclusively, or even mainly, a collection of laws, and this one, where it appears that the leading lights of Old English legislative history, Alfred and Wulfstan, were driven by compulsions beyond the requirements of mere efficiency; that the inspiration of even twelfth-century law-books lay as much in the Arts as the Law syllabus. Third, and again on the other hand, ideological commitment to literacy might equally drive efforts to implement the royal will. Written law was Biblical and Roman, Holy and Imperial. Those models demanded, the first urgently, that what angered God as well as the community be punished in the name of both. The gist of chapters 4–6 reinforces the message of chapter 3: the recording of law was not intimately tied to its enforcement, was for the most part beyond the horizons of who lived with its effects. Yet the lesson of

231   Southern, 'England in the Twelfth Century Renaissance', pp. 174–7; with his 'From Schools to University', pp. 12–21.
232   *Quadr.* II Pr. 14:1 (*Gesetze* I, p. 543); Sharpe, 'Prefaces of "Quadripartitus"', p. 172.
233   Barker, 'Ivo of Chartres', p. 21; Somerville, 'Papal excerpts in Arsenal MS 713B', pp. 177–80.
234   Radding, *Origins*, pp. 114, 163–4.

Part III will be that that law was enforced. These results are not contradictory. A king inspired to make written law was by that token encouraged to direct the disputes and disorders of his people. If most of his subjects were unaffected by his sporadic activity in the one sphere, they were left with no doubt of his involvement in the other.

CHAPTER 7

Conclusion: Legislative Mentalities

Part II of this book has concerned the nature of the evidence for the earliest phase of English legal history. Since chapter 4, it has addressed what has always and understandably been regarded as the primary evidence, the legislation of early English kings. Discussion has been so extended and so elliptical because the texts are anything but straightforward vehicles of historical evidence. Like all literary products of a culture adjusting to the technology of script, they are deeply problematic as to conception, preservation, and so function. The objective throughout has therefore been to take as little as possible for granted; above all, to avoid the temptation to substitute for what the evidence actually said and did more modern notions of what it should have been saying or doing. That is why the texts have been viewed not in a chronological or analytical framework, either of which are impositions by retrospective intelligence, but from as close as historians may get to contemporary angles of vision: reports (or absence thereof) by narrative sources or recorded lawsuits; scribal priorities in the compilation and arrangement of the materials; ideologies detectable from the texts themselves and from related genres. That is also why, if the undertaking that this part of the book would eschew speculative flights has been honoured at least as much in breach as in observance, it can yet be claimed that the speculations ventured have attempted to make sense of the evidence as it stands. Whether or not the materials have been explained, they have at least not been explained away.

Clearly, it is time to see what conclusions emerge from the several hundred foregoing pages. What is one now to think that Anglo-Saxon law-codes were trying to do? What did they in fact do? The emphasis hitherto has been on the difficulties in the way of accepting that they did all that they claimed to be doing, all that they might be expected to have done. They rarely behaved and were seldom treated like the programme for the day-to-day conduct of society and the remedy of its mundane disorders that they purported to be. But this is a paradoxical outcome for an argument that put a premium on the evidence as it actually confronts the commentator. Besides, care has so far been taken not to foreclose on more instantly obvious ways of understanding the position. By way of insisting that options are still open, the first thing this summary should do is to stress that the materials *can* be interpreted in a way that is not only more obvious but also internally consistent, deduced from rather than imposed on the evidence, and inherently plausible.[1]

Such an approach might take as a point of departure the analogy drawn at the end of chapter 4 (pp. 262–3) between law-codes and charters. Most Old English charters survive only in cartularies. In their original form, they were of course entered on individual pieces of parchment. Well over a hundred of these are extant. There may have been an incentive to keep 'originals' alongside cartulary copies as evidence of title. There was no such incentive with the primal forms of legislation. Once incorporated into a collection (chapter 4, pp. 224–53), or some other more numinous context even better equipped to withstand temporal abrasion (pp. 181–97), individual texts might just as well be discarded. Discarded they could quite easily have been, if, as hinted more than once in chapter 4 (pp. 181–2, 248, 263), laws were circulated on single-sheets in parchment folders. In those circumstances, it would not be surprising that the one text certainly extant in original form is a writ confirming the specific rights of Londoners (chapter 5, pp. 398–9); or that what otherwise looks most like a code in current condition is the very latest vernacular copy to survive (chapter 4, pp. 253–5).

It would also be no surprise that only some codes are preserved in pre-conquest books: Alfred-Ine, I and II Æthelstan, I Edmund, II–IV Edgar, V–VIII and X Æthelred, Cnut 1018 and 1020, *Ymb Æwbricas*, the *Geþyncðu* group, and *Grið*; plus, accepting that Nowell and Wanley had access to Old English manuscripts since lost (chapter 4, pp. 258–9, 260–2) V Æthelstan, IX Æthelred and *Iudex*.[2] Other things that would make equally good sense are that knowledge of Æthelred's legislation after 1008 or of Cnut's before Christmas 1020 depends upon liturgical or homiletic volumes more or less closely linked with Wulfstan (chapter 4, pp. 190–210); or that legislation by Edgar and Æthelred which does appear to have existed, survives only as fragments or not at all (chapter 3, pp. 125–8, chapter 5, pp. 321, 328, 369–70, chapter 6, pp. 442–4).[3] From accepting that, it is not a large step towards maintaining that important pronouncements could have vanished altogether – much as some critical judicial reforms of Charlemagne seem to have done (chapter 2, pp. 88–9). Nor would it be any occasion for a raised eyebrow that legislation was so consistently overlooked by chroniclers of events until William of Malmesbury's enquiring eye lit upon an Anglo-Saxon legal collection (chapter 3, pp. 137–8).

There would, moreover, be no mystery about the anomalous form taken by many extant texts. If law-codes passed around in sheafs of loose parchments, they would naturally have been reshuffled. Not only were 'official' texts at risk of being broken up and mixed with tangentially related matter, as with 'IV Æthelred' (chapter 5, pp. 322–3, 371–2). They would also tend to acquire appendages: extended glosses like *Be Blaserum* or *Ordal*; semi-official (at least) manifestos like *Hundred* and perhaps the 'Alfred-Guthrum Appendix'; locally focused pieces like *Dunsæte*; sketches of forensic morality like *Iudex*; or indeed

---

1   This approach is perhaps most powerfully exemplified by Keynes, 'Royal Government and the Written Word'; see also Campbell, 'Observations on English Government', 'Significance of the Anglo-Norman State', and 'Late Anglo-Saxon State', pp. 58–9, 62.

2   See chapter 5, pp. 265–6, 291–5, 309, 313–15, 317, 332–7, 346–7, 372–3, 382, 391–2, 394.

3   See also the possible signs of lost legislation by Æthelstan in his Grately code: chapter 5, n. 172.

tracts with little if any legal content like *Rectitudines* and *Gerefa* (chapter 5, pp. 367–8, 373–4, 378–9, 379–80, 381–2, 382–3, 387–9). It could at the same time be predicted, given Wulfstan's obsessive convictions, that laws copied by his scribes would be liable to be remoulded as homilies, and to be distributed beside other designs for an idealized society (chapter 4, pp. 198–209, chapter 5, pp. 331–6). One could even argue (but probably would not) that, in the light of other manifestations of Alfredian eggheadedness, it might almost be expected that a code from his pen would be abnormally prone to ideological impulses.

The way is thereby opened to belief that pre-conquest England was something like a *pays du droit écrit* after all. Its kings may have made law much like Henry II or even Edward I. However, the odds were stacked against the survival of their efforts. Monkish piety, alien ignorance and neglect, the hazards of damp, fire or bookworm conspired to distort or blot out what they and their servants did in pursuit of the goals to which they undoubtedly aspired.

This, to labour the point, is a wholly rational approach to the shortcomings of the evidence. But there are two reasons why it does not in last resort convince. The first harks back to points made in chapters 4 and 5. Because other works by Alfred and Wulfstan are extant, it is possible to identify their personal contributions as law-makers (chapter 5, pp. 273–7, 339–45). This made Alfred a very abnormal king indeed. But granted that Wulfstan became unusually learned in the law 'of God and world' (chapter 4, pp. 213–24, chapter 5, pp. 341–5, 355–64), all that was immediately exceptional about him were his distinctive style and script. Cathedral libraries were the usual transmitters of legislative materials to later ages, even if Worcester did more than most (chapter 4, pp. 182–224). Wulfhelm and Oda of Canterbury, the Ælfheahs of Winchester and Lyfing of Crediton, Maurice of London, Ernulf of Rochester and Gerard of Hereford and York may have done some of the same things as Wulfstan (chapter 4, pp. 167–81, 223, 235–6, 245–53, chapter 5, pp. 294–300, chapter 6, pp. 472–3). There is every reason why bishops should have played so prominent a role. Quite apart from their training in the law of God and of His Church, the Old English kingdom expected much of them. They jointly presided over shire-courts (chapter 3, pp. 152–6). When a reeve fell down in his duty to implement the Grately decrees, Æthelstan expected the local bishop to collect the disobedience-fine.[4] Yet it was these juridically active persons, committed by their profession to the ideal of written law, who imparted the spin with which texts passed down to posterity, and who left the gaps that posterity could not make good (chapter 5, pp. 414–15). If bishops were so insouciant as regards the integrity of the royal will, would ealdormen and reeves have been more sollicitous?

The second consideration looks further back in this volume, to chapter 2. One of its main messages was that though the Carolingians earnestly endeavoured to emulate the standards of government by *lex scripta* set in the past by Rome (and Israel), and maintained up to a point by neighbouring regimes in southern Europe, they were ultimately unable to measure up to them (pp. 46–53, 66–70,

---

4   II As 25:1; in the margin of Professor Whitelock's copy of *Laws* (At), which I possess through the generosity of Dr Keynes, stands the pertinent pencilled question, 'why not the ealdorman?'

79–81, 86–92). This North-South contrast is certainly not a matter of differential rates of manuscript survival. More reported law-cases survive from the *Regnum Italiae* than any one other part of the Frankish dominions, and more from 'Gothia' than most (table 2.2); but there are many fewer copies of Visigothic or Lombard legislation or of Italian capitularies than of *comparabilia* from north of the Alps and Pyrenees (table 2.1). The essence of the contrast is that southern law and politics were – and had for long been – tuned in a more literate key than northern; as a result, legal texts and manuscripts were easier to use; and as a result of that, they *were* more readily used. The simplest and most plausible explanation for the contrast is the vitality of the Roman notarial tradition in parts of the world where other symptoms of *Romanitas* lingered longest (chapter 2, pp. 89–90).

Yet if one turns to a comparison of Frankish with English manifestations, it is almost all in the former's favour. English texts had one great advantage: they were in the language of everyday life (chapter 2, pp. 41–2, 101). But they were regularly reproduced in continuous prose, clauses either being provided scriptorially (chapter 4, pp. 189–90, chapter 5, pp. 341, 350); or, if conceivably official in origin, then decidedly unhelpful (chapter 5, pp. 267–9, 300, 304–5). Copies of Frankish *leges* and capitularies, by contrast, stayed consistently faithful to a titular or capitular structure that there is every reason to think original. Frankish law books were, for the most part, just that: unadulterated by extraneous matter (chapter 2, pp. 60–1). Anglo-Saxon law books, on the other hand, were always primarily about something else (chapter 4, pp. 262–3). There was a Frankish *lex* for every 'gens'; Kent and Wessex alone had anything comparable, and 'laws' of Mercia and the Danelaw came to life only in the twelfth century (chapter 5, 408–11, chapter 6, p. 466). Roughly ten times as many royal pronouncements are known from Francia 740–890 as from England 886–1066. Copies of laws are fifteen times more numerous in the one than the other. From no part of the English kingdom are there even hints of cited written law like those detectable from the central regions of the Frankish realm (chapter 2, pp. 39, 79, chapter 3, pp. 143, 160). The only part of Francia that was as limited in its range of evidence as England was the area east of the Rhine and north of the Danube (chapter 2, p. 92). What lowland Britain had in common with that region was not only related language or 'blood and bone', but also the most residual of inheritances from the Roman past.

In conjuring up a map of Europe's post-Roman legal culture, therefore, one can envisage deeply hatched arenas of *lex scripta* south of the Alps and Pyrenees, shading off as the eye moves up, though not sharply till one gets north of the Danube and the Loire-Saône watershed, and less sharply beyond the latter than the former. In such terms, southern England is merely stippled, the North effectively 'blank'.[5] Pursuing Bloch's image for a moment, 'it is not hard to recognize' in these gradations the varying depth of Rome's imprint: not upon ideals, for the *élites* of sub-Roman Europe shared a hankering after its *exempla*, but upon the common practice of society. In these terms too, it is no longer possible to explain the limits of Anglo-Saxon evidence by invoking the hazards of its battle

5   This is of course to adapt a famous passage in Bloch, *Feudal Society*, pp. 445–6.

for survival. English patterns were part of a wider picture, and one that makes historical sense.

Thus, the first, and for the purposes of the overall project the central, conclusion suggested by this study is that early medieval England was not a *pays du droit écrit*, either in the way that some other parts of Europe were at the time, or that it was itself later. Odd as this seems in the light of the fact that a fair amount of secular legislation was issued in tenth-century England, as against almost none overseas, it is the conclusion indicated by comparing the evidence with that from other times and places.[6] Legal prose reached almost lawyerly standards under Æthelred, at the same time as royal charters became prone to raise legal issues (chapter 5, pp. 324–6). But had this juristic culture attained the depth of Pavia's (chapter 6, pp. 468–70), it could hardly have been so comprehensively hijacked by Wulfstan's sermonizing. Yet this is to say what Anglo-Saxon law-codes did *not* do. It is unfortunately a bit harder to say precisely what they *did*. What they *were*, perhaps above all, was an index of governing mentalities. Viewed that way, the totality of the evidence has a coherence which it lacks when seen as the fruit of a system of written law. If Alfred's *domboc* was planned as an epitome of God's Covenant with the people to whom He had given lowland Britain, the contradictions between traditional West Saxon law, standing in Ine's name, and the adjustments introduced by Alfred himself under the purported influence of other traditions were by comparison unimportant. The device of dividing the law of Wessex into 120 chapters was positively neat (chapter 5, pp. 266–9, 278–80). No less rational was that this lawbook should be laid beside the record of the conquest of southern England in its earliest copy; and beside the history of God's conquest of the conquerors in one made seventy years later (chapter 4, pp. 166–7, 180).

Alfred's people having been inducted into the Solomonic programme which, as he and Asser said, the king set for himself (chapter 3, pp. 119–24, chapter 6, pp. 427–9), his successors operated like the empire-builders they conceived themselves to be. Imitating Franks as well as Romans, they issued edicts to exalt God's Church and to repress society's disorders (chapter 3, pp. 128–9, chapter 6, pp. 438–45). When Archbishop Wulfstan deduced from mounting disturbances in the cosmos that God had found the results wanting, and indeed that Creation as a whole might now lie open to the ravages of Antichrist, he of course concentrated on the essentials of Christian morality; and when the opportunity came to redraft God's Covenant with the English, the laws of Cnut's predecessors were naturally accompanied by repeated warnings of the ineluctability of Divine Judgement (chapter 5, pp. 355–65, chapter 6, pp. 453–65). Since, moreover, the aims of law and homily were the same, they were logically found sharing the same format within the same codices. Hardly less reasonable was that laws with so solemn a purpose should be inserted in liturgical volumes, even Gospel-books (chapter 4, pp. 190–7). Finally, the laws of England, which had served as a fixed point amidst the disruptions of the 1016 conquest (chapter 3, pp. 129–33), could (so far as possible) be reassembled as one anchor in the cyclonic conditions

---

6 Significantly, the only secular legislation on the continent contemporary with that of Alfred and his successors was issued by the Ottonians and Salians for Italy: *Constitutiones*, ed. Weiland, 13, 16, 21–3, 32, 37, 45, 52–4. English and German patterns will be compared in chapter 14.

created by that of 1066 (chapter 4, pp. 224–53, chapter 5, pp. 404–13). At the same time, early glimpses of the world of Learned Law opening up to the South inspired new intellectual ambitions in those who sought to delineate their character or to record their history (chapter 3, pp. 137–4, chapter 6, pp. 465–70).

Among this perspective's virtues is that political ideologies offer a better explanation than (say) the oscillations of social order why legislation should have been resumed after a century or two by Alfred and then been discontinued after 1023, remaining episodic throughout the period between (chapter 6, pp. 448–9). The most ideologically sensitized kings and royal advisers were precisely those most prone to issue codes – or at any rate codes that their servants troubled to keep. Another more important virtue is that it does not sunder the outlook that supplied the evidence from that of lawmakers themselves. The laws of pre-Angevin England are viewed as outgrowths of a legal culture at a particular stage of development rather than as levers of an inevitably rudimentary legal system. The effect is to stress the seriousness of the enterprise on which rulers were engaged, rather than the natural limitations of the response to so grand a design from their subjects; to cut the ground from under lofty condescension towards the 'barbarity' of the epoch, while obviating the need felt by great scholars of an earlier age to switch responsibility for the state of the texts from governments who would have known what they were doing to 'scribes' who did not.[7] Does it follow that early English law and law-making remained fundamentally oral in character? Presumably; that is the implication of lawsuits wherein written law played no part, even when the nature of the case gave it an opening (chapter 3, pp. 148, 150). At the same time, it is hard to say quite what 'orality' would mean, given the availability of so many texts. The point is emphatically not that texts did not matter, but that they did not resonate as they might have. This chapter and volume should in any case finish by insisting what does not follow from their argument.

One thing that certainly need not follow is that legislation was exclusively visionary. There were times when commentators after 1066 seem to part company from reality, as noted in chapter 6 (pp. 465–8); but that chapter also observed (p. 429) that Alfred's point would have been wholly lost if the law that he set beside God's were not recognizable to his audience. It would not have been possible for Wulfstan and Cnut to invoke 'Edgar's law', nor would the Northumbrian rebels have demanded 'Cnut's' (chapter 3, pp. 129–34), nor finally would Norman conquerors have appealed to 'Edward's' (chapter 5, pp. 397–401), if principles and practices decreed after 899 had not been accepted by the English as their own. In that oxymoronical sense, pre-conquest legislation may be evidence of English *law*, even if not an infallible guide to English *law-making*.

A second deduction that is not warranted by the proposition that legal culture was not fully literate is that law was 'merely' customary. Perceptions of Europe's past have paid a high price for the fact that writing came to it alongside most of what else is thought 'civilized' in the legionary's knapsack. In the field of legal history, Roman convictions that law is either written ('lex') or custom ('mos'), passed on as it was by Isidore even before the twelfth century (chapter 2,

7   Wormald, 'Lex Scripta . . . ', pp. 117–19 (pp. 15–18).

pp. 43–4, chapter 6, pp. 466–7), has cast a long shadow. Yet law can innovate without being written down. Over the aeons of prehistory, it must have done.[8] To draw a sharp line between eras irradiated with the written evidence that is a historian's stock-in-trade and an archaeologist's prehistoric gloaming hinders understanding of periods which were transitional and by that token extended. The early medieval West was not prehistoric, but nor was it fully historic. It was proto-historic. That does not mean that its rulers were semi-effective. It means that government zeal had less – less not no – need of textual tools. On the whole, it seems unlikelier that the 'lex' of Edgar described by Lantfred was an oral *ukase* (chapter 3, pp. 125–8) than that it was the written counterpart to his 'fourth' code, fragments of which survive (chapter 5, pp. 320–1, 369–70). On the other hand, Alfred's 'oath and pledge' seems to have made an appearance before it was taken up by his laws (chapter 5, pp. 283–4), and nothing suggests that it had done so in writing. Much of this volume has dwelt on the apparent failure of written law to do the job that it would be expected to. Yet the second section of chapter 3 discovered that the degree to which kings were able to dictate to their subjects did not by any means always depend on the use of written instructions.

The importance of this is that it resurrects the point made in concluding chapter 6 (pp. 475–6), which will be the central point of Volume II. The development of English *law* from Alfred to Cnut and beyond did not run along the tracks that *legislation* marked out, but it did run in parallel with them. However constricted the ultimate effects of Mosaic or Roman example on the legislative tradition, its impact on the law enforced was profound. So a volume whose thesis is that tenth-century English legislation could not compare in range or sophistication with Frankish, still less Spanish or Italian, can end by stating what looks like its antithesis. In the tenth century, the law of English kings intruded into their subjects' lives to an extent that had no Anglo-Saxon precedent. It also had no European parallel. This was a time when official activity began to run down after 945 in the hitherto robust Italian state; when the purview of the Visigothic Code, once by exceptionally aggressive definition the sole admissable Spanish law, was eroded by grants of *fueros*; when a Flemish lady could grant away 'the power of discipline according to legal process which once belonged to royal majesty'; when the rights exercised in Burgundy by the Counts of Mâcon were rapidly dwindling; when (it must be said) one of the few parts of the continent where Carolingian organization remained in good fettle was Normandy; and when historians even of the *Reich* like to stress the elements of informality and consensus in its networks of power.[9] On the continent, the gulf between the age of the *Volksrechte* and that of the Learned Laws was opening (chapter 1, pp. 15, 20). English law was meanwhile moving to the position where, metaphorically if not literally, the king's writ would run throughout his realm.

---

8   Wormald, 'Frederic William Maitland', p. 22 (pp. 65–6).
9   Wickham, *Early Medieval Italy*, pp. 179–81; Collins, *Early Medieval Spain*, pp. 247–8; Dunbabin, *France in the Making*, p. 58; James, *Origins of France*, pp. 192–6; Bates, *Normandy before 1066*, pp. 162–72; Reuter, *Germany in the early Middle Ages*, pp 89–94, 191–220. These points are selected from general surveys by leading modern English scholars (and friends): I have over-simplified them of course, and the next volume will have to take on board recent 'revisionist' trends in this area (cf. Bisson, '"Feudal Revolution", Debate'). But the contrast with England will be found to stand.

Bibliography

This bibliography is at the same time a bibliographical *index*; that is to say, items are followed by the references to the *chapter and footnote* in which they are cited (any item mentioned in pages of the text proper will of course be found in the General Index as appropriate). Following the Sources Section (II) will be found a Subsidiary Concordance/Index (i) for my LS/'Lawsuits', and Subsidiary Indices for citations of (ii) Anglo-Saxon Charters, (iii) Anglo-Saxon Laws (defined as texts in Liebermann's *Gesetze* I), and (iv) Frankish Capitularies. Citations of *Quadripartitus* as text are in Subsidiary Index (iii), but below are citations of its several MSS.

I MANUSCRIPTS

Copenhagen, Kongelige Bibliotek, Gl. Kgl. Saml.
  MS 1595 4°. **Ch. 4, table 4.4, nn.** 204, 233
  MS 1943.4°. **Ch. 2, n.** 193
Exeter, Cathedral Library
  MS 3501 (the 'Exeter Book'). **Ch. 4, nn.** 55, 240
Florence, Laurenziana, s.n. ('Littera Pisana'). **Ch. 2, nn.** 144, 207
Fulda, Landesbibliothek
  MS D I. **Ch. 2, n.** 172
Geneva, Univbib.
  MS 50. **Ch. 2, n.** 180
Gotha Forschungsbibliothek
  MS Memb. I 84. **Ch. 2, nn.** 124–5, 130, 132, 134–6, 200, 202
The Hague, Rijksmuseum Meermanno-Westreenianum
  MS 10 D 2: cf. Berlin Sttsbib. Phillips MS 1762
Halberstadt, Bib. Domgymnasiums, s.n. **Ch. 2, nn.** 144, 207
Hamburg Staats- und Universitätsbibliothek, Cod. 141a in scrinio. **Ch. 2, n.** 193
Heiligenkreuz, Stiftsbibliothek
  MS 217. **Ch. 2, nn.** 125, 200
Hereford, Cathedral Library
  MS P.1.ii. **Ch. 4, n.** 103
Huntington Library, San Marino, California 30/B5 c.15142. **Ch. 4, n.** 384
Ivrea, Biblioteca Capitolare
  MS XXXIII. **Ch. 2, nn.** 201, 292
  MS XXXIV. **Ch. 2, nn.** 201, 292
Kassel, Gesamthochschul-Bibliothek, etc. 4°
  MS theol. 1. **Ch. 2, n.** 185
Laon, Bibliothèque Municipale
  MS 201. **Ch. 2, n.** 185
  MS 265. **Ch. 2, n.** 185
Leiden, Bibliotheek der Rijksuniversiteit
  BPL MS 114. **Ch. 2, n.** 148
  MS Voss. latina O. 86. **Ch. 2, nn.** 158, 180
  MS Voss. latina Q. 119. **Ch. 2, nn.** 146, 166, 178, 193–4; ch. 6, n. 194
Le Havre, Bibliothèque municipale
  MS 330. **Ch. 4, n.** 185
León, Archivio Catedralicio
  MS 15. **Ch. 2, nn.** 50, 144
Lichfield, Cathedral Library
  MS Lich. 1. **Ch. 4, n.** 103
London, British Library
  Additional MS 10546 (the Moutier-Grandval Bible). **Ch. 2, n.** 130
  Additional MS 16413. **Ch. 2, n.** 204

Additional MS 22398. **Ch. 2, nn.** 157, 193–4
Additional MS 34652 (f. 2). **Ch. 4, nn.** 42–3
Additional MS 43703 ['Nw1–2']. **Ch. 4, table 4.1, nn.** 42–78, 259, 265, 374, 384; **Ch. 5, table 5.1, nn.** 5–6, 119, 130–5, 160, 162–3, 532
Additional MS 47967 (the 'Tollemache' Orosius). **Ch. 4, nn.** 14–15, 21
Additional MS 49366 ['Hk']. **Ch. 4, nn.** 276, 305, 311–12; **ch. 5, table 5.2, nn.** 160, 162, 208, 272–3, 418, 550, 557, 664–5, 675, 682; **ch. 6, n.** 226
Additional MS 57337 (the 'Anderson' Pontifical). **Ch. 4, nn.** 130, 133
Additional MS 61735. **Ch. 4, n.** 103
Burney MS 277 ['Bu']. **Ch. 4, table 4.1, nn.** 357–60; **ch. 5, n.** 6
Cotton MS
  Caligula A.xv. **Ch. 4, nn.** 100, 102
  Claudius A.iii ['K']. **Ch. 4, table 4.1, nn.** 114–35
  Claudius A.iv. **Ch. 4, n.** 365
  Claudius B.iv. **Ch. 4, n.** 191
  Claudius D.ii ['K2']. **Ch. 4, nn.** 81, 304; **ch. 5, nn.** 140, 148, 631
  Cleopatra B.xiii. **Ch. 6, n.** 118
  Domitian i. **Ch. 4, nn.** 100, 102
  Domitian viii ['Dm']. **Ch. 4, nn.** 319–21, 324
  Faustina A.ii. **Ch. 4, n.** 365
  Faustina A.x. **Ch. 4, n.** 100
  Faustina B.iv. **Subsidiary Index (i), no.** 177
  Faustina B.vi. **Ch. 4, n.** 117
  Galba A.ii, iii. **Ch. 4, n.** 100
  Galba A.xiv + Nero A.ii, ff. 3–13. **Ch. 4, nn.** 100–1
  Galba A.xviii. **Ch. 4, nn.** 23–4
  Julius A.vi. **Ch. 4, n.** 26
  Julius C.ii. **Ch. 4, nn.** 245–6
  Nero A i ['G']. **Ch. 1, n.** 20; **ch. 3, n.** 82; **ch. 4, tables 4.1, 4.2, 4.4, nn.** 97, 147–64, 178, 199, 210–11, 213–14, 229, 240–63, 268, 356, 370; **ch. 5, table 5.1, nn.** 6, 87, 206–7, 319–21, 323, 333, 340, 361, 371, 386, 404–5, 410, 415–16, 603; **ch. 6, n.** 154
  Nero C.ix **Ch. 4, n.** 365
  Nero D.x. **Ch. 4, n.** 365
  Nero E.i + London, British Library, Additional MSS 37777, 46204

['F']. Ch. 4, table 4.1, nn. 82–95, 117; ch. 5, n. 248

Otho A.x. Ch. 3, n. 82; ch. 4, nn. 361–6

Otho A.xii. Ch. 4, n. 100

Otho B.xi ['Ot']. Ch. 3, n. 90; ch. 4, table 4.1, nn. 41–78, 272; ch. 5, table 5.1, nn. 6, 130, 132, 163

Otho C.i. Ch. 4, n. 103

Otho D.viii. Ch. 4, n. 365

Otho E.xiii. Ch. 6, nn. 10, 13

Tiberius A.ii. Ch. 4, nn. 25, 103, 114, 117

Tiberius A.iii. Ch. 3, n. 71; ch. 4, nn.100, 253; ch. 5, nn. 316, 380, 535

Tiberius B.v. Ch. 4, nn. 23, 103, 117, 337

Titus A.xxvii ['T']. Ch. 4, nn. 302, 305, 311, 318; ch. 5, n. 272, 550, 557, 631, 637

Titus D.xxvi, xxvii. Ch. 4, nn. 100–2, 189

Vespasian A.i (the 'Vespasian Psalter'). Ch. 4, n. 26

Vespasian A.xiv. Ch. 4, n. 108; ch. 6, nn. 125, 176

Vespasian B.xxiv. Ch. 4, n. 19

Vespasian D.ii. Ch. 6, n. 128

Vitellius A.vii. Ch. 6, n. 118

Vitellius E.xviii. Ch. 4, nn. 100–1, 103

Egerton MSS 2832 + 269 + Paris Bibliothèque Nationale MS latina 4633. Ch. 2, nn. 193–4

Harley MS 55 ['A']. Ch. 4, table 4.1, nn. 79, 96–113, 266, 271, 341–52; ch. 5, n. 227–8, 415–16, 418, 440

Harley MS 208. Ch. 4, n. 95

Harley MS 746. Ch. 5, nn. 665, 682

Harley MS 1704. Ch. 5, n. 682

Harley MS 2965 (the 'Book of Nunnaminster'). Ch. 4, nn. 13, 24

Harley MS 6018. Ch. 4, nn. 86, 90

Royal MS 1.D.ix. Ch. 4, n. 103

Royal MS 1.E.vi Ch. 4, n. 81

Royal MS 2.B.v. Ch. 4, n. 103

Royal MS 11.B.ii ['R']. Ch. 4, nn. 301, 309, 311, 317; ch. 5, table 5.2, nn. 140, 148, 272–3, 306, 418, 550, 557

Royal 12.D.xvii ('Bald's Leechbook'). Ch. 4, nn. 61–4

Stowe MS 2. Ch. 4, n. 185

Stowe MS 944 (the New Minster *Liber Vitae*). Ch. 4, nn. 33, 36, 103, 188

BL, Printed Books, Henry Davis Collection 59 ['Nw4']. Ch. 4, n. 381

London, Lambeth Palace Library MS 149. Ch. 4, n. 240

Lyon, Bibliothèque de la Ville MS 375. Ch. 2, n. 173

Manchester, John Rylands Library MS latina 155 + London, British Library, Additional MS 14252 ['Rs']. Ch. 4, nn. 303, 307; ch. 5, nn. 140, 148

MS latina 420 ['M']. Ch. 4, nn. 276, 300, 305, 310–11; ch. 5, table 5.2, nn. 138, 160, 162, 208, 272–3, 550, 557; ch. 6, n. 226

Milan, Archivio Civico Storico MS Trivulziano 688. Ch. 2, n. 207

Milan, Biblioteca Ambrosiana MS A.46 inf. Ch. 2, nn. 154, 190

Modena, Biblioteca Capitolare MS O.I.2. Ch. 2, nn. 12, 124–5, 128–33, 149, 200, 202

MS O.II.2. Ch. 2, n. 204

Montecassino, Archivio dell' Abbazia MS 125. Ch. 2, n. 204

Montpellier, Bibliothèque Interuniversitaire (Section Médecine) MS 84. Ch. 2, n. 37

MS H 136. Ch. 2, nn. 168, 172, 193–4

München, Staatsbibliothek MS latina 3519. Ch. 2, n. 207

MS latina 3853. Ch. 2, nn. 125, 200

MS latina 4115. Ch. 2, nn. 177, 188

MS latina 4460. Ch. 2, n. 206

MS latina 5260. Ch. 2, n. 207

MS latina 6360. Ch. 2, n. 190

MS latina 14468. Ch. 2, n. 184

MS latina 14508. Ch. 2, nn. 162, 185

MS latina 19415 (I–II). Ch. 2, n. 206

MS latina 19416. Ch. 2, nn. 205, 292

MS latina 22501. Ch. 2, n. 144

MS latina 29555/1 etc. Ch. 2. nn. 203, 207

MS latina 29555/2. Ch. 2, n. 121

München, Universitätsbibliothek MS 8° 132. Ch. 2, nn. 26, 179

Münster, Staatsarchiv msc. MS VII. 5201. Ch. 2, nn. 193–4

Naples, Biblioteca Nazionale MS IV.A.8. Ch. 2, nn. 144, 207

Novara, Biblioteca Capitolare MS XV. Ch. 2, n. 204

MS XXX. Ch. 2, n. 204

Nürnberg, Stadbibliothek MS Cent. V, App. 96. Ch. 2, nn. 192, 194

Oxford, Bodleian Library
  Additional MS D.82. Ch. 4, n. 363
  MS Arch. Selden B.16. Ch. 3, nn. 85–6
  MS Auct. D.2.16. Ch. 4, n. 103
  MS Auct. F.4.32. Ch. 4, n. 24
  MS Barlow 37. Ch. 4, table 4.4, nn. 204,
    207; ch. 6, n. 156
  MS Bodley 343. Ch. 4, n. 237
  MS Bodley 579 (the 'Leofric' missal). Ch.
    4, nn. 103, 130
  MS Bodley 718. Ch. 4, nn. 209, 216–17,
    240
  MS Digby 13. Ch. 5, n. 637
  MS Gough London 54. Ch. 4, n. 42
  MS Hatton 20. Ch. 4, n. 105
  MS Hatton 42. Ch. 4, nn. 216, 218; ch.
    5, n. 196
  MS Hatton 113–14. Ch. 4, nn. 172, 237;
    ch. 6, n. 129
  MS Junius 27 (the 'Junius Psalter'). Ch.
    4, nn. 14–15, 22–3, 26
  MS Junius 85–6. Ch. 4, n. 100
  MS Junius 121. Ch. 4, n. 237; ch. 5, nn.
    453, 584; ch. 6, n. 154
  MS Laud misc. 126. Ch. 2, n. 182
  MS Laud misc. 482. Ch. 4, n. 237
  MS Laud misc. 509 + BL, Cotton MS
    Vespasian D.xxi. Ch. 4, n. 81
  MS Rawlinson C.641 ['Rl']. Ch. 4, table
    4.8, n. 339; ch 5, nn. 621, 635, 637,
    682
  (Printed Books) 4ᵗᵒ L.5 Jur. Seld. Ch. 4, n.
    384
  (Printed Books) Vet. A.3 c. 196. Ch. 4,
    table 4.1, nn.367–70; ch. 5, n. 227
Oxford, Corpus Christi College
  MS 197. Ch. 4, n. 103
Oxford, Oriel College
  MS 46 ['Or']. Ch. 4, nn. 81, 304
Oxford, St John's College 17 + British
    Library, Cotton MS Nero C.vii, ff. 80–4.
    Ch. 4, nn. 81, 100, 102
Paris, Bibliothèque Nationale
  MS latina 943 (the 'Dunstan'/'Sherborne'
    Pontifical). Ch. 4, nn. 103, 130, 133,
    240
  MS latina 2718. Ch. 2, nn. 168, 170–1,
    188
  MS latina 2796. Ch. 2, n. 162
  MS latina 3182. Ch. 2, n. 192; ch. 6, n.
    10
  MS latina 3878 + Weimar, Hauptsarchiv,
    Depositum Hardenberg, frag. 9. Ch.
    2, nn. 125, 200
  MS latina 4280a. Ch. 2. n. 154
  MS latina 4403b. Ch. 2, n. 172

MS latina 4404. Ch. 2, nn. 174, 178,
  193–4
MS latina 4408. Ch. 2, n. 168
MS latina 4409. Ch. 2, nn. 162, 172,
  178; ch. 6, n. 194
MS latina 4416. Ch. 2, n. 168
MS latina 4417. Ch. 2, n. 193
MS latina 4418. Ch. 2, nn. 112, 146,
  168, 175, 178, 207
MS latina 4568. Ch. 2, n. 207
MS latina 4613. Ch. 2, nn. 201–2
MS latina 4626. Ch. 2, n. 160; ch. 6, n.
  194
MS latina 4627. Ch. 2, nn. 162, 168
MS latina 4628. Ch. 2, nn. 193–4
MS latina 4628a. Ch. 2, nn. 157, 192,
  194; ch. 4, nn. 17, 78; ch. 6, n. 194
MS latina 4629. Ch. 2, nn. 148, 174,
  193–4
MS latina 4632. Ch. 2, nn. 159, 193
MS latina 4634. Ch. 2, nn. 154, 190
MS latina 4635. Ch. 2, n. 203
MS latina 4636. Ch. 2, nn. 154, 190
MS latina 4637. Ch. 2, nn. 154, 190
MS latina 4638. Ch. 2, n. 155
MS latina 4758. Ch. 2, nn. 173, 189
MS latina 4759. Ch. 2, n. 189
MS latina 4759a. Ch. 2, n. 180
MS latina 4760. Ch. 2, n. 157; ch. 6, n.
  194
MS latina 4761/1+2. Ch. 2, n. 191
MS latina 4762. Ch. 2, n. 190
MS latina 4771. Ch. 5, nn. 637, 682
MS latina 4787. Ch. 2, n. 189
MS latina 4788. Ch. 2, nn. 145, 192, 194
MS latina 4789. Ch. 2, n. 180
MS latina 4995. Ch. 2, nn. 96, 192, 194;
  ch. 6, n. 194
MS latina 5095. Ch. 2, n. 190
MS latina 5577. Ch. 2, n. 185
MS latina 8801. Ch. 2, nn. 146, 180
MS latina 9643. Ch. 2, nn. 33, 144
MS latina 9653. Ch. 2, nn. 173, 178; ch.
  6, n. 194
MS latina 9654. Ch. 2, nn. 146, 163–4,
  178
MS latina 10575 (the 'Ecgberht'
  Pontifical). Ch. 4, nn. 103, 131–2
MS latina 10753. Ch. 2, nn. 162, 173,
  193
MS latina 10754. Ch. 2, nn. 160, 192,
  194
MS latina 10756. Ch. 2, n. 168
MS latina 10758. Ch. 2, nn. 156, 178,
  192, 194; ch. 4, nn. 17, 78; ch. 6, n.
  194

MS latina 12021. Ch. 2, n. 144
MS latina 12097. Ch. 2, n. 144
MS latina 12161. Ch. 2, nn. 50, 144, 344
MS latina 12205. Ch. 2, n. 171
MS latina 12475. Ch. 2, n. 144
MS latina 18237 (I–III). Ch. 2, nn. 145, 180; ch. 6, n. 194
MS latina 18238 (I/III–II). Ch. 2, nn. 145, 192
MS latina 18239. Ch. 2, n. 191
MS n.a. latina 204. Ch. 2, nn. 168, 171, 188, 193–4
Rochester DC, s.n. ('*Textus Roffensis*', ['H']). Ch. 2, nn. 320, 322, 348; ch. 3, n. 82; ch. 4, tables 4.1, 4.8, 4.9, nn. 264, 269–70, 272, 287, 314, 327–40, 359–60, 383–4; ch. 5, tables 5.1, 5.2, nn. 6, 20, 107, 109, 131, 133, 135–6, 142, 149, 152, 160, 162, 205, 208, 269–70, 274, 278, 418, 494–6, 539, 551, 563, 585, 590–1, 597, 619, 621, 634–5, 637, 642; ch. 6, n. 212
Rome, Biblioteca Vallicelliana
MS A.5. Ch. 2, n. 204
Rome, San Paolo fuori le mura, s.n. ('Bible of St Paul's without the Walls'). Ch. 3, n. 25
Rouen, Bibliothèque municipale
MS A.27 (368) (the 'Lanalet' Pontifical). Ch. 4, nn. 105, 130, 132–3
MS U.109 (1382). Ch. 4, table 4.4, nn. 204, 208, 234
MS Y.7 (369) (The 'Benedictional of Archbishop Robert'). Ch. 4, nn. 130, 132–3
St Gallen, Stiftsbibliothek
MS 222. Ch. 2, n. 185
MS 338. Ch. 2, n. 189
MS 675. Ch. 2, n. 185
MS 722. Ch. 2, nn. 172, 207–8
MS 727. Ch. 2, nn. 137, 153–4
MS 728. Ch. 2, n. 193
MS 729. Ch. 2, nn. 168, 173, 189
MS 730. Ch. 2, nn. 63, 144
MS 731 (the 'Wandalgarius' codex). Ch. 2, nn. 130, 173, 189
MS 733. Ch. 2, nn. 187–8
MS 1395. Ch. 2, nn. 144, 207
Sankt Paul im Lavanttal, Archiv des Benediktinerstiftes
MS 4/1 (St Paul-in- Kärnten MS xxv.4.8). Ch. 2, nn. 198, 202
St Petersburg, Publicnaja Biblioteka
MS Q.v.II. 11. Ch. 2, nn. 192, 194

Schaffhausen, Stadtbibliothek
MS Min. 75. Ch. 2, n. 157
Stuttgart, Württembergische Landesbibliothek
MS HB VI 112. Ch. 2, n. 190
MS iur. 4º 134. Ch. 2, nn. 205, 207
University of California, Los Angeles
MS 170/529. Ch. 4, n. 305
Utrecht, Bibliothek der Rijksuniversiteit
Script. Eccl. MS 484 (the 'Utrecht Psalter'). Ch. 2, n. 130
Valenciennes, Bibliothèque Municipale
MS 162. Ch. 2, n. 116
Vatican, Biblioteca Apostolica
Barberini MS latina 679. Ch. 2, n. 185
Chigi MS F.IV.75. Ch. 2, n. 201
MS Palatina latina 289. Ch. 2, n. 183
MS Palatina latina 582. Ch. 2, nn. 163–4, 178, 190
MS Palatina latina 583. Ch. 2, nn. 137, 153
MS Palatina latina 773. Ch. 2, n. 180
MS Palatina latina 973. Ch. 2, n. 154
Codex Reginensis latina 69. Ch. 2, n. 185
Codex Reginensis latina 263. Ch. 2, n. 203
Codex Reginensis latina 291. Ch. 2, n. 155
Codex Reginensis latina 520. Ch. 2, nn. 192, 194
Codex Reginensis latina 846. Ch. 2, nn. 168, 172, 178; ch. 6, n. 194
Codex Reginensis latina 852. Ch. 2, n. 168
Codex Reginensis latina 857. Ch. 2, nn. 168, 178, 188
Codex Reginensis latina 886. Ch. 2, nn. 33, 144
Codex Reginensis latina 946 ['Vr']. Ch. 4, table 4.1, nn. 353–6
Codex Reginensis latina 974. Ch. 2, nn. 153–4, 190
Codex Reginensis latina 991. Ch. 2, nn. 161, 168, 178, 195
Codex Reginensis latina 1023. Ch. 2, n. 154
Codex Reginensis latina 1024. Ch. 2, nn. 63, 144
Codex Reginensis latina 1050. Ch. 2, nn. 173, 178, 193; ch. 6, n. 194
Codex Reginensis latina 1128. Ch. 2, nn. 173, 178, 189; ch. 6, n. 194

Vatican, Biblioteca Apostolica (*cont.*)
　Codex Reginensis latina 1431. Ch. 2, n.
　　168
　MS Vaticana latina 1339. Ch. 2, n. 204
　MS Vaticana latina 3827. Ch. 2, n. 185
　MS Vaticana latina 4982. Ch. 2, n. 155
　MS Vaticana latina 5359. Ch. 2, n. 203
　MS Vaticana latina 5751. Ch. 2, n. 185
　MS Vaticana latina 5766. Ch. 2, nn. 33,
　　144
Vercelli, Biblioteca Capitolare Eusebiana
　MS XV. Ch. 2, n. 204
　MS CXVII (the 'Vercelli Book'). Ch. 6, n.
　　129
　MS CLXXIV. Ch. 2, n. 204
　MS CLXXXVIII. Ch. 2, n. 144
Verona, Biblioteca Capitolare
　MS XXXVIII (36). Ch. 2, nn. 144, 207
　MS LXII (60). Ch. 2, nn. 144, 207
Warsaw, Biblioteka Uniwersytecka
　MS 1. Ch. 2, nn. 168, 171–2
Wien, Österreichische Nationalbibliothek
　MS 406. Ch. 2, n. 206
　MS 2232. Ch. 2, n. 185

Wolfenbüttel, Herzog August Bibliothek
　MS Aug. 4⁰ 50.2. Ch. 2, nn. 192, 194
　MS Blankenberg 130. Ch. 2, nn.
　　201–2, 207, 292
　MS Gud. latina 299. Ch. 2, nn. 193–4
　MS Gud. latina 327. Ch. 2, n. 189
　MS Helmst. 254. Ch. 2, n. 186
　MS Helmst. 454. Ch. 2, n. 371
　MS Helmst. 496a. Ch. 2, n. 181
　MS Helmst. 513. Ch. 2, nn. 179, 203
　MS Helmst. 532 (III). Ch. 2, n. 207
　MS Weißenburg 97. Ch. 2, nn. 63, 172
Worcester, Cathedral Library
　MS Q. 5. Ch. 4, nn. 100, 102
Yale University (New Haven), Beinecke
　　Library MS 413.
　　Ch. 2, nn. 155, 164
York, Minster Library
　MS Add. 1 (the 'York Gospels'). Ch. 4,
　　table 4.1, nn. 95, 137–46; ch. 5, nn.
　　380, 613
Zürich, Staatsarchiv
　MS C VI 3. Ch. 2, n. 144.

II SOURCES

Sources are ordered by the first significant word(s) (other than definite or indefinite articles, numerals, first names, titles like 'Bishop', 'King', 'St', etc.) of the (short) title cited in the Notes; this is normally that which appears on the title page of the preferred edition, except that the names of authors (Einhard, William of Malmesbury) are usually Anglicized. For indexation of Biblical citations, see *Biblia Sacra*. Translations are into English unless otherwise specified.

Abbo of Fleury, 'Collectio Canonum', *PL* CXXXIX, cols 471–508. Ch. 6, nn. 145, 147–8

Abbo of Fleury, 'Liber Apologeticus', *PL* CXXXIX, cols 461–72. Ch. 6, n. 165

Abbo of Fleury, 'Passio S. Eadmundi', edited by M. Winterbottom, *Three Lives of English Saints* (Toronto Medieval Latin Texts, 1972), pp. 65–87: see Subsidiary Index (i).

Abbo von Saint-Germain des Près, 22 Predigten: kritische Ausgabe und Kommentar, edited by U. Önnerfors (Lateinische Sprache und Literatur des Mittelalters 16, Frankfurt, 1985). Ch. 4, tables 4.4, 4.5, n. 199; ch. 6, n. 177

Abingdon: see *Charters, Chronicon.*

Acta Sanctorum Ordinis Sancti Benedicti, edited by J. Mabillon (9 vols, Paris, 1668–1701). Ch. 2, n. 232

Acts and Monuments: see *Foxe*

Adalbéron de Laon, Poème au Roi Robert, edited and translated (French) by C. Carozzi (Classiques de l' histoire de France au Moyen Age 32, Paris, 1979). Ch. 6, nn. 159, 161–3

Adémar of Chabannes, Chronique, edited by J. Chavanon (Collection de textes pour servir à l' étude et l'enseignement de l'histoire, Paris, 1897). Ch. 6, n. 140

Adso, De Ortu et Tempore Antichristi, edited by D. Verhelst (CCCM XLV, 1976), pp. 1–30. Ch 4, table 4.4, n. 235; ch. 6, n. 128

'Ælfrici abbatis epistula ad monachos Egneshamnenses directa', edited by H. Nocent, *Corpus Consuetudinum*, ed. Hallinger, VII.3, pp. 149–85. Ch. 4, n. 220

Ælfric's Catholic Homilies, The Second Series, edited by M. Godden (EETS S.S. 5, Oxford, 1979). Ch. 2, n. 330; ch. 4, table 4.5; ch. 6, nn. 128, 156

Ælfric's Lives of Saints, edited and translated by W.W. Skeat (2 vols, EETS 94, 114, Oxford, 1890–1900, repr. 1966). Ch. 6, n. 158

Ælfric, 'On the Old and New Testament' and 'Epilogue', *The Old English Heptateuch*, ed. Crawford, pp. 1–75. Ch. 2, n. 326; ch. 6, nn. 158, 165

Ælfric: see also *Hirtenbriefe.*

Aeneid: see *Vergil.*

Æthelgifu: see *Will.*

Æthelweard: see *Chronicle.*

Agobard, 'De divinis sententiis contra iudicium Dei', edited by L. van Acker, *Agobardi Lugdunensis Opera Omnia* (CCSM LII, 1981), pp. 29–49. Ch. 2, nn. 99, 217; ch. 6, n. 31

Agobard of Lyons, Epistolae, edited by E. Dümmler (MGH, Epistolae Karolini Aevi III, Berlin, 1899), pp. 150–239. Ch. 2, nn. 99, 217; ch. 3, n. 25; ch. 6, n. 31

Alcuin, 'Enchiridion seu Expositio ... in Psalmos ... Graduales', *PL* C, cols 569–638. Ch. 6, n. 4

Alcuin, Epistolae, edited by E. Dümmler (MGH, Epistolae Karolini Aevi II, Berlin, 1895), pp. 1–493. Ch. 2, nn. 171, 370–3; ch. 3, n. 27; ch. 4, table 4.4; ch. 5, nn. 83–4, 195, 215–16; ch. 6, nn. 176–7

Alcuin, 'Liber de virtutibus et vitiis ad Widonem Comitem', *PL* CI, cols 613–38. Ch. 2, nn. 127, 151, 213; ch. 4, n. 41, ch. 5, nn. 531–6

Alfred the Great. Asser's Life of King Alfred and other contemporary sources, translated with introduction and notes by S. Keynes and M. Lapidge (London, 1983). Ch. 3, nn. 7, 12, 14, 28; ch. 4, n. 47; ch. 5, nn. 88, 93; ch. 6, n. 40

King Alfred's West Saxon Version of Gregory's Pastoral Care, edited and translated by H. Sweet (EETS 45, London, 1871). Ch. 2, n. 330; ch. 5, nn. 32, 34, 38–9, 63–5, 73, 108; ch. 6, nn. 18, 47–9, 51

King Alfred's Old English Version of Boethius De Consolatione Philosophiae, edited by W.J. Sedgefield (Oxford, 1899); translated *idem* (Oxford, 1900). Ch. 5, nn. 63, 73; ch. 6, nn. 19, 45, 158

King Alfred's Version of St Augustine's "Soliloquies", edited by T. Carnicelli (Cambridge, Ma, 1969). Ch. 5, n. 73; ch. 6, n. 46

Das altenglische Bußbuch (sog. Confessionale Pseudo-Egberti), edited by R. Spindler (Leipzig, 1934). Ch. 4, table 4.5, nn. 237–8

Die altenglische Version des Halitgarschen Bubuches (sogenannte Poenitentiale Pseudo-Ecgberti), edited by J. Raith (Grein-Wülker, Bibliothek der angelsächsischen Prosa XIII, 2nd edn, Darmstadt, 1964). Ch. 4, table 4.5, nn. 237–8; ch. 5, n. 379

Die alt- und mittelenglischen Apollonius-Bruchstücke, mit dem Text der Historia Apollonii nach der englischen Handschriftengruppe, edited by J. Raith (Munich, 1956). Ch. 4, nn. 181–2, 184

Amalarius, *De ecclesiasticis officiis* (= *Liber Officialis*), edited by J.M. Hanssens, *Amalarii Episcopi Opera Liturgica Omnia* (3 vols, Studi e Testi 138–40, Vatican, 1948–50) II. Ch. 4, table 4.4, n. 234

Amalarius, *Eclogae de Ordine Romano*, ed. Hanssens, *Amalarii Opera Liturgica* III, pp. 225–65. Ch. 4, table 4.4, n. 221

Ancient Laws and Institutes of England, edited by B. Thorpe (folio edition, London, 1840); see also 'Excerptiones Egberti', 'Penitential of (pseudo-) Theodore'. Ch. 1, n. 103; ch. 4, tables 4.2, 4.4, 4.5, nn. 148, 206, 213–14, 231, 236; ch. 5, nn. 7, 20, 129, 262, 463, 502, 505, 522, 547, 550, 571, 579, 596, 604

An Ancient Manuscript of the Eighth or Ninth Century formerly belonging to St Mary's Abbey or Nunnaminster, Winchester, edited by W. de Gray Birch (Hampshire Record Society 2, 1889). Ch. 4, n. 13

Andreas and the Fates of the Apostles, edited by K.R. Brooks (Oxford, 1961). ch. 4, n. 202

Anglo-Saxon Charters, edited and translated by A.J. Robertson (Cambridge, 2nd edn, 1956); see also Subsidiary Indices (i), (ii). Ch. 3, nn. 110, 114–15, 122; ch. 4, nn. 65, 99, 104, 121; ch. 5, n. 255

Anglo-Saxon Charters. An Annotated List and Bibliography, edited by P.H. Sawyer (Royal Historical Society Handbooks, London, 1968); revised edition by S. Kelly and S. Keynes (Royal Historical Society, forthcoming); see Subsidiary Indices (i), (ii).

'Anglo-Saxon Chronicle': these sources are cited by *corrected* year (supplied from the translation in *EHD I, II*) followed by appropriate text *siglum/a* (so '1066D' for the nearest to a contemporary English account of the Battle of Hastings); and, unless otherwise stated, from *Two of the Saxon Chronicles Parallel*, edited by J. Earle and C. Plummer (2 vols, Oxford, 1892–9): see also Subsidiary Index (i). Ch. 2, n. 326; ch. 3, nn. 41, 48–9, 51–2, 59–60, 63–5, 77, 90, 109; ch. 4, nn. 10, 31, 34, 41, 43, 105, 124–5; ch. 5, nn. 96, 384, 399, 622; ch. 6, table 6.2, nn. 72, 86, 88, 90, 110, 119, 133, 139

The Anglo-Saxon Chronicle MS A, edited by J. Bately (The Anglo-Saxon Chronicle, a Collaborative Edition 3, general editors D. Dumville and S. Keynes, Cambridge, 1986). Ch. 4, nn. 3, 5–7, 18, 24, 31–2, 34, 45; ch. 5, n. 199

The Anglo-Saxon Chronicle MS D, edited by G.C. Cubbin (Anglo-Saxon Chronicle 6, general editors D. Dumville and S. Keynes, Cambridge, 1996). Ch. 3, n. 49

Anglo-Saxon Ely. Records of Ely Abbey and its benefactors in the tenth and eleventh centuries, edited and translated by S. Keynes and A. Kennedy (forthcoming); see also Subsidary Index (i). **Ch. 3, nn. 126–7, 131, 139, 150; ch. 4, nn. 125, 127; ch. 6, n. 72**

The Anglo-Saxon Minor Poems, edited by E.V.K. Dobbie (The Anglo-Saxon Poetic Records 6, New York, 1942). **Ch. 4, nn. 48, 69–71, 76, 118, 121, 166, 179**

Two Anglo-Saxon Pontificals (the Egbert and Sidney Sussex Pontificals), edited by H.M.J. Banting (Henry Bradshaw Society CIV, London, 1989 for 1985–7). **Ch. 4, nn. 131–2, 134, 200; ch. 5, n. 553; ch. 6, n. 115**

Anglo-Saxon Wills, edited and translated by D. Whitelock (Cambridge, 1930); see also Subsidiary Indices (i) and (ii). **Ch. 5, n. 372**

Anglo-Saxon Writs, edited and translated by F. Harmer (2nd edn, Stamford, 1989); see also Subsidiary Indices (i) and (ii). **Ch. 3, nn. 123, 144–6; ch. 5, n. 395; ch. 6, n. 60**

Annales Fuldenses, edited by F. Kurze (MGH, Scriptores rerum Germanicarum in usum scholarum, 1891). **Ch. 5, n. 100; ch. 6, n. 111**

Annales Laureshamenses, edited by G.H. Pertz (MGH, Scriptores in folio I, 1826), pp. 19–39. **Ch. 2, n. 86.**

Annales Regni Francorum, edited by F. Kurze (MGH, Scriptores rerum Germanicarum in usum scholarum, 1895). **Ch. 2, n. 230; ch. 6, n. 111**

Annales de Saint-Bertin, edited by F. Grat *et al.* (Société de l' histoire de France, Paris, 1964). **Ch. 2, n. 102; ch. 5, n. 100; ch. 6, n. 111**

'Annales de Wintonia', in *Annales Monastici*, edited by H.R. Luard (5 vols, RS 36, 1864–9) II, pp. 1–125: see also Susidiary Index (i). **Ch. 3, n. 92**

The Annals of St Neots with Vita Prima Sancti Neoti, edited by D. Dumville and M. Lapidge, (The Anglo-Saxon Chronicle, a Collaborative Edition 17, general editors D. Dumville and S. Keynes, Cambridge, 1985). **Ch. 3, nn. 9, 11, 89**

Ansegisus: see *Kapitulariensammlung.*

Antiphonaire monastique de Worcester, edited by A. Mocquereau (Paléographie musicale. Les Principaux manuscrits de Chant XII nos. 104–18, Paris, 1922–5). **Ch. 4, n. 84**

Apollonius: see *Alt- und mittelenglischen, Old English.*

'Appendix Eclogae' and 'Nomos Mosaïkos', in L. Burgmann and Sp. Troianos (editors), *Fontes Minores iuris Byzantini* III (general editor D. Simon, Frankfurt, 1979), pp. 24–167. **Ch. 6, n. 8**

Arbeo, Vita et Passio S. Haimhrammi Martyris, edited and translated (German) by B. Bischoff (Munich, 1953). **Ch. 2, n. 341**

ARCHAIONOMIA sive de priscis anglorum legibus libri, sermone Anglico, vetustate antiquissimo, aliquot abhinc seculis conscripti, atque nunc demum, magno iurisperitorum, et amantium antiquitatis omnium commodo e tenebris in lucem vocati, Gulielmo Lambardo interprete (London, 1568); reprinted with *Leges Henrici Primi* (edited by R. Twysden) and other Anglo-Norman texts, by A. Whelock (Cambridge, 1644). **Ch. 1, n. 102; ch. 4, nn. 97, 265, 342–3, 373–84; ch. 5, nn. 7, 20, 135, 139, 262, 412, 522**

Asser's Life of King Alfred, edited by W.H. Stevenson (2nd edn, with introduction by D. Whitelock, Oxford, 1959). **Ch. 3, nn. 5, 7–8, 12, 14–15, 72; ch. 5, n. 96**

Astronomer: see *Thegan.*

Atto of Vercelli, *De Pressuris Ecclesiasticis*, edited by J. Bauer, *Die Schrift 'De Pressuris Ecclesiasticis' des Bischofs Atto von Vercelli* (Tübingen, 1975). **Ch. 4, table 4.4, n. 232**

Bald's Leechbook (BM, Royal Manuscript 12.D.xvii), edited by C.E. Wright and R. Quirk (EEMSF 5, 1955). **Ch. 4, n. 62**

Bedae Venerabilis, Expositio Actuum Apostolorum et Retractatio, edited by M.L.W. Laistner (Cambridge, Ma, 1933; repr. Bedae Venerabilis Opera II, Opera Exegetica, CCSL CXXI ii 4, 1983). **Ch. 6, nn. 3–4**

Bedae Venerabilis, De Templo Libri II, edited by D. Hurst (Bedae Venerabilis Opera II, Opera Exegetica, CCSL CXIXA ii 2A, 1969). **Ch. 6, n. 4**

Bedae Venerabilis in Marci Evangelium Expositio, edited by D. Hurst (Bedae Venerabilis Opera II, Opera Exegetica, CCSL CXX ii 3, 1960). **Ch. 4, n. 84**

Bede's Ecclesiastical History of the English People, edited and translated by B. Colgrave and R.A.B. Mynors (Oxford Medieval Texts, Oxford, 1969). **Ch. 2, n. 1; ch. 3, nn. 29, 41; ch. 4, table 4.4, nn. 40, 70, 77; ch. 6, nn. 96, 178**

Bede, 'Historia Abbatum', *Venerabilis Baedae Opera*, ed. Plummer, I, pp. 364–87. **Ch. 2, n. 2**

Venerabilis Baedae Opera Historica, edited by C. Plummer (2 vols, Oxford, 1896): see Bede, *Bede's Ecclesiastical History*.

Bede: see also Epistola, *Historiae*, *Old English*.

S. Benedict: see *Miraculis*.

Benedicti Capitularia, edited by G.H. Pertz (MGH, Leges in folio II(ii), 1837), pp. 17–158. **Ch. 2, nn. 152, 154, 190; ch. 6, nn. 9, 21**

The Benedictional of Archbishop Robert, edited by H.A. Wilson (Henry Bradshaw Society XXIV, London, 1903). **Ch. 4, nn. 130, 132–3; ch. 6, n. 117**

The Benedictine Office, edited by J.M. Ure (Edinburgh University Publications in Language and Literature 11, 1957). **Ch. 4, table 4.3, nn. 166, 174, 179**

Beowulf, edited by F. Klaeber (3rd edn, Lexington, Ma, 1950). **Ch. 2, n. 360**

Biblia Sacra iuxta Vulgatam Versionem, edited by R. Weber *et al.* (2 vols, Stuttgart, 1969). **Ch. 2, n. 219; ch. 3, nn. 15–16, 23; ch. 5, nn. 38, 173; ch. 6, nn. 3, 11, 15–18, 20–2, 28, 42, 135**

Bibliothèque Nationale. Catalogue Générale des Manuscrits Latins, edited by Ph. Lauer, M. Thomas, D. Bloch, J. Sclaver *et al.* (7 vols + tables [to no. 3835], Paris, 1939–91). **Ch. 2, n. 170; ch. 6, n. 10**

William Blackstone, Commentaries on the Laws of England. A Facsimile of the First Edition of 1765–9, edited by T. Katz *et al.* (4 vols, Chicago, 1979). **Ch. 1, nn. 5–10, 17**

Boethius, The Consolation of Philosophy, edited and translated by S.J. Tester (Loeb series, 2nd edn, 1973). **Ch. 6, n. 19**

Die Briefe des heiligen Bonifatius und Lullus, edited by M. Tangl (MGH, Epistolae Selectae in usum scholarum I, Berlin, 1916). **Ch. 2, n. 319**

Burchard, 'Decretorum Libri XX', *PL* CXL, cols 537–1058. **Ch. 4, table 4.4; ch. 6, nn. 146–7**

Burchard, 'Lex Familiae Wormatiensis Ecclesiae', ed. Weiland, *Constitutiones*, pp. 639–44. **Ch. 6, n. 148**

The Burgundian Code, translated by K.F. Drew (Philadelphia, 1949). **Ch. 2, n. 45**

Burton Abbey: see *Charters*.

Die Bußordnungen der abendländischen Kirche, edited by H. Wasserschleben (Halle, 1851). **Ch. 4, table 4.4, n. 206; ch. 6, n. 142**

Byrhtferth of Ramsey, The Lives of Oswald and Ecgwine, edited and translated by M. Lapidge (Oxford Medieval Texts, Oxford, forthcoming): see also Subsidiary Index (i). **Ch. 3, nn. 39, 149**

Caesar, Gallic War, edited and translated by H.J. Edwards (Loeb series, 1917). **Ch. 1, n. 45**

Caesarius of Arles, Sermones, edited by G. Morin (2 vols, CCSL CIII–CIV, 1953). **Ch. 5, n. 196**

Canones Wallici (= *Excerpta de libris Francorum et Romanorum*), *Irish Penitentials*, ed. Bieler, pp. 136–49. **Ch. 2, n. 285; ch. 4, table 4.4**

Capitula Episcoporum I, edited by P. Brommer (MGH, 1984); II, edited by R. Pokorny and M. Stratmann (MGH, 1995): see Ghaerbald, Hinkmar, Radulf, Theodulf.

Capitulare de Villis. Cod. Guelf. 254 Helmst. der Herzog August Bibliothek Wolfenbüttel, edited by C-R. Brühl (Dokumente der deutschen Geschichte in Faksimiles I(1), Stuttgart, 1971). **Ch. 2, n. 186**

Capitularia Regum Francorum, edited by A. Boretius and V. Krause (2 vols, MGH, Legum Sectio II, 1883–97): see also Subsidiary Index (iv). **Ch. 2, nn. 89, 96**

Cartulaire de l'Abbaye de Gorze, edited by A. d' Herbomez (Mettensia II, 1898). **Ch. 2, n. 228**

Cartulaire de l' abbaye de Redon, edited by A. de Courson (Collection de Documents inédits sur l' Histoire de France, Paris, 1863). **Ch. nn. 227, 229, 272, 282–3, 286**

Two Cartularies of the Benedictine Abbeys of Muchelney and Athelney, edited by E.H. Bates, Somerset Record Society 14, 1899): see Subsidiary Indices (i), (ii).

Cartularium Monasterii de Rameseia, edited by W.H. Hart and P.A. Lyons (3 vols, RS 79, 1884–93): see Subsidiary Index (i).

Cartularium Saxonicum, edited by W. de Gray Birch (3+ vols, London, 1885–99): see Subsidiary Indices (i), (ii).

Cassiodorus Senator, Variae, edited by T. Mommsen (MGH, Auctores Antiquissimi XII, Berlin, 1894). Ch. 2, n. 47

Cassiodorus: Variae, translated by S.J.B. Barnish (Translated Texts for Historians 12, Liverpool, 1992). Ch. 2, n. 47

Catalogue: see *Bibliothèque Nationale*.

Catalogus Librorum Manuscriptorum Bibliothecae Wigorniensis, made by Patrick Young, librarian to James I, edited by I. Atkins and N.R. Ker (Cambridge, 1944). Ch. 4, n. 89

Charlemagne. Translated Sources, edited by P.D. King (Kendal, 1987). Ch. 2, n. 86

Chartae Latinae Antiquiores, general editors A. Brückner, R. Marichal *et al.* (46 vols, Zürich, 1954–95). Ch. 2, n. 38

Charters of Abingdon Abbey, edited by S.E. Kelly (2 vols, Anglo-Saxon Charters VII, British Academy, Oxford, 1999): see also Subsidiary Index (i). Ch. 3, n. 104

Charters of Burton Abbey, edited by P.H. Sawyer (Anglo-Saxon Charters II, British Academy, Oxford, 1979): see also Subsidiary Index (i). Ch. 6, n. 81

Charters of Rochester, edited by A. Campbell (Anglo-Saxon Charters I, British Academy, Oxford, 1973): see also Subsidiary Index (i). Ch. 4, n. 328

Charters of Selsey, edited by S.E. Kelly (Anglo-Saxon Charters VI, British Academy, Oxford, 1997): see Subsidiary Index (i).

Charters of Shaftesbury Abbey, edited by S.E. Kelly (Anglo-Saxon Charters V, British Academy, Oxford, 1996): see also Subsidiary Index (i). Ch. 5, n. 373

Charters of Sherborne Abbey, edited by M.A. O'Donovan (Anglo-Saxon Charters III, British Academy, Oxford, 1988): see Subsidiary Index (i)

Charters: see also *Select*.

'Les Chartes de l' Abbaye de Nouaillé', edited by P. de Monsabert, *Archives Historiques de Poitou* xlix (1936), pp. 1–401. Ch. 2, n. 228

'Chronica Pontificum Ecclesiae Eboracensis', *Historians of the Church of York*, ed. Raine, II, pp. 312–445. Ch. 3, n. 52

The Chronicle of Æthelweard, edited and translated by A. Campbell (Nelson's Medieval Texts, Edinburgh, 1962). Ch. 3, n. 82; ch. 4, nn. 364, 366

The Chronicle of John of Worcester, edited and translated by R.R. Darlington, J. Bray and P. McGurk (3 vols, Oxford Medieval Texts, Oxford, 1995-): see also Subsidiary Index (i). Ch. 3, nn. 50, 64, 72–6; ch. 5, nn. 224, 398, 622; ch. 6, table 6.2

Chronicle of Robert of Torigny, Chronicles IV, ed. Howlett. Ch. 5, n. 622

Chronicle: see also 'Anglo-Saxon', *Waltham*.

Chronicles of the reigns of Stephen, Henry II and Richard I, edited by R. Howlett (4 vols, RS 82, 1884–9): see *Chronicle of Robert, Historia Ricardi*.

Chronicon Abbatiae de Evesham, edited by W.D. Macray (RS 29, 1863): see also Subsidiary Index (i). Ch. 3, n. 151

Chronicon Abbatiae Rameseiensis, edited by W.D. Macray (RS 83, 1886): see also Subsidiary Index (i). Ch. 3, nn. 89, 141–2, 144

Chronicon Monasterii de Abingdon, edited by J. Stevenson (2 vols, RS 2, 1858): see Subsidiary Indices (i), (ii).

The Claudius Pontificals, edited by D.H. Turner (Henry Bradshaw Society XCVII, London, 1971 (for 1964)). Ch. 4, nn. 115–17, 121, 130–4; ch. 5, n. 553

Codex Diplomaticus Aevi Saxonici, edited by J.M. Kemble (6 vols, London, 1839–48): see Subsidiary Indices (i), (ii).

Codice Diplomatico Longobardo I–II, edited by L. Schiaparelli (Fonti per la storia dell' Italia, Rome, 1929–33). Ch. 2, nn. 295–7, 306

Codice Diplomatico Longobardo III(1), IV (1), edited by C-R. Brühl (Fonti per la Storia dell' Italia, Rome, 1973, 1981). Ch. 2, nn. 292–3, 295–6, 306

Codice Diplomatico Longobardo V, edited by H. Zielinski (Fonti per la storia dell' Italia, Rome, 1986). **Ch. 2, nn. 295–6, 302**

Codices Latini Antiquiores, edited by E.A. Lowe (11 vols + Supplement, Oxford, 1934–71). **Ch. 2, nn. 33, 37, 50, 63, 143–4, 172, 179, 207, 344**

[Codicis] Theodosiani Libri XVI cum Constitutionibus Sirmondianis, et Leges Novellae ad Theodosianum Pertinentes, edited by T. Mommsen and P.M. Meyer (2 vols in 3, 3rd edn, Berlin, 1962). **Ch. 2, nn. 32–3, 51–2, 143–4; ch. 5, n. 94**

Collatio: see *Mosaicarum*.

Collectio Canonum Hibernensis: see *Irische Kanonensammlung*.

Collectio Capitularium Ansegisi: see *Kapitulariensammlung*.

A Collection of the Laws and Canons of the Church of England ..., translated by J. Johnson (London, 1720; new edn, 2 vols, Library of Anglo-Catholic Theology, Oxford, 1850). **Ch. 4, nn. 204, 213**

Concilia Aevi Karolini (MGH, Legum Sectio III, 1906 - [series still in progress]). **Ch. 4, table 4.4, n. 206; ch. 6, n. 50**

Concilia, Decreta, Leges, Constitutiones in re Ecclesiarum Orbis Britanniae, edited by Sir Henry Spelman (London, 1639). **Ch. 4, nn. 214–15; ch. 5, n. 604**

Concilia Galliae, 511–695, edited by C. de Clercq (CCSL CXLVIIIA, 1963). **Ch. 2, nn. 346–7**

Concilia Magnae Britanniae et Hiberniae AD 446–1717, edited by D. Wilkins (4 vols, London, 1737). **Ch. 4, n. 236**

Concilios Visigóticos e Hispano-romanos, edited by J. Vives (España cristiana I, Madrid/Barcelona, 1963). **Ch. 4, table 4.4, n. 206**

Constitutiones et Acta Publica Imperatorum et Regum I, edited by L. Weiland (MGH, Legum Sectio IV, 1893). **Ch. 7, n. 6**

'"Constitutions" of Archbishop Oda', *Councils and Synods*, ed. Whitelock *et al.*, I, pp. 67–74. **Ch. 2, n. 371; ch. 5, nn. 195, 213–14, 216**

The Copenhagen Wulfstan Collection, edited by J.E. Cross and J. Morrish Tunberg (EEMSF XXV, 1993). **Ch. 4, nn. 108, 155, 162, 233**

Corpus Consuetudinum Monasticarum, edited by K. Hallinger (13–14 vols, series in progress, Siegburg, 1963-): see 'Ælfrici epistula'.

Corpus Iuris Civilis, edited by T. Mommsen *et al.* (3 vols: I, *Institutiones, Digesta*; II, *Codex Iustinianus*; III, *Novellae*; 14th edn, Berlin, 1967); *Digest* repr. and translated by A. Watson (4 vols, Philadelphia, 1985); among innumerable translations of *Institutes*, the latest is by J.A.C. Thomas (Amsterdam, 1975). **Ch. 2, nn. 31, 144, 172, 207; ch. 3, nn. 47, 86; ch. 5, n. 68**

Councils and Ecclesiastical Documents relating to Great Britain and Ireland, edited by A.W. Haddan and W. Stubbs, (3 vols, Oxford, 1869–78, repr., 1964). **Ch. 4, table 4.4, n. 206; ch. 5, n. 449; ch. 6, n. 96**

Councils & Synods with Other Documents relating to the English Church. I, A.D. 871–1204, edited by D. Whitelock *et al.* (2 vols, Oxford, 1981). **Ch. 2, n. 371; ch. 3, nn. 44, 70; ch. 4, nn. 47, 367, 370; ch. 5, nn. 35, 338, 343, 363, 371, 392–3, 400, 489, 554, 570, 579, 584, 604, 606, 618, 621; ch. 6, nn. 40, 52, 85, 141, 144**

The Crawford Collection of Early Charters and Documents, edited by A.S. Napier and W.H. Stevenson (Oxford, 1895): see Subsidiary Indices (i), (ii).

S. Cuthberht: see 'Miraculis'

Decretales pseudo-isidorianae et Capitula Angrilamni, edited by P. Hinschius (Leipzig, 1863). **Ch. 4, table 4.4, n. 206; ch. 5, n. 94; ch. 6, nn. 29, 213**

Defensor, Liber Scintillarum, edited by H. Rochais (CCSL CXVII i, 1957), pp. 1–308. **Ch. 2, n. 187; ch. 4, table 4.4, n. 235**

Diplomata of Arnolf, Charlemagne, Lothar, Louis the German, etc.: see *Urkunden*.

Diplomata of Charles the Bald, Eudes, Louis II, etc.: see *Recueil*.

I Diplomi di Lodovico II: see *Urkunden Ludwigs II*.

Domesday Book, edited by A. Farley (London, 1783); the text is cited by its MS folio nos and cols; but also by the section nos of the county-by-county Phillimore edition (general editor, John Morris, Chichester, 1975–86): see also Subsidiary Index (i). **Ch. 1, n. 15; ch. 3, nn. 102, 142; ch. 5, nn. 484, 647, 685; ch. 6, nn. 63, 95**

'Dominic of Evesham, "Vita S. Ecgwini Episcopi et Confessoris"', edited by M. Lapidge, *Analecta Bollandiana* 96 (1978), pp. 65–104: see also Subsidiary Index (i). **Ch. 3, n. 151**

Ducange, Glossarium mediae et infimae Latinitatis, edited by L. Favre (10 vols, Paris, 1883–7). **Ch. 4, n. 40**

S. Dunstan: see 'Vita'.

The Durham Collectar, edited by A. Correa (Henry Bradshaw Society CVII, London, 1992). **Ch. 5, n. 497**

The Durham Ritual, edited by T.J. Brown (EEMSF XVI, 1969). **Ch. 5, n. 497; ch. 6, table 6.2, n. 66**

Eadmer, Historia Novorum in Anglia, edited by M. Rule (RS 81, 1884). **Ch. 3, nn. 69, 71; ch. 5, n. 622**

Ecclesiae Occidentalis Monumenta Iuris Antiquissima, edited by C.H. Turner and E. Schwartz (2 vols, Oxford, 1899–1939). **Ch. 4, table 4.4, n. 206**

The Ecclesiastical History of Ordericus Vitalis, edited and translated by M. Chibnall (6 vols, Oxford Medieval Texts, Oxford, 1969–80). **Ch. 3, nn. 70, 76; ch. 5, n. 622**

Ecloga Leonis et Constantini cum Appendice, edited by A.G. Montferratus (Athens, 1889), translated by E.H. Freshfield, *A Manual of Roman Law: The Ecloga.* (Cambridge, 1926). **Ch. 2, n. 31; ch. 6, n. 8**

'Edictum Theodorici Regis', edited by J. Baviera, in S. Riccobono *et al.* (editors), *Fontes Iuris Romani Anteiustiniani* (3 vols, 2nd edn, Florence, 1968–9) II, pp. 683–710. **Ch. 2, n. 47**

S. Edith: see 'Vita'.

Edward King and Martyr, edited by C. Fell (Leeds Texts and Monographs n.s. 3, Leeds 1971). **Ch. 5, n. 373**

Einhard, Vita Karoli Magni, edited by O. Holder-Egger (MGH, Scriptores rerum Germanicarum in usum scholarum, 6th edn, 1911). **Ch. 2, nn. 87, 104, 157; ch. 3, n. 3; ch. 6, n. 107**

An Eleventh-Century Anglo-Saxon Illustrated Miscellany: BL Cotton Tiberius B.v, Part I, edited by P. McGurk (EEMSF XXI, 1983). **Ch. 4, nn. 23, 34, 117, 337**

Encomium Emmae Reginae, edited and translated by A. Campbell (Camden Society, 3rd series LXXII, London 1949; repr. with supplementary introduction by S. Keynes, Camden Classic reprints 4, Cambridge 1998). **Ch. 3, n. 40**

English Historical Documents, Vol. I, c. 550–1042, edited and translated by D. Whitelock (2nd edn, London, 1979). **Ch. 3, nn. 37, 48, 90, 95; ch. 4, nn. 10, 41; ch. 5, nn. 20, 100, 132, 149, 202, 227, 260, 274, 314, 338, 363, 462, 502, 506, 510, 554, 580–1, 604; ch. 6, table 6.2, n. 88**

English Historical Documents, Vol. II, 1042–1189, edited and translated by D.C. Douglas (2nd edn, London, 1980). **Ch. 5, nn. 559, 634**

English Lawsuits from William I to Richard I, edited by R.C. van Caenegem (2 vols, Selden Society 106–7, London, 1990–1). **Ch. 3, n. 150; ch. 4, n. 263; ch. 5, n. 486**

Epistola Bede ad Ecgbertum Episcopum, *Venerabilis Baedae Opera*, ed. Plummer, I, pp. 405–23. **Ch. 2, n. 329**

Epistolae aevi Merovingici collectae, edited by W. Gundlach, (MGH, Epistolae Merovingici et Karolini Aevi I, Berlin, 1892). **Ch. 2, n. 149**

Ernulf, 'De Incestis Coniugiis', PL CLXIII, cols 1457–74. **Ch. 6, nn. 221–2**

L' Estoire des Engleis by Geffrei Gaimar, edited by A. Bell (Anglo-Norman Texts xiv–xvi, Oxford, 1960): see also Subsidiary Index (i). **Ch. 3, nn. 90–1**

Lestorie des Engles by Geffrei Gaimar, edited and translated by T.D. Hardy and C.T. Martin (2 vols, RS 91, 1888–9). **Ch. 3, n. 91**

Evesham: see *Chronicon*.

'Excerptiones Egberti, Eboracensis Archiepiscopi, e dictis et canonibus sanctorum patrum concinnatae', *Ancient Laws*, ed. Thorpe, pp. 326–41; or Aronstam, 'Latin Tradition' (*III MODERN COMMENTARY s.n.*), pp. 54–128. **Ch. 4, tables 4.1, 4.2, 4.4, nn. 159, 204, 206, 213–17, 229–30; ch. 5, n. 378; ch. 6, nn. 141, 147**

Facsimiles of Ancient Charters in the British Museum, edited by E.A. Bond (4 vols, London, 1873–8): see also Subsidiary Index (ii). **Ch. 3, n. 116**

Facsimiles of Anglo-Saxon Manuscripts, edited by W.B. Sanders (3 vols, Ordnance Survey, Southampton, 1878–84): see also Subsidiary Index (ii). **Ch. 3, n. 97**

Facsimiles of English Royal Writs to A.D. 1100, presented to V.H. Galbraith, edited by T.A.M. Bishop and P. Chaplais (Oxford, 1957). **Ch. 3, n. 97; ch. 5, n. 616**

Fleury: see *Recueil*.

Folcwin, Gesta abbatum S. Bertini Sithensium, edited by O. Holder-Egger (MGH Scriptores in folio XIII, 1881), pp. 600–73. **Ch. 5, n. 202**

Fontes Minores iuris Byzantini: see 'Appendix Eclogae'.

Formulae Merowingici et Karolini Aevi, edited by K. Zeumer (MGH, Legum Sectio V, 1886). **Ch. 2, nn. 39, 84, 170, 172, 242–4, 258, 263, 265, 267, 270, 274, 303, 309–10**

Sir John Fortescue, In Praise of the Laws of England, edited by S. Lockwood, *Fortescue, On the Laws and Governance of England* (Cambridge Texts in the History of Political Thought, general editors R. Geuss and Q. Skinner, Cambridge, 1997). **Ch. 1, n. 18**

The Fourth Book of the Chronicle of Fredegar with its continuations, edited and translated by J.M. Wallace-Hadrill (Nelson's Medieval Classics, Edinburgh, 1960). **Ch. 2, n. 346**

R. Fowler (editor), 'A Late Old English Handbook for the Use of a Confessor', *Anglia* LXXXIII (1965), pp. 1–34. **Ch. 4, tables 4.3, 4.4, n. 179; ch. 5, table 5.4, nn. 407, 425**

John Foxe, Acts and Monuments, 4th edition revised and corrected by J. Pratt (4 vols, London, 1843). **Ch. 1, n. 17**

Freising: see *Traditionen*.

Frithegod, Breviloquium vitae beati Wilfredi; Wulfstan Cantor Narratio metrica de Sancto Swithuno, edited by A. Campbell (Zürich, 1950). **Ch. 3, n. 29; ch. 6, table 6.2**

Gaimar: see *L' Estoire, Lestorie*.

Geoffrey of Monmouth: see *Historia Regum*.

Germania: see *Tacitus*.

Die Gesetze der Angelsachsen, edited and translated (German) by F. Liebermann (3 vols: I, *Text und Übersetzung*; IIi, *Wörterbuch*; IIii, *Sachglossar*; III, *Einleitung . . . Erklärungen*; Halle, 1903, 1906/12, 1916; repr. Aalen, 1960); see also Subsidiary Index (iii). **Ch. 1, nn. 2, 96, 99, 101, 106–7, 109–10, 112; ch. 3, nn. 10, 13, 69, 88; ch. 4, nn. 1–2, 38, 41, 44, 82, 96, 109, 111, 114, 147, 165, 193, 196, 224, 241, 258, 261, 264, 285, 288–9, 298, 311, 327, 338, 341, 351–3, 357, 359, 361, 375, 377, 379; ch. 5, nn. 3–4, 7, 9, 13, 15, 18, 20, 23, 47, 59, 63, 73–4, 76, 85, 90, 99, 101, 107, 129, 135–6, 142, 149, 160, 179, 195, 213, 215, 218, 221, 227, 229, 248, 262, 264, 268–9, 274, 278, 289, 291, 310, 312, 318–19, 326–7, 341, 346, 358, 360–1, 404, 410, 412, 414, 416, 420, 438, 459, 461, 463, 469–70, 472, 474, 476, 485, 494, 497, 501, 503, 505, 507, 521–2, 524, 527, 539, 541, 543, 548–9, 555, 557, 563, 569, 571, 579, 584, 597, 604, 606, 620, 631, 634, 636–9, 644, 652, 656, 659, 661, 663, 665–6, 668, 674, 680–1, 687, 690; ch. 6, nn. 11, 24, 28, 39, 41, 72, 79, 85, 88, 97, 118, 232**

Die Gesetze der Angelsachsen, edited by R. Schmid (2nd edn, Leipzig, 1858) (1st edn, 1832). **Ch. 1, n. 104; ch. 4, n. 298; ch. 5, nn. 7, 9, 20, 23, 129, 262, 461, 505, 515, 522, 547, 571, 579, 604**

Die Gesetze des Karolingerreiches 714–911. III: Sachsen, Thüringer, Chamaven und Friesen, edited by K.A. Eckhardt (2nd edn, Germanenrechte, Göttingen, 1953). **Ch. 2, nn. 90, 318; ch. 5, nn. 82, 85**

Die Gesetze der Langobarden/Leges Langobardorum 643–866, edited and translated (German) by F. Beyerle (2nd edn [Latin only], Germanenrechte n.f. 3, Witzenhausen, 1962). **Ch. 2, n. 21**

The Gesta Guillelmi of William of Poitiers, edited and translated by R.H.C. Davis and Marjorie Chibnall (Oxford Medieval Texts, Oxford, 1998). **Ch. 3, nn. 41, 46, 76; ch. 5, n. 615**

Gesta Pontificum Cameracensium, edited by L.C. Bethmann (MGH Scriptores in folio VII, 1846), pp. 393–487. **Ch. 6, nn. 160, 162**

Ghaerbald von Lüttich, 'Erstes Kapitular', *Capitula Episcoporum* I, ed. Brommer, pp. 3–21. **Ch. 4, table 4.4, nn. 209, 215, 217; ch. 5, n. 378**

Rodulfus Glaber, The Five Books of the Histories, edited by J. France (with N. Bulst and P. Reynolds, Oxford Medieval Texts, Oxford, 1989). **Ch. 6, n. 140**

Glanvill: see *Treatise*.

Gorze: see *Cartulaire*.

Goscelin: see 'Translatio', 'Vita Mildrethae'.

Grégoire le Grand, Règle Pastorale, edited and translated (French) by B. Judic, F. Rommel and C. Morel (2 vols, Sources Chrétiennes 381, Paris, 1992). **Ch. 5, n. 38; ch. 6, nn. 48–9**

Gregory the Great: see also *Bischof Wærferths*.

Gregory of Tours, Decem Libri Historiarum, edited by B. Krusch and W. Levison (MGH, Scriptores rerum Merovingicarum I, 2nd edn, 1952). **Ch. 3, n. 3**

Guildhall: see *Munimenta*.

Sir Matthew Hale, The History of the Common Law of England, edited with an introduction by C.M. Gray (Chicago, 1971). **Ch. 1, nn. 11–13**

Die Heiligen Englands, edited by F. Liebermann (Hannover, 1889). **Ch. 4, table 4.3, nn. 166, 176, 188**

Heming, Chartularium ecclesiae Wigorniensis, edited by T. Hearne (Oxford, 1723): see Subsidiary Index (i).

Heinrici II et Arduini Diplomata, edited by H. Breßlau *et al.* (MGH, Diplomata Regum et Imperatorum Germaniae III, 1900–3). **Ch. 3, n. 113**

Henry I: see *Leges*.

Henry ... of Huntingdon, Historia Anglorum, edited and translated by D. Greenway (Oxford Medieval Texts, Oxford, 1996). **Ch. 3, nn. 77, 88; ch. 5, nn. 622, 637**

Heptateuch, Hexateuch: see *Old English*.

Hermann, 'Liber de Miraculis Sancti Eadmundi', *Memorials of St Edmund's*, ed. Arnold, I, pp. 26–92: see also Subsidiary Index (i). **Ch. 3, n. 89**

Hincmar, 'Ad episcopos regni ... pro Carlomanno rege', *PL* CXXV, cols 1007–18. **Ch. 6, n. 37**

Hincmar, 'Explanatio in Ferculum Salomonis', *PL* CXXV, cols 817–34. **Ch. 6, n. 32**

Hincmar, 'Opusculum LV capitulorum adversus Hincmarum Laudunensem', *PL* CXXVI, cols 282–494. **Ch. 5, n. 94; ch. 6, nn. 32–3, 35–6**

Hincmar, 'De regis persona et regio ministerio', *PL* CXXV, cols 833–56. **Ch. 3, n. 21**

Hincmar, 'Vita Sancti Remigii', *PL* CXXV, cols 1129–88. **Ch. 6, n. 34**

Hinkmar von Reims, De Divortio Lotharii Regis et Theutbergae Reginae, edited by L. Böhringer (MGH Legum Sectio III, Concilia IV, supplementum I, 1992). **Ch. 5, n. 71; ch. 6, nn. 15, 31, 33, 35**

Hinkmar, 'Kapitularen', *Capitula Episcoporum* II, ed. Pokorny and Stratmann, pp. 3–89. **Ch. 6, n. 36**

Hinkmar von Reims, De Ordine Palatii, edited and translated (German) by T. Gross and R. Schieffer (MGH, Fontes Iuris Germanici Antiqui in usum scholarum III, 2nd edn, 1980). **Ch. 2, n. 213; ch. 3, nn. 19, 21–2; ch. 6, nn. 37, 39**

Die Hirtenbriefe Ælfrics, edited by B. Fehr (Bibliothek der angelsächsischen Prosa IX, general editors C.W.M. Grein and R.P. Wülker, repr. with supplement to the introduction by P. Clemoes, Darmstadt, 1966). **Ch. 4, tables 4.2, 4.4, 4.5, nn. 148, 200, 215, 222, 224, 237; ch. 6, nn. 141, 143–4, 158, 165**

The Historia Regum Britanniae of Geoffrey of Monmouth. I, Bern, Burgerbibliothek, MS 568, edited by N. Wright (Cambridge, 1985). **Ch. 3, n. 87; ch. 4, n. 302**

Historia Ricardi ... Hagustaldensis, Chronicles III, ed. Howlett, pp. 137–78. **Ch. 5, n. 622**

Historiae Ecclesiasticae Gentis Anglorum Libri V. A Venerabili Beda Presbytero scripti ... Ab Augustissimo veterum Anglo-Saxonum Rege ... Alfredo examinati, eiusque paraphrasi Saxonica eleganter explicati ... Quibus ... Saxonicam Chronologiam ... nunquam antea in lucem editam, nunc quoque primo Latine versam contexuimus ... , [edited and] published by A. Whelock (Cambridge, 1643). **Ch. 4, n. 42**

Historians of the Church of York and its Archbishops, edited by J. Raine (3 vols, RS 71, 1871–94): see 'Chronica Pontificum', 'Vita S. Oswaldi'

'Historiola de primordiis episcopatus Somersetensis', edited by J. Hunter, *Ecclesiastical documents, I. A brief history of the bishoprick of Somerset* (Camden Society, London, 1840): see Subsidiary Index (i).

The Homilies of Wulfstan, edited by D. Bethurum (Oxford, 1957). Ch. 4, tables 4.1. 4.2, 4.3, 4.4, 4.5, nn. 136, 142, 153, 158, 165, 177, 193, 199, 224, 235; ch. 5, tables 5.3, 5.4, nn. 334, 347, 349, 366, 368, 438, 452, 599; ch. 6, nn. 125–7, 130, 173–5, 177

Hrabanus Maurus, 'De Clericorum Institutione', *PL* CVII, cols 293–420. Ch. 4, table 4.4, nn. 233–4

Hrabanus Maurus, 'Commentaria in Exodum', *PL* CVIII, cols 9–248. Ch. 6, n. 5

Hrabanus (Maurus), Epistolae, edited by E. Dümmler (MGH, Epistolae Karolini Aevi III, Berlin, 1899), pp. 379–516. Ch. 2, n. 9

Hrabanus Maurus, 'Liber de Oblatione Puerorum', *PL* CVII, cols 419–40. Ch. 2, n. 317

R. Hübner, 'Gerichtsurkunden der fränkischen Zeit': see *III MODERN COMMENTARY s.n.*

Hugh the Chanter, The History of the Church of York 1066–1127, edited and translated by C. Johnson (2nd edn, revised by M. Brett *et al.*, Oxford Medieval Texts, 1990). Ch. 6, nn. 207, 227

Die 'Institutes of Polity, Civil and Ecclesiastical': ein Werk Erzbischof Wulfstans von York, edited by K. Jost (Schweizer Anglistische Arbeiten 47, general editors O. Funke and H. Straumann, Bern, 1959). Ch. 4, tables 4.1, 4.2, 4.3, 4.4, 4.5, nn. 152, 158–9, 163, 165, 178, 193; ch. 5, table 5.4, nn. 322, 407, 440, 453, 568, 584, 599–600, 604; ch. 6, nn. 153–8, 178

Die irische Kanonensammlung, edited by H. Wasserschleben (2nd edn, Leipzig, 1885). Ch. 3, n. 13; ch. 4, table 4.4; ch. 6, n. 156

The Irish Penitentials, edited and translated by L. Bieler (Scriptores Latini Hiberniae V, Dublin, Institute for Advanced Studies, 1963): see *Canones Wallici*, 'Synodus', 'Three Irish Canons'.

Isidore of Seville, Chronica maiora, edited by T. Mommsen (MGH, Auctores Antiquissimi XI, Chronica Minora II, Berlin, 1894), pp. 391–481. Ch. 2, n. 346

Isidore of Seville, Etymologiarum sive Originum Libri XX, edited by W.M. Lindsay (2 vols, Oxford, 1911). Ch. 2, nn. 80, 149; ch. 6, n. 191

Isidore of Seville, Historia Gothorum . . ., edited by T. Mommsen (MGH, Auct. Ant. XI, as above), pp. 241–304. Ch. 2, n. 43

Isidore of Seville, 'Liber Numerorum qui in sanctis scripturis occurrunt', *PL* LXXXIII, cols 179–200. Ch. 6, n. 5

Isidore of Seville, 'Libri Sententiarum' *PL* LXXXIII, cols 537–738. Ch. 2, n. 213; ch. 4, table 4.4

Isidore of Seville, 'Quaestiones in . . . Exodum', *PL* LXXXIII, cols 287–322. Ch. 6, n. 5

Ivo of Chartres, 'Epistolae', *PL* CLXII, cols 11–296. Ch. 6, n. 221

Ivo of Chartres, 'Prologus', *PL* CLXI, cols 47–60. Ch. 6, nn. 222, 224

John of Worcester: see *Chronicle*.

Jonas of Orléans, 'De Institutione Laicali', *PL* CVI, cols 121–280. Ch. 2, n. 213

Jonas d' Orleans et son 'De Institutione Regia', edited by J. Reviron (L' Église et l' État au haut Moyen Age, editor H-X. Arquillière, Paris, 1930), pp. 119–94. Ch. 3, n. 25

Justinian: see *Corpus Iuris*.

Die Kapitulariensammlung des Ansegis (Collectio Capitularium Ansegisi), edited by G. Schmitz (MGH, Capitularia Regum Francorum, N.S. I, 1996); see also Subsidiary Index (iv). Ch. 2, nn. 118–20, 123, 152, 154, 157; ch. 3, n. 18; ch. 4, table 4.4; ch. 5, nn. 70, 82, 128, 197, 216, 238, 241, 243, 295, 447

Lambarde: see *ARCHAIONOMIA*.

Late Merovingian France. History and Hagiography, 640–720, translated with commentary by P. Fouracre and R. Gerberding (Manchester, Medieval Sources, 1996). Ch. 2, n. 82

The Law of Hywel Dda. Law texts from Medieval Wales, edited and translated by D. Jenkins (Llandysul, 1986). Ch. 5, n. 95

Laws of the Alamans and Bavarians, translated by T.J. Rivers (Philadelphia, 1977). Ch. 2, nn. 26, 28, 80

The Laws of the Earliest English Kings, edited and translated by F.L. Attenborough (Cambridge, 1922). Ch. 5, nn. 7, 20, 462, 496; ch. 7, n. 4

The Laws of the Kings of England from Edmund to Henry I, edited and translated by A.J. Robertson (Cambridge, 1925). Ch. 5, n. 662

The Laws of the Salian Franks, translated by K.F. Drew (Philadelphia, 1991). Ch. 2, nn. 14, 64

Laws of the Salian and Ripuarian Franks, translated by T. J. Rivers (New York, 1986). Ch. 2, n. 24

Leechdoms, Wortcunning and Starcraft of Early England, edited by O. Cockayne (3 vols, RS 35, 1864–6). Ch. 4, nn. 48, 61, 63–4, 100; ch. 5, nn. 490, 547

Leges Alamannorum, edited by K.A. Eckhardt (I, *Einführung u. Recensio Chlothariana (Pactus)*; II, *Recensio Lantfridiana (Lex)* (Germanenrechte n.f., Westgermanisches Recht, Göttingen, 1958, 1962). Ch. 2, table 2.3, nn. 28, 78, 92, 340

Leges Alamannorum, edited by K. Lehmann (MGH, Legum Sectio I, V(1), 1888; 2nd edn, revised by K.A. Eckhardt, 1966). Ch. 2, nn. 28, 341, 347

Leges Alamannorum et Baiwariorum, edited by J. Merkel (MGH, Leges in folio III, 1863). Ch. 2, nn. 8, 27

Leges Anglo-Saxonicae Ecclesiasticae et Civiles, edited by D. Wilkins (London, 1721). Ch. 1, nn. 8, 102; ch. 5, nn. 7, 129, 262, 522

Leges Burgundionum, edited by L.R. de Salis (MGH, Legum Sectio I, II(1) (1892). Ch. 2, nn. 45–6, 53–4, 173, 180

Leges Henrici Primi, edited and translated by L.J. Downer (Oxford, 1972). Ch. 5, nn. 686–7; ch. 6, nn. 188, 214

Leges Langobardorum, edited by F, Bluhme (with A. Boretius) (MGH, Leges in folio IV, 1868). Ch. 2, table 2.3, nn. 21–2, 51, 54–5, 57, 71, 82–3, 306–7, 325, 335, 337, 348; ch. 3, nn. 17, 113; ch. 5, 69, 197; ch. 6, nn. 196, 201, 206

Leges Visigothorum, edited by K. Zeumer (MGH, Legum Sectio I, I, 1902). Ch. 2, nn. 43, 49–50, 54–5, 71, 82, 344; ch. 5, n. 197

The Leofric Missal as used in the Cathedral of Exeter . . ., edited by F.E. Warren (Oxford, 1883). Ch. 4, n. 130; ch. 6, n. 115

The Letters of Frederic William Maitland, edited by C.H.S. Fifoot (Selden Society Supplementary Series 1, London, 1965). Ch. 1, nn. 60–1, 69, 77

The Letters of Frederic William Maitland, Volume II, edited by P.N.R. Zutshi (Selden Society Supplementary Series 11, London, 1995). Ch. 1, n. 61

Lex Baiuariorum, edited by E. de Schwind (MGH, Legum Sectio I, V(2), 1926). Ch. 2, table 2.3, nn. 26–7, 54, 80–2, 96, 341, 344, 347

Lex Baiuvariorum. Lichtdruckwiedergabe der Ingolstädter Handschrift . . ., edited by K. Beyerle (München, 1926). Ch. 2, nn. 26, 179

Lex Frisionum, edited and translated (German) by K.A. and W.A. Eckhardt (MGH, Fontes Iuris Germanici Antiqui in usum scholarum XII, 1982). Ch. 2, n. 90; ch. 5, nn. 82, 90

Lex Ribuaria, edited by F. Beyerle and R. Buchner (MGH, Legum Sectio I, III(2), 1951). Ch. 2, table 2.3, nn. 24–5, 92, 96, 150, 157, 180, 213, 216, 342, 348; ch. 5, n. 700

Lex Ribuaria, edited by K.A. Eckhardt (I, *Austrasisches Recht im 7ten Jahrhundert*; II, *Lex Ribuaria*) (Germanenrechte n.f., Westgermanisches Recht, Göttingen, 1959, 1966). Ch. 2, nn. 24, 90, 344

Lex Romana Visigothorum, edited by G. Hänel (Leipzig, 1848; repr. Aalen, 1962). Ch. 2, nn. 34, 172, 344; ch. 3, n. 85; ch. 5, nn. 94, 227

Lex Salica: 100-Titel Text; *Pactus Legis Salicae I, Einführung*; *I2, Systematischer Text*; *II1, 65-titel Text*; *II2, Kapitularien und 70-titel Text*, edited by K.A. Eckhardt (Germanenrechte n.f., Westgermanisches Recht, Göttingen, 1953, 1954, 1957, 1955, 1956). Ch. 2, nn. 14, 58, 65, 93, 95, 150, 169

(Pactus) Legis Salicae, Lex Salica, edited by K.A. Eckhardt (MGH, Legum Sectio I, IV (i–ii) (1962–9)). Ch. 1, n. 105; ch. 2, table 2.3, nn. 14, 16–20, 58–61, 63–5, 67–8, 72–6, 84, 94–5, 143, 146, 150, 157–8, 172–3, 177, 180, 189, 247, 274, 335, 342, 364; ch. 3, n. 17; ch. 5, n. 511

Liber Eliensis, edited by E.O. Blake (Camden Society 3rd series XCII, London, 1962); see also Subsidiary Index (i). Ch. 3, nn 126, 128, 131, 138–9, 150; ch. 4, n. 127; ch. 5, nn. 391; ch. 6, table 6.2, n. 72

Liber Historiae Francorum, edited by B. Krusch (MGH, Scriptores rerum Merovingicarum II, 1888), pp. 215–328. **Ch. 2, nn. 60–1, 158**

Liber Legis Langobardorum Papiensis dictus, edited by A. Boretius, *Leg. Lang.*, pp. 290–585 (with Boretius' introduction, pp. xlvi–xcviii). **Ch. 6, nn. 196–201, 206, 210**

Liber Monasterii de Hyda, edited by E. Edwards (RS 45, 1866): see Subsidiary Indices (i), (ii).

Liber Psalmorum. The West Saxon Psalms, edited by J.W. Bright and R.L. Ramsay (Boston, 1907). **Ch. 5, nn. 63, 73; ch. 6, n. 46**

The Liber Vitae of the New Minster and Hyde Abey Winchester, edited by S. Keynes (EEMSF XXVI, 1996). **Ch. 4, nn. 36, 188–9; ch. 5, n. 203**

Liber Vitae. Register and Martyrology of New Minster and Hyde Abbey Winchester, edited by W. de Gray Birch (Hampshire Record Society 6, 1892). **Ch. 4, nn. 33, 36**

Liebermann, without further gloss, normally refers to *Gesetze der Angelsachsen*.

The Life of King Edward the Confessor, edited and translated by F. Barlow (Nelson's Medieval Texts, Edinburgh, 1962). **Ch. 3, nn. 42, 44, 64; ch. 6, table 6.2**

'The Life of St Edburga of Winchester', ed. Ridyard, *Royal Saints of Anglo-Saxon England* (see *III MODERN COMMENTARY s.n.*), pp. 253–308: see also Subsidiary Index (i). **Ch. 3, nn. 147–8**

The Lombard Laws, translated by K.F. Drew (Philadelphia, 1973). **Ch. 2, n. 21**

Loup de Ferrières, Correspondance, edited and translated (French) by L. Levillain (2 vols, Classiques de l'histoire de France au Moyen Age 10, 16, 2nd edn, 1964). **Ch. 2, nn. 9, 140, 317; ch. 3, n. 25**

Lupus of Ferrières, Epistolae, edited by E. Dümmler (MGH, Epistolae Karolini Aevi IV, Berlin, 1902–25), pp. 1–126. **Ch. 2, nn. 9, 140, 317; ch. 3, n. 25**

Manaresi: see *I Placiti*.

Mansi, Sacrorum Conciliorum Nova et Amplissima Collectio (31 vols, Florence/ Venice, 1759–98). **Ch. 6, n. 138**

Materials for the History of Thomas Becket, edited by J.C. Robertson and J.B. Sheppard (7 vols, RS 67, 1875–85). **Ch. 3, n. 70**

Matthew Paris, Chronica Maiora, edited by H.R. Luard (7 vols, RS 57, 1872–83). **Ch. 3, n. 37**

Memorials of Saint Dunstan, edited by W. Stubbs (RS 63, 1874): see also 'Vita S. Dunstani'. **Ch. 6, n. 119**

Memorials of St Edmund's Abbey, edited by T. Arnold (3 vols, RS 96, 1890–6): see Hermann, Samson.

St Mildrith: see 'Translatio', 'Vita'.

[Ex] Miraculis Sancti Benedicti, edited by O. Holder-Egger (MGH, Scriptores in folio XV, 1887–8). **Ch. 2, nn. 4, 7, 211–12, 231–2**

'De Miraculis et Translationibus Sancti Cuthberti', edited by T. Arnold, *Symeoni Monachi Opera Omnia* (2 vols, RS 75, 1882–5): see Subsidiary Index (i).

The Mirror of Justices, edited by W.J. Whittaker, with an introduction by F.W. Maitland (Selden Society 7, 1895). **Ch. 1, n. 18**

Mordek, *Bibliotheca capitularium*: see *III MODERN COMMENTARY s.n.*

Mosaicarum et Romanarum Legum Collatio, edited by T. Mommsen (Collectio Librorum iuris Romani antejustiniani in usum scholarum, edited by P. Krüger *et al.*, 3 vols, Berlin, 1884–90) III, pp. 107–98; translated by M. Hyamson, *Mosaicarum et Romanarum Legum Collatio (with Introduction, Facsimile and Translation of the Berlin Codex, Notes and Appendices* (Oxford, 1913). **Ch. 6, nn. 7, 15**

Munimenta Gildhallae Londoniensis, edited by H.T. Riley (3 vols in 4, RS 12, 1859–62). **Ch. 4, n. 67**

Narratio de S. Swithuno: see *Frithegod*

St Neots: see *Annals*.

New Minster: see *Liber Vitae*.

'Nomos Mosaïkos': see 'Appendix Eclogae'.

Novum Testamentum . . . Latine, edited by J. Wordsworth, H.J. White and H.F.D. Sparks (3 vols, Oxford, 1889–1954). **Ch. 6, n. 28**

Nunnaminster: see *Ancient Manuscript*.

The Old English Apollonius of Tyre, edited by P. Goolden (Oxford English Monographs, general editors J.R.R. Tolkien, F.P. Wilson and H. Gardner, 1958). Ch. 4, table 4.3, nn. 166, 181–2

The Old English Version of Bede's Ecclesiastical History, edited by T. Miller (2 vols, EETS 95, 110, London, 1890–98). Ch. 2, n. 360; ch. 4, n. 40; ch. 5, nn. 17, 35

The Old English Version of the Heptateuch, edited by S. Crawford (EETS 160, Oxford, 1922). Ch. 4, table 4.3, nn. 166, 175; ch. 6, n. 158

The Old English Illustrated Hexateuch (BM Cotton Claudius B.iv), edited by C.R. Dodwell and P. Clemoes (EEMSF XVIII, 1974). Ch. 4, n. 191

The Old English Orosius, edited by J. Bately (EETS S.S. 6, Oxford, 1980). Ch. 2, n. 360; ch. 5, nn. 17, 30; ch. 6, n. 26

Ordericus Vitalis: see *Ecclesiastical*.

Les Ordines Romani, edited by M. Andrieu (5 vols, Spicilegium Sacrum Lovaniense 11, 23–4, 38–9, 1931–61). Ch. 4, table 4.4, n. 198

Ordnance Survey, *Britain before the Norman Conquest* (Southampton, 1973). Ch. 6, map, n. 68

Paulus Orosius, Historiarum adversum paganos libri VII, edited by C. Zangemeister (Vienna, 1882). Ch. 6, n. 26

Orosius: see also *Old English*.

Papsturkunden, 896–1046, edited by H. Zimmermann (2 vols, Österreichischen Akademie der Wissenschaften, Philosophisch-historische Klasse, Denkschriften 174, 177, Vienna, 1984–5). Ch. 3, n. 140

The Parker Chronicle and Laws, edited by R. Flower and H. Smith (EETS 208, Oxford 1941, repr. 1973). Ch. 4, nn. 2, 5

Passiones Leudegarii, edited by B. Krusch (MGH, Scriptores rerum Merovingicarum V, 1910), pp. 249–362; see also *Late Merovingian France*. Ch. 2, n. 82

Paul the Deacon, Historia Langobardorum, edited by L. Bethmann and G. Waitz (MGH, Scriptores rerum Langobardicarum, 1878). Ch. 2, nn. 111, 131; ch. 3, nn. 82, 86

'Penitential of (pseudo-) Theodore'/'Liber Poenitentialis Theodori Archiepiscopi', *Ancient Laws*, ed. Thorpe, pp. 277–306. Ch. 4, tables 4.2, 4.4, nn. 231, 238; ch. 6, n. 143

Placita Anglo-Normannica: Law-cases from William I to Richard I, edited by M.M. Bigelow (London, 1879). Ch. 1, n. 15

I Placiti del "Regnum Italiae", edited by C. Manaresi (3 vols, Fonti per la Storia dell' Italia, Rome, 1955–60). Ch. 2, nn. 292, 294–5, 298–9, 302–4, 306–8

Poetae Latini aevi Karolini I, edited by E. Dümmler (MGH, Poetarum Latinorum Medii Aevi, Berlin, 1881). Ch. 2, nn. 111, 213; ch. 3, n. 25; ch. 6, n. 25

Poetae Latini aevi Karolini IV(3), edited by K. Strecker (MGH, Poetarum Latinorum Medii Aevi, Berlin, 1923). Ch. 2, n. 8

The Political Songs of England from the Reign of John to that of Edward II, edited by T. Wright (Camden Society VI, 1839). Ch. 6, n. 158

Pontifical of Egbert, Sidney Sussex: see *Anglo-Saxon Pontificals*.

Pontificale Lanaletense, edited by G.H. Doble (Henry Bradshaw Society LXXIV, London, 1937). Ch. 4, nn. 130, 132–3

Pseudo-Cyprianus, De XII abusivis saeculi, edited by S. Hellmann (Texte und Untersuchungen zur Geschichte der altchristlichen Literatur 34(i), general editors A. Harnack and C. Schmidt, Leipzig, 1910), pp. 1–60. Ch. 3, n. 21; ch. 6, n. 119

Quadripartitus: ed. Liebermann, *Ein englisches Rechtsbuch*: see *III MODERN COMMENTARY s.n.*; or *Gesetze* I, pp. 529–46, etc.: see Subsidiary Index (iii).

Radulf von Bourges, 'Kapitular', *Capitula Episcoporum* I, ed. Brommer, pp. 227–68. Ch. 4, table 4.4

Ramsey: see *Cartularium, Chronicon*.

Recueil des Actes de Charles II le chauve, roi de France, edited by G. Tessier *et al.* (3 vols, Chartes et Diplômes, Académie des Inscriptions et Belles-Lettres, Paris, 1943–55). Ch. 2, nn. 225, 229, 255, 272

Recueil des Actes d' Eudes, roi de France, edited by G. Tessier and R-H. Bautier (Chartes et Diplômes etc., Paris, 1967). **Ch. 2, nn. 225, 280**

Recueil des Actes de Louis II le Bègue, Louis III et Carloman, rois de France, edited by R-H. Bautier *et al.* (Chartes et Diplômes etc., Paris 1978). **Ch. 2, n. 225**

Recueil des Chartes de l' Abbaye de Saint-Benôit-sur-Loire, edited by M. Prou and A. Vidier (2 vols, Société historique et archéologique du Gâtinais V–VI, Paris/Orléans, 1900–32). **Ch. 2, nn. 229, 232, 238–41, 263, 275–6, 278, 313**

The Red Book of the Exchequer, edited by H. Hall (3 vols, RS 99, 1896). **Ch. 3, n. 84; ch. 5, nn. 621, 631, 688**

Redon: see *Cartulaire*.

Regensburg: see *Traditionen*.

Regesta Alsatiae Aevi Merovingici et Karolini, 496–918, edited by A. Brückner (Strasburg, 1949). **Ch. 2, n. 224**

Regesta Regum Anglo-Normannorum, edited by H.W.C. Davis (Vol. I, Oxford, 1913), C. Johnson and H.A. Cronne (Vol. II, 1956), Cronne and R.H.C. Davis (Vols III–IV, 1968–9). **Ch. 4, n. 297; ch. 5, nn. 615, 621, 624; ch. 6, nn. 60–1, 110**

Regularis Concordia, edited and translated by T. Symons (Nelson's Medieval Classics, Edinburgh, 1953). **Ch. 3, n. 71; ch. 4, table 4.4, nn. 168–9; ch. 5, n. 246**

Report on the Manuscripts of Lord Middleton preserved at Wollaton Hall, Nottinghamshire, edited by W.H. Stevenson (Historical Manuscripts Commission, 1911). **Ch. 4, n. 90**

Richard fitz Nigel, Dialogue of the Exchequer edited and translated by C. Johnson (Oxford Medieval Texts, revised edn, Oxford, 1983). **Ch. 5, n. 679**

Richard of Hexham: see *Historia*.

Robert of Torigny: see *Chronicle*.

Rochester: see *Charters, Textus*.

Sallust, edited and translated by J.C. Rolfe (Loeb series, 2nd edn, 1931). **Ch. 3, n. 45**

Samson, 'Opus de Miraculis Sancti Ædmundi', ed. Arnold, *Memorials of St Edmund's*, I, pp. 107–208. **Ch. 3, n. 89**

R. Schmid: see *Gesetze der Angelsachsen*.

Sedulius Scottus, Liber de Rectoribus Christianis, edited by S. Hellmann (Quellen und Untersuchungen zur lateinischen Philologie des Mittelalters 1 (i), general editor L. Traube, Munich, 1906), pp. 1–91. **Ch. 3, n. 25; ch. 4, table 4.4; ch. 6, n. 156**

Select Charters and other Illustrations of English Constitutional History, from the earliest times to the reign of Edward I, edited by W. Stubbs (9th edn, revised by H.W.C. Davis, Oxford, 1913). **Ch. 5, n. 634; ch. 6, n. 61**

Select English Historical Documents of the Ninth and Tenth Centuries, edited and translated by F.E. Harmer (Cambridge, 1914): see also Subsidiary Index (i). **Ch. 3, n. 95; ch. 5, n. 93**

Selsey: see *Charters*.

Sermo Lupi ad Anglos, edited by D. Whitelock (London, 3rd edn, 1963). **Ch. 4, nn. 127, 136, 182; ch. 5, nn. 322, 366, 372, 393, 426, 442, 572, 594, 602; ch. 6, nn. 173–5**

Shaftesbury: see *Charters*.

Sherborne: see *Charters*.

Sidonius Apollinaris, Poems and Letters, edited and translated by W.B. Anderson (2 vols, Loeb series, 1936–65). **Ch. 2, n. 44; ch. 3, n. 46**

Smaragdus, 'Via Regia', PL CII, cols 931–70. **Ch. 3, n. 24**

Statutes of the Realm, The Record Commission (9 vols + indices, London, 1810–28). **Ch. 3, n. 67**

Suetonius, edited and translated by J.C. Rolfe (2 vols, Loeb series, 1951). **Ch. 2, n. 91**

Suger, Vie de Louis VI le Gros, edited and translated (French) by H. Waquet (Classiques de l'histoire de France au Moyen Age 11, Paris, 1929). **Ch. 5, n. 622**

'Synodus I Sancti Patricii', *Irish Penitentials*, ed. Bieler, pp. 54–9. **Ch. 4, table 4.4**

Tacitus, 'De Origine et Situ Germanorum', edited by M. Winterbottom and R.M. Ogilive, *Cornelii Taciti Opera Minora* (Oxford, 1975). **Ch. 2, n. 338**

J. Tardif, 'Un Abrégé Juridique des Étymologes d' Isidore de Seville', *Mélanges Julien Havet* (Paris, 1895), pp. 659–81. **Ch. 2, n. 133**

Textes et documents d' histoire du Moyen Age, V^e–Xe siècles, edited and translated (French) by P. Riché and G. Tate (2 vols, Paris, 1974–6). **Ch. 2, n. 126**

Textes relatifs aux institutions privées et publiques aux époques merovingienne et carolingienne (Institutions privées), edited by M. Thévenin (Collection des textes pour servir à l' étude et l' enseignement d' histoire, Paris, 1887). **Ch. 2, nn. 126, 229, 250, 272**

Textus Roffensis, edited by P.H. Sawyer (2 vols, EEMSF VII, XI, 1957, 1962). **Ch. 2, nn. 320, 322, 348; ch. 4, nn. 327, 329, 335; ch. 6, n. 219**

Thegan, Gesta Hludowici Imperatoris; Astronomer, Vita Hludowici Imperatoris, edited and translated (German) by E. Tremp (MGH, Scriptores rerum Germanicarum in usum scholarum LXIV, 1995). **Ch. 2, nn. 157, 266; ch. 3, nn. 3, 20, 101**

The Theodosian Code and Novels and the Sirmondian Constitutions, translated by C. Pharr (Princeton, 1952). **Ch. 2, n. 32**

Theodosius II: see [*Codicis*] *Theodosiani*.

Theodulf von Orleans, 'Kapitularen', *Capitula Episcoporum* I, ed. Brommer, pp. 73–184. **Ch. 4, table 4.4; ch. 6, n. 29**

Theodulfi Capitula in England, edited by H. Sauer (Texte und Untersuchungen zur englischen Philologie 8, general editors H. Gneuss and W. Weiß, Munich, 1978). **Ch. 5, n. 65**

Thesaurus Latinae Linguae (10 vols, still in progress, Leipzig and Stuttgart, 1900-). **Ch. 4, n. 40**

Thévenin: see *Textes*.

'Three Irish Canons', *Irish Penitentials*, ed. Bieler, pp. 182–3. **Ch. 4, table 4.4**

Tiberius B.v: see *Eleventh-Century*.

Die Traditionen des Hochstifts Freising, edited by T. Bitterauf (2 vols, Quellen zur bayrischen Geschichte IV–V, Munich, 1905–9). **Ch. 2, nn. 228–9, 233, 272, 290**

Die Traditionen des Hochstiftes Regensburg und des Klosters St Emmeram, edited by J. Widemann (Quellen zur bayrischen Geschichte n.f. 8, 1943). **Ch. 2, n. 228**

'Translatio S. Mildrethae': D.W. Rollason, 'Goscelin of Canterbury's Account of the Translation and Miracles of St Mildrith', *Med. Stud.* 48 (1986), pp. 139–210: see Subsidiary Index (i).

The Treatise on the laws and customs of the realm of England commonly called Glanvill, edited and translated by G.D.G. Hall (Oxford Medieval Texts, 2nd edn with a note on further reading by M.T. Clanchy, Oxford, 1993). **Ch. 3, n. 47**

Die Urkunden Arnolfs, edited by P. Kehr (MGH, Diplomata regum Germaniae ex stirpe Karolinorum III, Berlin, 1955). **Ch. 2, n. 229**

Die Urkunden Lothars I und Lothars II, edited by T. Schieffer (MGH, Diplomatum Karolinorum III, Berlin, 1966). **Ch. 2, nn. 229, 292, 303**

Die Urkunden Ludwigs II, edited by K. Wanner (MGH, Diplomatum Karolinorum IV, Munich, 1994). Also published as *I Diplomi Lodovico II* (Fonti per la Storia dell' Italia medievale, Rome, 1994). **Ch. 2, nn. 292, 295, 303**

Die Urkunden Ludwigs des deutschen, Karlmanns und Ludwigs des jüngeren, edited by P. Kehr (MGH, Diplomata regum Germaniae ex stirpe Karolinorum I, Berlin, 1934). **Ch. 2, nn. 225, 229, 265, 268, 270**

Die Urkunden Pippins, Karlmanns und Karls des Großen, edited by E. Mühlbacher (MGH, Diplomatum Karolinorum I, 1906). **Ch. 2, nn. 65, 219, 225, 233, 267, 292, 303**

The Usatges of Barcelona. The fundamental law of Catalonia, translated with an introduction and notes by D.J. Kagay (University of Pennsylvania, Middle Ages Series, general editor E. Peters, Philadelphia, 1994). **Ch. 5, n. 456**

The Vercelli Homilies and Related Texts, edited by D.G. Scragg (EETS 300, Oxford, 1992). **Ch. 6, n. 129**

Vergil, Aeneid, edited by R.D. Williams (2 vols, London, 1972). **Ch. 3, n. 45**

The Visigothic Code, translated by S.P. Scott (Boston, 1910). **Ch. 2, n. 49**

'Vita Sancti Dunstani Auctore B', *Memorials of Saint Dunstan*, ed. Stubbs, pp. 3–52. **Ch. 4, n. 37; ch. 6, table 6.2, n. 67**

'Vita S. Dunstani auctore Osberno', *Memorials of Saint Dunstan*, ed. Stubbs, pp. 69–161: see also Subsidiary Index (i). **Ch. 3, nn. 44, 71, 150**

Vita S. Ecgwini: see Byrhtferth, 'Dominic'.

Vita S. Edburgae: see Life.

'Vita S. Edithae Virginis', edited by A. Wilmart, 'La légende de Sainte Edithe ... par le moine Goscelin', *Analecta Bollandiana* 56 (1938), pp. 5–101, 265–307: see also Subsidiary Index (i). **Ch. 3, n. 39**

Vita Edwardi: see *Life of King Edward*

'Vita Sancti Kenelmi', edited by and translated by R.C. Love, *Three Eleventh Century Anglo-Saxon Saints' Lives* (Oxford Medieval Texts, 1996): see Subsidiary Index (i).

Vita Sancti Lebuini, edited by A. Hofmeister (MGH Scriptores in folio XXX(2), Leipzig, 1934), pp. 789–95. **Ch. 5, n. 680**

'Vita ... Mildrethae', edited by D.W. Rollason, *The Mildrith Legend. A Study in Early Medieval Hagiography in England* (Studies in the Early History of Britain, general editor N. Brooks, Leicester, 1982), pp. 105–43. **Ch. 3, n. 45**

'Vita S. Oswaldi archiepiscopi Eboracensis', *Historians of the Church of York*, ed. Raine, I, 399–475. **Ch. 3, nn. 39, 44, 71; ch. 5, n. 372; ch. 6, n. 110.** See also *Byrhtferth*.

Vita S. Wulfstani, edited by R.R. Darlington (Camden Society, 3rd series XL, 1928). **Ch. 6, n. 110**

Bischof Wærferths von Worcester Übersetzung der Dialoge Gregors des Großen, edited by H. Hecht (Bibliothek der angelsächsischen Prosa V, general editors C.M.W. Grein and R.P. Wülker, Leipzig, 1900). **Ch. 5, nn. 35, 65**

The Waltham Chronicle, edited and translated by L. Watkiss and M. Chibnall (Oxford Medieval Texts, Oxford, 1994): see also Subsidiary Index (i). **Ch. 3, n. 153**

Welsh Medieval Law, edited and translated by A.W. Wade-Evans (Oxford, 1909); see also *Law of Hywel Dda*. **Ch. 5, n. 95**

Whelock: see *Archaionomia, Historiae Ecclesiasticae.*

Widukind, Rerum gestarum Saxonicarum libri tres, edited by H-E. Lohmann and P. Hirsch (MGH, Scriptores rerum Germanicarum in usum scholarum, 5th edn, 1935). **Ch. 2, n. 318; ch. 3, n. 4**

D. Wilkins: see *Leges Anglo-Saxonicae.*

The Will of Æthelgifu, edited and translated by D. Whitelock (Roxburghe Club, Oxford, 1968): see Subsidiary Index (i).

William of Malmesbury, The Early History of Glastonbury, edited and translated by J. Scott (Woodbridge, 1981). **Ch. 4, n. 103**

William of Malmesbury, De Gestis Pontificum Anglorum, edited by N.E.S.A. Hamilton (RS 52, 1870): see also Subsidiary Index (i). **Ch. 4, n. 385; ch. 5, n. 201**

William of Malmesbury, De Gestis Regum Anglorum, edited by W. Stubbs (2 vols, RS 90, 1887–9): see also Subsidiary Index (i). **Ch. 1, n. 30; ch. 3, nn. 59–60, 73, 77–83, 85; ch. 5, nn. 201, 398, 529, 619, 622; ch. 6, table 6.2**

William of Poitiers: see *Gesta Guillelmi.*

Wulfstan of Winchester, Life of St Æthelwold, edited and translated by M. Lapidge and M. Winterbottom (Oxford Medieval Texts, Oxford, 1991): see also Subsidiary Index (i). **Ch. 3, n. 29; ch. 4, nn. 37, 87**

Wulfstan's Canons of Edgar, edited by R. Fowler (EETS 266, Oxford, 1972). **Ch. 4, table 4.3, nn. 179, 192; ch. 5, tables 5.3, 5.4, nn. 108, 349, 368, 394, 407, 459, 579, 603–4, 611; ch. 6, n. 141**

A Wulfstan Manuscript. Cotton Nero A.i, edited by H.R. Loyn (EEMSF XVII, 1971). **Ch. 1, n. 20; ch. 4, table 4.2, nn. 107, 147, 149–51, 158, 163, 210, 243–50, 255, 263, 343**

Wulfstan, Sammlung der ihm zugeschriebenen Homilien, nebst Untersuchung uber ihrer Echtheit, edited by A.S. Napier (Sammlung englischer Denkmäler im kritischen Ausgaben IV, Berlin, 1883). **Ch. 4, tables 4.2, 4.3, 4.4, nn. 141, 165, 177–8, 180, 193, 224; ch. 5,** table 5.4, nn. 230, 312, 316–18, 331–2, 336, 344, 366, 389, 393, 438–9, 471, 611; ch. 6, nn. 129–30, 178

Wulfstan: see also *Copenhagen, Homilies, Institutes, Sermo Lupi*.

Young, Patrick: see *Catalogus*.

The York Gospels: a facsimile with introductory essays, edited by N. Barker (Roxburghe Club, London, 1986). **Ch. 4, nn. 137–41, 146**

SUBSIDIARY SOURCE INDICES

(i) *Summary Concordance of 'Anglo-Saxon Lawsuits' ('LS')*

Cf. chapter 3, n. 93; editions have been updated as appropriate; dates are those of the *documents*; references are to S* (the as yet unpublished revised 'Sawyer') when the new entry materially affects views of the charter, e.g. its date.

1. S 1429 (BCS 156), 736x7   **Ch. 4, n. 79**

2. S 1256 (*Shaft. Ch.* 1(b)), 759   **Ch. 4, n. 79**

3. S 1257 (BCS 241), 781

4. S 1430+1260+1432 (BCS 256, 308, RoASCh 4), 789, 803, 822x3   **Ch. 6, n. 62**

5. S 137 (BCS 269), 794

6. S 1258 (BCS 291), 798   **Ch. 4, n. 79**

7. S 158+1435 (*Sels. Ch.* 14–15), 801, 825

8. S 1431 (BCS 309), 803   **Ch. 6, n. 96**

9. S 1431 (BCS 309), 803   **Ch. 6, n. 96**

10. S 1431 (BCS 309), 803   **Ch. 6, n. 96**

11. S 1187 (BCS 313), 804   **Ch. 3, n. 93; ch. 4, n. 79**

12. S 1433 (BCS 379), 824   **Ch. 3, n. 93; ch. 4, n. 79**

13. S 1434 (BCS 378), 824   **Ch. 4, n. 79**

14. S* 1436 (BCS 384), 825   **Ch. 3, n. 96; ch. 6, n. 96**

15. S 1437 (RoASCh 5), 825   **Ch. 5, n. 490; ch. 6, n. 62**

16. S* 1438 (BCS 421), 838–9

17. S 192 (BCS 430), 840

18. S 1439 (BCS 445), 844   **Ch. 3, n. 96**

19. S 1439 (BCS 445), 844   **Ch. 3, n. 96**

20. S 1507 (HaSD 11), 879x88   **Ch. 3, n. 98**

21. S 1441 (HaSD 14), 896

22. S 1442 (BCS 575), 897   **Ch. 3, n. 98**

23. S 1445 (HaSD 18), 900x24   **Ch. 3, nn. 95–103**

24. S 1445 (HaSD 18), 900x24   **Ch. 3, nn. 8, 95–103**

25. S 1445 (HaSD 18), 900x24   **Ch. 3, nn. 95–103; ch. 5, n. 478.**

26. S 1445 (HaSD 18), 900x24   **Ch. 3, nn. 95–103; ch. 6, table 6.2**

27. S 362 (BCS 595), 901   **Ch. 3, n. 106**

28. S 1446 (HaSD 150), c. 903   **Ch. 6, n. 56**

29. S* 375 (BCS 623), 909   **Ch. 3, n. 106; ch. 6, n. 92**

30. S* 414–15 (BCS 670–1), 931   **Ch. 3, n. 106; ch. 5, n. 201**

31. S 443 (BCS 727), 938   **Ch. 3, n. 106; ch. 5, n. 199**

32. S 1211 (HaSD 23), c. 959   **Ch. 3, n. 131**

33. S 1211 (HaSD 23), c. 959

34. S 1211 (HaSD 23), c. 959   **Ch. 3, n. 140; ch. 6, table 6.2**

35. S 1211 (HaSD 23), c. 959   **Ch. 3, n. 140**

36. S* 687 (*Ab. Ch.* 86), 960   **Ch. 3, n. 106**

37. S* 753 (BCS 1198), 967   **Ch. 3, nn. 102, 106**

38. S 1447 (RoASCh 44), 968   **Ch. 5, n. 549**

39. S 1447 (RoASCh 44), 968   **Ch. 3, n. 140; ch. 5, n. 549**

40. S 1447 (RoASCh 44), 968   **Ch. 5, n. 549**

41. S 792 (BCS 1297), 973   **Ch. 3, nn. 102, 106; ch. 4, n. 125**

42. S* 796 (BCS 1301), 974

43. S* 1377 (RoASCh 37), 963x75   **Ch. 4, n. 127**

44. S* 842 (*Liber de Hyda*, ed. Edwards, pp. 215–27), 982. **Ch. 3, nn. 106, 114**

45. S* 1457 (RoASCh 59), 980x87   Ch. 3, n. 93

46. S* 1457 (RoASCh 59), 980x87   Ch. 3, nn. 93, 114, 140; ch. 6, table 6.2

47. S* 1458 (RoASCh 41), *c.* 995   Ch. 3, nn. 114, 140

48. S 869 (*Liber de Hyda*, ed. Edwards, pp. 238–42), 988   Ch. 3, nn. 106, 114; ch. 6, table 6.2

49. S 1454 (RoASCh 66), 990   Ch. 3, nn. 114–25

50. RoASCh 40, 966x92   Ch. 3, nn. 114, 138

51. RoASCh 40, 966x92   Ch. 3, nn. 114, 138

52. RoASCh 40, 966x92   Ch. 3, n. 114

53. S 1453 (RoASCh 54), 972x92   Ch. 4, nn. 99, 104, 124, 126

54. S 883 (*Ab. Ch.* 125), 995   Ch. 3, nn. 106, 114

55. S 884 (*Cartularies of Muchelney and Athelney*, ed. Bates, 14), 995 Ch. 3, nn. 114

56. S* 886 (*Ab. Ch.* 126), 995   Ch. 3, nn. 102, 106, 114

57. S 877 (*Liber de Hyda*, ed. Edwards, pp. 242–3, RoASCh 63), 996   Ch. 3, nn. 106, 114, 131; ch. 6, table 6.2

58. S 877 (*Liber de Hyda*, ed. Edwards, pp. 242–3, RoASCh 63), 996 Ch. 3, nn. 106, 114, 131; ch. 6, table 6.2

59. S 891 (KCD 698), 997   Ch. 3, nn. 114, 140; ch. 5, nn. 304, 342; ch.6, table 6.1, nn. 69–70, 94

60. S 893 (*Roch. Ch.* 32), 998   Ch. 3, nn. 106, 114, 140; ch. 5, n. 373; ch.6, table 6.2

61. S* 892 (*Crawf. Coll.* 8), 998   Ch. 3, nn. 102, 106, 114

62. S 939 (WhW 16(ii)), 995x9   Ch. 3, nn. 99, 114; ch. 6, table 6.2

63. S 896+937 (*Ab. Ch.* 128–9), 999   Ch. 3, nn. 106, 108, 114, 140; ch. 6, table 6.2

64. S 937 (*Ab. Ch.* 129), ?999   Ch. 3, nn. 102, 106, 114

65. S 1497 (*Will of Æthelgifu*, ed. Whitelock), 985x1002   Ch. 6, n. 86

66. S 1242 (HaWr 108), 995x1002

67. S 1242 (HaWr 108), 995x1002   Ch. 3, nn. 114, 140

68. S 901 (*Ab. Ch.* 132), 1002   Ch. 3, nn. 106, 114; ch. 5, n. 492

69. S 1456 (RoASCh 69), 995x1005   Ch. 3, nn. 93, 114, 123

70. S 911 (KCD 714), 1005   Ch. 3, nn. 106, 114; ch. 5, n. 492

71. S 916+926 (*Crawf. Coll.* 11, *Roch. Ch.* 33), 1007, 1012   Ch. 3, nn. 106, 114

72. (a) S* 918 (*Ab. Ch.* 135), 1008   Ch. 3, nn. 106, 114, 140
    (b) S 934 (*Ab. Ch.* 137), 1012   Ch. 3, nn. 106, 114

73. S 923 (*Burt. Ch.* 33), 1011   Ch. 3, nn. 102, 106, 114; ch. 5, n. 492

74. S 1383+1422 (*Sherb. Ch.* 13–14), 1001x12, 1012   Ch. 3, n. 114

75. S 926 (*Roch. Ch.* 33), 1012   Ch. 3, nn. 106, 114

76. S 927 (*Ab. Ch.* 136), 1012   Ch. 3, nn. 104–14; ch. 6, table 6.2

77. S 1460 (RoASCh 83), 1010x23   Ch. 5, n. 549

78. S* 1462a (KCD 803), 1017x27   Ch. 5, n. 492

79. S 991 (HaWr 48), 1017x30   Ch. 3, n. 106

80. S 1462 (RoASCh 78), 1016x35

81. S 1223 (KCD 938), 1033x38   Ch. 3, nn. 106, 114

82. S 1527 (WhW 24), 1000x38

83. S 1467 (RoASCh 91), 1038x40   Ch. 3, n. 97

84. S 1472 (RoASCh 102), 1044x45   Ch. 3, n. 118

85. S 1474 (*Sherb. Ch.* 17), 1045x46

86. S 1404 (*Ab. Ch.* 143 + *Chronicon de Abingdon*, ed. Stevenson, pp. 457–9, 475–7) 1045x48

87. S 1123 (HaWr 79), 1049   Ch. 3, n. 146

88. S 1229 (RoASCh 96), 1042x52

89. S 1077 (HaWr 17), 1052   Ch. 3, n. 146

90. S 1408 (KCD 805), 1052x6

91. S 1029 (KCD 808), 1060

92. S 1090 (HaWr 35), 1053x61   Ch. 3, n. 146

93. S* 1110 (HaWr 62, *Cartularium de Rameseia* , ed. Hart and Lyons I, p. 188), 1055x65

94. S 1026 (KCD 801, *Chronicon Evesham*, ed. McCray, pp. 45–6, 93–4), '1055'   Ch. 3, nn. 102, 131

95. S 1241 (HaWr 72), 1066x75

96. *DB* i 78d (*Dorset* 19:14)   Ch. 3, n. 146

97. *DB* i 252d (*Shropshire* 3d:7)

98. *DB* i 252d (*Shropshire* 3d:7)

99. *DB* i 376b (*Lincolnshire* CW:12)

100. *DB* ii 2b (*Essex* 1:3)   Ch. 3, n. 102

101. *DB* ii 310b–311a, cf. 313a, 342b (*Suffolk* 6:79, 6:92, 7:114)

102. *DB* ii 401b–402a (*Suffolk* 27:7)   **Ch. 3, nn. 102, 146**

103. *Heming, Chartularium*, ed. Hearne, pp. 260–1   **Ch. 3, n. 131**

104. *Heming, Chartularium*, ed. Hearne, pp. 264–5   **Ch. 3, n. 130**

105. *Heming, Chartularium*, ed. Hearne, pp. 267–8   **Ch. 3, n. 130**

106. *Heming, Chartularium*, ed. Hearne, p. 275

107. *Lib. Æth.* 5 (*Lib. El.*, ed. Blake, ii 7)   **Ch. 3, nn. 114, 128**

108. *Lib. Æth.* 5 (*Lib. El.*, ed. Blake, ii 7)   **Ch. 3, nn. 114, 128, 130, 139**

109. *Lib. Æth.* 6 (*Lib. El.*, ed. Blake, ii 8)   **Ch. 3, nn. 114, 128, 139**

110. *Lib. Æth.* 8 (*Lib. El.*, ed. Blake, ii 10   **Ch. 3, nn. 114, 128–30, 135, 139**

111. *Lib. Æth.* 10 (*Lib. El.*, ed. Blake, ii 11)   **Ch. 3, nn. 114, 128, 135, 139; ch. 6, table 6.2**

112. *Lib. Æth.* 11 (*Lib. El.*, ed. Blake, ii 11)   **Ch. 3, nn. 114, 128, 130, 135,137**

113. *Lib. Æth.* 14 (*Lib. El.*, ed. Blake, ii 11a)   **Ch. 3, nn. 114, 128–9**

114. *Lib. Æth.* 14 (*Lib. El.*, ed. Blake, ii 11a)   **Ch. 3, nn. 114, 128–30, 137**

115. *Lib. Æth.* 15 (*Lib. El.*, ed. Blake, ii 12)   **Ch. 3, nn. 114, 128–30, 137, 139**

116. *Lib. Æth.* 27 (*Lib. El.*, ed. Blake, ii 18)   **Ch. 3, nn. 126–39**

117. *Lib. Æth.* 28 (*Lib. El.*, ed. Blake, ii 18)   **Ch. 3, nn. 114, 126–39**

118. *Lib. Æth.* 29 (*Lib. El.*, ed. Blake, ii 19)   **Ch. 3, n. 128**

119. *Lib. Æth.* 29 (*Lib. El.*, ed. Blake, ii 19)   **Ch. 3, nn. 114, 128, 130, 139**

120. *Lib. Æth.* 34 (*Lib. El.*, ed. Blake, ii 24)   **Ch. 3, nn. 114, 126–39**

121. *Lib. Æth.* 35 (*Lib. El.*, ed. Blake, ii 25)   **Ch. 3, nn. 114, 128, 135, 137,139**

122. *Lib. Æth.* 38 (*Lib. El.*, ed. Blake, ii 27)   **Ch. 3, nn. 114, 128–31, 139**

123. *Lib. Æth.* 39 (*Lib. El.*, ed. Blake, ii 30)   **Ch. 3, nn. 114, 128–9**

124. *Lib. Æth.* 42 (*Lib. El.*, ed. Blake, ii 32)   **Ch. 3, n. 128**

125. *Lib. Æth.* 42 (*Lib. El.*, ed. Blake, ii 32)   **Ch. 3, nn. 128, 130–1**

126. *Lib. Æth.* 43 (*Lib. El.*, ed. Blake, ii 33)   **Ch. 3, nn. 114, 128, 130–1, 139**

127. *Lib. Æth.* 42 (*Lib. El.*, ed. Blake, ii 32)   **Ch. 3, nn. 102, 128–9**

128. *Lib. Æth.* 44 (*Lib. El.*, ed. Blake, ii 33)   **Ch. 3, nn. 114, 128–9, 138**

129. *Lib. Æth.* 45 (*Lib. El.*, ed. Blake, ii 34)   **Ch. 3, nn. 102, 128**

130. *Lib. Æth.* 45 (*Lib. El.*, ed. Blake, ii 34)   **Ch. 3, nn. 114, 128–9, 135, 139**

131. *Lib. Æth.* 54 (*Lib. El.*, ed. Blake, ii 43)   **Ch. 3, n. 128**

132. *Lib. Æth.* 60 (*Lib. El.*, ed. Blake, ii 49b)   **Ch. 3, nn. 102, 128–9**

133. *Chronicon de Abingdon*, ed. Stevenson, I, pp. 88–90   **Ch. 3, n. 94**

134. *Chronicon de Abingdon*, ed. Stevenson, I, pp. 459–60

135. *Lib. El.*, ed. Blake, ii 96   **Ch. 3, nn. 128, 130**

136. *Chron. Ram.* 25   **Ch. 3, n. 130**

137. *Chron. Ram.* 25   **Ch. 3, nn. 114, 130, 140**

138. *Chron. Ram.* 28   **Ch. 3, n. 114**

139. *Chron. Ram.* 28   **Ch. 3, n. 114**

140. *Chron. Ram.* 47   **Ch. 3, nn. 130, 140**

141. *Chron. Ram.* 47   **Ch. 3, nn. 114, 130**

142. *Chron. Ram.* 47   **Ch. 3, nn. 114, 130**

143. *Chron. Ram.* 49   **Ch. 3, n. 114**

144. *Chron. Ram.* 74

145. *Chron. Ram.* 74   **Ch. 3, nn. 150, 154**

146. *Chron. Ram.* 75   **Ch. 3, n. 130**

147. *Chron. Ram.* 90

148. *Chron. Ram.* 92

149. *Chron. Ram.* 96–8   **Ch. 3, nn. 144–5**

150. *Chron. Ram.* 103   **Ch. 3, n. 142**

151. 'Historiola … episcopatus Somersetensis', ed. Hunter, p. 17

152. *Chronicon Evesham*, ed. McCray, pp. 79–82   **Ch. 3, nn. 114, 130–1, 140**

153. *Chronicon Evesham*, ed. McCray, pp. 93–4 (and 45–6)

154. Lantfred 25 (Lapidge, *Cult of St Swithun*)   **Ch. 3, nn. 102, 154**

155. Lantfred 26 (Lapidge, *Cult of St Swithun*)   **Ch. 3, n. 102**

156. Lantfred 27 (Lapidge, *Cult of St Swithun*)   **Ch. 3, nn. 102, 154**

157. Abbo, 'Passio S. Eadmundi' 15   **Ch. 3, nn. 102, 150, 154**

158. Wulfstan, 'Life of St Æthelwold' 46   **Ch. 3, nn. 102, 114, 154**

159. Byrhtferth, 'Life of St Ecgwine' iv 10 (Lapidge, *Byrhtferth*) + *Chronicon Evesham*, pp. 42–4   **Ch. 3, nn. 149–51, 154**

160. ASC 1020CDE   **Ch. 6, table 6.2**

161. ASC 1049C   **Ch. 6, table 6.2**

162. ASC 1051DE   **Ch. 6, table 6.2**

163. ASC 1052CDE   **Ch. 6, table 6.2**

164. ASC 1055CDE   **Ch. 6, table 6.2**

165. ASC 1065C   **Ch. 6, table 6.2**

166. 'Vita S. Kenelmi', 18, pp. 72–5   Ch. 3, nn. 150, 154
167. 'Vita S. Kenelmi', 19, pp. 74–5   Ch. 3, nn. 150, 154
168. 'Vita S. Dunstani' auct. Osbern, i 36   Ch. 3, nn. 94, 114
169. 'Vita S. Edithae' ii 5   Ch. 3, nn. 102, 114, 150, 154
170. 'Translatio S. Mildrethae' 18
171. Hermann, 'Liber De Miraculis S. Eadmundi' 2   Ch. 3, nn. 102, 150, 154
172. *Chronicon Evesham*, pp. 41–2   Ch. 3, nn. 114, 140, 150, 154

173. 'De Miraculis S. Cuthberti' 5   Ch. 3, nn. 64, 150, 154
174. 'Vita S. Dunstani' auct. Eadmer, i 27   Ch. 3, n. 114
175. *JW* II, pp. 530–3
176. William of Malmesbury, *Gest. Pont.* ii 82
177. 'Miracula S. Albani' (BL Cotton MS Faustina B iv, ff. 22v – 23v)   Ch. 3, nn. 150, 154
177a 'Life of St Edburga' 6   Ch. 3, nn. 94, 147–8
178. *Waltham Chronicle* 24   Ch. 3, nn. 102, 153–4

(ii)   *Index of citations of Anglo-Saxon Charters (S, S*)*

S 283   Ch. 6, n. 56
S 286   Ch. 6, nn. 56, 108
S* 286a   Ch. 6, n. 108
S 287–288   Ch. 6, n. 56
S 290   Ch. 6, nn. 56, 108
S 292   Ch. 6, n. 56
S 293   Ch. 6, nn. 56, 108
S 294   Ch. 6, n. 108
S* 294a–294b   Ch. 6, n. 108
S 296   Ch. 6, nn. 56, 108
S 297   Ch. 6, n. 56
S 298   Ch. 6, nn. 56, 108
S 300   Ch. 6, n. 56
S 302   Ch. 6, nn. 56, 108
S 303–305   Ch. 6, nn. 56, 108, 112
S 306   Ch. 6, nn. 56, 108
S 307–308   Ch. 6, nn. 56, 108, 112
S 309–311   Ch. 6, nn. 56, 108
S 329–332   Ch. 6, n. 56
S 333   Ch. 6, nn. 56, 108
S* 334   Ch. 2, n. 376; ch. 6, nn. 56, 66
S 335–336, 338   Ch. 6, n. 56
S* 338a   Ch. 6, n. 56
S 340   Ch. 6, n. 56
S* 342   Ch. 2, n. 376; ch. 6, nn. 56, 66
S 345   Ch. 6, n. 56
S 347   Ch. 6, n. 108
S 350   Ch. 6, n. 56
S 352   Ch. 6, n. 108
S 359   Ch. 4, n. 35; ch. 6, table 6.2, n. 92
S 362   Ch. 3, n. 106
S 364   Ch. 6, table 6.2, n. 92
S 366   Ch. 6, table 6.2
S 368   Ch. 3, n. 98; ch. 6, table 6.2, n. 92
S 369   Ch. 3, n. 148; ch. 6, n. 92
S 372–373   Ch. 6, table 6.2
S 374   Ch. 4, n. 35; ch. 6, table 6.2, n. 92
S* 375   Ch. 3, n. 106; ch. 6, n. 92
S 379   Ch. 5, n. 200; ch. 6, table 6.2
S 391   Ch. 6, table 6.2
S 392   Ch. 6, n. 102
S 394, 399, 400, 403, 405   Ch. 6, table 6.2
S 406   Ch. 6, n. 102
S 407, 412–413   Ch. 5, n. 174; ch. 6, table 6.2
S* 414–415   Ch. 3, n. 106; ch. 5, n. 201
S 416   Ch. 5, n. 174; ch. 6, table 6.2, nn. 69, 76, 103
S 417   Ch. 5, n. 174; ch. 6, table 6.2
S 418   Ch. 5, nn. 174, 200, 203; ch. 6, table 6.2, n. 76
S* 418a   Ch. 5, n. 174; ch. 6, table 6.2
S 419   Ch. 5, nn. 174, 200; ch. 6, table 6.2 n. 76
S 420   Ch. 6, table 6.2

S 422   Ch. 5, nn. 174, 200; ch. 6, table 6.2, n. 76
S 423   Ch. 5, n. 200; ch. 6, table 6.2, n. 76
S 425   Ch. 5, n. 174; ch. 6, table 6.2
S 426   Ch. 5, n. 174; ch. 6, table 6.2, n. 80
S 427   Ch. 6, table 6.2, nn. 69, 76
S 429–431   Ch. 6, n. 103
S 434   Ch. 5, nn. 174, 201; ch. 6, table 6.2, n. 75
S 435–436   Ch. 5, n. 201; ch. 6, table 6.2, n. 75
S 437, 441   Ch. 6, n. 103
S 443   Ch. 3, n. 106; ch. 5, n. 199
S 447   Ch. 4, nn. 12, 25
S 449   Ch. 4, n. 19
S 450   Ch. 6, table 6.2
S 451   Ch. 5, n. 486
S 455   Ch. 4, n. 103
S 456–457   Ch. 5, n. 486
S 464   Ch. 4, nn. 12, 25
S 472–473, 479   Ch. 6, table 6.2, nn. 56, 86
S 484   Ch. 6, n. 86
S 495   Ch. 4, n. 19
S 497   Ch. 4, nn. 12, 25
S 505   Ch. 6, table 6.2, n. 85
S 510   Ch. 4, nn. 12, 25
S 511   Ch. 6, table 6.2
S 512   Ch. 4, n. 12
S 520   Ch. 6, table 6.2, n. 56
S 528, 535   Ch. 4, nn. 12, 25
S 537   Ch. 6, table 6.2
S 539 = S* 338a
S 548   Ch. 6, n. 102
S 549   Ch. 6, table 6.2, nn. 56, 102
S 550   Ch. 6, n. 102
S 552   Ch. 4, nn. 12, 25
S* 552a   Ch. 6, table 6.2
S 569   Ch. 6, n. 102
S 571   Ch. 6, n. 54
S 572   Ch. 6, n. 102
S 590, 598   Ch. 6, n. 104
S 607, 611   Ch. 6, table 6.2
S 633   Ch. 6, table 6.2, nn. 56, 102
S 636   Ch. 4, n. 11
S 646   Ch. 6, table 6.2, n. 68
S 658, 667   Ch. 6, table 6.2
S 670   Ch. 6, n. 54
S 674–679   Ch. 6, n. 91
S* 687   Ch. 3, n. 106
S 712   Ch. 4, n. 126; ch. 6, n. 90
S* 712a   Ch. 6, n. 90
S 716   Ch. 4, n. 124; ch. 6, n. 90
S 731   Ch. 3, n. 74; ch. 6, n. 54
S 732–4, 738   Ch. 6, n. 90
S 745   Ch. 5, n. 260

S 751   Ch. 6, n. 92
S* 753   Ch. 3, nn. 102, 106
S 775   Ch. 6, nn. 92, 102
S 776   Ch. 6, table 6.2
S 779   Ch. 6, table 6.2, n. 90
S 781   Ch. 6, n. 66
S 782   Ch. 4, n. 125; ch. 5, n. 260; ch. 6, n. 92
S 783   Ch. 6, n. 54
S 792   Ch. 3, nn. 102, 106; ch. 4, n. 125
S 795   Ch. 6, n. 92
S 802, 806   Ch. 6, table 6.2
S 813   Ch. 4, n. 103
S 830   Ch. 6, table 6.2
S 842   Ch. 3, nn. 106, 114
S 850   Ch. 5, n. 373
S 856   Ch. 4, n. 280
S 862   Ch. 6, n. 70
S 864   Ch. 3, n. 140
S 866   Ch. 5, n. 373
S 867   Ch. 6, n. 70
S 869   Ch. 3, nn. 106, 114; ch. 6, table 6.2
S 873   Ch. 6, table 6.2
S 876   Ch. 3, n. 140; ch. 5, n. 297; ch. 6, table 6.1, nn. 53, 69, 94
S 877   Ch. 3, nn. 106, 114, 131; ch. 6, table 6.2
S 878   Ch. 5, n. 304
S 883   Ch. 3, nn. 106, 114
S 884   Ch. 3, n. 114
S 885   Ch. 3, n. 140; ch. 5, n. 373
S* 886   Ch. 3, nn. 102, 106, 114
S 888   Ch. 3, n. 140; ch. 5, n. 373
S 889   Ch. 3, n. 140; ch. 5, n. 342
S 890   Ch. 6, table 6.2
S 891   Ch. 3, nn. 114, 140; ch. 5, nn. 298, 304, 342; ch. 6, table 6.1, nn. 69–70, 94
S* 892   Ch. 3, nn. 102, 106, 114
S 893   Ch. 3, nn. 106, 114, 140; ch. 5, n. 373; ch. 6, table 6.2
S 894   Ch. 6, n. 54
S 896   Ch. 3, nn. 106, 108, 114, 140; ch. 6, table 6.2
S 899   Ch. 5, nn. 304, 342, 373
S 901   Ch. 3, nn. 106, 114; ch. 5, n. 492
S 903   Ch. 5, n. 342
S 904   Ch. 5, nn. 304, 373
S 905   Ch. 6, table 6.2
S 906   Ch. 5, n. 304; ch. 6, n. 70
S 909   Ch. 6, table 6.2
S 911   Ch. 3, nn. 106, 114; ch. 5, nn. 342, 492; ch. 6, n. 70
S 915   Ch. 6, table 6.2
S 916   Ch. 3, nn. 106, 114
S* 918   Ch. 3, nn. 106, 114, 140
S 919, 920–921   Ch. 5, n. 342

S 923   Ch. 3, nn. 102, 106, 114; ch. 5, n. 492
S 926   Ch. 3, nn. 106, 114; ch. 5, n. 373
S 927   Ch. 3, nn. 104–14; ch. 6, table 6.2
S 928   Ch. 5, n. 342
S* 931a–931b   Ch. 6, table 6.2
S 934   Ch. 3, nn. 106, 114
S 937   Ch. 3, nn. 102, 106, 108, 114, 140; ch. 5, n. 342; ch. 6, table 6.2
S 939   Ch. 3, nn. 99, 114; ch. 6, table 6.2
S 942   Ch. 5, n. 342
S 951   Ch. 4, n. 122; ch. 5, n. 342
S 953   Ch. 4, n. 122
S 956   Ch. 4, n. 122; ch. 5, n. 373; ch. 6, table 6.2
S 958   Ch. 6, table 6.2
S 959   Ch. 4, n. 122
S 960–961   Ch. 4, nn. 122, 127
S 962   Ch. 4, n. 122
S 963   Ch. 4, n. 280
S 964   Ch. 4, n. 122
S 965   Ch. 5, n. 411; ch. 6, n. 54
S 967–969, 975   Ch. 4, n. 122
S 976   Ch. 5, n. 411
S 980   Ch. 4, n. 122
S 981   Ch. 3, n. 99; ch. 6, table 6.2
S 985   Ch. 6, n. 60
S 991   Ch. 3, n. 106
S 993   Ch. 6, table 6.2
S 994   Ch. 4, n. 122
S 1001–1002, 1006–1007   Ch. 4, n. 122
S 1008   Ch. 4, n. 11
S 1010   Ch. 4, n. 122
S 1011   Ch. 6, n. 54
S 1012   Ch. 4, n. 122
S 1015   Ch. 5, n. 373
S 1018, 1021   Ch. 6, table 6.2
S 1026   Ch. 3, nn. 102, 131
S 1028   Ch. 5, n. 373
S 1041   Ch. 4, n. 473; ch. 6, n. 54
S 1042   Ch. 6, table 6.2
S 1043   Ch. 6, n. 54
S 1068–1070, 1073–1074, 1076–1078, 1090   Ch. 3, n. 146
S 1109   Ch. 6, n. 60
S 1123   Ch. 3, n. 146
S 1165   Ch. 6, nn. 56, 108
S 1167–1168   Ch. 6, n. 108
S 1169   Ch. 6, nn. 56, 108
S 1170–1171, 1180   Ch. 6, n. 108
S 1184   Ch. 6, n. 56
S* 1186a   Ch. 2, n. 376
S 1187   Ch. 3, n. 93; ch. 4, n. 79
S 1194   Ch. 3, n. 117; ch. 6, nn. 56, 108
S 1205   Ch. 3, n. 98
S 1208   Ch. 6, table 6.2

S 1211 Ch. 3, nn. 131, 140; ch. 6, table 6.2

S 1222 Ch. 4, nn. 121–2

S 1223 Ch. 3, nn. 106, 114

S 1242 Ch. 3, nn. 114, 140

S 1245 Ch. 6, nn. 56, 108

S 1248–1249 Ch. 6, n. 108

S 1256, 1258 Ch. 4, n. 79

S 1264 Ch. 6, n. 56

S 1266–1267 Ch. 4, nn. 56, 108

S 1273–1274 Ch. 6, n. 56

S 1284 Ch. 3, nn. 98, 100; ch. 4, n. 35; ch. 6, table 6.2

S 1285 Ch. 4, n. 35

S 1286 Ch. 4, n. 35; ch. 6, table 6.2, n. 92

S 1294 Ch. 6, n. 54

S 1328 Ch. 6, table 6.2

S 1368 Ch. 3, n. 118

S* 1377 Ch. 4, n. 127

S 1384 Ch. 4, n. 162

S 1410 Ch. 6, n. 108

S 1417 Ch. 5, n. 203

S 1429 Ch. 4, n. 79

S 1430 Ch. 6, n. 62

S* 1431–1431b Ch. 6, n. 96

S 1433 Ch. 3, n. 93; ch. 4, n. 79

S 1434 Ch. 4, n. 79

S* 1436 Ch. 3, n. 96; ch. 6, n. 96

S 1437 Ch. 5, n. 490; ch. 6, n. 62

S 1439 Ch. 3, n. 96

S 1441 Ch. 6, n. 56

S 1442 Ch. 3, n. 98

S 1443 Ch. 3, n. 148; ch. 4, n. 35

S 1445 Ch. 3, nn. 8, 95–103; ch. 6, table 6.2, nn. 56, 92

S 1446 Ch. 6, n. 56

S 1447 Ch. 3, n. 140; ch. 5, n. 549

S 1453 Ch. 4, nn. 99, 104, 124, 126

S 1454 Ch. 3, nn. 114–25

S 1456 Ch. 3, nn. 93, 114, 123

S* 1457 Ch. 3, nn. 93, 114, 140; ch. 6, table 6.2

S* 1458 Ch. 3, nn. 114, 140

S 1459 Ch. 5, n. 554

S 1460 Ch. 5, n. 549

S 1461 Ch. 3, n. 118; ch. 5, n. 554

S* 1462a Ch. 5, n. 492

S 1463 Ch. 4, nn. 122, 127; ch. 6, table 6.2

S 1465 Ch. 4, n. 122; ch. 6, table 6.2

S 1467 Ch. 3, n. 97

S 1471 Ch. 6, table 6.2

S 1472 Ch. 3, nn. 117–18

S 1473 Ch. 3, n. 118

S 1478 Ch. 3, n. 99; ch. 6, table 6.2

S 1497 Ch. 6, n. 86

S 1507 Ch. 6, n. 56

S 1509 Ch. 5, n. 203

S 1520–1521 Ch. 3, n. 99

S 1555 Ch. 4, n. 278

S 1604 Ch. 6, table 6.2

S 1606 Ch. 6, n. 86

S 1628 Ch. 6, n. 56

S 1660 Ch. 4, n. 123

S 1792 Ch. 6, table 6.2

S 1797 Ch. 3, n. 98

S* 1810d Ch, 6, table 6.2, n. 86

S 1862 Ch. 3, n. 117

(iii) *Index of citations of Old English law-codes (Gesetze I, etc.)*

Abt Ch. 2, table 2.3, nn. 322–50, 366; ch. 4, tables 4.1, 4.8, 4.9, n. 384; ch. 5, table 5.4, nn. 28, 34, 55, 75, 77, 85–7, 120, 222, 357, 438, 597

Af Ch. 2, nn. 322, 324, 330, 337, 369–70; ch. 3, table 3.1, nn. 79, 82, 112, 133, 148; ch. 4, tables 4.1, 4.6, 4.7, 4.8, 4.9, nn. 38–9, 45–6, 48–9, 252, 262, 269, 282–3, 286, 289–91, 318, 336, 360, 384; ch. 5, table 5.4, nn. 1–99, 102, 117–18, 120, 123–5, 130, 171, 183, 186, 189, 209, 222, 227, 287, 370, 374, 421, 427, 438, 504, 537, 551, 587, 643, 646, 649, 660, 697; ch. 6, nn. 1–52, 170, 183

AGu Ch. 1, n. 21; ch. 3, table 3.1; ch. 4, tables 4.1, 4.6, 4.7. 4.9, nn. 267, 275, 283; ch. 5, nn. 44, 57, 100–105, 524, 551; ch. 6, n. 72

App. AGu Ch. 3, table 3.1; ch. 4, tables 4.1, 4.7, 4.9; ch. 5, nn. 515–21; ch. 6, n. 72

I As Ch. 3, table 3.1, n. 82; ch. 4, tables 4.1, 4.2, 4.3, 4.7, 4.9, nn. 158, 246, 371; ch. 5, table 5.1, nn. 119, 129, 162, 173–6, 182–3, 193–4, 233, 239–40, 292, 348, 368, 499, 625–6; ch. 6, table 6.1

II As Ch. 3, table 3.1, n. 134; ch. 4, tables 4.1, 4.6, 4.7, 4.8, 4.9, nn. 49, 53–7, 269–72, 286, 292; ch. 5, tables 5.1, 5.4, nn. 3, 5–6, 104, 122, 129–34, 139, 141, 143–4, 147, 156, 159–67, 170–2, 182–3,

610, 626, 629, 644, 647–9, 658–9, 676; ch. 6, table 6.1

Cn 1018 Ch. 3, table 3.1, nn. 53, 55–6, 61; ch. 4, tables 4.1, 4.3, n. 178; ch. 5, table 5.4, nn. 230, 315, 327, 332, 336–8, 367, 371, 382, 384–90, 435, 443, 491, 588, 596; ch. 6, table 6.1

Cn 1020 Ch. 3, table 3.1, n. 54; ch. 4, table 4.1, n. 144; ch. 5, table 5.4, nn. 119, 382, 384, 392–7, 625

Cn 1027 Ch. 3, table 3.1, n. 73; ch. 5, nn. 398–403, 411, 625

Cons. Cn Ch. 3, table 3.1; ch. 4, tables 4.1, 4.7, 4.9; ch. 5, nn. 227, 408, 415–16, 418, 440, 653–60, 682; ch. 6, n. 182

Duns. Ch. 3, table 3.1; ch. 4, table 4.1, 4.6, 4.7, 4.9, nn. 267, 279; ch. 5, nn. 100, 104, 184, 264, 522–30, 542, 551

ECf Ch. 1, nn. 14, 21, 24, 106; ch. 3, table 3.1, nn. 43, 59; ch. 4, tables 4.1, 4.7, 4.9; ch. 5, nn. 470, 677–8, 680–5; ch. 6, nn. 182, 187

II Eg Ch. 3, table 3.1, n. 57; ch. 4, tables 4.1, 4.2, 4.3, 4.7, 4.9, nn. 97, 110–11, 113, 246, 254, 257, 262, 266, 342–4, 367, 369–70; ch. 5, table 5.4, nn. 3, 13, 206, 228–9, 232–5, 240–1, 257, 348, 368–9, 470–1, 604, 649; ch. 6, table 6.1, n. 87

III Eg Ch. 1, n. 19; ch. 3, table 3.1, nn. 61, 121, 137; ch. 4, tables 4.1, 4.2, 4.3, 4.7, 4.9, nn. 97, 109–11, 113, 246, 254, 257, 262, 266, 342–4, 351, 370; ch. 5, table 5.4, nn. 3, 119, 206, 212, 227–9, 232–4, 236, 242, 244–5, 257–9, 375, 388, 428, 505, 507, 514, 517, 537, 604, 626; ch. 6, table 6.1, n. 87

IV Eg Ch. 3, table 3.1, nn. 31–2, 136; ch. 4, tables 4.1, 4.4, nn. 83, 90, 92, 112, 117, 126; ch. 5, nn. 104, 119, 157, 226, 247–60, 292, 343, 397, 460, 478–80, 505, 528, 544, 626; ch. 6, table 6.1, nn. 87–9, 91–2

EGu Ch. 3, table 3.1, nn. 34, 61; ch. 4, tables 4.1, 4.6, 4.7, 4.8, 4.9, nn. 275, 314; ch. 5, tables 5.3, 5.4, nn. 100, 122, 130, 227, 337, 349, 368, 448, 459, 464, 491, 570–9, 650; ch. 6, n. 141

I Em Ch, 3, table 3.1, n. 82; ch. 4, tables 4.1, 4.2, 4.3, 4.6, 4.7, 4.8, 4.9, nn. 158, 267, 283; ch. 5, nn. 157, 205–7, 209–10, 217, 222, 239, 368, 376, 424, 448, 493; ch. 6, table 6.1, nn. 82, 85

II Em Ch. 3, table 3.1; ch. 4, tables 4.1, 4.6, 4.7, 4.8, 4.9; ch. 5, table 5.5, nn. 109, 119, 122, 204–5, 208, 210–12, 217,

222, 233, 257, 376, 439, 502, 625–6; ch. 6, table 6.1, n. 82

III Em Ch. 3, table 3.1; ch. 4, tables 4.1, 4.7, 4.9; ch. 5, nn. 209–10, 212, 218–20, 223, 242, 244, 376, 437, 507, 509–10, 520, 538, 543, 550, 643; ch. 6, table 6.1, n. 82

Episc. Ch. 4, tables 4.1, 4.7, 4.9, n. 315; ch. 5, table 5.1, nn. 459, 584, 618

I Ew Ch. 2, nn. 322, 328; ch. 3, table 3.1, n. 134; ch. 4, tables 4.1, 4.6, 4.7, 4.8, 4.9; ch. 5, table 5.4, nn. 104, 107–11, 113, 116, 119–20, 122, 164, 171, 183, 209, 242, 537, 626; ch. 6, table 6.1

II Ew Ch. 2, n. 328; ch. 3, table 3.1; ch. 4, tables 4.1, 4.6, 4.7, 4.8, 4.9; ch. 5, nn. 13, 109–11, 113–16, 119–20, 122, 223, 233, 242, 244, 464, 507, 519, 537, 543, 626; ch. 6, table 6.1, nn. 72–3

Excom. Ch. 4, tables 4.1, 4.5, 4.8, 4.9, n. 196; ch. 5, n. 459

Forf. Ch. 3, table 3.1; ch. 4, tables 4.1, 4.6, 4.7, 4.8, 4.9, n. 273; ch. 5, nn. 268, 473–9, 503, 505

Ger. Ch. 3, table 3.1; ch. 4, tables 4.1, 4.6, 4.9, nn. 277, 282; ch. 5, nn. 557–61, 564, 567–8

Geþyn. Ch. 3, table 3.1; ch. 4, tables 4.1, 4.3, 4.7, 4.8, 4.9, nn. 178, 317; ch. 5, table 5.4, nn. 580, 583–5, 590–4, 619, 652; ch. 6, n. 178

Grið Ch. 3, table 3.1; ch. 4, tables 4.1, 4.2, nn. 160, 246, 251; ch. 5, table 5.4, nn. 87, 262, 357, 427, 438, 478, 575–6, 595–602, 650; ch. 6, n. 153

Had. Ch. 3, table 3.1; ch. 4, tables 4.1, 4.3, 4.7, 4.8, 4.9, nn. 178, 315; ch. 5, tables 5.1, 5.4, nn. 575, 581–2

Hl Ch. 2, nn. 323–4, 327, 330, 352, 354, 366; ch. 4, tables 4.1, 4.8, 4.9; ch. 5, nn. 222, 542

Hn Ch. 3, table 3.1; ch. 4, table 4.7; ch. 5, nn. 227, 470, 671, 686–700; ch. 6, nn. 180, 182–5, 188–91, 193, 213–14

Hn com Ch. 3, table 3.1; ch. 4, tables 4.1, 4.7, 4.9; ch. 5, nn. 632–3; ch. 6, n. 61

Hn Lond Ch. 4, table 4.7; ch. 5, nn. 630, 688

Hn mon Ch. 3, table 3.1; ch. 5, n. 632; ch. 6, nn. 61, 122

Hu. Ch. 3, table 3.1, n. 134; ch. 4, tables 4.1, 4.6, 4.7, 4.9, n. 273; ch. 5, nn. 106, 119–20, 242, 292, 459, 467, 505–14

Ine Ch. 2, nn. 324, 327, 330, 358–63, 365–8; ch. 3, nn. 78, 82, 103, 112, 148; ch. 4, tables 4.1, 4.6, 4.7, 4.8, 4.9, nn.

(iv)   *Index of citations of Frankish Capitularies (numbered as in* Cap.*)*

22   Ch. 2, nn. 82, 98, 105, 108, 113, 116, 181, 187, 194, 213, 372, 374; ch. 4, table 4.4, n. 218; ch. 5, nn. 70, 128, 216, 241

23   Ch. 2, nn. 108, 161, 187

24   Ch. 2, n. 166

25   Ch. 2, n. 105

26   Ch. 2, nn. 109, 183; ch. 5, n. 82

27   Ch. 2, nn. 109, 183

28   Ch. 2, n. 223

29   Ch. 2, n. 108

31   Ch. 2, n. 185

32   Ch. 2, nn. 89, 186

33   Ch. 2, nn. 105, 109, 116, 201, 213–14, 254; ch. 3, n. 18

34   Ch. 2, nn. 108, 164

35   Ch. 2, n. 213

36   Ch. 5, n. 378

39   Ch. 2, nn. 66, 96, 150, 157, 174, 250, 254; ch. 5, nn. 82, 243

40   Ch. 2, nn. 96, 157, 174, 214

41   Ch. 2, nn. 96, 150, 180

42   Ch. 2, n. 183

43–44   Ch. 2, nn. 109, 150, 194; ch. 5, nn. 238, 447

48–49   Ch. 2, n. 163

50   Ch. 2, n. 117

51–52   Ch. 2, nn. 108, 163; ch. 5, nn. 82, 447

53   Ch. 2, nn. 108, 163

56   Ch. 2, n. 254

57   Ch. 2, nn. 150, 194

58   Ch. 2, nn. 105, 163, 216, 254

59   Ch. 2, n. 163

61–63   Ch. 2, nn. 108, 213; ch. 5, nn. 128, 243

64–65   Ch. 2, nn. 108, 163, 245; ch. 3, n. 19; ch. 5, nn. 82, 243

66   Ch. 5, n. 216

67   Ch. 2, nn. 150, 174, 194; ch. 5, n. 216

68   Ch. 2, n. 96

69   Ch. 3, n. 19

71–72   Ch. 2, nn. 108, 163

73   Ch. 2, n. 163

74   Ch. 2, n. 109, 273; ch. 5, n. 447

76   Ch. 2, n. 261

77   Ch. 2, n. 105

78   Ch. 2, n. 183

80   Ch. 2, nn. 214, 245–6

82   Ch. 2, nn. 174, 192, 194

85   Ch. 2, n. 105

88   Ch. 2, n. 103

89   Ch. 2, nn. 103, 187

90–91   Ch. 2, n. 103

92–93   Ch. 2, nn. 89, 103

94   Ch. 2, nn. 103, 187; ch. 5, n. 82

95   Ch. 2, n. 103; ch. 5, n. 85

97   Ch. 2, nn. 103, 187

98   Ch. 2, nn. 88, 103; ch. 5, n. 85

99–103, 105   Ch. 2, n. 103

116   Ch. 2, n. 105

118   Ch. 2, n. 183

121   Ch. 2, n. 108

128   Ch. 2, n. 186

129   Ch. 2, n. 292

134–135   Ch. 2, nn. 97, 218

136   Ch. 2, nn. 97, 170

137   Ch. 2, nn. 97–8, 170

138   Ch. 2, nn. 97, 170, 220

139   Ch. 2, nn. 97–8, 170, 218, 220; ch. 5, nn. 82, 197, 447

140   Ch. 2, nn. 97, 170, 254

141   Ch. 2, nn. 97, 170, 213, 218

142   Ch. 2, nn. 97, 254

143–145   Ch. 2, n. 170

146   Ch. 3, n. 19

150   Ch. 2, nn. 98, 109, 116–17, 201, 213–14

151   Ch. 4, n. 214

155   Ch. 2, n. 269

156   Ch. 2, n. 245

157–158   Ch. 2, nn. 103, 199

159–162   Ch. 2, n. 103

163–165   Ch. 2, nn. 103, 199, 203

166–168   Ch. 2, n. 103

170   Ch. 5, n. 246

181   Ch. 2, n. 199

184   Ch. 2, n. 98

185   Ch. 2, n. 98; ch. 3, n. 19

186   Ch. 2, nn. 98, 108

187–190   Ch. 2, n. 98

191   Ch. 2, nn. 98, 122

192   Ch. 2, nn. 98, 122, 213–14; ch. 3, n. 19

193   Ch. 2, nn. 98, 122; ch. 5, n. 82

196   Ch. 3, n. 23

198   Ch. 2, n. 99

201–202   Ch. 2, nn. 103, 203

203   Ch. 2, n. 103

204   Ch. 2, nn. 100, 103; ch. 5, nn. 82, 100

205   Ch. 2, nn. 100, 103; ch. 3, n. 66; ch. 5, n. 100

206–208   Ch. 2, nn. 100, 103; ch. 5, n. 100

209–210   Ch. 2, nn. 103, 135

211   Ch. 2, n. 103

212–213   Ch. 2, nn. 103, 135

214–215   Ch. 2, n. 103

216–217   Ch. 2, nn. 103, 132

218–219   Ch. 2, n. 103

220   Ch. 2, nn. 100, 103

III MODERN COMMENTARY

Indexed as in I, II. Cross-references to '*work*, ed. X' designate a publication appearing in *II SOURCES*; 'X (ed.), *work* indicates one elsewhere in this section. Works by the same author are cited in chronological order of publication. Where articles are reprinted in authors' collected editions, footnotes usually contain page-references to the latter, added in brackets.

H. Aarsleff, *The Study of Language in England, 1780–1860* (Princeton, 1967).   **Ch. 1, n. 41**

R.R. Abels, *Lordship and Military Obligation in Anglo-Saxon England* (London, 1988).   **Ch. 6, n. 168**

H. Adams *et al.*, *Essays in Anglo-Saxon Law* (Boston, 1876).   **Ch. 1, nn. 52–5**

S.R. Airlie, 'The Political Behaviour of the Secular Magnates in Francia, 829–79' (Oxford, D.Phil., 1985).   **Ch. 2, n. 281**

S.R. Airlie, 'The Aristocracy', in McKitterick (ed.), *New Cambridge Medieval History*, pp. 431–50.   **Ch. 2, n. 315**

J.J.G. Alexander, 'The Illumination', in *York Gospels*, ed. Barker, pp. 65–79. **Ch. 4, n. 139**

J.J.G. Alexander and M.T. Gibson (editors), *Medieval Learning and Literature. Studies presented to Richard William Hunt* (Oxford, 1976): see Bischoff, Southern.

J. Allen, *Inquiry into the Rise and Growth of the Royal Prerogative in England* (London, 1829).   **Ch. 1, nn. 33, 35**

R. Allnatt 'The History of the New Minster, Winchester, and its estates, 900–1200' (Oxford, M.Litt., 1990).   **Ch. 4, n. 36**

G. Althoff, *Amicitiae und Pacta: Bündnis, Einung, Politik und Gebetsgedenkung im beginnenden 10. Jahrhundert* (Hannover, 1992).   **Ch. 6, n. 76**

K. von Amira, *Germanisches Recht* (2 vols, 4th edn revised by K.A. Eckhardt, Berlin, 1960); originally published as 'Grundriss des germanischen Rechts', in H. Paul, *Grundriss der germanischen Philologie* (Straßburg, 1890). **Ch 1, n. 63; ch. 6, n. 39**

P. Amory, 'The meaning and purpose of ethnic terminology in the Burgundian Laws', *EME* 2 (1993), pp. 1–28.   **Ch. 2, n. 46**

T. Anderson Jr., 'Roman military colonies in Gaul, Salian Ethnogenesis and the forgotten meaning of *Pactus Legis Salicae* 59.5', *EME* 4 (1995), pp. 129–44. **Ch. 2, nn. 48, 85**

H.H. Anton, *Fürstenspiegel und Herrscherethos in der Karolingerzeit* (Bonner historischer Forschungen 32, Bonn, 1968).   **Ch. 3, n. 25**

E. Archibald, *Apollonius of Tyre: Medieval and Renaissance Themes and Variations* (Cambridge, 1991).   **Ch. 4, nn. 181, 183–4**

R. Aronstam, 'The Latin Canonical Tradition in late Anglo-Saxon England: the *Excerptiones Egberti*' (Columbia, Ph.D., 1974).   **Ch. 4, table 4.4, nn. 193, 208, 213, 217, 224**

R. Aronstam, 'Recovering Hucarius: a historiographical study in early English canon law', *Bulletin of Medieval Canon Law* n.s. 5 (1975), pp. 117–22.   **Ch. 4, n. 217**

R. Aronstam. 'Penitential pilgrimages to Rome in the early Middle Ages', *Archivum Historiae Pontificiae* 13 (1975), pp. 65–83.   **Ch. 4, n. 206**

E.E. Barker, 'The Cottonian Fragments of Æthelweard's *Chronicle*', *BIHR* XXIV (1951), pp. 46–62.   **Ch. 4, nn. 364, 366**

L. Barker, 'Ivo of Chartres and the Anglo-Norman Cultural Tradition', *ANS* XIII (1990/1), pp. 15–33.   **Ch. 6, nn. 217–18, 221, 227, 233**

F. Barlow, *Edward the Confessor* (London, 1970).   **Ch. 3, nn. 43, 63**

F. Barlow, *The English Church 1066–1154* (London, 1979).   **Ch. 3, n. 70; ch.4, n. 297; ch. 6, n. 226**

F. Barlow, *William Rufus* (London, 1983).   **Ch. 6, n. 61**

B. Barr, 'The History of the Volume', in *York Gospels*, ed. Barker, pp. 101–17.   **Ch. 4, nn. 138, 146**

J. Barrow, 'The Chronology of Forgery Production at Worcester from *c*. 1000 to the Early Twelfth Century', in N.P. Brooks and Barrow (editors), *Saint Wulfstan of Worcester* (forthcoming).   **Ch. 6, n. 76**

R. Bartlett, *Trial by Fire and Water.The Medieval Judicial Ordeal* (Oxford, 1986).   **Ch. 2, nn. 217, 219; ch. 4, n. 40**

J. Bately, 'The Old English Orosius: The Question of Dictation', *Anglia* 84 (1966), pp. 255–304.   **Ch. 5, n. 30**

J. Bately, 'King Alfred and the Old English Translation of Orosius', *Anglia* 88 (1970), pp. 433–59.   **Ch. 5, nn. 30–3, 37–8, 41–2, 44–5, 48–9, 53–6, 58, 60, 62, 65–6**

J. Bately, 'The Compilation of the Anglo-Saxon Chronicle, 60 BC to AD 890: Vocabulary as Evidence', *PBA* LXIV (1978), pp. 93–127.   **Ch. 5, nn. 30, 34**

J. Bately, 'Lexical evidence for the authorship of the prose psalms in the Paris Psalter', *ASE* 10 (1981), pp. 69–95.   **Ch. 5, nn. 30, 34, 36–7, 43, 46–7, 49–52, 57, 59, 61, 63–4, 66**

J. Bately, 'The Literary Prose of King Alfred's Reign: Translation or Transformation?', *OEN* Subsidia 10 (1984).   **Ch. 6, nn. 6, 11, 43**

J. Bately, 'Old English Prose before and during the reign of Alfred', *ASE* 17 (1988), pp. 93–138.   **Ch. 4, n. 63**

J. Bately, *The Anglo-Saxon Chronicle, Texts and textual relationships*, (Reading Medieval Studies, Monograph 3, 1991).   **Ch. 4, n. 18**

J. Bately, 'John Joscelyn and the Laws of the Anglo-Saxon Kings', in Korhammer *et al.* (eds), *Words, Texts and Manuscripts*, pp. 435–66.   **Ch. 4, nn. 245, 342–3**

D. Bates, *Normandy before 1066* (London, 1982).   **Ch. 3, n. 70; ch. 7, n. 9**

D. Bates, *William the Conqueror* (London, 1989).   **Ch. 6, n. 110**

M. Bateson, 'A Worcester Cathedral Book of Ecclesiastical Collections made *c*. 1000 AD', *EHR* X (1895), pp. 712–31.   **Ch. 4, nn. 204, 206, 229**

M. Becher, *Eid und Herrschaft.Untersuchungen zum Herrscherethos Karls des Großen* (Sigmaringen, 1993).   **Ch. 2, n. 273**

W. Bergmann, 'Untersuchungen zu den Gerichtsurkunden der Merowingerzeit', *Arch. Dip.* 22 (1976), pp. 1–186.   **Ch. 2, nn. 303, 311–12**

W. Bergmann, 'Die Formulae Andecavenses, eine Formelsammlung auf der Grenze zwischen Antike und Mittelalter', *Arch. Dip.* 24 (1978), pp. 1–53.   **Ch. 2, n. 40**

W. Bergmann, 'Fortleben des antiken Notariats im Frühmittelalter', in P-J. Schuler *et al.* (editors), *Tradition und Gegenwart. Festschrift zum 175-jährigen Bestehen eines badischen Notarstandes* (Karlsruhe, 1981), pp. 23–35.   **Ch. 2, n. 40**

D.S. Berkowitz, *John Selden's Formative Years. Politics and Society in Early Seventeenth-Century England* (Washington, 1988).   **Ch. 4, n. 98**

E. Besta, 'Le Fonti dell' Editto di Rotari', *Atti del primo Congresso internazionale di Studi Longobardi* (Spoleto, 1952), pp. 51–69.   **Ch. 2, n. 70**

D. Bethurum, 'Archbishop Wulfstan's Commonplace Book', *Proceedings of the Modern Language Association of America* LVII (1942), pp. 916–929.   **Ch. 4, nn. 156, 204, 235**

D. Bethurum, 'Six anonymous Old English Codes', *Journal of English and Germanic Philology* XLIX (1950), pp. 449–63.   **Ch. 1, n. 127; ch. 5, nn. 589, 593**

D. Bethurum, 'Episcopal Magnificence in the Eleventh Century', in S.B. Greenfield (editor), *Studies in Old English Literature in Honor of Arthur G. Brodeur* (Eugene, 1963), pp. 162–71.   **Ch. 5, n. 565**

H. Beumann *et al.*, *Karl der Große. Lebenswerk und Nachleben* (5 vols, Düsseldorf, 1965–8): see Bischoff, Ganshof.

F. Beyerle, 'Über Normtypen und Erweiterungen der Lex Salica', *ZSS germ. Abt* XLIV (1924), pp. 394–419.   **Ch. 2, nn. 70, 333; ch. 5, n. 23**

F. Beyerle, 'Die süddeutschen Leges und die merowingische Gesetzgebung (Volksrechtliche Studien II)', *ZSS germ. Abt.* XLIX (1929), pp. 264–432. **Ch. 2, nn. 339, 347**

J. Biancalana, 'For Want of Justice: Legal Reforms of Henry II', *Columbia Law Review* 88 (1988), pp. 433–536. **Ch. 1, n. 83**

M. Biddle (editor), *Winchester in the Early Middle Ages: an Edition and Discussion of the Winton Domesday* (Winchester Studies I, general editor M. Biddle, Oxford, 1976). **Ch. 6, n. 64**

M. Biddle, 'Seasonal Festivals and Residence: Winchester, Westminster and Gloucester in the tenth to twelfth centuries', *ANS* VIII (1985/6), pp. 51–72. **Ch. 6, nn. 54, 110, 122**

F.M. Biggs, T.D. Hill and P.E. Szarmach (editors), *Sources of Anglo-Saxon Literary Culture: a Trial Version* (Medieval and Renaissance Texts and Studies 74, Binghamton, 1990); see also Wormald, 'LAWS'. **Ch. 4, n. 202; ch. 5, n. 535**

D.A. Binchy, 'The Linguistic and Historical Value of the Irish Law Tracts', *PBA* 29 (1943), pp. 195–227; repr. in *Celtic Law Papers (introductory to Welsh medieval law and government)* (International Commission for the History of Representative and Parliamentary Institutions XLII, Aberystwyth, 1971, Brussels, 1973), pp. 73–107. **Ch. 1, n. 3**

D.A. Binchy, 'Celtic Suretyship, a fossilized Indo-European institution?' *Irish Jurist* n.s. 7 (1972), pp. 360–72. **Ch. 5, n. 95**

B. Bischoff, 'Manuscripts in the Age of Charlemagne', in *idem* (translated and edited by M. Gorman), *Manuscripts and Libraries in the Age of Charlemagne* (Cambridge, 1994), pp. 20–55 (originally 'Panorama der Handschriftenüberlieferung aus der Zeit Karls des Großen', in Beumann *et al.* (eds), *Karl der Große, II Das Geistige Leben*, pp. 233–54; repr. in *Mittelalterliche Studien* III, pp. 5–38). **Ch. 2, n. 148**

B. Bischoff, 'The Court Library under Louis the Pious', *Manuscripts and Libraries* (as above), pp. 76–92 (originally 'Die Hofbibliothek unter Ludwig dem Frommen', in Alexander and Gibson (eds), *Medieval Learning and Literature*, pp. 3–22; repr. in *Mittelalterliche Studien* I, p. 170–86). **Ch. 2, nn. 167, 175**

B. Bischoff, *Mittelalterliche Studien. Ausgewählte Aufsätze zur Schriftkunde und Literaturgeschichte* (3 vols, Stuttgart, 1966–81): see above.

B. Bischoff (translated by D. O'Croinin and D. Ganz), *Latin Palaeography. Antiquity and the Middle Ages* (Cambridge, 1990). **Ch. 2, n. 167**

E. Bishop, *Liturgica Historica: Papers on the Liturgy and Religious Life of the Western Church* (Oxford, 1918). **Ch. 4, n. 15**

T.A.M. Bishop, *English Caroline Minuscule* (Oxford Palaeographical Handbooks, general editors R.W. Hunt, C.H. Roberts and F. Wormald, Oxford, 1971). **Ch. 4, nn. 91, 139, 185**

T.N. Bisson, 'The "Feudal Revolution"', *PP* 142 (1994), pp. 6–42; followed by 'Debate' (D. Barthélemy, S.D. White, T. Reuter, C. Wickham, T.N. Bisson), *PP* 152 (1996), pp. 196–223, 155 (1997), pp. 177–225. **Ch. 1, n. 87; ch. 6, nn. 131, 138, 171; ch. 7, n. 9**

M. Blackburn, 'Mints, Burhs and the Grately Code cap. 14: 2', in Hill and Rumble (eds), *Defence of Wessex*, pp. 160–75. **Ch. 6, nn. 77–8**

W. Blackstone, *Commentaries*: see *II SOURCES*.

M. Bloch (translated by L.A. Manyon), *Feudal Society* (London, 1961). **Ch. 7, n. 5**

C.E. Blunt, 'The Coinage of Æthelstan, 924–39: a Survey', *BNJ* XLII (special Volume for the seventieth birthday of Christopher Evelyn Blunt, edited by M. Dolley, J. Porteous and H.E. Pagan, 1974). **Ch. 6, nn. 79, 81, 121**

C.E. Blunt, B.H.I.H. Stewart and C.S.S. Lyon, *Coinage in Tenth-Century England: from Edward the Elder to Edgar's Reform* (Oxford, 1989). **Ch. 6, n. 78**

W.F. Bolton, 'How Boethian is Alfred's *Boethius*?', in Szarmach (ed.), *Studies in earlier Old English Prose*, pp. 153–68. **Ch. 3, n. 28; ch. 6, n. 6**

A-M. la Bonnardière, 'En marge de la "Biblia Augustiniana": une "Retractatio"', *Revue des études Augustiniennes* 10 (1964), pp. 305–7. **Ch. 6, n. 28**

E. Boshof, *Erzbischof Agobard von Lyon* (Cologne, 1969). **Ch. 2, n. 99**

J. Bossy (editor), *Disputes and Settlements.Law and Human Relations in the West* (Cambridge, 1983): see Clanchy, James.

J. Bosworth, with T. Toller (and supplement by A. Campbell), *An Anglo-Saxon Dictionary* (2 vols, Oxford repr., 1972). **Ch. 5, nn. 469, 473, 485**

F. Bougard, *La Justice dans le Royaume d' Italie de la fin du VIIIe siècle au début du XIe siècle* (Bibliothèque des écoles françaises d' Athènes et de Rome 291, Rome, 1995). **Ch. 2, nn. 118, 142, 187, 203, 295, 299–300, 305, 307**

M. Boynton and S. Reynolds, 'The author of the Fonthill Letter', *ASE* 25 (1996), pp. 91–5. **Ch. 3. n. 98**

R. Brady, *A Complete History of England from the first entrance of the Romans ... Unto the End of the Reign of Henry III* (London, 1685). **Ch. 1, nn. 25–7**

P. Brand, *The Origins of the English Legal Profession* (Oxford, 1992). **Ch. 6, n. 208**

B. Brassington, 'Studies in the *Nachleben* of Ivo of Chartres: the Influence of his Prologue on Several Panormia-Derived Collections', *Monumenta Iuris Canonici*, Series C: Subsidia 10 (1997), pp. 63–82. **Ch. 6, n. 222**

M. Brett, 'John of Worcester and his contemporaries', in Davis and Wallace-Hadrill (eds), *Writing of History in the Middle Ages* (Oxford, 1981), pp. 101–26. **Ch. 3, nn. 72–3; ch. 5, n. 398**

M. Brett, 'Forgery at Rochester', in *Fälschungen in Mittelalter* IV (Diplomatische Fälschungen II), pp. 397–412. **Ch. 4, n. 328**

M. Brett, 'The *Collectio Lanfranci* and its Competitors', in L. Smith and B. Ward (editors), *Intellectual Life in the Middle Ages: Essays presented to Margaret Gibson* (London, 1992), pp. 157–74. **Ch. 6, nn. 212–13, 218**

M. Brett, 'Urban II and the collections attributed to Ivo of Chartres', *Monumenta Iuris Canonici*, Series C: Subsidia 9 (1992), pp. 27–46. **Ch. 6, nn. 214–16**

M. Brett, 'The sources and influence of Paris Bibliothèque de l' Arsenal MS 713*', *Monumenta Iuris Canonici*, Series C: Subsidia 10 (1997), pp. 149–67. **Ch. 6, nn. 214, 216**

C.N.L. Brooke, 'Geoffrey of Monmouth as a historian', in Brooke *et al.* (eds), *Church and Government*, pp. 77–91. **Ch. 3, n. 87**

C.N.L. Brooke *et al.* (editors), *Church and Government in the Middle Ages: Essays presented to C.R. Cheney on his 70th Birthday* (Cambridge, 1976): see Brooke, Foreville.

C.N.L. Brooke, *The Medieval Idea of Marriage* (Oxford, 1991). **Ch. 5, n. 553**

Z.N. Brooke, *The English Church and the Papacy, from the Conquest to the Reign of John* (Cambridge, 1931). **Ch. 6, nn. 212, 218**

N. Brooks, 'The pre-conquest charters of Christ Church Canterbury', (Oxford, D. Phil., 1969). **Ch. 4, n. 117**

N. Brooks, 'The development of military obligations in eighth- and ninth-century England', in Clemoes and Hughes (eds), *England Before the Conquest*, pp. 69–84. **Ch. 2, n. 375; ch. 5, n. 374**

N. Brooks, 'Arms, Status and Warfare in Late-Saxon England', in Hill (ed.), *Ethelred*, pp. 81–103. **Ch. 5, n. 441**

N. Brooks *et al.*, 'A New Charter of King Edgar', *ASE* 13 (1984), pp. 137–55. **Ch. 6, n. 90**

N. Brooks, *The Early History of the Church of Canterbury* (Studies in the Early History of Britain, general editor N. Brooks, Leicester, 1984). **Ch. 4, nn. 122, 139; ch. 6, n. 96**

N. Brooks, 'The West Saxon hidage and the "Appendix"', in Hill and Rumble (eds), *Defence of Wessex*, pp. 87–92. **Ch. 4, n. 66**

N. Brooks and C. Cubitt (editors), *St Oswald of Worcester: Life and Influence* (Studies in the Early History of Britain, general editor N. Brooks, Leicester, 1996): see Dyer, Lapidge.

E.A.R. Brown, 'Georges Duby and the Three Orders', *Viator* 17 (1986), pp. 51–64. **Ch. 6, nn. 159, 167**

J. Brückmann, 'Latin Manuscript Pontificals and Benedictionals in England and Wales', *Traditio* 29 (1973), pp. 391–458. **Ch. 4, n. 130**

C-R. Brühl, 'Fränkischer Krönungsbrauch und das Problem der "Festkrönungen"', *HZ* 194 (1962), pp. 265–326. **Ch. 6, n. 111**

C-R. Brühl, 'The Town as a Political Centre: General Survey', in M.W. Barley (editor), *European Towns: their Archaeology and Early History* (Council for British Archaeology, London, 1977), pp. 419–30. **Ch. 6, n. 64**

C-R. Brühl, 'Kronen und Krönungsbrauch im frühen und höhen Mittelalter', *HZ* 234 (1982), pp. 1–31. **Ch. 6, nn. 111, 120**

M-B. Brugière, *Littérature et Droit dans la Gaule du Ve siècle* (Toulouse, 1974). **Ch. 2, n. 44**

M-B. Brugière, 'Réflexions sur la Crise de la Justice en Occident à la fin de l' Antiquité: l'apport de la littérature', *La Giustizia* I, pp. 165–223. **Ch. 2, nn. 44, 56**

H. Brunner, 'Zeugen und Inquisitionsbeweis der karolingischen Zeit', *Sitzungsberichte der Wiener Akademie der Wissenschaften*, ph.-hist. Kl. LI (Vienna, 1865). Ch. 1, n. 79

H. Brunner, *Die Entstehung der Schwurgerichte* (Berlin, 1872). Ch. 1, nn. 79–80

H. Brunner, 'The Sources of English Law', in *Select Essays in Anglo-American Legal History*, edited by a committee of the Association of American Law Schools (3 vols, Cambridge, 1908) II, pp. 7–52; originally published as 'Überblick über die Geschichte der französischen, normannischen und englischen Rechtsquellen', in F. von Holtzendorff (editor), *Encyclopädie der Rechtswissenschaft* (Leipzig, 3rd edn, 1877), pp. 229–67. Ch. 1, nn. 63–5, 73, 89

H. Brunner, 'Über ein verschollenes merowingisches Königsgesetz des 7. Jahrhunderts', *Sitzungsberichte der königlichen preußischen Akademie der Wissenschaften* XXXIX (Berlin, 1901), pp. 932–55. Ch. 2, nn. 339–40

H. Brunner, *Deutsche Rechtsgeschichte* (2 vols, 2nd edn, completed by C. Fr. von Schwerin, Leipzig, 1906, 1928). Ch. 1, nn. 40, 63; ch. 2, nn. 197, 216, 222, 250

R. Buchner, *Die Rechtsquellen* (Beiheft zu Wattenbach-Levison, *Deutschlands Geschischtsquellen im Mittelalter*, Weimar, 1953). Ch. 2, n. 39

R. Buchner, 'Die römischen und die germanischen Wesenszüge in der neuen politischen Ordnung des Abendlandes', *Sett. Spol.* V (1958), pp. 223–69. Ch. 2, n. 345

T.M. Buck, *Admonitio und Praedicatio. Zur religiös-pastoralen Dimension von Kapitularien und kapituliennähen Texte (507–814)* (Freiburger Beiträge zur mittelalterlichen Geschichte 9, general editor H. Mordek, Frankfurt, 1997). Ch. 2, n. 108

A. Bühler, 'Capitularia Relecta. Studien zur Entstehung und Überlieferung der Kapitularien Karls des Großen und Ludwigs des Frommen', *Arch. Dip.* 32 (1986), pp. 305–501. Ch. 2, nn. 106, 110, 142, 164, 202

A. Bühler, 'Wort und Schrift im karolingischen Recht', *Archiv für Kulturgeschichte* 72 (1990), pp. 275–96. Ch. 2, nn, 86, 110, 117

D.A. Bullough, 'Leo, *qui apud Hlotharium magni loci habebatur*, et le gouvernement du *Regnum Italiae* à l'époque carolingienne', *Le Moyen Age* 3 (1961), pp. 221–45. Ch. 2, n. 298

D.A. Bullough, 'Anglo-Saxon Institutions and Early English Society', *Annali della fondazione italiana per la storia amministrativa* 2 (1965), pp. 645–59. Ch. 5, n. 77

D.A. Bullough, *The Age of Charlemagne* (London, 1965). Ch. 2, n. 64

D.A. Bullough, '*Europae Pater*: Charlemagne and his achievement in the light of recent scholarship', *EHR* LXXXV (1970), pp. 59–105. Ch. 2, n. 297

D.A. Bullough, 'The Educational Tradition in England from Alfred to Ælfric: teaching *utriusque linguae*', *Sett. Spol.* XIX (1972), pp. 453–94. Ch. 5, n. 185

E. Burke, 'An Essay towards an Abridgement of English History', in *The Works of Edmund Burke* (6 vols, London, 1901–2) VI, pp. 184–422. Ch. 1, n. 31

J.W. Burrow, 'The "Village Community" and the Uses of History in Late Nineteenth-Century England', in N. McKendrick (editor), *Historical Perspectives. Studies in English Thought and Society in Honour of J.H. Plumb* (Cambridge, 1974), pp. 255–84. Ch. 1, n. 66

R.C. van Caenegem, *Royal Writs in England from the Conquest to Glanvill* (Selden Society 77, London, 1958–9). Ch. 1, n. 122

R.C. van Caenegem, *The Birth of the English Common Law* (Cambridge, 2nd edn, 1988). Ch. 1, n. 92

J. Calmette, 'Un jugement original de Wifred le velu pour l'abbaye d'Amer', *Bibliothèque de l'École des Chartes* LXVII (1906), pp. 60–9. Ch. 2, n. 258

H.M. Cam, 'The Evolution of the Medieval English Franchise', *Speculum* XXXII (1957), pp. 427–42, repr. in her *Law-Finders and Law-Makers in Medieval England* (London, 1962), pp. 22–43. Ch. 1, n. 116; ch. 3, n. 138

M.L. Cameron, 'Bald's *Leechbook*: its sources and their use in its compilation', *ASE* 12 (1983), pp. 153–82. Ch. 4, nn. 62, 100

J. Campbell, 'Observations on English Government from the Tenth to the Twelfth Century', *TRHS* 5th series 25 (1975), pp. 39–54; repr. in his *Essays*, pp. 155–70. Ch. 1, nn. 111, 125; ch. 5, nn. 197, 483; ch. 7, n. 1

J. Campbell, 'England, France, Flanders and Germany: some Comparisons and Connections', in Hill (ed.), *Ethelred*, pp. 255–70, repr. in his *Essays*, pp. 191–207. **Ch. 6, n. 137**

J. Campbell, 'Bede's Words for Places', in P.H. Sawyer (editor), *Places, Names and Graves* (Leeds, 1979), pp. 34–54; repr. in his *Essays*, pp. 99–119. **Ch. 5, n. 35**

J. Campbell, 'The Significance of the Anglo-Norman State in the Administrative History of Western Europe', in Paravicini and Werner (eds), *Histoire Comparée de l'Administration*, pp. 117–34; repr. in his *Essays*, pp. 171–89. **Ch. 2, n. 105; ch. 5, n. 632; ch. 7, n. 1**

J. Campbell, 'Some Twelfth-Century Views of the Anglo-Saxon Past, *Peritia* 3 (1984), pp. 131–50; repr. in his *Essays*, pp. 209–28.   **Ch. 3, nn. 68, 83; ch. 6,n. 230**

J. Campbell, *Essays in Anglo-Saxon History* (London, 1986): see above.

J. Campbell, 'Asser's *Life of Alfred*', in C. Holdsworth and T.N. Wiseman (editors), *The Inheritance of Historiography, 350–900* (Exeter Studies in History 12, Exeter, 1986), pp. 117–35. **Ch. 3, nn. 6, 28**

J. Campbell, *Stubbs and the English State* (Stenton Lecture 21, Reading, 1989). **Ch. 1, n. 56**

J. Campbell, 'The Late Anglo-Saxon State: A Maximum View', *PBA* LXXXVII (1994), pp. 39–65. **Ch. 1, n. 125; ch. 5, n. 632; ch. 7, n. 1**

J. Campbell, 'The United Kingdom of England', in A. Grant and K.J. Stringer (editors), *Uniting the Kingdom?* (London, 1995), pp. 31–47. **Ch. 6, n. 101**

J. Campbell, 'Taking directions in Anglo-Saxon history from a forgotten Oxford prophet (E.W. Robertson)' (forthcoming). **Ch. 1, n. 37**

J. Campbell (editor), *The Anglo-Saxons* (Oxford, 1982). **Ch. 6, nn. 113, 121**

J.I. Catto, 'Andrew Horn: law and history in fourteenth-century England', in Davis and Wallace-Hadrill (eds), *Writing of History in the Middle Ages*, pp. 367–91. **Ch. 1, n. 18; ch. 4, nn. 304, 307**

H.M. Chadwick, *Studies on Anglo-Saxon Institutions* (Cambridge, 1905). **Ch. 1, n. 109; ch. 2, n. 368; ch. 5, n. 586**

H.M. Chadwick, *The Origin of the English Nation* (Cambridge, 1907). **Ch. 3, n. 94**

P. Chaplais, 'The original charters of Herbert and Gervase, abbots of Westminster (1121–1157)', in P.M. Barnes and C.F. Slade (editors), *A Medieval Miscellany for Doris Mary Stenton* (Pipe Roll Society N.S. XXXVI, London, 1962), pp. 89–110; repr. in his *Essays*, XVIII. **Ch. 3, n. 148**

P. Chaplais, 'The Authenticity of the Royal Anglo-Saxon Diplomas of Exeter', *BIHR* XXXIX (1966), pp. 1–34, repr. with Addenda in his *Essays*, XV. **Ch. 4, n. 240**

P. Chaplais, 'The Origin and Authenticity of the Royal Anglo-Saxon Diploma', *Journal of the Society of Archivists* III (1965–9), pp. 48–61. **Ch. 4, n. 12; ch. 6, nn. 55, 58**

P. Chaplais, 'The Anglo-Saxon Chancery: from the Diploma to the Writ', *Journal of the Society of Archivists* III (1965–9), pp. 160–76. **Ch. 3, n. 123; ch. 5, n. 395**

P. Chaplais, 'Some Early Anglo-Saxon Charters on Single Sheets: Originals or Copies?', *Journal of the Society of Archivists* III (1965–9), pp. 315–36. **Ch. 6, n. 58**

P. Chaplais, *Essays in Medieval Diplomacy and Administration* (London, 1981): see above.

T.M. Charles-Edwards, *Early Irish and Welsh Kinship* (Oxford, 1993). **Ch. 1, nn. 43–4; ch. 2, n. 368**

C. Chase (editor), *Two Alcuin Letter-Books* (Toronto Medieval Latin Texts 5, 1975). **Ch. 6, n. 176**

M.T. Clanchy, 'Law and Love in the Middle Ages', in Bossy (ed.), *Disputes and Settlements*, pp. 47–67. **Ch. 1, n. 124; ch. 3, n. 143**

P. Classen, 'Kaiserreskript und Königsurkunde. Diplomatische Studien zum römisch-germanisch Kontinuitätsproblem I–II', *Arch. Dip.* 1 (1955), pp. 1–87; 2 (1956), pp. 1–115. **Ch. 2, n. 311**

P. Classen, 'Die Verträge von Verdun und von Coulaines 843 als politische Grundlagen des westfränkischen Reiches', *HZ* 196 (1963), pp. 1–35. **Ch. 2, n. 101**

P. Classen, 'Fortleben und Wandel spätrömischen Urkundenwesens im frühen Mittelalter', in *idem* (ed.) *Recht und Schrift*, pp. 13–54. **Ch. 2, n. 311**

P. Classen (editor), *Recht und Schrift im Mittelalter* (Vorträge und Forschungen der Konstanzer Arbeitskreis für mittelalterliche Geschichte XXIII, 1977): see Classen, Nehlsen.

R.W. Clement, 'The Production of the *Pastoral Care*: King Alfred and his Helpers', in Szarmach (ed.), *Studies in Earlier Old English Prose*, pp. 129–52. Ch. 5, nn. 30, 66

P. Clemoes, *Interactions of Thought and Language in Old English Poetry* (Cambridge Studies in Anglo-Saxon England 12, general editors S. Keynes and M. Lapidge, Cambridge, 1995). Ch. 5, n. 541

P. Clemoes and K. Hughes (editors), *England Before the Conquest. Studies in Primary Sources Presented to Dorothy Whitelock* (Cambridge, 1971): see Brooks, Dolley, Ker.

R. Collins, *Early Medieval Spain. Unity in Diversity, 400–1000* (New Studies in Medieval History, general editor M. Keen, London, 1983). Ch. 2, nn. 43, 48; ch. 7, n. 9

R. Collins, '"*Sicut lex Gothorum continet*": law and charters in ninth- and tenth-century León and Catalonia', *EHR* C (1985), pp. 489–512. Ch. 2, nn. 257, 259–60

R. Collins, 'Visigothic law and regional custom in disputes in early medieval Spain', in *Disputes*, pp. 85–104. Ch. 2, n. 257

R. Collins, 'Deception and Misrepresentation in early eighth century Frankish historiography: two case studies', in Jarnut *et al.* (eds), *Karl Martell*, pp. 227–47. Ch. 2, n. 141

P. Conner, *Anglo-Saxon Exeter: A Tenth-Century Cultural History* (Studies in Anglo-Saxon History IV, general editor D.N. Dumville, Woodbridge, 1993). Ch. 4, nn. 226, 240

G. Constable, 'The Orders of Society', in his *Three Studies in Medieval Religious and Social Thought* (Cambridge, 1995), pp. 249–360. Ch. 6, n. 159

E. Cortese, *Il Rinascimento Giuridico Medievale* (Rome, 1992). Ch. 6, n. 228

H.E.J. Cowdrey, 'The Peace and Truce of God in the Eleventh Century', *PP* 46 (1970), pp. 42–67, repr. in his *Popes, Monks and Crusaders*, VII. Ch. 6, n. 138

H.E.J. Cowdrey, 'The Anglo-Norman *Laudes Regiae*', *Viator* XIII (1981), pp. 37–78, repr. in his *Popes, Monks and Crusaders*, VIII. Ch. 6, n. 110

H.E.J. Cowdrey, *Popes, Monks and Crusaders* (London, 1984): see above.

P. Cramer, 'Ernulf of Rochester and Early Anglo-Norman Canon Law', *JEH* 40 (1989), pp. 483–510. Ch. 6, nn. 218, 221, 223

J. Crick, *The Historia Regum Britanniae of Geoffrey of Monmouth, III: A Summary Catalogue of the Manuscripts* (Cambridge, 1989). Ch. 4, n. 302

J.E. Cross, 'Wulfstan's *De Anticristo* in a twelfth-century Worcester manuscript', *ASE* 20 (1991), pp. 203–20. Ch. 6, n. 128

J.E. Cross, 'A Newly Identified Manuscript of Wulfstan's "Commonplace Book": Rouen Bibliothèque Municipale 1382 (U 109), fols 173r–98v', *Journal of Medieval Latin* 2 (1992), pp. 63–83. Ch. 4, nn. 192, 203–4, 208, 222, 234

J.E. Cross and J. Morrish Tunberg (eds), *Copenhagen Wulfstan*: see II SOURCES.

J.E. Cross and A. Hamer, 'Ælfric's letters and the *Excerptiones Ecgberhti*', in Roberts *et al.* (eds), *Alfred the Wise*, pp. 5–13. Ch. 4, n. 215

C. Cubitt, *Anglo-Saxon Church Councils c. 650–c. 850* (Studies in the Early History of Britain, general editor N. Brooks, Leicester, 1995). Ch. 2, nn. 372–3; ch. 3, n. 156; ch. 6, n. 96

E.R. Curtius (translated by W.R. Trask), *European Literature and the Latin Middle Ages* (repr. London, 1979). Ch. 3, n. 45

R. Dammery, 'The Law-Code of King Alfred the Great: a Study, Edition and Translation' (Cambridge, Ph. D., 1991). Ch. 4, nn. 265, 268; ch. 5, nn. 7, 17

R. Dammery, 'Editing the Anglo-Saxon Laws: Felix Liebermann and Beyond', in D.G. Scragg and P. Szarmach (editors), *The Editing of Old English* (Woodbridge, 1994), pp. 251–61. Ch. 1, n. 107; ch. 4, n. 375; ch. 5, nn. 340, 603

S. Daniel, *The Collection of the History of England* (London, 1634). Ch. 1, nn. 22–4

R.R. Darlington, 'Ecclesiastical Reform in the Late Old English Period', *EHR* LI (1936), pp. 385–428. Ch. 5, n. 213

D. Daube, *Forms of Roman Legislation* (Oxford, 1956). Ch. 2, n. 333; ch. 5, nn. 23, 169

D. Daube, *Roman Law. Linguistic, Social and Philosophical Aspects* (Edinburgh, 1969). Ch. 5, n. 168

R.R. Davies, *The Matter of Britain and the Matter of England* (Oxford, 1996). Ch. 3, n. 87

W. Davies, 'Disputes, their conduct and their settlement in the village communities of eastern Brittany in the ninth century', in S. Humphreys (editor), *History and Anthropology I(2), The Discourse of Law* (London, 1985), pp. 289–312.   **Ch. 2, n. 227**

W. Davies, 'People and places in dispute in ninth-century Brittany', in *Disputes*, pp. 65–84.   **Ch. 2, nn. 222, 227, 234, 284, 286–7, 310**

W. Davies, 'Forgery in the Cartulaire de Redon', in *Fälschungen im Mittelalter* IV (Diplomatischer Fälschungen II), pp. 265–74.   **Ch. 2, n. 283**

W. Davies, *Small Worlds. The Village Community in Early Medieval Brittany* (London, 1988).   **Ch. 2, nn. 227, 256, 283**

W. Davies, 'Composition of the Redon Cartulary', *Francia* 17 (1990), pp. 69–90.   **Ch. 2, n. 227**

W. Davies and P. Fouracre (editors), *The Settlement of Disputes in Early Medieval Europe* (Cambridge, 1986): see also Collins, Davies, Fouracre, Morris, Nelson, Wickham, Wood, Wormald.   **Ch. 2, n. 310; ch. 3, n. 120**

W. Davies and P. Fouracre (editors), *Property and Power in the early Middle Ages* (Cambridge, 1995): see Nelson, Wood.

H.W.C. Davis, 'The Anglo-Saxon Laws', *EHR* XXVIII (1913), pp. 417–30.   **Ch. 1, nn. 109, 113**

R.H.C. Davis and J.M. Wallace-Hadrill (editors), *The Writing of History in the Middle Ages: Essays presented to Richard William Southern* (Oxford, 1981): see Brett, Catto.

J. Devisse, *Hincmar et la Loi* (Université de Dakar, Publications de la section d'Histoire 5, 1962).   **Ch. 2, p. 207; ch. 6, nn. 15, 30**

J. Devisse, 'Essai sur l'histoire d'une expression qui a fait fortune: *consilium et auxilium* au IXᵉ siècle', *Le Moyen Age* 74 (1968), pp. 179–205.   **Ch. 2, n. 101**

J. Devisse, *Hincmar Archevêque de Reims 845–82* (3 vols, Geneva, 1975–6).   **Ch. 2, nn. 101, 207, 279; ch. 6, n. 30**

O. Dickau, 'Studien zur Kanzlei und zum Urkundenwesen Kaiser Ludwigs des Frommen I–II', *Arch. Dip.* 34 (1988), pp. 3–156; 35 (1989), pp. 1–170.   **Ch. 2, n. 171**

A. Dihle, *Die Goldene Regel: eine Einführung in die Geschichte der antiken und frühmittelalterlichen Vulgärethik* (Göttingen, 1962).   **Ch. 6, n. 28**

G. Dilcher, 'Gesetzgebung als Rechtserneuerung: eine Studie zum Selbstverständnis der mittelalterlichen *Leges*', in A. Fink *et al.* (editors), *Rechtsgeschichte als Kulturgeschichte: Festschrift für Adalbert Erler zum 70 Geburtstag* (Aalen, 1976), pp. 13–35.   **Ch. 5, nn. 68, 660**

H.G. Dirksen, 'Über die Collatio Legum Mosaicarum et Romanarum.Anhang: Hinkmar, Erzbischof von Rheims als Kenner der Quellen des römishcen Rechts', in his *Hinterlassene Schriften zur Kritik und Auslegung der Quellen römischer Rechtsgeschichte und Alterthumskunde* (edited by F.D. Sanio, 2 vols, Leipzig, 1871) II, pp. 130–41.   **Ch. 6, n. 15**

G. Dolezalek, *Verzeichnis der Handschriften zum römischen Recht bis 1600* (4 vols, Frankfurt, 1972).   **Ch. 2, n. 143**

R.H.M. Dolley and D.M. Metcalf, 'The reform of the English coinage under Eadgar', in Dolley (editor), *Anglo-Saxon Coins. Studies presented to F.M. Stenton on the occasion of his 80th birthday* (London, 1961), pp. 136–68.   **Ch. 3, n. 37**

R.H.M. Dolley, 'The nummular brooch from Sulgrave', in Clemoes and Hughes (eds), *England Before the Conquest*, pp. 333–49.   **Ch. 6, n. 134**

R.H.M. Dolley, 'An Introduction to the Coinage of Æthelræd II', in Hill (ed.), *Ethelred*, pp. 115–33.   **Ch. 6, n. 98**

E. Drage, 'Bishop Leofric and Exeter Cathedral 1050–72: a reassessment of the manuscript evidence' (Oxford, D.Phil., 1978).   **Ch. 4, n. 227; ch. 6, n. 118**

R. Drögereit, 'Gab es eine angelsächsische Königskanzlei?', *Archiv für Urkundenforschung* 13 (1935), pp. 335–436.   **Ch. 4, n. 12; ch. 6, n. 55**

G. Duby, *L'An Mil* (Paris, 1967).   **Ch. 6, n. 138**

G. Duby, *Les trois ordres ou l'imaginaire du féodalisme* (Paris, 1978); translated by A. Goldhammer, *The Three Orders.Feudal Society Imagined* (Chicago, 1980).   **Ch. 6, nn. 159, 162–5, 167, 169**

D.N. Dumville, 'The Anglian collection of royal genealogies and regnal lists', *ASE* 5 (1976), pp. 23–50. **Ch. 4, nn. 20, 337**

D.N. Dumville, 'The Catalogue Texts', in *An Eleventh-Century Illustrated Miscellany*, ed. McGurk, pp. 55–7. **Ch. 4, nn. 23, 337**

D.N. Dumville, 'On the dating of the early Breton law-codes', *Études Celtiques* 21 (1984), pp. 207–21. **Ch. 2, n. 285**

D.N. Dumville, 'The West Saxon Genealogical Regnal List and the Chronology of early Wessex', *Peritia* 4 (1985), pp. 21–66. **Ch. 4, n. 43**

D.N. Dumville, 'The West Saxon genealogical regnal list: Manuscripts and Texts', *Anglia* 104 (1986), pp. 1–32. **Ch. 4, nn. 42, 75**

D.N. Dumville, 'English Square minuscule script: the background and earliest phases', *ASE* 16 (1987), pp. 147–79. **Ch 4, nn. 21, 24, 27, 29**

D.N. Dumville, 'The treaty of Alfred and Guthrum', in his *Wessex and England*, pp. 1–27. **Ch. 5, nn. 100, 105**

D.N. Dumville, 'The Anglo-Saxon Chronicle and the Origins of English Square Minuscule Script', in his *Wessex and England*, pp. 55–139. **Ch. 4, nn. 3, 5–9, 12, 21, 24, 26, 38**

D.N. Dumville, 'Between Alfred the Great and Edgar the Peacemaker: Æthelstan, first king of England', in his *Wessex and England*, pp. 141–71. **Ch. 6, n. 74**

D.N. Dumville, *Wessex and England from Alfred to Edgar* (Studies in Anglo-Saxon History III, general editor D.N. Dumville, Woodbridge, 1992): see above.

D.N. Dumville, *Liturgy and the Ecclesiastical History of Late Anglo-Saxon England* (Studies in Anglo-Saxon History V, general editor D.N. Dumville, Woodbridge, 1992). **Ch. 4, nn. 20, 23, 26–7, 29, 34, 89, 103, 105, 115, 120, 128–9, 133–4, 209, 231, 240, 338; ch. 5, n. 497; ch. 6, n. 118**

D.N. Dumville, *English Caroline Script and Monastic History. Studies in Benedictinism* (Studies in Anglo-Saxon History VI, general editor D.N. Dumville, Woodbridge, 1993). **Ch. 4, nn. 139, 228, 231, 237**

D.N. Dumville, 'English Square minuscule script: the mid-century phases', *ASE* 23 (1994), pp. 133–64. **Ch. 4, nn. 20, 27**

J. Dunbabin, *France in the Making, 843–1180* (Oxford, 1985). **Ch. 7, n. 9**

A.A.M. Duncan, revised edition of W.C. Dickinson, *Scotland from the Earliest Times to 1603* (Edinburgh, 1978). **Ch. 5, n. 586**

C. Dyer, 'St Oswald and 10,000 West Midland Peasants', in Brooks and Cubitt (eds), *St Oswald of Worcester*, pp. 174–93. **Ch. 5, nn. 559, 565**

O. Eberhardt, *Via Regia. Der Fürstenspiegel Smaragds von St Mihiel und seine literarische Gattung* (Münstersche Mittelalterschriften 28, general editors H. Belting, K. Hauck *et al.*, Munich, 1977). **Ch. 3, nn. 24, 27**

K.A. Eckhardt, *Leges Alamannorum*; *Pactus Legis Salicae*; *Lex Ribuaria*, etc.: see II *SOURCES, sub tit.*

W.A. Eckhardt, *Die Kapitulariensammlung Bischof Ghaerbalds von Lüttich* (Deutschrechtliches Archiv 5, Göttingen, 1955). **Ch. 2, n. 191**

W.A. Eckhardt, 'Die Capitularia Missorum Specialia von 802', *DA* 12 (1956), pp. 498–516. **Ch. 2, nn. 165, 246**

W. Edelstein, *Eruditio und Sapientia. Weltbild und Erziehung in der Karolingerzeit* (Freiburg, 1965). **Ch. 3, n. 27**

H. Edwards, *The Charters of the early West Saxon Kingdom* (British Archaeological Reports, British Series 198, Oxford, 1988). **Ch. 2, n. 359**

A. Ellegård and G. Åkerström-Hougen (editors), *Rome and the North* (Studies in Mediterranean Archaeology and Literature 135, Jonsered, 1996): see Wood, Wormald.

P. Ellis, *Welsh Tribal Law and Custom* (2 vols, Oxford, 1926). **Ch. 3, n. 95**

A.B. Emden, *A Biographical Register of the University of Cambridge to 1500* (Cambridge, 1963). **Ch. 4, n. 249**

A.B. Emden, *A Biographical Register of the University of Oxford to A.D. 1500* (3 vols, Oxford, 1957). **Ch. 4, nn. 249, 268**

S. Esders, *Römische Rechtstradition und merowingisches Königtum. Zum Rechtscharakter politischer Herrschaft in Burgund im 6. und 7. Jahrhundert* (Veröffentlichungen des Max-Planck–Instituts für Geschichte 134, Göttingen, 1997). **Ch. 2, nn. 76, 173**

Fälschungen im Mittelalter (6 vols, MGH Schriften 33, 1988–9): see Brett, Davies.

C. Fell, 'Unfrið: an approach to a definition', *Saga Book of the Viking Society* XXI (1982–3), pp. 85–100.   **Ch. 5, nn. 285, 293**

J. Fleckenstein, *Die Hofkapelle der deutschen Könige* (2 vols, Stuttgart, 1959, 1966).   **Ch. 4, n. 30**

R. Fleming, 'Christ Church's Sisters and Brothers: An Edition and Discussion of Canterbury Obituary Lists', in M.A. Meyer (editor), *The Culture of Christendom. Essays in medieval history in commemoration of Denis L.T. Bethell* (London, 1993), pp. 115–53.   **Ch. 4, n. 122**

V. Flint, 'The *Historia Regum Britanniae* of Geoffrey of Monmouth: parody and its purpose. A suggestion', *Speculum* LIV (1979), pp. 447–68.   **Ch. 3, n. 87**

R. Flower, 'Laurence Nowell and a recovered Anglo-Saxon poem', *British Museum Quarterly* VIII (1934–5), pp. 130–2.   **Ch. 4, n. 42**

R. Flower, 'Laurence Nowell and the discovery of England in Tudor Times', *PBA* XXI (1935), pp. 47–73.   **Ch. 4, nn. 42, 374–5**

R. Flower, 'The Text of the Burghal Hidage', *London Medieval Studies* I (1937), pp. 60–4.   **Ch. 4, nn. 42, 50; ch. 5, n. 488**

H. Focillon, *The Year 1000* (1952, English translation, New York, 1971).   **Ch. 6, n. 138**

M. Förster, 'Altenglische Predigtsquellen', *Arch. SNSL* CXXII (1912), pp. 246–62; with 'Nachtrag', *ibid.* CXXIX (1912), p. 49.   **Ch. 5, n. 535**

G. Folliet, 'Le plus ancien témoin du *De gratia et libero arbitrio* et du *De correptione et gratia* (MS Paris BN lat. 12205), *Scriptorium* L (1996), pp. 88–97.   **Ch. 2, n. 171**

R. Foreville, 'The Synod of the Province of Rouen in the eleventh and twelfth centuries', in Brooke *et al.* (eds), *Church and Government in the Middle Ages*, pp. 19–39.   **Ch. 3, n. 70**

J. Fontaine, *Isidore de Seville et la Culture Classique dans l' Espagne Wisigothique* (2 vols, Études Augustiniennes, Paris, 1959).   **Ch. 6, n. 191**

P. Fouracre, '"Placita" and the settlement of disputes in later Merovingian Francia', in *Disputes*, pp. 23–43.   **Ch. 2, n. 274; ch. 3, n. 131**

P. Fouracre, 'Carolingian Justice: the Rhetoric of Improvement and Contexts of Abuse', *La Giustizia* I, pp. 771–803.   **Ch. 2, n. 234**

P. Fournier, 'Le *Liber ex Lege Moysi* et les tendances bibliques du Droit canonique Irlandais', *Revue Celtique* 30 (1909), pp. 221–34.   **Ch. 6, n. 10**

P. Fournier and G. Le Bras, *Histoire des Collections Canoniques en Occident depuis les Fausses Décrétales jusqu'au Décret de Gratien* (2 vols, Paris, 1931).   **Ch. 6, nn. 147, 149, 215–16**

A.J. Frantzen, *The Literature of Penance in Anglo-Saxon England* (New Brunswick, 1983).   **Ch. 4, nn. 209, 231, 236–7**

A.J. Frantzen, *King Alfred* (Twayne's English Authors, general editor G.D. Economou, Boston, 1986).   **Ch. 5, n. 66; ch. 6, nn. 1, 6, 11, 43**

E.A. Freeman, *The History of the Norman Conquest of England, its Causes and its Results* (6 vols, Oxford, 3rd edn, 1877–9).   **Ch. 1, n. 59; ch. 5, n. 457**

E. Freise, 'Studien zum Einzugsbereich der Klostergemeinschaft von Fulda', in K. Schmid (editor), *Die Klostergemeinschaft von Fulda im früheren Mittelalter* (3 vols in 5, Münstersche Mittelalterschriften 8 , general editors H. Belting, K. Hauck *et al.*, Munich, 1978) II(3).   **Ch. 2, n. 317**

H. Fuhrmann, 'Zum Vorwort des Dekrets Bischof Burchards von Wurms', in *Societá, Istituzioni, Spiritualitá. Studi in onore di Cinzio Violante* (2 vols, Centro Italiano di Studi sull' alto Medioevo, 1994) I, pp. 383–93.   **Ch. 6, n. 146**

V.H. Galbraith, 'Who Wrote Asser's Life of Alfred?', in *idem*, *An Introduction to the Study of History* (London, 1964), pp. 88–128.   **Ch. 3, n. 5; ch. 6, n. 44**

F.L. Ganshof, 'Recherches sur les capitulaires', *Revue historique de Droit français et étranger* série IV, 35 (1957), pp. 33–87, 196–246.   **Ch. 2, nn. 106, 110, 196**

F.L. Ganshof, 'Charlemagne's programme of imperial government', in his *Carolingians and the Frankish Monarchy*, pp. 55–85.   **Ch. 3, n. 18**

F.L. Ganshof, 'The use of the written word in Charlemagne's administration', in his *Carolingians and the Frankish Monarchy*, pp. 125–42.   **Ch. 2, n. 105**

F.L. Ganshof (translated by J. Sondheimer), *The Carolingians and the Frankish Monarchy* (London, 1971): see above.

F.L. Ganshof, 'Charlemagne and the Administration of Justice', translated from his paper in Beumann *et al.* (eds), *Karl der Große* I, pp. 394–419, by B. and M. Lyon, *Frankish Institutions under Charlemagne* (New York, 1968), pp. 72–97, 161–83.   Ch. 2, nn. 222, 245–6, 309

F.L. Ganshof, 'Contribution à l'étude de l'application du Droit Romain et des Capitulaires dans la Monarchie Franque sous les Carolingiens', *Studi in Onore di Edoardo Volterra* (6 vols, Milan, 1971) III, pp. 585–603.   Ch. 2, nn. 4–5, 215, 218, 222, 245

D. Ganz, 'Bureaucratic Shorthand and Merovingian Learning', in Wormald *et al.* (eds), *Ideal and Reality*, pp. 58–75.   Ch. 2, nn. 170, 267

D. Ganz, 'The Debate on Predestination', in M.T. Gibson and J.L. Nelson (editors), *Charles the Bald. Court and Kingdom* (2nd edn, Aldershot, 1990), pp. 283–302.   Ch. 2, n. 317

D. Ganz and W. Goffart, 'Charters Earlier than 800 from French Collections', *Speculum* LXV (1990), pp. 906–32.   Ch. 2, nn. 41, 312

G. Garnett, '"Franci et Angli": the legal distinctions between peoples after the Conquest', *ANS* VIII (1986), pp. 109–37.   Ch. 4, n. 296; ch. 5, nn. 620, 642, 651

G. Garnett and J. Hudson (editors), *Law and Government in Medieval England and Normandy. Essays in Honour of Sir James Holt* (Cambridge, 1994): see Sharpe, Wormald.

M. McC. Gatch, 'King Alfred's Version of Augustine's *Soliloquia*: Some Suggestions on its Rationale and Unity', in Szarmach (ed.), *Studies in Earlier Old English Prose*, pp. 17–45. Ch. 6, n. 6

J. Gaudemet, 'L'Apport du Droit Romain aux institutions ecclésiales (XIᵉ–XIIᵉ s.)', *Miscellanea del centro di studi medievali* XI (1986), pp. 174–97.   Ch. 6, n. 224

P. Geary, *Before France and Germany. The Creation and Transformation of the Merovingian World* (Oxford, 1988).   Ch. 2, n. 62

P. Geary, 'Extra-judicial Means of Conflict Resolution', *La Giustizia* I, pp. 569–605. Ch. 2, n. 314

M. Gelling, *The West Midlands in the Early Middle Ages* (Studies in the Early History of Britain, general editor N. Brooks, Leicester, 1992).   Ch. 5, nn. 522, 525–6

R.A. Gerberding, *The Rise of the Carolingians and the Liber Historiae Francorum* (Oxford Historical Monographs, Oxford, 1987).   Ch. 4, n. 36

M.T. Gibson, *Lanfranc of Bec* (Oxford, 1978).   Ch. 6, nn. 192, 209

J.T. Gilchrist, 'The relationship between the Collection in Four Books and the Collection in Seventy-four Titles', *Bulletin of Medieval Canon Law* n.s. 12 (1982), pp. 13–30.   Ch. 6, n. 216

J. Gillingham, 'The Introduction of Knight Service into England', *ANS* IV (1981/2), pp. 53–64.   Ch. 6, n. 60

J. Gillingham, 'The Context and Purposes of Geoffrey of Monmouth's *History of the Kings of Britain*', *ANS* XIII (1990/1), pp. 99–118.   Ch. 3, n. 87

J. Gillingham, 'Kingship, Chivalry and Love. Political and Cultural Values in the earliest history written in French: Geoffrey Gaimar's *Estoire des Engleis*', in C.W. Hollister (editor), *Anglo-Norman Political Culture and the Twelfth-Century Renaissance* (Woodbridge, 1995), pp. 33–58.   Ch. 3, n. 90; ch. 5, n. 669

M. Gluckman, 'The Peace in the Feud', in his *Custom and Conflict in Africa* (Oxford, 1956), pp. 1–26.   Ch. 2, n. 338

H. Gneuss, 'The Origin of Standard Old English and Æthelwold's School at Winchester', *ASE* 1 (1972), pp. 63–83.   Ch. 5, n. 305

H. Gneuss, 'A preliminary list of manuscripts written or owned in England up to 1100', *ASE* 9 (1981), pp. 1–60.   Ch. 4, nn. 81, 95; ch. 6, n. 10

H. Gneuss, 'Liturgical Books in Anglo-Saxon England', in Lapidge and Gneuss (eds), *Learning and Literature*, pp. 91–141.   Ch. 4, n. 129

M. Godden, 'Apocalypse and Invasion in Late Anglo-Saxon England', in Godden, D. Gray and T. Hoad (editors), *From Anglo-Saxon to Early Middle English: Studies presented to E.G. Stanley* (Oxford, 1994), pp. 130–62.   Ch. 4, n. 153; ch. 5, n. 324; ch. 6, nn. 127, 130, 173–5, 177

M. Godden, 'Wærferth and King Alfred: the Fate of the Old English *Dialogues*', in Roberts, Nelson and Godden (eds), *Alfred the Wise*, pp. 35–51.   **Ch. 5, n. 35**

P. Godman, *Poetry of the Carolingian Renaissance* (London, 1985).   **Ch. 2, n. 213**

P. Godman and R. Collins (editors), *Charlemagne's Heir. New Perspectives on the Reign of Louis the Pious (814–40)* (Oxford, 1990): see Guillot, Johanek, Schmitz.

J. Goebel, *Felony and Misdemeanour* (vol. I only, New York, 1937; repr. with introduction by E. Peters, Philadelphia, 1976).   **Ch. 1, nn. 40, 119**

W. Goffart, *The Le Mans Forgeries. A Chapter from the History of Church Property in the Ninth Century* (Harvard Historical Studies LXXVI, 1966).   **Ch. 2, n. 273**

E. Goldberg, 'Popular Revolt, Dynastic Politics, and Aristocratic Factionalism in the Early Middle Ages: the Saxon *Stellinga* reconsidered', *Speculum* LXX (1995), pp. 467–501. **Ch. 2, n. 318**

A. Gransden, *Historical Writing in England c. 550 to c. 1307* (London, 1974).   **Ch. 3, nn. 2, 68, 83, 92; ch. 4, n. 322**

F. Graus, 'Die Rolle der Gewalt bei den Anfängen des Feudalismus und die "Gefangenenbefreiungen" der merowingischen Hagiographie', *Jahrbuch für Wirtschaftsgeschichte* 1 (1961), pp. 61–156.   **Ch. 2, n. 232; ch. 3, n. 155**

J.A. Green, *The Government of England under Henry I* (Cambridge studies in medieval life and thought 4th series 3, Cambridge, 1986).   **Ch. 6, n. 122**

J.A. Green, *English Sheriffs to 1154* (London, 1990).   **Ch. 5, n. 615**

J. Greenberg, 'The Confessor's Laws and the Radical Face of the Ancient Constitution', *EHR* CIV (1989), pp. 611–37.   **Ch. 1, nn. 15, 27**

J. Greenberg and L. Marin, 'Politics and Memory: Sharnborn's Case and the Role of the Norman Conquest in Stuart Political Thought', in H. Nenner (editor), *Politics and the political imagination in later Stuart Britain; essays presented to Lois Green Schwoerer* (Rochester N.Y., 1997), pp. 121–42.   **Ch. 1, n.15**

M. Gretsch, 'The Benedictine Rule in Old English, a Document of Bishop Æthelwold's Reform Politics', in Korhammer *et al.* (eds), *Words, Texts and Manuscripts*, pp. 131–58. **Ch. 4, n. 190**

M. Gretsch, 'The language of the Fonthill Letter', *ASE* 23 (1994), pp. 57–102.   **Ch. 3, n. 98**

P. Grierson, 'Grimbald of St Bertin's', *EHR* LV (1940), pp. 529–61.   **Ch. 6, n. 40**

P. Grierson, 'La fonction sociale de la monnaie en Angleterre aux VIIᵉ et VIIIᵉ siècles', *Sett. Spol.* VIII (1961), pp. 341–62.   **Ch. 5, n. 77**

P. Grierson, Presidential Address, *Numismatic Chronicle*, 7th series II (1962), pp. i–xvii. **Ch. 3, n. 38**

P. Grierson and M. Blackburn, *Medieval European Coinage; with a catalogue of the coins in the Fitzwilliam Museum Cambridge. I, The Early Middle Ages (Fifth to Tenth Centuries)* (Cambridge, 1986).   **Ch. 5, n. 77**

J. Grimm, *Deutsche Rechtsalterthümer* (4th enlarged edn by A. Heusler and R. Hübner, 2 vols, Leipzig, 1899).   **Ch. 1, nn. 40, 42**

J. Guerout, 'Le testament de Sainte Fare: matériaux pour l'étude et l'édition critique … ', *Revue d'histoire ecclésiastique* 60 (1965), pp. 761–821.   **Ch. 2, n. 85**

O. Guillot, 'Une *ordinatio* méconnue. Le Capitulaire de 823–825', in Godman and Collins (eds), *Charlemagne's Heir*, pp. 455–86.   **Ch. 2, n. 98**

S.L. Guterman, *From Personal to Territorial Law: Aspects of the History and Structure of the Western Legal-Constitutional Tradition* (New York, 1972).   **Ch. 2, n. 5**

M. Hale, *History of the Common Law*: see *II SOURCES*.

H. Hallam, *View of the State of Europe during the Middle Ages* (2 vols, London, 1818; 11th edn in 3 vols, London, 1856).   **Ch. 1, nn. 33–5, 95**

B. Hamilton, 'Prester John and the Three Kings of Cologne', in Mayr-Harting and Moore (eds), *Studies presented to R.H.C. Davis*, pp. 177–91.   **Ch. 4, n. 308**

C. Hammer, '*Lex Scripta* in Early Medieval Bavaria: use and abuse of the *lex Baiuvariorum*', in E.B. King and S.J. Ridyard (editors), *Law in Mediaeval Life and Thought* (Sewanee Mediaeval Studies, editor E.B. King, Sewanee, 1990), pp. 185–95. **Ch. 2, n. 290**

C. Hammer, 'Land sales in eighth- and ninth-century Bavaria: legal, economic and social aspects', *EME* 6 (1997), pp. 47–76. **Ch. 2, n. 290**

C. Hammer, 'The Handmaid's Tale: Morganatic Relationships in Early-Mediaeval Bavaria' (forthcoming). **Ch. 2, n. 288**

J. Hannig, *Consensus Fidelium. Frühfeudale Interpretationen des Verhältnisses von Königtum und Adel am Beispiel des Frankenreiches* (Monographien zur Geschichte des Mittelalters 27, Stuttgart, 1982). **Ch. 2, n. 102**

J. Hannig, 'Pauperiores vassi de infra palatio? Zur Entstehung der karolingischen Königsbotenorganisation', *MIÖG* 91 (1983), pp. 309–74. **Ch. 2, nn. 166, 216, 246**

M. Hare, 'Kings, crowns and festivals: the origins of Gloucester as a royal ceremonial centre', *Transactions of the Bristol and Gloucestershire Archaeological Society* CXV (1997), pp. 41–78. **Ch. 3, n. 52; ch. 6, nn. 110, 120, 122**

J. Harries, 'Sidonius Apollinaris, Rome and the barbarians: a climate of treason?', in J. Drinkwater and H. Elton (editors), *Fifth-Century Gaul: a Crisis of Identity?* (Cambridge, 1992), pp. 298–308. **Ch. 2, n. 44**

J. Harries, 'The Background to the Code', in Harries and Wood (eds), *Theodosian Code*, pp. 1–16. **Ch. 2, n. 32**

J. Harries and I.N. Wood (editors), *The Theodosian Code. Studies in the Imperial Law of Late Antiquity* (London, 1993): see Harries, Matthews, Wood.

C.R. Hart, *The Early Charters of Eastern England* (Leicester, 1966). **Ch. 4, n. 125**

C.R. Hart, 'Athelstan "Half-king" and his Family' *ASE* 2 (1973), pp. 115–44; revised in his *The Danelaw* (London, 1992), pp. 569–604. **Ch. 6, nn. 89, 91**

C.R. Hart, 'The East Anglian Chronicle', *Journal of Medieval History* 7 (1981), pp. 249–82. **Ch. 3, n. 11**

C.R. Hart, 'Byrhtferth's Northumbrian Chronicle', *EHR* XCVII (1982), pp. 558–82. **Ch. 3, n. 51**

W. Hartmann, 'Die Kanonessammlung der Handschrift Rom, Biblioteca Vallicelliana, B.89', *Bulletin of Medieval Canon Law* n.s. 17 (1987), pp. 45–64. **Ch. 6, n. 216**

W. Hartmann, 'Rechtskenntnis und Rechtsverständnis bei den Laien des früheren Mittelalters', in H. Mordek (editor), *Aus Archiven und Bibliotheken. Festschrift für Raymund Kottje zum 65. Geburtstag* (Frankfurt, 1992), pp. 1–20. **Ch. 2, n. 316**

P.D.A. Harvey, 'Rectitudines Singularum Personarum and Gerefa', *EHR* CVIII (1993), pp. 1–22. **Ch. 4, n. 277; ch. 5, nn. 559–60, 562, 565, 569**

H. Hayashi, 'The Lost Laws of Anglo-Saxon Kings', in his *Essays in Anglo-Saxon Law* (2 vols, privately printed, Tokyo, 1990–2). **Ch. 2, n. 369**

H.D. Hazeltine, 'Felix Liebermann', *PBA* XXIV (1939), pp. 319–59. **Ch. 1, nn. 97, 114**

T. Head and R. Landes (editors), *The Peace of God. Social Violence and Religious Response in France around the year 1000* (Ithaca, 1992). **Ch. 6, nn. 138, 140, 171**

R.H. Helmholz, 'The Learned Laws in "Pollock and Maitland" ', in Hudson (ed.), *History of English Law*, pp. 145–69. **Ch. 1, n. 94**

E. Heymann, 'Felix Liebermann', *ZSS*, germ Abt. XLVI (1926), pp. xxiii–xxxix. **Ch. 1, nn. 97, 114**

G. Hickes, *Antiquae Literaturae Septentrionalis Libri Duo* (Oxford, 1705). **Ch. 4, n. 98**

C. Hicks (editor), *England in the Eleventh Century. Proceedings of the 1990 Harlaxton Symposium* (Harlaxton Medieval Studies II, Stamford, 1992): see Loyn, Pfaff, Wilcox.

J. Higgitt, 'Glastonbury, Dunstan, Monasticism and Manuscripts', *Art History* 2 (1979), pp. 275–90. **Ch. 4, n. 24**

C. Hill, 'The Norman Yoke', in his *Puritanism and Revolution* (London, 1958), pp. 50–122. **Ch. 1, n. 16**

D. Hill, 'The Burghal Hidage: The Establishment of a Text', *Med. Arch.* XIII (1969), pp. 84–92. **Ch. 4, nn. 65–6**

D. Hill (editor), *Ethelred the Unready. Papers from the Millenary Conference* (British Archaeological Reports, British Series 59, Oxford, 1978): see Brooks, Campbell, Dolley, Wormald.

D. Hill, *An Atlas of Anglo-Saxon England* (Oxford, 1981). **Ch. 4, n. 65**

D. Hill, 'The nature of the figures'; 'The Calculation and the purpose of the Burghal Hidage', in Hill and Rumble (eds), *Defence of Wessex*, pp. 74–87, 92–7. **Ch. 4, n. 65**

D. Hill and A. Rumble (editors), *The defence of Wessex. The Burghal Hidage and Anglo-Saxon fortifications* (Manchester, 1996): see Brooks, Hill, Rumble, Wormald.

J. Hill, 'The "Regularis Concordia" and its Latin and Old English Reflexes', *Revue Bénédictine* 101 (1991), pp. 299–315.   **Ch. 4, nn. 169, 187, 190, 220**

R.H. Hodgkin, *A History of the Anglo-Saxons* (2 vols, Oxford, 3rd edn, 1952).   **Ch. 3, n. 18; ch. 5, n. 99**

T. Hodgkin, *The History of England from the earliest times to the Norman Conquest* (The Political History of England I, London, 1897).   **Ch. 5, n. 99**

H. Hoffmann, *Gottesfriede und Treuga Dei* (MGH Schriften 20, 1964).   **Ch. 6, n. 138**

H. Hoffmann and R. Pokorny, *Das Dekret des Bischofs Burchard von Wurms* (MGH Hilfsmittel 12, Munich, 1991).   **Ch. 6, n. 147**

W. Hofstetter, 'Winchester and the standardization of Old English vocabulary', *ASE* 17 (1988), pp. 139–61.   **Ch. 5, n. 305**

C. Hohler, 'Some Service Books of the Later Saxon Church', in D. Parsons (editor), *Tenth-Century Studies. Essays in Commemoration of the Council of Winchester and 'Regularis Concordia'* (Chichester, 1975), pp. 60–83, 217–27.   **Ch. 4, nn. 108, 211; ch. 6, nn. 114, 141**

A. Holder, *Lex Salica Emendata nach dem Codex von Trier-Leijden (Vossianus Lat. Oct. 86)* (Leipzig, 1880).   **Ch. 2, n. 158**

W. Holdsworth, *A History of English Law* (17 vols, 7th edn edited by A.L. Goodhart and H.G. Hanbury, with a new introduction by S.B. Chrimes, London, 1956; 1st edn 1903–52).   **Ch. 1, nn. 115–17**

W. Holdsworth, *Historians of Anglo-American Law* (New York, 1928).   **Ch. 1, n. 113**

C.W. Hollister, 'London's first Charter of Liberties: Is it Genuine?', *Jnl Med. Hist.* 6 (1980), pp. 289–306, repr. in his *Monarchy, Magnates and Institutions in the Anglo-Norman World* (London, 1986), pp. 191–208.   **Ch. 5, n. 630**

J.C. Holt, 'The Origins of the Constitutional Tradition in England', in his *Magna Carta and Medieval Government* (International Commission for the History of Representative and Parliamentary Opinion LXVIII, London, 1985), pp. 1–22.   **Ch. 3, n. 67; ch. 4, nn. 268, 306; ch. 5, n. 623**

J.C. Holt, *Magna Carta* (Cambridge, 2nd edn, 1992).   **Ch. 5, n. 442**

A.M. Honoré, *Tribonian* (London, 1978).   **Ch. 2, n. 31**

A.M. Honoré, *Emperors and Lawyers* (London, 1981).   **Ch. 2, n. 42**

A.M. Honoré, 'The Making of the Theodosian Code', *ZSS* rom. Abt. CIII (1986), pp. 133–222.   **Ch. 2, n. 42**

C. Hough, 'Women and the Law in Early Anglo-Saxon England' (Nottingham, Ph.D., 1993).   **Ch. 2, n. 321**

C. Hough, 'A Reappraisal of Æthelberht 84', *Nottingham Medieval Studies* XXXVII (1993), pp. 1–6.   **Ch. 2, n. 343**

C. Hough, 'The early Kentish "divorce laws": a reconsideration of Æthelberht, chs. 79 and 80', *ASE* 23 (1994), pp. 19–34.   **Ch. 2, n. 343**

D.R. Howlett, *British Books in Biblical Style* (Dublin, 1997).   **Ch. 4, n. 72; ch. 6, n. 11**

J. Hudson, 'Administration, Family and Perceptions of the Past in Late Twelfth Century England: Richard fitz Nigel and the Dialogue of the Exchequer', in P. Magdalino (editor), *The Perception of the Past in Twelfth-Century Europe* (London, 1992), pp. 75–98.   **Ch. 3, n. 63; ch. 5, n. 458**

J. Hudson, *Land, Law, and Lordship in Anglo-Norman England* (Oxford, 1994).   **Ch. 1, n. 83**

J. Hudson, *The Formation of the English Common Law. Law and Society in England from the Norman Conquest to Magna Carta* (London, 1996).   **Ch. 1, n. 83**

J. Hudson, 'Maitland and Anglo-Norman Law', in Hudson (ed.), *History of English Law*, pp. 21–46.   **Ch. 1, nn. 2, 72; ch. 5, nn. 691, 694; ch. 6, n. 179**

J. Hudson (editor), *The History of English Law. Centenary Essays on "Pollock and Maitland"* (Cambridge, 1996): see Helmholz, Hudson, White, Wormald.

R. Hübner, 'Gerichtsurkunden der fränkischen Zeit. I. Die Gerichtsurkunden aus Deutschland und Frankreich bis zum Jahre 1000'; 'II. Die Gerichtsurkunden aus Italien bis zum Jahre 1150', *ZSS*, germ. Abt. XII (1891) App., pp. 1–118, XIV (1893) App., pp. 1–258 (separately reprinted, Aalen, 1971).   **Ch. 2, nn. 72, 222–5, 228–30, 232–3, 238–42, 250, 252–3, 255–8, 260–3, 265, 267–75, 280, 282–3, 286–94, 296–9, 302–4, 306–8, 310**

D. Hume, *The History of England from the Invasion of Julius Caesar to the Revolution in 1688* (8 vols, new and corrected edn, London, 1770).   **Ch. 1, n. 30**

R.W. Hunt, W.A. Pantin and R.W. Southern (editors), *Studies in Medieval History presented to Frederick Maurice Powicke* (Oxford, 1948): see Ker, Southern.

N. Hurnard, 'The Anglo-Norman Franchises', *EHR* LXIV (1949), pp. 289–322, 433–60.   **Ch. 3, n. 138**

P. Hyams, 'The Common Law and the French Connection', *ANS* IV (1981/2), pp. 77–92.   **Ch. 6, n. 186**

P.R. Hyams, 'Feud in Medieval England', *Haskins Society Journal* 3 (1991), pp. 1–21.   **Ch. 1, n. 124**

A. Iglesia Ferreirós, 'La Creacion del Derecho en Cataluña, *Anuario de Historia del Derecho Español* XLVII (1977), pp. 99–423.   **Ch. 2, nn. 226, 260**

D. Iogna-Prat, 'Le "Baptême" du Schéma des Trois Ordres Fonctionels. L'apport de l'école d'Auxerre dans la seconde moitié du IXᵉ siècle', *Annales: Économies, Sociétés, Civilisations* 41 (1986), pp. 101–26   **Ch. 6, nn. 159, 164**

D. Iogna-Prat, *Agni Immaculati. Recherches sur les sources hagiographiques relatives à saint Maieul de Cluny (954–94)* (Paris, 1988).   **Ch. 6, nn. 164–5**

K-U. Jäschke, 'Frühmittelalterliche Festkrönungen? Überlegungen zu Terminologie und Methode', *HZ* 211 (1970), pp. 556–88.   **Ch. 6, n. 111**

E. James, '"Beati Pacifici": Bishops and the Law in sixth-century Gaul', in Bossy, ed., *Disputes and Settlements*, pp. 25–46.   **Ch. 2, n. 232**

E. James, *The Origins of France. From Clovis to the Capetians, 500–1000* (New Studies in Medieval History, general editor M. Keen, London, 1982).   **Ch. 7, n. 9**

E. James, *The Franks* (Peoples of Europe, general editors J. Campbell and B. Cunliffe, Oxford, 1988).   **Ch. 2, n. 69**

M.R. James, *A Descriptive Catalogue of the Manuscripts in the Library of Corpus Christi College Cambridge*, (2 vols, Cambridge, 1911–12).   **Ch. 4, nn. 197, 201, 268**

M.R. James (and F. Taylor), *A Descriptive Catalogue of the Latin Manuscripts in the John Rylands Library Manchester* I (Manchester, 1921).   **Ch. 4, n. 303**

J. Jarnut *et al.* (editors), *Karl Martell in seiner Zeit* (Beihefte der Francia 37, 1994): see Collins, Mordek.

R. Jayatilaka, 'The *Regula Sancti Benedicti* in late Anglo-Saxon England: the manuscripts and their readers' (Oxford, D.Phil., 1997).   **Ch. 4, nn. 100, 190**

P. Johanek, 'Probleme einer zukünftigen Edition der Urkunden Ludwigs des Frommen', in Godman and Collins (eds), *Charlemagne's Heir*, pp. 409–24.   **Ch. 2, nn. 264, 266**

J.E.A. Joliffe, *Pre-feudal England. The Jutes* (Oxford, 1933).   **Ch. 2, n. 345**

E. John, 'Orbis Britanniae and the Anglo-Saxon Kings', in his *Orbis Britanniae and Other Studies* (Leicester, 1966), pp. 1–63.   **Ch. 6, n. 101**

E. John, 'The World of Abbot Ælfric', in Wormald *et al.* (eds), *Ideal and Reality*, pp. 300–16.   **Ch. 6, n. 165**

K. Jost, 'Einige Wulfstantexte und ihre Quellen', *Anglia*, 44 (1932), pp. 265–315.   **Ch. 5, n. 334**

K. Jost, *Wulfstanstudien* (Schweizer Anglistische Arbeiten 23, general editors E. Dieth *et al.*, Bern, 1950).   **Ch. 4, n. 142; ch. 5, nn. 318, 329, 334, 336, 338, 344, 346, 385, 394, 612; ch. 6, nn. 129, 142**

W. Kapelle, *The Norman Conquest of the North. The Region and Its Transformation, 1000–1135* (London, 1979).   **Ch. 3, n. 64**

B. Kasten, 'Erbrechtliche Verfügungen des 8. und 9. Jahrhunderts. Zugleich ein Beitrag zur Organisation und zur Schriftlichkeit bei der Verwaltung adeliger Grundherrschaften am Beispiel des Grafen Heccard aus Burgund', *ZSS germ. Abt.* CVII (1990), pp. 236–338.   **Ch. 2, nn. 269, 275–6, 278**

E. Kaufmann, '*Quod paganorum tempore observabant*. Ist der Titel 58 der Lex Salica (Pactus) eine Neuschöpfung der Merowinger?', in K. Hauck *et al.* (editors), *Sprache und*

Recht. Beiträge zur Kulturgeschichte des Mittelalters. Festschrift für Ruth Schmidt-Wiegand zum 60. Geburtstag (Berlin, 1986), pp. 374–90.   Ch. 2, n. 95

H. Keller, 'I Placiti nella storiografia degli ultimi cento anni', *Fonti Medioevali e problematica storiografica* (Atti del Congresso internazionale tenuto in occasione del 90° anniversario della fondazione dell' Istituto storico italiano, Istituto storico italiano per il medioevo I, Rome, 1976), pp. 41–68.   Ch. 6, nn. 222, 295

S. Kelly, 'Anglo-Saxon Lay Society and the Written Word', in McKitterick (ed.), *Uses of Literacy*, pp. 36–62.   Ch. 5, n. 545

S. Kelly, *Royal Styles in Anglo-Saxon Diplomas* (privately printed, Cambridge, 1992).   Ch. 6, n. 101

J.M. Kemble, *The Saxons in England* (2 vols, London, 1849, reissue by W. de Gray Birch, London, 1876).   Ch. 1, nn. 46–51; ch. 4, n. 67; ch. 5, n. 505

A.G. Kennedy, 'Cnut's law code of 1018', *ASE* 11 (1983), pp. 57–81.   Ch. 3, nn. 48, 53; ch. 5, nn. 336, 385–6, 394, 406, 435

A.G. Kennedy, 'Law and Litigation in the *Libellus Æthelwoldi episcopi*', *ASE* 24 (1995), pp. 131–83.   Ch. 3, nn. 137–8

N.R. Ker, 'Membra Disiecta', *British Museum Quarterly* XII (1938), pp. 130–5.   Ch. 4, nn. 81, 114

N.R. Ker, 'Membra Disiecta, Second Series', *British Museum Quarterly* XIV (1939–40), pp. 79–86.   Ch. 4, nn. 42, 81, 85, 87, 91

N.R. Ker, 'Hemming's Cartulary', in Hunt, Pantin and Southern (eds), *Studies presented to Powicke* (Oxford, 1948), pp. 49–75.   Ch. 4, nn. 89, 108

N.R. Ker, 'Liber Custumarum and other Manuscripts formerly at the Guildhall', *Guildhall Miscellany* I (3) (1954), pp. 37–45.   Ch. 4, nn. 81, 304

N.R. Ker, *Catalogue of Manuscripts containing Anglo-Saxon* (2nd edn with supplement [*ASE* 5 (1976), pp. 121–31], Oxford, 1990).   Ch. 1, n. 127; ch. 3, nn. 71, 82; ch. 4, nn. 1–3, 7, 9, 11, 41–2, 53, 61, 64, 80–2, 88, 91, 95–6, 100–102, 105, 114, 117, 137, 147, 165–7, 171–2, 186, 193, 195, 219, 221, 224–5, 227, 231, 241, 246, 249–50, 253, 255, 263–5, 285, 327, 341, 353, 357–8, 361, 363, 365, 367, 372; ch. 5, nn. 341, 380; ch. 6, n. 118

N.R. Ker, *English Manuscripts in the Century after the Norman Conquest* (Oxford, 1960).   Ch. 4, n. 330

N.R. Ker, 'The Handwriting of Archbishop Wulfstan', in Clemoes and Hughes (eds), *England before the Conquest*, pp. 315–31.   Ch. 1, n. 127; ch. 4, nn. 108, 113, 119, 138, 218; ch. 5, n. 320

F. Kerff, *Der Quadripartitus. Ein Handbuch der karolingischen Kirchenreform* (Quellen und Forschungen zum Recht im Mittelalter 1, general editors R. Kottje and H. Mordek, Sigmaringen, 1982).   Ch. 4, nn. 209, 216

S. Keynes, *The Diplomas of King Æthelred 'the Unready', 978–1016* (Cambridge Studies in medieval life and thought, 3rd series 13, 1980).   Ch. 3, nn. 36, 104–7, 110–11, 140; ch. 4, nn. 19, 123, 146, 328; ch. 5, nn. 297–8, 314, 342, 373; ch. 6, nn. 54, 59, 70–1, 99–100

S. Keynes, *Anglo-Saxon Manuscripts and Other Items of Related Interest in the Library of Trinity College, Cambridge* (privately printed for the International Society of Anglo-Saxonists conference at Cambridge, 1985).   Ch. 4, n. 24

S. Keynes, 'King Æthelstan's books', in Lapidge and Gneuss (eds), *Learning and Literature*, pp. 143–201.   Ch. 4, nn. 25, 28, 117

S. Keynes, 'The Additions in Old English', in *York Gospels*, ed. Barker, pp. 81–99.   Ch. 4, nn. 124, 126, 137–8, 140–1; ch. 5, nn. 380, 394, 471, 613; ch. 6, nn. 90, 93

S. Keynes, 'Regenbald the Chancellor', *ANS* X (1987/8), pp. 185–222.   Ch. 6, n. 59

S. Keynes, 'Royal government and the written word in late Anglo-Saxon England', in McKitterick (ed.), *Uses of Literacy*, pp. 226–57.   Ch. 3, nn. 98, 116, 123; ch. 4, nn. 275, 294; ch. 5, nn. 101, 154, 200, 345; ch. 7, n. 1

S. Keynes, 'Crime and Punishment in the reign of King Æthelred the Unready', in Wood and Lund (eds), *People and Places*, pp. 67–81.   Ch. 3, n. 134

S. Keynes, 'The Historical Context of the Battle of Maldon', in D. Scragg (editor), *The Battle of Maldon* (Oxford, 1991), pp. 81–113.   Ch. 5, nn. 265, 283

S. Keynes, 'The Fonthill Letter', in Korhammer *et al.* (eds), *Words, Texts and Manuscripts*, pp. 53–97.   Ch. 3, nn. 95, 98

S. Keynes, 'Cnut's Earls', in Rumble (ed.), *Reign of Cnut*, pp. 43–88.   **Ch. 4, nn. 122, 240; ch. 5, n. 392**

S. Keynes, 'The "Dunstan B" charters', *ASE* 23 (1994), pp. 165–93.   **Ch. 5, n. 220; ch. 6, n. 54**

S. Keynes, 'The West Saxon Charters of King Æthelwulf and his Sons', *EHR* CIX (1994), pp. 1109–49.   **Ch. 4, n. 35; ch. 6, n. 56**

S. Keynes (ed.), *Liber Vitae of the New Minster*: see *II. SOURCES*.

S. Keynes, *An Atlas of Attestations in Anglo-Saxon Charters, c. 670–1066* (Department of Anglo-Saxon, Norse and Celtic, Cambridge, 1998)   **Ch. 3, n. 110; ch. 4, nn. 35, 122–3, 280; ch. 5, nn. 154, 203, 304**

S. Keynes, 'King Alfred and the Mercians', in M.A.S. Blackburn and D.N. Dumville (editors), *Kings, Currency and Alliances. History and coinage of Southern England in the Ninth Century* (Studies in Anglo-Saxon History IX, general editor D.N. Dumville, Woodbridge, 1998), pp. 1–45.   **Ch. 5, n. 105**

W. Kienast, 'Das Fortleben des Gotischen Rechtes in Südfrankreich und Katalonien', in his *Studien über die französischen Volkstämme des Frühmittelalters* (Pariser historischer Studien VII, Stuttgart, 1968), pp. 151–70.   **Ch. 2, n. 260**

P.D. King, *Law and Society in the Visigothic Kingdom* (Cambridge Studies in Medieval Life and Thought, 3rd series 5, Cambridge, 1972).   **Ch. 2, n. 255**

P.D. King, 'King Chindasvind and the First Territorial Law-code of the Visigothic Kingdom', in E. James (editor), *Visigothic Spain: New Approaches* (Oxford, 1980), pp. 131–57.   **Ch. 2, nn. 47, 50**

V. King, 'Ealdred, Archbishop of York: the Worcester Years', *ANS* XVIII (1995/6), pp. 123–37.   **Ch. 3, n. 52**

H. Kleinknecht and W. Gutbrod, *Law* (Biblical Key words, from G. Kittel, *Theologisches Wörterbuch zum neuen Testament*), translated by D.M. Barton and P.R. Ackroyd (London, 1962).   **Ch. 5, n. 24**

H. Kleinschmidt, *Untersuchungen über das englische Königtum im 10. Jahrhundert* (Göttinger Bausteine zur Geschichtswissenschaft 49, general editors H. Goetting *et al.*, Göttingen, 1979).   **Ch. 6, n. 101**

H. Kleinschmidt, 'Die Titulaturen englischer Könige im 10. und 11. Jahrhundert', in H. Wolfram and A. Scharer (editors), *Intitulatio III. Lateinische Herrschertitel und Herrschertitulaturen vom 7. zum 13. Jahrhundert* (MÖIG Ergänzungsband XXIX, Vienna, 1988), pp. 75–129.   **Ch. 6, n. 101**

H-W. Klewitz, 'Die Festkrönungen der deutschen Könige', *ZSS*, kan. Abt. 28 (1939), pp. 48–96.   **Ch. 6, nn. 110–11, 120**

F. Kluge, 'Fragment eines angelsächsischen Briefes', *Englische Studien* VIII (1884), pp. 62–3.   **Ch. 4, n. 73; ch. 5, n. 489**

D. Knowles, C.N.L. Brooke and V. London, editors, *The Heads of Religious Houses, England and Wales, 940–1216* (Cambridge, 1972).   **Ch. 4, n. 189**

M. Korhammer *et al.* (editors), *Words, Texts and Manuscripts. Studies in Anglo-Saxon Culture presented to Helmut Gneuss on the occasion of his sixty-fifth Birthday* (Cambridge, 1992): see Bately, Gretsch, Keynes.

D. Korte, *Untersuchungen zu Inhalt, Stil und Technik angelsächsischer Gesetze und Rechtsbücher des 6. bis 12. Jahrhunderts* (Archiv für vergleichende Kulturwissenschaft 10, editor C. Helfer, Meisenheim, 1974).   **Ch. 2, nn. 351, 361; ch. 5, nn. 19, 22–3, 112, 434, 684, 696; ch. 6, nn. 187, 189**

R. Kottje, *Studien zum Einfluß des alten Testamentes auf Recht und Liturgie des frühen Mittelalters (6.–8. Jahrhundert)* (Bonner historische Forschungen 23, general editor S. Skalweit, Bonn, 1970).   **Ch. 5, n. 196; ch. 6, n. 10**

R. Kottje, 'Die Lex Baiuvariorum - das Recht der Baiern', in Mordek (ed.), *Überlieferung und Geltung*, pp. 9–23.   **Ch. 2, nn. 139, 180, 206**

R. Kottje, 'Zum Geltungsbereich der Lex Alamannorum', in H. Beumann and W. Schröder (editors), *Die Transalpinen Verbindungen der Bayern, Alemannen und Franken bis zum 10. Jahrhundert* ('Nationes'. Historische und philologische Untersuchungen zur Entstehung der europäischen Nationen im Mittelalter 6, Sigmaringen, 1987), pp. 359–77.   **Ch. 2, nn. 139, 180, 206**

A. Krah, *Absetzungsverfahren als Spiegelbild von Königsmacht. Untersuchungen zum Kräfteverhältnis zwischen Königtum und Adel im Karolingerreich und seinen Nachfolgestaaten* (Untersuchungen zur deutschen Staats- und Rechtsgeschichte, n.f. 26, general editors A. Erler *et al.*, Aalen, 1987).   Ch. 2, nn. 10, 230, 270, 292

K. Kröschell, 'Recht und Rechtsbegriff in 12ten Jahrhundert', *Probleme des 12ten Jahrhunderts* (Vorträge und Forschungen des Konstanzer Arbeitskreis für mittelalterliche Geschichte XII, Konstanz, 1968), pp. 309–35.   Ch. 6, n. 228

B. Krusch, 'Neue forschungen über die drei oberdeutschen Leges: Bajuvariorum, Alamannorum, Ribuariorum', *Abhandlungen der Gesellschaft der Wissenschaften zu Göttingen* XX(1) (1927), pp. 1–208.   Ch. 2, nn. 26, 28, 58, 339–40

S. Kuttner, 'The Revival of Jurisprudence', in R.L. Benson and G. Constable (editors), *Renaissance and Renewal in the Twelfth Century* (Oxford, 1982), pp. 299–323.   Ch. 6. n. 228

W. Lambarde, *Archion, or, a Commentary upon the High Courts of Justice in England* (London, 1592).   Ch. 1, nn. 10, 19–20

Lambarde: see *II SOURCES, ARCHAIONOMIA*

P. Landau, 'Das Dekret des Ivo von Chartres', *ZSS* kan. Abt. LXX (1984), pp. 1–44. Ch. 6, n. 218

P. Landau, 'Ivo von Chartres', *Theologische Realenzyklopädie* 16, pp. 422–7.   Ch. 6, n. 215

M. Lapidge, 'Three Latin poems from Æthelwold's school at Winchester', *ASE* 1 (1972), pp. 85–137.   Ch. 3, n. 29

M. Lapidge, 'The Medieval Hagiography of St Ecgwine', *Vale of Evesham Historical Society, Research Papers* 6 (1977), pp. 77–93.   Ch. 3, n. 149

M. Lapidge, 'Byrhtferth and the *Vita S. Ecgwini*', *Med. Stud.* XLI (1979), pp. 331–53.   Ch. 3, n. 149; ch. 4, nn. 87, 91

M. Lapidge, 'Some Latin poems as evidence for the reign of Athelstan', *ASE* 9 (1981), pp. 61–98.   Ch. 5, n. 529

M. Lapidge, 'Byrhtferth of Ramsey and the early sections of the *Historia Regum* attributed to Symeon of Durham', *ASE* 10 (1982), pp. 97–122.   Ch. 3, n. 51; ch. 6, n. 118

M. Lapidge, 'Ealdred of York and MS. Cotton Vitellius E.xii', *Yorkshire Archaeological Journal* 55 (1983), pp. 11–25.   Ch. 3, n. 52; ch. 6, n. 110

M. Lapidge, 'A tenth-century metrical calendar from Ramsey', *Revue Bénédictine* 94 (1984), pp. 326–69.   Ch. 4, n. 34

M. Lapidge, 'The School of Theodore and Hadrian', *ASE* 15 (1986), pp. 45–72.   Ch. 4, n. 77

M. Lapidge, 'Æthelwold as Scholar and Teacher', in Yorke (ed.), *Bishop Æthelwold*, pp. 89–117.   Ch. 3, n. 29

M. Lapidge, *Bede the Poet* (Jarrow Lecture, 1993).   Ch. 4, n. 172

M. Lapidge, 'Byrhtferth and Oswald', in Brooks and Cubitt (eds), *St Oswald*, pp. 64–83. Ch. 3, n. 39

M. Lapidge (ed.), *Byrhtferth of Ramsey, The Lives of Oswald and Ecgwine*: see *II SOURCES, Byrhtferth*.

M. Lapidge, *The Cult of St Swithun* (Winchester Studies IV(2), general editor M. Biddle, forthcoming).   Ch. 3, n. 29

M. Lapidge and H. Gneuss (editors), *Learning and Literature in Anglo-Saxon England. Studies presented to Peter Clemoes on the occasion of his sixty-fifth birthday* (Cambridge, 1985): see Gneuss, Keynes.

M. Lares, *Bible et Civilisation Anglaise. Contribution à l'étude des elements d'Ancien Testament dans la Civilisation Vieille Anglaise* (Lille, Service de reproduction des thèses, 1975).   Ch. 6, n. 20

C.H. Lawrence, *Saint Edmund of Abingdon. A Study in Hagiography and History* (Oxford, 1960).   Ch. 4, n. 268

M.K. Lawson, 'The Collection of Danegeld and Heregeld in the reigns of Æthelred II and Cnut', *EHR* XCIX (1984), pp. 721–38.   Ch. 5, n. 409

M.K. Lawson, '"Those Stories Look True": levels of taxation in the reigns of Æthelred II and Cnut', *EHR* CIV (1989), pp. 385–406.   Ch. 5, n. 396

M.K. Lawson, 'Archbishop Wulfstan and the Homiletic Element in the Laws of Æthelred II and Cnut', *EHR* CVII (1992), pp. 565–86; repr. in Rumble (ed.), *Reign of Cnut*, pp. 141–64. **Ch. 4, n. 157; Ch. 5, nn. 213, 335, 379, 381, 442, 454; Ch. 6, nn. 134, 137**

M.K. Lawson, *Cnut. The Danes in England in the Early Eleventh Century* (London, 1993). **Ch. 4, n. 122; Ch. 5, nn. 382, 384, 392, 399–400**

B.A. Lees, *Alfred the Great, the Truth Teller, Maker of England* (Heroes of the Nations, London, 1919) **Ch. 5, n. 99**

P.S. Leicht, *Storia del Diritto italiano. Le Fonti* (Milan, 1939). **Ch. 6, n. 197**

R. Le Jan, *Famille et Pouvoir dans le Monde Franc (VIIᵉ–Xᵉ siècle). Essai d'anthropologie sociale* (Histoire Ancienne et Médiévale 33, Paris, 1995). **Ch. 2, nn. 228, 276**

R. Le Jan, 'Justice royale et pratiques sociales dans le royaume franc au IXᵉ siècle', *La Giustizia* II, pp. 47–90. **Ch. 2, nn. 213, 272**

P. Lendinara, 'The Kentish Laws', in J. Hines (editor), *The Anglo-Saxons, from the Migration Period to the eighth century. An ethnographic perspective* (San Marino, 1997), pp. 211–43. **Ch. 2, n. 332**

V. Leroquais, *Les Pontificaux Manuscrits des Bibliothèques publiques de France* (3 vols, Paris, 1937). **Ch. 4, n. 130**

L. Levillain, 'Les Nibelungen historiques et leurs alliances de famille', *Annales du Midi* XLIX (1937), pp. 337–407, L (1938), pp. 5–66. **Ch. 2, nn. 141, 246, 276, 281**

E. Levy, *West Roman Vulgar Law. The Law of Property* (Memoirs of the American Philosophical Society 29, Philadelphia, 1951). **Ch. 2, n. 35**

E. Levy, 'Weströstlisches Vulgarrecht und Justinian', *ZSS* rom. Abt LXXVI (1959), pp. 1–36; reprinted in his *Gesammelte Schriften* I, pp. 264–88. **Ch. 2, n. 35**

E. Levy, 'The Vulgarization of Roman Law in the Early Middle Ages, as illustrated by successive recensions of the *Pauli Sententiae*', *Medievalia et Humanistica* I (1943), pp. 14–40; repr. in his *Gesammelte Schriften* I, pp. 220–47. **Ch. 2, n. 36**

E. Levy, *Gesammelte Schriften* (2 vols, Köln-Graz, 1963): see above.

C.P. Lewis, 'An Introduction to the Herefordshire Domesday' *The Herefordshire Domesday* (*Domesday Book*, general editor A. Williams, Alecto Historical Editions, London, 1988), pp. 1–22. **Ch. 6, n. 522**

K.J. Leyser, *Rule and Conflict in an Early Medieval Society. Ottonian Saxony* (London, 1979). **Ch. 6, nn. 105, 111**

K.J. Leyser, 'The Tenth-Century Condition', in idem, *Medieval Germany and its Neighbours 900–1250* (London, 1984), pp. 1–9. **Ch. 6, n. 139**

K. Leyser, 'The Ottonians and Wessex', translated and revised from its original German (*FMS* 17 (1983), pp. 73–97), in his *Communications and Power* I, pp. 73–104. **Ch. 6, n. 105**

K. Leyser, 'Early Medieval Canon Law and the Beginnings of Knighthood', in L. Fenske *et al.* (editors), *Institutionen, Kultur und Gesellschaft. Festschrift für Josef Fleckenstein zu seinem 65. Geburtstag* (Sigmaringen, 1984); repr. in his *Communications and Power* I, pp. 51–71. **Ch. 6, nn. 159, 169**

K. Leyser, 'On the Eve of the First European Revolution', in his *Communications and Power* II, pp. 1–19. **Ch. 6, n. 171**

K. Leyser (edited by T. Reuter), *Communications and Power in Medieval Europe* (2 vols, London, 1994): see above.

F. Liebermann, 'Die Abfassungszeit der Leges Henrici', *Forschungen zur deutschen Geschichte* 16 (1876), pp. 582–6. **Ch. 1, n. 98**

F. Liebermann, 'Ein ungedrucktes Vorwort zu den Leges Henrici Primi', *ZSS* germ Abt. III (1882), pp. 127–37. **Ch. 1, n. 98**

F. Liebermann, 'Zu den Gesetzen der Angelsachsen', *ZSS* germ Abt. V (1884), pp. 198–226. **Ch. 1, n. 100**

F. Liebermann, *Quadripartitus. Ein englisches Rechtsbuch von 1114* (Halle, 1892): see also Subsidiary Index (iii). **Ch. 4, nn. 298, 311, 321; ch. 5, n. 516; ch. 6, n. 226**

F. Liebermann, 'On the Instituta Cnuti aliorumque Regum Anglorum', *TRHS* N.S. 7 (1893), pp. 77–107. **Ch. 5, nn. 638, 646**

F. Liebermann, *Consiliatio Cnuti, eine Übertragung angelsächsischer Gesetze aus dem zwölften Jahrhundert* (Halle, 1893). **Ch. 5, nn. 654–6**

F. Liebermann, *Über Pseudo-Cnut's Constitutiones de Foresta* (Halle, 1894).   **Ch. 5, n. 661**

F. Liebermann, *Über die Leges Anglorum Saeculo xiii ineunte Londoniis collectae* (Halle, 1894).   **Ch. 3, n. 88; Ch. 4, nn. 67, 306–7; Ch. 5, n. 516**

F. Liebermann, 'Kesselfang bei den Westsachsen im 7ten Jahrhundert', *Sitzungsberichte der königlichen Akademie der Wissenschaften zu Berlin* (1896), pp. 829–35.   **Ch. 4, n. 40**

F. Liebermann, *Über die Leges Edwardi Confessoris* (Halle, 1896).   **Ch. 5, nn. 683, 685**

F. Liebermann, 'Wulfstan und Cnut', *Arch. SNSL* CIII (1899), pp. 47–54.   **Ch. 1, n. 126; Ch. 5, n. 346**

F. Liebermann, 'Matrosenstellung aus Landgütern der Kirche London', *Arch. SNSL* CIV (1900), pp. 17–24.   **Ch. 4, n. 268**

F. Liebermann, 'Über die Leis Willelme', *Arch. SNSL* CVI (1901), pp. 113–38.   **Ch. 5, n. 662**

F. Liebermann, *Über das englische Rechtsbuch Leges Henrici* (Halle, 1901).   **Ch. 5, n. 687**

F. Liebermann, 'De accusatoribus aus Pseudo-Isidor', *Deutsche Zeitschrift für Kirchenrecht* XI (1902), pp. 1–5.   **Ch. 6, n. 212**

F. Liebermann (ed.), *Gesetze der Angelsachsen*: see *II SOURCES*.

F. Liebermann, review of Asser, *Deutsche Literaturzeitung* XXV (1904), cols 480–4.   **Ch. 3, n. 10**

F. Liebermann, 'King Alfred and Mosaic Law', *Transactions of the Jewish Historical Society* VI (1912), pp. 21–31.   **Ch. 6, n. 18**

F. Liebermann, 'A Contemporary Manuscript of the "Leges Anglorum Londoniis Collectae"', *EHR* XXVIII (1913), pp. 732–45.   **Ch. 4. nn. 303, 307**

F. Liebermann, 'Über die Gesetze Ines von Wessex', in *Mélanges d' histoire offerts à M. Ch. Bémont* (Paris, 1913), pp. 21–42.   **Ch. 5, n. 15**

F. Liebermann, *The National Assembly in the Anglo-Saxon Period* (London, 1913).   **Ch. 5, n. 213; Ch. 6, nn. 57, 59, 71, 108**

F. Liebermann, 'Ist Lambardes Text der Gesetze Æthelstans neuzeitliche Fälschung?', *Beiblatt zur Anglia. Mitteilungen über englische Sprache und Literatur und über englischen Unterricht* XXXV (1924), pp. 214–18.   **Ch. 4, n. 371**

F. Liebermann (with A.A. Arnold), 'Notes on the *Textus Roffensis*', *Archaeologia Cantiana* XXIII (1898), pp. 94–112.   **Ch. 4, n. 327**

D. Liebs, *Die Jurisprudenz im spätantiken Italien (260 - 640 n. Chr.)* (Freiburger rechtsgeschichtliche Abhandlungen n.f. 8, Berlin, 1987).   **Ch. 2, n. 30**

D. Liebs, 'Römische Juristen der Merowinger' in G. Köbler and H. Nehlsen (editors), *Wirkungen europäischer Rechtskultur. Festschrift für Karl Kröschell zu seinem 70. Geburtstag* (München, 1998), pp. 635–66.   **Ch. 2, n. 76**

E. Liggins, 'The Authorship of the Old English Orosius', *Anglia* 88 (1970), pp. 289–322.   **Ch. 5, n. 37**

R.S. Lopez, 'Byzantine Law in the seventh century and its reception by the Germans and the Arabs, *Byzantion* XVI (1942–3), pp. 445–61.   **Ch. 5, n. 197**

F. Lot and L. Halphen, *La règne de Charles le Chauve: I, 840–51* (Vol. I only, Bibliothèque de l' école des hautes études 175, Paris, 1909).   **Ch. 3, n. 66**

H.R. Loyn (ed.), *Wulfstan MS*: see *II SOURCES*.

H.R. Loyn, 'Wales and England in the Tenth Century: the Context of the Æthelstan Charters', *Welsh History Review* XIV (1983), pp. 283–301, repr. in his *Society and Peoples*, pp. 173–99.   **Ch. 6, n. 81**

H.R. Loyn, 'Peter's Pence', *Friends of Lambeth Palace Library Annual Report* (1984), pp. 10–20, repr. in his *Society and Peoples*, pp. 241–58.   **Ch. 5, n. 472**

H.R. Loyn, *Society and Peoples. Studies in the History of England and Wales, c. 600–1200* (London, 1992): see above.

H.R. Loyn, '*De Iure Domini Regis*. A Comment on Royal Authority in eleventh-century England', in Hicks (ed.), *England in the Eleventh Century*, pp. 17–24.   **Ch. 5, n. 693**

N. Lund, 'King Edgar and the Danelaw', *Medieval Scandinavia* 9 (1976), pp. 181–95.   **Ch. 3, n. 62; Ch. 5, nn. 256, 302**

N. Lund, 'Peace and Non-peace in the Viking Age – Ottar in Biarma-land, the Rus in Byzantium, and Danes and Norwegians in England', in J. Knirk (editor), *Proceedings of the Tenth Viking Congress (Larkollen, Norway, 1985)* (Universitetets Oldsaksamlings Skrifter n.r. 9, Oslo, 1987), pp. 255–69.   **Ch. 5, n. 265**

A. Lutz, *Die Version G der angelsächsischen Chronik, Rekonstruktion und Edition* (Texte und Untersuchungen zur englischen Philologie 11, general editors H. Gneuss and W. Weiß, Munich, 1981).   **Ch. 4, nn. 41–3, 46, 48–9**

G. Lysaght, 'Fleury and St Benedict: Monastery and Patron Saint (640–877)' (Oxford, D.Phil., 1984).   **Ch. 2, nn. 211, 231**

K. McCone, *Pagan Past and Christian Present in Early Irish Literature* (Maynooth Monographs 3, Naas, 1990).   **Ch. 1, n. 44**

P. McGurk (ed.), *Eleventh-Century Illustrated Miscellany*: see *II SOURCES*.

P. McGurk, 'The Palaeography', in *York Gospels*, ed. Barker, pp. 37–42.   **Ch. 4, pp. 139–40**

P. McGurk (ed.), *Chronicle of John of Worcester*: see *II SOURCES*.

E.A. McIntyre, 'Early twelfth-century Worcester Cathedral Priory, with special reference to the manuscripts written there' (Oxford, D. Phil., 1978).   **Ch. 4, nn. 87, 91**

R. McKitterick, *The Carolingians and the Written Word* (Cambridge, 1989).   **Ch. 2, nn. 105, 110, 115, 126–7, 130, 139, 141–2, 169, 208**

R. McKitterick, 'Zur Herstellung von Kapitularien: Die Arbeit des Leges-Skriptoriums', *MÖIG* 101 (1993), pp. 3–16.   **Ch. 2, nn. 167, 171**

R. McKitterick, 'Introduction', in *idem* (ed.), *New Cambridge Medieval History II*, pp. 3–17.   **Ch. 2, n. 318**

R. McKitterick (editor), *The Uses of Literacy in Early Mediaeval Europe* (Cambridge, 1990): see Kelly, Keynes, Nelson, I. Wood.

R. McKitterick (editor), *The New Cambridge Medieval History of Europe. II, c. 700–c. 900* (Cambridge, 1995): see Airlie, Shepard.

T. Madox, *The History and Antiquities of the Exchequer* (London, 1711).   **Ch. 1, n. 95**

E. Magnou-Nortier, *Foi et Fidélité. Recherches sur l' évolution des liens personels chez les Francs du VIIe–IXe siècle* (Publications de l'Université de Toulouse-le Mirail série A 28, 1976).   **Ch. 2, n. 101**

E. Magnou-Nortier, 'Note sur l'expression *Iustitiam Facere* dans les Capitulaires Carolingiens', in M. Sot, C. Lepelley *et al.* (editors), *Haut Moyen Age: Culture, Éducation et Société. Études offertes à Pierre Riché* (Paris, 1990), pp. 249–64.   **Ch. 2, n. 315**

F.W. Maitland, *Domesday Book and Beyond* (new edn with foreword by J.C. Holt, Cambridge, 1987).   **Ch. 1, nn. 2, 70, 72, 84–5, 88, 116; Ch. 4, n. 67; Ch. 5, n. 693**

F.W. Maitland, *Collected Papers*, edited by H.A.L. Fisher (3 vols, Cambridge, 1911).   **Ch. 1, nn. 61–2, 64–5, 70–3, 76–8, 86, 89–90, 108; Ch. 5, n. 692**

F.W. Maitland, *Selected Historical Essays*, edited by H. Cam (Cambridge, 1957).   **Ch. 1, nn. 70, 115; Ch. 5, n. 127**

F. de Marini Avonzo, 'Diritto e Giustizia nell' Occidente Tardoantico', *La Giustizia* I, pp. 105–25.   **Ch. 2, n. 221**

E. Mason, *St Wulfstan of Worcester c. 1008–1095* (Oxford, 1990).   **Ch. 4, n. 164**

J.F. Matthews, 'The Making of the Text', in Harries and Wood (eds), *Theodosian Code*, pp. 19–44.   **Ch. 2, n. 32**

K. von Maurer, 'Über angelsächsische Rechtsverhältnisse', *Kritische Überschau der deutschen Gesetzgebung* I (1853), pp. 47–120, 405–31, II (1854), pp. 30–68, 388–440, III (1856), pp. 26–61.   **Ch. 1, n. 99**

H. Mayr-Harting, 'Saxons, Danes and Normans, 409–1154: Overview', in C. Haigh (editor), *The Cambridge Historical Encyclopedia of Great Britain and Ireland* (Cambridge, 1985), pp. 54–8.   **Ch. 3, n. 15**

H. Mayr-Harting, *Ottonian Book Illumination. An Historical Study* (2 vols, London, 1991).   **Ch. 2, nn. 134, 138; Ch. 6, n. 136**

H. Mayr-Harting, 'Charlemagne, the Saxons and the Imperial Coronation of 800', *EHR* CXI (1996), pp. 1113–33.   **Ch. 2, n. 318**

H. Mayr-Harting and R.I. Moore (editors), *Studies in Medieval History presented to R.H.C. Davis* (Oxford, 1985): see Hamilton, Rollason, Wickham.

A.L. Meaney, 'Alfred, the Patriarch and the White Stone', *AUMLA: Journal of the Australasian Universities Language and Literature Assoc.* XLIX (1978), pp. 65–79.   Ch. 4, n. 63

A.L. Meaney, 'Variant versions of Old English Medical Remedies and the Compilation of Bald's Leechbook', *ASE* 13 (1984), pp. 235–68.   Ch. 4, nn. 62, 100

B. Merta, 'Politische Theorie in den Königsurkunden Pippins', *MÖIG* 100 (1992), pp. 117–31.   Ch. 2, n. 65

M.D. Metcalf, *Coinage in Ninth-Century Northumbria (The Tenth Oxford Symposium on Coinage and Monetary History)* (British Archaeological Reports, British Series 180, Oxford, 1987).   Ch. 5, n. 587

F. Millar, *The Emperor in the Roman World (31 BC-AD 337)* (London, 1977).   Ch. 2, n. 42

E. Miller, *The Abbey and Bishopric of Ely. The Society of an Ecclesiastical Estate from the Tenth Century to the Early Fourteenth Century* (Cambridge Studies in Medieval Life and Thought N.S. 1, Cambridge, 1951).   Ch. 3, n. 138

S.F.C. Milsom, *Historical Foundations of the Common Law* (London, 1969).   Ch. 1, n. 118

S.F.C. Milsom, 'F.W. Maitland', *PBA* LXVI (1980), pp. 265–81.   Ch. 1, n. 82

B. Mitchell, *Old English Syntax* (2 vols, Oxford, 1985).   Ch. 2, n. 333

H. Moisl, 'Some Aspects of the Relationship between Secular and Ecclesiastical Learning in Ireland and England in the early post-conversion period' (Oxford, D.Phil., 1979).   Ch. 1, n. 45

H. Moisl, 'Kingship and Orally Transmitted *Stammestradition* among the Lombards and Franks', in H. Wolfram and A. Schwarcz (editors), *Die Bayern und ihre Nachbarn* I (Österreichische Akademie der Wissenschaften, philosophisch-historische Klasse, Denkschriften 179, Wien, 1985), pp. 111–19.   Ch. 2, n. 104

R.I. Moore, 'Family, Community and Cult on the Eve of the Gregorian Reform'. *TRHS* 5th series 30 (1980), pp. 49–69.   Ch. 6, n. 171

H. Mordek, 'Karolingische Kapitularien', in *idem* (ed.), *Überlieferung und Geltung*, pp. 25–50.   Ch. 2, nn. 106, 110, 121, 197

H. Mordek, 'Weltliches Recht im Kloster Weißenburg/Elsaß: Hinkmar von Rheims und die Kapitulariensammlung des Cod. Sélestat, Bibliothèque Humaniste, 14 (104)', in M. Borgolte and H. Spilling (editors), *Festschrift für Johanne Autenrieth zu ihrem 65. Geburtstag* (Sigmaringen, 1988), pp. 69–85.   Ch. 2, n. 155

H. Mordek, 'Ein Freiburger Kapitularienfragment', *DA* 48 (1992), pp. 609–13.   Ch. 2, n. 128

H. Mordek, 'Die Hedenen als politische Kraft im austrasischen Frankenreich', in Jarnut *et al.* (eds), *Karl Martell*, pp. 345–66.   Ch. 2, nn. 62, 77

H. Mordek, 'Ein Bildnis König Bernhards von Italien? Zum Frontispiz in Cod. St Paul (Kärnten), Stiftsbibliothek, 4/1', in *Societá, Istituzioni, Spiritualitá. Studi in onore de Cinzio Violante* (Spoleto, 1994), pp. 547–55.   Ch. 2, n. 198

H. Mordek, 'Frühmittelalterliche Gesetzgeber und Iustitia in Miniaturen weltlicher Rechtshandschriften', *La Giustizia* I, pp. 997–1052.   Ch. 2, nn. 8–9, 129–30, 134, 173–4, 181, 198, 210

H. Mordek, *Bibliotheca capitularium regum Francorum manuscripta. Überlieferung und Traditionszusammenhang der fränkischen Herrschererlasse* (MGH Hilfsmittel 15, Munich, 1995).   Ch. 2, nn. 12, 96, 116, 121, 123, 125, 128–9, 132–7, 142–3, 145, 147–9, 152–6, 159–60, 163, 166, 170–2, 174, 176, 179–80, 182–3, 185, 187, 189–90, 195, 198–204, 208, 292, 318, 347; ch. 5, n. 246

H. Mordek, 'Kapitularien und Schriftlichkeit', in R. Schieffer (editor), *Schriftkultur und Reichsverwaltung unter den Karolingern* (Abhandlungen der Nordrhein-Westfälischen Akademie der Wissenschaften 97, 1996), pp. 34–66.   Ch. 2, nn. 110, 130, 171

H. Mordek, 'Ein exemplarischer Rechtsstreit: Hinkmar von Reims und Neuilly-Saint-Front', *ZSS* kan. Abt. LXXXIII (1997), pp. 86–112.   Ch. 2, nn. 10, 279

H. Mordek (editor), *Überlieferung und Geltung normativer Texte des frühen und hohen Mittelalters* (Quellen und Forschungen zum Recht im Mittelalter, general editors R. Kottje and H. Mordek, 4, Sigmaringen, 1986): see Kottje, Mordek

P. Morison, 'The Miraculous and French Society *circa* 950–1100' (Oxford, D.Phil., 1986). Ch. 3, n. 155

C. Morris, 'William I and the church courts', *EHR* LXXXII (1967), pp. 449–63.   Ch. 3, n. 70; ch. 5, n. 618

R. Morris, 'Dispute Settlement in the Byzantine Provinces in the tenth century', in *Disputes*, pp. 125–47.   Ch. 3, n. 152

J. Morrish, 'King Alfred's Letter as a Source on Learning in England in the Ninth Century', in Szarmach (ed.), *Studies in Earlier Old English Prose*, pp. 87–107.   Ch. 3, n. 98

F. Mütherich, 'Frühmittelalterliche Rechtshandschriften', *Festschrift für Hermann Fillitz zum 70. Geburtstag* (Aachener Kunstblätter 60, 1994), pp. 79–86.   Ch. 2, nn. 130, 163, 174

A. Murray, *Reason and Society in the Middle Ages* (Oxford, 1978).   Ch. 6, nn. 159, 169, 172

A.C. Murray, *Germanic Kinship Structure. Studies in Law and Society in Antiquity and the early Middle Ages* (Studies and Texts 65, Pontifical Institute of Mediaeval Studies, Toronto, 1983).   Ch. 2, nn. 48, 58, 85

A.C. Murray, 'From Roman to Frankish Gaul: "Centenarii" and "Centenae" in the Administration of the Merovingian Kingdom', *Traditio* XLIV (1988), pp. 59–100.   Ch. 2, n. 75

A.C. Murray, 'Immunity, Nobility and the *Edict of Paris*', *Speculum* LXIX (1994), pp. 18–39.   Ch. 2, n. 76

C. Neff, 'Scandinavian Elements in the Wantage Code of Æthelred II', *Journal of Legal History* 10 (1989), pp. 285–316.   Ch. 5, nn. 291, 299, 303

H. Nehlsen, *Sklavenrecht zwischen Antike und Mittelalter. Germanisches und römisches Recht in den germanischen Rechtsaufzeichnungen* (Göttinger Studien zur Rechtsgeschichte 7, Göttingen, 1972).   Ch. 2, n. 248

H. Nehlsen, 'Zur Aktualität und Effektivität germanischer Rechtsaufzeichnungen', in Classen (ed.), *Recht und Schrift*, pp. 449–502.   Ch. 2, nn. 75, 249, 260

H. Nehlsen, 'Karl-August Eckhardt+', *ZSS* germ. Abt CIV (1987), pp. 497–536.   Ch. 2, n. 58

H. Nehlsen, 'Entstehung des öffentlichen Strafrechts bei den germanischen Stämmen', in K. Kröschell (editor), *Gerichtslauben-Vorträge. Festkolloquium zum fünfundsiebzigsten Geburtstag von Hans Thieme* (Sigmaringen, 1983), pp. 3–16.   Ch. 2, n. 76

K. Nehlsen-von Stryk, *Die boni homines des frühen Mittelalters* (Freiburger rechtsgeschichtliche Abhandlungen n.f. 2, Berlin, 1981).   Ch. 2, n. 310

J.L. Nelson, 'On the Limits of the Carolingian Renaissance', in D. Baker (editor), *Renaissance and Renewal in Christian History* (Studies in Church History 14, Oxford, 1977), pp. 51–69; repr. in her *Politics and Ritual*, pp. 49–67.   Ch. 2, n. 315

J.L. Nelson, 'Kingship, Law and Liturgy in the Political Thought of Hincmar of Rheims', *EHR* XCII (1977), pp. 241–79; repr. in *Politics and Ritual*, pp. 133–71.   Ch. 2, n. 101; Ch. 6, n. 30

J.L. Nelson, 'Inauguration rituals', in *EMK*, pp. 50–71; repr. in *Politics and Ritual*, pp. 283–307.   Ch. 6, n. 92

J.L. Nelson, 'The Earliest Surviving Royal *Ordo*: Some Liturgical and Historical Aspects', in B. Tierney and P. Linehan (editors), *Authority and Power: Studies in Medieval Law and Government Presented to Walter Ullmann* (Cambridge, 1980), pp. 29–48; repr. in *Politics and Ritual*, pp. 341–60.   Ch. 6, nn. 113, 115

J.L. Nelson, 'The Rites of the Conqueror', *ANS* IV (1981/2), pp. 117–32; repr. in *Politics and Ritual*, pp. 375–401.   Ch. 3, n. 52

J.L. Nelson, 'Legislation and Consensus in the reign of Charles the Bald', in Wormald *et al.* (eds), *Ideal and Reality*, pp. 202–27; repr. in *Politics and Ritual*, pp. 91–116.   Ch. 2, nn. 102, 155

J.L. Nelson, 'The Second English *Ordo*', in *Politics and Ritual*, pp. 361–74.   Ch. 6, nn. 100, 114, 117

J.L. Nelson, *Politics and Ritual in Early Medieval Europe* (London, 1986): see also above. Ch. 3, n. 25

J.L. Nelson, 'Dispute Settlement in Carolingian West Francia', in *Disputes*, pp. 45–64; repr. in her *Frankish World*, pp. 51–74.   Ch. 2, nn. 5–6, 222, 237, 242, 251, 265, 275, 281, 310

J.L. Nelson, 'Wealth and Wisdom: the politics of Alfred the Great', in J. Rosenthal (editor), *Kings and Kingship* (Acta XI, Center for Medieval and Early Renaissance Studies, State University of New York, 1987), pp. 31–52.   Ch. 6, nn. 43, 52

J.L. Nelson, 'Literacy in Carolingian Government', in McKitterick (ed.), *Uses of Literacy*, pp. 258–96; repr. in her *Frankish World*, pp. 1–36.   Ch. 2, nn. 5–6

J.L. Nelson, 'Reconstructing a royal family: Reflections on Alfred, from Asser chapter 2', in Wood and Lund (eds), *People and Places*, pp. 47–66.   Ch. 4, n. 33

J.L. Nelson, *Charles the Bald* (The Medieval World, general editor D. Bates, London, 1992).   Ch. 2, nn. 13, 281

J.L. Nelson, 'The Political Ideas of Alfred of Wessex' in A. Duggan (editor), *Kings and Kingship in Medieval Europe* (King's College London Medieval Studies X, general editor J Bately, London, 1993), pp. 125–58.   Ch. 6, nn. 43, 166

J.L. Nelson, 'The wary widow', in Davies and Fouracre (eds), *Property and Power*, pp. 82–113.   Ch. 2, n. 276

J.L. Nelson, *The Frankish World, 750–900* (London, 1996): see also above.   Ch. 2, n. 114

J.L. Nelson, '" ... sicut olim gens Francorum ... nunc gens Anglorum": Fulk's Letter to Alfred revisited', in Roberts *et al.* (eds), *Alfred the Wise*, pp. 135–44.   Ch. 6, n. 40

J.L. Nelson, 'Kings with Justice; Kings without Justice: an Early Medieval Paradox', *La Giustizia* II, pp. 797–826.   Ch. 2, nn. 129, 315

J.E. Niermeyer, *Mediae Latinitatis Lexicon Minus* (Leiden, 1976).   Ch. 2, n. 86

F. Noble, *Offa's Dyke Reviewed*, edited by M. Gelling (British Archaeological Reports, British Series 114, Oxford 1983).   Ch. 4, n. 279; ch. 5, n. 522

T.F.X. Noble, 'The monastic ideal as a model for empire: the case of Louis the Pious', *Revue Bénédictine* 86 (1976), pp. 235–50.   Ch. 2, n. 97

B. O'Brien, 'Propaganda, Forgery and the Orality of English Law: the Becket conflict and the invention of the myth *of lex non scripta*', in J.A. Bush and A. Wijffels (editors), *Learning the Law. Teaching and Transmission of Law in England, 1150–1900* (London, 1999), pp. 1–16.

B. O'Brien, *God's Peace and King's Peace. The Laws of Edward the Confessor* (Philadelphia, 1999)   Ch. 1, nn. 26, 106; ch. 5, nn. 650, 653, 677. 680–1; ch. 6, n. 187

D. Ó'Corráin, L Breatnach and A. Breen, 'The Laws of the Irish', *Peritia* 3 (1984), pp. 382–438.   Ch. 6, n. 10

M. O'Donovan, 'An interim revision of episcopal dates for the province of Canterbury, 850–950, part II', *ASE* 2 (1973), pp. 91–113.   Ch. 4, n. 31

O.G. Oexle, 'Die funktionale Dreiteilung der "Gesellschaft" bei Adlabero von Laon. Deutungsgeschemata der sozialen Wirklichkeit im früheren Mittelalter, *FMS* 12 (1978), pp. 1–54.   Ch. 6, nn. 159, 169

O.G. Oexle, 'Die "Wirklichkeit" und das "Wissen". Ein Blick auf das sozialgeschichtliche Oeuvre von Georges Duby', *HZ* 232 (1981), pp. 61–91.   Ch. 6, n. 159

L. Oliver, 'The Language of the Early English Laws' (Harvard, Ph.D., 1995).   Ch. 2. nn. 321, 332

P.P. O'Neill, 'The Old English Introductions to the Prose Psalms of the Paris Psalter: Sources, Structure and Composition', *Studies in Philology* 78 (5) (1981), pp. 20–38.   Ch. 6, n. 46

E. Ortigues, 'L' Élaboration de la théorie des trois ordres chez Haymon d' Auxerre', *Francia* 14 (1986), pp. 27–43.   Ch. 6, nn. 159, 164

K. Otten, *König Alfreds Boethius* (Studien zur englischen Philologie 3, general editors G. Müller-Schwefe and F. Schubel, Tübingen, 1964).   Ch. 6, nn. 6, 43

R.I. Page, 'The Parker Register and Matthew Parker's Anglo-Saxon manuscripts', *Transactions of the Cambridge Bibliographical Society* VIII (1981), pp. 1–17.   Ch. 4, n. 4

R.I. Page, '*Gerefa*: Some problems of Meaning', in A. Bammesberger (editor), *Problems of Old English lexicography: studies in memory of Angus Cameron* (Regensburg, 1985), pp. 211–28.   Ch. 4, n. 281; ch. 5, n. 564

R.I. Page, *Matthew Parker and his Books* (Kalamazoo, 1993).   Ch. 4, n. 173

F. Palgrave, *The Rise and Progress of the English Commonwealth. Anglo-Saxon Period*

(The Anglo-Saxon Policy, and the Institutions Arising out of laws and usages which prevailed before the Conquest) (2 vols, London, 1832).   Ch. 1, nn. 33–6, 39, 42, 91; ch. 5, n. 75

W. Paravicini and K-F. Werner (editors), *Histoire Comparée de l'Administration (IVᵉ–XVIIIᵉ siècles)* (Beihefte der Francia 9, 1980): see Campbell, Werner.

M.B. Parkes, 'The palaeography of the Parker manuscript of the *Chronicle*, laws and Sedulius, and historiography at Winchester in the late ninth and tenth centuries', *ASE 5* (1976), pp. 149–71; supplemented by 'A fragment of an early-tenth-century Anglo-Saxon manuscript and its significance', *ASE 12* (1983), pp. 129–40.   Ch. 4, nn. 3–4, 7, 12, 75

F. Patetta, 'Sull' introduzione in Italia della Collezione d' Ansegiso, e sulla data del cosi detto Capitulare Mantuanum Duplex attribuito all' anno 787', in his *Studi sulle fonti giuridiche medievali* (edited by G. Astuti, Turin, 1967), pp. 719–28.   Ch. 2, n. 89

D. Pelteret, *Slavery in Early Medieval England. From the Reign of Alfred until the Twelfth Century* (Studies in Anglo-Saxon History VII, general editor D.N. Dumville, Woodbridge, 1995).   Ch. 6, n. 142

P. Périn, 'The Undiscovered Grave of King Clovis (+511)', in M. Carver (editor), *The Age of Sutton Hoo* (Woodbridge, 1992), pp. 255–64.   Ch. 6, n. 346

R.W. Pfaff, 'Eadui Basan, Scriptorum Princeps?', *England in the Eleventh Century*, ed. Hicks, pp. 267–84.   Ch. 4, n. 139

P.E. Pieler, 'Byzantinische Rechtsliteratur', in H. Hunger (editor), *Die hochsprachliche profane Literatur der Byzantiner* (Byzantinische Handbuch V, 2 vols, Munich, 1978) II, pp. 341–480.   Ch. 6. n. 8

T.F.T. Plucknett, *A Concise History of the Common Law* (London, 5th edn, 1956).   Ch. 1, n. 118

C. Plummer, *Life and Times of Alfred the Great* (Oxford, 1902).   Ch. 1, n. 1; ch. 3, n. 18; ch. 5, n. 99

J.G.A. Pocock, *The Ancient Constitution and the Feudal Law. A Study of English Historical Thought in the Seventeenth Century* (Cambridge, 1957).   Ch. 1, nn. 16, 26

F. Pollock and F.W. Maitland, *The History of English Law to the accession of Edward I* (2 vols, reissue edited by S.F.C. Milsom, Cambridge, 1968).   Ch. 1, nn. 2, 4, 67–8, 70, 72, 74–5, 81, 91–2, 95; ch. 5, nn. 90, 127, 455, 694; ch. 6, nn. 188, 202

J-P. Poly, 'La corde au cou: les Francs, la France et la loi Salique', *Genèse de l'état moderne en Mediterranée. Approches historiques et anthropologique des pratiques et des representations* (Collection de l'école française de Rome 168, Rome, 1993), pp. 287–320.   Ch. 2, nn. 62, 325

J-P. Poly and E. Bournazel (translated by C. Higgitt), *The Feudal Transformation 900–1200* (New York, 1991).   Ch. 6, n. 138

T.E. Powell, 'The "Three Orders" of Society in Anglo-Saxon England', *ASE 23* (1994), pp. 103–32.   Ch. 6, nn. 158–9, 167

F. Prinz, *Frühes Mönchtum im Frankenreich* (Munich, 1965).   Ch. 2, n. 209

H. Pryce, 'Duw yn lle mach: Briduw yng nghyfraith Hywel', in T.M. Charles-Edwards, et al., (editors), *Lawyers and Laymen. Studies in the History of Law presented to Professor Dafydd Jenkins on his Seventy-fifth Birthday* (Cardiff, 1986), pp. 47–71.   Ch. 5, n. 95

C.F. Radding, *The Origins of Medieval Jurisprudence. Pavia and Bologna 850–1150* (New Haven, 1988).   Ch. 6, nn. 195, 197–201, 203, 205, 210, 234

C.F. Radding, 'Vatican Latin 1406, Mommsen's MS S, and the Reception of the Digest in the Middle Ages', *ZSS rom. Abt. CX* (1993), pp. 501–51.   Ch. 6, nn. 195, 203, 210

C.F. Radding, 'The Geography of Learning in Early Eleventh-Century Europe: Lanfranc of Bec and Berengar of Tours Revisited', *Bullettino dell' Istituto Storico Italiano per il Medio Evo 98* (1992), pp. 145–72.   Ch. 6, n. 210

C.M. Radding, '"Petre te appellat Martinus". Eleventh-century Judicial Procedure as seen through the glosses of Walcausus', *La Giustizia II*, pp. 827–61.   Ch. 6, nn. 195, 198, 200

P. Rahtz, *The Saxon and Medieval Palaces at Cheddar* (British Archaeological Reports, British Series 65, Oxford, 1979).   Ch. 6, n. 65

P. Rapin de Thoyras, *Histoire d' Angleterre* (10 vols, the Hague, 1724); translated by N. Tindal (15 vols, London, 1726–31).   Ch. 1, nn. 28–9

J. Reeves, *History of the English Law from the time of the Saxons, to the end of the Reign of Philip and Mary* (4 vols, London, 1787); Reeves' *History of the English Law, from the Time of the Romans to the end of the reign of Elizabeth*, edited by W.F. Finlayson (3 vols, London, 1869).   **Ch. 1, nn. 38–9, 42**

T. Reuter, *Germany in the Early Middle Ages, 800–1056* (Longman History of Germany, London, 1991).   **Ch, 7, n. 9.**

R.E. Reynolds, *The Ordinals of Christ from their Origins to the Twelfth Century* (Beiträge zur Geschichte und Quellenkunde des Mittelalters 7, general editor H. Fuhrmann, Berlin 1978).   **Ch. 4, n. 131**

S. Reynolds, *Kingdoms and Communities in Western Europe, 900–1300* (Oxford, 2nd edn, 1996).   **Ch. 2, nn. 326; ch. 3, n. 66; ch. 6, n. 228**

S. Reynolds, *Fiefs and Vassals. The Medieval Evidence Reinterpreted* (Oxford, 1994).   **Ch. 6, n. 204**

M.P. Richards, 'The Manuscript Contexts of the Old English Laws', in Szarmach (ed.), *Studies in Earlier Old English Prose*, pp. 171–92.   **Ch. 4, nn. 1, 69, 295**

M.P. Richards, *Texts and Their Traditions in the Medieval Library of Rochester Cathedral Priory* (Philadelphia, Transactions of the American Philosophical Society 78 (3), 1988).   **Ch. 4, n. 327; ch. 6, n. 219**

M. Richards, 'Elements of a Written Standard in the Old English Laws', in J.B. Trahern Jr (editor), *Standardizing English. Essays in the History of Language Change* (Tennessee Studies in Literature 31, 1989).   **Ch. 2, n. 333**

H.G. Richardson and G.O. Sayles, *The Governance of Medieval England from the Conquest to Magna Carta* (Edinburgh, 1963).   **Ch. 6, n. 110**

H.G. Richardson and G.O. Sayles, *Law and Legislation from Æthelberht to Magna Carta* (Edinburgh, 1966).   **Ch. 2, n. 325; ch. 5, nn. 279, 299, 483, 617, 643, 662, 666–8, 675, 681; ch. 6, n. 124**

P. Riché, 'Les bibliothèques de trois aristocrates laics carolingiens', *Le Moyen Age 69* (1963), pp. 87–104.   **Ch. 2, nn. 126, 141**

P. Riché, *Enseignement du Droit en Gaule du VIe au XIe siècle* (IRMAe I.5.b.*bb*, 1965).   **Ch. 2, n. 36; ch. 6, n. 194**

P. Riché, *De l'éducation antique à l'éducation chevaleresque* (Paris, 1968).   **Ch. 3, n. 27**

S.J. Ridyard, *The Royal Saints of Anglo-Saxon England. A Study of West Saxon and East Anglian Cults* (Cambridge studies in medieval life and thought, 4th series 9, Cambridge, 1988).   **Ch. 5, n. 373**

J. Roberts, J.L. Nelson and M. Godden (editors), *Alfred the Wise. Studies in honour of Janet Bately on the occasion of her sixty-fifth birthday* (Cambridge, 1997): see Cross and Hamer, Godden, Nelson, Stanley, Wormald.

E.W. Robertson, *Historical Essays in Connexion with the Land, the Church, Etc.* (Edinburgh, 1872).   **Ch. 1, n. 37**

F.C. Robinson, 'Old English Literature in its Most Immediate Context', in J.D. Niles (editor), *Old English Literature in Context. Ten Essays* (Cambridge, 1980), pp. 11–29.   **Ch. 4, n. 69**

H-A. Roll, *Zur Geschichte der Lex Salica-Forschung* (Untersuchungen zur deutschen Staats- und Rechtsgeschichte n.f. 17, Aalen, 1972).   **Ch. 2, n. 58**

D.W. Rollason, 'Lists of saints' resting-places in Anglo-Saxon England', *ASE* 7 (1978), pp. 61–93.   **Ch. 4, n. 188**

D. Rollason, 'The Miracles of St Benedict: a Window on Early Medieval France', in Mayr-Harting and Moore (eds), *Studies presented to R.H.C. Davis*, pp. 73–90.   **Ch. 2, n. 211**

A. Rumble (editor), *The Reign of Cnut: King of England, Denmark and Norway* (Leicester, 1994): see Keynes, Lawson, Sawyer.

A. Rumble, 'The known manuscripts of the Burghal Hidage', in Hill and Rumble (eds), *Defence of Wessex*, pp. 36–58.   **Ch. 4, nn. 41, 307**

H. Sauer, 'Zur Überlieferung und Anlage von Erzbischof Wulfstans "Handbuch"', *DA* 36 (1980), pp. 341–84.   **Ch. 4, nn. 193, 204–5, 207, 222–3, 231–2**

H. Sauer, 'Die Exkommunikationsriten aus Wulfstans Handbuch und Liebermanns Gesetze', in C. Pollner *et al.* (editors), *Bright is the Ring of Words. Festschrift für Horst Weinstock zum 65. Geburtstag* (Bonn, 1996), pp. 283–307.   **Ch. 4, nn. 196–7**

N. Saul, 'Murder and Justice Medieval Style. The Pashley Case, 1327–8', *History Today* 34 (August 1984), pp. 30–5. **Ch. 3, n. 131**

F.C. von Savigny, *Geschichte des römischen Rechts im Mittelalter* (2nd edn, 7 vols, Heidelberg, 1834–51). **Ch. 1, n. 42; ch. 6, n. 15**

P.H. Sawyer (ed.), *Textus Roffensis*: see *II SOURCES*.

P.H. Sawyer, 'Baldersby, Borup and Bruges: the Rise of Northern Europe', *University of Leeds Review* 16 (1973), pp. 75–96. **Ch. 3, n. 38**

P.H. Sawyer, *From Roman Britain to Norman England* (London, 1978). **Ch. 5, n. 77**

P.H. Sawyer, 'The Royal *Tun* in Pre-Conquest England', in Wormald *et al.* (eds), *Ideal and Reality*, pp. 273–99. **Ch. 6, nn. 53, 63–4, 95**

P.H. Sawyer, 'The Bloodfeud in Fact and Fiction', *Acta Jutlandica* LXIII(2) (1987), pp. 27–38. **Ch. 2, nn. 67, 338**

P.H. Sawyer, 'Cnut's Scandinavian empire', in Rumble (ed.), *Reign of Cnut*, pp. 10–22. **Ch. 5, n. 411**

P. Sawyer, 'The Last Scandinavian Kings of York', *Northern History* XXXI (1995), pp. 39–44. **Ch. 6, nn. 83–4**

P.H. Sawyer and I.N. Wood (editors), *Early Medieval Kingship* (Leeds, 1977): see Nelson, Wormald.

A. Scharer, 'The writing of history at King Alfred's court', *EME* 5 (1996), pp. 177–206. **Ch. 3, nn. 5, 15**

R. Schmid (ed.), *Gesetze der Angelsachsen*: see *II SOURCES*.

R. Schmidt-Wiegand, 'Die kritische Ausgabe der Lex Salica – noch immer ein Problem?', *ZSS* germ. Abt. LXXVI (1959), pp. 301–19. **Ch. 2, n. 58**

R. Schmidt-Wiegand, 'Die volksprachigen Wörter der Leges barbarorum als Ausdruck sprachlicher Interferenz', *FMS* 13 (1979), pp. 56–87. **Ch. 2, n. 66**

R. Schmidt-Wiegand, 'Recht und Ewa. Die Epoche des althochdeutschen in ihrer Bedeutung für die Geschichte der deutschen Rechtssprache', in R. Bergmann *et al.* (editors), *Althochdeutsch* (Heidelberg, 1987) II, pp. 937–58. **Ch. 2, n. 330**

G. Schmitz, 'Zur Überlieferung von Thegans Vita Hludowici und der Kapitulariensammlung des Ansegis', *Rheinische Vierteljahresblätter* 44 (1980), pp. 1–15. **Ch. 2, n. 157**

G. Schmitz, 'Wucher in Laon. Eine neue Quelle zu Karl dem Kahlen und Hinkmar von Rheims', *DA* 37 (1981), pp. 529–58. **Ch. 6, n. 38**

G. Schmitz, 'The Capitulary Legislation of Louis the Pious', in Godman and Collins (eds), *Charlemagne's Heir*, pp. 425–36; in full, 'Zur Kapitulariengesetzgebung Ludwigs des Frommen', *DA* 42 (1986), pp. 471–516. **Ch. 2, nn. 97, 118**

G. Schmitz, 'Intelligente Schreiber. Beobachtungen aus Ansegis- und Kapitularienhandschriften', in H. Mordek (editor), *Papsttum, Kirche und Recht. Festschrift für Horst Fuhrmann zum 65. Geburtstag* (Tübingen, 1991), pp. 79–93. **Ch. 2, n. 159**

G. Schmitz (ed.), *Kapitulariensammlung*: see *II SOURCES*.

R. Schneider, 'Zur rechtlichen Bedeutung der Kapitularientexte', *DA* 23 (1967), pp. 273–94. **Ch. 2, n. 117**

Cl-D. Schott, 'Der Stand der Leges-Forschung', *FMS* 13 (1979), pp. 29–55. **Ch. 2, n. 29**

Cl-D. Schott, 'Zur Geltung der Lex Alamannorum', in P. Fried and W-D. Sick (editors), *Die historische Landschaft zwischen Lech und Vogesen* (Veröffentlichungen des alemannischen Instituts Freiburg LIX, etc., 1988), pp. 75–105. **Ch. 2, nn. 8, 210**

Cl-D. Schott, 'Traditionelle Formen der Konfliktlösung in der Lex Burgundionum', *La Giustizia* I, pp. 933–61. **Ch. 2, n. 45**

J.R. Schwyter, *Old English Legal Language; the lexical field of theft* (Northwestern European language evolution, supplementary vol. 15, Odense, 1996). **Ch. 5, nn. 117, 168**

J.R. Schwyter, 'Syntax and Style in the Anglo-Saxon Law-Codes', in C. Ehler and U. Schaefer (editors), *Verschriftung – Verschriftlichung: Aspekte des Medienwechsels in verschiedenen Kulturen und Epochen* (ScriptOralia, Tübingen, 1998), pp. 186–228. **Ch. 2, nn. 333, 351, 361; Ch. 5, nn. 23, 112, 164, 209, 236–7, 284, 430**

W.G. Searle, *Onomasticon Anglo-Saxonicum* (Cambridge, 1897). **Ch. 6, n. 92**

W. Sellert, 'Aufzeichnung des Rechts und Gesetz', in *idem* (editor), *Das Gesetz in Spätantike und frühem Mittelalter* (Abhandlungen der Akademie der Wissenschaften in Göttingen 196, 1992), pp. 67–102.   **Ch. 2, n. 110**

J. Semmler, 'Reichsidee und kirchliche Gesetzgebungebung', *Zeitschrift für Kirchengeschichte* 71 (1960), pp. 37–65.   **Ch. 2, n. 99**

R. Sharpe, 'The Prefaces of *Quadripartitus*', in Garnett and Hudson (eds), *Law and Government in Medieval England and Normandy*, pp. 148–72.   **Ch. 4, nn. 299, 313, 325; ch. 5, nn. 660, 679, 689, 692; ch. 6, nn. 184, 190, 225, 232**

J. Shepard, 'Slavs and Bulgars', in McKitterick (ed.), *New Cambridge Medieval History II*, pp. 228–48.   **Ch. 2, n. 350**

T.A. Shippey, 'Wealth and Wisdom in King Alfred's *Preface* to the Old English *Pastoral Care*', *EHR* XCIV (1979), pp. 346–55.   **Ch. 6, n. 43**

I. Short, 'Patrons and Polyglots: French Literature in Twelfth-Century England', *ANS* XIV (1991/2), pp. 229–49.   **Ch. 3, n. 90; ch. 5, nn. 665, 669**

I. Short, 'Gaimar's Epilogue and Geoffrey of Monmouth's *Liber Vetustissimus*', *Speculum* LXIX (1994), pp. 323–43.   **Ch. 3, n. 90**

H. Siems, *Studien zur Lex Frisionum* (Abhandlungen zur rechtswissenschaftlichen Grundlagenforschung 42, Munich, 1980).   **Ch. 2, n. 90**

H. Siems, *Handel und Wucher im Spiegel frühmittelalterlicher Rechtsquellen* (MGH Schriften 35, 1992).   **Ch. 2, n. 115; ch. 6, n. 38**

H. Siems, 'Textbearbeitung und Umgang mit Rechtstexten im Frühmittelalter. Zur Umgestaltung der Leges im Liber Legum des Lupus', in H. Siems *et al.* (editors), *Recht im frühmittelalterliche Gallien* (Köln, 1995), pp. 29–72.   **Ch. 2, nn. 11, 19, 23, 25, 27**

A.W.B. Simpson, 'The Laws of Ethelbert', in M.S. Arnold *et al.* (editors), *On the Laws and Customs of England. Essays in Honor of Samuel E. Thorne* (Chapel Hill, 1981), pp. 3–17.   **Ch. 2, n. 337**

K. Sisam, 'The Authenticity of Certain Texts in Lambarde's *Archaionomia* 1568', repr. from *Modern Language Review* xviii (1923), xx (1925), in his *Studies*, pp. 232–58.   **Ch. 4, nn. 367, 371**

K. Sisam, *Studies in the History of Old English Literature* (Oxford, 1953).   **Ch. 4, nn. 69, 71, 76, 105; ch. 5, nn. 36, 338, 371**

T. Smith, *Catalogus Librorum Manuscriptorum Bibliothecae Cottonianae* (Oxford, 1696).   **Ch. 4, nn. 86, 90, 362, 365**

A.P. Smyth, *Scandinavian York and Dublin* (2 vols, Dublin 1975–9).   **Ch. 6, nn. 83, 85–6**

A.P. Smyth, *King Alfred the Great* (Oxford, 1995).   **Ch. 3, nn. 5, 11, 101**

R. Somerville, 'Papal Excerpts in Arsenal MS 713B', *Monumenta Iuris Canonici*, Series C: Subsidia 10 (1997), pp. 169–84.   **Ch. 6, n. 233**

R.W. Southern, 'Lanfranc of Bec and Berengar of Tours', in Hunt, Pantin and Southern (eds), *Studies presented to Powicke*, pp. 27–48.   **Ch. 6, n. 209**

R.W. Southern, *The Making of the Middle Ages* (London, 1953).   **Ch. 6, n. 192**

R.W. Southern, *Saint Anselm and his Biographer. A Study of Monastic Life and Thought, 1059–c. 1130* (Cambridge, 1963).   **Ch. 3, n. 71**

R.W. Southern, 'The place of England in the Twelfth Century Renaissance', in his *Medieval Humanism and Other Studies* (Oxford, 1970), pp. 158–80.   **Ch. 3, n. 68; ch. 6, n. 231**

R.W. Southern, 'Aspects of the European Tradition of Historical Writing: 1. The Classical Tradition from Einhard to Geoffrey of Monmouth', *TRHS* 5th series 20 (1970), pp. 173–96.   **Ch. 3, n. 45**

R.W. Southern, 'Aspects of the European Tradition of Historical Writing: 4. The Sense of the Past', *TRHS* 5th series 23 (1973), pp. 243–63.   **Ch. 3, n. 83; ch. 4, n. 340**

R.W. Southern, 'Master Vacarius and the Beginning of an English Academic Tradition', in Alexander and Gibson (eds), *Medieval Learning and Literature*, pp. 257–86.   **Ch. 6, n. 211**

R.W. Southern, 'From Schools to University', in J. Catto (editor), *The History of the University of Oxford I* (general editor, T.H. Aston, Oxford, 1984), pp. 1–36.   **Ch. 6, n. 231**

H. Spelman, *Glossarium Archaiologicum Continens Latino-Barbara, Peregrina, Obsoleta ac Novatae Significationis Vocabula …* (London, 3rd edn, 1678).   **Ch. 1, nn. 15, 21, 26**

H. Spelman, *Reliquiae Spelmannianae. The Posthumous Works of Sir Henry Spelman Kt, Relating to the Laws and Antiquities of England*, edited by E. Gibson (London, 1698; 2nd edn, 1723, with *English Works Published in his Lifetime*, 1727).   **Ch. 1, n. 15**

J. Spelman, *Ælfredi Magni Anglorum Regis Invictissimi Vita tribus libris comprehensa* (in Latin translation by members of University College Oxford, Oxford, 1678); *The Life of King Alfred the Great* (original English version (1643), edited by T. Hearne, Oxford, 1709).   **Ch. 1, nn. 21, 30**

R. Sprandel, *Ivo von Chartres und seine Stellung in der Kirchengeschichte* (Pariser historische Studien 1, Stuttgart, 1962).   **Ch. 6, nn. 215, 224**

M. Springer, 'Gab es ein Volk der Salier?', in D. Geuenich *et al.* (editors), *Nomen et Gens. Zur historischen Aussagekraft frühmittelalterlicher Personennamen* (Berlin, 1997), pp. 59–83.   **Ch. 2, n. 68**

R.C. Stacey, 'Law and Order in the *Very* Old West: England and Ireland in the Early Middle Ages', in B.T. Hudson and V. Ziegler (editors), *Crossed Paths. Methodological Approaches in the Celtic Aspect of the European Middle Ages* (Lanham Mr, 1991), pp. 39–60.   **Ch. 1, n. 44**

P. Stafford, 'The King's Wife in Wessex 800–1066', *PP* 91 (1981), pp. 3–27.   **Ch. 4, n. 33**

P. Stafford, 'The laws of Cnut and the history of Anglo-Saxon royal promises', *ASE* 10 (1981), pp. 173–90.   **Ch. 5, nn. 440–2, 629**

P. Stafford, *Queen Emma and Queen Edith. Queenship and Women's Power in Eleventh-Century England* (Oxford, 1997).   **Ch. 4, n. 123**

E.G. Stanley, 'The Glorification of Alfred King of Wessex (from the publication of Sir John Spelman's *Life*, 1689 and 1709, to the publication of Reinhold Pauli's, 1851', *Poetica* 12 (1981), pp. 103–33; repr. in idem, *A Collection of Papers with Emphasis on Old English Literature* (Publications of the Dictionary of Old English 3, Toronto, 1987), pp. 410–41.   **Ch. 1, nn. 5, 21**

E.G. Stanley, 'On the Laws of King Alfred: the End of the Preface and the Beginning of the Laws', in Roberts *et al.* (eds), *Alfred the Wise*, pp. 211–21.   **Ch. 2, n. 369; ch. 5, nn. 74, 541**

E.G. Stanley, 'Trial by Jury, and how Later Ages Perceive its Origin – Perhaps in Anglo-Saxon England', in M.J. Toswell (editor), *The Laws and the Prophets in the Middle Ages and the Renaissance* (forthcoming).   **Ch. 1, n. 5**

E.G. Stanley, 'Die angelsächsische Rechtspflege – und wie man sie später aufgefaßt hat' (forthcoming).   **Ch. 1, n. 5**

E. Steinwenter, 'Die Briefe des Qu. Aur. Symmachus als Rechtsquelle', *ZSS*, rom. Abt. LXXIV (1957), pp. 1–25.   **Ch. 2, n. 221**

D.M. Stenton, *English Justice between the Norman Conquest and the Great Charter, 1066–1215* (London, 1965).   **Ch. 1, nn. 120–2**

F.M. Stenton, 'The South-western element in the Old English Chronicle', in A.G. Little and F.M. Powicke (editors), in D.M. Stenton (editor), *Preparatory to Anglo-Saxon England. Being the Collected Papers of Frank Merry Stenton* (Oxford, 1970), pp. 106–15.   **Ch. 4, n. 24**

F.M. Stenton, *The Latin Charters of the Anglo-Saxon Period* (Oxford, 1955).   **Ch. 3, n. 105**

F.M. Stenton, *Anglo-Saxon England* (3rd edn, Oxford History of England, general editor G.N. Clark, Oxford, 1971).   **Ch. 1, nn. 118, 128; ch. 3, n. 62; ch. 5, nn. 99, 202, 225, 299; ch. 6, n. 124**

W.H. Stevenson, 'Yorkshire Surveys and other Eleventh-Century Documents in the York Gospels', *EHR* XXVII (1912), pp. 1–25.   **Ch. 5, n. 395**

I. Stewart, 'Coinage and Recoinage after Edgar's Reform', in K. Jonsson (editor), *Studies in Anglo-Saxon Coinage* (Stockholm, 1989), pp. 457–85.   **Ch. 3, n. 38; ch. 6, n. 98**

W. Stubbs, *The Constitutional History of England in its Origin and Development* (revised edn, 3 vols, Oxford, 1880).   **Ch. 1, nn. 56–8**

M.J. Swanton, *Anglo-Saxon Prose* (London, 1975).   **Ch. 4, n. 181; ch. 5, n. 559; ch. 6, n. 153**

P. Szarmach, 'The Meaning of Alfred's *Preface* to the *Pastoral Care*', *Mediaevalia* 6 (Special volume in honor of Bernard F. Huppé, 1980), pp. 57–86.   **Ch. 6, n. 43**

P. Szarmach (editor), *Studies in Earlier Old English Prose* (Albany, 1986): see Bolton, Clement, Gatch, Richards.

J.P.S. Tatlock, *The Legendary History of Britain. Geoffrey of Monmouth's Historia Regum Britanniae and Its Early Vernacular Versions* (Berkeley, 1950).   **Ch. 3, n. 87**

F. Taylor, *Supplementary Handlist of Western Manuscripts in the John Rylands Library 1937* (Manchester, 1937).   **Ch. 4, n. 300**

E. Temple, *Anglo-Saxon Manuscripts 900–1066* (A Survey of Manuscripts illuminated in the British Isles 2, general editor J.J.G. Alexander, London, 1976).   **Ch. 4, n. 22**

G. Theuerkauf, *Lex, Speculum, Compendium Iuris. Rechtsaufzeichnung und Rechtsbewußtsein in Norddeutschland vom 8. bis 16. Jahrhundert* (Forschungen zur deutschen Rechtsgeschichte 6, Cologne, 1968).   **Ch. 2, n. 318**

G. Theuerkauf, 'Burchard von Wurms und die Rechtskunde seiner Zeit', *FMS* 2 (1968), pp. 144–61.   **Ch. 2, n. 316; ch. 6, n. 148**

E.A. Thompson, *The Goths in Spain* (Oxford, 1969).   **Ch. 2, n. 255**

R.M. Thomson, 'William of Malmesbury as historian and man of letters', *JEH* 29 (1978), pp. 387–413, repr. with modifications in *idem, William of Malmesbury* (Woodbridge, 1987), pp. 11–38.   **Ch. 3, nn. 83, 85–6**

B. Thorpe (ed.), *Ancient Laws and Institutes of England*: see *II SOURCES*.

J-O. Tjäder, *Die nichtliterarischen lateinischen Papyri Italiens aus der Zeit 445–700* (3 vols, Skrifta utgivna av Svenska Institutet i Rom 4° XIX, Lund, 1954–82).   **Ch. 2, nn. 38, 302**

R. Torkar, 'Zu den ae. Medizinaltexten in Otho B.xi und Royal 12 D.xvii. Mit einer Edition der Unica (Ker, No. 180 art. 11 a–d)', *Anglia* 94 (1976), pp. 319–38.   **Ch. 4, n. 62**

R. Torkar, *Eine altenglische Übersetzung von Alcuins De Virtutibus et Vitiis, Kap 20 (Liebermanns Judex). Untersuchungen und Textausgabe* (Texte und Untersuchungen zur englischen Philologie 7, general editors H. Gneuss and W. Weiß, Munich, 1981).   **Ch. 4, nn. 38, 41–3, 46–51, 53–4, 56, 58–9, 246, 257, 260, 383; ch. 5, nn. 5–6, 472, 531–6**

T.F. Tout, 'Felix Liebermann', *History* n.s. X (1926), pp. 311–19.   **Ch. 1, n. 108**

E. Treharne, 'A unique Old English formula for excommunication from Cambridge, Corpus Christi College 303', *ASE* 24 (1995), pp. 185–211.   **Ch. 4, n. 196**

M. Treschow, 'The Prologue to Alfred's Law Code: Instruction in the Spirit of Mercy'. *Florilegium* 13 (1994), pp. 79–110.   **Ch. 6, n. 10**

M.H. Turk, *The Legal Code of Alfred the Great* (Halle, 1893).   **Ch. 5, nn. 7, 14, 74; ch. 6, nn. 1, 28**

S. Turner, *The History of the Anglo-Saxons* (2 vols, 2nd edn, London, 1807).   **Ch. 1, n. 32**

S. Turner, *History of England from the Norman Conquest to the Accession of Edward I* (London, 1814).   **Ch. 1, n. 32**

W. Turpin, 'The Law Codes and Late Roman Law', *Revue Internationale des Droits de l'Antiquité* 3rd series XXXII (1985), pp. 339–53.   **Ch. 2, n. 42**

W. Ullmann, 'On the Influence of Geoffrey of Monmouth in English History', in C. Bauer *et al.* (editors), *Speculum Historiale. Geschichte im Spiegel von Geschichtsschreibung und Geschichtsdeutung ... Johannes Spörl dargebracht* (Freiburg, 1965), pp. 257–76.   **Ch. 3, n. 88**

P. Vinogradoff, *English Society in the Eleventh Century. Essays in English Medieval History* (Oxford, 1908).   **Ch. 1, n. 121**

P. Vinogradoff, *Roman Law in Medieval Europe* (2nd edn, Oxford, 1929).   **Ch. 2, n. 5**

Λ. de Vogüé (editor), *La Règle de Saint Benoit* (6 vols, Sources Chrétiennes 181–6, Paris, 1971–2).   **Ch. 2, n. 312**

H. Vollrath, *Die Synoden Englands bis 1066* (Konziliengeschichte, general editor W. Brandmüller, Reihe A: Darstellungen, Paderborn, 1985).   **Ch. 2, n. 372; ch. 3, n. 94; ch. 5, n. 363**

R. Volpini, 'Placiti del "Regnum Italie" (saec. IX–XI). Primi Contributi per un nuovo censimento', in P. Zerbi (editor), *Contributi dell' Istituto di Storia Medioevale* 3 (Milan, 1975), pp. 245–520.   **Ch. 2, n. 292**

E. Volterra, 'Western post-classical Lawschools', *Cambridge Law Journal* X (1949), pp. 196–207.   **Ch. 2, n. 36**

S. Walker, 'A Context for "Brunanburh"?' in T. Reuter (editor), *Warriors and Churchmen in the High Middle Ages. Essays presented to Karl Leyser* (London, 1992), pp. 21–39. Ch. 6, n. 81

J.M. Wallace-Hadrill, 'The Franks and the English in the Ninth Century: some common historical interests', *History* XXXV (1949), pp. 202–18; repr. in *EMH*, pp. 201–16. Ch. 6, n. 2

J.M. Wallace-Hadrill, 'The Bloodfeud of the Franks', *BJRL* XLI (1958–9), pp. 459–87; repr. in his *Long-Haired Kings*, pp. 121–47. Ch. 2, nn. 67, 338

J.M. Wallace-Hadrill, '*Gothia* and *Romania*', *BJRL* XLIV (1961–2), pp. 213–37; repr. in his *Long-Haired Kings*, pp. 25–48. Ch. 2, n. 37

J.M. Wallace-Hadrill, *The Long-Haired Kings, and other studies in Frankish History* (London, 1962): see also above. Ch. 2, n. 79

J.M. Wallace-Hadrill, 'The *Via Regia* of the Carolingian Age', in B. Smalley (editor), *Trends in Medieval Political Thought* (Oxford, 1965), pp. 22–41; repr. in *EMH*, pp. 181–200. Ch. 6, nn. 27, 30

J.M. Wallace-Hadrill, review of I. Haselbach, *Aufstieg und Herrschaft der Karlinger in der Darstellung der sogenannten Annales Mettenses priores*, *EHR* LXXXVI (1971), pp. 154–6. Ch. 4, n. 36

J.M. Wallace-Hadrill, *Early Germanic Kingship in England and on the Continent* (Oxford, 1971). Ch. 2, nn. 2, 82; ch. 3, n. 28; ch. 5, n. 68; ch. 6, n. 47

J.M. Wallace-Hadrill, *Early Medieval History* (Oxford, 1975): see above.

J.M. Wallace-Hadrill, *The Frankish Church* (Oxford, 1983). Ch. 3, n. 25; ch. 5, n. 553; ch. 6, n. 30

J.M. Wallace-Hadrill, *Bede's Ecclesiastical History of the English People. A Historical Commentary* (Oxford Medieval Texts, Oxford, 1988). Ch. 2, n. 2

L. Wallach, *Alcuin and Charlemagne* (Cornell Studies in Classical Philology XII, general editors H. Caplan *et al.*, Ithaca, 1957). Ch. 5, n. 536

H. Wanley, *Antiquae Literaturae Septentrionalis Liber Alter, seu Humphredi Wanleii Librorum Vett. Septentrionalium, qui in Angliae Bibliothecis extant, nec non multorum Vett. Codd. Septentrionalium alibi extantium Catalogus Historico-Criticus* (Oxford, 1705). Ch. 4, nn. 42, 52–3, 55, 75, 90, 100, 362, 365

P.L. Ward, 'An Early Version of the Anglo-Saxon Coronation Ceremony', *EHR* LVII (1942), pp. 345–61. Ch. 6, n. 116

G.F. Warner and J.P. Gilson, *Catalogue of Western Manuscripts in the old Royal and King's Collections* (4 vols, London, 1921). Ch. 4, n. 301

A. Watson, *The Library of Sir Simonds D'Ewes* (London, 1966). Ch. 4, n. 98

T. Webber, 'Salisbury and the Exon Domesday: Some Observations Concerning the Origin of Exeter Cathedral MS 3500', *English Manuscript Studies* I (1989), pp. 1–18. Ch. 6, n. 229

T. Webber, *Scribes and Scholars at Salisbury Cathedral, c. 1075–c. 1125* (Oxford, 1992). Ch. 6, n. 229

F. Weinisch, *Spezifisch anglisches Wortgut in den nordhumbrischen Interlinearglossierungen des Lukasevangeliums* (Anglistische Forschungen 132, Heidelberg, 1979). Ch. 5, n. 36

K-F. Werner, 'Missus-Marchio-Comes. Entre l' administration centrale et l' administration locale de l' empire carolingien', in Paravicini and Werner (eds), *Histoire Comparée de l'Administration*, pp. 191–239. Ch. 2, nn. 105, 246

S.D. White, 'Kinship and Lordship in Early Medieval England: the story of Sigeberht, Cynewulf and Cyneheard', *Viator* 20 (1989), pp. 1–18. Ch. 5, n. 96

S.D. White, 'Proposing the Ordeal and Avoiding it: Strategy and Power in W. French Litigation, 1050–1110', in T.N. Bisson (editor), *Cultures of Power: Lordship, Status and Process in Twelfth-Century Europe* (Philadelphia, 1995), pp. 89–123. Ch. 2, n. 217

S.D. White, 'Clotild's Revenge: Politics, Kinship and Ideology in the Merovingian Blood Feud', in S.K. Cohn Jr and S.A. Epstein (editors), *Portraits of Medieval and Renaissance Living. Essays in Memory of D. Herlihy* (Ann Arbor, 1996), pp. 107–30. Ch. 2, nn. 67, 338

S.D. White, 'Maitland on Family and Kinship', in Hudson (ed.), *History of English Law*, pp. 91–113. Ch. 1, nn. 66, 93

D. Whitelock, 'Wulfstan and the so-called Laws of Edward and Guthrum', *EHR* LVI (1941), pp. 1–21.   **Ch. 5, n. 572**

D. Whitelock, 'Archbishop Wulfstan, Homilist and Statesman', *TRHS* 4th series 24 (1942), pp. 25–45.   **Ch. 4, n. 145, 156, 204, 223; ch. 6, n. 125**

D. Whitelock, 'Wulfstan and the Laws of Cnut', *EHR* LXIII (1948), pp. 433–52.   **Ch. 1, n. 127; ch. 3, nn. 53, 58–9; ch. 5, nn. 385–6, 406**

D. Whitelock, 'Wulfstan's authorship of Cnut's Laws', *EHR* LXX (1955), pp. 72–85.   **Ch. 3, nn. 53, 58; ch. 5, nn. 385, 394, 396**

D. Whitelock, 'The Dealings of the Kings of England with Northumbria in the Tenth and Eleventh Centuries', in P. Clemoes (editor), *The Anglo-Saxons. Studies presented to Bruce Dickins* (Cambridge, 1959), pp. 70–88.   **Ch. 4, nn. 93, 123; ch. 6, nn. 84, 90, 99**

D. Whitelock, 'The Old English Bede', *PBA* XLVIII (1962), pp. 57–90.   **Ch. 5, n. 35**

D. Whitelock, 'Wulfstan at York', in J.B. Bessinger Jr. & R.P. Creed (editors), *Franciplegius: Medieval and linguistic studies in Honor of Francis Peabody Magoun* (New York, 1965), pp. 214–31.   **Ch. 4, nn. 94–5, 123, 161, 163–4**

D. Whitelock, 'William of Malmesbury on the works of King Alfred', in D.A. Pearsall and R.A. Waldron (editors), *Medieval Literature and Civilization: Studies in memory of G.N. Garmonsway* (London, 1968), pp. 78–93.   **Ch. 3, n. 79**

D. Whitelock, 'Wulfstan *Cantor* and Anglo-Saxon law', in A.H. Orrick (editor), *Nordica et Anglica. Studies in Honor of Stefán Einarsson* (The Hague, 1968), pp. 83–92.   **Ch. 3, nn. 30, 34**

D. Whitelock, 'The Authorship of the Account of King Edgar's Establishment of Monasteries', in J.L. Rosier (editor), *Philological Essays. Studies in Old and Middle English Language and Literature in Honour of Herbert Dean Meritt* (The Hague, 1968), pp. 125–36.   **Ch. 5, n. 260**

D. Whitelock, 'The list of chapter headings in the Old English Bede', in R.B. Burlin and E.B. Irving (editors), *Old English Studies in Honour of John C. Pope* (Toronto, 1974), pp. 263–84.   **Ch. 5, n. 17**

D. Whitelock, 'Some Charters in the Name of King Alfred', in M.H. King and W.M. Stevens (editors), *Saints, Scholars and Heroes. Studies in Medieval Culture in honour of Charles W. Jones* (Collegeville, Minnesota, 1979), pp. 77–98.   **Ch. 3, n. 101**

C. Wickham, *Early Medieval Italy. Central Power and Local Society 400–1000* (New Studies in Medieval History, general editor M. Keen, London, 1981).   **Ch. 2, nn. 57, 83, 306; ch. 7, n. 9**

C. Wickham, 'Lawyers' Time: History and Memory in Tenth and Eleventh-Century Italy', in Mayr-Harting and Moore (eds), *Studies presented to R.H.C. Davis*, pp. 53–71.   **Ch. 6, n. 197**

C. Wickham, 'Land disputes and their social framework in Lombard-Carolingian Italy, 700–900', in *Disputes*, pp. 105–24.   **Ch. 2, nn. 292, 295, 301; ch. 3, n. 152**

C. Wickham, 'European Forests in the Early Middle Ages: Landscape and Land Clearance', *Sett. Spol.* XXXVII (1990), pp. 479–548.   **Ch. 6, n. 67**

F. Wieacker, *Allgemeine Zustände und Rechtszustände gegen Ende des weströmischen Reichs* (*IRMAe* I.2.a, 1963).   **Ch. 2, n. 35**

J. Wilcox, 'Napier's "Wulfstan" Homilies XL and XLII: two anonymous works from Winchester?', *JEGP* XC (1991), pp. 1–19.   **Ch. 6, n. 129**

J. Wilcox, 'The dissemination of Wulfstan's homilies: the Wulfstan tradition in eleventh-century vernacular preaching', in Hicks (ed.), *England in the Eleventh Century*, pp. 199–217.   **Ch. 4, nn. 177, 180; ch. 5, n. 318; ch. 6, n. 129**

D. Wilkins: see *II SOURCES, Leges Anglo-Saxonicae.*

N. Wilkins, *Catalogue des manuscrits français de la bibliothèque Parker* (Cambridge, 1993).   **Ch. 4, n. 268**

A. Williams, '*Princeps Merciorum gentis*: the family, career and connections of Ælfhere, ealdorman of Mercia, 956–83', *ASE* 10 (1982), pp. 143–72.   **Ch. 6, n. 89**

G.H. Williams, *The Norman Anonymous of 1100 AD* (Harvard Theological Studies XVIII, Cambridge, Ma, 1951).   **Ch. 2, n. 227**

G.H. Williams, *The Norman Anonymous of 1100 AD* (Harvard Theological Studies XVIII, Cambridge, Ma, 1951). **Ch. 2, n. 227**

B. Woledge and I. Short, 'Liste provisoire de mss du XIIᵉ siècle contenant des textes en langue francaise', *Romania* CII (1981), pp. 1–17. **Ch. 5, n. 665**

H. Wolfram (translated by T.J. Dunlap), *History of the Goths* (Berkeley, 1988). **Ch. 2, n. 47**

I.N. Wood, 'Disputes in late fifth- and sixth-century Gaul: some problems', in *Disputes*, pp. 7–22. **Ch. 2, nn. 40, 217**

I.N. Wood, *The Merovingian North Sea* (Occasional Papers on Medieval Topics 1, Alingsås, 1983). **Ch. 2, n. 348**

I.N. Wood, 'Administration, Law and Culture in Merovingian Gaul', in McKitterick (ed.), *Uses of Literacy*, pp. 63–81. **Ch. 2, nn. 84, 344**

I.N. Wood, '*Nachleben*: the Code in the Middle Ages'; 'The Code in Merovingian Gaul', in Harries and and Wood (eds), *Theodosian Code*, pp. 159–77. **Ch. 2, nn. 33, 45**

I.N. Wood, *The Merovingian Kingdoms, 450–751* (London, 1994). **Ch. 2, nn. 59, 70, 73, 75, 79–80, 82**

I.N. Wood, 'Teutsind, Witlaic and the history of Merovingian *precaria*', in Davies and Fouracre (eds), *Property and Power*, pp. 31–52. **Ch. 2, n. 277**

I.N. Wood, 'Roman Law in the Barbarian Kingdoms', in Ellegård and Åkerström-Hougen (eds), *Rome and the North*, pp. 5–14. **Ch. 2, nn. 33, 62**

I.N. Wood and N. Lund (editors), *People and Places in Northern Europe, 500–1600. Studies presented to Peter Hayes Sawyer* (Woodbridge, 1991): see Keynes, Nelson, Wormald.

M. Wood, 'The Making of King Æthelstan's Empire: an English Charlemagne?', in Wormald *et al.* (eds), *Ideal and Reality*, pp. 250–72. **Ch. 4, nn. 28, 37; ch. 6, n. 105**

F. Wormald, 'Decorated Initials in English MSS from A.D. 900 to 1100', *Archaeologia* XCI (1945), pp. 107–35. **Ch. 4, nn. 14, 22**

[C.] P. Wormald, 'The Uses of Literacy in Anglo-Saxon England and its Neighbours', *TRHS* 5th series 27 (1977), pp. 95–114. **Ch. 2, n. 350; ch. 5, n. 158**

[C.] P. Wormald, '*Lex Scripta* and *Verbum Regis*: Legislation and Germanic Kingship from Euric to Cnut', *EMK*, pp. 105–38; repr. in *Legal Culture*, pp. 1–43. **Ch. 2, nn. 3, 15, 44, 89, 93–4, 110, 117, 197, 249, 260, 290, 349; ch. 5, n. 121; ch. 7, n. 7**

[C.] P. Wormald, 'Æthelred the Lawmaker', in Hill (ed.), *Ethelred*, pp. 47–80. **Ch. 5, nn. 261, 286, 296, 325, 338, 343, 367, 371, 378; ch. 6, nn. 98, 119**

[C.] P. Wormald, *Bede and the Conversion of England: the Charter Evidence* (Jarrow Lecture, 1984). **Ch. 6, n. 58**

[C.] P. Wormald, 'Charters, law and the settlement of disputes in Anglo-Saxon England', in *Disputes*, pp. 149–68; repr. in *Legal Culture*, pp. 289–311. **Ch. 1, nn. 67, 122; ch. 3, nn. 93, 107; ch. 4, n. 79; ch. 5, n. 545**

[C.] P. Wormald, 'A Handlist of Anglo-Saxon Lawsuits', *ASE* 17 (1988), pp. 247–81; repr. in *Legal Culture*, pp. 253–87. See also Subsidiary Index (i). **Ch. 1, n. 122; ch. 2, n. 320; ch. 3, nn. 93–4, 106, 114, 121, 141, 143, 147, 156; ch. 6, n. 62**

[C.] P. Wormald, 'Liebermann, Felix', in J. Cannon *et al.* (editors), *The Blackwell Dictionary of Historians* (Oxford, 1988), pp. 245–7. **Ch. 1, n. 97**

[C.] P. Wormald, 'Æthelwold and his Continental Counterparts: Contact, Comparison, Contrast', in Yorke (ed.), *Bishop Æthelwold*, pp. 13–42. **Ch. 6, n. 106**

[C.] P. Wormald, 'In Search of King Offa's "Law-code", in Wood and Lund (eds), *People and Places*, pp. 25–45; repr. in *Legal Culture*, pp. 201–24. **Ch. 2, nn. 107, 369, 372–3; ch. 5, nn. 35, 215**

[C.] P. Wormald, *How do we know so much about Anglo-Saxon Deerhurst?* (Deerhurst Lecture, 1991). **Ch. 3, n. 49**

[C.] P. Wormald, '"*Quadripartitus*"', in Garnett and Hudson (eds), *Law and Government in Medieval England and Normandy*, pp. 111–47; repr. in *Legal Culture*, pp. 81–114. **Ch. 1, n. 98; ch. 4, nn. 299, 305, 307, 311–12, 315, 319–21, 323–4, 326; ch. 5, nn. 306, 636, 665, 687, 689; ch. 6, nn. 225, 230**

[C.] P. Wormald, '*Engla Lond*: the Making of an Allegiance', *Journal of Historical*

Sociology 7 (1994), pp. 1–24; repr. in *Legal Culture*, pp. 359–82.   Ch. 4, n. 73; ch. 6, n. 176

[C.] P. Wormald, '*Laga Eadwardi*: the *Textus Roffensis* in context', ANS XVII (1994/5), pp. 243–66; repr. in *Legal Culture*, pp. 115–37.   Ch. 4, nn. 331, 333–4, 336, 339; ch. 5, n. 635; ch. 6, nn. 220, 223–4

[C.] P. Wormald, '"*Inter Cetera Bona* … *Genti Suae*": Law-making and Peace-Keeping in the earliest English Kingdoms', *La Giustizia* I, pp. 963–96; repr. in *Legal Culture*, pp. 179–99.   Ch. 2, nn. 3, 29, 321, 333–5, 351, 356, 361, 363; ch. 5, nn. 23, 25

[C.] P. Wormald, 'BL, Cotton MS Otho B. xi: a supplementary note', in Hill and Rumble (eds), *Defence of Wessex*, pp. 59–68; repr. in *Legal Culture*, pp. 71-80.   Ch. 4, nn. 41, 57, 60, 63, 68, 71, 73–4

[C.] P. Wormald, '*Exempla Romanorum*: the Earliest English Legislation in Context', in Ellegård and Åkerström-Hougen (eds), *Rome and the North*, pp. 15–27.   Ch. 2, nn. 3, 29, 363

[C.] P. Wormald, 'Maitland and Anglo-Saxon Law: Beyond Domesday Book', in Hudson (ed.), *History of English Law*, pp. 1–20.   Ch. 1, nn. 2, 60, 70; ch. 6, n. 179

[C.] P. Wormald, 'The Lambarde Problem: Eighty Years On', in Roberts, Nelson and Godden (eds), *Alfred the Wise*, pp. 237–75; repr. in *Legal Culture*, pp. 139–78.   Ch. 4, nn. 265, 373, 375–6, 378, 380, 382, 384; ch. 5, nn. 6, 132, 139

[C.] P. Wormald, 'Giving God and King their Due: Conflict and its Regulation in the early English State', *La Giustizia* II, pp. 549–92; repr. in *Legal Culture*, pp. 333–57.   Ch. 1, n. 123; ch. 3, nn. 115–16, 191–21, 124–5, 137–8, 143; ch. 5, n. 215

[C.] P. Wormald, 'Frederic William Maitland and the earliest English Law', *Law and History Review* 16 (1998), pp. 1–25; repr. in *Legal Culture*, pp. 45–69.   Ch. 1, nn. 60–1, 66, 70–7, 81, 86–9, 95; ch. 6, n. 179; ch. 7, n. 8

[C.] P. Wormald, 'Archbishop Wulfstan and the Holiness of Society', in D. Pelteret (editor), *Anglo Saxon History. Basic Readings* (New York, 2000, pp. 191–224); repr. in *Legal Culture*, pp. 225–51.   Ch. 4, nn. 108, 143, 151, 204, 207–8, 212, 214–16; ch. 5, nn. 565, 573, 609

[C.] P. Wormald, *Legal Culture in the Early Medieval West. Law as Text, Image, and Experience* (London, 1999): see above.

[C.] P. Wormald, 'Kings and Kingship', in P. Fouracre (editor), *The New Cambridge Medieval History of Europe I, c. 500–c. 700* (Cambridge, forthcoming).   Ch. 2, n. 29

[C.] P. Wormald, 'LAWS', in Biggs *et al.* (eds), *Sources of Anglo-Saxon Literary Culture* (forthcoming).   Ch. 4, n. 204; ch. 5, nn. 349, 368, 452; ch. 6, n. 153

[C.] P. Wormald, D. Bullough and R. Collins (editors), *Ideal and Reality in Frankish and Anglo-Saxon Society. Studies presented to J.M. Wallace-Hadrill* (Oxford, 1983): see Ganz, John, Nelson, Sawyer, M. Wood.

R. Wright, *Late Latin and Early Romance in Spain and Carolingian France* (ARCA Classical and Medieval Texts, Papers and Monographs 8, 1982).   Ch. 2, n. 115

J. Wuest, *Die 'Leis Willelme': Untersuchungen zur ältesten Gesetzbuch in französischer Sprache* (Romanica Helvetica 79, Bern, 1969).   Ch. 5, nn. 662, 666

B. Yorke, 'Æthelwold and the Politics of the Tenth Century', in Yorke (ed.), *Bishop Æthelwold*, pp. 65–88.   Ch. 6, n. 100

B. Yorke (editor), *Bishop Æthelwold, His Career and Influence* (Woodbridge, 1988): see Lapidge, Wormald, Yorke.

J. Yver, 'Les caractères originaux du groupe de Coûtumes de l'Ouest de la France', *Revue Historique de Droit français et étranger* XXIX (1951), pp. 18–79.   Ch. 6, n. 186

J. Yver, 'Les deux groupes de Coûtumes de Nord', *Revue du Nord* XXXV (1953), pp. 197–220, XXXVI (1954), pp. 5–36.   Ch. 6, n. 186

K. Zeumer, 'Zur Geschichte der westgothischen Gesetzgebung I–III', *Neues Archiv* XXIII (1897–8), pp. 419–516, XXIV (1898–9), pp. 39–122, 571–630.   Ch. 2, n. 43; ch. 5, n. 69

J. Zupitza, 'Ein weiteres Bruchstück der Regula concordia in altenglischer Sprache', *Arch. SNSL* LXXXIV (1890), pp. 1–24.   Ch. 4, table 4.3, nn. 166, 168, 190

Index

This Index relates mainly to the *text*. For material in Notes or Tables reference should be made to the relevant sections of the *Bibliographical Index*, cross-references to which may be 'taken as read'; however, points of substance not adequately screened thereby are covered below. Sources or modern authorities are indexed here only if discussed at length in the text (as in chapter 1), or when invoked without corresponding annotation; discussions of particularly significant manuscripts are here indexed under 'law books, Old English, specific.'